LEAVES OF GRASS

AUTHORITATIVE TEXTS
PREFACES
WHITMAN ON HIS ART
CRITICISM

WALT WHITMAN

LEAVES OF GRASS

AUTHORITATIVE TEXTS

PREFACES

WHITMAN ON HIS ART

CRITICISM

➤➤◄◄

Edited by

SCULLEY BRADLEY

PROFESSOR EMERITUS
THE UNIVERSITY OF PENNSYLVANIA

HAROLD W. BLODGETT

PROFESSOR EMERITUS
UNION COLLEGE

W · W · NORTON & COMPANY

New York · London

W. W. Norton & Company, Inc., 500 Fifth Avenue, New York, N.Y. 10110

Copyright © 1973 by W. W. Norton & Company, Inc.

Copyright © 1965 by New York University

Reprinted by arrangement with New
York University Press

Library of Congress Cataloging in Publication Data

Whitman, Walt, 1819–1892.
Leaves of grass.

(A Norton critical edition)
Bibliography: p.
I. Bradley, Edward Sculley, 1897–ed.
II. Blodgett, Harold William, 1900–ed.
III. Title.
PS3201   1972   811'.3   72–5156
ISBN 0-393-04354-1
ISBN 0-393-09388-3 {pbk.}

GRATEFUL ACKNOWLEDGMENT IS MADE TO
MR. CHARLES E. FEINBERG,
WHOSE ASSISTANCE MADE POSSIBLE THE ILLUSTRATIONS
IN THIS VOLUME AND WHO ALSO MADE
AVAILABLE TO THE PUBLISHER THE RESOURCES
OF THE FEINBERG COLLECTION.

Printed in the United States of America

1 2 3 4 5 6 7 8 9 0

Contents

The Text of *Leaves of Grass, 1891–1892*

Epigraph: Come, said my Soul

Inscriptions

By the Roadside

Drum-Taps

Memories of President Lincoln

PREFATORY LETTER AND A BACKWARD GLANCE O'ER TRAVEL'D ROADS

Old Age Echoes

Other Poetic Writings

POEMS EXCLUDED FROM "LEAVES OF GRASS"

PASSAGES EXCLUDED FROM "LEAVES OF GRASS" POEMS

UNPUBLISHED POEMS

UNCOLLECTED MANUSCRIPT FRAGMENTS

Preface

This edition of *Leaves of Grass* presents the whole body of Walt Whitman's poems, together with a wide selection from surviving fragments. The basic text is that of the last and ninth edition, over which Whitman himself presided, with the insistence that all future printings should be a "copy and facsimile" of his final arrangement, arrived at through almost incessant accretion, emendation, and manipulation from the first twelve poems, untitled and unsigned, of the 1855 edition to the authorized 1891–92 edition of three hundred and eighty-nine poems.

The editors have not only honored Whitman's injunction to preserve the authorized text as he left it, but they also present here the forty-five poems and twenty-eight passages from poems which he chose to exclude from his successive editions in the process of developing groups in an order that did not become fixed until he arrived at his seventh edition in 1881. Some of the poems are so impressive in originality and power that the poet may have regretted their exclusion. The editors also present twenty-two poems never before published, forty-three poems posthumously published and here collected for the first time, and sixty fragments of poems selected from manuscript, either intended as additions to poems now in *Leaves of Grass* or composed as parts of poems never to be completed.

In their preparation of the Variorum Edition, the editors verified the 1890–91 text by collation of the texts of all of Whitman's editions, and examined all extant poetic manuscripts. They are able therefore to include in the footnotes of this edition those textual and manuscript variants which throw light upon the interpretation of particular passages. They have also implemented the poet's own statements of intent by printing in this edition, not only the "Backward Glance O'er Travel'd Roads" in the position to which the poet first assigned it, but for the first time all of the prefaces, including the 1856 letter to Emerson— all these in their original texts, and showing later variants. The Introduction provides a full account of the growth of *Leaves of Grass*, of the authorized poems, the excluded poems and passages, the uncollected poems and fragments, the unpublished poems, and the problems of text and manuscript attendant thereto.

Finally, this edition provides a selection of criticism. The editors have brought within the allowable space some thirty essays, selected both because they illustrate a remarkable range and because in themselves they possess excellence. For a history of Whitman's critical fortunes, see Harold Blodgett's essay, "The Critical Response." In addition the editors include, under the title "Whitman on His Art," the poet's own informal comment expressed in adjurations to himself on notebook pages, in letters to friends, in conversations, and in occasional newspaper pieces.

Unlike many poets, Whitman did not engage in formal literary analysis. In fact he was at pains to disavow the "literary," which he associated with the "genteel," and avoided shop talk. But actually he was profoundly engaged with a radical determination to express a new poetry which should be the vehicle of his overpowering vision; and his sense of aesthetic values, set forth so vividly in the 1855 preface, was always sensitive and operative. His manuscripts, of which an example appears in this edition, reveal how constantly he revised, how he tried to follow the severe standards he had proposed for himself—"no ornamental similes at all—not one: perfect transparent clearness sanity, and health. . . ." He was possessed by a vision, a state of mind and feeling that made the words possible, and it was out of the urgency of this vision and his desire to share it with the reader that there came the expressive power for his task. Aesthetics interested him only as the means to his purpose, and his purpose was to reveal the eligibility of his reader for the immortal and the good, not to make a poem for its own sake, although if he succeeded, the poem was worthy for its own sake. Elsewhere Whitman said (see "Starting from Paumanok," lines 131–33) that he shared three greatnesses— Love, Democracy, and Religion.

It is this visionary aspect of Whitman's poetry that survives all the diverse currents of interpretation that have flowed from more than a century of criticism. He himself emphasizes it, not only in the formal pronouncements but in the first anonymous review wherein he boasts that he does not satisfy the reader, but leaves him "the taste of the Paradisaic tree of the knowledge of good and evil, never to be erased again." We have no occasion to expatiate on the essays here printed, but it is notable that the intrinsic quality of Whitman most insisted upon in recent criticism is just this,—his visionary grasp of a world that, without the redemptive power which he celebrates, is in exceeding peril.

Our indebtedness to others is immense, and we cannot hope to give its full measure. With Charles E. Feinberg and our colleagues on the editorial board we share the aid and strength of a mutual enterprise. We have enjoyed, too, the fullest cooperation and interest of the directors of libraries and the collectors who have Whitman manuscripts and rare editions in their charge. Specific identification of sources is, in each instance, acknowledged in the text, but we particularly wish here to record our appreciation to the following—Library of Congress: Roy P. Basler, Director, Reference Department; Henry J. Dubester, Chief, General Reference and Bibliographical Division; David C. Mearns, Curator of Manuscripts; and C. Carroll Hollis, Specialist in American Cultural History. Duke University Library: Thomas M. Simkins, Curator of Rare Books. University of Virginia: Clifton Waller Barrett, donor of the American Literature Collection; Francis L. Berkeley, Jr., Executive Assistant to the President; and Anne Freudenberg, Acting Curator of Manuscripts. Yale University Library: Donald C. Gallup, Curator, Collection of American Literature. New York Public Library: the late John D. Gordan, Curator, Berg Collection; and Lewis Stark, Chief of the Reserve Division. The late T. Edward Hanley, Bradford, Pennsylvania, whose Whitman MSS are now in the collection of the University of Texas. Henry E. Huntington Library: Herbert C. Schulz, Curator of Manuscripts. Boston Public Library: Zoltan Haraszti, Keeper of Rare Books. Pierpont Morgan Library: Herbert Cahoon, Curator of Autograph MSS. Rutgers University Library: Donald F. Cameron, Director. Brown University Library: Roger E. Stoddard, Assistant Librarian. Houghton Library, Harvard University. Ohio Wesleyan University: Dr. John H. Lancaster, Librarian and Custodian of the William D. Bayley Collection; Ernest F. Amy, Professor Emeritus. University of California: Livezey Collection. Mills College, Oakland, California. Rollins College, Florida.

Particularly, we are sensible of the generous assistance of our own institutions and collaborative agencies in providing financial support for our enterprise, and we wish to express our gratitude: to the John Simon Guggenheim Memorial Foundation for a fellowship to implement the search for manuscripts; to Union College for a succession of grants to assist manuscript collation; to the American Philosophical Society for assistance in the work of collation of texts for the Variorum; to the University of Pennsylvania for annual grants of the Faculty Research Committee and for the assignment of research assistants during the progress of the entire *Leaves of Grass* editions; to the Rare Book Collection of the University of Pennsylvania for supplying us with first editions, duplicating services, and generous space allocations, and particularly to Dr. Neda M. Westlake, Director of the Rare Book Collection, for her continuous supervision of the research as a special project of the Rare Book Collection, and to Mrs. Susan Baldwin of her staff; to the staff of the Library of Union College, and particularly to the former Librarian, Helmer L. Webb, and the present Librarian, Edwin K. Tolan, for unstinted interest in providing materials and facilities for our project; to Arthur Golden, of City College, New York, for his generous cooperation in furnishing copies of his invaluable diplomatic transcript of Whitman's annotated "Blue Copy" of *Leaves of Grass* 1860.

The editors are fully aware that this listing is inadequate to the proper recognition of the support and encouragement they have received from a host of friends, colleagues, and lovers of poetry, both within and without the professional world of scholarship. It may be accounted as a tribute to America's great poet and as an instance of the largeness of spirit on which he himself relied.

Harold W. Blodgett
Sculley Bradley

The Text of
Leaves of Grass

1891–1892

Leaves of Grass

Including
SANDS AT SEVENTY... *1st Annex*,
GOOD-BYE MY FANCY... *2d Annex*,
A BACKWARD GLANCE O'ER TRAVEL'D ROADS,
and Portrait from Life.

COME, said my Soul,
Such verses for my Body let us write, (for we are one,)
That should I after death invisibly return,
Or, long, long hence, in other spheres,
There to some group of mates the chants resuming,
(Tallying Earth's soil, trees, winds, tumultuous waves,)
Ever with pleas'd smile I may keep on,
Ever and ever yet the verses owning—as, first, I here and now,
Signing for Soul and Body, set to them my name,

Walt Whitman

PHILADELPHIA
DAVID McKAY, PUBLISHER
23 SOUTH NINTH STREET
1891-'2

Soul] First printed in the Christmas number of the New
York *Daily Graphic*, Dec., 1874, then in the New York
Tribune, Feb. 19, 1876, this poem, signed by WW, became
the title-page epigraph of LG 1876, LG 1882 (Camden),
CPP 1888, and finally LG 1891-2 where it was restored after
having disappeared from the title-pages of LG 1881 and
1883–84. Numerous MSS (Barrett, Berg, BPL, Hunting-
ton) show elaborate revision. See CW,X,131–4 for earlier
versions, originally transcribed by W. S. Kennedy in *The
Conservator*, June, 1896.

Introduction

THE GROWTH OF "LEAVES OF GRASS"

In the Variorum Edition, which presents for the first time all the poems of *Leaves of Grass* in chronological order, a full analysis is made of the almost incessant revision, reordering, and augmentation that culminated in the final 1881 arrangement. It is pertinent here briefly to characterize and outline this process, which has often been described by mutually exclusive images—a cathedral constructed from a blueprint in the poet's mind, or a tree growing from year to year, its rings marking the successive editions. A better image is one the poet used in a postcard to his friend William Douglas O'Connor, March 5, 1889, upon sending him the 1888 one-volume *Complete Poems & Prose:* "I can hardly tell why, but feel very positively that if anything can justify my revolutionary attempts & utterances, it is such *ensemble*—like a great city to modern civilization & a whole combined clustering paradoxical identity a man, a woman . . . "

Actually the successive nine editions of the poet's lifetime grew out of his vivid sense of endless materials, a creative pressure welling from profound depths, and a boundless acceptance which expressed itself in an urgent inclusiveness rather than in the artful limits of deliberate design. In franker moments the poet recognized this. In a very late note, December 6, 1891, he speaks of "hackling" at *Leaves of Grass* for *thirty-six* years, of its "cumulous" character, even its "jaggedness." And more than once he testified to his intuitive approach. "I do not suppose," he said, "that I shall ever again have the *afflatus* I had in writing the first *Leaves of Grass*," and he spoke of his experiment as a radical utterance out of the abysms of the Soul. In such phrases Whitman was describing the workings of the creative mind, which plans and constructs indeed with the impassioned power of discovery.

The poet was receptive to its promptings. He had to wait upon the event, and in his case, the event was the whole life of his nation. So Whitman was surely justified in insisting upon identifying the growth of his *Leaves* with the growth of his country. He had new things to say, new approaches, shifts of insight and mood as he and his land developed: "as I have lived in fresh lands, inchoate, and in a revolutionary age, future-founding," he wrote in his 1876 Preface, "I have felt to identify the points of that age, these lands, in my recitatives . . . Within my time the United States have emerg'd from nebulous vagueness and suspense, to full orbic, (though varied) decision . . . Out of that stretch of time . . . my Poems too have found genesis."

Here, in outline summary, is the record: The twelve poems of LG 1855, in which the introductory poem, to be called "Song of Myself," is longer than the other eleven poems taken together, boldly eschew all distinction of title, and indeed the whole design seems to emphasize the singleness of the poet's song—variations upon one utterance. In the second edition, LG 1856, Whitman began to count his poems. He added twenty—among them some of his best—and in his exuberant letter to Emerson, really his 1856 Preface, he boasts that he will keep on until he has made a hundred and then several hundred, perhaps a thousand! He also fashioned titles, some absurdly long, some reduced to a syllable—"Clef Poem," or "Bunch Poem." It was an odd and yet arresting table of contents from a writer uncommitted to a pattern.

Within the next four years his now intense creative energy produced no less than 124 poems for his third edition, LG 1860, making 156 in all; and yet at the same time he was hopefully pondering, as a kind of "wander-teacher," a program of lectures corresponding with his *Leaves*, to reach his countrymen if his poems should not. LG 1860 was the first to display a group arrangement of sorts, emphasized by eccentric typography; and yet an examination of his manuscripts shows (*vide* Bowers) that probably as late as 1859 Whitman had had no decisive intention whatever of dividing his poems into groups. The compelling factor was his sudden focusing upon two special themes, and later a third: the celebration of comradeship in "Calamus," of procreation in "Children of Adam," and of the nation at war in *Drum-Taps*. Such new demands led the poet to observe (in the *Saturday Press*, January 7, 1860) that *Leaves of Grass* had not yet really been published at all—he was slowly trying his hand at the structure he had undertaken. And these three groups did possess a homogeneity so vital that through all succeeding editions they remained essentially undisturbed by the considerable shifting to which the poet subjected them—so considerable, indeed, that only thirty-eight of the seventy-one pieces in the 1865–1866 *Drum-Taps* and "Sequel to Drum-Taps" were held in place, thirty-three poems being eventually dispersed into no less than nine other groups. To return to the third edition, its remaining clusters—the remarkable "Chants Democratic," the numbered "Leaves of Grass," and the "Messenger Leaves"—demonstrated no survival value *as groups*, and so disappeared. The poet had no certain structural plan, and this uncertainty, deepening under the perturbation of a personal crisis, even led him, in three of the 1860 poems, to question whether he should go on.

But of course he was bound to go on, and plans multiplied. Late in 1860 his Boston publisher announced a separate volume, *Banner at Daybreak*, but it never appeared. In an MS draft of an unpublished preface originally dated May 31, 1861, the poet complained, "the paths to the house are made, but where is the house itself?" But when presently the poems of *Drum-Taps* began to form under the immediate stress of war, the poet grew in confidence. "I *must* be continually bringing out poems—now is the hey day," he wrote on November 17, 1863, to his publisher, Eldridge, and much of his creative concentration may be sensed from the annotations that crowd the pages of his third edition toward his next. Fortunately these annotations are extant in the LG 1860 "Blue Copy," now in the Lion Collection—the very volume, WW averred, (Traubel, III, 474) which James Harlan, secretary of the Interior, had surreptitiously examined before he dismissed the poet from his Washington clerkship. "Transfer to Drum-Taps?" the poet questions at the top of a page, or "Out—out altogether" he scrawls in the margin of others, and some annotations indicate that he was pondering still other volumes or groupings under such titles as "Leaves-Droppings" or "Pioneers."

The book *Drum-Taps* (1865), turning upon the pivotal issue of the Civil War, was very important to the poet both as document and· as art, and with its "Sequel" (1865–1866), he began the practice of developing supplements with their own pagination, to be bound up with the parent volume or issued separately. In August, 1866, he wrote to Abby Price of going to New York to bring out a new and much better edition of *Leaves of Grass*—"that unkillable work." This was to be the fourth edition of 1867, which he designated in the Bucke biography as beginning the order and classification eventually settled upon. Yet this order, more flexible than in LG 1860, is notably casual, and not so much an advance in thematic sequence as in variety of content. The supplements—now augmented by "Songs Before Parting"—were so variously combined with the major text that LG 1867 exists in four different forms. Of the various groupings, only "Calamus" and "Children of Adam" were "clusters" in Whitman's sense of that word: only these fifty-six poems, exclusive of the supplements, possessed an unmistakable consistency of theme. Seventy-six of the other poems were distributed among untitled groups, and the remaining twenty-six were arranged in a series of four "Leaves of Grass" groups and one group of "Thoughts," carried over intact from the "Thoughts" of 1860. No patent unity of theme distinguished the "Leaves of Grass" groups—the title being a mere convenience—and in later editions the poems comprising them were thoroughly scattered.

With all its supplements, LG 1867 included 236 poems, only fifty-seven short of the 293 which were to compose the final arrangement of 1881. And very soon—as early as May, 1869—Whitman began to hint of his final edition, and of turning to religious themes. These speculations occupied his thoughts in both the 1872 and 1876 Prefaces: *Leaves of Grass* he felt to be as complete as he could make it, and its "surplusage" might become a supplementary volume, the voice—as he wrote in 1872—of "a composite, electric, democratic personality," or—as he put it in 1876—"of those convictions which make the unseen Soul govern absolutely at last."

These aims, really explicit from the first, were purposefully stressed in later poems—superbly so in "Passage to India"—but the structural problem was not solved. Indeed it could not be. Instead there was the improvising of an arrangement for a body of work already largely complete. The 1871 *Leaves of Grass*, with only nine new poems, was formed into twenty-two groups, sixteen of them titled—some simply as "Leaves of Grass"—and the other six untitled. The 1871 pamphlet *Passage to India*, with only twenty-two of its seventy-four poems new, was formed into six titled groups and three untitled, the poet at once binding it in as a supplement in LG 1872.

Five years after the 1871 edition appeared LG 1876, identical except for a few intercalations. Its companion volume, *Two Rivulets*, was a medley of prose, fourteen new poems under the "Two Rivulets" title, four "Centennial Songs," seven poems under the title piece, "As a Strong Bird on Pinions Free," and the 1871 collection, *Passage to India*. Undoubtedly Whitman had made a practical solution of the problem of arranging a two-volume edition to signalize the centennial year, but his perplexity had been pressing. A notebook belonging to the mid-1870's addresses questions to himself: "Qu—whether to make a new Vol of these pieces including *Whispers of Heavenly Death?*—qu—whether to finish up *Leaves of Grass* in one Vol—*Drum-Taps* in another . . . —*Whispers* etc in another."

The questions ended in mid-air, but the poet now resolved to end his problem by a thorough reshuffling of all his poems into the final arrangement of 1881, a process in which several group titles (some very good, for Whitman had a gift for titles) disappear, their contents absorbed into the surviving groups. The cluster "Inscriptions," first faintly suggested in 1867, is an appropriate introduction, although certain announcement poems elsewhere are quite as inscriptive as these. Such groups as "Birds of Passage," "By the Roadside," "Autumn Rivulets," and "From Noon to Starry Night" do possess a casual consonance of theme, but attempts to demonstrate a rule of logical continuity in them are embarrassed by too many exceptions. On the other hand, two of the groups carrying over from *Passage to India*—"Sea-Drift" (formerly "Sea-Shore Memories") and "Whispers of Heavenly Death" are very closely knit, and so is the final group "Songs of Parting," sounding a farewell with poems that had appeared over a period of more than twenty years. The sense of departure had haunted Whitman's pages ever since "So Long!" had closed the 1860 edition. For the rest, there are the three stalwarts—"Children of Adam," "Calamus," and "Drum-Taps," together with the twenty-five major poems to which the poet gave the importance of standing by themselves. Perhaps it should be noted that in this whole process not only have groups constantly shifted, but also the poems within the groups, so that a given poem may have appeared in three or four different groups from 1860 to 1881. There was to be no more shifting, but there would be addition: the sixty-five poems of "Sands at Seventy," first separately published in *November Boughs* (1888), and the thirty-one poems of "Goodbye My Fancy," first separately published in 1891. Both "annexes" were to round out the 1891–1892 edition, the poet's sole authorized text.

This is the poet's structure—neither the "Leaves" in the order of their growth nor the cathedral of prefigured design. These figures were ideals which gave solace and strength to a task which had often to face a bleak reality of contingency and crisis. Certain comment, arguing from the 1881 arrangement, has attributed to Whitman a prescience which robs him of his true stature. It is just as erroneous to argue, as some critics have, that the poet's constant revisions, shiftings, and insertions betray indecisiveness or uncertainty. There is never any doubt of a purpose kept consciously in view, an aim never deviated from; nor is there doubt that Whitman intended and achieved structure. Still, it was a structure that grew as the poet grew, that was adapted to the necessities he met and molded by the pressures his own life felt—its materials altered, added to, subtracted from, transposed as time and need required. And so it was alive. The construction of *Leaves of Grass* is best to be regarded, not as a hierarchic system of themes, but as resourceful editing by a man who was obliged to be his own publisher for most of his life, who serenely confronted a hostile literary market, who enjoyed little benefit of professional advice, and who nevertheless essentially achieved what he had set out to do. It took resolution—the resolution of the poet who told himself, "Now voyager sail thou forth to seek and find."

THE POEMS OF THE CANON

Yet in one's absorption with the tortuous process by which the poet arrived at his final structure—the preferred and authorized text of 1891–1892 —one should not fail to acknowledge the impressive and, on the whole, triumphal advance of the poet's genius in its hard-won path.

To begin in 1855 with "Song of Myself," untitled and in no signal way distinguished from its accompanying eleven poems, was directly to assert without skirmish or equivocation the basic theme of this poet's creative intent: to improve and transform life (the poet as maker and reformer), to discern and set forth its miraculousness (the poet as celebrator), and to sing the transcendence of human love, envisioned as divine (the poet as lover). The companion poems of the first edition were—as in a sense were also the future poems of *Leaves of Grass*—an extension of the prime purpose, celebration of the individual, of the nation, and of spiritual possibility. So, for example, we have (employing the final titles) "A Song for Occupations," the poem of daily work which in later editions was to undergo severe revision; "To Think of Time," also to be much revised but even now strongly anticipating "Crossing Brooklyn Ferry" in its poignant concern with time and death; "The Sleepers," powerfully original in imaginative grasp—a twentieth century poem in its penetration into subconscious states; "I Sing the Body Electric," an announcement poem, really, for what was to be one of the great groups of the third edition; "Faces," of audacious imagery, limning both the victorious and the broken; "Song of the Answerer," to be fused later with a kindred poem largely derived from the 1855 Preface; and "There was a Child Went Forth," simple and profound in its

Lockean grasp of the relation of experience to knowledge.

His ambition undaunted by massive indifference toward his first edition, the poet prefaced his second by the brash exuberance of his "Dear Master" letter to Emerson—a kind of *Democratic Vistas* in embryo, calling for identity, for national character, and individuality. He now had twenty new poems to strengthen his poetic evangelism, and remarkable poems some of them were, including the strange "Poem of the Propositions of Nakedness" (later "Respondez!"), which he was to exclude, retaining two passages as mementos of a passionate deviation into irony. Four of the poems derive much of their being from the poetic storehouse of the 1855 Preface—notably the somewhat confused "Poem of Many in One" ("By Blue Ontario's Shore"), which elaborates the thesis of the American Bard for America, an outburst to be greatly modified in later editions; and "Poem of the Last Explanations of Prudence" ("Song of Prudence"), an Emersonian meditation on value.

Other salient—and successful—compositions are "Poem of Salutation" ("Salut au Monde!"), a vigorously expressive recognition of the peoples of the earth, their cultures and religions; the assuring and intimate "To You"; the buoyant "Poem of the Road" ("Song of the Open Road"), the most famous of the invitation poems; and "Broad-Axe Poem" ("Song of the Broad-Axe"), with its flawless opening lines and its evocation of the shapes of America, among which the poet at first included himself. Two of the bold new poems, "A Woman Waits for Me" and "Spontaneous Me," were to find their fitting place in the "Enfans d'Adam" of the third edition. But the most beautiful poem of the second edition was "Sun-Down Poem" ("Crossing Brooklyn Ferry"), with its descriptions of the "glories strung like beads on my smallest sights and hearings," and its vision, penetrating beyond time and appearance to an eternal and changeless reality.

The thirty-two poems of the first two editions were a prelude to an extraordinary burst of creative energy in the next three years. Indeed by June, 1857 (the date is surmised by Dr. Bucke), WW made a cryptic reference to "the three hundred and sixty-five" as the goal he had set himself for the "Great Construction of the New Bible" (*N and F*, p. 57). Whether the figure refers to poems or days, we do not know, but in a letter of the following July 20 he speaks of wanting to bring out a third edition, for which he already has a hundred poems. We know, too, from manuscript evidence that even before this date he was working on poems that were to appear in *LG* 1860. His failure to publish his third edition in 1857 may be attributed to a number of reasons —perhaps his absorption in the editorship of the *Brooklyn Times*, perhaps the difficulty of finding a publisher in a year of business depression, perhaps his own financial straits. At any rate it seems fortunate, in retrospect, that Thayer and Eldridge were not to make the enthusiastic offer that eventuated in the third edition until February 10, 1860, for early in 1859 the poet experienced another access of poetic energy whose source seems to be a profound need that changed the current of his important opening poem, "Proto-Leaf" ("Starting from Paumanok") and produced two great new clusters—"Calamus" and "Enfans d'Adam." With the encouragement of publishers who believed in him and with 124 poems added to the existing 32, he was now for the first time to arrange his poems into a structural pattern which should emphasize the basic themes—as he announced them in "Proto-Leaf"—of "the greatness of Love and Democracy—and the greatness of Religion."

"Proto-Leaf" is not only an announcement of themes, but a moving declaration that the poet "will write the evangel-poem of comrades and of love"; and this he does in the forty-five new poems of the "Calamus" cluster which in their sensibility and candor are art of a high order, superior in delicacy to the more literal-seeming "Enfans d'Adam," which WW was to defend in his famous talk with Emerson on Boston Common and also in his prose piece, "A Memorandum at a Venture." This group of fifteen poems, twelve of which were new, was introduced by the brilliant "To the Garden the World," evoking the figure of Adam, who with conscious art appears again in the final poem of the cluster.

The other clusters were less successful, and so did not survive. The twenty-one "Chants Democratic," advertising themselves in subtitle as "Native American," displayed a certain confident strength, derived in part from six poems of the earlier editions, and also one interesting failure, "Apostroph," a curious exercise in ecstatic exclamation. These poems were to be widely dispersed, as were those of the group of twenty-four simply titled "Leaves of Grass," which opened with a remarkable confession later to be called "As I Ebb'd with the Ocean of Life." The poet, addressing the ocean as father and rejecting "all the blab whose echoes recoil upon me," avows in humility the terrible burden of trying to penetrate the meaning of existence. "O I perceive I have not understood anything—not a single object—and that no man ever can." One more cluster, "Messenger Leaves," does have a single theme to hold its fifteen poems together, in the sense that they are indeed all messages, beginning with the moving "To You" of the second edition, but their sequence was not to be maintained—the poet assuming in later editions, perhaps, that the whole of *Leaves of Grass* is a message, properly considered.

In comparative estimates, few would question that the finest single achievement of the third edition is "Out of the Cradle," first published as "A Child's Reminiscence" in the New York *Saturday Press*, December 24, 1859, and in LG 1860 as "A Word Out of the Sea." Its variants are worth special study, for the poet worked long on this poem, which has been characterized by D. H. Lawrence as "the perfect utterance of a concentrated, spontaneous soul." Whether or not the poet here sublimated a personal grief over the loss of a lover, it is certain that he revealed his own poetic birth. "My own songs awakened from that hour."

The 1860 edition closed, strangely for a poet scarcely turned forty, with a note of leave-taking: the seemingly casual "So Long!" which announces what shall come after him and ends with an exalted farewell: "Remember my words

—I love you—I depart from materials, / I am as one disembodied, triumphant, dead." Altogether, as Roy Harvey Pearce has declared in his facsimile edition, LG 1860 is a great book—he believes the poet's greatest. But Whitman's greatness was not yet expended.

He was to experience a great new source of poetic inspiration—the Civil War—of which the 1865 *Drum-Taps* and its 1865–1866 "Sequel" were the consequence. Despite the circumstance that a number of these seventy-one poems were probably composed before the actual conflict, and that many of them were later dispersed into other groups, they derive their strength and centrality from the poet's total commitment to the tremendous crisis of his beloved democracy. He wrote them, as he put it, "on the field, in the hospitals, as I worked with the soldier boys . . . ," and later he averred, "Without those three or four years and the experiences they gave, *Leaves of Grass* would not now be existing." We cannot accept this statement in view of such achievements as "Song of Myself," "Crossing Brooklyn Ferry," and "Out of the Cradle Endlessly Rocking," but we see what the poet meant when we consider his equally remarkable statement in a letter on *Drum-Taps* to William Douglas O'Connor, January 6, 1865: "It is in my opinion superior to Leaves of Grass—certainly more perfect as a work of art . . ." He goes on to stress such qualities as proportion, control, and the removal of all verbal superfluity.

Drum-Taps, then, was a highly conscious achievement in craft. Working with great materials on a task that he said had haunted him—"the pending action of this *Time & Land we swim in*"—Whitman found artistic resources in himself which were quite unrecognized in the poetic practices of the day, and, incidentally, unperceived by two young reviewers of *Drum-Taps*, William Dean Howells and Henry James, both of whom complained of the poet's lack of art. These resources manifested themselves in an ability at stark depiction of war scenes, whose realism in such poems as "A Sight in Camp . . ." or "The Wound-Dresser" look forward to the specificity of a Crane or a Hemingway; and in sharply etched vignettes such as "Cavalry Crossing a Ford" or "An Army Corps on the March," which reveal an artist's fascination with the sight and show of war. But even more than descriptive power or objective reporting, the poems evince another quality which informs their aesthetic sensibility— the compassion and love which, lifted above the desperation of some of the "Calamus" poems, animates the whole enterprise with a sympathetic imaginativeness whose richest expression is the great threnody, "When Lilacs Last in the Dooryard Bloom'd,—"the most sweet and sonorous nocturne," exclaimed Swinburne, "ever chanted in the church of the world." Some critics consider this to be Whitman's greatest poem; some disagree, feeling a sense of artifice in its deployment of symbols; but certainly it may stand as the high point of the poet's personal engagement with war and with the issues of his nation, commemorating not alone the death of a great hero but the heroic and the truly great in humanity.

But if the Lincoln elegy is the high point, what is to be said of WW's poetic performance thereafter—the new verses of the six editions of LG still to come, as well as certain poems in separate publication? It has become almost a cliché of one school of Whitman criticism to stress not only a falling-off of poetic energy (which was to be expected), but a regrettable change of intent, the complaint being that in later years Whitman the visionary was overtaken by Whitman the prophet—that the poet was conquered by the propagandist. There is directness in this charge, and some evidence to support it, but one should heed the poet's own insistence that he wanted a full, not a partial judgment upon his work—that he was not to be known as a piece of something but as a totality (Traubel, I, 272). When we consider Whitman's totality, we are persuaded of its genuineness and of its steady adherence to a crowning purpose, painstakingly detailed in "A Backward Glance . . .": to "formulate a poem whose every thought or fact should directly or indirectly be or connive at an implicit belief in the wisdom, health, mystery, beauty of every process, every concrete object, every human or other existence, not only consider'd from the point of view of all, but of each."

Let us briefly summarize the record from this point. After the *Drum-Taps* poems, and exclusive of the two annexes, "Sands at Seventy" and "Good-bye My Fancy," Whitman was to publish nearly ninety poems. It must be said that, taken together, they give an impression of appetite for life, of unwaning poetic interest, and a high degree of distinctive performance despite the hazards and disabilities of the oncoming years. More than a fourth of them are short lyrics of less than eight or ten lines, some of them designed for the introductory "Inscriptions" cluster; a number, such as "Outlines for a Tomb" or "O Star of France" are poems of occasion; several, of which the greatest is "The Return of the Heroes" (originally "A Carol of Harvest, for 1867"), deal with the still harrowing memory of the war and the crucial problems for democratic society left in its wake. In fact, the problems as well as the potentialities of democracy were to furnish the substance of three major poems which WW composed in response to public invitation, poems which furnished, too, a certain temptation for the poet to act as America's official voice. These were "Song of the Exposition" (American Institute, New York, 1871), "Thou Mother with Thy Equal Brood" (Dartmouth College, 1872), and "Song of the Universal" (Tufts College, 1874). Of these the last is the best, if only that in expressing his theme— the reaffirmation of his idealism—the poet uses a pattern that is direct, terse, almost epigrammatic. In the first, and to a lesser extent in the second of these public poems, the poet is occasionally betrayed into a Polonius-like sententiousness, so earnest a spokesman for America that he sounds at times more like her agent than her lover. Yet even here the bold, original image may be found. Who else could speak of installing the Muse among the kitchenware?

The most distinguished poem of the later period is "Passage to India," first separately published in 1871, and then incorporated into LG 1872 and TR 1876. Writing with characteristic exultation in the achievement of three great advances in communication—the opening of the Suez Canal, the completion of the continental railway system in his own country, and the laying of the Atlantic and Pacific cables—the poet moves swiftly to his great dream of international brotherhood, and so to his "passage to more than India," the venturing of the soul into the seas of God. As with his "Proud Music of the Storm," "The Mystic Trumpeter," "Prayer of Columbus," and "Song of the Redwood Tree," the poet in "Passage to India" finds and skillfully employs images of strength, love, and endurance which lift his expression into poetry beautifully free from the encumbrance of rhetoric.

The impressive poems of Whitman's later years illustrate, then, the turn of direction and emphasis which he himself noted in both his 1872 and 1876 Prefaces—the singing of the "unseen Soul" and "Spiritual Law." These poems were destined never to fill the "further, equally needed Volume" the poet had projected, but nevertheless they found their proper place in the parent— and only—*Leaves of Grass*. Included among them were not only the longer poems of major effort but such exquisite brief lyrics as "Darest Thou Now O Soul," "Whispers of Heavenly Death," "On the Beach at Night," and "The Last Invocation."

Finally, let us remind ourselves that this poet never—even toward the end, when he was bedridden and helpless—lost his power over his own idiom. It informs his expression to the last—in, for example, such poems of the annexes as "A Prairie Sunset," "Old Salt Kossabone," "Twilight," and "Fancies at Navesink." "Garrulous to the very last," he cheerfully wrote. Garrulous, yes, but also possessed to the very last with his own gift and self.

POEMS AND PASSAGES EXCLUDED FROM "LEAVES OF GRASS"

An important category of Whitman's complete poems in the present edition is represented in two collections: "Poems Excluded from *Leaves of Grass*" and "Passages Excluded from *Leaves of Grass* Poems." (See these headings in Table of Contents for locations.) As in the case of those *Leaves of Grass* poems which Whitman finally retained, these texts have also been established in this edition by a new collation of all LG volumes authorized by Whitman from 1855 to 1891–1892, including the concurrent "Supplements" and "Clusters" from *Drum Taps* (1865) to *Good-Bye My Fancy* (1891). This new collation of texts appears in *Leaves of Grass: A Variorum Edition*, a work in preparation by the present editors in this edition of *Collected Writings of Walt Whitman*.

An earlier variorum prepared by Oscar Lovell Triggs appeared as an appendix to *Leaves of Grass* in *Complete Writings of Walt Whitman* (New York, 1902). Emory Holloway, in his familiar *Leaves of Grass*, Inclusive Edition (1924), added four poems to the twenty-five "Rejected Poems" in the Triggs Appendix, and reprinted the same twenty-nine in the appendix to his "Nonesuch Press Edition" of the *Leaves* (*ca.* 1938). The present editors have preferred to refer to these as "Excluded Poems" and we have been able to add sixteen, bringing the total to forty-five, while making alterations and amplifications in the texts as presented by Triggs. From the close study of these poems one gets the impression that they have been unduly neglected and that they will gain approval and importance by their association, in the present edition, with the groups of poems not before collected or surviving in manuscript unpublished. They deserve comparison with the canon poems of LG, from which they were excluded for reasons not always unfavorable to their merits.

The complete collation of LG texts and supplements also identified the large number of lines, fragments, and passages of larger scope which Whitman excluded from LG poems in the process of revision, not primarily because he disapproved of them as creative work. Triggs also showed many such passages in his variorum, remote from and subordinated to the *Leaves of Grass* poems. The present editors were impressed by the genuine insight and poetic merit, the poem-like unity and independence, of many of the excluded passages; of these we chose, frankly, those that pleased us most, twenty-eight in number, to stand as a separate group in association with the other *Leaves of Grass* texts. The student will find the entire body of excluded lines, passages, and poems in the variorum to be published in this edition. We have had to supply titles for all these passages, of course, and for eight of the forty-five excluded poems.

We have called these "excluded," instead of continuing the familiar term, "rejected," because we find the latter to be somewhat pejorative, and unjustified in view of the value of many of these pieces as creations, revelations, doctrines, or precepts, or as stages in the growth of the poet or his work. Each of these passages has the merit that it was once judged by the poet worthy to be included in *Leaves of Grass*, where a number remained for a decade or two. They are integral to *Leaves of Grass* considered as a construct of Whitman's mind through a period of years, and they are enormously valuable either to the scholar or to the general reader interested in the growth of Whitman's art, mind, methods of composition, and critical interpretation of life. We have attempted to facilitate this critical approach by subtending to each poem or passage the dates of first and last appearance in an LG edition; also, our first footnote gives the provenance and life history of the passage and whatever commentary may seem to be useful.

A number of the excluded poems, particularly those originating in the 1860 *Leaves*, appeared only in one edition, like that attractive image, "In the New Garden," to which reference will be made below. More poems of early origin —such as "Think of the Soul," "Respondez!", and "Thought"—continued to reappear for as long as twenty years without fundamental alterations. Like previous editors, we chose to show each of these in the text of its last appearance, unless special circumstances, explained by a note, required another choice. Since the exclusions range in date from 1860 to 1891, the last texts of these poems are not consistent in formal conventions, because Whitman was experimenting during this period with changes of style involving the use of asterisks, points, dashes, brackets, foreign words, neologisms and classical derivatives, the elision of the "e" before "d" in past-tense constructions, and the like. We have not attempted regularization, preferring these poems to appear in their natural diversity, each representing the characteristics of the edition from which it was extracted. The same diversity will appear, of course, in the formal style of the passages excluded from poems.

Really complex questions developed in choosing the appropriate text to be honored when a poem, during the course of its life, had been fragmented by the poet's borrowing from it lines used in later poems; or when it had been changed by the exclusion of some secondary theme, or had been divided into two or more poems, of which one or more were later excluded; or when, as happened, two early poems had been combined to form a third, which then might have been excluded but in fact was actually retained in the canon. All of these changes occurred, and others also, which, however defensible on creative grounds, are calculated to dismay the editor who must choose one text, or one stage of the text, for publication. The present editors frequently made a choice at variance with that of Triggs, who generally—but not consistently—favored the latest text that appeared, and who usually excluded from his text of a "rejected" poem all those passages that had appeared in poems in the final 1881 *Leaves*. We have attempted to treat each poem as a separate problem, and since this edition is meant to serve the reader primarily—the scholar will also use the Variorum Edition—we chose in each case the text that gives the completest idea of the original poem, with an accompanying note which in most cases will enable the attentive student to reconstruct the changes that occurred in its text.

The comparison of texts of these excluded poems made clear that, as in the case of the *Leaves of Grass* poems in general, Whitman worked prodigiously at their improvement in manuscript and in various forms of trial run before he included them in the *Leaves*. His "exclusion" of the poem from the *Leaves* did not necessarily indicate its rejection for creative shortcomings. Like other poems similarly revised, some of these were shifted from "cluster" to "cluster," from 1856 to 1881, in the poet's persistent effort to secure unity and order among the topics of his great book. As the footnotes will show, other reasons for excluding poems and passages were certain changes in his own ideas or convictions, or in his attitude toward the propriety or usefulness of emphasizing them; changes in the temper of the times because of the changing conditions of a war-torn country; and changes that occurred about 1871 in the meanings to be emphasized in his book as a whole. In short, the idea that the excluded poems and passages were necessarily of inferior creative value to those retained should not be lightly accepted. Whitman continued to borrow lines from excluded poems, as from early manuscripts that he had frugally hoarded, long after he had set them aside.

As was said, the poet's borrowing of lines from a previous poem produced one of the difficult textual problems. For example, "Debris," a luxuriant poem of sixty lines, appears only in LG 1860. By 1872 nearly half its lines had been distributed among seven new poems, of which six survived in the final collection of *Leaves of Grass* (1881). A seventh LG poem, "Stronger Lessons," a couplet borrowed from "Debris," appeared in *November Boughs* (1888) and was transferred to the "First Annex" of the 1891–2 edition. In accord, presumably, with his general practice, Triggs published only what he regarded as the undistributed remnant of "Debris"—thirty-five lines (by our count it would be only thirty-one). What has come down to readers in Triggs's edition is neither "Debris" nor any poem that Whitman authorized. The present edition gives the complete 1860 text of sixty lines, with a note showing the distribution of lines to other poems. The excluded poem, "States," appeared only in the 1860 edition, but the reader acquainted with *Leaves of Grass* will recognize the last three stanzas with particular pleasure. Whitman borrowed these stanzas, adding a refrain to each of the first two in LG 1867 and thereby created his most admired "Calamus" poem, "For you, O Democracy." Of the original "States," Triggs published only the first thirty-five lines, omitting the seven-line conclusion which the poet had transposed. But Whitman had borrowed even earlier, in 1865, the nineteen lines from "States" that form the body of the memorable Civil War poem, "Over the Carnage Rose Prophetic a Voice," which also remained in the final LG selection. Triggs must have forgotten this—he mentions the transposition in his variorum—but had he remembered it, the application of his editorial principle would have reduced the poem to a disorderly remnant of sixteen lines. The present text represents the original forty-two lines of the 1860 text, showing "States" as a poem of independent merits.

Certain poems, which in the earlier versions were a fusion or contrast of two or more themes, were revised by the cancellation of a secondary theme, thereby emphasizing the principal motif. "Great Are the Myths" (1855) which in 1860 numbered seventy-one lines, was reduced, in LG 1867, to forty-nine lines by the cancellation of three sections. This eliminated the secondary theme, which dealt with the accumulation of belief in human values, tested by the duration of historical time. In the shortened version this poem, important in conception but weak in its execution, was not excluded until the definitive selection of 1881. The present text is the uncut version of 1860, seventy-one lines, in which the interest of a paradox is contributed by the minor theme. By following the instruction of the footnote, the reader may compare the two versions. Triggs, with consistency, gave the abbreviated version of forty-nine lines, apparently unaware that four of these lines were actually retained in 1881, as the "new" poem, "Youth, Day, Old Age, and Night."

Similarly, "Says" contained two themes each appearing antiphonally in a series of eight stanzas. In his mood of postwar reconciliation the poet cancelled, in LG 1867, the four stanzas condemning the system of slavery and its intellectual hypocrisies, leaving only the theme of democratic individualism. Although the poem was now deprived of any of its interesting tension, it was not excluded until the 1881 edition. Since none of the poem appeared in the final selection, Triggs was consistent in publishing the entire 1860 text, in spite of the exclusions of 1867. The present edition of the same text shows, in the note. the verbal changes that occurred in the title and in the abbreviated text.

Unlike "Says," several of the poems ultimately excluded were improved by pruning and fundamental revision. Two noteworthy examples are "Poem of Remembrances for a Girl or a Boy of These States" (1856), and "Apostroph" (1860); each yielded in revision a much better short poem which was excluded in 1881, although each possessed sufficient independence and interest to justify its retention. In 1867 the poet rejected the first twenty-one lines of "Poem of Remembrances . . ." and retained the last twenty-three, with some revision, as "Think of the Soul." In the present edition, the rejected first half of the original poem is shown in its latest text (1860) and "Think of the Soul" follows in its latest text (1867), so that both the poem as a whole and the derivative poem are available to the reader. A somewhat different editorial problem was that of "Apostroph," an unwieldy and declamatory poem of the 1860 edition. Its aforementioned derivative, the impressive "O Sun of Real Peace," was based primarily on the last nineteen lines of the original. The two versions are so different in effect, however, that it seemed better to the present editors, as to their predecessors, to reproduce the entire last text of both the parent and the derived poem, in succession.

Triggs's extreme application of his rule, that lines surviving in poems of the final *LG* 1881 could not be shown in the text of the related excluded poems, caused at least two good poems to disappear completely from the *Leaves of Grass* collections. Their lines were indeed consumed by four poems of the 1881 canon, a fact not surprising, considering that these despoiled ancestors comprised collectively only ten lines to begin with. The two poems are "Thoughts —2" and "Thoughts—4" (see notes to these poems). For the first time in any collection we show them as they originally appeared in the 1860 Cluster, "Thoughts," which included seven valuable small poems. Numbers "2" and "4" each had an independent vitality, and it seems appropriate to restore them. A similar reward of the new collation was the rediscovery, in *LG* 1867, of the first version of "When I Read the Book" (*q.v.* in "Excluded Poems"). This is, of course, familiar as the title of the ninth of the poems among the initial "Inscriptions" section of the *Leaves;* and Triggs's principle of choice would have barred it from his collection. In the original form, however, the single last line, at once epigrammatic and profound, raises the poem to the top level of Whitman's dramatic intensity. In transferring it to the "Inscriptions" in 1871, he replaced this line with three lines which by comparison are only honest, prosaic exposition.

In retrospect the editors would add a comment, perhaps out of context, in praise of the pioneer textual work that Oscar Lovell Triggs accomplished in analyzing the *Leaves of Grass* editions. With respect to the lacunae in his "rejected poems" collection, it may be presumed that he defined his purpose as the simple collection of all lines and fragments, from any *LG* edition, which were not represented in the final *LG* selection. The present editors have a different purpose: the faithful reproduction of the most complete and satisfactory text, for the general reader, of every poem excluded from *LG* or its supplements.

The previous discussion of textual problems made reference to the literary values that a number of these poems possess. That so many of them are impressive is the more noteworthy when one considers that the present collection is defined as complete, without discrimination on the ground of merit. However, the "Passages excluded from *Leaves of Grass* Poems" include only the best of those which combine a certain independence and formal unity with poetic values. Unlike the excluded poems, the excluded passages did not impose on the editors any necessity for making a complete collection. The Variorum in its completeness will show that many worthy passages still remained in discard. The jewel of them all, perhaps, was left unused in the remnant of "Debris," lines 35–43 (*q.v.*) which may be recalled by its central line, "I will take an egg out of the robin's nest in the orchard." This is the kind of nature lyric—simple, rapt, and luminous—that the young Sandburg learned, perhaps from Whitman, to make out of common things and the common speech of the people.

Numerous trial manuscripts of passages finally dropped from poems of *Leaves of Grass* survived at the poet's death, some of them to be transcribed in Bucke's familiar *Notes and Fragments* before appearing again in Triggs's variorum. Of these, the "Black Lucifer" poem proved at once the most baffling and the most meritorious. In the present edition it appears with the first-line title, "Now Lucifer Was Not Dead," in a text resulting from the collation of the successive editions of "The Sleepers," one of Whitman's major poems, in which the Lucifer canto remained from 1855 until 1876. It is evidently an invective parable against slavery, predicting the Negro's inevitable revenge, and its concluding metaphor (*q.v.*), although terrifying even a century later, is one of Whitman's greatest. Conjecturally, it was canceled from "The Sleepers" because the revisions of that poem had made it an embodiment of human love in which revenge had no place, and because of Whitman's sense of reconciliation after the war, which influenced his revision of several other poems. Another excluded canto of "The Sleepers," "O Hot-Cheek'd and Blushing" (as named by its first line) is also one of Whitman's most creative passages, in which, again, symbol, emotion, and subject are in effective balance. It contains perhaps the most subtle sexual imagery of all Whitman's poems (see note), but by 1876 it also was inappropriate in the context of the parent poem and out of harmony with Whitman's objective treatment of sexual themes in this late period. In the same spirit, much earlier, was one of his most memorable passages, the three-stanza introduction for "You Felons on Trial in Courts," when it first appeared in 1860. In this edition, under its first-line title, "O Bitter Sprig," this indeed seems to be a "confession sprig," as the poet said, and he may have been influenced to exclude it in the next edition because of his hard-won caution suggesting greater objectivity, or less intimacy, in treating sexual themes. In 1859, in the manuscript of "Once I Passed Through a Populous City," he had changed the lover from a man to a woman; and in the 1860 edition, three good poems open to the same sort of criticism were not again published. They appear in the present collection: See "Who Is Now Reading This," "I Thought that Knowledge Alone Would Suffice," and "Hours Continuing Long." One can think of no good reason, however, for Whitman's excluding, after 1860, the excellent little poem, "In the New Garden," which provides a compatible twin for another 1860 poem, "As Adam Early in the Morning," that finally came to rest as the last of the "Children of Adam" cluster. The "new garden" contained the "new Adam," seeking "this moment, . . . the woman of the future," in contrast with the first Adam of the other poem. Among other small poems in this collection which show interesting evidence of Whitman's craftsmanship, "To You" (see note) is particularly recommended because the poet rescued it from mawkishness by inserting a single line; and also "To the Reader at Parting," which Whitman rehabilitated almost by sleight-of-hand, then excluded after all.

The editors have no desire to gild the lilies which the reader might otherwise gather unblemished, but since they have made a value choice among many interesting excluded passages, it is probable that certain values should be identified. A good many of these passages seem to be felicitous expressions of some prevalent theme or quality in *Leaves of Grass*. A number of them illustrate Whitman's practical idealism, or his almost metaphysical concept of reality. One such theme is the function of the poet as bard or prophet; however, in "Facts Showered Over with Light" he includes, with the poet, the "literat," the writer in general, the man of ideas and expressive power. "As he emits himself facts are showered over with light, . . . Each precise object," whether common or refined, "gleams with unmatched beauty." There is a serenely controlled power in this expression of a familiar credo dropped by the wayside. Metaphysical indeed, besides manifesting beauty and power, is Whitman's quite unusually explicit expression of faith in personal survival beyond death (cf. "A Thought of the Clef of Eternity"). Metaphysical to the point of being Emersonian is the quatrain (cf. "You Dumb, Beautiful Ministers"), which was deleted from "Crossing Brooklyn Ferry," possibly because it too explicitly defined a motif in the poem more subtly expressed in another passage. Still, even in the excluded passage, the identification of spiritual with material realities is by no means superficial.

A significant number of worthy passages were canceled from the poems apparently because the luxuriance of Whitman's perception had defied the scope of the book to contain, even in the form of inventories, all the good things he had found in the abundance of daily life. Hence the tally of "Old Forever New Things," excluded from "A Song for Occupations," reproduces by the free association of carefully selected common things the immediate sense of the physical world of the workman of New York a century ago. "What Do You Hear, Walt Whitman?" excluded from "Salut an Monde," is a diapason of the sounds of gusto and delight with which mankind makes its "salute to the world" of nature and primitive activity. Almost enough musical themes for a symphony are suggested in this passage alone. These are the sounds that man knew—and made—from the beginning of his existence. Also primordial are the questions that this prodigal poet dropped by the wayside in "The Teeming Mother of Mothers" (from "I Sing the Body Electric")—simple questions which suddenly subsume all the individual responsibilities for the continuity of being.

Other passages are small poems in which suddenly we find some aspect of our protean poet himself—superficially comic or deeply moved, as the case may be. Comic certainly, when we realize that "His Shape Arises" (from "Song of the Broad-Axe"), which begins as an impressive description of the heroic shape of the "New Man," gradually takes on the unmistakable aspect of the young poet's picture of himself; he may have suppressed it for that reason. However, in "Readers to Come," our title for the excluded stanzas from "Poets to Come," one suddenly feels the pathos of Whitman's situation—a genuine poet, under the compulsion of a mission and a message, who found apparently none to hear, unless they lay still asleep behind the locked doors of tomorrow. "Give Me the Clue" may suggest a personal dimension involving the poet with the bereaved mockingbird, mourning for the loss of a "beloved" mate in "Out of the Cradle Endlessly Rocking," from which this stanza was excluded—but why?

These and many more values found by the editors in the poems and passages excluded from *Leaves of Grass*, resulted in the determination to edit them in depth, and to give them a place closely associated with the canon poems of *Leaves of Grass* in this comprehensive edition of the poems that Whitman created after the beginning of the *Leaves*.

THE UNCOLLECTED POEMS

Among the poet's many jottings for titles were "Leaves Supervened" or "Plus-Leaves,"—i.e., leaves additional or leaves to be added. He wrote with such abundance that he knew selection to be an unceasing problem, as it is indeed that of any artist, but with him a particularly pressing one, for he had a gradually developing schema within which to direct his essential purpose—to celebrate the individual (himself as symbol), the nation, and his intuition of final things. To conform to this purpose, he had worked out through the years, as we have seen, a structure which was essentially complete by 1881. To this he adhered faithfully, but he had much left over—much that was good as well as some that was negligible, and—practically speaking—he could not bring himself to throw anything away even if he could find no place for it. It is a great mistake to think of Whitman as an uncritical genius whose prodigality led him into wastefulness. So it is that we find poems and fragments outside the canon, both in unpublished and in published MSS. Of the sixty-five "Uncollected Poems" presented here, forty-three have been printed—thirty-six in books, seven in periodicals.

A few of these poems—notably "Pictures"—may be regarded as preliminary sketches which in both subject and technique prefigure the accomplishment manifest in *Leaves of Grass*. Others are indeed "additional"—not workings of themes later amplified in *Leaves of Grass*, but subjects or promptings which the poet decided not to include in his canon. Such a poem, for example, is "The Two Vaults," suggested by the scene in Pfaff's underground Broadway restaurant, where the poet, as in more than one "Leaves of Grass" poem, is caught by the doubt of reality. A few of the poems have such distinction that one imagines the poet must have been reluctant to reject them. Consider, for instance, the powerful scorn of "Scantlings," the poignance of the lyric, "Of Your Soul," the exultant dedication of "To an Exclusive." Yet the poet knew that the same ideas, the same fervor, were already present in the *Leaves* of his final choice.

The "Uncollected Poems" range in time from compositions that antedate the first edition to the early 1880's, and their range of interest and topic is roughly that of *Leaves of Grass* itself—from the "celebrations" of 1855–1860 to the absorption in the great war, to the themes of union and nationalism thereafter, and near the end to the delicate grace of "Wood Odors." The manuscripts exist in many collections and in many forms, but notably in the poet's invaluable notebooks and the scattered leaves that Dr. Bucke faithfully gathered in *Notes and Fragments*.

Twenty-two of the sixty-five "Uncollected Poems" are here published for the first time, from eight separate manuscript collections, ranging from the banal "A Soul Duet," which in all probability dates from the 1840's, to the appealing "Champagne in Ice," which if not poetry, is a human document of interest penned cheerfully in the extremities of age. Several deal with the war days whose immediacy never failed in the poet's mind; all of them relate to his basic themes which he tried to summarize in one of them, "Last Words." In the poet's judgment they were not momentous enough or artful enough to be honored by inclusion in *Leaves of Grass*, but all—as do the other uncollected poems—testify to a persistent exertion of idiom and interest.

THE UNCOLLECTED MANUSCRIPT FRAGMENTS

The poetic fragments encountered by the forager into Whitman manuscripts are of two sorts according to the status given them by the poet. On the one hand are the passages definitely related to the poems of the LG canon as alternative or additional readings; on the other are the passages related to compositions that would have become poems in *Leaves of Grass* if the poet's power had fulfilled his intention. The poet's work was incessant, and such lines as these were his daily exercise. The fragments related to the LG poems are of course to be collated in the variorum edition, and they are also drawn upon in the annotations of this edition as they may serve to illustrate a point or elucidate the text. The other fragments—"outside" the *Leaves*, so to speak—are here selected for reader's interest; they also will be fully represented in the variorum edition.

A few of the fragments can be roughly dated by subject (*vide* the war poems) or by the circumstances of being written on identifiable stationery or letterhead, but with most of them the time of composition is only a matter of guesswork. A good guess would be the period 1847–1860, for both in tone and theme they are akin to the earlier poems. If it be asked how one can always be sure that a given passage *is* a fragment rather than a complete poem, the answer is simply that one can't. When the poet leaves a MS passage without title, this may be an indication that it is only a fragment, for he usually titled his poems or numbered them in the original composition, but this rule cannot be relied upon. But the problem does not press: one feels reasonably confident that a particular cluster of lines achieves aesthetic wholeness, or that—as here—the composition is a fragment to await completion. Even so, the lines may elicit delight.

THE MANUSCRIPT SOURCES

A notable advantage of this edition is that it is the first fully to take into account and employ the resources of the considerable accumulation of the poet's manuscripts, held in many public and private collections. After Whitman died his surviving unattached literary materials were distributed, as is well known, into the custody of three literary executors, Dr. Richard Maurice Bucke, Thomas B. Harned, and Horace Traubel. Of the three Dr. Bucke was the only one to undertake the responsibility of editing those MSS which had come into his hands. His *Notes and Fragments* (1899) is invaluable; and, considering that he was not a professional scholar, his editing is admirably faithful to its responsibilities. There are errors, to be sure, but they are few.

Since this major distribution of the poet's MSS, they have passed through many hands and are widely scattered. They are of many sorts and their variety is formidable: notes and ideas toward poems, often jotted down with lists of titles; working notes and phrases; trial lines; rough drafts; amended drafts; fair copies for the printer—even, on occasion, longhand copies for souvenir purposes—of poems already printed. They exist in many conditions and forms: in the invaluable notebooks of few or many pages which the poet habitually carried about with him, on tax forms or other "waste paper," economically garnered, on the backs of letters and opened envelopes, on wrapping paper and on scrap paper of all sorts. A single page of MS may be written on as many as six or seven strips of paper pasted together, and the medium may be of four or five kinds—pencil, blue crayon, black ink, lighter ink, red ink—and sometimes the revisions and deletions are so crowded and intricate that the MS is a pastiche of line and color. Also, a MS may exist in an orderly succession of sheets on which the lines are neatly transcribed.

This rich store is, of course, specifically drawn upon for line-by-line collation in the Variorum Edition, but its value to the Reader's Edition is salient as well—not only in aiding interpretation of certain passages but also in furnishing, on occasion, variant readings that illuminate beyond the power of the immediate text. For instance, we learn from manuscript that "Starting from Paumanok" was first titled "Premonition," and that the "Calamus" poem "We Two Boys Together Clinging" originally carried the exotic title "Razzia," an Arabic word meaning "raid" or "foray." We learn, too, that in "Song of Myself" the magnificent phrase "Far-swooping elbow'd earth" was first "Earth of far arms," and that in the same passage "Still nodding night" was originally "Still slumberous night." And had the poet retained his MS revision of the title and first line of "A Woman Waits for Me"—"A Woman America Knows (or Shall Yet Know)"—the poem would not, perhaps, have had the inference of assignation which some critics erroneously found in it.

These are illustrations among many of how our annotations have often profited by MS sources. More important, no less than twenty-two poems are here printed from MS for the first time, as well as a large number of selected fragments, a full presentation of which will be the province of the Variorum Edition. In his 1902 variorum readings, Oscar L. Triggs drew rather fitfully and without identification upon MS sources introduced by the phrase: "Early manuscript readings of lines in this section." He was faithful to his editorial responsibility, but he did not have access to all sources; and both the Reader's Edition and the Variorum Edition, concerned to scrutinize all MS resources extant and available, take account of much that he did not note.

William Carlos Williams, whose interesting comments on Whitman were sometimes affected by inadequate knowledge, once said: "Whitman didn't have the training to construct his verses after a conscious mold which would have given him power over them to turn them this way, then that, at will. He only knew how to give them birth and to release them to go their own way." (*Leaves of Grass One Hundred Years After*, ed. by Milton Hindus, p. 23). How wrong he was the MSS show—they show, indeed, that the poet released his verses only after he had recast them again and again to find the form he wanted.

THE PREFACES

This edition of *Leaves of Grass* gives more than the usual attention to Whitman's prefaces and to the writings functioning as prefaces in *Leaves of Grass* editions of 1855, 1856, 1872, 1876, and 1891–2. These writings are not all shown in consecutive order; "A Backward Glance . . . " is retained in the position which it occupied in the text which we have honored, the *Leaves of Grass* dated 1891–2, in which Whitman placed "A Backward Glance O'er Travel'd Roads" after the text of the poems and included the note which approved that edition, with this essay, for future publication. It seems to have gone without comment that "A Backward Glance . . . " first appeared in this position—with the same injunction—in the *Leaves* of 1889, but since the poet then supposed, with apparent good reason, that this edition was his last before death, the authorization of the final arrangement is only made more compelling. In the 1889 edition, Whitman also commemorated his seventieth birthday by prefacing the retrospective essay with a "Letter to the Reader," which was so serene in facing imminent mortality, so "garrulous to the very last," and so characteristic of the mood of those last years in which he made the few but important decisions affecting the final construction of his book, that the present editors have included it, as prefatory to "A Backward Glance . . . " in this edition also. The remainder of the prefaces appear consecutively as a group. We have annotated them with the object of emphasizing their values for the general reader of Whitman's poetry. These essays, in chronological order, usefully explicate Whitman's concept of the unity existing between the poet, his art, his experience, and his theory of nature; they mark, also, certain stages in his construction of what he supposed could become a single poem composed of poems. We wish also to call renewed attention to the values of the earliest preface, which appeared in the first *Leaves of Grass* (1855).

Like Wordsworth's introduction to the second issue of *Lyrical Ballads* in 1800, Whitman's preface to the first *Leaves of Grass* edition influenced the changing course of poetry by predicting and defining the functions of the poet and the form and range of poetry in the age to come. Unlike Wordsworth, Whitman did not live to know that he measurably succeeded; his poetry was so advanced in psychological and social insight, and so radically sophisticated in form and symbolism, that younger poets did not recognize their indebtedness until after 1915. Whitman's first preface was a radical prose composition, poised on the very brink of lyrical communication. A bit more of tension in the metaphors, a heightening of the rhythmic regulation, and the emotional forces were ready to go into independent orbit. And they did so.

They did so, from one angle of vision, because Whitman extracted numerous lines and groups of lines from this preface, to be rewritten, paraphrased, or even transcribed into poems which appeared for the most part in the *Leaves* of 1856 or 1860. None of these derivatives are among Whitman's masterpieces, although "By Blue Ontario's Shore" and "Song of the Answerer," after indispensable revisions, took a position among those poems which support the meaning of *Leaves of Grass* as a whole. Much more importantly, the Preface of 1855 went into independent orbit as an impassioned prose masterpiece. The ingenuous force and fervor which expressed a radical creed, and perhaps a revelation—with but a handful of poems for illustration—is now seen to have been prophetic with respect to Whitman's final accomplishment and the acceptance, in the present century, of his psychological basis and his organic structure of poetry. Certainly Whitman in his full accomplishment remained faithful to his creed. Numerous critics have observed Traubel's report that the poet more than thirty years later expressed doubt concerning the continuing importance of his first preface, but his remark is not disparaging in view of Whitman's knowledge that every idea in the 1855 Preface had been somewhere translated into his poems. The poems of the 1855 edition likewise give the impression of being a spontaneous first expression of an overwhelming and sudden discovery affecting the poet's theory of man's personality and the nature of existence. The Preface and the poems of 1855 are in remarkable accord; literary history knows very few examples of such consistency between the art and the theory of a creative writer. From all points of view this essay is among the great writings of American literature. Of Whitman's critical pronouncements, only "A Backward Glance O'er Travel'd Roads," his last recapitulation of his poetry, has so much material value, and even that lacks the stylistic felicity of the first preface.

The long neglect of the special values of the 1855 Preface may justify the special emphasis upon it in this edition. In 1882 and in later collections of his prose, Whitman published an abbreviated version, shorter by some 328 equivalent lines, or nearly one-third the original bulk. Most of the cancellations apparently resulted from the poet's desire to omit certain lines of prose which had been translated into the poems. For whatever reason, his revisions diminished the essay's lyric *élan* and its exciting vigor as a manifesto. The shorter version, as finally published in the poet's *Complete Prose Works* (1892), is included in the present collection in the second volume of *Prose Works 1892*, where it is collated with all earlier texts.

The present version is the entire 1855 text, printed from a facsimile, including the punctuation, which represents Whitman's earlier practice. Our notes identify the lines of the essay which were borrowed for the eight poems most affected, and they also give the lines which Whitman inserted in later editions of this preface. The reader is referred to the first note on the text of this preface for further detail.

The second edition, *Leaves of Grass* (1856), had no preface in the accepted sense, yet we have no doubt that Whitman's open letter to Emerson, which followed the poems in this overstuffed little book, was intended by its author to serve the function of a preface; the well-publicized fact that Emerson had generously praised the first *Leaves* was sufficient to capture the attention of every informed reader. Except for the epistolary opening and closing paragraphs, this letter has the character of an introduction, calling attention to certain ideas already strongly expressed in the poetry of the volume. In part it is a searching, rebellious satire on the failure of American society, in spite of the principles of its famous revolutionary foundation, to develop the concept of individualism at the level of great leadership and new revelations. In consistency with the same idea, the essay calls for the development of an American literature that shall be "inherent"—not simply nationalistic; that shall produce poets able to reveal, in American life, "the indefinable hard something that is Nature." Finally, and in the same vein, this essay is perhaps Whitman's most explicit and fullest prose exposition of his belief that the sexual nature of man is the source of creativeness and individualism and must be made illustrious—this on psychological grounds only lately familiar in twentieth-century American thought. This open letter was Whitman's reply to the familiar letter that Emerson had sent him on July 21, 1855, praising the first edition of *Leaves of Grass* with unequivocal and characteristic understanding of the full meaning of these poems and with knowledge that they would offend readers in general. Having within three months been "persuaded" by editor Charles A. Dana to make Emerson's letter public in the New York *Tribune*, Whitman now replied by this open letter, dated August 1856, and he printed the two letters together in the 1856 *Leaves* in an appendix entitled "Leaves Droppings." Still without asking Emerson's permission, as if bent on social suicide, the Brooklyn poet had the spine of the volume ornamented with a gold-stamped copy of Emerson's words from the letter: "I Greet you at the / Beginning of A / Great Career / R. W. Emerson /. Emerson, it is reported, only remarked to Samuel Longfellow that Whitman "has done a strange rude thing," but he remained his staunch friend. The reader will find other specific information in the note on the text, "Letter to Emerson, 1856."

The Preface of 1872, originally the introduction to the small volume of poems entitled *As a Strong Bird on Pinions Free*, and the Preface of 1876, which was prepared for the "Centennial" volume, *Two Rivulets*, are in the present edition brought into close association with each other by the footnotes. Like the "Preface 1855" and "A Backward Glance O'er Travel'd Roads," the prefaces of 1872 and 1876 may be found in numerous collections of Whitman's poems and prose, but none of these have been annotated. As a whole, these prefaces constitute a progressive revelation of Whitman the man and poet, but the prefaces of 1872 and 1876 have an additional interest for the reader and critic. They show that Whitman, during these years, was going through a "midchannel" crisis of illness and confused aims. He had not yet quite realized that, whether from illness or other causes, his great period of creativity had closed, indeed had begun to close about 1867. In Preface 1872 he declared an intention to write another book, parallel to *Leaves of Grass*. The former work had established, he thought, the theme of democratic individualism; the companion volume was to be dedicated to the theme of the democratic society and in particular to its religious values. "As A Strong Bird on Pinions Free," he thought, might prove to be the beginning of this new cycle. Very likely a few poems of the early 1870's—certainly "Passage to India" and "Prayer of Columbus"—were related to the plan, but as our notes make clear, Whitman was destined never to regain the health and creative imagination that, from 1850 to 1865, had supported an astonishing creativity and originality.

This commentary on the prefaces began with a reference to "A Backward Glance O'er Travel'd Roads," and we should return at least briefly to it, as the last to be completed of all Whitman's major essays in self-criticism. Its first appearance in *November Boughs* (1888) was prepared for by a number of trial runs of its related major themes in a succession of essays over a period of several years, and this complex process of growth is indicated in the textual footnotes of the present edition. The essay is so familiar that, although it is the most generous in its information among the articles functioning as prefaces, it may be treated somewhat less fully than Preface 1855. Generally speaking, it divides into two related subjects: the personality of the poet in the perspective of the history of his times, of which he believed the Civil War to be the central event; and secondly, his theory of poetry, involving the recognition of that experience which excited his creativity and gave him, for a time, a dedication which seemed to represent the inspiration of some vast power outside him. It was pointed out above that the present edition of "A Backward Glance . . . " is supported, as in the 1889 *Leaves*, by the prefatory "Letter to the Reader." This, and the "Letter to Emerson, 1856," have not previously appeared in an edition of Whitman's prefaces.

THE TEXT AND THE NOTES

The selection of the text to be honored in any edition is of first concern; but in fact the text reproduced here had already been identified by the same editors in their work on *A Variorum Edition of Leaves of Grass*, which will appear later, in two companion volumes with the present work, as part of the total edition of *The Collected Writings of Walt Whitman*. By definition the *Variorum Edition* deals strictly and exhaustively with all textual variants and evidence that may be derived from the collation of all extant texts of each poem. The present "Reader's Edition" intends only to show the honored text without interruption, for the satisfaction of the reader. For the satisfaction of the reader-turned-student, footnotes for each poem summarize the history of the text, clarify foreign or archaic expressions, and identify allusions now generally unfamiliar.

The text was printed directly from a photographic facsimile, which was corrected for mechanical defects. As was said above, this edition is one of the two issues of 1891–2, containing the prefatory note recommending that future editions be "a copy and facsimile, indeed of the text of these . . . pages." The contents of the edition are indicated by its bibliographical description: **Leaves of Grass**/Including/SANDS AT SEVENTY . . . *1st Annex,*/GOOD-BYE MY FANCY . . . *2nd Annex,*/A BACKWARD GLANCE O'ER TRAVEL'D ROADS,/*and Portrait from Life.*//*Walt Whitman* [facsimile autograph] beneath the poem, "Come, said my Soul,"//PHILADEL-PHIA/DAVID MCKAY, PUBLISHER/23 SOUTH NINTH STREET/1891–2//

As Whitman bibliographers have noted, this issue appears in two forms, with identical title pages, contents, and pagination but different in binding. One form is bound in heavy paper, the covers plain, the spine showing only a pasted-on label on which is printed the title and the author's name, the covers usually grey in color or dark chocolate brown (called the "brownstone front" by Whitman's familiars). Of the softbound issue, only a small number were hurriedly bound up in advance of the whole edition so that the bedfast author could autograph copies as Christmas gifts for his friends. They were available in November. However, the report that Whitman's increasing weakness pre-

vented him from completing his task is sustained by the survival of copies for-
warded on behalf of the poet by Horace Traubel. The early copy at the Univer-
sity of Pennsylvania, inscribed to J. W. Wallace in Whitman's hand but not
dated, must have been mailed in mid-November, 1891, since it reached Wallace
at his home in Bolton, England about December 17 (J. Johnston and J. W.
Wallace, *Visits to Walt Whitman* . . . , London, 1917, p. 231). The bulk
of the 1891–2 edition was the second form, bound in dark green cloth; the
covers are plain, the spine gold-stamped with the title and the names of author
and publisher. No copy bearing Whitman's autograph has been seen, although
a copy in Gay W. Allen's collection bears the acquisition date of "May/92"
and the poet lived until March 26. The term, "deathbed edition" has been
applied to both issues, but more appropriately to the softbound form.

Many of these facts have long been known, but it has not previously been
reported that the softbound issue does not contain the verbal changes and
mechanical variants which first appeared in Whitman's revised *Leaves of Grass*
in 1888 and 1889. These revisions did appear, however, in the hardbound
issue of 1891–2. The differences between the two issues have been verified by
the comparison of a significant number of copies of each form in several col-
lections, and by the thorough examination of the Feinberg MS of the volume
as made up for the printer, in which loose signatures of LG 1889 constitute
the copy for the canon poems and show the corrections of 1888 and 1889 which
appear only in the clothbound issue of 1891–2, not in softbound copies.
Therefore the present editors have honored, in the text of this volume, that of
the green cloth hardbound issue of 1891–2. Important variants between the
two issues—those which affect the meaning—are shown in the footnotes.

The preparation of the Variorum, which will report all variants of every
kind, also sorted out the successive texts of the "Poems Excluded from *Leaves
of Grass*" and "Passages Excluded from Poems of *Leaves of Grass*," two sepa-
rate sections following the *Leaves of Grass*, 1891–2, in this edition. The new
Variorum provided information reflected in the report of the textual history in
notes to the poems of the *Leaves of Grass* canon.

Whitman's prefaces, like the poems, created the problem of selecting the
text to be honored. We chose in all cases the first edition texts which appeared
in the volumes of Whitman's poems that they heralded. Read consecutively in
this arrangement they represent in their way the poet's *apologia*, his stirring
critical defense of what he knew was then a radical poetry. We hope they will
again make available for a new generation the immediate urgency of this poetry
in its first appearance, and demonstrate its continuing relationship to the Ameri-
can ideology. Never before have all these pieces appeared together in associa-
tion with the complete text of the *Leaves of Grass*. Not even Whitman, in
Complete Prose Works, 1892, included the prefatorial "Letter to Emerson"
1856 or the "Letter to the Reader" of 1889. All the other prefaces appear
in the present *Collected Writings*, *Prose Works*, *1892*, but necessarily in their
last edition texts. Professor Floyd Stovall has edited them so as to show by

footnotes what were their first-edition sources, while we here have edited the
first edition texts with reference to their last-edition derivatives—a calculated
dualism of *a quo* and *ad quem* in these *Collected Writings of Walt Whitman*.

Among mechanical characteristics which should be noted in this text is
the treatment of run-on or spill-over lines in the canon poems of *Leaves of
Grass*. This body of Whitman's poems retained unchanged the same pagi-
nations and type-face established by the plates of the Boston edition of 1881
until the poet's last edition of 1891–2; Whitman's verbal alterations during
this period were accommodated to the existing space. Whether or not the
breaking of the run-on lines was arbitrary or represented at times a rhythmic
device, we have retained the evidence by following the 1891–2 edition scrupu-
lously in this respect. Exceptions occur in no more than a score of instances
when the spill-over is a hyphenated remnant of the last word of the entire
poetic line. We have not indicated the numbering of stanzas, or groups of
stanzas, except for the last edition, our present text. However, since our
pagination is different from that of the 1891–2 edition, we were able to re-
store the space between stanzas whenever a stanza break occurring in ear-
lier editions was accidentally obscured in the texts of 1881 and later by the
ending of a stanza at the last line of a page. The failure of twentieth-century
editions to do this resulted in some severe distortions. For example, the restora-
tion of "To the Man-of-War Bird" in a three-stanza form (instead of two)
contributes to the understanding of its dramatic development and its rhythmic
pattern. The characteristics treated above do not apply, of course, to the
excluded poems or fragments, or to uncollected poems, because they vary with
respect to typography, stanza divisions, and spill-overs from one edition, or
one MS, to another. Our selections of the best text for poems not in the canon
therefore led to inconsistencies in the poetry outside the 1891 *Leaves*. Also, the
typography of our titles here is not Whitman's but is standard in this entire
edition of *Collected Writings*.

With respect to footnotes we have not employed index numbers above the
line of text, preferring to identify the footnote by the corresponding line-
number in the text, followed by a key word in that line. Whitman's original
texts identified his notes by asterisks. Therefore, Whitman's notes are re-
produced here with the asterisk only, thus differentiating them from the
editors' notes. We call attention also to the dating of the literature of this edition.
In all cases the dates, if known, will appear below the concluding line of text,
the date at the left margin representing the first appearance in print and the
date at the right margin indicating the appearance of the writing in its last
approved form as shown. Date of composition, if known, will appear in the
first footnote (the headnote or title-note) and more detailed information dating
the publications may also appear in the same place. This use of the headnote
has been especially necessary in dating the poems excluded from early issues.
We commonly abbreviate the title and date of a Whitman edition: LG 1860
(*Leaves of Grass*); DT 1865 (*Drum-Taps*); CPW 1892 (*Complete Prose*

Works). In addition, for a clothbound or hardbound volume, or for a paper-bound edition, find respectively "hb" and "sb"; but see complete "list of abbreviations" following.

This edition represents a very genuine collaboration, continued with increasing pleasure over a number of years, during which both editors were burdened with quite different and competing responsibilities. Every editorial decision, whether involving the form or the contents of this book, has resulted from consultation and agreement. Notes and prefatory essays represent in each instance initiation by one collaborator and review by the other. Our mutual indebtedness to many institutions, libraries and individuals has been gratefully acknowledged in the Preface.

Note to the 1968 edition: A number of errors occurred in the first impression of The Comprehensive Reader's Edition. These have now been silently corrected, and a few of the notes have been enlarged or revised.

Abbreviations

CPP	*Complete Poems & Prose of Walt Whitman, 1855–1888* (1888)
CPSP	*Complete Poetry and Selected Prose and Letters*, Nonesuch Edition, ed. by Emory Holloway (1938)
CPW	Whitman, *Complete Prose Works* (1892)
CT	Complete Text
CW	*Complete Writings of Walt Whitman*, ed. by R. M. Bucke and others, 10 vols. (1902)
DAB	*Dictionary of American Biography*
DNB	*Dictionary of National Biography* (British)
Doheny	Estelle Doheny Collection, Doheny Memorial Library, St. John's Seminary, Camarillo, California
Donaldson	Thomas Donaldson, *Walt Whitman the Man* (1896)
DT	Whitman, *Drum-Taps* (1865–1866)
Duke	Library of Duke University: Trent Collection
DV	Whitman, *Democratic Vistas* (1871)
EA	*Etudes Anglaises*
EJ	*English Journal*
ELH	*Journal of English Literary History*
ESQ	*Emerson Society Quarterly*
Expli	*Explicator*
Faner	Robert D. Faner, *Walt Whitman and Opera* (1951)
FBW	William Sloane Kennedy, *The Fight of a Book for the World* (1926)
FCI	*Faint Clews and Indirections* (Trent MS Collection), ed. by Clarence Gohdes and Rollo G. Silver (1949)
Feinberg	Charles E. Feinberg Collection
Furness	Clifton J. Furness, *Walt Whitman's Workshop* (1928)
GBF	Whitman, *Good-Bye My Fancy* (1891)
GF	*Gathering of the Forces*, ed. by Cleveland Rogers and John Black, 2 vols. (1920)
Gilchrist	Herbert H. Gilchrist, *Anne Gilchrist: Her Life and Writings* (1887)
Glicksberg	Charles I. Glicksberg, *Walt Whitman and the Civil War* (1933)
Handbook	Gay Wilson Allen, *Walt Whitman Handbook* (1946)
Hanley	T. E. Hanley Collection, University of Texas
Harned	*The Letters of Anne Gilchrist and Walt Whitman*, ed. by Thomas B. Harned (1918)
HLQ	*Huntington Library Quarterly*
Holloway	Emory Holloway, *Whitman: An Interpretation in Narrative* (1926)
— —	See *CPSP*
— —	See *Inclusive LG*

——	See *UPP*
Houghton	Houghton Library, Harvard University
Huntington	Henry E. Huntington Library, San Marino, California
Imprints	*Leaves of Grass Imprints* (1860)
Inclusive *LG*	*Leaves of Grass*, Inclusive Edition, ed. by Emory Holloway (1924 *et seq.*)
In Re	*In Re Walt Whitman*, ed. by Horace L. Traubel, R. M. Bucke, T. B. Harned (1893)
ISL	*I Sit and Look Out*, ed. by Emory Holloway and Vernolian Schwartz (1932)
Kennedy	William Sloan Kennedy, *Reminiscences of Walt Whitman* (1896)
——	See *FBW*
——	See *WDC*
LC	Library of Congress
LC *Whitman*	*Walt Whitman: Catalog Based upon the Collections of the Library of Congress* (1955)
LG	*Leaves of Grass* (*LG*, *LG* 1860, etc.)
Lion	Oscar Lion Collection, New York Public Library
Livezey	Livezey Collection, University of California
Memoranda	Whitman, *Memoranda During the War* (1875)
Miller	James E. Miller, Jr., *A Critical Guide to Leaves of Grass* (1857)
MLN	*Modern Language Notes*
Morgan	Pierpont Morgan Library, New York City
Mott	Frank Luther Mott, *A History of American Magazines*, 4 vols.
N and F	*Notes and Fragments*, ed. by R. M. Bucke (1899): republished, *CW*, Vol. IX
NB	Whitman, *November Boughs* (1888)
NED	*New English Dictionary*
NEQ	*New England Quarterly*
NYD	*New York Dissected*, ed. Emory Holloway and Ralph Adimari (1936)
NYPL	New York Public Library; See Berg, See Lion
PBSA	*Publications of the Bibliographical Society of America*
Pennsylvania	University of Pennsylvania Library, Philadelphia
Perry	Bliss Perry, *Walt Whitman* (1906)
PI	Whitman, *Passage to India* (1871)
PMLA	*Publications of the Modern Language Ass'n*
PT	Partial text
SB	*Studies in Bibliography*
SDC	Whitman, *Specimen Days & Collect* (1882)
Texas	Library of the University of Texas: Hanley
Traubel	Horace Traubel, *With Walt Whitman in Camden*, 3 vols.

	(1906–1914); Vol. IV, ed. by Sculley Bradley (1953): Vol. V, ed. by Gertrude Traubel (in press)
TR	Whitman, *Two Rivulets* (1876)
Trent	Trent Memorial Collection; cf. Duke
TSE	*Tulane Studies in English*
UPP	*The Uncollected Poetry and Prose of Walt Whitman*, 2 vols. ed. by Emory Holloway (1921)
Va.	Library of the University of Virginia, Charlottesville
Visits	*Visits to Walt Whitman in 1890–1891 by two Lancashire Friends*, John Johnston and J. W. Wallace (London, 1917; New York, 1918)
WD	Whitman, *The Wound Dresser*, ed. by R. M. Bucke (1898)
WDC	Whitman, *Walt Whitman's Diary in Canada*, ed. by William Sloane Kennedy (1904)
Wells	Carolyn Wells and Alfred F. Goldsmith, *A Concise Bibliography of the Works of Walt Whitman* (1922)
WW	Walt Whitman
WWM	Gay W. Allen and E. Allen, *Walt Whitman as Man, Poet and Legend* (1960)
WWN	*Walt Whitman Newsletter*, Vol I, 1–4, (New York University Press,) 1955
WWP	*Walt Whitman Poems*, ed. by Gay W. Allen and Charles T. Davis (1955)
WWR	*Walt Whitman Review* (successor to the *Newsletter*), Wayne State University Press, Vol. II *et seq.* (1956–)
Yale	Yale Collection of American Literature

Inscriptions.

One's-Self I Sing.

One's-Self I sing, a simple separate person,
Yet utter the word Democratic, the word En-Masse.

Of physiology from top to toe I sing,
Not physiognomy alone nor brain alone is worthy for the Muse, I
     say the Form complete is worthier far,
The Female equally with the Male I sing.

Of Life immense in passion, pulse, and power,
Cheerful, for freest action form'd under the laws divine,
The Modern Man I sing.

  1867   *1871*

As I Ponder'd in Silence.

As I ponder'd in silence,
Returning upon my poems, considering, lingering long,

INSCRIPTIONS] First became a group title for the opening nine poems of LG 1871. In LG 1881 the group was increased to the present twenty-four poems, of which one was new.

SING] This poem is a shorter rendering of the "Inscription" italicized on the frontispiece of LG 1867, and reprinted in the "Sands at Seventy" group of NB (1888) under the title, "Small the Theme of my Chant." The present version was first printed in LG 1871. Both versions were derived from drafts in seven small notebooks which WW had fastened into his own copy of the first edition of LG, and which were edited by Clifton Joseph Furness in 1929. See Furness, "Introductions intended for American editions of Leaves of Grass," 115–137, and "Appendix," 165–174.

    1. One's-Self] WW "sings" of man's identity, his innermost being, not his self in the usual sense.

    2. En-Masse] WW was fond of this borrowed word, using it in his first poem, "Song of Myself" (line 478).

SILENCE] In this and the next poem WW begins a use of *italics* whose flexibility and variety the student will find interesting to note as he proceeds through LG. Here the form is question and answer, but in the following poem it is imagined response. In "Song of the Redwood-Tree," as in "Out of the Cradle . . ." and "Out of the Rolling Ocean . . . ," it is direct first person. In the thrush song of "When Lilacs Last . . ." it is a voice overheard, and so on.

A Phantom arose before me with distrustful aspect,
Terrible in beauty, age, and power,
5 The genius of poets of old lands,
As to me directing like flame its eyes,
With finger pointing to many immortal songs,
And menacing voice, *What singest thou?* it said,
Know'st thou not there is but one theme for ever-enduring bards?
10 *And that is the theme of War, the fortune of battles,*
The making of perfect soldiers.

Be it so, then I answer'd,
I too haughty Shade also sing war, and a longer and greater one
*   than any,*
Waged in my book with varying fortune, with flight, advance and
*   retreat, victory deferr'd and wavering,*
(Yet methinks certain, or as good as certain, at the last,) the field
15 *   the world,*
For life and death, for the Body and for the eternal Soul,
Lo, I too am come, chanting the chant of battles,
I above all promote brave soldiers.
     1871   1871

In Cabin'd Ships at Sea.

In cabin'd ships at sea,
The boundless blue on every side expanding,
With whistling winds and music of the waves, the large imperious
        waves,
Or some lone bark buoy'd on the dense marine,
5 Where joyous full of faith, spreading white sails,
She cleaves the ether mid the sparkle and the foam of day, or
        under many a star at night,
By sailors young and old haply will I, a reminiscence of the land,
        be read,
In full rapport at last.

SEA] First published in the 1871 "Inscriptions" in the positions they now occupy,
both this poem and the preceding "As I Ponder'd in Silence" are concerned with the
destiny of LG. W. S. Kennedy, WW's friend and commentator, said (*Conservator*,
No. 12, February, 1907, p. 184) that this poem was suggested by a passage in
Pindar's fifth ode:

> "Speed thou, my dulcet lay,
>   In every bark and pinnace o'er the deep."

Here are our thoughts, voyagers' thoughts,
Here not the land, firm land, alone appears, may then by them be
*   said,*   10
The sky o'erarches here, we feel the undulating deck beneath our
*   feet,*
We feel the long pulsation, ebb and flow of endless motion,
The tones of unseen mystery, the vague and vast suggestions of the
*   briny world, the liquid-flowing syllables,*
The perfume, the faint creaking of the cordage, the melancholy
*   rhythm,*
The boundless vista and the horizon far and dim are all here,   15
And this is ocean's poem.

Then falter not O book, fulfil your destiny,
You not a reminiscence of the land alone,
You too as a lone bark cleaving the ether, purpos'd I know not
    whither, yet ever full of faith,
Consort to every ship that sails, sail you!   20
Bear forth to them folded my love, (dear mariners, for you I fold
    it here in every leaf;)
Speed on my book! spread your white sails my little bark athwart
    the imperious waves,
Chant on, sail on, bear o'er the boundless blue from me to every
    sea,
This song for mariners and all their ships.
  1871   *1871*

To Foreign Lands.

I heard that you ask'd for something to prove this puzzle the New
    World,
And to define America, her athletic Democracy,
Therefore I send you my poems that you behold in them what you
    wanted.
  1860   *1871*

Note the structural regularity of this poem: three stanzas of eight iambic lines each, beginning and ending with shorter lines.
    6. ether] The element which, according to Aristotle, filled the rarefied upper spaces.
    14. cordage] The ropes in the rigging of a ship.
    LANDS] First appeared among the "Messenger Leaves" group of LG 1860.

To a Historian.

You who celebrate bygones,
Who have explored the outward, the surfaces of the races, the life
        that has exhibited itself,
Who have treated of man as the creature of politics, aggregates,
        rulers and priests,
I, habitan of the Alleghanies, treating of him as he is in himself
        in his own rights,
Pressing the pulse of the life that has seldom exhibited itself, (the
5   great pride of man in himself,)
Chanter of Personality, outlining what is yet to be,
I project the history of the future.

1860   1871

To Thee Old Cause.

To thee old cause!
Thou peerless, passionate, good cause,
Thou stern, remorseless, sweet idea,
Deathless throughout the ages, races, lands,
5 After a strange sad war, great war for thee,
(I think all war through time was really fought, and ever will be
        really fought, for thee,)
These chants for thee, the eternal march of thee.

(A war O soldiers not for itself alone,
Far, far more stood silently waiting behind, now to advance in
        this book.)

HISTORIAN] Compare this poem with its inflated first version, "Chants Demo-
cratic" No. 10, LG 1860.
    4. habitan of the Alleghanies] "habitan" is apparently the poet's coinage, per-
haps derived from "habitant," a native of Canada (or Louisiana) of French descent.
The Alleghenies are the oldest mountains in the United States; thus WW is
allegorically identifying himself with the ancient geologic past of his land. "Alle-
ghanies" is Whitman's own spelling.
    CAUSE] WW frequently refers—in similar phrase—to "the good old cause," and
comes closest to defining it in the 1860 "To a Certain Cantatrice" as "the progress
and freedom of the race." In addressing the cause as "Thou orb of many orbs!" the
poet employs the word in the older sense of "sphere of activity." In "Whitman and the
'Good Old Cause,'" (AL, 34 (November, 1962), 400–403), Clarence Gohdes offers
evidence to show why the poet could take for granted that his contemporaries would

Thou orb of many orbs! 10
Thou seething principle! thou well-kept, latent germ! thou centre!
Around the idea of thee the war revolving,
With all its angry and vehement play of causes,
(With vast results to come for thrice a thousand years,)
These recitatives for thee,—my book and the war are one, 15
Merged in its spirit I and mine, as the contest hinged on thee,
As a wheel on its axis turns, this book unwitting to itself,
Around the idea of thee.

1871   1881

Eidólons.

        I met a seer,
Passing the hues and objects of the world,
The fields of art and learning, pleasure, sense,
        To glean eidólons.

        Put in thy chants said he, 5
No more the puzzling hour nor day, nor segments, parts, put in,
Put first before the rest as light for all and entrance-song of all,
        That of eidólons.

        Ever the dim beginning,
Ever the growth, the rounding of the circle, 10
Ever the summit and the merge at last, (to surely start again,)
        Eidólons! eidólons!

understand the phrase. See also WW's MS note on the "good old cause" in N and F,
55.
        EIDÓLONS] First published in the New York *Tribune*, Feb. 19, 1876, then in *TR*
(1876), and transferred to "Inscriptions" in 1881. WW entered in his MS "Notebook
on Words" (Feinberg): "Ei-do-lon (Gr) phantom—the *image* of a Helen at Troy
instead of real flesh and blood woman." Years later he told Traubel, "It is the custom
everywhere to pronounce the word *ei*dolons: I always make it ei*dó*lons: this is right,
too. I make considerable use of the word." (Traubel, III, 131). WW employs the
word as a refrain to express the concept, central in *LG*, that behind all appearance is
soul, the ultimate reality, eternal and changeless. W. S. Kennedy (*FBW*, 181–182)
suggests the influence of Balfour Stewart and P. G. Tait's *The Unseen Universe*
(1875), whose thesis is "that each organic or inorganic object on the earth makes, in
the process of its growth, a delicate facsimile register of itself on the living sensitive
ether that lies immediately around it and bathes and interpenetrates its every atom."

Ever the mutable,
Ever materials, changing, crumbling, re-cohering,
15   Ever the ateliers, the factories divine,
          Issuing eidólons.

Lo, I or you,
Or woman, man, or state, known or unknown,
We seeming solid wealth, strength, beauty build,
20   But really build eidólons.

The ostent evanescent,
The substance of an artist's mood or savan's studies long,
Or warrior's, martyr's, hero's toils,
          To fashion his eidólon.

25   Of every human life,
(The units gather'd, posted, not a thought, emotion, deed, left out,)
The whole or large or small summ'd, added up,
          In its eidólon.

The old, old urge,
30   Based on the ancient pinnacles, lo, newer, higher pinnacles,
From science and the modern still impell'd,
          The old, old urge, eidólons.

The present now and here,
America's busy, teeming, intricate whirl,
35   Of aggregate and segregate for only thence releasing,
          To-day's eidólons.

These with the past,
Of vanish'd lands, of all the reigns of kings across the sea,
Old conquerors, old campaigns, old sailors' voyages,
40   Joining eidólons.

Densities, growth, façades,
Strata of mountains, soils, rocks, giant trees,
Far-born, far-dying, living long, to leave,
          Eidólons everlasting.

21. ostent] A token or portent.

Exaltè, rapt, ecstatic,
The visible but their womb of birth,
Of orbic tendencies to shape and shape and shape,
    The mighty earth-eidólon.   45

    All space, all time,
(The stars, the terrible perturbations of the suns,   50
Swelling, collapsing, ending, serving their longer, shorter use,)
    Fill'd with eidólons only.

    The noiseless myriads,
The infinite oceans where the rivers empty,
The separate countless free identities, like eyesight,   55
    The true realities, eidólons.

    Not this the world,
Nor these the universes, they the universes,
Purport and end, ever the permanent life of life,
    Eidólons, eidólons.   60

    Beyond thy lectures learn'd professor,
Beyond thy telescope or spectroscope observer keen, beyond all
    mathematics,
Beyond the doctor's surgery, anatomy, beyond the chemist with
    his chemistry,
    The entities of entities, eidólons.

    Unfix'd yet fix'd,   65
Ever shall be, ever have been and are,
Sweeping the present to the infinite future,
    Eidólons, eidólons, eidólons.

    The prophet and the bard,
Shall yet maintain themselves, in higher stages yet,   70
Shall mediate to the Modern, to Democracy, interpret yet to them,
    God and eidólons.

    And thee my soul,
Joys, ceaseless exercises, exaltations,
Thy yearning amply fed at last, prepared to meet,   75
    Thy mates, eidólons.

Thy body permanent,
The body lurking there within thy body,
The only purport of the form thou art, the real I myself,
80   An image, an eidólon.

Thy very songs not in thy songs,
No special strains to sing, none for itself,
But from the whole resulting, rising at last and floating,
        A round full-orb'd eidólon.
    1876   *1876*

For Him I Sing.

For him I sing,
I raise the present on the past,
(As some perennial tree out of its roots, the present on the past,)
With time and space I him dilate and fuse the immortal laws,
5   To make himself by them the law unto himself.
    1871   *1871*

When I Read the Book.

When I read the book, the biography famous,
And is this then (said I) what the author calls a man's life?
And so will some one when I am dead and gone write my life?
(As if any man really knew aught of my life,
Why even I myself I often think know little or nothing of my real
5   life,
Only a few hints, a few diffused faint clews and indirections
I seek for my own use to trace out here.)
    1867   *1871*

SING] First appeared in the "Inscriptions" of LG 1871.
  BOOK] The first (and more powerful) version of this poem in LG 1867 was
limited to five lines, the first four as they are now, the fifth completing the paren-
thesis: As if you, O cunning Soul, did not keep your secret well!). The MS (Lion)
shows many variants.
  STUDIES] First appeared in the 1865 *Drum-Taps*, and was transferred to "In-

Beginning My Studies.

Beginning my studies the first step pleas'd me so much,
The mere fact consciousness, these forms, the power of motion,
The least insect or animal, the senses, eyesight, love,
The first step I say awed me and pleas'd me so much,
I have hardly gone and hardly wish'd to go any farther,   5
But stop and loiter all the time to sing it in ecstatic songs.

1865   *1871*

Beginners.

How they are provided for upon the earth, (appearing at intervals,)
How dear and dreadful they are to the earth,
How they inure to themselves as much as to any—what a paradox
     appears their age,
How people respond to them, yet know them not,
How there is something relentless in their fate all times,   5
How all times mischoose the objects of their adulation and re-
     ward,
And how the same inexorable price must still be paid for the same
     great purchase.

1860   *1860*

To the States.

To the States or any one of them, or any city of the States, *Resist
     much, obey little,*
Once unquestioning obedience, once fully enslaved,
Once fully enslaved, no nation, state, city of this earth, ever after-
     ward resumes its liberty.

1860   *1881*

scriptions" in 1871.
    BEGINNERS] This distinguished little poem, which first appeared in LG 1860,
shows WW's power to withhold and challenge. The word "beginners" is to be taken
in no obvious sense: the beginners are the great innovators.
    TO THE STATES] First titled "Walt Whitman's Caution," this poem was one of
the "Messenger Leaves" of LG 1860; and, appropriately, one of the "Songs of Insur-
rection" of the 1871 and 1876 editions.

On Journeys through the States.

On journeys through the States we start,
(Ay through the world, urged by these songs,
Sailing henceforth to every land, to every sea,)
We willing learners of all, teachers of all, and lovers of all.

We have watch'd the seasons dispensing themselves and passing
5   on,
And have said, Why should not a man or woman do as much as
         the seasons, and effuse as much?

We dwell a while in every city and town,
We pass through Kanada, the North-east, the vast valley of the
         Mississippi, and the Southern States,
We confer on equal terms with each of the States,
10 We make trial of ourselves and invite men and women to hear,
We say to ourselves, Remember, fear not, be candid, promulge the
         body and the soul,
Dwell a while and pass on, be copious, temperate, chaste, mag-
         netic,
And what you effuse may then return as the seasons return,
And may be just as much as the seasons.

      1860   *1871*

To a Certain Cantatrice.

Here, take this gift,
I was reserving it for some hero, speaker, or general,

THROUGH THE STATES] No. 17 of the "Chants Democratic" of LG 1860, this
poem was dropped from the 1867 edition, and then restored in the 1871 *Passage to
India*, also in the "Passage to India" annexes of LG 1872 and the 1876 *Two Rivulets*.
The poet's theme is accurately conveyed in an MS title he was not to use—"Wander-
Teachers" (Bowers, 164).
      8. Kanada] This spelling of "Canada"—and its adjectival form, "Kanadian"—is
consistent in LG, and purely idiosyncratic.
      CANTATRICE] One of the "Messenger Leaves" of LG 1860, this poem was trans-
ferred to "Songs of Insurrection" in 1871 and 1876, and to "Inscriptions" in 1881.
The tribute is addressed to Madame Marietta Alboni, great coloratura soprano, who
in the New York season of 1852–1853 appeared in ten operas, every one attended by
the poet, as he proudly testified (CW, IV, 26).

One who should serve the good old cause, the great idea, the prog-
    ress and freedom of the race,
Some brave confronter of despots, some daring rebel;
But I see that what I was reserving belongs to you just as much as
    to any.   5

1860   *1871*

Me Imperturbe.

Me imperturbe, standing at ease in Nature,
Master of all or mistress of all, aplomb in the midst of irrational things,
Imbued as they, passive, receptive, silent as they,
Finding my occupation, poverty, notoriety, foibles, crimes, less im-
    portant than I thought,
Me toward the Mexican sea, or in the Mannahatta or the Tennessee,
    or far north or inland,   5
A river man, or a man of the woods, or of any farm-life of these
    States or of the coast, or the lakes or Kanada,
Me wherever my life is lived, O to be self-balanced for contingen-
    cies,
To confront night, storms, hunger, ridicule, accidents, rebuffs, as
    the trees and animals do.

1860   *1881*

Savantism.

Thither as I look I see each result and glory retracing itself and
    nestling close, always obligated,
Thither hours, months, years—thither trades, compacts, establish-
    ments, even the most minute,

IMPERTURBE] No. 18 of the "Chants Democratic" of LG 1860, this poem was
transferred to "Inscriptions" in 1881. It is remindful of the counsels to himself which
WW often entered in his notebooks, and is little changed from the original MS.

    5. Mannahatta] This Indian name for his city so pleased WW that he used it
many times in his poetry. Irving had also popularized it in his *Knickerbocker's His-
tory of New York* (1809), Book III, chap. I: " . . . the lovely island of Manna-
hatta." The name is an Algonquian word, meaning "large island" (*Proceedings of the
New York State Historical Association*, 1906, pp. 13–14, "Indian Geographical
Names").

    SAVANTISM] This 1860 poem was transferred to *Passage to India* in 1871, and
hence to the "Passage to India" annexes of LG 1872 and the 1876 *Two Rivulets*, and
to "Inscriptions" in 1881. "Savantism" may be interpreted as the wisdom which
perceives the relationship and indebtedness of all appearance to its spiritual source.

Thither every-day life, speech, utensils, politics, persons, estates;
Thither we also, I with my leaves and songs, trustful, admirant,
5   As a father to his father going takes his children along with him.
   1860   1860

The Ship Starting.

Lo, the unbounded sea,
On its breast a ship starting, spreading all sails, carrying even her
     moonsails,
The pennant is flying aloft as she speeds she speeds so stately—
     below emulous waves press forward,
They surround the ship with shining curving motions and foam.
   1865   1881

I Hear America Singing.

I hear America singing, the varied carols I hear,
Those of mechanics, each one singing his as it should be blithe
     and strong,
The carpenter singing his as he measures his plank or beam,
The mason singing his as he makes ready for work, or leaves off
     work,
The boatman singing what belongs to him in his boat, the deck-
5   hand singing on the steamboat deck,
The shoemaker singing as he sits on his bench, the hatter singing
     as he stands,
The wood-cutter's song, the ploughboy's on his way in the morn-
     ing, or at noon intermission or at sundown,
The delicious singing of the mother, or of the young wife at work,
     or of the girl sewing or washing,

STARTING] Originally an 1865 *Drum-Taps* poem, "The Ship Starting" was grouped with ". . . Paumanok" in 1871 and 1876, and was transferred to "Inscriptions" in 1881.

SINGING] This poem was first published in LG 1860 as No. 20 of "Chants Democratic"; and for the next edition, 1867, WW had achieved the title and the first line we now know, an inspired improvement upon the original "American mouthsongs!" The poem was transferred to "Inscriptions" in 1881. Inevitably it has received many musical adaptations—notably as a cantata for mixed voices by Harvey B. Gaul (1925) and by George Kleinsinger (1941). Also it became the title song of a group of WW's poems for mixed voices by Normand Lockwood (1954).

BESIEGED] Originally this poem constituted the last four lines of an eight-line

Each singing what belongs to him or her and to none else,
The day what belongs to the day—at night the party of young
      fellows, robust, friendly,   10
Singing with open mouths their strong melodious songs.
    1860   *1867*

What Place Is Besieged?

What place is besieged, and vainly tries to raise the siege?
Lo, I send to that place a commander, swift, brave, immortal,
And with him horse and foot, and parks of artillery,
And artillery-men, the deadliest that ever fired gun.
    1860   *1867*

Still Though the One I Sing.

Still though the one I sing,
(One, yet of contradictions made,) I dedicate to Nationality,
I leave in him revolt, (O latent right of insurrection! O quench-
      less, indispensable fire!)
    1871   *1871*

Shut Not Your Doors.

Shut not your doors to me proud libraries,
For that which was lacking on all your well-fill'd shelves, yet
      needed most, I bring,
Forth from the war emerging, a book I have made,
The words of my book nothing, the drift of it every thing,

poem printed as "Calamus" No. 31 in *LG* 1860. In the next edition, 1867, it appeared
under its present title, and the first four lines of the original piece also became a
separate piece under the title, "Here, Sailor!" now "What Ship Puzzled at Sea."
"What Place is Besieged?" was transferred to "Inscriptions" in 1881.

    SING] This was the introductory poem (and the only new one) of a group of six
labelled "Songs of Insurrection" which WW arranged for the 1871 and 1876 editions,
then became one of the "Inscriptions" in 1881.

    DOORS] First a *Drum-Taps* poem, this piece was much improved in revision,
achieving its final—and best—form in the 1881 "Inscriptions." Among the changes
was the dropping of four lines in the 1871 version to become in 1881 part of another
poem, "As they Draw to a Close."

5   A book separate, not link'd with the rest nor felt by the intellect,
But you ye untold latencies will thrill to every page.

    1865   *1881*

Poets to Come.

Poets to come! orators, singers, musicians to come!
Not to-day is to justify me and answer what I am for,
But you, a new brood, native, athletic, continental, greater than
       before known,
Arouse! for you must justify me.

5   I myself but write one or two indicative words for the future,
I but advance a moment only to wheel and hurry back in the
       darkness.

I am a man who, sauntering along without fully stopping, turns a
       casual look upon you and then averts his face,
Leaving it to you to prove and define it,
Expecting the main things from you.

    1860   *1867*

To You.

Stranger, if you passing meet me and desire to speak to me, why
       should you not speak to me?
And why should I not speak to you?

    1860   *1860*

     COME] Originally No. 14 of "Chants Democratic," LG 1860, this poem was
shortened and improved in 1867, transferred to "The Answerer" group in 1871 and
1876, and finally to "Inscriptions" in 1881.

     YOU] The last of the "Messenger Leaves" of LG 1860, this poem was transferred
to "Inscriptions" in 1881.

     READER] This final poem of the "Inscriptions" group was one of the seventeen
new poems in LG 1881.

     PAUMANOK] The introductory poem of the 1860 edition, under the title "Proto-
Leaf," this fervent announcement of the poet's theme and purpose was originally
entitled "Premonition," as the MS (Barrett) shows. See Bowers, 2–36, which also

Thou Reader.

Thou reader throbbest life and pride and love the same as I,
Therefore for thee the following chants.

1881   *1881*

Starting from Paumanok.

1

Starting from fish-shape Paumanok where I was born,
Well-begotten, and rais'd by a perfect mother,
After roaming many lands, lover of populous pavements,
Dweller in Mannahatta my city, or on southern savannas,
Or a soldier camp'd or carrying my knapsack and gun, or a miner
    in California,   5
Or rude in my home in Dakota's woods, my diet meat, my drink
    from the spring,
Or withdrawn to muse and meditate in some deep recess,
Far from the clank of crowds intervals passing rapt and happy,
Aware of the fresh free giver the flowing Missouri, aware of mighty
    Niagara,

prints (40–56) a WW notebook of 1856 (Feinberg) containing many first-draft
lines for this poem, whose composition was begun immediately after the appearance
of the first edition of LG. Its present title first appeared in the 1867 edition, which
contains more revisions than any other. These revisions are of considerable interest
and should be studied. The poem was placed in its present position, immediately
following the "Inscriptions" group, in LG 1871. It is itself an extended "Inscription,"
as the original titles "Premonition" and "Proto-Leaf" also suggest. But it is much
more than an announcement of intent; like "Song of Myself" it is both a mythic and
personal portrait of the poet—the new man of the Western World. For commentary,
see Allen, *Handbook*, 38–40; and Miller, 192–196.
    4. Mannahatta] Cf. note, line 5, "Me Imperturbe."

10   Aware of the buffalo herds grazing the plains, the hirsute and
         strong-breasted bull,
     Of earth, rocks, Fifth-month flowers experienced, stars, rain, snow,
         my amaze,
     Having studied the mocking-bird's tones and the flight of the
         mountain-hawk,
     And heard at dawn the unrivall'd one, the hermit thrush from the
         swamp-cedars,
     Solitary, singing in the West, I strike up for a New World.

                        2

15   Victory, union, faith, identity, time,
     The indissoluble compacts, riches, mystery,
     Eternal progress, the kosmos, and the modern reports.

     This then is life,
     Here is what has come to the surface after so many throes and
         convulsions.

20   How curious! how real!
     Underfoot the divine soil, overhead the sun.

     See revolving the globe,
     The ancestor-continents away group'd together,
     The present and future continents north and south, with the
         isthmus between.

25   See, vast trackless spaces,
     As in a dream they change, they swiftly fill,
     Countless masses debouch upon them,
     They are now cover'd with the foremost people, arts, institutions,
         known.

     See, projected through time,
30   For me an audience interminable.

     With firm and regular step they wend, they never stop,
     Successions of men, Americanos, a hundred millions,

     13. heard at dawn] The softbound issue, unlike the present hardbound issue of
the 1891–2 text, reads "dusk," as in editions previous to 1888.
     38. Libertad!] This Spanish word for "freedom" or "Liberty" is a favorite bor-

One generation playing its part and passing on,
Another generation playing its part and passing on in its turn,
With faces turn'd sideways or backward towards me to listen,   35
With eyes retrospective towards me.

3

Americanos! conquerors! marches humanitarian!
Foremost! century marches! Libertad! masses!
For you a programme of chants.

Chants of the prairies,   40
Chants of the long-running Mississippi, and down to the Mexican
          sea,
Chants of Ohio, Indiana, Illinois, Iowa, Wisconsin and Minnesota,
Chants going forth from the centre from Kansas, and thence equi-
          distant,
Shooting in pulses of fire ceaseless to vivify all.

4

Take my leaves America, take them South and take them North,   45
Make welcome for them everywhere, for they are your own off-
          spring,
Surround them East and West, for they would surround you,
And you precedents, connect lovingly with them, for they connect
          lovingly with you.

I conn'd old times,
I sat studying at the feet of the great masters,   50
Now if eligible O that the great masters might return and study me.

In the name of these States shall I scorn the antique?
Why these are the children of the antique to justify it.

5

Dead poets, philosophs, priests,
Martyrs, artists, inventors, governments long since,   55

rowing, appearing frequently in *LG.*
    54 philosophs] WW was fond of this variant of "philosopher," from the French
"philosophe," a term often referring to the popular quasi-philosophers of the 18th
century French Enlightenment.

Language-shapers on other shores,
Nations once powerful, now reduced, withdrawn, or desolate,
I dare not proceed till I respectfully credit what you have left
  wafted hither,
I have perused it, own it is admirable, (moving awhile among it,)
Think nothing can ever be greater, nothing can ever deserve more
60 than it deserves,
Regarding it all intently a long while, then dismissing it,
I stand in my place with my own day here.

Here lands female and male,
Here the heir-ship and heiress-ship of the world, here the flame of
  materials,
65 Here spirituality the translatress, the openly-avow'd,
The ever-tending, the finalè of visible forms,
The satisfier, after due long-waiting now advancing,
Yes here comes my mistress the soul.

6

The soul,
Forever and forever—longer than soil is brown and solid—longer
70 than water ebbs and flows.

I will make the poems of materials, for I think they are to be the
  most spiritual poems,
And I will make the poems of my body and of mortality,
For I think I shall then supply myself with the poems of my soul
  and of immortality.

I will make a song for these States that no one State may under
  any circumstances be subjected to another State,
And I will make a song that there shall be comity by day and by
75 night between all the States, and between any two of them,
And I will make a song for the ears of the President, full of weap-
  ons with menacing points,

  66. finalè] Properly, finale; the error was introduced in the Rees Welsh edition,
1882.
  78–81] This four-line passage was added in LG 1867. Compare with the eleventh

And behind the weapons countless dissatisfied faces;
And a song make I of the One form'd out of all,
The fang'd and glittering One whose head is over all,
Resolute warlike One including and over all,   80
(However high the head of any else that head is over all.)

I will acknowledge contemporary lands,
I will trail the whole geography of the globe and salute courte-
      ously every city large and small,
And employments! I will put in my poems that with you is hero-
      ism upon land and sea,
And I will report all heroism from an American point of view.   85

I will sing the song of companionship,
I will show what alone must finally compact these,
I believe these are to found their own ideal of manly love, indi-
      cating it in me,
I will therefore let flame from me the burning fires that were
      threatening to consume me,
I will lift what has too long kept down those smouldering fires,   90
I will give them complete abandonment,
I will write the evangel-poem of comrades and of love,
For who but I should understand love with all its sorrow and joy?
And who but I should be the poet of comrades?

                      7

I am the credulous man of qualities, ages, races,   95
I advance from the people in their own spirit,
Here is what sings unrestricted faith.

Omnes! omnes! let others ignore what they may,
I make the poem of evil also, I commemorate that part also,
I am myself just as much evil as good, and my nation is—and I
      say there is in fact no evil,   100
(Or if there is I say it is just as important to you, to the land or
      to me, as any thing else.)

stanza of "Pioneers! O Pioneers!" in which the "fang'd and warlike mistress" is
evidently the flag waving over the warlike procession.
   98. Omnes!] Latin plural: "all"; here the meaning is extended to suggest "the
all."

I too, following many and follow'd by many, inaugurate a religion,
    I descend into the arena,
(It may be I am destin'd to utter the loudest cries there, the win-
    ner's pealing shouts,
Who knows? they may rise from me yet, and soar above every thing.)

105   Each is not for its own sake,
I say the whole earth and all the stars in the sky are for religion's
    sake.

I say no man has ever yet been half devout enough,
None has ever yet adored or worship'd half enough,
None has begun to think how divine he himself is, and how cer-
    tain the future is.

I say that the real and permanent grandeur of these States must
110   be their religion,
Otherwise there is no real and permanent grandeur;
(Nor character nor life worthy the name without religion,
Nor land nor man or woman without religion.)

8

What are you doing young man?
115   Are you so earnest, so given up to literature, science, art, amours?
These ostensible realities, politics, points?
Your ambition or business whatever it may be?

It is well—against such I say not a word, I am their poet also,
But behold! such swiftly subside, burnt up for religion's sake,
For not all matter is fuel to heat, impalpable flame, the essential
120   life of the earth,
Any more than such are to religion.

9

What do you seek so pensive and silent?
What do you need camerado?
Dear son do you think it is love?

123. camerado] This favorite word of WW for "comrade"—to be used in *LG* seven
times, beginning with "Song of Myself"—is neither the present French *camarade*
nor the Spanish *camarada*, but, as Louise Pound noted in "Walt Whitman and the
French Language," *American Speech*, 1 (May, 1926), 424, "an old English form of

Listen dear son—listen America, daughter or son,   125
It is a painful thing to love a man or woman to excess, and yet it
     satisfies, it is great,
But there is something else very great, it makes the whole coincide,
It, magnificent, beyond materials, with continuous hands sweeps
     and provides for all.

          10

Know you, solely to drop in the earth the germs of a greater
     religion,
The following chants each for its kind I sing.   130

My comrade!
For you to share with me two greatnesses, and a third one rising
     inclusive and more resplendent,
The greatness of Love and Democracy, and the greatness of Reli-
     gion.

Melange mine own, the unseen and the seen,
Mysterious ocean where the streams empty,   135
Prophetic spirit of materials shifting and flickering around me,
Living beings, identities now doubtless near us in the air that we
     know not of,
Contact daily and hourly that will not release me,
These selecting, these in hints demanded of me.

Not he with a daily kiss onward from childhood kissing me,   140
Has winded and twisted around me that which holds me to him,
Any more than I am held to the heavens and all the spiritual
     world,
After what they have done to me, suggesting themes.

O such themes—equalities! O divine average!
Warblings under the sun, usher'd as now, or at noon, or set-
     ting,   145

the Spanish word which he had from the Waverley novels."
   133. Religion] With these three "greatnesses" WW summarized, in 1860, the
essential themes of LG.
   134. Melange] French: a mixture; here the commingled elements in the following
lines.

Strains musical flowing through ages, now reaching hither,
I take to your reckless and composite chords, add to them, and
  cheerfully pass them forward.

11

As I have walk'd in Alabama my morning walk,
I have seen where the she-bird the mocking-bird sat on her nest
  in the briers hatching her brood.

150 I have seen the he-bird also,
I have paus'd to hear him near at hand inflating his throat and
  joyfully singing.

And while I paus'd it came to me that what he really sang for was
  not there only,
Nor for his mate nor himself only, nor all sent back by the echoes,
But subtle, clandestine, away beyond,
155 A charge transmitted and gift occult for those being born.

12

Democracy! near at hand to you a throat is now inflating itself
  and joyfully singing.

Ma femme! for the brood beyond us and of us,
For those who belong here and those to come,
I exultant to be ready for them will now shake out carols stronger
  and haughtier than have ever yet been heard upon earth.

160 I will make the songs of passion to give them their way,
And your songs outlaw'd offenders, for I scan you with kindred
  eyes, and carry you with me the same as any.

I will make the true poem of riches,
To earn for the body and the mind whatever adheres and goes
  forward and is not dropt by death;
I will effuse egotism and show it underlying all, and I will be the
  bard of personality,

157. Ma femme!] WW addresses Democracy as "Ma femme!" in two other poems
of 1860—"For You O Democracy" and "France: the 18th Year of these States."

And I will show of male and female that either is but the equal
    of the other,   165
And sexual organs and acts! do you concentrate in me, for I am
    determin'd to tell you with courageous clear voice to prove
    you illustrious,
And I will show that there is no imperfection in the present, and
    can be none in the future,
And I will show that whatever happens to anybody it may be
    turn'd to beautiful results,
And I will show that nothing can happen more beautiful than
    death,
And I will thread a thread through my poems that time and events
    are compact,   170
And that all the things of the universe are perfect miracles, each
    as profound as any.

I will not make poems with reference to parts,
But I will make poems, songs, thoughts, with reference to ensemble,
And I will not sing with reference to a day, but with reference to
    all days,
And I will not make a poem nor the least part of a poem but has
    reference to the soul,   175
Because having look'd at the objects of the universe, I find there
    is no one nor any particle of one but has reference to the soul.

13

Was somebody asking to see the soul?
See, your own shape and countenance, persons, substances, beasts,
    the trees, the running rivers, the rocks and sands.

All hold spiritual joys and afterwards loosen them;
How can the real body ever die and be buried?   180

Of your real body and any man's or woman's real body,
Item for item it will elude the hands of the corpse-cleaners and
    pass to fitting spheres,
Carrying what has accrued to it from the moment of birth to the
    moment of death.

166. illustrious] This line was transferred to its present position in 1871. Origi-
nally it followed line 85.
    Section 13] See N and F, 27, No. 65, for MS variant of this section.

Not the types set up by the printer return their impression, the
    meaning, the main concern,
Any more than a man's substance and life or a woman's substance
185   and life return in the body and the soul,
Indifferently before death and after death.

Behold, the body includes and is the meaning, the main concern,
    and includes and is the soul;
Whoever you are, how superb and how divine is your body, or any
    part of it!

14

Whoever you are, to you endless announcements!

190   Daughter of the lands did you wait for your poet?
Did you wait for one with a flowing mouth and indicative hand?
Toward the male of the States, and toward the female of the States,
Exulting words, words to Democracy's lands.

Interlink'd, food-yielding lands!
195   Land of coal and iron! land of gold! land of cotton, sugar, rice!
Land of wheat, beef, pork! land of wool and hemp! land of the
    apple and the grape!
Land of the pastoral plains, the grass-fields of the world! land of
    those sweet-air'd interminable plateaus!
Land of the herd, the garden, the healthy house of adobie!
Lands where the north-west Columbia winds, and where the south-
    west Colorado winds!
200   Land of the eastern Chesapeake! land of the Delaware!
Land of Ontario, Erie, Huron, Michigan!
Land of the Old Thirteen! Massachusetts land! land of Vermont
    and Connecticut!
Land of the ocean shores! land of sierras and peaks!
Land of boatmen and sailors! fishermen's land!
205   Inextricable lands! the clutch'd together! the passionate ones!
The side by side! the elder and younger brothers! the bony-limb'd!

198. adobie] WW's spelling in all editions of this poem, here and in line 221. *Cf.*
"Song of Myself," line 323, n.

The great women's land! the feminine! the experienced sisters
    and the inexperienced sisters!
Far breath'd land! Arctic braced! Mexican breez'd! the diverse!
    the compact!
The Pennsylvanian! the Virginian! the double Carolinian!
O all and each well-loved by me! my intrepid nations! O I at
    any rate include you all with perfect love!   210
I cannot be discharged from you! not from one any sooner than
    another!
O death! O for all that, I am yet of you unseen this hour with
    irrepressible love,
Walking New England, a friend, a traveler,
Splashing my bare feet in the edge of the summer ripples on Pau-
    manok's sands,
Crossing the prairies, dwelling again in Chicago, dwelling in every
    town,   215
Observing shows, births, improvements, structures, arts,
Listening to orators and oratresses in public halls,
Of and through the States as during life, each man and woman
    my neighbor,
The Louisianian, the Georgian, as near to me, and I as near to
    him and her,
The Mississippian and Arkansian yet with me, and I yet with any
    of them,   220
Yet upon the plains west of the spinal river, yet in my house of
    adobie,
Yet returning eastward, yet in the Seaside State or in Maryland,
Yet Kanadian cheerily braving the winter, the snow and ice wel-
    come to me,
Yet a true son either of Maine or of the Granite State, or the Nar-
    ragansett Bay State, or the Empire State,
Yet sailing to other shores to annex the same, yet welcoming every
    new brother,   225
Hereby applying these leaves to the new ones from the hour they
    unite with the old ones,
Coming among the new ones myself to be their companion and
    equal, coming personally to you now,
Enjoining you to acts, characters, spectacles, with me.

213. traveler] The softbound issue, unlike the present hardbound issue of the
1891–2 text, reads "traveller."

15

With me with firm holding, yet haste, haste on.

230 For your life adhere to me,
    (I may have to be persuaded many times before I consent to give
        myself really to you, but what of that?
    Must not Nature be persuaded many times?)

No dainty dolce affettuoso I,
Bearded, sun-burnt, gray-neck'd, forbidding, I have arrived,
235 To be wrestled with as I pass for the solid prizes of the universe,
For such I afford whoever can persevere to win them.

16

On my way a moment I pause,
Here for you! and here for America!
Still the present I raise aloft, still the future of the States I
        harbinge glad and sublime,
And for the past I pronounce what the air holds of the red
240   aborigines.

The red aborigines,
Leaving natural breaths, sounds of rain and winds, calls as of birds
        and animals in the woods, syllabled to us for names,
Okonee, Koosa, Ottawa, Monongahela, Sauk, Natchez, Chatta-
        hoochee, Kaqueta, Oronoco,
Wabash, Miami, Saginaw, Chippewa, Oshkosh, Walla-Walla,
Leaving such to the States they melt, they depart, charging the
245   water and the land with names.

17

Expanding and swift, henceforth,
Elements, breeds, adjustments, turbulent, quick and audacious,
A world primal again, vistas of glory incessant and branching,

---

233. dolce affettuoso] Two Italian words familiar as directions in music, suggest-
ing sweet, dainty sentiment by contrast with the following lines.
    239. harbinge] Foretell.
    257. Kaw] Originally, a tribe of Siouan Indians after whom the state of Kansas is
named. The Kaw is also a river in Kansas.

A new race dominating previous ones and grander far, with new
      contests,
New politics, new literatures and religions, new inventions and arts.   250

These, my voice announcing—I will sleep no more but arise,
You oceans that have been calm within me! how I feel you, fathom-
      less, stirring, preparing unprecedented waves and storms.

18

See, steamers steaming through my poems,
See, in my poems immigrants continually coming and landing,
See, in arriere, the wigwam, the trail, the hunter's hut, the flat-boat,
      the maize-leaf, the claim, the rude fence, and the backwoods
      village,   255
See, on the one side the Western Sea and on the other the Eastern
      Sea, how they advance and retreat upon my poems as upon
      their own shores,
See, pastures and forests in my poems—see, animals wild and
      tame—see, beyond the Kaw, countless herds of buffalo
      feeding on short curly grass,
See, in my poems, cities, solid, vast, inland, with paved streets,
      with iron and stone edifices, ceaseless vehicles, and commerce,
See, the many-cylinder'd steam printing-press—see, the electric
      telegraph stretching across the continent,
See, through Atlantica's depths pulses American Europe reaching,
      pulses of Europe duly return'd,   260
See, the strong and quick locomotive as it departs, panting, blowing
      the steam-whistle,
See, ploughmen ploughing farms—see, miners digging mines—
      see, the numberless factories,
See, mechanics busy at their benches with tools—see from among
      them superior judges, philosophs, Presidents, emerge, drest
      in working dresses,
See, lounging through the shops and fields of the States, me well-
      belov'd, close-held by day and night,
Here the loud echoes of my songs there—read the hints come at last.   265

Section 18] Note the comparative recency of some of the inventions here cited:
the rotary printing press, 1846; the electric telegraph, 1832; the steam locomotive,
1829.
260. Atlantica's] Originally Atlantica was one of the names for Atlantis or Ata-
lantis, fabled island in the Atlantic ocean. Here, it is WW's poetic name for the
Atlantic.

19

O camerado close! O you and me at last, and us two only.
O a word to clear one's path ahead endlessly!
O something ecstatic and undemonstrable! O music wild!
O now I triumph—and you shall also;
O hand in hand—O wholesome pleasure—O one more desirer
270   and lover!
O to haste firm holding—to haste, haste on with me.

    (1856) 1860   1881

Song of Myself.

1

I celebrate myself, and sing myself,
And what I assume you shall assume,
For every atom belonging to me as good belongs to you.

I loafe and invite my soul,
5   I lean and loafe at my ease observing a spear of summer grass.

    Section 19] The reader should compare this section with its first 1860 version, in
which the "Calamus" sentiment of "adhesiveness" is expressed in lines that were
dropped from all succeeding editions. Both the first (1855) edition and the third
(1860) edition are now available in inexpensive reprints.
    MYSELF] This poem, untitled and unsectioned in 1855, occupied more than half
of the first edition of LG. In 1856 it was titled "Poem of Walt Whitman, an
American"; in the 1860 and succeeding editions it was titled simply "Walt Whitman"
until in 1881 it became "Song of Myself." As the variorum readings indicate, its
evolution, beginning in the notebooks of 1847–1848 (see UPP, II, 69–86), and
continuing with many revisions through seven editions, was not complete until 1881,
although the poet never altered the poem fundamentally, restricting himself to
changes in diction and rhythm. "Song of Myself" is essentially the epitome of the
poet's "haughty" song, sure in its intent; and what to early commentators seemed a

My tongue, every atom of my blood, form'd from this soil, this
        air,
Born here of parents born here from parents the same, and their
        parents the same,
I, now thirty-seven years old in perfect health begin,
Hoping to cease not till death.

Creeds and schools in abeyance,   10
Retiring back a while sufficed at what they are, but never forgotten,
I harbor for good or bad, I permit to speak at every hazard,
Nature without check with original energy.

        2

Houses and rooms are full of perfumes, the shelves are crowded
        with perfumes,
I breathe the fragrance myself and know it and like it,   15
The distillation would intoxicate me also, but I shall not let it.

The atmosphere is not a perfume, it has no taste of the distillation,
        it is odorless,
It is for my mouth forever, I am in love with it,
I will go to the bank by the wood and become undisguised and
        naked,
I am mad for it to be in contact with me.   20

The smoke of my own breath,
Echoes, ripples, buzz'd whispers, love-root, silk-thread, crotch and
        vine,
My respiration and inspiration, the beating of my heart, the pass-
        ing of blood and air through my lungs,

kind of chaos of poetic exuberance is now recognized as deliberate structure—perhaps
an early modern example of the method of free association, but artful and controlled
in its reporting of what comes into awareness. The movement of "Song of Myself" is
circular rather than progressive, returning upon itself in evocation of ecstasy and
confession, of identification and recognition, of rapturous union with earth and
spirit—truly a celebration both personal and universal. See Allen, *Handbook*, 114–
121; Blodgett, "Teaching 'Song of Myself,' " *ESQ*, I Quarter, 1961, 2–3; Kallsen,
" 'Song of Myself': Logical Unity through Analogy," *W.V.U.B.*, IX, 33–40; Miller,
" 'Song of Myself' as Inverted Mystical Experience," *PMLA*, LXX, 631–661; Strauch,
"The Structure of Walt Whitman's 'Song of Myself,' " *EJ*, XXVII, 597–607.

    20. me] The symbolism of this passage, lines 14–20, suggests the opposition
between experience from shelved books and experience from Nature—a Words-
worthian concept. See Alice L. Cooke, "A Note on Whitman's Symbolism in 'Song of
Myself,' " *MLN*, LXV, 228–232.

The sniff of green leaves and dry leaves, and of the shore and
    dark-color'd sea-rocks, and of hay in the barn,
The sound of the belch'd words of my voice loos'd to the eddies
25   of the wind,
A few light kisses, a few embraces, a reaching around of arms,
The play of shine and shade on the trees as the supple boughs
    wag,
The delight alone or in the rush of the streets, or along the fields
    and hill-sides,
The feeling of health, the full-noon trill, the song of me rising from
    bed and meeting the sun.

Have you reckon'd a thousand acres much? have you reckon'd
30   the earth much?
Have you practis'd so long to learn to read?
Have you felt so proud to get at the meaning of poems?

Stop this day and night with me and you shall possess the origin
    of all poems,
You shall possess the good of the earth and sun, (there are millions
    of suns left,)
You shall no longer take things at second or third hand, nor look
35   through the eyes of the dead, nor feed on the spectres in books,
You shall not look through my eyes either, nor take things from me,
You shall listen to all sides and filter them from your self.

3

I have heard what the talkers were talking, the talk of the begin-
    ning and the end,
But I do not talk of the beginning or the end.

40 There was never any more inception than there is now,
Nor any more youth or age than there is now,
And will never be any more perfection than there is now,
Nor any more heaven or hell than there is now.

34. millions of suns left] WW was stirred by astronomical immensity, and his
grasp of solar data was advanced for his day. He was probably influenced by the
New York lectures of the Cincinnati astronomer, Ormsby MacKnight Mitchel in
December, 1847. See Joseph Beaver, *Walt Whitman—Poet of Science* (1951), 44,
63 ff.

49. entretied] A carpenter's term meaning "cross-braced," as between two joists

Urge and urge and urge,
Always the procreant urge of the world.

Out of the dimness opposite equals advance, always substance and   45
   increase, always sex,
Always a knit of identity, always distinction, always a breed of life.

To elaborate is no avail, learn'd and unlearn'd feel that it is so.

Sure as the most certain sure, plumb in the uprights, well entretied,
   braced in the beams,
Stout as a horse, affectionate, haughty, electrical,   50
I and this mystery here we stand.

Clear and sweet is my soul, and clear and sweet is all that is not
   my soul.

Lack one lacks both, and the unseen is proved by the seen,
Till that becomes unseen and receives proof in its turn.

Showing the best and dividing it from the worst age vexes age,   55
Knowing the perfect fitness and equanimity of things, while they
   discuss I am silent, and go bathe and admire myself.

Welcome is every organ and attribute of me, and of any man
   hearty and clean,
Not an inch nor a particle of an inch is vile, and none shall be
   less familiar than the rest.

I am satisfied—I see, dance, laugh, sing;
As the hugging and loving bed-fellow sleeps at my side through
   the night, and withdraws at the peep of the day with
   stealthy tread,   60
Leaving me baskets cover'd with white towels swelling the house
   with their plenty,
Shall I postpone my acceptation and realization and scream at my eyes,

or walls. Here WW is drawing upon the vernacular of his experience as a house
builder with his father.
   55. age] In the first four editions of *LG*, a comma was placed between "worst"
and "age," narrowing the sense.
   60. tread] The 1855 version of this line is explicit: "As God comes a loving bed-
fellow and sleeps at my side all night and close on the peep of the day,"

That they turn from gazing after and down the road,
And forthwith cipher and show me to a cent,
Exactly the value of one and exactly the value of two, and which
65   is ahead?

4

Trippers and askers surround me,
People I meet, the effect upon me of my early life or the ward
      and city I live in, or the nation,
The latest dates, discoveries, inventions, societies, authors old and
      new,
My dinner, dress, associates, looks, compliments, dues,
70 The real or fancied indifference of some man or woman I love,
The sickness of one of my folks or of myself, or ill-doing or loss or
      lack of money, or depressions or exaltations,
Battles, the horrors of fratricidal war, the fever of doubtful news,
      the fitful events;
These come to me days and nights and go from me again,
But they are not the Me myself.

75 Apart from the pulling and hauling stands what I am,
Stands amused, complacent, compassionating, idle, unitary,
Looks down, is erect, or bends an arm on an impalpable certain
      rest,
Looking with side-curved head curious what will come next,
Both in and out of the game and watching and wondering at it.

Backward I see in my own days where I sweated through fog with
80   linguists and contenders,
I have no mockings or arguments, I witness and wait.

5

I believe in you my soul, the other I am must not abase itself to you,
And you must not be abased to the other.

64. show me to a cent] Reads "show to me a cent" from 1881 to 1888; corrected
by WW in LG 1889. Appears correctly in the present hardbound form of LG
1891–2, but not in the softbound issue of this edition.
    Section 5] The debate between the soul and the body, a fixed convention of
medieval literature, influenced later writers. Generally the soul and the body were

Loafe with me on the grass, loose the stop from your throat,
Not words, not music or rhyme I want, not custom or lecture, not
     even the best,   85
Only the lull I like, the hum of your valvèd voice.

I mind how once we lay such a transparent summer morning,
How you settled your head athwart my hips and gently turn'd over
     upon me,
And parted the shirt from my bosom-bone, and plunged your
     tongue to my bare-stript heart,
And reach'd till you felt my beard, and reach'd till you held my feet.   90

Swiftly arose and spread around me the peace and knowledge that
     pass all the argument of the earth,
And I know that the hand of God is the promise of my own,
And I know that the spirit of God is the brother of my own,
And that all the men ever born are also my brothers, and the
     women my sisters and lovers,
And that a kelson of the creation is love,   95
And limitless are leaves stiff or drooping in the fields,
And brown ants in the little wells beneath them,
And mossy scabs of the worm fence, heap'd stones, elder, mullein
     and poke-weed.

6

A child said *What is the grass?* fetching it to me with full hands;
How could I answer the child? I do not know what it is any
     more than he.   100

I guess it must be the flag of my disposition, out of hopeful green
     stuff woven.

Or I guess it is the handkerchief of the Lord,
A scented gift and remembrancer designedly dropt,
Bearing the owner's name someway in the corners, that we may
     see and remark, and say *Whose?*

regarded as opposites and enemies, one good, one evil. But in this mystical union of
body and soul, expressed in erotic imagery, the poet experiences immediate intuitive
revelation. It is remarkable that the mystical state is achieved not by rejecting the
physical senses but by their joyous consummation with the spiritual. *Cf.* section 21,
line 1, and section 48, lines 1 and 2.

105 Or I guess the grass is itself a child, the produced babe of the
       vegetation.

Or I guess it is a uniform hieroglyphic,
And it means, Sprouting alike in broad zones and narrow zones,
Growing among black folks as among white,
Kanuck, Tuckahoe, Congressman, Cuff, I give them the same, I
       receive them the same.

110 And now it seems to me the beautiful uncut hair of graves.

Tenderly will I use you curling grass,
It may be you transpire from the breasts of young men,
It may be if I had known them I would have loved them,
It may be you are from old people, or from offspring taken soon
       out of their mothers' laps,
115 And here you are the mothers' laps.

This grass is very dark to be from the white heads of old mothers,
Darker than the colorless beards of old men,
Dark to come from under the faint red roofs of mouths.

O I perceive after all so many uttering tongues,
And I perceive they do not come from the roofs of mouths for
120   nothing.

I wish I could translate the hints about the dead young men and
       women,
And the hints about old men and mothers, and the offspring taken
       soon out of their laps.

What do you think has become of the young and old men?
And what do you think has become of the women and children?

125 They are alive and well somewhere,
The smallest sprout shows there is really no death,
And if ever there was it led forward life, and does not wait at the
       end to arrest it,
And ceas'd the moment life appear'd.

      109. same] "Kanuck"—French Canadian; "Tuckahoe"—tidewater Virginian who

All goes onward and outward, nothing collapses,
And to die is different from what any one supposed, and luckier.   130

7

Has any one supposed it lucky to be born?
I hasten to inform him or her it is just as lucky to die, and I
      know it.

I pass death with the dying and birth with the new-wash'd babe,
      and am not contain'd between my hat and boots,
And peruse manifold objects, no two alike and every one good,
The earth good and the stars good, and their adjuncts all good.   135

I am not an earth nor an adjunct of an earth,
I am the mate and companion of people, all just as immortal and
      fathomless as myself,
(They do not know how immortal, but I know.)

Every kind for itself and its own, for me mine male and female,
For me those that have been boys and that love women,   140
For me the man that is proud and feels how it stings to be
      slighted,
For me the sweet-heart and the old maid, for me mothers and the
      mothers of mothers,
For me lips that have smiled, eyes that have shed tears,
For me children and the begetters of children.

Undrape! you are not guilty to me, nor stale nor discarded,   145
I see through the broadcloth and gingham whether or no,
And am around, tenacious, acquisitive, tireless, and cannot be
      shaken away.

8

The little one sleeps in its cradle,
I lift the gauze and look a long time, and silently brush away flies
      with my hand.

The youngster and the red-faced girl turn aside up the bushy hill,   150
I peeringly view them from the top.

eats "tuckahoe," a brown fungus sometimes called "Virginia truffle"; "Cuff"—a Ne-
gro.

The suicide sprawls on the bloody floor of the bedroom,
I witness the corpse with its dabbled hair, I note where the pistol
        has fallen.

The blab of the pave, tires of carts, sluff of boot-soles, talk of the
        promenaders,
The heavy omnibus, the driver with his interrogating thumb, the
155   clank of the shod horses on the granite floor,
The snow-sleighs, clinking, shouted jokes, pelts of snow-balls,
The hurrahs for popular favorites, the fury of rous'd mobs,
The flap of the curtain'd litter, a sick man inside borne to the
        hospital,
The meeting of enemies, the sudden oath, the blows and fall,
The excited crowd, the policeman with his star quickly working
160   his passage to the centre of the crowd,
The impassive stones that receive and return so many echoes,
What groans of over-fed or half-starv'd who fall sunstruck or in
        fits,
What exclamations of women taken suddenly who hurry home and
        give birth to babes,
What living and buried speech is always vibrating here, what howls
        restrain'd by decorum,
Arrests of criminals, slights, adulterous offers made, acceptances,
165   rejections with convex lips,
I mind them or the show or resonance of them—I come and I
        depart.

9

The big doors of the country barn stand open and ready,
The dried grass of the harvest-time loads the slow-drawn wagon,
The clear light plays on the brown gray and green intertinged,
170   The armfuls are pack'd to the sagging mow.

I am there, I help, I came stretch'd atop of the load,
I felt its soft jolts, one leg reclined on the other,

188. feet] The preceding four lines are based upon a painting entitled "The
Trapper's Bride," by the Baltimore artist, Alfred Jacob Miller (1810–1874). See
Edgeley W. Todd, "Indian Pictures and Two Whitman Poems," *HLQ*, XIX, 1–11.
Section 10 is in its entirety a good instance of WW's customary mingling of his own

I jump from the cross-beams and seize the clover and timothy,
And roll head over heels and tangle my hair full of wisps.

10

Alone far in the wilds and mountains I hunt, 175
Wandering amazed at my own lightness and glee,
In the late afternoon choosing a safe spot to pass the night,
Kindling a fire and broiling the fresh-kill'd game,
Falling asleep on the gather'd leaves with my dog and gun by my
      side.

The Yankee clipper is under her sky-sails, she cuts the sparkle and
      scud, 180
My eyes settle the land, I bend at her prow or shout joyously from
      the deck.

The boatmen and clam-diggers arose early and stopt for me,
I tuck'd my trowser-ends in my boots and went and had a good
      time;
You should have been with us that day round the chowder-kettle.

I saw the marriage of the trapper in the open air in the far west, *See footnote* 185
      the bride was a red girl, *188*
Her father and his friends sat near cross-legged and dumbly
      smoking, they had moccasins to their feet and large thick
      blankets hanging from their shoulders,
On a bank lounged the trapper, he was drest mostly in skins, his
      luxuriant beard and curls protected his neck, he held his
      bride by the hand,
She had long eyelashes, her head was bare, her coarse straight
      locks descended upon her voluptuous limbs and reach'd to
      her feet.

The runaway slave came to my house and stopt outside,
I heard his motions crackling the twigs of the woodpile, 190

experience with extrapolated experience like the bard or ballader of old—the clam-
ming incident from his actual youth, the runaway slave episode probably experienced
or witnessed, the imagined experience of the hunters (from literary or actual hear-
say), and the extrapolation of the Indian bride by the agency of a painting. All with
the ballad "I."

Through the swung half-door of the kitchen I saw him limpsy and
     weak,
And went where he sat on a log and led him in and assured him,
And brought water and fill'd a tub for his sweated body and bruis'd
     feet,
And gave him a room that enter'd from my own, and gave him
     some coarse clean clothes,
195 And remember perfectly well his revolving eyes and his awkwardness,
And remember putting plasters on the galls of his neck and ankles;
He staid with me a week before he was recuperated and pass'd
     north,
I had him sit next me at table, my fire-lock lean'd in the corner.

11

Twenty-eight young men bathe by the shore,
200 Twenty-eight young men and all so friendly;
Twenty-eight years of womanly life and all so lonesome.

She owns the fine house by the rise of the bank,
She hides handsome and richly drest aft the blinds of the window.

Which of the young men does she like the best?
205 Ah the homeliest of them is beautiful to her.

Where are you off to, lady? for I see you,
You splash in the water there, yet stay stock still in your room.

Dancing and laughing along the beach came the twenty-ninth bather,
The rest did not see her, but she saw them and loved them.

The beards of the young men glisten'd with wet, it ran from their
210   long hair,
Little streams pass'd all over their bodies.

Section 11] This parable—WW's first—is audacious for its time, and extraordi-
narily delicate in its sensitive recognition of loneliness and desire. In his essay on
Whitman in *The New Spirit* (1890), p. 104 of the Modern Library edition, Havelock
Ellis pays tribute to the Homeric simplicity and grandeur of the poet's expression in
this episode. The reader may find symbolic significance in the number "twenty-

An unseen hand also pass'd over their bodies,
It descended tremblingly from their temples and ribs.

The young men float on their backs, their white bellies bulge to
    the sun, they do not ask who seizes fast to them,
They do not know who puffs and declines with pendant and bend-
    ing arch,   215
They do not think whom they souse with spray.

12

The butcher-boy puts off his killing-clothes, or sharpens his knife
    at the stall in the market,
I loiter enjoying his repartee and his shuffle and break-down.

Blacksmiths with grimed and hairy chests environ the anvil,
Each has his main-sledge, they are all out, there is a great heat in
    the fire.   220

From the cinder-strew'd threshold I follow their movements,
The lithe sheer of their waists plays even with their massive arms,
Overhand the hammers swing, overhand so slow, overhand so
    sure,
They do not hasten, each man hits in his place.

13

The negro holds firmly the reins of his four horses, the block swags
    underneath on its tied-over chain,   225
The negro that drives the long dray of the stone-yard, steady and
    tall he stands pois'd on one leg on the string-piece,
His blue shirt exposes his ample neck and breast and loosens over
    his hip-band,
His glance is calm and commanding, he tosses the slouch of his
    hat away from his forehead,

eight" as the lunar cycle.
  218. shuffle and break-down] Shuffle is a slow (or adagio) dance with sliding
movements; break-down is a rollicking, noisy dance. Both were then familiar in
popular entertainment and minstrelsy.
  226. string-piece] Long piece of heavy squared timber used in shoring or construc-
tion.

The sun falls on his crispy hair and mustache, falls on the black
      of his polish'd and perfect limbs.

I behold the picturesque giant and love him, and I do not stop
230   there,
I go with the team also.

In me the caresser of life wherever moving, backward as well as
      forward sluing,
To niches aside and junior bending, not a person or object missing,
Absorbing all to myself and for this song.

Oxen that rattle the yoke and chain or halt in the leafy shade,
235   what is that you express in your eyes?
It seems to me more than all the print I have read in my life.

My tread scares the wood-drake and wood-duck on my distant and
      day-long ramble,
They rise together, they slowly circle around.

I believe in those wing'd purposes,
240 And acknowledge red, yellow, white, playing within me,
And consider green and violet and the tufted crown intentional,
And do not call the tortoise unworthy because she is not something
      else,
And the jay in the woods never studied the gamut, yet trills pretty
      well to me,
And the look of the bay mare shames silliness out of me.

14

245 The wild gander leads his flock through the cool night,
Ya-honk he says, and sounds it down to me like an invitation,
The pert may suppose it meaningless, but I listening close,
Find its purpose and place up there toward the wintry sky.

The sharp-hoof'd moose of the north, the cat on the house-sill,
      the chickadee, the prairie-dog,

   267. king-pin] A much extended spoke of the pilot wheel, providing greater
leverage in strong currents.

The litter of the grunting sow as they tug at her teats, 250
The brood of the turkey-hen and she with her half-spread wings,
I see in them and myself the same old law.

The press of my foot to the earth springs a hundred affections,
They scorn the best I can do to relate them.

I am enamour'd of growing out-doors, 255
Of men that live among cattle or taste of the ocean or woods,
Of the builders and steerers of ships and the wielders of axes and
mauls, and the drivers of horses,
I can eat and sleep with them week in and week out.

What is commonest, cheapest, nearest, easiest, is Me,
Me going in for my chances, spending for vast returns, 260
Adorning myself to bestow myself on the first that will take me,
Not asking the sky to come down to my good will,
Scattering it freely forever.

15

The pure contralto sings in the organ loft,
The carpenter dresses his plank, the tongue of his foreplane whistles
its wild ascending lisp, 265
The married and unmarried children ride home to their Thanks-
giving dinner,
The pilot seizes the king-pin, he heaves down with a strong arm,
The mate stands braced in the whale-boat, lance and harpoon are
ready,
The duck-shooter walks by silent and cautious stretches,
The deacons are ordain'd with cross'd hands at the altar, 270
The spinning-girl retreats and advances to the hum of the big
wheel,
The farmer stops by the bars as he walks on a First-day loafe and
looks at the oats and rye,
The lunatic is carried at last to the asylum a confirm'd case,
(He will never sleep any more as he did in the cot in his mother's
bed-room;)

272. First-day] Quaker designation for Sunday. loafe] Whitman's spelling for
"loaf," a time of loafing, or idle spell.

275   The jour printer with gray head and gaunt jaws works at his case,
      He turns his quid of tobacco while his eyes blurr with the manuscript;
      The malform'd limbs are tied to the surgeon's table,
      What is removed drops horribly in a pail;
      The quadroon girl is sold at the auction-stand, the drunkard nods
          by the bar-room stove,
      The machinist rolls up his sleeves, the policeman travels his beat,
280   the gate-keeper marks who pass,
      The young fellow drives the express-wagon, (I love him, though
         I do not know him;)
      The half-breed straps on his light boots to compete in the race,
      The western turkey-shooting draws old and young, some lean on
         their rifles, some sit on logs,
      Out from the crowd steps the marksman, takes his position, levels
         his piece;
285   The groups of newly-come immigrants cover the wharf or levee,
      As the woolly-pates hoe in the sugar-field, the overseer views them
         from his saddle,
      The bugle calls in the ball-room, the gentlemen run for their part-
         ners, the dancers bow to each other,
      The youth lies awake in the cedar-roof'd garret and harks to the
         musical rain,
      The Wolverine sets traps on the creek that helps fill the Huron,
      The squaw wrapt in her yellow-hemm'd cloth is offering moccasins
290   and bead-bags for sale,
      The connoisseur peers along the exhibition-gallery with half-shut
         eyes bent sideways,
      As the deck-hands make fast the steamboat the plank is thrown for
         the shore-going passengers,
      The young sister holds out the skein while the elder sister winds it
         off in a ball, and stops now and then for the knots,
      The one-year wife is recovering and happy having a week ago
         borne her first child,
      The clean-hair'd Yankee girl works with her sewing-machine or in
295   the factory or mill,
      The paving-man leans on his two-handed rammer, the reporter's
         lead flies swiftly over the note-book, the sign-painter is
         lettering with blue and gold,

     275. jour-printer] Journeyman printer.

The canal boy trots on the tow-path, the book-keeper counts at
      his desk, the shoemaker waxes his thread,
The conductor beats time for the band and all the performers
      follow him,
The child is baptized, the convert is making his first professions,
The regatta is spread on the bay, the race is begun, (how the
      white sails sparkle!)   300
The drover watching his drove sings out to them that would
      stray,
The pedler sweats with his pack on his back, (the purchaser hig-
      gling about the odd cent;)
The bride unrumples her white dress, the minute-hand of the clock
      moves slowly,
The opium-eater reclines with rigid head and just-open'd lips,
The prostitute draggles her shawl, her bonnet bobs on her tipsy
      and pimpled neck,   305
The crowd laugh at her blackguard oaths, the men jeer and wink
      to each other,
(Miserable! I do not laugh at your oaths nor jeer you;)
The President holding a cabinet council is surrounded by the great
      Secretaries,
On the piazza walk three matrons stately and friendly with twined
      arms,
The crew of the fish-smack pack repeated layers of halibut in the
      hold,   310
The Missourian crosses the plains toting his wares and his cattle,
As the fare-collector goes through the train he gives notice by the
      jingling of loose change,
The floor-men are laying the floor, the tinners are tinning the roof,
      the masons are calling for mortar,
In single file each shouldering his hod pass onward the laborers;
Seasons pursuing each other the indescribable crowd is gather'd,
      it is the fourth of Seventh-month, (what salutes of cannon
      and small arms!)   315
Seasons pursuing each other the plougher ploughs, the mower
      mows, and the winter-grain falls in the ground;
Off on the lakes the pike-fisher watches and waits by the hole in
      the frozen surface,

---

289. Wolverine] Native of Michigan.
315. fourth of Seventh-month] Quaker designation for the Fourth of July.

The stumps stand thick round the clearing, the squatter strikes
　　　deep with his axe,
Flatboatmen make fast towards dusk near the cotton-wood or
　　　pecan-trees,
Coon-seekers go through the regions of the Red river or through
　　　those drain'd by the Tennessee, or through those of the
320　　　Arkansas,
Torches shine in the dark that hangs on the Chattahooche or
　　　Altamahaw,
Patriarchs sit at supper with sons and grandsons and great-grandsons
　　　around them,
In walls of adobie, in canvas tents, rest hunters and trappers after
　　　their day's sport,
The city sleeps and the country sleeps,
325　The living sleep for their time, the dead sleep for their time,
The old husband sleeps by his wife and the young husband sleeps
　　　by his wife;
And these tend inward to me, and I tend outward to them,
And such as it is to be of these more or less I am,
And of these one and all I weave the song of myself.

16

330　I am of old and young, of the foolish as much as the wise,
Regardless of others, ever regardful of others,
Maternal as well as paternal, a child as well as a man,
Stuff'd with the stuff that is coarse and stuff'd with the stuff that
　　　is fine,
One of the Nation of many nations, the smallest the same and the
　　　largest the same,
A Southerner soon as a Northerner, a planter nonchalant and
335　　　hospitable down by the Oconee I live,
A Yankee bound my own way ready for trade, my joints the
　　　limberest joints on earth and the sternest joints on earth,
A Kentuckian walking the vale of the Elkhorn in my deer-skin
　　　leggings, a Louisianian or Georgian,
A boatman over lakes or bays or along coasts, a Hoosier, Badger,
　　　Buckeye;

---

321. Chattahooche or Altamahaw] Southern rivers. The first (from which Whit-
man omits a final "e") forms a boundary between Georgia and Alabama and Georgia
and Florida; the second is in Georgia.

323. adobie] In 1855 "abode;" in 1856, "adobe;" from 1860, "adobie." *Cf.* "Start-
ing from Paumanok," line 198, n.

At home on Kanadian snow-shoes or up in the bush, or with
      fishermen off Newfoundland,
At home in the fleet of ice-boats, sailing with the rest and tacking,   340
At home on the hills of Vermont or in the woods of Maine, or the
      Texan ranch,
Comrade of Californians, comrade of free North-Westerners, (loving
      their big proportions,)
Comrade of raftsmen and coalmen, comrade of all who shake
      hands and welcome to drink and meat,
A learner with the simplest, a teacher of the thoughtfullest,
A novice beginning yet experient of myriads of seasons,   345
Of every hue and caste am I, of every rank and religion,
A farmer, mechanic, artist, gentleman, sailor, quaker,
Prisoner, fancy-man, rowdy, lawyer, physician, priest.

I resist any thing better than my own diversity,
Breathe the air but leave plenty after me,   350
And am not stuck up, and am in my place.

(The moth and the fish-eggs are in their place,
The bright suns I see and the dark suns I cannot see are in their
      place,
The palpable is in its place and the impalpable is in its place.)

17

These are really the thoughts of all men in all ages and lands, they
      are not original with me,   355
If they are not yours as much as mine they are nothing, or next
      to nothing,
If they are not the riddle and the untying of the riddle they are
      nothing,
If they are not just as close as they are distant they are nothing.

This is the grass that grows wherever the land is and the water is,
This the common air that bathes the globe.   360

   338. Hoosier, Badger, Buckeye] Nicknames for people from Indiana, Wisconsin,
and Ohio respectively.

18

With music strong I come, with my cornets and my drums,
I play not marches for accepted victors only, I play marches for
    conquer'd and slain persons.

Have you heard that it was good to gain the day?
I also say it is good to fall, battles are lost in the same spirit in
    which they are won.

365 I beat and pound for the dead,
I blow through my embouchures my loudest and gayest for them.

Vivas to those who have fail'd!
And to those whose war-vessels sank in the sea!
And to those themselves who sank in the sea!
370 And to all generals that lost engagements, and all overcome heroes!
And the numberless unknown heroes equal to the greatest heroes
    known!

19

This is the meal equally set, this the meat for natural hunger,
It is for the wicked just the same as the righteous, I make appoint-
    ments with all,
I will not have a single person slighted or left away,
375 The kept-woman, sponger, thief, are hereby invited,
The heavy-lipp'd slave is invited, the venerealee is invited;
There shall be no difference between them and the rest.

This is the press of a bashful hand, this the float and odor of hair,
This the touch of my lips to yours, this the murmur of yearning,
380 This the far-off depth and height reflecting my own face,
This the thoughtful merge of myself, and the outlet again.

Do you guess I have some intricate purpose?
Well I have, for the Fourth-month showers have, and the mica on
    the side of a rock has.

366. embouchures] Mouthpieces of wind instruments. Also, the shape of the
mouth and lips in blowing.

Do you take it I would astonish?
Does the daylight astonish? does the early redstart twittering
    through the woods?   385
Do I astonish more than they?

This hour I tell things in confidence,
I might not tell everybody, but I will tell you.

20

Who goes there? hankering, gross, mystical, nude;
How is it I extract strength from the beef I eat?   390

What is a man anyhow? what am I? what are you?

All I mark as my own you shall offset it with your own,
Else it were time lost listening to me.

I do not snivel that snivel the world over,
That months are vacuums and the ground but wallow and filth.   395

Whimpering and truckling fold with powders for invalids, con-
    formity goes to the fourth-remov'd,
I wear my hat as I please indoors or out.

Why should I pray? why should I venerate and be ceremonious?

Having pried through the strata, analyzed to a hair, counsel'd with
    doctors and calculated close,
I find no sweeter fat than sticks to my own bones.   400

In all people I see myself, none more and not one a barley-corn
    less,
And the good or bad I say of myself I say of them.

I know I am solid and sound,
To me the converging objects of the universe perpetually flow,
All are written to me, and I must get what the writing means.   405

396. fold with powders] Powdered medicine was then folded in doses in small
papers prepared by the physician.

I know I am deathless,
I know this orbit of mine cannot be swept by a carpenter's
    compass,
I know I shall not pass like a child's carlacue cut with a burnt
    stick at night.

I know I am august,
410 I do not trouble my spirit to vindicate itself or be understood,
I see that the elementary laws never apologize,
(I reckon I behave no prouder than the level I plant my house by,
    after all.)

I exist as I am, that is enough,
If no other in the world be aware I sit content,
415 And if each and all be aware I sit content.

One world is aware and by far the largest to me, and that is
    myself,
And whether I come to my own to-day or in ten thousand or ten
    million years,
I can cheerfully take it now, or with equal cheerfulness I can wait.

My foothold is tenon'd and mortis'd in granite,
420 I laugh at what you call dissolution,
And I know the amplitude of time.

21

I am the poet of the Body and I am the poet of the Soul,
The pleasures of heaven are with me and the pains of hell are
    with me,
The first I graft and increase upon myself, the latter I translate
    into a new tongue.

425 I am the poet of the woman the same as the man,
And I say it is as great to be a woman as to be a man,
And I say there is nothing greater than the mother of men.

---

408. carlacue] A variant of "curlicue," something fancifully curled, as a flourish
in writing.
433–445.] The ms draft (Lion) of this passage shows that its superb phrasing was
not immediately achieved. Originally "Still nodding night . . ." was "Still slumber-

I chant the chant of dilation or pride,
We have had ducking and deprecating about enough,
I show that size is only development.   430

Have you outstript the rest? are you the President?
It is a trifle, they will more than arrive there every one, and still
      pass on.

I am he that walks with the tender and growing night,
I call to the earth and sea half-held by the night.

Press close bare-bosom'd night—press close magnetic nourishing
      night!   435
Night of south winds—night of the large few stars!
Still nodding night—mad naked summer night.

Smile O voluptuous cool-breath'd earth!
Earth of the slumbering and liquid trees!
Earth of departed sunset—earth of the mountains misty-topt!   440
Earth of the vitreous pour of the full moon just tinged with blue!
Earth of shine and dark mottling the tide of the river!
Earth of the limpid gray of clouds brighter and clearer for my
      sake!
Far-swooping elbow'd earth—rich apple-blossom'd earth!
Smile, for your lover comes.   445

Prodigal, you have given me love—therefore I to you give love!
O unspeakable passionate love.

22

You sea! I resign myself to you also—I guess what you mean,
I behold from the beach your crooked inviting fingers,
I believe you refuse to go back without feeling of me,   450
We must have a turn together, I undress, hurry me out of sight of
      the land,
Cushion me soft, rock me in billowy drowse,
Dash me with amorous wet, I can repay you.

ous night . . ."; "O voluptuous cool-breath'd earth!" was "O voluptuous procreant
Earth!"; "vitreous pour of the full moon . . ." was "vitreous fall of the
full moon . . ."; and "Far-swooping elbow'd earth . . ." was "Earth of far
arms . . ."

Sea of stretch'd ground-swells,
455 Sea breathing broad and convulsive breaths,
Sea of the brine of life and of unshovell'd yet always-ready graves,
Howler and scooper of storms, capricious and dainty sea,
I am integral with you, I too am of one phase and of all phases.

Partaker of influx and efflux I, extoller of hate and conciliation,
460 Extoller of amies and those that sleep in each others' arms.

I am he attesting sympathy,
(Shall I make my list of things in the house and skip the house
    that supports them?)

I am not the poet of goodness only, I do not decline to be the
    poet of wickedness also.

What blurt is this about virtue and about vice?
465 Evil propels me and reform of evil propels me, I stand indifferent,
My gait is no fault-finder's or rejecter's gait,
I moisten the roots of all that has grown.

Did you fear some scrofula out of the unflagging pregnancy?
Did you guess the celestial laws are yet to be work'd over and
    rectified?

470 I find one side a balance and the antipodal side a balance,
Soft doctrine as steady help as stable doctrine,
Thoughts and deeds of the present our rouse and early start.

This minute that comes to me over the past decillions,
There is no better than it and now.

What behaved well in the past or behaves well to-day is not such
475   a wonder,

464–476.] In their reconciliation of apparent opposites, these lines suggest the
influence of Hegel, in whose dialectic WW was much interested. See CW, IV, 312–
322, and IX, 167–174. To what extent WW followed Hegel is controversial. See
Mody C. Boatright, "Whitman and Hegel," *University of Texas Studies in English*,
Bulletin IX (July 8, 1929), 134–150; and Olive W. Parsons, "Whitman the Non-
Hegelian," PMLA, LVIII (December, 1943) 1073–1093.
  486. stonecrop] A hardy sedum, some varieties long esteemed in folk medicine as

The wonder is always and always how there can be a mean man
    or an infidel.

23

Endless unfolding of words of ages!
And mine a word of the modern, the word En-Masse.

A word of the faith that never balks,
Here or henceforward it is all the same to me, I accept Time abso-
    lutely.   480

It alone is without flaw, it alone rounds and completes all,
That mystic baffling wonder alone completes all.

I accept Reality and dare not question it,
Materialism first and last imbuing.

Hurrah for positive science! long live exact demonstration!   485
Fetch stonecrop mixt with cedar and branches of lilac,
This is the lexicographer, this the chemist, this made a grammar
    of the old cartouches,
These mariners put the ship through dangerous unknown seas,
This is the geologist, this works with the scalpel, and this is a
    mathematician.

Gentlemen, to you the first honors always!   490
Your facts are useful, and yet they are not my dwelling,
I but enter by them to an area of my dwelling.

Less the reminders of properties told my words,
And more the reminders they of life untold, and of freedom and
    extrication,

a vulnerary or healing for wounds; it is here "mixt with cedar"—a tree long associated
with graveyards and comfort for the bereaved—as in WW's threnody to Lincoln
(*q.v.*) where the lilac functions (as here) as a symbol of love and male comradeship.
    487. cartouches] Scroll-shaped carvings especially prevalent on ancient columns
and entablatures. The Egyptian cartouches on memorials to monarchs bore hiero-
glyphs of importance in establishing the language. In the mid-fifties WW was a
frequenter and publicist of Dr. Henry Abbott's Museum of Egyptian Antiquities on
Broadway. See *NYD*, 27–40.

And make short account of neuters and geldings, and favor men
495   and women fully equipt,
And beat the gong of revolt, and stop with fugitives and them that
          plot and conspire.

24

Walt Whitman, a kosmos, of Manhattan the son,
Turbulent, fleshy, sensual, eating, drinking and breeding,
No sentimentalist, no stander above men and women or apart from
          them,
500   No more modest than immodest.

Unscrew the locks from the doors!
Unscrew the doors themselves from their jambs!

Whoever degrades another degrades me,
And whatever is done or said returns at last to me.

Through me the afflatus surging and surging, through me the cur-
505   rent and index.

I speak the pass-word primeval, I give the sign of democracy,
By God! I will accept nothing which all cannot have their coun-
          terpart of on the same terms.

Through me many long dumb voices,
Voices of the interminable generations of prisoners and slaves,
510   Voices of the diseas'd and despairing and of thieves and dwarfs,
Voices of cycles of preparation and accretion,
And of the threads that connect the stars, and of wombs and of
          the father-stuff,
And of the rights of them the others are down upon,
Of the deform'd, trivial, flat, foolish, despised,
515   Fog in the air, beetles rolling balls of dung.

---

497. son] Through the first three editions this line read "Walt Whitman, an
American, one of the roughs, a kosmos." "Kosmos" was then a word of particular
import, hypothesizing the sublime order of the universe, and befitting an Emersonian,
as WW was. Briefly, in 1867, the word was dropped, and the line became "Walt
Whitman am I, of mighty Manhattan the son:" then restored to read "Walt
Whitman am I, a Kosmos, of mighty Manhattan the son." Finally, in 1881 the poet,
triumphing over rhetoric, achieved the present reading.

Through me forbidden voices,
Voices of sexes and lusts, voices veil'd and I remove the veil,
Voices indecent by me clarified and transfigur'd.

I do not press my fingers across my mouth,
I keep as delicate around the bowels as around the head and heart,   520
Copulation is no more rank to me than death is.

I believe in the flesh and the appetites,
Seeing, hearing, feeling, are miracles, and each part and tag of me
        is a miracle.

Divine am I inside and out, and I make holy whatever I touch or
        am touch'd from,
The scent of these arm-pits aroma finer than prayer,   525
This head more than churches, bibles, and all the creeds.

If I worship one thing more than another it shall be the spread of
        my own body, or any part of it,
Translucent mould of me it shall be you!
Shaded ledges and rests it shall be you!
Firm masculine colter it shall be you!   530
Whatever goes to the tilth of me it shall be you!
You my rich blood! your milky stream pale strippings of my life!
Breast that presses against other breasts it shall be you!
My brain it shall be your occult convolutions!
Root of wash'd sweet-flag! timorous pond-snipe! nest of guarded
        duplicate eggs! it shall be you!   535
Mix'd tussled hay of head, beard, brawn, it shall be you!
Trickling sap of maple, fibre of manly wheat, it shall be you!
Sun so generous it shall be you!
Vapors lighting and shading my face it shall be you!
You sweaty brooks and dews it shall be you!   540
Winds whose soft-tickling genitals rub against me it shall be you!

  505. afflatus] Latin *afflare*, *afflatum*, to breathe or blow on. In this context, a divine
impartation of power or inspiration.
  530. colter] In non-symbolic terms the colter is the prong which directs the plow
into the turf.
  531. tilth] Cultivation or tillage of the soil.
  535. sweet flag . . . pond-snipe . . . duplicate eggs] The imagery of this line
is, of course, phallic.

Broad muscular fields, branches of live oak, loving lounger in my
    winding paths, it shall be you!
Hands I have taken, face I have kiss'd, mortal I have ever
    touch'd, it shall be you.

I dote on myself, there is that lot of me and all so luscious,
545 Each moment and whatever happens thrills me with joy,
I cannot tell how my ankles bend, nor whence the cause of my
    faintest wish,
Nor the cause of the friendship I emit, nor the cause of the friend-
    ship I take again.

That I walk up my stoop, I pause to consider if it really be,
A morning-glory at my window satisfies me more than the meta-
    physics of books.

550 To behold the day-break!
The little light fades the immense and diaphanous shadows,
The air tastes good to my palate.

Hefts of the moving world at innocent gambols silently rising,
    freshly exuding,
Scooting obliquely high and low.

555 Something I cannot see puts upward libidinous prongs,
Seas of bright juice suffuse heaven.

The earth by the sky staid with, the daily close of their junction,
The heav'd challenge from the east that moment over my head,
The mocking taunt, See then whether you shall be master!

25

560 Dazzling and tremendous how quick the sun-rise would kill me,
If I could not now and always send sun-rise out of me.

We also ascend dazzling and tremendous as the sun,
We found our own O my soul in the calm and cool of the day-
    break.

550–559.] In this passage, the procreative impulse of the individual (lines 528–543)

My voice goes after what my eyes cannot reach,
With the twirl of my tongue I encompass worlds and volumes of
    worlds. 565

Speech is the twin of my vision, it is unequal to measure itself,
It provokes me forever, it says sarcastically,
Walt you contain enough, why don't you let it out then?

Come now I will not be tantalized, you conceive too much of
    articulation,
Do you not know O speech how the buds beneath you are folded? 570
Waiting in gloom, protected by frost,
The dirt receding before my prophetical screams,
I underlying causes to balance them at last,
My knowledge my live parts, it keeping tally with the meaning of
    all things,
Happiness, (which whoever hears me let him or her set out in
    search of this day.) 575

My final merit I refuse you, I refuse putting from me what I really
    am,
Encompass worlds, but never try to encompass me,
I crowd your sleekest and best by simply looking toward you.

Writing and talk do not prove me,
I carry the plenum of proof and every thing else in my face, 580
With the hush of my lips I wholly confound the skeptic.

26

Now I will do nothing but listen,
To accrue what I hear into this song, to let sounds contribute
    toward it.

I hear bravuras of birds, bustle of growing wheat, gossip of flames,
    clack of sticks cooking my meals,
I hear the sound I love, the sound of the human voice, 585
I hear all sounds running together, combined, fused or following,

gives way to the cosmic energies symbolized in the sunrise (lines 550–559).
  580. plenum] Fullness.

Sounds of the city and sounds out of the city, sounds of the day
      and night,
Talkative young ones to those that like them, the loud laugh of
      work-people at their meals,
The angry base of disjointed friendship, the faint tones of the sick,
The judge with hands tight to the desk, his pallid lips pronoun-
590   cing a death-sentence,
The heave'e'yo of stevedores unlading ships by the wharves, the
      refrain of the anchor-lifters,
The ring of alarm-bells, the cry of fire, the whirr of swift-streak-
      ing engines and hose-carts with premonitory tinkles and
      color'd lights,
The steam-whistle, the solid roll of the train of approaching cars,
The slow march play'd at the head of the association marching
      two and two,
(They go to guard some corpse, the flag-tops are draped with
595   black muslin.)

I hear the violoncello, ('tis the young man's heart's complaint,)
I hear the key'd cornet, it glides quickly in through my ears,
It shakes mad-sweet pangs through my belly and breast.

I hear the chorus, it is a grand opera,
600   Ah this indeed is music—this suits me.

A tenor large and fresh as the creation fills me,
The orbic flex of his mouth is pouring and filling me full.

I hear the train'd soprano (what work with hers is this?)
The orchestra whirls me wider than Uranus flies,
It wrenches such ardors from me I did not know I possess'd
605   them,
It sails me, I dab with bare feet, they are lick'd by the indolent
      waves,
I am cut by bitter and angry hail, I lose my breath,
Steep'd amid honey'd morphine, my windpipe throttled in fakes
      of death,
At length let up again to feel the puzzle of puzzles,
610   And that we call Being.

604. Uranus] The seventh planet, long believed the most remote: the Greek
personification of Heaven.

27

To be in any form, what is that?
(Round and round we go, all of us, and ever come back thither,)
If nothing lay more develop'd the quahaug in its callous shell
      were enough.

Mine is no callous shell,
I have instant conductors all over me whether I pass or stop,   615
They seize every object and lead it harmlessly through me.

I merely stir, press, feel with my fingers, and am happy,
To touch my person to some one else's is about as much as I can
      stand.

28

Is this then a touch? quivering me to a new identity,
Flames and ether making a rush for my veins,   620
Treacherous tip of me reaching and crowding to help them,
My flesh and blood playing out lightning to strike what is hardly
      different from myself,
On all sides prurient provokers stiffening my limbs,
Straining the udder of my heart for its withheld drip,
Behaving licentious toward me, taking no denial,   625
Depriving me of my best as for a purpose,
Unbuttoning my clothes, holding me by the bare waist,
Deluding my confusion with the calm of the sunlight and pasture-
      fields,
Immodestly sliding the fellow-senses away,
They bribed to swap off with touch and go and graze at the edges
      of me,   630
No consideration, no regard for my draining strength or my anger,
Fetching the rest of the herd around to enjoy them a while,
Then all uniting to stand on a headland and worry me.

The sentries desert every other part of me,
They have left me helpless to a red marauder,
They all come to the headland to witness and assist against me.   635

608. fakes] The turns or coils of a rope.
613. quahaug] An Atlantic coast clam.

I am given up by traitors,
I talk wildly, I have lost my wits, I and nobody else am the
　　　greatest traitor,
I went myself first to the headland, my own hands carried me
　　　there.

You villain touch! what are you doing? my breath is tight in its
640　　　throat,
Unclench your floodgates, you are too much for me.

29

Blind loving wrestling touch, sheath'd hooded sharp-tooth'd
　　　touch!
Did it make you ache so, leaving me?

Parting track'd by arriving, perpetual payment of perpetual loan,
645　Rich showering rain, and recompense richer afterward.

Sprouts take and accumulate, stand by the curb prolific and vital,
Landscapes projected masculine, full-sized and golden.

30

All truths wait in all things,
They neither hasten their own delivery nor resist it,
650　They do not need the obstetric forceps of the surgeon,
The insignificant is as big to me as any,
　(What is less or more than a touch?)

Logic and sermons never convince,
The damp of the night drives deeper into my soul.

655　(Only what proves itself to every man and woman is so,
Only what nobody denies is so.)

---

664. pismire] An ant.
670–683.] Cf. lines 670–671 with WW's notebook observation: "The soul or spirit
transmits itself into all matter—into rocks, and can live the life of a rock—into the
sea, and can feel itself the sea—into the oak, or other tree—into an animal, and feel
itself a horse, a fish, or bird—into the earth—into the motions of the suns and stars"

A minute and a drop of me settle my brain,
I believe the soggy clods shall become lovers and lamps,
And a compend of compends is the meat of a man or woman,
And a summit and flower there is the feeling they have for each
      other,   660
And they are to branch boundlessly out of that lesson until it
      becomes omnific,
And until one and all shall delight us, and we them.

31

I believe a leaf of grass is no less than the journey-work of the stars,
And the pismire is equally perfect, and a grain of sand, and the
      egg of the wren,
And the tree-toad is a chef-d'œuvre for the highest,   665
And the running blackberry would adorn the parlors of heaven,
And the narrowest hinge in my hand puts to scorn all machinery,
And the cow crunching with depress'd head surpasses any statue,
And a mouse is miracle enough to stagger sextillions of infidels.

I find I incorporate gneiss, coal, long-threaded moss, fruits, grains,
      esculent roots,   670
And am stucco'd with quadrupeds and birds all over,
And have distanced what is behind me for good reasons,
But call any thing back again when I desire it.

In vain the speeding or shyness,
In vain the plutonic rocks send their old heat against my approach,   675
In vain the mastodon retreats beneath its own powder'd bones,
In vain objects stand leagues off and assume manifold shapes,
In vain the ocean settling in hollows and the great monsters lying
      low,
In vain the buzzard houses herself with the sky,
In vain the snake slides through the creepers and logs,   680
In vain the elk takes to the inner passes of the woods,
In vain the razor-bill'd auk sails far north to Labrador,
I follow quickly, I ascend to the nest in the fissure of the cliff.

(*UPP*, II, 64). The passage as a whole reflects the concepts of the evolution of species
popularized by Darwin's *Origin of Species* four years later. See Loren Eiseley, *The
Darwin Century* (1959), 48–69.

  675. plutonic rocks] Solidified from the molten conglomerate deep in the earth,
here associated with the earliest (Archeozoic) earth history.

32

I think I could turn and live with animals, they are so placid and
    self-contain'd,
685 I stand and look at them long and long.

They do not sweat and whine about their condition,
They do not lie awake in the dark and weep for their sins,
They do not make me sick discussing their duty to God,
Not one is dissatisfied, not one is demented with the mania of
    owning things,
Not one kneels to another, nor to his kind that lived thousands of
690   years ago,
Not one is respectable or unhappy over the whole earth.

So they show their relations to me and I accept them,
They bring me tokens of myself, they evince them plainly in their
    possession.

I wonder where they get those tokens,
695 Did I pass that way huge times ago and negligently drop them?

Myself moving forward then and now and forever,
Gathering and showing more always and with velocity,
Infinite and omnigenous, and the like of these among them,
Not too exclusive toward the reachers of my remembrancers,
700 Picking out here one that I love, and now go with him on brotherly terms.

A gigantic beauty of a stallion, fresh and responsive to my caresses,
Head high in the forehead, wide between the ears,
Limbs glossy and supple, tail dusting the ground,
Eyes full of sparkling wickedness, ears finely cut, flexibly moving.

705 His nostrils dilate as my heels embrace him,
His well-built limbs tremble with pleasure as we race around and
    return.

698. omnigenous] Of all kinds.

    Section 33] WW's so-called "cataloguing," brilliantly illustrated in lines 717–
797, as in many later passages of LG, used to be occasionally cited as evidence of his
"barbarism" or naïveté as an artist. Now this aspect of his technique is generally
recognized for what it is—the powerful employment of a great imagination which
delights to celebrate "God in every object" with loving, exact art. Among articles on
this subject, note especially Mattie Swayne, "Whitman's Catalogue Rhetoric,"
University of Texas Studies in English, No. 412 (July 8, 1941), 162–178; and

I but use you a minute, then I resign you, stallion,
Why do I need your paces when I myself out-gallop them?
Even as I stand or sit passing faster than you.

33

Space and Time! now I see it is true, what I guess'd at,   710
What I guess'd when I loaf'd on the grass,
What I guess'd while I lay alone in my bed,
And again as I walk'd the beach under the paling stars of the
    morning.

My ties and ballasts leave me, my elbows rest in sea-gaps,
I skirt sierras, my palms cover continents,   715
I am afoot with my vision.

By the city's quadrangular houses—in log huts, camping with lumbermen,
Along the ruts of the turnpike, along the dry gulch and rivulet bed,
Weeding my onion-patch or hoeing rows of carrots and parsnips,
    crossing savannas, trailing in forests,
Prospecting, gold-digging, girdling the trees of a new purchase,   720
Scorch'd ankle-deep by the hot sand, hauling my boat down the
    shallow river,
Where the panther walks to and fro on a limb overhead, where
    the buck turns furiously at the hunter,
Where the rattlesnake suns his flabby length on a rock, where the
    otter is feeding on fish,
Where the alligator in his tough pimples sleeps by the bayou,
Where the black bear is searching for roots or honey, where the
    beaver pats the mud with his paddle-shaped tail;   725
Over the growing sugar, over the yellow-flower'd cotton plant, over
    the rice in its low moist field,
Over the sharp-peak'd farm house, with its scallop'd scum and
    slender shoots from the gutters,

Detlev W. Schumann, "Enumerative Style and Its Significance in Whitman, Rilke,
Werfel," *MLQ*, III (June, 1942), 171–204.
   710. guess'd at] Read "guessed" in the softbound form of this edition. The hard-
bound issue, which is followed here, reflects WW's elision of this "e" in the two
previous editions (1888–9).
   727. scallop'd scum . . . shoots] The rain-washed sediment on the roof of old
farm houses. Such houses often sustained weeds on their roofs, much in the European
tradition.

Over the western persimmon, over the long-leav'd corn, over the
     delicate blue-flower flax,
Over the white and brown buckwheat, a hummer and buzzer there
     with the rest,
Over the dusky green of the rye as it ripples and shades in the
730   breeze;
Scaling mountains, pulling myself cautiously up, holding on by low
     scragged limbs,
Walking the path worn in the grass and beat through the leaves of
     the brush,
Where the quail is whistling betwixt the woods and the wheat-lot,
Where the bat flies in the Seventh-month eve, where the great gold-
     bug drops through the dark,
Where the brook puts out of the roots of the old tree and flows to
735   the meadow,
Where cattle stand and shake away flies with the tremulous shud-
     dering of their hides,
Where the cheese-cloth hangs in the kitchen, where andirons
     straddle the hearth-slab, where cobwebs fall in festoons
     from the rafters;
Where trip-hammers crash, where the press is whirling its cylinders,
Wherever the human heart beats with terrible throes under its
     ribs,
Where the pear-shaped balloon is floating aloft, (floating in it my-
740   self and looking composedly down,)
Where the life-car is drawn on the slip-noose, where the heat
     hatches pale-green eggs in the dented sand,
Where the she-whale swims with her calf and never forsakes it,
Where the steam-ship trails hind-ways its long pennant of smoke,
Where the fin of the shark cuts like a black chip out of the water,
745 Where the half-burn'd brig is riding on unknown currents,
Where shells grow to her slimy deck, where the dead are corrupt-
     ing below;
Where the dense-starr'd flag is borne at the head of the regiments,
Approaching Manhattan up by the long-stretching island,
Under Niagara, the cataract falling like a veil over my countenance,

741. life-car] A water-tight vehicle traveling along a rope strung from aloft on a
ship, for the purpose of removing passengers, usually in a disaster.
752. bull-dances] A slang term for "buffalo-dance," originally danced by Indians.

Upon a door-step, upon the horse-block of hard wood outside,   750
Upon the race-course, or enjoying picnics or jigs or a good game
    of base-ball,
At he-festivals, with blackguard gibes, ironical license, bull-dances,
    drinking, laughter,
At the cider-mill tasting the sweets of the brown mash, sucking
    the juice through a straw,
At apple-peelings wanting kisses for all the red fruit I find,
At musters, beach-parties, friendly bees, huskings, house-raisings;   755
Where the mocking-bird sounds his delicious gurgles, cackles,
    screams, weeps,
Where the hay-rick stands in the barn-yard, where the dry-stalks
    are scatter'd, where the brood-cow waits in the hovel,
Where the bull advances to do his masculine work, where the stud
    to the mare, where the cock is treading the hen,
Where the heifers browse, where geese nip their food with short
    jerks,
Where sun-down shadows lengthen over the limitless and lonesome
    prairie,   760
Where herds of buffalo make a crawling spread of the square
    miles far and near,
Where the humming-bird shimmers, where the neck of the long-
    lived swan is curving and winding,
Where the laughing-gull scoots by the shore, where she laughs her
    near-human laugh,
Where bee-hives range on a gray bench in the garden half hid by
    the high weeds,
Where band-neck'd partridges roost in a ring on the ground with
    their heads out,   765
Where burial coaches enter the arch'd gates of a cemetery,
Where winter wolves bark amid wastes of snow and icicled trees,
Where the yellow-crown'd heron comes to the edge of the marsh
    at night and feeds upon small crabs,
Where the splash of swimmers and divers cools the warm noon,
Where the katy-did works her chromatic reed on the walnut-tree
    over the well,   770

754. apple-peelings] The use of this term in LG is perhaps the earliest in print,
although "apple-paring" appeared as early as 1819. See William D. Templeman, "On
Whitman's Apple-peelings," PQ, XXXV (April, 1956), 200–202.
    755. musters] A localism, now rare, for assemblages of people.

Through patches of citrons and cucumbers with silver-wired leaves,
Through the salt-lick or orange glade, or under conical firs,
Through the gymnasium, through the curtain'd saloon, through the
        office or public hall;
Pleas'd with the native and pleas'd with the foreign, pleas'd with
        the new and old,
775 Pleas'd with the homely woman as well as the handsome,
Pleas'd with the quakeress as she puts off her bonnet and talks
        melodiously,
Pleas'd with the tune of the choir of the whitewash'd church,
Pleas'd with the earnest words of the sweating Methodist preach-
        er, impress'd seriously at the camp-meeting;
Looking in at the shop-windows of Broadway the whole forenoon,
        flatting the flesh of my nose on the thick plate glass,
Wandering the same afternoon with my face turn'd up to the
780   clouds, or down a lane or along the beach,
My right and left arms round the sides of two friends, and I in the
        middle;
Coming home with the silent and dark-cheek'd bush-boy, (behind
        me he rides at the drape of the day,)
Far from the settlements studying the print of animals' feet, or
        the moccasin print,
By the cot in the hospital reaching lemonade to a feverish patient,
785 Nigh the coffin'd corpse when all is still, examining with a candle;
Voyaging to every port to dicker and adventure,
Hurrying with the modern crowd as eager and fickle as any,
Hot toward one I hate, ready in my madness to knife him,
Solitary at midnight in my back yard, my thoughts gone from me
        a long while,
Walking the old hills of Judæa with the beautiful gentle God by
790   my side,
Speeding through space, speeding through heaven and the stars,
Speeding amid the seven satellites and the broad ring, and the
        diameter of eighty thousand miles,
Speeding with tail'd meteors, throwing fire-balls like the rest,
Carrying the crescent child that carries its own full mother in
        its belly,
795 Storming, enjoying, planning, loving, cautioning,

782. drape of the day] close of day.

Backing and filling, appearing and disappearing,
I tread day and night such roads.

I visit the orchards of spheres and look at the product,
And look at quintillions ripen'd and look at quintillions green.

I fly those flights of a fluid and swallowing soul,   800
My course runs below the soundings of plummets.

I help myself to material and immaterial,
No guard can shut me off, no law prevent me.

I anchor my ship for a little while only,
My messengers continually cruise away or bring their returns to me.   805

I go hunting polar furs and the seal, leaping chasms with a pike-
        pointed staff, clinging to topples of brittle and blue.

I ascend to the foretruck,
I take my place late at night in the crow's-nest,
We sail the arctic sea, it is plenty light enough,
Through the clear atmosphere I stretch around on the wonderful
        beauty,   810
The enormous masses of ice pass me and I pass them, the scenery
        is plain in all directions,
The white-topt mountains show in the distance, I fling out my
        fancies toward them,
We are approaching some great battle-field in which we are soon
        to be engaged,
We pass the colossal outposts of the encampment, we pass with
        still feet and caution,
Or we are entering by the suburbs some vast and ruin'd city,   815
The blocks and fallen architecture more than all the living cities
        of the globe.

I am a free companion, I bivouac by invading watchfires,
I turn the bridegroom out of bed and stay with the bride myself,
I tighten her all night to my thighs and lips.

806. topples] Dictionaries do not list a noun form of this word; the poet is appar-
ently referring to an overhanging protrusion of ice which has "toppled" from above.

820   My voice is the wife's voice, the screech by the rail of the stairs,
They fetch my man's body up dripping and drown'd.

I understand the large hearts of heroes,
The courage of present times and all times,
How the skipper saw the crowded and rudderless wreck of the
      steam-ship, and Death chasing it up and down the storm,
How he knuckled tight and gave not back an inch, and was faith-
825   ful of days and faithful of nights,
And chalk'd in large letters on a board, *Be of good cheer, we will
      not desert you;*
How he follow'd with them and tack'd with them three days and
      would not give it up,
How he saved the drifting company at last,
How the lank loose-gown'd women look'd when boated from the
      side of their prepared graves,
How the silent old-faced infants and the lifted sick, and the sharp-
830   lipp'd unshaved men;
All this I swallow, it tastes good, I like it well, it becomes mine,
I am the man, I suffer'd, I was there.

The disdain and calmness of martyrs,
The mother of old, condemn'd for a witch, burnt with dry wood,
      her children gazing on,
The hounded slave that flags in the race, leans by the fence, blow-
835   ing, cover'd with sweat,
The twinges that sting like needles his legs and neck, the mur-
      derous buckshot and the bullets,
All these I feel or am.

I am the hounded slave, I wince at the bite of the dogs,
Hell and despair are upon me, crack and again crack the marksmen,
I clutch the rails of the fence, my gore dribs, thinn'd with the
840   ooze of my skin,
I fall on the weeds and stones,
The riders spur their unwilling horses, haul close,

832. there] The shipwreck here described was that of the *San Francisco*, which
sailed from New York December 22, 1853, bound for South America, and was
caught in a gale within a few hundred miles of the city. From December 23 until
January 5 she was helpless, 150 being at one time washed away in a single sea. The
disaster was reported in the New York *Weekly Tribune* of January 21, 1854, a copy

Taunt my dizzy ears and beat me violently over the head with
    whip-stocks.

Agonies are one of my changes of garments,
I do not ask the wounded person how he feels, I myself become
    the wounded person,   845
My hurts turn livid upon me as I lean on a cane and observe.

I am the mash'd fireman with breast-bone broken,
Tumbling walls buried me in their debris,
Heat and smoke I inspired, I heard the yelling shouts of my com-
    rades,
I heard the distant click of their picks and shovels,   850
They have clear'd the beams away, they tenderly lift me forth.

I lie in the night air in my red shirt, the pervading hush is for my
    sake,
Painless after all I lie exhausted but not so unhappy,
White and beautiful are the faces around me, the heads are bared
    of their fire-caps,
The kneeling crowd fades with the light of the torches.   855

Distant and dead resuscitate,
They show as the dial or move as the hands of me, I am the clock
    myself.

I am an old artillerist, I tell of my fort's bombardment,
I am there again.

Again the long roll of the drummers,   860
Again the attacking cannon, mortars,
Again to my listening ears the cannon responsive.

I take part, I see and hear the whole,
The cries, curses, roar, the plaudits for well-aim'd shots,
The ambulanza slowly passing trailing its red drip,   865

of which was later found among WW's effects. See Bucke, "Notes on the Text of
'Leaves of Grass,'" *Conservator*, vol. 7 (May, 1896), 40.
   840. dribs] Obsolete: "dribbles" (cf. "drips").
   865. ambulanza] Apparently Whitman's incorrect Spanish for "ambulance." The
proper form is "ambulancia."

Workmen searching after damages, making indispensable repairs,
The fall of grenades through the rent roof, the fan-shaped explo-
      sion,
The whizz of limbs, heads, stone, wood, iron, high in the air.

Again gurgles the mouth of my dying general, he furiously waves
      with his hand,
870   He gasps through the clot *Mind not me—mind—the entrenchments.*

34

Now I tell what I knew in Texas in my early youth,
(I tell not the fall of Alamo,
Not one escaped to tell the fall of Alamo,
The hundred and fifty are dumb yet at Alamo,)
'Tis the tale of the murder in cold blood of four hundred and
875   twelve young men.

Retreating they had form'd in a hollow square with their baggage
      for breastworks,
Nine hundred lives out of the surrounding enemy's, nine times
      their number, was the price they took in advance,
Their colonel was wounded and their ammunition gone,
They treated for an honorable capitulation, receiv'd writing and
      seal, gave up their arms and march'd back prisoners of war.

880   They were the glory of the race of rangers,
Matchless with horse, rifle, song, supper, courtship,
Large, turbulent, generous, handsome, proud, and affectionate,
Bearded, sunburnt, drest in the free costume of hunters,
Not a single one over thirty years of age.

The second First-day morning they were brought out in squads
885   and massacred, it was beautiful early summer,
The work commenced about five o'clock and was over by eight.

875. men] This is the tale of the massacre by the Mexican enemy of Captain
Fannin and his company of 371 Texans after their surrender at Goliad, March 27,
1836. See Louis J. Wortham, *A History of Texas* (1924) III, 239–265.

885. second First-day] Sunday in the parlance of the Quakers, who strongly
influenced WW's youth. Their pacifist inclination unites with the ideas of Sunday in
strong contrast with the massacre here described.

899. me] This line first appeared in the 1867 edition; in the three earlier editions

None obey'd the command to kneel,
Some made a mad and helpless rush, some stood stark and
    straight,
A few fell at once, shot in the temple or heart, the living and dead
    lay together,
The maim'd and mangled dug in the dirt, the new-comers saw
    them there, 890
Some half-kill'd attempted to crawl away,
These were despatch'd with bayonets or batter'd with the blunts
    of muskets,
A youth not seventeen years old seiz'd his assassin till two more
    came to release him,
The three were all torn and cover'd with the boy's blood.

At eleven o'clock began the burning of the bodies; 895
That is the tale of the murder of the four hundred and twelve
    young men.

35

Would you hear of an old-time sea-fight?
Would you learn who won by the light of the moon and stars?
List to the yarn, as my grandmother's father the sailor told it to me.

Our foe was no skulk in his ship I tell you, (said he,) 900
His was the surly English pluck, and there is no tougher or truer,
    and never was, and never will be;
Along the lower'd eve he came horribly raking us.

We closed with him, the yards entangled, the cannon touch'd,
My captain lash'd fast with his own hands.

We had receiv'd some eighteen pound shots under the water, 905
On our lower-gun-deck two large pieces had burst at the first fire,
    killing all around and blowing up overhead.

the poet had asked, "Did you read in the seabooks of the oldfashioned frigate-
fight?" Actually, his sources were both the tales told him by his maternal grand-
mother Naomi Van Velsor, whose father, Capt. John Williams, had served under
John Paul Jones, and the account by Jones himself in a letter to Benjamin Franklin
about the battle on September 23, 1779 between his *BonHomme Richard* and the
British *Serapis* off Flamborough Head. This letter, printed in *Old South Leaflets*
(Boston, n.d.), VII, 36–39, is followed by WW with close parallelism. See David
Goodale, "Some of Walt Whitman's Borrowings," *AL*, X, 202–213.

Fighting at sun-down, fighting at dark,
Ten o'clock at night, the full moon well up, our leaks on the gain,
      and five feet of water reported,
The master-at-arms loosing the prisoners confined in the after-hold
      to give them a chance for themselves.

910   The transit to and from the magazine is now stopt by the sentinels,
They see so many strange faces they do not know whom to trust.

Our frigate takes fire,
The other asks if we demand quarter?
If our colors are struck and the fighting done?

915   Now I laugh content, for I hear the voice of my little captain,
We have not struck, he composedly cries, *we have just begun our
      part of the fighting.*

Only three guns are in use,
One is directed by the captain himself against the enemy's main-
      mast,
Two well serv'd with grape and canister silence his musketry and
      clear his decks.

920   The tops alone second the fire of this little battery, especially the main-top,
They hold out bravely during the whole of the action.

Not a moment's cease,
The leaks gain fast on the pumps, the fire eats toward the powder-
      magazine.

One of the pumps has been shot away, it is generally thought we
      are sinking.

925   Serene stands the little captain,
He is not hurried, his voice is neither high nor low,
His eyes give more light to us than our battle-lanterns.

Toward twelve there in the beams of the moon they surrender to us.

36

Stretch'd and still lies the midnight,
930   Two great hulls motionless on the breast of the darkness,

Our vessel riddled and slowly sinking, preparations to pass to the
    one we have conquer'd,
The captain on the quarter-deck coldly giving his orders through
    a countenance white as a sheet,
Near by the corpse of the child that serv'd in the cabin,
The dead face of an old salt with long white hair and carefully
    curl'd whiskers,
The flames spite of all that can be done flickering aloft and below,   935
The husky voices of the two or three officers yet fit for duty,
Formless stacks of bodies and bodies by themselves, dabs of flesh
    upon the masts and spars,
Cut of cordage, dangle of rigging, slight shock of the soothe of
    waves,
Black and impassive guns, litter of powder-parcels, strong scent,
A few large stars overhead, silent and mournful shining,   940
Delicate sniffs of sea-breeze, smells of sedgy grass and fields by the
    shore, death-messages given in charge to survivors,
The hiss of the surgeon's knife, the gnawing teeth of his saw,
Wheeze, cluck, swash of falling blood, short wild scream, and long,
    dull, tapering groan,
These so, these irretrievable.

37

You laggards there on guard! look to your arms!   945
In at the conquer'd doors they crowd! I am possess'd!
Embody all presences outlaw'd or suffering,
See myself in prison shaped like another man,
And feel the dull unintermitted pain.

For me the keepers of convicts shoulder their carbines and keep
    watch,   950
It is I let out in the morning and barr'd at night.

Not a mutineer walks handcuff'd to jail but I am handcuff'd to
    him and walk by his side,
(I am less the jolly one there, and more the silent one with sweat
    on my twitching lips.)

Not a youngster is taken for larceny but I go up too, and am tried
    and sentenced.

955 Not a cholera patient lies at the last gasp but I also lie at the last
        gasp,
My face is ash-color'd, my sinews gnarl, away from me people
        retreat.

Askers embody themselves in me and I am embodied in them,
I project my hat, sit shame-faced, and beg.

38

Enough! enough! enough!
960 Somehow I have been stunn'd. Stand back!
Give me a little time beyond my cuff'd head, slumbers, dreams,
        gaping,
I discover myself on the verge of a usual mistake.

That I could forget the mockers and insults!
That I could forget the trickling tears and the blows of the bludg-
        eons and hammers!
That I could look with a separate look on my own crucifixion and
965   bloody crowning.

I remember now,
I resume the overstaid fraction,
The grave of rock multiplies what has been confided to it, or to
        any graves,
Corpses rise, gashes heal, fastenings roll from me.

I troop forth replenish'd with supreme power, one of an average
970   unending procession,
Inland and sea-coast we go, and pass all boundary lines,
Our swift ordinances on their way over the whole earth,
The blossoms we wear in our hats the growth of thousands of years.

Eleves, I salute you! come forward!
975 Continue your annotations, continue your questionings.

958. I project my hat] The beggar then commonly extended his hat to receive
alms.
974. Eleves] French: pupils or disciples.

39

The friendly and flowing savage, who is he?
Is he waiting for civilization, or past it and mastering it?

Is he some Southwesterner rais'd out-doors? is he Kanadian?
Is he from the Mississippi country? Iowa, Oregon, California?
The mountains? prairie-life, bush-life? or sailor from the sea?   980

Wherever he goes men and women accept and desire him,
They desire he should like them, touch them, speak to them, stay
          with them.

Behavior lawless as snow-flakes, words simple as grass, uncomb'd
          head, laughter, and naivetè,
Slow-stepping feet, common features, common modes and ema-
          nations,
They descend in new forms from the tips of his fingers,   985
They are wafted with the odor of his body or breath, they fly out
          of the glance of his eyes.

40

Flaunt of the sunshine I need not your bask—lie over!
You light surfaces only, I force surfaces and depths also.

Earth! you seem to look for something at my hands,
Say, old top-knot, what do you want?   990

Man or woman, I might tell how I like you, but cannot,
And might tell what it is in me and what it is in you, but cannot,
And might tell that pining I have, that pulse of my nights and
          days.

Behold, I do not give lectures or a little charity,
When I give I give myself.   995

990. old top-knot] This epithet was familiar in frontier humor as a comic, half-
affectionate term for an Indian, whose tuft of hair or ornament on top of the head was
characteristic of certain tribes. Perhaps we have here a conscious echo from the
reference to the "friendly and flowing savage" of line 976.

You there, impotent, loose in the knees,
Open your scarf'd chops till I blow grit within you,
Spread your palms and lift the flaps of your pockets,
I am not to be denied, I compel, I have stores plenty and to spare,
1000 And any thing I have I bestow.

I do not ask who you are, that is not important to me,
You can do nothing and be nothing but what I will infold you.

To cotton-field drudge or cleaner of privies I lean,
On his right cheek I put the family kiss,
1005 And in my soul I swear I never will deny him.

On women fit for conception I start bigger and nimbler babes,
(This day I am jetting the stuff of far more arrogant republics.)

To any one dying, thither I speed and twist the knob of the door,
Turn the bed-clothes toward the foot of the bed,
1010 Let the physician and the priest go home.

I seize the descending man and raise him with resistless will,
O despairer, here is my neck,
By God, you shall not go down! hang your whole weight upon me.

I dilate you with tremendous breath, I buoy you up,
1015 Every room of the house do I fill with an arm'd force,
Lovers of me, bafflers of graves.

Sleep—I and they keep guard all night,
Not doubt, not decease shall dare to lay finger upon you,
I have embraced you, and henceforth possess you to myself,
1020 And when you rise in the morning you will find what I tell you is so.

41

I am he bringing help for the sick as they pant on their backs,
And for strong upright men I bring yet more needed help.

---

997. scarf'd chops] Scarified or channeled, hence lined or "worn-down" face.
1018. decease] This word was misprinted as "disease" in the 1902 CW, and the error seems to have been repeated in most later editions.
1032. image] Kronos: the Titan, son of Uranus and Gaea, who dethroned his father

I heard what was said of the universe,
Heard it and heard it of several thousand years;
It is middling well as far as it goes—but is that all?   1025

Magnifying and applying come I,
Outbidding at the start the old cautious hucksters,
Taking myself the exact dimensions of Jehovah,
Lithographing Kronos, Zeus his son, and Hercules his grandson,
Buying drafts of Osiris, Isis, Belus, Brahma, Buddha,   1030
In my portfolio placing Manito loose, Allah on a leaf, the crucifix
    engraved,
With Odin and the hideous-faced Mexitli and every idol and image,
Taking them all for what they are worth and not a cent more,
Admitting they were alive and did the work of their days,
(They bore mites as for unfledg'd birds who have now to rise and
    fly and sing for themselves,)   1035
Accepting the rough deific sketches to fill out better in myself,
    bestowing them freely on each man and woman I see,
Discovering as much or more in a framer framing a house,
Putting higher claims for him there with his roll'd-up sleeves driving
    the mallet and chisel,
Not objecting to special revelations, considering a curl of smoke
    or a hair on the back of my hand just as curious as any
    revelation,
Lads ahold of fire-engines and hook-and-ladder ropes no less to
    me than the gods of the antique wars,   1040
Minding their voices peal through the crash of destruction,
Their brawny limbs passing safe over charr'd laths, their white
    foreheads whole and unhurt out of the flames;
By the mechanic's wife with her babe at her nipple interceding for
    every person born,
Three scythes at harvest whizzing in a row from three lusty angels
    with shirts bagg'd out at their waists,
The snag-tooth'd hostler with red hair redeeming sins past and to
    come,   1045
Selling all he possesses, traveling on foot to fee lawyers for his
    brother and sit by him while he is tried for forgery;

and was in turn dethroned by his son, Zeus. Osiris: Egyptian god of the lower world.
Isis: Egyptian goddess of fertility, sister and wife of Osiris. Belus: legendary king
of Assyria. Manito: Nature spirit of the Algonquian Indians. Mexitli: Aztec god of
war. Brahma, in Hindu religion, the supreme soul of the universe. Odin, in Norse
mythology, the god of war.

What was strewn in the amplest strewing the square rod about
      me, and not filling the square rod then,
The bull and the bug never worshipp'd half enough,
Dung and dirt more admirable than was dream'd,
The supernatural of no account, myself waiting my time to be one
1050   of the supremes,
The day getting ready for me when I shall do as much good as
      the best, and be as prodigious;
By my life-lumps! becoming already a creator,
Putting myself here and now to the ambush'd womb of the shadows.

42

A call in the midst of the crowd,
1055 My own voice, orotund sweeping and final.

Come my children,
Come my boys and girls, my women, household and intimates,
Now the performer launches his nerve, he has pass'd his prelude
      on the reeds within.

Easily written loose-finger'd chords—I feel the thrum of your
      climax and close.

1060 My head slues round on my neck,
Music rolls, but not from the organ,
Folks are around me, but they are no household of mine.

Ever the hard unsunk ground,
Ever the eaters and drinkers, ever the upward and downward sun,
      ever the air and the ceaseless tides,
1065 Ever myself and my neighbors, refreshing, wicked, real,
Ever the old inexplicable query, ever that thorn'd thumb, that
      breath of itches and thirsts,

1048. The bull and the bug] Probably chosen as common objects; yet the bull was
worshipped in Greece as the embodiment of Dionysus, and also held sacred by the
Egyptians and believed by the Moslems to support the earth on its back. The
scarabaeus, a dung beetle, was the model for ikons of the Egyptian sun god,
Khepera.
1066. thorn'd thumb] WW's version of the familiar metaphor, "thorn in the flesh,"
an image of vexation.

Ever the vexer's *hoot! hoot!* till we find where the sly one hides
    and bring him forth,
Ever love, ever the sobbing liquid of life,
Ever the bandage under the chin, ever the trestles of death.

LIVING DEAD

Here and there with dimes on the eyes walking,   1070
To feed the greed of the belly the brains liberally spooning,
Tickets buying, taking, selling, but in to the feast never once going,
Many sweating, ploughing, thrashing, and then the chaff for pay-
    ment receiving,
A few idly owning, and they the wheat continually claiming.

MOTLYIAN

This is the city and I am one of the citizens,   1075
Whatever interests the rest interests me, politics, wars, markets,
    newspapers, schools,
The mayor and councils, banks, tariffs, steamships, factories, stocks,
    stores, real estate and personal estate.

The little plentiful manikins skipping around in collars and tail'd
    coats,
I am aware who they are, (they are positively not worms or fleas,)
I acknowledge the duplicates of myself, the weakest and shallowest
    is deathless with me,   1080
What I do and say the same waits for them,
Every thought that flounders in me the same flounders in them.

I know perfectly well my own egotism,
Know my omnivorous lines and must not write any less,
And would fetch you whoever you are flush with myself.   1085

Not words of routine this song of mine,
But abruptly to question, to leap beyond yet nearer bring;
This printed and bound book—but the printer and the printing-
    office boy?

1069. trestles] The supports on which the dead lie; the same image is employed in
"Beat! Beat! Drums!"
1070. dimes on the eyes] The phrase powerfully combines the previous image of
death (dimes keep the eye-lids closed until the funeral) and that of greed, following.
Cf. E. A. Robinson's sonnet on Aaron Stark:

    A miser was he, with a miser's nose,
    And eyes like little dollars in the dark.

The well-taken photographs—but your wife or friend close and
      solid in your arms?
The black ship mail'd with iron, her mighty guns in her turrets—
1090   but the pluck of the captain and engineers?
In the houses the dishes and fare and furniture—but the host and
      hostess, and the look out of their eyes?
The sky up there—yet here or next door, or across the way?
The saints and sages in history—but you yourself?
Sermons, creeds, theology—but the fathomless human brain,
1095 And what is reason? and what is love? and what is life?

43

I do not despise you priests, all time, the world over,
My faith is the greatest of faiths and the least of faiths,
Enclosing worship ancient and modern and all between ancient
      and modern,
Believing I shall come again upon the earth after five thousand
      years,
Waiting responses from oracles, honoring the gods, saluting the
1100 sun,
Making a fetich of the first rock or stump, powowing with sticks in
      the circle of obis,
Helping the llama or brahmin as he trims the lamps of the idols,
Dancing yet through the streets in a phallic procession, rapt and
      austere in the woods a gymnosophist,
Drinking mead from the skull-cup, to Shastas and Vedas admirant,
      minding the Koran,
Walking the teokallis, spotted with gore from the stone and knife,
1105   beating the serpent-skin drum,
Accepting the Gospels, accepting him that was crucified, knowing
      assuredly that he is divine,
To the mass kneeling or the puritan's prayer rising, or sitting
      patiently in a pew,

1101. obis] Properly, "obi" or "obeah," sorcery of African origin, formerly practiced
by Negroes in the British West Indies, the Guianas, and the southeastern United
States.
1102. llama] Properly, "lama," Tibetan high priest.
1103. gymnosophist] Member of an ancient Hindu sect of ascetics who wore little or
no clothing.

Ranting and frothing in my insane crisis, or waiting dead-like till
    my spirit arouses me,
Looking forth on pavement and land, or outside of pavement and
    land,
Belonging to the winders of the circuit of circuits.   1110

One of that centripetal and centrifugal gang I turn and talk like a
    man leaving charges before a journey.

Down-hearted doubters dull and excluded,
Frivolous, sullen, moping, angry, affected, dishearten'd, atheistical,
I know every one of you, I know the sea of torment, doubt,
    despair and unbelief.

How the flukes splash!   1115
How they contort rapid as lightning, with spasms and spouts of
    blood!

Be at peace bloody flukes of doubters and sullen mopers,
I take my place among you as much as among any,
The past is the push of you, me, all, precisely the same,
And what is yet untried and afterward is for you, me, all, precisely
    the same.   1120

I do not know what is untried and afterward,
But I know it will in its turn prove sufficient, and cannot fail.

Each who passes is consider'd, each who stops is consider'd, not
    a single one can it fail.

It cannot fail the young man who died and was buried,
Nor the young woman who died and was put by his side,   1125
Nor the little child that peep'd in at the door, and then drew back
    and was never seen again,

1104. Shastas and Vedas] Shastas (properly "shastras") and Vedas are collections
of the ancient sacred literature of Hinduism.
1105. teokallis] Aztec temples, usually built upon a truncated pyramid.
1111. gang] In the obsolescent sense of a group of people traveling in the same
direction; not then a disparaging term.
1117. bloody flukes] As the flukes (tail fins) of a stricken whale.

Nor the old man who has lived without purpose, and feels it with
       bitterness worse than gall,
Nor him in the poor house tubercled by rum and the bad dis-
       order,
Nor the numberless slaughter'd and wreck'd, nor the brutish koboo
       call'd the ordure of humanity,
1130   Nor the sacs merely floating with open mouths for food to slip in,
Nor any thing in the earth, or down in the oldest graves of the
       earth,
Nor any thing in the myriads of spheres, nor the myriads of
       myriads that inhabit them,
Nor the present, nor the least wisp that is known.

44

It is time to explain myself—let us stand up.

1135   What is known I strip away,
I launch all men and women forward with me into the Unknown.

The clock indicates the moment—but what does eternity indicate?

We have thus far exhausted trillions of winters and summers,
There are trillions ahead, and trillions ahead of them.

1140   Births have brought us richness and variety,
And other births will bring us richness and variety.

I do not call one greater and one smaller,
That which fills its period and place is equal to any.

Were mankind murderous or jealous upon you, my brother, my
       sister?
1145   I am sorry for you, they are not murderous or jealous upon me,
All has been gentle with me, I keep no account with lamentation,
(What have I to do with lamentation?)

I am an acme of things accomplish'd, and I an encloser of things
       to be.

1129. koboo] A native of Palembang on the east coast of Sumatra. See T. O.
Mabbott, *Expli.*, XI, 34.
1148–1169.] Cf. note for lines 670–683.

My feet strike an apex of the apices of the stairs,
On every step bunches of ages, and larger bunches between the
     steps,   1150
All below duly travel'd, and still I mount and mount.

Rise after rise bow the phantoms behind me,
Afar down I see the huge first Nothing, I know I was even there,
I waited unseen and always, and slept through the lethargic mist,
And took my time, and took no hurt from the fetid carbon.   1155

Long I was hugg'd close—long and long.

Immense have been the preparations for me,
Faithful and friendly the arms that have help'd me.

Cycles ferried my cradle, rowing and rowing like cheerful boatmen,
For room to me stars kept aside in their own rings,   1160
They sent influences to look after what was to hold me.

Before I was born out of my mother generations guided me,
My embryo has never been torpid, nothing could overlay it.

For it the nebula cohered to an orb,
The long slow strata piled to rest it on,   1165
Vast vegetables gave it sustenance,
Monstrous sauroids transported it in their mouths and deposited
    it with care.

All forces have been steadily employ'd to complete and delight me,
Now on this spot I stand with my robust soul.

45

O span of youth! ever-push'd elasticity!   1170
O manhood, balanced, florid and full.

My lovers suffocate me,
Crowding my lips, thick in the pores of my skin,
Jostling me through streets and public halls, coming naked to me
    at night,

1167. sauroids] Sauria, prehistoric mammoth reptiles, thought according to legend
to carry their eggs in their mouths—a folk superstition which, with respect to snakes,
has survived to modern times.

Crying by day *Ahoy!* from the rocks of the river, swinging and
1175   chirping over my head,
Calling my name from flower-beds, vines, tangled underbrush,
Lighting on every moment of my life,
Bussing my body with soft balsamic busses,
Noiselessly passing handfuls out of their hearts and giving them
            to be mine.

Old age superbly rising! O welcome, ineffable grace of dying
1180   days!

Every condition promulges not only itself, it promulges what grows
            after and out of itself,
And the dark hush promulges as much as any.

I open my scuttle at night and see the far-sprinkled systems,
And all I see multiplied as high as I can cipher edge but the rim
            of the farther systems.

1185 Wider and wider they spread, expanding, always expanding,
Outward and outward and forever outward.

My sun has his sun and round him obediently wheels,
He joins with his partners a group of superior circuit,
And greater sets follow, making specks of the greatest inside them.

1190 There is no stoppage and never can be stoppage,
If I, you, and the worlds, and all beneath or upon their surfaces,
            were this moment reduced back to a pallid float, it would
            not avail in the long run,
We should surely bring up again where we now stand,
And surely go as much farther, and then farther and farther.

A few quadrillions of eras, a few octillions of cubic leagues, do not
            hazard the span or make it impatient,
1195 They are but parts, any thing is but a part.

See ever so far, there is limitless space outside of that,
Count ever so much, there is limitless time around that.

1181. promulges] Archaic form of "promulgate," to make known, to make wide-
spread.

My rendezvous is appointed, it is certain,
The Lord will be there and wait till I come on perfect terms,
The great Camerado, the lover true for whom I pine will be there.   1200

46

I know I have the best of time and space, and was never measured
       and never will be measured.

I tramp a perpetual journey, (come listen all!)
My signs are a rain-proof coat, good shoes, and a staff cut from
       the woods,
No friend of mine takes his ease in my chair,
I have no chair, no church, no philosophy,   1205
I lead no man to a dinner-table, library, exchange,
But each man and each woman of you I lead upon a knoll,
My left hand hooking you round the waist,
My right hand pointing to landscapes of continents and the public
       road.

Not I, not any one else can travel that road for you,   1210
You must travel it for yourself.

It is not far, it is within reach,
Perhaps you have been on it since you were born and did not
       know,
Perhaps it is everywhere on water and on land.

Shoulder your duds dear son, and I will mine, and let us hasten
       forth,   1215
Wonderful cities and free nations we shall fetch as we go.

If you tire, give me both burdens, and rest the chuff of your hand
       on my hip,
And in due time you shall repay the same service to me,
For after we start we never lie by again.

This day before dawn I ascended a hill and look'd at the crowded
       heaven,   1220

1217. chuff] English dialectical adjective meaning "chubby" or "fat"; here converted
into a noun referring to the heel of the hand.

And I said to my spirit *When we become the enfolders of those
　　orbs, and the pleasure and knowledge of every thing in
　　them, shall we be fill'd and satisfied then?*
And my spirit said *No, we but level that lift to pass and continue
　　beyond.*

You are also asking me questions and I hear you,
I answer that I cannot answer, you must find out for yourself.

1225　Sit a while dear son,
Here are biscuits to eat and here is milk to drink,
But as soon as you sleep and renew yourself in sweet clothes, I
　　kiss you with a good-by kiss and open the gate for your
　　egress hence.

Long enough have you dream'd contemptible dreams,
Now I wash the gum from your eyes,
You must habit yourself to the dazzle of the light and of every
1230　　moment of your life.

Long have you timidly waded holding a plank by the shore,
Now I will you to be a bold swimmer,
To jump off in the midst of the sea, rise again, nod to me, shout,
　　and laughingly dash with your hair.

47

I am the teacher of athletes,
He that by me spreads a wider breast than my own proves the
1235　　width of my own,
He most honors my style who learns under it to destroy the
　　teacher. *If you meet the Buddha on the road kill him*

The boy I love, the same becomes a man not through derived
　　power, but in his own right,
Wicked rather than virtuous out of conformity or fear,
Fond of his sweetheart, relishing well his steak,
Unrequited love or a slight cutting him worse than sharp steel
1240　　cuts,
First-rate to ride, to fight, to hit the bull's eye, to sail a skiff, to
　　sing a song or play on the banjo,

Preferring scars and the beard and faces pitted with small-pox
      over all latherers,
And those well-tann'd to those that keep out of the sun.

I teach straying from me, yet who can stray from me?
I follow you whoever you are from the present hour,   1245
My words itch at your ears till you understand them.

I do not say these things for a dollar or to fill up the time while I
      wait for a boat,
(It is you talking just as much as myself, I act as the tongue of
      you,
Tied in your mouth, in mine it begins to be loosen'd.)

I swear I will never again mention love or death inside a house,   1250
And I swear I will never translate myself at all, only to him or her
      who privately stays with me in the open air.

If you would understand me go to the heights or water-shore,
The nearest gnat is an explanation, and a drop or motion of waves
      a key,
The maul, the oar, the hand-saw, second my words.

No shutter'd room or school can commune with me,   1255
But roughs and little children better than they.

The young mechanic is closest to me, he knows me well,
The woodman that takes his axe and jug with him shall take me
      with him all day,
The farm-boy ploughing in the field feels good at the sound of my
      voice,
In vessels that sail my words sail, I go with fishermen and seamen
      and love them.   1260

The soldier camp'd or upon the march is mine,
On the night ere the pending battle many seek me, and I do not
      fail them,
On that solemn night (it may be their last) those that know me
      seek me.

My face rubs to the hunter's face when he lies down alone in his
      blanket,

1265   The driver thinking of me does not mind the jolt of his wagon,
The young mother and old mother comprehend me,
The girl and the wife rest the needle a moment and forget where
      they are,
They and all would resume what I have told them.

48

I have said that the soul is not more than the body,
1270   And I have said that the body is not more than the soul,
And nothing, not God, is greater to one than one's self is,
And whoever walks a furlong without sympathy walks to his own
      funeral drest in his shroud,
And I or you pocketless of a dime may purchase the pick of the
      earth,
And to glance with an eye or show a bean in its pod confounds
      the learning of all times,
And there is no trade or employment but the young man following
1275   it may become a hero,
And there is no object so soft but it makes a hub for the wheel'd
      universe,
And I say to any man or woman, Let your soul stand cool and
      composed before a million universes.

And I say to mankind, Be not curious about God,
For I who am curious about each am not curious about God,
(No array of terms can say how much I am at peace about God
1280   and about death.)

I hear and behold God in every object, yet understand God not
      in the least,
Nor do I understand who there can be more wonderful than
      myself.

Why should I wish to see God better than this day?
I see something of God each hour of the twenty-four, and each
      moment then,

1290. accoucheur] Midwife, obstetrician; note also "the elder-hand" below.
1292–1293.] These lines are echoed by Thomas Wolfe in his story "The Four Lost

In the faces of men and women I see God, and in my own face in
    the glass, *supra* 1285
I find letters from God dropt in the street, and every one is sign'd
    by God's name,
And I leave them where they are, for I know that wheresoe'er I go,
Others will punctually come for ever and ever.

49

And as to you Death, and you bitter hug of mortality, it is idle to
    try to alarm me.

To his work without flinching the accoucheur comes, *Birth* 1290
I see the elder-hand pressing receiving supporting,
I recline by the sills of the exquisite flexible doors,
And mark the outlet, and mark the relief and escape.

And as to you Corpse I think you are good manure, but that does
    not offend me,
I smell the white roses sweet-scented and growing, 1295
I reach to the leafy lips, I reach to the polish'd breasts of melons.

And as to you Life I reckon you are the leavings of many deaths,
(No doubt I have died myself ten thousand times before.)

I hear you whispering there O stars of heaven,
O suns—O grass of graves—O perpetual transfers and pro-
    motions, 1300
If you do not say any thing how can I say any thing?

Of the turbid pool that lies in the autumn forest,
Of the moon that descends the steeps of the soughing twilight,
Toss, sparkles of day and dusk—toss on the black stems that
    decay in the muck,
Toss to the moaning gibberish of the dry limbs. 1305

I ascend from the moon, I ascend from the night,
I perceive that the ghastly glimmer is noonday sunbeams reflected,

Men": "As we leaned on the sills of evening, as we stood in the frames of the
marvellous doors . . ."

And debouch to the steady and central from the offspring great or
    small.

50 *Lots of "it's"*

There is that in me—I do not know what it is—but I know it is
    in me.

1310 Wrench'd and sweaty—calm and cool then my body becomes,
I sleep—I sleep long.

I do not know it—it is without name—it is a word unsaid,
It is not in any dictionary, utterance, symbol.

Something it swings on more than the earth I swing on,
1315 To it the creation is the friend whose embracing awakes me.

Perhaps I might tell more. Outlines! I plead for my brothers
    and sisters.

Do you see O my brothers and sisters?
It is not chaos or death—it is form, union, plan—it is eternal
    life—it is Happiness.

51

The past and present wilt—I have fill'd them, emptied them,
1320 And proceed to fill my next fold of the future.

Listener up there! what have you to confide to me?
Look in my face while I snuff the sidle of evening,
(Talk honestly, no one else hears you, and I stay only a minute
    longer.)

Do I contradict myself?
1325 Very well then I contradict myself,
(I am large, I contain multitudes.)

1308. debouch] Emerge. Cf. The French, "bouche," a mouth; and note the "flexible
doors" (l.1293). "I" is apparently the subject of the verb, and if so, "offspring"
may be interpreted as "point of departure."
1318. Happiness] For an interpretation of this passage as mystical intuition, see
Clarence Gohdes, "Section 50 of Whitman's 'Song of Myself,'" MLN, LXXV, 653–656.
1322. snuff the sidle of evening] Cf. the colloquial phrase, to "snuff out" (extin-
guish) a light—in this case the sidelong glimmer of evening.

I concentrate toward them that are nigh, I wait on the door-slab.

Who has done his day's work? who will soonest be through with
     his supper?
Who wishes to walk with me?

Will you speak before I am gone? will you prove already too late?   1330

52

The spotted hawk swoops by and accuses me, he complains of my
     gab and my loitering.

I too am not a bit tamed, I too am untranslatable,
I sound my barbaric yawp over the roofs of the world.

The last scud of day holds back for me,
It flings my likeness after the rest and true as any on the shadow'd
     wilds,   1335
It coaxes me to the vapor and the dusk.

I depart as air, I shake my white locks at the runaway sun,
I effuse my flesh in eddies, and drift it in lacy jags.

I bequeath myself to the dirt to grow from the grass I love,
If you want me again look for me under your boot-soles.   1340

You will hardly know who I am or what I mean,
But I shall be good health to you nevertheless,
And filter and fibre your blood.

Failing to fetch me at first keep encouraged,
Missing me one place search another,   1345
I stop somewhere waiting for you.

1855   *1881*

1324–1325. contradict myself] Cf. Emerson's "A foolish consistency is the hobgoblin
of little minds, adored by little statesmen and philosophers and divines" ("Self-
Reliance," *Essays: First Series*, 1841).
1346. you] Through a series of bold images—the hawk, the meteor-like scud or loose
eddies of evening mist, the dirt which nourishes the grass—the poet leaves the reader
with his legacy of great natural force, untranslatable but found everywhere—in the
sky or under foot.

Children of Adam.

To the Garden the World.

To the garden the world anew ascending,
Potent mates, daughters, sons, preluding,
The love, the life of their bodies, meaning and being,
Curious here behold my resurrection after slumber,
5   The revolving cycles in their wide sweep having brought me again,
Amorous, mature, all beautiful to me, all wondrous,
My limbs and the quivering fire that ever plays through them, for
       reasons, most wondrous,
Existing I peer and penetrate still,
Content with the present, content with the past,
10 By my side or back of me Eve following,
Or in front, and I following her just the same.

1860   *1867*

ADAM] In two of his notes toward poems WW set forth his ideas for this group. One reads: "A string of Poems (short, etc.), embodying the amative love of woman—the same as Live Oak Leaves do the passion of friendship for man." (MS unlocated; N and F, 169, No. 63). The other, evidently written after the "Live Oak Leaves" had been replaced by "Calamus" as a symbol, is more explicit: "Theory of a Cluster of Poems the same *to the passion of Woman-Love* as the "Calamus-Leaves" are to adhesiveness, manly love. Full of animal-fire, tender, burning,—the tremulous ache, delicious, yet such a torment. The swelling elate and vehement, that will not be denied. Adam, as a central figure and type. One piece presenting a vivid picture (in connection with the spirit) of a fully complete, well-developed man, eld, bearded, swart, fiery,—as a more than rival of the youthful type-hero of novels and love poems" (Trent; N and F, 124, No. 142).

Under the title "Enfans d'Adam" the group first appeared in LG 1860 as fifteen poems, twelve of which were new. In the 1867 edition the title was changed to "Children of Adam," and one of the poems, "In the New Garden, in all the Parts," was dropped. In 1871 the fourteen poems of the preceding edition were retained, together with two transfers from the *Drum-Taps* poems, to make a total of sixteen; thereafter the group remained unchanged, although the present order is slightly different from that of the original. WW was formally to defend this group in his "A Memorandum at a Venture," *North American Review* (June, 1882) CXXXIV, 456–450, as a few months earlier he had defended it in talk with Emerson on the Boston

From Pent-up Aching Rivers.

From pent-up aching rivers,
From that of myself without which I were nothing,
From what I am determin'd to make illustrous, even if I stand
     sole among men,
From my own voice resonant, singing the phallus,
Singing the song of procreation,   5
Singing the need of superb children and therein superb grown
     people,
Singing the muscular urge and the blending,
Singing the bedfellow's song, (O resistless yearning!
O for any and each the body correlative attracting!
O for you whoever you are your correlative body! O it, more than   10
     all else, you delighting!)
From the hungry gnaw that eats me night and day,
From native moments, from bashful pains, singing them,
Seeking something yet unfound though I have diligently sought it
     many a long year,
Singing the true song of the soul fitful at random,
Renascent with grossest Nature or among animals,   15
Of that, of them and what goes with them my poems informing,
Of the smell of apples and lemons, of the pairing of birds,
Of the wet of woods, of the lapping of waves,

Common. He is reported by Traubel as remarking, " 'Children of Adam' stumps the
worst and the best; I have even tried hard to see if it might not as I grow older or
experience new moods stump me; I have even almost deliberately tried to retreat. But
it would not do. When I tried to take those pieces out of the scheme the whole scheme
came down about my ears" (Traubel, i, 3).

    WORLD] Two MS versions of this poem, under the title "Leaves-Droppings," are
in the Barrett collection (see *WWM*, 58), and as WW's second note on the "Children
of Adam" group indicates, "Adam, as a central figure and type," is here made the
controlling symbol of the group, the subject of its first poem and its last. The poet
left this fine poem unaltered through the successive editions.

    RIVERS] Originally "Enfans d'Adam" No. 2 in the 1860 edition, this poem took
its present title in the next edition (1867) from what had been its tenth line,
although the poet had tentatively entered the title "Song of Procreation" in his MS
revisions. It is a daring and original celebration of the drive of sex, not only the
procreative instinct but the whole appetite for the context of creation—the smell of
apples, the wet of woods. The poem remained comparatively unchanged although a
few lines were later omitted, including, in 1881, the passage:

           Singing what, to the Soul, entirely redeemed her,
              the faithful one, the prostitute, who detained
              me when I went to the city;
           Singing the song of prostitutes.

Of the mad pushes of waves upon the land, I them chanting,
20   The overture lightly sounding, the strain anticipating,
The welcome nearness, the sight of the perfect body,
The swimmer swimming naked in the bath, or motionless on his
      back lying and floating,
The female form approaching, I pensive, love-flesh tremulous
      aching,
The divine list for myself or you or for any one making,
25   The face, the limbs, the index from head to foot, and what it
      arouses,
The mystic deliria, the madness amorous, the utter abandonment,
(Hark close and still what I now whisper to you,
I love you, O you entirely possess me,
O that you and I escape from the rest and go utterly off, free and
      lawless,
30   Two hawks in the air, two fishes swimming in the sea not more
      lawless than we;)
The furious storm through me careering, I passionately trembling,
The oath of the inseparableness of two together, of the woman
      that loves me and whom I love more than my life, that oath
      swearing,
(O I willingly stake all for you,
O let me be lost if it must be so!
35   O you and I! what is it to us what the rest do or think?
What is all else to us? only that we enjoy each other and exhaust
      each other if it must be so;)
From the master, the pilot I yield the vessel to,
The general commanding me, commanding all, from him permis-
      sion taking,
From time the programme hastening, (I have loiter'd too long as
      it is,)
40   From sex, from the warp and from the woof,
From privacy, from frequent repinings alone,
From plenty of persons near and yet the right person not near,
From the soft sliding of hands over me and thrusting of fingers
      through my hair and beard,

40. warp . . . woof] Associated with the word "sex," the interweaving vertical
and horizontal strands on a loom suggest masculine and feminine opposites.

ELECTRIC] No. 5 of the twelve poems of the 1855 edition, "I Sing the Body
Electric," untitled and unsectioned, became "Poem of the Body" in the 1856 edition,
augmented with the remarkable anatomical inventory which now concludes the

From the long sustain'd kiss upon the mouth or bosom,
From the close pressure that makes me or any man drunk, fainting
    with excess,   45
From what the divine husband knows, from the work of fatherhood,
From exultation, victory and relief, from the bedfellow's embrace
    in the night,
From the act-poems of eyes, hands, hips and bosoms,
From the cling of the trembling arm,
From the bending curve and the clinch,   50
From side by side the pliant coverlet off-throwing,
From the one so unwilling to have me leave, and me just as unwilling
    to leave,
(Yet a moment O tender waiter, and I return,)
From the hour of shining stars and dropping dews,
From the night a moment I emerging flitting out,   55
Celebrate you act divine and you children prepared for,
And you stalwart loins.

   1860   *1881*

I Sing the Body Electric.

1

I sing the body electric,
The armies of those I love engirth me and I engirth them,
They will not let me off till I go with them, respond to them,
And discorrupt them, and charge them full with the charge of the
    soul.

Was it doubted that those who corrupt their own bodies conceal
    themselves?   5

poem. The poet's MS notes thereon are now in the Trent Duke collection (*N and F*,
172, No. 84). In 1860 the poem became "Enfans d'Adam" No. 3 with a few minor
revisions; and in 1867 it acquired its present sectioning and title, which was also its
opening line. There were minor changes in 1871 and 1881. What the poet sang—
lovingly, boldly to the limit of specificity—was this world's body, in whose movements
he found insatiable delight; but also, as he tells us repeatedly, he is singing the soul.

And if those who defile the living are as bad as they who defile
    the dead?
And if the body does not do fully as much as the soul?
And if the body were not the soul, what is the soul?

2

The love of the body of man or woman balks account, the body
    itself balks account,
10   That of the male is perfect, and that of the female is perfect.

The expression of the face balks account,
But the expression of a well-made man appears not only in his
    face,
It is in his limbs and joints also, it is curiously in the joints of his
    hips and wrists,
It is in his walk, the carriage of his neck, the flex of his waist and
    knees, dress does not hide him,
The strong sweet quality he has strikes through the cotton and
15   broadcloth,
To see him pass conveys as much as the best poem, perhaps more,
You linger to see his back, and the back of his neck and shoul-
    der-side.

The sprawl and fulness of babes, the bosoms and heads of women,
    the folds of their dress, their style as we pass in the street,
    the contour of their shape downwards,
The swimmer naked in the swimming-bath, seen as he swims
    through the transparent green-shine, or lies with his face
    up and rolls silently to and fro in the heave of the water,
The bending forward and backward of rowers in row-boats,
20   the horseman in his saddle,
Girls, mothers, house-keepers, in all their performances,
The group of laborers seated at noon-time with their open dinner-
    kettles, and their wives waiting,
The female soothing a child, the farmer's daughter in the garden
    or cow-yard,
The young fellow hoeing corn, the sleigh-driver driving his six
    horses through the crowd,

The wrestle of wrestlers, two apprentice-boys, quite grown, lusty,
    good-natured, native-born, out on the vacant lot at sun-
    down after work, 25
The coats and caps thrown down, the embrace of love and resistance,
The upper-hold and under-hold, the hair rumpled over and blind-
    ing the eyes;
The march of firemen in their own costumes, the play of mascu-
    line muscle through clean-setting trowsers and waist-straps,
The slow return from the fire, the pause when the bell strikes
    suddenly again, and the listening on the alert,
The natural, perfect, varied attitudes, the bent head, the curv'd
    neck and the counting; 30
Such-like I love—I loosen myself, pass freely, am at the mother's
    breast with the little child,
Swim with the swimmers, wrestle with wrestlers, march in line with
    the firemen, and pause, listen, count.

3

I knew a man, a common farmer, the father of five sons,
And in them the fathers of sons, and in them the fathers of sons.

This man was of wonderful vigor, calmness, beauty of person, 35
The shape of his head, the pale yellow and white of his hair and
    beard, the immeasurable meaning of his black eyes, the
    richness and breadth of his manners,
These I used to go and visit him to see, he was wise also,
He was six feet tall, he was over eighty years old, his sons were
    massive, clean, bearded, tan-faced, handsome,
They and his daughters loved him, all who saw him loved him,
They did not love him by allowance, they loved him with personal
    love, 40
He drank water only, the blood show'd like scarlet through the
    clear-brown skin of his face,
He was a frequent gunner and fisher, he sail'd his boat himself,
    he had a fine one presented to him by a ship-joiner,
    he had fowling-pieces presented to him by men that loved him,
When he went with his five sons and many grand-sons to hunt or
    fish, you would pick him out as the most beautiful and
    vigorous of the gang,

You would wish long and long to be with him, you would wish to
    sit by him in the boat that you and he might touch each
    other.

4

45   I have perceiv'd that to be with those I like is enough,
To stop in company with the rest at evening is enough,
To be surrounded by beautiful, curious, breathing, laughing flesh
    is enough,
To pass among them or touch any one, or rest my arm ever so
    lightly round his or her neck for a moment, what is this
    then?
I do not ask any more delight, I swim in it as in a sea.

There is something in staying close to men and women and look-
    ing on them, and in the contact and odor of them, that
50   pleases the soul well,
All things please the soul, but these please the soul well.

5

This is the female form,
A divine nimbus exhales from it from head to foot,
It attracts with fierce undeniable attraction,
I am drawn by its breath as if I were no more than a helpless
55   vapor, all falls aside but myself and it,
Books, art, religion, time, the visible and solid earth, and what was
    expected of heaven or fear'd of hell, are now consumed,
Mad filaments, ungovernable shoots play out of it, the response
    likewise ungovernable,
Hair, bosom, hips, bend of legs, negligent falling hands all dif-
    fused, mine too diffused,
Ebb stung by the flow and flow stung by the ebb, love-flesh swel-
    ling and deliciously aching,
Limitless limpid jets of love hot and enormous, quivering jelly of
60   love, white-blow and delirious juice,
Bridegroom night of love working surely and softly into the pros-
    trate dawn,
Undulating into the willing and yielding day,
Lost in the cleave of the clasping and sweet-flesh'd day.

This the nucleus—after the child is born of woman, man is born
    of woman,
This the bath of birth, this the merge of small and large, and the
    outlet again. 65

Be not ashamed women, your privilege encloses the rest, and is the
    exit of the rest,
You are the gates of the body, and you are the gates of the soul.

The female contains all qualities and tempers them,
She is in her place and moves with perfect balance,
She is all things duly veil'd, she is both passive and active, 70
She is to conceive daughters as well as sons, and sons as well as
    daughters.

As I see my soul reflected in Nature,
As I see through a mist, One with inexpressible completeness,
    sanity, beauty,
See the bent head and arms folded over the breast, the Female
    I see.

6

The male is not less the soul nor more, he too is in his place, 75
He too is all qualities, he is action and power,
The flush of the known universe is in him,
Scorn becomes him well, and appetite and defiance become him
    well,
The wildest largest passions, bliss that is utmost, sorrow that is
    utmost become him well, pride is for him,
The full-spread pride of man is calming and excellent to the soul, 80
Knowledge becomes him, he likes it always, he brings every thing
    to the test of himself,
Whatever the survey, whatever the sea and the sail he strikes
    soundings at last only here,
(Where else does he strike soundings except here?)

The man's body is sacred and the woman's body is sacred,
No matter who it is, it is sacred—is it the meanest one in the
    laborers' gang?
Is it one of the dull-faced immigrants just landed on the wharf? 85

Each belongs here or anywhere just as much as the well-off, just
    as much as you,
Each has his or her place in the procession.

(All is a procession,
90   The universe is a procession with measured and perfect motion.)

Do you know so much yourself that you call the meanest ignorant?
Do you suppose you have a right to a good sight, and he or she
    has no right to a sight?
Do you think matter has cohered together from its diffuse float,
    and the soil is on the surface, and water runs and vegeta-
    tion sprouts,
For you only, and not for him and her?

7

95 A man's body at auction,
   (For before the war I often go to the slave-mart and watch the
     sale,)
I help the auctioneer, the sloven does not half know his business.

Gentlemen look on this wonder,
Whatever the bids of the bidders they cannot be high enough for it,
For it the globe lay preparing quintillions of years without one
100   animal or plant,
For it the revolving cycles truly and steadily roll'd.

In this head the all-baffling brain,
In it and below it the makings of heroes.

Examine these limbs, red, black, or white, they are cunning in
    tendon and nerve,
105 They shall be stript that you may see them.

Exquisite senses, life-lit eyes, pluck, volition,
Flakes of breast-muscle, pliant backbone and neck, flesh not
    flabby, good-sized arms and legs,
And wonders within there yet.

    96. sale] This line was added in 1881.

Within there runs blood,
The same old blood! the same red-running blood! 110
There swells and jets a heart, there all passions, desires, reachings,
    aspirations,
(Do you think they are not there because they are not express'd in
    parlors and lecture-rooms?)

This is not only one man, this the father of those who shall be
    fathers in their turns,
In him the start of populous states and rich republics,
Of him countless immortal lives with countless embodiments and
    enjoyments. 115

How do you know who shall come from the offspring of his off-
    spring through the centuries?
(Who might you find you have come from yourself, if you could
    trace back through the centuries?)

8

A woman's body at auction,
She too is not only herself, she is the teeming mother of mothers,
She is the bearer of them that shall grow and be mates to the
    mothers. 120

Have you ever loved the body of a woman?
Have you ever loved the body of a man?
Do you not see that these are exactly the same to all in all nations
    and times all over the earth?

If any thing is sacred the human body is sacred,
And the glory and sweet of a man is the token of manhood
    untainted,
And in man or woman a clean, strong, firm-fibred body, is more 125
    beautiful than the most beautiful face.

Have you seen the fool that corrupted his own live body? or the
    fool that corrupted her own live body?
For they do not conceal themselves, and cannot conceal themselves.

9

O my body! I dare not desert the likes of you in other men and
      women, nor the likes of the parts of you,
I believe the likes of you are to stand or fall with the likes of the
130   soul, (and that they are the soul,)
I believe the likes of you shall stand or fall with my poems, and
      that they are my poems,
Man's, woman's, child's, youth's, wife's, husband's, mother's, father's,
      young man's, young woman's poems,
Head, neck, hair, ears, drop and tympan of the ears,
Eyes, eye-fringes, iris of the eye, eyebrows, and the waking or
      sleeping of the lids,
Mouth, tongue, lips, teeth, roof of the mouth, jaws, and the jaw-
135   hinges,
Nose, nostrils of the nose, and the partition,
Cheeks, temples, forehead, chin, throat, back of the neck, neck-
      slue,
Strong shoulders, manly beard, scapula, hind-shoulders, and the
      ample side-round of the chest,
Upper-arm, armpit, elbow-socket, lower-arm, arm-sinews, arm-
      bones,
Wrist and wrist-joints, hand, palm, knuckles, thumb, forefinger,
140   finger-joints, finger-nails,
Broad breast-front, curling hair of the breast, breast-bone, breast-side,
Ribs, belly, backbone, joints of the backbone,
Hips, hip-sockets, hip-strength, inward and outward round, man-
      balls, man-root,
Strong set of thighs, well carrying the trunk above,
145 Leg-fibres, knee, knee-pan, upper-leg, under-leg,
Ankles, instep, foot-ball, toes, toe-joints, the heel;
All attitudes, all the shapeliness, all the belongings of my or your
      body or of any one's body, male or female,
The lung-sponges, the stomach-sac, the bowels sweet and clean,
The brain in its folds inside the skull-frame,
150 Sympathies, heart-valves, palate-valves, sexuality, maternity,

ME] Originally an 1856 poem with the title "Poem of Procreation" and becoming
"Enfans d'Adam" No. 4 in 1860, "A Woman Waits for me" took its present title from
its first line in 1867. Had WW honored the title and first line he had tentatively
ventured in his 1860 MS revisions, "A woman America knows (or shall yet know)—

Womanhood, and all that is a woman, and the man that comes
    from woman,
The womb, the teats, nipples, breast-milk, tears, laughter, weeping,
    love-looks, love-perturbations and risings,
The voice, articulation, language, whispering, shouting aloud,
Food, drink, pulse, digestion, sweat, sleep, walking, swimming,
Poise on the hips, leaping, reclining, embracing, arm-curving and
    tightening,   155
The continual changes of the flex of the mouth, and around the
    eyes,
The skin, the sunburnt shade, freckles, hair,
The curious sympathy one feels when feeling with the hand the
    naked meat of the body,
The circling rivers the breath, and breathing it in and out,
The beauty of the waist, and thence of the hips, and thence down-
    ward toward the knees,   160
The thin red jellies within you or within me, the bones and the
    marrow in the bones,
The exquisite realization of health;
O I say these are not the parts and poems of the body only, but
    of the soul,
O I say now these are the soul!

1855   1881

A Woman Waits for Me.

A woman waits for me, she contains all, nothing is lacking,
Yet all were lacking if sex were lacking, or if the moisture of the
    right man were lacking.

Sex contains all, bodies, souls,
Meanings, proofs, purities, delicacies, results, promulgations,
Songs, commands, health, pride, the maternal mystery, the seminal
    milk,   5
All hopes, benefactions, bestowals, all the passions, loves, beauties,
    delights of the earth,

she contains all, nothing is lacking," his poem would probably have earned less
opprobrium than it did then, with its seeming suggestion of assignation. Later
changes were minor: a few lines were omitted, notably "O I will fetch bully breeds of
children yet!"

All the governments, judges, gods, follow'd persons of the earth,
These are contain'd in sex as parts of itself and justifications of
      itself.

Without shame the man I like knows and avows the deliciousness
      of his sex,
10   Without shame the woman I like knows and avows hers.

Now I will dismiss myself from impassive women,
I will go stay with her who waits for me, and with those women
      that are warm-blooded and sufficient for me,
I see that they understand me and do not deny me,
I see that they are worthy of me, I will be the robust husband
      of those women.

15   They are not one jot less than I am,
They are tann'd in the face by shining suns and blowing winds,
Their flesh has the old divine suppleness and strength,
They know how to swim, row, ride, wrestle, shoot, run, strike,
      retreat, advance, resist, defend themselves,
They are ultimate in their own right—they are calm, clear, well-
      possess'd of themselves.

20   I draw you close to me, you women,
I cannot let you go, I would do you good,
I am for you, and you are for me, not only for our own sake, but
      for others' sakes,
Envelop'd in you sleep greater heroes and bards,
They refuse to awake at the touch of any man but me.

25   It is I, you women, I make my way,
I am stern, acrid, large, undissuadable, but I love you,
I do not hurt you any more than is necessary for you,
I pour the stuff to start sons and daughters fit for these States, I
      press with slow rude muscle,
I brace myself effectually, I listen to no entreaties,

SPONTANEOUS ME] Oddly titled "Bunch Poem" (after its final image) when it
appeared in the 1856 edition, this poem became No. 5 of the "Enfans d'Adam" group
in 1860, and in 1867 took its present title from the first line, which was added in
1860. Another addition of 1860, the phrase "my Adamic and fresh daughters,"

I dare not withdraw till I deposit what has so long accumulated
    within me.   30

Through you I drain the pent-up rivers of myself,
In you I wrap a thousand onward years,
On you I graft the grafts of the best-beloved of me and America,
The drops I distil upon you shall grow fierce and athletic girls,
    new artists, musicians, and singers,
The babes I beget upon you are to beget babes in their turn,   35
I shall demand perfect men and women out of my love-spendings,
I shall expect them to interpenetrate with others, as I and you
    interpenetrate now,
I shall count on the fruits of the gushing showers of them, as I
    count on the fruits of the gushing showers I give now,
I shall look for loving crops from the birth, life, death, immortality,
    I plant so lovingly now.

    1856   *1871*

Spontaneous Me.

Spontaneous me, Nature,
The loving day, the mounting sun, the friend I am happy with,
The arm of my friend hanging idly over my shoulder,
The hillside whiten'd with blossoms of the mountain ash,
The same late in autumn, the hues of red, yellow, drab, purple,
    and light and dark green,   5
The rich coverlet of the grass, animals and birds, the private
    untrimm'd bank, the primitive apples, the pebble-stones,
Beautiful dripping fragments, the negligent list of one after an-
    other as I happen to call them to me or think of them,
The real poems, (what we call poems being merely pictures,)
The poems of the privacy of the night, and of men like me,
This poem drooping shy and unseen that I always carry, and that
    all men carry,   10
(Know once for all, avow'd on purpose, wherever are men like
    me, are our lusty lurking masculine poems,)

relates it to the "Adam" image which informs the whole group. Intense and frank in
sexual imagery, it is remarkable for its time. In his "Blue Copy" revisions of the 1860
edition, WW had marked the tenth line for deletion, but he retained it, and indeed
marked the poem "satisfactory—Jan. '65."

Love-thoughts, love-juice, love-odor, love-yielding, love-climbers,
     and the climbing sap,
Arms and hands of love, lips of love, phallic thumb of love, breasts
     of love, bellies press'd and glued together with love,
Earth of chaste love, life that is only life after love,
The body of my love, the body of the woman I love, the body
15   of the man, the body of the earth,
Soft forenoon airs that blow from the south-west,
The hairy wild-bee that murmurs and hankers up and down, that
     gripes the full-grown lady-flower, curves upon her with
     amorous firm legs, takes his will of her, and holds himself
     tremulous and tight till he is satisfied;
The wet of woods through the early hours,
Two sleepers at night lying close together as they sleep, one with an
     arm slanting down across and below the waist of the other,
The smell of apples, aromas from crush'd sage-plant, mint, birch-
20   bark,
The boy's longings, the glow and pressure as he confides to me
     what he was dreaming,
The dead leaf whirling its spiral whirl and falling still and content
     to the ground,
The no-form'd stings that sights, people, objects, sting me with,
The hubb'd sting of myself, stinging me as much as it ever can
     any one,
The sensitive, orbic, underlapp'd brothers, that only privileged
25   feelers may be intimate where they are,
The curious roamer the hand roaming all over the body, the
     bashful withdrawing of flesh where the fingers soothingly
     pause and edge themselves,
The limpid liquid within the young man,
The vex'd corrosion so pensive and so painful,
The torment, the irritable tide that will not be at rest,
30 The like of the same I feel, the like of the same in others,
The young man that flushes and flushes, and the young woman
     that flushes and flushes,
The young man that wakes deep at night, the hot hand seeking to
     repress what would master him,

---

17. lady-flower] The generic suggestion of "female" is enriched by popular memory of the "Lady's Slipper," the familiar little orchid of field and garden, formally named *Cypripedium*, "Venus' Foot."

24. hubb'd] Centered, as in a wheel's hub; and *cf.* "no-form'd," just above.

JOY] Originally No. 6 of the "Enfans d'Adam" group, this poem took its present

The mystic amorous night, the strange half-welcome pangs, visions,
    sweats,
The pulse pounding through palms and trembling encircling
    fingers, the young man all color'd, red, ashamed, angry;
The souse upon me of my lover the sea, as I lie willing and naked,   35
The merriment of the twin babes that crawl over the grass in the
    sun, the mother never turning her vigilant eyes from them,
The walnut-trunk, the walnut-husks, and the ripening or ripen'd
    long-round walnuts,
The continence of vegetables, birds, animals,
The consequent meanness of me should I skulk or find myself
    indecent, while birds and animals never once skulk or
    find themselves indecent,
The great chastity of paternity, to match the great chastity of
    maternity,   40
The oath of procreation I have sworn, my Adamic and fresh
    daughters,
The greed that eats me day and night with hungry gnaw, till I
    saturate what shall produce boys to fill my place when I
    am through,
The wholesome relief, repose, content,
And this bunch pluck'd at random from myself,
It has done its work—I toss it carelessly to fall where it may.   45

    1856   *1867*

One Hour to Madness and Joy.

One hour to madness and joy! O furious! O confine me not!
(What is this that frees me so in storms?
What do my shouts amid lightnings and raging winds mean?)

O to drink the mystic deliria deeper than any other man!
O savage and tender achings! (I bequeath them to you my
    children,
I tell them to you, for reasons, O bridegroom and bride.)   5

title from the first line, added in 1867. Another significant change for the 1867
edition was the dropping, after line 7, of the lover's adjuration:
            Know, I am a man, attracting, at any time, her I
                but look upon, or touch with the tips of my fingers,
            Or that touches my face, or leans against me.)
After 1867 the text remained as it is, except for minor changes.

O to be yielded to you whoever you are, and you to be yielded to
    me in defiance of the world!
O to return to Paradise! O bashful and feminine!
O to draw you to me, to plant on you for the first time the lips of
    a determin'd man.

10 O the puzzle, the thrice-tied knot, the deep and dark pool, all
    untied and illumin'd!
O to speed where there is space enough and air enough at last!
To be absolv'd from previous ties and conventions, I from mine
    and you from yours!
To find a new unthought-of nonchalance with the best of Nature!
To have the gag remov'd from one's mouth!
15 To have the feeling to-day or any day I am sufficient as I am.

O something unprov'd! something in a trance!
To escape utterly from others' anchors and holds!
To drive free! to love free! to dash reckless and dangerous!
To court destruction with taunts, with invitations!
20 To ascend, to leap to the heavens of the love indicated to me!
To rise thither with my inebriate soul!
To be lost if it must be so!
To feed the remainder of life with one hour of fulness and freedom!
With one brief hour of madness and joy.

1860   *1881*

Out of the Rolling Ocean the Crowd.

Out of the rolling ocean the crowd came a drop gently to me,
Whispering *I love you, before long I die,*
I have travel'd a long way merely to look on you to touch you,
For I could not die till I once look'd on you,
5 *For I fear'd I might afterward lose you.*

CROWD] This poem, probably composed in the early 1860's, was originally a
Drum-Taps poem (1865), and was transferred to the "Children of Adam" group in
1871. It seems remarkably to anticipate the WW-Anne Gilchrist episode, and was
actually addressed, according to Ellen O'Connor, to Mrs. Juliette H. Beach of
Albion, N. Y. who had written a favorable notice of the third edition of LG which had
earned the wrath of her husband, who substituted a hostile review in the *Saturday
Press* of June 2, 1860. This story was corroborated by Clara Barrus, John Burroughs'
biographer. See UPP, I, lviii, note 15, and Allen, 260–262. Before 1881 the poem's

Now we have met, we have look'd, we are safe,
Return in peace to the ocean my love,
I too am part of that ocean my love, we are not so much sepa-
     rated,
Behold the great rondure, the cohesion of all, how perfect!
But as for me, for you, the irresistible sea is to separate us,   10
As for an hour carrying us diverse, yet cannot carry us diverse for-
     ever;
Be not impatient—a little space—know you I salute the air, the
     ocean and the land,
Every day at sundown for your dear sake my love.

     1865   1881

Ages and Ages Returning at Intervals.

Ages and ages returning at intervals,
Undestroy'd, wandering immortal,
Lusty, phallic, with the potent original loins, perfectly sweet,
I, chanter of Adamic songs,
Through the new garden the West, the great cities calling,   5
Deliriate, thus prelude what is generated, offering these, offering
     myself,
Bathing myself, bathing my songs in Sex,
Offspring of my loins.

     1860   1867

We Two, How Long We Were Fool'd.

We two, how long we were fool'd,
Now transmuted, we swiftly escape as Nature escapes,
We are Nature, long have we been absent, but now we return,
We become plants, trunks, foliage, roots, bark,

two sections were numbered, the second being enclosed within parentheses. Note the
characteristic use of italics for direct address.

     INTERVALS] In 1860, No. 12 of the "Enfans d'Adam" group, this poem remained
unchanged through later editions except for the capitalizing of the word "Sex" in
1867, at which time it assumed its present title.

     FOOL'D] In 1860, No. 7 of the "Enfans d'Adam" group, this poem began with the
line "You and I—what the earth is, we are," which was dropped in 1867 when the
poem took its title from the present first line. Another line was also dropped, and
there were further minor changes.

5   We are bedded in the ground, we are rocks,
We are oaks, we grow in the openings side by side,
We browse, we are two among the wild herds spontaneous as
       any,
We are two fishes swimming in the sea together,
We are what locust blossoms are, we drop scent around lanes
       mornings and evenings,
10   We are also the coarse smut of beasts, vegetables, minerals,
We are two predatory hawks, we soar above and look down,
We are two resplendent suns, we it is who balance ourselves orbic
       and stellar, we are as two comets,
We prowl fang'd and four-footed in the woods, we spring on
       prey,
We are two clouds forenoons and afternoons driving overhead,
We are seas mingling, we are two of those cheerful waves rolling
15   over each other and interwetting each other,
We are what the atmosphere is, transparent, receptive, pervious,
       impervious,
We are snow, rain, cold, darkness, we are each product and
       influence of the globe,
We have circled and circled till we have arrived home again, we
       two,
We have voided all but freedom and all but our own joy.

1860   *1881*

O Hymen! O Hymenee!

O hymen! O hymenee! why do you tantalize me thus?
O why sting me for a swift moment only?
Why can you not continue? O why do you now cease?
Is it because if you continued beyond the swift moment you
       would soon certainly kill me?

1860   *1867*

HYMENEE!] This poem was No. 13 of the "Enfans d'Adam" in 1860, taking its
present title in 1867. Both the title and the substance of the poem may have been
suggested to WW by a passage in George Sand's *The Countess of Rudolstadt*, a
novel he regarded as a masterpiece. See Esther Shephard, *Walt Whitman's Pose*,
178–180.

LOVE] No. 14 of the "Enfans d'Adam" group in 1860, this poem took its present
title in 1867 and remained unchanged except for the addition of "amorous" in the first
line.

I Am He That Aches with Love.

I am he that aches with amorous love;
Does the earth gravitate? does not all matter, aching, attract all
          matter?
So the body of me to all I meet or know.

1860   *1867*

Native Moments.

Native moments—when you come upon me—ah you are here
          now,
Give me now libidinous joys only,
Give me the drench of my passions, give me life coarse and rank,
To-day I go consort with Nature's darlings, to-night too,
I am for those who believe in loose delights, I share the midnight
          orgies of young men,   5
I dance with the dancers and drink with the drinkers,
The echoes ring with our indecent calls, I pick out some low person
          for my dearest friend,
He shall be lawless, rude, illiterate, he shall be one condemn'd by
          others for deeds done,
I will play a part no longer, why should I exile myself from my
          companions?
O you shunn'd persons, I at least do not shun you,   10
I come forthwith in your midst, I will be your poet,
I will be more to you than to any of the rest.

1860   *1881*

Once I Pass'd through a Populous City.

Once I pass'd through a populous city imprinting my brain for
          future use with its shows, architecture, customs, traditions,

MOMENTS] This poem, No. 8 of the "Enfans d'Adam" group in 1860, took its
present title in 1867 and has remained unchanged except for the dropping in 1881 of
the phrase "I take for my love some prostitute—" after "indecent calls" in the seventh
line. The MS (Barrett) reveals other rejected phrases: "Give me fierce pleasures
only! Give me the weedy luxuriance!"

CITY] This poem, No. 9 of the "Enfans d'Adam" group, has remained unchanged
through all the editions, but its MS (Barrett; printed in UPP II, 102 and Bowers, 64)
significantly alters the whole import of the poem, whose present reading had led

Yet now of all that city I remember only a woman I casually met
     there who detain'd me for love of me,
Day by day and night by night we were together—all else has
     long been forgotten by me,
I remember I say only that woman who passionately clung to me,
5 Again we wander, we love, we separate again,
Again she holds me by the hand, I must not go,
I see her close beside me with silent lips sad and tremulous.

    1860   *1861*

I Heard You Solemn-Sweet Pipes of the Organ.

I heard you solemn-sweet pipes of the organ as last Sunday morn
     I pass'd the church,
Winds of autumn, as I walk'd the woods at dusk I heard your
     long-stretch'd sighs up above so mournful,
I heard the perfect Italian tenor singing at the opera, I heard the
     soprano in the midst of the quartet singing;
Heart of my love! you too I heard murmuring low through one
     of the wrists around my head,
Heard the pulse of you when all was still ringing little bells last
5   night under my ear.

    1861   *1867*

Facing West from California's Shores.

Facing west from California's shores,
Inquiring, tireless, seeking what is yet unfound,

early biographers to infer a New Orleans "romance." The second line of the MS
reads:

        But now of all that city I remember only the man
           who wandered with me, there, for love of me,

and the fourth line reads, in part:

        —I remember, I say, only one rude and ignorant
        man

    ORGAN] Originally, this poem reflected the sentiments of love and war appro-
priate to the time of its first appearance, in the New York *Leader*, October 12, 1861,
under the title "Little Bells Last Night," and beginning:

        War-suggesting trumpets, I heard you.

I, a child, very old, over waves, towards the house of maternity,
    the land of migrations, look afar,
Look off the shores of my Western sea, the circle almost circled;
For starting westward from Hindustan, from the vales of Kashmere,   5
From Asia, from the north, from the God, the sage, and the
    hero,
From the south, from the flowery peninsulas and the spice islands,
Long having wander'd since, round the earth having wander'd,
Now I face home again, very pleas'd and joyous,
(But where is what I started for so long ago?   10
And why is it yet unfound?)

1860   *1867*

As Adam Early in the Morning.

As Adam early in the morning,
Walking forth from the bower refresh'd with sleep,
Behold me where I pass, hear my voice, approach,
Touch me, touch the palm of your hand to my body as I pass,
Be not afraid of my body.   5

1861   *1867*

The opening three lines and a seventh were omitted when WW again printed it in the "Sequel to Drum-Taps," 1865–1866; and with no further alterations it was transferred to the "Children of Adam" group in 1871.

    SHORES] No. 10 of the 1860 "Enfans d'Adam," this poem acquired its title and first line in 1867. The MS version (Barrett) begins with the present third line, under the title, "Hindustan, from the Western Sea." In his characteristic role as wanderer, the bard is here symbolic of the race, with its Asian beginnings and westward advance to its return full circle.

    MORNING] The final (No. 15) poem of the "Enfans d'Adam" group. The first line, "Early in the morning," was altered in 1867 to its present reading so that the controlling symbol, Adam in the Garden, is the specific image of the entire poem.

Calamus.

In Paths Untrodden.

In paths untrodden,
In the growth by margins of pond-waters,
Escaped from the life that exhibits itself,
From all the standards hitherto publish'd, from the pleasures,
        profits, conformities,
5   Which too long I was offering to feed my soul,
Clear to me now standards not yet publish'd, clear to me that my
        soul,
That the soul of the man I speak for rejoices in comrades,
Here by myself away from the clank of the world,

CALAMUS] Of all the groups in LG, the "Calamus" poems, first appearing in the text in 1860, possess the closest autonomy, held together by a sentiment of manly attachment ("adhesiveness" was WW's term) which some readers find more intimate and compelling than that of "Children of Adam." Their beginning may be surmised in an MS cluster of twelve poems (out of sequence in their present position) which appear originally to have been intended for a commemorative notebook, of like pen and ink and marked by Roman numerals. These poems reveal a story of attachment and renunciation whose symbol at first was not "Calamus" but "Live Oak with Moss." See Bowers, lxiii–lxxiv.

For the benefit of his English editor, W. M. Rossetti, WW defined his symbol as follows: " 'Calamus' is a common word here. It is the very large & aromatic grass, or rush, growing about water-ponds in the valleys—spears about three feet high—often called 'sweet flag'—grows all over the Northern and Middle States . . . The recherché or ethereal sense of the term, as used in my book, arises probably from the actual Calamus presenting the biggest & hardiest kind of spears of grass—and their fresh, acquatic, pungent bouquet." (Corr. I, 347). That the symbol also possessed a specific sexual significance is apparent from its use five years earlier in "Song of Myself" (see line 535). To John Addington Symonds, who inquired whether the "Calamus" sentiment was homo-erotic, WW gave an emphatic denial, alleging his normal sexuality. (See Blodgett, 61–69 and 205–208.)

Both in *Democratic Vistas* and in his 1876 Preface to LG, WW was at pains to insist that the meaning of "Calamus" resides mainly in its political significance,—e.g., "It is to the development, identification, and general prevalence of that fervid comradeship, (the adhesive love, at least rivaling the amative love hitherto possessing imaginative literature, if not going beyond it,) that I look for the counterbalance and offset of our materialistic and vulgar American democracy, and for the spiritualization thereof." However mistaken such a hope, there is no question that for the poet the "Calamus" sentiment possessed a power both tragic and idealistic, from whose

Tallying and talk'd to here by tongues aromatic,
No longer abash'd, (for in this secluded spot I can respond as I
      would not dare elsewhere,)   10
Strong upon me the life that does not exhibit itself, yet contains
      all the rest,
Resolv'd to sing no songs to-day but those of manly attachment,
Projecting them along that substantial life,
Bequeathing hence types of athletic love,
Afternoon this delicious Ninth-month in my forty-first year,   15
I proceed for all who are or have been young men,
To tell the secret of my nights and days,
To celebrate the need of comrades.

    1860   *1867*

Scented Herbage of My Breast.

Scented herbage of my breast,
Leaves from you I glean, I write, to be perused best afterwards,
Tomb-leaves, body-leaves growing up above me above death,

inner turmoil was to emerge compassion, sympathy, and balance.
    Through the remaining six editions of *LG*, this group of poems retained its
identity with surprisingly little change. The forty-five poems of 1860 were reduced
in 1867 to forty-two, with three poems rejected; in 1871 one poem was added and
four were transferred to *Passage to India* to make a total of thirty-nine, which is
the number retained for the final arrangement of 1881.
    UNTRODDEN] In all editions this resolute announcement opens the "Calamus"
group, taking its present title in 1867 although in the revisions of his 1860 copy WW
had considered the alternate title, "By the Calamus Pond I Wander." Three different
MSS (Trent, Barrett, and *N and F*, 1, 45, No. 149), offer variant readings, including
the lines:

        And now I care not to walk the earth unless a
           friend walk by my side,
        And now I dare sing no other songs only those
           of lovers,

    15. Ninth-month in my forty-first year] September, 1859.
    BREAST] The second of the 1860 "Calamus" group, this poem remained substan-
tially unchanged except for the dropping in 1881 of the following line after the
present seventh line:

        O burning and throbbing—surely all will one
           day be accomplished;

The intricate symbolism of the "emblematic and capricious blades" is difficult to
follow—even the poet (line 22) cries that they serve him not, but it is clear that in
this poignant confession love has led him to think of death as a deliverance. D. H.
Lawrence, reflecting upon this poem (see *Studies in Classic American Literature*,
1922) remarks that "Whitman is a very great poet, of the end of life." The exultant
celebrator of life is also the solicitor of death, which to him is not morbid, but

Perennial roots, tall leaves, O the winter shall not freeze you
 delicate leaves,

Every year shall you bloom again, out from where you retired you
5 shall emerge again;

O I do not know whether many passing by will discover you or
 inhale your faint odor, but I believe a few will;

O slender leaves! O blossoms of my blood! I permit you to tell
 in your own way of the heart that is under you,

O I do not know what you mean there underneath yourselves, you
 are not happiness,

You are often more bitter than I can bear, you burn and sting me,

Yet you are beautiful to me you faint tinged roots, you make me
10 think of death,

Death is beautiful from you, (what indeed is finally beautiful except
 death and love?)

O I think it is not for life I am chanting here my chant of lovers,
 I think it must be for death,

For how calm, how solemn it grows to ascend to the atmosphere
 of lovers,

Death or life I am then indifferent, my soul declines to prefer,

15 (I am not sure but the high soul of lovers welcomes death most,)

Indeed O death, I think now these leaves mean precisely the same
 as you mean,

Grow up taller sweet leaves that I may see! grow up out of my
 breast!

Spring away from the conceal'd heart there!

Do not fold yourself so in your pink-tinged roots timid leaves!

20 Do not remain down there so ashamed, herbage of my breast!

Come I am determin'd to unbare this broad breast of mine, I
 have long enough stifled and choked;

Emblematic and capricious blades I leave you, now you serve me
 not,

I will say what I have to say by itself,

I will sound myself and comrades only, I will never again utter a
 call only their call,

---

beautiful. Esther Shephard has made the interesting discovery that in his concept of
tomb leaves growing out of his breast, WW was influenced by poring over illustra-
tions in Ippolito Rosellini's account of the Egyptians (Pisa, 1844) which show the
burial chamber of Osiris, from whose mummy are sprouting leaves of grain. WW
had seen the plates of the book in the Astor Library and wrote of it in *Life
Illustrated*, December 8, 1855. See Shephard, "Possible Sources of Some of Whit-

I will raise with it immortal reverberations through the States,   25
I will give an example to lovers to take permanent shape and
      will through the States,
Through me shall the words be said to make death exhilarating,
Give me your tone therefore O death, that I may accord with it,
Give me yourself, for I see that you belong to me now above all,
      and are folded inseparably together, you love and death are,
Nor will I allow you to balk me any more with what I was calling life,   30
For now it is convey'd to me that you are the purports essential,
That you hide in these shifting forms of life, for reasons, and that
      they are mainly for you,
That you beyond them come forth to remain, the real reality,
That behind the mask of materials you patiently wait, no matter
      how long,
That you will one day perhaps take control of all,   35
That you will perhaps dissipate this entire show of appearance,
That may-be you are what it is all for, but it does not last so very long,
But you will last very long.

1860   1881

Whoever You Are Holding Me Now in Hand.

Whoever you are holding me now in hand,
Without one thing all will be useless,
I give you fair warning before you attempt me further,
I am not what you supposed, but far different.

Who is he that would become my follower?   5
Who would sign himself a candidate for my affections?

The way is suspicious, the result uncertain, perhaps destructive,
You would have to give up all else, I alone would expect to be
      your sole and exclusive standard,
Your novitiate would even then be long and exhausting,

man's Ideas and Symbols in *Hermes Mercurius Trismegistus* and Other Works,"
MLQ, XIV, 60–81.
    HAND] This poem, the third of the 1860 "Calamus" group, underwent no substan-
tial change after taking its present title in 1867, although in his 1860 MS revisions
the poet had considered the title "These leaves conning, you con at peril." In the role
of prophet or redeemer, the poet makes his absolute demands upon his followers,
offering challenges rather than assurances.

The whole past theory of your life and all conformity to the lives
10   around you would have to be abandon'd,
Therefore release me now before troubling yourself any further, let
       go your hand from my shoulders,
Put me down and depart on your way.

Or else by stealth in some wood for trial,
Or back of a rock in the open air,
(For in any roof'd room of a house I emerge not, nor in com-
15   pany,
And in libraries I lie as one dumb, a gawk, or unborn, or dead,)
But just possibly with you on a high hill, first watching lest any
       person for miles around approach unawares,
Or possibly with you sailing at sea, or on the beach of the sea or
       some quiet island,
Here to put your lips upon mine I permit you,
20   With the comrade's long-dwelling kiss or the new husband's kiss,
For I am the new husband and I am the comrade.

Or if you will, thrusting me beneath your clothing,
Where I may feel the throbs of your heart or rest upon your hip,
Carry me when you go forth over land or sea;
25   For thus merely touching you is enough, is best,
And thus touching you would I silently sleep and be carried
       eternally.

But these leaves conning you con at peril,
For these leaves and me you will not understand,
They will elude you at first and still more afterward, I will
       certainly elude you,
Even while you should think you had unquestionably caught me,
30   behold!
Already you see I have escaped from you.

For it is not for what I have put into it that I have written this
       book,

----

22. clothing] The poet identifies himself with his book in the first 26 lines;
however, in ll. 27–38 he becomes the commentator.

DEMOCRACY] In 1860 this poem was part of "Calamus" No. 5, a fifteen-stanza
poem of forty-two lines. In 1865 lines from the first twelve stanzas were rearranged,
with additions, to make the *Drum-Taps* poem "Over the Carnage Rose Prophetic a

Nor is it by reading it you will acquire it,
Nor do those know me best who admire me and vauntingly praise
    me,
Nor will the candidates for my love (unless at most a very few)
    prove victorious,   35
Nor will my poems do good only, they will do just as much evil,
    perhaps more,
For all is useless without that which you may guess at many times
    and not hit, that which I hinted at;
Therefore release me and depart on your way.

   1860   *1881*

For You O Democracy.

Come, I will make the continent indissoluble,
I will make the most splendid race the sun ever shone upon,
I will make divine magnetic lands,
       With the love of comrades,
         With the life-long love of comrades.   5

I will plant companionship thick as trees along all the rivers of
    America, and along the shores of the great lakes, and all
    over the prairies,
I will make inseparable cities with their arms about each other's
    necks,
       By the love of comrades,
        By the manly love of comrades.

For you these from me, O Democracy, to serve you ma femme!   10
For you, for you I am trilling these songs.

   1860   *1881*

Voice"; in 1867 the present poem was made from the last three stanzas, with the
repetend added, and entitled "A Song." Under this title it again appeared in 1871 and
1876, and with the present title in 1881. In 1902 the first twelve stanzas in their
original form were reprinted among the "Rejected Poems" under the title, "[States],"
q.v. below: "Poems Excluded from *Leaves of Grass*."

These I Singing in Spring.

These I singing in spring collect for lovers,
(For who but I should understand lovers and all their sorrow and
        joy?
And who but I should be the poet of comrades?)
Collecting I traverse the garden the world, but soon I pass the
        gates,
5   Now along the pond-side, now wading in a little, fearing not the
        wet,
Now by the post-and-rail fences where the old stones thrown there,
        pick'd from the fields, have accumulated,
(Wild-flowers and vines and weeds come up through the stones
        and partly cover them, beyond these I pass,)
Far, far in the forest, or sauntering later in summer, before I think
        where I go,
Solitary, smelling the earthy smell, stopping now and then in the
        silence,
10 Alone I had thought, yet soon a troop gathers around me,
Some walk by my side and some behind, and some embrace my
        arms or neck,
They the spirits of dear friends dead or alive, thicker they come,
        a great crowd, and I in the middle,
Collecting, dispensing, singing, there I wander with them,
Plucking something for tokens, tossing toward whoever is near me,
15 Here, lilac, with a branch of pine,
Here, out of my pocket, some moss which I pull'd off a live-oak
        in Florida as it hung trailing down,
Here, some pinks and laurel leaves, and a handful of sage,
And here what I now draw from the water, wading in the pond-
        side,
(O here I last saw him that tenderly loves me, and returns again
        never to separate from me,
And this, O this shall henceforth be the token of comrades, this
20   calamus-root shall,

SPRING] The antecedent of "These" is apparently the "tokens" (line 14) which
the poet collects for lovers, but of them all only the calamus root, drawn from the
water by the pond-side, possesses a special significance for those who "love as I
myself am capable of loving." In his 1860 MS emendations, WW considered, but
fortunately abandoned, the sentimental title, "As I walk alone at candlelight." The

Interchange it youths with each other! let none render it back!)
And twigs of maple and a bunch of wild orange and chestnut,
And stems of currants and plum-blows, and the aromatic cedar,
These I compass'd around by a thick cloud of spirits,
Wandering, point to or touch as I pass, or throw them loosely from me,   25
Indicating to each one what he shall have, giving something to
    each;
But what I drew from the water by the pond-side, that I reserve,
I will give of it, but only to them that love as I myself am capable
    of loving.

1860   *1867*

Not Heaving from my Ribb'd Breast Only.

Not heaving from my ribb'd breast only,
Not in sighs at night in rage dissatisfied with myself,
Not in those long-drawn, ill-supprest sighs,
Not in many an oath and promise broken,
Not in my wilful and savage soul's volition,   5
Not in the subtle nourishment of the air,
Not in this beating and pounding at my temples and wrists,
Not in the curious systole and diastole within which will one day cease,
Not in many a hungry wish told to the skies only,
Not in cries, laughter, defiances, thrown from me when alone far
    in the wilds,   10
Not in husky pantings through clinch'd teeth,
Not in sounded and resounded words, chattering words, echoes,
    dead words,
Not in the murmurs of my dreams while I sleep,
Nor the other murmurs of these incredible dreams of every day,
Nor in the limbs and senses of my body that take you and
    dismiss you continually—not there,   15
Not in any or all of them O adhesiveness! O pulse of my life!
Need I that you exist and show yourself any more than in these songs.

1860   *1867*

poem took its present title in 1867, and remained unchanged thereafter.
    ONLY] No. 6 of the "Calamus" group in 1860, this poem remained unchanged
through all editions, taking its title in 1867.
    16. adhesiveness] This is a phrenological term, meaning the propensity for friend-
ship. See Edward Hungerford, "Walt Whitman and His Chart of Bumps," *AL*, II,
350–384 (January, 1931).

Terrible Doubt of Appearances.

Of the terrible doubt of appearances,
Of the uncertainty after all, that we may be deluded,
That may-be reliance and hope are but speculations after all,
That may-be identity beyond the grave is a beautiful fable only,
May-be the things I perceive, the animals, plants, men, hills,
5   shining and flowing waters,
The skies of day and night, colors, densities, forms, may-be these
        are (as doubtless they are) only apparitions, and the real
        something has yet to be known,
(How often they dart out of themselves as if to confound me and
        mock me!
How often I think neither I know, nor any man knows, aught of
        them,)
May-be seeming to me what they are (as doubtless they indeed
        but seem) as from my present point of view, and might
        prove (as of course they would) nought of what they
        appear, or nought anyhow, from entirely changed points
        of view;
To me these and the like of these are curiously answer'd by my
10   lovers, my dear friends,
When he whom I love travels with me or sits a long while holding
        me by the hand,
When the subtle air, the impalpable, the sense that words and
        reason hold not, surround us and pervade us,
Then I am charged with untold and untellable wisdom, I am
        silent, I require nothing further,
I cannot answer the question of appearances or that of identity
        beyond the grave,
15 But I walk or sit indifferent, I am satisfied,
He ahold of my hand has completely satisfied me.

1860   *1867*

APPEARANCES] Compare with lines 32–33 of "Scented Herbage of my Breast" in which the "real reality" is contrasted with "these shifting forms of life." Here the same idea—that only love confirms reality—is developed into powerful form. This "Calamus" No. 7 was given its present title in 1867. It is interesting that in his 1860 revisions WW deleted the syntactically involved line 9, and then decided to let it stand.

METAPHYSICS] This poem, added to the "Calamus" group in 1871, sublimates the sentiment of "adhesiveness" to lofty universal principle. A MS draft (BPL) has the

The Base of All Metaphysics.

And now gentlemen,
A word I give to remain in your memories and minds,
As base and finalè too for all metaphysics.

(So to the students the old professor,
At the close of his crowded course.)   5

Having studied the new and antique, the Greek and Germanic
        systems,
Kant having studied and stated, Fichte and Schelling and Hegel,
Stated the lore of Plato, and Socrates greater than Plato,
And greater than Socrates sought and stated, Christ divine having
        studied long,
I see reminiscent to-day those Greek and Germanic systems,   10
See the philosophies all, Christian churches and tenets see,
Yet underneath Socrates clearly see, and underneath Christ the
        divine I see,
The dear love of man for his comrade, the attraction of friend to
        friend,
Of the well-married husband and wife, of children and parents,
Of city for city and land for land.   15

1871   1871

Recorders Ages Hence.

Recorders ages hence,
Come, I will take you down underneath this impassive exterior, I
        will tell you what to say of me,

title, "The Professor's Answer." An assiduous note taker, WW had a general, not a
dialectical, interest in philosophy. See Olive W. Parsons, "Whitman the Non-
Hegelian," PMLA, LVIII (December, 1943) 1073–1093.
    HENCE] Both the MS (Barrett) and the 1860 text of this poem began with the
following two lines, dropped in 1867 when it took its present title and form:

> You bards of ages hence! when you refer to me,
>   mind not so much my poems,
> Nor speak of me that I prophesied of The States,
>   and led them the way of their glories;

    3. finalè] The incorrect use of an accent was introduced in the Osgood LG 1881
and prevails in all later editions, including the final LG 1892.

Publish my name and hang up my picture as that of the tenderest
    lover,

The friend the lover's portrait, of whom his friend his lover was
    fondest,

Who was not proud of his songs, but of the measureless ocean of
5   love within him, and freely pour'd it forth,

Who often walk'd lonesome walks thinking of his dear friends, his
    lovers,

Who pensive away from one he lov'd often lay sleepless and dissat-
    isfied at night,

Who knew too well the sick, sick dread lest the one he lov'd
    might secretly be indifferent to him,

Whose happiest days were far away through fields, in woods, on
    hills, he and another wandering hand in hand, they twain
    apart from other men,

Who oft as he saunter'd the streets curv'd with his arm the shoul-
    der of his friend, while the arm of his friend rested upon
10   him also.

1860   *1867*

When I Heard at the Close of the Day.

When I heard at the close of the day how my name had been
    receiv'd with plaudits in the capitol, still it was not a happy
    night for me that follow'd,

And else when I carous'd, or when my plans were accomplish'd,
    still I was not happy,

But the day when I rose at dawn from the bed of perfect health,
    refresh'd, singing, inhaling the ripe breath of autumn,

When I saw the full moon in the west grow pale and disappear in
    the morning light,

When I wander'd alone over the beach, and undressing bathed,
5   laughing with the cool waters, and saw the sun rise,

And when I thought how my dear friend my lover was on his way
    coming, O then I was happy,

DAY] Both this poem ("Calamus" No. 11) and the preceding poem ("Calamus"
No. 10) were originally indicated with Roman numerals III and VII respectively in
the series of twelve poems, apparently so numbered in MS (Barrett) in order to
commemorate a single episode. This poem remained unchanged after taking its
present title in 1867.

O then each breath tasted sweeter, and all that day my food
      nourish'd me more, and the beautiful day pass'd well,
And the next came with equal joy, and with the next at evening
      came my friend,
And that night while all was still I heard the waters roll slowly
      continually up the shores,
I heard the hissing rustle of the liquid and sands as directed to
      me whispering to congratulate me,   10
For the one I love most lay sleeping by me under the same cover
      in the cool night,
In the stillness in the autumn moonbeams his face was inclined
      toward me,
And his arm lay lightly around my breast—and that night I was
      happy.

1860   *1867*

Are You the New Person Drawn toward Me?

Are you the new person drawn toward me?
To begin with take warning, I am surely far different from what
      you suppose;
Do you suppose you will find in me your ideal?
Do you think it so easy to have me become your lover?
Do you think the friendship of me would be unalloy'd satisfaction?   5
Do you think I am trusty and faithful?
Do you see no further than this façade, this smooth and tolerant
      manner of me?
Do you suppose yourself advancing on real ground toward a real
      heroic man?
Have you no thought O dreamer that it may be all maya, illusion?

1860   *1867*

ME] The MS (Barrett) of this "Calamus" No. 12 has a more intimate title, "To
a new personal admirer." In his 1860 revisions WW had made the marginal notation
for the whole poem, "Out without fail," but instead he dropped the final two and
one-half lines of the 1860 text, and reprinted it in the next edition under the present
title.

Roots and Leaves Themselves Alone.

Roots and leaves themselves alone are these,
Scents brought to men and women from the wild woods and
    pond-side,
Breast-sorrel and pinks of love, fingers that wind around tighter
    than vines,
Gushes from the throats of birds hid in the foliage of trees as the
    sun is risen,
5 Breezes of land and love set from living shores to you on the living
    sea, to you O sailors!
Frost-mellow'd berries and Third-month twigs offer'd fresh to
    young persons wandering out in the fields when the winter
    breaks up,
Love-buds put before you and within you whoever you are,
Buds to be unfolded on the old terms,
If you bring the warmth of the sun to them they will open and
    bring form, color, perfume, to you,
If you become the aliment and the wet they will become flowers,
10   fruits, tall branches and trees.

1860   1867

Not Heat Flames Up and Consumes.

Not heat flames up and consumes,
Not sea-waves hurry in and out,
Not the air delicious and dry, the air of ripe summer, bears lightly
    along white down-balls of myriads of seeds,
Wafted, sailing gracefully, to drop where they may;

ALONE] WW improved the 1867 text of this "Calamus" No. 13 by dropping the
first two lines and the last three from the poem. The opening lines of the 1860 text
had read:
             Calamus taste,
           (For I must change the strain—these are not to
               be pensive leaves, but leaves of joy,)
and the original MS (Barrett) title was "Buds."
    CONSUMES] This "Calamus" No. 14, unchanged since it took its present title in
1867, was originally, as the MS (Barrett) shows, numbered I in the Roman numeral

Not these, O none of these more than the flames of me, consum-
    ing, burning for his love whom I love,   5
O none more than I hurrying in and out;
Does the tide hurry, seeking something, and never give up? O I
    the same,
O nor down-balls nor perfumes, nor the high rain-emitting clouds,
    are borne through the open air,
Any more than my soul is borne through the open air,
Wafted in all directions O love, for friendship, for you.   10

  1860   *1867*

Trickle Drops.

Trickle drops! my blue veins leaving!
O drops of me! trickle, slow drops,
Candid from me falling, drip, bleeding drops,
From wounds made to free you whence you were prison'd,
From my face, from my forehead and lips,   5
From my breast, from within where I was conceal'd, press forth
    red drops, confession drops,
Stain every page, stain every song I sing, every word I say, bloody
    drops,
Let them know your scarlet heat, let them glisten,
Saturate them with yourself all ashamed and wet,
Glow upon all I have written or shall write, bleeding drops,   10
Let it all be seen in your light, blushing drops.

  1860   *1867*

City of Orgies.

City of orgies, walks and joys,
City whom that I have lived and sung in your midst will one day
    make you illustrious,

series already referred to, and it carried the title "Calamus-Leaves," altered from a
still earlier title, "Live Oak, with Moss."

    DROPS] The first line of this "Calamus" No. 15 was added in 1867. There were
no further changes. The 1860 MS (Barrett) has the title "Confession Drops," which
supports the meaning of line 6.

    ORGIES] Compare this poem with the *Drum-Taps* poem, "City of Ships," also
celebrating Manhattan, but with a different emphasis. In the MS (Barrett), the
name of the city is not given. The poem, originally "Calamus" No. 18, has remained
unchanged since it took its title in 1867.

Not the pageants of you, not your shifting tableaus, your specta-
    cles, repay me,
Not the interminable rows of your houses, nor the ships at the
    wharves,
Nor the processions in the streets, nor the bright windows with goods in
    them,
5 Nor to converse with learn'd persons, or bear my share in the soiree
    or feast;
Not those, but as I pass O Manhattan, your frequent and swift
    flash of eyes offering me love,
Offering response to my own—these repay me,
Lovers, continual lovers, only repay me.

1860   *1867*

Behold This Swarthy Face.

Behold this swarthy face, these gray eyes,
This beard, the white wool unclipt upon my neck,
My brown hands and the silent manner of me without charm;
Yet comes one a Manhattanese and ever at parting kisses me
    lightly on the lips with robust love,
And I on the crossing of the street or on the ship's deck give a
5   kiss in return,
We observe that salute of American comrades land and sea,
We are those two natural and nonchalant persons.

1860   *1871*

I Saw in Louisiana a Live-Oak Growing.

I saw in Louisiana a live-oak growing,
All alone stood it and the moss hung down from the branches,
Without any companion it grew there uttering joyous leaves of
    dark green,
And its look, rude, unbending, lusty, made me think of myself,

FACE] WW improved the 1860 version of this "Calamus," No. 19 by omitting for
the next edition the opening two-line stanza:

        Mind you the timid models of the rest, the
            majority?
        Long I minded them, but hence I will not—for
            I have adopted models for myself, and now
            offer them to The Lands.

But I wonder'd how it could utter joyous leaves standing alone
    there without its friend near, for I knew I could not,   5
And I broke off a twig with a certain number of leaves upon it,
    and twined around it a little moss,
And brought it away, and I have placed it in sight in my room,
It is not needed to remind me as of my own dear friends,
(For I believe lately I think of little else than of them,)
Yet it remains to me a curious token, it makes me think of manly
    love;   10
For all that, and though the live-oak glistens there in Louisiana
    solitary in a wide flat space,
Uttering joyous leaves all its life without a friend a lover near,
I know very well I could not.

1860   1867

To a Stranger.

Passing stranger! you do not know how longingly I look upon
    you,
You must be he I was seeking, or she I was seeking, (it comes to
    me as of a dream,)
I have somewhere surely lived a life of joy with you,
All is recall'd as we flit by each other, fluid, affectionate, chaste,
    matured,
You grew up with me, were a boy with me or a girl with me,   5
I ate with you and slept with you, your body has become not yours
    only nor left my body mine only,
You give me the pleasure of your eyes, face, flesh, as we pass, you
    take of my beard, breast, hands, in return,
I am not to speak to you, I am to think of you when I sit alone
    or wake at night alone,
I am to wait, I do not doubt I am to meet you again,
I am to see to it that I do not lose you.   10

1860   1867

    GROWING] Two MSS of this poem (Barrett, Berg) show little revision except for
line rearrangement. It is numbered 11 in the Roman numeral series and No. 20 of
the 1860 "Calamus" group, receiving its title and final text in 1867. Despite its
intensity, biographical significance is not a necessary inference.

    STRANGER] The MS (Barrett) of this poem, "Calamus" No. 22, gives it the pres-
ent title, printed in 1867 without further changes.

This Moment Yearning and Thoughtful.

This moment yearning and thoughtful sitting alone,
It seems to me there are other men in other lands yearning
   and thoughtful,
It seems to me I can look over and behold them in Germany,
   Italy, France, Spain,
Or far, far away, in China, or in Russia or Japan, talking other
   dialects,
5 And it seems to me if I could know those men I should become
   attached to them as I do to men in my own lands,
O I know we should be brethren and lovers,
I know I should be happy with them.

  1860   .   *1881*

I Hear It Was Charged Against Me.

I hear it was charged against me that I sought to destroy institu-
   tions,
But really I am neither for nor against institutions,
(What indeed have I in common with them? or what with the
   destruction of them?)
Only I will establish in the Mannahatta and in every city of these
   States inland and seaboard,
And in the fields and woods, and above every keel little or large
   that dents the water,
5 Without edifices or rules or trustees or any argument,
The institution of the dear love of comrades.

  1860   *1867*

THOUGHTFUL] This "Calamus" No. 23 was designated in MS (Barrett) as IV in
Roman numerals. In 1867 a line following the present fourth line,

    It seems to me they are as wise, beautiful,
      benevolent, as any in my own lands;—

was dropped, and in 1881 the present lines 3 and 4 were constructed from the former
line 3.
  ME] In 1860 the first line of this "Calamus" No. 24 was in present tense. There
were no further changes after the poem took its title in 1867.

The Prairie-Grass Dividing.

The prairie-grass dividing, its special odor breathing,
I demand of it the spiritual corresponding,
Demand the most copious and close companionship of men,
Demand the blades to rise of words, acts, beings,
Those of the open atmosphere, coarse, sunlit, fresh, nutritious,   5
Those that go their own gait, erect, stepping with freedom and
        command, leading not following,
Those with a never-quell'd audacity, those with sweet and lusty
        flesh clear of taint,
Those that look carelessly in the faces of Presidents and governors,
        as to say *Who are you?*
Those of earth-born passion, simple, never constrain'd, never
        obedient,
Those of inland America.   10

1860   1867

When I Peruse the Conquer'd Fame.

When I peruse the conquer'd fame of heroes and the victories
        of mighty generals, I do not envy the generals,
Nor the President in his Presidency, nor the rich in his great
        house,
But when I hear of the brotherhood of lovers, how it was with
        them,
How together through life, through dangers, odium, unchanging,
        long and long,
Through youth and through middle and old age, how unfaltering,
        how affectionate and faithful they were,   5

1. charged against me] The poem is to be taken, not as a reaction to a specific
charge, but as the spirited rhetorical challenge of a man whose visionary utterance is
not to be confined by the institutional.
    DIVIDING] In 1860 the first line of this "Calamus" No. 25 read "own" for
"special"; and "choice and chary of its love-power," followed "taint," in line 7. The
poem took its present title and form in 1867.
    FAME] WW considered the title, "When I perused the fame of heroes" in his
1860 MS revisions of this "Calamus" No. 28, but gave it the present title in 1867.
There were very minor alterations in 1871.

Then I am pensive—I hastily walk away fill'd with the bitterest
    envy.

1860   *1871*

We Two Boys Together Clinging.

We two boys together clinging,
One the other never leaving,
Up and down the roads going, North and South excursions
    making,
Power enjoying, elbows stretching, fingers clutching,
5 Arm'd and fearless, eating, drinking, sleeping, loving,
No law less than ourselves owning, sailing, soldiering, thieving,
    threatening,
Misers, menials, priests alarming, air breathing, water drinking, on
    the turf or the sea-beach dancing,
Cities wrenching, ease scorning, statutes mocking, feebleness chas-
    ing,
Fulfilling our foray.

1860   *1867*

A Promise to California.

A promise to California,
Or inland to the great pastoral Plains, and on to Puget sound and
    Oregon;
Sojourning east a while longer, soon I travel toward you, to remain,
    to teach robust American love,
For I know very well that I and robust love belong among you,
    inland, and along the Western sea;

CLINGING] The following line, dropped in 1867, appeared after the present
seventh line in the 1860 text of this "Calamus" No. 26:

> With birds singing—With fishes swimming—With
> trees branching and leafing,

In the Barrett MS WW headed the poem with the exotic title "Razzia," a word
of Arabic origin meaning "raid" or "foray." The poem took its present title in
1867.

CALIFORNIA] The MS (Barrett) of this "Calamus" No. 30 makes no mention of
California, the first line reading "A promise to Indiana, Nebraska, Kansas, Iowa,

For these States tend inland and toward the Western sea, and I
    will also.   5
1860   *1867*

Here the Frailest Leaves of Me.

Here the frailest leaves of me and yet my strongest lasting,
Here I shade and hide my thoughts, I myself do not expose them,
And yet they expose me more than all my other poems.
1860   *1871*

No Labor-Saving Machine.

No labor-saving machine,
Nor discovery have I made,
Nor will I be able to leave behind me any wealthy bequest to
      found a hospital or library,
Nor reminiscence of any deed of courage for America,
Nor literary success nor intellect, nor book for the book-shelf,
But a few carols vibrating through the air I leave,   5
For comrades and lovers.
1860   *1881*

A Glimpse.

A glimpse through an interstice caught,
Of a crowd of workmen and drivers in a bar-room around the
      stove late of a winter night, and I unremark'd seated in a
      corner,

Minnesota, and others:" nor is there any mention in the text of "robust American
love." The poem took its present title in 1867.

    ME] The 1860 text of this "Calamus" No. 44 opened with the following line (not
in the Barrett MS), "Here my last words, and the most baffling," subsequently
dropped in 1867. The poem took its present title in 1867.

    MACHINE] The opening phrase of the sixth line of this "Calamus," No. 33,
reading "Only these carols," was changed in 1867 to read "Only a few carols," and in
1881 to "But a few carols." It took its present title in 1867.

    GLIMPSE] The first line of this "Calamus" No. 29 was very slightly revised in
1867, and 1860 MS revisions indicate that WW had considered the more extended
title, "A Glimpse Caught Through an Interstice."

Of a youth who loves me and whom I love, silently approaching
      and seating himself near, that he may hold me by the hand,
A long while amid the noises of coming and going, of drinking
      and oath and smutty jest,
There we two, content, happy in being together, speaking little,
5   perhaps not a word.

1860   *1867*

A Leaf for Hand in Hand.

A leaf for hand in hand;
You natural persons old and young!
You on the Mississippi and on all the branches and bayous of the
      Mississippi!
You friendly boatmen and mechanics! you roughs!
5 You twain! and all processions moving along the streets!
I wish to infuse myself among you till I see it common for you to
      walk hand in hand.

1860   *1867*

Earth, My Likeness.

Earth, my likeness,
Though you look so impassive, ample and spheric there,
I now suspect that is not all;
I now suspect there is something fierce in you eligible to burst forth,
5 For an athlete is enamour'd of me, and I of him,
But toward him there is something fierce and terrible in me eligible
      to burst forth,
I dare not tell it in words, not even in these songs.

1860   *1867*

    HAND] WW's MS version (Barrett) of this "Calamus" No. 37 (see Bowers,
112) may be preferred to its first text (1860) which, incidentally, included in line 2
the phrase, "You on the Eastern Sea, and you on the Western!" dropped in 1867
when the poem took its present title and form.
    LIKENESS] In the Barrett MS this "Calamus" No. 36 is numbered XI, but in
another MS (Feinberg) it is marked as VI. The poem took its present title in 1867,
but otherwise remained unchanged.
    DREAM] Compare this "Calamus" No. 34 with the Barrett MS reading (Bowers,

I Dream'd in a Dream.

I dream'd in a dream I saw a city invincible to the attacks of the
     whole of the rest of the earth,
I dream'd that was the new city of Friends,
Nothing was greater there than the quality of robust love, it led
     the rest,
It was seen every hour in the actions of the men of that city,
And in all their looks and words.   5

1860   1867

What Think You I Take My Pen in Hand?

What think you I take my pen in hand to record?
The battle-ship, perfect-model'd, majestic, that I saw pass the
     offing to-day under full sail?
The splendors of the past day? or the splendor of the night that
     envelops me?
Or the vaunted glory and growth of the great city spread around
     me?—no;
But merely of two simple men I saw to-day on the pier in the
     midst of the crowd, parting the parting of dear friends,   5
The one to remain hung on the other's neck and passionately
     kiss'd him,
While the one to depart tightly prest the one to remain in his
     arms.

1860   1881

To the East and to the West.

To the East and to the West,
To the man of the Seaside State and of Pennsylvania,

114), whose phrasing is simpler and more direct. It is numbered IX in the Roman
numeral series. The poem has remained unchanged since it took its present title
in 1867.
     HAND] The Barrett MS of this "Calamus" No. 32 shows it to be VI in the
Roman numeral series. It has remained unchanged since it took its present title in
1867, except for the substitution in 1881 of "But merely" for "But I record" in the
beginning of the fifth line.
     WEST] In 1860 the first line of this "Calamus" No. 35 read "To you of New
England"; this was excluded under the present title in 1867.

To the Kanadian of the north, to the Southerner I love,
These with perfect trust to depict you as myself, the germs are in
    all men,
I believe the main purport of these States is to found a superb
5   friendship, exaltè, previously unknown,
Because I perceive it waits, and has been always waiting, latent in
    all men.

1860   *1867*

Sometimes with One I Love.

Sometimes with one I love I fill myself with rage for fear I effuse
    unreturn'd love,
But now I think there is no unreturn'd love, the pay is certain one
    way or another,
(I loved a certain person ardently and my love was not return'd,
Yet out of that I have written these songs.)

1860   *1867*

To a Western Boy.

Many things to absorb I teach to help you become eleve of mine;
Yet if blood like mine circle not in your veins,
If you be not silently selected by lovers and do not silently select
    lovers,
Of what use is it that you seek to become eleve of mine?

1860   *1881*

LOVE] Both the MS (Barrett) and the 1860 text of this "Calamus" No. 39 conclude with a third line, as follows:

> Doubtless I could not have perceived the universe,
> or written one of my poems, if I had not freely
> given myself to comrades, to love.

The poem took its title and present reading in 1867.
BOY] The MS (Barrett) of this "Calamus" No. 42 shows it to be XII in the Roman numeral series. It received its present title and an opening line, "O Boy of the West!" in 1867, which was dropped, with some further minor revision, in 1881.
    1. eleve] Pupil.

Fast Anchor'd Eternal O Love!

Fast-anchor'd eternal O love! O woman I love!
O bride! O wife! more resistless than I can tell, the thought of
    you!
Then separate, as disembodied or another born,
Ethereal, the last athletic reality, my consolation,
I ascend, I float in the regions of your love O man,   5
O sharer of my roving life.

1860   *1867*

Among the Multitude.

Among the men and women the multitude,
I perceive one picking me out by secret and divine signs,
Acknowledging none else, not parent, wife, husband, brother,
    child, any nearer than I am,
Some are baffled, but that one is not—that one knows me.

Ah lover and perfect equal,   5
I meant that you should discover me so by faint indirections,
And I when I meet you mean to discover you by the like in you.

1860   *1881*

O You Whom I Often and Silently Come.

O you whom I often and silently come where you are that I may
    be with you,

LOVE!] Both in Barrett MS and in the 1860 text, the first line of this "Calamus"
No. 38 read, "Primeval my love for the woman I love." In all editions, "Fast-anchor'd"
lacks the hyphen in the title.

MULTITUDE] This "Calamus" No. 41 is but slightly revised from its original
in the Barrett MS and 1860 text. It took its present title in 1867. Note the echo of
line 6 in the phrase, "faint clews and indirections" in the 1867 "Inscription," "When I
Read the Book."

COME] This "Calamus" No. 43 whose MS (Barrett) designates it as X of the
Roman numeral series, has remained unchanged through all the editions, taking its
present title in 1867.

As I walk by your side or sit near, or remain in the same room
    with you,
Little you know the subtle electric fire that for your sake is play-
    ing within me.

    1860   *1867*

That Shadow My Likeness.

That shadow my likeness that goes to and fro seeking a liveli-
    hood, chattering, chaffering,
How often I find myself standing and looking at it where it
    flits,
How often I question and doubt whether that is really me;
But among my lovers and caroling these songs,
5   O I never doubt whether that is really me.

    1860   *1881*

Full of Life Now.

Full of life now, compact, visible,
I, forty years old the eighty-third year of the States,
To one a century hence or any number of centuries hence,
To you yet unborn these, seeking you.

5   When you read these I that was visible am become invisible,
Now it is you, compact, visible, realizing my poems, seeking me,
Fancying how happy you were if I could be with you and become
    your comrade;
Be it as if I were with you. (Be not too certain but I am now with you.)

    1860   *1871*

    LIKENESS] The gist of this poem, "Calamus" No. 40, is contained in three lines
jotted down in an 1859 notebook (LC 89) transcribed in UPP II, 91. It took its title
in 1867, and its fourth line was slightly revised in 1881.
    1. chaffering] Bantering. This is a meaning, long in use, from "chaffer" (noun,
fl. ca. 1850), a banterer or a joker at the expense of others (Partridge, *A Dictionary
of Slang and Unconventional English*).
    NOW] The MS (Barrett) of this "Calamus" No. 45 contains the rejected opening
line:

        Throwing far, throwing over the head of death, I,
           full of affection,

and its second line (now the first and second lines) reads "thirty-eight years old the
eighty-first year of The States," indicating that WW composed the poem in 1857. It

Salut Au Monde!

1

O take my hand Walt Whitman!
Such gliding wonders! such sights and sounds!
Such join'd unended links, each hook'd to the next,
Each answering all, each sharing the earth with all.

What widens within you Walt Whitman?   5
What waves and soils exuding?
What climes? what persons and cities are here?
Who are the infants, some playing, some slumbering?
Who are the girls? who are the married women?
Who are the groups of old men going slowly with their arms about
    each other's necks?
What rivers are these? what forests and fruits are these?   10
What are the mountains call'd that rise so high in the mists?
What myriads of dwellings are they fill'd with dwellers?

2

Within me latitude widens, longitude lengthens,
Asia, Africa, Europe, are to the east—America is provided for in
    the west,   15
Banding the bulge of the earth winds the hot equator,

took its present title in 1867; it was slightly revised then, and also in 1871.
    MONDE!] The third poem of the second edition of LG 1856, under the title "Poem
of Salutation," this poem took its present title in 1860. In his 1855 Preface WW had
said of the American bard that "to him the other continents arrive as contributions";
and so, early in the development of LG, he undertook to express a world vision—
"within me latitude widens, longitude lengthens"—which tempered and balanced his
nationalism. His revisions were fairly constant, but preserved the general proportion.
Notably, he added in 1860 the effective salutation of the closing four lines, and for
the final 1881 version he removed, with discrimination, quite a number of lines that
were descriptive of the United States, so limiting his point of view outward from
America to other lands. In composing his poem, WW was much influenced by his
reading of Volney's *Ruins*. See David Goodale, "Some of Walt Whitman's Borrow-
ings," *AL*, X, 202–213.

Curiously north and south turn the axis-ends,
Within me is the longest day, the sun wheels in slanting rings, it
　　　does not set for months,
Stretch'd in due time within me the midnight sun just rises above
　　　the horizon and sinks again,
20　Within me zones, seas, cataracts, forests, volcanoes, groups,
Malaysia, Polynesia, and the great West Indian islands.

3

What do you hear Walt Whitman?

I hear the workman singing and the farmer's wife singing,
I hear in the distance the sounds of children and of animals early
　　　in the day,
25　I hear emulous shouts of Australians pursuing the wild horse,
I hear the Spanish dance with castanets in the chestnut shade, to
　　　the rebeck and guitar,
I hear continual echoes from the Thames,
I hear fierce French liberty songs,
I hear of the Italian boat-sculler the musical recitative of old
　　　poems,
I hear the locusts in Syria as they strike the grain and grass with
30　　　the showers of their terrible clouds,
I hear the Coptic refrain toward sundown, pensively falling on the
　　　breast of the black venerable vast mother the Nile,
I hear the chirp of the Mexican muleteer, and the bells of the
　　　mule,
I hear the Arab muezzin calling from the top of the mosque,
I hear the Christian priests at the altars of their churches, I hear
　　　the responsive base and soprano,
I hear the cry of the Cossack, and the sailor's voice putting to sea
35　　　at Okotsk,
I hear the wheeze of the slave-coffle as the slaves march on, as
　　　the husky gangs pass on by twos and threes, fasten'd together
　　　with wrist-chains and ankle-chains,

---

　　34. base] Properly, "bass," in harmonic music the lower range of instrument or
voice; cf. "soprano," above.
　　35. Okotsk] Seaport of eastern Siberia.
　　36. slave-coffle] Slave caravan.
　　50. Chian Shahs, Altays, Ghauts] Mountain systems in China, Siberia, and

I hear the Hebrew reading his records and psalms,
I hear the rhythmic myths of the Greeks, and the strong legends
  of the Romans,
I hear the tale of the divine life and bloody death of the beautiful
  God the Christ,
I hear the Hindoo teaching his favorite pupil the loves, wars,
  adages, transmitted safely to this day from poets who wrote
  three thousand years ago. 40

  4

What do you see Walt Whitman?
Who are they you salute, and that one after another salute you?

I see a great round wonder rolling through space,
I see diminute farms, hamlets, ruins, graveyards, jails, factories,
  palaces, hovels, huts of barbarians, tents of nomads upon
  the surface,
I see the shaded part on one side where the sleepers are sleeping,
  and the sunlit part on the other side,
I see the curious rapid change of the light and shade, 45
I see distant lands, as real and near to the inhabitants of them as
  my land is to me.

I see plenteous waters,
I see mountain peaks, I see the sierras of Andes where they range,
I see plainly the Himalayas, Chian Shahs, Altays, Ghauts, 50
I see the giant pinnacles of Elbruz, Kazbek, Bazardjusi,
I see the Styrian Alps, and the Karnac Alps,
I see the Pyrenees, Balks, Carpathians, and to the north the
  Dofrafields, and off at sea mount Hecla,
I see Vesuvius and Etna, the mountains of the Moon, and the
  Red mountains of Madagascar,
I see the Lybian, Arabian, and Asiatic deserts,
I see huge dreadful Arctic and Antarctic icebergs, 55

British India respectively.
 51. Elbruz, Kazbek, Bazardjusi] Mountain peaks in the Caucasus.
 52. Styrian . . . Karnac Alps] Austrian and Italian Alps.
 53. mount Hecla] Volcano in southwest Iceland.
 54. mountains of the Moon] A range placed by Ptolemy in the interior of Africa.

I see the superior oceans and the inferior ones, the Atlantic and
        Pacific, the sea of Mexico, the Brazilian sea, and the sea
        of Peru,
The waters of Hindustan, the China sea, and the gulf of Guinea,
The Japan waters, the beautiful bay of Nagasaki land-lock'd in its
        mountains,
The spread of the Baltic, Caspian, Bothnia, the British shores, and
60   the bay of Biscay,
The clear-sunn'd Mediterranean, and from one to another of its
        islands,
The White sea, and the sea around Greenland.

I behold the mariners of the world,
Some are in storms, some in the night with the watch on the look-
        out,
65 Some drifting helplessly, some with contagious diseases.

I behold the sail and steamships of the world, some in clusters in
        port, some on their voyages,
Some double the cape of Storms, some cape Verde, others capes
        Guardafui, Bon, or Bajadore,
Others Dondra head, others pass the straits of Sunda, others cape
        Lopatka, others Behring's straits,
Others cape Horn, others sail the gulf of Mexico or along Cuba
        or Hayti, others Hudson's bay or Baffin's bay,
Others pass the straits of Dover, others enter the Wash, others the
        firth of Solway, others round cape Clear, others the Land's
70   End,
Others traverse the Zuyder Zee or the Scheld,
Others as comers and goers at Gibraltar or the Dardanelles,
Others sternly push their way through the northern winter-packs,
Others descend or ascend the Obi or the Lena,

59. Nagasaki] Reads "Nagusaki" in the softbound, but not in the hardbound
issue of 1891–2. The error occurred in 1881, was corrected in *LG* 1889.
    67. cape of Storms] The name given by Bartholomeu Dias to the Cape of Good
Hope. cape Verde] Westernmost point of Africa. Guardafui] Northeastern extremity
of the Somali country, Africa. Bon] Northeast Tunis, Africa. Bajadore] Unidenti-
fied.
    68. Dondra head] Southernmost cape of Ceylon. straits of Sunda] Sea passage
separating Sumatra and Java. cape Lopatka] Southern extremity of Kamchatka.
    71. Scheld] River of France, Belgium, and the Netherlands, flowing to the North
Sea. Now spelled Schelde or Scheldt.
    74. Obi] Inlet of Arctic Ocean, north of Siberia. Lena] One of the chief rivers of

Others the Niger or the Congo, others the Indus, the Burampooter
      and Cambodia,   75
Others wait steam'd up ready to start in the ports of Australia,
Wait at Liverpool, Glasgow, Dublin, Marseilles, Lisbon, Naples,
      Hamburg, Bremen, Bordeaux, the Hague, Copenhagen,
Wait at Valparaiso, Rio Janeiro, Panama.

5

I see the tracks of the railroads of the earth,
I see them in Great Britain, I see them in Europe,   80
I see them in Asia and in Africa.

I see the electric telegraphs of the earth,
I see the filaments of the news of the wars, deaths, losses, gains,
      passions, of my race.

I see the long river-stripes of the earth,
I see the Amazon and the Paraguay,   85
I see the four great rivers of China, the Amour, the Yellow River,
      the Yiang-tse, and the Pearl,
I see where the Seine flows, and where the Danube, the Loire, the
      Rhone, and the Guadalquiver flow,
I see the windings of the Volga, the Dnieper, the Oder,
I see the Tuscan going down the Arno, and the Venetian along
      the Po,
I see the Greek seaman sailing out of Egina bay.   90

6

I see the site of the old empire of Assyria, and that of Persia, and
      that of India,
I see the falling of the Ganges over the high rim of Saukara.

Siberia.
   75. Niger or the Congo] African rivers. Indus, the Burampooter and Cambodia]
Asian rivers.
     86. Amour] Whitman's spelling for Amur, a river of East Asia.
     87. Guadalquiver] River in southern Spain.
     88. Oder] One of the chief rivers of Germany.
     92. Saukara] Probably a misspelling for "Sankara" in WW's source, reflected in
his MS and in the first edition of the poem, 1856. Sankara is a familiar alternative
name for Siva, in ancient Hindu literature the male divinity associated with both
destruction and rebirth, hence fertility. From the head of Siva, or Sankara, sprang
the Ganges, cascading over "the high rim" of his hair, which was piled in rows

I see the place of the idea of the Deity incarnated by avatars in
  human forms,
I see the spots of the successions of priests on the earth, oracles,
  sacrificers, brahmins, sabians, llamas, monks, muftis, ex-
  horters,
I see where druids walk'd the groves of Mona, I see the mistletoe
95 and vervain,
I see the temples of the deaths of the bodies of Gods, I see the
  old signifiers.

I see Christ eating the bread of his last supper in the midst of
  youths and old persons,
I see where the strong divine young man the Hercules toil'd faith-
  fully and long and then died,
I see the place of the innocent rich life and hapless fate of the
  beautiful nocturnal son, the full-limb'd Bacchus,
I see Kneph, blooming, drest in blue, with the crown of feathers
100 on his head,
I see Hermes, unsuspected, dying, well-belov'd, saying to the
  people *Do not weep for me,*
This is not my true country, I have lived banish'd from my true
  country, I now go back there,
I return to the celestial sphere where every one goes in his turn.

    7

I see the battle-fields of the earth, grass grows upon them and
  blossoms and corn,
105 I see the tracks of ancient and modern expeditions.

of curls above the brow. The present line and the next are the remnant of four in
the MS, which substantiate the idea above:
  The Sanscrit—the ancient poems and laws;
  The idea of Gods incarnated by their avatars in man and woman;
  The falling of the waters of the Ganges over the high rim of Saukara;
  The poems descended safely to this day from poets of three thousand years ago.
For the identification of Sankara (Shankara) with Siva (Shiva) see p. 22, and for
the fall of the Ganges see p. 104, in P. Thomas, *Epics, Myths, and Legends of
India*, Bombay, 1940, third ed., n.d.
  93. avatars] The incarnation of the deity by an avatar in human form occurs in
several religions, including the Hindu and Egyptian.
  94. sabians] Originally, a semi-Christian sect of Babylonia; later a semi-Moslem
sect of Mesopotamia. llamas] Properly, "lamas," Tibetan priests. muftis] Official

I see the nameless masonries, venerable messages of the unknown
     events, heroes, records of the earth.

I see the places of the sagas,
I see pine-trees and fir-trees torn by northern blasts,
I see granite bowlders and cliffs, I see green meadows and lakes,
I see the burial-cairns of Scandinavian warriors,   110
I see them raised high with stones by the marge of restless oceans,
       that the dead men's spirits when they wearied of their quiet
       graves might rise up through the mounds and gaze on the
       tossing billows, and be refresh'd by storms, immensity,
       liberty, action.

I see the steppes of Asia,
I see the tumuli of Mongolia, I see the tents of Kalmucks and
     Baskirs,
I see the nomadic tribes with herds of oxen and cows,
I see the table-lands notch'd with ravines, I see the jungles and
     deserts,   115
I see the camel, the wild steed, the bustard, the fat-tail'd sheep,
     the antelope, and the burrowing wolf.

I see the highlands of Abyssinia,
I see flocks of goats feeding, and see the fig-tree, tamarind, date,
And see fields of teff-wheat and places of verdure and gold.

I see the Brazilian vaquero,   120
I see the Bolivian ascending mount Sorata,

expounders of Mohammedan law.
  95. groves of Mona] Latin name of Anglesea, county of North Wales. vervain] A
European mallow, like mistletoe a legendary association with Druid worship.
  100. Kneph] In Egyptian mythology, a god with the body of a man and the head of
a sheep.
  101. Hermes] In Greek mythology the messenger of the gods. WW took this
passage about Kneph and Hermes almost literally from Volney's *Ruins*. See Goodale,
op. cit., 213.
  110, 111. warriors] These lines about the Scandinavian warriors were directly
developed from a newspaper clipping found in one of WW's notebooks. See Bucke, N
and F, 43n.
  113. Kalmucks and Baskirs] Nomadic tribes of Mongolia.
  119. teff-wheat] An Abyssinian grain plant.

I see the Wacho crossing the plains, I see the incomparable rider
    of horses with his lasso on his arm,
I see over the pampas the pursuit of wild cattle for their hides.

8

I see the regions of snow and ice,
125 I see the sharp-eyed Samoiede and the Finn,
I see the seal-seeker in his boat poising his lance,
I see the Siberian on his slight-built sledge drawn by dogs,
I see the porpoise-hunters, I see the whale-crews of the south Pa-
    cific and the north Atlantic,
I see the cliffs, glaciers, torrents, valleys, of Switzerland—I mark
    the long winters and the isolation.

I see the cities of the earth and make myself at random a part of
130   them,
I am a real Parisian,
I am a habitan of Vienna, St. Petersburg, Berlin, Constantinople,
I am of Adelaide, Sidney, Melbourne,
I am of London, Manchester, Bristol, Edinburgh, Limerick,
I am of Madrid, Cadiz, Barcelona, Oporto, Lyons, Brussels, Berne,
135   Frankfort, Stuttgart, Turin, Florence,
I belong in Moscow, Cracow, Warsaw, or northward in Christiania
    or Stockholm, or in Siberian Irkutsk, or in some street in
    Iceland,
I descend upon all those cities, and rise from them again.

10

I see vapors exhaling from unexplored countries,
I see the savage types, the bow and arrow, the poison'd splint, the
    fetich, and the obi.

140 I see African and Asiatic towns,
I see Algiers, Tripoli, Derne, Mogadore, Timbuctoo, Monrovia,
I see the swarms of Pekin, Canton, Benares, Delhi, Calcutta, Tokio,

---

    122. Wacho] A member of a Caddoan Indian tribe, Texas.
    Section 8] In 1881 WW excluded a former section 8, transposing seven of its
eight lines to "A Paumanok Picture" (see note, p. 460). Former section 9 then be-
came section 8 and the number 9 was cancelled from the sequence.
    125. Samoiede] A member of the Samoyedes, a neo-Siberian tribe in the region of
the Altai mountains.
    143. Kruman] Tribesman of Liberia, West Africa.

I see the Kruman in his hut, and the Dahoman and Ashantee-man
    in their huts,
I see the Turk smoking opium in Aleppo,
I see the picturesque crowds at the fairs of Khiva and those of
    Herat,   145
I see Teheran, I see Muscat and Medina and the intervening sands,
    I see the caravans toiling onward,
I see Egypt and the Egyptians, I see the pyramids and obelisks,
I look on chisell'd histories, records of conquering kings, dynasties,
    cut in slabs of sand-stone, or on granite-blocks,
I see at Memphis mummy-pits containing mummies embalm'd,
    swathed in linen cloth, lying there many centuries,
I look on the fall'n Theban, the large-ball'd eyes, the side-drooping
    neck, the hands folded across the breast.   150

I see all the menials of the earth, laboring,
I see all the prisoners in the prisons,
I see the defective human bodies of the earth,
The blind, the deaf and dumb, idiots, hunchbacks, lunatics,
The pirates, thieves, betrayers, murderers, slave-makers of the earth, 155
The helpless infants, and the helpless old men and women.

I see male and female everywhere,
I see the serene brotherhood of philosophs,
I see the constructiveness of my race,
I see the results of the perseverance and industry of my race,   160
I see ranks, colors, barbarisms, civilizations, I go among them, I
    mix indiscriminately,
And I salute all the inhabitants of the earth.

    11

You whoever you are!
You daughter or son of England!
You of the mighty Slavic tribes and empires! you Russ in Russia! 165
You dim-descended, black, divine-soul'd African, large, fine-
    headed, nobly-form'd, superbly destin'd, on equal terms
    with me!

   145. Khiva] Former khanate in western Asia, now in the USSR. Herat] City of
northwestern Afghanistan.
   146. Teheran] Capital of Iran. Muscat] Capital of Oman, Arabia. Medina] City in
Hejaz, Saudi Arabia.

You Norwegian! Swede! Dane! Icelander! you Prussian!
You Spaniard of Spain! you Portuguese!
You Frenchwoman and Frenchman of France!
You Belge! you liberty-lover of the Netherlands! (you stock
170   whence I myself have descended;)
You sturdy Austrian! you Lombard! Hun! Bohemian! farmer of
           Styria!
You neighbor of the Danube!
You working-man of the Rhine, the Elbe, or the Weser! you
           working-woman too!
You Sardinian! you Bavarian! Swabian! Saxon! Wallachian!
           Bulgarian!
175 You Roman! Neapolitan! you Greek!
You lithe matador in the arena at Seville!
You mountaineer living lawlessly on the Taurus or Caucasus!
You Bokh horse-herd watching your mares and stallions feeding!
You beautiful-bodied Persian at full speed in the saddle shooting
           arrows to the mark!
180 You Chinaman and Chinawoman of China! you Tartar of Tartary!
You women of the earth subordinated at your tasks!
You Jew journeying in your old age through every risk to stand
           once on Syrian ground!
You other Jews waiting in all lands for your Messiah!
You thoughtful Armenian pondering by some stream of the Eu-
           phrates! you peering amid the ruins of Nineveh! you
           ascending mount Ararat!
You foot-worn pilgrim welcoming the far-away sparkle of the
185   minarets of Mecca!
You sheiks along the stretch from Suez to Bab-el-mandeb ruling
           your families and tribes!
You olive-grower tending your fruit on fields of Nazareth, Damas-
           cus, or lake Tiberias!

171. Styria] A province of southeastern Austria.
173. Weser] River in Germany.
174. Swabian] Native of Swabia, now a district of southwestern Bavaria. Wal-
lachian] Native of Wallachia, now a part of Romania.
177. Taurus] A mountain range in southern Asia Minor, in Turkey. Caucasus]
Mountain range between the Black Sea and the Caspian.
178. Bokh] Referring to Bokhara, a part of the Uzbek Republic, USSR, formerly a
khanate of central Asia.
186. Bab-el-mandeb] A strait connecting the Red Sea with the Indian Ocean.
187. lake Tiberias] The Sea of Galilee in Palestine.

You Thibet trader on the wide inland or bargaining in the shops
    of Lassa!
You Japanese man or woman! you liver in Madagascar, Ceylon,
    Sumatra, Borneo!
All you continentals of Asia, Africa, Europe, Australia, indifferent
    of place!   190
All you on the numberless islands of the archipelagoes of the sea!
And you of centuries hence when you listen to me!
And you each and everywhere whom I specify not, but include
    just the same!
Health to you! good will to you all, from me and America sent!

Each of us inevitable,   195
Each of us limitless—each of us with his or her right upon the
    earth,
Each of us allow'd the eternal purports of the earth,
Each of us here as divinely as any is here.

      12

You Hottentot with clicking palate! you woolly-hair'd hordes!
You own'd persons dropping sweat-drops or blood-drops!   200
You human forms with the fathomless ever-impressive counte-
    nances of brutes!
You poor koboo whom the meanest of the rest look down upon
    for all your glimmering language and spirituality!
You dwarf'd Kamtschatkan, Greenlander, Lapp!
You Austral negro, naked, red, sooty, with protrusive lip, groveling,
    seeking your food!
You Caffre, Berber, Soudanese!   205
You haggard, uncouth, untutor'd Bedowee!
You plague-swarms in Madras, Nankin, Kaubul, Cairo!

  199. Hottentot with clicking palate] The word "Hottentot" in WW's day and later
connoted the uncouth or primitive, as "clicking palate" also suggests primitive
articulation.
  202. koboo] Kubu, one of a primitive Malayan forest tribe of south-central Suma-
tra.
  203. Kamtschatkan] Native of Kamchatka, a peninsula in northeastern Siberia.
  206. Bedowee] Bedouin, a nomadic Arabian.
  207. Madras] State and capital of southeastern India. Nankin] A city in southeast-
ern China, former capital, usually spelled Nanking. Kaubul] Kabul, capital of
Afghanistan.

You benighted roamer of Amazonia! you Patagonian! you Feejee-
     man!
I do not prefer others so very much before you either,
I do not say one word against you away back there where you
210   stand,
     (You will come forward in due time to my side.)

13

My spirit has pass'd in compassion and determination around the
     whole earth,
I have look'd for equals and lovers and found them ready for me
     in all lands,
I think some divine rapport has equalized me with them.

You vapors, I think I have risen with you, moved away to distant
215   continents, and fallen down there, for reasons,
I think I have blown with you you winds;
You waters I have finger'd every shore with you,
I have run through what any river or strait of the globe has run
     through,
I have taken my stand on the bases of peninsulas and on the high
     embedded rocks, to cry thence:

220 *Salut au monde!*
What cities the light or warmth penetrates I penetrate those cities
     myself,
All islands to which birds wing their way I wing my way myself.

Toward you all, in America's name,
I raise high the perpendicular hand, I make the signal,
225 To remain after me in sight forever,
For all the haunts and homes of men.

  1856   *1881*

ROAD] Entitled "Poem of the Road" in 1856 and 1860, and taking its present title
in 1867, this famous second-edition poem underwent only slight revision, one line
being added in 1881 and ten others being dropped either in 1871 or in 1881. Of all
WW's poems, it perhaps best meets the expectation of the general reader with its
elation, its buoyant invitation to adventure, and its confident promise. Yet, as in all
the greater poems, its power resides in its symbolic import without diminution of the
literal and realistic. W. S. Kennedy has surmised that WW found inspiration for

Song of the Open Road.

1

Afoot and light-hearted I take to the open road,
Healthy, free, the world before me,
The long brown path before me leading wherever I choose.

Henceforth I ask not good-fortune, I myself am good-fortune,
Henceforth I whimper no more, postpone no more, need nothing,   5
Done with indoor complaints, libraries, querulous criticisms,
Strong and content I travel the open road.

The earth, that is sufficient,
I do not want the constellations any nearer,
I know they are very well where they are,   10
I know they suffice for those who belong to them.

(Still here I carry my old delicious burdens,
I carry them, men and women, I carry them with me wherever I go,
I swear it is impossible for me to get rid of them,
I am fill'd with them, and I will fill them in return.)   15

2

You road I enter upon and look around, I believe you are not all
          that is here,
I believe that much unseen is also here.

this poem in a passage from George Sand's novel *Consuelo:* "What is there more
beautiful than a road? It is the symbol and the image of an active and varied
life . . . And then that road is the passage of Humanity, the route of the Uni-
verse . . . So far as the sight can read, the road is a land of liberty . . ." (see
Conservator, February, 1907, 184–185).

          6. criticisms] This line was added in 1881. WW's continued illness confirmed
his belief that he must now consider LG completed. *Cf.* "Prefaces," 1872 and 1876.

Here the profound lesson of reception, nor preference nor denial,
The black with his woolly head, the felon, the diseas'd, the illiterate
      person, are not denied;
The birth, the hasting after the physician, the beggar's tramp, the
20   drunkard's stagger, the laughing party of mechanics,
The escaped youth, the rich person's carriage, the fop, the eloping
      couple,
The early market-man, the hearse, the moving of furniture into the
      town, the return back from the town,
They pass, I also pass, any thing passes, none can be interdicted,
None but are accepted, none but shall be dear to me.

3

25   You air that serves me with breath to speak!
You objects that call from diffusion my meanings and give them
      shape!
You light that wraps me and all things in delicate equable showers!
You paths worn in the irregular hollows by the roadsides!
I believe you are latent with unseen existences, you are so dear
      to me.

30   You flagg'd walks of the cities! you strong curbs at the edges!
You ferries! you planks and posts of wharves! you timber-lined
      sides! you distant ships!
You rows of houses! you window-pierc'd façades! you roofs!
You porches and entrances! you copings and iron guards!
You windows whose transparent shells might expose so much!
35   You doors and ascending steps! you arches!
You gray stones of interminable pavements! you trodden crossings!
From all that has touch'd you I believe you have imparted to
      yourselves, and now would impart the same secretly to me,
From the living and the dead you have peopled your impassive
      surfaces, and the spirits thereof would be evident and
      amicable with me.

4

The earth expanding right hand and left hand,
40   The picture alive, every part in its best light,
The music falling in where it is wanted, and stopping where it is
      not wanted,

The cheerful voice of the public road, the gay fresh sentiment of
      the road.

O highway I travel, do you say to me *Do not leave me?*
Do you say *Venture not—if you leave me you are lost?*
Do you say *I am already prepared, I am well-beaten and un-
      denied, adhere to me?*   45

O public road, I say back I am not afraid to leave you, yet I love
      you,
You express me better than I can express myself,
You shall be more to me than my poem.

I think heroic deeds were all conceiv'd in the open air, and all
      free poems also,
I think I could stop here myself and do miracles,   50
I think whatever I shall meet on the road I shall like, and who-
      ever beholds me shall like me,
I think whoever I see must be happy.

5

From this hour I ordain myself loos'd of limits and imaginary
      lines,
Going where I list, my own master total and absolute,
Listening to others, considering well what they say,   55
Pausing, searching, receiving, contemplating,
Gently, but with undeniable will, divesting myself of the holds
      that would hold me.

I inhale great draughts of space,
The east and the west are mine, and the north and the south are
      mine.

I am larger, better than I thought,   60
I did not know I held so much goodness.

All seems beautiful to me,
I can repeat over to men and women You have done such good
      to me I would do the same to you,
I will recruit for myself and you as I go,

65 I will scatter myself among men and women as I go,
I will toss a new gladness and roughness among them,
Whoever denies me it shall not trouble me,
Whoever accepts me he or she shall be blessed and shall bless me.

6

Now if a thousand perfect men were to appear it would not amaze
      me,
Now if a thousand beautiful forms of women appear'd it would
70   not astonish me.

Now I see the secret of the making of the best persons,
It is to grow in the open air and to eat and sleep with the earth.

Here a great personal deed has room,
(Such a deed seizes upon the hearts of the whole race of men,
Its effusion of strength and will overwhelms law and mocks all
75   authority and all argument against it.)

Here is the test of wisdom,
Wisdom is not finally tested in schools,
Wisdom cannot be pass'd from one having it to another not
          having it,
Wisdom is of the soul, is not susceptible of proof, is its own proof,
80 Applies to all stages and objects and qualities and is content,
Is the certainty of the reality and immortality of things, and the
          excellence of things;
Something there is in the float of the sight of things that provokes
          it out of the soul.

Now I re-examine philosophies and religions,
They may prove well in lecture-rooms, yet not prove at all under
          the spacious clouds and along the landscape and flowing
          currents.

85 Here is realization,
Here is a man tallied—he realizes here what he has in him,

---

82. float] The "float of the sight of things" suggests the "flood" or "flowing" of
the appearances that provoke wisdom (call it forth) out of the soul. Cf. line 62,
"Crossing Brooklyn Ferry." Particularly WW would be aware of the meaning of

The past, the future, majesty, love—if they are vacant of you,
    you are vacant of them.

Only the kernel of every object nourishes;
Where is he who tears off the husks for you and me?
Where is he that undoes stratagems and envelopes for you and me?   90

Here is adhesiveness, it is not previously fashion'd, it is apropos;
Do you know what it is as you pass to be loved by strangers?
Do you know the talk of those turning eye-balls?

7

Here is the efflux of the soul,
The efflux of the soul comes from within through embower'd
    gates, ever provoking questions,   95
These yearnings why are they? these thoughts in the darkness
    why are they?
Why are there men and women that while they are nigh me the
    sunlight expands my blood?
Why when they leave me do my pennants of joy sink flat and lank?
Why are there trees I never walk under but large and melodious
    thoughts descend upon me?
(I think they hang there winter and summer on those trees and
    always drop fruit as I pass;)   100
What is it I interchange so suddenly with strangers?
What with some driver as I ride on the seat by his side?
What with some fisherman drawing his seine by the shore as I
    walk by and pause?
What gives me to be free to a woman's and man's good-will?
    what gives them to be free to mine?

8

The efflux of the soul is happiness, here is happiness,   105
I think it pervades the open air, waiting at all times,
Now it flows unto us, we are rightly charged.

"float" as the footlights on the stage, i.e. a flood of light.
    86. tallied] Colloquially, "added up." Sometimes WW used the word in the
further sense of "to evaluate or estimate."
    91. apropos] Meaning here, in the context, "appropriate" or "timely."

Here rises the fluid and attaching character,
The fluid and attaching character is the freshness and sweetness
      of man and woman,
(The herbs of the morning sprout no fresher and sweeter every
      day out of the roots of themselves, than it sprouts fresh
      and sweet continually out of itself.)

Toward the fluid and attaching character exudes the sweat of the
      love of young and old,
From it falls distill'd the charm that mocks beauty and attainments,
Toward it heaves the shuddering longing ache of contact.

9

Allons! whoever you are come travel with me!
Traveling with me you find what never tires.

The earth never tires,
The earth is rude, silent, incomprehensible at first, Nature is rude
      and incomprehensible at first,
Be not discouraged, keep on, there are divine things well envelop'd,
I swear to you there are divine things more beautiful than words
      can tell.

Allons! we must not stop here,
However sweet these laid-up stores, however convenient this dwell-
      ing we cannot remain here,
However shelter'd this port and however calm these waters we
      must not anchor here,
However welcome the hospitality that surrounds us we are per-
      mitted to receive it but a little while.

10

Allons! the inducements shall be greater,
We will sail pathless and wild seas,
We will go where winds blow, waves dash, and the Yankee clipper
      speeds by under full sail.

114. Allons!] French: "Let us go!" In the succeeding canto, it becomes martial.
129. formules] French: "formulas." In his "Blue Copy" revisions of the 1860

Allons! with power, liberty, the earth, the elements,
Health, defiance, gayety, self-esteem, curiosity;
Allons! from all formules!
From your formules, O bat-eyed and materialistic priests.   130

The stale cadaver blocks up the passage—the burial waits no
          longer.

Allons! yet take warning!
He traveling with me needs the best blood, thews, endurance,
None may come to the trial till he or she bring courage and health,
Come not here if you have already spent the best of yourself,   135
Only those may come who come in sweet and determin'd bodies,
No diseas'd person, no rum-drinker or venereal taint is permitted
          here.

(I and mine do not convince by arguments, similes, rhymes,
We convince by our presence.)

          11

Listen! I will be honest with you,   140
I do not offer the old smooth prizes, but offer rough new prizes,
These are the days that must happen to you:
You shall not heap up what is call'd riches,
You shall scatter with lavish hand all that you earn or achieve,
You but arrive at the city to which you were destin'd, you hardly
          settle yourself to satisfaction before you are call'd by an
          irresistible call to depart,   145
You shall be treated to the ironical smiles and mockings of those
          who remain behind you,
What beckonings of love you receive you shall only answer with
          passionate kisses of parting,
You shall not allow the hold of those who spread their reach'd
          hands toward you.

          12

Allons! after the great Companions, and to belong to them!
They too are on the road—they are the swift and majestic men—
          they are the greatest women,   150

edition of LG, WW deleted this and the following two lines, but retained them in the
1867 edition nevertheless.

Enjoyers of calms of seas and storms of seas,
Sailors of many a ship, walkers of many a mile of land,
Habituès of many distant countries, habituès of far-distant dwellings,
Trusters of men and women, observers of cities, solitary toilers,
155   Pausers and contemplators of tufts, blossoms, shells of the shore,
Dancers at wedding-dances, kissers of brides, tender helpers of
    children, bearers of children,
Soldiers of revolts, standers by gaping graves, lowerers-down of
    coffins,
Journeyers over consecutive seasons, over the years, the curious
    years each emerging from that which preceded it,
Journeyers as with companions, namely their own diverse phases,
160   Forth-steppers from the latent unrealized baby-days,
Journeyers gayly with their own youth, journeyers with their
    bearded and well-grain'd manhood,
Journeyers with their womanhood, ample, unsurpass'd, content,
Journeyers with their own sublime old age of manhood or woman-
    hood,
Old age, calm, expanded, broad with the haughty breadth of the
    universe,
165   Old age, flowing free with the delicious near-by freedom of death.

13

Allons! to that which is endless as it was beginningless,
To undergo much, tramps of days, rests of nights,
To merge all in the travel they tend to, and the days and nights
    they tend to,
Again to merge them in the start of superior journeys,
170   To see nothing anywhere but what you may reach it and pass it,
To conceive no time, however distant, but what you may reach it
    and pass it,
To look up or down no road but it stretches and waits for you,
    however long but it stretches and waits for you,
To see no being, not God's or any, but you also go thither,
To see no possession but you may possess it, enjoying all without
    labor or purchase, abstracting the feast yet not abstracting
    one particle of it,
To take the best of the farmer's farm and the rich man's elegant
    villa, and the chaste blessings of the well-married couple,
175   and the fruits of orchards and flowers of gardens,

To take to your use out of the compact cities as you pass through,
To carry buildings and streets with you afterward wherever you go,
To gather the minds of men out of their brains as you encounter
    them, to gather the love out of their hearts,
To take your lovers on the road with you, for all that you leave
    them behind you,
To know the universe itself as a road, as many roads, as roads for
    traveling souls.   180

All parts away for the progress of souls,
All religion, all solid things, arts, governments—all that was or is
    apparent upon this globe or any globe, falls into niches and
    corners before the procession of souls along the grand roads
    of the universe.

Of the progress of the souls of men and women along the grand
    roads of the universe, all other progress is the needed
    emblem and sustenance.

Forever alive, forever forward,
Stately, solemn, sad, withdrawn, baffled, mad, turbulent, feeble,
    dissatisfied,   185
Desperate, proud, fond, sick, accepted by men, rejected by men,
They go! they go! I know that they go, but I know not where
    they go,
But I know that they go toward the best—toward something
    great.

Whoever you are, come forth! or man or woman come forth!
You must not stay sleeping and dallying there in the house,
    though you built it, or though it has been built for you.   190

Out of the dark confinement! out from behind the screen!
It is useless to protest, I know all and expose it.

Behold through you as bad as the rest,
Through the laughter, dancing, dining, supping, of people,
Inside of dresses and ornaments, inside of those wash'd and
    trimm'd faces,   195
Behold a secret silent loathing and despair.

No husband, no wife, no friend, trusted to hear the confession,
Another self, a duplicate of every one, skulking and hiding it goes,
Form!ess and wordless through the streets of the cities, polite and
    bland in the parlors,
200 In the cars of railroads, in steamboats, in the public assembly,
Home to the houses of men and women, at the table, in the bed-
    room, everywhere,
Smartly attired, countenance smiling, form upright, death under
    the breast-bones, hell under the skull-bones,
Under the broadcloth and gloves, under the ribbons and artificial
    flowers,
Keeping fair with the customs, speaking not a syllable of itself,
205 Speaking of any thing else but never of itself.

14

Allons! through struggles and wars!
The goal that was named cannot be countermanded.

Have the past struggles succeeded?
What has succeeded? yourself? your nation? Nature?
Now understand me well—it is provided in the essence of things
    that from any fruition of success, no matter what, shall
210   come forth something to make a greater struggle necessary.

My call is the call of battle, I nourish active rebellion,
He going with me must go well arm'd,
He going with me goes often with spare diet, poverty, angry
    enemies, desertions.

15

Allons! the road is before us!
It is safe—I have tried it—my own feet have tried it well—be
215   not detain'd!

FERRY] This was the "Sun-Down Poem" of the second edition, the most distin-
guished of the new poems of 1856, taking its present title in 1860. It is possible that
WW began its composition even before the first edition went to press, for many of its
lines are entered into one of his notebooks of the period. See *An 1855–56 Notebook
Toward the Second Edition of Leaves of Grass*, ed. by Harold W. Blodgett (1959).
The revisions through the various editions—some fourteen lines were dropped and
quite a number of phrases amended—reveal the constant improvement in a composi-

Let the paper remain on the desk unwritten, and the book on the
    shelf unopen'd!
Let the tools remain in the workshop! let the money remain
    unearn'd!
Let the school stand! mind not the cry of the teacher!
Let the preacher preach in his pulpit! let the lawyer plead in the
    court, and the judge expound the law.

Camerado, I give you my hand!   220
I give you my love more precious than money,
I give you myself before preaching or law;
Will you give me yourself? will you come travel with me?
Shall we stick by each other as long as we live?

1856   1881

Crossing Brooklyn Ferry.

1

Flood-tide below me! I see you face to face!
Clouds of the west—sun there half an hour high—I see you
    also face to face.

Crowds of men and women attired in the usual costumes, how
    curious you are to me!
On the ferry-boats the hundreds and hundreds that cross, return-
    ing home, are more curious to me than you suppose,

tion whose first version evidenced mastery of artistic power. With exalted and
sustained inspiration the poet presents a transcendent reality unlimited by the tyr-
anny of time or person or space, a poetic demonstration of the power of appear-
ances—"dumb, beautiful ministers"—to affirm the soul. Philosophical in theme, the
poem is yet profoundly personal—his own daily experience made illustrious—and its
strength lies in its aesthetic vision. For a detailed analysis, see Stanley K. Coffman's
" 'Crossing Brooklyn Ferry': A Note on the Catalogue Technique in Whitman's
Poetry." MP, LI, 225–232.

And you that shall cross from shore to shore years hence are
　　　more to me, and more in my meditations, than you might
5　　　suppose.

　　　2

The impalpable sustenance of me from all things at all hours of
　　　the day,
The simple, compact, well-join'd scheme, myself disintegrated,
　　　every one disintegrated yet part of the scheme,
The similitudes of the past and those of the future,
The glories strung like beads on my smallest sights and hearings,
　　　on the walk in the street and the passage over the river,
10　The current rushing so swiftly and swimming with me far away,
The others that are to follow me, the ties between me and them,
The certainty of others, the life, love, sight, hearing of others.

Others will enter the gates of the ferry and cross from shore to
　　　shore,
Others will watch the run of the flood-tide,
Others will see the shipping of Manhattan north and west, and
15　　　the heights of Brooklyn to the south and east,
Others will see the islands large and small;
Fifty years hence, others will see them as they cross, the sun half
　　　an hour high,
A hundred years hence, or ever so many hundred years hence,
　　　others will see them,
Will enjoy the sunset, the pouring-in of the flood-tide, the falling-
　　　back to the sea of the ebb-tide.

　　　3

20　It avails not, time nor place—distance avails not,
I am with you, you men and women of a generation, or ever so
　　　many generations hence,
Just as you feel when you look on the river and sky, so I felt,
Just as any of you is one of a living crowd, I was one of a crowd,
Just as you are refresh'd by the gladness of the river and the
　　　bright flow, I was refresh'd,

28. Twelfth-month sea-gulls] WW's use of the Quaker designation for the days

Just as you stand and lean on the rail, yet hurry with the swift
      current, I stood yet was hurried,   25
Just as you look on the numberless masts of ships and the thick-
      stemm'd pipes of steamboats, I look'd.

I too many and many a time cross'd the river of old,
Watched the Twelfth-month sea-gulls, saw them high in the air
      floating with motionless wings, oscillating their bodies,
Saw how the glistening yellow lit up parts of their bodies and left
      the rest in strong shadow,
Saw the slow-wheeling circles and the gradual edging toward the
      south,   30
Saw the reflection of the summer sky in the water,
Had my eyes dazzled by the shimmering track of beams,
Look'd at the fine centrifugal spokes of light round the shape of
      my head in the sunlit water,
Look'd on the haze on the hills southward and south-westward,
Look'd on the vapor as it flew in fleeces tinged with violet,   35
Look'd toward the lower bay to notice the vessels arriving,
Saw their approach, saw aboard those that were near me,
Saw the white sails of schooners and sloops, saw the ships at anchor,
The sailors at work in the rigging or out astride the spars,
The round masts, the swinging motion of the hulls, the slender
      serpentine pennants,   40
The large and small steamers in motion, the pilots in their pilot-
      houses,
The white wake left by the passage, the quick tremulous whirl of
      the wheels,
The flags of all nations, the falling of them at sunset,
The scallop-edged waves in the twilight, the ladled cups, the
      frolicsome crests and glistening,
The stretch afar growing dimmer and dimmer, the gray walls of
      the granite storehouses by the docks,   45
On the river the shadowy group, the big steam-tug closely flank'd
      on each side by the barges, the hay-boat, the belated
      lighter,
On the neighboring shore the fires from the foundry chimneys
      burning high and glaringly into the night,

and months often produced a more musical phrase.
   33. centrifugal spokes of light] An aureole available to anyone.

Casting their flicker of black contrasted with wild red and yellow
    light over the tops of houses, and down into the clefts of
    streets.

4

These and all else were to me the same as they are to you,
50 I loved well those cities, loved well the stately and rapid river,
The men and women I saw were all near to me,
Others the same—others who look back on me because I look'd
    forward to them,
(The time will come, though I stop here to-day and to-night.)

5

What is it then between us?
55 What is the count of the scores or hundreds of years between us?

Whatever it is, it avails not—distance avails not, and place avails
    not,
I too lived, Brooklyn of ample hills was mine,
I too walk'd the streets of Manhattan island, and bathed in the
    waters around it,
I too felt the curious abrupt questionings stir within me,
60 In the day among crowds of people sometimes they came upon me,
In my walks home late at night or as I lay in my bed they came
    upon me,
I too had been struck from the float forever held in solution,
I too had receiv'd identity by my body,
That I was I knew was of my body, and what I should be I knew
    I should be of my body.

6

65 It is not upon you alone the dark patches fall,
The dark threw its patches down upon me also,
The best I had done seem'd to me blank and suspicious,
My great thoughts as I supposed them, were they not in reality
    meagre?
Nor is it you alone who know what it is to be evil,
70 I am he who knew what it was to be evil,

I too knitted the old knot of contrariety,
Blabb'd, blush'd, resented, lied, stole, grudg'd,
Had guile, anger, lust, hot wishes I dared not speak,
Was wayward, vain, greedy, shallow, sly, cowardly, malignant,
The wolf, the snake, the hog, not wanting in me,   75
The cheating look, the frivolous word, the adulterous wish, not
    wanting,
Refusals, hates, postponements, meanness, laziness, none of these
    wanting,
Was one with the rest, the days and haps of the rest,
Was call'd by my nighest name by clear loud voices of young men
    as they saw me approaching or passing,
Felt their arms on my neck as I stood, or the negligent leaning of
    their flesh against me as I sat,   80
Saw many I loved in the street or ferry-boat or public assembly,
    yet never told them a word,
Lived the same life with the rest, the same old laughing, gnawing,
    sleeping,
Play'd the part that still looks back on the actor or actress,
The same old role, the role that is what we make it, as great as we
    like,
Or as small as we like, or both great and small.   85

                    7

Closer yet I approach you,
What thought you have of me now, I had as much of you—I laid
    in my stores in advance,
I consider'd long and seriously of you before you were born.

Who was to know what should come home to me?
Who knows but I am enjoying this?   90
Who knows, for all the distance, but I am as good as looking at
    you now, for all you cannot see me?

                    8

Ah, what can ever be more stately and admirable to me than mast-
    hemm'd Manhattan?

    89–91.] Cf. endings, "Song of Myself" and "So Long."

River and sunset and scallop-edg'd waves of flood-tide?
The sea-gulls oscillating their bodies, the hay-boat in the twilight,
    and the belated lighter?
What gods can exceed these that clasp me by the hand, and with
    voices I love call me promptly and loudly by my nighest
95   name as I approach?
What is more subtle than this which ties me to the woman or man
    that looks in my face?
Which fuses me into you now, and pours my meaning into you?

We understand then do we not?
What I promis'd without mentioning it, have you not accepted?
What the study could not teach—what the preaching could not
100   accomplish is accomplish'd, is it not?

9

Flow on, river! flow with the flood-tide, and ebb with the ebb-
    tide!
Frolic on, crested and scallop-edg'd waves!
Gorgeous clouds of the sunset! drench with your splendor me, or
    the men and women generations after me!
Cross from shore to shore, countless crowds of passengers!
Stand up, tall masts of Mannahatta! stand up, beautiful hills of
105   Brooklyn!
Throb, baffled and curious brain! throw out questions and answers!
Suspend here and everywhere, eternal float of solution!
Gaze, loving and thirsting eyes, in the house or street or public
    assembly!
Sound out, voices of young men! loudly and musically call me by
    my nighest name!
110 Live, old life! play the part that looks back on the actor or actress!
Play the old role, the role that is great or small according as one
    makes it!
Consider, you who peruse me, whether I may not in unknown
    ways be looking upon you;
Be firm, rail over the river, to support those who lean idly, yet
    haste with the hasting current;
Fly on, sea-birds! fly sideways, or wheel in large circles high in
    the air;

Receive the summer sky, you water, and faithfully hold it till all
    downcast eyes have time to take it from you! 115
Diverge, fine spokes of light, from the shape of my head, or any
    one's head, in the sunlit water!
Come on, ships from the lower bay! pass up or down, white-sail'd
    schooners, sloops, lighters!
Flaunt away, flags of all nations! be duly lower'd at sunset!
Burn high your fires, foundry chimneys! cast black shadows at
    nightfall! cast red and yellow light over the tops of the
    houses!

Appearances, now or henceforth, indicate what you are, 120
You necessary film, continue to envelop the soul,
About my body for me, and your body for you, be hung our
    divinest aromas,
Thrive, cities—bring your freight, bring your shows, ample and
    sufficient rivers,
Expand, being than which none else is perhaps more spiritual,
Keep your places, objects than which none else is more lasting. 125

You have waited, you always wait, you dumb, beautiful ministers,
We receive you with free sense at last, and are insatiate hence-
    forward,
Not you any more shall be able to foil us, or withhold yourselves
    from us,
We use you, and do not cast you aside—we plant you perma-
    nently within us,
We fathom you not—we love you—there is perfection in you also, 130
You furnish your parts toward eternity,
Great or small, you furnish your parts toward the soul.

1856   1881

Song of the Answerer.

1

Now list to my morning's romanza, I tell the signs of the Answerer,
To the cities and farms I sing as they spread in the sunshine
    before me.

A young man comes to me bearing a message from his brother,
How shall the young man know the whether and when of his
    brother?
5 Tell him to send me the signs.

And I stand before the young man face to face, and take his right
    hand in my left hand and his left hand in my right hand,
And I answer for his brother and for men, and I answer for him
    that answers for all, and send these signs.

Him all wait for, him all yield up to, his word is decisive and final,
Him they accept, in him lave, in him perceive themselves as amid
    light,
10 Him they immerse and he immerses them.

Beautiful women, the haughtiest nations, laws, the landscape,
    people, animals,
The profound earth and its attributes and the unquiet ocean, (so
    tell I my morning's romanza,)

ANSWERER] For the 1881 edition this poem was created from what had been two
separate poems, the first section having originally been one of the twelve untitled
poems of the first edition, becoming "Poem of the Poet" in the second edition, "Leaves
of Grass No. 3" in the third, and in the fourth "Now List to My Morning Romanza,"
a title taken from the then added two-line opening passage, and retained until the
second section and present title were added in 1881. The second section began in 1856
as "Poem of The Singers and of The Words of Poems," became "Leaves of Grass

All enjoyments and properties and money, and whatever money
    will buy,
The best farms, others toiling and planting and he unavoidably
    reaps,
The noblest and costliest cities, others grading and building and
    he domiciles there,   15
Nothing for any one but what is for him, near and far are for him,
    the ships in the offing,
The perpetual shows and marches on land are for him if they are
    for anybody.

He puts things in their attitudes,
He puts to-day out of himself with plasticity and love,
He places his own times, reminiscences, parents, brothers and
    sisters, associations, employment, politics, so that the rest
    never shame them afterward, nor assume to command
    them.   20

He is the Answerer,
What can be answer'd he answers, and what cannot be answer'd
    he shows how it cannot be answer'd.

A man is a summons and challenge,
(It is vain to skulk—do you hear that mocking and laughter? do
    you hear the ironical echoes?)

Books, friendships, philosophers, priests, action, pleasure, pride,
    beat up and down seeking to give satisfaction,   25
He indicates the satisfaction, and indicates them that beat up and
    down also.

Whichever the sex, whatever the season or place, he may go freshly
    and gently and safely by day or by night,
He has the pass-key of hearts, to him the response of the prying
    of hands on the knobs.

No. 6" in the third edition, and "The Indications" in the fourth, fifth, and sixth
editions, until in 1881 it took its present position. The joining of the two poems
is obviously appropriate, for the Poet of the second section is the Answerer
of the first; and in fact the two were consecutive in the editions of 1871 and
1876. As it now stands, the composition is the result of not a little revision. From the
first section the last four lines were dropped in 1867; and some lines of the second
section were adapted from the 1855 Preface.
    1. romanza] Italian: ballad or air.

His welcome is universal, the flow of beauty is not more welcome
        or universal than he is,
30 The person he favors by day or sleeps with at night is blessed.

Every existence has its idiom, every thing has an idiom and tongue,
He resolves all tongues into his own and bestows it upon men, and
        any man translates, and any man translates himself also,
One part does not counteract another part, he is the joiner, he
        sees how they join.

He says indifferently and alike *How are you friend?* to the
        President at his levee,
And he says *Good-day my brother*, to Cudge that hoes in the
35   sugar-field,
And both understand him and know that his speech is right.

He walks with perfect ease in the capitol,
He walks among the Congress, and one Representative says to
        another, *Here is our equal appearing and new*.

Then the mechanics take him for a mechanic,
And the soldiers suppose him to be a soldier, and the sailors that
40   he has follow'd the sea,
And the authors take him for an author, and the artists for an
        artist,
And the laborers perceive he could labor with them and love them,
No matter what the work is, that he is the one to follow it or has
        follow'd it,
No matter what the nation, that he might find his brothers and
        sisters there.

45 The English believe he comes of their English stock,
A Jew to the Jew he seems, a Russ to the Russ, usual and near,
        removed from none.

Whoever he looks at in the traveler's coffee-house claims him,
The Italian or Frenchman is sure, the German is sure, the Spaniard
        is sure, and the island Cuban is sure,

   35. Cudge] A common name then for a Negro field hand. Cf. "Cuff," line 109,
"Song of Myself."

The engineer, the deck-hand on the great lakes, or on the Missis-
sippi or St. Lawrence or Sacramento, or Hudson or Pau-
manok sound, claims him.

The gentleman of perfect blood acknowledges his perfect blood,   50
The insulter, the prostitute, the angry person, the beggar, see
themselves in the ways of him, he strangely transmutes them,
They are not vile any more, they hardly know themselves they are
so grown.

2

The indications and tally of time,
Perfect sanity shows the master among philosophs,
Time, always without break, indicates itself in parts,   55
What always indicates the poet is the crowd of the pleasant com-
pany of singers, and their words,
The words of the singers are the hours or minutes of the light or
dark, but the words of the maker of poems are the general
light and dark,
The maker of poems settles justice, reality, immortality,
His insight and power encircle things and the human race,
He is the glory and extract thus far of things and of the human
race.   60

The singers do not beget, only the Poet begets,
The singers are welcom'd, understood, appear often enough, but
rare has the day been, likewise the spot, of the birth of the
maker of poems, the Answerer,
(Not every century nor every five centuries has contain'd such a
day, for all its names.)

The singers of successive hours of centuries may have ostensible
names, but the name of each of them is one of the singers,
The name of each is, eye-singer, ear-singer, head-singer, sweet-
singer, night-singer, parlor-singer, love-singer, weird-singer,
or something else.   65

All this time and at all times wait the words of true poems,
The words of true poems do not merely please,

The true poets are not followers of beauty but the august masters
    of beauty;
The greatness of sons is the exuding of the greatness of mothers
    and fathers,
70   The words of true poems are the tuft and final applause of science.

Divine instinct, breadth of vision, the law of reason, health, rudeness
    of body, withdrawnness,
Gayety, sun-tan, air-sweetness, such are some of the words of poems.

The sailor and traveler underlie the maker of poems, the Answerer,
The builder, geometer, chemist, anatomist, phrenologist, artist, all
    these underlie the maker of poems, the Answerer.

75   The words of the true poems give you more than poems,
They give you to form for yourself poems, religions, politics, war,
    peace, behavior, histories, essays, daily life, and every
    thing else,
They balance ranks, colors, races, creeds, and the sexes,
They do not seek beauty, they are sought,
Forever touching them or close upon them follows beauty, longing,
    fain, love-sick.

They prepare for death, yet are they not the finish, but rather the
80   outset,
They bring none to his or her terminus or to be content and full,
Whom they take they take into space to behold the birth of stars,
    to learn one of the meanings,
To launch off with absolute faith, to sweep through the ceaseless
    rings and never be quiet again.

1855, 1856   *1881*

70. tuft] A small flexible cluster, but in WW's figure, suggesting a culminating
adornment, familiar in the male bird's crest or the Indian's feathered topknot. This
line is one of several adapted from the 1855 Preface.

74. phrenologist] Phrenology then occupied a place in public imagination later to
be taken by the infant science of psychology.

FEUILLAGE] French for "foliage," here used symbolically as a universal particu-
lar, like leaves of grass. WW himself interpreted this poem in the first paragraph of
a letter he wrote offering it to *Harper's Magazine* January 7, 1860: "The theory of 'A
Chant of National Feuillage' is to bring in, (devoting a line, or two or three lines to
each,) a comprehensive collection of touches, locales, incidents, idiomatic scenes,
from every section, South, West, North, East, Kanada, Texas, Maine, Virginia, the

Our Old Feuillage.

Always our old feuillage!
Always Florida's green peninsula—always the priceless delta of
      Louisiana—always the cotton-fields of Alabama and Texas,
Always California's golden hills and hollows, and the silver moun-
      tains of New Mexico—always soft-breath'd Cuba,
Always the vast slope drain'd by the Southern sea, inseparable with
      the slopes drain'd by the Eastern and Western seas,
The area the eighty-third year of these States, the three and a half
      millions of square miles,   5
The eighteen thousand miles of sea-coast and bay-coast on the
      main, the thirty thousand miles of river navigation,
The seven millions of distinct families and the same number of
      dwellings—always these, and more, branching forth into
      numberless branches,
Always the free range and diversity—always the continent of
      Democracy;
Always the prairies, pastures, forests, vast cities, travelers, Kanada,
      the snows;
Always these compact lands tied at the hips with the belt stringing
      the huge oval lakes;   10
Always the West with strong native persons, the increasing density
      there, the habitans, friendly, threatening, ironical, scorning
      invaders;

Mississippi Valley, etc, etc, etc.—all intensely fused to the urgency of compact America, 'America always'—all in a vein of graphic, short, clear, hasting along—as having a huge bouquet to collect, and quickly taking and binding in every characteristic subject that offers itself—making a compact, the-whole-surrounding, *National Poem*, after its sort, after my own style." The poem was rejected. Although it appeared in the 1860 edition as "Chants Democratic" No. 4, the MS (Barrett) shows that it was composed, at least in part, as early as 1856. The poem has undergone little change. In 1867 it was titled "American Feuillage," and it first took its present title in 1881.

    5. eighty-third year] The MS reads "Eightieth year," indicating that the poem was worked upon as early as 1856.

All sights, South, North, East—all deeds, promiscuously done at
    all times,
All characters, movements, growths, a few noticed, myriads unno-
    ticed,
Through Mannahatta's streets I walking, these things gathering,
On interior rivers by night in the glare of pine knots, steamboats
15   wooding up,
Sunlight by day on the valley of the Susquehanna, and on the
    valleys of the Potomac and Rappahannock, and the valleys
    of the Roanoke and Delaware,
In their northerly wilds beasts of prey haunting the Adirondacks
    the hills, or lapping the Saginaw waters to drink,
In a lonesome inlet a sheldrake lost from the flock, sitting on the
    water rocking silently,
In farmers' barns oxen in the stable, their harvest labor done, they
    rest standing, they are too tired,
Afar on arctic ice the she-walrus lying drowsily while her cubs play
20   around,
The hawk sailing where men have not yet sail'd, the farthest polar
    sea, ripply, crystalline, open, beyond the floes,
White drift spooning ahead where the ship in the tempest dashes,
On solid land what is done in cities as the bells strike midnight
    together,
In primitive woods the sounds there also sounding, the howl of the
    wolf, the scream of the panther, and the hoarse bellow of
    the elk,
In winter beneath the hard blue ice of Moosehead lake, in summer
25   visible through the clear waters, the great trout swimming,
In lower latitudes in warmer air in the Carolinas the large black
    buzzard floating slowly high beyond the tree tops,
Below, the red cedar festoon'd with tylandria, the pines and
    cypresses growing out of the white sand that spreads far
    and flat,
Rude boats descending the big Pedee, climbing plants, parasites
    with color'd flowers and berries enveloping huge trees,
The waving drapery on the live-oak trailing long and low, noise-
    lessly waved by the wind,

27. tylandria] Properly, tillandsia, or Spanish moss.
28. Pedee] Name given to the Yadkin river after it enters South Carolina.

The camp of Georgia wagoners just after dark, the supper-fires
    and the cooking and eating by whites and negroes,   30
Thirty or forty great wagons, the mules, cattle, horses, feeding
    from troughs,
The shadows, gleams, up under the leaves of the old sycamore-
    trees, the flames with the black smoke from the pitch-pine
    curling and rising;
Southern fishermen fishing, the sounds and inlets of North Caro-
    lina's coast, the shad-fishery and the herring-fishery, the
    large sweep-seines, the windlasses on shore work'd by
    horses, the clearing, curing, and packing-houses;
Deep in the forest in piney woods turpentine dropping from the
    incisions in the trees, there are the turpentine works,
There are the negroes at work in good health, the ground in all
    directions is cover'd with pine straw;   35
In Tennessee and Kentucky slaves busy in the coalings, at the
    forge, by the furnace-blaze, or at the corn-shucking,
In Virginia, the planter's son returning after a long absence, joy-
    fully welcom'd and kiss'd by the aged mulatto nurse,
On rivers boatmen safely moor'd at nightfall in their boats under
    shelter of high banks,
Some of the younger men dance to the sound of the banjo or
    fiddle, others sit on the gunwale smoking and talking;
Late in the afternoon the mocking-bird, the American mimic,
    singing in the Great Dismal Swamp,   40
There are the greenish waters, the resinous odor, the plenteous
    moss, the cypress-tree, and the juniper-tree;
Northward, young men of Mannahatta, the target company from
    an excursion returning home at evening, the musket-muz-
    zles all bear bunches of flowers presented by women;
Children at play, or on his father's lap a young boy fallen asleep,
    (how his lips move! how he smiles in his sleep!)
The scout riding on horseback over the plains west of the Missis-
    sippi, he ascends a knoll and sweeps his eyes around;
California life, the miner, bearded, dress'd in his rude costume,
    the stanch California friendship, the sweet air, the graves
    one in passing meets solitary just aside the horse-path;   45

---

40. Great Dismal Swamp] Marshy region north of Albemarle Sound, North
Carolina.

Down in Texas the cotton-field, the negro-cabins, drivers driving
　　　mules or oxen before rude carts, cotton bales piled on
　　　banks and wharves;
Encircling all, vast-darting up and wide, the American Soul, with
　　　equal hemispheres, one Love, one Dilation or Pride;
In arriere the peace-talk with the Iroquois the aborigines, the
　　　calumet, the pipe of good-will, arbitration, and indorse-
　　　ment,
The sachem blowing the smoke first toward the sun and then
　　　toward the earth,
The drama of the scalp-dance enacted with painted faces and
50　　　guttural exclamations,
The setting out of the war-party, the long and stealthy march,
The single file, the swinging hatchets, the surprise and slaughter
　　　of enemies;
All the acts, scenes, ways, persons, attitudes of these States,
　　　reminiscences, institutions,
All these States compact, every square mile of these States without
　　　excepting a particle;
Me pleas'd, rambling in lanes and country fields, Paumanok's
55　　　fields,
Observing the spiral flight of two little yellow butterflies shuffling
　　　between each other, ascending high in the air,
The darting swallow, the destroyer of insects, the fall traveler
　　　southward but returning northward early in the spring,
The country boy at the close of the day driving the herd of cows
　　　and shouting to them as they loiter to browse by the road-
　　　side,
The city wharf, Boston, Philadelphia, Baltimore, Charleston, New
　　　Orleans, San Francisco,
60　　The departing ships when the sailors heave at the capstan;
Evening—me in my room—the setting sun,
The setting summer sun shining in my open window, showing the
　　　swarm of flies, suspended, balancing in the air in the centre
　　　of the room, darting athwart, up and down, casting swift
　　　shadows in specks on the opposite wall where the shine is;

48. arriere] French: properly arrière, "behind," "in the rear," but here meaning
"in the past."
67. sporades] Designating both "the scattered islands"—Greek isles in the Ae-
gean, with a capital "S"—and the sporadic stars not belonging to any constellation.
70. Nueces] River in southwestern Texas. Brazos] River in Texas, southwest of

The athletic American matron speaking in public to crowds of
      listeners,
Males, females, immigrants, combinations, the copiousness, the
      individuality of the States, each for itself—the money-
      makers,
Factories, machinery, the mechanical forces, the windlass, lever,
      pulley, all certainties,   65
The certainty of space, increase, freedom, futurity,
In space the sporades, the scatter'd islands, the stars—on the
      firm earth, the lands, my lands,
O lands! all so dear to me—what you are, (whatever it is,) I
      putting it at random in these songs, become a part of that,
      whatever it is,
Southward there, I screaming, with wings slow flapping, with the
      myriads of gulls wintering along the coasts of Florida,
Otherways there atwixt the banks of the Arkansaw, the Rio
      Grande, the Nueces, the Brazos, the Tombigbee, the Red
      River, the Saskatchawan or the Osage, I with the spring
      waters laughing and skipping and running,   70
Northward, on the sands, on some shallow bay of Paumanok, I
      with parties of snowy herons wading in the wet to seek
      worms and aquatic plants,
Retreating, triumphantly twittering, the king-bird, from piercing
      the crow with its bill, for amusement—and I triumphantly
      twittering,
The migrating flock of wild geese alighting in autumn to refresh
      themselves, the body of the flock feed, the sentinels out-
      side move around with erect heads watching, and are from
      time to time reliev'd by other sentinels—and I feeding
      and taking turns with the rest,
In Kanadian forests the moose, large as an ox, corner'd by
      hunters, rising desperately on his hind-feet, and plunging
      with his fore-feet, the hoofs as sharp as knives—and I,
      plunging at the hunters, corner'd and desperate,
In the Mannahatta, streets, piers, shipping, store-houses, and the
      countless workmen working in the shops,   75

Galveston. Tombigbee] River in eastern Mississippi and western Alabama.
71–73] Such lines as these on the behavior of birds testify to WW's close observa-
tion. In a letter of August 24, 1879, John Burroughs, who had been composing an
article on "Nature and the Poets," confessed: "I cannot catch you in any mistake, as I
wish I could, for that is my game." (Traubel, III, 260)

176 LEAVES OF GRASS

And I too of the Mannahatta, singing thereof—and no less in
    myself than the whole of the Mannahatta in itself,
Singing the song of These, my ever-united lands—my body no
    more inevitably united, part to part, and made out of a
    thousand diverse contributions one identity, any more than
    my lands are inevitably united and made ONE IDENTITY;
Nativities, climates, the grass of the great pastoral Plains,
Cities, labors, death, animals, products, war, good and evil—
    these me,
These affording, in all their particulars, the old feuillage to me
    and to America, how can I do less than pass the clew of
    the union of them, to afford the like to you?
Whoever you are! how can I but offer you divine leaves, that you
    also be eligible as I am?
How can I but as here chanting, invite you for yourself to collect
    bouquets of the incomparable feuillage of these States?

80

1860   1881

A Song of Joys.

O to make the most jubilant song!
Full of music—full of manhood, womanhood, infancy!
Full of common employments—full of grain and trees.

O for the voices of animals—O for the swiftness and balance of
    fishes!

JOYS] Entitled "Poem of Joys" when it first appeared in 1860, and "Poems of
Joy" in 1867, the poem reverted to its first title in 1871 and 1876 and took its present
title in 1881. Based on personal reminiscences, but designed, like "Song of the Open
Road," to celebrate the American experience generally, the poem underwent consider-
able alteration by excision, addition, and transposition. The most notable addition
was that in 1871 of a passage (lines 121 through 133) which may indicate a fresh

O for the dropping of raindrops in a song!   5
O for the sunshine and motion of waves in a song!

O the joy of my spirit—it is uncaged—it darts like lightning!
It is not enough to have this globe or a certain time,
I will have thousands of globes and all time.

O the engineer's joys! to go with a locomotive!   10
To hear the hiss of steam, the merry shriek, the steam-whistle, the
    laughing locomotive!
To push with resistless way and speed off in the distance.

O the gleesome saunter over fields and hillsides!
The leaves and flowers of the commonest weeds, the moist fresh
    stillness of the woods,
The exquisite smell of the earth at daybreak, and all through the
    forenoon.   15

O the horseman's and horsewoman's joys!
The saddle, the gallop, the pressure upon the seat, the cool gurgling
    by the ears and hair.

O the fireman's joys!
I hear the alarm at dead of night,
I hear bells, shouts! I pass the crowd, I run!   20
The sight of the flames maddens me with pleasure.

O the joy of the strong-brawn'd fighter, towering in the arena in
    perfect condition, conscious of power, thirsting to meet his
    opponent.

O the joy of that vast elemental sympathy which only the human
    soul is capable of generating and emitting in steady and
    limitless floods.

access of confidence after the tribulations of the Civil War. The MSS show that WW
had been working upon this theme since the early 1850's. For example, he made the
following entry in a pre-1855 notebook (LC Whitman, 85): "Poem incarnating the
mind of an old man, whose life has been magnificently developed—the wildest and
most exuberant joy—the utterance of hope and floods of anticipation—faith in what-
ever happens—but all enfolded on Joy Joy Joy which underlies and overtops the
whole effusion."

O the mother's joys!
The watching, the endurance, the precious love, the anguish, the
25   patiently yielded life.

O the joy of increase, growth, recuperation,
The joy of soothing and pacifying, the joy of concord and harmony.

O to go back to the place where I was born,
To hear the birds sing once more,
30   To ramble about the house and barn and over the fields once more,
And through the orchard and along the old lanes once more.

O to have been brought up on bays, lagoons, creeks, or along the
          coast,
To continue and be employ'd there all my life,
The briny and damp smell, the shore, the salt weeds exposed at
          low water,
35   The work of fishermen, the work of the eel-fisher and clam-fisher;
I come with my clam-rake and spade, I come with my eel-spear,
Is the tide out? I join the group of clam-diggers on the flats,
I laugh and work with them, I joke at my work like a mettlesome
          young man;
In winter I take my eel-basket and eel-spear and travel out on foot
          on the ice—I have a small axe to cut holes in the ice,
Behold me well-clothed going gayly or returning in the afternoon,
40   my brood of tough boys accompanying me,
My brood of grown and part-grown boys, who love to be with no
          one else so well as they love to be with me,
By day to work with me, and by night to sleep with me.

Another time in warm weather out in a boat, to lift the lobster-pots
          where they are sunk with heavy stones, (I know the
          buoys,)
O the sweetness of the Fifth-month morning upon the water as I
          row just before sunrise toward the buoys,
I pull the wicker pots up slantingly, the dark green lobsters are
          desperate with their claws as I take them out, I insert
45   wooden pegs in the joints of their pincers,

35. clam-fisher] Lines 28–47 reflect actual memories of the poet's boyhood and the
Long Island shore, where clamming and fishing were then local industries. Cf. "Song

I go to all the places one after another, and then row back to the
     shore,
There in a huge kettle of boiling water the lobsters shall be boil'd
     till their color becomes scarlet.

Another time mackerel-taking,
Voracious, mad for the hook, near the surface, they seem to fill the
     water for miles;
Another time fishing for rock-fish in Chesapeake bay, I one of the   50
     brown-faced crew;
Another time trailing for blue-fish off Paumanok, I stand with
     braced body,
My left foot is on the gunwale, my right arm throws far out the
     coils of slender rope,
In sight around me the quick veering and darting of fifty skiffs,
     my companions.

O boating on the rivers,
The voyage down the St. Lawrence, the superb scenery, the
     steamers,   55
The ships sailing, the Thousand Islands, the occasional timber-raft
     and the raftsmen with long-reaching sweep-oars,
The little huts on the rafts, and the steam of smoke when they
     cook supper at evening.

(O something pernicious and dread!
Something far away from a puny and pious life!
Something unproved! something in a trance!   60
Something escaped from the anchorage and driving free.)

O to work in mines, or forging iron,
Foundry casting, the foundry itself, the rude high roof, the ample
     and shadow'd space,
The furnace, the hot liquid pour'd out and running.

O to resume the joys of the soldier!   65
To feel the presence of a brave commanding officer—to feel his
     sympathy!

of Myself," lines 182–184.
     44. Fifth-month] In Quaker parlance, the month of May.

To behold his calmness—to be warm'd in the rays of his smile!
To go to battle—to hear the bugles play and the drums beat!
To hear the crash of artillery—to see the glittering of the bayonets
      and musket-barrels in the sun!
70 To see men fall and die and not complain!
To taste the savage taste of blood—to be so devilish!
To gloat so over the wounds and deaths of the enemy.

O the whaleman's joys! O I cruise my old cruise again!
I feel the ship's motion under me, I feel the Atlantic breezes fan-
      ning me,
I hear the cry again sent down from the mast-head, *There—she*
75 *   blows!*
Again I spring up the rigging to look with the rest—we descend,
      wild with excitement,
I leap in the lower'd boat, we row toward our prey where he lies,
We approach stealthy and silent, I see the mountainous mass,
      lethargic, basking,
I see the harpooneer standing up, I see the weapon dart from his
      vigorous arm;
O swift again far out in the ocean the wounded whale, settling,
80   running to windward, tows me,
Again I see him rise to breathe, we row close again,
I see a lance driven through his side, press'd deep, turn'd in
      the wound,
Again we back off, I see him settle again, the life is leaving him
      fast,
As he rises he spouts blood, I see him swim in circles narrower
      and narrower, swiftly cutting the water—I see him die,
He gives one convulsive leap in the centre of the circle, and then
85   falls flat and still in the bloody foam.

O the old manhood of me, my noblest joy of all!
My children and grand-children, my white hair and beard,
My largeness, calmness, majesty, out of the long stretch of my life.

O ripen'd joy of womanhood! O happiness at last!
I am more than eighty years of age, I am the most venerable
90   mother,
How clear is my mind—how all people draw nigh to me!

What attractions are these beyond any before? what bloom more
    than the bloom of youth?
What beauty is this that descends upon me and rises out of me?

O the orator's joys!
To inflate the chest, to roll the thunder of the voice out from the
    ribs and throat,   95
To make the people rage, weep, hate, desire, with yourself,
To lead America—to quell America with a great tongue.

O the joy of my soul leaning pois'd on itself, receiving identity
    through materials and loving them, observing characters
    and absorbing them,
My soul vibrated back to me from them, from sight, hearing, touch,
    reason, articulation, comparison, memory, and the like,
The real life of my senses and flesh transcending my senses and flesh,   100
My body done with materials, my sight done with my material eyes,
Proved to me this day beyond cavil that it is not my material eyes
    which finally see,
Nor my material body which finally loves, walks, laughs, shouts,
    embraces, procreates.

O the farmer's joys!
Ohioan's, Illinoisian's, Wisconsinese', Kanadian's, Iowan's, Kan-
    sian's, Missourian's, Oregonese' joys!   105
To rise at peep of day and pass forth nimbly to work,
To plough land in the fall for winter-sown crops,
To plough land in the spring for maize,
To train orchards, to graft the trees, to gather apples in the fall.

O to bathe in the swimming-bath, or in a good place along shore,   110
To splash the water! to walk ankle-deep, or race naked along the
    shore.

O to realize space!
The plenteousness of all, that there are no bounds,
To emerge and be of the sky, of the sun and moon and flying
    clouds, as one with them.

O the joy of a manly self-hood!   115
To be servile to none, to defer to none, not to any tyrant known
    or unknown,

To walk with erect carriage, a step springy and elastic,
To look with calm gaze or with a flashing eye,
To speak with a full and sonorous voice out of a broad chest,
To confront with your personality all the other personalities of the
120   earth.

Know'st thou the excellent joys of youth?
Joys of the dear companions and of the merry word and laughing
        face?
Joy of the glad light-beaming day, joy of the wide-breath'd games?
Joy of sweet music, joy of the lighted ball-room and the dancers?
125 Joy of the plenteous dinner, strong carouse and drinking?

Yet O my soul supreme!
Know'st thou the joys of pensive thought?
Joys of the free and lonesome heart, the tender, gloomy heart?
Joys of the solitary walk, the spirit bow'd yet proud, the suffering
        and the struggle?
The agonistic throes, the ecstasies, joys of the solemn musings day
130   or night?
Joys of the thought of Death, the great spheres Time and Space?
Prophetic joys of better, loftier love's ideals, the divine wife, the
        sweet, eternal, perfect comrade?
Joys all thine own undying one, joys worthy thee O soul.

O while I live to be the ruler of life, not a slave,
135 To meet life as a powerful conqueror,
No fumes, no ennui, no more complaints or scornful criticisms,
To these proud laws of the air, the water and the ground, proving
        my interior soul impregnable,
And nothing exterior shall ever take command of me.

For not life's joys alone I sing, repeating—the joy of death!
The beautiful touch of Death, soothing and benumbing a few
140   moments, for reasons,
Myself discharging my excrementitious body to be burn'd, or
        render'd to powder, or buried,
My real body doubtless left to me for other spheres,

130. agonistic] In its primary Greek meaning, relating to the contest in athletics **or**
the arts.

My voided body nothing more to me, returning to the purifications,
  further offices, eternal uses of the earth.

O to attract by more than attraction!
How it is I know not—yet behold! the something which obeys
  none of the rest,   145
It is offensive, never defensive—yet how magnetic it draws.

O to struggle against great odds, to meet enemies undaunted!
To be entirely alone with them, to find how much one can stand!
To look strife, torture, prison, popular odium, face to face!
To mount the scaffold, to advance to the muzzles of guns with
  perfect nonchalance!   150
To be indeed a God!

O to sail to sea in a ship!
To leave this steady unendurable land,
To leave the tiresome sameness of the streets, the sidewalks and
  the houses,
To leave you O you solid motionless land, and entering a ship,   155
To sail and sail and sail!

O to have life henceforth a poem of new joys!
To dance, clap hands, exult, shout, skip, leap, roll on, float on!
To be a sailor of the world bound for all ports,
A ship itself, (see indeed these sails I spread to the sun and air,)   160
A swift and swelling ship full of rich words, full of joys.

1860   1881

Song of the Broad-Axe.

1

Weapon shapely, naked, wan,
Head from the mother's bowels drawn,
Wooded flesh and metal bone, limb only one and lip only one,
Gray-blue leaf by red-heat grown, helve produced from a little
      seed sown,
5 Resting the grass amid and upon,
To be lean'd and to lean on.

Strong shapes and attributes of strong shapes, masculine trades,
      sights and sounds,
Long varied train of an emblem, dabs of music,
Fingers of the organist skipping staccato over the keys of the
      great organ.

2

10 Welcome are all earth's lands, each for its kind,
Welcome are lands of pine and oak,
Welcome are lands of the lemon and fig,
Welcome are lands of gold,
Welcome are lands of wheat and maize, welcome those of the
      grape,

BROAD-AXE] Entitled "Broad-Axe Poem" in 1856 and "Chants Democratic" No. 2
in 1860, this poem took its present title in 1867. From the 390 lines of the first version
to the 254 of its final form, it has been much revised, although the superb first six
lines and indeed the whole poem's essential quality was achieved in the 1856 text.
The most considerable change is the disappearance after 1860 of eighteen lines, just
before its final section, which exuberantly described the idealized "shape" of the poet
himself, "arrogant, masculine, naive, rowdyish . . ." Among the several MSS re-
lated to this poem is a single sheet on which are set down in three separate columns
about 400 words of jottings about the broad-axe and its role in history (Trent, N and
F, 1:97, 33–34.) To WW the broad-axe is an emblem—the emblem of a "long

Welcome are lands of sugar and rice,   15
Welcome the cotton-lands, welcome those of the white potato
    and sweet potato,
Welcome are mountains, flats, sands, forests, prairies,
Welcome the rich borders of rivers, table-lands, openings,
Welcome the measureless grazing-lands, welcome the teeming soil
    of orchards, flax, honey, hemp;
Welcome just as much the other more hard-faced lands,   20
Lands rich as lands of gold or wheat and fruit lands,
Lands of mines, lands of the manly and rugged ores,
Lands of coal, copper, lead, tin, zinc,
Lands of iron—lands of the make of the axe.

3

The log at the wood-pile, the axe supported by it,   25
The sylvan hut, the vine over the doorway, the space clear'd for a
    garden,
The irregular tapping of rain down on the leaves after the storm
    is lull'd,
The wailing and moaning at intervals, the thought of the sea,
The thought of ships struck in the storm and put on their beam
    ends, and the cutting away of masts,
The sentiment of the huge timbers of old-fashion'd houses and
    barns,   30
The remember'd print or narrative, the voyage at a venture of
    men, families, goods,
The disembarkation, the founding of a new city,
The voyage of those who sought a New England and found it, the
    outset anywhere,
The settlements of the Arkansas, Colorado, Ottawa, Willamette,
The slow progress, the scant fare, the axe, rifle, saddle-bags;   35

varied train" which is the poem itself, powerfully setting forth the attributes and
shapes which the great instrument, both builder and destroyer, symbolizes—the
creative strength of man deriving from the confident, independent masculinity and
femininity which the poem celebrates. Note the artistic skill of the opening trochaic
lines with their subtle pattern of sound and imagery in which the weapon becomes
personal and alive. Jean Catel has surmised that Alfred B. Street's "Song of the Axe"
(*Graham's Magazine*, April, 1855) may be a source for this poem. See *Rythme et
iangage dans la I'ᵉ Édition des "Leaves of Grass"* (1855), 75–76. See also Stanley K.
Coffman's exposition of stanza 1, section 1 in *Expl*, XII, 39.

   34. Ottawa] River in Canada between Ontario and Quebec. Willamette] River in
western Oregon, flowing into the Columbia river.

The beauty of all adventurous and daring persons,
The beauty of wood-boys and wood-men with their clear un-
      trimm'd faces,
The beauty of independence, departure, actions that rely on
      themselves,
The American contempt for statutes and ceremonies, the bound-
      less impatience of restraint,
The loose drift of character, the inkling through random types,
40   the solidification;
The butcher in the slaughter-house, the hands aboard schooners
      and sloops, the raftsman, the pioneer,
Lumbermen in their winter camp, daybreak in the woods, stripes
      of snow on the limbs of trees, the occasional snapping,
The glad clear sound of one's own voice, the merry song, the
      natural life of the woods, the strong day's work,
The blazing fire at night, the sweet taste of supper, the talk, the
      bed of hemlock-boughs and the bear-skin;
45 The house-builder at work in cities or anywhere,
The preparatory jointing, squaring, sawing, mortising,
The hoist-up of beams, the push of them in their places, laying
      them regular,
Setting the studs by their tenons in the mortises according as they
      were prepared,
The blows of mallets and hammers, the attitudes of the men,
      their curv'd limbs,
Bending, standing, astride the beams, driving in pins, holding on
50   by posts and braces,
The hook'd arm over the plate, the other arm wielding the axe,
The floor-men forcing the planks close to be nail'd,
Their postures bringing their weapons downward on the bearers,
The echoes resounding through the vacant building;
55 The huge storehouse carried up in the city well under way,
The six framing-men, two in the middle and two at each end,
      carefully bearing on their shoulders a heavy stick for a
      cross-beam,
The crowded line of masons with trowels in their right hands
      rapidly laying the long side-wall, two hundred feet from
      front to rear,

---

    45. house-builder] Lines 45–72 reflect the poet's youthful experience as a carpen-
ter, his love of the trustworthy tools, the well-joined wood, the familiar excitement of

The flexible rise and fall of backs, the continual click of the
      trowels striking the bricks,
The bricks one after another each laid so workmanlike in its
      place, and set with a knock of the trowel-handle,
The piles of materials, the mortar on the mortar-boards, and the
      steady replenishing by the hod-men;   60
Spar-makers in the spar-yard, the swarming row of well-grown
      apprentices,
The swing of their axes on the square-hew'd log shaping it toward
      the shape of a mast,
The brisk short crackle of the steel driven slantingly into the pine,
The butter-color'd chips flying off in great flakes and slivers,
The limber motion of brawny young arms and hips in easy cos-
      tumes,   65
The constructor of wharves, bridges, piers, bulk-heads, floats,
      stays against the sea;
The city fireman, the fire that suddenly bursts forth in the close-
      pack'd square,
The arriving engines, the hoarse shouts, the nimble stepping and
      daring,
The strong command through the fire-trumpets, the falling in line,
      the rise and fall of the arms forcing the water,
The slender, spasmic, blue-white jets, the bringing to bear of the
      hooks and ladders and their execution,   70
The crash and cut away of connecting wood-work, or through
      floors if the fire smoulders under them,
The crowd with their lit faces watching, the glare and dense
      shadows;
The forger at his forge-furnace and the user of iron after him,
The maker of the axe large and small, and the welder and tem-
      perer,
The chooser breathing his breath on the cold steel and trying the
      edge with his thumb,   75
The one who clean-shapes the handle and sets it firmly in the
      socket;
The shadowy processions of the portraits of the past users also,
The primal patient mechanics, the architects and engineers,
The far-off Assyrian edifice and Mizra edifice,

the fire in that fire-prone age.
    79. Mizra] Egyptian, after "Mizraim," Biblical name for Egypt.

80 The Roman lictors preceding the consuls,
  The antique European warrior with his axe in combat,
  The uplifted arm, the clatter of blows on the helmeted head,
  The death-howl, the limpsy tumbling body, the rush of friend and
    foe thither,
  The siege of revolted lieges determin'd for liberty,
  The summons to surrender, the battering at castle gates, the truce
85   and parley,
  The sack of an old city in its time,
  The bursting in of mercenaries and bigots tumultuously and
    disorderly,
  Roar, flames, blood, drunkenness, madness,
  Goods freely rifled from houses and temples, screams of women in
    the gripe of brigands,
  Craft and thievery of camp-followers, men running, old persons
90   despairing,
  The hell of war, the cruelties of creeds,
  The list of all executive deeds and words just or unjust,
  The power of personality just or unjust.

    4

  Muscle and pluck forever!
95 What invigorates life invigorates death,
  And the dead advance as much as the living advance,
  And the future is no more uncertain than the present,
  For the roughness of the earth and of man encloses as much as
    the delicatesse of the earth and of man,
  And nothing endures but personal qualities.

100 What do you think endures?
  Do you think a great city endures?
  Or a teeming manufacturing state? or a prepared constitution? or
    the best built steamships?
  Or hotels of granite and iron? or any chef-d'œuvres of engineering,
    forts, armaments?

  80. lictors] Minor Roman officials who carried the fasces (rods and axe), symbol
of authority, in procession.
  98. delicatesse] (properly délicatesse) French: delicacy. On WW's loan words
and neologisms, see Louise Pound, "Walt Whitman's Neologisms," *American Mer-cury*, IV (February, 1925), 199–201, and "Walt Whitman and the French Lan-guage," *AS*, 1 (May, 1926), 421–430.

Away! these are not to be cherish'd for themselves,
They fill their hour, the dancers dance, the musicians play for
      them,   105
The show passes, all does well enough of course,
All does very well till one flash of defiance.

A great city is that which has the greatest men and women,
If it be a few ragged huts it is still the greatest city in the whole
      world.

     5

The place where a great city stands is not the place of stretch'd
      wharves, docks, manufactures, deposits of produce merely,   110
Nor the place of ceaseless salutes of new-comers or the anchor-
      lifters of the departing,
Nor the place of the tallest and costliest buildings or shops selling
      goods from the rest of the earth,
Nor the place of the best libraries and schools, nor the place where
      money is plentiest,
Nor the place of the most numerous population.

Where the city stands with the brawniest breed of orators and
      bards,   115
Where the city stands that is belov'd by these, and loves them in
      return and understands them,
Where no monuments exist to heroes but in the common words
      and deeds,
Where thrift is in its place, and prudence is in its place,
Where the men and women think lightly of the laws,
Where the slave ceases, and the master of slaves ceases,   120
Where the populace rise at once against the never-ending audacity
      of elected persons,
Where fierce men and women pour forth as the sea to the whistle
      of death pours its sweeping and unript waves,

    108. greatest men and women] Although Marxist critics have claimed WW, his
individualistic ideality, typically concentrated here in sections 4 and 5, is clearly
rooted in the Jeffersonian idealism which flourished in his early environment.
    118. prudence] Cf. "Song of Prudence" and note thereon. To WW prudence was
not merely a pragmatic virtue, but intrinsic and inseparable in every virtuous
thought or deed, recalling its original association with "providence."

Where outside authority enters always after the precedence of
     inside authority,
Where the citizen is always the head and ideal, and President,
     Mayor, Governor and what not, are agents for pay,
Where children are taught to be laws to themselves, and to depend
125   on themselves,
Where equanimity is illustrated in affairs,
Where speculations on the soul are encouraged,
Where women walk in public processions in the streets the same
     as the men,
Where they enter the public assembly and take places the same as
     the men;
130 Where the city of the faithfulest friends stands,
Where the city of the cleanliness of the sexes stands,
Where the city of the healthiest fathers stands,
Where the city of the best-bodied mothers stands,
There the great city stands.

6

135 How beggarly appear arguments before a defiant deed!
How the floridness of the materials of cities shrivels before a man's
     or woman's look!

All waits or goes by default till a strong being appears;
A strong being is the proof of the race and of the ability of the
     universe,
When he or she appears materials are overaw'd,
140 The dispute on the soul stops,
The old customs and phrases are confronted, turn'd back, or laid
     away.

What is your money-making now? what can it do now?
What is your respectability now?
What are your theology, tuition, society, traditions, statute-books,
     now?
145 Where are your jibes of being now?
Where are your cavils about the soul now?

7

A sterile landscape covers the ore, there is as good as the best for
     all the forbidding appearance.

There is the mine, there are the miners,
The forge-furnace is there, the melt is accomplish'd, the hammers-
      men are at hand with their tongs and hammers,
What always served and always serves is at hand.   150

Than this nothing has better served, it has served all,
Served the fluent-tongued and subtle-sensed Greek, and long ere
      the Greek,
Served in building the buildings that last longer than any,
Served the Hebrew, the Persian, the most ancient Hindustanee,
Served the mound-raiser on the Mississippi, served those whose
      relics remain in Central America,   155
Served Albic temples in woods or on plains, with unhewn pillars
      and the druids,
Served the artificial clefts, vast, high, silent, on the snow-cover'd
      hills of Scandinavia,
Served those who time out of mind made on the granite walls
      rough sketches of the sun, moon, stars, ships, ocean waves,
Served the paths of the irruptions of the Goths, served the pas-
      toral tribes and nomads,
Served the long distant Kelt, served the hardy pirates of the Baltic,   160
Served before any of those the venerable and harmless men of
      Ethiopia,
Served the making of helms for the galleys of pleasure and the
      making of those for war,
Served all great works on land and all great works on the sea,
For the mediæval ages and before the mediæval ages,
Served not the living only then as now, but served the dead.   165

8

I see the European headsman,
He stands mask'd, clothed in red, with huge legs and strong naked
      arms,
And leans on a ponderous axe.

(Whom have you slaughter'd lately European headsman?
Whose is that blood upon you so wet and sticky?)   170

I see the clear sunset of the martyrs,
I see from the scaffolds the descending ghosts,

156. Albic] English, from "Albion," ancient name for England.

Ghosts of dead lords, uncrown'd ladies, impeach'd ministers,
  rejected kings,
Rivals, traitors, poisoners, disgraced chieftains and the rest.

175 I see those who in any land have died for the good cause,
The seed is spare, nevertheless the crop shall never run out,
(Mind you O foreign kings, O priests, the crop shall never run out.)

I see the blood wash'd entirely away from the axe,
Both blade and helve are clean,
They spirt no more the blood of European nobles, they clasp no
180 more the necks of queens.

I see the headsman withdraw and become useless,
I see the scaffold untrodden and mouldy, I see no longer any axe
  upon it,
I see the mighty and friendly emblem of the power of my own
  race, the newest, largest race.

9

(America! I do not vaunt my love for you,
185 I have what I have.)

The axe leaps!
The solid forest gives fluid utterances,
They tumble forth, they rise and form,
Hut, tent, landing, survey,
190 Flail, plough, pick, crowbar, spade,
Shingle, rail, prop, wainscot, jamb, lath, panel, gable,
Citadel, ceiling, saloon, academy, organ, exhibition-house, li-
  brary,
Cornice, trellis, pilaster, balcony, window, turret, porch,
Hoe, rake, pitchfork, pencil, wagon, staff, saw, jack-plane, mallet,
  wedge, rounce,
195 Chair, tub, hoop, table, wicket, vane, sash, floor,
Work-box, chest, string'd instrument, boat, frame, and what not,
Capitols of States, and capitol of the nation of States,

---

194. rounce] Handle of a hand press.

Long stately rows in avenues, hospitals for orphans or for the poor
 or sick,
Manhattan steamboats and clippers taking the measure of all seas.

The shapes arise!   200
Shapes of the using of axes anyhow, and the users and all that
 neighbors them,
Cutters down of wood and haulers of it to the Penobscot or Ken-
 nebec,
Dwellers in cabins among the Californian mountains or by the little
 lakes, or on the Columbia,
Dwellers south on the banks of the Gila or Rio Grande, friendly
 gatherings, the characters and fun,
Dwellers along the St. Lawrence, or north in Kanada, or down by
 the Yellowstone, dwellers on coasts and off coasts,   205
Seal-fishers, whalers, arctic seamen breaking passages through the
 ice.

The shapes arise!
Shapes of factories, arsenals, foundries, markets,
Shapes of the two-threaded tracks of railroads,
Shapes of the sleepers of bridges, vast frameworks, girders, arches,   210
Shapes of the fleets of barges, tows, lake and canal craft, river craft,
Ship-yards and dry-docks along the Eastern and Western seas, and
 in many a bay and by-place,
The live-oak kelsons, the pine planks, the spars, the hackmatack-
 roots for knees,
The ships themselves on their ways, the tiers of scaffolds, the
 workmen busy outside and inside,
The tools lying around, the great auger and little auger, the adze,
 bolt, line, square, gouge, and bead-plane.   215

10

The shapes arise!
The shape measur'd, saw'd, jack'd, join'd, stain'd,
The coffin-shape for the dead to lie within in his shroud,

---

213. hackmatack-roots] Larch or juniper roots; the "knees" are structural mem-
bers of bent wood which bear strains.

The shape got out in posts, in the bedstead posts, in the posts of
        the bride's bed,
The shape of the little trough, the shape of the rockers beneath,
220   the shape of the babe's cradle,
The shape of the floor-planks, the floor-planks for dancers' feet,
The shape of the planks of the family home, the home of the
        friendly parents and children,
The shape of the roof of the home of the happy young man and
        woman, the roof over the well-married young man and
        woman,
The roof over the supper joyously cook'd by the chaste wife, and
        joyously eaten by the chaste husband, content after his day's work.

225   The shapes arise!
The shape of the prisoner's place in the court-room, and of him
        or her seated in the place,
The shape of the liquor-bar lean'd against by the young rum-
        drinker and the old rum-drinker,
The shape of the shamed and angry stairs trod by sneaking foot-
        steps,
The shape of the sly settee, and the adulterous unwholesome
        couple,
The shape of the gambling-board with its devilish winnings and
230   losings,
The shape of the step-ladder for the convicted and sentenced
        murderer, the murderer with haggard face and pinion'd arms,
The sheriff at hand with his deputies, the silent and white-lipp'd
        crowd, the dangling of the rope.

The shapes arise!
Shapes of doors giving many exits and entrances,
235   The door passing the dissever'd friend flush'd and in haste,
The door that admits good news and bad news,
The door whence the son left home confident and puff'd up,
The door he enter'd again from a long and scandalous absence,
        diseas'd, broken down, without innocence, without means.

        11

Her shape arises,
240   She less guarded than ever, yet more guarded than ever,

EXPOSITION] Composed in response to the invitation of the American Institute to
read a poem at the opening of its fortieth Annual Exhibition in New York City,

The gross and soil'd she moves among do not make her gross and
    soil'd,
She knows the thoughts as she passes, nothing is conceal'd from her,
She is none the less considerate or friendly therefor,
She is the best belov'd, it is without exception, she has no reason
    to fear and she does not fear,
Oaths, quarrels, hiccupp'd songs, smutty expressions, are idle to
    her as she passes,   245
She is silent, she is possess'd of herself, they do not offend her,
She receives them as the laws of Nature receive them, she is strong,
She too is a law of Nature—there is no law stronger than she is.

       12

The main shapes arise!
Shapes of Democracy total, result of centuries,   250
Shapes ever projecting other shapes,
Shapes of turbulent manly cities,
Shapes of the friends and home-givers of the whole earth,
Shapes bracing the earth and braced with the whole earth.

  1856   *1881*

Song of the Exposition.

      1

(Ah little recks the laborer,
How near his work is holding him to God,
The loving Laborer through space and time.)

After all not to create only, or found only,
But to bring perhaps from afar what is already founded,   5
To give it our own identity, average, limitless, free,

September 7, 1871, this piece was published in the same year as a booklet under the
title *After All, Not to Create Only* following its appearance in a dozen newspapers,

To fill the gross the torpid bulk with vital religious fire,
Not to repel or destroy so much as accept, fuse, rehabilitate,
To obey as well as command, to follow more than to lead,
10   These also are the lessons of our New World;
While how little the New after all, how much the Old, Old World!

Long and long has the grass been growing,
Long and long has the rain been falling,
Long has the globe been rolling round.

2

15   Come Muse migrate from Greece and Ionia,
Cross out please those immensely overpaid accounts,
That matter of Troy and Achilles' wrath, and Æneas', Odysseus'
          wanderings,
Placard "Removed" and "To Let" on the rocks of your snowy
          Parnassus,
Repeat at Jerusalem, place the notice high on Jaffa's gate and on
          Mount Moriah,
The same on the walls of your German, French and Spanish
20   castles, and Italian collections,
For know a better, fresher, busier sphere, a wide, untried domain
          awaits, demands you.

3

Responsive to our summons,
Or rather to her long-nurs'd inclination,

including the Washington *Daily Morning Chronicle*, the New York *Evening Post*, and the Springfield *Republican*, on the occasion of its presentation at the Exhibition. In fact, WW did his best to publicize the event, furnishing copy himself, and later defending the poem anonymously against a prevailingly hostile press. One editorial (New York *Globe*, September 7, 1871) boasted of the poet's foreign reputation with details which WW himself must have supplied, if indeed he were not the actual author. See Allen, 432–435 and Traubel, I, 324–329. The poem appeared under its first title at the end of the 1872 *Leaves of Grass*, and in the *Two Rivulets* of 1876 under its present title, "Song of the Exposition," prefaced by an editorial. For the final 1881 text, the poem was improved by the addition of the opening three lines and the deletion of some twenty lines, but it remains one of WW's comparative failures because it does not surmount its own rhetoric. The theme was valid, and peculiarly the poet's own in its insistence upon exalting "the present and the real" and teaching "the average man the glory of his daily walk and trade," but the stridency of tone and the bathos of some of the phrasing were painfully unapparent to the poet.

          13–14. round] W. S. Kennedy (*Conservator*, February, 1907, 184) has suggested

Join'd with an irresistible, natural gravitation,
She comes! I hear the rustling of her gown,   25
I scent the odor of her breath's delicious fragrance,
I mark her step divine, her curious eyes a-turning, rolling,
Upon this very scene.

The dame of dames! can I believe then,
Those ancient temples, sculptures classic, could none of them
      retain her?   30
Nor shades of Virgil and Dante, nor myriad memories, poems,
      old associations, magnetize and hold on to her?
But that she's left them all—and here?

Yes, if you will allow me to say so,
I, my friends, if you do not, can plainly see her,
The same undying soul of earth's, activity's, beauty's, heroism's
      expression,
Out from her evolutions hither come, ended the strata of her   35
      former themes,
Hidden and cover'd by to-day's, foundation of to-day's,
Ended, deceas'd through time, her voice by Castaly's fountain,
Silent the broken-lipp'd Sphynx in Egypt, silent all those century-
      baffling tombs,
Ended for aye the epics of Asia's, Europe's helmeted warriors,
      ended the primitive call of the muses,   40
Calliope's call forever closed, Clio, Melpomene, Thalia dead,
Ended the stately rhythmus of Una and Oriana, ended the quest
      of the holy Graal,

that these lines are an echo of the clown's song at the end of *Twelfth Night:*

> A great while ago the world began,
> With hey, ho, the wind and the rain,

17. wanderings] These are, of course, references to the Homeric epics.
18. Parnassus] A peak in southern Greece, sacred to the Muses and hence a symbol of the realm of poetry.
19. Jaffa's gate] Jaffa is a seaport in Israel. Mount Moriah] Hill of Jerusalem on which Solomon's temple was built.
30. retain] This word is "restrain" both in MS and in the 1871 edition.
38. Castaly's fountain] A spring on Mount Parnassus whose waters were thought to be a source of poetic inspiration.
41. Calliope's . . . Clio, Melpomene, Thalia] Respectively, the muses of epic poetry, history, tragedy, and comedy.
42. Una] The character who symbolizes true religion in Book I of Spenser's *Faerie Queene.* Oriana] A character in the romance *Amadis of Gaul*, also the name

Jerusalem a handful of ashes blown by the wind, extinct,
The Crusaders' streams of shadowy midnight troops sped with the
      sunrise,
45   Amadis, Tancred, utterly gone, Charlemagne, Roland, Oliver gone,
Palmerin, ogre, departed, vanish'd the turrets that Usk from its
      waters reflected,
Arthur vanish'd with all his knights, Merlin and Lancelot and
      Galahad, all gone, dissolv'd utterly like an exhalation;
Pass'd! pass'd! for us, forever pass'd, that once so mighty world,
      now void, inanimate, phantom world,
Embroider'd, dazzling, foreign world, with all its gorgeous legends,
      myths,
Its kings and castles proud, its priests and warlike lords and
50   courtly dames,
Pass'd to its charnel vault, coffin'd with crown and armor on,
Blazon'd with Shakspere's purple page,
And dirged by Tennyson's sweet sad rhyme.

I say I see, my friends, if you do not, the illustrious emigré,
      (having it is true in her day, although the same, changed,
      journey'd considerable,)
Making directly for this rendezvous, vigorously clearing a path for
55   herself, striding through the confusion,
By thud of machinery and shrill steam-whistle undismay'd,
Bluff'd not a bit by drain-pipe, gasometers, artificial fertilizers,
Smiling and pleas'd with palpable intent to stay,
She's here, install'd amid the kitchen ware!

      4

60   But hold—don't I forget my manners?
To introduce the stranger, (what else indeed do I live to chant
      for?) to thee Columbia;

given by Elizabethan poets to Queen Elizabeth. Holy Graal] More commonly spelled
"Grail," the legendary cup used by Jesus at the Last Supper.
    45. Amadis] Hero of medieval romances. Tancred] Norman leader of the first
Crusade. Charlemagne] King of the Franks, 800–814 A.D. Roland] Legendary hero
of the Charlemagne exploits. Oliver] A friend of Roland and one of Charlemagne's
twelve peers.
    46. Palmerin] Hero of the Portuguese romance, *Palmerin of England*. Usk]
River of Wales and England, associated with Arthurian legend.
    47. Arthur] Legendary king of Britain, sixth century A.D., founder of the Round

In liberty's name welcome immortal! clasp hands,
And ever henceforth sisters dear be both.

Fear not O Muse! truly new ways and days receive, surround you,
I candidly confess a queer, queer race, of novel fashion,   65
And yet the same old human race, the same within, without,
Faces and hearts the same, feelings the same, yearnings the same,
The same old love, beauty and use the same.

5

We do not blame thee elder World, nor really separate ourselves
      from thee,
(Would the son separate himself from the father?)   70
Looking back on thee, seeing thee to thy duties, grandeurs,
      through past ages bending, building,
We build to ours to-day.

Mightier than Egypt's tombs,
Fairer than Grecia's, Roma's temples,
Prouder than Milan's statued, spired cathedral,   75
More picturesque than Rhenish castle-keeps,
We plan even now to raise, beyond them all,
Thy great cathedral sacred industry, no tomb,
A keep for life for practical invention.

As in a waking vision,   80
E'en while I chant I see it rise, I scan and prophesy outside
      and in,
Its manifold ensemble.

Around a palace, loftier, fairer, ampler than any yet,
Earth's modern wonder, history's seven outstripping,

Table. Merlin] Magician and seer, helper of King Arthur. Lancelot] Bravest among
King Arthur's knights, lover of Queen Guinevere. Galahad] Noblest of the knights
of the Round Table, son of Lancelot and Elaine.
      53. rhyme.] Tennyson's romances, *Idylls of the King*, 1859–1885, were then—it
should be remembered—strictly contemporary.
      83–90. palace] These lines are descriptive of the famous exhibition structures of
the time—the great Crystal Palace of London, built to house the International Ex-
hibition of 1851, and the American Crystal Palace opened in 1853 to house a World's
Fair at what is now Bryant Park, New York City.

85 High rising tier on tier with glass and iron façades,
    Gladdening the sun and sky, enhued in cheerfulest hues,
    Bronze, lilac, robin's-egg, marine and crimson,
    Over whose golden roof shall flaunt, beneath thy banner Freedom,
    The banners of the States and flags of every land,
90 A brood of lofty, fair, but lesser palaces shall cluster.

    Somewhere within their walls shall all that forwards perfect human
        life be started,
    Tried, taught, advanced, visibly exhibited.

    Not only all the world of works, trade, products,
    But all the workmen of the world here to be represented.

95 Here shall you trace in flowing operation,
    In every state of practical, busy movement, the rills of civilization,
    Materials here under your eye shall change their shape as if by
        magic,
    The cotton shall be pick'd almost in the very field,
    Shall be dried, clean'd, ginn'd, baled, spun into thread and cloth
        before you,
    You shall see hands at work at all the old processes and all the
100   new ones,
    You shall see the various grains and how flour is made and then
        bread baked by the bakers,
    You shall see the crude ores of California and Nevada passing on
        and on till they become bullion,
    You shall watch how the printer sets type, and learn what a com-
        posing-stick is,
    You shall mark in amazement the Hoe press whirling its cylinders,
        shedding the printed leaves steady and fast,
    The photograph, model, watch, pin, nail, shall be created before
105   you.

    In large calm halls, a stately museum shall teach you the infinite
        lessons of minerals,
    In another, woods, plants, vegetation shall be illustrated—in
        another animals, animal life and development.

    104. Hoe press] Rotary press invented in 1846 by Richard March Hoe, and on
display at the Exposition.
    112. Pharos] Lighthouse near Alexandria, Egypt, one of the seven wonders of the
ancient world, as were also the Gardens of Babylon.

One stately house shall be the music house,
Others for other arts—learning, the sciences, shall all be here,
None shall be slighted, none but shall here be honor'd, help'd,
    exampled.   110

6

(This, this and these, America, shall be *your* pyramids and obelisks,
Your Alexandrian Pharos, gardens of Babylon,
Your temple at Olympia.)

The male and female many laboring not,
Shall ever here confront the laboring many,   115
With precious benefits to both, glory to all,
To thee America, and thee eternal Muse.

And here shall ye inhabit powerful Matrons!
In your vast state vaster than all the old,
Echoed through long, long centuries to come,   120
To sound of different, prouder songs, with stronger themes,
Practical, peaceful life, the people's life, the People themselves,
Lifted, illumin'd, bathed in peace—elate, secure in peace.

7

Away with themes of war! away with war itself!
Hence from my shuddering sight to never more return that show
    of blacken'd, mutilated corpses!   125
That hell unpent and raid of blood, fit for wild tigers or for lop-
    tongued wolves, not reasoning men,
And in its stead speed industry's campaigns,
With thy undaunted armies, engineering,
Thy pennants labor, loosen'd to the breeze,
Thy bugles sounding loud and clear.   130

113. temple at Olympia] In ancient Elis, Greece, famous for colossal statue of Zeus
by Phidias.
124. war] Cf. "As I Ponder'd in Silence," where the war of bloodshed is supplanted
by the war of ideas. Here the poet suggests that technology will conquer war.

Away with old romance!
Away with novels, plots and plays of foreign courts,
Away with love-verses sugar'd in rhyme, the intrigues, amours of
    idlers,
Fitted for only banquets of the night where dancers to late music
    slide,
135   The unhealthy pleasures, extravagant dissipations of the few,
With perfumes, heat and wine, beneath the dazzling chandeliers.

To you ye reverent sane sisters,
I raise a voice for far superber themes for poets and for art,
To exalt the present and the real,
140   To teach the average man the glory of his daily walk and trade,
To sing in songs how exercise and chemical life are never to be
    baffled,
To manual work for each and all, to plough, hoe, dig,
To plant and tend the tree, the berry, vegetables, flowers,
For every man to see to it that he really do something, for every
    woman too;
145   To use the hammer and the saw, (rip, or cross-cut,)
To cultivate a turn for carpentering, plastering, painting,
To work as tailor, tailoress, nurse, hostler, porter,
To invent a little, something ingenious, to aid the washing, cook-
    ing, cleaning,
And hold it no disgrace to take a hand at them themselves.

150   I say I bring thee Muse to-day and here,
All occupations, duties broad and close,
Toil, healthy toil and sweat, endless, without cessation,
The old, old practical burdens, interests, joys,
The family, parentage, childhood, husband and wife,
155   The house-comforts, the house itself and all its belongings,
Food and its preservation, chemistry applied to it,
Whatever forms the average, strong, complete, sweet-blooded man
    or woman, the perfect longeve personality,
And helps its present life to health and happiness, and shapes its soul,
For the eternal real life to come.

131. romance] Persistently anti-romantic both in poetry and prose criticism, WW associated his idea of romanticism with intrigues, amours, and the extravagant dissipation of an effete civilization.

137. sane sisters] The nine Muses.

With latest connections, works, the inter-transportation of the world,   160
Steam-power, the great express lines, gas, petroleum,
These triumphs of our time, the Atlantic's delicate cable,
The Pacific railroad, the Suez canal, the Mont Cenis and Gothard
       and Hoosac tunnels, the Brooklyn bridge,
This earth all spann'd with iron rails, with lines of steamships
       threading every sea,
Our own rondure, the current globe I bring.   165

8

And thou America,
Thy offspring towering e'er so high, yet higher Thee above all
       towering,
With Victory on thy left, and at thy right hand Law;
Thou Union holding all, fusing, absorbing, tolerating all,
Thee, ever thee, I sing.   170

Thou, also thou, a World,
With all thy wide geographies, manifold, different, distant,
Rounded by thee in one—one common orbic language,
One common indivisible destiny for All.

And by the spells which ye vouchsafe to those your ministers in
       earnest,   175
I here personify and call my themes, to make them pass before ye.

Behold, America! (and thou, ineffable guest and sister!)
For thee come trooping up thy waters and thy lands;
Behold! thy fields and farms, thy far-off woods and mountains,
As in procession coming.   180

Behold, the sea itself,
And on its limitless, heaving breast, the ships;
See, where their white sails, bellying in the wind, speckle the green
       and blue,

157. longeve] Long-lasting.
163. Mont Cenis . . . Gothard . . . Hoosac tunnels] Respectively, an 8-mile tunnel joining France and Italy through Alpine Mount Cenis; a 9¼-mile tunnel beneath St. Gotthard pass between Switzerland and Italy; a 4½-mile tunnel in Massachusetts on the Fitchburg railroad.

See, the steamers coming and going, steaming in or out of port,
185   See, dusky and undulating, the long pennants of smoke.

Behold, in Oregon, far in the north and west,
Or in Maine, far in the north and east, thy cheerful axemen,
Wielding all day their axes.

Behold, on the lakes, thy pilots at their wheels, thy oarsmen,
190   How the ash writhes under those muscular arms!

There by the furnace, and there by the anvil,
Behold thy sturdy blacksmiths swinging their sledges,
Overhand so steady, overhand they turn and fall with joyous clank,
Like a tumult of laughter.

195   Mark the spirit of invention everywhere, thy rapid patents,
Thy continual workshops, foundries, risen or rising,
See, from their chimneys how the tall flame-fires stream.

Mark, thy interminable farms, North, South,
Thy wealthy daughter-states, Eastern and Western,
The varied products of Ohio, Pennsylvania, Missouri, Georgia,
200   Texas, and the rest,
Thy limitless crops, grass, wheat, sugar, oil, corn, rice, hemp, hops,
Thy barns all fill'd, the endless freight-train and the bulging
       storehouse,
The grapes that ripen on thy vines, the apples in thy orchards,
Thy incalculable lumber, beef, pork, potatoes, thy coal, thy gold
       and silver,
205   The inexhaustible iron in thy mines.

All thine O sacred Union!
Ships, farms, shops, barns, factories, mines,
City and State, North, South, item and aggregate,
We dedicate, dread Mother, all to thee!

210   Protectress absolute, thou! bulwark of all!
For well we know that while thou givest each and all, (generous
       as God,)
Without thee neither all nor each, nor land, home,
Nor ship, nor mine, nor any here this day secure,
Nor aught, nor any day secure.

9

And thou, the Emblem waving over all!   215
Delicate beauty, a word to thee, (it may be salutary,)
Remember thou hast not always been as here to-day so comfortably
    ensovereign'd,
In other scenes than these have I observ'd thee flag,
Not quite so trim and whole and freshly blooming in folds of stain-
    less silk,
But I have seen thee bunting, to tatters torn upon thy splinter'd staff,   220
Or clutch'd to some young color-bearer's breast with desperate hands,
Savagely struggled for, for life or death, fought over long,
'Mid cannons' thunder-crash and many a curse and groan and yell,
    and rifle-volleys cracking sharp,
And moving masses as wild demons surging, and lives as nothing
    risk'd,
For thy mere remnant grimed with dirt and smoke and sopp'd in
    blood,   225
For sake of that, my beauty, and that thou might'st dally as now
    secure up there,
Many a good man have I seen go under.

Now here and these and hence in peace, all thine O Flag!
And here and hence for thee, O universal Muse! and thou for them!
And here and hence O Union, all the work and workmen thine!   230
None separate from thee—henceforth One only, we and thou,
(For the blood of the children, what is it, only the blood
    maternal?
And lives and works, what are they all at last, except the roads to
    faith and death?)

While we rehearse our measureless wealth, it is for thee, dear
    Mother,
We own it all and several to-day indissoluble in thee;   235
Think not our chant, our show, merely for products gross or lucre
    —it is for thee, the soul in thee, electric, spiritual!
Our farms, inventions, crops, we own in thee! cities and States in
    thee!
Our freedom all in thee! our very lives in thee!

   1871   *1881*

Song of the Redwood-Tree.

1

A California song,
A prophecy and indirection, a thought impalpable to breathe as air,
A chorus of dryads, fading, departing, or hamadryads departing,
A murmuring, fateful, giant voice, out of the earth and sky,
5 Voice of a mighty dying tree in the redwood forest dense.

Farewell my brethren,
Farewell O earth and sky, farewell ye neighboring waters,
My time has ended, my term has come.

Along the northern coast,
10 Just back from the rock-bound shore and the caves,
In the saline air from the sea in the Mendocino country,
With the surge for base and accompaniment low and hoarse,
With crackling blows of axes sounding musically driven by strong
   arms,
Riven deep by the sharp tongues of the axes, there in the redwood
   forest dense,
15 I heard the mighty tree its death-chant chanting.

The choppers heard not, the camp shanties echoed not,
The quick-ear'd teamsters and chain and jack-screw men heard
   not,
As the wood-spirits came from their haunts of a thousand years to
   join the refrain,
But in my soul I plainly heard.

REDWOOD-TREE] WW composed this poem in the fall of 1873, asking and re-
ceiving $100 for it from *Harper's Magazine*, which printed it in its issue of February,
1874. It next appeared among the "Centennial Songs" of the 1876 *Two Rivulets*, and
then in LG 1881, remaining unchanged in title and also—except for one or two
words—in text. Among the MS drafts (Barrett and Trent) is WW's own note to
himself on its theme: "The spinal idea of the poem I (the tree) have fill'd my time and
fill'd it grandly All is prepared for you—my termination comes prophecy [*sic*] a great
race—great as the mountains and the trees Intersperse with *italic* (first person
speaking) the same as in 'Out of the Cradle endlessly rocking.'" To Rudolf Schmidt

Murmuring out of its myriad leaves,   20
Down from its lofty top rising two hundred feet high,
Out of its stalwart trunk and limbs, out of its foot-thick bark,
That chant of the seasons and time, chant not of the past only
       but the future.

You untold life of me,
And all you venerable and innocent joys,   25
Perennial hardy life of me with joys 'mid rain and many a
       summer sun,
And the white snows and night and the wild winds;
O the great patient rugged joys, my soul's strong joys unreck'd by
       man,
(For know I bear the soul befitting me, I too have consciousness,
       identity,
And all the rocks and mountains have, and all the earth,)   30
Joys of the life befitting me and brothers mine,
Our time, our term has come.

Nor yield we mournfully majestic brothers,
We who have grandly fill'd our time;
With Nature's calm content, with tacit huge delight,   35
We welcome what we wrought for through the past,
And leave the field for them.

For them predicted long,
For a superber race, they too to grandly fill their time,
For them we abdicate, in them ourselves ye forest kings!   40
In them these skies and airs, these mountain peaks, Shasta,
       Nevadas,
These huge precipitous cliffs, this amplitude, these valleys, far Yosemite,
To be in them absorb'd, assimilated.

Then to a loftier strain,
Still prouder, more ecstatic rose the chant,   45

WW wrote, March 4, 1874, that he had written the poem "to idealize our great
Pacific half of America, (the future *better half*)—" (Corr. II, 282). A diplomatic
reprint of two MSS. (Barrett-Va.) of the poem, one rough and the other comparatively
finished, is presented by Fredson Bowers in PBSA, L (1st Quarter, 1956), 53–85.
    11. Mendocino] California coastal county north of San Francisco.
    16. shanties] Suggesting both huts and work-songs.
    41. Shasta] Mountain peak in Siskiyou County, California. Nevadas] Sierra
Nevada, mountain range in eastern California.

As if the heirs, the deities of the West,
Joining with master-tongue bore part.

Not wan from Asia's fetiches,
Nor red from Europe's old dynastic slaughter-house,
(Area of murder-plots of thrones, with scent left yet of wars and
50   *scaffolds everywhere,)*
But come from Nature's long and harmless throes, peacefully
          builded thence,
These virgin lands, lands of the Western shore,
To the new culminating man, to you, the empire new,
You promis'd long, we pledge, we dedicate.

55   *You occult deep volitions,*
You average spiritual manhood, purpose of all, pois'd on yourself,
          giving not taking law,
You womanhood divine, mistress and source of all, whence life
          and love and aught that comes from life and love,
You unseen moral essence of all the vast materials of America,
          (age upon age working in death the same as life,)
You that, sometimes known, oftener unknown, really shape and
          mould the New World, adjusting it to Time and Space,
You hidden national will lying in your abysms, conceal'd but ever
60   *alert,*
You past and present purposes tenaciously pursued, may-be uncon-
          scious of yourselves,
Unswerv'd by all the passing errors, perturbations of the surface;
You vital, universal, deathless germs, beneath all creeds, arts,
          statutes, literatures,
Here build your homes for good, establish here, these areas entire,
          lands of the Western shore,
65   *We pledge, we dedicate to you.*

For man of you, your characteristic race,
Here may he hardy, sweet, gigantic grow, here tower proportion-
          ate to Nature,
Here climb the vast pure spaces unconfined, uncheck'd by wall or
          roof,

    55–65. volitions] An early working draft (Trent-Duke) of this eleven-line passage
is printed in *FCI*, 8–9.

Here laugh with storm or sun, here joy, here patiently inure,
Here heed himself, unfold himself, (not others' formulas heed,)
  here fill his time,   70
To duly fall, to aid, unreck'd at last,
To disappear, to serve.

Thus on the northern coast,
In the echo of teamsters' calls and the clinking chains, and the
  music of choppers' axes,
The falling trunk and limbs, the crash, the muffled shriek, the
  groan,   75
Such words combined from the redwood-tree, as of voices ecstatic,
  ancient and rustling,
The century-lasting, unseen dryads, singing, withdrawing,
All their recesses of forests and mountains leaving,
From the Cascade range to the Wahsatch, or Idaho far, or Utah,
To the deities of the modern henceforth yielding,   80
The chorus and indications, the vistas of coming humanity, the
  settlements, features all,
In the Mendocino woods I caught.

2

The flashing and golden pageant of California,
The sudden and gorgeous drama, the sunny and ample lands,
The long and varied stretch from Puget sound to Colorado south, 85
Lands bathed in sweeter, rarer, healthier air, valleys and mountain
  cliffs,
The fields of Nature long prepared and fallow, the silent, cyclic
  chemistry,
The slow and steady ages plodding, the unoccupied surface ripen-
  ing, the rich ores forming beneath;
At last the New arriving, assuming, taking possession,
A swarming and busy race settling and organizing everywhere, 90
Ships coming in from the whole round world, and going out to
  the whole world,
To India and China and Australia and the thousand island para-
  dises of the Pacific,

  79. Cascade] Range of mountains in Oregon, Washington, and British Colum-
bia. Wahsatch] More commonly Wasatch, a range in northern Utah and southeast-
ern Idaho.

Populous cities, the latest inventions, the steamers on the rivers,
    the railroads, with many a thrifty farm, with machinery,
And wool and wheat and the grape, and diggings of yellow gold.

3

95 But more in you than these, lands of the Western shore,
  (These but the means, the implements, the standing-ground,)
  I see in you, certain to come, the promise of thousands of years,
    till now deferr'd,
  Promis'd to be fulfill'd, our common kind, the race.

The new society at last, proportionate to Nature,
In man of you, more than your mountain peaks or stalwart trees
100   imperial,
In woman more, far more, than all your gold or vines, or even
    vital air.

Fresh come, to a new world indeed, yet long prepared,
I see the genius of the modern, child of the real and ideal,
Clearing the ground for broad humanity, the true America, heir
    of the past so grand,
105 To build a grander future.

1874   1881

OCCUPATIONS] The second of the twelve untitled poems of the first edition. It was subsequently "Poem of The Daily Work of The Workmen and Workwomen of These States" (1856), No. 3 of the "Chants Democratic" (1860), "To Workingmen" (1867), and "Carol of Occupations" (1871 and 1876); in 1881 it received its present title. WW worked at it persistently, regarding it as a major pronouncement. In the MS revisions of his 1860 text he suggested such titles as "Song of Trades and Implements" or "Chant of Mechanics," and although he wrote on the title page, "This is satisfactory as it now is, Dec. 7, 1864," he marked for deletion much of what is now the fifth section, and labeled the final section "out without fail!" Section 5 contained 65 lines in 1855, was expanded to 80 lines in 1860, and finally reduced to

A Song for Occupations.

1

A song for occupations!
In the labor of engines and trades and the labor of fields I find
      the developments,
And find the eternal meanings.

Workmen and Workwomen!
Were all educations practical and ornamental well display'd out
      of me, what would it amount to?   5
Were I as the head teacher, charitable proprietor, wise statesman,
      what would it amount to?
Were I to you as the boss employing and paying you, would that
      satisfy you?

The learn'd, virtuous, benevolent, and the usual terms,
A man like me and never the usual terms.

Neither a servant nor a master I,   10
I take no sooner a large price than a small price, I will have my
      own whoever enjoys me,
I will be even with you and you shall be even with me.

If you stand at work in a shop I stand as nigh as the nighest in
      the same shop,

its present 38. The 178 lines of the original poem became 196 in 1856, 205 in 1860,
158 in 1871 and 1876, and finally 151. The general effect was to shorten the
catalogues and diminish the sense of intimacy. For example, the opening passage
(dropped in 1881) began:

> Come closer to me,
> Push close my lovers and take the best I possess,
> Yield closer and closer and give me the best you
>   possess.

Compare lines 1309–1313, "Song of Myself," with lines 44–48 of this "Song" for
examples of the consistency in spirit of the first *Leaves*.

If you bestow gifts on your brother or dearest friend I demand as
  good as your brother or dearest friend,
If your lover, husband, wife, is welcome by day or night, I must
15   be personally as welcome,
If you become degraded, criminal, ill, then I become so for your
  sake,
If you remember your foolish and outlaw'd deeds, do you think
  I cannot remember my own foolish and outlaw'd deeds?
If you carouse at the table I carouse at the opposite side of the
  table,
If you meet some stranger in the streets and love him or her, why
  I often meet strangers in the street and love them.

20   Why what have you thought of yourself?
  Is it you then that thought yourself less?
  Is it you that thought the President greater than you?
  Or the rich better off than you? or the educated wiser than you?

(Because you are greasy or pimpled, or were once drunk, or a
  thief,
25   Or that you are diseas'd, or rheumatic, or a prostitute,
  Or from frivolity or impotence, or that you are no scholar and
  never saw your name in print,
  Do you give in that you are any less immortal?)

          2

  Souls of men and women! it is not you I call unseen, unheard,
  untouchable and untouching,
  It is not you I go argue pro and con about, and to settle whether
  you are alive or no,
30   I own publicly who you are, if nobody else owns.

  Grown, half-grown and babe, of this country and every country, in-
  doors and out-doors, one just as much as the other, I see,
  And all else behind or through them.

  The wife, and she is not one jot less than the husband,
  The daughter, and she is just as good as the son,
35   The mother, and she is every bit as much as the father.

Offspring of ignorant and poor, boys apprenticed to trades,
Young fellows working on farms and old fellows working on farms,
Sailor-men, merchant-men, coasters, immigrants,
All these I see, but nigher and farther the same I see,
None shall escape me and none shall wish to escape me. 40

I bring what you much need yet always have,
Not money, amours, dress, eating, erudition, but as good,
I send no agent or medium, offer no representative of value, but
    offer the value itself.

There is something that comes to one now and perpetually,
It is not what is printed, preach'd, discussed, it eludes discussion
    and print, 45
It is not to be put in a book, it is not in this book,
It is for you whoever you are, it is no farther from you than your
    hearing and sight are from you,
It is hinted by nearest, commonest, readiest, it is ever provoked
    by them.

You may read in many languages, yet read nothing about it,
You may read the President's message and read nothing about it
    there, 50
Nothing in the reports from the State department or Treasury
    department, or in the daily papers or weekly papers,
Or in the census or revenue returns, prices current, or any
    accounts of stock.

3

The sun and stars that float in the open air,
The apple-shaped earth and we upon it, surely the drift of them
    is something grand,
I do not know what it is except that it is grand, and that it is
    happiness, 55
And that the enclosing purport of us here is not a speculation or
    bon-mot or reconnoissance,
And that it is not something which by luck may turn out well for
    us, and without luck must be a failure for us,
And not something which may yet be retracted in a certain
    contingency.

The light and shade, the curious sense of body and identity, the
    greed that with perfect complaisance devours all things,
The endless pride and outstretching of man, unspeakable joys
60   and sorrows,
The wonder every one sees in every one else he sees, and the
    wonders that fill each minute of time forever,
What have you reckon'd them for, camerado?
Have you reckon'd them for your trade or farm-work? or for the
    profits of your store?
Or to achieve yourself a position? or to fill a gentleman's leisure,
    or a lady's leisure?

Have you reckon'd that the landscape took substance and form
65   that it might be painted in a picture?
Or men and women that they might be written of, and songs sung?
Or the attraction of gravity, and the great laws and harmonious
    combinations and the fluids of the air, as subjects for the savans?
Or the brown land and the blue sea for maps and charts?
Or the stars to be put in constellations and named fancy names?
Or that the growth of seeds is for agricultural tables, or agricul-
70   ture itself?

Old institutions, these arts, libraries, legends, collections, and the
    practice handed along in manufactures, will we rate them
    so high?
Will we rate our cash and business high? I have no objection,
I rate them as high as the highest—then a child born of a
    woman and man I rate beyond all rate.

We thought our Union grand, and our Constitution grand,
75 I do not say they are not grand and good, for they are,
I am this day just as much in love with them as you,
Then I am in love with You, and with all my fellows upon the
    earth.

We consider bibles and religions divine—I do not say they are
    not divine,

67. savans] WW's spelling for "savants," learned men. Cf. "philosophs."
78. bibles] Not capitalized: any book regarded as authoritative.

I say they have all grown out of you, and may grow out of you
  still,
It is not they who give the life, it is you who give the life,   80
Leaves are not more shed from the trees, or trees from the earth,
  than they are shed out of you.

4

The sum of all known reverence I add up in you whoever you are,
The President is there in the White House for you, it is not you
  who are here for him,
The Secretaries act in their bureaus for you, not you here for them,
The Congress convenes every Twelfth-month for you,   85
Laws, courts, the forming of States, the charters of cities, the
  going and coming of commerce and mails, are all for you.

List close my scholars dear,
Doctrines, politics and civilization exurge from you,
Sculpture and monuments and any thing inscribed anywhere are
  tallied in you,
The gist of histories and statistics as far back as the records reach
  is in you this hour, and myths and tales the same,   90
If you were not breathing and walking here, where would they
  all be?
The most renown'd poems would be ashes, orations and plays
  would be vacuums.

All architecture is what you do to it when you look upon it,
(Did you think it was in the white or gray stone? or the lines of
  the arches and cornices?)

All music is what awakes from you when you are reminded by the
  instruments,   95
It is not the violins and the cornets, it is not the oboe nor the
  beating drums, nor the score of the baritone singer singing
  his sweet romanza, nor that of the men's chorus, nor that
  of the women's chorus,
It is nearer and farther than they.

  88. exurge] To rise or come into view. Usually "exsurge." WW's form is cited in
N.E.D.
88–97.] Cf. lines 82–88 of "A Song of the Rolling Earth."

5

Will the whole come back then?
Can each see signs of the best by a look in the looking-glass? is
    there nothing greater or more?
100   Does all sit there with you, with the mystic unseen soul?

Strange and hard that paradox true I give,
Objects gross and the unseen soul are one.

House-building, measuring, sawing the boards,
Blacksmithing, glass-blowing, nail-making, coopering, tin-roofing,
    shingle-dressing,
Ship-joining, dock-building, fish-curing, flagging of sidewalks by
105   flaggers,
The pump, the pile-driver, the great derrick, the coal-kiln and
    brick-kiln,
Coal-mines and all that is down there, the lamps in the darkness,
    echoes, songs, what meditations, what vast native thoughts
    looking through smutch'd faces,
Iron-works, forge-fires in the mountains or by river-banks, men
    around feeling the melt with huge crowbars, lumps of ore,
    the due combining of ore, limestone, coal,
The blast-furnace and the puddling-furnace, the loup-lump at the
    bottom of the melt at last, the rolling-mill, the stumpy
    bars of pig-iron, the strong clean-shaped T-rail for rail-
    roads,
Oil-works, silk-works, white-lead-works, the sugar-house, steam-
110   saws, the great mills and factories,
Stone-cutting, shapely trimmings for façades or window or door-
    lintels, the mallet, the tooth-chisel, the jib to protect the
    thumb,
The calking-iron, the kettle of boiling vault-cement, and the fire
    under the kettle,
The cotton-bale, the stevedore's hook, the saw and buck of the
    sawyer, the mould of the moulder, the working-knife of
    the butcher, the ice-saw, and all the work with ice,

109. loup-lump] The pasty mass of iron at the bottom of the melt—the product
sought in the smelting process.

The work and tools of the rigger, grappler, sail-maker, block-
    maker,
Goods of gutta-percha, papier-maché, colors, brushes, brush-
    making, glazier's implements,   115
The veneer and glue-pot, the confectioner's ornaments, the
    decanter and glasses, the shears and flat-iron,
The awl and knee-strap, the pint measure and quart measure, the
    counter and stool, the writing-pen of quill or metal, the
    making of all sorts of edged tools,
The brewery, brewing, the malt, the vats, every thing that is done
    by brewers, wine-makers, vinegar-makers,
Leather-dressing, coach-making, boiler-making, rope-twisting, dis-
    tilling, sign-painting, lime-burning, cotton-picking, electro-
    plating, electrotyping, stereotyping,
Stave-machines, planing-machines, reaping-machines, ploughing-
    machines, thrashing-machines, steam wagons,   120
The cart of the carman, the omnibus, the ponderous dray,
Pyrotechny, letting off color'd fireworks at night, fancy figures and
    jets;
Beef on the butcher's stall, the slaughter-house of the butcher, the
    butcher in his killing-clothes,
The pens of live pork, the killing-hammer, the hog-hook, the
    scalder's tub, gutting, the cutter's cleaver, the packer's maul,
    and the plenteous winterwork of pork-packing,
Flour-works, grinding of wheat, rye, maize, rice, the barrels and
    the half and quarter barrels, the loaded barges, the high
    piles on wharves and levees,   125
The men and the work of the men on ferries, railroads, coasters,
    fish-boats, canals;
The hourly routine of your own or any man's life, the shop, yard,
    store, or factory,
These shows all near you by day and night—workman! whoever
    you are, your daily life!
In that and them the heft of the heaviest—in that and them far
    more than you estimated, (and far less also,)
In them realities for you and me, in them poems for you and me,   130
In them, not yourself—you and your soul enclose all things, re-
    gardless of estimation,

111. jib] Projecting shield.

In them the development good—in them all themes, hints, possi-
bilities.

I do not affirm that what you see beyond is futile, I do not advise
you to stop,
I do not say leadings you thought great are not great,
135   But I say that none lead to greater than these lead to.

                         6

Will you seek afar off? you surely come back at last,
In things best known to you finding the best, or as good as the
best,
In folks nearest to you finding the sweetest, strongest, lovingest,
Happiness, knowledge, not in another place but this place, not for
another hour but this hour,
Man in the first you see or touch, always in friend, brother,
140   nighest neighbor—woman in mother, sister, wife,
The popular tastes and employments taking precedence in poems
or anywhere,
You workwomen and workmen of these States having your own
divine and strong life,
And all else giving place to men and women like you.

When the psalm sings instead of the singer,
145   When the script preaches instead of the preacher,
When the pulpit descends and goes instead of the carver that
carved the supporting desk,
When I can touch the body of books by night or by day, and
when they touch my body back again,
When a university course convinces like a slumbering woman and
child convince,
When the minted gold in the vault smiles like the night-watchman's
daughter,

EARTH] This 1856 poem underwent comparatively slight revision except for its
title and beginning. The changes in title themselves indicate successive emphasis
upon the sayers, the words, and the earth: "Poem of The Sayers of The Words of
The Earth" (1856); "To the Sayers of Words" (1860, 1867); "Carol of Words"
(1871, 1876); "A Song of the Rolling Earth" (1881). The opening two lines,
dropped in 1881, provided an explicit clue for the reader:

Earth, round, rolling, compact—suns, moons, ani-
mals—all these are words,
Watery, vegetable, sauroid advances—beings, pre-

When warrantee deeds loafe in chairs opposite and are my friendly
    companions,   150
I intend to reach them my hand, and make as much of them as
    I do of men and women like you.

    1855   *1881*

A Song of the Rolling Earth.

1

A song of the rolling earth, and of words according,
Were you thinking that those were the words, those upright lines?
    those curves, angles, dots?
No, those are not the words, the substantial words are in the
    ground and sea,
They are in the air, they are in you.

Were you thinking that those were the words, those delicious sounds
    out of your friends' mouths?   5
No, the real words are more delicious than they.

Human bodies are words, myriads of words,
(In the best poems re-appears the body, man's or woman's, well-
    shaped, natural, gay,
Every part able, active, receptive, without shame or the need of
    shame.)

monitions, lispings of the future—these
are vast words.
In his MS emendations of the 1860 "Blue Copy" text, WW proposed changing the
opening to "This rolling earth is the word to be said," but withdrew the alteration,
and the lines were retained through 1876. Some of his greatest lines are in this poem,
a poetic demonstration of the transcendentalist doctrine expounded by Emerson in
Nature, Part IV, "Language" (1836): "Language is a . . . use which Nature
subserves to man. Nature is the vehicle of thought . . . Words are signs of natural
facts."

10   Air, soil, water, fire—those are words,
      I myself am a word with them—my qualities interpenetrate with
              theirs—my name is nothing to them,
      Though it were told in the three thousand languages, what would
              air, soil, water, fire, know of my name?

      A healthy presence, a friendly or commanding gesture, are words,
              sayings, meanings,
      The charms that go with the mere looks of some men and women,
              are sayings and meanings also.

15   The workmanship of souls is by those inaudible words of the earth,
      The masters know the earth's words and use them more than
              audible words.

      Amelioration is one of the earth's words,
      The earth neither lags nor hastens,
      It has all attributes, growths, effects, latent in itself from the jump,
      It is not half beautiful only, defects and excrescences show just as
20   much as perfections show.

      The earth does not withhold, it is generous enough,
      The truths of the earth continually wait, they are not so conceal'd
              either,
      They are calm, subtle, untransmissible by print,
      They are imbued through all things conveying themselves willingly,
25   Conveying a sentiment and invitation, I utter and utter,
      I speak not, yet if you hear me not of what avail am I to you?
      To bear, to better, lacking these of what avail am I?

      (Accouche! accouchez!
      Will you rot your own fruit in yourself there?
30   Will you squat and stifle there?)

      19. from the jump] For Biblical analogy of the primordial word, consider John
      I: 1: "In the beginning was the Word . . . and the Word was God."
          28. Accouche! accouchez!] French: properly "Accouchée! accouchez!"—i.e.,
      "You pregnant one! be delivered!"
          44. interminable sisters] The sisters, the "ceaseless cotillons," are the stars and
      planets, among whom is the earth, the "beautiful sister we know," the whole passage,
      lines 44–72, being governed by the figure of time, the consequence of celestial

The earth does not argue,
Is not pathetic, has no arrangements,
Does not scream, haste, persuade, threaten, promise,
Makes no discriminations, has no conceivable failures,
Closes nothing, refuses nothing, shuts none out,   35
Of all the powers, objects, states, it notifies, shuts none out.

The earth does not exhibit itself nor refuse to exhibit itself, pos-
          sesses still underneath,
Underneath the ostensible sounds, the august chorus of heroes, the
          wail of slaves,
Persuasions of lovers, curses, gasps of the dying, laughter of young
          people, accents of bargainers,
Underneath these possessing words that never fail.   40

To her children the words of the eloquent dumb great mother
          never fail,
The true words do not fail, for motion does not fail and reflection
          does not fail,
Also the day and night do not fail, and the voyage we pursue does
          not fail.

Of the interminable sisters,
Of the ceaseless cotillons of sisters,   45
Of the centripetal and centrifugal sisters, the elder and younger
          sisters,
The beautiful sister we know dances on with the rest.

With her ample back towards every beholder,
With the fascinations of youth and the equal fascinations of age,
Sits she whom I too love like the rest, sits undisturb'd,   50
Holding up in her hand what has the character of a mirror, while
          her eyes glance back from it,

motion. Cf. the poem "Days" by Emerson, whose "daughters of time" regard man
with "scorn" for his paltry use of their gifts. By contrast, WW's unending cotillions
of "sisters" dance by—the one (line 50), the "twenty-four" (line 55), the "three
hundred and sixty-five" (line 63), making luminous the faces of men and things,
"embracing man" and "all" on "the divine ship."

45. cotillons] This is the French form for a brisk ballroom dance of the 19th
century, also used in LG 1881 and in the 1902 CW, but in the LG editions of
1856, 1860, 1867, 1871, 1872, and 1876 the English "cotillions" appears.

Glance as she sits, inviting none, denying none,
Holding a mirror day and night tirelessly before her own face.

Seen at hand or seen at a distance,
55 Duly the twenty-four appear in public every day,
Duly approach and pass with their companions or a companion,
Looking from no countenances of their own, but from the counte-
nances of those who are with them,
From the countenances of children or women or the manly coun-
tenance,
From the open countenances of animals or from inanimate things,
From the landscape or waters or from the exquisite apparition of
60 the sky,
From our countenances, mine and yours, faithfully returning them,
Every day in public appearing without fail, but never twice with
the same companions.

Embracing man, embracing all, proceed the three hundred and
sixty-five resistlessly round the sun;
Embracing all, soothing, supporting, follow close three hundred
and sixty-five offsets of the first, sure and necessary as they.

65 Tumbling on steadily, nothing dreading,
Sunshine, storm, cold, heat, forever withstanding, passing, carrying,
The soul's realization and determination still inheriting,
The fluid vacuum around and ahead still entering and dividing,
No balk retarding, no anchor anchoring, on no rock striking,
70 Swift, glad, content, unbereav'd, nothing losing,
Of all able and ready at any time to give strict account,
The divine ship sails the divine sea.

2

Whoever you are! motion and reflection are especially for you,
The divine ship sails the divine sea for you.

Whoever you are! you are he or she for whom the earth is solid
75 and liquid,
You are he or she for whom the sun and moon hang in the sky,

96. that which responds love] WW sometimes coined an intransitive verb into a

For none more than you are the present and the past,
For none more than you is immortality.

Each man to himself and each woman to herself, is the word of
      the past and present, and the true word of immortality;
No one can acquire for another—not one,   80
Not one can grow for another—not one.

The song is to the singer, and comes back most to him,
The teaching is to the teacher, and comes back most to him,
The murder is to the murderer, and comes back most to him,
The theft is to the thief, and comes back most to him,   85
The love is to the lover, and comes back most to him,
The gift is to the giver, and comes back most to him—it cannot
      fail,
The oration is to the orator, the acting is to the actor and actress
      not to the audience,
And no man understands any greatness or goodness but his own,
      or the indication of his own.

3

I swear the earth shall surely be complete to him or her who shall
      be complete,   90
The earth remains jagged and broken only to him or her who
      remains jagged and broken.

I swear there is no greatness or power that does not emulate
      those of the earth,
There can be no theory of any account unless it corroborate the
      theory of the earth,
No politics, song, religion, behavior, or what not, is of account, unless it
      compare with the amplitude of the earth,
Unless it face the exactness, vitality, impartiality, rectitude of the
      earth.   95

I swear I begin to see love with sweeter spasms than that which
      responds love,
It is that which contains itself, which never invites and never
      refuses.

transitive form; actually the translation of the Latin roots is transitive, i.e., to
"promise back" love.

I swear I begin to see little or nothing in audible words,
All merges toward the presentation of the unspoken meanings
          of the earth,
Toward him who sings the songs of the body and of the truths
100   of the earth,
Toward him who makes the dictionaries of words that print can-
          not touch.

I swear I see what is better than to tell the best,
It is always to leave the best untold.

When I undertake to tell the best I find I cannot,
105   My tongue is ineffectual on its pivots,
My breath will not be obedient to its organs,
I become a dumb man.

The best of the earth cannot be told anyhow, all or any is best,
It is not what you anticipated, it is cheaper, easier, nearer,
110   Things are not dismiss'd from the places they held before,
The earth is just as positive and direct as it was before,
Facts, religions, improvements, politics, trades, are as real as before,
But the soul is also real, it too is positive and direct,
No reasoning, no proof has establish'd it,
115   Undeniable growth has establish'd it.

          4

These to echo the tones of souls and the phrases of souls,
(If they did not echo the phrases of souls what were they then?
If they had not reference to you in especial what were they then?)

I swear I will never henceforth have to do with the faith that tells
          the best,
120   I will have to do only with that faith that leaves the best untold.

Say on, sayers! sing on, singers!
Delve! mould! pile the words of the earth!
Work on, age after age, nothing is to be lost,
It may have to wait long, but it will certainly come in use,
When the materials are all prepared and ready, the architects shall
125   appear.

I swear to you the architects shall appear without fail,
I swear to you they will understand you and justify you,
The greatest among them shall be he who best knows you, and
        encloses all and is faithful to all,
He and the rest shall not forget you, they shall perceive that you
        are not an iota less than they,
You shall be fully glorified in them.   130

 1856   *1881*

Youth, Day, Old Age and Night.

Youth, large, lusty, loving—youth full of grace, force, fascination,
Do you know that Old Age may come after you with equal grace,
        force, fascination?

Day full-blown and splendid—day of the immense sun, action,
        ambition, laughter,
The Night follows close with millions of suns, and sleep and
        restoring darkness.

 1855   *1881*

NIGHT] This poem is composed of four lines retained from the 1855 poem "Great
are the Myths" when it was excluded from *LG* 1881. They had been lines 19 through
22 of the original piece, which was the final poem of the first edition.

Birds of Passage.

Song of the Universal.

1

Come said the Muse,
Sing me a song no poet yet has chanted,
Sing me the universal.

In this broad earth of ours,
5   Amid the measureless grossness and the slag,
Enclosed and safe within its central heart,
Nestles the seed perfection.

By every life a share or more or less,
None born but it is born, conceal'd or unconceal'd the seed is
      waiting.

2

10   Lo! keen-eyed towering science,
As from tall peaks the modern overlooking,
Successive absolute fiats issuing.

PASSAGE] This group, new to WW's final 1881 arrangement, appears under a
title which admirably suggests an abiding element in his poetry—the sense of flight
and change. Although the seven component poems each appeared in a different
group in various earlier editions of *LG*, they now acquire a casual unity of tone be-
cause each deals with movement—whether of the evolution of cultural perfection, or
westward expansion, or the search for one's own identity, or the vicissitudes of
history.

UNIVERSAL] Written in response to the invitation (March 20, 1874) of a group
of young men at Tufts College to deliver a poem at Commencement, this piece was
recited June 17 *in absentia* because WW's illness prevented his personal ap-

Yet again, lo! the soul, above all science,
For it has history gather'd like husks around the globe,
For it the entire star-myriads roll through the sky.   15

In spiral routes by long detours,
(As a much-tacking ship upon the sea,)
For it the partial to the permanent flowing,
For it the real to the ideal tends.

For it the mystic evolution,   20
Not the right only justified, what we call evil also justified.

Forth from their masks, no matter what,
From the huge festering trunk, from craft and guile and tears,
Health to emerge and joy, joy universal.

Out of the bulk, the morbid and the shallow,   25
Out of the bad majority, the varied countless frauds of men and
       states,
Electric, antiseptic yet, cleaving, suffusing all,
Only the good is universal.

3

Over the mountain-growths disease and sorrow,
An uncaught bird is ever hovering, hovering,   30
High in the purer, happier air.

From imperfection's murkiest cloud,
Darts always forth one ray of perfect light,
One flash of heaven's glory.

pearance. The poem received nearly simultaneous publication in several newspa-
pers—the New York *Daily Graphic* and *Evening Post* on June 17, the Springfield
Republican on June 18, the New York *World* on June 19, and the Camden *New
Republic* on June 20. Its first book appearance was among the "Centennial Songs" of
the 1876 *Two Rivulets*, companion volume to LG. Composed in the wake of personal
trials, notably WW's paralytic stroke January 23, 1873 and the death of his mother
the following May 23, it is a strong reaffirmation of faith, its ideal of perfection's
culmination being strongly affected by the poet's reading of Hegel. See Allen, 460.
The MS drafts (Yale and Berg) show much working over.
    19. real to the ideal] In the sense of substance and idea.

35   To fashion's, custom's discord,
To the mad Babel-din, the deafening orgies,
Soothing each lull a strain is heard, just heard,
From some far shore the final chorus sounding.

O the blest eyes, the happy hearts,
40   That see, that know the guiding thread so fine,
Along the mighty labyrinth.

4

And thou America,
For the scheme's culmination, its thought and its reality,
For these (not for thyself) thou hast arrived.

45   Thou too surroundest all,
Embracing carrying welcoming all, thou too by pathways broad
          and new,
To the ideal tendest.

The measur'd faiths of other lands, the grandeurs of the past,
Are not for thee, but grandeurs of thine own,
50   Deific faiths and amplitudes, absorbing, comprehending all,
All eligible to all.

All, all for immortality,
Love like the light silently wrapping all,
Nature's amelioration blessing all,
55   The blossoms, fruits of ages, orchards divine and certain,
Forms, objects, growths, humanities, to spiritual images ripening.

Give me O God to sing that thought,
Give me, give him or her I love this quenchless faith,
In Thy ensemble, whatever else withheld withhold not from us,
60   Belief in plan of Thee enclosed in Time and Space,
Health, peace, salvation universal.

59. Thy ensemble] A transcendental concept, rife in WW's youth, was the integrated ensemble of all microcosms in the grand single macrocosm of Being.
PIONEERS!] First published in numbered stanzas in the 1865 *Drum-Taps*, again in the 1867 "Drum-Taps" annex, and in 1871 and 1876 among a *Leaves of Grass* group entitled "Marches Now the War is Over," this poem, with its strong trochaic

Is it a dream?
Nay but the lack of it the dream,
And failing it life's lore and wealth a dream,
And all the world a dream.   65

1874   *1881*

Pioneers! O Pioneers!

   Come my tan-faced children,
Follow well in order, get your weapons ready,
Have you your pistols? have you your sharp-edged axes?
      Pioneers! O pioneers!

   For we cannot tarry here,   5
We must march my darlings, we must bear the brunt of danger,
We the youthful sinewy races, all the rest on us depend,
      Pioneers! O pioneers!

   O you youths, Western youths,
So impatient, full of action, full of manly pride and friendship,   10
Plain I see you Western youths, see you tramping with the fore-
      most,
      Pioneers! O pioneers!

   Have the elder races halted?
Do they droop and end their lesson, wearied over there beyond
      the seas?
We take up the task eternal, and the burden and the lesson,   15
      Pioneers! O pioneers!

   All the past we leave behind,
We debouch upon a newer mightier world, varied world,
Fresh and strong the world we seize, world of labor and the march,
      Pioneers! O pioneers!   20

beat, is obviously designed to be a marching song. Recalling "Eidólons" in its stanza
structure, it is one of the more than a dozen *LG* poems which, in the regularity of their
meter, are atypical of WW. Charles B. Willard has called attention to the influence
of Tennyson's "Ulysses" upon this poem. (*WWN*, II, 9–10.)

   18. debouch] To emerge from a narrow pass into open country. Cf. WW's use of
this word in "Song of Myself," section 49, the last line.

We detachments steady throwing,
Down the edges, through the passes, up the mountains steep,
Conquering, holding, daring, venturing as we go the unknown ways,
     Pioneers! O pioneers!

25   We primeval forests felling,
We the rivers stemming, vexing we and piercing deep the mines
     within,
We the surface broad surveying, we the virgin soil upheaving,
     Pioneers! O pioneers!

     Colorado men are we,
From the peaks gigantic, from the great sierras and the high
30   plateaus,
From the mine and from the gully, from the hunting trail we come,
     Pioneers! O pioneers!

     From Nebraska, from Arkansas,
Central inland race are we, from Missouri, with the continental
     blood intervein'd,
All the hands of comrades clasping, all the Southern, all the
35   Northern,
     Pioneers! O pioneers!

     O resistless restless race!
O beloved race in all! O my breast aches with tender love for all!
O I mourn and yet exult, I am rapt with love for all,
40   Pioneers! O pioneers!

     Raise the mighty mother mistress,
Waving high the delicate mistress, over all the starry mistress,
     (bend your heads all,)
Raise the fang'd and warlike mistress, stern, impassive, weapon'd
     mistress,
     Pioneers! O pioneers!

45   See my children, resolute children,
By those swarms upon our rear we must never yield or falter,
Ages back in ghostly millions frowning there behind us urging,
     Pioneers! O pioneers!

74. suns and planets] Erroneously printed as "sons" in the 1881 revision and

On and on the compact ranks,
With accessions ever waiting, with the places of the dead quickly
   fill'd,   50
Through the battle, through defeat, moving yet and never stopping,
  Pioneers! O pioneers!

  O to die advancing on!
Are there some of us to droop and die? has the hour come?
Then upon the march we fittest die, soon and sure the gap is fill'd, 55
  Pioneers! O pioneers!

  All the pulses of the world,
Falling in they beat for us, with the Western movement beat,
Holding single or together, steady moving to the front, all for us,
  Pioneers! O pioneers!   60

  Life's involv'd and varied pageants,
All the forms and shows, all the workmen at their work,
All the seamen and the landsmen, all the masters with their slaves,
  Pioneers! O pioneers!

  All the hapless silent lovers,   65
All the prisoners in the prisons, all the righteous and the wicked,
All the joyous, all the sorrowing, all the living, all the dying,
  Pioneers! O pioneers!

  I too with my soul and body,
We, a curious trio, picking, wandering on our way,   70
Through these shores amid the shadows, with the apparitions
   pressing,
  Pioneers! O pioneers!

  Lo, the darting bowling orb!
Lo, the brother orbs around, all the clustering suns and planets,
All the dazzling days, all the mystic nights with dreams,   75
  Pioneers! O pioneers!

  These are of us, they are with us,
All for primal needed work, while the followers there in embryo
   wait behind,

thereafter until *LG* 1889. The 1891–2 hardbound issue reads "suns," but the soft
bound issue of that date retained the error.

We to-day's procession heading, we the route for travel clearing,
80   Pioneers! O pioneers!

O you daughters of the West!
O you young and elder daughters! O you mothers and you wives!
Never must you be divided, in our ranks you move united,
            Pioneers! O pioneers!

85   Minstrels latent on the prairies!
(Shrouded bards of other lands, you may rest, you have done
            your work,)
Soon I hear you coming warbling, soon you rise and tramp amid us,
            Pioneers! O pioneers!

Not for delectations sweet,
90 Not the cushion and the slipper, not the peaceful and the studious,
Not the riches safe and palling, not for us the tame enjoyment,
            Pioneers! O pioneers!

Do the feasters gluttonous feast?
Do the corpulent sleepers sleep? have they lock'd and bolted doors?
95 Still be ours the diet hard, and the blanket on the ground,
            Pioneers! O pioneers!

Has the night descended?
Was the road of late so toilsome? did we stop discouraged nodding
            on our way?
Yet a passing hour I yield you in your tracks to pause oblivious,
100   Pioneers! O pioneers!

Till with sound of trumpet,
Far, far off the daybreak call—hark! how loud and clear I hear
            it wind,
Swift! to the head of the army!—swift! spring to your places,
            Pioneers! O pioneers!

1865   *1881*

YOU] In 1856 this poem appeared under the title "Poem of You, Whoever You
Are," and in 1860 as "To You, Whoever You are." In 1867 it was simply "Leaves
of Grass" No. 4, and from 1871 it has carried its present title. Although three lines

To You.

Whoever you are, I fear you are walking the walks of dreams,
I fear these supposed realities are to melt from under your feet
     and hands,
Even now your features, joys, speech, house, trade, manners,
       troubles, follies, costume, crimes, dissipate away from you,
Your true soul and body appear before me,
They stand forth out of affairs, out of commerce, shops, work,
       farms, clothes, the house, buying, selling, eating, drinking,
       suffering, dying.   5

Whoever you are, now I place my hand upon you, that you be my
     poem,
I whisper with my lips close to your ear,
I have loved many women and men, but I love none better than
     you.

O I have been dilatory and dumb,
I should have made my way straight to you long ago,   10
I should have blabb'd nothing but you, I should have chanted
       nothing but you.

I will leave all and come and make the hymns of you,
None has understood you, but I understand you,
None has done justice to you, you have not done justice to your-
     self,
None but has found you imperfect, I only find no imperfection in
     you,
None but would subordinate you, I only am he who will never   15
       consent to subordinate you,
I only am he who places over you no master, owner, better, God,
       beyond what waits intrinsically in yourself.

Painters have painted their swarming groups and the centre-figure
     of all,

have been dropped from the first text, it has undergone but slight revision, and it
remains a striking instance of WW's intimate address directly to the reader, some-
what in the manner of teacher to disciple. Here the teacher encourages one of the
"divine average" to discover and respect his own personal identity.

From the head of the centre-figure spreading a nimbus of gold-
color'd light,
But I paint myriads of heads, but paint no head without its nim-
bus of gold-color'd light,
20   From my hand from the brain of every man and woman it streams,
effulgently flowing forever.

O I could sing such grandeurs and glories about you!
You have not known what you are, you have slumber'd upon
yourself all your life,
Your eyelids have been the same as closed most of the time,
25   What you have done returns already in mockeries,
(Your thrift, knowledge, prayers, if they do not return in mock-
eries, what is their return?)

The mockeries are not you,
Underneath them and within them I see you lurk,
I pursue you where none else has pursued you,
Silence, the desk, the flippant expression, the night, the accustom'd
routine, if these conceal you from others or from yourself,
30   they do not conceal you from me,
The shaved face, the unsteady eye, the impure complexion, if these
balk others they do not balk me,
The pert apparel, the deform'd attitude, drunkenness, greed, pre-
mature death, all these I part aside.

There is no endowment in man or woman that is not tallied in
you,
There is no virtue, no beauty in man or woman, but as good is in
you,
35   No pluck, no endurance in others, but as good is in you,
No pleasure waiting for others, but an equal pleasure waits for you.

As for me, I give nothing to any one except I give the like care-
fully to you,

---

19. gold-color'd light] Note that WW endowed the head of the "average" man
with its nimbus also in "Crossing Brooklyn Ferry," line 116.
44. hopples] Hobbles or fetters.
45. promulges] Publishes, sets forth. Cf. "promulgates," a more formal word,
which has recently been preferred.

I sing the songs of the glory of none, not God, sooner than I
     sing the songs of the glory of you.

Whoever you are! claim your own at any hazard!
These shows of the East and West are tame compared to you,   40
These immense meadows, these interminable rivers, you are
     immense and interminable as they,
These furies, elements, storms, motions of Nature, throes of appar-
     ent dissolution, you are he or she who is master or mistress
     over them,
Master or mistress in your own right over Nature, elements, pain,
     passion, dissolution.

The hopples fall from your ankles, you find an unfailing sufficiency,
Old or young, male or female, rude, low, rejected by the rest,
     whatever you are promulges itself,   45
Through birth, life, death, burial, the means are provided, nothing
     is scanted,
Through angers, losses, ambition, ignorance, ennui, what you are
     picks its way.

1856   *1881*

France,

The 18th Year of these States.

A great year and place,
A harsh discordant natal scream out-sounding, to touch the
     mother's heart closer than any yet.

I walk'd the shores of my Eastern sea,
Heard over the waves the little voice,
Saw the divine infant where she woke mournfully wailing, amid the
     roar of cannon, curses, shouts, crash of falling buildings,   5
Was not so sick from the blood in the gutters running, nor from
     the single corpses, nor those in heaps, nor those borne
     away in the tumbrils,

FRANCE] Unchanged in title since its first appearance in the 1860 edition, this
poem was appropriately included in a small group entitled "Songs of Insurrection" in
the editions of 1871 and 1876. WW is, of course, commemorating the year 1794 of
the French Revolution, the climactic year of the Revolutionary Tribunal. The text has
undergone but slight revision from its first MS reading (Barrett).

Was not so desperate at the battues of death—was not so shock'd
    at the repeated fusillades of the guns.

Pale, silent, stern, what could I say to that long-accrued retribu-
    tion?
Could I wish humanity different?
10   Could I wish the people made of wood and stone?
Or that there be no justice in destiny or time?

O Liberty! O mate for me!
Here too the blaze, the grape-shot and the axe, in reserve, to
    fetch them out in case of need,
Here too, though long represt, can never be destroy'd,
15   Here too could rise at last murdering and ecstatic,
Here too demanding full arrears of vengeance.

Hence I sign this salute over the sea,
And I do not deny that terrible red birth and baptism,
But remember the little voice that I heard wailing, and wait with
    perfect trust, no matter how long,
And from to-day sad and cogent I maintain the bequeath'd cause,
20   as for all lands,
And I send these words to Paris with my love,
And I guess some chansonniers there will understand them,
For I guess there is latent music yet in France, floods of it,
O I hear already the bustle of instruments, they will soon be
    drowning all that would interrupt them,
25   O I think the east wind brings a triumphal and free march,
It reaches hither, it swells me to joyful madness,
I will run transpose it in words, to justify it,
I will yet sing a song for you ma femme.

   1860   *1871*

Myself and Mine.

Myself and mine gymnastic ever,
To stand the cold or heat, to take good aim with a gun, to sail a
    boat, to manage horses, to beget superb children,

    7. battues] The beaten, the wantonly slaughtered, as of helpless crowds.
    22. chansonniers] Song writers.
    28. ma femme] Literally, my woman; here, Democracy, personified.
    MINE] In 1860 this poem was No. 10 of the "Leaves of Grass" group, and in
1867 it was No. 2 of another group so named. With the 1871, 1872, and 1876 edi-

To speak readily and clearly, to feel at home among common
    people,
And to hold our own in terrible positions on land and sea.

Not for an embroiderer,   5
(There will always be plenty of embroiderers, I welcome them also,)
But for the fibre of things and for inherent men and women.

Not to chisel ornaments,
But to chisel with free stroke the heads and limbs of plenteous
    supreme Gods, that the States may realize them walking
    and talking.

Let me have my own way,   10
Let others promulge the laws, I will make no account of the laws,
Let others praise eminent men and hold up peace, I hold up
    agitation and conflict,
I praise no eminent man, I rebuke to his face the one that was
    thought most worthy.

(Who are you? and what are you secretly guilty of all your life?
Will you turn aside all your life? will you grub and chatter all
    your life?   15
And who are you, blabbing by rote, years, pages, languages,
    reminiscences,
Unwitting to-day that you do not know how to speak properly a
    single word?)

Let others finish specimens, I never finish specimens,
I start them by exhaustless laws as Nature does, fresh and modern
    continually.

I give nothing as duties,   20
What others give as duties I give as living impulses,
(Shall I give the heart's action as a duty?)

Let others dispose of questions, I dispose of nothing, I arouse
    unanswerable questions,

tions it was included in the "Passage to India" supplement with its present title.
WW dropped the two original opening lines in 1867 for the present opening line, and
at the same time deleted—just before the present line 26—two lines confessing "the
evil I really am." In its announcement of personal intent it could well be one of the
"Inscriptions" poems.
    11. promulge] Promulgate. Cf. "To You," line 45, note.

Who are they I see and touch, and what about them?
What about these likes of myself that draw me so close by tender
25   directions and indirections?

I call to the world to distrust the accounts of my friends, but
          listen to my enemies, as I myself do,
I charge you forever reject those who would expound me, for I
          cannot expound myself,
I charge that there be no theory or school founded out of me,
I charge you to leave all free, as I have left all free.

30   After me, vista!
O I see life is not short, but immeasurably long,
I henceforth tread the world chaste, temperate, an early riser, a
          steady grower,
Every hour the semen of centuries, and still of centuries.

I must follow up these continual lessons of the air, water, earth,
35   I perceive I have no time to lose.

          1860   *1881*

Year of Meteors.

          (1859–60.)

Year of meteors! brooding year!
I would bind in words retrospective some of your deeds and signs,
I would sing your contest for the 19th Presidentiad,
I would sing how an old man, tall, with white hair, mounted the
          scaffold in Virginia,
5   (I was at hand, silent I stood with teeth shut close, I watch'd,
I stood very near you old man when cool and indifferent, but
          trembling with age and your unheal'd wounds you mounted
          the scaffold;)

METEORS] In 1865 and 1867 this poem was in *Drum-Taps;* in 1871, 1872, and
1876 in a "Leaves of Grass" group, from which it was transferred to the present
group in 1881. Printed in *N and F*, item 184, pp. 51–52, are two MS fragments (Berg
and Feinberg) in which WW describes two meteor showers: one, November 13,
1833, in a prose paragraph, and the other, November 12–13, 1858, in five trial lines
which may have been intended for his "Pictures" poem.
    3. 19th Presidentiad] The 1860 Lincoln-Douglas electoral contest.

I would sing in my copious song your census returns of the States,
The tables of population and products, I would sing of your ships
      and their cargoes,
The proud black ships of Manhattan arriving, some fill'd with
      immigrants, some from the isthmus with cargoes of gold,
Songs thereof would I sing, to all that hitherward comes would I
      welcome give,   10
And you would I sing, fair stripling! welcome to you from me,
      young prince of England!
(Remember you surging Manhattan's crowds as you pass'd with
      your cortege of nobles?
There in the crowds stood I, and singled you out with attachment;)
Nor forget I to sing of the wonder, the ship as she swam up my
      bay,
Well-shaped and stately the Great Eastern swam up my bay, she
      was 600 feet long,   15
Her moving swiftly surrounded by myriads of small craft I forget
      not to sing;
Nor the comet that came unannounced out of the north flaring in
      heaven,
Nor the strange huge meteor-procession dazzling and clear shoot-
      ing over our heads,
(A moment, a moment long it sail'd its balls of unearthly light
      over our heads,
Then departed, dropt in the night, and was gone;)   20
Of such, and fitful as they, I sing—with gleams from them would
      I gleam and patch these chants,
Your chants, O year all mottled with evil and good—year of
      forebodings!
Year of comets and meteors transient and strange—lo! even here
      one equally transient and strange!
As I flit through you hastily, soon to fall and be gone, what is this
      chant,
What am I myself but one of your meteors?   25

1865   *1881*

    4. old man] John Brown the abolitionist, hanged for treason, December 2, 1859
at Charles Town, Va.
    11. fair stripling] Edward, Prince of Wales, who visited New York City on
October 11, 1860. WW made a notebook entry on his visit (*LC* Whitman, No. 92).
See "Prince of Wales" in *Fragments*.
    15. Great Eastern] Famous British iron steamship, of later tragic history, which
reached New York City June 28, 1860 on her maiden Atlantic crossing.

With Antecedents.

1

With antecedents,
With my fathers and mothers and the accumulations of past
    ages,
With all which, had it not been, I would not now be here, as I
    am,
With Egypt, India, Phenicia, Greece and Rome,
5   With the Kelt, the Scandinavian, the Alb and the Saxon,
With antique maritime ventures, laws, artisanship, wars and jour-
    neys,
With the poet, the skald, the saga, the myth, and the oracle,
With the sale of slaves, with enthusiasts, with the troubadour, the
    crusader, and the monk,
With those old continents whence we have come to this new
    continent,
10 With the fading kingdoms and kings over there,
With the fading religions and priests,
With the small shores we look back to from our own large and
    present shores,
With countless years drawing themselves onward and arrived at
    these years,
You and me arrived—America arrived and making this year,
15 This year! sending itself ahead countless years to come.

2

O but it is not the years—it is I, it is You,
We touch all laws and tally all antecedents,
We are the skald, the oracle, the monk and the knight, we easily
    include them and more,
We stand amid time beginningless and endless, we stand amid evil
    and good,
20 All swings around us, there is as much darkness as light,

ANTECEDENTS] The first publication of this poem was in the New York *Saturday Press*, January 14, 1860, under the title, "You and Me and To-day." In the 1860 *LG* it is No. 7 of the "Chants Democratic," taking its present title from 1867 on. The MS

The very sun swings itself and its system of planets around us,
Its sun, and its again, all swing around us.

As for me, (torn, stormy, amid these vehement days,)
I have the idea of all, and am all and believe in all,
I believe materialism is true and spiritualism is true, I reject no part.   25

(Have I forgotten any part? any thing in the past?
Come to me whoever and whatever, till I give you recogni-
          tion.)

I respect Assyria, China, Teutonia, and the Hebrews,
I adopt each theory, myth, god, and demi-god,
I see that the old accounts, bibles, genealogies, are true, without
          exception,   30
I assert that all past days were what they must have been,
And that they could no-how have been better than they were,
And that to-day is what it must be, and that America is,
And that to-day and America could no-how be better than they
          are.

                          3
In the name of these States and in your and my name, the
          Past,   35
And in the name of these States and in your and my name, the
          Present time.

I know that the past was great and the future will be great,
And I know that both curiously conjoint in the present time,
(For the sake of him I typify, for the common average man's
          sake, your sake if you are he,)
And that where I am or you are this present day, there is the
          centre of all days, all races,   40
And there is the meaning to us of all that has ever come of races
          and days, or ever will come.

1860   *1881*

(Barrett-Va.) proposes two other titles: "Poemet," deleted for "Evolutions." The
parenthetical phrase of line 23, "(torn, stormy, even as I, amid these vehement
days,)" was added in 1867.
          5. the Alb] Man of Albion, i.e. England.

A Broadway Pageant.

1

Over the Western sea hither from Niphon come,
Courteous, the swart-cheek'd two-sworded envoys,
Leaning back in their open barouches, bare-headed, impassive,
Ride to-day through Manhattan.

5   Libertad! I do not know whether others behold what I behold,
In the procession along with the nobles of Niphon, the errand-
      bearers,
Bringing up the rear, hovering above, around, or in the ranks
      marching,
But I will sing you a song of what I behold Libertad.

When million-footed Manhattan unpent descends to her pavements,
When the thunder-cracking guns arouse me with the proud roar
10   I love,
When the round-mouth'd guns out of the smoke and smell I love
      spit their salutes,
When the fire-flashing guns have fully alerted me, and heaven-
      clouds canopy my city with a delicate thin haze,
When gorgeous the countless straight stems, the forests at the
      wharves, thicken with colors,
When every ship richly drest carries her flag at the peak,
15   When pennants trail and street-festoons hang from the windows,

PAGEANT] This poem was first printed in the New York *Times*, June 27, 1860,
under the title "The Errand-Bearers," in commemoration of the parade down Broad-
way eleven days before of the Japanese embassy, which had come to America to work
on treaty arrangements between America and Japan. The title, and the Quaker phrase
in the subtitle—"16th 6th Month, Year 84 of The States"—were changed when the
poem appeared in the 1865 *Drum-Taps* as "A Broadway Pageant (Reception Japa-
nese Embassy, June 16, 1860)." The *Drum-Taps* text was but slightly changed
from the newspaper text, but a significant revision of the opening lines was made for
the 1871 and succeeding texts. Omitted was the fourth line phrase "Lesson-giving

When Broadway is entirely given up to foot-passengers and foot-
      standers, when the mass is densest,
When the façades of the houses are alive with people, when eyes
      gaze riveted tens of thousands at a time,
When the guests from the islands advance, when the pageant
      moves forward visible,
When the summons is made, when the answer that waited thou-
      sands of years answers,
I too arising, answering, descend to the pavements, merge with
      the crowd, and gaze with them.   20

      2

Superb-faced Manhattan!
Comrade Americanos! to us, then at last the Orient comes.

To us, my city,
Where our tall-topt marble and iron beauties range on opposite
      sides, to walk in the space between,
To-day our Antipodes comes.   25

The Originatress comes,
The nest of languages, the bequeather of poems, the race of eld,
Florid with blood, pensive, rapt with musings, hot with passion,
Sultry with perfume, with ample and flowing garments,
With sunburnt visage, with intense soul and glittering eyes,   30
The race of Brahma comes.

See my cantabile! these and more are flashing to us from the
      procession,
As it moves changing, a kaleidoscope divine it moves changing
      before us.

princes," and in general the emphasis was shifted from deference to the Orient to the
role of America as the mistress of a new world-democracy. In this sense "A Broad-
way Pageant" is a precursor of "Passage to India."
      1. Niphon] Commonly Nippon, Japanese name for Japan.
      5. Libertad] Spanish: liberty. In WW's usage it is also the personification of
freedom.
      27. race of eld] People of olden time.
      32. cantabile] Properly, an adjective meaning "flowing" or "songlike," but WW
uses it as a noun, meaning "melodious song."

For not the envoys nor the tann'd Japanee from his island only,
Lithe and silent the Hindoo appears, the Asiatic continent itself
35   appears, the past, the dead,
The murky night-morning of wonder and fable inscrutable,
The envelop'd mysteries, the old and unknown hive-bees,
The north, the sweltering south, eastern Assyria, the Hebrews, the
          ancient of ancients,
Vast desolated cities, the gliding present, all of these and more are
          in the pageant-procession.

40   Geography, the world, is in it,
The Great Sea, the brood of islands, Polynesia, the coast beyond,
The coast you henceforth are facing—you Libertad! from your
          Western golden shores,
The countries there with their populations, the millions en-masse
          are curiously here,
The swarming market-places, the temples with idols ranged along
          the sides or at the end, bonze, brahmin, and llama,
45   Mandarin, farmer, merchant, mechanic, and fisherman,
The singing-girl and the dancing-girl, the ecstatic persons, the
          secluded emperors,
Confucius himself, the great poets and heroes, the warriors, the
          castes, all,
Trooping up, crowding from all directions, from the Altay moun-
          tains,
From Thibet, from the four winding and far-flowing rivers of
          China,
From the southern peninsulas and the demi-continental islands,
50   from Malaysia,
These and whatever belongs to them palpable show forth to me,
          and are seiz'd by me,
And I am seiz'd by them, and friendlily held by them,
Till as here them all I chant, Libertad! for themselves and for
          you.

For I too raising my voice join the ranks of this pageant,
55   I am the chanter, I chant aloud over the pageant,
I chant the world on my Western sea,
I chant copious the islands beyond, thick as stars in the sky,

44. bonze, brahmin, and llama] Respectively Buddhist monk of Japan, member
of the priestly Hindu caste, and Tibetan priest (properly spelled "lama").

I chant the new empire grander than any before, as in a vision it
    comes to me,
I chant America the mistress, I chant a greater supremacy,
I chant projected a thousand blooming cities yet in time on those
    groups of sea-islands,   60
My sail-ships and steam-ships threading the archipelagoes,
My stars and stripes fluttering in the wind,
Commerce opening, the sleep of ages having done its work, races
    reborn, refresh'd,
Lives, works resumed—the object I know not—but the old, the
    Asiatic renew'd as it must be,
Commencing from this day surrounded by the world.   65

3

And you Libertad of the world!
You shall sit in the middle well-pois'd thousands and thousands of
    years,
As to-day from one side the nobles of Asia come to you,
As to-morrow from the other side the queen of England sends her
    eldest son to you.

The sign is reversing, the orb is enclosed,   70
The ring is circled, the journey is done,
The box-lid is but perceptibly open'd, nevertheless the perfume
    pours copiously out of the whole box.

Young Libertad! with the venerable Asia, the all-mother,
Be considerate with her now and ever hot Libertad, for you are all,
Bend your proud neck to the long-off mother now sending mes-
    sages over the archipelagoes to you,   75
Bend your proud neck low for once, young Libertad.

Were the children straying westward so long? so wide the tramping?
Were the precedent dim ages debouching westward from Paradise
    so long?
Were the centuries steadily footing it that way, all the while
    unknown, for you, for reasons?

   69. eldest son] Edward, Prince of Wales, later Edward VII, whose 1860 visit to
America is referred to in "Year of Meteors."

They are justified, they are accomplish'd, they shall now be turn'd
80   the other way also, to travel toward you thence,
They shall now also march obediently eastward for your sake
          Libertad.

1860   1881

Sea-Drift.

Out of the Cradle Endlessly Rocking.

Out of the cradle endlessly rocking,
Out of the mocking-bird's throat, the musical shuttle,
Out of the Ninth-month midnight,
Over the sterile sands and the fields beyond, where the child
          leaving his bed wander'd alone, bareheaded, barefoot,
5   Down from the shower'd halo,

SEA-DRIFT] This group of eleven poems, compiled in LG 1881, included the seven poems of the "Sea-Shore Memories" cluster in the 1871 Passage to India, two new poems, and two poems transferred from the 1876 Two Rivulets. The new group is one of the poet's most consonant arrangements, held together by the impression, deep in childhood memory, of the sea and the beach, an influence which is at the heart of his acceptance of the tragic in life.

ROCKING] First published (MS Berg) under the title "A Child's Reminiscence" in the Christmas number (December 24, 1859) of the New York Saturday Press, whose editor, Henry Clapp, was WW's friend and companion in the Pfaff Restaurant coterie. The long proem, called "Pre-Verse," syntactically a single sentence, was followed by "Reminiscence," in thirty-five numbered stanzas. With concurrent revisions the poem appeared prominently in all LG or Passage to India editions; the present authorized text appeared in LG 1881. The revisions of 1860 merit close study, while those of 1867 greatly improved the phrasing. In LG 1860 and 1867 the title was "A Word Out of the Sea." Under its present title it headed the "Sea-Shore Memories" group in Passage to India in 1871 and until that supplement was consolidated with LG in 1881.

WW himself probably wrote the editorial notice of the poem in the same issue of the Saturday Press: "Our readers may, if they choose, consider as our Christmas or New Year's present to them, the curious warble, by Walt Whitman, of 'A Child's

Up from the mystic play of shadows twining and twisting as if
    they were alive,
Out from the patches of briers and blackberries,
From the memories of the bird that chanted to me,
From your memories sad brother, from the fitful risings and fall-
    ings I heard,
From under that yellow half-moon late-risen and swollen as if with
    tears,   10
From those beginning notes of yearning and love there in the
    mist,
From the thousand responses of my heart never to cease,
From the myriad thence-arous'd words,
From the word stronger and more delicious than any,
From such as now they start the scene revisiting,   15
As a flock, twittering, rising, or overhead passing,
Borne hither, ere all eludes me, hurriedly,
A man, yet by these tears a little boy again,
Throwing myself on the sand, confronting the waves,
I, chanter of pains and joys, uniter of here and hereafter,   20
Taking all hints to use them, but swiftly leaping beyond them,
A reminiscence sing.

Once Paumanok,
When the lilac-scent was in the air and Fifth-month grass was
    growing,

Reminiscence,' on our First Page. Like the 'Leaves of Grass,' the purport of this wild
and plaintive song, well-enveloped, and eluding definition, is positive and unquestion-
able, like the effect of music.

    The piece will bear reading many times—perhaps, indeed only comes forth, as
from recesses, by many repetitions.

    In "All About a Mocking Bird" (*Saturday Press*, January 7, 1860), WW
defended the poem against a charge in the Cincinnati *Daily Commercial* (December
28, 1859) that the poem is meaningless. The poem is profoundly autobiographical in
that its theme goes to the very center of the poet's experience—how he became a poet
and how his songs awoke. Whether or not it is based on a personal loss is not known,
but surely its interpretation of love and death relates it to the "Calamus" themes.
Helen Price recalled that WW had read it to her family as early as 1858. (See
Bucke, 29.) Swinburne called it ". . . the most lovely and wonderful thing I have
read for years and years . . . there is such beautiful skill and subtle power in every
word of it." An excellent article is Leo Spitzer's " 'Explication de Texte' Applied to
Walt Whitman's 'Out of the Cradle Endlessly Rocking,' " (*ELH*, XVI, 229–249).

    3. Ninth-month] The Quaker designation for September may here suggest the
human cycle of fertility and birth, in contrast with "sterile sands" in the next
line.

    23. Paumanok] WW was especially fond of this Indian name for Long Island as
closely associated with his childhood memories.

25 Up this seashore in some briers,
  Two feather'd guests from Alabama, two together,
  And their nest, and four light-green eggs spotted with brown,
  And every day the he-bird to and fro near at hand,
  And every day the she-bird crouch'd on her nest, silent, with
          bright eyes,
  And every day I, a curious boy, never too close, never disturbing
30   them,
  Cautiously peering, absorbing, translating.

  Shine! shine! shine!
  Pour down your warmth, great sun!
  While we bask, we two together.

35 *Two together!*
  Winds blow south, or winds blow north,
  Day come white, or night come black,
  Home, or rivers and mountains from home,
  Singing all time, minding no time,
40 *While we two keep together.*

  Till of a sudden,
  May-be kill'd, unknown to her mate,
  One forenoon the she-bird crouch'd not on the nest,
  Nor return'd that afternoon, nor the next,
45 Nor ever appear'd again.

  And thenceforward all summer in the sound of the sea,
  And at night under the full of the moon in calmer weather,
  Over the hoarse surging of the sea,
  Or flitting from brier to brier by day,
50 I saw, I heard at intervals the remaining one, the he-bird,
  The solitary guest from Alabama.

  Blow! blow! blow!
  Blow up sea-winds along Paumanok's shore;
  I wait and I wait till you blow my mate to me.

55 Yes, when the stars glisten'd,
  All night long on the prong of a moss-scallop'd stake,

  32. shine] Comparison with earlier versions shows WW's success in improving
the lyrics (printed in italics) which resemble birdsong; especially the characteristic

Down almost amid the slapping waves,
Sat the lone singer wonderful causing tears.

He call'd on his mate,
He pour'd forth the meanings which I of all men know. 60

Yes my brother I know,
The rest might not, but I have treasur'd every note,
For more than once dimly down to the beach gliding,
Silent, avoiding the moonbeams, blending myself with the shadows,
Recalling now the obscure shapes, the echoes, the sounds and
  sights after their sorts, 65
The white arms out in the breakers tirelessly tossing,
I, with bare feet, a child, the wind wafting my hair,
Listen'd long and long.

Listen'd to keep, to sing, now translating the notes,
Following you my brother. 70

Soothe! soothe! soothe!
Close on its wave soothes the wave behind,
And again another behind embracing and lapping, every one close,
But my love soothes not me, not me.

Low hangs the moon, it rose late, 75
It is lagging—O I think it is heavy with love, with love.

O madly the sea pushes upon the land,
With love, with love.

O night! do I not see my love fluttering out among the breakers?
What is that little black thing I see there in the white? 80

Loud! loud! loud!
Loud I call to you, my love!
High and clear I shoot my voice over the waves,
Surely you must know who is here, is here,
You must know who I am, my love.

85

reiteration of phrase, the varied vocalic modulation of the cadences, and the staccato
"twittering" accentuation (lines 80, 91–92, 110, for example).

Low-hanging moon!
What is that dusky spot in your brown yellow?
O it is the shape, the shape of my mate!
O moon do not keep her from me any longer.

90 Land! land! O land!
Whichever way I turn, O I think you could give me my mate
        back again if you only would,
For I am almost sure I see her dimly whichever way I look.

O rising stars!
Perhaps the one I want so much will rise, will rise with some
        of you.

95 O throat! O trembling throat!
Sound clearer through the atmosphere!
Pierce the woods, the earth,
Somewhere listening to catch you must be the one I want.

Shake out carols!
100 Solitary here, the night's carols!
Carols of lonesome love! death's carols!
Carols under that lagging, yellow, waning moon!
O under that moon where she droops almost down into the sea!
O reckless despairing carols.

105 But soft! sink low!
Soft! let me just murmur,
And do you wait a moment you husky-nois'd sea,
For somewhere I believe I heard my mate responding to me,
So faint, I must be still, be still to listen,
But not altogether still, for then she might not come immediately
110   to me.

Hither my love!
Here I am! here!
With this just-sustain'd note I announce myself to you,
This gentle call is for you my love, for you.

115 Do not be decoy'd elsewhere,
That is the whistle of the wind, it is not my voice,

130. aria] See Robert D. Faner's *Walt Whitman and Opera*, 1951, especially pp.

That is the fluttering, the fluttering of the spray,
Those are the shadows of leaves.

O darkness! O in vain!
O I am very sick and sorrowful.   120

O brown halo in the sky near the moon, drooping upon the sea!
O troubled reflection in the sea!
O throat! O throbbing heart!
And I singing uselessly, uselessly all the night.

O past! O happy life! O songs of joy!   125
In the air, in the woods, over fields,
Loved! loved! loved! loved! loved!
But my mate no more, no more with me!
We two together no more.

The aria sinking,   130
All else continuing, the stars shining,
The winds blowing, the notes of the bird continuous echoing,
With angry moans the fierce old mother incessantly moaning,
On the sands of Paumanok's shore gray and rustling,
The yellow half-moon enlarged, sagging down, drooping, the face
     of the sea almost touching,   135
The boy ecstatic, with his bare feet the waves, with his hair the
     atmosphere dallying,
The love in the heart long pent, now loose, now at last tumultu-
     ously bursting,
The aria's meaning, the ears, the soul, swiftly depositing,
The strange tears down the cheeks coursing,
The colloquy there, the trio, each uttering,   140
The undertone, the savage old mother incessantly crying,
To the boy's soul's questions sullenly timing, some drown'd secret
     hissing,
To the outsetting bard.

Demon or bird! (said the boy's soul,)
Is it indeed toward your mate you sing? or is it really to me?   145
For I, that was a child, my tongue's use sleeping, now I have
     heard you,

173–177, for an analysis of WW's use of this opera form.

Now in a moment I know what I am for, I awake,
And already a thousand singers, a thousand songs, clearer, louder
      and more sorrowful than yours,
A thousand warbling echoes have started to life within me, never
      to die.

150   O you singer solitary, singing by yourself, projecting me,
O solitary me listening, never more shall I cease perpetuating
      you,
Never more shall I escape, never more the reverberations,
Never more the cries of unsatisfied love be absent from me,
Never again leave me to be the peaceful child I was before what
      there in the night,
155   By the sea under the yellow and sagging moon,
The messenger there arous'd, the fire, the sweet hell within,
The unknown want, the destiny of me.

O give me the clew! (it lurks in the night here somewhere,)
O if I am to have so much, let me have more!

160   A word then, (for I will conquer it,)
The word final, superior to all,
Subtle, sent up—what is it?—I listen;
Are you whispering it, and have been all the time, you sea-
      waves?
Is that it from your liquid rims and wet sands?

165   Whereto answering, the sea,
Delaying not, hurrying not,
Whisper'd me through the night, and very plainly before day-
      break,
Lisp'd to me the low and delicious word death,
And again death, death, death, death,

LIFE] Probably composed in 1859; first published as "Bardic Symbols" in the
Atlantic Monthly, April, 1860; in LG 1860 it appeared as No. 1 of the "Leaves of
Grass" with the restoration of lines 59–60, whose realism had caused editor James
Russell Lowell to request their omission from the magazine, in which WW was so
eager to appear that he uncharacteristically acceded. (See Corr, I, 47–48.) In LG
1867, the title restated the first line, "Elemental Drifts," later dropped. It was so
called in the cluster, "Sea-Shore Memories," of *Passage to India*, 1871 to 1876, and
was given its present title and position in 1881. The MSS (Houghton and Barrett)

Hissing melodious, neither like the bird nor like my arous'd child's
    heart, 170
But edging near as privately for me rustling at my feet,
Creeping thence steadily up to my ears and laving me softly all
    over,
Death, death, death, death, death.

Which I do not forget,
But fuse the song of my dusky demon and brother,
That he sang to me in the moonlight on Paumanok's gray beach, 175
With the thousand responsive songs at random,
My own songs awaked from that hour,
And with them the key, the word up from the waves,
The word of the sweetest song and all songs,
That strong and delicious word which, creeping to my feet, 180
(Or like some old crone rocking the cradle, swathed in sweet
    garments, bending aside,)
The sea whisper'd me.

1859 *1881*

As I Ebb'd with the Ocean of Life.

1

As I ebb'd with the ocean of life,
As I wended the shores I know,
As I walk'd where the ripples continually wash you Paumanok,
Where they rustle up hoarse and sibilant,
Where the fierce old mother endlessly cries for her castaways, 5
I musing late in the autumn day, gazing off southward,
Held by this electric self out of the pride of which I utter poems,
Was seiz'd by the spirit that trails in the lines underfoot,

and printed variants show persistent, though minor, revision.

    The poem is remarkable in its poignant admission of self-doubt and frustration; in the period of its composition WW, having left his editorial post on the Brooklyn *Times*, was unemployed and insecure. Yet the mood of this poem is not that of personal discontent so much as recognition of the "tears of things" in the human condition. It is not the poet alone who identifies himself with the sands and drift, who seeks the consolation of the father, and who at the end is thrown helpless on the shore like a drowned corpse; it is humankind. Other poems—for example, "On the Beach at Night"—make their answer.

The rim, the sediment that stands for all the water and all the
    land of the globe.

Fascinated, my eyes reverting from the south, dropt, to follow
    those slender windrows,
Chaff, straw, splinters of wood, weeds, and the sea-gluten,
Scum, scales from shining rocks, leaves of salt-lettuce, left by the
    tide,
Miles walking, the sound of breaking waves the other side of me,
Paumanok there and then as I thought the old thought of likenesses,
These you presented to me you fish-shaped island,
As I wended the shores I know,
As I walk'd with that electric self seeking types.

2

As I wend to the shores I know not,
As I list to the dirge, the voices of men and women wreck'd,
As I inhale the impalpable breezes that set in upon me,
As the ocean so mysterious rolls toward me closer and closer,
I too but signify at the utmost a little wash'd-up drift,
A few sands and dead leaves to gather,
Gather, and merge myself as part of the sands and drift.

O baffled, balk'd, bent to the very earth,
Oppress'd with myself that I have dared to open my mouth,
Aware now that amid all that blab whose echoes recoil upon me I
    have not once had the least idea who or what I am,
But that before all my arrogant poems the real Me stands yet
    untouch'd, untold, altogether unreach'd,
Withdrawn far, mocking me with mock-congratulatory signs and
    bows,
With peals of distant ironical laughter at every word I have written,
Pointing in silence to these songs, and then to the sand beneath.

I perceive I have not really understood any thing, not a single
    object, and that no man ever can,
Nature here in sight of the sea taking advantage of me to dart
    upon me and sting me,
Because I have dared to open my mouth to sing at all.

14. likenesses] The correspondence, in transcendental terms, between the
"wash'd-up drift" and the poet himself.

3

You oceans both, I close with you,   35
We murmur alike reproachfully rolling sands and drift, knowing
    not why,
These little shreds indeed standing for you and me and all.

You friable shore with trails of debris,
You fish-shaped island, I take what is underfoot,
What is yours is mine my father.   40

I too Paumanok,
I too have bubbled up, floated the measureless float, and been
    wash'd on your shores,
I too am but a trail of drift and debris,
I too leave little wrecks upon you, you fish-shaped island.

I throw myself upon your breast my father,   45
I cling to you so that you cannot unloose me,
I hold you so firm till you answer me something.

Kiss me my father,
Touch me with your lips as I touch those I love,
Breathe to me while I hold you close the secret of the murmuring
    I envy.   50

4

Ebb, ocean of life, (the flow will return,)
Cease not your moaning you fierce old mother,
Endlessly cry for your castaways, but fear not, deny not me,
Rustle not up so hoarse and angry against my feet as I touch you
    or gather from you.

I mean tenderly by you and all,   55
I gather for myself and for this phantom looking down where we
    lead, and following me and mine.

    27. all that blab] Cf. the "barbaric yawp" of line 1333 of "Song of Myself."
    45. my father] Paumanok, the island, his natal land, is here the father symbol as
the ocean is the "fierce old mother."

Me and mine, loose windrows, little corpses,
Froth, snowy white, and bubbles,
(See, from my dead lips the ooze exuding at last,
60   See, the prismatic colors glistening and rolling,)
Tufts of straw, sands, fragments,
Buoy'd hither from many moods, one contradicting another,
From the storm, the long calm, the darkness, the swell,
Musing, pondering, a breath, a briny tear, a dab of liquid or soil,
65   Up just as much out of fathomless workings fermented and thrown,
A limp blossom or two, torn, just as much over waves floating,
       drifted at random,
Just as much for us that sobbing dirge of Nature,
Just as much whence we come that blare of the cloud-trumpets,
We, capricious, brought hither we know not whence, spread out
       before you,
70   You up there walking or sitting,
Whoever you are, we too lie in drifts at your feet.

     1860   *1881*

Tears.

Tears! tears! tears!
In the night, in solitude, tears,
On the white shore dripping, dripping, suck'd in by the sand,
Tears, not a star shining, all dark and desolate,
5   Moist tears from the eyes of a muffled head;
O who is that ghost? that form in the dark, with tears?
What shapeless lump is that, bent, crouch'd there on the sand?
Streaming tears, sobbing tears, throes, choked with wild cries;
O storm, embodied, rising, careering with swift steps along the
       beach!

59. (See] This and the following line were excised from the *Atlantic Monthly* copy.

     TEARS] This was one of seven new poems added to LG 1867, where it appeared as No. 2 of a "Leaves of Grass" cluster. In 1871 and 1876 it was transferred to the new "Sea-Shore Memories" group of *Passage to India*. In "The Fundamental Metrical Principle in Whitman's Poetry," *AL*, X, 437–459, Sculley Bradley has analyzed the remarkable accentual symmetry of this poem.

     MAN-OF-WAR-BIRD] This poem first appeared in the London *Athenaeum*, April 1, 1876; it was an intercalation in some copies of LG 1876, again appeared in the

O wild and dismal night storm, with wind—O belching and des-
    perate!   10
O shade so sedate and decorous by day, with calm countenance
    and regulated pace,
But away at night as you fly, none looking—O then the unloosen'd
    ocean,
Of tears! tears! tears!
    1867   *1871*

To the Man-of-War-Bird.

Thou who hast slept all night upon the storm,
Waking renew'd on thy prodigious pinions,
(Burst the wild storm? above it thou ascended'st,
And rested on the sky, thy slave that cradled thee,)
Now a blue point, far, far in heaven floating,   5
As to the light emerging here on deck I watch thee,
(Myself a speck, a point on the world's floating vast.)

Far, far at sea,
After the night's fierce drifts have strewn the shore with wrecks,
With re-appearing day as now so happy and serene,   10
The rosy and elastic dawn, the flashing sun,
The limpid spread of air cerulean,
Thou also re-appearest.

Thou born to match the gale, (thou art all wings,)
To cope with heaven and earth and sea and hurricane,   15
Thou ship of air that never furl'st thy sails,
Days, even weeks untired and onward, through spaces, realms
    gyrating,
At dusk that look'st on Senegal, at morn America,
That sport'st amid the lightning-flash and thunder-cloud,

Philadelphia *Progress* of November 16, 1878 with a headnote passage from Jules
Michelet's *The Bird* (English translation, 1869), and was finally placed among the
"Sea-Drift" group in 1881. The poem is practically a paraphrase of the English
translation of the French original, although WW acknowledges indebtedness only in
the *Progress* publication. Adeline Knapp was the first to note the parallel in the
Critic, XLIV, 467–468. WW had read Michelet in English as early as April, 1847,
and was much influenced by his work, particularly *The People* (English translation,
1845). The whole relationship is reviewed by Gay W. Allen in "Walt Whitman and
Jules Michelet," *EA*, I, 230–237.
    18. Senegal] Territory in French West Africa. Now a republic.

20   In them, in thy experiences, had'st thou my soul,
      What joys! what joys were thine!
       1876   *1881*

Aboard at a Ship's Helm.

Aboard at a ship's helm,
A young steersman steering with care.

Through fog on a sea-coast dolefully ringing,
An ocean-bell—O a warning bell, rock'd by the waves.

5   O you give good notice indeed, you bell by the sea-reefs ringing,
     Ringing, ringing, to warn the ship from its wreck-place.

For as on the alert O steersman, you mind the loud admonition,
The bows turn, the freighted ship tacking speeds away under her
            gray sails,
The beautiful and noble ship with all her precious wealth speeds
            away gayly and safe.

10   But O the ship, the immortal ship! O ship aboard the ship!
      Ship of the body, ship of the soul, voyaging, voyaging, voyaging.
       1867   *1881*

On the Beach at Night.

On the beach at night,
Stands a child with her father,
Watching the east, the autumn sky.

Up through the darkness,
5   While ravening clouds, the burial clouds, in black masses spreading,
     Lower sullen and fast athwart and down the sky,

20–21.] Cf. final stanza of Shelley's "To a Skylark" for reversal of the sentiment of
these lines.
    HELM] No. 3 of a "Leaves of Grass" group in the 1867 edition, this poem took its
present title in the "Sea-Shore Memories" group of *Passage to India* (1871). In 1881
it was finally consolidated with *LG* in the "Sea-Drift" cluster.
    NIGHT] This poem, under its present title, first appeared in the "Sea-Shore
Memories" of *Passage to India* (1871), and was transferred to the "Sea-Drift" group

Amid a transparent clear belt of ether yet left in the east,
Ascends large and calm the lord-star Jupiter,
And nigh at hand, only a very little above,
Swim the delicate sisters the Pleiades.   10

From the beach the child holding the hand of her father,
Those burial-clouds that lower victorious soon to devour all,
Watching, silently weeps.

Weep not, child,
Weep not, my darling,   15
With these kisses let me remove your tears,
The ravening clouds shall not long be victorious,
They shall not long possess the sky, they devour the stars only in
        apparition,
Jupiter shall emerge, be patient, watch again another night, the
        Pleiades shall emerge,
They are immortal, all those stars both silvery and golden shall
        shine out again,   20
The great stars and the little ones shall shine out again, they
        endure,
The vast immortal suns and the long-enduring pensive moons
        shall again shine.

Then dearest child mournest thou only for Jupiter?
Considerest thou alone the burial of the stars?

Something there is,   25
 (With my lips soothing thee, adding I whisper,
I give thee the first suggestion, the problem and indirection,)
Something there is more immortal even than the stars,
 (Many the burials, many the days and nights, passing away,)
Something that shall endure longer even than lustrous Jupiter,   30
Longer than sun or any revolving satellite,
Or the radiant sisters the Pleiades.

1871   *1881*

in 1881. Cf. Wordsworth's 1807 sonnet, "It is a beauteous evening, calm and free" for
an interesting analogy in sensibility.
    10. delicate sisters the Pleiades] "Sisters" read "brothers" in 1871 and 1876,
being corrected in 1881 to conform with the Grecian myth about the Pleiades, the
seven daughters of Atlas who were placed by Zeus among the stars; hence the name
given to a group of stars in the constellation Taurus.
    32. sisters] Read "brothers" in 1871 and 1876. See note above.

The World below the Brine.

The world below the brine,
Forests at the bottom of the sea, the branches and leaves,
Sea-lettuce, vast lichens, strange flowers and seeds, the thick tangle,
    openings, and pink turf,
Different colors, pale gray and green, purple, white, and gold, the
    play of light through the water,
Dumb swimmers there among the rocks, coral, gluten, grass, rushes,
5   and the aliment of the swimmers,
Sluggish existences grazing there suspended, or slowly crawling
    close to the bottom,
The sperm-whale at the surface blowing air and spray, or disporting
    with his flukes,
The leaden-eyed shark, the walrus, the turtle, the hairy sea-leopard,
    and the sting-ray,
Passions there, wars, pursuits, tribes, sight in those ocean-depths,
    breathing that thick-breathing air, as so many do,
The change thence to the sight here, and to the subtle air breathed
10   by beings like us who walk this sphere,
The change onward from ours to that of beings who walk other
    spheres.

    1860   *1871*

On the Beach at Night Alone.

On the beach at night alone,
As the old mother sways her to and fro singing her husky song,
As I watch the bright stars shining, I think a thought of the clef
    of the universes and of the future.

BRINE] No. 16 of the "Leaves of Grass" group of the 1860 edition, and No. 4 of
a group of the same name in 1867, this poem received its present title in 1871 when it
was placed in the "Sea-Shore Memories" group of *Passage to India*. Its MS (Barrett)
is simply headed "Leaf.—" In 1881 it was transferred to the present position.

ALONE] As the "Clef Poem" ("clef" here used in the sense of "clue" or "key") of
LG 1856, and No. 12 of the "Leaves of Grass" group of LG 1860, this poem was
more than twice the length of its present version, and the "thought of the clef of
the universes" is presented as an extended, candidly personal reflection. In 1867, as
No. 1 of a "Leaves of Grass" cluster, the poem was radically revised to its present
form, and in 1871 it took its present title as one of the "Sea-Shore Memories" of

A vast similitude interlocks all,
All spheres, grown, ungrown, small, large, suns, moons, planets, 5
All distances of place however wide,
All distances of time, all inanimate forms,
All souls, all living bodies though they be ever so different, or in
      different worlds,
All gaseous, watery, vegetable, mineral processes, the fishes, the
      brutes,
All nations, colors, barbarisms, civilizations, languages, 10
All identities that have existed or may exist on this globe, or any
      globe,
All lives and deaths, all of the past, present, future,
This vast similitude spans them, and always has spann'd,
And shall forever span them and compactly hold and enclose them.

   1856   *1881*

Song for All Seas, All Ships.

1

To-day a rude brief recitative,
Of ships sailing the seas, each with its special flag or ship-signal,
Of unnamed heroes in the ships—of waves spreading and spread-
      ing far as the eye can reach,
Of dashing spray, and the winds piping and blowing,
And out of these a chant for the sailors of all nations, 5
Fitful, like a surge.

Of sea-captains young or old, and the mates, and of all intrepid
      sailors,

Passage to India. In LG 1881 it was transferred to the "Sea-Drift" group.
   4. similitude] This concept is Hegelian, similar to Emerson's transcendental
view that the great macrocosm contains all microcosms—perhaps is the sum of them.
See note, lines 464–476, "Song of Myself," for Hegelian influence on WW.
   SHIPS] This poem, first printed in the New York *Daily Graphic*, April 4, 1873,
under the title "Sea Captains, Young or Old," was written in commemoration of two
recent marine disasters: the British steamer *Northfleet* was sunk January 22, 1873 in
a collision off Dungeness with a loss of 300; and the White Star steamer *Atlantic* was
wrecked off Nova Scotia, April 1, 1873, with a loss of 547. Under its present title the
poem appeared as one of the four "Centennial Songs" of the 1876 *Two Rivulets*, and
finally in the "Sea-Drift" group of LG 1881.

Of the few, very choice, taciturn, whom fate can never surprise
      nor death dismay,
Pick'd sparingly without noise by thee old ocean, chosen by thee,
Thou sea that pickest and cullest the race in time, and unitest
10   nations,
Suckled by thee, old husky nurse, embodying thee,
Indomitable, untamed as thee.

(Ever the heroes on water or on land, by ones or twos appearing,
Ever the stock preserv'd and never lost, though rare, enough for
      seed preserv'd.)

       2

15 Flaunt out O sea your separate flags of nations!
Flaunt out visible as ever the various ship-signals!
But do you reserve especially for yourself and for the soul of man
      one flag above all the rest,
A spiritual woven signal for all nations, emblem of man elate above
      death,
Token of all brave captains and all intrepid sailors and mates,
20   And all that went down doing their duty,
Reminiscent of them, twined from all intrepid captains young or old,
A pennant universal, subtly waving all time, o'er all brave sailors,
All seas, all ships.

    1873   *1881*

Patroling Barnegat.

Wild, wild the storm, and the sea high running,
Steady the roar of the gale, with incessant undertone muttering,
Shouts of demoniac laughter fitfully piercing and pealing,
Waves, air, midnight, their savagest trinity lashing,
5 Out in the shadows there milk-white combs careering,
On beachy slush and sand spirts of snow fierce slanting,

    BARNEGAT] This poem was first printed in *The American*, June, 1880, reprinted
in *Harper's Monthly*, April, 1881, and finally in its present position in LG 1881. The
MS drafts (Feinberg) indicate much reworking. Barnegat Bay, a large salt inlet
about thirty miles long, is off the coast of Ocean County, N. J. where WW some-
times visited during his Camden days.

Where through the murk the easterly death-wind breasting,
Through cutting swirl and spray watchful and firm advancing,
(That in the distance! is that a wreck? is the red signal flaring?)
Slush and sand of the beach tireless till daylight wending,   10
Steadily, slowly, through hoarse roar never remitting,
Along the midnight edge by those milk-white combs careering,
A group of dim, weird forms, struggling, the night confronting,
That savage trinity warily watching.

1880   1881

After the Sea-Ship.

After the sea-ship, after the whistling winds,
After the white-gray sails taut to their spars and ropes,
Below, a myriad myriad waves hastening, lifting up their necks,
Tending in ceaseless flow toward the track of the ship,
Waves of the ocean bubbling and gurgling, blithely prying,   5
Waves, undulating waves, liquid, uneven, emulous waves,
Toward that whirling current, laughing and buoyant, with curves,
Where the great vessel sailing and tacking displaced the surface,
Larger and smaller waves in the spread of the ocean yearnfully
     flowing,
The wake of the sea-ship after she passes, flashing and frolicsome
     under the sun,   10
A motley procession with many a fleck of foam and many fragments,
Following the stately and rapid ship, in the wake following.

1874   1881

SEA-SHIP] This poem was first published in the Christmas number of the New York *Daily Graphic*, December, 1874, under the title, "In the Wake Following." The MS (Mills College) indicates many variants and has still another title, "Waves in the Vessel's Wake." The poem took its present title in the 1876 *Two Rivulets*, and in LG 1881 became one of the "Sea-Drift" group.

By the Roadside.

A Boston Ballad.

(1854.)

To get betimes in Boston town I rose this morning early,
Here's a good place at the corner, I must stand and see the show.

Clear the way there Jonathan!
Way for the President's marshal—way for the government cannon!
Way for the Federal foot and dragoons, (and the apparitions
5   copiously tumbling.)

I love to look on the Stars and Stripes, I hope the fifes will play
       Yankee Doodle.
How bright shine the cutlasses of the foremost troops!
Every man holds his revolver, marching stiff through Boston town.

A fog follows, antiques of the same come limping,
Some appear wooden-legged, and some appear bandaged and
10   bloodless.

Why this is indeed a show—it has called the dead out of the
       earth!
The old graveyards of the hills have hurried to see!

ROADSIDE] The two opening poems of this group are from the first edition of 1855, and three were newly written for the final 1881 arrangement. Sixteen are poems from LG 1860, five from the 1865 *Drum-Taps*, one from LG 1867, and two from the 1871 *Passage to India*. The title "By the Roadside" suggests no especial assignment of theme whatever, unless the poet meant to evoke the notion of "wayside" topics as they strike the mind during one's passage through life. What we have here seems at first to be simply poetic miscellany: poems of rebellion, of stern admonition, of the questioning of life's meaning, of idealistic vision, of announcement, of descriptive intent. The group is truly a melange held together by the common bond of the poet's experience as roadside observer—passive, but alert and continually recording.

BALLAD] Untitled as one of the twelve poems of the first edition, this piece was

Phantoms! phantoms countless by flank and rear!
Cock'd hats of mothy mould—crutches made of mist!
Arms in slings—old men leaning on young men's shoulders.   15

What troubles you Yankee phantoms? what is all this chattering
 of bare gums?
Does the ague convulse your limbs? do you mistake your crutches
 for firelocks and level them?

If you blind your eyes with tears you will not see the President's
 marshal,
If you groan such groans you might balk the government cannon.

For shame old maniacs—bring down those toss'd arms, and let
 your white hair be,   20
Here gape your great grandsons, their wives gaze at them from
 the windows,
See how well dress'd, see how orderly they conduct themselves.

Worse and worse—can't you stand it? are you retreating?
Is this hour with the living too dead for you?

Retreat then—pell-mell!   25
To your graves—back—back to the hills old limpers!
I do not think you belong here anyhow.

But there is one thing that belongs here—shall I tell you what it
 is, gentlemen of Boston?

I will whisper it to the Mayor, he shall send a committee to
 England,
They shall get a grant from the Parliament, go with a cart to the
 royal vault,   30

called in 1856 "Poem of Apparitions in Boston, the 78th Year of These States"; in 1860, "A Boston Ballad, the 78th Year of These States"; in 1867, "To Get Betimes in Boston Town"; and in 1871 received its present title. It belonged to no group before 1881. One of the earliest of the 1855 poems, it was probably composed in June, 1854, during the indignant public excitement at the arrest and trial in Boston of the fugitive slave, Anthony Burns, shortly after the passage of the Kansas-Nebraska bill. It is melodramatic and bold, but its harsh satire is not native to Whitman's verse, and its rhythms are gawky, although curiously appropriate. See Stephen D. Malin, " 'A Boston Ballad' and the Boston Riot," *WWR*, IX (September, 1963) 51–57.

 3. Jonathan] Common name for the New England rustic or Yankee, first popularized by Royall Tyler's comedy, *The Contrast* (1787).

Dig out King George's coffin, unwrap him quick from the grave-
    clothes, box up his bones for a journey,
Find a swift Yankee clipper—here is freight for you, black-bellied
    clipper,
Up with your anchor—shake out your sails—steer straight toward
    Boston bay.

Now call for the President's marshal again, bring out the govern-
    ment cannon,
35   Fetch home the roarers from Congress, make another procession,
    guard it with foot and dragoons.

This centre-piece for them;
Look, all orderly citizens—look from the windows, women!

The committee open the box, set up the regal ribs, glue those that
    will not stay,
Clap the skull on top of the ribs, and clap a crown on top of the
    skull.

You have got your revenge, old buster—the crown is come to its
40   own, and more than its own.

Stick your hands in your pockets, Jonathan—you are a made
    man from this day,
You are mighty cute—and here is one of your bargains.

1854   *1871*

Europe,

The 72d and 73d Years of These States.

Suddenly out of its stale and drowsy lair, the lair of slaves,
Like lightning it le'pt forth half startled at itself,
Its feet upon the ashes and the rags, its hands tight to the throats
    of kings.

EUROPE] This poem is the earliest of the twelve of 1855, being first published in
the New York *Daily Tribune* of June 21, 1850 under the title "Resurgemus," with
different line arrangement and occasionally different phrasing. In LG 1855 it was, of
course, untitled; in 1856 it was "Poem of The Dead Young Men of Europe, the 72nd
and 73rd Years of These States;" and in 1860 it took its present title. It belonged to
no group until it was placed among the "Songs of Insurrection" in 1871 and 1876,

O hope and faith!
O aching close of exiled patriots' lives!
O many a sicken'd heart!
Turn back unto this day and make yourselves afresh.

And you, paid to defile the People—you liars, mark!
Not for numberless agonies, murders, lusts,
For court thieving in its manifold mean forms, worming from his
    simplicity the poor man's wages,
For many a promise sworn by royal lips and broken and laugh'd
    at in the breaking,

Then in their power not for all these did the blows strike revenge,
    or the heads of the nobles fall;
The People scorn'd the ferocity of kings.

But the sweetness of mercy brew'd bitter destruction, and the
    frighten'd monarchs come back,
Each comes in state with his train, hangman, priest, tax-gatherer,
Soldier, lawyer, lord, jailer, and sycophant.

Yet behind all lowering stealing, lo, a shape,
Vague as the night, draped interminably, head, front and form, in
    scarlet folds,
Whose face and eyes none may see,
Out of its robes only this, the red robes lifted by the arm,
One finger crook'd pointed high over the top, like the head of a
    snake appears.

Meanwhile corpses lie in new-made graves, bloody corpses of
    young men,
The rope of the gibbet hangs heavily, the bullets of princes are
    flying, the creatures of power laugh aloud,
And all these things bear fruits, and they are good.

and it was transferred to the present group in 1881. It was inspired, of course, by the
year of revolution, 1848, when Louis Philippe was dethroned in France and a second
Republic set up February 26; when Ferdinand I of Austria abdicated in favor of his
nephew Franz Josef; when freedom was proclaimed in Hungary under Kossuth; and
when there were also revolts in Ireland, Lombardy, Venice, Denmark, and Schleswig-
Holstein.

25 Those corpses of young men,
Those martyrs that hang from the gibbets, those hearts pierc'd by
    the gray lead,
Cold and motionless as they seem live elsewhere with unslaugh-
    ter'd vitality.

They live in other young men O kings!
They live in brothers again ready to defy you,
30 They were purified by death, they were taught and exalted.

Not a grave of the murder'd for freedom but grows seed for free-
    dom, in its turn to bear seed,
Which the winds carry afar and re-sow, and the rains and the
    snows nourish.

Not a disembodied spirit can the weapons of tyrants let loose,
But it stalks invisibly over the earth, whispering, counseling,
    cautioning.

35 Liberty, let others despair of you—I never despair of you.

Is the house shut? is the master away?
Nevertheless, be ready, be not weary of watching,
He will soon return, his messengers come anon.

1850   *1871*

A Hand-Mirror.

Hold it up sternly—see this it sends back, (who is it? is it
    you?)
Outside fair costume, within ashes and filth,
No more a flashing eye, no more a sonorous voice or springy
    step,
Now some slave's eye, voice, hands, step,
5 A drunkard's breath, unwholesome eater's face, venerealee's flesh,
Lungs rotting away piecemeal, stomach sour and cankerous,

HAND-MIRROR] This poem has remained unchanged and with the same title
since its first appearance in the 1860 edition. The MS (Barrett) shows that its
original title, deleted, was "Looking-Glass."
GODS] When this poem was first published in *Passage to India*, 1871, and again

Joints rheumatic, bowels clogged with abomination,
Blood circulating dark and poisonous streams,
Words babble, hearing and touch callous,
No brain, no heart left, no magnetism of sex;   10
Such from one look in this looking-glass ere you go hence,
Such a result so soon—and from such a beginning!

    1860   *1860*

Gods.

Lover divine and perfect Comrade,
Waiting content, invisible yet, but certain,
Be thou my God.

Thou, thou, the Ideal Man,
Fair, able, beautiful, content, and loving,   5
Complete in body and dilate in spirit,
Be thou my God.

O Death, (for Life has served its turn,)
Opener and usher to the heavenly mansion,
Be thou my God.   10

Aught, aught of mightiest, best I see, conceive, or know,
(To break the stagnant tie—thee, thee to free, O soul,)
Be thou my God.

All great ideas, the races' aspirations,
All heroisms, deeds of rapt enthusiasts,   15
Be ye my Gods.

Or Time and Space,
Or shape of Earth divine and wondrous,
Or some fair shape I viewing, worship,
Or lustrous orb of sun or star by night,   20
Be ye my Gods.

    1871   *1881*

in 1876, it opened with two lines, dropped in the present 1881 version:

        Thought of the Infinite—the All—
        Be thou my God.

Also dropped was an invocation to "thee, Old Cause" in the fifth stanza.

Germs.

Forms, qualities, lives, humanity, language, thoughts,
The ones known, and the ones unknown, the ones on the stars,
The stars themselves, some shaped, others unshaped,
Wonders as of those countries, the soil, trees, cities, inhabitants,
     whatever they may be,
Splendid suns, the moons and rings, the countless combinations
5   and effects,
Such-like, and as good as such-like, visible here or anywhere,
     stand provided for in a handful of space, which I extend
     my arm and half enclose with my hand,
That containing the start of each and all, the virtue, the germs
     of all.

    1860   *1871*

Thoughts.

Of ownership—as if one fit to own things could not at pleasure
     enter upon all, and incorporate them into himself or herself;
Of vista—suppose some sight in arriere through the formative
     chaos, presuming the growth, fulness, life, now attain'd on
     the journey,
(But I see the road continued, and the journey ever continued;)
Of what was once lacking on earth, and in due time has become
     supplied—and of what will yet be supplied,
Because all I see and know I believe to have its main purport in
5   what will yet be supplied.

    1860   *1881*

GERMS] In LG 1860 this poem was "Leaves of Grass" No. 19, and in 1867 it was
No. 2 of the "Leaves of Grass" in the annex, "Songs Before Parting." It was entitled
"Germs" in 1871 and finally placed in the cluster "By the Roadside" in 1881. The MS
(Barrett) has the title, "As of Origins." The "germs" are a strikingly concentrated
figure of the transcendental "each and all." Cf. Emerson's poem, "Each and All."

THOUGHTS] In LG 1860 and 1867, a six-line poem identified only as "No. 2" of
the cluster, "Thoughts." This consisted of the present lines 2 to 5, preceded by the
couplet:

               Of waters, forests, hills;
               Of the earth at large, whispering through medium
                  of me;

In LG 1871 the poem became seven lines, WW having superimposed the present

When I Heard the Learn'd Astronomer.

When I heard the learn'd astronomer,
When the proofs, the figures, were ranged in columns before me,
When I was shown the charts and diagrams, to add, divide, and
      measure them,
When I sitting heard the astronomer where he lectured with much
      applause in the lecture-room,
How soon unaccountable I became tired and sick,   5
Till rising and gliding out I wander'd off by myself,
In the mystical moist night-air, and from time to time,
Look'd up in perfect silence at the stars.

1865   *1865*

Perfections.

Only themselves understand themselves and the like of themselves,
As souls only understand souls.

1860   *1860*

O Me! O Life!

O me! O life! of the questions of these recurring,
Of the endless trains of the faithless, of cities fill'd with the
      foolish,
Of myself forever reproaching myself, (for who more foolish than
      I, and who more faithless?)

first line (previously the initial line of "Thoughts No. 4"); in LG 1881 WW dropped
the couplet (the initial lines of 1860, seen above) reducing the poem finally to the
present five lines. The original poems, "Thoughts," No. 2 and No. 4, will be found
in this volume under the heading, "Poems Excluded from LG."

ASTRONOMER] A *Drum-Taps* poem in 1865 and 1867, this much-anthologized
piece was in the "Songs of Parting" group of LG in 1871 and 1876 and was included
in the present group in 1881.

PERFECTIONS] This poem first appeared in the 1860 edition and was reprinted
without change in all succeeding editions.

LIFE!] This poem first appeared in the 1865–1866 *Sequel to Drum-Taps*, and
remained unchanged until in LG 1881 the word "will" in the last line was changed to
"may."

Of eyes that vainly crave the light, of the objects mean, of the
    struggle ever renew'd,
Of the poor results of all, of the plodding and sordid crowds I
5   see around me,
Of the empty and useless years of the rest, with the rest me inter-
    twined,
The question, O me! so sad, recurring—What good amid these,
    O me, O life?

    Answer.

That you are here—that life exists and identity,
That the powerful play goes on, and you may contribute a verse.

    1865–6   *1881*

To a President.

All you are doing and saying is to America dangled mirages,
You have not learn'd of Nature—of the politics of Nature you
    have not learn'd the great amplitude, rectitude, impartiality,
You have not seen that only such as they are for these States,
And that what is less than they must sooner or later lift off from
    these States.

    1860   *1860*

I Sit and Look Out.

I sit and look out upon all the sorrows of the world, and upon all
    oppression and shame,
I hear secret convulsive sobs from young men at anguish with
    themselves, remorseful after deeds done,
I see in low life the mother misused by her children, dying,
    neglected, gaunt, desperate,

PRESIDENT] This poem began as one of the "Messenger Leaves" of LG 1860, and
remained unchanged. The president addressed is no doubt James Buchanan, who at
this time represented to the poet a democratic failure, soon to be redeemed by
Abraham Lincoln.

    OUT] "Leaves of Grass" No. 17 in LG 1860; No. 5 in another group so named in
LG 1867. The poem's present title appeared in 1871, when it was also in a "Leaves of
Grass" group; it was transferred in 1881 to "By the Roadside." The MS (Barrett)
has the title "Leaf.—"

I see the wife misused by her husband, I see the treacherous
    seducer of young women,
I mark the ranklings of jealousy and unrequited love attempted to
    be hid, I see these sights on the earth,   5
I see the workings of battle, pestilence, tyranny, I see martyrs and
    prisoners,
I observe a famine at sea, I observe the sailors casting lots who
    shall be kill'd to preserve the lives of the rest,
I observe the slights and degradations cast by arrogant persons
    upon laborers, the poor, and upon negroes, and the like;
All these—all the meanness and agony without end I sitting look
    out upon,
See, hear, and am silent.   10

  1860   1871

To Rich Givers.

What you give me I cheerfully accept,
A little sustenance, a hut and garden, a little money, as I rendez-
    vous with my poems,
A traveler's lodging and breakfast as I journey through the States,
    —why should I be ashamed to own such gifts? why to
    advertise for them?
For I myself am not one who bestows nothing upon man and woman,
For I bestow upon any man or woman the entrance to all the gifts
    of the universe.   5

  1860   1881

The Dalliance of the Eagles.

Skirting the river road, (my forenoon walk, my rest,)
Skyward in air a sudden muffled sound, the dalliance of the eagles,

---

GIVERS] Under this title, one of the "Messenger Leaves" of LG 1860. The poem
was ungrouped in LG 1867, placed among the "Songs of Parting" in 1871 and 1876,
and in the present group in 1881.

EAGLES] This poem was first printed in *Cope's Tobacco Plant* for November,
1880, and is one of the new poems of LG 1881. The MSS (Barrett, LC Whitman,
Feinberg) show much reworking. According to Clara Barrus, WW, who had never
witnessed the mating of eagles, wrote the poem from a description given him by John
Burroughs, who observed the occurrence in the early 1860's at Marlboro on the
Hudson River (Barrus, xxiv, 169–170).

The rushing amorous contact high in space together,
The clinching interlocking claws, a living, fierce, gyrating wheel,
5   Four beating wings, two beaks, a swirling mass tight grappling,
In tumbling turning clustering loops, straight downward falling,
Till o'er the river pois'd, the twain yet one, a moment's lull,
A motionless still balance in the air, then parting, talons loosing,
Upward again on slow-firm pinions slanting, their separate diverse
     flight,
10 She hers, he his, pursuing.

    1880   *1881*

Roaming in Thought.

(*After reading* HEGEL.)

Roaming in thought over the Universe, I saw the little that is
    Good steadily hastening towards immortality,
And the vast all that is call'd Evil I saw hastening to merge itself
    and become lost and dead.

    1881   *1881*

A Farm Picture.

Through the ample open door of the peaceful country barn,
A sunlit pasture field with cattle and horses feeding,
And haze and vista, and the far horizon fading away.

    1865   *1871*

THOUGHT] Like the preceding poem, this two-line piece was new to this group
and the 1881 edition. WW felt that his own idealism was affirmed by Hegel's, whose
dialectic—thesis, antithesis, and synthesis—is essentially illustrated by these lines.
The poet's own notes on Hegel were based mainly on two secondary sources:
F. H. Hedge's *The Prose Writers of Germany* (1849) and Joseph Gostwick's *German
Literature* (1854). See Sister Mary Eleanor, "Hedge's *Prose Writers of Germany* as
a source of Whitman's Knowledge of German Philosophy," *MLN*, LXI (June, 1946),
381–388; and W. B. Fulghum, Jr., "Whitman's Debt to Joseph Gostwick," *AL*, XII
(January, 1941), 491–496. For contrasting views of Hegel's influence on WW, see
Mody C. Boatright, "Whitman and Hegel," *TxSF*, No. 9 (July 8, 1929), 134–150,
and Olive W. Parsons, "Whitman the Non-Hegelian," *PMLA*, LVIII (December,
1943), 1073–1093.

A Child's Amaze.

Silent and amazed even when a little boy,
I remember I heard the preacher every Sunday put God in his
    statements,
As contending against some being or influence.

1865   *1867*

The Runner.

On a flat road runs the well-train'd runner,
He is lean and sinewy with muscular legs,
He is thinly clothed, he leans forward as he runs,
With lightly closed fists and arms partially rais'd.

1867   *1867*

Beautiful Women.

Women sit or move to and fro, some old, some young,
The young are beautiful—but the old are more beautiful than the
    young.

1860   *1871*

Mother and Babe.

I see the sleeping babe nestling the breast of its mother,
The sleeping mother and babe—hush'd, I study them long and
    long.

1865   *1867*

PICTURE] Only the first two lines comprised this poem when it appeared in 1865 and in the LG 1867 annex as one of the "*Drum-Taps.*" In LG 1871 and 1876 it was ungrouped; in LG 1881 it was given its present position.

AMAZE] A *Drum-Taps* poem of 1865 and LG 1867 annex; ungrouped in LG 1871 and 1876; added to the present group in 1881.

RUNNER] First appeared in LG 1867; ungrouped in all editions until included in the present group in 1881.

WOMEN] These two lines formed a stanza of the poem "Debris" in LG 1860, were reprinted under the title "Picture" in LG 1867, took the present title in LG 1871, and were incorporated into "By the Roadside" in LG 1881.

BABE] This poem first appeared in the 1865 *Drum-Taps*, then in the LG 1867 annex, ungrouped in LG 1871 and 1876, and added to the present group in 1881.

Thought.

Of obedience, faith, adhesiveness;
As I stand aloof and look there is to me something profoundly
            affecting in large masses of men following the lead of those
            who do not believe in men.

1860   *1860*

Visor'd.

A mask, a perpetual natural disguiser of herself,
Concealing her face, concealing her form,
Changes and transformations every hour, every moment,
Falling upon her even when she sleeps.

1860   *1867*

Thought.

Of Justice—as if Justice could be any thing but the same ample
            law, expounded by natural judges and saviors,
As if it might be this thing or that thing, according to decisions.

1860   *1860*

Gliding O'er All.

Gliding o'er all, through all,
Through Nature, Time, and Space,
As a ship on the waters advancing,

THOUGHT] This was No. 7 of the "Thoughts" in LG 1860, was reprinted in 1867
in the same position; took the title "Thought" in LG 1871 and 1876, ungrouped; and
was placed in "By the Roadside" in LG 1881. Its MS (Huntington) numbers the
"Thought" as "59."

VISOR'D] These four lines formed a stanza of the poem "Debris" in LG 1860; they
constituted a poem with the present title, and ungrouped, in LG 1867, 1871, and
1876; and were placed in "By the Roadside" in LG 1881.

THOUGHT] These two lines were originally the third and fourth lines of the
four-line poem, "No. 4" of the "Thoughts" in LG 1860 and 1867. In 1871, 1872, and
1876 the poem appeared in *Passage to India*, and in 1881 it was transferred to "By
the Roadside."

The voyage of the soul—not life alone,
Death, many deaths I'll sing.   5
  1871   *1871*

Hast Never Come to Thee an Hour.

Hast never come to thee an hour,
A sudden gleam divine, precipitating, bursting all these bubbles,
        fashions, wealth?
These eager business aims—books, politics, art, amours,
To utter nothingness?
  1881   *1881*

Thought.

Of Equality—as if it harm'd me, giving others the same chances
        and rights as myself—as if it were not indispensable to
        my own rights that others possess the same.
  1860   *1871*

To Old Age.

I see in you the estuary that enlarges and spreads itself grandly as
        it pours in the great sea.
  1860   *1860*

Locations and Times.

Locations and times—what is it in me that meets them all, when-
        ever and wherever, and makes me at home?

ALL] This poem first appeared as the epigraph on the title page of *Passage to
India* in 1871, 1872, and 1876, and was transferred to the present group in 1881.
    HOUR] A new poem of the 1881 edition. The MS (Barrett) shows two separate
drafts on a single leaf, with much revision.
    THOUGHT] This poem was the second line of "Thoughts" No. 4 in the 1860 and
1867 editions; in 1871, 1872, and 1876 it was printed in *Passage to India* as a
separate poem under the present title, and transferred to "By the Roadside" in
1881.
    AGE] In 1860 this poem was one of the "Messenger Leaves"; in 1867 it appeared
ungrouped; in 1871, 1872, and 1876 it was transferred to *Passage to India;* and in
1881 to the present group.
    TIMES] This poem, first printed as No. 22 of the 1860 "Leaves of Grass" group,

Forms, colors, densities, odors—what is it in me that corresponds
    with them?

1860   *1871*

Offerings.

A thousand perfect men and women appear,
Around each gathers a cluster of friends, and gay children and
    youths, with offerings.

1860   *1871*

To the States,

    To Identify the 16th, 17th, or 18th Presidentiad.

Why reclining, interrogating? why myself and all drowsing?
What deepening twilight—scum floating atop of the waters,
Who are they as bats and night-dogs askant in the capitol?
What a filthy Presidentiad! (O South, your torrid suns! O North,
    your arctic freezings!)
Are those really Congressmen? are those the great Judges? is that
5   the President?

is actually a revision of four lines, 133–136, dropped after 1856 from the 1856
"Sun-Down Poem," now "Crossing Brooklyn Ferry." In 1867 it appeared in the
annex, "Songs Before Parting"; in 1871, 1872, and 1876 it was transferred under the
present title to *Passage to India,* and in 1881 to "By the Roadside."

    OFFERINGS] In the 1860 edition this poem was the seventh stanza of "Debris";
in 1867 it was a separate poem entitled "Picture"; in 1871 and 1876 it acquired its
present title as a *Passage to India* poem, and it was transferred to "By the Roadside"
in 1881.

    STATES] One of the "Messenger Leaves" of the 1860 edition, this poem was
reprinted without change in all following editions. WW himself indicates in the MS
notes of his "Blue Copy" edition that he composed it in the three years "1857-8-9."
The "16th, 17th, or 18th Presidentiad" refers to the administrations of Fillmore,
Pierce, and Buchanan, toward which the passionate scorn of the poet found expres-
sion not alone in these verses, but also in his political pamphlet, "The Eighteenth
Presidency!" unpublished during his lifetime. See Edward F. Grier, *Walt Whitman:
The Eighteenth Presidency: A Critical Text* (1956).

    DRUM-TAPS] WW's earliest reference to *Drum-Taps* is in a letter of March 31,
1863, in which he asks his mother to look after the MS, but he was at work on some
of the poems by 1860 or earlier, when he was considering the printing of a collection,
Banner at Day-Break, some of whose titles were later identified as *Drum-Taps* poems
(see Allen, 267). WW said *Drum-Taps* was "put together by fits and starts, on the
field, in the hospitals, as I worked with the soldier boys . . ." (Traubel, II, 137);
and after much persistence against odds, he sent the book to press in May, 1865. The
first issue was a thin book of 72 pages containing 53 poems, one of which was the
short twelve-line "Hush'd be the Camps To-day" about the burial of Lincoln. The

Then I will sleep awhile yet, for I see that these States sleep, for
    reasons;
(With gathering murk, with muttering thunder and lambent shoots
    we all duly awake,
South, North, East, West, inland and seaboard, we will surely
    awake.)

1860   *1860*

Drum-Taps.

First O Songs for a Prelude.

First O songs for a prelude,
Lightly strike on the stretch'd tympanum pride and joy in my city,
How she led the rest to arms, how she gave the cue,
How at once with lithe limbs unwaiting a moment she sprang,

great Lincoln elegy, "When Lilacs Last in the Dooryard Bloom'd," was the first of 18
more poems published as "Sequel to Drum-Taps (since the Preceding Came from the
Press)," and bound into the second issue of *Drum-Taps*. Five hundred copies were
printed, and the reviews were comparatively few and unenthusiastic, notably those
by two bright young men of the future, William Dean Howells and Henry James,
just turned twenty-eight and twenty-two years respectively. Such a response saddened
the poet, who—as he told O'Connor—felt that *Drum-Taps* was superior as a work
of art to LG. Despite the distinction, WW was profoundly aware that *Drum-Taps*
was a part of LG, that indeed the experience of the war had given identity
and homogeneity to the whole. He was to say as much years later in "A Backward
Glance. . . ." For the publishing history of *Drum-Taps*, see the introduction,
xxxiv–xlv, of F. De Wolfe Miller's facsimile edition of *Drum-Taps* (1959).

Because of its subject matter *Drum-Taps* preserved more autonomy through the
successive editions of LG than most of the groups, despite many changes, as the notes
indicate. From the first the group was not limited to war poems, at least 20 of the 71
poems in *Drum-Taps* and in the "Sequel" having nothing to do with the theme
suggested by the title; and these—notably "Out of the Rolling Ocean the Crowd" and
"Chanting the Square Deific"—were, after 1865–1866, placed elsewhere. Of the 53
Drum-Taps poems of 1865, only 29 are retained in the final 1881 grouping; and of
the 18 poems of the "Sequel," only 9 are retained. The others were shifted, often more
than once, to other groups. To put the situation in another way, of the 43 poems now
in "Drum-Taps," 38 were either in the original *Drum-Taps* or in the "Sequel," and
only 5 originated elsewhere. In his final arrangement, the poet attained a concentra-
tion not before achieved.

PRELUDE] In 1865 and 1867 this introductory poem was simply entitled "Drum-

5 (O superb! O Manhattan, my own, my peerless!
O strongest you in the hour of danger, in crisis! O truer than steel!)
How you sprang—how you threw off the costumes of peace with
   indifferent hand,
How your soft opera-music changed, and the drum and fife were
   heard in their stead,
How you led to the war, (that shall serve for our prelude, songs
   of soldiers,)
10 How Manhattan drum-taps led.

Forty years had I in my city seen soldiers parading,
Forty years as a pageant, till unawares the lady of this teeming
   and turbulent city,
Sleepless amid her ships, her houses, her incalculable wealth,
With her million children around her, suddenly,
15 At dead of night, at news from the south,
Incens'd struck with clinch'd hand the pavement.

A shock electric, the night sustain'd it,
Till with ominous hum our hive at daybreak pour'd out its myriads.

From the houses then and the workshops, and through all the
   doorways,
20 Leapt they tumultuous, and lo! Manhattan arming.

To the drum-taps prompt,
The young men falling in and arming,
The mechanics arming, (the trowel, the jack-plane, the black-
   smith's hammer, tost aside with precipitation,)
The lawyer leaving his office and arming, the judge leaving the
   court,
The driver deserting his wagon in the street, jumping down,
25   throwing the reins abruptly down on the horses' backs,
The salesman leaving the store, the boss, book-keeper, porter, all
   leaving;

Taps"; in 1871 and 1876, it was preceded by four lines in italics which served as an
epigraph for the whole group:

    Aroused and angry,
    I thought to beat the alarum, and urge relentless
     war;

Squads gather everywhere by common consent and arm,
The new recruits, even boys, the old men show them how to wear
     their accoutrements, they buckle the straps carefully,
Outdoors arming, indoors arming, the flash of the musket-barrels,
The white tents cluster in camps, the arm'd sentries around, the
     sunrise cannon and again at sunset,   30
Arm'd regiments arrive every day, pass through the city, and
     embark from the wharves,
(How good they look as they tramp down to the river, sweaty,
     with their guns on their shoulders!
How I love them! how I could hug them, with their brown faces
     and their clothes and knapsacks cover'd with dust!)
The blood of the city up—arm'd! arm'd! the cry everywhere,
The flags flung out from the steeples of churches and from all the
     public buildings and stores,   35
The tearful parting, the mother kisses her son, the son kisses his
     mother,
(Loth is the mother to part, yet not a word does she speak to
     detain him,)
The tumultuous escort, the ranks of policemen preceding, clearing
     the way,
The unpent enthusiasm, the wild cheers of the crowd for their
     favorites,
The artillery, the silent cannons bright as gold, drawn along,
     rumble lightly over the stones,   40
(Silent cannons, soon to cease your silence,
Soon unlimber'd to begin the red business;)
All the mutter of preparation, all the determin'd arming,
The hospital service, the lint, bandages and medicines,
The women volunteering for nurses, the work begun for in earnest,
     no mere parade now;   45
War! an arm'd race is advancing! the welcome for battle, no
     turning away;
War! be it weeks, months, or years, an arm'd race is advancing
     to welcome it.

            But soon my fingers fail'd me, my face droop'd,
                and I resign'd myself.
            To sit by the wounded and soothe them, or silently
                watch the dead.

In 1881 the poem took its first line for its title, and the epigraph became the fourth,
fifth, and sixth lines of "The Wound-Dresser."

Mannahatta a-march—and it's O to sing it well!
It's O for a manly life in the camp.

50　And the sturdy artillery,
　　The guns bright as gold, the work for giants, to serve well the guns,
　　Unlimber them! (no more as the past forty years for salutes for
　　　　　　courtesies merely,
　　Put in something now besides powder and wadding.)

　　And you lady of ships, you Mannahatta,
55　Old matron of this proud, friendly, turbulent city,
　　Often in peace and wealth you were pensive or covertly frown'd
　　　　　　amid all your children,
　　But now you smile with joy exulting old Mannahatta.

　　1865　　　　　　　　　　　　　　　　　　　　　*1881*

Eighteen Sixty-One.

　　Arm'd year—year of the struggle,
　　No dainty rhymes or sentimental love verses for you terrible year,
　　Not you as some pale poetling seated at a desk lisping cadenzas
　　　　　　piano,
　　But as a strong man erect, clothed in blue clothes, advancing,
　　　　　　carrying a rifle on your shoulder,
5　With well-gristled body and sunburnt face and hands, with a knife
　　　　　　in the belt at your side,
　　As I heard you shouting loud, your sonorous voice ringing across
　　　　　　the continent,
　　Your masculine voice O year, as rising amid the great cities,
　　Amid the men of Manhattan I saw you as one of the workmen,
　　　　　　the dwellers in Manhattan,
　　Or with large steps crossing the prairies out of Illinois and
　　　　　　Indiana,
10　Rapidly crossing the West with springy gait and descending the
　　　　　　Alleghanies,

　　SIXTY-ONE] In all editions before 1881, the title of this poem was in figures,
"1861." WW attempted to sell it, October 1, 1861, to the *Atlantic* for $20, but James
Russell Lowell, the editor, turned it down with the odd excuse that before he could
use it, its interest, "which is of the present,—would have passed." See Corr I, 57, and

Or down from the great lakes or in Pennsylvania, or on deck
    along the Ohio river,
Or southward along the Tennessee or Cumberland rivers, or at
    Chattanooga on the mountain top,
Saw I your gait and saw I your sinewy limbs clothed in blue,
    bearing weapons, robust year,
Heard your determin'd voice launch'd forth again and again,
Year that suddenly sang by the mouths of the round-lipp'd cannon,   15
I repeat you, hurrying, crashing, sad, distracted year.

   1865   *1881*

Beat! Beat! Drums!

Beat! beat! drums!—blow! bugles! blow!
Through the windows—through doors—burst like a ruthless
    force,
Into the solemn church, and scatter the congregation,
Into the school where the scholar is studying;
Leave not the bridegroom quiet—no happiness must he have
    now with his bride,   5
Nor the peaceful farmer any peace, ploughing his field or gathering
    his grain,
So fierce you whirr and pound you drums—so shrill you bugles
    blow.

Beat! beat! drums!—blow! bugles! blow!
Over the traffic of cities—over the rumble of wheels in the
    streets;
Are beds prepared for sleepers at night in the houses? no sleepers
    must sleep in those beds,   10
No bargainers' bargains by day—no brokers or speculators—
    would they continue?
Would the talkers be talking? would the singer attempt to sing?
Would the lawyer rise in the court to state his case before the
    judge?
Then rattle quicker, heavier drums—you bugles wilder blow.

Traubel, II, 213.
    DRUMS!] This stirring call to arms was first published simultaneously, September 28, 1861, in both *Harper's Weekly* and the New York *Leader*. Note the skill with which WW, by spondaic and anapaestic emphasis, imposes his martial rhythm.

15   Beat! beat! drums!—blow! bugles! blow!
Make no parley—stop for no expostulation,
Mind not the timid—mind not the weeper or prayer,
Mind not the old man beseeching the young man,
Let not the child's voice be heard, nor the mother's entreaties,
Make even the trestles to shake the dead where they lie awaiting
20   the hearses,
So strong you thump O terrible drums—so loud you bugles blow.

1861   *1867*

From Paumanok Starting I Fly Like a Bird.

From Paumanok starting I fly like a bird,
Around and around to soar to sing the idea of all,
To the north betaking myself to sing there arctic songs,
To Kanada till I absorb Kanada in myself, to Michigan then,
To Wisconsin, Iowa, Minnesota, to sing their songs, (they are
5   inimitable;)
Then to Ohio and Indiana to sing theirs, to Missouri and Kansas
      and Arkansas to sing theirs,
To Tennessee and Kentucky, to the Carolinas and Georgia to sing
      theirs,
To Texas and so along up toward California, to roam accepted
      everywhere;
To sing first, (to the tap of the war-drum if need be,)
10   The idea of all, of the Western world one and inseparable,
And then the song of each member of these States.

1865   *1867*

Song of the Banner at Daybreak.

Poet.

O a new song, a free song,
Flapping, flapping, flapping, flapping, by sounds, by voices clearer,

BIRD] This poem appeared in *Drum-Taps* under this title in all editions.
DAYBREAK] Since in 1861 "Banner at Day-Break" was advertised by WW's
publishers, Thayer and Eldridge, as the title poem of a book he had in preparation, it
is clear that the poet worked on this poem at least four years before *Drum-Taps* was
published (see Allen, 267). In 1871 and 1876 it was transferred to another group,

By the wind's voice and that of the drum,
By the banner's voice and child's voice and sea's voice and father's
  voice,
Low on the ground and high in the air,   5
On the ground where father and child stand,
In the upward air where their eyes turn,
Where the banner at daybreak is flapping.

Words! book-words! what are you?
Words no more, for hearken and see,   10
My song is there in the open air, and I must sing,
With the banner and pennant a-flapping.

I'll weave the chord and twine in,
Man's desire and babe's desire, I'll twine them in, I'll put in life,
I'll put the bayonet's flashing point, I'll let bullets and slugs whizz, 15
(As one carrying a symbol and menace far into the future,
Crying with trumpet voice, *Arouse and beware! Beware and
  arouse!*)
I'll pour the verse with streams of blood, full of volition, full of joy,
Then loosen, launch forth, to go and compete,
With the banner and pennant a-flapping.   20

  Pennant.

Come up here, bard, bard,
Come up here, soul, soul,
Come up here, dear little child,
To fly in the clouds and winds with me, and play with the measure-
  less light.

  Child.

Father what is that in the sky beckoning to me with long finger? 25
And what does it say to me all the while?

"Bathed in War's Perfume," which was abandoned in 1881.
  The poem is exceptional in *LG* in that it possesses a formal literary pattern which
the poet fortunately did not again attempt—a kind of dramatic colloquy in which the
poet, at beginning and end, instructs himself, and is instructed, to sing the idealism
of war. Despite its exemplary theme, the poem is oversententious, and a number of
revisions in later editions did not essentially improve it.

Father.

Nothing my babe you see in the sky,
And nothing at all to you it says—but look you my babe,
Look at these dazzling things in the houses, and see you the
  money-shops opening,
And see you the vehicles preparing to crawl along the streets with
30 goods;
These, ah these, how valued and toil'd for these!
How envied by all the earth.

Poet.

Fresh and rosy red the sun is mounting high,
On floats the sea in distant blue careering through its channels,
On floats the wind over the breast of the sea setting in toward
35 land,
The great steady wind from west or west-by-south,
Floating so buoyant with milk-white foam on the waters.

But I am not the sea nor the red sun,
I am not the wind with girlish laughter,
Not the immense wind which strengthens, not the wind which
40 lashes,
Not the spirit that ever lashes its own body to terror and death,
But I am that which unseen comes and sings, sings, sings,
Which babbles in brooks and scoots in showers on the land,
Which the birds know in the woods mornings and evenings,
And the shore-sands know and the hissing wave, and that banner
45 and pennant,
Aloft there flapping and flapping.

Child.

O father it is alive—it is full of people—it has children,
O now it seems to me it is talking to its children,
I hear it—it talks to me—O it is wonderful!
50 O it stretches—it spreads and runs so fast—O my father,
It is so broad it covers the whole sky.

Father.

Cease, cease, my foolish babe,
What you are saying is sorrowful to me, much it displeases me;
Behold with the rest again I say, behold not banners and pennants
     aloft,
But the well-prepared pavements behold, and mark the solid-wall'd
     houses.   55

Banner and Pennant.

Speak to the child O bard out of Manhattan,
To our children all, or north or south of Manhattan,
Point this day, leaving all the rest, to us over all—and yet we
     know not why,
For what are we, mere strips of cloth profiting nothing,
Only flapping in the wind?   60

Poet.

I hear and see not strips of cloth alone,
I hear the tramp of armies, I hear the challenging sentry,
I hear the jubilant shouts of millions of men, I hear Liberty!
I hear the drums beat and the trumpets blowing,
I myself move abroad swift-rising flying then,   65
I use the wings of the land-bird and use the wings of the sea-bird,
     and look down as from a height,
I do not deny the precious results of peace, I see populous cities
     with wealth incalculable,
I see numberless farms, I see the farmers working in their fields
     or barns,
I see mechanics working, I see buildings everywhere founded,
     going up, or finish'd,
I see trains of cars swiftly speeding along railroad tracks drawn
     by the locomotives,   70
I see the stores, depots, of Boston, Baltimore, Charleston, New
     Orleans,
I see far in the West the immense area of grain, I dwell awhile
     hovering,
I pass to the lumber forests of the North, and again to the South-
     ern plantation, and again to California;

Sweeping the whole I see the countless profit, the busy gatherings,
      earn'd wages,
75   See the Identity formed out of thirty-eight spacious and haughty
      States, (and many more to come,)
See forts on the shores of harbors, see ships sailing in and out;
Then over all, (aye! aye!) my little and lengthen'd pennant
      shaped like a sword,
Runs swiftly up indicating war and defiance—and now the hal-
      yards have rais'd it,
Side of my banner broad and blue, side of my starry banner,
80   Discarding peace over all the sea and land.

      Banner and Pennant.

Yet louder, higher, stronger, bard! yet farther, wider cleave!
No longer let our children deem us riches and peace alone,
We may be terror and carnage, and are so now,
Not now are we any one of these spacious and haughty States,
      (nor any five, nor ten,)
85   Nor market nor depot we, nor money-bank in the city,
But these and all, and the brown and spreading land, and the
      mines below, are ours,
And the shores of the sea are ours, and the rivers great and small,
And the fields they moisten, and the crops and the fruits are ours,
Bays and channels and ships sailing in and out are ours—while
      we over all,
Over the area spread below, the three or four millions of square
90   miles, the capitals,
The forty millions of people,—O bard! in life and death supreme,
We, even we, henceforth flaunt out masterful, high up above,
Not for the present alone, for a thousand years chanting through you,
This song to the soul of one poor little child.

      Child.

95   O my father I like not the houses,
They will never to me be any thing, nor do I like money,
But to mount up there I would like, O father dear, that banner I
      like,
That pennant I would be and must be.

Father.

Child of mine you fill me with anguish,
To be that pennant would be too fearful,   100
Little you know what it is this day, and after this day, forever,
It is to gain nothing, but risk and defy every thing,
Forward to stand in front of wars—and O, such wars!—what
      have you to do with them?
With passions of demons, slaughter, premature death?

Banner.

Demons and death then I sing,   105
Put in all, aye all will I, sword-shaped pennant for war,
And a pleasure new and ecstatic, and the prattled yearning of
      children,
Blent with the sounds of the peaceful land and the liquid wash
      of the sea,
And the black ships fighting on the sea envelop'd in smoke,
And the icy cool of the far, far north, with rustling cedars and
      pines,   110
And the whirr of drums and the sound of soldiers marching, and
      the hot sun shining south,
And the beach-waves combing over the beach on my Eastern
      shore, and my Western shore the same,
And all between those shores, and my ever running Mississippi
      with bends and chutes,
And my Illinois fields, and my Kansas fields, and my fields of
      Missouri,
The Continent, devoting the whole identity without reserving an
      atom,   115
Pour in! whelm that which asks, which sings, with all and the
      yield of all,
Fusing and holding, claiming, devouring the whole,
No more with tender lip, nor musical labial sound,
But out of the night emerging for good, our voice persuasive no
      more,
Croaking like crows here in the wind.   120

Poet.

My limbs, my veins dilate, my theme is clear at last,
Banner so broad advancing out of the night, I sing you haughty
          and resolute,
I burst through where I waited long, too long, deafen'd and
          blinded,
My hearing and tongue are come to me, (a little child taught me,)
125 I hear from above O pennant of war your ironical call and demand,
Insensate! insensate! (yet I at any rate chant you,) O banner!
Not houses of peace indeed are you, nor any nor all their pros-
          perity, (if need be, you shall again have every one of those
          houses to destroy them,
You thought not to destroy those valuable houses, standing fast,
          full of comfort, built with money,
May they stand fast, then? not an hour except you above them
          and all stand fast;)
O banner, not money so precious are you, not farm produce you,
130   nor the material good nutriment,
Nor excellent stores, nor landed on wharves from the ships,
Not the superb ships with sail-power or steam-power, fetching and
          carrying cargoes,
Nor machinery, vehicles, trade, nor revenues—but you as hence-
          forth I see you,
Running up out of the night, bringing your cluster of stars, (ever-
          enlarging stars,)
Divider of daybreak you, cutting the air, touch'd by the sun,
135   measuring the sky,
(Passionately seen and yearn'd for by one poor little child,
While others remain busy or smartly talking, forever teaching
          thrift, thrift;)
O you up there! O pennant! where you undulate like a snake
          hissing so curious,
Out of reach, an idea only, yet furiously fought for, risking bloody
          death, loved by me,
So loved—O you banner leading the day with stars brought from
140   the night!

DEEPS] This poem has always remained in "Drum-Taps" under this title, and
with no revision. Vehement and stirring, it was probably composed in the early days
of recruiting, and its sentiment, turning from nature's dauntlessness to man's, is

Valueless, object of eyes, over all and demanding all—(absolute
    owner of all)—O banner and pennant!
I too leave the rest—great as it is, it is nothing—houses,
    machines are nothing—I see them not,
I see but you, O warlike pennant! O banner so broad, with stripes,
    I sing you only,
Flapping up there in the wind.

1865   1881

Rise O Days from Your Fathomless Deeps.

1

Rise O days from your fathomless deeps, till you loftier, fiercer
    sweep,
Long for my soul hungering gymnastic I devour'd what the earth
    gave me,
Long I roam'd the woods of the north, long I watch'd Niagara
    pouring,
I travel'd the prairies over and slept on their breast, I cross'd the
    Nevadas, I cross'd the plateaus,
I ascended the towering rocks along the Pacific, I sail'd out to
    sea,   5
I sail'd through the storm, I was refresh'd by the storm,
I watch'd with joy the threatening maws of the waves,
I mark'd the white combs where they career'd so high, curling
    over,
I heard the wind piping, I saw the black clouds,
Saw from below what arose and mounted, (O superb! O wild as
    my heart, and powerful!)   10
Heard the continuous thunder as it bellow'd after the lightning,
Noted the slender and jagged threads of lightning as sudden and
    fast amid the din they chased each other across the sky;
These, and such as these, I, elate, saw—saw with wonder, yet
    pensive and masterful,
All the menacing might of the globe uprisen around me,
Yet there with my soul I fed, I fed content, supercilious.   15

echoed in the later "Give Me the Splendid Silent Sun." Note too, in stanza 3, the
poet's exultant relief from the "doubt nauseous" that had plagued him when his
beloved cities had been the scene of futile political bickering.

2

'Twas well, O soul—'twas a good preparation you gave me,
Now we advance our latent and ampler hunger to fill,
Now we go forth to receive what the earth and the sea never
      gave us,
Not through the mighty woods we go, but through the mightier
      cities,
20   Something for us is pouring now more than Niagara pouring,
Torrents of men, (sources and rills of the Northwest are you
      indeed inexhaustible?)
What, to pavements and homesteads here, what were those storms
      of the mountains and sea?
What, to passions I witness around me to-day? was the sea risen?
Was the wind piping the pipe of death under the black clouds?
Lo! from deeps more unfathomable, something more deadly and
25   savage,
Manhattan rising, advancing with menacing front—Cincinnati,
      Chicago, unchain'd;
What was that swell I saw on the ocean? behold what comes here,
How it climbs with daring feet and hands—how it dashes!
How the true thunder bellows after the lightning—how bright
      the flashes of lightning!
How Democracy with desperate vengeful port strides on, shown
30   through the dark by those flashes of lightning!
(Yet a mournful wail and low sob I fancied I heard through the
      dark,
In a lull of the deafening confusion.)

3

Thunder on! stride on, Democracy! strike with vengeful stroke!
And do you rise higher than ever yet O days, O cities!

---

33. stroke!] This poem, like "Beat! Beat! Drums!" and perhaps others of the war poems, suggests to some readers a fundamental inconsistency in the poet of "Reconciliation," who also asserted that "a kelson of the creation is love." The argument on this poem might consider certain contrary evidence. Lines 31–32 are poignantly aware of the "mournful wail and low sob" amid the strong, passionate thunder. Also, many believed that the issue was in fact the survival of democracy itself. Finally, the naturalistic view that good and evil are compounded in all reality, one of WW's recurrent themes, is established here by references to the violence inherent in nature (cf. stanza 1 and the concluding lines, 40–48). Is the poet in fact an approving

Crash heavier, heavier yet O storms! you have done me good,   35
My soul prepared in the mountains absorbs your immortal strong
        nutriment,
Long had I walk'd my cities, my country roads through farms,
        only half satisfied,
One doubt nauseous undulating like a snake, crawl'd on the
        ground before me,
Continually preceding my steps, turning upon me oft, ironically
        hissing low;
The cities I loved so well I abandon'd and left, I sped to the
        certainties suitable to me,   40
Hungering, hungering, hungering, for primal energies and Nature's
        dauntlessness,
I refresh'd myself with it only, I could relish it only,
I waited the bursting forth of the pent fire—on the water and air
        I waited long;
But now I no longer wait, I am fully satisfied, I am glutted,
I have witness'd the true lightning, I have witness'd my cities electric,   45
I have lived to behold man burst forth and warlike America rise,
Hence I will seek no more the food of the northern solitary wilds,
No more the mountains roam or sail the stormy sea.

        1865   1867

Virginia—The West.

The noble sire fallen on evil days,
I saw with hand uplifted, menacing, brandishing,
(Memories of old in abeyance, love and faith in abeyance,)
The insane knife toward the Mother of All.

The noble son on sinewy feet advancing,   5
I saw, out of the land of prairies, land of Ohio's waters and of
        Indiana,

participant or a recording observer?
    WEST] This satire on Virginia's secession from the Democracy which she helped
to create, as compared to the loyalty of the Americans from the new West, was not
one of the Civil War poems of *Drum-Taps* in 1865, and it was not added to that
section until 1881. It is perhaps more closely related to the title poem of the volume in
which it first appeared in 1872—"As a Strong Bird on Pinions Free," later called
"Thou Mother with thy Equal Brood" in *LG* 1881. This poem (*q.v.*) celebrated a
varied chain of different states, yet one identity only. "Virginia—The West" was first
printed in the March, 1872, issue of *The Kansas Magazine*.

To the rescue the stalwart giant hurry his plenteous offspring,
Drest in blue, bearing their trusty rifles on their shoulders.

Then the Mother of All with calm voice speaking,
As to you Rebellious, (I seemed to hear her say,) why strive
10   against me, and why seek my life?
When you yourself forever provide to defend me?
For you provided me Washington—and now these also.

1872   1881

City of Ships.

City of ships!
(O the black ships! O the fierce ships!
O the beautiful sharp-bow'd steam-ships and sail-ships!)
City of the world! (for all races are here,
5   All the lands of the earth make contributions here;)
City of the sea! city of hurried and glittering tides!
City whose gleeful tides continually rush or recede, whirling in
          and out with eddies and foam!
City of wharves and stores—city of tall façades of marble and
          iron!
Proud and passionate city—mettlesome, mad, extravagant city!
Spring up O city—not for peace alone, but be indeed yourself,
10   warlike!
Fear not—submit to no models but your own O city!
Behold me—incarnate me as I have incarnated you!
I have rejected nothing you offer'd me—whom you adopted I have adopted,
Good or bad I never question you—I love all—I do not con-
          demn any thing,
15   I chant and celebrate all that is yours—yet peace no more,
In peace I chanted peace, but now the drum of war is mine,
War, red war is my song through your streets, O city!

1865   1867

SHIPS] Always in *Drum-Taps* under this title, and without revision.
   STORY] With very minor revision, and under the same title, this poem has
remained in the "Drum-Taps" group in all editions. Its story commemorates the
Battle of Long Island, August 27, 1776, which took place in the region of Washing-
ton Park (Fort Greene), when fortifications raised by rebel troops delayed enemy
progress until Washington could make his retreat safely across the East River. WW

The Centenarian's Story.

Volunteer of 1861–2, (at Washington Park, Brooklyn, assisting the Centenarian.)

Give me your hand old Revolutionary,
The hill-top is nigh, but a few steps, (make room gentlemen,)
Up the path you have follow'd me well, spite of your hundred and
    extra years,
You can walk old man, though your eyes are almost done,
Your faculties serve you, and presently I must have them serve me. 5

Rest, while I tell what the crowd around us means,
On the plain below recruits are drilling and exercising,
There is the camp, one regiment departs to-morrow,
Do you hear the officers giving their orders?
Do you hear the clank of the muskets? 10

Why what comes over you now old man?
Why do you tremble and clutch my hand so convulsively?
The troops are but drilling, they are yet surrounded with smiles,
Around them at hand the well-drest friends and the women,
While splendid and warm the afternoon sun shines down, 15
Green the midsummer verdure and fresh blows the dallying
    breeze,
O'er proud and peaceful cities and arm of the sea between.

But drill and parade are over, they march back to quarters,
Only hear that approval of hands! hear what a clapping!

As wending the crowds now part and disperse—but we old man, 20
Not for nothing have I brought you hither—we must remain,
You to speak in your turn, and I to listen and tell.

describes this episode briefly in No. 11 of the "Brooklyniana" articles which he ran at intervals in the *Brooklyn Standard*, 1861–1862 (see *UPP*, II, 267–268). According to family tradition, one of the sons of Nehemiah Whitman, WW's great grandfather, lost his life fighting as a rebel lieutenant in this action. It is evident that this is one of the early-composed poems of the group, for it is listed under the title "Washington's First Battle" in the 1860 announcement for WW's never-published volume *Banner at Day-Break*. See note on "Drum-Taps."

The Centenarian.

When I clutch'd your hand it was not with terror,
But suddenly pouring about me here on every side,
And below there where the boys were drilling, and up the slopes
25   they ran,
And where tents are pitch'd, and wherever you see south and
      south-east and south-west,
Over hills, across lowlands, and in the skirts of woods,
And along the shores, in mire (now fill'd over) came again and
      suddenly raged,
As eighty-five years a-gone no mere parade receiv'd with applause
      of friends,
But a battle which I took part in myself—aye, long ago as it is,
30   I took part in it,
Walking then this hilltop, this same ground.

Aye, this is the ground,
My blind eyes even as I speak behold it re-peopled from graves,
The years recede, pavements and stately houses disappear,
35 Rude forts appear again, the old hoop'd guns are mounted,
I see the lines of rais'd earth stretching from river to bay,
I mark the vista of waters, I mark the uplands and slopes;
Here we lay encamp'd, it was this time in summer also.

As I talk I remember all, I remember the Declaration,
40 It was read here, the whole army paraded, it was read to us here,
By his staff surrounded the General stood in the middle, he held
      up his unsheath'd sword,
It glitter'd in the sun in full sight of the army.

'Twas a bold act then—the English war-ships had just arrived,
We could watch down the lower bay where they lay at anchor,
45 And the transports swarming with soldiers.

A few days more and they landed, and then the battle.

39. Declaration] The Declaration of Independence, adopted the preceding July 4, was signed by members of Congress on August 2, only about three weeks before the battle.

41. General] General George Washington no doubt read the Declaration to the troops some time after August 2 (see note above). But he was quartered in New York, General Headquarters of his army; General Putnam remained in immediate

Twenty thousand were brought against us,
A veteran force furnish'd with good artillery.

I tell not now the whole of the battle,
But one brigade early in the forenoon order'd forward to engage
    the red-coats,   50
Of that brigade I tell, and how steadily it march'd,
And how long and well it stood confronting death.

Who do you think that was marching steadily sternly confronting
    death?
It was the brigade of the youngest men, two thousand strong,
Rais'd in Virginia and Maryland, and most of them known per-
    sonally to the General.   55

Jauntily forward they went with quick step toward Gowanus' waters,
Till of a sudden unlook'd for by defiles through the woods, gain'd
    at night,
The British advancing, rounding in from the east, fiercely playing
    their guns,
That brigade of the youngest was cut off and at the enemy's mercy.

The General watch'd them from this hill,   60
They made repeated desperate attempts to burst their environment,
Then drew close together, very compact, their flag flying in the
    middle,
But O from the hills how the cannon were thinning and thinning
    them!

It sickens me yet, that slaughter!
I saw the moisture gather in drops on the face of the General.   65
I saw how he wrung his hands in anguish.

Meanwhile the British manœuvr'd to draw us out for a pitch'd
    battle,
But we dared not trust the chances of a pitch'd battle.

command at the battle scene on Brooklyn Heights.

    45. transports] These activities occurred at nearby Staten Island, completely
occupied by the British commander, General Howe, who had been steadily reinforced
by the fleet for several weeks.
    56. Gowanus' waters] Gowanus Bay is immediately to the southwest of the
battleground.

We fought the fight in detachments,
Sallying forth we fought at several points, but in each the luck was
70   against us,
Our foe advancing, steadily getting the best of it, push'd us back
   to the works on this hill,
Till we turn'd menacing here, and then he left us.

That was the going out of the brigade of the youngest men, two
   thousand strong,
Few return'd, nearly all remain in Brooklyn.

75 That and here my General's first battle,
No women looking on nor sunshine to bask in, it did not conclude
   with applause,
Nobody clapp'd hands here then.

But in darkness in mist on the ground under a chill rain,
Wearied that night we lay foil'd and sullen,
While scornfully laugh'd many an arrogant lord off against us
80   encamp'd,
Quite within hearing, feasting, clinking wineglasses together over
   their victory.

So dull and damp and another day,
But the night of that, mist lifting, rain ceasing,
Silent as a ghost while they thought they were sure of him, my
   General retreated.

85 I saw him at the river-side,
Down by the ferry lit by torches, hastening the embarcation;
My General waited till the soldiers and wounded were all pass'd
   over,
And then, (it was just ere sunrise,) these eyes rested on him for
   the last time.

Every one else seem'd fill'd with gloom,
90 Many no doubt thought of capitulation.

  84. retreated] Washington's "strategic" retreats set a new pattern of battle logis-
tics, but this first time he had the assistance of his enemy, General Howe. Howe's
astonishing apathy was to become legendary. In this first instance he had only to

But when my General pass'd me,
As he stood in his boat and look'd toward the coming sun,
I saw something different from capitulation.

Terminus.

Enough, the Centenarian's story ends,
The two, the past and present, have interchanged,   95
I myself as connecter, as chansonnier of a great future, am now
  speaking.

And is this the ground Washington trod?
And these waters I listlessly daily cross, are these the waters he
  cross'd,
As resolute in defeat as other generals in their proudest triumphs?

I must copy the story, and send it eastward and westward,   100
I must preserve that look as it beam'd on you rivers of Brooklyn.

See—as the annual round returns the phantoms return,
It is the 27th of August and the British have landed,
The battle begins and goes against us, behold through the smoke
  Washington's face,
The brigade of Virginia and Maryland have march'd forth to inter-
  cept the enemy,   105
They are cut off, murderous artillery from the hills plays upon
  them,
Rank after rank falls, while over them silently droops the flag,
Baptized that day in many a young man's bloody wounds,
In death, defeat, and sisters', mothers' tears.

Ah, hills and slopes of Brooklyn! I perceive you are more valuable
  than your owners supposed;   110
In the midst of you stands an encampment very old,
Stands forever the camp of that dead brigade.

1865   *1881*

send a warship or two into the East River and prevent the Americans' retreat to New
York.
 104. Following an earlier punctuation, the softbound issue of 1891–2 reads: "The
battle begins, and goes against us behold . . ." .

Cavalry Crossing a Ford.

A line in long array where they wind betwixt green islands,
They take a serpentine course, their arms flash in the sun—hark
      to the musical clank,
Behold the silvery river, in it the splashing horses loitering stop to
      drink,
Behold the brown-faced men, each group, each person a picture,
      the negligent rest on the saddles,
5   Some emerge on the opposite bank, others are just entering the
      ford—while,
Scarlet and blue and snowy white,
The guidon flags flutter gayly in the wind.

1865   *1871*

Bivouac on a Mountain Side.

I see before me now a traveling army halting,
Below a fertile valley spread, with barns and the orchards of
      summer,
Behind, the terraced sides of a mountain, abrupt, in places rising
      high,
Broken, with rocks, with clinging cedars, with tall shapes dingily
      seen,
5   The numerous camp-fires scatter'd near and far, some away up on
      the mountain,
The shadowy forms of men and horses, looming, large-sized,
      flickering,
And over all the sky—the sky! far, far out of reach, studded,
      breaking out, the eternal stars.

1865   *1871*

FORD] This poem remained unchanged through all the editions except for the
adding of line 6 in 1871. F. O. Matthiessen in *American Renaissance*, 1941, noted
that many of WW's poems were like the genre painting of certain Dutch and
Flemish painters, rendered in words; the subject homely and quiet, the selection of
details suggesting the movement of life arrested for a moment, and perhaps intimat-
ing but not depicting a story. A representative group of these were assembled by the
poet at this point; see the present poem and these following: "Bivouac on a Mountain
Side," "An Army Corps on the March," "By the Bivouac's Fitful Flame," "A Sight in
Camp in the Daybreak Gray and Dim," "As Toilsome I Wandered Virginia's
Woods," "I Saw Old General at Bay," and "Look Down Fair Moon."

An Army Corps on the March.

With its cloud of skirmishers in advance,
With now the sound of a single shot snapping like a whip, and
    now an irregular volley,
The swarming ranks press on and on, the dense brigades press
    on,
Glittering dimly, toiling under the sun—the dust-cover'd men,
In columns rise and fall to the undulations of the ground,   5
With artillery interspers'd—the wheels rumble, the horses sweat,
As the army corps advances.

1865–6   *1871*

By the Bivouac's Fitful Flame.

By the bivouac's fitful flame,
A procession winding around me, solemn and sweet and slow—but
    first I note,
The tents of the sleeping army, the fields' and woods' dim
    outline,
The darkness lit by spots of kindled fire, the silence,
Like a phantom far or near an occasional figure moving,   5
The shrubs and trees, (as I lift my eyes they seem to be stealthily
    watching me,)
While wind in procession thoughts, O tender and wondrous thoughts,
Of life and death, of home and the past and loved, and of those
    that are far away;
A solemn and slow procession there as I sit on the ground,
By the bivouac's fitful flame.   10

1865   *1867*

4. Following an earlier punctuation subtly different in meaning, the softbound issue of 1891–2 reads: "each group, each person, a picture, . . ." .

SIDE] This poem remained unchanged through all the editions except that in 1871 the phrase in line 7 "studded with the eternal stars" was revised to the present reading. See note, "Cavalry Crossing a Ford," above.

MARCH] First printed in "Sequel to Drum-Taps," 1865–1866, and in the 1867 "Drum-Taps" annex under the title "An Army on the March," this poem took its present title in 1871 when the final line "As the army resistless advances" was revised to the present reading. See note, "Cavalry Crossing a Ford," above.

FLAME] This poem has remained unchanged through all the editions. See note, "Cavalry Crossing a Ford," above.

Come Up from the Fields Father.

Come up from the fields father, here's a letter from our Pete,
And come to the front door mother, here's a letter from thy dear
      son.

Lo, 'tis autumn,
Lo, where the trees, deeper green, yellower and redder,
Cool and sweeten Ohio's villages with leaves fluttering in the
5   moderate wind,
Where apples ripe in the orchards hang and grapes on the trellis'd
      vines,
(Smell you the smell of the grapes on the vines?
Smell you the buckwheat where the bees were lately buzzing?)

Above all, lo, the sky so calm, so transparent after the rain, and
      with wondrous clouds,
Below too, all calm, all vital and beautiful, and the farm prospers
10   well.

Down in the fields all prospers well,
But now from the fields come father, come at the daughter's call,
And come to the entry mother, to the front door come right away.

Fast as she can she hurries, something ominous, her steps
      trembling,
15 She does not tarry to smooth her hair nor adjust her cap.

Open the envelope quickly,
O this is not our son's writing, yet his name is sign'd,
O a strange hand writes for our dear son, O stricken mother's soul!
All swims before her eyes, flashes with black, she catches the main
      words only,

FATHER] This poem, which—like the following, "Vigil Strange . . ."—has long
been a favorite of this group and often anthologized, illustrates WW's power of vivid
realization of a scene even though single lines or phrases may seem deficient in poetic
quality. The poem remained in "Drum-Taps" unchanged through all editions.
    6. Where apples . . .] This line echoes an observation WW made to his
mother in a letter of June 30, 1863 describing a passing cavalry regiment: "Alas,
how many of these healthy handsome rollicking young men will lie cold in death,

Sentences broken, *gunshot wound in the breast, cavalry skirmish,*
    taken to hospital, 20
At present low, but will soon be better.

Ah now the single figure to me,
Amid all teeming and wealthy Ohio with all its cities and farms,
Sickly white in the face and dull in the head, very faint,
By the jamb of a door leans. 25

Grieve not so, dear mother, (the just-grown daughter speaks
    through her sobs,
The little sisters huddle around speechless and dismay'd,)
See, dearest mother, the letter says Pete will soon be better.

Alas poor boy, he will never be better, (nor may-be needs to be
    better, that brave and simple soul,)
While they stand at home at the door he is dead already, 30
The only son is dead.

But the mother needs to be better,
She with thin form presently drest in black,
By day her meals untouch'd, then at night fitfully sleeping, often
    waking,
In the midnight waking, weeping, longing with one deep longing, 35
O that she might withdraw unnoticed, silent from life escape and
    withdraw,
To follow, to seek, to be with her dear dead son.

  1865   *1867*

Vigil Strange I Kept on the Field One Night.

Vigil strange I kept on the field one night;
When you my son and my comrade dropt at my side that day,
One look I but gave which your dear eyes return'd with a look I
    shall never forget,

before the apples ripe in the orchards." Corr., 1, 114.
    NIGHT] Superior in poetic skill to the preceding poem, with which it is closely
allied, this poem, a monologue both lyrical and dramatic, is artfully controlled and
profoundly felt. An excellent analysis may be found in James E. Miller, *A Critical
Guide to Leaves of Grass* (1957), 157–160. It is to be recalled that many young
boys were present in the ranks both North and South, some of them under age. The
poem remained in "Drum-Taps" practically unchanged through all editions.

One touch of your hand to mine O boy, reach'd up as you lay on
    the ground,

5   Then onward I sped in the battle, the even-contested battle,

Till late in the night reliev'd to the place at last again I made my
    way,

Found you in death so cold dear comrade, found your body son
    of responding kisses, (never again on earth responding,)

Bared your face in the starlight, curious the scene, cool blew the
    moderate night-wind,

Long there and then in vigil I stood, dimly around me the battle-
    field spreading,

10 Vigil wondrous and vigil sweet there in the fragrant silent night,

But not a tear fell, not even a long-drawn sigh, long, long I gazed,

Then on the earth partially reclining sat by your side leaning my
    chin in my hands,

Passing sweet hours, immortal and mystic hours with you dearest
    comrade—not a tear, not a word,

Vigil of silence, love and death, vigil for you my son and my
    soldier,

15 As onward silently stars aloft, eastward new ones upward stole,

Vigil final for you brave boy, (I could not save you, swift was your
    death,

I faithfully loved you and cared for you living, I think we shall
    surely meet again,)

Till at latest lingering of the night, indeed just as the dawn
    appear'd,

My comrade I wrapt in his blanket, envelop'd well his form,

Folded the blanket well, tucking it carefully over head and care-
20   fully under feet,

And there and then and bathed by the rising sun, my son in his
    grave, in his rude-dug grave I deposited,

Ending my vigil strange with that, vigil of night and battle-field
    dim,

Vigil for boy of responding kisses, (never again on earth
    responding,)

Vigil for comrade swiftly slain, vigil I never forget, how as day
    brighten'd,

UNKNOWN] This poem and the following, "A Sight in Camp . . . ," among
others, report the scenes of war with an authenticity which in the 1860's anticipated
the realism of Stephen Crane and—much later—Ernest Hemingway. Their moder-
nity, unappreciated at the time, was achieved by on-the-spot notation—in this in-

I rose from the chill ground and folded my soldier well in his
    blanket,   25
And buried him where he fell.
   1865   *1867*

A March in the Ranks Hard-Prest, and the Road Unknown.

A march in the ranks hard-prest, and the road unknown,
A route through a heavy wood with muffled steps in the darkness,
Our army foil'd with loss severe, and the sullen remnant retreating,
Till after midnight glimmer upon us the lights of a dim-lighted
    building,
We come to an open space in the woods, and halt by the dim-
    lighted building,   5
'Tis a large old church at the crossing roads, now an impromptu
    hospital,
Entering but for a minute I see a sight beyond all the pictures and
    poems ever made,
Shadows of deepest, deepest black, just lit by moving candles and
    lamps,
And by one great pitchy torch stationary with wild red flame and
    clouds of smoke,
By these, crowds, groups of forms vaguely I see on the floor, some
    in the pews laid down,   10
At my feet more distinctly a soldier, a mere lad, in danger of
    bleeding to death, (he is shot in the abdomen,)
I stanch the blood temporarily, (the youngster's face is white as
    a lily,)
Then before I depart I sweep my eyes o'er the scene fain to
    absorb it all,
Faces, varieties, postures beyond description, most in obscurity,
    some of them dead,
Surgeons operating, attendants holding lights, the smell of ether,
    the odor of blood,   15
The crowd, O the crowd of the bloody forms, the yard outside
    also fill'd,

stance, in a Washington hospital notebook of 1863–1864 (LC Whitman, 101).
Glicksberg (pp. 123–125) has transcribed the notebook pages, with their trial lines,
upon which WW drew for the particular scene evoked in the poem. It has remained
unchanged in the "Drum-Taps" group through all editions.

Some on the bare ground, some on planks or stretchers, some in
    the death-spasm sweating,
An occasional scream or cry, the doctor's shouted orders or calls,
The glisten of the little steel instruments catching the glint of the
    torches,
20 These I resume as I chant, I see again the forms, I smell the odor,
Then hear outside the orders given, *Fall in, my men, fall in;*
But first I bend to the dying lad, his eyes open, a half-smile gives
    he me,
Then the eyes close, calmly close, and I speed forth to the
    darkness,
Resuming, marching, ever in darkness marching, on in the ranks,
25 The unknown road still marching.

   1865   *1867*

A Sight in Camp in the Daybreak Gray and Dim.

A sight in camp in the daybreak gray and dim,
As from my tent I emerge so early sleepless,
As slow I walk in the cool fresh air the path near by the hospital
    tent,
Three forms I see on stretchers lying, brought out there untended
    lying,
5 Over each the blanket spread, ample brownish woolen blanket,
Gray and heavy blanket, folding, covering all.

Curious I halt and silent stand,
Then with light fingers I from the face of the nearest the first just
    lift the blanket;
Who are you elderly man so gaunt and grim, with well-gray'd
    hair, and flesh all sunken about the eyes?
10 Who are you my dear comrade?

     DIM] In a notebook of 1862–1863 (LC Whitman 94) the poet entered the idea
for this poem together with its penultimate line: "Sight at daybreak in camp in front
of the hospital tent Three dead men lying, each with a blanket spread over him—I
lift up one and look at the young man's face, calm and yellow. 'Tis strange!
    (Young man: I think this face of yours the face of my dead Christ.)" *UPP*, II,
93. The poem has remained in the "Drum-Taps" group practically unchanged.

Then to the second I step—and who are you my child and
    darling?
Who are you sweet boy with cheeks yet blooming?

Then to the third—a face nor child nor old, very calm, as of
    beautiful yellow-white ivory;
Young man I think I know you—I think this face is the face
    of the Christ himself,
Dead and divine and brother of all, and here again he lies.   15
   1865   *1867*

As Toilsome I Wander'd Virginia's Woods.

As toilsome I wander'd Virginia's woods,
To the music of rustling leaves kick'd by my feet, (for 'twas
    autumn,)
I mark'd at the foot of a tree the grave of a soldier;
Mortally wounded he and buried on the retreat, (easily all could
    I understand,)
The halt of a mid-day hour, when up! no time to lose—yet this
    sign left,
On a tablet scrawl'd and nail'd on the tree by the grave,   5
Bold, cautious, true, and my loving comrade.

Long, long I muse, then on my way go wandering,
Many a changeful season to follow, and many a scene of life,
Yet at times through changeful season and scene, abrupt, alone,
    or in the crowded street,
Comes before me the unknown soldier's grave, comes the inscrip-
    tion rude in Virginia's woods,   10
Bold, cautious, true, and my loving comrade.
   1865   *1867*

      WOODS] This poem has remained unchanged in "Drum-Taps" through all editions.
Characteristically, as in many other poems of this group, the sense of direct experi-
ence is strongly evoked.

Not the Pilot.

Not the pilot has charged himself to bring his ship into port,
    though beaten back and many times baffled;
Not the pathfinder penetrating inland weary and long,
By deserts parch'd, snows chill'd, rivers wet, perseveres till he
    reaches his destination,
More than I have charged myself, heeded or unheeded, to com-
    pose a march for these States,
5 For a battle-call, rousing to arms if need be, years, centuries
    hence.

1860   *1881*

Year That Trembled and Reel'd Beneath Me.

Year that trembled and reel'd beneath me!
Your summer wind was warm enough, yet the air I breathed
    froze me,
A thick gloom fell through the sunshine and darken'd me,
Must I change my triumphant songs? said I to myself,
5 Must I indeed learn to chant the cold dirges of the baffled?
And sullen hymns of defeat?

1865   *1867*

The Wound-Dresser.

1

An old man bending I come among new faces,
Years looking backward resuming in answer to children,

PILOT] This poem first appeared untitled in the 1860 group "Debris," and was
given its present title in 1867. In LG 1871 it was transferred to "Drum-Taps" with a
revision of the final line, which was again improved for the final version of LG
1881. The announcement of purpose in the fourth line may refer to the forthcoming
Drum-Taps, but more likely to the whole LG—battle call for centuries hence.

ME] This poem has remained unchanged in "Drum-Taps" through all editions.
The "Year" may be 1863–1864, which saw many critical actions. See, for example,
WW's piece in SDC, "The Wounded from Chancellorsville," dated May, 1863.

WOUND-DRESSER] In its first three editions, 1865, 1867, and 1871, this poem was

Come tell us old man, as from young men and maidens that love
    me,
(Arous'd and angry, I'd thought to beat the alarum, and urge
    relentless war,
But soon my fingers fail'd me, my face droop'd and I resign'd
    myself,   5
To sit by the wounded and soothe them, or silently watch the
    dead;)
Years hence of these scenes, of these furious passions, these
    chances,
Of unsurpass'd heroes, (was one side so brave? the other was
    equally brave;)
Now be witness again, paint the mightiest armies of earth,
Of those armies so rapid so wondrous what saw you to tell us?   10
What stays with you latest and deepest? of curious panics,
Of hard-fought engagements or sieges tremendous what deepest
    remains?

    2

O maidens and young men I love and that love me,
What you ask of my days those the strangest and sudden your
    talking recalls,
Soldier alert I arrive after a long march cover'd with sweat and
    dust,   15
In the nick of time I come, plunge in the fight, loudly shout in
    the rush of successful charge,
Enter the captur'd works—yet lo, like a swift-running river they
    fade,
Pass and are gone they fade—I dwell not on soldiers' perils or
    soldiers' joys,
(Both I remember well—many the hardships, few the joys, yet I
    was content.)

entitled "The Dresser," receiving its present title in 1876. It has always remained in
the "Drum-Taps" group, and its content is a faithful description of WW's ministra-
tions to the war-wounded in Washington hospitals. In fact lines 4, 5, and 6, which
first appeared in 1871 and 1876 as a prefatory epigraph for the whole "Drum-
Taps" group, are WW's recognition of his true role as the compassionate comforter
of all soldiers, North and South, the poet of "Reconciliation" (1865), who knew that
"war and all its deeds of carnage must in time be utterly lost." In 1898 his executor,
Richard Maurice Bucke, used this title for his edition of WW's letters to soldiers
during the war.

20   But in silence, in dreams' projections,
      While the world of gain and appearance and mirth goes on,
      So soon what is over forgotten, and waves wash the imprints off
          the sand,
      With hinged knees returning I enter the doors, (while for you up
          there,
      Whoever you are, follow without noise and be of strong heart.)

25   Bearing the bandages, water and sponge,
      Straight and swift to my wounded I go,
      Where they lie on the ground after the battle brought in,
      Where their priceless blood reddens the grass the ground,
      Or to the rows of the hospital tent, or under the roof'd hospital,
30   To the long rows of cots up and down each side I return,
      To each and all one after another I draw near, not one do I miss,
      An attendant follows holding a tray, he carries a refuse pail,
      Soon to be fill'd with clotted rags and blood, emptied, and fill'd
          again.

      I onward go, I stop,
35   With hinged knees and steady hand to dress wounds,
      I am firm with each, the pangs are sharp yet unavoidable,
      One turns to me his appealing eyes—poor boy! I never knew
          you,
      Yet I think I could not refuse this moment to die for you, if that
          would save you.

3

      On, on I go, (open doors of time! open hospital doors!)
      The crush'd head I dress, (poor crazed hand tear not the bandage
40   away,)
      The neck of the cavalry-man with the bullet through and through
          I examine,
      Hard the breathing rattles, quite glazed already the eye, yet life
          struggles hard,
      (Come sweet death! be persuaded O beautiful death!
      In mercy come quickly.)

45   From the stump of the arm, the amputated hand,
      I undo the clotted lint, remove the slough, wash off the matter
          and blood,

     AMERICA] Until 1881 the title of this poem, taken from its first line, was "Long,

Back on his pillow the soldier bends with curv'd neck and side-
    falling head,
His eyes are closed, his face is pale, he dares not look on the
    bloody stump,
And has not yet look'd on it.

I dress a wound in the side, deep, deep,   50
But a day or two more, for see the frame all wasted and sinking,
And the yellow-blue countenance see.

I dress the perforated shoulder, the foot with the bullet-wound,
Cleanse the one with a gnawing and putrid gangrene, so sicken-
    ing, so offensive,
While the attendant stands behind aside me holding the tray and
    pail.   55

I am faithful, I do not give out,
The fractur'd thigh, the knee, the wound in the abdomen,
These and more I dress with impassive hand, (yet deep in my
    breast a fire, a burning flame.)

4

Thus in silence in dreams' projections,
Returning, resuming, I thread my way through the hospitals,   60
The hurt and wounded I pacify with soothing hand,
I sit by the restless all the dark night, some are so young,
Some suffer so much, I recall the experience sweet and sad,
(Many a soldier's loving arms about this neck have cross'd and
    rested,
Many a soldier's kiss dwells on these bearded lips.)   65
    1865   *1881*

Long, Too Long America.

Long, too long America,
Traveling roads all even and peaceful you learn'd from joys and
    prosperity only,

Too Long, O Land." Both title and first line were then revised to the present
reading.

But now, ah now, to learn from crises of anguish, advancing, grap-
     pling with direst fate and recoiling not,
And now to conceive and show to the world what your children
     en-masse really are,
(For who except myself has yet conceiv'd what your children
5   en-masse really are?)

1865   *1881*

Give Me the Splendid Silent Sun.

1

Give me the splendid silent sun with all his beams full-dazzling,
Give me juicy autumnal fruit ripe and red from the orchard,
Give me a field where the unmow'd grass grows,
Give me an arbor, give me the trellis'd grape,
Give me fresh corn and wheat, give me serene-moving animals
5   teaching content,
Give me nights perfectly quiet as on high plateaus west of the
     Mississippi, and I looking up at the stars,
Give me odorous at sunrise a garden of beautiful flowers where I
     can walk undisturb'd,
Give me for marriage a sweet-breath'd woman of whom I should
     never tire,
Give me a perfect child, give me away aside from the noise of the
     world a rural domestic life,
Give me to warble spontaneous songs recluse by myself, for my
10   own ears only,
Give me solitude, give me Nature, give me again O Nature your
     primal sanities!

These demanding to have them, (tired with ceaseless excitement,
     and rack'd by the war-strife,)
These to procure incessantly asking, rising in cries from my heart,
While yet incessantly asking still I adhere to my city,

SUN] This poem was steadily reprinted without change until LG 1881, when the
penultimate line was relieved of its final phrase, "with varied chorus and light of the
sparkling eyes." The poem is artful in its initial reiteration, the rhythmic balance and
tonality of its lines, the antiphonal contrast of its two stanzas, the graphic precision
of each visual image, and the effect of free association among them, inducing as a

Day upon day and year upon year O city, walking your streets,   15
Where you hold me enchain'd a certain time refusing to give me
      up,
Yet giving to make me glutted, enrich'd of soul, you give me
      forever faces;
(O I see what I sought to escape, confronting, reversing my cries,
I see my own soul trampling down what it ask'd for.)

     2

Keep your splendid silent sun,   20
Keep your woods O Nature, and the quiet places by the
      woods,
Keep your fields of clover and timothy, and your corn-fields and
      orchards,
Keep the blossoming buckwheat fields where the Ninth-month
      bees hum;
Give me faces and streets—give me these phantoms incessant
      and endless along the trottoirs!
Give me interminable eyes—give me women—give me comrades
      and lovers by the thousand!   25
Let me see new ones every day—let me hold new ones by the
      hand every day!
Give me such shows—give me the streets of Manhattan!
Give me Broadway, with the soldiers marching—give me the
      sound of the trumpets and drums!
(The soldiers in companies or regiments—some starting away,
      flush'd and reckless,
Some, their time up, returning with thinn'd ranks, young, yet very
      old, worn, marching, noticing nothing;)   30
Give me the shores and wharves heavy-fringed with black
      ships!
O such for me! O an intense life, full to repletion and varied!
The life of the theatre, bar-room, huge hotel, for me!
The saloon of the steamer! the crowded excursion for me! the
      torchlight procession!

whole the recognition of contrast between the serene delights of nature and the
turbulence of war-excited city streets. An MS fragment (Trent)—"Give me some-
thing savage and luxuriant . . . Give me large, full-voiced men"—suggests the
theme.
    24. trottoirs] French: **sidewalks.**

The dense brigade bound for the war, with high piled military
35　　　wagons following;
People, endless, streaming, with strong voices, passions, pageants,
Manhattan streets with their powerful throbs, with beating drums
　　　as now,
The endless and noisy chorus, the rustle and clank of muskets,
　　　(even the sight of the wounded,)
Manhattan crowds, with their turbulent musical chorus!
40　Manhattan faces and eyes forever for me.

　　1865　　　　　　　　　　　　　　　　　　　　　1881

Dirge for Two Veterans.

　　　The last sunbeam
Lightly falls from the finish'd Sabbath,
On the pavement here, and there beyond it is looking,
　　　Down a new-made double grave.

5　　　Lo, the moon ascending,
Up from the east the silvery round moon,
Beautiful over the house-tops, ghastly, phantom moon,
　　　Immense and silent moon.

　　　I see a sad procession,
10　And I hear the sound of coming full-key'd bugles,
All the channels of the city streets they're flooding,
　　　As with voices and with tears.

　　　I hear the great drums pounding,
And the small drums steady whirring,
15　And every blow of the great convulsive drums,
　　　Strikes me through and through.

　　　For the son is brought with the father,
(In the foremost ranks of the fierce assault they fell,

TWO VETERANS] First appearing in the "Sequel to Drum-Taps," 1865–1866, this elegy has remained unchanged in all editions. One of the few poems of LG which employ regular stanzaic form, its artistry has been highly praised—among others, by John Bailey, WW's English biographer, who characterizes it as "incomparably fine." In it the solemnity of loss corresponds with the drum beat of a dead-march, and with the plaintive tonality of lines unrhymed or dissonant. Note, for example, the initial consonantal rhyme of sunbeam > Sabbath; the assonantal associations of they're

Two veterans son and father dropt together,
    And the double grave awaits them.)   20

    Now nearer blow the bugles,
And the drums strike more convulsive,
And the daylight o'er the pavement quite has faded,
    And the strong dead-march enwraps me.

    In the eastern sky up-buoying,   25
The sorrowful vast phantom moves illumin'd,
('Tis some mother's large transparent face,
    In heaven brighter growing.)

    O strong dead-march you please me!
O moon immense with your silvery face you soothe me!   30
O my soldiers twain! O my veterans passing to burial!
    What I have I also give you.

    The moon gives you light,
And the bugles and the drums give you music,
And my heart, O my soldiers, my veterans,   35
    My heart gives you love.

  1865–6   *1867*

Over the Carnage Rose Prophetic a Voice.

Over the carnage rose prophetic a voice,
Be not dishearten'd, affection shall solve the problems of freedom
    yet,
Those who love each other shall become invincible,
They shall yet make Columbia victorious.

Sons of the Mother of All, you shall yet be victorious,   5
You shall yet laugh to scorn the attacks of all the remainder of
    the earth.

flooding > tears, of pounding > whirring > drums > through, of father > fell >
together; and the remarkable 4-line reiteration (stanza 2) of "moon," modified by
two adjectives in analyzed rhyme—"ascending" and "silent."

    VOICE] All but the first and last lines of this poem were originally part of the 1860
"Calamus" No. 5, here rearranged. Its present form has remained unchanged since
its inclusion in the 1865 *Drum-Taps*. Plainly WW hoped that the sentiment of
"manly affection" would be the cohering principle of the nation in time of peril.

No danger shall balk Columbia's lovers,
If need be a thousand shall sternly immolate themselves for one.

One from Massachusetts shall be a Missourian's comrade,
From Maine and from hot Carolina, and another an Oregonese,
10   shall be friends triune,
More precious to each other than all the riches of the earth.

To Michigan, Florida perfumes shall tenderly come,
Not the perfumes of flowers, but sweeter, and wafted beyond death.

It shall be customary in the houses and streets to see manly
        affection,
15 The most dauntless and rude shall touch face to face lightly,
The dependence of Liberty shall be lovers,
The continuance of Equality shall be comrades.

These shall tie you and band you stronger than hoops of iron,
I, ecstatic, O partners! O lands! with the love of lovers tie you.

20 (Were you looking to be held together by lawyers?
Or by an agreement on a paper? or by arms?
Nay, nor the world, nor any living thing, will so cohere.)

1860   *1867*

I Saw Old General at Bay.

I saw old General at bay,
(Old as he was, his gray eyes yet shone out in battle like stars,)
His small force was now completely hemm'd in, in his works,
He call'd for volunteers to run the enemy's lines, a desperate
        emergency,
I saw a hundred and more step forth from the ranks, but two or
5   three were selected,

BAY] Unchanged in "Drum-Taps" through all editions, this poem celebrates the heroic tradition of war. "Old General" is a prototype, not to be identified.
    5. ranks,] This comma, broken by repeated printings, shows as a period in LG 1888 and later issues.

I saw them receive their orders aside, they listen'd with care, the
      adjutant was very grave,
I saw them depart with cheerfulness, freely risking their lives.

   1865   *1867*

The Artilleryman's Vision.

While my wife at my side lies slumbering, and the wars are over
      long,
And my head on the pillow rests at home, and the vacant mid-
      night passes,
And through the stillness, through the dark, I hear, just hear, the
      breath of my infant,
There in the room as I wake from sleep this vision presses upon me;
The engagement opens there and then in fantasy unreal, 5
The skirmishers begin, they crawl cautiously ahead, I hear the
      irregular snap! snap!
I hear the sounds of the different missiles, the short *t-h-t! t-h-t!*
      of the rifle-balls,
I see the shells exploding leaving small white clouds, I hear the
      great shells shrieking as they pass,
The grape like the hum and whirr of wind through the trees,
      (tumultuous now the contest rages,)
All the scenes at the batteries rise in detail before me again, 10
The crashing and smoking, the pride of the men in their pieces,
The chief-gunner ranges and sights his piece and selects a fuse of
      the right time,
After firing I see him lean aside and look eagerly off to note the
      effect;
Elsewhere I hear the cry of a regiment charging, (the young
      colonel leads himself this time with brandish'd sword,)
I see the gaps cut by the enemy's volleys, (quickly fill'd up, no
      delay,) 15
I breathe the suffocating smoke, then the flat clouds hover low
      concealing all;
Now a strange lull for a few seconds, not a shot fired on either side,

VISION] Originally "The Veteran's Vision," this poem took its present title, with
other very minor changes, in 1871. It is essentially based on some thirty MS lines set
down by WW in a Washington notebook of 1862–1863 (LC 94). They are trans-
cribed in Glicksberg, 121–123.

Then resumed the chaos louder than ever, with eager calls and
    orders of officers,
While from some distant part of the field the wind wafts to my
    ears a shout of applause, (some special success,)
And ever the sound of the cannon far or near, (rousing even in
    dreams a devilish exultation and all the old mad joy in the
20   depths of my soul,)
And ever the hastening of infantry shifting positions, batteries,
    cavalry, moving hither and thither,
(The falling, dying, I heed not, the wounded dripping and red I
    heed not, some to the rear are hobbling,)
Grime, heat, rush, aide-de-camps galloping by or on a full run,
With the patter of small arms, the warning *s-s-t* of the rifles, (these
    in my vision I hear or see,)
25 And bombs bursting in air, and at night the vari-color'd rockets.

    1865   *1881*

Ethiopia Saluting the Colors.

Who are you dusky woman, so ancient hardly human,
With your woolly-white and turban'd head, and bare bony feet?
Why rising by the roadside here, do you the colors greet?

('Tis while our army lines Carolina's sands and pines,
5 Forth from thy hovel door thou Ethiopia com'st to me,
As under doughty Sherman I march toward the sea.)

Me master years a hundred since from my parents sunder'd,
A little child, they caught me as the savage beast is caught,
Then hither me across the sea the cruel slaver brought.

COLORS] WW composed this poem in 1867 with the title "Ethiopia Commenting,"
and submitted it September 7 to the *Galaxy* magazine for $25. Although he thought
it was accepted, it was never printed, and he withdrew it on November 2, 1868. See
Corr I, 337, 341, 354; II, 21, 69. It first appeared in LG in 1871 and again in 1876
under its present title, accompanied by the subtitle "(A Reminiscence of 1864)," and
within the group, later dropped, entitled "Bathed in War's Perfume." It was transfer-
red to "Drum-Taps" in 1881. Note that the poem not only employs regular stanzaic
structure but also both internal and terminal rhyme.

No further does she say, but lingering all the day,   10
Her high-borne turban'd head she wags, and rolls her darkling
    eye,
And courtesies to the regiments, the guidons moving by.

What is it fateful woman, so blear, hardly human?
Why wag your head with turban bound, yellow, red and green?
Are the things so strange and marvelous you see or have seen?   15
  1871   *1881*

Not Youth Pertains to Me.

Not youth pertains to me,
Nor delicatesse, I cannot beguile the time with talk,
Awkward in the parlor, neither a dancer nor elegant,
In the learn'd coterie sitting constrain'd and still, for learning
    inures not to me,
Beauty, knowledge, inure not to me—yet there are two or three
    things inure to me,   5
I have nourish'd the wounded and sooth'd many a dying soldier,
And at intervals waiting or in the midst of camp,
Composed these songs.
  1865   *1871*

Race of Veterans.

Race of veterans—race of victors!
Race of the soil, ready for conflict—race of the conquering march!
(No more credulity's race, abiding-temper'd race,)
Race henceforth owning no law but the law of itself,
Race of passion and the storm.   5
  1865–6   *1871*

ME] Compare the last two lines of this poem, revised in 1871, with the original
1865 *Drum-Taps* version:

    And at intervals I have strung together a few songs,
    Fit for war, and the life of the camp.

VETERANS] A "Sequel" poem of the 1865–1866 *Drum-Taps*, this piece was
placed in the group "Marches Now the War is Over" in 1871 and 1876, with its first
line "Race of veterans!" expanded by the phrase "race of victors!" The poem was
returned to "Drum-Taps" in 1881.

World Take Good Notice.

World take good notice, silver stars fading,
Milky hue ript, weft of white detaching,
Coals thirty-eight, baleful and burning,
Scarlet, significant, hands off warning,
5   Now and henceforth flaunt from these shores.

1865   *1881*

O Tan-Faced Prairie-Boy.

O tan-faced prairie-boy,
Before you came to camp came many a welcome gift,
Praises and presents came and nourishing food, till at last among
       the recruits,
You came, taciturn, with nothing to give—we but look'd on each
       other,
5   When lo! more than all the gifts of the world you gave me.

1865   *1867*

Look Down Fair Moon.

Look down fair moon and bathe this scene,
Pour softly down night's nimbus floods on faces ghastly, swollen,
       purple,

NOTICE] This poem has remained unchanged since its appearance in the 1865
Drum-Taps, although in 1871 and 1876 it was transferred to the group "Bathed in
War's Perfume," then returned to "Drum-Taps" in 1881. An earlier MS (Yale)
version was published in facsimile by J. H. Johnston in the *Century Magazine*, Vol.
59 (February, 1911), 532:

Rise, lurid stars.

Rise, lurid stars, woolly white no more;
Change, angry cloth—weft of the silver stars no more;
Orbs blushing scarlet—thirty-four stars, red as flame,
     On the blue bunting this day we sew.

World take good notice, silver stars have vanished;
Orbs now of scarlet—mortal coals, all aglow,
Dots of molten iron, wakeful and ominous,
     On the blue bunting henceforth appear.

See "Excluded Poems" for another MS (Feinberg) reading, so different as to

On the dead on their backs with arms toss'd wide,
Pour down your unstinted nimbus sacred moon.

1865   *1881*

Reconciliation.

Word over all, beautiful as the sky,
Beautiful that war and all its deeds of carnage must in time be
    utterly lost,
That the hands of the sisters Death and Night incessantly softly
    wash again, and ever again, this soil'd world;
For my enemy is dead, a man divine as myself is dead,
I look where he lies white-faced and still in the coffin—I draw
    near,
Bend down and touch lightly with my lips the white face in the
    coffin.

5

1865–6   *1881*

How Solemn as One by One.

(*Washington City*, 1865.)

How solemn as one by one,
As the ranks returning worn and sweaty, as the men file by where
    I stand,

---

constitute still a third version.

    3. Coals thirty-eight] The MS version lists "thirty four stars," which would
place its composition between January 29, 1861, the date of admission of Kansas,
the thirty-fourth state, and June 19, 1863, the date of admission of West Virginia,
the thirty-fifth state. The 1865 text reads "coals thirty-six," since Nevada, the thirty-
sixth state, was admitted October 31, 1864. The thirty-eighth state, Colorado, was
admitted August 1, 1876.

    PRAIRIE-BOY] This poem has remained in "Drum-Taps" unchanged through all
editions.

    MOON] This poem has remained in "Drum-Taps" unchanged through all edi-
tions to 1881, when "their" was excluded before "arms" in the third line.

    RECONCILIATION] This justly famous poem was first printed in the "Sequel to
Drum-Taps, 1865–1866," and remained unchanged except for the exclusion, in 1881,
of the pronoun "I" opening the last line.

    ONE] This poem was one of the "Sequel" pieces of 1865–1866, and has remained
in "Drum-Taps" in all editions. The title note (*Washington City*, 1865.) was added
in 1871.

As the faces the masks appear, as I glance at the faces studying the
    masks,
(As I glance upward out of this page studying you, dear friend,
    whoever you are,)
How solemn the thought of my whispering soul to each in the
5   ranks, and to you,
I see behind each mask that wonder a kindred soul,
O the bullet could never kill what you really are, dear friend,
Nor the bayonet stab what you really are;
The soul! yourself I see, great as any, good as the best,
10 Waiting secure and content, which the bullet could never kill,
Nor the bayonet stab O friend.

    1865–6   *1871*

As I Lay with My Head in Your Lap Camerado.

As I lay with my head in your lap camerado,
The confession I made I resume, what I said to you and the open
    air I resume,
I know I am restless and make others so,
I know my words are weapons full of danger, full of death,
For I confront peace, security, and all the settled laws, to unsettle
5   them,
I am more resolute because all have denied me than I could ever
    have been had all accepted me,
I heed not and have never heeded either experience, cautions,
    majorities, nor ridicule,
And the threat of what is call'd hell is little or nothing to me,
And the lure of what is call'd heaven is little or nothing to me;
Dear camerado! I confess I have urged you onward with me, and
10   still urge you, without the least idea what is our destination,
Or whether we shall be victorious, or utterly quell'd and defeated.

    1865–6   *1881*

CAMERADO] Another "Sequel" poem of 1865–1866, this piece was transferred in
1871 and 1876 to a "Leaves of Grass" group, and returned to "Drum-Taps" in 1881,
improved by the exclusion of a parenthetical passage which had followed line 4:

    (Indeed I am myself the real soldier;
    It is not he, there, with his bayonet, and not the
      red-striped artilleryman;).

CLUSTER] This poem was first published in the group "Bathed in War's Perfume"

Delicate Cluster.

Delicate cluster! flag of teeming life!
Covering all my lands—all my seashores lining!
Flag of death! (how I watch'd you through the smoke of battle
  pressing!
How I heard you flap and rustle, cloth defiant!)
Flag cerulean—sunny flag, with the orbs of night dappled!   5
Ah my silvery beauty—ah my woolly white and crimson!
Ah to sing the song of you, my matron mighty!
My sacred one, my mother.
 1871   1871

To a Certain Civilian.

Did you ask dulcet rhymes from me?
Did you seek the civilian's peaceful and languishing rhymes?
Did you find what I sang erewhile so hard to follow?
Why I was not singing erewhile for you to follow, to understand—
  nor am I now;
(I have been born of the same as the war was born,   5
The drum-corps' rattle is ever to me sweet music, I love well the
  martial dirge,
With slow wail and convulsive throb leading the officer's funeral;)
What to such as you anyhow such a poet as I? therefore leave my
  works,
And go lull yourself with what you can understand, and with piano-
  tunes,
For I lull nobody, and you will never understand me.   10
 1865   1871

of the 1871 edition of LG, and transferred to "Drum-Taps" in 1881.
 CIVILIAN] In the 1865 Drum-Taps this defiant poem was composed of six lines
only, from the first of which it took its title. In 1871 and 1876 it was included in the
Supplement, "Passage to India," in the group "Ashes of Soldiers," with its present title
and the addition of lines 2, 5, 6, and 7, as well as the phrase "with piano-tunes" in
line 9. In 1881 the poem was returned to "Drum-Taps." At least one biographer has
speculated that the poet was here confronting a particular person, but there is no
evidence to this effect.

Lo, Victress on the Peaks.

Lo, Victress on the peaks,
Where thou with mighty brow regarding the world,
(The world O Libertad, that vainly conspired against thee,)
Out of its countless beleaguering toils, after thwarting them all,
5   Dominant, with the dazzling sun around thee,
Flauntest now unharm'd in immortal soundness and bloom—lo, in
          these hours supreme,
No poem proud, I chanting bring to thee, nor mastery's rapturous
          verse,
But a cluster containing night's darkness and blood-dripping
          wounds,
And psalms of the dead.

    1865–6   *1881*

Spirit Whose Work Is Done.

(*Washington City*, 1865.)

Spirit whose work is done—spirit of dreadful hours!
Ere departing fade from my eyes your forests of bayonets;
Spirit of gloomiest fears and doubts, (yet onward ever unfaltering
          pressing,)
Spirit of many a solemn day and many a savage scene—electric
          spirit,
5   That with muttering voice through the war now closed, like a tire-
          less phantom flitted,
Rousing the land with breath of flame, while you beat and beat
          the drum,
Now as the sound of the drum, hollow and harsh to the last,
          reverberates round me,

PEAKS] This poem, one of the "Sequel" poems of 1865–1866, was placed with minor revisions in the group "Bathed in War's Perfume" in 1871 and 1876, and returned to "Drum-Taps" in 1881. "Victress" or "Libertad" is of course the poet's personification of freedom. This is one of the poems in which WW seems to have developed a pattern of line-lengths which corresponds to the undulations of the thought.

As your ranks, your immortal ranks, return, return from the battles,
As the muskets of the young men yet lean over their shoulders,
As I look on the bayonets bristling over their shoulders,   10
As those slanted bayonets, whole forests of them appearing in the
      distance, approach and pass on, returning homeward,
Moving with steady motion, swaying to and fro to the right and
      left,
Evenly lightly rising and falling while the steps keep time;
Spirit of hours I knew, all hectic red one day, but pale as death
      next day,
Touch my mouth ere you depart, press my lips close,   15
Leave me your pulses of rage—bequeath them to me—fill me
      with currents convulsive,
Let them scorch and blister out of my chants when you are gone,
Let them identify you to the future in these songs.

    1865–6   *1881*

Adieu to a Soldier.

Adieu O soldier,
You of the rude campaigning, (which we shared,)
The rapid march, the life of the camp,
The hot contention of opposing fronts, the long manœuvre,
Red battles with their slaughter, the stimulus, the strong terrific
      game,   5
Spell of all brave and manly hearts, the trains of time through you
      and like of you all fill'd,
With war and war's expression.

Adieu dear comrade,
Your mission is fulfill'd—but I, more warlike,
Myself and this contentious soul of mine,   10
Still on our own campaigning bound,
Through untried roads with ambushes opponents lined,

DONE] This poem first appeared in the "Sequel" of 1865–1866, and with minor revision has remained in "Drum-Taps" through all editions. The title note "(*Washington City*, 1865.)" was added in 1871.

SOLDIER] This poem was first published in 1871 in the group "Marches Now the War is Over," and was transferred to "Drum-Taps" in 1881. Of particular interest is WW's identification of his own mission with the hazards of war.

Through many a sharp defeat and many a crisis, often baffled,
Here marching, ever marching on, a war fight out—aye here,
15   To fiercer, weightier battles give expression.

    1871   1871

Turn O Libertad.

Turn O Libertad, for the war is over,
From it and all henceforth expanding, doubting no more, resolute,
    sweeping the world,
Turn from lands retrospective recording proofs of the past,
From the singers that sing the trailing glories of the past,
From the chants of the feudal world, the triumphs of kings, slavery,
5   caste,
Turn to the world, the triumphs reserv'd and to come—give up
    that backward world,
Leave to the singers of hitherto, give them the trailing past,
But what remains remains for singers for you—wars to come are
    for you,
(Lo, how the wars of the past have duly inured to you, and the
    wars of the present also inure;)
Then turn, and be not alarm'd O Libertad—turn your undying
10   face,
To where the future, greater than all the past,
Is swiftly, surely preparing for you.

    1865   1871

To the Leaven'd Soil They Trod.

To the leaven'd soil they trod calling I sing for the last,
(Forth from my tent emerging for good, loosing, untying the tent-
    ropes,)

LIBERTAD] In the *Drum-Taps* of 1865 and 1867 the first line of this poem
read, "Turn, O Libertad, no more doubting." Then in 1871 and 1876, when it was
transferred to the group "Marches Now the War is Over," the first line was revised to
its present reading and the second line added. These changes emphasize WW's
persistent conviction that the American historical experience marked an epochal
change in the entire course of world history. Liberty (Libertad) of the individual
was won by the Revolution; it was confirmed at last for all the people, however
obscure, by the Civil War. Before, the poet notes, history was feudalism, kings.

In the freshness the forenoon air, in the far-stretching circuits and
    vistas again to peace restored,
In the fiery fields emanative and the endless vistas beyond, to the
    South and the North,
To the leaven'd soil of the general Western world to attest my
    songs,   5
To the Alleghanian hills and the tireless Mississippi,
To the rocks I calling sing, and all the trees in the woods,
To the plains of the poems of heroes, to the prairies spreading
    wide,
To the far-off sea and the unseen winds, and the sane impalpable
    air;
And responding they answer all, (but not in words,)   10
The average earth, the witness of war and peace, acknowledges
    mutely,
The prairie draws me close, as the father to bosom broad the son,
The Northern ice and rain that began me nourish me to the end,
But the hot sun of the South is to fully ripen my songs.

1865–6   *1881*

slavery, caste, but "wars to come are for you, . . . O Libertad."
    TROD] From its first publication in the "Sequel" of 1865–1866, this poem has
remained the terminal piece of the "Drum-Taps" series, with its purpose to call the
"leaven'd sod" to attest the poet's songs. For the final 1881 text the second line, "Not
cities, nor man alone, nor war, nor the dead," was dropped; and the seventh line was
revised, not for the better, to become the present eleventh line. However, the revision
does retain the beautiful phrase "the average earth," on which the emotional force of
the poem greatly depends. For in a sense the diverse culture of this continent was
first "averaged" by the Civil War.

Memories of President Lincoln.

When Lilacs Last in the Dooryard Bloom'd.

1

When lilacs last in the dooryard bloom'd,
And the great star early droop'd in the western sky in the night,
I mourn'd, and yet shall mourn with ever-returning spring.

Ever-returning spring, trinity sure to me you bring,
5   Lilac blooming perennial and drooping star in the west,
And thought of him I love.

LINCOLN] The four poems comprising this group were first brought together in the 1871 and 1876 "Passage to India" annex under the title "President Lincoln's Burial Hymn." They were finally grouped under the present title in 1881.
BLOOM'D] This great threnody, called by Swinburne "the most sweet and sonorous nocturne ever chanted in the church of the world," was composed in the weeks immediately following Lincoln's assassination, April 14, 1865, to become the title poem of the "Sequel" of eighteen poems comprising twenty-four pages, which was printed in the fall to be bound in with *Drum-Taps.* In 1871 and 1876 it headed the group entitled "President Lincoln's Burial Hymn" which was given its present title in the final grouping of 1881. A few minor revisions were made both in 1871 and 1881. For example in 1871 the refrain—the carol of the bird—was italicized for the first time, and the felicitous phrase "retrievements out of the night" was added to line 198. In the Feinberg Collection are two MS pages containing a list of about ninety words expressive of sorrow, evidently compiled by the poet in working on his elegy, and also there are six small notebook pages of MS jottings on the hermit thrush. "He is deeply interested in what I tell him of the Hermit Thrush," wrote John Burroughs to Myron B. Benton in September, 1865, "and says he has used largely the information I have given him in one of his principal poems" (Barrus, 24).
Such evidences are interesting, but can throw little light upon the processes which produced this masterpiece. Its secret lies profoundly in the depths of the poet's own involvement, and yet it is controlled and objective in its accomplishment. The subtle counterpoint of the three basic symbols—the lilacs of perennial spring (the poet's love), the fallen western star (Lincoln), the song of the hermit thrush (the chant of death), as well as the complex interplay of subsidiary symbols; the universalizing of the poet's grief; the evocation of the awesome procession of death; the ecstatic and reconciling carol which is a lyric within a lyric—all these are composed into a mighty structure of genius. It is a structure which resembles music in that it is its own being, its own experience of emotion that matters,—not its "meaning."

2

O powerful western fallen star!
O shades of night—O moody, tearful night!
O great star disappear'd—O the black murk that hides the star!
O cruel hands that hold me powerless—O helpless soul of me!   10
O harsh surrounding cloud that will not free my soul.

3

In the dooryard fronting an old farm-house near the white-wash'd
     palings,
Stands the lilac-bush tall-growing with heart-shaped leaves of rich
     green,
With many a pointed blossom rising delicate, with the perfume
     strong I love,
With every leaf a miracle—and from this bush in the dooryard,   15
With delicate-color'd blossoms and heart-shaped leaves of rich
     green,
A sprig with its flower I break.

WW's observation of Lincoln as the representative democratic man, the living symbol in many respects of his own message to America, was unremitting. See the several notations on Lincoln in *Specimen Days*, and his memorial lectures, "Death of Abraham Lincoln," SDC (1882), and "Abraham Lincoln," NB (1888). Lincoln died on the morning of April 15, 1865, and after remaining in Washington until April 21, his body was carried in the long procession through American cities, including Baltimore, Harrisburg, Philadelphia, New York, Albany, Buffalo, Cleveland, Columbus, Indianapolis, and Chicago. Interment took place at Springfield, Ill., on May 4.

1. lilacs] The lilac's almost universal adaptability, combined with its beauty, made it the most familiar American dooryard shrub. In ancient design, especially in Persian art and literature, the lilac flower, with its heart-shaped leaves and its lobed, paniculated spire of blossoms, acquired erotic significance as a masculine principle. In WW's plant symbolism of male comradeship—calamus, sweet flag, maple, bearded moss, etc.—the lilac occasionally appears, but here it achieves the loftiest transcendence in its dedication to the national martyr.

Speaking in his Lincoln lecture of the fateful day, April 14, WW said: "I remember where I was stopping at the time, the season being advanced, there were many lilacs in full bloom. By one of those caprices that enter and give tinge to events without being at all a part of them, I find myself always reminded of the great tragedy of that day by the sight and odor of these blossoms." CW, v, 246.

Confirming this association, without reference to WW, Julia Taft, friend from childhood of Lincoln's children, reports of her brother, the surgeon, Colonel Charles S. Taft, who tended the dying President through the night, "The yard of the house . . . was full of blossoming lilacs, and as long as Charlie Taft lived the scent of lilacs . . . brought back the black horror of that dreadful night." Julia Taft Bayne, *Tad Lincoln's Father* (1931), 202–204.

2. great star] Venus, low in the western sky at this time. See WW's comment in SPC (*Prose Works*, 1, 187–188, Coll W).

4

In the swamp in secluded recesses,
A shy and hidden bird is warbling a song.

20   Solitary the thrush,
The hermit withdrawn to himself, avoiding the settlements,
Sings by himself a song.

Song of the bleeding throat,
Death's outlet song of life, (for well dear brother I know,
25   If thou wast not granted to sing thou would'st surely die.)

5

Over the breast of the spring, the land, amid cities,
Amid lanes and through old woods, where lately the violets peep'd
    from the ground, spotting the gray debris,
Amid the grass in the fields each side of the lanes, passing the
    endless grass,
Passing the yellow-spear'd wheat, every grain from its shroud in
    the dark-brown fields uprisen,
30   Passing the apple-tree blows of white and pink in the orchards,
Carrying a corpse to where it shall rest in the grave,
Night and day journeys a coffin.

6

Coffin that passes through lanes and streets,
Through day and night with the great cloud darkening the land,
35   With the pomp of the inloop'd flags with the cities draped in black,
With the show of the States themselves as of crape-veil'd women
    standing,
With processions long and winding and the flambeaus of the night,
With the countless torches lit, with the silent sea of faces and the
    unbared heads,
With the waiting depot, the arriving coffin, and the sombre faces,
With dirges through the night, with the thousand voices rising
40   strong and solemn,
With all the mournful voices of the dirges pour'd around the coffin,

The dim-lit churches and the shuddering organs—where amid
    these you journey,
With the tolling tolling bells' perpetual clang,
Here, coffin that slowly passes,
I give you my sprig of lilac. 45

7

(Nor for you, for one alone,
Blossoms and branches green to coffins all I bring,
For fresh as the morning, thus would I chant a song for you O
    sane and sacred death.

All over bouquets of roses,
O death, I cover you over with roses and early lilies, 50
But mostly and now the lilac that blooms the first,
Copious I break, I break the sprigs from the bushes,
With loaded arms I come, pouring for you,
For you and the coffins all of you O death.)

8

O western orb sailing the heaven, 55
Now I know what you must have meant as a month since I
    walk'd,
As I walk'd in silence the transparent shadowy night,
As I saw you had something to tell as you bent to me night after
    night,
As you droop'd from the sky low down as if to my side, (while
    the other stars all look'd on,)
As we wander'd together the solemn night, (for something I know
    not what kept me from sleep,) 60
As the night advanced, and I saw on the rim of the west how full
    you were of woe,
As I stood on the rising ground in the breeze in the cool trans-
    parent night,
As I watch'd where you pass'd and was lost in the netherward
    black of the night,
As my soul in its trouble dissatisfied sank, as where you sad orb,
Concluded, dropt in the night, and was gone. 65

9

Sing on there in the swamp,
O singer bashful and tender, I hear your notes, I hear your call,
I hear, I come presently, I understand you,
But a moment I linger, for the lustrous star has detain'd me,
70   The star my departing comrade holds and detains me.

10

O how shall I warble myself for the dead one there I loved?
And how shall I deck my song for the large sweet soul that has
        gone?
And what shall my perfume be for the grave of him I love?

Sea-winds blown from east and west,
Blown from the Eastern sea and blown from the Western sea, till
        there on the prairies meeting,
These and with these and the breath of my chant,
I'll perfume the grave of him I love.

11

O what shall I hang on the chamber walls?
And what shall the pictures be that I hang on the walls,
80   To adorn the burial-house of him I love?

Pictures of growing spring and farms and homes,
With the Fourth-month eve at sundown, and the gray smoke lucid
        and bright,
With floods of the yellow gold of the gorgeous, indolent, sinking
        sun, burning, expanding the air,
With the fresh sweet herbage under foot, and the pale green leaves
        of the trees prolific,
In the distance the flowing glaze, the breast of the river, with a
85   wind-dapple here and there,
With ranging hills on the banks, with many a line against the sky,
        and shadows,
And the city at hand with dwellings so dense, and stacks of chim-
        neys,

And all the scenes of life and the workshops, and the workmen
      homeward returning.

12

Lo, body and soul—this land,
My own Manhattan with spires, and the sparkling and hurrying
      tides, and the ships,   90
The varied and ample land, the South and the North in the light,
      Ohio's shores and flashing Missouri,
And ever the far-spreading prairies cover'd with grass and corn.

Lo, the most excellent sun so calm and haughty,
The violet and purple morn with just-felt breezes,
The gentle soft-born measureless light,   95
The miracle spreading bathing all, the fulfill'd noon,
The coming eve delicious, the welcome night and the stars,
Over my cities shining all, enveloping man and land.

13

Sing on, sing on you gray-brown bird,
Sing from the swamps, the recesses, pour your chant from the
      bushes,   100
Limitless out of the dusk, out of the cedars and pines.

Sing on dearest brother, warble your reedy song,
Loud human song, with voice of uttermost woe.

O liquid and free and tender!
O wild and loose to my soul—O wondrous singer!   105
You only I hear—yet the star holds me, (but will soon depart,)
Yet the lilac with mastering odor holds me.

14

Now while I sat in the day and look'd forth,
In the close of the day with its light and the fields of spring, and
      the farmers preparing their crops,
In the large unconscious scenery of my land with its lakes and
      forests,   110

In the heavenly aerial beauty, (after the perturb'd winds and the
    storms,)
Under the arching heavens of the afternoon swift passing, and the
    voices of children and women,
The many-moving sea-tides, and I saw the ships how they
    sail'd,
And the summer approaching with richness, and the fields all busy
    with labor,
And the infinite separate houses, how they all went on, each with
115   its meals and minutia of daily usages,
And the streets how their throbbings throbb'd, and the cities pent
    —lo, then and there,
Falling upon them all and among them all, enveloping me with the
    rest,
Appear'd the cloud, appear'd the long black trail,
And I knew death, its thought, and the sacred knowledge of
    death.

120 Then with the knowledge of death as walking one side of me,
And the thought of death close-walking the other side of me,
And I in the middle as with companions, and as holding the
    hands of companions,
I fled forth to the hiding receiving night that talks not,
Down to the shores of the water, the path by the swamp in the
    dimness,
125 To the solemn shadowy cedars and ghostly pines so still.

And the singer so shy to the rest receiv'd me,
The gray-brown bird I know receiv'd us comrades three,
And he sang the carol of death, and a verse for him I love.

From deep secluded recesses,
130 From the fragrant cedars and the ghostly pines so still,
Came the carol of the bird.

And the charm of the carol rapt me,
As I held as if by their hands my comrades in the night,
And the voice of my spirit tallied the song of the bird.

135. *death*] In the first 1865–1866 version, the song of the bird was not distin-
guished by italics. In 1871 the italics were used, and the song had its own subtitle,

Come lovely and soothing death,   135
Undulate round the world, serenely arriving, arriving,
In the day, in the night, to all, to each,
Sooner or later delicate death.

Prais'd be the fathomless universe,
For life and joy, and for objects and knowledge curious,   140
And for love, sweet love—but praise! praise! praise!
For the sure-enwinding arms of cool-enfolding death.

Dark mother always gliding near with soft feet,
Have none chanted for thee a chant of fullest welcome?
Then I chant it for thee, I glorify thee above all,   145
I bring thee a song that when thou must indeed come, come unfal-
        teringly.

Approach strong deliveress,
When it is so, when thou hast taken them I joyously sing the dead,
Lost in the loving floating ocean of thee,
Laved in the flood of thy bliss O death.   150

From me to thee glad serenades,
Dances for thee I propose saluting thee, adornments and feast-
        ings for thee,
And the sights of the open landscape and the high-spread sky are
        fitting,
And life and the fields, and the huge and thoughtful night.

The night in silence under many a star,   155
The ocean shore and the husky whispering wave whose voice I
        know,
And the soul turning to thee O vast and well-veil'd death,
And the body gratefully nestling close to thee.

Over the tree-tops I float thee a song,
Over the rising and sinking waves, over the myriad fields and the
        prairies wide,   160
Over the dense-pack'd cities all and the teeming wharves and ways,
I float this carol with joy, with joy to thee O death.

"Death Carol," which was dropped in 1881. Compare this lyrical refrain with the
songs of the bird in "Out of the Cradle Endlessly Rocking" and the tree in "Song of
the Redwood Tree."

15

To the tally of my soul,
Loud and strong kept up the gray-brown bird,
165 With pure deliberate notes spreading filling the night.

Loud in the pines and cedars dim,
Clear in the freshness moist and the swamp-perfume,
And I with my comrades there in the night.

While my sight that was bound in my eyes unclosed,
170 As to long panoramas of visions.

And I saw askant the armies,
I saw as in noiseless dreams hundreds of battle-flags,
Borne through the smoke of the battles and pierc'd with missiles
   I saw them,
And carried hither and yon through the smoke, and torn and
   bloody,
175 And at last but a few shreds left on the staffs, (and all in silence,)
And the staffs all splinter'd and broken.

I saw battle-corpses, myriads of them,
And the white skeletons of young men, I saw them,
I saw the debris and debris of all the slain soldiers of the war,
180 But I saw they were not as was thought,
They themselves were fully at rest, they suffer'd not,
The living remain'd and suffer'd, the mother suffer'd,
And the wife and the child and the musing comrade suffer'd,
And the armies that remain'd suffer'd.

16

185 Passing the visions, passing the night,
Passing, unloosing the hold of my comrades' hands,
Passing the song of the hermit bird and the tallying song of my
   soul,

---

171. askant] Cf. "askance," obliquely.

CAPTAIN!] This is the most widely known and least characteristic poem that WW ever published. It appeared first in the New York *Saturday Press*, November 4, 1865, next in the *Drum-Taps* "Sequel," and then, with several revisions, in the *Passage to India* of 1871 and 1876. It was returned to "Drum-Taps" with no further changes in

Victorious song, death's outlet song, yet varying ever-altering song,
As low and wailing, yet clear the notes, rising and falling, flooding
    the night,
Sadly sinking and fainting, as warning and warning, and yet again
    bursting with joy,   190
Covering the earth and filling the spread of the heaven,
As that powerful psalm in the night I heard from recesses,
Passing, I leave thee lilac with heart-shaped leaves,
I leave thee there in the door-yard, blooming, returning with
    spring.

I cease from my song for thee,   195
From my gaze on thee in the west, fronting the west, communing
    with thee,
O comrade lustrous with silver face in the night.

Yet each to keep and all, retrievements out of the night,
The song, the wondrous chant of the gray-brown bird,
And the tallying chant, the echo arous'd in my soul,   200
With the lustrous and drooping star with the countenance full
    of woe,
With the holders holding my hand nearing the call of the bird,
Comrades mine and I in the midst, and their memory ever to
    keep, for the dead I loved so well,
For the sweetest, wisest soul of all my days and lands—and this
    for his dear sake,
Lilac and star and bird twined with the chant of my soul,   205
There in the fragrant pines and the cedars dusk and dim.

1865–6   *1881*

O Captain! My Captain!

O Captain! my Captain! our fearful trip is done,
The ship has weather'd every rack, the prize we sought is won,
The port is near, the bells I hear, the people all exulting,

1881. The MS readings (Feinberg) show much reworking, and to Traubel the poet confessed that he did not feel at ease with its regularity of form in stanza, meter, and rhyme. He also expressed humorous irritation that the poem had succeeded with the public as his other poems had not. "I'm almost sorry I ever wrote the poem." See Traubel, II, 304, 332–334.

While follow eyes the steady keel, the vessel grim and daring;
5   But O heart! heart! heart!
          O the bleeding drops of red,
             Where on the deck my Captain lies,
               Fallen cold and dead.

O Captain! my Captain! rise up and hear the bells;
10 Rise up—for you the flag is flung—for you the bugle trills,
For you bouquets and ribbon'd wreaths—for you the shores
      a-crowding,
For you they call, the swaying mass, their eager faces turning;
          Here Captain! dear father!
            This arm beneath your head!
15   It is some dream that on the deck,
                You've fallen cold and dead.

My Captain does not answer, his lips are pale and still,
My father does not feel my arm, he has no pulse nor will,
The ship is anchor'd safe and sound, its voyage closed and done,
20 From fearful trip the victor ship comes in with object won;
          Exult O shores, and ring O bells!
            But I with mournful tread,
             Walk the deck my Captain lies,
              Fallen cold and dead.

1865–6   *1871*

Hush'd Be the Camps To-day.

(*May 4, 1865.*)

Hush'd be the camps to-day,
And soldiers let us drape our war-worn weapons,
And each with musing soul retire to celebrate,
Our dear commander's death.

TO-DAY] WW was able to include this poem in his 1865 *Drum-Taps* before the
addition of the "Sequel," but his title note read, "A. L. Buried April 19, 1865,"
evidently under the misapprehension that interment, as well as the funeral, was to
take place in Washington. In the 1871 and 1876 editions he corrected the note to the
present reading, and also made a number of changes in the final stanza. An analysis

No more for him life's stormy conflicts,   5
Nor victory, nor defeat—no more time's dark events,
Charging like ceaseless clouds across the sky.

But sing poet in our name,
Sing of the love we bore him—because you, dweller in camps,
    know it truly.

As they invault the coffin there,   10
Sing—as they close the doors of earth upon him—one verse,
For the heavy hearts of soldiers.

1865   *1871*

This Dust Was Once the Man.

This dust was once the man,
Gentle, plain, just and resolute, under whose cautious hand,
Against the foulest crime in history known in any land or age,
Was saved the Union of these States.

1871   *1871*

of the MS (Rutgers) of this poem is made by Oral S. Coad in the *Journal of the Rutgers University Library*, II (December, 1938), 6–10.

MAN] This poem was first published in 1871 in the "President Lincoln's Burial Hymn" group of *Passage to India*, and again in 1876 in the *Two Rivulets* supplement of the same title. It remained unchanged when it was transferred to "Drum-Taps" in 1881.

By Blue Ontario's Shore.

1

By blue Ontario's shore,
As I mused of these warlike days and of peace return'd, and the
    dead that return no more,
A Phantom gigantic superb, with stern visage accosted me,
Chant me the poem, it said, *that comes from the soul of America,*
    chant me the carol of victory,
5   *And strike up the marches of Libertad, marches more powerful yet,*
And sing me before you go the song of the throes of Democracy.

(Democracy, the destin'd conqueror, yet treacherous lip-smiles
    everywhere,
And death and infidelity at every step.)

2

A Nation announcing itself,
10   I myself make the only growth by which I can be appreciated,
I reject none, accept all, then reproduce all in my own forms.

SHORE] In theme and intent this poem is essentially the poetical equivalent of the
1855 Preface, from which, in its present form, it draws more than sixty of its
lines—and many more in the earlier editions. In it WW identifies the purpose of his
poetry with the aspiration and potentiality of his country; in it he presents himself as
the bard of his people with a mandate from the Muse—the Phantom of the opening
lines.
    Of all his poems, this poem has undergone the most extensive and ceaseless revi-
sion. It originated as one of the twenty new poems of the second edition under the title
"Poem of Many in One," about one-fourth of its then 280 lines being transfers from
the 1855 Preface. In 1860 it was the opening "No. 1" of the "Chants Democratic," 20
lines being dropped and some 8 added. In *LG* 1867, the fourth edition, the title
became "As I Sat Alone by Blue Ontario's Shore," and notable sections were added—
the opening one and several others—which reflect the poet's experiences and reflec-
tions upon the Civil War and expand the text to 337 lines. In the 1871 and 1876 text
the alterations were far fewer, although the additions brought the poem to 345 lines.
Finally, in 1881, the poem took its present title, and some 10 lines were dropped,
including the interesting observation, which had first appeared in the preceding
edition, that "As a wheel turns on its axle, so I find my chants turning finally on the
war." The student is advised to make a study of the many variants. Notes on the

A breed whose proof is in time and deeds,
What we are we are, nativity is answer enough to objections,
We wield ourselves as a weapon is wielded,
We are powerful and tremendous in ourselves,   15
We are executive in ourselves, we are sufficient in the variety of
          ourselves,
We are the most beautiful to ourselves and in ourselves,
We stand self-pois'd in the middle, branching thence over the
          world,
From Missouri, Nebraska, or Kansas, laughing attacks to scorn.

Nothing is sinful to us outside of ourselves,   20
Whatever appears, whatever does not appear, we are beautiful or
          sinful in ourselves only.

(O Mother—O Sisters dear!
If we are lost, no victor else has destroy'd us,
It is by ourselves we go down to eternal night.)

          3
Have you thought there could be but a single supreme?
There can be any number of supremes—one does not counter-   25
          vail another any more than one eyesight countervails
          another, or one life countervails another.

"Preface 1855" in this volume indicate the lines in that essay which were transposed
in some form into this poem.
    A prose paragraph turned up by Traubel (Traubel, II, 57) seems to express, as
WW agreed, the idea from which the poem originally advanced:
    "A song America demands that breathes her native air—an utterance to invigor-
ate Democracy. Democracy, the destined conqueror—(yet treacherous lip-smiles
everywhere, and death and infidelity at every step.) Of such a song let me, (for I
have had that dream,) initiate here the NOVICE'S ATTEMPT,—and bravos to the
bards, who coming after me, do better far."
    1. shore] In this first section, first added in the 1867 edition, compare the
address of the Phantom with its original text:
          Chant me a poem, it said, *of the range of the high Soul*
                    of Poets.
          And chant of the welcome bards that breathe but my
                    native air—invoke those bards;
          And chant me, before you go, the Song of the throes of
                    Democracy.
    22. O Mother] Here, as in later references, the Nation personified, representing
also Democracy. Sisters] The States, as elsewhere in *LG*.

All is eligible to all,
All is for individuals, all is for you,
No condition is prohibited, not God's or any.

30   All comes by the body, only health puts you rapport with the universe.

Produce great Persons, the rest follows.

4

Piety and conformity to them that like,
Peace, obesity, allegiance, to them that like,
I am he who tauntingly compels men, women, nations,
35   Crying, Leap from your seats and contend for your lives!

I am he who walks the States with a barb'd tongue, questioning
     every one I meet,
Who are you that wanted only to be told what you knew before?
Who are you that wanted only a book to join you in your nonsense?

(With pangs and cries as thine own O bearer of many children,
40   These clamors wild to a race of pride I give.)

O lands, would you be freer than all that has ever been before?
If you would be freer than all that has been before, come listen
     to me.

Fear grace, elegance, civilization, delicatesse,
Fear the mellow sweet, the sucking of honey-juice,
45   Beware the advancing mortal ripening of Nature,
Beware what precedes the decay of the ruggedness of states and
     men.

5

Ages, precedents, have long been accumulating undirected
     materials,
America brings builders, and brings its own styles.

     31. follows] In the 1867 edition, the following scornful passage, later dropped,
was here inserted:

           America isolated I sing;
           I say that works made here in the spirit of other
               lands, are so much poison to These States.

The immortal poets of Asia and Europe have done their work
    and pass'd to other spheres,
A work remains, the work of surpassing all they have done.   50

America, curious toward foreign characters, stands by its own at
    all hazards,
Stands removed, spacious, composite, sound, initiates the true
    use of precedents,
Does not repel them or the past or what they have produced
    under their forms,
Takes the lesson with calmness, perceives the corpse slowly borne
    from the house,
Perceives that it waits a little while in the door, that it was fittest
    for its days,   55
That its life has descended to the stalwart and well-shaped heir
    who approaches,
And that he shall be fittest for his days.

Any period one nation must lead,
One land must be the promise and reliance of the future.

These States are the amplest poem,   60
Here is not merely a nation but a teeming Nation of nations,
Here the doings of men correspond with the broadcast doings of
    the day and night,
Here is what moves in magnificent masses careless of particulars,
Here are the roughs, beards, friendliness, combativeness, the soul
    loves,
Here the flowing trains, here the crowds, equality, diversity, the
    soul loves.   65

6

Land of lands and bards to corroborate!
Of them standing among them, one lifts to the light a west-bred
    face,   65

> How dare these insects assume to write poems for
>   America?
> For our armies, and the offspring following the
>   armies.

    53. Does not repel] Beginning with this phrase, the remainder of this section and
most of the following section 6 is composed from the 1855 Preface, *q.v.*, Notes.

To him the hereditary countenance bequeath'd both mother's and
     father's,
His first parts substances, earth, water, animals, trees,
70 Built of the common stock, having room for far and near,
Used to dispense with other lands, incarnating this land,
Attracting it body and soul to himself, hanging on its neck with
     incomparable love,
Plunging his seminal muscle into its merits and demerits,
Making its cities, beginnings, events, diversities, wars, vocal in him,
75 Making its rivers, lakes, bays, embouchure in him,
Mississippi with yearly freshets and changing chutes, Columbia,
     Niagara, Hudson, spending themselves lovingly in him,
If the Atlantic coast stretch or the Pacific coast stretch, he stretch-
     ing with them North or South,
Spanning between them East and West, and touching whatever is
     between them,
Growths growing from him to offset the growths of pine, cedar,
     hemlock, live-oak, locust, chestnut, hickory, cottonwood,
     orange, magnolia,
80 Tangles as tangled in him as any canebrake or swamp,
He likening sides and peaks of mountains, forests coated with
     northern transparent ice,
Off him pasturage sweet and natural as savanna, upland, prairie,
Through him flights, whirls, screams, answering those of the fish-
     hawk, mocking-bird, night-heron, and eagle,
His spirit surrounding his country's spirit, unclosed to good and
     evil,
Surrounding the essences of real things, old times and present
85   times,
Surrounding just found shores, islands, tribes of red aborigines,
Weather-beaten vessels, landings, settlements, embryo stature and
     muscle,
The haughty defiance of the Year One, war, peace, the formation
     of the Constitution,
The separate States, the simple elastic scheme, the immigrants,
The Union always swarming with blatherers and always sure and
90   impregnable,

    73. seminal] In the 1856, 1860, and 1867 editions, this adjective was, erroneously,
"semitic." So also in "Preface 1855".
    75. embouchure] The mouth of a river, here used as a verb.

The unsurvey'd interior, log-houses, clearings, wild animals, hunt-
    ers, trappers,
Surrounding the multiform agriculture, mines, temperature, the
    gestation of new States,
Congress convening every Twelfth-month, the members duly
    coming up from the uttermost parts,
Surrounding the noble character of mechanics and farmers, espe-
    cially the young men,
Responding their manners, speech, dress, friendships, the gait they
    have of persons who never knew how it felt to stand in the
    presence of superiors,   95
The freshness and candor of their physiognomy, the copiousness
    and decision of their phrenology,
The picturesque looseness of their carriage, their fierceness when
    wrong'd,
The fluency of their speech, their delight in music, their curiosity,
    good temper and open-handedness, the whole composite
    make,
The prevailing ardor and enterprise, the large amativeness,
The perfect equality of the female with the male, the fluid move-
    ment of the population,   100
The superior marine, free commerce, fisheries, whaling, gold-dig-
    ging,
Wharf-hemm'd cities, railroad and steamboat lines intersecting all
    points,
Factories, mercantile life, labor-saving machinery, the Northeast,
    Northwest, Southwest,
Manhattan firemen, the Yankee swap, southern plantation life,
Slavery—the murderous, treacherous conspiracy to raise it upon
    the ruins of all the rest,   105
On and on to the grapple with it—Assassin! then your life or
    ours be the stake, and respite no more.

7

(Lo, high toward heaven, this day,
Libertad, from the conqueress' field return'd,

88. Year One] The first year of American Independence.
99. amativeness] Phrenological term for "sexual love."
107. this day] Section 7, beginning with this line, was added in 1867, its MS being
pasted by the poet in his "Blue Copy" 1860 edition.

I mark the new aureola around your head,
110   No more of soft astral, but dazzling and fierce,
With war's flames and the lambent lightnings playing,
And your port immovable where you stand,
With still the inextinguishable glance and the clinch'd and lifted fist,
And your foot on the neck of the menacing one, the scorner
      utterly crush'd beneath you,
The menacing arrogant one that strode and advanced with his
115   senseless scorn, bearing the murderous knife,
The wide-swelling one, the braggart that would yesterday do so
      much,
To-day a carrion dead and damn'd, the despised of all the earth,
An offal rank, to the dunghill maggots spurn'd.)

8

Others take finish, but the Republic is ever constructive and ever
      keeps vista,
Others adorn the past, but you O days of the present, I adorn
120   you,
O days of the future I believe in you—I isolate myself for your
      sake,
O America because you build for mankind I build for you,
O well-beloved stone-cutters, I lead them who plan with decision
      and science,
Lead the present with friendly hand toward the future.

125   (Bravas to all impulses sending sane children to the next age!
But damn that which spends itself with no thought of the stain,
      pains, dismay, feebleness, it is bequeathing.)

9

I listened to the Phantom by Ontario's shore,
I heard the voice arising demanding bards,
By them all native and grand, by them alone can these States be
      fused into the compact organism of a Nation.

To hold men together by paper and seal or by compulsion is no
130   account,

123. science] This line and about twenty lines following in sections 9 and 10
originated in the 1855 Preface, *q.v.*, Notes.

That only holds men together which aggregates all in a living
      principle, as the hold of the limbs of the body or the fibres
      of plants.

Of all races and eras these States with veins full of poetical stuff
      most need poets, and are to have the greatest, and use
      them the greatest,
Their Presidents shall not be their common referee so much as
      their poets shall.

(Soul of love and tongue of fire!
Eye to pierce the deepest deeps and sweep the world!   135
Ah Mother, prolific and full in all besides, yet how long barren,
      barren?)

10

Of these States the poet is the equable man,
Not in him but off from him things are grotesque, eccentric, fail
      of their full returns,
Nothing out of its place is good, nothing in its place is bad,
He bestows on every object or quality its fit proportion, neither
      more nor less,   140
He is the arbiter of the diverse, he is the key,
He is the equalizer of his age and land,
He supplies what wants supplying, he checks what wants checking,
In peace out of him speaks the spirit of peace, large, rich, thrifty,
      building populous towns, encouraging agriculture, arts,
      commerce, lighting the study of man, the soul, health,
      immortality, government,
In war he is the best backer of the war, he fetches artillery as good
      as the engineer's, he can make every word he speaks draw
      blood,   145
The years straying toward infidelity he witholds by his steady
      faith,
He is no arguer, he is judgment, (Nature accepts him absolutely,)
He judges not as the judge judges but as the sun falling round a
      helpless thing,

137. equable man] The portrait of the poet sketched in this section may be found
in the sixth paragraph of the 1855 Preface, *q.v.*, Notes.

As he sees the farthest he has the most faith,
150 His thoughts are the hymns of the praise of things,
In the dispute on God and eternity he is silent,
He sees eternity less like a play with a prologue and denouement,
He sees eternity in men and women, he does not see men and
      women as dreams or dots.

For the great Idea, the idea of perfect and free individuals,
155 For that, the bard walks in advance, leader of leaders,
The attitude of him cheers up slaves and horrifies foreign despots.

Without extinction is Liberty, without retrograde is Equality,
They live in the feelings of young men and the best women,
(Not for nothing have the indomitable heads of the earth been
      always ready to fall for Liberty.)

              11
160 For the great Idea,
That, O my brethren, that is the mission of poets.

Songs of stern defiance ever ready,
Songs of the rapid arming and the march,
The flag of peace quick-folded, and instead the flag we know,
165 Warlike flag of the great Idea.

(Angry cloth I saw there leaping!
I stand again in leaden rain your flapping folds saluting,
I sing you over all, flying beckoning through the fight—O the
      hard-contested fight!
The cannons ope their rosy-flashing muzzles—the hurtled balls
      scream,
The battle-front forms amid the smoke—the volleys pour incessant
170   from the line,
Hark, the ringing word *Charge!*—now the tussle and the furious
      maddening yells,
Now the corpses tumble curl'd upon the ground,
Cold, cold in death, for precious life of you,
Angry cloth I saw there leaping.)

    160. great Idea] This section was added in 1867.

12

Are you he who would assume a place to teach or be a poet here
    in the States? 175
The place is august, the terms obdurate.

Who would assume to teach here may well prepare himself body
    and mind,
He may well survey, ponder, arm, fortify, harden, make lithe him-
    self,
He shall surely be question'd beforehand by me with many and
    stern questions.

Who are you indeed who would talk or sing to America? 180
Have you studied out the land, its idioms and men?
Have you learn'd the physiology, phrenology, politics, geography,
    pride, freedom, friendship of the land? its substratums and
    objects?
Have you consider'd the organic compact of the first day of the
    first year of Independence, sign'd by the Commissioners,
    ratified by the States, and read by Washington at the head
    of the army?
Have you possess'd yourself of the Federal Constitution?
Do you see who have left all feudal processes and poems behind
    them, and assumed the poems and processes of Democracy? 185
Are you faithful to things? do you teach what the land and sea,
    the bodies of men, womanhood, amativeness, heroic angers,
    teach?
Have you sped through fleeting customs, popularities?
Can you hold your hand against all seductions, follies, whirls, fierce
    contentions? are you very strong? are you really of the
    whole People?
Are you not of some coterie? some school or mere religion?
Are you done with reviews and criticisms of life? animating now
    to life itself? 190
Have you vivified yourself from the maternity of these States?
Have you too the old ever-fresh forbearance and impartiality?
Do you hold the like love for those hardening to maturity? for the
    last-born? little and big? and for the errant?

What is this you bring my America?
Is it uniform with my country? 195

Is it not something that has been better told or done before?

Have you not imported this or the spirit of it in some ship?

Is it not a mere tale? a rhyme? a prettiness?—is the good old
　　　cause in it?

Has it not dangled long at the heels of the poets, politicians,
　　　literats, of enemies' lands?

200　Does it not assume that what is notoriously gone is still here?

Does it answer universal needs? will it improve manners?

Does it sound with trumpet-voice the proud victory of the Union
　　　in that secession war?

Can your performance face the open fields and the seaside?

Will it absorb into me as I absorb food, air, to appear again in my
　　　strength, gait, face?

Have real employments contributed to it? original makers, not
205　　　mere amanuenses?

Does it meet modern discoveries, calibres, facts, face to face?

What does it mean to American persons, progresses, cities? Chi-
　　　cago, Kanada, Arkansas?

Does it see behind the apparent custodians the real custodians
　　　standing, menacing, silent, the mechanics, Manhattanese,
　　　Western men, Southerners, significant alike in their apathy,
　　　and in the promptness of their love?

Does it see what finally befalls, and has always finally befallen, each
　　　temporizer, patcher, outsider, partialist, alarmist, infidel,
　　　who has ever ask'd any thing of America?

210　What mocking and scornful negligence?

The track strew'd with the dust of skeletons,

By the roadside others disdainfully toss'd.

13

Rhymes and rhymers pass away, poems distill'd from poems pass
　　　away,

The swarms of reflectors and the polite pass, and leave ashes,

Admirers, importers, obedient persons, make but the soil of litera-
215　　　ture,

America justifies itself, give it time, no disguise can deceive it or
　　　conceal from it, it is impassive enough,

Only toward the likes of itself will it advance to meet them,

213. away] This line and several others in section 13 originated in the 1855
Preface, *q.v.*, Notes.

If its poets appear it will in due time advance to meet them,
    there is no fear of mistake,
(The proof of a poet shall be sternly deferr'd till his country
    absorbs him as affectionately as he has absorb'd it.)

He masters whose spirit masters, he tastes sweetest who results
    sweetest in the long run,   220
The blood of the brawn beloved of time is unconstraint;
In the need of songs, philosophy, an appropriate native grand-
    opera, shipcraft, any craft,
He or she is greatest who contributes the greatest original prac-
    tical example.

Already a nonchalant breed, silently emerging, appears on the
    streets,
People's lips salute only doers, lovers, satisfiers, positive knowers,   225
There will shortly be no more priests, I say their work is done,
Death is without emergencies here, but life is perpetual emer-
    gencies here,
Are your body, days, manners, superb? after death you shall be
    superb,
Justice, health, self-esteem, clear the way with irresistible power;
How dare you place any thing before a man?   230

14

Fall behind me States!
A man before all—myself, typical, before all.

Give me the pay I have served for,
Give me to sing the songs of the great Idea, take all the rest,
I have loved the earth, sun, animals, I have despised riches,   235
I have given alms to every one that ask'd, stood up for the stupid
    and crazy, devoted my income and labor to others,
Hated tyrants, argued not concerning God, had patience and
    indulgence toward the people, taken off my hat to nothing
    known or unknown,
Gone freely with powerful uneducated persons and with the young,
    and with the mothers of families,

---

  231. States!] Many of the lines in section 14 originated in the 1855 Preface,
q.v., Notes.

Read these leaves to myself in the open air, tried them by trees,
    stars, rivers,
240 Dismiss'd whatever insulted my own soul or defiled my body,
Claim'd nothing to myself which I have not carefully claim'd for
    others on the same terms,
Sped to the camps, and comrades found and accepted from every
    State,
(Upon this breast has many a dying soldier lean'd to breathe his
    last,
This arm, this hand, this voice, have nourish'd, rais'd, restored,
245 To life recalling many a prostrate form;)
I am willing to wait to be understood by the growth of the taste
    of myself,
Rejecting none, permitting all.

(Say O Mother, have I not to your thought been faithful?
Have I not through life kept you and yours before me?)

15

250 I swear I begin to see the meaning of these things,
It is not the earth, it is not America who is so great,
It is I who am great or to be great, it is You up there, or any one,
It is to walk rapidly through civilizations, governments, theories,
Through poems, pageants, shows, to form individuals.

255 Underneath all, individuals,
I swear nothing is good to me now that ignores individuals,
The American compact is altogether with individuals,
The only government is that which makes minute of individuals,
The whole theory of the universe is directed unerringly to one
    single individual—namely to You.

(Mother! with subtle sense severe, with the naked sword in your
260   hand,
I saw you at last refuse to treat but directly with individuals.)

16

Underneath all, Nativity,
I swear I will stand by my own nativity, pious or impious so be it;

273. you and me] Compare MS reading of twenty lines (N and F, 14–15, item 27)

I swear I am charm'd with nothing except nativity,
Men, women, cities, nations, are only beautiful from nativity.   265

Underneath all is the Expression of love for men and women,
(I swear I have seen enough of mean and impotent modes of
      expressing love for men and women,
After this day I take my own modes of expressing love for men
      and women.)

I swear I will have each quality of my race in myself,
(Talk as you like, he only suits these States whose manners favor
      the audacity and sublime turbulence of the States.)   270

Underneath the lessons of things, spirits, Nature, governments,
      ownerships, I swear I perceive other lessons,
Underneath all to me is myself, to you yourself, (the same monoto-
      nous old song.)

17

O I see flashing that this America is only you and me,
Its power, weapons, testimony, are you and me,
Its crimes, lies, thefts, defections, are you and me,   275
Its Congress is you and me, the officers, capitols, armies, ships, are
      you and me,
Its endless gestations of new States are you and me,
The war, (that war so bloody and grim, the war I will henceforth
      forget), was you and me,
Natural and artificial are you and me,
Freedom, language, poems, employments, are you and me,   280
Past, present, future, are you and me.

I dare not shirk any part of myself,
Not any part of America good or bad,
Not to build for that which builds for mankind,
Not to balance ranks, complexions, creeds, and the sexes,   285
Not to justify science nor the march of equality,
Nor to feed the arrogant blood of the brawn belov'd of time.

with section 17.

I am for those that have never been master'd,
For men and women whose tempers have never been master'd,
290   For those whom laws, theories, conventions, can never master.

I am for those who walk abreast with the whole earth,
Who inaugurate one to inaugurate all.

I will not be outfaced by irrational things,
I will penetrate what it is in them that is sarcastic upon me,
295   I will make cities and civilizations defer to me,
This is what I have learnt from America—it is the amount, and it
        I teach again.

(Democracy, while weapons were everywhere aim'd at your breast,
I saw you serenely give birth to immortal children, saw in dreams
        your dilating form,
Saw you with spreading mantle covering the world.)

18

300   I will confront these shows of the day and night,
I will know if I am to be less than they,
I will see if I am not as majestic as they,
I will see if I am not as subtle and real as they,
I will see if I am to be less generous than they,
I will see if I have no meaning, while the houses and ships have
305   meaning,
I will see if the fishes and birds are to be enough for themselves,
        and I am not to be enough for myself.

I match my spirit against yours you orbs, growths, mountains,
        brutes,
Copious as you are I absorb you all in myself, and become the
        master myself,
America isolated yet embodying all, what is it finally except
        myself?
310   These States, what are they except myself?

I know now why the earth is gross, tantalizing, wicked, it is for my
        sake,
I take you specially to be mine, you terrible, rude forms.

316. shore] This section was added in 1867.

(Mother, bend down, bend close to me your face,
I know not what these plots and wars and deferments are for,
I know not fruition's success, but I know that through war and
       crime your work goes on, and must yet go on.)   315

19

Thus by blue Ontario's shore,
While the winds fann'd me and the waves came trooping toward
       me,
I thrill'd with the power's pulsations, and the charm of my theme
       was upon me,
Till the tissues that held me parted their ties upon me.

And I saw the free souls of poets,   320
The loftiest bards of past ages strode before me,
Strange large men, long unwaked, undisclosed, were disclosed to
       me.

20

O my rapt verse, my call, mock me not!
Not for the bards of the past, not to invoke them have I launch'd
       you forth,
Not to call even those lofty bards here by Ontario's shores,   325
Have I sung so capricious and loud my savage song.

Bards for my own land only I invoke,
(For the war the war is over, the field is clear'd,)
Till they strike up marches henceforth triumphant and onward,
To cheer O Mother your boundless expectant soul.   330

Bards of the great Idea! bards of the peaceful inventions! (for
       the war, the war is over!)
Yet bards of latent armies, a million soldiers waiting ever-ready,
Bards with songs as from burning coals or the lightning's fork'd
       stripes!
Ample Ohio's, Kanada's bards—bards of California! inland
       bards—bards of the war!
You by my charm I invoke.   335
    1856   *1881*

   323. not!] This section was added in 1867.

Reversals.

Let that which stood in front go behind,
Let that which was behind advance to the front,
Let bigots, fools, unclean persons, offer new propositions,
Let the old propositions be postponed,
5   Let a man seek pleasure everywhere except in himself,
Let a woman seek happiness everywhere except in herself.

1856   *1881*

Autumn Rivulets.

As Consequent, Etc.

As consequent from store of summer rains,
Or wayward rivulets in autumn flowing,
Or many a herb-lined brook's reticulations,
Or subterranean sea-rills making for the sea,
5   Songs of continued years I sing.

REVERSALS] The six lines composing this poem were originally part of a 57-line poem of 1856, "Poem of the Propositions of Nakedness," in which WW, expressing a mood—rare for him—of ironic sarcasm, proposed the reversal of his own affirmations. This 1856 poem became No. 5 of the "Chants Democratic" of 1860; was again retitled "Respondez" in 1867, 1871, and 1876; and then was rejected in 1881 except for "Reversals" and another three lines to be called "Transpositions." See "Respondez" in the section of "Excluded Poems" below.

RIVULETS] The thirty-eight poems of this group, new to the final 1881 arrangement, draw upon no less than nine separate editions, from the two 1855 poems to the four here published for the first time. In between are five of 1856, twelve of 1860, three of 1865, one of 1867, five of the 1871 *Passage to India*, one of the 1872 *As a Strong Bird on Pinions Free and Other Poems*, and four of the 1876 *Two Rivulets*. As a group these poems are devoted to no common theme or progression of idea, and they are also disparate in quality. They have perhaps the prevailing mood of retrospective recall, of mature evaluation, and the autumnal wisdom of experience. In short, "Autumn Rivulets" constitute a range, not a focus of the poet's interest.

CONSEQUENT, *etc.*] This introductory poem, new to LG in 1881, carries forward the metaphor of the group title, the only one of the thirty-eight overtly to do so. However, other poems in the cluster also project the mood of the title, such as "The City

Life's ever-modern rapids first, (soon, soon to blend,
With the old streams of death.)

Some threading Ohio's farm-fields or the woods,
Some down Colorado's cañons from sources of perpetual snow,
Some half-hid in Oregon, or away southward in Texas,   10
Some in the north finding their way to Erie, Niagara, Ottawa,
Some to Atlantica's bays, and so to the great salt brine.

In you whoe'er you are my book perusing,
In I myself, in all the world, these currents flowing,
All, all toward the mystic ocean tending.   15

Currents for starting a continent new,
Overtures sent to the solid out of the liquid,
Fusion of ocean and land, tender and pensive waves,
(Not safe and peaceful only, waves rous'd and ominous too,
Out of the depths the storm's abysmic waves, who knows whence?   20
Raging over the vast, with many a broken spar and tatter'd sail.)

Or from the sea of Time, collecting vasting all, I bring,
A windrow-drift of weeds and shells.

O little shells, so curious-convolute, so limpid-cold and voiceless,
Will you not little shells to the tympans of temples held,   25
Murmurs and echoes still call up, eternity's music faint and far,
Wafted inland, sent from Atlantica's rim, strains for the soul of the
     prairies,

Dead-House," "This Compost," "Unnamed Lands," "Outlines for a Tomb," "Laws
for Creation," "To a Common Prostitute," "Kosmos," and "Who Learns My Lesson
Complete." Although "As Consequent, etc." is new to the 1881 edition, two of its
passages are transferred, as the footnotes indicate, from two poems of the 1876 TR,
now rejected for use here. The imagery of the poem is intricate. The "wayward
rivulets" are both WW's own poems and the fructifying currents of the continent;
the "little shells," cast up from the sea of Time, are also the tidings of his poems,
made out of his life and years; and the "windrow-drift of weeds and shells" are a
double metaphor: the poet's discoveries—weeds and shells—being distributed like a
windrow on the sea and then drifting ashore to form another line, a "windrow-
drift."

     13. perusing] Lines 13–15 were originally lines 10–12 of "Two Rivulets" in the
1876 TR.
     16. new] Lines 16–21 were originally lines 13–18 of the 1876 "Or from That Sea
of Time."
     22. bring] Lines 22–33 were originally lines 1–12 of the 1876 "Or from That
Sea of Time."
     22. collecting vasting] "To vast"—short for "avast"—meant "to stop" or "to
give up." Perhaps the meaning is "bringing everything to the end of its voyage.

Whisper'd reverberations, chords for the ear of the West joyously
    sounding,
Your tidings old, yet ever new and untranslatable,
30 Infinitesimals out of my life, and many a life,
  (For not my life and years alone I give—all, all I give,)
These waifs from the deep, cast high and dry,
Wash'd on America's shores?

1876, 1881   *1881*

The Return of the Heroes.

1

For the lands and for these passionate days and for myself,
Now I awhile retire to thee O soil of autumn fields,
Reclining on thy breast, giving myself to thee,
Answering the pulses of thy sane and equable heart,
5 Tuning a verse for thee.

O earth that hast no voice, confide to me a voice,
O harvest of my lands—O boundless summer growths,
O lavish brown parturient earth—O infinite teeming womb,
A song to narrate thee.

2

10 Ever upon this stage,
Is acted God's calm annual drama,
Gorgeous processions, songs of birds,
Sunrise that fullest feeds and freshens most the soul,

HEROES] This poem was first published in *The Galaxy*, September, 1867, under
the title, "A Carol of Harvest for 1867," and reprinted in *Tinsley's Magazine* (Lon-
don) the following month. Then, with a number of revisions, it was published in the
1871 *Passage to India*. The same text appeared in the "Passage to India" supplement
of the 1876 *TR* with an added headnote: "In all History, antique or modern, the
grandest achievement yet for political Humanity—grander even than the triumph
of THIS UNION over Secession—was the return, disbanding, and peaceful disinte-
gration from compact military organization, back into agricultural and civil employ-
ments, of the vast Armies, the two millions of embattled men of America—a prob-
lem reserved for Democracy, our day and land, to promptly solve." After some fur-
ther revision the poem appeared in *LG* 1881 with present title and text, which has
dropped the original opening passage:

The heaving sea, the waves upon the shore, the musical, strong
     waves,
The woods, the stalwart trees, the slender, tapering trees,   15
The liliput countless armies of the grass,
The heat, the showers, the measureless pasturages,
The scenery of the snows, the winds' free orchestra,
The stretching light-hung roof of clouds, the clear cerulean and
     the silvery fringes,
The high dilating stars, the placid beckoning stars,   20
The moving flocks and herds, the plains and emerald meadows,
The shows of all the varied lands and all the growths and products.

3

Fecund America—to-day,
Thou art all over set in births and joys!
Thou groan'st with riches, thy wealth clothes thee as a swathing-
     garment,   25
Thou laughest loud with ache of great possessions,
A myriad-twining life like interlacing vines binds all thy vast
     demesne,
As some huge ship freighted to water's edge thou ridest into
     port,
As rain falls from the heaven and vapors rise from earth, so have
     the precious values fallen upon thee and risen out of thee;
Thou envy of the globe! thou miracle!   30
Thou, bathed, choked, swimming in plenty,
Thou lucky Mistress of the tranquil barns,
Thou Prairie Dame that sittest in the middle and lookest out upon
     thy world, and lookest East and lookest West,

> A song of the grass and fields!
> A song of the soil, and the good green grass!
> A song no more of the city streets;
> A song of the soil of fields.
>
> A song with the smell of sun-dried hay, where the
>   nimble pitchers handle the pitch-fork;
> A song tasting of new wheat, and of fresh-husk'd
>   maize.

Examination of the Barrett MS suggests that themes for two separate poems—
the abundant harvest of 1867 and the return of the soldiers—had been skillfully
united in a single poem which sensitively associated the tilled fields of the fecund
land with the red fields of war. See Fredson Bowers' analysis of the MS in *MP*, LII,
No. 1 (August, 1954), 29–51.

Dispensatress, that by a word givest a thousand miles, a million
      farms, and missest nothing,
Thou all-acceptress—thou hospitable, (thou only art hospitable as
35   God is hospitable.)

       4

When late I sang sad was my voice,
Sad were the shows around me with deafening noises of hatred
      and smoke of war;
In the midst of the conflict, the heroes, I stood,
Or pass'd with slow step through the wounded and dying.

40   But now I sing not war,
Nor the measur'd march of soldiers, nor the tents of camps,
Nor the regiments hastily coming up deploying in line of battle;
No more the sad, unnatural shows of war.

Ask'd room those flush'd immortal ranks, the first forth-stepping
      armies?
45   Ask room alas the ghastly ranks, the armies dread that follow'd.

(Pass, pass, ye proud brigades, with your tramping sinewy legs,
With your shoulders young and strong, with your knapsacks and
      your muskets;
How elate I stood and watch'd you, where starting off you
      march'd.

Pass—then rattle drums again,
50   For an army heaves in sight, O another gathering army,
Swarming, trailing on the rear, O you dread accruing army,
O you regiments so piteous, with your mortal diarrhœa, with your
      fever,
O my land's maim'd darlings, with the plenteous bloody bandage
      and the crutch,
Lo, your pallid army follows.)

   56. and lanes,] We have restored the comma, which was destroyed in an earlier
printing.

5

But on these days of brightness,   55
On the far-stretching beauteous landscape, the roads and lanes,
  the high-piled farm-wagons, and the fruits and barns,
Should the dead intrude?

Ah the dead to me mar not, they fit well in Nature,
They fit very well in the landscape under the trees and grass,
And along the edge of the sky in the horizon's far margin.   60

Nor do I forget you Departed,
Nor in winter or summer my lost ones,
But most in the open air as now when my soul is rapt and at
  peace, like pleasing phantoms,
Your memories rising glide silently by me.

6

I saw the day the return of the heroes,   65
(Yet the heroes never surpass'd shall never return,
Them that day I saw not.)

I saw the interminable corps, I saw the processions of armies,
I saw them approaching, defiling by with divisions,
Streaming northward, their work done, camping awhile in clusters
  of mighty camps.   70

No holiday soldiers—youthful, yet veterans,
Worn, swart, handsome, strong, of the stock of homestead and
  workshop,
Harden'd of many a long campaign and sweaty march,
Inured on many a hard-fought bloody field.

A pause—the armies wait,   75
A million flush'd embattled conquerors wait,
The world too waits, then soft as breaking night and sure as dawn,
They melt, they disappear.

65. I saw the day] WW gives an eyewitness account of the soldiers' return to
Washington in two of his *Specimen Days* entries: "The Armies Returning" of May
7, 1865 and "The Grand Review" of May 23.

Exult O lands! victorious lands!
80   Not there your victory on those red shuddering fields,
But here and hence your victory.

Melt, melt away ye armies—disperse ye blue-clad soldiers,
Resolve ye back again, give up for good your deadly arms,
Other the arms the fields henceforth for you, or South or North,
85   With saner wars, sweet wars, life-giving wars.

7

Loud O my throat, and clear O soul!
The season of thanks and the voice of full-yielding,
The chant of joy and power for boundless fertility.

All till'd and untill'd fields expand before me,
90   I see the true arenas of my race, or first or last,
Man's innocent and strong arenas.

I see the heroes at other toils,
I see well-wielded in their hands the better weapons.

I see where the Mother of All,
95   With full-spanning eye gazes forth, dwells long,
And counts the varied gathering of the products.

Busy the far, the sunlit panorama,
Prairie, orchard, and yellow grain of the North,
Cotton and rice of the South and Louisianian cane,
100   Open unseeded fallows, rich fields of clover and timothy,
Kine and horses feeding, and droves of sheep and swine,
And many a stately river flowing and many a jocund brook,
And healthy uplands with herby-perfumed breezes,
And the good green grass, that delicate miracle the ever-recurring
          grass.

8

105   Toil on heroes! harvest the products!
Not alone on those warlike fields the Mother of All,
With dilated form and lambent eyes watch'd you.

114. machines,] We have restored the comma, which was not present in *LG* 1889

Toil on heroes! toil well! handle the weapons well!
The Mother of All, yet here as ever she watches you.

Well-pleased America thou beholdest,   110
Over the fields of the West those crawling monsters,
The human-divine inventions, the labor-saving implements;
Beholdest moving in every direction imbued as with life the
      revolving hay-rakes,
The steam-power reaping-machines and the horse-power machines,
The engines, thrashers of grain and cleaners of grain, well sepa-
      rating the straw, the nimble work of the patent pitchfork,   115
Beholdest the newer saw-mill, the southern cotton-gin, and the
      rice-cleanser.

Beneath thy look O Maternal,
With these and else and with their own strong hands the heroes
      harvest.

All gather and all harvest,
Yet but for thee O Powerful, not a scythe might swing as now in
      security,   120
Not a maize-stalk dangle as now its silken tassels in peace.

Under thee only they harvest, even but a wisp of hay under thy
      great face only,
Harvest the wheat of Ohio, Illinois, Wisconsin, every barbed spear
      under thee,
Harvest the maize of Missouri, Kentucky, Tennessee, each ear in
      its light-green sheath,
Gather the hay to its myriad mows in the odorous tranquil barns,   125
Oats to their bins, the white potato, the buckwheat of Michigan,
      to theirs;
Gather the cotton in Mississippi or Alabama, dig and hoard the
      golden the sweet potato of Georgia and the Carolinas,
Clip the wool of California or Pennsylvania,
Cut the flax in the Middle States, or hemp or tobacco in the
      Borders,
Pick the pea and the bean, or pull apples from the trees or bunches
      of grapes from the vines,   130

and the 1891–2 hardbound issue honored here. It appears in the softbound issue and
in texts from 1881 to 1888.

Or aught that ripens in all these States or North or South,
Under the beaming sun and under thee.

1867   *1881*

There Was a Child Went Forth.

There was a child went forth every day,
And the first object he look'd upon, that object he became,
And that object became part of him for the day or a certain part
    of the day,
Or for many years or stretching cycles of years.

5   The early lilacs became part of this child,
And grass and white and red morning-glories, and white and red
       clover, and the song of the phœbe-bird,
And the Third-month lambs and the sow's pink-faint litter, and
       the mare's foal and the cow's calf,
And the noisy brood of the barnyard or by the mire of the pond-
       side,
And the fish suspending themselves so curiously below there, and
       the beautiful curious liquid,
And the water-plants with their graceful flat heads, all became part
10   of him.

The field-sprouts of Fourth-month and Fifth-month became part
       of him,
Winter-grain sprouts and those of the light-yellow corn, and the
       esculent roots of the garden,
And the apple-trees cover'd with blossoms and the fruit afterward,
       and wood-berries, and the commonest weeds by the road,
And the old drunkard staggering home from the outhouse of the
       tavern whence he had lately risen,
15 And the schoolmistress that pass'd on her way to the school,
And the friendly boys that pass'd, and the quarrelsome boys,

FORTH] The tenth poem of the first edition, this much-anthologized lyric under-
went moderate but constant revision in later texts. In 1856 it was entitled, "Poem of
the Child That Went Forth, and Always Goes Forth, Forever and Forever"; in 1860,
"Leaves of Grass No. 9"; in 1867 "No. 1" of another *LG* group; and since 1871 it has
had its present title.
    The poem irresistibly suggests autobiography in its vivid identification of the

And the tidy and fresh-cheek'd girls, and the barefoot negro boy
    and girl,
And all the changes of city and country wherever he went.

His own parents, he that had father'd him and she that had con-
    ceiv'd him in her womb and birth'd him,
They gave this child more of themselves than that,   20
They gave him afterward every day, they became part of him.

The mother at home quietly placing the dishes on the supper-
    table,
The mother with mild words, clean her cap and gown, a whole-
    some odor falling off her person and clothes as she walks by,
The father, strong, self-sufficient, manly, mean, anger'd, unjust,
The blow, the quick loud word, the tight bargain, the crafty lure,   25
The family usages, the language, the company, the furniture, the
    yearning and swelling heart,
Affection that will not be gainsay'd, the sense of what is real, the
    thought if after all it should prove unreal,
The doubts of day-time and the doubts of night-time, the curious
    whether and how,
Whether that which appears so is so, or is it all flashes and specks?
Men and women crowding fast in the streets, if they are not flashes
    and specks what are they?   30
The streets themselves and the façades of houses, and goods in
    the windows,
Vehicles, teams, the heavy-plank'd wharves, the huge crossing at
    the ferries,
The village on the highland seen from afar at sunset, the river
    between,
Shadows, aureola and mist, the light falling on roofs and gables of
    white or brown two miles off,
The schooner near by sleepily dropping down the tide, the little
    boat slack-tow'd astern,   35
The hurrying tumbling waves, quick-broken crests, slapping,

growing child with his own experience. Yet the poet universalized his testimony; a
final line, dropped in 1867 read: "And these become of him or her that peruses them
now." Tennyson's line in "Ulysses"—"I am a part of all that I have met"—makes the
same point. A handsome children's edition of this poem, with pictures by Zhenya Gay,
was published in 1943.
    27. unreal] Compare the thought of this and the following three lines with that of
the 1860 poem, "Of the Terrible Doubt of Appearances."

The strata of color'd clouds, the long bar of maroon-tint away
    solitary by itself, the spread of purity it lies motionless in,
The horizon's edge, the flying sea-crow, the fragrance of salt
    marsh and shore mud,
These became part of that child who went forth every day, and
    who now goes, and will always go forth every day.

1855   *1871*

Old Ireland.

Far hence amid an isle of wondrous beauty,
Crouching over a grave an ancient sorrowful mother,
Once a queen, now lean and tatter'd seated on the ground,
Her old white hair drooping dishevel'd round her shoulders,
5 At her feet fallen an unused royal harp,
Long silent, she too long silent, mourning her shrouded hope and
      heir,
Of all the earth her heart most full of sorrow because most full of
    love.

Yet a word ancient mother,
You need crouch there no longer on the cold ground with fore-
    head between your knees,
10 O you need not sit there veil'd in your old white hair so dishevel'd,
For know you the one you mourn is not in that grave,
It was an illusion, the son you love was not really dead,
The Lord is not dead, he is risen again young and strong in
    another country,
Even while you wept there by your fallen harp by the grave,
15 What you wept for was translated, pass'd from the grave,
The winds favor'd and the sea sail'd it,
And now with rosy and new blood,
Moves to-day in a new country.

1861   *1867*

IRELAND] First appeared in the *New York Leader*, November 2, 1861, collected
in *Drum-Taps* 1865, and remained unchanged in all LG editions. Some variants occur
in the magazine text—for example, the phrase "an armed man" after "to-day" in the
final line. The Fenian Brotherhood, an Irish-American revolutionary society, was
founded in the United States in 1858; in the decade 1851–1860, one and a half million
Irish, faced with famine and poverty, emigrated to America, while the total remaining

The City Dead-House.

By the city dead-house by the gate,
As idly sauntering wending my way from the clangor,
I curious pause, for lo, an outcast form, a poor dead prostitute
      brought,
Her corpse they deposit unclaim'd, it lies on the damp brick
      pavement,
The divine woman, her body, I see the body, I look on it alone,   5
That house once full of passion and beauty, all else I notice not,
Nor stillness so cold, nor running water from faucet, nor odors
      morbific impress me,
But the house alone—that wondrous house—that delicate fair
      house—that ruin!
That immortal house more than all the rows of dwellings ever
      built!
Or white-domed capitol with majestic figure surmounted, or all
      the old high-spired cathedrals,   10
That little house alone more than them all—poor, desperate
      house!
Fair, fearful wreck—tenement of a soul—itself a soul,
Unclaim'd, avoided house—take one breath from my tremulous
      lips,
Take one tear dropt aside as I go for thought of you,
Dead house of love—house of madness and sin, crumbled,
      crush'd,   15
House of life, erewhile talking and laughing—but ah, poor house,
      dead even then,
Months, years, an echoing, garnish'd house—but dead, dead,
      dead.

1867   1881

---

population of Ireland was less than six million.

    DEAD-HOUSE] This poem was first published in the 1867 *LG*, and has remained substantially unchanged in text and title. Still very popular was a poem by Thomas Hood, "The Bridge of Sighs" (1844), which depicts and ponders in an insistent dactylic rhythm a suicide prostitute, while the author properly maintains aesthetic distance from the subject. Compare WW's poem, which is obviously different.

This Compost.

1

Something startles me where I thought I was safest,
I withdraw from the still woods I loved,
I will not go now on the pastures to walk,
I will not strip the clothes from my body to meet my lover the sea,
5   I will not touch my flesh to the earth as to other flesh to renew me.

O how can it be that the ground itself does not sicken?
How can you be alive you growths of spring?
How can you furnish health you blood of herbs, roots, orchards, grain?
Are they not continually putting distemper'd corpses within you?
10   Is not every continent work'd over and over with sour dead?

Where have you disposed of their carcasses?
Those drunkards and gluttons of so many generations?
Where have you drawn off all the foul liquid and meat?
I do not see any of it upon you to-day, or perhaps I am deceiv'd,
I will run a furrow with my plough, I will press my spade through
15   the sod and turn it up underneath,
I am sure I shall expose some of the foul meat.

2

Behold this compost! behold it well!
Perhaps every mite has once form'd part of a sick person—yet behold!
The grass of spring covers the prairies,
20   The bean bursts noiselessly through the mould in the garden,
The delicate spear of the onion pierces upward,
The apple-buds cluster together on the apple-branches,

COMPOST] First published in *LG* 1856 under the arresting title, "Poem of Wonder at The Resurrection of The Wheat"; appeared with revisions in *LG* 1860 as "Leaves of Grass" No. 4; present title in 1867, and completed text, 1881. The poem has undergone much revision, and a sizable MS fragment (Trent), printed in *FCI*, 9–11, shows early stages. A sentence in the chapter "Spring" of Thoreau's *Walden,*

The resurrection of the wheat appears with pale visage out of its
     graves,
The tinge awakes over the willow-tree and the mulberry-tree,
The he-birds carol mornings and evenings while the she-birds sit
     on their nests,   25
The young of poultry break through the hatch'd eggs,
The new-born of animals appear, the calf is dropt from the cow,
     the colt from the mare,
Out of its little hill faithfully rise the potato's dark green leaves,
Out of its hill rises the yellow maize-stalk, the lilacs bloom in the
     dooryards,
The summer growth is innocent and disdainful above all those
     strata of sour dead.   30

What chemistry!
That the winds are really not infectious,
That this is no cheat, this transparent green-wash of the sea
     which is so amorous after me,
That it is safe to allow it to lick my naked body all over with its
     tongues,
That it will not endanger me with the fevers that have deposited
     themselves in it,   35
That all is clean forever and forever,
That the cool drink from the well tastes so good,
That blackberries are so flavorous and juicy,
That the fruits of the apple-orchard and the orange-orchard, that
     melons, grapes, peaches, plums, will none of them poison me,
That when I recline on the grass I do not catch any disease,   40
Though probably every spear of grass rises out of what was once
     a catching disease.

Now I am terrified at the Earth, it is that calm and patient,
It grows such sweet things out of such corruptions,
It turns harmless and stainless on its axis, with such endless
     successions of diseas'd corpses,

published just two years before, expresses a thought of striking similarity: "There
was a dead horse in the hollow by the path to my home which compelled me
sometimes to go out of my way, especially in the night when the air was heavy, but
the assurance it gave me of the strong appetite and inviolable health of Nature was
my compensation for this." Both in form and subject this poem is essential Whitman,
one of his best. Cf. also "Song of Myself," section 49, lines 1294–1298.

45 It distills such exquisite winds out of such infused fetor,
It renews with such unwitting looks its prodigal, annual, sumptu-
ous crops,
It gives such divine materials to men, and accepts such leavings
from them at last.

1856   1881

To a Foil'd European Revolutionaire.

Courage yet, my brother or my sister!
Keep on—Liberty is to be subserv'd whatever occurs;
That is nothing that is quell'd by one or two failures, or any num-
ber of failures,
Or by the indifference or ingratitude of the people, or by any
unfaithfulness,
5   Or the show of the tushes of power, soldiers, cannon, penal statutes.

What we believe in waits latent forever through all the continents,
Invites no one, promises nothing, sits in calmness and light, is
positive and composed, knows no discouragement,
Waiting patiently, waiting its time.

(Not songs of loyalty alone are these,
10   But songs of insurrection also,
For I am the sworn poet of every dauntless rebel the world over,
And he going with me leaves peace and routine behind him,
And stakes his life to be lost at any moment.)

The battle rages with many a loud alarm and frequent advance
and retreat,
15   The infidel triumphs, or supposes he triumphs,
The prison, scaffold, garroté, handcuffs, iron necklace and lead-
balls do their work,
The named and unnamed heroes pass to other spheres,

REVOLUTIONAIRE] When first published in *LG* 1856 with several of its lines
transferred from the 1855 Preface, this poem had the flamboyant title, "Liberty
Poem for Asia, Africa, Europe, America, Australia, Cuba, and The Archipelagoes of
the Sea." In 1860 and 1867 it became "To a Foiled Revolter or Revoltress," and in
1871 it took its present title. It is evident that the poet meant, as he added in 1871, to
be the voice "of every dauntless rebel the world over." The text was much revised in

The great speakers and writers are exiled, they lie sick in distant
  lands,
The cause is asleep, the strongest throats are choked with their
  own blood,
The young men droop their eyelashes toward the ground when
  they meet;   20
But for all this Liberty has not gone out of the place, nor the
  infidel enter'd into full possession.

When liberty goes out of a place it is not the first to go, nor the
  second or third to go,
It waits for all the rest to go, it is the last.

When there are no more memories of heroes and martyrs,
And when all life and all the souls of men and women are dis-
  charged from any part of the earth,   25
Then only shall liberty or the idea of liberty be discharged from
  that part of the earth,
And the infidel come into full possession.

Then courage European revolter, revoltress!
For till all ceases neither must you cease.

I do not know what you are for, (I do not know what I am for
  myself, nor what any thing is for,)   30
But I will search carefully for it even in being foil'd,
In defeat, poverty, misconception, imprisonment—for they too
  are great.

Did we think victory great?
So it is—but now it seems to me , when it cannot be help'd, that
  defeat is great,
And that death and dismay are great.   35

 1856   *1881*

LG editions from 1860 to 1871.
  In the fifth and sixth editions of 1871 and 1876 this poem was one of six placed in
a special group called "Songs of Insurrection," a division not retained in later editions.
   5. tushes] Variant of "tusks" or "teeth."
   16. garroté]Erroneous accent added in *CPP* 1888; repeated in hardbound text of
LG 1891–2, but not in the softbound issue.

Unnamed Lands.

Nations ten thousand years before these States, and many times
    ten thousand years before these States,
Garner'd clusters of ages that men and women like us grew up and
    travel'd their course and pass'd on,
What vast-built cities, what orderly republics, what pastoral tribes
    and nomads,
What histories, rulers, heroes, perhaps transcending all others,
5   What laws, customs, wealth, arts, traditions,
What sort of marriage, what costumes, what physiology and
    phrenology,
What of liberty and slavery among them, what they thought of
    death and the soul,
Who were witty and wise, who beautiful and poetic, who brutish
    and undevelop'd,
Not a mark, not a record remains—and yet all remains.

O I know that those men and women were not for nothing, any
10   more than we are for nothing,
I know that they belong to the scheme of the world every bit as
    much as we now belong to it.

Afar they stand, yet near to me they stand,
Some with oval countenances learn'd and calm,
Some naked and savage, some like huge collections of insects,
15   Some in tents, herdsmen, patriarchs, tribes, horsemen,
Some prowling through woods, some living peaceably on farms,
    laboring, reaping, filling barns,
Some traversing paved avenues, amid temples, palaces, factories,
    libraries, shows, courts, theatres, wonderful monuments.

LANDS] This poem was first published in LG 1860 under its present title. The
Barrett MS (Bowers, 220–224) and the sucessive texts indicate moderate revision.
An early prose MS draft of factual backgrounds (Trent: "The most immense part of
ancient history is altogether unknown," etc.) contains several lines later used in the
poem (see N and F, 76–77). However, the real theme of the poem is not the past
existence of unnamed lands and civilizations, but the poet's faith that they are
somehow perpetuated.

PRUDENCE] Except for the two opening lines, this 1856 poem is taken, practically
in its entirety, from the 1855 Preface, and has undergone but minor changes since. In
LG 1856 it was called "Poem of the Last Explanation of Prudence," in LG 1860
"Leaves of Grass" No. 5, and in the following three editions the title was the poem's

Are those billions of men really gone?
Are those women of the old experience of the earth gone?
Do their lives, cities, arts, rest only with us?   20
Did they achieve nothing for good for themselves?

I believe of all those men and women that fill'd the unnamed
      lands, every one exists this hour here or elsewhere, invisible
      to us,
In exact proportion to what he or she grew from in life, and out
      of what he did or she did, felt, became, loved, sinn'd, in life.

I believe that was not the end of those nations or any person of
      them, any more than this shall be the end of my nation, or
      of me;
Of their languages, governments, marriage, literature, products,
      games, wars, manners, crimes, prisons, slaves, heroes, poets,   25
I suspect their results curiously await in the yet unseen world,
      counterparts of what accrued to them in the seen world,
I suspect I shall meet them there,
I suspect I shall there find each old particular of those unnamed
      lands.

1860   *1881*

Song of Prudence.

Manhattan's streets I saunter'd pondering,
On Time, Space, Reality—on such as these, and abreast with
      them Prudence.

The last explanation always remains to be made about prudence,
Little and large alike drop quietly aside from the prudence that
      suits immortality.

first line (*q.v.*). In 1881 it took its present title and position.
      One of the most Emersonian of WW's poems, it may have been influenced by
Emerson's lecture on "Prudence" (*Essays: First Series*, 1841). Emerson's observa-
tion that Prudence is "the outmost action of the inward life" and that "everything in
nature, even motes and feathers, go by law and not by luck" strongly supports the
poem. A scrap of prose MS (Feinberg) complains that "spiritual prudence" is
"nearly altogether omitted in modern formulas, & in the atmosphere of poems & all
the literary products."
      4. suits immortality] Although prudence is now familiarly referred to pragmatic
caution in worldly affairs, its basic meaning, as here, is "wisdom conducing to moral
virtue and discipline."

5   The soul is of itself,
    All verges to it, all has reference to what ensues,
    All that a person does, says, thinks, is of consequence,
    Not a move can a man or woman make, that affects him or her in
           a day, month, any part of the direct lifetime, or the hour
           of death,
    But the same affects him or her onward afterward through the
           indirect lifetime.

10 The indirect is just as much as the direct,
    The spirit receives from the body just as much as it gives to the
           body, if not more.

    Not one word or deed, not venereal sore, discoloration, privacy
           of the onanist,
    Putridity of gluttons or rum-drinkers, peculation, cunning, betrayal,
           murder, seduction, prostitution,
    But has results beyond death as really as before death.

    Charity and personal force are the only investments worth any
15   thing.

    No specification is necessary, all that a male or female does, that is
           vigorous, benevolent, clean, is so much profit to him or her,
    In the unshakable order of the universe and through the whole
           scope of it forever.

    Who has been wise receives interest,
    Savage, felon, President, judge, farmer, sailor, mechanic, literat,
           young, old, it is the same,
20 The interest will come round—all will come round.

    Singly, wholly, to affect now, affected their time, will forever affect,
           all of the past and all of the present and all of the future,
    All the brave actions of war and peace,
    All help given to relatives, strangers, the poor, old, sorrowful, young
           children, widows, the sick, and to shunn'd persons,
    All self-denial that stood steady and aloof on wrecks, and saw
           others fill the seats of the boats,
    All offering of substance or life for the good old cause, or for a
25   friend's sake, or opinion's sake,

    19. judge] The word "prostitute" appeared between "judge" and "farmer" in
1856 only.

All pains of enthusiasts scoff'd at by their neighbors,
All the limitless sweet love and precious suffering of mothers,
All honest men baffled in strifes recorded or unrecorded,
All the grandeur and good of ancient nations whose fragments we
      inherit,
All the good of the dozens of ancient nations unknown to us by
      name, date, location,   30
All that was ever manfully begun, whether it succeeded or no,
All suggestions of the divine mind of man or the divinity of his
      mouth, or the shaping of his great hands,
All that is well thought or said this day on any part of the globe,
      or on any of the wandering stars, or on any of the fix'd
      stars, by those there as we are here,
All that is henceforth to be thought or done by you whoever you
      are, or by any one,
These inure, have inured, shall inure, to the identities from which
      they sprang, or shall spring.   35

Did you guess any thing lived only its moment?
The world does not so exist, no parts palpable or impalpable so
      exist,
No consummation exists without being from some long previous
      consummation, and that from some other,
Without the farthest conceivable one coming a bit nearer the
      beginning than any.

Whatever satisfies souls is true;   40
Prudence entirely satisfies the craving and glut of souls,
Itself only finally satisfies the soul,
The soul has that measureless pride which revolts from every lesson
      but its own.

Now I breathe the word of the prudence that walks abreast with
      time, space, reality,
That answers the pride which refuses every lesson but its own.   45

What is prudence is indivisible,
Declines to separate one part of life from every part,
Divides not the righteous from the unrighteous or the living from
      the dead,
Matches every thought or act by its correlative,

50 Knows no possible forgiveness or deputed atonement,
Knows that the young man who composedly peril'd his life and
     lost it has done exceedingly well for himself without doubt,
That he who never peril'd his life, but retains it to old age in
     riches and ease, has probably achiev'd nothing for himself
     worth mentioning,
Knows that only that person has really learn'd who has learn'd to
     prefer results,
Who favors body and soul the same,
55 Who perceives the indirect assuredly following the direct,
Who in his spirit in any emergency whatever neither hurries nor
     avoids death.

1856   *1881*

The Singer in the Prison.

1

> *O sight of pity, shame and dole!*
> *O fearful thought—a convict soul.*

Rang the refrain along the hall, the prison,
Rose to the roof, the vaults of heaven above,
Pouring in floods of melody in tones so pensive sweet and strong
5   the like whereof was never heard,
Reaching the far-off sentry and the armed guards, who ceas'd their
     pacing,
Making the hearer's pulses stop for ecstasy and awe.

2

The sun was low in the west one winter day,
When down a narrow aisle amid the thieves and outlaws of the
     land,
(There by the hundreds seated, sear-faced murderers, wily counter-
10   feiters,

PRISON] This poem was first published in the *Saturday Evening Visitor* (Wash-
ington), December 25, 1869, before inclusion in the 1871 *Passage to India* and
succeeding editions of LG. In the present text (1881) WW excluded the two-
line refrain after the first canto and each quatrain of the hymn.

Gather'd to Sunday church in prison walls, the keepers round,
Plenteous, well-armed, watching with vigilant eyes,)
Calmly a lady walk'd holding a little innocent child by either
　　　hand,
Whom seating on their stools beside her on the platform,
She, first preluding with the instrument a low and musical prelude,　　15
In voice surpassing all, sang forth a quaint old hymn.

　　　A soul confined by bars and bands,
　　　Cries, help! O help! and wrings her hands,
　　　Blinded her eyes, bleeding her breast,
　　　Nor pardon finds, nor balm of rest.　　20

　　　Ceaseless she paces to and fro,
　　　O heart-sick days! O nights of woe!
　　　Nor hand of friend, nor loving face,
　　　Nor favor comes, nor word of grace.

　　　It was not I that sinn'd the sin,　　25
　　　The ruthless body dragg'd me in;
　　　Though long I strove courageously,
　　　The body was too much for me.

　　　Dear prison'd soul bear up a space,
　　　For soon or late the certain grace;　　30
　　　To set thee free and bear thee home,
　　　The heavenly pardoner death shall come.

　　　　　Convict no more, nor shame, nor dole!
　　　　　Depart—a God-enfranchis'd soul!

3

The singer ceas'd,　　35
One glance swept from her clear calm eyes o'er all those upturn'd
　　　faces,
Strange sea of prison faces, a thousand varied, crafty, brutal,
　　　seam'd and beauteous faces,

The poem celebrates the 1869 concert of the famous singer Parepa-Rosa in Sing Sing Prison, a performance said to have been attended by the poet himself. (See *In Re*, 370.) It is one of the few poems in LG inspired by an occasion or making any use of conventional versification. Frankly sentimental, it is burdened with clichés. MS in Huntington.

Then rising, passing back along the narrow aisle between them,
While her gown touch'd them rustling in the silence,
40 She vanish'd with her children in the dusk.

While upon all, convicts and armed keepers ere they stirr'd,
(Convict forgetting prison, keeper his loaded pistol,)
A hush and pause fell down a wondrous minute,
With deep, half-stifled sobs and sound of bad men bow'd and
    moved to weeping,
45 And youth's convulsive breathings, memories of home,
The mother's voice in lullaby, the sister's care, the happy childhood,
The long-pent spirit rous'd to reminiscence;
A wondrous minute then—but after in the solitary night, to many,
    many there,
Years after, even in the hour of death, the sad refrain, the tune,
    the voice, the words,
50 Resumed, the large calm lady walks the narrow aisle,
The wailing melody again, the singer in the prison sings,

> *O sight of pity, shame and dole!*
> *O fearful thought—a convict soul.*

1869   1881

Warble for Lilac-Time.

Warble me now for joy of lilac-time, (returning in reminiscence,)
Sort me O tongue and lips for Nature's sake, souvenirs of earliest
    summer,
Gather the welcome signs, (as children with pebbles or stringing
    shells,)
Put in April and May, the hylas croaking in the ponds, the elastic
    air,
5 Bees, butterflies, the sparrow with its simple notes,
Blue-bird and darting swallow, nor forget the high-hole flashing
    his golden wings,

LILAC-TIME] First published in *The Galaxy*, May, 1870 (MS in Berg). Re-
printed with concurrent slight revisions in *Passage to India*, 1871; in the *Daily
Graphic*, May 12, 1873; in the "Passage to India" group of LG 1872 and TR 1876;
and with eight lines cancelled, in its present form in LG 1881. One of WW's most
successful lyrics, this "jocund and sparkling" spring song also suggests the emotional
range of the lilac symbol (cf. note, "When Lilacs Last in the Dooryard Bloom'd").
TOMB] First published in *The Galaxy*, January, 1870, under the title, "Brother
of all, with Generous Hand." Reprinted in *Passage to India*, 1871; in the "Passage to

The tranquil sunny haze, the clinging smoke, the vapor,
Shimmer of waters with fish in them, the cerulean above,
All that is jocund and sparkling, the brooks running,
The maple woods, the crisp February days and the sugar-making,   10
The robin where he hops, bright-eyed, brown-breasted,
With musical clear call at sunrise, and again at sunset,
Or flitting among the trees of the apple-orchard, building the nest
    of his mate,
The melted snow of March, the willow sending forth its yellow-
    green sprouts,
For spring-time is here! the summer is here! and what is this
    in it and from it?   15
Thou, soul, unloosen'd—the restlessness after I know not what;
Come, let us lag here no longer, let us be up and away!
O if one could but fly like a bird!
O to escape, to sail forth as in a ship!
To glide with thee O soul, o'er all, in all, as a ship o'er the waters;   20
Gathering these hints, the preludes, the blue sky, the grass, the
    morning drops of dew,
The lilac-scent, the bushes with dark green heart-shaped leaves,
Wood-violets, the little delicate pale blossoms called innocence,
Samples and sorts not for themselves alone, but for their atmos-
    phere,
To grace the bush I love—to sing with the birds,   25
A warble for joy of lilac-time, returning in reminiscence.

    1870   *1881*

Outlines for a Tomb.

  (*G. P., Buried 1870.*)

    1

What may we chant, O thou within this tomb?
What tablets, outlines, hang for thee, O millionnaire?

India" group of *LG* 1872 and *TR* 1876; and in 1881 under its present title with thirty
of its seventy-nine lines cancelled. An early MS (Trent), printed in *N and F*, 44–45,
item 147, shows some resemblance to the poem in its presentation of "tableaus," a
favorite device with WW.

    2. millionnaire] George Peabody (1795–1869), philanthropist, who died in
London, November 4, 1869, his body being returned by British warship to his native
Danvers, Mass., in January, 1870. He founded the Peabody museums at Yale and
Harvard.

The life thou lived'st we know not,
But that thou walk'dst thy years in barter, 'mid the haunts of
      brokers,
5   Nor heroism thine, nor war, nor glory.

2

Silent, my soul,
With drooping lids, as waiting, ponder'd,
Turning from all the samples, monuments of heroes.

While through the interior vistas,
10   Noiseless uprose, phantasmic, (as by night Auroras of the north,)
Lambent tableaus, prophetic, bodiless scenes,
Spiritual projections.

In one, among the city streets a laborer's home appear'd,
After his day's work done, cleanly, sweet-air'd, the gaslight burning,
15   The carpet swept and a fire in the cheerful stove.

In one, the sacred parturition scene,
A happy painless mother birth'd a perfect child.

In one, at a bounteous morning meal,
Sat peaceful parents with contented sons.

20   In one, by twos and threes, young people,
Hundreds concentring, walk'd the paths and streets and roads,
Toward a tall-domed school.

In one a trio beautiful,
Grandmother, loving daughter, loving daughter's daughter, sat,
25   Chatting and sewing.

In one, along a suite of noble rooms,
'Mid plenteous books and journals, paintings on the walls, fine
      statuettes,
Were groups of friendly journeymen, mechanics young and old,
Reading, conversing.

MASK] First published in the New York *Tribune*, Feb. 19, 1876, then in *Two
Rivulets* (1876), a companion volume to LG, and in WW's "Centennial Edition" of

All, all the shows of laboring life,   30
City and country, women's, men's and children's,
Their wants provided for, hued in the sun and tinged for once
          with joy,
Marriage, the street, the factory, farm, the house-room, lodging-
          room,
Labor and toil, the bath, gymnasium, playground, library, college,
The student, boy or girl, led forward to be taught,   35
The sick cared for, the shoeless shod, the orphan father'd and
          mother'd,
The hungry fed, the houseless housed;
(The intentions perfect and divine,
The workings, details, haply human.)

          3
O thou within this tomb,   40
From thee such scenes, thou stintless, lavish giver,
Tallying the gifts of earth, large as the earth,
Thy name an earth, with mountains, fields and tides.

Nor by your streams alone, you rivers,
By you, your banks Connecticut,   45
By you and all your teeming life old Thames,
By you Potomac laving the ground Washington trod, by you
          Patapsco,
You Hudson, you endless Mississippi—nor you alone,
But to the high seas launch, my thought, his memory.

    1870   1881

          Out from behind This Mask.

          (*To Confront a Portrait.*)

              1

Out from behind this bending rough-cut mask,
These lights and shades, this drama of the whole,

LG in that year. The poem was WW's description of a portrait in LG 1876, facing
"The Wound-Dresser," (*q.v.*, above, among the "Drum-Taps" poems). This portrait,

This common curtain of the face contain'd in me for me, in you
    for you, in each for each,
(Tragedies, sorrows, laughter, tears—O heaven!
5 The passionate teeming plays this curtain hid!)
This glaze of God's serenest purest sky,
This film of Satan's seething pit,
This heart's geography's map, this limitless small continent, this
    soundless sea;
Out from the convolutions of this globe,
This subtler astronomic orb than sun or moon, than Jupiter, Venus,
10   Mars,
This condensation of the universe, (nay here the only universe,
Here the idea, all in this mystic handful wrapt;)
These burin'd eyes, flashing to you to pass to future time,
To launch and spin through space revolving sideling, from these
    to emanate,
15 To you whoe'er you are—a look.

2

A traveler of thoughts and years, of peace and war,
Of youth long sped and middle age declining,
(As the first volume of a tale perused and laid away, and this the
    second,
Songs, ventures, speculations, presently to close,)
20 Lingering a moment here and now, to you I opposite turn,
As on the road or at some crevice door by chance, or open'd win-
    dow,
Pausing, inclining, baring my head, you specially I greet,

not present in the 1892 edition here reproduced, was printed from a handsome
engraving on wood, by W. J. Linton, of a photograph of the poet made by G. C.
Potter in Washington in 1871. It was to his poetic self-portrait that WW referred,
not to the artist's engraving, in a preview to *TR* that he wrote appearing in the New
York *Daily Tribune*, February 19, 1876: "Whitman gives his own portrait from life
in the book—a large, bending, gray-haired man, 'looking at you.'" See Blodgett,
"Whitman and the Linton Portrait," *WWN*, IV (September, 1958), 90–91. No
ambiguity was present in the subtitle to the poem as published in 1876, which read:
"To confront My Portrait, illustrating 'the *Wound-Dresser*,' in LEAVES OF GRASS." In
1881, the present subtitle was substituted and minor verbal alterations were made to
produce the present, final text.
    13. burin'd eyes] "Burin'd" is a technical term meaning "cut by the burin," an

To draw and clinch your soul for once inseparably with mine,
Then travel travel on.

1876   *1881*

Vocalism.

1

Vocalism, measure, concentration, determination, and the divine
      power to speak words;
Are you full-lung'd and limber-lipp'd from long trial? from vigor-
      ous practice? from physique?
Do you move in these broad lands as broad as they?
Come duly to the divine power to speak words?
For only at last after many years, after chastity, friendship, procrea-
      tion, prudence, and nakedness,   5
After treading ground and breasting river and lake,
After a loosen'd throat, after absorbing eras, temperaments, races,
      after knowledge, freedom, crimes,
After complete faith, after clarifyings, elevations, and removing
      obstructions,
After these and more, it is just possible there comes to a man, a
      woman, the divine power to speak words;
Then toward that man or that woman swiftly hasten all—none
      refuse, all attend,   10
Armies, ships, antiquities, libraries, paintings, machines, cities,
      hate, despair, amity, pain, theft, murder, aspiration, form in
      close ranks,
They debouch as they are wanted to march obediently through
      the mouth of that man or that woman.

engraver's tool.

    VOCALISM] A fusion of two poems in 1881, each of which had developed inde-
pendently in all editions since LG 1860. There they had both first appeared—the first
stanza of the present poem as "No. 12" in the "Chants Democratic" cluster; the
second stanza as "No. 21" in a "Leaves of Grass" cluster. With intervening changes
in phrasing and titles, the poem of stanza 1 above became "To Oratists" in LG 1872 to
1876, where the second stanza also appeared as a separate poem, "Voices." In the
conflation of 1881, the first stanza lost thirteen lines while the second stanza dropped
two. The fusion was then successful, for both parts celebrate the same theme—the
power of the voice, which had so attracted the poet in his earlier days that he had
seriously considered the possibility of becoming an orator. See Asselineau, 94–96.
The MSS of both stanzas (Barrett) are printed in Bowers, 154–158; 182.

2

O what is it in me that makes me tremble so at voices?
Surely whoever speaks to me in the right voice, him or her I shall
     follow,
As the water follows the moon, silently, with fluid steps, anywhere
15   around the globe.

All waits for the right voices;
Where is the practis'd and perfect organ? where is the develop'd
     soul?
For I see every word utter'd thence has deeper, sweeter, new
     sounds, impossible on less terms.

I see brains and lips closed, tympans and temples unstruck,
20   Until that comes which has the quality to strike and to unclose,
Until that comes which has the quality to bring forth what lies
     slumbering forever ready in all words.

1860   *1881*

To Him That Was Crucified.

My spirit to yours dear brother,
Do not mind because many sounding your name do not under-
     stand you,
I do not sound your name, but I understand you,
I specify you with joy O my comrade to salute you, and to salute
     those who are with you, before and since, and those to
     come also,

    14–15. globe] These two lines were used by George Eliot as an epigraph for
chapter 29, book 4 of her novel Daniel Deronda (1876). For her interest in WW, see
Blodgett, 169–171.
    CRUCIFIED] This poem was first published, under this title, in the "Messenger
Leaves" group of the 1860 *LG*, and has remained unchanged except for the dropping
in 1881 of the parenthetical phrase "(there are others also)" at the end of the third
line. The opening lines are plainly a reference to the figure of Christ, the poem
quickly broadening its meaning to include all crucified ones, of whom the poet is the
comrade and brother.
    COURTS] First published as "Leaves of Grass" No. 13 in *LG* 1860, beginning with
eight lines removed from all succeeding editions (see below; also in appended section
of "Rejected Poems and Passages"):

        O bitter sprig! Confession sprig!
        In the bouquet I give you place also—I bind you in,

That we all labor together transmitting the same charge and suc-
    cession,   5

We few equals indifferent of lands, indifferent of times,
We, enclosers of all continents, all castes, allowers of all theologies,
Compassionaters, perceivers, rapport of men,
We walk silent among disputes and assertions, but reject not the
    disputers nor any thing that is asserted,
We hear the bawling and din, we are reach'd at by divisions, jeal-
    ousies, recriminations on every side,   10
They close peremptorily upon us to surround us, my comrade,
Yet we walk unheld, free, the whole earth over, journeying up and
    down till we make our ineffaceable mark upon time and the
    diverse eras,
Till we saturate time and eras, that the men and women of races,
    ages to come, may prove brethren and lovers as we are.

1860   1881

You Felons on Trial in Courts.

You felons on trial in courts,
You convicts in prison-cells, you sentenced assassins chain'd and
    handcuff'd with iron,
Who am I too that I am not on trial or in prison?
Me ruthless and devilish as any, that my wrists are not chain'd
    with iron, or my ankles with iron?

You prostitutes flaunting over the trottoirs or obscene in your
    rooms,   5
Who am I that I should call you more obscene than myself?

                    Proceeding no further till, humbled publicly,
                    I give fair warning, once for all.

                    I own that I have been sly, thievish, mean, a prevari-
                      cator, greedy, derelict,
                    And I own that I remain so yet.
                    What foul thought but I think it—or have in me the
                      stuff out of which it is thought?
                    What in darkness in bed at night, alone or with a
                      companion?

    There were no other significant changes after 1860, although the confession note
was also struck by a revision of title which WW made in his 1860 "Blue Copy" but
never honored: "Sprig of Confession."

O culpable! I acknowledge—I exposé!
(O admirers, praise not me—compliment not me—you make
    me wince,
I see what you do not—I know what you do not.)

10   Inside these breast-bones I lie smutch'd and choked,
Beneath this face that appears so impassive hell's tides continually
    run,
Lusts and wickedness are acceptable to me,
I walk with delinquents with passionate love,
I feel I am of them—I belong to those convicts and prostitutes
    myself,
15   And henceforth I will not deny them—for how can I deny myself?

    1860   *1867*

Laws for Creations.

Laws for creations,
For strong artists and leaders, for fresh broods of teachers and
    perfect literats for America,
For noble savans and coming musicians.

All must have reference to the ensemble of the world, and the
    compact truth of the world,
There shall be no subject too pronounced—all works shall illus-
5   trate the divine law of indirections.

What do you suppose creation is?
What do you suppose will satisfy the soul, except to walk free and
    own no superior?
What do you suppose I would intimate to you in a hundred ways,
    but that man or woman is as good as God?

CREATIONS] First appeared in *LG* 1860 as "No. 13" in the cluster, "Chants
Democratic." In *LG* 1867, the poem was reduced from eighteen to eleven lines,
resulting in the present text, much improved in concentration and effectiveness.
Preserved in the Barrett collection are extensive MS notes and drafts for this poem,
which are printed in *N and F*, 22–23, item 48; also an early MS draft of the whole,
printed in Bowers, 158–160, with the rejected title, "American Laws."

PROSTITUTE] One of the "Messenger Leaves" of the 1860 *LG*, and unchanged in
all succeeding editions, this poem has acquired a certain notoriety in having in an
earlier period been frequently cited for censorship. In his MS (Huntington) WW

And that there is no God any more divine than Yourself?
And that that is what the oldest and newest myths finally mean?   10
And that you or any one must approach creations through such
    laws?

1860   1871

To a Common Prostitute.

Be composed—be at ease with me—I am Walt Whitman, liberal
    and lusty as Nature,
Not till the sun excludes you do I exclude you,
Not till the waters refuse to glisten for you and the leaves to rustle
    for you, do my words refuse to glisten and rustle for you.

My girl I appoint with you an appointment, and I charge you that
    you make preparation to be worthy to meet me,
And I charge you that you be patient and perfect till I come.   5

Till then I salute you with a significant look that you do not forget
    me.

1860   1860

I Was Looking a Long While.

I was looking a long while for Intentions,
For a clew to the history of the past for myself, and for these
    chants—and now I have found it,
It is not in those paged fables in the libraries, (them I neither
    accept nor reject,)
It is no more in the legends than in all else,
It is in the present—it is this earth to-day,   5

had originally written "My love" for "My girl" in the fourth line, and "kiss on your
lips" for "significant look" in the sixth. The poet may have thought of this poem as a
variation upon the Biblical account of the woman taken in adultery (John 8:
8–11).

    WHILE] This poem was first published as "Chants Democratic" No. 19 in LG
1860, and took its present title in 1867. Only minor revisions appear in the compari-
son of printed texts and the MS (Barrett), printed by Bowers, 168. At least three
years before publication, trial drafts of four of its lines were entered in an 1856–1857
notebook (Feinberg). As an announcement of purpose, it could well have been an
"Inscriptions" poem.

It is in Democracy—(the purport and aim of all the past,)
It is the life of one man or one woman to-day—the average man
     of to-day,
It is in languages, social customs, literatures, arts,
It is in the broad show of artificial things, ships, machinery, poli-
     tics, creeds, modern improvements, and the interchange of
     nations,
10   All for the modern—all for the average man of to-day.
    1860   1881

Thought.

Of persons arrived at high positions, ceremonies, wealth, scholar-
     ships, and the like;
(To me all that those persons have arrived at sinks away from
     them, except as it results to their bodies and souls,
So that often to me they appear gaunt and naked,
And often to me each one mocks the others, and mocks himself or
     herself,
And of each one the core of life, namely happiness, is full of the
5   rotten excrement of maggots,
And often to me those men and women pass unwittingly the true
     realities of life, and go toward false realities,
And often to me they are alive after what custom has served them,
     but nothing more,
And often to me they are sad, hasty, unwaked sonnambules walk-
     ing the dusk.)
    1860   1871

Miracles.

Why, who makes much of a miracle?
As to me I know of nothing else but miracles,

THOUGHT] This poem was first published as No. 3 of the "Thoughts" group of
LG 1860, and has remained unchanged under this title in all succeeding editions. MS
in Huntington.
    8. sonnambules] French: sleepwalkers.
    MIRACLES] Appeared as "Poem of Perfect Miracles" in LG 1856 and as "Leaves
of Grass" No. 8 in LG 1860; present title in 1867. Persistent revision to 1881 short-
ened it by eleven lines. The theme of the poem had long been on the poet's mind: in a
pre-1855 notebook (LC Whitman, 85) he had written, "We hear of miracles.—But

Whether I walk the streets of Manhattan,
Or dart my sight over the roofs of houses toward the sky,
Or wade with naked feet along the beach just in the edge of the
    water, 5
Or stand under trees in the woods,
Or talk by day with any one I love, or sleep in the bed at night
    with any one I love,
Or sit at table at dinner with the rest,
Or look at strangers opposite me riding in the car,
Or watch honey-bees busy around the hive of a summer forenoon, 10
Or animals feeding in the fields,
Or birds, or the wonderfulness of insects in the air,
Or the wonderfulness of the sundown, or of stars shining so quiet
    and bright,
Or the exquisite delicate thin curve of the new moon in spring;
These with the rest, one and all, are to me miracles, 15
The whole referring, yet each distinct and in its place.

To me every hour of the light and dark is a miracle,
Every cubic inch of space is a miracle,
Every square yard of the surface of the earth is spread with the same,
Every foot of the interior swarms with the same. 20

To me the sea is a continual miracle,
The fishes that swim—the rocks—the motion of the waves—
    the ships with men in them,
What stranger miracles are there?

1856   1881

Sparkles from the Wheel.

Where the city's ceaseless crowd moves on the livelong day,
Withdrawn I join a group of children watching, I pause aside with
    them.

what is there that is not a miracle?" Surpassing this poem in fervor are several
revelations in early sections of "Song of Myself," culminating with the miracle of a
mouse in section 31, q.v.

  WHEEL] First appeared, with the present title and text, in a "Leaves of Grass"
group of the 1871 *Passage to India*. MS scraps (Feinberg) contain trial lines, and
the MS of the complete poem (Barrett) is printed by Bowers, 254–256. Older
readers will remember the fascination of city children by the itinerant knife-grinder
and his treadle wheel; the poem illustrates WW's brilliant power to create a vignette

By the curb toward the edge of the flagging,
A knife-grinder works at his wheel sharpening a great knife,
Bending over he carefully holds it to the stone, by foot and knee,
With measur'd tread he turns rapidly, as he presses with light but
              firm hand,
Forth issue then in copious golden jets,
Sparkles from the wheel.

The scene and all its belongings, how they seize and affect me,
The sad sharp-chinn'd old man with worn clothes and broad
              shoulder-band of leather,
Myself effusing and fluid, a phantom curiously floating, now here
              absorb'd and arrested,
The group, (an unminded point set in a vast surrounding,)
The attentive, quiet children, the loud, proud, restive base of the
              streets,
The low hoarse purr of the whirling stone, the light-press'd blade,
Diffusing, dropping, sideways-darting, in tiny showers of gold,
Sparkles from the wheel.

              1871   1871

To a Pupil.

Is reform needed? is it through you?
The greater the reform needed, the greater the Personality you
              need to accomplish it.

You! do you not see how it would serve to have eyes, blood,
              complexion, clean and sweet?
Do you not see how it would serve to have such a body and soul
              that when you enter the crowd an atmosphere of desire
              and command enters with you, and every one is impress'd
              with your Personality?

of such scenes, in which, however, the point of view is not entirely objective—the
poet, an "arrested phantom," bringing in himself as observer, conscious perhaps of
himself as being also a maker of sparkles from the wheel. Compare some of these
qualities in Robert Frost's "The Grindstone."
    PUPIL] One of the "Messenger Leaves" of LG 1860, this poem has remained

O the magnet! the flesh over and over!   5
Go, dear friend, if need be give up all else, and commence to-day
      to inure yourself to pluck, reality, self-esteem, definiteness,
      elevatedness,
Rest not till you rivet and publish yourself of your own Personality.

  1860   *1867*

Unfolded Out of the Folds.

Unfolded out of the folds of the woman man comes unfolded,
      and is always to come unfolded,
Unfolded only out of the superbest woman of the earth is to come
      the superbest man of the earth,
Unfolded out of the friendliest woman is to come the friendliest
      man,
Unfolded only out of the perfect body of a woman can a man be
      form'd of perfect body,
Unfolded only out of the inimitable poems of woman can come
      the poems of man, (only thence have my poems come;)   5
Unfolded out of the strong and arrogant woman I love, only
      thence can appear the strong and arrogant man I love,
Unfolded by brawny embraces from the well-muscled woman I
      love, only thence come the brawny embraces of the man,
Unfolded out of the folds of the woman's brain come all the folds
      of the man's brain, duly obedient,
Unfolded out of the justice of the woman all justice is unfolded,
Unfolded out of the sympathy of the woman is all sympathy;   10
A man is a great thing upon the earth and through eternity, but
      every jot of the greatness of man is unfolded out of
      woman;
First the man is shaped in the woman, he can then be shaped in
      himself.

  1856   *1881*

virtually unchanged through all the editions, and the MS (Barrett), printed in
Bowers, 188, shows practically no variations.

    FOLDS] First appeared in LG 1856 as "Poem of Women"; in 1860 and 1867
identified only by its number in a "Leaves of Grass" cluster; present title in LG 1871
and thereafter, with only slight revision. Its emphasis on the eugenic role of women
is characteristic.

What Am I After All.

What am I after all but a child, pleas'd with the sound of my own
  name? repeating it over and over;
I stand apart to hear—it never tires me.

To you your name also;
Did you think there was nothing but two or three pronunciations
  in the sound of your name?

1860   *1867*

Kosmos.

Who includes diversity and is Nature,
Who is the amplitude of the earth, and the coarseness and sex-
  uality of the earth, and the great charity of the earth, and
  the equilibrium also,
Who has not look'd forth from the windows the eyes for nothing,
  or whose brain held audience with messengers for nothing,
Who contains believers and disbelievers, who is the most majestic
  lover,
Who holds duly his or her triune proportion of realism, spiritualism,
  and of the æsthetic or intellectual,
Who having consider'd the body finds all its organs and parts
  good,
Who, out of the theory of the earth and of his or her body under-
  stands by subtle analogies all other theories,

ALL] In LG 1860 this poem was "Leaves of Grass" No. 22, and in LG 1867, No. 4 in the "Songs Before Parting" supplement; with present title in 1871 as a *Passage to India* poem. In both the Barrett MS (Bowers, 184) and the 1860 text is a second line, dropped in 1867:

  I cannot tell why it affects me so much, when
    I hear it from women's voices, and from men's
    voices, or from my own voice.

KOSMOS] Usually meaning "an ordered universe," Kosmos is here applied to an individual possessing a systematic, inclusive harmony—as also in "Song of Myself," section 24, line 1. Identical in title and text in the Barrett MS (Bowers, 224–226), in LG 1860, and all later editions, except that the terminal phrase of line 7, "all other theories," was added in 1867.

LIKE] WW first saw the Missouri when he returned from his residence in New Orleans, June, 1848; and again on his Western trip in 1879. Printed in *Drum-*

The theory of a city, a poem, and of the large politics of these
      States;
Who believes not only in our globe with its sun and moon, but in
      other globes with their suns and moons,
Who, constructing the house of himself or herself, not for a day
      but for all time, sees races, eras, dates, generations,   10
The past, the future, dwelling there, like space, inseparable to-
      gether.

1860   *1867*

Others May Praise What They Like.

Others may praise what they like;
But I, from the banks of the running Missouri, praise nothing in
      art or aught else,
Till it has well inhaled the atmosphere of this river, also the
      western prairie-scent,
And exudes it all again.

1865   *1881*

Who Learns My Lesson Complete?

Who learns my lesson complete?
Boss, journeyman, apprentice, churchman and atheist,
The stupid and the wise thinker, parents and offspring, merchant,
      clerk, porter and customer,

Taps (1865), and with minor revisions in "Drum-Taps" 1867, *Passage to India*
(1871), and the "Passage to India" supplement, 1872 and 1876, before inclusion in
LG 1881.
    COMPLETE] The eleventh of the twelve untitled poems of LG 1855. In 1856
titled "Lesson Poem," it was in LG 1860 and 1867 "Leaves of Grass" No. 11 and No. 3
respectively; in *Passage to India* (1871) under the present title, and so in LG 1881.
Considerably revised, the poem was most interestingly altered in line 21, which
in the first three editions had read:

    And how I was not palpable once, but am now—and was born on the last
      day of May in the Year 43 of America—and passed from a babe, in
      the creeping trance of three summers and three winters, to articulate
      and walk—all this is equally wonderful,
    And that I grew six feet high, and that I have become a man thirty-six
      years old in the Year 79 of America, and that I am here anyhow, are
      all equally wonderful,

Editor, author, artist, and schoolboy—draw nigh and commence;
5   It is no lesson—it lets down the bars to a good lesson,
And that to another, and every one to another still.

The great laws take and effuse without argument,
I am of the same style, for I am their friend,
I love them quits and quits, I do not halt and make salaams.

I lie abstracted and hear beautiful tales of things and the reasons
10   of things,
They are so beautiful I nudge myself to listen.

I cannot say to any person what I hear—I cannot say it to myself
       —it is very wonderful.

It is no small matter, this round and delicious globe moving so
       exactly in its orbit for ever and ever, without one jolt or the
       untruth of a single second,
I do not think it was made in six days, nor in ten thousand years,
       nor ten billions of years,
Nor plann'd and built one thing after another as an architect
15   plans and builds a house.

I do not think seventy years is the time of a man or woman,
Nor that seventy millions of years is the time of a man or woman,
Nor that years will ever stop the existence of me, or any one else.

Is it wonderful that I should be immortal? as every one is im-
       mortal;
I know it is wonderful, but my eyesight is equally wonderful, and
       how I was conceived in my mother's womb is equally
20   wonderful,
And pass'd from a babe in the creeping trance of a couple of
       summers and winters to articulate and walk—all this is
       equally wonderful.

TESTS] First printed with the present title in LG 1860, and in all succeeding
editions without change. The "tests" in this pronouncement seem to be the intuitive

And that my soul embraces you this hour, and we affect each
      other without ever seeing each other, and never perhaps to
      see each other, is every bit as wonderful.

And that I can think such thoughts as these is just as wonderful,
And that I can remind you, and you think them and know them
      to be true, is just as wonderful.

And that the moon spins round the earth and on with the earth, is
      equally wonderful,
And that they balance themselves with the sun and stars is equally
      wonderful.

1855   *1867*

25

Tests.

All submit to them where they sit, inner, secure, unapproachable
      to analysis in the soul,
Not traditions, not the outer authorities are the judges,
They are the judges of outer authorities and of all traditions,
They corroborate as they go only whatever corroborates them-
      selves, and touches themselves;
For all that, they have it forever in themselves to corroborate far
      and near without one exception.

1860   *1860*

5

The Torch.

On my Northwest coast in the midst of the night a fishermen's
      group stands watching,
Out on the lake that expands before them, others are spearing
      salmon,
The canoe, a dim shadowy thing, moves across the black water,
Bearing a torch ablaze at the prow.

1865   *1871*

judgments of the soul. MS in Huntington.
    TORCH] First published in *Drum-Taps* 1865, this memorable vignette remained
unchanged after slight revision in the text of 1871.

O Star of France.

1870–71.

O star of France,
The brightness of thy hope and strength and fame,
Like some proud ship that led the fleet so long,
Beseems to-day a wreck driven by the gale, a mastless hulk,
5 And 'mid its teeming madden'd half-drown'd crowds,
Nor helm nor helmsman.

Dim smitten star,
Orb not of France alone, pale symbol of my soul, its dearest
    hopes,
The struggle and the daring, rage divine for liberty,
Of aspirations toward the far ideal, enthusiast's dreams of brother-
10   hood,
Of terror to the tyrant and the priest.

Star crucified—by traitors sold,
Star panting o'er a land of death, heroic land,
Strange, passionate, mocking, frivolous land.

Miserable! yet for thy errors, vanities, sins, I will not now rebuke
15   thee,
Thy unexampled woes and pangs have quell'd them all,
And left thee sacred.

In that amid thy many faults thou ever aimedst highly,
In that thou wouldst not really sell thyself however great the price,
20 In that thou surely wakedst weeping from thy drugg'd sleep,
In that alone among thy sisters thou, giantess, didst rend the ones
    that shamed thee,
In that thou couldst not, wouldst not, wear the usual chains,

FRANCE] In the Franco-Prussian War, 1870–1871, the defeat of France was
acknowledged by the Treaty of Frankfort, May 10, 1871; ratification by the new
French reactionary government provoked a bloody insurrection of the Commune of
Paris, May 21–28. This poem was first published June, 1871, in *The Galaxy*, which
paid WW $25 (Corr. II, 121). It was collected in *As a Strong Bird on Pinions Free
and Other Poems* (1872), reprinted in *Two Rivulets* (1876), and revised in LG
1881. The MS in the British Museum agrees with that in the Franco-American

This cross, thy livid face, thy pierced hands and feet,
The spear thrust in thy side.

O star! O ship of France, beat back and baffled long!   25
Bear up O smitten orb! O ship continue on!

Sure as the ship of all, the Earth itself,
Product of deathly fire and turbulent chaos,
Forth from its spasms of fury and its poisons,
Issuing at last in perfect power and beauty,   30
Onward beneath the sun following its course,
So thee O ship of France!

Finish'd the days, the clouds dispel'd,
The travail o'er, the long-sought extrication,
When lo! reborn, high o'er the European world,   35
(In gladness answering thence, as face afar to face, reflecting ours
         Columbia,)
Again thy star O France, fair lustrous star,
In heavenly peace, clearer, more bright than ever,
Shall beam immortal.

1871   1880

The Ox-Tamer.

In a far-away northern county in the placid pastoral region,
Lives my farmer friend, the theme of my recitative, a famous
         tamer of oxen,
There they bring him the three-year-olds and the four-year-olds to
         break them,
He will take the wildest steer in the world and break him and
         tame him,
He will go fearless without any whip where the young bullock
         chafes up and down the yard,   5

Museum at Blerancourt, as does the magazine text, in giving the final line as "Shall
rise immortal." All texts of the poem preceding that of LG 1881 are divided into four
stanzas.
    OX-TAMER] First published in the New York *Daily Graphic*, December, 1874,
in a miscellany of prose and verse called "A Christmas Garland," but apparently
composed as early as 1860, for it is one of ten poems listed by Thayer and Eldridge in
an advertisement of that year for the never-published *Banner at Daybreak*. (See
Allen, 267.) The poem appeared in *Two Rivulets* (1876) and in LG 1881.

The bullock's head tosses restless high in the air with raging eyes,
Yet see you! how soon his rage subsides—how soon this tamer
      tames him;
See you! on the farms hereabout a hundred oxen young and old,
      and he is the man who has tamed them,
They all know him, all are affectionate to him;
10 See you! some are such beautiful animals, so lofty looking;
Some are buff-color'd, some mottled, one has a white line running
      along his back, some are brindled,
Some have wide flaring horns (a good sign)—see you the
      bright hides,
See, the two with stars on their foreheads—see, the round bodies
      and broad backs,
How straight and square they stand on their legs—what fine
      sagacious eyes!
How they watch their tamer—they wish him near them—how
15   they turn to look after him!
What yearning expression! how uneasy they are when he moves
      away from them;
Now I marvel what it can be he appears to them, (books, politics,
      poems, depart—all else departs,)
I confess I envy only his fascination—my silent, illiterate friend,
Whom a hundred oxen love there in his life on farms,
20 In the northern county far, in the placid pastoral region.

    1874   *1881*

An Old Man's Thought of School.

For the Inauguration of a Public School, Camden, New Jersey, 1874.

An old man's thought of school,
An old man gathering youthful memories and blooms that youth
      itself cannot.

    SCHOOL] First published in the New York *Daily Graphic*, November 3, 1874,
with the headnote: "The following poem was recited personally by the author
Saturday afternoon, October 31, at the inauguration of the fine new Cooper Public
School, Camden, New Jersey." Collected in *Two Rivulets* (1876), somewhat im-
proved by the omission of three rather prosy lines in the final stanza, and included in
LG 1881.
    14. Fox] George Fox, 1624–1691, British reformer and founder of the Society of
Friends.

Now only do I know you,
O fair auroral skies—O morning dew upon the grass!

And these I see, these sparkling eyes,   5
These stores of mystic meaning, these young lives,
Building, equipping like a fleet of ships, immortal ships,
Soon to sail out over the measureless seas,
On the soul's voyage.

Only a lot of boys and girls?   10
Only the tiresome spelling, writing, ciphering classes?
Only a public school?

Ah more, infinitely more;
(As George Fox rais'd his warning cry, "Is it this pile of brick
      and mortar, these dead floors, windows, rails, you call the
      church?
Why this is not the church at all—the church is living, ever living
      souls.")   15

And you America,
Cast you the real reckoning for your present?
The lights and shadows of your future, good or evil?
To girlhood, boyhood look, the teacher and the school.

1874   1881

Wandering at Morn.

Wandering at morn,
Emerging from the night from gloomy thoughts, thee in my
      thoughts,
Yearning for thee harmonious Union! thee, singing bird divine!
Thee coil'd in evil times my country, with craft and black dismay,
      with every meanness, treason thrust upon thee,

MORN] First published in the New York *Daily Graphic*, March 15, 1873,
entitled "The Singing Thrush," and dated Washington, March 10. The MS (Fein-
berg), signed and dated Washington, February 28, 1873, shows two discarded
titles—"The Future Song" and "The Singing Bird," and also two lines printed in the
magazine text, but not in the 1876 *Two Rivulets* or in LG 1881, in which the poem
appeared under its present title.
      4. evil times] This was a year of financial panic and depression, precipitated by
the failure of the banking house of Jay Cooke.

This common marvel I beheld—the parent thrush I watch'd feed-
ing its young,
The singing thrush whose tones of joy and faith ecstatic,
Fail not to certify and cheer my soul.

There ponder'd, felt I,
If worms, snakes, loathsome grubs, may to sweet spiritual songs
be turn'd,
If vermin so transposed, so used and bless'd may be,
Then may I trust in you, your fortunes, days, my country;
Who knows but these may be the lessons fit for you?
From these your future song may rise with joyous trills,
Destin'd to fill the world.

1873   1881

Italian Music in Dakota.

["*The Seventeenth—the finest Regimental Band I ever heard.*"]

Through the soft evening air enwinding all,
Rocks, woods, fort, cannon, pacing sentries, endless wilds,
In dulcet streams, in flutes' and cornets' notes,
Electric, pensive, turbulent, artificial,
(Yet strangely fitting even here, meanings unknown before,
Subtler than ever, more harmony, as if born here, related here,
Not to the city's fresco'd rooms, not to the audience of the opera
house,
Sounds, echoes, wandering strains, as really here at home,
Sonnambula's innocent love, trios with *Norma's* anguish,
And thy ecstatic chorus *Poliuto;*)

DAKOTA] This poem, new to LG 1881, is a memorial of WW's western trip of
1879. Never actually in the Dakotas, the poet may have heard the "Seventeenth
Regimental Band" while it was on tour in the region he traveled. MS in Yale.
    9. *Sonnambula's* innocent love] In Vincenzo Bellini's *La Sonnambula* (The
Sleepwalker, 1831), the innocent heroine, Amina, is falsely accused of unfaithfulness
when she walks asleep into the room of a strange man. Her affronted fiancé ultimately
realizes the truth of the situation, and the lovers are happily united.
    Norma's anguish] In Bellini's *Norma* (1831) the heroine, a high priestess of a
Druid temple, breaks her vows by falling in love with Pollione, a Roman proconsul.
When he is unfaithful to her, she incites her people against him, but love makes her
powerless to implement her revenge. Pollione, moved by her love, renounces his own
perfidy. Together they immolate themselves in a funeral pyre.
    10. *Poliuto*] Opera by Gaetano Donizetti (1797–1848). Donizetti was famous

Ray'd in the limpid yellow slanting sundown,
Music, Italian music in Dakota.

While Nature, sovereign of this gnarl'd realm,
Lurking in hidden barbaric grim recesses,
Acknowledging rapport however far remov'd,   15
(As some old root or soil of earth its last-born flower or fruit,)
Listens well pleas'd.

1881   1881

With All Thy Gifts.

With all thy gifts America,
Standing secure, rapidly tending, overlooking the world,
Power, wealth, extent, vouchsafed to thee—with these and like
        of these vouchsafed to thee,
What if one gift thou lackest? (the ultimate human problem never
        solving,)
The gift of perfect women fit for thee—what if that gift of gifts
        thou lackest?   5
The towering feminine of thee? the beauty, health, completion,
        fit for thee?
The mothers fit for thee?

1873   1881

My Picture-Gallery.

In a little house keep I pictures suspended, it is not a fix'd house,
It is round, it is only a few inches from one side to the other;

for his choral power, his "rare skill in writing for the voice" (*Encyclopedia Britannica*).
    GIFTS] First published in the New York *Daily Graphic*, March 6, 1873, then in
TR (1876) and *LG* 1881. The MS (Feinberg) shows no verbal difference.
    PICTURE-GALLERY] The poet's round house is, of course, the dwelling of his
mind, within which the "cicerone" guides us among the pictures of memory. The
symbolism may remind us of the considerably different employment in Poe's "The
Haunted Palace" (1839), where disorder has conquered the guide. First published in
The American, October 30, 1880, and then in *LG* 1881, this poem originated as a
small part of a pre-1855 twenty-nine-page notebook, entitled "Pictures," with the
injunction, "break all this into Pictures." Passages are reflected in several *LG* poems
and fragments. See Holloway, *Pictures* (1927) and "Uncollected Poems" below; MS
Notebook (Yale); MS of this poem (Barrett).

Yet behold, it has room for all the shows of the world, all memo-
     ries!
Here the tableaus of life, and here the groupings of death;
5   Here, do you know this? this is cicerone himself,
With finger rais'd he points to the prodigal pictures.

    1880   *1881*

The Prairie States.

A newer garden of creation, no primal solitude,
Dense, joyous, modern, populous millions, cities and farms,
With iron interlaced, composite, tied, many in one,
By all the world contributed—freedom's and law's and thrift's
     society,
5   The crown and teeming paradise, so far, of time's accumulations,
To justify the past.

    1880   *1881*

STATES] The MS of this poem, dated from Camden, March 15, 1880, was
published in facsimile in *The Art Autograph*, May, 1880, having been sent there,
according to WW's MS note on an earlier MS copy (Hanley) "for the Irish famine."
The poem was first collected in LG 1881.

STORM] Published as "Proud Music of the Sea-Storm" in *The Atlantic Monthly*,
February, 1869. WW had asked Emerson to offer it to the editor, James T. Fields,
and he was paid $100 (Corr. II, 71–73). It was the second, and last, Whitman poem
to appear in the *Atlantic*. Asked why he had appealed to Emerson, WW replied:
"For several reasons, I may say. But the best reason I had was in his own suggestion
that I should permit him to do such things for me when the moment seemed ripe for
it." (Traubel, II, 22). WW referred to his achievement in one of his anonymous
pieces for the Washington *Star*, January 18, 1869: "The Atlantic for February
contains a long poem from his sturdy pen, and one of the very best, to our notion, that
he has yet written." With present title and one significant revision—the insertion of
the phrase, "bridging the way from Life to Death" in the penultimate line—the poem
appeared in the 1871 *Passage to India*, the 1876 *Two Rivulets*, and LG 1881.

Critics have praised the musical pattern of this poem—its symphonic structure
(Handbook, 199–200) and its similarity to an operatic overture (Faner, 153–154)—
and such comparisons are provocative; yet it is clear that its essential being resides in

Proud Music of the Storm.

1

Proud music of the storm,
Blast that careers so free, whistling across the prairies,
Strong hum of forest tree-tops—wind of the mountains,
Personified dim shapes—you hidden orchestras,
You serenades of phantoms with instruments alert,   5
Blending with Nature's rhythmus all the tongues of nations;
You chords left as by vast composers—you choruses,
You formless, free, religious dances—you from the Orient,
You undertone of rivers, roar of pouring cataracts,
You sounds from distant guns with galloping cavalry,   10
Echoes of camps with all the different bugle-calls,
Trooping tumultuous, filling the midnight late, bending me power-
        less,
Entering my lonesome slumber-chamber, why have you seiz'd me?

2

Come forward O my soul, and let the rest retire,
Listen, lose not, it is toward thee they tend,   15

its dramatic dedication, brought brilliantly to a climax in the final passage:

> Poems bridging the way from Life to Death, vaguely wafted in
>   night air, uncaught, unwritten,
> Which let us go forth in the bold day and write.

In the beginning, the poet is seized by the music, not alone of physical Nature, but of the "hidden orchestras" of human actions, past and present, which in the varied forms of festival, war, balladry, and all the passionate chants of life, are celebrated in the second section of the poem. Then in the third section the poet dwells delightedly on his own musical experience, an experience presently extended to the music of the wide world, heard or imagined, until he cries, "Give me to hold all sounds . . . Fill me with all the voices of the universe. . . ." Then, awakened from his trance, he knows that he has found his "clew" to go forth to "tally" life, refreshed and cheered. One great surmise remains—now in mid-career he feels a new "rhythmus" to fit the poems he has yet to write. Thus "Proud Music of the Storm" announces a new phase in which, as noted in both the 1872 and 1876 prefaces, WW turns to the sphere of "Spiritual Law." The poem is a fitting prelude for "Passage to India." For an extensive analysis see Sydney J. Krause, "Whitman, Music, and *Proud Music of the Storm*," PMLA, LXXII (September, 1957), 705–721.

Parting the midnight, entering my slumber-chamber,
For thee they sing and dance O soul.

A festival song,
The duet of the bridegroom and the bride, a marriage-march,
20　With lips of love, and hearts of lovers fill'd to the brim with love,
The red-flush'd cheeks and perfumes, the cortege swarming full of
　　　　friendly faces young and old,
To flutes' clear notes and sounding harps' cantabile.

Now loud approaching drums,
Victoria! see'st thou in powder-smoke the banners torn but flying?
　　　　the rout of the baffled?
25　Hearest those shouts of a conquering army?

(Ah soul, the sobs of women, the wounded groaning in agony,
The hiss and crackle of flames, the blacken'd ruins, the embers
　　　　of cities,
The dirge and desolation of mankind.)

Now airs antique and mediæval fill me,
30　I see and hear old harpers with their harps at Welsh festivals,
I hear the minnesingers singing their lays of love,
I hear the minstrels, gleemen, troubadours, of the middle ages.

Now the great organ sounds,
Tremulous, while underneath, (as the hid footholds of the earth,
35　On which arising rest, and leaping forth depend,
All shapes of beauty, grace and strength, all hues we know,
Green blades of grass and warbling birds, children that gambol
　　　　and play, the clouds of heaven above,)
The strong base stands, and its pulsations intermits not,
Bathing, supporting, merging all the rest, maternity of all the
　　　　rest,

---

22. cantabile] Music in song-like style, appropriate to the wedding procession.
24. Victoria] England's queen. Perhaps a reference to the Crimean War and the charge of the Light Brigade at Balaklava, October 25, 1854; perhaps a taunting reference to the triumphant Northern armies (1865) in the light of British "neutrality."
34–39. while underneath . . . maternity of all the rest] The symbolism in these lines is interesting: that the base (bass) notes of a musical phrase represent the maternal basic strength of the whole harmony of creation.

And with it every instrument in multitudes,   40
The players playing, all the world's musicians,
The solemn hymns and masses rousing adoration,
All passionate heart-chants, sorrowful appeals,
The measureless sweet vocalists of ages,
And for their solvent setting earth's own diapason,   45
Of winds and woods and mighty ocean waves,
A new composite orchestra, binder of years and climes, ten-fold
    renewer,
As of the far-back days the poets tell, the Paradiso,
The straying thence, the separation long, but now the wandering
    done,
The journey done, the journeyman come home,   50
And man and art with Nature fused again.

Tutti! for earth and heaven;
(The Almighty leader now for once has signal'd with his wand.)

The manly strophe of the husbands of the world,
And all the wives responding.   55

The tongues of violins,
(I think O tongues ye tell this heart, that cannot tell itself,
This brooding yearning heart, that cannot tell itself.)

3

Ah from a little child,
Thou knowest soul how to me all sounds became music,   60
My mother's voice in lullaby or hymn,
(The voice, O tender voices, memory's loving voices,
Last miracle of all, O dearest mother's, sister's, voices;)
The rain, the growing corn, the breeze among the long-leav'd corn,
The measur'd sea-surf beating on the sand,   65

    48. Paradiso] The third part of Dante's *Divina Commedia*, in which the great
Italian poet and his Beatrice together ascend to their sphere in Heaven, the "wander-
ing done" (line 49).
    52. Tutti!] Literally, "all, entire!"—a command to the instruments, "all to-
gether!" as signaled by the orchestra leader of line 53, after the straying from
"Paradiso" and the journey home again.
    54. strophe] Now usually "stanza," but here, as in the Greek choral dance, one in
a succession of corresponding movements.

The twittering bird, the hawk's sharp scream,
The wild-fowl's notes at night as flying low migrating north or
 south,
The psalm in the country church or mid the clustering trees, the
 open air camp-meeting,
The fiddler in the tavern, the glee, the long-strung sailor-song,
70 The lowing cattle, bleating sheep, the crowing cock at dawn.

All songs of current lands come sounding round me,
The German airs of friendship, wine and love,
Irish ballads, merry jigs and dances, English warbles,
Chansons of France, Scotch tunes, and o'er the rest,
75 Italia's peerless compositions.

Across the stage with pallor on her face, yet lurid passion,
Stalks Norma brandishing the dagger in her hand.

I see poor crazed Lucia's eyes' unnatural gleam,
Her hair down her back falls loose and dishevel'd.

80 I see where Ernani walking the bridal garden,
Amid the scent of night-roses, radiant, holding his bride by the
 hand,
Hears the infernal call, the death-pledge of the horn.

To crossing swords and gray hairs bared to heaven,
The clear electric base and baritone of the world,
85 The trombone duo, Libertad forever!

75. Italia's peerless compositions] The opera, in which WW's interest was inex-
haustible.
77. Norma] The heroine of Vincenzo Bellini's opera of the same name. Cf. note,
line 9, "Italian Music in Dakota." Norma, brandishing her dagger against her lover,
is enacting the climactic scene of the opera.
78. Lucia] The heroine of Gaetano Donizetti's opera, *Lucia di Lammermoor.*
Tricked into marriage with a man she does not love, Lucia murders him and
collapses into madness.
80. Ernani] The hero of Giuseppe Verdi's opera of the same name. Ernani's
secret adoration of a court lady betrothed to a Spanish grandee leads him into a
typically complex love intrigue ending in his tragic suicide.
83–85] A reference to the great trombone duet from Bellini's opera, *I Puritani.*
89. Fernando] The hero of Donizetti's opera *La Favorita.* Lines 86–89 describe
one of the poet's most loved scenes, in which Fernando is in despair, believing his
beloved Leonora has deceived him by becoming the king's mistress.
90. Amina] Soprano role in Bellini's *La Sonnambula.* See note, line 9, "Italian

From Spanish chestnut trees' dense shade,
By old and heavy convent walls a wailing song,
Song of lost love, the torch of youth and life quench'd in despair,
Song of the dying swan, Fernando's heart is breaking.

Awaking from her woes at last retriev'd Amina sings,   90
Copious as stars and glad as morning light the torrents of her joy.

(The teeming lady comes,
The lustrious orb, Venus contralto, the blooming mother,
Sister of loftiest gods, Alboni's self I hear.)

4

I hear those odes, symphonies, operas,   95
I hear in the *William Tell* the music of an arous'd and angry
          people,
I hear Meyerbeer's *Huguenots*, the *Prophet*, or *Robert*,
Gounod's *Faust*, or Mozart's *Don Juan*.

I hear the dance-music of all nations,
The waltz, some delicious measure, lapsing, bathing me in bliss,   100
The bolero to tinkling guitars and clattering castanets.

I see religious dances old and new,
I hear the sound of the Hebrew lyre,
I see the crusaders marching bearing the cross on high, to the
          martial clang of cymbals,

Music in Dakota."
     93. lustrious] In its first appearance (*Atlantic Monthly*, February, 1869), read
"lustrous." If "lustrious" is in fact a typographical error, it persisted through nine
LG issues during WW's lifetime, to become "lustrous" once, in 76.2 TR (not in the
"Centennial") and afterward only posthumously, in LG 1897 and later. Conjecturally
(cf. lustrous > illustrious) to WW the wordworker, Alboni was both the incom-
parably lustrous Venus and the illustrious songstress. See note, 94.
     94. Alboni] Marietta Alboni, great operatic prima-donna, introduced to New
York during the summer of 1852. WW attended all of her performances and regarded
her singing as the most moving of his musical experiences.
     96. *William Tell*] Rossini's famous opera about the Swiss hero was first produced
in 1829.
     97. Meyerbeer] Giacomo Meyerbeer (1791–1863) produced his romantic operas,
Robert le Diable, *Les Huguenots*, and *Le Prophète* in Paris in 1831, 1836, and 1849
respectively.
     98.] Gounod's *Faust*, an opera based upon Goethe's great poem, was produced in
Paris in 1859; Mozart's *Don Juan* (properly, *Don Giovanni*) was produced in Prague
29 Oct., 1787.

I hear dervishes monotonously chanting, interspers'd with frantic
105   shouts, as they spin around turning always towards Mecca,
I see the rapt religious dances of the Persians and the Arabs,
Again, at Eleusis, home of Ceres, I see the modern Greeks dancing,
I hear them clapping their hands as they bend their bodies,
I hear the metrical shuffling of their feet.

I see again the wild old Corybantian dance, the performers
110   wounding each other,
I see the Roman youth to the shrill sound of flageolets throwing
      and catching their weapons,
As they fall on their knees and rise again.

I hear from the Mussulman mosque the muezzin calling,
I see the worshippers within, nor form nor sermon, argument nor
      word,
115 But silent, strange, devout, rais'd, glowing heads, ecstatic faces.

I hear the Egyptian harp of many strings,
The primitive chants of the Nile boatmen,
The sacred imperial hymns of China,
To the delicate sounds of the king, (the stricken wood and stone,)
120 Or to Hindu flutes and the fretting twang of the vina,
A band of bayaderes.

5

Now Asia, Africa leave me, Europe seizing inflates me,
To organs huge and bands I hear as from vast concourses of
      voices,
Luther's strong hymn *Eine feste Burg ist unser Gott*,
125 Rossini's *Stabat Mater dolorosa*,

107. Eleusis] Ancient Grecian city, northwest of Athens. Ceres] In Roman my-
thology, goddess of the harvest.
110. Corybantian] The Corybants were revelling attendants of the Phrygian god-
dess, Cybele, whom the Greeks adopted from the ancients and associated with
Aphrodite and Dionysus in rites celebrating the wild delights of nature.
119. king] Ancient Chinese musical instrument made of resonant stones hung in a
wooden frame, and struck with a hammer.
120. vina] Hindu musical instrument of the zither family.
121. bayaderes] Indian dancing girls.
124. Luther's . . . hymn] "A strong refuge is our God."
125. *Stabat Mater dolorosa*] Title of oratorio. Literally, "The sorrowing mother

Or floating in some high cathedral dim with gorgeous color'd
      windows,
The passionate *Agnus Dei* or *Gloria in Excelsis*.

Composers! mighty maestros!
And you, sweet singers of old lands, soprani, tenori, bassi!
To you a new bard caroling in the West,   130
Obeisant sends his love.

(Such led to thee O soul,
All senses, shows and objects, lead to thee,
But now it seems to me sound leads o'er all the rest.)

I hear the annual singing of the children in St. Paul's cathedral,   135
Or, under the high roof of some colossal hall, the symphonies,
      oratorios of Beethoven, Handel, or Haydn,
The *Creation* in billows of godhood laves me.

Give me to hold all sounds, (I madly struggling cry,)
Fill me with all the voices of the universe,
Endow me with their throbbings, Nature's also,   140
The tempests, waters, winds, operas and chants, marches and
      dances,
Utter, pour in, for I would take them all!

6

Then I woke softly,
And pausing, questioning awhile the music of my dream,
And questioning all those reminiscences, the tempest in its fury,   145
And all the songs of sopranos and tenors,
And those rapt oriental dances of religious fervor,
And the sweet varied instruments, and the diapason of organs,

was standing."
   127. *Agnus Dei . . . Gloria in Excelsis*] Titles of hymns. Literally, "Lamb of
God," "Glory in the Highest."
   137. *Creation*] *The Creation* is a famous oratorio by Franz Joseph Haydn.
   140. throbbings] The typographical error "thobbings" occurred in the LG
1881 plates. Correction was made in CPP 1888, in LG 1889 and the hardbound issue
of 1891–2 (the present text) but not in the softbound issue of that date.
   142. take them all!] In WW's graphic description (lines 102–142) of various
consummations of religious experience, there is an advance from the frenzied ecstasy
of ancient rites to the "billows of godhood," the high spirituality of the greatest
composers.

And all the artless plaints of love and grief and death,
I said to my silent curious soul out of the bed of the slumber-
150   chamber,
Come, for I have found the clew I sought so long,
Let us go forth refresh'd amid the day,
Cheerfully tallying life, walking the world, the real,
Nourish'd henceforth by our celestial dream.

155 And I said, moreover,
Haply what thou hast heard O soul was not the sound of winds,
Nor dream of raging storm, nor sea-hawk's flapping wings nor
          harsh scream,
Nor vocalism of sun-bright Italy,
Nor German organ majestic, nor vast concourse of voices, nor
          layers of harmonies,
Nor strophes of husbands and wives, nor sound of marching
160   soldiers,
Nor flutes, nor harps, nor the bugle-calls of camps,
But to a new rhythmus fitted for thee,
Poems bridging the way from Life to Death, vaguely wafted in
          night air, uncaught, unwritten,
Which let us go forth in the bold day and write.

1869   *1881*

INDIA] This poem was published in 1871 as the title piece of a paper-bound
volume of 120 pages, including seventy-five poems, of which twenty-three were new.
It appeared also in cloth-bound publication and as a supplement bound into LG 1871
without new pagination; so also in LG 1872 and *Two Rivulets*, 1876. Then, with very
slight revision, these poems were incorporated among the poems of LG 1881. This
culminating achievement of his later years was apparently the poet's launching song
for his unfulfilled project, a "further Volume" which should sing "the unseen Soul" as
LG sang "the Body and Existence" (1876 Preface). WW continued: "*Passage to
India*, and its cluster, are but freer vent and fuller expression to what, from the first,
and so throughout, more or less lurks in my writings, underneath every page, every
line, everywhere."
    The poem emerged from a long foreground and from a number of separate
compositions. In a small notebook (Lion) of fourteen leaves, WW jotted down ideas
for the poem, emphasizing Columbus as his heroic symbol. (Diplomatic transcript
by Fredson Bowers, BNYPL, July, 1957, 348–352; also transcribed in Traubel, IV,
399–400.) One leaf (Va.), entitled "Fables," which began as an independent poem,
was later incorporated into the second section of this poem. A version of section 5,
entitled "Thou Vast Rondure Swimming in Space" (see lines 81–115 and cf. MS
facsimile, GF, I, 260), was submitted in 1868–1869 to both *The Fortnightly Review*
and *The Atlantic Monthly*, but never printed. (Corr. II, 77). A MS (Lion) of
twenty-three leaves, incorporating pasted-on proof slips from both "Fables" and
"Thou Vast Rondure . . . ," gives evidence that lines 182–223 were first conceived
as an independent poem under the title, "O Soul, Thou Pleaseth Me." (See Fredson
Bowers, BNYPL, Vol. 61, 319–348, for diplomatic text.) A Harvard MS of twenty-
one leaves is evidently a fair copy of the Lion MS. (For diplomatic text, see Bowers,

Passage to India.

1

Singing my days,
Singing the great achievements of the present,
Singing the strong light works of engineers,
Our modern wonders, (the antique ponderous Seven outvied,)
In the Old World the east the Suez canal,   5
The New by its mighty railroad spann'd,
The seas inlaid with eloquent gentle wires;
Yet first to sound, and ever sound, the cry with thee O soul,
The Past! the Past! the Past!

The Past—the dark unfathom'd retrospect!   10
The teeming gulf—the sleepers and the shadows!
The past—the infinite greatness of the past!

MP, LI, November, 1953, 102–117).

At the beginning of his poem, the poet evokes the public interest in recent great achievements of communication—the opening of the Suez Canal, the junction of the Union and Central Pacific transcontinental railroads, and the laying of the Atlantic and Pacific cables. But this was not another "poem of materials"; the poet passes swiftly to his noble dream of international brotherhood, and to the great climax of his poem, the passage to more than India, the fearless venturing of the soul to the seas of God. To Traubel WW said, referring to "Passage to India," "There's more of me, the essential ultimate me, in that than in any of the poems. There is no philosophy, consistent or inconsistent, in that poem . . . but the burden of it is evolution—the one thing escaping the other—the unfolding of cosmic purposes" (Traubel, I, 156–157). For detailed analysis of the poem's movement and imagery, see Stanley K. Coffman, Jr., "Form and Meaning in Whitman's 'Passage to India,'" *PMLA*, LXX (June, 1955), 337–349. For a more generalized interpretation, see John Lovell, Jr., "Appreciating Whitman: 'Passage to India,' *MLQ*, XXI (June, 1960), 131–141.

4. Seven] The Seven Wonders of the World of ancient times were the Egyptian pyramids, the Mausoleum at Halicarnassus, the Temple of Artemis at Ephesus, the Hanging Gardens of Babylon, the Colossus of Rhodes, the statue of Zeus at Olympia, and the lighthouse at Alexandria.

5. Suez] The Suez Canal, joining the Mediterranean and Red Seas, was begun April, 1859, and opened November 17, 1869.

6. railroad] The Union Pacific and the Central Pacific railroads were joined at Promontory, Utah, May 10, 1869.

7. wires] The laying of the Atlantic cable was successfully completed in 1866.

For what is the present after all but a growth out of the past?
(As a projectile form'd, impell'd, passing a certain line, still keeps
                on,
15   So the present, utterly form'd, impell'd by the past.)

             2

Passage O soul to India!
Eclaircise the myths Asiatic, the primitive fables.

Not you alone proud truths of the world,
Nor you alone ye facts of modern science,
20   But myths and fables of eld, Asia's, Africa's fables,
The far-darting beams of the spirit, the unloos'd dreams,
The deep diving bibles and legends,
The daring plots of the poets, the elder religions;
O you temples fairer than lilies pour'd over by the rising sun!
O you fables spurning the known, eluding the hold of the known,
25   mounting to heaven!
You lofty and dazzling towers, pinnacled, red as roses, burnish'd
                with gold!
Towers of fables immortal fashion'd from mortal dreams!
You too I welcome and fully the same as the rest!
You too with joy I sing.

30   Passage to India!
Lo, soul, seest thou not God's purpose from the first?
The earth to be spann'd, connected by network,
The races, neighbors, to marry and be given in marriage,
The oceans to be cross'd, the distant brought near,
35   The lands to be welded together.

A worship new I sing,
You captains, voyagers, explorers, yours,
You engineers, you architects, machinists, yours,
You, not for trade or transportation only,
40   But in God's name, and for thy sake O soul.

17. Eclaircise] French: clarify.
18. world] Lines 18–29 were once intended, as our headnote indicates, to be a
separate poem under the title, "Fables."

3

Passage to India!
Lo soul for thee of tableaus twain,
I see in one the Suez canal initiated, open'd,
I see the procession of steamships, the Empress Eugenie's leading
   the van,
I mark from on deck the strange landscape, the pure sky, the
   level sand in the distance,   45
I pass swiftly the picturesque groups, the workmen gather'd,
The gigantic dredging machines.

In one again, different, (yet thine, all thine, O soul, the same,)
I see over my own continent the Pacific railroad surmounting
   every barrier,
I see continual trains of cars winding along the Platte carrying
   freight and passengers,   50
I hear the locomotives rushing and roaring, and the shrill steam-
   whistle,
I hear the echoes reverberate through the grandest scenery in the
   world,
I cross the Laramie plains, I note the rocks in grotesque shapes,
   the buttes,
I see the plentiful larkspur and wild onions, the barren, colorless,
   sage-deserts,
I see in glimpses afar or towering immediately above me the
   great mountains, I see the Wind river and the Wahsatch
   mountains,   55
I see the Monument mountain and the Eagle's Nest, I pass the
   Promontory, I ascend the Nevadas,
I scan the noble Elk mountain and wind around its base,
I see the Humboldt range, I thread the valley and cross the river,
I see the clear waters of lake Tahoe, I see forests of majestic
   pines,
Or crossing the great desert, the alkaline plains, I behold enchant-
   ing mirages of waters and meadows,   60
Marking through these and after all, in duplicate slender lines,

44. Eugenie's] The Empress Eugénie, wife of Napoleon III, was on *L'Aigle*, the
ship leading the procession in the ceremonies opening the Suez canal.
49. barrier] Lines 49–63 are descriptive of the railroad route from Omaha to San
Francisco.

Bridging the three or four thousand miles of land travel,
Tying the Eastern to the Western sea,
The road between Europe and Asia.

65 (Ah Genoese thy dream! thy dream!
Centuries after thou art laid in thy grave,
The shore thou foundest verifies thy dream.)

4

Passage to India!
Struggles of many a captain, tales of many a sailor dead,
70 Over my mood stealing and spreading they come,
Like clouds and cloudlets in the unreach'd sky.

Along all history, down the slopes,
As a rivulet running, sinking now, and now again to the surface
    rising,
A ceaseless thought, a varied train—lo, soul, to thee, thy sight,
    they rise,
75 The plans, the voyages again, the expeditions;
Again Vasco de Gama sails forth,
Again the knowledge gain'd, the mariner's compass,
Lands found and nations born, thou born America,
For purpose vast, man's long probation fill'd,
80 Thou rondure of the world at last accomplish'd.

5

O vast Rondure, swimming in space,
Cover'd all over with visible power and beauty,
Alternate light and day and the teeming spiritual darkness,
Unspeakable high processions of sun and moon and countless
    stars above,
85 Below, the manifold grass and waters, animals, mountains, trees,
With inscrutable purpose, some hidden prophetic intention,
Now first it seems my thought begins to span thee.

65. Genoese] Christopher Columbus. Cf. "Prayer of Columbus," the poem follow-
ing this.
76. Vasco de Gama] Correctly, da Gama: Portuguese navigator, first European

Down from the gardens of Asia descending radiating,
Adam and Eve appear, then their myriad progeny after them,
Wandering, yearning, curious, with restless explorations,   90
With questionings, baffled, formless, feverish, with never-happy
      hearts,
With that sad incessant refrain, *Wherefore unsatisfied soul?* and
      Whither O mocking life?

Ah who shall soothe these feverish children?
Who justify these restless explorations?
Who speak the secret of impassive earth?   95
Who bind it to us? what is this separate Nature so unnatural?
What is this earth to our affections? (unloving earth, without a
        throb to answer ours,
Cold earth, the place of graves.)

Yet soul be sure the first intent remains, and shall be carried out,
Perhaps even now the time has arrived.   100

After the seas are all cross'd, (as they seem already cross'd,)
After the great captains and engineers have accomplish'd their
      work,
After the noble inventors, after the scientists, the chemist, the
      geologist, ethnologist,
Finally shall come the poet worthy that name,
The true son of God shall come singing his songs.   105

Then not your deeds only O voyagers, O scientists and inventors,
      shall be justified,
All these hearts as of fretted children shall be sooth'd,
All affection shall be fully responded to, the secret shall be told,
All these separations and gaps shall be taken up and hook'd and
      link'd together,
The whole earth, this cold, impassive, voiceless earth, shall be
      completely justified,   110
Trinitas divine shall be gloriously accomplish'd and compacted by
      the true son of God, the poet,
(He shall indeed pass the straits and conquer the mountains,

to sail around Africa to India (1497–1498).
  81. Rondure] In view of the unity of lines 81–115, it is not surprising that WW
offered this passage to the magazines for independent prepublication. Cf. headnote.

He shall double the cape of Good Hope to some purpose,)
Nature and Man shall be disjoin'd and diffused no more,
115   The true son of God shall absolutely fuse them.

6

Year at whose wide-flung door I sing!
Year of the purpose accomplish'd!
Year of the marriage of continents, climates and oceans!
(No mere doge of Venice now wedding the Adriatic,)
I see O year in you the vast terraqueous globe given and giving
120   all,
Europe to Asia, Africa join'd, and they to the New World,
The lands, geographies, dancing before you, holding a festival
      garland,
As brides and bridegrooms hand in hand.

Passage to India!
125   Cooling airs from Caucasus far, soothing cradle of man,
The river Euphrates flowing, the past lit up again.

Lo soul, the retrospect brought forward,
The old, most populous, wealthiest of earth's lands,
The streams of the Indus and the Ganges and their many af-
      fluents,
130   (I my shores of America walking to-day behold, resuming all,)
The tale of Alexander on his warlike marches suddenly dying,
On one side China and on the other side Persia and Arabia,
To the south the great seas and the bay of Bengal,
The flowing literatures, tremendous epics, religions, castes,
Old occult Brahma interminably far back, the tender and junior
135   Buddha,
Central and southern empires and all their belongings, possessors,

---

119. doge of Venice] At the pinnacle of the power of Venice, the Doge annually performed a ceremonial wedding of the city to the sea by throwing a ring into the Adriatic.

126. Euphrates] The valley of the Euphrates is, traditionally, the cradle of Western civilization, and hypothetically associated with Noah's flood.

131. Alexander] Alexander the Great died on his return journey from an invasion of India (323 B.C.).

137. Tamerlane . . . Aurungzebe] Three hundred years apart in time, Tamerlane (1336?–1405), "Prince of Destruction," led wars of conquest in Turkey, Persia, India, and Russia; and Aurungzebe (1618–1707), emperor of Hindustan and self-

The wars of Tamerlane, the reign of Aurungzebe,
The traders, rulers, explorers, Moslems, Venetians, Byzantium, the
     Arabs, Portuguese,
The first travelers famous yet, Marco Polo, Batouta the Moor,
Doubts to be solv'd, the map incognita, blanks to be fill'd,   140
The foot of man unstay'd, the hands never at rest,
Thyself O soul that will not brook a challenge.

The mediæval navigators rise before me,
The world of 1492, with its awaken'd enterprise,
Something swelling in humanity now like the sap of the earth in
     spring,   145
The sunset splendor of chivalry declining.

And who art thou sad shade?
Gigantic, visionary, thyself a visionary,
With majestic limbs and pious beaming eyes,
Spreading around with every look of thine a golden world,   150
Enhuing it with gorgeous hues.

As the chief histrion,
Down to the footlights walks in some great scena,
Dominating the rest I see the Admiral himself,
(History's type of courage, action, faith,)   155
Behold him sail from Palos leading his little fleet,
His voyage behold, his return, his great fame,
His misfortunes, calumniators, behold him a prisoner, chain'd,
Behold his dejection, poverty, death.

(Curious in time I stand, noting the efforts of heroes,   160
Is the deferment long? bitter the slander, poverty, death?
Lies the seed unreck'd for centuries in the ground? lo, to God's
     due occasion,

styled "Conqueror of the World," to some extent made good this boast in neighboring
Mohammedan and Indian principalities.

  139. Marco Polo, Batouta] Both Marco Polo (1254–1324), Venetian traveler
who penetrated into far Cathay, and Batouta (1303–1377), a traveler in Africa and
Asia, were agents of mercantile expansion.

  154. Admiral] Columbus, "Admiral of the Ocean Sea." Cf., above, "the chief
histrion" (actor) and "the world of 1492." See also line 65, note.

  156. Palos] Spanish seaport from which Columbus sailed on August 3, 1492.
Regarding the misfortunes of his last years (cf. lines 158–164), see WW's "Prayer
of Columbus" (following), in which one may perceive an autobiographical overtone.

Uprising in the night, it sprouts, blooms,
And fills the earth with use and beauty.)

7

165   Passage indeed O soul to primal thought,
Not lands and seas alone, thy own clear freshness,
The young maturity of brood and bloom,
To realms of budding bibles.

O soul, repressless, I with thee and thou with me,
170   Thy circumnavigation of the world begin,
Of man, the voyage of his mind's return,
To reason's early paradise,
Back, back to wisdom's birth, to innocent intuitions,
Again with fair creation.

8

175   O we can wait no longer,
We too take ship O soul,
Joyous we too launch out on trackless seas,
Fearless for unknown shores on waves of ecstasy to sail,
Amid the wafting winds, (thou pressing me to thee, I thee to me,
        O soul,)
180   Caroling free, singing our song of God,
Chanting our chant of pleasant exploration.

With laugh and many a kiss,
(Let others deprecate, let others weep for sin, remorse, humilia-
        tion,)
O soul thou pleasest me, I thee.

185   Ah more than any priest O soul we too believe in God,
But with the mystery of God we dare not dally.

O soul thou pleasest me, I thee,
Sailing these seas or on the hills, or waking in the night,
Thoughts, silent thoughts, of Time and Space and Death, like
       waters flowing,

182. kiss] This passage (lines 182–223) was one of several ultimate components

Bear me indeed as through the regions infinite, 190
Whose air I breathe, whose ripples hear, lave me all over,
Bathe me O God in thee, mounting to thee,
I and my soul to range in range of thee.

O Thou transcendent,
Nameless, the fibre and the breath, 195
Light of the light, shedding forth universes, thou centre of them,
Thou mightier centre of the true, the good, the loving,
Thou moral, spiritual fountain—affection's source—thou reser-
    voir,
(O pensive soul of me—O thirst unsatisfied—waitest not there?
Waitest not haply for us somewhere there the Comrade perfect?) 200
Thou pulse—thou motive of the stars, suns, systems,
That, circling, move in order, safe, harmonious,
Athwart the shapeless vastnesses of space,
How should I think, how breathe a single breath, how speak, if,
    out of myself,
I could not launch, to those, superior universes? 205

Swiftly I shrivel at the thought of God,
At Nature and its wonders, Time and Space and Death,
But that I, turning, call to thee O soul, thou actual Me,
And lo, thou gently masterest the orbs,
Thou matest Time, smilest content at Death, 210
And fillest, swellest full the vastnesses of Space.

Greater than stars or suns,
Bounding O soul thou journeyest forth;
What love than thine and ours could wider amplify?
What aspirations, wishes, outvie thine and ours O soul? 215
What dreams of the ideal? what plans of purity, perfection,
    strength?
What cheerful willingness for others' sake to give up all?
For others' sake to suffer all?

Reckoning ahead O soul, when thou, the time achiev'd,
The seas all cross'd, weather'd the capes, the voyage done, 220
Surrounded, copest, frontest God, yieldest, the aim attain'd,

of "Passage to India" which originated as independent poems (see headnote). It was entitled "O Soul, Thou Pleaseth Me."

As fill'd with friendship, love complete, the Elder Brother found,
The Younger melts in fondness in his arms.

9

Passage to more than India!
225 Are thy wings plumed indeed for such far flights?
O soul, voyagest thou indeed on voyages like those?
Dispostest thou on waters such as those?
Soundest below the Sanscrit and the Vedas?
Then have thy bent unleash'd.

230 Passage to you, your shores, ye aged fierce enigmas!
Passage to you, to mastership of you, ye strangling problems!
You, strew'd with the wrecks of skeletons, that, living, never
      reach'd you.

Passage to more than India!
O secret of the earth and sky!
235 Of you O waters of the sea! O winding creeks and rivers!
Of you O woods and fields! of you strong mountains of my land!
Of you O prairies! of you gray rocks!
O morning red! O clouds! O rain and snows!
O day and night, passage to you!

240 O sun and moon and all you stars! Sirius and Jupiter!
Passage to you!

Passage, immediate passage! the blood burns in my veins!
Away O soul! hoist instantly the anchor!
Cut the hawsers—haul out—shake out every sail!
245 Have we not stood here like trees in the ground long enough?

228. Sanscrit and the Vedas] The ancient Hindu holy books, the Vedas, written in
Sanskrit, became, in translation, influential in the age of Emerson, Thoreau, and
Whitman.

    COLUMBUS] This poem was first published in *Harper's Magazine*, March, 1874,
WW asking and receiving $60 (Corr. II, 259). It appeared in *Two Rivulets*
(1876), and finally, improved by omission of two mediocre lines and a phrase from
another line, in *LG* 1881. A MS (Feinberg) of some twenty scraps of paper of
varying sizes shows considerable reworking of trial lines. WW wrote to Ellen
O'Connor, "as I see it now I shouldn't wonder if I have unconsciously put a sort of
autobiographical dash in it" (Corr. II, 272). This was conscious understatement,

Have we not grovel'd here long enough, eating and drinking like
    mere brutes?
Have we not darken'd and dazed ourselves with books long enough?

Sail forth—steer for the deep waters only,
Reckless O soul, exploring, I with thee, and thou with me,
For we are bound where mariner has not yet dared to go,   250
And we will risk the ship, ourselves and all.

O my brave soul!
O farther farther sail!
O daring joy, but safe! are they not all the seas of God?
O farther, farther, farther sail!   255

   1871   *1881*

Prayer of Columbus.

A batter'd, wreck'd old man,
Thrown on this savage shore, far, far from home,
Pent by the sea and dark rebellious brows, twelve dreary months,
Sore, stiff with many toils, sicken'd and nigh to death,
I take my way along the island's edge,   5
Venting a heavy heart.

and another woman admirer, Mrs. Anne Gilchrist, made the identification explicit:
"You too have sailed over stormy seas to your goal—surrounded with mocking
disbelievers—you too have paid the great price of health—our Columbus" (Harned,
108). On January 23 of the preceding year, WW had suffered a paralytic stroke;
just four months later, May 23, he had lost his mother; and during the 1870's, despite
occasional placement of poems in the magazines, he was feeling the public neglect.
He, too, was battered, wrecked, and sore. But the deep purport linking this poem
with "Passage to India" (cf. lines 143–164) is the poet's profoundly felt need of
divine sanction for his work, his body of poetry which had come from the "potent,
felt, interior command," for which he, as Columbus, prays. See WW's prefatory note
to the 1876 *Two Rivulets* text.

I am too full of woe!
Haply I may not live another day;
I cannot rest O God, I cannot eat or drink or sleep,
10   Till I put forth myself, my prayer, once more to Thee,
Breathe, bathe myself once more in Thee, commune with Thee,
Report myself once more to Thee.

Thou knowest my years entire, my life,
My long and crowded life of active work, not adoration merely;
15   Thou knowest the prayers and vigils of my youth,
Thou knowest my manhood's solemn and visionary meditations,
Thou knowest how before I commenced I devoted all to come to
            Thee,
Thou knowest I have in age ratified all those vows and strictly
            kept them,
Thou knowest I have not once lost nor faith nor ecstasy in Thee,
20   In shackles, prison'd, in disgrace, repining not,
Accepting all from Thee, as duly come from Thee.

All my emprises have been fill'd with Thee,
My speculations, plans, begun and carried on in thoughts of Thee,
Sailing the deep or journeying the land for Thee;
25   Intentions, purports, aspirations mine, leaving results to Thee.

O I am sure they really came from Thee,
The urge, the ardor, the unconquerable will,
The potent, felt, interior command, stronger than words,
A message from the Heavens whispering to me even in sleep,
30   These sped me on.

By me and these the work so far accomplish'd,
By me earth's elder cloy'd and stifled lands uncloy'd, unloos'd,
By me the hemispheres rounded and tied, the unknown to the known.

The end I know not, it is all in Thee,
35   Or small or great I know not—haply what broad fields, what lands,
Haply the brutish measureless human undergrowth I know,
Transplanted there may rise to stature, knowledge worthy Thee,

    20. repining not] Columbus' dark years—his imprisonment after the third voy-
age, the death of Isabella, the neglect by Ferdinand, the poverty and physical
afflictions—were known to WW through the pages of Washington Irving's *Life and
Voyages of Christopher Columbus* (1828), available in the 1861 Putnam edition of

Haply the swords I know may there indeed be turn'd to reaping-
          tools,
Haply the lifeless cross I know, Europe's dead cross, may bud and
          blossom there.

One effort more, my altar this bleak sand;   40
That Thou O God my life hast lighted,
With ray of light, steady, ineffable, vouchsafed of Thee,
Light rare untellable, lighting the very light,
Beyond all signs, descriptions, languages;
For that O God, be it my latest word, here on my knees,   45
Old, poor, and paralyzed, I thank Thee.

My terminus near,
The clouds already closing in upon me,
The voyage balk'd, the course disputed, lost,
I yield my ships to Thee.   50

My hands, my limbs grow nerveless,
My brain feels rack'd, bewilder'd,
Let the old timbers part, I will not part,
I will cling fast to Thee, O God, though the waves buffet me,
Thee, Thee at least I know.   55

Is it the prophet's thought I speak, or am I raving?
What do I know of life? what of myself?
I know not even my own work past or present,
Dim ever-shifting guesses of it spread before me,
Of newer better worlds, their mighty parturition,   60
Mocking, perplexing me.

And these things I see suddenly, what mean they?
As if some miracle, some hand divine unseal'd my eyes,
Shadowy vast shapes smile through the air and sky,
And on the distant waves sail countless ships,   65
And anthems in new tongues I hear saluting me.

1874   1881

the *Works* and elsewhere. In fact, in the MS prose jottings (Feinberg) for this
poem, he transcribes several phrases verbatim from Irving's terminal essay, "Obser-
vations on the Character of Columbus."
    23. thoughts of Thee,] The eroded comma was restored in the present edition.

The Sleepers.

1

I wander all night in my vision,
Stepping with light feet, swiftly and noiselessly stepping and
  stopping,
Bending with open eyes over the shut eyes of sleepers,
Wandering and confused, lost to myself, ill-assorted, contradic-
  tory,
5 Pausing, gazing, bending, and stopping.

How solemn they look there, stretch'd and still,
How quiet they breathe, the little children in their cradles.

The wretched features of ennuyés, the white features of corpses,
  the livid faces of drunkards, the sick-gray faces of onanists,
The gash'd bodies on battle-fields, the insane in their strong-door'd
   rooms, the sacred idiots, the new-born emerging from
   gates, and the dying emerging from gates,
10 The night pervades them and infolds them.

SLEEPERS] The Fourth of the untitled twelve of the first edition, this poem was
called "Night Poem" in 1856, "Sleep-Chasings" in 1860 and 1867, and "The Sleepers"
since 1871. It has undergone much revision, particularly in the withdrawal of
difficult but interesting passages, not so much for aesthetic as for discretionary
reasons; and of all WW's poems it may be said that this one most repays study of the
first 1855 text. It is a powerful and original composition, one of the poet's most
imaginative, and also one of the most esoteric. It is perhaps the only surrealist
American poem of the nineteenth century, remarkable in its anticipation of later
experiment. Bucke, WW's first official biographer and a professional student of the
mind, was able in 1883 to characterize "The Sleepers" accurately as "a representation
of the mind during sleep—of connected, half-connected, and disconnected thoughts
and feelings as they occur in dreams, some commonplace, some weird, some voluptu-
ous, and all given with the true and strange emotional accompaniments that belong
to them. Sometimes (and these are the most astonishing parts of the poem) the

The married couple sleep calmly in their bed, he with his palm on
     the hip of the wife, and she with her palm on the hip of
     the husband,
The sisters sleep lovingly side by side in their bed,
The men sleep lovingly side by side in theirs,
And the mother sleeps with her little child carefully wrapt.

The blind sleep, and the deaf and dumb sleep,   15
The prisoner sleeps well in the prison, the runaway son sleeps,
The murderer that is to be hung next day, how does he sleep?
And the murder'd person, how does he sleep?

The female that loves unrequited sleeps,
And the male that loves unrequited sleeps,   20
The head of the money-maker that plotted all day sleeps,
And the enraged and treacherous dispositions, all, all sleep.

I stand in the dark with drooping eyes by the worst-suffering and
     the most restless,
I pass my hands soothingly to and fro a few inches from them,
The restless sink in their beds, they fitfully sleep.   25

Now I pierce the darkness, new beings appear,
The earth recedes from me into the night,
I saw that it was beautiful, and I see that what is not the earth is
     beautiful.

I go from bedside to bedside, I sleep close with the other sleepers
     each in turn,

vague emotions, without thought, that occasionally arise in sleep, are given as they
actually occur, apart from any idea—the words having in the intellectual sense no
meaning, but arousing, as music does, the state of feeling intended" (Bucke, 171–
172). John Burroughs, on the other hand, confessed that he could not understand the
poem, and he spoke for many (*Whitman: A Study*, 5). Perhaps the poet himself
could not have explicated certain aspects of his vision, but the main theme is
unmistakable and moving. In the world of night the poet is both the dreamer and
participant in the dreams of others; he identifies his consciousness with theirs—the
whole experience becoming essentially one in which the darkness, symbolic of spirit-
ual fulfillment, is an agent of invigoration and renewal. The penetration, the audacity
of metaphor, the psychological insight of this poem, with its engagement of sexual
fantasy, was unmatched in its time and challenges the best achievements—in this
kind—of ours. For explication, see Allen and Davis, 141–143; and Miller, 130–141.
    26. Now I pierce] With this line the poet's vision deepens; he not only dreams
but also experiences "the dreams of the other dreamers" with whom he identifies.

30   I dream in my dream all the dreams of the other dreamers,
And I become the other dreamers.

I am a dance—play up there! the fit is whirling me fast!

I am the ever-laughing—it is new moon and twilight,
I see the hiding of douceurs, I see nimble ghosts whichever way
      I look,
Cache and cache again deep in the ground and sea, and where it
35   is neither ground nor sea.

Well do they do their jobs those journeymen divine,
Only from me can they hide nothing, and would not if they could,
I reckon I am their boss and they make me a pet besides,
And surround me and lead me and run ahead when I walk,
To lift their cunning covers to signify me with stretch'd arms, and
40   resume the way;
Onward we move, a gay gang of blackguards! with mirth-shouting
       music and wild-flapping pennants of joy!

I am the actor, the actress, the voter, the politician,
The emigrant and the exile, the criminal that stood in the box,
He who has been famous and he who shall be famous after to-day,
The stammerer, the well-form'd person, the wasted or feeble
45   person.

I am she who adorn'd herself and folded her hair expectantly,
My truant lover has come, and it is dark.

Double yourself and receive me darkness,
Receive me and my lover too, he will not let me go without
      him.

50   I roll myself upon you as upon a bed, I resign myself to the dusk.

---

    34. douceurs] French; plural form of "delight" or "sweetness," but here, delight. From this line to the end of the passage (line 41) the poet subtly suggests the pleasures of erotic participation.

    35. Cache] French: a hiding place

    40. cunning] Used here in the sense of the Germanic root: "knowing," or "possessed of ability"; note that the covered ones "signify"—make signs to—the speaker.

    46. I am she] In this episode there seem to be three identities: "she," the lover, and the darkness, a profound generative force of which "she" is aware, before and

He whom I call answers me and takes the place of my lover,
He rises with me silently from the bed.

Darkness, you are gentler than my lover, his flesh was sweaty and
      panting,
I feel the hot moisture yet that he left me.

My hands are spread forth, I pass them in all directions,   55
I would sound up the shadowy shore to which you are journeying.

Be careful darkness! already what was it touch'd me?
I thought my lover had gone, else darkness and he are one,
I hear the heart-beat, I follow, I fade away.

      2

I descend my western course, my sinews are flaccid,   60
Perfume and youth course through me and I am their wake.

It is my face yellow and wrinkled instead of the old woman's,
I sit low in a straw-bottom chair and carefully darn my grandson's
      stockings.

It is I too, the sleepless widow looking out on the winter mid-
      night,
I see the sparkles of starshine on the icy and pallid earth.   65

A shroud I see and I am the shroud, I wrap a body and lie in the
      coffin,
It is dark here under ground, it is not evil or pain here, it is blank
      here, for reasons.

(It seems to me that every thing in the light and air ought to be
      happy,

after the "lover" is received.
    60. I descend] With this line the poet begins to identify himself with a series of
dream episodes in which death and loss are projected by the struggle of the brave
swimmer, the wrecked ship, and—in three scenes from actuality—the Battle at
Brooklyn Heights, the farewell of Washington to his troops, and the visit of the red
squaw to the old homestead.   western course] The concept of the movement of race
and culture from east to west was generally reflected in LG. Cf. "Facing West from
California's Shores."

Whoever is not in his coffin and the dark grave let him know he
    has enough.)

3

I see a beautiful gigantic swimmer swimming naked through the
70   eddies of the sea,
His brown hair lies close and even to his head, he strikes out with
    courageous arms, he urges himself with his legs,
I see his white body, I see his undaunted eyes,
I hate the swift-running eddies that would dash him head-fore-
    most on the rocks.

What are you doing you ruffianly red-trickled waves?
Will you kill the courageous giant? will you kill him in the prime
75   of his middle age?

Steady and long he struggles,
He is baffled, bang'd, bruis'd, he holds out while his strength holds
    out,
The slapping eddies are spotted with his blood, they bear him
    away, they roll him, swing him, turn him,
His beautiful body is borne in the circling eddies, it is continually
    bruis'd on rocks,
80 Swiftly and out of sight is borne the brave corpse.

4

I turn but do not extricate myself,
Confused, a past-reading, another, but with darkness yet.

The beach is cut by the razory ice-wind, the wreck-guns sound,
The tempest lulls, the moon comes floundering through the drifts.

I look where the ship helplessly heads end on, I hear the burst as
    she strikes, I hear the howls of dismay, they grow fainter
85   and fainter.

90. defeat at Brooklyn] After the Battle of Brooklyn Heights, August 27, 1776,
in which the Americans were decisively worsted, Washington skillfully managed to

I cannot aid with my wringing fingers,
I can but rush to the surf and let it drench me and freeze
        upon me.

I search with the crowd, not one of the company is wash'd to us
        alive,
In the morning I help pick up the dead and lay them in rows in
        a barn.

5

Now of the older war-days, the defeat at Brooklyn,   90
Washington stands inside the lines, he stands on the intrench'd
        hills amid a crowd of officers,
His face is cold and damp, he cannot repress the weeping drops,
He lifts the glass perpetually to his eyes, the color is blanch'd from
        his cheeks,
He sees the slaughter of the southern braves confided to him by
        their parents.

The same at last and at last when peace is declared,   95
He stands in the room of the old tavern, the well-belov'd soldiers
        all pass through,
The officers speechless and slow draw near in their turns,
The chief encircles their necks with his arm and kisses them on
        the cheek,
He kisses lightly the wet cheeks one after another, he shakes
        hands and bids good-by to the army.

6

Now what my mother told me one day as we sat at dinner
        together,   100
Of when she was a nearly grown girl living home with her parents
        on the old homestead.

A red squaw came one breakfast-time to the old homestead,
On her back she carried a bundle of rushes for rush-bottoming
        chairs,

ferry his troops across to New York to prevent total disaster. WW wrote of the
episode in his "Brooklyniana" sketches. (See *UPP*, II, 267 ff.)

Her hair, straight, shiny, coarse, black, profuse, half-envelop'd her
      face,
Her step was free and elastic, and her voice sounded exquisitely
105   as she spoke.

My mother look'd in delight and amazement at the stranger,
She look'd at the freshness of her tall-borne face and full and
      pliant limbs,
The more she look'd upon her she loved her,
Never before had she seen such wonderful beauty and purity,
She made her sit on a bench by the jamb of the fireplace, she
110   cook'd food for her,
She had no work to give her, but she gave her remembrance and
      fondness.

The red squaw staid all the forenoon, and toward the middle of
      the afternoon she went away,
O my mother was loth to have her go away,
All the week she thought of her, she watch'd for her many a
      month,
115 She remember'd her many a winter and many a summer,
But the red squaw never came nor was heard of there again.

7

A show of the summer softness—a contact of something unseen
      —an amour of the light and air,
I am jealous and overwhelm'd with friendliness,
And will go gallivant with the light and air myself.

120 O love and summer, you are in the dreams and in me,
Autumn and winter are in the dreams, the farmer goes with his
      thrift,
The droves and crops increase, the barns are well-fill'd.

Elements merge in the night, ships make tacks in the dreams,
The sailor sails, the exile returns home,
The fugitive returns unharm'd, the immigrant is back beyond
125   months and years,

    117. A show] The two final sections, 7 and 8, illustrate the great theme of return
and retrievement under the ministration of the night, the "mother," in whom the poet

The poor Irishman lives in the simple house of his childhood
        with the well-known neighbors and faces,
They warmly welcome him, he is barefoot again, he forgets he is
        well off,
The Dutchman voyages home, and the Scotchman and Welshman
        voyage home, and the native of the Mediterranean voy-
        ages home,
To every port of England, France, Spain, enter well-fill'd ships,
The Swiss foots it toward his hills, the Prussian goes his way, the
        Hungarian his way, and the Pole his way,   130
The Swede returns, and the Dane and Norwegian return.

The homeward bound and the outward bound,
The beautiful lost swimmer, the ennuyé, the onanist, the female
        that loves unrequited, the money-maker,
The actor and actress, those through with their parts and those
        waiting to commence,
The affectionate boy, the husband and wife, the voter, the nominee
        that is chosen and the nominee that has fail'd,   135
The great already known and the great any time after to-day,
The stammerer, the sick, the perfect-form'd, the homely,
The criminal that stood in the box, the judge that sat and sen-
        tenced him, the fluent lawyers, the jury, the audience,
The laugher and weeper, the dancer, the midnight widow, the red
        squaw,
The consumptive, the erysipalite, the idiot, he that is wrong'd,   140
The antipodes, and every one between this and them in the dark,
I swear they are averaged now—one is no better than the other,
The night and sleep have liken'd them and restored them.

I swear they are all beautiful,
Every one that sleeps is beautiful, every thing in the dim light is
        beautiful,   145
The wildest and bloodiest is over, and all is peace.

Peace is always beautiful,
The myth of heaven indicates peace and night.

lay so long, and whom he loves as much as he does the "rich running day." Compare
the last lines, 177–184, with the earlier passage on darkness, 46–54, and see note on
line 46.

The myth of heaven indicates the soul,
The soul is always beautiful, it appears more or it appears less, it
150   comes or it lags behind,
It comes from its embower'd garden and looks pleasantly on
      itself and encloses the world,
Perfect and clean the genitals previously jetting, and perfect and
      clean the womb cohering,
The head well-grown proportion'd and plumb, and the bowels and
      joints proportion'd and plumb.

The soul is always beautiful,
155 The universe is duly in order, every thing is in its place,
What has arrived is in its place and what waits shall be in its place,
The twisted skull waits, the watery or rotten blood waits,
The child of the glutton or venerealee waits long, and the child
      of the drunkard waits long, and the drunkard himself waits
      long,
The sleepers that lived and died wait, the far advanced are to go on
      in their turns, and the far behind are to come on in
      their turns,
The diverse shall be no less diverse, but they shall flow and unite
160   —they unite now.

8

The sleepers are very beautiful as they lie unclothed,
They flow hand in hand over the whole earth from east to west as
      they lie unclothed,
The Asiatic and African are hand in hand, the European and
      American are hand in hand,
Learn'd and unlearn'd are hand in hand, and male and female are
      hand in hand,
The bare arm of the girl crosses the bare breast of her lover, they
165   press close without lust, his lips press her neck,
The father holds his grown or ungrown son in his arms with meas-
      ureless love, and the son holds the father in his arms with
      measureless love,
The white hair of the mother shines on the white wrist of the
      daughter,

TRANSPOSITIONS] This poem was reconstructed in 1881 from three lines—46,
44, and 22 (in that order)—of the poem "Respondez," dropped in 1881, and origi-

The breath of the boy goes with the breath of the man, friend is
    inarm'd by friend,
The scholar kisses the teacher and the teacher kisses the scholar,
    the wrong'd is made right,
The call of the slave is one with the master's call, and the master
    salutes the slave,   170
The felon steps forth from the prison, the insane becomes sane,
    the suffering of sick persons is reliev'd,
The sweatings and fevers stop, the throat that was unsound is
    sound, the lungs of the consumptive are resumed, the poor
    distress'd head is free,
The joints of the rheumatic move as smoothly as ever, and
    smoother than ever,
Stiflings and passages open, the paralyzed become supple,
The swell'd and convuls'd and congested awake to themselves
    in condition,   175
They pass the invigoration of the night and the chemistry of the
    night, and awake.

I too pass from the night,
I stay a while away O night, but I return to you again and love you.

Why should I be afraid to trust myself to you?
I am not afraid, I have been well brought forward by you,   180
I love the rich running day, but I do not desert her in whom I lay
    so long,
I know not how I came of you and I know not where I go with
    you, but I know I came well and shall go well.

I will stop only a time with the night, and rise betimes,
I will duly pass the day O my mother, and duly return to you.

  1855   *1881*

Transpositions.

Let the reformers descend from the stands where they are forever

nally titled (1856) as "Poem of the Propositions of Nakedness." See notes on "Re-
spondez" in the section of "Excluded Poems," below.

bawling—let an idiot or insane person appear on each of
the stands;
Let judges and criminals be transposed—let the prison-keepers be
put in prison—let those that were prisoners take the keys;
Let them that distrust birth and death lead the rest.

1856   *1881*

To Think of Time.

1

To think of time—of all that retrospection,
To think of to-day, and the ages continued henceforward.

Have you guess'd you yourself would not continue?
Have you dreaded these earth-beetles?
5   Have you fear'd the future would be nothing to you?

Is to-day nothing? is the beginningless past nothing?
If the future is nothing they are just as surely nothing.

To think that the sun rose in the east—that men and women
were flexible, real, alive—that every thing was alive,
To think that you and I did not see, feel, think, nor bear our part,
10 To think that we are now here and bear our part.

2

Not a day passes, not a minute or second without an accouche-
ment,
Not a day passes, not a minute or second without a corpse.

TIME] The third of the untitled twelve of the first edition, this poem was named
"Burial Poem" in 1856, "Burial" in 1860 and 1867, and "To Think of Time" since
1871. Like "The Sleepers" it has been considerably revised, although unchanged in
essentials, and a comparison of the various editions is interesting. As the earlier titles
suggest, this poem poses the question of death, which absorbed such nineteenth
century poets as Poe, Tennyson, Bryant, Wordsworth, and Dickinson. WW's poem,
less complex than his other great poem dealing with time and death, "Crossing

The dull nights go over and the dull days also,
The soreness of lying so much in bed goes over,
The physician after long putting off gives the silent and terrible
     look for an answer,   15
The children come hurried and weeping, and the brothers and
     sisters are sent for,
Medicines stand unused on the shelf, (the camphor-smell has long
     pervaded the rooms,)
The faithful hand of the living does not desert the hand of the
     dying,
The twitching lips press lightly on the forehead of the dying,
The breath ceases and the pulse of the heart ceases,   20
The corpse stretches on the bed and the living look upon it,
It is palpable as the living are palpable.

The living look upon the corpse with their eyesight,
But without eyesight lingers a different living and looks curiously
     on the corpse.

3

To think the thought of death merged in the thought of materials,   25
To think of all these wonders of city and country, and others taking
     great interest in them, and we taking no interest in them.

To think how eager we are in building our houses,
To think others shall be just as eager, and we quite indifferent.

(I see one building the house that serves him a few years, or
     seventy or eighty years at most,
I see one building the house that serves him longer than that.)   30

Slow-moving and black lines creep over the whole earth—they
     never cease—they are the burial lines,
He that was President was buried, and he that is now President
     shall surely be buried.

Brooklyn Ferry," is nonetheless powerful in its blunt immediacy. Its unevasive confrontation of the reader with the temporality of possessions and materials, and with the ironic fact of transience within seeming permanence, is remindful of Emerson's "Hamatreya." The black lines of burial creep over the whole earth. Yet the poet's affirmation is unequivocal; the goal of good is unmistakable. Nothing dies. Everything has a soul, and the poet does not walk toward annihilation. The exquisite scheme is for immortality.

4

A reminiscence of the vulgar fate,
A frequent sample of the life and death of workmen,
35   Each after his kind.

Cold dash of waves at the ferry-wharf, posh and ice in the river,
    half-frozen mud in the streets,
A gray discouraged sky overhead, the short last daylight of
    December,
A hearse and stages, the funeral of an old Broadway stage-driver,
    the cortege mostly drivers.

Steady the trot to the cemetery, duly rattles the death-bell,
The gate is pass'd, the new-dug grave is halted at, the living alight,
40   the hearse uncloses,
The coffin is pass'd out, lower'd and settled, the whip is laid on
    the coffin, the earth is swiftly shovel'd in,
The mound above is flatted with the spades—silence,
A minute—no one moves or speaks—it is done,
He is decently put away—is there any thing more?

He was a good fellow, free-mouth'd, quick-temper'd, not bad-
45   looking,
Ready with life or death for a friend, fond of women, gambled,
    ate hearty, drank hearty,
Had known what it was to be flush, grew low-spirited toward the
    last, sicken'd, was help'd by a contribution,
Died, aged forty-one years—and that was his funeral.

Thumb extended, finger uplifted, apron, cape, gloves, strap, wet-
    weather clothes, whip carefully chosen,
Boss, spotter, starter, hostler, somebody loafing on you, you loafing
50   on somebody, headway, man before and man behind,
Good day's work, bad day's work, pet stock, mean stock, first out,
    last out, turning-in at night,
To think that these are so much and so nigh to other drivers, and
    he there takes no interest in them.

36. posh] Imitative of sound made by walking through slush. WW's use of this
word in this line is cited in Webster's Unabridged Dictionary.
38. stage-driver] Probably WW, who made friends of stage drivers, had attended
the funeral of one. See "Omnibus Jaunts and Drivers" in *Specimen Days* (*Prose*

5

The markets, the government, the working-man's wages, to think
      what account they are through our nights and days,
To think that other working-men will make just as great account
      of them, yet we make little or no account.

The vulgar and the refined, what you call sin and what you call
      goodness, to think how wide a difference,   55
To think the difference will still continue to others, yet we lie
      beyond the difference.

To think how much pleasure there is,
Do you enjoy yourself in the city? or engaged in business? or
      planning a nomination and election? or with your wife and
      family?
Or with your mother and sisters? or in womanly housework? or
      the beautiful maternal cares?
These also flow onward to others, you and I flow onward,   60
But in due time you and I shall take less interest in them.

Your farm, profits, crops—to think how engross'd you are,
To think there will still be farms, profits, crops, yet for you of
      what avail?

6

What will be will be well, for what is is well,
To take interest is well, and not to take interest shall be well.   65

The domestic joys, the daily housework or business, the building
      of houses, are not phantasms, they have weight, form,
      location,
Farms, profits, crops, markets, wages, government, are none of
      them phantasms,
The difference between sin and goodness is no delusion,
The earth is not an echo, man and his life and all the things of
      his life are well-consider'd.

Works, I, 18–19, Coll W).
    41. whip] The driver's whip, according to custom, was buried with him.
    49–51.] The three lines following are interesting in their employment of terms of
the driver's trade which now belong to the past.

You are not thrown to the winds, you gather certainly and safely
      around yourself,
70   Yourself! yourself! yourself, for ever and ever!

7

It is not to diffuse you that you were born of your mother and
      father, it is to identify you,
It is not that you should be undecided, but that you should be decided,
Something long preparing and formless is arrived and form'd in you,
75   You are henceforth secure, whatever comes or goes.

The threads that were spun are gather'd, the weft crosses the warp,
      the pattern is systematic.

The preparations have every one been justified,
The orchestra have sufficiently tuned their instruments, the baton
      has given the signal.

The guest that was coming, he waited long, he is now housed,
He is one of those who are beautiful and happy, he is one of those
80   that to look upon and be with is enough.

The law of the past cannot be eluded,
The law of the present and future cannot be eluded,
The law of the living cannot be eluded, it is eternal,
The law of promotion and transformation cannot be eluded,
85   The law of heroes and good-doers cannot be eluded,
The law of drunkards, informers, mean persons, not one iota
      thereof can be eluded.

8

Slow moving and black lines go ceaselessly over the earth,
Northerner goes carried and Southerner goes carried, and they on
      the Atlantic side and they on the Pacific,
And they between, and all through the Mississippi country, and
      all over the earth.

The great masters and kosmos are well as they go, the heroes and
90   good-doers are well,

The known leaders and inventors and the rich owners and pious
     and distinguish'd may be well,
But there is more account than that, there is strict account of
     all.

The interminable hordes of the ignorant and wicked are not
     nothing,
The barbarians of Africa and Asia are not nothing,
The perpetual successions of shallow people are not nothing as
     they go.   95

Of and in all these things,
I have dream'd that we are not to be changed so much, nor the
     law of us changed,
I have dream'd that heroes and good-doers shall be under the
     present and past law,
And that murderers, drunkards, liars, shall be under the present
     and past law,
For I have dream'd that the law they are under now is enough.   100

And I have dream'd that the purpose and essence of the known
     life, the transient,
Is to form and decide identity for the unknown life, the permanent.

If all came but to ashes of dung,
If maggots and rats ended us, then Alarum! for we are betray'd,
Then indeed suspicion of death.   105

Do you suspect death? if I were to suspect death I should die
     now,
Do you think I could walk pleasantly and well-suited toward
     annihilation?

Pleasantly and well-suited I walk,
Whither I walk I cannot define, but I know it is good,
The whole universe indicates that it is good,   110
The past and the present indicate that it is good.

How beautiful and perfect are the animals!
How perfect the earth, and the minutest thing upon it!
What is called good is perfect, and what is called bad is just as
     perfect,

The vegetables and minerals are all perfect, and the imponderable
115   fluids perfect;
Slowly and surely they have pass'd on to this, and slowly and surely
          they yet pass on.

          9
I swear I think now that every thing without exception has an
          eternal soul!
The trees have, rooted in the ground! the weeds of the sea have!
          the animals!

I swear I think there is nothing but immortality!
That the exquisite scheme is for it, and the nebulous float is for it,
120   and the cohering is for it!
And all preparation is for it—and identity is for it—and life and
          materials are altogether for it!

     1855   *1881*

     DEATH] This group first appeared in *Passage to India* (1871) as a cluster of
thirteen poems. In 1881 the poet added five poems, also from *Passage to India*, to
make up the present eighteen. In this final grouping, the consonance of theme is
maintained—the exploration of the "unknown region" of spiritual law and the accept-
ance of death as a fulfillment and a new beginning. One of these poems originated in
LG 1856, nine in *LG* 1860, two in the 1865 *Drum-Taps*, and six in *LG* 1871. As early
as November 22, 1867 the poet had written to his English admirer, William M.
Rossetti, "It is quite certain that I shall add to my next edition (carrying out my plan
from the first,) a brief cluster of pieces, born of thoughts on the deep themes of
Death & Immortality" (*Corr.* II, 350). Five of the poems had their first appearance
in the English *Broadway Magazine* for October, 1868: "Whispers of Heavenly
Death," "Darest Thou Now O Soul," "A Noiseless Patient Spider," "The Last
Invocation," and "Pensive and Faltering"; and by 1870, according to MS evidence (a

Whispers of Heavenly Death.

Darest Thou Now O Soul.

Darest thou now O soul,
Walk out with me toward the unknown region,
Where neither ground is for the feet nor any path to follow?

No map there, nor guide,
Nor voice sounding, nor touch of human hand, 5
Nor face with blooming flesh, nor lips, nor eyes, are in that land.

I know it not O soul,
Nor dost thou, all is a blank before us,
All waits undream'd of in that region, that inaccessible land.

Till when the ties loosen, 10
All but the ties eternal, Time and Space,
Nor darkness, gravitation, sense, nor any bounds bounding us.

Then we burst forth, we float,
In Time and Space O soul, prepared for them,

booklet in the Feinberg Collection), he was considering these pieces, with eight more, either for a separate book or for a supplement that might be bound into a later edition of LG. See Harold W. Blodgett, "Whitman's *Whisperings*," WWR, VII (March, 1962).

SOUL] Appeared in *Broadway Magazine* (London), October, 1868, the second of five numbered poems under the single title, "Whispers of Heavenly Death." Cf. note above. They had been submitted in response to solicitation from G. Routledge and Sons, December 28, 1867 (Traubel, I, 263), to whom WW replied December 30, 1867 and again January 17 and February 19, 1868, accepting $50 in gold for the poems after an asking price of $120. (Corr. I, 355; II, 13, 17–18). The poem was printed in *Passage to India* (1871), in the "Passage to India" supplement of LG 1871 and of *Two Rivulets* (1876); and in the present text (1881) with the word "bounding" in the twelfth line as a revision for "bound." The division into three-line stanzas gives an impressive sense of regularity.

Equal, equipt at last, (O joy! O fruit of all!) them to fulfil O
15   soul.

      1868   1881

Whispers of Heavenly Death.

Whispers of heavenly death murmur'd I hear,
Labial gossip of night, sibilant chorals,
Footsteps gently ascending, mystical breezes wafted soft and low,
Ripples of unseen rivers, tides of a current flowing, forever flowing,
(Or is it the plashing of tears? the measureless waters of human
5   tears?)

I see, just see skyward, great cloud-masses,
Mournfully slowly they roll, silently swelling and mixing,
With at times a half-dimm'd sadden'd far-off star,
Appearing and disappearing.

10 (Some parturition rather, some solemn immortal birth;
On the frontiers to eyes impenetrable,
Some soul is passing over.)

      1868   1871

DEATH] This poem was the first of the *Broadway* poems of October, 1868. See
above. It remained unchanged in the 1871 and 1876 "Passage to India" supplement,
and in 1881.
      DEIFIC] First printed in "Sequel to Drum-Taps" (1865–1866), but WW wrote
trial passages on the theme earlier than *LG* 1855, e.g., see "Pictures" ("Uncol-
lected Poems," below). Another trial passage begins: "Two antique records . . ."
(notebook, 1860–1861, LC Whitman, 91, published in *UPP* 11, 91–92, and
in "Uncollected Poems"; trial titles were "Quadrel," 1860, for the never-published
Banner at Daybreak, and "Quadriune" or "Deus Quadriune," written on the contents
page of an *LG* 1860 ("Blue Copy," Lion). The long-meditated poem of 1865–1866
remained unaltered until the final edition except for two slight changes in *LG*
1881—the substitution, in line 5, of "Time, old" for "Time" and the exclusion, after
the present line 21, of the following line:

      (Conqueror yet—for before me all the armies and soldiers of the earth
            shall yet bow—and all the weapons of war become impotent.)

      Of this poem WW remarked, "It would be hard to give the idea mathematical
expression: the idea of spiritual equity—the north, south, east, west of the constituted
universe (even the soul universe)—the four sides as sustaining the universe (the
supernatural something): this is not the poem but the idea back of the poem or below
the poem. I am lame enough trying to explain it in other words—the idea seems to fit
its own words better than mine. You see, at the time the poem wrote itself: now I am
trying to write it" (Traubel, I, 156).
      WW here ignores theological creed or doctrine. Like Emerson's gnomic

Chanting the Square Deific.

1

Chanting the square deific, out of the One advancing, out of the
     sides,
Out of the old and new, out of the square entirely divine,
Solid, four-sided, (all the sides needed,) from this side Jehovah
     am I,
Old Brahm I, and I Saturnius am;
Not Time affects me—I am Time, old, modern as any,   5
Unpersuadable, relentless, executing righteous judgments,
As the Earth, the Father, the brown old Kronos, with laws,
Aged beyond computation, yet ever new, ever with those mighty
     laws rolling,
Relentless I forgive no man—whoever sins dies—I will have
     that man's life;
Therefore let none expect mercy—have the seasons, gravitation,
     the appointed days, mercy? no more have I,   10
But as the seasons and gravitation, and as all the appointed days
     that forgive not,

"Brahma," this poem deals with the principles, moral and myth-making, which have
been constant and compounded in mankind's universal experience of spiritual or
moral reality. Four principles appear, each in a separate canto: first, the elder God,
uncreated creator, whose being is soul, law, authority and time, as symbolized by
Jehovah, Brahma, Saturnius, Kronos; second, the principle of love—herald, messen-
ger, and intercessor, the master of miracle and sacrifice, typified by Christ, Hermes,
and Hercules. Emblem of revolt, pride, and guilt, Satan (Hebrew, "enemy") is abun-
dantly represented in the fallen gods and angels, demons and devils in the myths of
man's spiritual adventure. Finally, the reconciling principle of the universal spirit,
"Santa Spirita," pervades all—God, Savior, and Satan. For further analysis, see
George L. Sixbey, "Chanting the Square Deific—a Study in Whitman's Religion,"
AL, IX (May, 1937), 171–195.

    3. Jehovah] In this context, one notes in Hebrew scriptures the persistence of
these attributions: the divinity of the Godhead; the Word or the One; the lawgiver;
and the "consolator."

    4. Brahm] Brahma: in Hindu theology the supreme spirit of the universe, the
timeless and uncreated creator, hence incomparable. Saturnius] Saturn: in Roman
mythology the Titan who preceded Jupiter as head of the Olympian hierarchy. Son
of the primordial Uranus, he was the first of the gods concerned for humanity; as god
of seedtime and harvest and as lawgiver, he produced the first "golden age" for
mankind.

    7. Kronus] Cronus: in Greek mythology one of the most ancient gods, whom the
Romans confused with Saturn (see above). Born of the father-god, Uranus, whom
he overthrew to rule in his place, he was identified with time and the ancients'
discovery of it.

I dispense from this side judgments inexorable without the least
     remorse.

2

Consolator most mild, the promis'd one advancing,
With gentle hand extended, the mightier God am I,
Foretold by prophets and poets in their most rapt prophecies and
15   poems,
From this side, lo! the Lord Christ gazes—lo! Hermes I—lo!
     mine is Hercules' face,
All sorrow, labor, suffering, I, tallying it, absorb in myself,
Many times have I been rejected, taunted, put in prison, and
     crucified, and many times shall be again,
All the world have I given up for my dear brothers' and sisters'
     sake, for the soul's sake,
Wending my way through the homes of men, rich or poor, with
20   the kiss of affection,
For I am affection, I am the cheer-bringing God, with hope and
     all-enclosing charity,
With indulgent words as to children, with fresh and sane words,
     mine only,
Young and strong I pass knowing well I am destin'd myself to an
     early death;
But my charity has no death—my wisdom dies not, neither early
     nor late,
25 And my sweet love bequeath'd here and elsewhere never dies.

3

Aloof, dissatisfied, plotting revolt,
Comrade of criminals, brother of slaves,
Crafty, despised, a drudge, ignorant,
With sudra face and worn brow, black, but in the depths of my
     heart, proud as any,
30 Lifted now and always against whoever scorning assumes to rule me,

---

29. sudra] The Sudra is the lowest Hindu caste.
36. Santa Spirita] The Holy Spirit. The familiar Christian phrases—"Spirito
Santo" (Italian) and "Spiritus Sanctus" (Latin)—differ from WW's in being mascu-
line and in the usual Latinic word order. If not an example of linguistic ignorance, as
some suggest, WW's phrase is an inspired homonymous invention, affirming at once

Morose, full of guile, full of reminiscences, brooding, with many
    wiles,
(Though it was thought I was baffled and dispel'd, and my wiles
    done, but that will never be,)
Defiant, I, Satan, still live, still utter words, in new lands duly
    appearing, (and old ones also,)
Permanent here from my side, warlike, equal with any, real as any,
Nor time nor change shall ever change me or my words.   35

4

Santa Spirita, breather, life,
Beyond the light, lighter than light,
Beyond the flames of hell, joyous, leaping easily above hell,
Beyond Paradise, perfumed solely with mine own perfume,
Including all life on earth, touching, including God, including
    Saviour and Satan,   40
Ethereal, pervading all, (for without me what were all? what were
    God?)
Essence of forms, life of the real identities, permanent, positive,
    (namely the unseen,)
Life of the great round world, the sun and stars, and of man,
    I, the general soul,
Here the square finishing, the solid, I the most solid,
Breathe my breath also through these songs.   45

1865–6   *1881*

Of Him I Love Day and Night.

Of him I love day and night I dream'd I heard he was dead,
And I dream'd I went where they had buried him I love, but he
    was not in that place,
And I dream'd I wander'd searching among burial-places to find
    him,
And I found that every place was a burial-place;

the secular spirit and the lofty meaning of this fourth canto.
    NIGHT] Originally entitled "Calamus No. 17" (LG 1860, Barrett MS "Poemet"),
the poem acquired its present title in LG 1867. Transferred in 1871 from LG "Cala-
mus" to the new supplement, "Passage to India," appropriately, since it is more
concerned with "whispers of heavenly death" than with manly love.

The houses full of life were equally full of death, (this house is
5   now,)
The streets, the shipping, the places of amusement, the Chicago,
        Boston, Philadelphia, the Mannahatta, were as full of the
        dead as of the living,
And fuller, O vastly fuller of the dead than of the living;
And what I dream'd I will henceforth tell to every person and age,
And I stand henceforth bound to what I dream'd,
And now I am willing to disregard burial-places and dispense
10   with them,
And if the memorials of the dead were put up indifferently every-
        where, even in the room where I eat or sleep, I should be
        satisfied,
And if the corpse of any one I love, or if my own corpse, be
        duly render'd to powder and pour'd in the sea, I shall be
        satisfied,
Or if it be distributed to the winds I shall be satisfied.

1860   *1867*

Yet, Yet, Ye Downcast Hours.

Yet, yet, ye downcast hours, I know ye also,
Weights of lead, how ye clog and cling at my ankles,
Earth to a chamber of mourning turns—I hear the o'erweening,
        mocking voice,
Matter is conqueror—matter, triumphant only, continues onward.

5   Despairing cries float ceaselessly toward me,
The call of my nearest lover, putting forth, alarm'd, uncertain,
The sea I am quickly to sail, come tell me,
Come tell me where I am speeding, tell me my destination.

I understand your anguish, but I cannot help you,
I approach, hear, behold, the sad mouth, the look out of the eyes,
10   your mute inquiry,

HOURS] The second and third stanzas first appeared in *LG* 1860 as sections 5 and
6 of "Debris"; they reappeared in *LG* 1867 as the poem, "Despairing Cries." In 1871
the first stanza and present title were added when the poem appeared among the
"Whispers of Heavenly Death" in *Passage to India* (1871). In his revised *LG* "Blue
Copy," WW noted marginally: "tr[transfer] to Religious Leaves."
    ME] Appeared in *LG* 1860 as the final section of "Debris." In *LG* 1867 were
added the first line and the title, and the final clauses of the third and fifth lines, all

Whither I go from the bed I recline on, come tell me;
Old age, alarm'd, uncertain—a young woman's voice, appealing
      to me for comfort;
A young man's voice, *Shall I not escape?*

1860   *1871*

As If a Phantom Caress'd Me.

As if a phantom caress'd me,
I thought I was not alone walking here by the shore;
But the one I thought was with me as now I walk by the shore,
      the one I loved that caress'd me,
As I lean and look through the glimmering light, that one has
      utterly disappear'd,
And those appear that are hateful to me and mock me.   5

1860   *1867*

Assurances.

I need no assurances, I am a man who is pre-occupied of his
      own soul;
I do not doubt that from under the feet and beside the hands and
      face I am cognizant of, are now looking faces I am not
      cognizant of, calm and actual faces,
I do not doubt but the majesty and beauty of the world are latent
      in any iota of the world,
I do not doubt I am limitless, and that the universes are limitless,
      in vain I try to think how limitless,
I do not doubt that the orbs and the systems of orbs play their
      swift sports through the air on purpose, and that I shall one
      day be eligible to do as much as they, and more than they,   5
I do not doubt that temporary affairs keep on and on millions of
      years,

conforming with the poet's revisions in his so-called "Blue Copy" of *LG* 1860.

    ASSURANCES] First appeared in *LG* 1856 as sixteen lines, entitled "Faith Poem," and again without textual change in *LG* 1860, there entitled No. 7 among a "Leaves of Grass" cluster. In *LG* 1867, pruned to twelve lines by exclusion of four declarations, it appeared with the present title in the new cluster, "Songs before Parting." Transferred in 1871 to the "Whispers of Heavenly Death" cluster in *Passage to India*, where the present twelve-line text resulted from the exclusion of two lines in favor of two then added. The essential purport of the poem remained unchanged.

I do not doubt interiors have their interiors, and exteriors have
      their exteriors, and that the eyesight has another eyesight,
      and the hearing another hearing, and the voice another
      voice,
I do not doubt that the passionately-wept deaths of young men
      are provided for, and that the deaths of young women and
      the deaths of little children are provided for,
(Did you think Life was so well provided for, and Death, the pur-
      port of all Life, is not well provided for?)
I do not doubt that wrecks at sea, no matter what the horrors of
      them, no matter whose wife, child, husband, father, lover,
10   has gone down, are provided for, to the minutest points,
I do not doubt that whatever can possibly happen anywhere at
      any time, is provided for in the inherences of things,
I do not think Life provides for all and for Time and Space, but I
      believe Heavenly Death provides for all.

1856   *1871*

Quicksand Years.

Quicksand years that whirl me I know not whither,
Your schemes, politics, fail, lines give way, substances mock and
      elude me,
Only the theme I sing, the great and strong-possess'd soul, eludes
      not,
One's-self must never give way—that is the final substance—
      that out of all is sure,
5 Out of politics, triumphs, battles, life, what at last finally remains?
When shows break up what but One's-Self is sure?

1865   *1871*

YEARS] The long first line doubled as title in the first appearance, *Drum-Taps* 1865, and in the "Drum-Taps" supplement to LG 1867. Transferred with present title to the "Whispers of Heavenly Death" cluster, *Passage to India* (1871). For two earlier MS drafts from an 1862–1863 notebook (LC Whitman, 94), see Glicksberg, 125–126.

4. substance] The concept of a "final substance" was reflected in ancient magic, alchemy, and science, and may be said to survive in modern nuclear research.

ME] Originally No. 21 of "Calamus," in LG 1860. Present title in 1867; transferred to the present group in *Passage to India* (1871). Original text unrevised

That Music Always Round Me.

That music always round me, unceasing, unbeginning, yet long
    untaught I did not hear,
But now the chorus I hear and am elated,
A tenor, strong, ascending with power and health, with glad notes
    of daybreak I hear,
A soprano at intervals sailing buoyantly over the tops of immense
    waves,
A transparent base shuddering lusciously under and through the
    universe,   5
The triumphant tutti, the funeral wailings with sweet flutes and
    violins, all these I fill myself with,
I hear not the volumes of sound merely, I am moved by the
    exquisite meanings,
I listen to the different voices winding in and out, striving, contend-
    ing with fiery vehemence to excel each other in emotion;
I do not think the performers know themselves—but now I think
    I begin to know them.

1860   *1867*

What Ship Puzzled at Sea.

What ship puzzled at sea, cons for the true reckoning?
Or coming in, to avoid the bars and follow the channel a perfect
    pilot needs?
Here, sailor! here, ship! take aboard the most perfect pilot,
Whom, in a little boat, putting off and rowing, I hailing you offer.

1860   *1881*

except by insertion of "That" before the first line, a revision by WW in the "Blue
Copy," LG 1860. The poem is WW's direct recognition of the power of music in his
inspiration.
    6. tutti] Italian: musical notation for full tonality of all instruments played
simultaneously. See also note on line 52, "Proud Music of the Storm."
    SEA] In LG 1860, the first four lines of "Calamus" No. 31, but in LG 1867 a
separate poem entitled "Here, Sailor!" and so also in the present cluster in the
"*Passage to India*" supplements in LG 1871 and *Two Rivulets* (1876). The present
title appeared in LG 1881.

A Noiseless Patient Spider.

A noiseless patient spider,
I mark'd where on a little promontory it stood isolated,
Mark'd how to explore the vacant vast surrounding,
It launch'd forth filament, filament, filament, out of itself,
5 Ever unreeling them, ever tirelessly speeding them.

And you O my soul where you stand,
Surrounded, detached, in measureless oceans of space,
Ceaselessly musing, venturing, throwing, seeking the spheres to
  connect them,
Till the bridge you will need be form'd, till the ductile anchor
  hold,
10 Till the gossamer thread you fling catch somewhere, O my soul.

1868   *1881*

O Living Always, Always Dying.

O living always, always dying!
O the burials of me past and present,
O me while I stride ahead, material, visible, imperious as ever;
O me, what I was for years, now dead, (I lament not, I am
  content;)
5 O to disengage myself from those corpses of me, which I turn
  and look at where I cast them,

SPIDER] First appeared in *Broadway Magazine* (London), October, 1868, the
third of five numbered poems printed under the single title, "Whispers of Heavenly
Death," which survived as the title of the cluster in which this poem appeared in the
"*Passage to India*" supplements of 1871 and 1876. In *LG* 1881 the final revision is
the substitution of "detached" for a second "surrounded" in line 7. An untitled MS
version in a Washington notebook of 1862–1863 (LC Whitman, 94) is significantly
different (see *UPP*, II, 93). There the spider's symbolic outreaching filaments express
the "Calamus" sentiment; the poet's effortless rededication of the published version
shows brilliant artistry and impressive sublimation.

DYING] No. 27 of the "Calamus" group in *LG* 1860, this poem took its present title
in 1867, was placed in the "*Passage to India*" supplement in 1871 and 1876, and in
the "Whispers" cluster in *LG* 1881. The 1860 text began:

To pass on, (O living! always living!) and leave the corpses
    behind.

1860   1867

To One Shortly to Die.

From all the rest I single out you, having a message for you,
You are to die—let others tell you what they please, I cannot
    prevaricate,
I am exact and merciless, but I love you—there is no escape for
    you.

Softly I lay my right hand upon you, you just feel it,
I do not argue, I bend my head close and half envelop it,   5
I sit quietly by, I remain faithful,
I am more than nurse, more than parent or neighbor,
I absolve you from all except yourself spiritual bodily, that is eter-
    nal, you yourself will surely escape,
The corpse you will leave will be but excrementitious.

The sun bursts through in unlooked-for directions,   10
Strong thoughts fill you and confidence, you smile,
You forget you are sick, as I forget you are sick,
You do not see the medicines, you do not mind the weeping
    friends, I am with you,
I exclude others from you, there is nothing to be commiserated,
I do not commiserate, I congratulate you.   15

1860   1871

O Love!
O dying—always dying!

Present reading of the first line in LG 1867. The MS (Barrett) has the title, "Leaf."
DIE] Originally one of the "Messenger Leaves" of LG 1860, this poem remained
unchanged except for line 8, to which the clause, "you yourself will surely escape,"
was added in 1871 with the poem's transfer to the *Passage to India* supplement. It
was finally merged with the "Whispers" in LG 1881. Of the two MSS (Barrett) one is
the present text, but the other, a MS fragment, gives the following variant:

I must not deceive you—you are to die,
I am melancholy and stern, but I love you—there
    is no escape for you.—
I do not know your destination, but I know it is
    real and perfect.

Night on the Prairies.

Night on the prairies,
The supper is over, the fire on the ground burns low,
The wearied emigrants sleep, wrapt in their blankets;
I walk by myself—I stand and look at the stars, which I think now
      I never realized before.

5   Now I absorb immortality and peace,
I admire death and test propositions.

How plenteous! how spiritual! how resumé!
The same old man and soul—the same old aspirations, and the
      same content.

I was thinking the day most splendid till I saw what the not-day
      exhibited,
I was thinking this globe enough till there sprang out so noiseless
10   around me myriads of other globes.

Now while the great thoughts of space and eternity fill me I will
      measure myself by them,
And now touch'd with the lives of other globes arrived as far
      along as those of the earth,
Or waiting to arrive, or pass'd on farther than those of the earth,
I henceforth no more ignore them than I ignore my own life,
15   Or the lives of the earth arrived as far as mine, or waiting to arrive.

PRAIRIES] First appeared as No. 15 of the cluster, "Leaves of Grass," in LG 1860; reprinted with WW's revisions ("Blue Copy," LG 1860) as No. 3 of a "Leaves of Grass" group in LG 1867, and with present title in the supplement, *Passage to India*, 1871 and 1876, and in LG 1881 as one of the "Whispers" cluster. The poet had not yet visited the prairie country when he composed his poem, nor when he added the emigrant camp passage (lines 2 and 3) in 1867. An interesting literary influence upon the thought of this poem was Joseph Blanco White's sonnet, "Night," of which Dr. Bucke found WW's clipping. White (1775–1841) was an English Unitarian clergyman, admired by Coleridge.

7. resumé] French: correctly, résumé, "summed up." WW's linguistic borrowings are sometimes effective (see note on "Santa Spirita" in "Chanting the Square Deific," above). Others, as in the present instance, leave something to be desired—perhaps an English equivalent.

9. not-day] Cf. in philosophy the classic distinction between the "me" and the "not-me" as two entities within the whole of reality. WW's magnificent dichotomy

O I see now that life cannot exhibit all to me, as the day cannot,
I see that I am to wait for what will be exhibited by death.

1860   1871

Thought.

As I sit with others at a great feast, suddenly while the music is
      playing,
To my mind, (whence it comes I know not,) spectral in mist of
      a wreck at sea,
Of certain ships, how they sail from port with flying streamers and
      wafted kisses, and that is the last of them,
Of the solemn and murky mystery about the fate of the President,
Of the flower of the marine science of fifty generations founder'd
      off the Northeast coast and going down—of the steamship
      Arctic going down,   5
Of the veil'd tableau—women gather'd together on deck, pale,
      heroic, waiting the moment that draws so close—O the
      moment!
A huge sob—a few bubbles—the white foam spirting up—and
      then the women gone,
Sinking there while the passionless wet flows on—and I now
      pondering, Are those women indeed gone?
Are souls drown'd and destroy'd so?
Is only matter triumphant?   10

1860   1871

---

mounts in stages of contrast: of earth-light with what is beyond earth's darkness; of
measurable space with eternal time; of earth-life with life on other globes; and
finally, of knowledge of life with knowledge of death.

    THOUGHT] Appeared in LG 1860 and 1867 as No. 5 of a cluster of poems entitled
"Thoughts." With the addition of the present lines 3 and 4, it appeared as a separate
poem in the supplement, *Passage to India*, in 1871, 1872, and 1876. With no
further change, it appeared in the present cluster of the final 1881 LG text.

    2. spectral] In its context WW's word has double meaning: the following
pictures are like a spectre, but also have the quality of an image cast by the broken
spectrum falling upon the mist.

    4. President] The steamer *President* sailed from New York to Liverpool, March
11, 1841, with 136 persons on board, and was never heard from again.

    5. Arctic] The steamer *Arctic*, sailing from Liverpool to New York, collided
with the French steamer, *Vesta*, on September 27, 1854, in a fog forty miles off Cape
Race, Newfoundland; 350 were lost, including many women and children.

The Last Invocation.

At the last, tenderly,
From the walls of the powerful fortress'd house,
From the clasp of the knitted locks, from the keep of the well-
    closed doors,
Let me be wafted.

5   Let me glide noiselessly forth;
With the key of softness unlock the locks—with a whisper,
Set ope the doors O soul.

Tenderly—be not impatient,
(Strong is your hold O mortal flesh,
10   Strong is your hold O love.)
    1868   *1871*

As I Watch'd the Ploughman Ploughing.

As I watch'd the ploughman ploughing,
Or the sower sowing in the fields, or the harvester harvesting,
I saw there too, O life and death, your analogies;
(Life, life is the tillage, and Death is the harvest according.)
    1871   *1871*

INVOCATION] The fourth of the five numbered poems first printed in the London *Broadway Magazine*, October, 1868. (See note on "Whispers of Heavenly Death.") Next it appeared in the present group in the 1871 *Passage to India;* it was reprinted in LG 1872, in *Two Rivulets* (1876), and finally, unaltered, in 1881. Of superb lyrical skill, it has often been set to music by modern composers—among them, Frank Bridge (1919), Percival Garratt (1920) and James H. Rogers (1919). In the words of John Livingston Lowes (*Convention and Revolt in Poetry*, 1919), the reader who will "let the words beat their own time" may find the clue to WW's practice of constructing stanzas on the basis of repetitive accentual patterns of rhythm.

    3. keep] This archaic noun refers to the deep underground vaults of a dungeon or castle.

    PLOUGHING] This poem was first published in the 1871 *Passage to India*, again in that supplement in LG 1872 and *Two Rivulets*, 1876, finally in LG 1881,—each time in the cluster, "Whisperings of Heavenly Death." Remaining unchanged, it is one of the most successfully sustained of WW's little gnomic poems, the entire structure being a harmonious, functional vehicle for the fundamental aphorism (line 4).

    FALTERING] The last of the five numbered poems first printed in the London *Broadway Magazine*, October, 1868, this remained unchanged in the present group in the 1871 *Passage to India*, in LG 1872, in *Two Rivulets* (1876), and in the final LG 1881. Pertinent here again is the concluding comment in the note on "Ploughing," above.

Pensive and Faltering.

Pensive and faltering,
The words *the Dead* I write,
For living are the Dead,
(Haply the only living, only real,
And I the apparition, I the spectre.)   5

1868   1871

Thou Mother with Thy Equal Brood.

1

Thou Mother with thy equal brood,
Thou varied chain of different States, yet one identity only,
A special song before I go I'd sing o'er all the rest,
For thee, the future.

BROOD] In response to the invitation—not entirely guileless—of a group of Dartmouth seniors to deliver their Commencement poem, June 26, 1872, WW composed "As a Strong Bird on Pinions Free," presented it in Hanover with only fair success, then published it that year as the title poem of a small volume containing seven other poems. This volume, without new pagination, became a supplement, bound in with *Two Rivulets* (1876). WW incorporated this poem in LG 1881 with minor revisions, adding the present first canto of four stanzas, which in ASB 1872 had appeared as "One Song, America, Before I Go." Its first stanza, increased to four lines, reiterated the new title here, and intensified its purport.

Although the Dartmouth occasion had been arranged with evident intent to annoy the faculty, WW took it in good faith as justifying his claim to national attention; indeed he wrote a flamboyant press release for the Washington papers, which refused to run it (see Perry, 205–210). For the volume of 1872, WW wrote an important preface reviewing his past hopes and present plans with eloquent candor. This poem has deserved attention as a central statement of WW's convictions about the role of the "equal brood" of the states in American democracy, and the future of that democracy in the world order. The power of the idealism has overcome the rhetoric. For an account of WW's Dartmouth reception, see Perry, 203–210, and Harold W. Blodgett, "Walt Whitman's Dartmouth Visit," *Dartmouth Alumni Magazine*, Vol. 25 (February, 1933), 13–15. MSS include a notebook with five pages of jottings on the theme (Yale), some fragments of the poem (LC and Barrett), and the complete MS of the printer's copy of 1872 (Berg).

5   I'd sow a seed for thee of endless Nationality,
I'd fashion thy ensemble including body and soul,
I'd show away ahead thy real Union, and how it may be accomplish'd.

The paths to the house I seek to make,
But leave to those to come the house itself.

10   Belief I sing, and preparation;
As Life and Nature are not great with reference to the present only,
But greater still from what is yet to come,
Out of that formula for thee I sing.

2

As a strong bird on pinions free,
15   Joyous, the amplest spaces heavenward cleaving,
Such be the thought I'd think of thee America,
Such be the recitative I'd bring for thee.

The conceits of the poets of other lands I'd bring thee not,
Nor the compliments that have served their turn so long,
Nor rhyme, nor the classics, nor perfume of foreign court or
20   indoor library;
But an odor I'd bring as from forests of pine in Maine, or breath
of an Illinois prairie,
With open airs of Virginia or Georgia or Tennessee, or from Texas
uplands, or Florida's glades,
Or the Saguenay's black stream, or the wide blue spread of
Huron,
With presentment of Yellowstone's scenes, or Yosemite,
And murmuring under, pervading all, I'd bring the rustling sea-
25   sound,
That endlessly sounds from the two Great Seas of the world.

And for thy subtler sense subtler refrains dread Mother,
Preludes of intellect tallying these and thee, mind-formulas fitted
for thee, real and sane and large as these and thee,

47. ship of Democracy] Compare WW's use of this image with Longfellow's in
the 1850 poem, "The Building of the Ship," whose most famous passage begins

Thou! mounting higher, diving deeper than we knew, thou
    transcendental Union!
By thee fact to be justified, blended with thought,   30
Thought of man justified, blended with God,
Through thy idea, lo, the immortal reality!
Through thy reality, lo, the immortal idea!

3

Brain of the New World, what a task is thine,
To formulate the Modern—out of the peerless grandeur of the
    modern,   35
Out of thyself, comprising science, to recast poems, churches, art,
(Recast, may-be discard them, end them—may-be their work is
    done, who knows?)
By vision, hand, conception, on the background of the mighty
    past, the dead,
To limn with absolute faith the mighty living present.

And yet thou living present brain, heir of the dead, the Old
    World brain,   40
Thou that lay folded like an unborn babe within its folds so long,
Thou carefully prepared by it so long—haply thou but unfoldest
    it, only maturest it,
It to eventuate in thee—the essence of the by-gone time contain'd
    in thee,
Its poems, churches, arts, unwitting to themselves, destined with
    reference to thee;
Thou but the apples, long, long, long a-growing,   45
The fruit of all the Old ripening to-day in thee.

4

Sail, sail thy best, ship of Democracy,
Of value is thy freight, 'tis not the Present only,
The Past is also stored in thee,
Thou holdest not the venture of thyself alone, not of the Western
    continent alone,   50
Earth's *résumé* entire floats on thy keel O ship, is steadied by thy
    spars,

"Thou, too, sail on, O Ship of State!" WW's stanza was given separate publication in
the New York *Tribune*, February 19, 1876, under the title "Ship of Democracy."

With thee Time voyages in trust, the antecedent nations sink or
 swim with thee,
With all their ancient struggles, martyrs, heroes, epics, wars, thou
 bear'st the other continents,
Theirs, theirs as much as thine, the destination-port triumphant;
Steer then with good strong hand and wary eye O helmsman, thou
55 carriest great companions,
Venerable priestly Asia sails this day with thee,
And royal feudal Europe sails with thee.

5

Beautiful world of new superber birth that rises to my eyes,
Like a limitless golden cloud filling the western sky,
60 Emblem of general maternity lifted above all,
Sacred shape of the bearer of daughters and sons,
Out of thy teeming womb thy giant babes in ceaseless procession
 issuing,
Acceding from such gestation, taking and giving continual strength
 and life,
World of the real—world of the twain in one,
World of the soul, born by the world of the real alone, led to
65 identity, body, by it alone,
Yet in beginning only, incalculable masses of composite precious
 materials,
By history's cycles forwarded, by every nation, language, hither
 sent,
Ready, collected here, a freer, vast, electric world, to be con-
 structed here,
(The true New World, the world of orbic science, morals, litera-
 tures to come,)
Thou wonder world yet undefined, unform'd, neither do I define
70 thee,
How can I pierce the impenetrable blank of the future?
I feel thy ominous greatness evil as well as good,
I watch thee advancing, absorbing the present, transcending the
 past,
I see thy light lighting, and thy shadow shadowing, as if the
 entire globe,
75 But I do not undertake to define thee, hardly to comprehend thee,

62. teeming womb] Oscar Cargill (*Intellectual America*, New York, 1941) be-

I but thee name, thee prophesy, as now,
I merely thee ejaculate!

Thee in thy future,
Thee in thy only permanent life, career, thy own unloosen'd mind,
    thy soaring spirit,
Thee as another equally needed sun, radiant, ablaze, swift-moving,
    fructifying all,   80
Thee risen in potent cheerfulness and joy, in endless great
    hilarity,
Scattering for good the cloud that hung so long, that weigh'd so
    long upon the mind of man,
The doubt, suspicion, dread, of gradual, certain decadence of man;
Thee in thy larger, saner brood of female, male—thee in thy
    athletes, moral, spiritual, South, North, West, East,
(To thy immortal breasts, Mother of All, thy every daughter, son,
    endear'd alike, forever equal,)   85
Thee in thy own musicians, singers, artists, unborn yet, but cer-
    tain,
Thee in thy moral wealth and civilization, (until which thy proud-
    est material civilization must remain in vain,)
Thee in thy all-supplying, all-enclosing worship—thee in no single
    bible, saviour, merely,
Thy saviours countless, latent within thyself, thy bibles incessant
    within thyself, equal to any, divine as any,
(Thy soaring course thee formulating, not in thy two great wars,
    nor in thy century's visible growth,   90
But far more in these leaves and chants, thy chants, great Mother!)
Thee in an education grown of thee, in teachers, studies, students,
    born of thee,
Thee in thy democratic fêtes en-masse, thy high original festivals,
    operas, lecturers, preachers,
Thee in thy ultimata, (the preparations only now completed, the
    edifice on sure foundations tied,)
Thee in thy pinnacles, intellect, thought, thy topmost rational joys,
    thy love and godlike aspiration,   95
In thy resplendent coming literati, thy full-lung'd orators, thy
    sacerdotal bards, kosmic savans,
These! these in thee, (certain to come,) to-day I prophesy.

lieves that this is the "one poem that ties him [WW] most completely to his times" as
"the natural voice of breeding and prolific America, the Priapus of the new continent."

6

Land tolerating all, accepting all, not for the good alone, all good
for thee,
Land in the realms of God to be a realm unto thyself,
100 Under the rule of God to be a rule unto thyself.

(Lo, where arise three peerless stars,
To be thy natal stars my country, Ensemble, Evolution, Freedom,
Set in the sky of Law.)

Land of unprecedented faith, God's faith,
105 Thy soil, thy very subsoil, all upheav'd,
The general inner earth so long so sedulously draped over, now
hence for what it is boldly laid bare,
Open'd by thee to heaven's light for benefit or bale.

Not for success alone,
Not to fair-sail unintermitted always,
The storm shall dash thy face, the murk of war and worse than
110 war shall cover thee all over,
(Wert capable of war, its tug and trials? be capable of peace, its
trials,
For the tug and mortal strain of nations come at last in prosper-
ous peace, not war;)
In many a smiling mask death shall approach beguiling thee, thou
in disease shalt swelter,
The livid cancer spread its hideous claws, clinging upon thy
breasts, seeking to strike thee deep within,
Consumption of the worst, moral consumption, shall rouge thy
115 face with hectic,
But thou shalt face thy fortunes, thy diseases, and surmount them
all,
Whatever they are to-day and whatever through time they may be,
They each and all shall lift and pass away and cease from thee,

PICTURE] From *LG* 1856 through *LG* 1876, these seven lines constituted canto
8 of "Salut au Monde!" together with an opening line now dropped. Then, with a
sure aesthetic instinct, the poet transferred them, almost without revision, to his 1881
edition as a single poem. In his 1902 "Variorum Readings," Oscar Lovell Triggs had
noted the dropping of the lines without recognizing their happy reappearance. From
the beginning, WW was able to transmit without discussion the meaning of such

While thou, Time's spirals rounding, out of thyself, thyself still
     extricating, fusing,
Equable, natural, mystical Union thou, (the mortal with immortal
     blent,)   120
Shalt soar toward the fulfilment of the future, the spirit of the
     body and the mind,
The soul, its destinies.

The soul, its destinies, the real real,
(Purport of all these apparitions of the real;)
In thee America, the soul, its destinies,   125
Thou globe of globes! thou wonder nebulous!
By many a throe of heat and cold convuls'd, (by these thyself
     solidifying,)
Thou mental, moral orb—thou New, indeed new, Spiritual World!
The Present holds thee not—for such vast growth as thine,
For such unparallel'd flight as thine, such brood as thine,   130
The FUTURE only holds thee and can hold thee.

   1872   *1881*

A Paumanok Picture

Two boats with nets lying off the sea-beach, quite still,
Ten fishermen waiting—they discover a thick school of moss-
     bonkers—they drop the join'd seine-ends in the water,
The boats separate and row off, each on its rounding course to the
     beach, enclosing the mossbonkers,
The net is drawn in by a windlass by those who stop ashore,
Some of the fishermen lounge in their boats, others stand ankle-
     deep in the water, pois'd on strong legs,   5
The boats partly drawn up, the water slapping against them,
Strew'd on the sand in heaps and windrows, well out from the
     water, the green-back'd spotted mossbonkers.

   1881   *1881*

quiet scenes, which have been compared with genre painting. Such scenes are dis-
played with virtuosity in *Drum-Taps* (1865).
    2. mossbonkers] Also "mossbunkers." The menhaden, a fish used for bait, or
converted into oil and fertilizer.
    3. its rounding course] Having joined the ends of two seine nets offshore, the
boats return to the shore with the free ends, in opposite directions around a semi-
circle, trapping the fish in the looped nets.

From Noon to Starry Night.

Thou Orb Aloft Full-Dazzling.

Thou orb aloft full-dazzling! thou hot October noon!
Flooding with sheeny light the gray beach sand,
The sibilant near sea with vistas far and foam,
And tawny streaks and shades and spreading blue;
5   O sun of noon refulgent! my special word to thee.

Hear me illustrious!
Thy lover me, for always I have loved thee,
Even as basking babe, then happy boy alone by some wood edge,
      thy touching-distant beams enough,
Or man matured, or young or old, as now to thee I launch my
      invocation.

10   (Thou canst not with thy dumbness me deceive,
I know before the fitting man all Nature yields,
Though answering not in words, the skies, trees, hear his voice—
      and thou O sun,
As for thy throes, thy perturbations, sudden breaks and shafts of
      flame gigantic,
I understand them, I know those flames, those perturbations well.)

NIGHT] It is difficult to find an unmistakable unifying principle in this cluster, which is new to the final 1881 arrangement of *LG*, and one may sensibly conclude that the poet had none in mind. It is a miscellany both in source and theme, its twenty-two poems being brought together from seven different editions, 1855 to 1881. Here is the 1855 "Faces," a poem so salient that one wonders why WW did not give it a place to itself in the final arrangement, as he did to twenty-five other poems. Here also is the 1856 "Excelsior," a sort of confident catechism whose position has often shifted in the editions. Here are six brief poems of "inscriptive" intent from the third edition, and four from the *Drum-Taps* group. Nearly half of the poems are late arrivals—five, in fact, are new to the 1881 edition. However lacking in unity of theme or period of creation, the group as a whole is prevailingly reflective or retrospective, and characterized by lyric power and truth. At times the lyric satisfaction is only sporadic in a poem, as at the beginning of "Thou Orb Aloft *. . .*" or the end of "All is Truth." In the most noteworthy examples, chiefly shorter poems, the lyric propriety is nobly sustained,—as in "To a Locomotive in Winter," "Mannahatta," "Spirit that Form'd this Scene," and "By Broad Potomac's Shore." Fittingly, the poet closes with "A Clear Midnight," excellent little coda of four lines, a strain appropriate to his

Thou that with fructifying heat and light,   15
O'er myriad farms, o'er lands and waters North and South,
O'er Mississippi's endless course, o'er Texas' grassy plains, Kana-
    da's woods,
O'er all the globe that turns its face to thee shining in space,
Thou that impartially infoldest all, not only continents, seas,
Thou that to grapes and weeds and little wild flowers givest so
    liberally,   20
Shed, shed thyself on mine and me, with but a fleeting ray out of
    thy million millions,
Strike through these chants.

Nor only launch thy subtle dazzle and thy strength for these,
Prepare the later afternoon of me myself—prepare my lengthen-
    ing shadows,
Prepare my starry nights.   25

1881   *1881*

Faces.

1

Sauntering the pavement or riding the country by-road, lo, such
    faces!
Faces of friendship, precision, caution, suavity, ideality,
The spiritual-prescient face, the always welcome common benevo-
    lent face,

concluding group, "Songs of Parting," which follows.

FULL-DAZZLING] Published in *The American,* June 4, 1881, under the title "A Summer Invocation"; included under its present title in LG 1881. In a diary note of May, 1881 (*Walt Whitman's Diary in Canada,* ed. by W. S. Kennedy, 58–59), WW records: "Received back to-day the MS of the little piece of "A Summer's Invocation," which I had sent to H's [Harper's] magazine. The editor said he returned it because his readers wouldn't understand any meaning to it." Yet the poem is clearly a hymn to the sun, invoking its creative "fructifying light" to "strike through these chants" into the twilight and "starry nights" of his descending life. It is one of the better poems of the autumnal years. In the MS (LC Whitman 29) the poet suggests several other titles, including "Sun-up" and "A Seashore Invocation."

FACES] The sixth of the untitled twelve of the first edition, this poem was "Poem of Faces" in 1856, "Leaf of Faces" in 1860, "A Leaf of Faces" in 1867, and "Faces" since 1871. Both the surviving MS fragments (Barrett, Trent) and the revisions through the seven editions to 1881 show constant, but minor, reworking. The poet, always intent on the balance of real with ideal, with brilliant imagery limns the faces of actuality, but his insistence is on fulfillment, and his final images are those of victory and fruition.

The face of the singing of music, the grand faces of natural law-
   yers and judges broad at the back-top,
The faces of hunters and fishers bulged at the brows, the shaved
5   blanch'd faces of orthodox citizens,
The pure, extravagant, yearning, questioning artist's face,
The ugly face of some beautiful soul, the handsome detested or
   despised face,
The sacred faces of infants, the illuminated face of the mother of
   many children,
The face of an amour, the face of veneration,
10 The face as of a dream, the face of an immobile rock,
The face withdrawn of its good and bad, a castrated face,
A wild hawk, his wings clipp'd by the clipper,
A stallion that yielded at last to the thongs and knife of the gelder.

Sauntering the pavement thus, or crossing the ceaseless ferry, faces
   and faces and faces,
15 I see them and complain not, and am content with all.

   2

Do you suppose I could be content with all if I thought them
   their own finalè?

This now is too lamentable a face for a man,
Some abject louse asking leave to be, cringing for it,
Some milk-nosed maggot blessing what lets it wrig to its hole.

20 This face is a dog's snout sniffing for garbage,
Snakes nest in that mouth, I hear the sibilant threat.

This face is a haze more chill than the arctic sea,
Its sleepy and wabbling icebergs crunch as they go.

  19. wrig] A shortened form, now obsolete, of "wriggle."
  20. sniffing] Appeared as "sniffling" in *LG* 1860 only; corrected by WW in his
"Blue Copy" revisions.
  23. wabbling] Spelled "wobbling" until *LG* 1881; colloquial; meaning "uncer-
tainly toppling back and forth."
  25. caoutchouc] Crude rubber.
  29. speculates] With the meaning, now rare, "to see, or contemplate."

This is a face of bitter herbs, this an emetic, they need no label,
And more of the drug-shelf, laudanum, caoutchouc, or hog's-lard.   25

This face is an epilepsy, its wordless tongue gives out the unearthly
      cry,
Its veins down the neck distend, its eyes roll till they show nothing
      but their whites,
Its teeth grit, the palms of the hands are cut by the turn'd-in
      nails,
The man falls struggling and foaming to the ground, while he
      speculates well.

This face is bitten by vermin and worms,   30
And this is some murderer's knife with a half-pull'd scabbard.

This face owes to the sexton his dismalest fee,
An unceasing death-bell tolls there.

3

Features of my equals would you trick me with your creas'd and
      cadaverous march?
Well, you cannot trick me.   35

I see your rounded never-erased flow,
I see 'neath the rims of your haggard and mean disguises.

Splay and twist as you like, poke with the tangling fores of fishes
      or rats,
You'll be unmuzzled, you certainly will.

I saw the face of the most smear'd and slobbering idiot they had
      at the asylum,   40
And I knew for my consolation what they knew not,
I knew of the agents that emptied and broke my brother,

---

38. splay] As verb: "spread open" or "cut open." fores] When Dr. Bucke asked
WW what he meant by this word, the poet answered, " 'fores': the front, the snout,
whatever" (Traubel, IV, 243). In nautical language, the word in WW's time meant
the "forward" part of anything; as for the "snout," those of fish and rat are similar in
outline.
    42. brother] WW's brother, Eddie, born in 1835, was a mental defective, cared
for by the poet, whom he was to outlive by eight months.

The same wait to clear the rubbish from the fallen tenement,
And I shall look again in a score or two of ages,
And I shall meet the real landlord perfect and unharm'd, every
45   inch as good as myself.

4

The Lord advances, and yet advances,
Always the shadow in front, always the reach'd hand bringing up
          the laggards.

Out of this face emerge banners and horses—O superb! I see
          what is coming,
I see the high pioneer-caps, see staves of runners clearing the way,
50   I hear victorious drums.

This face is a life-boat,
This is the face commanding and bearded, it asks no odds of the
          rest,
This face is flavor'd fruit ready for eating,
This face of a healthy honest boy is the programme of all good.

55   These faces bear testimony slumbering or awake,
They show their descent from the Master himself.

Off the word I have spoken I except not one—red, white, black,
          are all deific,
In each house is the ovum, it comes forth after a thousand years.

Spots or cracks at the windows do not disturb me,
60   Tall and sufficient stand behind and make signs to me,
I read the promise and patiently wait.

This is a full-grown lily's face,
She speaks to the limber-hipp'd man near the garden pickets,
Come here she blushingly cries, *Come nigh to me limber-hipp'd
          man,*

          49. staves] The staff of authority, from ancient times, was carried before rulers or
judges to clear the way.

Stand at my side till I lean as high as I can upon you,   65
Fill me with albescent honey, bend down to me,
Rub to me with your chafing beard, rub to my breast and
          shoulders.

5

The old face of the mother of many children,
Whist! I am fully content.

Lull'd and late is the smoke of the First-day morning,   70
It hangs low over the rows of trees by the fences,
It hangs thin by the sassafras and wild-cherry and cat-brier under
          them.

I saw the rich ladies in full dress at the soiree,
I heard what the singers were singing so long,
Heard who sprang in crimson youth from the white froth and the
          water-blue.   75

Behold a woman!
She looks out from her quaker cap, her face is clearer and more
          beautiful than the sky.

She sits in an armchair under the shaded porch of the farmhouse,
The sun just shines on her old white head.

Her ample gown is of cream-hued linen,   80
Her grandsons raised the flax, and her grand-daughters spun it
          with the distaff and the wheel.

The melodious character of the earth,
The finish beyond which philosophy cannot go and does not wish
          to go,
The justified mother of men.

   1855   1881

   76. woman] The poet may here be portraying his maternal grandmother, Naomi
Williams Van Velsor. See *FCI*, 44–45.

The Mystic Trumpeter.

1

Hark, some wild trumpeter, some strange musician,
Hovering unseen in air, vibrates capricious tunes to-night.

I hear thee trumpeter, listening alert I catch thy notes,
Now pouring, whirling like a tempest round me,
5 Now low, subdued, now in the distance lost.

2

Come nearer bodiless one, haply in thee resounds
Some dead composer, haply thy pensive life
Was fill'd with aspirations high, unform'd ideals,
Waves, oceans musical, chaotically surging,
That now ecstatic ghost, close to me bending, thy cornet echoing,
10   pealing,
Gives out to no one's ears but mine, but freely gives to mine,
That I may thee translate.

3

Blow trumpeter free and clear, I follow thee,
While at thy liquid prelude, glad, serene,
15 The fretting world, the streets, the noisy hours of day withdraw,
A holy calm descends like dew upon me,
I walk in cool refreshing night the walks of Paradise,
I scent the grass, the moist air and the roses;

TRUMPETER] First published in *The Kansas Magazine* for February, 1872,
which WW characterized in a letter to his brother Jeff of January 26, 1872 as "a new
magazine, same style as the Atlantic—intended *for Western thought* & reminiscences
etc—" (Corr. II, 157). Successively reprinted in the 1872 volume *As a Strong Bird
on Pinions Free*, in the 1876 *Two Rivulets*, and finally in its present position in *LG*
1881, where the sole change was the removal of the adjective "wild" before "alarums"
in line 43. Surviving MSS (Feinberg, Barrett, Trent, Hanley) show a great profu-
sion of trial phrases and reworking from the first note to its final form. (See *FCI*,
13–14).
    The theme is music's inspiration, the poet choosing the trumpet perhaps because

Thy song expands my numb'd imbonded spirit, thou freest,
    launchest me,
Floating and basking upon heaven's lake.   20

4

Blow again trumpeter! and for my sensuous eyes,
Bring the old pageants, show the feudal world.

What charm thy music works! thou makest pass before me,
Ladies and cavaliers long dead, barons are in their castle halls, the
    troubadours are singing,
Arm'd knights go forth to redress wrongs, some in quest of the
    holy Graal;   25
I see the tournament, I see the contestants incased in heavy
    armor seated on stately champing horses,
I hear the shouts, the sounds of blows and smiting steel;
I see the Crusaders' tumultuous armies—hark, how the cymbals
    clang,
Lo, where the monks walk in advance, bearing the cross on high.

5

Blow again trumpeter! and for thy theme,   30
Take now the enclosing theme of all, the solvent and the setting,
Love, that is pulse of all, the sustenance and the pang,
The heart of man and woman all for love,
No other theme but love—knitting, enclosing, all-diffusing love.

O how the immortal phantoms crowd around me!   35
I see the vast alembic ever working, I see and know the flames
    that heat the world,

it was—in the conch stage—one of the most ancient and primitive of instruments.
The general figure is the presence of music, inherent in nature, life, and the memory
of things. The first five cantos invoke the memory of past musicians, especially those
who bring back the romantic periods of history which embody the eternal dreams of
lovers. But in canto 6 begins an antiphonal theme—the heralding of war,—its
brigandage, ravage, and the consequent shame of mankind; and finally comes the
magnificent resolution of the concluding canto, wherein man is redeemed, society is
Utopian, and all is joy. For a personal interpretation of the poet's powerful sym-
bolism, see W. L. Werner, "Whitman's 'The Mystic Trumpeter' as Autobiography,"
AL, VII (January, 1936), 455–458.
    19. imbonded] Apparently a neologism, meaning "confined" or "fettered."

The glow, the blush, the beating hearts of lovers,
So blissful happy some, and some so silent, dark, and nigh to
    death;
Love, that is all the earth to lovers—love, that mocks time and
    space,
40 Love, that is day and night—love, that is sun and moon and stars,
Love, that is crimson, sumptuous, sick with perfume,
No other words but words of love, no other thought but love.

6

Blow again trumpeter—conjure war's alarums.

Swift to thy spell a shuddering hum like distant thunder rolls,
Lo, where the arm'd men hasten—lo, mid the clouds of dust the
45   glint of bayonets,
I see the grime-faced cannoneers, I mark the rosy flash amid the
    smoke, I hear the cracking of the guns;
Nor war alone—thy fearful music-song, wild player, brings every
    sight of fear,
The deeds of ruthless brigands, rapine, murder—I hear the cries
    for help!
I see ships foundering at sea, I behold on deck and below deck
    the terrible tableaus.

7

50 O trumpeter, methinks I am myself the instrument thou playest,
Thou melt'st my heart, my brain—thou movest, drawest, chan-
    gest them at will;
And now thy sullen notes send darkness through me,
Thou takest away all cheering light, all hope,
I see the enslaved, the overthrown, the hurt, the opprest of the
    whole earth,
I feel the measureless shame and humiliation of my race, it
55   becomes all mine,

47. player] Erroneously printed as "prayer" in the *LG* 1924 "Inclusive Edition"
and in several subsequent editions.

WINTER] First published in a preview of *Two Rivulets* in the New York *Daily
Tribune*, February 19, 1876 before the volume appeared; included without change in
its present position in *LG* 1881. Fourteen pages of MS working notes, trial lines, and
rough draft (Feinberg) show the poet's effort to embody his conception. Notes on the

Mine too the revenges of humanity, the wrongs of ages, baffled
        feuds and hatreds,
Utter defeat upon me weighs—all lost—the foe victorious,
(Yet 'mid the ruins Pride colossal stands unshaken to the last,
Endurance, resolution to the last.)

8

Now trumpeter for thy close,   60
Vouchsafe a higher strain than any yet,
Sing to my soul, renew its languishing faith and hope,
Rouse up my slow belief, give me some vision of the future,
Give me for once its prophecy and joy.

O glad, exulting, culminating song!   65
A vigor more than earth's is in thy notes,
Marches of victory—man disenthral'd—the conqueror at last,
Hymns to the universal God from universal man—all joy!
A reborn race appears—a perfect world, all joy!
Women and men in wisdom innocence and health—all joy!   70
Riotous laughing bacchanals fill'd with joy!
War, sorrow, suffering gone—the rank earth purged—nothing
        but joy left!
The ocean fill'd with joy—the atmosphere all joy!
Joy! joy! in freedom, worship, love! joy in the ecstasy of life!
Enough to merely be! enough to breathe!   75
Joy! joy! all over joy!

1872   *1881*

To a Locomotive in Winter.

Thee for my recitative,
Thee in the driving storm even as now, the snow, the winter-day
        declining,

intention of the poem include the following: "The two ideas of Power & Motion
(twins, dear to the modern) / Address the locomotive as personally inviting it /
Ring the bell all through & blow the whistle." The final MS draft is in the Boston
Public Library.
    Although very different as poets, both WW and Emily Dickinson, refusing the
romantic posture that science and industry are inimical to the Muse, were inspired by
the locomotive. Cf. Dickinson's "I like to see it lap the miles—."

Thee in thy panoply, thy measur'd dual throbbing and thy beat
    convulsive,
Thy black cylindric body, golden brass and silvery steel,
Thy ponderous side-bars, parallel and connecting rods, gyrating,
5   shuttling at thy sides,
Thy metrical, now swelling pant and roar, now tapering in the
    distance,
Thy great protruding head-light fix'd in front,
Thy long, pale, floating vapor-pennants, tinged with delicate
    purple,
The dense and murky clouds out-belching from thy smoke-stack,
Thy knitted frame, thy springs and valves, the tremulous twinkle
10   of thy wheels,
Thy train of cars behind, obedient, merrily following,
Through gale or calm, now swift, now slack, yet steadily careering;
Type of the modern—emblem of motion and power—pulse of
    the continent,
For once come serve the Muse and merge in verse, even as here
    I see thee,
15 With storm and buffeting gusts of wind and falling snow,
By day thy warning ringing bell to sound its notes,
By night thy silent signal lamps to swing.

Fierce-throated beauty!
Roll through my chant with all thy lawless music, thy swinging
    lamps at night,
Thy madly-whistled laughter, echoing, rumbling like an earth-
20   quake, rousing all,
Law of thyself complete, thine own track firmly holding,
(No sweetness debonair of tearful harp or glib piano thine,)
Thy trills of shrieks by rocks and hills return'd,
Launch'd o'er the prairies wide, across the lakes,
25 To the free skies unpent and glad and strong.

1876   *1881*

MAGNET-SOUTH] First printed in LG 1860, and in the July 15, 1860 issue of *The Southern Literary Messenger*, as "Longings for Home," the poem was reprinted unchanged in text and title through the editions of 1867, 1871, and 1876. In 1881 it received its present title and position, with two changes: "Tennessee" was dropped for "Kentucky" in line 19, and the following line after the present line 19 was also dropped: "An Arkansas prairie—a sleeping lake, or still bayou." WW's liking for

O Magnet-South.

O magnet-South! O glistening perfumed South! my South!
O quick mettle, rich blood, impulse and love! good and evil! O
      all dear to me!
O dear to me my birth-things—all moving things and the trees
      where I was born—the grains, plants, rivers,
Dear to me my own slow sluggish rivers where they flow, distant,
      over flats of silvery sands or through swamps,
Dear to me the Roanoke, the Savannah, the Altamahaw, the
      Pedee, the Tombigbee, the Santee, the Coosa and the
      Sabine,   5
O pensive, far away wandering, I return with my soul to haunt
      their banks again,
Again in Florida I float on transparent lakes, I float on the Okee-
      chobee, I cross the hummock-land or through pleasant
      openings or dense forests,
I see the parrots in the woods, I see the papaw-tree and the blos-
      soming titi;
Again, sailing in my coaster on deck, I coast off Georgia, I coast
      up the Carolinas,
I see where the live-oak is growing, I see where the yellow-pine,
      the scented bay-tree, the lemon and orange, the cypress,
      the graceful palmetto,   10
I pass rude sea-headlands and enter Pamlico sound through an
      inlet, and dart my vision inland;
O the cotton plant! the growing fields of rice, sugar, hemp!
The cactus guarded with thorns, the laurel-tree with large white
      flowers,
The range afar, the richness and barrenness, the old woods
      charged with mistletoe and trailing moss,
The piney odor and the gloom, the awful natural stillness, (here
      in these dense swamps the freebooter carries his gun, and
      the fugitive has his conceal'd hut;)   15

the South, recalling his New Orleans days, is of course genuine enough; yet the
passion expressed here, with its luxuriant phrasing, may seem faintly factitious, as if
for the occasion.
    5. Roanoke . . . Savannah . . . Altamahaw . . . Pedee . . . Tombigbee
. . . Santee . . . Coosa . . . Sabine] Rivers of the deep South.
    7. Okeechobee] Lake in south-central Florida.
    11. Pamlico sound] Channel between the coast and islands off North Carolina.

O the strange fascination of these half-known half-impassable
      swamps, infested by reptiles, resounding with the bellow
      of the alligator, the sad noises of the night-owl and the
      wild-cat, and the whirr of the rattlesnake,
The mocking-bird, the American mimic, singing all the forenoon,
      singing through the moon-lit night,
The humming-bird, the wild turkey, the raccoon, the opossum;
A Kentucky corn-field, the tall, graceful, long-leav'd corn, slender,
      flapping, bright green, with tassels, with beautiful ears each
      well-sheath'd in its husk;
O my heart! O tender and fierce pangs, I can stand them not, I
20   will depart;
O to be a Virginian where I grew up! O to be a Carolinian!
O longings irrepressible! O I will go back to old Tennessee and
      never wander more.

     1860   *1881*

Mannahatta.

I was asking for something specific and perfect for my city,
Whereupon lo! upsprang the aboriginal name.

Now I see what there is in a name, a word, liquid, sane, unruly,
      musical, self-sufficient,
I see that the word of my city is that word from of old,
5 Because I see that word nested in nests of water-bays, superb,
Rich, hemm'd thick all around with sailships and steamships, an
      island sixteen miles long, solid-founded,

MANNAHATTA] First appeared, with the present title, in *LG* 1860; reprinted in
LG 1867; incorporated in a "Leaves of Grass" group in *LG* 1871; and in the present
cluster in *LG* 1881 with three concluding lines—after line 17—that are substituted for
an excluded seven-line conclusion which is worth the attention of the student:

    The parades, processions, bugles playing, flags flying, drums beating;
    A million people—manners free and superb—open voices—hospitality—
        the most courageous and friendly young men;
    The free city! no slaves! no owners of slaves!
    The beautiful city, the city of hurried and sparkling waters! the city of
        spires and masts!
    The city nested in bays! my city!
    The city of such women, I am mad to be with them! I will return after
        death to be with them!
    The city of such young men, I swear I cannot live happy without I often
        go talk, walk, eat, drink, sleep, with them!

Numberless crowded streets, high growths of iron, slender, strong,
        light, splendidly uprising toward clear skies,
Tides swift and ample, well-loved by me, toward sundown,
The flowing sea-currents, the little islands, larger adjoining islands,
        the heights, the villas,
The countless masts, the white shore-steamers, the lighters, the
        ferry-boats, the black sea-steamers well-model'd,   10
The down-town streets, the jobbers' houses of business, the houses
        of business of the ship-merchants and money-brokers, the
        river-streets,
Immigrants arriving, fifteen or twenty thousand in a week,
The carts hauling goods, the manly race of drivers of horses, the
        brown-faced sailors,
The summer air, the bright sun shining, and the sailing clouds
        aloft,
The winter snows, the sleigh-bells, the broken ice in the river,
        passing along up or down with the flood-tide or ebb-tide,   15
The mechanics of the city, the masters, well-form'd, beautiful-
        faced, looking you straight in the eyes,
Trottoirs throng'd, vehicles, Broadway, the women, the shops and
        shows,
A million people—manners free and superb—open voices—
        hospitality—the most courageous and friendly young men,
City of hurried and sparkling waters! city of spires and masts!
City nested in bays! my city!   20

    1860   *1881*

All is Truth.

O me, man of slack faith so long,
Standing aloof, denying portions so long,

"Mannahatta" is unquestionably WW's city, and he is its bard. The MS (Barrett)
shows little variation from the text.
    2. aboriginal name] Cf. note, line 5, "Me Imperturbe."
    TRUTH] Appeared as "Leaves of Grass" No. 18 in LG 1860; as "Leaves of Grass"
No. 1 in the supplementary "Songs Before Parting" of LG 1867; again as part of
another "Leaves of Grass" group in LG 1871 but with its present title; and finally in
the present cluster in LG 1881. MS title, "As of the Truth" (Barrett). The text
remained unchanged except that, after LG 1860, WW dropped the interesting third
line: "Me with mole's eyes, unrisen to buoyancy and vision—unfree."
    WW's answer to Pilate's eternal question, "What is truth," was influenced by the
Hegelian idealism, reflected through Emerson, Coleridge, and other authors familiar
to his youth. The relation of truth > falsehood, like that of good > evil, presented to
the poet a genuine philosophic dichotomy, the two seemingly integral halves of the
whole being, like positive and negative, attracted by and dependent upon each other.

Only aware to-day of compact all-diffused truth,
Discovering to-day there is no lie or form of lie, and can be none,
    but grows as inevitably upon itself as the truth does upon
    itself,
Or as any law of the earth or any natural production of the earth
5   does.

(This is curious and may not be realized immediately, but it must
    be realized,
I feel in myself that I represent falsehoods equally with the rest,
And that the universe does.)

Where has fail'd a perfect return indifferent of lies or the truth?
Is it upon the ground, or in water or fire? or in the spirit of man?
10   or in the meat and blood?

Meditating among liars and retreating sternly into myself, I see
    that there are really no liars or lies after all,
And that nothing fails its perfect return, and that what are called
    lies are perfect returns,
And that each thing exactly represents itself and what has pre-
    ceded it,
And that the truth includes all, and is compact just as much as
    space is compact,
And that there is no flaw or vacuum in the amount of the truth—
15   but that all is truth without exception;
And henceforth I will go celebrate any thing I see or am,
And sing and laugh and deny nothing.

1860   *1871*

A Riddle Song.

That which eludes this verse and any verse,
Unheard by sharpest ear, unform'd in clearest eye or cunningest
    mind,

In the long run, WW says, in the "perfect return," each of these temporal microcosms
is comprised in the eternal macrocosm. The poem may express WW's personal
solution of this perplexing paradox, leaving him free to "sing and laugh and deny
nothing." See Emerson's poem, "Each and All."

    SONG] One of the new poems of the 1881 LG, "A Riddle Song" was first published
in *Forney's Progress*, Philadelphia, April 17, 1880, with acknowledgement to the

Nor lore nor fame, nor happiness nor wealth,
And yet the pulse of every heart and life throughout the world
     incessantly,
Which you and I and all pursuing ever ever miss,   5
Open but still a secret, the real of the real, an illusion,
Costless, vouchsafed to each, yet never man the owner,
Which poets vainly seek to put in rhyme, historians in prose,
Which sculptor never chisel'd yet, nor painter painted,
Which vocalist never sung, nor orator nor actor ever utter'd,   10
Invoking here and now I challenge for my song.

Indifferently, 'mid public, private haunts, in solitude,
Behind the mountain and the wood,
Companion of the city's busiest streets, through the assemblage,
It and its radiations constantly glide.   15

In looks of fair unconscious babes,
Or strangely in the coffin'd dead,
Or show of breaking dawn or stars by night,
As some dissolving delicate film of dreams,
Hiding yet lingering.   20

Two little breaths of words comprising it,
Two words, yet all from first to last comprised in it.

How ardently for it!
How many ships have sail'd and sunk for it!
How many travelers started from their homes and ne'er return'd!   25
How much of genius boldly staked and lost for it!
What countless stores of beauty, love, ventur'd for it!
How all superbest deeds since Time began are traceable to it—
    and shall be to the end!
How all heroic martyrdoms to it!
How, justified by it, the horrors, evils, battles of the earth!   30
How the bright fascinating lambent flames of it, in every age and
    land, have drawn men's eyes,

"Sunnyside Press" (WW's letter, May 9, 1880, to John Burroughs; Barrus, 191).
Dr. R. M. Bucke wrote to WW August 29, 1888 that he had been thinking over the
"Riddle Song" and had made up his mind that the answer was "good cause" or "old
cause." Traubel reports that the poet would not verify. "Horace, I made the puzzle:
it's not my business to solve" (Traubel, II, 228). In his *The Fight of a Book for the
World*, page 188, W. S. Kennedy ventures another guess,—that the "two words" are
"The Ideal."

Rich as a sunset on the Norway coast, the sky, the islands, and the
      cliffs,
Or midnight's silent glowing northern lights unreachable.

Haply God's riddle it, so vague and yet so certain,
35 The soul for it, and all the visible universe for it,
And heaven at last for it.

1880   1881

Excelsior.

Who has gone farthest? for I would go farther,
And who has been just? for I would be the most just person of
      the earth,
And who most cautious? for I would be more cautious,
And who has been happiest? O I think it is I—I think no one
      was ever happier than I,
5   And who has lavish'd all? for I lavish constantly the best I have,
And who proudest? for I think I have reason to be the proudest
      son alive—for I am the son of the brawny and tall-topt
      city,
And who has been bold and true? for I would be the boldest and
      truest being of the universe,
And who benevolent? for I would show more benevolence than
      all the rest,
And who has receiv'd the love of the most friends? for I know
      what it is to receive the passionate love of many friends,
And who possesses a perfect and enamour'd body? for I do not
      believe any one possesses a more perfect or enamour'd
10   body than mine,

EXCELSIOR] Appeared in LG 1856 with the title, "Poem of The Heart of The Son
of Manhattan Island," affirming its character as personal credo; entitled "Chants
Democratic No. 15" in LG 1860; present title in 1867. Appeared in 1871 in the
"Passage to India" supplement, and in LG 1881 in the present group. The shaping
process was interesting. Two lines suggested in LG 1860 "Blue Copy" revisions were
not added:

> And who has adopted the loftiest motto?
> O I will put my motto over it, as it is over the top of this Song!

The following line, the tenth of the 1856 text was dropped, after 1871 revision, in
1881:

> And who has projected beautiful words through the longest time? By God!
>   I will outvie him! I will say such words, they shall stretch through
>   longer time!

And who thinks the amplest thoughts? for I would surround those
    thoughts,
And who has made hymns fit for the earth? for I am mad with de-
    vouring ecstasy to make joyous hymns for the whole earth.

1856   1881

Ah Poverties, Wincings, and Sulky Retreats.

Ah poverties, wincings, and sulky retreats,
Ah you foes that in conflict have overcome me,
(For what is my life or any man's life but a conflict with foes, the
    old, the incessant war?)
You degradations, you tussle with passions and appetites,
You smarts from dissatisfied friendships, (ah wounds the sharpest
    of all!)   5
You toil of painful and choked articulations, you meannesses,
You shallow tongue-talks at tables, (my tongue the shallowest of
    any;)
You broken resolutions, you racking angers, you smother'd ennuis!
Ah think not you finally triumph, my real self has yet to come
    forth,
It shall yet march forth o'ermastering, till all lies beneath me,   10
It shall yet stand up the soldier of ultimate victory.

1865–6   1881

Thoughts.

Of public opinion,
Of a calm and cool fiat sooner or later, (how impassive! how
    certain and final!)

Still another line, the twelfth of the 1856 text, was dropped in 1871:

> And to whom has been given the sweetest from women, and paid them in
>   kind? For I will take the like sweets, and pay them in kind.

RETREATS] Appeared in "Sequel to Drum-Taps" (1865–6) and reprinted in
all later editions without change of title or text, except for the substitution, in LG 1881,
of "ultimate" for "unquestioned." During the crisis years of the early 1860's, the poet,
deeply perturbed but invincibly hopeful, entered into his notebooks just such adjura-
tion to himself as the sentiments here expressed.

THOUGHTS] Entitled "Thought" in LG 1860 and 1867, and "Thoughts" there-
after. In the 1860 LG "Blue Copy" revisions WW cancelled this poem, but he
retained it in all editions, with the minor revision of two words in 1881. The theme is
a common one with the poet—the celebration of democracy sustained by the intuitive
wisdom of the people as against the impotence of institutionalism.

Of the President with pale face asking secretly to himself, *What
will the people say at last?*
Of the frivolous Judge—of the corrupt Congressman, Governor,
Mayor—of such as these standing helpless and exposed,
5 Of the mumbling and screaming priest, (soon, soon deserted,)
Of the lessening year by year of venerableness, and of the dicta
of officers, statutes, pulpits, schools,
Of the rising forever taller and stronger and broader of the intui-
tions of men and women, and of Self-esteem and Per-
sonality;
Of the true New World—of the Democracies resplendent en-
masse,
Of the conformity of politics, armies, navies, to them,
Of the shining sun by them—of the inherent light, greater than
10   the rest,
Of the envelopment of all by them, and the effusion of all from
them.

1860   1881

Mediums.

They shall arise in the States,
They shall report Nature, laws, physiology, and happiness,
They shall illustrate Democracy and the kosmos,
They shall be alimentive, amative, perceptive,
5 They shall be complete women and men, their pose brawny and
supple, their drink water, their blood clean and clear,
They shall fully enjoy materialism and the sight of products, they
shall enjoy the sight of the beef, lumber, bread-stuffs, of
Chicago the great city,
They shall train themselves to go in public to become orators and
oratresses,

MEDIUMS] Originally as "Chants Democratic" No. 16 in LG 1860; present title
in 1867; transferred in 1871 to *Passage to India* and in LG 1881 to the present
cluster. The one significant variant shows only in the MS (Barrett)—"America"
instead of "Democracy" in the third line; the few revisions in the printed text were
minor. The poem was probably composed in the mid-1850's, being clearly related to
the prophetic tenor of the first poems.
  9. gospels] In its original meaning, "good tidings."
  LIFE] A *Drum-Taps* poem of 1865 and 1867; transferred in 1871 to the group,
"Marches Now the War is Over," and to the present cluster in 1881. There were

Strong and sweet shall their tongues be, poems and materials of
      poems shall come from their lives, they shall be makers
      and finders,
Of them and of their works shall emerge divine conveyers, to
      convey gospels,
Characters, events, retrospections, shall be convey'd in gospels,
      trees, animals, waters, shall be convey'd,   10
Death, the future, the invisible faith, shall all be convey'd.

  1860   *1871*

Weave in, My Hardy Life.

Weave in, weave in, my hardy life,
Weave yet a soldier strong and full for great campaigns to come,
Weave in red blood, weave sinews in like ropes, the senses, sight
      weave in,
Weave lasting sure, weave day and night the weft, the warp,
      incessant weave, tire not,
(We know not what the use O life, nor know the aim, the end,
      nor really aught we know,   5
But know the work, the need goes on and shall go on, the death-
      envelop'd march of peace as well as war goes on,)
For great campaigns of peace the same the wiry threads to weave,
We know not why or what, yet weave, forever weave.

  1865   *1881*

Spain, 1873–74.

Out of the murk of heaviest clouds,
Out of the feudal wrecks and heap'd-up skeletons of kings,
Out of that old entire European debris, the shatter'd mummeries,

---

minor verbal changes in *LG* 1871 and *LG* 1881 only.

    SPAIN, 1873–74] First printed in the New York *Daily Graphic*, March 24, 1873,
then in the 1876 *Two Rivulets*, and in *LG* 1881 in its present position. The attempt to
establish a constitutional republic in Spain produced a virtual condition of anarchy
from February, 1873, until January, 1874, but failed to prevent the restoration of the
Bourbons with the proclamation of Don Alfonso as king, December 29, 1874.
Sympathetic with the democratic revolution, WW reminds America of her own birth
from Freedom, and in the second stanza predicts the final victory of Democracy
everywhere.

Ruin'd cathedrals, crumble of palaces, tombs of priests,
Lo, Freedom's features fresh undimm'd look forth—the same
5   immortal face looks forth;
(A glimpse as of thy Mother's face Columbia,
A flash significant as of a sword,
Beaming towards thee.)

Nor think we forget thee maternal;
10 Lag'd'st thou so long? shall the clouds close again upon thee?
Ah, but thou hast thyself now appear'd to us—we know thee,
Thou hast given us a sure proof, the glimpse of thyself,
Thou waitest there as everywhere thy time.

     1873   *1881*

By Broad Potomac's Shore.

By broad Potomac's shore, again old tongue,
(Still uttering, still ejaculating, canst never cease this babble?)
Again old heart so gay, again to you, your sense, the full flush
          spring returning,
Again the freshness and the odors, again Virginia's summer sky,
          pellucid blue and silver,
5 Again the forenoon purple of the hills,
Again the deathless grass, so noiseless soft and green,
Again the blood-red roses blooming.

Perfume this book of mine O blood-red roses!
Lave subtly with your waters every line Potomac!
Give me of you O spring, before I close, to put between its
10   pages!
O forenoon purple of the hills, before I close, of you!
O deathless grass, of you!

     1872   *1881*

SHORE] This poem was first published as the last of the group of seven poems
composing the 1872 supplementary volume, *As a Strong Bird on Pinions Free*. It was
then reprinted in the 1872 *Two Rivulets*, and finally in its present position in LG
1881. Its lyric power, delicate beyond the clichés of sentiment, is sustained by
memory and experience in a troubled year (1872). The ravages of war were still
fresh, the Washington clerkship was interrupted by necessary trips away, and illness
threatened both the poet and his mother. No wonder his imagination was moved by
symbol—the "blood-red roses" for friendship and the "perfume" for memory.

From Far Dakota's Cañons.

June 25, 1876.

From far Dakota's cañons,
Lands of the wild ravine, the dusky Sioux, the lonesome stretch,
    the silence,
Haply to-day a mournful wail, haply a trumpet-note for heroes.

The battle-bulletin,
The Indian ambuscade, the craft, the fatal environment,   5
The cavalry companies fighting to the last in sternest heroism,
In the midst of their little circle, with their slaughter'd horses for
        breastworks,
The fall of Custer and all his officers and men.

Continues yet the old, old legend of our race,
The loftiest of life upheld by death,   10
The ancient banner perfectly maintain'd,
O lesson opportune, O how I welcome thee!

As sitting in dark days,
Lone, sulky, through the time's thick murk looking in vain for light,
    for hope,
From unsuspected parts a fierce and momentary proof,   15
(The sun there at the centre though conceal'd,
Electric life forever at the centre,)
Breaks forth a lightning flash.

Thou of the tawny flowing hair in battle,
I erewhile saw, with erect head, pressing ever in front, bearing a
    bright sword in thy hand,
Now ending well in death the splendid fever of thy deeds,   20
(I bring no dirge for it or thee, I bring a glad triumphal sonnet,)

CAÑONS] First named "A Death Sonnet for Custer" and published in the New
York *Tribune*, July 10, 1876. WW was paid $10 (see letter of July 18, 1876, Corr.
III, 54.) The poem appeared as an intercalation in some copies of *LG* 1876, and in its
present title and position in *LG* 1881. Five MS notebooks (Feinberg), working notes
and trial phrases show Custer's death in the Sioux massacre on the banks of the Lit-
tle Big Horn as inspiring heroism in a slack time—an idea the poet phrases in his
fourth stanza. There is a MS draft (Feinberg) of the complete poem, and a MS
draft (Berg) for the New York *Tribune* version.

Desperate and glorious, aye in defeat most desperate, most glorious,
After thy many battles in which never yielding up a gun or a color,
25 Leaving behind thee a memory sweet to soldiers,
Thou yieldest up thyself.

1876   1881

Old War-Dreams.

In midnight sleep of many a face of anguish,
Of the look at first of the mortally wounded, (of that indescribable
     look,)
Of the dead on their backs with arms extended wide,
         I dream, I dream, I dream.

5 Of scenes of Nature, fields and mountains,
Of skies so beauteous after a storm, and at night the moon so
         unearthly bright,
Shining sweetly, shining down, where we dig the trenches and
         gather the heaps,
         I dream, I dream, I dream.

Long have they pass'd, faces and trenches and fields,
Where through the carnage I moved with a callous composure,
10   or away from the fallen,
Onward I sped at the time—but now of their forms at night,
         I dream, I dream, I dream.

1865-6   1881

Thick-Sprinkled Bunting.

Thick-sprinkled bunting! flag of stars!
Long yet your road, fateful flag—long yet your road, and lined
     with bloody death,

WAR-DREAMS] This poem appeared in the "Sequel to Drum-Taps," 1865–1866,
and in the 1867 "Drum-Taps" annex under the title, "In Clouds Descending, in
Midnight Sleep," the opening phrase of the first line, which was revised to its present
form in 1871. The 1871 text, transferred to the "Ashes of Soldiers" group of *Passage
to India*, has the title, "In Midnight Sleep" together with other minor revisions.
Present title and position came in the 1881 LG. Note the regularity of stanza form
and the use of refrain.
BUNTING] Appeared in the 1865 *Drum-Taps* and the "Drum-Taps" supplement

For the prize I see at issue at last is the world,
All its ships and shores I see interwoven with your threads greedy
     banner;
Dream'd again the flags of kings, highest borne, to flaunt unrival'd?   5
O hasten flag of man—O with sure and steady step, passing
     highest flags of kings,
Walk supreme to the heavens mighty symbol—run up above
     them all,
Flag of stars! thick-sprinkled bunting!

   1865   *1881*

What Best I See in Thee.

To U. S. G. return'd from his World's Tour.

What best I see in thee,
Is not that where thou mov'st down history's great highways,
Ever undimm'd by time shoots warlike victory's dazzle,
Or that thou sat'st where Washington sat, ruling the land in peace,
Or thou the man whom feudal Europe feted, venerable Asia
     swarm'd upon,   5
Who walk'd with kings with even pace the round world's prome-
     nade;
But that in foreign lands, in all thy walks with kings,
Those prairie sovereigns of the West, Kansas, Missouri, Illinois,
Ohio's, Indiana's millions, comrades, farmers, soldiers, all to the
     front,
Invisibly with thee walking with kings with even pace the round
     world's promenade,   10
Were all so justified.

   1881   *1881*

to LG 1867, under the title, "Flag of stars, thick-sprinkled bunting," which was its
first line; in LG 1871 with the present title and first line, included in the "Bathed in
War's Perfume" cluster; and in LG 1881 in the present cluster. N and F, p. 46, item
153, is a printing of the MS with variant readings.

    THEE] First appeared in LG 1881. General Grant began his world tour in the
spring of 1877 upon completing his eight years as president; he returned in Septem-
ber, 1879, having been received in England, Europe, and the Far East with distin-
guished honors. WW's comment, "The Silent General" in *Specimen Days*, parallels
the sentiment of the poem (*Prose Works*, I, 226, Coll W).

Spirit That Form'd This Scene.

Written in Platte Cañon, Colorado.

Spirit that form'd this scene,
These tumbled rock-piles grim and red,
These reckless heaven-ambitious peaks,
These gorges, turbulent-clear streams, this naked freshness,
5   These formless wild arrays, for reasons of their own,
I know thee, savage spirit—we have communed together,
Mine too such wild arrays, for reasons of their own;
Was't charged against my chants they had forgotten art?
To fuse within themselves its rules precise and delicatesse?
The lyrist's measur'd beat, the wrought-out temple's grace—
10   column and polish'd arch forgot?
But thou that revelest here—spirit that form'd this scene,
They have remember'd thee.

1881   *1881*

As I Walk These Broad Majestic Days.

As I walk these broad majestic days of peace,
(For the war, the struggle of blood finish'd, wherein, O terrific
    Ideal,
Against vast odds erewhile having gloriously won,
Now thou stridest on, yet perhaps in time toward denser wars,
5   Perhaps to engage in time in still more dreadful contests, dangers,
Longer campaigns and crises, labors beyond all others,)
Around me I hear that eclat of the world, politics, produce,
The announcements of recognized things, science,
The approved growth of cities and the spread of inventions.

SCENE] First appeared in *LG* 1881, and in the *Critic*, September 10 of the same year. A memory of WW's Western trip in 1879, it may be compared with its prose counterpart, "An Egotistical Find," in *Specimen Days* (*Prose Works*, I, 210–11, Coll W). MS in Feinberg Collection.

7. such wild arrays] It is notable that in the lyric mastery of these lines, WW not only meets the charge of his critics, but demonstrates its falsity.

DAYS] Originally No. 21 of "Chants Democratic" in *LG* 1860; transferred to the "Songs Before Parting" supplement to *LG* 1867 under the title, "As I Walk Solitary, Unattended"; then to the cluster, "Marches Now the War is Over," in *LG* 1871 under its present title. Present position in 1881. It has undergone considerable change,

I see the ships, (they will last a few years,)   10
The vast factories with their foremen and workmen,
And hear the indorsement of all, and do not object to it.

But I too announce solid things,
Science, ships, politics, cities, factories, are not nothing,
Like a grand procession to music of distant bugles pouring,
   triumphantly moving, and grander heaving in sight,   15
They stand for realities—all is as it should be.

Then my realities;
What else is so real as mine?
Libertad and the divine average, freedom to every slave on the
   face of the earth,
The rapt promises and luminè of seers, the spiritual world, these
   centuries-lasting songs,   20
And our visions, the visions of poets, the most solid announce-
   ments of any.

 1860   *1881*

A Clear Midnight.

This is thy hour O Soul, thy free flight into the wordless,
Away from books, away from art, the day erased, the lesson done,
Thee fully forth emerging, silent, gazing, pondering the themes
   thou lovest best,
Night, sleep, death and the stars.

 1881   *1881*

notably in the addition in 1871 of the opening six lines prompted by the Civil War, and the exclusion in 1881 of a final passage of five lines probably not essential to the theme. A fundamental tenet is WW's subject here—that he regards the nonmaterial realities of idea and ideals as more real, more permanent, than the material realities, however much he celebrates their immediate utility.

 20. luminè] In context the meaning of this invented word is clear, but its derivation, whether from lumen, "light," or luminary, "a light-giving body," has not been elucidated.

 MIDNIGHT] First appeared in *LG* 1881. Its MS (LC Whitman 28) reproduced in Furness, p. 174, carries the MS note: "for end of poem." The last, revised MS draft (Feinberg) is written on the back of a letter dated December 2, 1880.

Songs of Parting.

As the Time Draws Nigh.

As the time draws nigh glooming a cloud,
A dread beyond of I know not what darkens me.

I shall go forth,
I shall traverse the States awhile, but I cannot tell whither or how
  long,
Perhaps soon some day or night while I am singing my voice will
5   suddenly cease.

O book, O chants! must all then amount to but this?
Must we barely arrive at this beginning of us?—and yet it is
  enough, O soul;
O soul, we have positively appear'd—that is enough.

1860   *1871*

PARTING] Of the seventeen poems in this final cluster, four are from LG 1860,
four from the 1865 *Drum-Taps*, six from the 1871 *Passage to India*, one from the
1872 *As a Strong Bird on Pinions Free*, and two are new to the 1881 edition. It is
not incongruous that they should have appeared over a period of more than twenty
years and in five different editions. The imminence of departure had entered the
poet's pages as early as 1860, when, moved by a sense of dread lest his songs should
cease, he recalled in "As the Time Draws Nigh" the joys he had taken in life. Now in
1881 this poem opens the final section with equal propriety, the personal note muted
by time. The three other 1860 poems still apply, most notably "So Long!" Equally
suitable here are the poems not yet distributed into other groups—poems from the
"Songs Before Parting" of LG 1867, the "Songs of Parting" of LG 1871, the "Now
Finalè to the Shore" of *Passage to India*, and four poems from the 1865 *Drum-Taps*. Two of this cluster of 1881 were new poems. Perhaps the most genuine of the
group—if we except the ceremonious "So Long!"—is "Song at Sunset," a carol of
adoration. In these lyrics, reflecting a life passed a century ago, today's reader may
find familiar the same terrifying pace of change, the same vast gulfs of ignorance,
the same world hopes and fears, the same knowledge that at the end one has little to
bequeath save only what is in memory, and that, from the discovery of "endless
Finalés," one knows that "in my end is my beginning." The poet wrought well with
his group, for only one who possesses greatly can relinquish greatly, and what we
feel at last is not the sense of the end, but of continued life.

Years of the Modern.

Years of the modern! years of the unperform'd!
Your horizon rises, I see it parting away for more august dramas,
I see not America only, not only Liberty's nation but other nations
      preparing,
I see tremendous entrances and exits, new combinations, the soli-
      darity of races,
I see that force advancing with irresistible power on the world's
      stage,   5
(Have the old forces, the old wars, played their parts? are the
      acts suitable to them closed?)
I see Freedom, completely arm'd and victorious and very haughty,
      with Law on one side and Peace on the other,
A stupendous trio all issuing forth against the idea of caste;
What historic denouements are these we so rapidly approach?
I see men marching and countermarching by swift millions,   10
I see the frontiers and boundaries of the old aristocracies broken,
I see the landmarks of European kings removed,
I see this day the People beginning their landmarks, (all others
      give way;)
Never were such sharp questions ask'd as this day,
Never was average man, his soul, more energetic, more like a God,   15

NIGH] The original poem of nineteen lines in LG 1860, entitled "To My Soul," was more than twice the present length, and far more intimate, taking note as in farewell of "the unspeakable love I interchanged with women," "the curious attachment of young men to me," and "the tracks which I leave, upon the side-walks and fields. . . ." The poet outlived the immediate crisis implicit in poems of 1860, and retained the more important, general human condition in his revisions. A MS (Barrett) of the early version associates the phrase, "suddenly at the height and close of my career," with the cloud that darkens, but otherwise varies little from the 1860 text. The poem next appeared in the LG 1867 supplement, "Songs Before Parting," cut practically to its present text, under the title, "As Nearing Departure." With little further revision in the 1871–1876 text, it was placed in the "Songs of Parting" group with the present title.

MODERN] First appeared in the 1865 Drum-Taps with the title, "Years of the Unperformed"; transferred with present title and minor textual alterations to the "Songs of Parting" group of LG 1872 and LG 1881. Holloway (CPSP) was the first to note that in fact about half of the poem's lines are taken directly from the final section, "The World's Portents, Issues, the 80th Year of These States," of WW's unpublished 1856 political tract, The Eighteenth Presidency! ed. by Edward F. Grier (Lawrence, Kansas, 1956), pp. 42–45.

11. aristocracies broken] From line 11 through line 24 the phrasing is taken from the final section of The Eighteenth Presidency!

Lo, how he urges and urges, leaving the masses no rest!
His daring foot is on land and sea everywhere, he colonizes the
     Pacific, the archipelagoes,
With the steamship, the electric telegraph, the newspaper, the
     wholesale engines of war,
With these and the world-spreading factories he interlinks all
     geography, all lands;
What whispers are these O lands, running ahead of you, passing
20   under the seas?
Are all nations communing? is there going to be but one heart to
     the globe?
Is humanity forming en-masse? for lo, tyrants tremble, crowns
     grow dim,
The earth, restive, confronts a new era, perhaps a general divine war,
No one knows what will happen next, such portents fill the days
     and nights;
Years prophetical! the space ahead as I walk, as I vainly try to
25   pierce it, is full of phantoms,
Unborn deeds, things soon to be, project their shapes around me,
This incredible rush and heat, this strange ecstatic fever of dreams
     O years!
Your dreams O years, how they penetrate through me! (I know
     not whether I sleep or wake;)
The perform'd America and Europe grow dim, retiring in shadow
     behind me,
The unperform'd, more gigantic than ever, advance, advance upon
30   me.

1865   1881

Ashes of Soldiers.

Ashes of soldiers South or North,
As I muse retrospective murmuring a chant in thought,
The war resumes, again to my sense your shapes,
And again the advance of the armies.

SOLDIERS] First published in the 1865 *Drum-Taps*, an elegy entitled "Hymn of
Dead Soldiers," shorter by ten lines than it is now. Transferred to the supplement,
Passage to India 1871, the poem was essentially altered by the addition of the
present first two stanzas, and, as "Ashes of Soldiers," became the title poem for a
cluster of the same name, with the following epigraph:

    Again a verse for sake of you,
    You soldiers in the ranks—you Volunteers,

Noiseless as mists and vapors,   5
From their graves in the trenches ascending,
From cemeteries all through Virginia and Tennessee,
From every point of the compass out of the countless graves,
In wafted clouds, in myriads large, or squads of twos or threes or
          single ones they come,
And silently gather round me.   10

Now sound no note O trumpeters,
Not at the head of my cavalry parading on spirited horses,
With sabres drawn and glistening, and carbines by their thighs, (ah
          my brave horsemen!
My handsome tan-faced horsemen! what life, what joy and pride,
With all the perils were yours.)   15

Nor you drummers, neither at reveillé at dawn,
Nor the long roll alarming the camp, nor even the muffled beat
          for a burial,
Nothing from you this time O drummers bearing my warlike drums.

But aside from these and the marts of wealth and the crowded
          promenade,
Admitting around me comrades close unseen by the rest and
          voiceless,   20
The slain elate and alive again, the dust and debris alive,
I chant this chant of my silent soul in the name of all dead
          soldiers.

Faces so pale with wondrous eyes, very dear, gather closer yet,
Draw close, but speak not.

Phantoms of countless lost,   25
Invisible to the rest henceforth become my companions,
Follow me ever—desert me not while I live.

Who bravely fighting, silent fell,
To fill unmention'd graves.

Without significant textual change, the poem retained its place in this supplement to
LG 1872 and *Two Rivulets* (1876). Final text and present position in LG 1881,
without the epigraph. A MS fragment (Feinberg) of seven lines, not used in the
poem's revision, also develops the "ashes" metaphor which now informs both the
opening and closing passages of this compassionate poem.

Sweet are the blooming cheeks of the living—sweet are the musi-
    cal voices sounding,
But sweet, ah sweet, are the dead with their silent eyes.

30 Dearest comrades, all is over and long gone,
But love is not over—and what love, O comrades!
Perfume from battle-fields rising, up from the fœtor arising.

Perfume therefore my chant, O love, immortal love,
Give me to bathe the memories of all dead soldiers,
35 Shroud them, embalm them, cover them all over with tender pride.

Perfume all—make all wholesome,
Make these ashes to nourish and blossom,
O love, solve all, fructify all with the last chemistry.

Give me exhaustless, make me a fountain,
That I exhale love from me wherever I go like a moist perennial
40   dew,
For the ashes of all dead soldiers South or North.

   1865   *1881*

Thoughts.

1

Of these years I sing,
How they pass and have pass'd through convuls'd pains, as through
    parturitions,
How America illustrates birth, muscular youth, the promise, the
    sure fulfilment, the absolute success, despite of people—
    illustrates evil as well as good,
The vehement struggle so fierce for unity in one's-self;
How many hold despairingly yet to the models departed, caste,
5   myths, obedience, compulsion, and to infidelity,

THOUGHTS] Originally two separate poems—"Chants Democratic" No. 9 and
No. 11 in LG 1860; combined in LG 1867 as sections 1 and 2 of "Thoughts" in the
supplement, "Songs Before Parting." With little further revision "Thoughts" ap-
peared in LG 1871 in the "Songs of Parting" cluster; present position in LG 1881. The
MSS (Barrett) of the two 1860 poems are closely followed in the texts. In the LG

How few see the arrived models, the athletes, the Western States,
    or see freedom or spirituality, or hold any faith in results,
(But I see the athletes, and I see the results of the war glorious
    and inevitable, and they again leading to other results.)

How the great cities appear—how the Democratic masses, turbu-
    lent, wilful, as I love them,
How the whirl, the contest, the wrestle of evil with good, the
    sounding and resounding, keep on and on,
How society waits unform'd, and is for a while between things
    ended and things begun,   10
How America is the continent of glories, and of the triumph of
    freedom and of the Democracies, and of the fruits of so-
    ciety, and of all that is begun,
And how the States are complete in themselves—and how all
    triumphs and glories are complete in themselves, to lead
    onward,
And how these of mine and of the States will in their turn be con-
    vuls'd, and serve other parturitions and transitions,
And how all people, sights, combinations, the democratic masses
    too, serve—and how every fact, and war itself, with all its
    horrors, serves,
And how now or at any time each serves the exquisite transition
    of death.   15

    2

Of seeds dropping into the ground, of births,
Of the steady concentration of America, inland, upward, to im-
    pregnable and swarming places,
Of what Indiana, Kentucky, Arkansas, and the rest, are to be,
Of what a few years will show there in Nebraska, Colorado,
    Nevada, and the rest,
(Or afar, mounting the Northern Pacific to Sitka or Aliaska,)   20
Of what the feuillage of America is the preparation for—and of
    what all sights, North, South, East and West, are,

1860 "Blue Copy" revisions, WW gave the title "Thought" to each, and indicated
their transfer (unfulfilled) to *Drum-Taps*. As stanzas of a single poem, they compose
a unified vision of "immense spiritual results" for Western Democracy.
    20. Sitka or Aliaska] Sitka is a town in southeastern Alaska on Baranof Island;
"Aliaska" is unidentified.

Of this Union welded in blood, of the solemn price paid, of the
   unnamed lost ever present in my mind;
Of the temporary use of materials for identity's sake,
Of the present, passing, departing—of the growth of completer
   men than any yet,
Of all sloping down there where the fresh free giver the mother,
25   the Mississippi flows,
Of mighty inland cities yet unsurvey'd and unsuspected,
Of the new and good names, of the modern developments, of
   inalienable homesteads,
Of a free and original life there, of simple diet and clean and
   sweet blood,
Of litheness, majestic faces, clear eyes, and perfect physique there,
Of immense spiritual results future years far West, each side of the
30   Anahuacs,
Of these songs, well understood there, (being made for that area,)
Of the native scorn of grossness and gain there,
(O it lurks in me night and day—what is gain after all to savage-
   ness and freedom?)

1860   1881

Song at Sunset.

Splendor of ended day floating and filling me,
Hour prophetic, hour resuming the past,
Inflating my throat, you divine average,
You earth and life till the last ray gleams I sing.

5   Open mouth of my soul uttering gladness,
Eyes of my soul seeing perfection,
Natural life of me faithfully praising things,
Corroborating forever the triumph of things.

Illustrious every one!
10 Illustrious what we name space, sphere of unnumber'd spirits,

30. Anahuacs] An Aztec name signifying the plateau valley in which the city of
Mexico is located. Crossing its highest part is a series of ranges, part of which is
called "Condillera de Anahuac." The sense of the line and the plural form indicates
that WW is referring to the mountain ranges.
SUNSET] This brilliant paean, first printed in LG 1860 as "Chants Democratic"

Illustrious the mystery of motion in all beings, even the tiniest
    insect,
Illustrious the attribute of speech, the senses, the body,
Illustrious the passing light—illustrious the pale reflection on the
    new moon in the western sky,
Illustrious whatever I see or hear or touch, to the last.

Good in all,   15
In the satisfaction and aplomb of animals,
In the annual return of the seasons,
In the hilarity of youth,
In the strength and flush of manhood,
In the grandeur and exquisiteness of old age,   20
In the superb vistas of death.

Wonderful to depart!
Wonderful to be here!
The heart, to jet the all-alike and innocent blood!
To breathe the air, how delicious!   25
To speak—to walk—to seize something by the hand!
To prepare for sleep, for bed, to look on my rose-color'd flesh!
To be conscious of my body, so satisfied, so large!
To be this incredible God I am!
To have gone forth among other Gods, these men and women I
    love.   30

Wonderful how I celebrate you and myself!
How my thoughts play subtly at the spectacles around!
How the clouds pass silently overhead!
How the earth darts on and on! and how the sun, moon, stars,
    dart on and on!
How the water sports and sings! (surely it is alive!)   35
How the trees rise and stand up, with strong trunks, with branches
    and leaves!
(Surely there is something more in each of the trees, some living
    soul.)

No. 8, received its present title in LG 1867 in the supplement, "Songs Before Part-
ing," p. 29, and was transferred to the "Songs of Parting" cluster in LG 1871. In
MS (Barrett) the title reads, "A Sunset Carol"; in WW's 1860 "Blue Copy" revisions
is the same title with two words in the margin opposite—"finale" and "religious."
The poem received but little revision. The poet Rilke called poetry "the past that
breaks out in our hearts." This poem is the poet's joyous affirmation of his whole life.

O amazement of things—even the least particle!
O spirituality of things!
O strain musical flowing through ages and continents, now reaching
40   me and America!
I take your strong chords, intersperse them, and cheerfully pass
        them forward.

I too carol the sun, usher'd or at noon, or as now, setting,
I too throb to the brain and beauty of the earth and of all the
        growths of the earth,
I too have felt the resistless call of myself.

45 As I steam'd down the Mississippi,
As I wander'd over the prairies,
As I have lived, as I have look'd through my windows my eyes,
As I went forth in the morning, as I beheld the light breaking in
        the east,
As I bathed on the beach of the Eastern Sea, and again on the
        beach of the Western Sea,
As I roam'd the streets of inland Chicago, whatever streets I have
50   roam'd,
Or cities or silent woods, or even amid the sights of war,
Wherever I have been I have charged myself with contentment
        and triumph.

I sing to the last the equalities modern or old,
I sing the endless finalés of things,
55 I say Nature continues, glory continues,
I praise with electric voice,
For I do not see one imperfection in the universe,
And I do not see one cause or result lamentable at last in the
        universe.

49. Western Sea] WW never reached the Pacific in his travels, but from the
times of the Greek navigators the "western sea" has been in the common stock of
poetry as a symbol for the far-off or unattainable. Cf. Tennyson's "Stars of the
western sea" in a song of *The Princess* (1847), familiar to WW.
    DEATH] An elegy to the poet's mother, Louisa Van Velsor Whitman, who died
May 23, 1873 in her seventy-eighth year, a period when WW himself—as the first
line intimates—felt perturbations of death. The poem is one of the seventeen new to

O setting sun! though the time has come,
I still warble under you, if none else does, unmitigated adoration.   60
    1860   *1881*

As at Thy Portals Also Death.

As at thy portals also death,
Entering thy sovereign, dim, illimitable grounds,
To memories of my mother, to the divine blending, maternity,
To her, buried and gone, yet buried not, gone not from me,
(I see again the calm benignant face fresh and beautiful still,   5
I sit by the form in the coffin,
I kiss and kiss convulsively again the sweet old lips, the cheeks,
    the closed eyes in the coffin;)
To her, the ideal woman, practical, spiritual, of all of earth, life,
    love, to me the best,
I grave a monumental line, before I go, amid these songs,
And set a tombstone here.   10
    1881   *1881*

My Legacy.

The business man the acquirer vast,
After assiduous years surveying results, preparing for departure,
Devises houses and lands to his children, bequeaths stocks, goods,
    funds for a school or hospital,
Leaves money to certain companions to buy tokens, souvenirs of
    gems and gold.

But I, my life surveying, closing,   5
With nothing to show to devise from its idle years,
Nor houses nor lands, nor tokens of gems or gold for my friends,

---

LG 1881.
    LEGACY] Originated as an epigraph entitled "Souvenirs of Democracy," introducing *As a Strong Bird on Pinions Free* (1872), which became a supplement incorporated with others in *Two Rivulets* (1876). With the present title in LG 1881, the poem shows considerable revision in the second stanza not shown in Triggs' "Variorum Readings" of 1902.
    7. friends] Following this line in the first 1871–1876 version, the poem continues:

Yet certain remembrances of the war for you, and after you,
And little souvenirs of camps and soldiers, with my love,
10   I bind together and bequeath in this bundle of songs.

1872   1881

Pensive on Her Dead Gazing.

Pensive on her dead gazing I heard the Mother of All,
Desperate on the torn bodies, on the forms covering the battle-
            fields gazing,
(As the last gun ceased, but the scent of the powder-smoke
            linger'd,)
As she call'd to her earth with mournful voice while she stalk'd,
Absorb them well O my earth, she cried, I charge you lose not
5   my sons, lose not an atom,
And you streams absorb them well, taking their dear blood,
And you local spots, and you airs that swim above lightly
            impalpable,
And all you essences of soil and growth, and you my rivers' depths,
And you mountain sides, and the woods where my dear children's
            blood trickling redden'd,
10 And you trees down in your roots to bequeath to all future trees,
My dead absorb or South or North—my young men's bodies
            absorb, and their precious precious blood,
Which holding in trust for me faithfully back again give me many
            a year hence,
In unseen essence and odor of surface and grass, centuries hence,
In blowing airs from the fields back again give me my darlings,
            give my immortal heroes,
Exhale me them centuries hence, breathe me their breath, let not
15   an atom be lost,

            Only these Souvenirs of Democracy—In them—in
                all my songs—behind me leaving,
            To You, whoever you are, (bathing, leavening this
                leaf especially with my breath—pressing on it
                a moment with my own hands;
            —Here! feel how the pulse beats in my wrists!—how
                my heart's-blood is swelling, contracting!)
            I will You, in all, Myself, with promise to never
                desert you,
            To which I sign my name,
                                            Walt Whitman

O years and graves! O air and soil! O my dead, an aroma sweet!
Exhale them perennial sweet death, years, centuries hence.

1865   1881

Camps of Green.

Not alone those camps of white, old comrades of the wars,
When as order'd forward, after a long march,
Footsore and weary, soon as the light lessens we halt for the night,
Some of us so fatigued carrying the gun and knapsack, dropping
     asleep in our tracks,
Others pitching the little tents, and the fires lit up begin to
     sparkle,   5
Outposts of pickets posted surrounding alert through the dark,
And a word provided for countersign, careful for safety,
Till to the call of the drummers at daybreak loudly beating the
     drums,
We rise up refresh'd, the night and sleep pass'd over, and resume
     our journey,
Or proceed to battle.   10

Lo, the camps of the tents of green,
Which the days of peace keep filling, and the days of war keep
     filling,
With a mystic army, (is it too order'd forward? is it too only halt-
     ing awhile,
Till night and sleep pass over?)

Now in those camps of green, in their tents dotting the world,   15
In the parents, children, husbands, wives, in them, in the old and
     young,

GAZING] In *Drum-Taps* (1865) and in the same supplement to LG 1867; trans-
ferred to the "Ashes of Soldiers" group in *Passage to India* (1871) with the insertion
of present line 3; finally, with minor textual revisions, in LG 1881 with present
shortened title instead of the whole first line.

GREEN] Appeared with the present title in *Drum-Taps* (1865) and in the same
supplement to LG 1867; transferred to the "Ashes of Soldiers" group in *Passage to
India* (1871), with minor revisions then and in its present relocation in LG 1881.

Sleeping under the sunlight, sleeping under the moonlight, content
      and silent there at last,
Behold the mighty bivouac-field and waiting-camp of all,
Of the corps and generals all, and the President over the corps
      and generals all,
And of each of us O soldiers, and of each and all in the ranks we
20   fought,
(There without hatred we all, all meet.)

For presently O soldiers, we too camp in our place in the bivouac-
      camps of green,
But we need not provide for outposts, nor word for the counter-
      sign,
Nor drummer to beat the morning drum.

   1865   *1881*

The Sobbing of the Bells.

(*Midnight, Sept. 19–20, 1881.*)

The sobbing of the bells, the sudden death-news everywhere,
The slumberers rouse, the rapport of the People,
(Full well they know that message in the darkness,
Full well return, respond within their breasts, their brains, the sad
      reverberations,)
The passionate toll and clang—city to city, joining, sounding,
5   passing,
Those heart-beats of a Nation in the night.

   1881   *1881*

BELLS] The poet was in Boston, supervising the printing of his 1881 edition of
LG, when the news came of President Garfield's death, near midnight, September 19,
1881, from an assassin's attack of the previous July 2. He first published the poem in
the Boston *Daily Globe*, September 27, 1881, and then inserted it in the 1881 edition
just before the last pages were stereotyped. The two MSS (Feinberg and Berg) were
both published in facsimile (cf. Traubel, II, 137, and Bucke, 55). The poem was
reprinted in *The Poets' Tribute to Garfield* (Cambridge, 1881). On WW's friend-
ship with Garfield, whom he had known in Washington when the latter was a young
congressman from Ohio, see Allen, 495.

CLOSE] First published in the 1871 *Passage to India*, entitled "Thought" in the
cluster "Now Finalè to the Shore," but without the present lines 7–10; these were

As They Draw to a Close.

As they draw to a close,
Of what underlies the precedent songs—of my aims in them,
Of the seed I have sought to plant in them,
Of joy, sweet joy, through many a year, in them,
(For them, for them have I lived, in them my work is done,)   5
Of many an aspiration fond, of many a dream and plan;
Through Space and Time fused in a chant, and the flowing eternal
  identity,
To Nature encompassing these, encompassing God—to the joy-
  ous, electric all,
To the sense of Death, and accepting exulting in Death in its
  turn the same as life,
The entrance of man to sing;   10
To compact you, ye parted, diverse lives,
To put rapport the mountains and rocks and streams,
And the winds of the north, and the forests of oak and pine,
With you O soul.

1871   *1881*

Joy, Shipmate, Joy!

Joy, shipmate, joy!
(Pleas'd to my soul at death I cry,)
Our life is closed, our life begins,
The long, long anchorage we leave,
The ship is clear at last, she leaps!   5

present in the preceding poem of the same group as the last four lines of "Shut Not
Your Doors." The seventh line of the original poem was dropped in *LG* 1881:

  O you, O mystery great!—to place on record faith
    in you, O death!

  JOY! WANT PORTALS CAROLS] All four of these poems were first published in
the 1871 *Passage to India* (though not in this order), in the group "Now Finalè to
the Shore," with present titles and texts.
  1. Joy] The reader may observe that this poem and the following three, conclud-
ing this cluster, emphasize a persistent motivation of the "Songs of Parting" (see
headnote to that title above), a theme dominant in the beginning in "As the Time
Draws Nigh," "Ashes of Soldiers," and "Song at Sunset."

She swiftly courses from the shore,
Joy, shipmate, joy.
    1871   1871

The Untold Want.

The untold want by life and land ne'er granted,
Now voyager sail thou forth to seek and find.
    1871   1871

Portals.

What are those of the known but to ascend and enter the
        Unknown?
And what are those of life but for Death?
    1871   1871

These Carols.

These carols sung to cheer my passage through the world I see,
For completion I dedicate to the Invisible World.
    1871   1871

Now Finalè to the Shore.

Now finalè to the shore,
Now, land and life finalè and farewell,

    SHORE] First published in the 1871 *Passage to India* in a group of the same title, the poem appeared in 1881 with present title and text. Twenty years after "Now Finalè . . ." was written, WW included it in *Good-bye My Fancy* (1891), except for the first line. It terminates the small essay, "A Death-Bouquet," and he introduces the poem with the following words: "Like an invisible breeze after a long and sultry day, death sometimes sets in at last, soothingly and refreshingly, almost vitally . . . It is a curious suggestion of immortality that the mental and emotional powers remain to their clearest through all, while the senses of pain and flesh-volitions are blunted or even gone."
    1. Now finalè] A peculiarity of the 1892 text is the use of the grave accent for "finale" in the title and in lines 1 and 2. The accent was, however, correctly omitted in this edition from the same word in "Song at Sunset," line 54 (*q.v.*). Cf. Paumanok, "66: finalè" from 82 to 1902.
    LONG!] This farewell poem—"My songs cease, I abandon them"—has terminated *LG* ever since the third edition (1860), although considerably revised in text, if not

Now Voyager depart, (much, much for thee is yet in store,)
Often enough hast thou adventur'd o'er the seas,
Cautiously cruising, studying the charts,   5
Duly again to port and hawser's tie returning;
But now obey thy cherish'd secret wish,
Embrace thy friends, leave all in order,
To port and hawser's tie no more returning,
Depart upon thy endless cruise old Sailor.   10

    1871   *1871*

So Long!

To conclude, I announce what comes after me.

I remember I said before my leaves sprang at all,
I would raise my voice jocund and strong with reference to con-
      summations.

When America does what was promis'd,
When through these States walk a hundred millions of superb
      persons,
When the rest part away for superb persons and contribute to them,   5
When breeds of the most perfect mothers denote America,
Then to me and mine our due fruition.

I have press'd through in my own right,
I have sung the body and the soul, war and peace have I sung,
      and the songs of life and death,
And the songs of birth, and shown that there are many births.   10

in essential meaning. For the 1867 edition twenty-one lines were cancelled, in
accordance with WW's revised *LG* 1860 "Blue Copy," and three lines were added in
the 1871 edition. WW excluded earlier passages that struck a brasher note, produc-
ing in the final revision a certain humility and quiet confidence in ultimate recogni-
tion: "When America does what was promis'd . . . Then to me and mine our due
fruition." Lines 53–54 and 64–65 are paraphrased from "Leaves of Grass" No. 24 in
LG 1860, which then became "Now Lift Me Close" in 1867; reappeared as "To the
Reader at Parting" in *Passage to India* (1871) and in successive combinations of
that supplement with *LG* 1872 and *TR* (1876); then was dropped alto-
gether. William Sloane Kennedy (*Fight of a Book for the World*, p. 110) notes
that WW was early in using the expression, "So Long!" and that when he asked the
poet to define it, he replied: "A salutation of departure, greatly used among sailors,
sports, and prostitutes. The sense of it is 'Till we meet again,'—conveying an
inference that somehow they will doubtless so meet, sooner or later."

I have offer'd my style to every one, I have journey'd with confi-
    dent step;
While my pleasure is yet at the full I whisper *So long!*
And take the young woman's hand and the young man's hand for
    the last time.

15   I announce natural persons to arise,
I announce justice triumphant,
I announce uncompromising liberty and equality,
I announce the justification of candor and the justification of
    pride.

I announce that the identity of these States is a single identity
    only,
20   I announce the Union more and more compact, indissoluble,
I announce splendors and majesties to make all the previous poli-
    tics of the earth insignificant.

I announce adhesiveness, I say it shall be limitless, unloosen'd,
I say you shall yet find the friend you were looking for.

I announce a man or woman coming, perhaps you are the one,
    (*So long!*)
I announce the great individual, fluid as Nature, chaste, affection-
25   ate, compassionate, fully arm'd.

I announce a life that shall be copious, vehement, spiritual, bold,
I announce an end that shall lightly and joyfully meet its transla-
    tion.

I announce myriads of youths, beautiful, gigantic, sweet-blooded,
I announce a race of splendid and savage old men.

30   O thicker and faster—(*So long!*)
O crowding too close upon me,
I foresee too much, it means more than I thought,
It appears to me I am dying.

22. adhesiveness] A phrenological term designating the faculty of friendship,
used by WW in his earlier poems to designate manly comradeship. There is much in

Hasten throat and sound your last,
Salute me—salute the days once more. Peal the old cry once
    more. 35

Screaming electric, the atmosphere using,
At random glancing, each as I notice absorbing,
Swiftly on, but a little while alighting,
Curious envelop'd messages delivering,
Sparkles hot, seed ethereal down in the dirt dropping, 40
Myself unknowing, my commission obeying, to question it never
    daring,
To ages and ages yet the growth of the seed leaving,
To troops out of the war arising, they the tasks I have set promul-
    ging,
To women certain whispers of myself bequeathing, their affection
    me more clearly explaining,
To young men my problems offering—no dallier I—I the mus-
    cle of their brains trying, 45
So I pass, a little time vocal, visible, contrary,
Afterward a melodious echo, passionately bent for, (death making
    me really undying,)
The best of me then when no longer visible, for toward that I have
    been incessantly preparing.

What is there more, that I lag and pause and crouch extended
    with unshut mouth?
Is there a single final farewell? 50

My songs cease, I abandon them,
From behind the screen where I hid I advance personally solely
    to you.

Camerado, this is no book,
Who touches this touches a man,
(Is it night? are we here together alone?) 55
It is I you hold and who holds you,
I spring from the pages into your arms—decease calls me forth.

his writings and attitude to suggest that later he broadened his reference to include
friendship between man and woman, and woman and woman as well.

O how your fingers drowse me,
Your breath falls around me like dew, your pulse lulls the tympans
     of my ears,
60 I feel immerged from head to foot,
Delicious, enough.

Enough O deed impromptu and secret,
Enough O gliding present—enough O summ'd-up past.

Dear friend whoever you are take this kiss,
65 I give it especially to you, do not forget me,
I feel like one who has done work for the day to retire awhile,
I receive now again of my many translations, from my avataras as-
     cending, while others doubtless await me,
An unknown sphere more real than I dream'd, more direct, darts
     awakening rays about me, *So long!*
Remember my words, I may again return,
70 I love you, I depart from materials,
I am as one disembodied, triumphant, dead.

1860   *1881*

---

67. avataras] A Sanskrit word (cf. English "avatar"): "incarnation" or "embodi-
ment"—in Hinduism associated with the appearances of the deity, Vishnu,
as Krishna.

    SEVENTY] In the editions of LG from 1860 to 1881, and in the supplementary
volumes, beginning with *Drum-Taps* (1865), the poet attempted—by the continuous
revision of the poems, by excluding some and adding some newly created, by
arranging and rearranging clusters of related poems under group titles frequently
altered or recombined—to achieve a topical organization referring to chronology only
as the typical sequence of experience in the life of the so-called "average" man,
spanning the nineteenth century as his own life almost did. He had come to think of
LG as a "single poem"; he had hoped to continue with another such, designed to
represent the spiritual anabasis of modern man. By 1881 his mounting infirmities
brought him to a halt with only "this bundle of songs" bequeathed "to the Invisible
World." By 1888 he had completed a number of new pieces, many of them for
newspaper or periodical publication, and a major prose essay, "A Backward Glance

FIRST ANNEX

Sands at Seventy.

Mannahatta.

My city's fit and noble name resumed,
Choice aboriginal name, with marvellous beauty, meaning,
A rocky founded island—shores where ever gayly dash the coming,
    going, hurrying sea waves.

1888   1888–9

Paumanok.

Sea-beauty! stretch'd and basking!
One side thy inland ocean laving, broad, with copious commerce,
    steamers, sails,
And one the Atlantic's wind caressing, fierce or gentle—mighty
    hulls dark-gliding in the distance.
Isle of sweet brooks of drinking-water—healthy air and soil!
Isle of the salty shore and breeze and brine!   5

1888   1888–9

O'er Travel'd Roads." (see below). These, with other prose pieces, appeared as a
book, *November Boughs* (1888), in which the poems were headed, "Sands at
Seventy." This title did not come easily; several MS collections (Berg, Trent, Yale)
possess scribblings of other possibilities—"Halcyon Days," "Sands on the Shores,"
"Carols at Candlelight," "Carols Closing Sixty-Nine," etc. The poems of *November
Boughs* appeared as an annex, "Sands at Seventy," in reprints of LG 1884, some with
a new title page dated 1888, and again in LG 1889, all with the new penultimate
poem, "Old Age's Lambent Peaks," as in the present text. In the 1891–1892 LG,
the following group was introduced by a title page, backed by a table of "Contents."
The title page read: "ANNEX / TO PRECEDING PAGES. / SANDS AT SEVENTY. / Copy-
right, 1888, by Walt Whitman. / (SEE 'NOVEMBER BOUGHS')." The pagination of
this group followed in sequence that of the preceding text.
    MANNAHATTA] First published in the New York *Herald*, February 27, 1888,
with the third line unitalicized.
    PAUMANOK] First published in the New York *Herald*, February 29, 1888. Cf.
WW's lengthy autobiographical poem, "Starting from Paumanok" (i.e., Long Is-
land).

From Montauk Point.

I stand as on some mighty eagle's beak,
Eastward the sea absorbing, viewing, (nothing but sea and sky,)
The tossing waves, the foam, the ships in the distance,
The wild unrest, the snowy, curling caps—that inbound urge
      and urge of waves,
5 Seeking the shores forever.
    1888   *1888–9*

To Those Who've Fail'd.

To those who've fail'd, in aspiration vast,
To unnam'd soldiers fallen in front on the lead,
To calm, devoted engineers—to over-ardent travelers—to pilots
      on their ships,
To many a lofty song and picture without recognition—I'd rear a
      laurel-cover'd monument,
5 High, high above the rest—To all cut off before their time,
Possess'd by some strange spirit of fire,
Quench'd by an early death.
    1888   *1888–9*

A Carol Closing Sixty-nine.

A carol closing sixty-nine—a *résumé*—a repetition,
My lines in joy and hope continuing on the same,
Of ye, O God, Life, Nature, Freedom, Poetry;
Of you, my Land—your rivers, prairies, States—you, mottled
      Flag I love,

POINT] First published in the New York *Herald*, March 1, 1888. The place is a headland at the eastern end of Long Island, familiar in WW's earliest youth.

FAIL'D] First published in the New York *Herald*, January 27, 1888, with "aspiration" in the plural. The MS (Berg) shows the title, "A laurel wreath to those who've fail'd."

SIXTY-NINE] First published in the New York *Herald*, May 21, 1888. WW's MS (Barrett) shows the note, "sent to Lippincott's," and the cancellation of two other titles: "Carols at nearing Seventy" and "A Carol-Cluster at 69."

SOLDIERS] First published in the New York *Herald*, March 18, 1888.

Your aggregate retain'd entire—Of north, south, east and west,
    your items all;   5
Of me myself—the jocund heart yet beating in my breast,
The body wreck'd, old, poor and paralyzed—the strange inertia
    falling pall-like round me,
The burning fires down in my sluggish blood not yet extinct,
The undiminish'd faith—the groups of loving friends.

    1888   *1888–9*

The Bravest Soldiers.

Brave, brave were the soldiers (high named to-day) who lived
    through the fight;
But the bravest press'd to the front and fell, unnamed, unknown.

    1888   *1888–9*

A Font of Type.

This latent mine—these unlaunch'd voices—passionate powers,
Wrath, argument, or praise, or comic leer, or prayer devout,
(Not nonpareil, brevier, bourgeois, long primer merely,)
These ocean waves arousable to fury and to death,
Or sooth'd to ease and sheeny sun and sleep,   5
Within the pallid slivers slumbering.

    1888   *1888–9*

As I Sit Writing Here.

As I sit writing here, sick and grown old,
Not my least burden is that dulness of the years, querilities,

---

TYPE] John Russell Young's *Men and Memories* (New York, 1901, p. 107)
contains a slightly different version of this poem which, says the editor, was sent to
Mr. Young marked "personal—don't print." First published in this group, in *Novem-
ber Boughs* (1888).
    3. long primer] The preceding are the names of types in the sizes from six to ten
points, then most in use.
    HERE] First published in the New York *Herald*, May 14, 1888. The word
"querilities," so spelled by WW in the second line, should be "querulities." The error
appeared both in the *Herald* and in *November Boughs*.

Ungracious glooms, aches, lethargy, constipation, whimpering
    ennui,
May filter in my daily songs.

  1888   *1888–9*

My Canary Bird.

Did we count great, O soul, to penetrate the themes of mighty
    books,
Absorbing deep and full from thoughts, plays, speculations?
But now from thee to me, caged bird, to feel thy joyous warble,
Filling the air, the lonesome room, the long forenoon,
5 Is it not just as great, O soul?

  1888   *1888–9*

Queries to My Seventieth Year.

Approaching, nearing, curious,
Thou dim, uncertain spectre—bringest thou life or death?
Strength, weakness, blindness, more paralysis and heavier?
Or placid skies and sun? Wilt stir the waters yet?
5 Or haply cut me short for good? Or leave me here as now,
Dull, parrot-like and old, with crack'd voice harping, screeching?

  1888   *1888–9*

The Wallabout Martyrs.

[In Brooklyn, in an old vault, mark'd by no special recognition, lie huddled at this moment the undoubtedly authentic remains of the stanchest and earliest revolutionary patriots from the British prison ships and prisons of the times of 1776–83, in and around New York, and from all over Long Island; originally buried—many thousands of them—in trenches in the Wallabout sands.]

Greater than memory of Achilles or Ulysses,
More, more by far to thee than tomb of Alexander,

BIRD] First published in the New York *Herald*, March 2, 1888.
    YEAR] First published in the New York *Herald*, May 2, 1888. MSS, Huntington
and Feinberg. The Feinberg version includes three lines not printed:

> Steep me in immobility
> As we grow old we narrow on ourselves concentrating
> Something to us unspeakably pensive in our own age—our sorrows—

    6. harping] In the more colloquial sense of tedious repetition.
    MARTYRS] First published in the New York *Herald*, March 16, 1888. MS in

Those cart loads of old charnel ashes, scales and splints of
    mouldy bones,
Once living men—once resolute courage, aspiration, strength,
The stepping stones to thee to-day and here, America.   5
    1888   *1888–9*

The First Dandelion.

Simple and fresh and fair from winter's close emerging,
As if no artifice of fashion, business, politics, had ever been,
Forth from its sunny nook of shelter'd grass—innocent, golden,
    calm as the dawn,
The spring's first dandelion shows its trustful face.
    1888   *1888–9*

America.

Centre of equal daughters, equal sons,
All, all alike endear'd, grown, ungrown, young or old,
Strong, ample, fair, enduring, capable, rich,
Perennial with the Earth, with Freedom, Law and Love,
A grand, sane, towering, seated Mother,   5
Chair'd in the adamant of Time.
    1888   *1888–9*

Memories.

How sweet the silent backward tracings!
The wanderings as in dreams—the meditation of old times re-
    sumed—their loves, joys, persons, voyages.
    1888   *1888–9*

Barrett. Wallabout Bay is at the bend of the East River, present site of the Brooklyn Navy Yard.

    DANDELION] First published in the New York *Herald*, March 12, 1888, a salute to spring which appeared the day after the beginning of the great blizzard of 1888. MS in Barrett.

    AMERICA] First published in the New York *Herald*, February 11, 1888. Cf. "Thou Mother with Thy Equal Brood"; also "To-day and Thee," below.

    MEMORIES] First published in this group in *November Boughs* (1888). MS in Feinberg.

To-day and Thee.

The appointed winners in a long-stretch'd game;
The course of Time and nations—Egypt, India, Greece and
    Rome;
The past entire, with all its heroes, histories, arts, experiments,
Its store of songs, inventions, voyages, teachers, books,
Garner'd for now and thee—To think of it!
The heirdom all converged in thee!

   1888   *1888–9*

After the Dazzle of Day.

After the dazzle of day is gone,
Only the dark, dark night shows to my eyes the stars;
After the clangor of organ majestic, or chorus, or perfect band,
Silent, athwart my soul, moves the symphony true.

   1888   *1888–9*

Abraham Lincoln, Born Feb. 12, 1809.

To-day, from each and all, a breath of prayer—a pulse of
    thought,
To memory of Him—to birth of Him.
    Publish'd Feb. 12, 1888.

   1888   *1888–9*

Out of May's Shows Selected.

Apple orchards, the trees all cover'd with blossoms;
Wheat fields carpeted far and near in vital emerald green;
The eternal, exhaustless freshness of each early morning;

    THEE] First published in the New York *Herald*, April 23, 1888. MS in **Barrett**.
    DAY] First published in the New York *Herald*, February 3, 1888. MS in **Fein-berg**.
    1809] First published in the New York *Herald*, February 12, 1888. WW gave his first public lecture on Lincoln on April 14, 1879, and gave others at intervals until 1890, including one in Philadelphia in 1886 and one in New York in 1887.
    SELECTED] First published in the New York *Herald*, May 10, 1888.

The yellow, golden, transparent haze of the warm afternoon sun;
The aspiring lilac bushes with profuse purple or white flowers.   5

1888   *1888–9*

Halcyon Days.

Not from successful love alone,
Nor wealth, nor honor'd middle age, nor victories of politics or
    war;
But as life wanes, and all the turbulent passions calm,
As gorgeous, vapory, silent hues cover the evening sky,
As softness, fulness, rest, suffuse the frame, like fresher, balmier
    air,   5
As the days take on a mellower light, and the apple at last hangs
       really finish'd and indolent-ripe on the tree,
Then for the teeming quietest, happiest days of all!
The brooding and blissful halcyon days!

1888   *1888–9*

Fancies at Navesink.

The Pilot in the Mist.

Steaming the northern rapids—(an old St. Lawrence reminis-
    cence,
A sudden memory-flash comes back, I know not why,
Here waiting for the sunrise, gazing from this hill;) *

    DAYS] First published in the New York *Herald*, January 29, 1888. MS in
Hanley.
    8. halcyon days] WW, bird watcher and naturalist, probably knew the Greek
fable that the *halkyon*, a mythical kingfisher, nested at sea and calmed the waves of
the winter solstice.
    NAVESINK] This group of eight poems, after rejection by W. H. Alden, editor of
Harper's (Traubel, I, 61), was first published in *Nineteenth Century*, August,

Again 'tis just at morning—a heavy haze contends with day-
    break,
Again the trembling, laboring vessel veers me—I press through
5   foam-dash'd rocks that almost touch me,
Again I mark where aft the small thin Indian helmsman
Looms in the mist, with brow elate and governing hand.
      *Navesink—a sea-side mountain, lower entrance of New York Bay.
   1885   *1888–9*

Had I the Choice.

Had I the choice to tally greatest bards,
To limn their portraits, stately, beautiful, and emulate at will,
Homer with all his wars and warriors—Hector, Achilles, Ajax,
Or Shakspere's woe-entangled Hamlet, Lear, Othello—Tenny-
    son's fair ladies,
Metre or wit the best, or choice conceit to wield in perfect
5   rhyme, delight of singers;
These, these, O sea, all these I'd gladly barter,
Would you the undulation of one wave, its trick to me transfer,
Or breathe one breath of yours upon my verse,
And leave its odor there.
   1885   *1888–9*

You Tides with Ceaseless Swell.

You tides with ceaseless swell! you power that does this work!
You unseen force, centripetal, centrifugal, through space's
    spread,
Rapport of sun, moon, earth, and all the constellations,
What are the messages by you from distant stars to us? what
    Sirius'? what Capella's?
What central heart—and you the pulse—vivifies all? what
5   boundless aggregate of all?
What subtle indirection and significance in you? what clue to
    all in you? what fluid, vast identity,
Holding the universe with all its parts as one—as sailing in a ship?
   1885   *1888–9*

1885. It takes its place with the "Sea-Drift" cluster, which it indeed surpasses with
respect to sustained unity of theme and mood, as evidence of the fascination of the
sea upon the poet's mind and art, and his sense of kinship with its rhythms.
Abundant MS material—fifty-four scraps and fragments at LC, eighteen pages at

Last of Ebb, and Daylight Waning.

Last of ebb, and daylight waning,
Scented sea-cool landward making, smells of sedge and salt
    incoming,
With many a half-caught voice sent up from the eddies,
Many a muffled confession—many a sob and whisper'd word,
As of speakers far or hid.   5

How they sweep down and out! how they mutter!
Poets unnamed—artists greatest of any, with cherish'd lost
    designs,
Love's unresponse—a chorus of age's complaints—hope's last
    words,
Some suicide's despairing cry, *Away to the boundless waste, and
    never again return.*

On to oblivion then!   10
On, on, and do your part, ye burying, ebbing tide!
On for your time, ye furious debouché!

1885   1888–9

And Yet Not You Alone.

And yet not you alone, twilight and burying ebb,
Nor you, ye lost designs alone—nor failures, aspirations;
I know, divine deceitful ones, your glamour's seeming;
Duly by you, from you, the tide and light again—duly the
    hinges turning,
Duly the needed discord-parts offsetting, blending,   5
Weaving from you, from Sleep, Night, Death itself,
The rhythmus of Birth eternal.

1885   1888–9

Proudly the Flood Comes In.

Proudly the flood comes in, shouting, foaming, advancing,
Long it holds at the high, with bosom broad outswelling,

Yale, other pages in Barrett, Berg, Hanley, Huntington—show how thoroughly WW
worked upon this series, composing, amending, and rejecting. There is manuscript
evidence that he had considered a grouping somewhat different from the one printed,
including some poems later separately placed. Navesink is a seaside elevation on the
New Jersey coast, at the lower entrance of New York Bay.

All throbs, dilates—the farms, woods, streets of cities—workmen
    at work,
Mainsails, topsails, jibs, appear in the offing—steamers' pennants
    of smoke—and under the forenoon sun,
Freighted with human lives, gaily the outward bound, gaily the
5   inward bound,
Flaunting from many a spar the flag I love.

    1885   *1888–9*

By That Long Scan of Waves.

By that long scan of waves, myself call'd back, resumed upon
    myself,
In every crest some undulating light or shade—some retrospect,
Joys, travels, studies, silent panoramas—scenes ephemeral,
The long past war, the battles, hospital sights, the wounded and
    the dead,
Myself through every by-gone phase—my idle youth—old age at
5   hand,
My three-score years of life summ'd up; and more, and past,
By any grand ideal tried, intentionless, the whole a nothing,
And haply yet some drop within God's scheme's ensemble—some
    wave, or part of wave,
Like one of yours, ye multitudinous ocean.

    1885   *1888–9*

Then Last of All.

Then last of all, caught from these shores, this hill,
Of you O tides, the mystic human meaning:
Only by law of you, your swell and ebb, enclosing me the same,
The brain that shapes, the voice that chants this song.

    1885   *1888–9*

    All] The "Fancies at Navesink" end with this poem.
    1884] Under the title, "If I Should Need to Name, O Western World," this poem
was first published in the Philadelphia *Press*, October 26, 1884. The opposing
candidates in 1884 were Blaine and Cleveland, Blaine suffering defeat after the
defection of Roscoe Conkling. "There is no question at issue of any importance,"
WW wrote—(the issues happened to be the tariff and Chinese exclusion)—"But," he
went on, "I like well the *fact* of all these national elections—have written a little poem
about it" (*Walt Whitman's Diary in Canada*, 1904, p. 73).

AN ALBUM OF WHITMAN PORTRAITS

1. Whitman aged 30. The poet dates the photograph 1849, Bucke 1856. The signed copy in the Feinberg Collection is here reproduced by permission.

2. Whitman aged 35 (1854); engraved frontispiece, first edition, *Leaves of Grass*, 1855. The engraver, S. Hollyer, signed the Pierpont Morgan Library copy here reproduced by permission.

3. Whitman, about 40 (1859); engraved frontispiece, third
edition, *Leaves of Grass*, 1860. Charles Hine, the painter of
the portrait, signed the copy in the Feinberg Collection, here
reproduced by permission.

Walt Whitman
Washington DC
1863

4. Whitman aged 43 (1862)? This photograph was sent by the poet to William Rossetti for Mrs. Gilchrist with the comment: "I confess to myself a perhaps capricious fondness for it." The Saunders catalog dates it 1862, but the signed copy in the Feinberg Collection, here reproduced by permission, is inscribed 1863.

5. Whitman aged 44 (1863). Engraving by T. Johnson from photograph by Gardner. The copy in the Feinberg Collection is here reproduced by permission.

6. Whitman aged 50 (1869). Photograph by Frank Pearsall. The signed copy in the Feinberg Collection is here reproduced by permission.

7. Whitman aged 53 (1872). Photograph by Frank Pearsall.
The signed copy in the Feinberg Collection is here repro-
duced by permission.

8. Whitman aged 61 (1880). Photograph by F. Gutekunst of
Philadelphia. The signed copy in the Feinberg Collection is
here reproduced by permission.

Walt Whitman 1887

9. Whitman aged 68 (1887). Photograph by George C. Cox. One of the poet's favorites. He called it "The Laughing Philosopher" and sent a copy to Tennyson. The signed copy in the Feinberg Collection is here reproduced by permission.

10. Whitman aged 69 (1888). Portrait in oils by Thomas Eakins. Reproduced by courtesy of the Pennsylvania Academy of the Fine Arts.

Walt Whitman
(Sculptor's profile)
May 1891

11. Whitman aged 72 (1891). Sculptor's profile photograph
by the painter Thomas Eakins, and so inscribed by Whitman
on the Feinberg copy here reproduced by permission. One of
the last photographs, May, 1891; frontispiece to *Good-Bye
My Fancy* (1891).

Election Day, November, 1884.

If I should need to name, O Western World, your powerfulest
    scene and show,
'Twould not be you, Niagara—nor you, ye limitless prairies—nor
    your huge rifts of canyons, Colorado,
Nor you, Yosemite—nor Yellowstone, with all its spasmic geyser-
    loops ascending to the skies, appearing and disappearing,
Nor Oregon's white cones—nor Huron's belt of mighty lakes—
    nor Mississippi's stream:
—This seething hemisphere's humanity, as now, I'd name—*the
    still small voice* vibrating—America's choosing day,   5
(The heart of it not in the chosen—the act itself the main, the
    quadriennial choosing,)
The stretch of North and South arous'd—sea-board and inland
    —Texas to Maine—the Prairie States—Vermont, Virginia,
    California,
The final ballot-shower from East to West—the paradox and con-
    flict,
The countless snow-flakes falling—(a swordless conflict,
Yet more than all Rome's wars of old, or modern Napoleon's:)
    the peaceful choice of all,   10
Or good or ill humanity—welcoming the darker odds, the dross:
—Foams and ferments the wine? it serves to purify—while the
    heart pants, life glows:
These stormy gusts and winds waft precious ships,
Swell'd Washington's, Jefferson's, Lincoln's sails.

1884   *1888–9*

With Husky-Haughty Lips, O Sea!

With husky-haughty lips, O sea!
Where day and night I wend thy surf-beat shore,

SEA!] First published in *Harper's Monthly*, March, 1884, which paid $50.
The poem is a record of WW's visit to Ocean Grove, New Jersey, for a week with
John Burroughs in September and October, 1883, when he jotted down some of its
phrases in a thirteen-page notebook (Lion). Several trial lines were also penciled on
a page with letterhead reading Sheldon House, Ocean Grove (Feinberg). Four more
MS pages (Yale) record variants and final draft. One discarded title is "By thine
own lips, O Sea." WW's remarkable sequence of "Fancies at Navesink," above, may

Imaging to my sense thy varied strange suggestions,
    (I see and plainly list thy talk and conference here,)
5 Thy troops of white-maned racers racing to the goal,
Thy ample, smiling face, dash'd with the sparkling dimples of the
        sun,
Thy brooding scowl and murk—thy unloos'd hurricanes,
Thy unsubduedness, caprices, wilfulness;
Great as thou art above the rest, thy many tears—a lack from all
        eternity in thy content,
    (Naught but the greatest struggles, wrongs, defeats, could make
10   thee greatest—no less could make thee,)
Thy lonely state—something thou ever seek'st and seek'st, yet
        never gain'st,
Surely some right withheld—some voice, in huge monotonous
        rage, of freedom-lover pent,
Some vast heart, like a planet's, chain'd and chafing in those
        breakers,
By lengthen'd swell, and spasm, and panting breath,
15 And rhythmic rasping of thy sands and waves,
And serpent hiss, and savage peals of laughter,
And undertones of distant lion roar,
    (Sounding, appealing to the sky's deaf ear—but now, rapport for
        once,
A phantom in the night thy confidant for once,)
20 The first and last confession of the globe,
Outsurging, muttering from thy soul's abysms,
The tale of cosmic elemental passion,
Thou tellest to a kindred soul.

    1884   *1888–9*

also have been influenced in part by this holiday. Burroughs (diary, September 29),
referring to a walk on the beach, noted,

> "there is something grainy and saline in him, as in the voice of the sea . . .
> sometimes his talk is . . . eliptical and unfinished; again there comes a long,
> splendid roll of thought that . . . swings you quite free from your moor-
> ings."

    4. here] This line was added, after magazine publication, for the 1888–1889
text, followed here.
    GRANT] When this poem was first published in *Harper's Weekly*, May 16, 1885,
General Grant was still living. The title was the poem's first line, and a second stanza
read:

Death of General Grant.

As one by one withdraw the lofty actors,
From that great play on history's stage eterne,
That lurid, partial act of war and peace—of old and new con-
    tending,
Fought out through wrath, fears, dark dismays, and many a long
    suspense;
All past—and since, in countless graves receding, mellowing,   5
Victor's and vanquish'd—Lincoln's and Lee's—now thou with
    them,
Man of the mighty days—and equal to the days!
Thou from the prairies!—tangled and many-vein'd and hard has
    been thy part,
To admiration has it been enacted!

  1885   1888–9

Red Jacket (from Aloft.)

  [Impromptu on Buffalo City's monument to, and re-burial of the old Iroquois
orator, October 9, 1884.]

Upon this scene, this show,
Yielded to-day by fashion, learning, wealth,
(Nor in caprice alone—some grains of deepest meaning,)
Haply, aloft, (who knows?) from distant sky-clouds' blended
    shapes,
As some old tree, or rock or cliff, thrill'd with its soul,   5
Product of Nature's sun, stars, earth direct—a towering human
    form,

        And still shall be:—resume thou hero heart!
        Strengthen to firmest day, O rosy dawn of hope!
        Tho dirge I started first, to joyful shout reverse—and thou O grave,
        Wait long and long!

Although Grant died July 23, 1885, the first version was reprinted in *The Critic*,
August 15, 1885. Present version, *November Boughs* (1888). A MS is in the library
of St. John's Seminary, Camarillo, Calif.

  ALOFT] First published in the Philadelphia *Press*, October 10, 1884, and also in
the *Transactions of the Buffalo Historical Society*, III, 1885. Red Jacket (1750–
1830), grand sachem of the Iroquois, is credited with turning Iroquois support to the
American side in the War of 1812. WW did not attend the ceremony here cele-
brated.

In hunting-shirt of film, arm'd with the rifle, a half-ironical smile
    curving its phantom lips,
Like one of Ossian's ghosts looks down.

    1884   *1888–9*

Washington's Monument, February, 1885.

Ah, not this marble, dead and cold:
Far from its base and shaft expanding—the round zones circling,
    comprehending,
Thou, Washington, art all the world's, the continents' entire—
    not yours alone, America,
Europe's as well, in every part, castle of lord or laborer's cot,
Or frozen North, or sultry South—the African's—the Arab's in
5   his tent,
Old Asia's there with venerable smile, seated amid her ruins;
(Greets the antique the hero new? 'tis but the same—the heir
    legitimate, continued ever,
The indomitable heart and arm—proofs of the never-broken
    line,
Courage, alertness, patience, faith, the same—e'en in defeat de-
    feated not, the same:)
10 Wherever sails a ship, or house is built on land, or day or night,
Through teeming cities' streets, indoors or out, factories or farms,
Now, or to come, or past—where patriot wills existed or exist,
Wherever Freedom, pois'd by Toleration, sway'd by Law,
Stands or is rising thy true monument.

    1885   *1888–9*

Of That Blithe Throat of Thine.

[More than eighty-three degrees north—about a good day's steaming distance to
the Pole by one of our fast oceaners in clear water—Greely the explorer heard the
song of a single snow-bird merrily sounding over the desolation.]
Of that blithe throat of thine from arctic bleak and blank,
I'll mind the lesson, solitary bird—let me too welcome chilling
    drifts,

8. Ossian's ghosts] Ossian was the legendary third-century Gaelic bard whose
poems James Macpherson (1736–1796) professed to translate in a rhythmic prose
influential in the romanticism of the eighteenth century.

1885] First published in the Philadelphia *Press*, February 22, 1885, under the
title "Ah, Not This Granite Dead and Cold." Of four MS pages (Morgan), three are
work sheets; another MS, privately owned (De Gruson) is printer's copy for the

E'en the profoundest chill, as now—a torpid pulse, a brain un-
          nerv'd,
Old age land-lock'd within its winter bay—(cold, cold, O cold!)
These snowy hairs, my feeble arm, my frozen feet,   5
For them thy faith, thy rule I take, and grave it to the last;
Not summer's zones alone—not chants of youth, or south's warm
          tides alone,
But held by sluggish floes, pack'd in the northern ice, the cumulus
          of years,
These with gay heart I also sing.

     1885   *1888–9*

Broadway.

What hurrying human tides, or day or night!
What passions, winnings, losses, ardors, swim thy waters!
What whirls of evil, bliss and sorrow, stem thee!
What curious questioning glances—glints of love!
Leer, envy, scorn, contempt, hope, aspiration!   5
Thou portal—thou arena—thou of the myriad long-drawn lines
          and groups!
(Could but thy flagstones, curbs, façades, tell their inimitable
          tales;
Thy windows rich, and huge hotels—thy side-walks wide;)
Thou of the endless sliding, mincing, shuffling feet!
Thou, like the parti-colored world itself—like infinite, teeming,
          mocking life!   10
Thou visor'd, vast, unspeakable show and lesson!

     1888   *1888–9*

To Get the Final Lilt of Songs.

To get the final lilt of songs,
To penetrate the inmost lore of poets—to know the mighty ones,

1888 *November Boughs.*
     THINE] First published in *Harper's Monthly*, January, 1885, which paid WW
$30. MSS in LC and Feinberg.
     BROADWAY] First published in the New York *Herald*, April 10, 1888. MS in
Barrett.
     SONGS] First published in the New York *Herald*, April 16, 1888, under the title,
"The Final Lilt of Songs."

Job, Homer, Eschylus, Dante, Shakspere, Tennyson, Emerson;
To diagnose the shifting-delicate tints of love and pride and
     doubt—to truly understand,
5 To encompass these, the last keen faculty and entrance-price,
Old age, and what it brings from all its past experiences.

   1888   *1888–9*

Old Salt Kossabone.

Far back, related on my mother's side,
Old Salt Kossabone, I'll tell you how he died:
(Had been a sailor all his life—was nearly 90—lived with his
     married grandchild, Jenny;
House on a hill, with view of bay at hand, and distant cape, and
     stretch to open sea;)
The last of afternoons, the evening hours, for many a year his
5   regular custom,
In his great arm chair by the window seated,
(Sometimes, indeed, through half the day,)
Watching the coming, going of the vessels, he mutters to himself
     —And now the close of all:
One struggling outbound brig, one day, baffled for long—cross-
     tides and much wrong going,
At last at nightfall strikes the breeze aright, her whole luck veer-
10   ing,
And swiftly bending round the cape, the darkness proudly enter-
     ing, cleaving, as he watches,
"She's free—she's on her destination"—these the last words—
     when Jenny came, he sat there dead,
Dutch Kossabone, Old Salt, related on my mother's side, far
     back.

   1888   *1888–9*

KOSSABONE] First published in the New York *Herald*, February 25, 1888. The MS (Feinberg), endorsed by the actress, Ellen Terry, was presented to her by the poet. "Dutch Kossabone" was the father of Mary Kossabone (c. 1745–c. 1792), who married Garrett Van Velsor (1742–1812). Their son, Major Cornelius Van Velsor (1768–1837), married Naomi Williams (d. 1826). The poet's mother, Louisa Van Velsor (1795–1873) was the daughter of this marriage.

TENOR] First published in the *Critic*, November 8, 1884. The poem is a tribute to Signor Pasquale Brignole, whose funeral in New York City, November 3, 1884, is

The Dead Tenor.

As down the stage again,
With Spanish hat and plumes, and gait inimitable,
Back from the fading lessons of the past, I'd call, I'd tell and
    own,
How much from thee! the revelation of the singing voice from
    thee!
(So firm—so liquid-soft—again that tremulous, manly timbre!   5
The perfect singing voice—deepest of all to me the lesson—trial
    and test of all:)
How through those strains distill'd—how the rapt ears, the soul
    of me, absorbing
Fernando's heart, *Manrico's* passionate call, *Ernani's*, sweet
    Gennaro's,
I fold thenceforth, or seek to fold, within my chants transmuting,
Freedom's and Love's and Faith's unloos'd cantabile,   10
(As perfume's, color's, sunlight's correlation:)
From these, for these, with these, a hurried line, dead tenor,
A wafted autumn leaf, dropt in the closing grave, the shovel'd
    earth,
To memory of thee.
   1884   *1888–9*

Continuities.

[From a talk I had lately with a German spiritualist.]

Nothing is ever really lost, or can be lost,
No birth, identity, form—no object of the world.
Nor life, nor force, nor any visible thing;
Appearance must not foil, nor shifted sphere confuse thy brain.
Ample are time and space—ample the fields of Nature.   5

recorded in a newspaper clipping attached to the MS (Hanley). WW himself
identified the singer on an envelope in which he mailed the poem to his friend,
William Douglas O'Connor.
    8. *Fernando's . . . Manrico's . . . Ernani's . . . Gennaro's*] Characters, re-
spectively in Donizetti's opera *La Favorita*, Verdi's *Il Trovatore*, Verdi's *Ernani*, and
Donizetti's *Lucrezia Borgia*.
    CONTINUITIES] First published in the New York *Herald*, March 20, 1888. MSS
include a work sheet of trial lines (Feinberg) and a complete draft (Barrett).

The body, sluggish, aged, cold—the embers left from earlier
    fires,
The light in the eye grown dim, shall duly flame again;
The sun now low in the west rises for mornings and for noons
      continual;
To frozen clods ever the spring's invisible law returns,
10 With grass and flowers and summer fruits and corn.

    1888   *1888–9*

Yonnondio.

[The sense of the word is *lament for the aborigines*. It is an Iroquois term; and
has been used for a personal name.]

A song, a poem of itself—the word itself a dirge,
Amid the wilds, the rocks, the storm and wintry night,
To me such misty, strange tableaux the syllables calling up;
Yonnondio—I see, far in the west or north, a limitless ravine,
    with plains and mountains dark,
5 I see swarms of stalwart chieftains, medicine-men, and warriors,
As flitting by like clouds of ghosts, they pass and are gone in the
    twilight,
(Race of the woods, the landscapes free, and the falls!
No picture, poem, statement, passing them to the future:)
Yonnondio! Yonnondio!—unlimn'd they disappear;
10 To-day gives place, and fades—the cities, farms, factories fade;
A muffled sonorous sound, a wailing word is borne through the
    air for a moment,
Then blank and gone and still, and utterly lost.

    1887   *1888–9*

Life.

Ever the undiscouraged, resolute, struggling soul of man;
(Have former armies fail'd? then we send fresh armies—and
    fresh again;)

YONNONDIO] First published in the *Critic*, November 26, 1887. The poem is
one of the many memorials of WW's interest in American names.

LIFE] First published in the New York *Herald*, April 15, 1888. A sheet of rough
draft lines (Feinberg) for this poem was used by the poet in a letter of May 7, 1888
to Robert Pearsall Smith, containing the postscript: "I see I have taken a sheet of
paper with a rambling first draft of one of my Herald yaps—but n'importe."

SOMEWHERE] First published in *Lippincott's Magazine*, November, 1887. A

Ever the grappled mystery of all earth's ages old or new;
Ever the eager eyes, hurrahs, the welcome-clapping hands, the
     loud applause;
Ever the soul dissatisfied, curious, unconvinced at last;   5
Struggling to-day the same—battling the same.

1888   *1888–9*

"Going Somewhere."

My science-friend, my noblest woman-friend,
(Now buried in an English grave—and this a memory-leaf for
     her dear sake,)
Ended our talk—"The sum, concluding all we know of old or
     modern learning, intuitions deep,
"Of all Geologies—Histories—of all Astronomy—of Evolution,
     Metaphysics all,
"Is, that we all are onward, onward, speeding slowly, surely
     bettering,
"Life, life an endless march, an endless army, (no halt, but it is   5
     duly over,)
"The world, the race, the soul—in space and time the universes,
"All bound as is befitting each—all surely going somewhere."

1887   *1888–9*

From the 1867 edition L. of G.
Small the Theme of My Chant.

Small the theme of my Chant, yet the greatest—namely, One's-
     Self—a simple, separate person. That, for the use of the
     New World, I sing.
Man's physiology complete, from top to toe, I sing. Not physi-
     ognomy alone, nor brain alone, is worthy for the Muse;—I
     say the Form complete is worthier far. The Female equally
     with the Male, I sing.

facsimile of the MS printer's copy is reproduced opposite page 75 of Thomas C. Donaldson's *Walt Whitman, the Man* (1896). The "science-friend" is Anne Gilchrist, who died November 29, 1885. The story of her relationship with WW is recounted in Blodgett, 87–102.

    CHANT] with minor variants this poem first appeared on the flyleaf before the poems of LG 1867, a shorter version later opening the "Inscriptions" group of LG 1871. See note to "One's-Self I Sing." MSS are in the Barrett, Dartmouth, LC, and Yale collections.

Nor cease at the theme of One's-Self. I speak the word of the
    modern, the word En-Masse.
My Days I sing, and the Lands—with interstice I knew of hap-
    less War.
(O friend, whoe'er you are, at last arriving hither to commence,
    I feel through every leaf the pressure of your hand, which I
5   return.
And thus upon our journey, footing the road, and more than once, and
    link'd together let us go.)

    1867   *1888–9*

True Conquerors.

Old farmers, travelers, workmen (no matter how crippled or
    bent,)
Old sailors, out of many a perilous voyage, storm and wreck,
Old soldiers from campaigns, with all their wounds, defeats and
    scars;
Enough that they've survived at all—long life's unflinching ones!
Forth from their struggles, trials, fights, to have emerged at all
5   —in that alone,
True conquerors o'er all the rest.

    1888   *1888–9*

The United States to Old World Critics.

Here first the duties of to-day, the lessons of the concrete,
Wealth, order, travel, shelter, products, plenty;
As of the building of some varied, vast, perpetual edifice,
Whence to arise inevitable in time, the towering roofs, the lamps,
5   The solid-planted spires tall shooting to the stars.

    1888   *1888–9*

CONQUERORS] First published in the New York *Herald*, February 15, 1888.
    CRITICS] First published in the New York *Herald*, May 8, 1888. Among the "old
world critics" who especially interested WW in the 1880's were Matthew Arnold,
Robert Buchanan, Thomas Carlyle, and Oscar Wilde. See Blodgett, *Walt Whitman
in England*, *passim*.

The Calming Thought of All.

That coursing on, whate'er men's speculations,
Amid the changing schools, theologies, philosophies,
Amid the bawling presentations new and old,
The round earth's silent vital laws, facts, modes continue.

1888 *1888–9*

Thanks in Old Age.

Thanks in old age—thanks ere I go,
For health, the midday sun, the impalpable air—for life, mere
    life,
For precious ever-lingering memories, (of you my mother dear
    —you, father—you, brothers, sisters, friends,)
For all my days—not those of peace alone—the days of war the
    same,
For gentle words, caresses, gifts from foreign lands,   5
For shelter, wine and meat—for sweet appreciation,
(You distant, dim unknown—or young or old—countless, un-
    specified, readers belov'd,
We never met, and ne'er shall meet—and yet our souls embrace,
    long, close and long;)
For beings, groups, love, deeds, words, books—for colors, forms,
For all the brave strong men—devoted, hardy men—who've for-
    ward sprung in freedom's help, all years, all lands,   10
For braver, stronger, more devoted men—(a special laurel ere I
    go, to life's war's chosen ones,
The cannoneers of song and thought—the great artillerists—the
    foremost leaders, captains of the soul:)
As soldier from an ended war return'd—As traveler out of
    myriads, to the long procession retrospective,
Thanks—joyful thanks!—a soldier's, traveler's thanks.

1888 *1888–9*

ALL] First published in the New York *Herald*, May 27, 1888.
AGE] One MS scrap (Hanley) is a rough draft of the first eight lines; another
(Huntington) of the last five. Although the Hanley MS bears WW's notation,
"published Nov. 25, '87," it was actually published Nov. 24, in the Philadelphia
Press. It was reprinted in the New York *World* Nov. 23, 1890, there entitled "Walt
Whitman's Thanksgiving."

Life and Death.

The two old, simple problems ever intertwined,
Close home, elusive, present, baffled, grappled.
By each successive age insoluble, pass'd on,
To ours to-day—and we pass on the same.
    1888   *1888–9*

The Voice of the Rain.

And who art thou? said I to the soft-falling shower,
Which, strange to tell, gave me an answer, as here translated:
I am the Poem of Earth, said the voice of the rain,
Eternal I rise impalpable out of the land and the bottomless sea,
Upward to heaven, whence, vaguely form'd, altogether changed,
5   and yet the same,
I descend to lave the drouths, atomies, dust-layers of the globe,
And all that in them without me were seeds only, latent, unborn;
And forever, by day and night, I give back life to my own
      origin, and make pure and beautify it:
(For song, issuing from its birth-place, after fulfilment, wander-
      ing,
10 Reck'd or unreck'd, duly with love returns.)
    1885   *1888–9*

Soon Shall the Winter's Foil Be Here.

Soon shall the winter's foil be here;
Soon shall these icy ligatures unbind and melt—A little while,
And air, soil, wave, suffused shall be in softness, bloom and
      growth—a thousand forms shall rise
From these dead clods and chills as from low burial graves.

DEATH] First published in the New York *Herald*, May 23, 1888.
RAIN] First published in *Outing*, August, 1885. In a proof sheet (Feinberg) of
this poem, the title "A Rain Enigma" is rejected.
HERE] First published in the New York *Herald*, February 21, 1888. MS in
Huntington.

Thine eyes, ears—all thy best attributes—all that takes cognizance
　　of natural beauty,　　　　　　　　　　　　　　　　　　　　　　5
Shall wake and fill. Thou shalt perceive the simple shows, the
　　delicate miracles of earth,
Dandelions, clover, the emerald grass, the early scents and flow-
　　ers,
The arbutus under foot, the willow's yellow-green, the blossom-
　　ing plum and cherry;
With these the robin, lark and thrush, singing their songs—the
　　flitting bluebird;
For such the scenes the annual play brings on.　　　　　　　　　10

　　1888　　　　　　　　　　　　　　　　　　　　　　*1888–9*

While Not the Past Forgetting.

While not the past forgetting,
To-day, at least, contention sunk entire—peace, brotherhood up-
　　risen;
For sign reciprocal our Northern, Southern hands,
Lay on the graves of all dead soldiers, North or South,
(Nor for the past alone—for meanings to the future,)　　　　　5
Wreaths of roses and branches of palm.

　　　　Publish'd May 30, 1888

　　　　　　　　　　　　　　　　　　　　　　　　1888–9

The Dying Veteran.

[A Long Island incident—early part of the present century.]

Amid these days of order, ease, prosperity,
Amid the current songs of beauty, peace, decorum,
I cast a reminiscence—(likely 'twill offend you,
I heard it in my boyhood;)—More than a generation since,

FORGETTING] WW's note on publication of this Decoration Day poem has not
been substantiated, its first appearance evidently being in *November Boughs* (1888).
The MS (Feinberg) is a work sheet of trial lines.
　　VETERAN] First published in *McClure's Magazine*, June, 1887. WW told Wil-
liam Sloane Kennedy (*Reminiscences of Walt Whitman*, p. 55) that he received $25
for it—"far more than it is worth." MS in Feinberg Collection.

5   A queer old savage man, a fighter under Washington himself,
     (Large, brave, cleanly, hot-blooded, no talker, rather spiritual-
              istic,
     Had fought in the ranks—fought well—had been all through the
              Revolutionary war,)
     Lay dying—sons, daughters, church-deacons, lovingly tending
              him,
     Sharping their sense, their ears, towards his murmuring, half-
              caught words:
10   "Let me return again to my war-days,
     To the sights and scenes—to forming the line of battle,
     To the scouts ahead reconnoitering,
     To the cannons, the grim artillery,
     To the galloping aids, carrying orders,
15   To the wounded, the fallen, the heat, the suspense,
     The perfume strong, the smoke, the deafening noise;
     Away with your life of peace!—your joys of peace!
     Give me my old wild battle-life again!"

     1887   1888–9

Stronger Lessons.

Have you learn'd lessons only of those who admired you, and
         were tender with you, and stood aside for you?
Have you not learn'd great lessons from those who reject you,
         and brace themselves against you? or who treat you with
         contempt, or dispute the passage with you?

     1860   1888–9

A Prairie Sunset.

Shot gold, maroon and violet, dazzling silver, emerald, fawn,
The earth's whole amplitude and Nature's multiform power con-
         sign'd for once to colors;
The light, the general air possess'd by them—colors till now un-
         known,

     LESSONS] These two lines were first published as part of "Debris" in LG 1860,
then separately with the present title in LG 1867, but not in succeeding editions
before November Boughs Annex 1888.
     SUNSET] First published in the New York Herald, March 9, 1888.

No limit, confine—not the Western sky alone—the high meri-
          dian—North, South, all,
Pure luminous color fighting the silent shadows to the last.   5
     1888   *1888–9*

Twenty Years.

Down on the ancient wharf, the sand, I sit, with a new-comer
          chatting:
He shipp'd as green-hand boy, and sail'd away, (took some sud-
          den, vehement notion;)
Since, twenty years and more have circled round and round,
While he the globe was circling round and round,—and now
          returns:
How changed the place—all the old land-marks gone—the
          parents dead;   5
(Yes, he comes back *to lay in port for good—to settle*—has a well-
          fill'd purse—no spot will do but this;)
The little boat that scull'd him from the sloop, now held in
          leash I see,
I hear the slapping waves, the restless keel, the rocking in the
          sand,
I see the sailor kit, the canvas bag, the great box bound with
          brass,
I scan the face all berry-brown and bearded—the stout-strong
          frame,   10
Dress'd in its russet suit of good Scotch cloth:
(Then what the told-out story of those twenty years? What of
          the future?)
     1888   *1888–9*

Orange Buds by Mail from Florida.

[Voltaire closed a famous argument by claiming that a ship of war and the grand
opera were proofs enough of civilization's and France's progress, in his day.]

A lesser proof than old Voltaire's, yet greater,
Proof of this present time, and thee, thy broad expanse,
          America,

YEARS] First published in *The Magazine of Art* (New York), July, 1888, and re-
printed in *The Magazine of Art* (New York), September, 1888.
     FLORIDA] First published in the New York *Herald*, March 19, 1888. MS in
Barrett.

To my plain Northern hut, in outside clouds and snow,
Brought safely for a thousand miles o'er land and tide,
5   Some three days since on their own soil live-sprouting,
Now here their sweetness through my room unfolding,
A bunch of orange buds by mail from Florida.

   1888   *1888–9*

Twilight.

The soft voluptuous opiate shades,
The sun just gone, the eager light dispell'd—(I too will soon be
     gone, dispell'd,)
A haze—nirwana—rest and night—oblivion.

   1887   *1888–9*

You Lingering Sparse Leaves of Me.

You lingering sparse leaves of me on winter-nearing boughs,
And I some well-shorn tree of field or orchard-row;
You tokens diminute and lorn—(not now the flush of May, or
     July clover-bloom—no grain of August now;)
You pallid banner staves—you pennants valueless—you over-
     stay'd of time,
5   Yet my soul-dearest leaves confirming all the rest,
The faithfulest—hardiest—last.

   1887   *1888–9*

Not Meagre, Latent Boughs Alone.

Not meagre, latent boughs alone, O songs! (scaly and bare,
     like eagles' talons,)

    TWILIGHT] First published in *Century* 35 (December, 1887) 264, the poet
receiving $10. WW told Traubel he had had a number of letters objecting to the
word "oblivion" as inconsistent with his philosophy. "But oblivion as I use it there
is just the word, both as furnishing sense and rhythm to the idea I had in mind"
(Traubel, I, 141). "Nirwana" (nirvana) in fact suggests in Indian Hinduism the
emancipation from temporal life in a union with the eternal, and in Buddhism a
spiritual beatification without transmigration.
    ME] First published in *Lippincott's Magazine*, November, 1887. LC has a page of
trial lines.
    ALONE] First published in *Lippincott's Magazine*, November, 1887. The MS

But haply for some sunny day (who knows?) some future spring,
      some summer—bursting forth,
To verdant leaves, or sheltering shade—to nourishing fruit,
Apples and grapes—the stalwart limbs of trees emerging—the
      fresh, free, open air,
And love and faith, like scented roses blooming.   5

1887   *1888–9*

The Dead Emperor.

To-day, with bending head and eyes, thou, too, Columbia,
Less for the mighty crown laid low in sorrow—less for the
      Emperor,
Thy true condolence breathest, sendest out o'er many a salt sea
      mile,
Mourning a good old man—a faithful shepherd, patriot.

    Publish'd March 10, 1888.
1888   *1888–9*

As the Greek's Signal Flame.

    [For Whittier's eightieth birthday, December 17, 1887.]

As the Greek's signal flame, by antique records told,
Rose from the hill-top, like applause and glory,
Welcoming in fame some special veteran, hero,
With rosy tinge reddening the land he'd served,
So I aloft from Mannahatta's ship-fringed shore,   5
Lift high a kindled brand for thee, Old Poet.

1887   *1888–9*

(Feinberg) is a fragment of the first two lines.

    EMPEROR] First published in the New York *Herald*, March 10, 1888. MSS are a
rough draft (Barrett) and printer's draft (Berg). The emperor, Wilhelm I of
Germany, died in Berlin, March 9, 1888. To his friends, who protested this salute,
WW replied, ". . . too many of the fellows forget that I include emperors, lords,
kingdoms, as well as presidents, workmen, republics" (Traubel, I, 22).

    FLAME] First published in the New York *Herald*, December 15, 1887; reprinted
in the Boston *Advertizer*, December 17. A facsimile of the MS is reproduced in *CW*,
X, 134–135. WW never met Whittier, but they corresponded. See Traubel, I,
127.

The Dismantled Ship.

In some unused lagoon, some nameless bay,
On sluggish, lonesome waters, anchor'd near the shore,
An old, dismasted, gray and batter'd ship, disabled, done,
After free voyages to all the seas of earth, haul'd up at last and
    hawser'd tight,
5 Lies rusting, mouldering.

    1888   *1888–9*

Now Precedent Songs, Farewell.

Now precedent songs, farewell—by every name farewell,
(Trains of a staggering line in many a strange procession,
    waggons,
From ups and downs—with intervals—from elder years, mid-age,
    or youth,)
"In Cabin'd Ships," or "Thee Old Cause" or "Poets to Come"
5 Or "Paumanok," "Song of Myself," "Calamus," or "Adam,"
Or "Beat! Beat! Drums!" or "To the Leaven'd Soil they
    Trod,"
Or "Captain! My Captain!" "Kosmos," "Quicksand Years,"
    or "Thoughts,"
"Thou Mother with thy Equal Brood," and many, many more
    unspecified,
From fibre heart of mine—from throat and tongue—(My life's
    hot pulsing blood,
The personal urge and form for me—not merely paper, automatic
10   type and ink,)
Each song of mine—each utterance in the past—having its long,
    long history,

SHIP] First printed in the New York *Herald*, February 23, 1888. WW said the
poem was suggested by a picture hanging in the parlor of his friend, Thomas B.
Harned (Traubel, I, 390). Another source is suggested by the fact that a rough draft
(Feinberg) of the poem was found in WW's copy of John G. C. Brainard's *Occa-
sional Pieces of Poetry* (New York, 1825) at pages 47–48, where is printed Brain-
ard's lyric, "The Captain—A Fragment," dealing with a legend of the sea. A facsimile
of the MS is reproduced (page 103) in Thomas C. Donaldson's *Walt Whitman, the
Man.* Another MS is owned by Dr. Max Thorek.

FAREWELL] WW's own note at the foot of the page is a clear record of the

Of life or death, or soldier's wound, of country's loss or safety,
(O heaven! what flash and started endless train of all! com-
        pared indeed to that!
What wretched shred e'en at the best of all!)

1888   *1888–9*

An Evening Lull.

After a week of physical anguish,
Unrest and pain, and feverish heat,
Toward the ending day a calm and lull comes on,
Three hours of peace and soothing rest of brain.*

1888   *1888–9*

* The two songs on this page are eked out during an afternoon, June, 1888,
in my seventieth year, at a critical spell of illness. Of course no reader and probably
no human being at any time will ever have such phases of emotional and solemn
action as these involve to me. I feel in them an end and close of all.

Old Age's Lambent Peaks.

The touch of flame—the illuminating fire—the loftiest look at
        last,
O'er city, passion, sea—o'er prairie, mountain, wood—the earth
        itself;
The airy, different, changing hues of all, in falling twilight,
Objects and groups, bearings, faces, reminiscences;
The calmer sight—the golden setting, clear and broad:
So much i' the atmosphere, the points of view, the situations
        whence we scan,
Bro't out by them alone—so much (perhaps the best) unreck'd
        before;
The lights indeed from them—old age's lambent peaks.

1888   *1889*

5

composition of this and the following poem. Traubel, I, 353–354, discusses the
circumstances, which did not warrant more than a casual choice of the poems cited.
See also Traubel, II, 10. First published in *November Boughs* (1888).

LULL] Traubel, II, 248–249, comments on the proofreading of this poem. First
published in *November Boughs* (1888). Whitman's note includes the poem
preceding.

PEAKS] First printed in the *Century*, September, 1888, this poem was not
among the "Sands at Seventy" poems in *November Boughs*, 1888, nor in CPP the
same year. It was first collected in the Annex of 1884–88A91 LG reprints and the
Birthday LG 1889. Upon hearing that his friend Harned liked the poem, WW said,
"So do I . . . to me it is an essential poem—it needed to be made" (Traubel, II,
289). MS in Barrett.

After the Supper and Talk.

After the supper and talk—after the day is done,
As a friend from friends his final withdrawal prolonging,
Good-bye and Good-bye with emotional lips repeating,
(So hard for his hand to release those hands—no more will they
　　meet,
5　No more for communion of sorrow and joy, of old and young,
A far-stretching journey awaits him, to return no more,)
Shunning, postponing severance—seeking to ward off the last
　　word ever so little,
E'en at the exit-door turning—charges superflous calling back—
　　e'en as he descends the steps,
Something to eke out a minute additional—shadows of nightfall
　　deepening,
Farewells, messages lessening—dimmer the forthgoer's visage
10　　and form,
Soon to be lost for aye in the darkness—loth, O so loth to de-
　　part!
Garrulous to the very last.

1887　　　　　　　　　　　　　　　　　　　　　　　　　1888–9

　　　TALK] first published in *Lippincott's Magazine*, November, 1887, after having
been rejected by H. M. Alden of *Harper's*, January 3, 1885 (Traubel, II, 211). Of
the MSS, the Feinberg is entitled "So Loth to Depart" (reproduced in facsimile, CW,
II, 322–323); the Barrett is an earlier draft.
　　2d ANNEX] This "Preface Note" was printed in LG 1891–1892 without change
from the plates of the separately-published miscellany, *Good-Bye My Fancy* (1891).

SECOND ANNEX

Good-bye My Fancy.

Preface Note to 2d Annex,

CONCLUDING L. OF G.—1891.

Had I not better withhold (in this old age and paralysis of me) such little tags and fringe-dots (maybe specks, stains,) as follow a long dusty journey, and witness it afterward? I have probably not been enough afraid of careless touches, from the first—and am not now—nor of parrot-like repetitions—nor platitudes and the commonplace. Perhaps I am too democratic for such avoidances. Besides, is not the verse-field, as originally plann'd by my theory, now sufficiently illustrated—and full time for me to silently retire?—(indeed amid no loud call or market for my sort of poetic utterance.)

In answer, or rather defiance, to that kind of well-put interrogation, here comes this little cluster, and conclusion of my preceding clusters. Though not at all clear that, as here collated, it is worth printing (certainly I have nothing fresh to write)—I while away the hours of my 72d year—hours of forced confinement in my den—by putting in shape this small old age collation:

Last droplets of and after spontaneous rain,
From many limpid distillations and past showers;
(Will they germinate anything? mere exhalations as they all are—
the land's and sea's—America's;
Will they filter to any deep emotion? any heart and brain?)

However that may be, I feel like improving to-day's opportunity and wind up. During the last two years I have sent out, in the lulls of illness

Its MS (Feinberg) is clearly written in black ink with comparatively little revision—an indication, as the text itself reveals—of the relaxation, even gaiety, which the poet confesses "I have in me perennially anyhow." The quatrain, "Last droplets . . ." is included in the "Excluded Poems and Passages" (*q.v.*).

FANCY] The thirty-one poems of the "Second Annex—Good-Bye My Fancy," in LG 1891–2, had in some cases first been seen in periodical publication; they were and exhaustion, certain chirps—lingering-dying ones probably (undoubtedly)—which now I may as well gather and put in fair type while able to see correctly—(for my eyes plainly warn me they are dimming, and my brain more and more palpably neglects or refuses, month after month, even slight tasks or revisions.)

In fact, here I am these current years 1890 and '91, (each successive fortnight getting stiffer and stuck deeper) much like some hard-cased dilapidated grim ancient shell-fish or time-bang'd conch (no legs, utterly non-locomotive) cast up high and dry on the shore-sands, helpless to move anywhere—nothing left but behave myself quiet, and while away the days yet assign'd, and discover if there is anything for the said grim and time-bang'd conch to be got at last out of inherited good spirits and primal buoyant centre-pulses down there deep somewhere within his gray-blurr'd old shell............(Reader, you must allow a little fun here—for one reason there are too many of the following poemets about death, &c., and for another the passing hours (July 5, 1890) are so sunny-fine. And old as I am I feel to-day almost a part of some frolicsome wave, or for sporting yet like a kid or kitten—probably a streak of physical adjustment and perfection here and now. I believe I have it in me perennially anyhow.)

Then behind all, the deep-down consolation (it is a glum one, but I dare not be sorry for the fact of it in the past, nor refrain from dwelling, even vaunting here at the end) that this late-years palsied old shorn and shell-fish condition of me is the indubitable outcome and growth, now near for 20 years along, of too over-zealous, over-continued bodily and emotional excitement and action through the times of 1862, '3, '4 and '5, visiting and waiting on wounded and sick army volunteers, both sides, in campaigns or contests, or after them, or in hospitals or fields south of Washington City, or in that place and elsewhere—those hot, sad, wrenching times—the army volunteers, all States,—or North or South—the

then brought together in the first section of a miscellany of poetry and prose entitled *Good-Bye My Fancy* (1891). Like the poems of the "First Annex—Sands at Seventy," which were published in the miscellany, *November Boughs* (1888), these were written, for the most part, after the poet had felt it necessary to complete the arrangement of his poetry as a whole in LG 1881, because of failing health and creativity as explained above (see note to "First Annex—Sands at Seventy"). Like the first annex, the second contains poems, if not so many, which have genuine merits and are related usefully to the themes of the 1881 volume. The text of LG 1891–92, including finally the present annex, was the last edition of LG to be published in the poet's lifetime. The complete MS of *Good-Bye My Fancy* is extant (Feinberg), fully assembled for the printer from proof sheets, clippings, and holograph leaves.

From the text of LG 1891–2, which is reproduced in the present edition, we wounded, suffering, dying—the exhausting, sweating summers, marches, battles, carnage—those trenches hurriedly heap'd by the corpse-thousands, mainly unknown—Will the America of the future—will this vast rich Union ever realize what itself cost, back there after all?—those hecatombs of battle-deaths—Those times of which, O far-off reader, this whole book is indeed finally but a reminiscent memorial from thence by me to you?

Sail Out for Good, Eidólon Yacht!

Heave the anchor short!
Raise main-sail and jib—steer forth,
O little white-hull'd sloop, now speed on really deep waters,
(I will not call it our concluding voyage,
But outset and sure entrance to the truest, best, maturest;)   5
Depart, depart from solid earth—no more returning to these
      shores,
Now on for aye our infinite free venture wending,
Spurning all yet tried ports, seas, hawsers, densities, gravitation,
Sail out for good, eidólon yacht of me!

   1891   *1891–2*

Lingering Last Drops.

And whence and why come you?

We know not whence, (was the answer,)
We only know that we drift here with the rest,

have excluded two pages (405–406) following the "First Annex—Sands at Seventy." These were printed on a single leaf, of which the recto read: "2D (ANNEX / GOOD-BYE MY FANCY. / Copyright, 1891, by WALT WHITMAN." / The verso (page 406) was the table of contents of this annex, now superseded by the contents page of the present edition.

    YACHT!] First published in *Lippincott's Magazine*, March, 1891, together with three other poems, "Sounds of the Winter," "The Unexpress'd," and "After the Argument,"—all under the general title, "Old-Age Echoes." Hanley has a page of rough draft, Barrett trial lines, and Feinberg the MS of the whole poem as well as a proof sheet with the deleted title, "Old Age Recitatives."

    9. eidólon] See the poem "Eidólons," above.

    DROPS] MS in Feinberg Collection. First published in *Good-Bye My Fancy* (1891).

That we linger'd and lagg'd—but were wafted at last, and are
    now here,
5   To make the passing shower's concluding drops.

    1891   *1891–2*

Good-bye My Fancy.

Good-bye* my fancy—(I had a word to say,
But 'tis not quite the time—The best of any man's word or say,
Is when its proper place arrives—and for its meaning,
I keep mine till the last.)

    1891   *1891–2*

    * Behind a Good-bye there lurks much of the salutation of another beginning—
to me, Development, Continuity, Immortality, Transformation, are the chiefest life-
meanings of Nature and Humanity, and are the *sine qua non* of all facts, and each fact.
    Why do folks dwell so fondly on the last words, advice, appearance, of the
departing? Those last words are not samples of the best, which involve vitality at its
full, and balance, and perfect control and scope. But they are valuable beyond
measure to confirm and endorse the varied train, facts, theories and faith of the
whole preceding life.

On, on the Same, Ye Jocund Twain!

On, on the same, ye jocund twain!
My life and recitative, containing birth, youth, mid-age years,
Fitful as motley-tongues of flame, inseparably twined and merged
    in one—combining all,
My single soul—aims, confirmations, failures, joys—Nor single
    soul alone,
I chant my nation's crucial stage, (America's, haply humanity's)
5   —the trial great, the victory great,
A strange *eclaircissement* of all the masses past, the eastern
    world, the ancient, medieval,
Here, here from wanderings, strayings, lessons, wars, defeats—
    here at the west a voice triumphant—justifying all,
A gladsome pealing cry—a song for once of utmost pride and
    satisfaction;

    FANCY] WW's "word to say" on this theme is really uttered in the poem of the
same title which closes the group. "Fancy" is here used in the sense of "creative
imagination," now obsolescent but often so employed in the times of Coleridge and
Poe. First published in *Good-Bye My Fancy* (1891).
    TWAIN!] MSS include an early draft and proof sheet (Hanley) and four pages

I chant from it the common bulk, the general average horde,
　　(the best no sooner than the worst)—And now I chant old
　　age,
(My verses, written first for forenoon life, and for the summer's,
　　autumn's spread,
I pass to snow-white hairs the same, and give to pulses winter-
　　cool'd the same;)
As here in careless trill, I and my recitatives, with faith and
　　love,
Wafting to other work, to unknown songs, conditions,
On, on, ye jocund twain! continue on the same!

1891   *1891–2*

My 71st Year.

After surmounting three-score and ten,
With all their chances, changes, losses, sorrows,
My parents' deaths, the vagaries of my life, the many tearing
　　passions of me, the war of '63 and '4,
As some old broken soldier, after a long, hot, wearying march,
　　or haply after battle,
To-day at twilight, hobbling, answering company roll-call, *Here*,
　　with vital voice,
Reporting yet, saluting yet the Officer over all.

1889   *1891–2*

Apparitions.

A vague mist hanging 'round half the pages:
(Sometimes how strange and clear to the soul,
That all these solid things are indeed but apparitions, concepts,
　　non-realities.)

1891   *1891–2*

(Feinberg), including trial lines, rough draft, and final draft, dated May 10, 1890.
First published in *Good-Bye My Fancy* (1891).
　　YEAR] First published in *Century*, November, 1889.
　　APPARITIONS] The Feinberg MS of "Good-Bye My Fancy" shows these three
lines as a holograph scrap pasted up for a third stanza of the poem "L. of G's Pur-
port." First published in *Good-Bye My Fancy* (1891).

The Pallid Wreath.

Somehow I cannot let it go yet, funereal though it is,
Let it remain back there on its nail suspended,
With pink, blue, yellow, all blanch'd, and the white now gray
　　　and ashy,
One wither'd rose put years ago for thee, dear friend;
5　But I do not forget thee. Hast thou then faded?
Is the odor exhaled? Are the colors, vitalities, dead?
No, while memories subtly play—the past vivid as ever;
For but last night I woke, and in that spectral ring saw thee,
Thy smile, eyes, face, calm, silent, loving as ever:
10　So let the wreath hang still awhile within my eye-reach,
It is not yet dead to me, nor even pallid.

　　1891　　　　　　　　　　　　　　　　　　　　*1891–2*

An Ended Day.

The soothing sanity and blitheness of completion,
The pomp and hurried contest-glare and rush are done;
Now triumph! transformation! jubilate!*

　　1891　　　　　　　　　　　　　　　　　　　　*1891–2*

* NOTE.—*Summer country life.—Several years.*—In my rambles and explorations I found a woody place near the creek, where for some reason the birds in happy mood seem'd to resort in unusual numbers. Especially at the beginning of the day, and again at the ending, I was sure to get there the most copious birdconcerts. I repair'd there frequently at sunrise—and also at sunset, or just before . . . Once the question arose in me: Which is the best singing, the first or the lattermost? The first always exhilarated, and perhaps seem'd more joyous and stronger; but I always felt the sunset or late afternoon sounds more penetrating and sweeter —seem'd to touch the soul—often the evening thrushes, two or three of them, responding and perhaps blending. Though I miss'd some of the mornings, I found myself getting to be quite strictly punctual at the evening utterances.

ANOTHER NOTE.—"He went out with the tide and the sunset," was a phrase I heard from a surgeon describing an old sailor's death under peculiarly gentle conditions.

During the Secession War, 1863 and '4, visiting the Army Hospitals around Washington, I form'd the habit, and continued it to the end, whenever the ebb or flood tide began the latter part of day, of punctually visiting those at that time populous wards of suffering men. Somehow (or I thought so) the effect of the hour was palpable. The badly wounded would get some ease, and would like to talk a little, or be talk'd to. Intellectual and emotional natures would be at their best:

Deaths were always easier; medicines seem'd to have better effect when given then, and a lulling atmosphere would pervade the wards.

Similar influences, similar circumstances and hours, day-close, after great battles, even with all their horrors. I had more than once the same experience on the fields cover'd with fallen or dead.

Old Age's Ship & Crafty Death's.

From east and west across the horizon's edge,
Two mighty masterful vessels sailers steal upon us:
But we'll make race a-time upon the seas—a battle-contest yet!
    bear lively there!
(Our joys of strife and derring-do to the last!)
Put on the old ship all her power to-day!   5
Crowd top-sail, top-gallant and royal studding-sails,
Out challenge and defiance—flags and flaunting pennants added,
As we take to the open—take to the deepest, freest waters.

1890   *1891-2*

To the Pending Year.

Have I no weapon-word for thee—some message brief and
    fierce?
(Have I fought out and done indeed the battle?) Is there no shot
    left,
For all thy affectations, lisps, scorns, manifold silliness?
Nor for myself—my own rebellious self in thee?

WREATH] First published in the *Critic*, January 10, 1891. The MS (Berg) has the poet's notation, "My friends, Can you use this in the Critic? The price is $5 . . . " In the first line, "funereal," the MS reading, was erroneously spelled "funeral" in the *Critic*. The error persisted in the collections, 91*GBF* and 91–2*LG*, both probably printed directly from a clipping of the *Critic* text, a procedure encouraged by WW's failing eyesight.

DAY] MS in Feinberg. First published in *Good-Bye My Fancy* (1891).

DEATH'S] First published in *Century*, February, 1890. MSS include a rough draft and proof sheet (Feinberg) and a printer's copy MS reproduced in facsimile in George M. Williamson's *Catalogue of a Collection of Books, Letters and Manuscripts, written by Walt Whitman* (1903).

YEAR] First published in the *Critic*, January 5, 1889, under the title, "To the Year 1889." Three MSS: an early draft varying widely from the printed version (Feinberg), a later draft (Lion), and a final draft (Yale).

5   Down, down, proud gorge!—though choking thee;
Thy bearded throat and high-borne forehead to the gutter;
Crouch low thy neck to eleemosynary gifts.

     1889   *1891–2*

Shakspere-Bacon's Cipher.

I doubt it not—then more, far more;
In each old song bequeath'd—in every noble page or text,
(Different—something unreck'd before—some unsuspected
     author,)
In every object, mountain, tree, and star—in every birth and
     life,
As part of each—evolv'd from each—meaning, behind the os-
5   tent,
A mystic cipher waits infolded.

     1891   *1891–2*

Long, Long Hence.

After a long, long course, hundreds of years, denials,
Accumulations, rous'd love and joy and thought,
Hopes, wishes, aspirations, ponderings, victories, myriads of
     readers,
Coating, compassing, covering—after ages' and ages' encrus-
     tations,
5   Then only may these songs reach fruition.

     1891   *1891–2*

Bravo, Paris Exposition!

Add to your show, before you close it, France,
With all the rest, visible, concrete, temples, towers, goods, ma-
     chines and ores,

CIPHER] MS, an early draft (Feinberg) with title, "The Mystic Cipher" and
subtitle "A hint for scientists." A proof sheet is reproduced in facsimile in Traubel, I,
180. First published in *The Cosmopolitan*, October, 1887. 1887, 142.
     HENCE] MS in Feinberg. First published in *Good-Bye My Fancy* (1891).
     EXPOSITION] First published in *Harper's Weekly*, September 28, 1889. MS and

Our sentiment wafted from many million heart-throbs, ethereal
     but solid,
(We grand-sons and great-grand-sons do not forget your grand-
     sires,)
From fifty Nations and nebulous Nations, compacted, sent over-
     sea to-day,   5
America's applause, love, memories and good-will.

  1889   *1891–2*

Interpolation Sounds.

[General Philip Sheridan was buried at the Cathedral, Washington, D. C. Au-
gust, 1888, with all the pomp, music and ceremonies of the Roman Catholic service.]

Over and through the burial chant,
Organ and solemn service, sermon, bending priests,
To me come interpolation sounds not in the show—plainly to
     me, crowding up the aisle and from the window,
Of sudden battle's hurry and harsh noises—war's grim game to
     sight and ear in earnest;
The scout call'd up and forward—the general mounted and his
     aids around him—the new-brought word—the instantaneous
     order issued;   5
The rifle crack—the cannon thud—the rushing forth of men
     from their tents;
The clank of cavalry—the strange celerity of forming ranks—
     the slender bugle note;
The sound of horses' hoofs departing—saddles, arms, accoutre-
     ments.

  1888   *1891–2*

NOTE.—CAMDEN, N. J., August 7, 1888.—Walt Whitman asks the *New York
Herald* "to add his tribute to Sheridan:"
    "In the grand constellation of five or six names, under Lincoln's Presidency, that
history will bear for ages in her firmament as marking the last life-throbs of secession,
and beaming on its dying gasps, Sheridan's will be bright. One consideration rising
out of the now dead soldier's example as it passes my mind, is worth taking notice of.
If the war had continued any long time these States, in my opinion, would have
shown and proved the most conclusive military talents ever evinced by any nation

proof in Feinberg. The Paris Exposition, whose most famous exhibit was the Eiffel
Tower, was open from May 6 through November 6, 1889.
    SOUNDS] First published in the New York *Herald*, August 12, 1888, under the
title, "Over and Through the Burial Chant." LC has an earlier MS draft, and Yale the
final MS of printer's copy, at the top of which WW has written the direction, "Put
this in the day of Sheridan's burial ceremonies."

on earth. That they possess'd a rank and file ahead of all other known in points of quality and limitlessness of number are easily admitted. But we have, too, the eligibility of organizing, handling and officering equal to the other. These two, with modern arms, transportation, and inventive American genius, would make the United States, with earnestness, not only able to stand the whole world, but conquer that world united against us."

To the Sun-Set Breeze.

Ah, whispering, something again, unseen,
Where late this heated day thou enterest at my window, door,
Thou, laving, tempering all, cool-freshing, gently vitalizing
Me, old, alone, sick, weak-down, melted-worn with sweat;
Thou, nestling, folding close and firm yet soft, companion bet-
5   ter than talk, book, art,
    (Thou hast, O Nature! elements! utterance to my heart beyond
            the rest—and this is of them,)
So sweet thy primitive taste to breathe within—thy soothing
            fingers on my face and hands,
Thou, messenger-magical strange bringer to body and spirit of
            me,
    (Distances balk'd—occult medicines penetrating me from head
            to foot,)
I feel the sky, the prairies vast—I feel the mighty northern
10   lakes,
I feel the ocean and the forest—somehow I feel the globe itself
            swift-swimming in space;
Thou blown from lips so loved, now gone—haply from endless
            store, God-sent,
    (For thou art spiritual, Godly, most of all known to my
            sense,)
Minister to speak to me, here and now, what word has never
            told, and cannot tell,
Art thou not universal concrete's distillation? Law's, all As-
15   tronomy's last refinement?
Hast thou no soul? Can I not know, identify thee?

1890   1891–2

BREEZE] First published in *Lippincott's Magazine*, December, 1890. Ezra Pound praised this poem in an unpublished essay (Yale), dated February 1, 1909: "And yet if a man has written lines like Whitman's to the 'sunset breeze' one has to love him. I think we have not yet paid enough attention to the deliberate artistry of the man, not

Old Chants.

An ancient song, reciting, ending,
Once gazing toward thee, Mother of All,
Musing, seeking themes fitted for thee,
Accept for me, thou saidst, *the elder ballads*,
And name for me before thou goest each ancient poet. 5

(Of many debts incalculable,
Haply our New World's chieftest debt is to old poems.)

Ever so far back, preluding thee, America,
Old chants, Egyptian priests, and those of Ethiopia,
The Hindu epics, the Grecian, Chinese, Persian, 10
The Biblic books and prophets, and deep idyls of the Naza-
    rene,
The Iliad, Odyssey, plots, doings, wanderings of Eneas,
Hesiod, Eschylus, Sophocles, Merlin, Arthur,
The Cid, Roland at Roncesvalles, the Nibelungen,
The troubadours, minstrels, minnesingers, skalds, 15
Chaucer, Dante, flocks of singing birds,
The Border Minstrelsy, the bye-gone ballads, feudal tales, essays,
    plays,
Shakspere, Schiller, Walter Scott, Tennyson,
As some vast wondrous weird dream-presences,
The great shadowy groups gathering around, 20
Darting their mighty masterful eyes forward at thee,
Thou! with as now thy bending neck and head, with courteous
    hand and word, ascending,
Thou! pausing a moment, drooping thine eyes upon them, blent
    with their music,
Well pleased, accepting all, curiously prepared for by them,
Thou enterest at thy entrance porch. 25

1891   *1891–2*

in details but in the large" (Herbert Bergman, "Ezra Pound and Walt Whitman,"
AL, XXVII (March, 1955), 60.
    CHANTS] First published in New York *Truth*, March 19, 1891. LC has a MS of the
first five lines, Feinberg of the entire poem, with the alternative title, "An ancient
song reciting."

A Christmas Greeting.

From a Northern Star-Group to a Southern. 1889–'90.

Welcome, Brazilian brother—thy ample place is ready;
A loving hand—a smile from the north—a sunny instant hail!
(Let the future care for itself, where it reveals its troubles, im-
      pedimentas,
Ours, ours the present throe, the democratic aim, the acceptance
      and the faith;)
To thee to-day our reaching arm, our turning neck—to thee
5   from us the expectant eye,
Thou cluster free! thou brilliant lustrous one! thou, learning well,
The true lesson of a nation's light in the sky,
(More shining than the Cross, more than the Crown,)
The height to be superb humanity.

1889   *1891–2*

Sounds of the Winter.

Sounds of the winter too,
Sunshine upon the mountains—many a distant strain
From cheery railroad train—from nearer field, barn, house,
The whispering air—even the mute crops, garner'd apples, corn,
Children's and women's tones—rhythm of many a farmer and
5   of flail,
An old man's garrulous lips among the rest, *Think not we give
      out yet,*
Forth from these snowy hairs we keep up yet the lilt.

1891   *1891–2*

GREETING] Sold by WW to S. S. McClure for $11.00, according to CB entry of Dec. 4, 1889. No record of publication. Both the MS in rough draft and the printer's copy in Feinberg Collection.

8. the Cross . . . the Crown] Two brilliant constellations in the Southern hemisphere; but WW's figure strongly recalls the historic failures of "cross and crown" in national destinies.

WINTER] First published in *Lippincott's Magazine*, March, 1891. Both Barrett

A Twilight Song.

As I sit in twilight late alone by the flickering oak-flame,
Musing on long-pass'd war-scenes—of the countless buried un-
    known soldiers,
Of the vacant names, as unindented air's and sea's—the un-
    return'd,
The brief truce after battle, with grim burial-squads, and the
    deep-fill'd trenches
Of gather'd dead from all America, North, South, East, West,
    whence they came up,   5
From wooded Maine, New-England's farms, from fertile Penn-
    sylvania, Illinois, Ohio,
From the measureless West, Virginia, the South, the Carolinas,
    Texas,
(Even here in my room-shadows and half-lights in the noiseless
    flickering flames,
Again I see the stalwart ranks on-filing, rising—I hear the
    rhythmic tramp of the armies;)
You million unwrit names all, all—you dark bequest from all the
    war,   10
A special verse for you—a flash of duty long neglected—your
    mystic roll strangely gather'd here,
Each name recall'd by me from out the darkness and death's
    ashes,
Henceforth to be, deep, deep within my heart recording, for
    many a future year,
Your mystic roll entire of unknown names, or North or
    South,
Embalm'd with love in this twilight song.   15

1890   1891–2

and Lion have MSS, Feinberg the proof sheet.
    SONG] First published in *Century* 40 (May 1890) 27, with the subtitle, "For
unknown buried soldiers, North and South." WW toiled much over this poem. No
less than five drafts, three of which are mainly worksheets, are in the Brown Library;
Huntington has a final draft; and Barrett three trial lines on the back of a letter
dated August 14, 1889.

When the Full-grown Poet Came.

When the full-grown poet came,
Out spake pleased Nature (the round impassive globe, with all
      its shows of day and night,) saying, *He is mine;*
But out spake too the Soul of man, proud, jealous and unrec-
      onciled, *Nay, he is mine alone;*
—Then the full-grown poet stood between the two, and took
      each by the hand;
5 And to-day and ever so stands, as blender, uniter, tightly hold-
      ing hands,
Which he will never release until he reconciles the two,
And wholly and joyously blends them.

1876   *1891–2*

Osceola.

[When I was nearly grown to manhood in Brooklyn, New York, (middle of 1838,) I met one of the return'd U. S. Marines from Fort Moultrie, S. C., and had long talks with him—learn'd the occurrence below described—death of Osceola. The latter was a young, brave, leading Seminole in the Florida war of that time—was surrender'd to our troops, imprison'd and literally died of "a broken heart," at Fort Moultrie. He sicken'd of his confinement—the doctor and officers made every allowance and kindness possible for him; then the close:]

When his hour for death had come,
He slowly rais'd himself from the bed on the floor,
Drew on his war-dress, shirt, leggings, and girdled the belt
      around his waist,
Call'd for vermilion paint (his looking-glass was held before
      him,)
5 Painted half his face and neck, his wrists, and back-hands.

CAME] One of four poems, cut from proofsheets and pasted on blank ends of pages in the "Centennial Edition" of LG 1876, the small edition bound in brown calf. It was printed in the same position (p. 359) in the second issue of LG 1876 (bound in half cream-colored calf), the final poem of the group, "Bathed in War's Perfume;" not included in LG 1881. This poem appeared in the volume, GBF 1891, p. 14, and was retained in the same position in 92, Second Annex, GBF—the only one of the 76 intercalations that was retained in 92. That the poet restored it to life in the present annex accords with his evident early approval in selecting it to appear in the New York *Tribune* of February 19, 1876 with his preview of his current LG edition. A MS fragment related to this poem is printed in Bucke, N and F, item 185, p. 22; also in *Wake* 7, item 33, p. 18.

OSCEOLA] First published in *Munson's Illustrated World*, April, 1890. MSS include a rough draft MS (Feinberg) and a later draft (Yale), probably printer's copy. The inspiration for the poem derives in part from a large print of Osceola given to WW by the artist, George Catlin. See Edgeley W. Todd, "Indian Pictures and

Put the scalp-knife carefully in his belt—then lying down, resting
    a moment,
Rose again, half sitting, smiled, gave in silence his extended
    hand to each and all,
Sank faintly low to the floor (tightly grasping the tomahawk
    handle,)
Fix'd his look on wife and little children—the last:

(And here a line in memory of his name and death.)   10
    1890   *1891–2*

A Voice from Death.

(The Johnstown, Penn., cataclysm, May 31, 1889.)

A voice from Death, solemn and strange, in all his sweep and
    power,
With sudden, indescribable blow—towns drown'd—humanity by
    thousands slain,
The vaunted work of thrift, goods, dwellings, forge, street, iron
    bridge,
Dash'd pell-mell by the blow—yet usher'd life continuing on,
(Amid the rest, amid the rushing, whirling, wild debris,   5
A suffering woman saved—a baby safely born!)

Although I come and unannounc'd, in horror and in pang,
In pouring flood and fire, and wholesale elemental crash, (this
    voice so solemn, strange,)
I too a minister of Deity.

Yea, Death, we bow our faces, veil our eyes to thee,   10
We mourn the old, the young untimely drawn to thee,

Two Whitman Poems," HLQ, XIX (November, 1955), 1–11.
    10. in memory] The date of Osceola's death, January 30, 1838, verifies WW's
date. A gallant young leader of the second Seminole War (1835–1837), he was
treacherously seized and imprisoned while conferring under an American truce
agreement. Although not otherwise abused, he died within four months, substantiat-
ing the widespread belief that his race could not survive either in slavery or in
captivity.
    DEATH] First published in the New York *World*, June 7, 1889, in front-page
position only a week after the flood. The printer's MS copy is in Yale. The Johnstown
flood was caused by the sudden collapse of a dam following unprecedented rains;
some 2,200 lives were lost, and property estimated at $12,000,000.

The fair, the strong, the good, the capable,
The household wreck'd, the husband and the wife, the engulf'd
      forger in his forge,
The corpses in the whelming waters and the mud,
The gather'd thousands to their funeral mounds, and thousands
15   never found or gather'd.

Then after burying, mourning the dead,
(Faithful to them found or unfound, forgetting not, bearing the
      past, here new musing,)
A day—a passing moment or an hour—America itself bends low,
Silent, resign'd, submissive.

20 War, death, cataclysm like this, America,
Take deep to thy proud prosperous heart.

E'en as I chant, lo! out of death, and out of ooze and slime,
The blossoms rapidly blooming, sympathy, help, love,
From West and East, from South and North and over sea,
25 Its hot-spurr'd hearts and hands humanity to human aid moves on;
And from within a thought and lesson yet.

Thou ever-darting Globe! through Space and Air!
Thou waters that encompass us!
Thou that in all the life and death of us, in action or in sleep!
30 Thou laws invisible that permeate them and all,
Thou that in all, and over all, and through and under all,
      incessant!
Thou! thou! the vital, universal, giant force resistless, sleepless,
      calm,
Holding Humanity as in thy open hand, as some ephemeral toy,
How ill to e'er forget thee!

35 For I too have forgotten,
(Wrapt in these little potencies of progress, politics, culture,
      wealth, inventions, civilization,)
Have lost my recognition of your silent ever-swaying power,
      ye mighty, elemental throes,

    LESSON] MS printer's copy with cancelled title "A Sufi Lesson" in Feinberg. The poem's idea is an accurate reflection of Sufi mysticism. First published in *Good-Bye My Fancy* (1891).

In which and upon which we float, and every one of us is
    buoy'd.

1889   *1891–2*

A Persian Lesson.

For his o'erarching and last lesson the greybeard sufi,
In the fresh scent of the morning in the open air,
On the slope of a teeming Persian rose-garden,
Under an ancient chestnut-tree wide spreading its branches,
Spoke to the young priests and students.   5

"Finally my children, to envelop each word, each part of the
    rest,
Allah is all, all, all—is immanent in every life and object,
May-be at many and many-a-more removes—yet Allah, Allah,
    Allah is there.

"Has the estray wander'd far? Is the reason-why strangely
    hidden?
Would you sound below the restless ocean of the entire world?   10
Would you know the dissatisfaction? the urge and spur of every
    life;
The something never still'd—never entirely gone? the invisible
    need of every seed?

"It is the central urge in every atom,
(Often unconscious, often evil, downfallen,)
To return to its divine source and origin, however distant,   15
Latent the same in subject and in object, without one exception."

1891   *1891–2*

The Commonplace.

The commonplace I sing;
How cheap is health! how cheap nobility!

1. sufi] A teacher of Sufism, a Persian mysticism with a complex symbolism
which has influenced poets and artists.
    COMMONPLACE] First published, in MS facsimile, in *Munson's Magazine*,
March, 1891. A rough draft (Feinberg) shows minor variations.

Abstinence, no falsehood, no gluttony, lust;
The open air I sing, freedom, toleration,
(Take here the mainest lesson—less from books—less from the
        schools,)
The common day and night—the common earth and waters,
Your farm—your work, trade, occupation,
The democratic wisdom underneath, like solid ground for all.

1891   *1891–2*

"The Rounded Catalogue Divine Complete."

[Sunday, —— — ——.—Went this forenoon to church. A college professor, Rev.
Dr. ——, gave us a fine sermon, during which I caught the above words; but the
minister included in his "rounded catalogue" letter and spirit, only the esthetic things,
and entirely ignored what I name in the following:]

The devilish and the dark, the dying and diseas'd,
The countless (nineteen-twentieths) low and evil, crude and
        savage,
The crazed, prisoners in jail, the horrible, rank, malignant,
Venom and filth, serpents, the ravenous sharks, liars, the disso-
        lute;
(What is the part the wicked and the loathesome bear within
        earth's orbic scheme?)
Newts, crawling things in slime and mud, poisons,
The barren soil, the evil men, the slag and hideous rot.

1891   *1891–2*

Mirages.

(*Noted verbatim after a supper-talk outdoors in Nevada with two old miners.*)

More experiences and sights, stranger, than you'd think for;
Times again, now mostly just after sunrise or before sunset,

COMPLETE] First published *in Good-Bye My Fancy* (1891). Both an earlier
draft and the final MS printer's copy are in Feinberg. The rough draft shows much
revision, and many lines not included in the final version. For example:

> Buried and hid beneath the mountains of soil . . .
> A lustrous sapphire blue, eternal, vital, slumbers
>   ready (what is the part the wicked and the
>   loathsome bear within the latent scheme?)

5. loathesome] Correctly, "loathsome."

MIRAGES] First published in *Good-Bye My Fancy* (1891). A MS printer's copy
in Feinberg. The subheading has no biographical relevance. The western limit of

Sometimes in spring, oftener in autumn, perfectly clear weather,
        in plain sight,
Camps far or near, the crowded streets of cities and the shop-
        fronts,
(Account for it or not—credit or not—it is all true,   5
And my mate there could tell you the like—we have often con-
        fab'd about it,)
People and scenes, animals, trees, colors and lines, plain as could
        be,
Farms and dooryards of home, paths border'd with box, lilacs
        in corners,
Weddings in churches, thanksgiving dinners, returns of long-
        absent sons,
Glum funerals, the crape-veil'd mother and the daughters,   10
Trials in courts, jury and judge, the accused in the box,
Contestants, battles, crowds, bridges, wharves,
Now and then mark'd faces of sorrow or joy,
(I could pick them out this moment if I saw them again,)
Show'd to me just aloft to the right in the sky-edge,   15
Or plainly there to the left on the hill-tops.

  1891   *1891–2*

L. of G.'s Purport.

Not to exclude or demarcate, or pick out evils from their formid-
        able masses (even to expose them,)
But add, fuse, complete, extend—and celebrate the immortal and
        the good.

Haughty this song, its words and scope,
To span vast realms of space and time,
Evolution—the cumulative—growths and generations.   5

WW's journeys was Denver, Colorado.
  PURPORT] First published in *Good-Bye My Fancy* (1891). MS evidence exists in
the LC and the Feinberg collections, that this poem, an old-age companion piece to
earlier statements of intent such as "One's-Self I Sing" and "Small the Theme of my
Chant," was actually first projected, in part, as three separate poems: the present lines
1 and 2 under the title, "L. of G.'s Purport"; lines 6, 7, 8, and 9 under the title, "My
Task"; and lines 10, 11, and 12 under the title, "Death Dogs My Steps." To these
three were added two lines under the title, "For Us Two, Reader Dear," which were
finally published in another part of *Good-Bye My Fancy*, p. 44. Another Feinberg
MS gives lines, printed also on page 44, under the title "L of G."

Begun in ripen'd youth and steadily pursued,
Wandering, peering, dallying with all—war, peace, day, and
    night absorbing,
Never even for one brief hour abandoning my task,
I end it here in sickness, poverty, and old age.

10   I sing of life, yet mind me well of death:
To-day shadowy Death dogs my steps, my seated shape, and
    has for years—
Draws sometimes close to me, as face to face.

    1891   *1891–2*

The Unexpress'd.

How dare one say it?
After the cycles, poems, singers, plays,
Vaunted Ionia's, India's—Homer, Shakspere—the long, long
    times' thick dotted roads, areas,
The shining clusters and the Milky Ways of stars—Nature's
    pulses reap'd,
5   All retrospective passions, heroes, war, love, adoration,
All ages' plummets dropt to their utmost depths,
All human lives, throats, wishes, brains—all experiences' utter-
    ance;
After the countless songs, or long or short, all tongues, all lands,
Still something not yet told in poesy's voice or print—something
    lacking,
10   (Who knows? the best yet unexpress'd and lacking.)

    1891   *1891–2*

Grand Is the Seen.

Grand is the seen, the light, to me—grand are the sky and
    stars,

UNEXPRESS'D] First published in *Lippincott's Magazine*, March, 1891. The Yale
MS bears WW's notation, "Sent to Alden Oct. 18 '90 100 asked rejected all
returned." A later draft (Feinberg) is written on the back of a letter dated September
25, 1889; the MS printer's copy (Barrett) contains also the holograph of two other
poems—"Sounds of the Winter" and "After the Argument." The three appeared
together in *Lippincott's* under the general title, "Old Age Echoes."
    SEEN] First published in *Good-Bye My Fancy*. In addition to the MS printer's
copy (Feinberg), there are three MS versions of this poem, one at LC, a later one at
Houghton, and a third—present whereabouts unknown—transcribed in *CW*, X, 130.

Grand is the earth, and grand are lasting time and space,
And grand their laws, so multiform, puzzling, evolutionary;
But grander far the unseen soul of me, comprehending, endow-
    ing all those,
Lighting the light, the sky and stars, delving the earth, sailing
    the sea,   5
(What were all those, indeed, without thee, unseen soul? of
    what amount without thee?)
More evolutionary, vast, puzzling, O my soul!
More multiform far—more lasting thou than they.

  1891   *1891–2*

Unseen Buds.

Unseen buds, infinite, hidden well,
Under the snow and ice, under the darkness, in every square or
    cubic inch,
Germinal, exquisite, in delicate lace, microscopic, unborn,
Like babes in wombs, latent, folded, compact, sleeping;
Billions of billions, and trillions of trillions of them waiting,   5
(On earth and in the sea—the universe—the stars there in the
    heavens,)
Urging slowly, surely forward, forming endless,
And waiting ever more, forever more behind.

  1891   *1891–2*

Good-bye My Fancy!

Good-bye my Fancy!
Farewell dear mate, dear love!
I'm going away, I know not where,
Or to what fortune, or whether I may ever see you again,
So Good-bye my Fancy.   5

None of the three contains the sixth line, which was inserted in the printer's copy.
    BUDS] First published in *Good-Bye My Fancy.* In *The Evolution of Walt Whit-man*, Roger Asselineau suggests, on page 14, that in the development of his book, WW's poems themselves germinated in the fashion here described. The MS printer's copy is extant (Feinberg).
    FANCY!] First published in *Good-Bye My Fancy.* In this farewell the poet rounds out the sense of self-communion, of colloquy with his *alter ego*, which may be thought of as his "demon," his poetic genius—a continuing dialogue with the self that began with "Song of Myself," notably the fifth canto. See note on "FANCY" under the third poem (same title) of this annex.

Now for my last—let me look back a moment;
The slower fainter ticking of the clock is in me,
Exit, nightfall, and soon the heart-thud stopping.

Long have we lived, joy'd, caress'd together;
10   Delightful!—now separation—Good-bye my Fancy.

Yet let me not be too hasty,
Long indeed have we lived, slept, filter'd, become really blended
     into one;
Then if we die we die together, (yes, we'll remain one,)
If we go anywhere we'll go together to meet what happens,
15   May-be we'll be better off and blither, and learn something,
May-be it is yourself now really ushering me to the true songs,
     (who knows?)
May-be it is you the mortal knob really undoing, turning—so
     now finally,
Good-bye—and hail! my Fancy.

    1891   *1891–2*

A Backward Glance o'er Travel'd Roads
and Prefatory Letter

Prefatory Letter to the Reader,
Leaves of Grass 1889

MAY 31, 1889.
CAMDEN, NEW JERSEY, U. S. AMERICA.

To-day completes my three-score-and-ten years—rounds and coheres the successive growths and stages of L. of G. with the following essay and (sort of) testament—my hurried epilogue of intentions-bequest—and gives me the crowning content, (for these lines are written at the last,) of feeling and definitely, perhaps boastfully, reiterating, For good or bad, plain or not-plain, I have held out and now concluded my utterance, entirely its own way; the main wonder being to me, of the foregoing 404 pages entire, amid their many faults and omissions, that (after looking over them leisurely and critically, as the last week, night and day,) they have adhered faithfully to, and carried out, for nearly 40 years, over many gaps, through thick and thin, peace and war, sickness and health, clouds and sunshine, my latent purposes, &c., even as measurably well and far as they do between these covers. (Nature evidently achieves specimens only—plants the seeds of suggestions—is not so intolerant of what is call'd evil—relies on *law* and *character* more than special cases or partialities; and in my little scope I have follow'd or tried to follow the lesson: . . Probably that is about all.)

Yes, to-day finishes my 70th year; and even if but the merest additional

5

10

15

---

1. three-score-and-ten] On his seventieth birthday, aged by illness and infirmity rather than by years, Whitman wrote this very characteristic letter to appear in the 1889 *Leaves of Grass*, which commemorated his last birthday, as he supposed. We have inserted it in its original position because it fixes historically the effective date of his determination to recommend that "A Backward Glance . . ." be included at the end of future editions of *LG* and that his final revised text be honored in any "future printing." This he did by means of the very specific footnote. Fortunately he was able to complete another miscellany, *Good-Bye My Fancy* (1891), and to add its poems as a "Second Annex" to the finally revised *LG* 1891–2, truly a "deathbed edition," which is reproduced in the present text. That edition, without this letter, repeated the footnote verbatim, except for the change from "422 pages" to 438, and gave it a more prominent position on the verso of the title page, where it also appears in the present edition.

15–16. the lesson] That of nature, whose "successive growths and stages" from "seeds of suggestions" often remind Whitman how *LG* grew from his "latent pur-

preface, (and not plain what tie-together it has with the following *Backward Glance*,) I suppose I must reel out something to celebrate my old birthday
20   anniversary, and for this special edition of the latest completest L. of G. utterance.* Printers send word, too, there is a blank here to be written up—and what with? . . . Probably I may as well transcribe and eke out this note by the following lines of a letter last week to a valued friend who demands to know my current personal condition: . . . "First asking pardon for long neglect—
25   The perfect physical health, strength, buoyancy, (and inward impetus to back them,) which were vouchsafed during my whole life, and especially throughout the Secession War period, (1860 to '66,) seem'd to wane after those years, and were closely track'd by a stunning paralytic seizure, and following physical debility and inertia, (laggardness, torpor, indifference, perhaps laziness,) which
30   put me low in 1873 and '4 and '5—then lifted a little, but have essentially remain'd ever since; several spirts or attacks—five or six of them, one time or another from 1876 onward, but gradually mainly overcome—till now, 1888 and '9, the worst and most obstinate seizure of all. . . . Upon the whole, however, and even at this, and though old and sick, I keep up, maintain fair spirits,
35   partially read and write—have publish'd last and full and revised editions of my poems and prose (records and results of youth and early and mid age—of absolute strength and health—o'erseen now during a lingering ill spell)—But have had a bad year, this last one—have run a varied gauntlet, chronic constipa-

---

* As there are now several editions of L. of G., different texts and dates, I wish to say that I prefer and recommend the present one, complete, for future printing,

---

poses." These reiterations, and the laborious revision in the MSS and successive editions, run counter to the theory that LG was originally planned as a whole. The present is one of the most concise and clear of WW's many pronouncements on this point.

21. a blank] The old printer and newsman whimsically remembered a constant affliction of his trade: "a blank here to be written up—and with what?" It may be part of the jest that he filled the blank with one of his countless letters dealing minutely and cheerfully with his appalling excretory and motor infirmities.

Roads] Appeared with the present title as the introduction to *November Boughs* (1888), a prose miscellany preceded by "Sands at Seventy," a cluster of new poems. The *November Boughs* volume was reissued in London (1889) and inserted in *Complete Poems and Prose* (1888) as a supplement without change of pagination. In LG 1889, *a* limited edition celebrating the poet's seventieth birthday, the new poems, "Sands at Seventy," appeared as an "Annex"; also "A Backward Glance . . ." was given its final position, following the completed poems as a retrospective essay.

Preceding "A Backward Glance . . . ," the poet included an untitled birthday letter to the reader, dated May 31, 1889, (see the text and footnote immediately above). Whitman's footnote to the letter was his first definition of the final text. Any "future printing, if there should be any; [should be] a copy and fac-simile," (as he had already told Horace Traubel: "leaving the book completely as I left it"). This footnote also appears with appropriate page references (as in LG 1891–2, our master text) on the verso of the present title page (*q.v.*). All footnotes by Whitman have been allowed to stand as in the original text, designated by his asterisk. All editions of "A Backward Glance . . ." from 1888 to 1891–2 were printed from the

tion, and then vertigo, bladder and gastric troubles, and the foremention'd
steady disability and inertia; bequests of the serious paralysis at Washington,   40
D. C., closing the Secession War—that seizure indeed the culmination of much
that preceded, and real source of all my woes since. During the past year, and
now, with all these, (a body and brain-action dull'd, while the spirit is perhaps
willing and live enough,) I get along more contentedly and comfortably than
you might suppose—sit here all day in my big, high, strong, rattan-bottom'd   45
chair (with great wolf-skin spread on the back in cool weather)—as writing to
you now on a tablet on my lap, may-be my last missives of love, memories and
cheer."

A Backward Glance O'er Travel'd Roads.

Perhaps the best of songs heard, or of any and all true love, or life's
fairest episodes, or sailors', soldiers' trying scenes on land or sea, is the *résumé*
of them, or any of them, long afterwards, looking at the actualities away back
past, with all their practical excitations gone. How the soul loves to float amid
such reminiscences!   5

So here I sit gossiping in the early candle-light of old age—I and my
book—casting backward glances over our travel'd road. After completing, as it

---

if there should be any; a copy and fac-simile, indeed, of the text of these 422 pages.
The subsequent interval which is so important to form'd and launch'd works, books
especially, has pass'd; and waiting till fully after that, I give these concluding words.   5n

same plates, without textual change except for the correction, in LG 1889, of two
typographical errors (see footnotes below). Pages were not renumbered until the
final LG 1891–2.

The essay was completed by May 28, 1888 and set in type three days later, on the
poet's sixty-ninth birthday. It resulted from several previous ventures in literary auto-
biography, the first of which was "A Backward Glance on My Own Road" (*The
Critic*, January 5, 1884). This article, on two dominant themes, foreshadowed the
two halves of the present essay. The second half of the *Critic* article was probably
derived from the poet's article, "How 'Leaves of Grass' Was Made," reported as
having appeared "in 1885, in *The New York Star*," but this title is now known only
by a posthumous article of the same name (allegedly reprinted from the *Star* as a
memorial to Whitman) in *Frank Leslie's Popular Monthly* (June, 1892). Every
paragraph of the *Leslie's* text had also appeared before the final draft of 1888, with
minor variants, in the poet's article, "How I Made a Book," Philadelphia *Press*,
July 11, 1886. Whitman then wrote the first half of his new essay, a revision of
the first half of the 1884 ancestor, and this appeared as "My Book and I" in *Lippin-
cott's Monthly Magazine* (January, 1887). Every paragraph of "A Backward Glance
O'er Travel'd Roads" appeared in some form in one of the preceding four articles.
For a textual study of these essays see *Walt Whitman's Backward Glances*, Edited,
with an Introduction by Sculley Bradley and John A. Stevenson (Philadelphia,
1947), and see the edition of the essay in *Prose* II, Coll W.

6. old age] WW was only sixty-seven; this passage appeared in "My Book and
I," *Lippincott's Monthly Magazine* (January, 1887); see first note above.

were, the journey—(a varied jaunt of years, with many halts and gaps, of
intervals—or some lengthen'd ship-voyage, wherein more than once the last
10   hour had apparently arrived, and we seem'd certainly going down—yet reaching
port in a sufficient way through all discomfitures at last)—After completing my
poems, I am curious to review them in the light of their own (at the time
unconscious, or mostly unconscious) intentions, with certain unfoldings of the
thirty years they seek to embody. These lines, therefore, will probably blend the
15   weft of first purposes and speculations, with the warp of that experience after-
wards, always bringing strange developments.

Result of seven or eight stages and struggles extending through nearly·
thirty years, (as I nigh my three-score-and-ten I live largely on memory,) I look
upon "Leaves of Grass," now finish'd to the end of its opportunities and
20   powers, as my definitive *carte visite* to the coming generations of the New
World,* if I may assume to say so. That I have not gain'd the acceptance of my
own time, but have fallen back on fond dreams of the future—anticipations—
("still lives the song, though Regnar dies")—That from a worldly and business
point of view "Leaves of Grass" has been worse than a failure—that public
25   criticism on the book and myself as author of it yet shows mark'd anger and
contempt more than anything else—("I find a solid line of enemies to you
everywhere,"—letter from W. S. K., Boston, May 28, 1884)—And that solely
for publishing it I have been the object of two or three pretty serious special
official buffetings—is all probably no more than I ought to have expected. I had
30   my choice when I commenc'd. I bid neither for soft eulogies, big money returns,
nor the approbation of existing schools and conventions. As fulfill'd, or partially
fulfill'd, the best comfort of the whole business (after a small band of the
dearest friends and upholders ever vouchsafed to man or cause—doubtless all
the more faithful and uncompromising—this little phalanx!—for being so few)
35   is that, unstopp'd and unwarp'd by any influence outside the soul within me, I
have had my say entirely my own way, and put it unerringly on record—the
value thereof to be decided by time.

In calculating that decision, William O'Connor and Dr. Bucke are far more
peremptory than I am. Behind all else that can be said, I consider "Leaves of
40   Grass" and its theory experimental—as, in the deepest sense, I consider our

* When Champollion, on his death-bed, handed to the printer the revised proof

17. stages and struggles] WW authorized fifteen editions or reprints of *LG* poems.
Those representing genuine "stages and struggles" were nine; 1855, 1856, 1860,
1867, 1871–2, 1876, 1881, 1888–9, and 1891–2. The Civil War poems, *Drum-
Taps* (1865), might also be so regarded.

23. though Regnar dies] From "Alfred the Harper" (stanza 14, 1.3), a long
ballad by John Sterling. King Alfred, disguised as a harper, appears at the feast of
the Danes, who had ravaged the English coast and destroyed Regnar, the British
defender; the Harper-King boldly praises him in the quoted line, then makes his
escape to return victorious in Regnar's name. John Sterling (1806–1844), was a
Scottish-born English poet, publisher, and curate, whose *Life* (1851) was written
by Carlyle. WW copied the phrase about Regnar in his notes. Cf. *N and F*, IV: 52,
p. 167.

American republic itself to be, with its theory. (I think I have at least enough philosophy not to be too absolutely certain of any thing, or any results.) In the second place, the volume is a *sortie*—whether to prove triumphant, and conquer its field of aim and escape and construction, nothing less than a hundred years from now can fully answer. I consider the point that I have positively gain'd a hearing, to far more than make up for any and all other lacks and withholdings. Essentially, *that* was from the first, and has remain'd throughout, the main object. Now it seems to be achiev'd, I am certainly contented to waive any otherwise momentous drawbacks, as of little account. Candidly and dispassionately reviewing all my intentions, I feel that they were creditable—and I accept the result, whatever it may be.

After continued personal ambition and effort, as a young fellow, to enter with the rest into competition for the usual rewards, business, political, literary, &c.—to take part in the great *mèlée*, both for victory's prize itself and to do some good—After years of those aims and pursuits, I found myself remaining possess'd, at the age of thirty-one to thirty-three, with a special desire and conviction. Or rather, to be quite exact, a desire that had been flitting through my previous life, or hovering on the flanks, mostly indefinite hitherto, had steadily advanced to the front, defined itself, and finally dominated everything else. This was a feeling or ambition to articulate and faithfully express in literary or poetic form, and uncompromisingly, my own physical, emotional, moral, intellectual, and æsthetic Personality, in the midst of, and tallying, the momentous spirit and facts of its immediate days, and of current America—and to exploit that Personality, identified with place and date, in a far more candid and comprehensive sense than any hitherto poem or book.

Perhaps this is in brief, or suggests, all I have sought to do. Given the Nineteenth Century, with the United States, and what they furnish as area and points of view, "Leaves of Grass" is, or seeks to be, simply a faithful and doubtless self-will'd record. In the midst of all, it gives one man's—the author's—identity, ardors, observations, faiths, and thoughts, color'd hardly at all with any decided coloring from other faiths or other identities. Plenty of songs had been sung—beautiful, matchless songs—adjusted to other lands than these—another spirit and stage of evolution; but I would sing, and leave out or put in,

of his "Egyptian Grammar," he said gayly, "Be careful of this—it is my *carte de visite* to posterity."

27. W.S.K.] William Sloane Kennedy (1850–1929), critic and biographer, a late disciple of Whitman, of whom he wrote *Reminiscences* (1896) and—concerning LG—*The Fight of a Book for the World* (1926).

38. O'Connor and . . . Bucke] William Douglas O'Connor wrote *The Good Gray Poet* (1866), the earliest "vindication" of WW; Richard Maurice Bucke wrote an early biographical study, *Walt Whitman* (1883); both were the poet's devoted friends.

54. *mèlée*] The first "e" appears as a blank white space in the first edition, *November Boughs* (1888); so also in the two early reprints, CPP 1888–9 and the London edition, NB 1889. In LG 1889 the word appeared as "mèleé." Posthumously corrected, "mêlée," in the Small, Maynard edition (1897), as Whitman had spelled it in his *Lippincott's* article, 1887 (see above).

75 quite solely with reference to America and to-day. Modern science and democ-
racy seem'd to be throwing out their challenge to poetry to put them in its
statements in contradistinction to the songs and myths of the past. As I see it
now (perhaps too late,) I have unwittingly taken up that challenge and made an
attempt at such statements—which I certainly would not assume to do now,
knowing more clearly what it means.

80 For grounds for "Leaves of Grass," as a poem, I abandon'd the conventional
themes, which do not appear in it: none of the stock ornamentation, or choice
plots of love or war, or high, exceptional personages of Old-World song;
nothing, as I may say, for beauty's sake—no legend, or myth, or romance, nor
euphemism, nor rhyme. But the broadest average of humanity and its identities
85 in the now ripening Nineteenth Century, and especially in each of their count-
less examples and practical occupations in the United States to-day.

One main contrast of the ideas behind every page of my verses, compared
with establish'd poems, is their different relative attitude towards God, towards
the objective universe, and still more (by reflection, confession, assumption,
90 &c.) the quite changed attitude of the ego, the one chanting or talking, towards
himself and towards his fellow-humanity. It is certainly time for America,
above all, to begin this readjustment in the scope and basic point of view of
verse; for everything else has changed. As I write, I see in an article on
Wordsworth, in one of the current English magazines, the lines, "A few weeks
95 ago an eminent French critic said that, owing to the special tendency to science
and to its all-devouring force, poetry would cease to be read in fifty years." But
I anticipate the very contrary. Only a firmer, vastly broader, new area begins to
exist—nay, is already form'd—to which the poetic genius must emigrate. What-
ever may have been the case in years gone by, the true use for the imaginative
100 faculty of modern times is to give ultimate vivification to facts, to science, and to
common lives, endowing them with the glows and glories and final illustrious-
ness which belong to every real thing, and to real things only. Without that
ultimate vivification—which the poet or other artist alone can give—reality
would seem incomplete, and science, democracy, and life itself, finally in vain.

105 Few appreciate the moral revolutions, our age, which have been profounder
far than the material or inventive or war-produced ones. The Nineteenth Cen-
tury, now well towards its close (and ripening into fruit the seeds of the two
preceding centuries*)—the uprisings of national masses and shiftings of
boundary-lines—the historical and other prominent facts of the United
110 States—the war of attempted Secession—the stormy rush and haste of nebulous

5n * The ferment and germination even of the United States to-day, dating back to,
and in my opinion mainly founded on, the Elizabethan age in English history, the

74. America and today] That *LG* represents "one man's" identification with the
"moral America" of his own experience is repeated in the context of the entire article
(cf. paragraph fourth from the last).

83. myth] cf. "Great Are The Myths," which WW excluded from *LG*. More
often than he remembered, he had referred in *LG* to the ancient heroic myths, and
unconsciously he contributed to a new American myth rooted in the folklore of an

forces—never can future years witness more excitement and din of action—
never completer change of army front along the whole line, the whole civilized
world. For all these new and evolutionary facts, meanings, purposes, new poetic
messages, new forms and expressions, are inevitable.

My Book and I—what a period we have presumed to span! those thirty   115
years from 1850 to '80—and America in them! Proud, proud indeed may we be,
if we have cull'd enough of that period in its own spirit to worthily waft a few
live breaths of it to the future!

Let me not dare, here or anywhere, for my own purposes, or any purposes,
to attempt the definition of Poetry, nor answer the question what it is. Like   120
Religion, Love, Nature, while those terms are indispensable, and we all give a
sufficiently accurate meaning to them, in my opinion no definition that has ever
been made sufficiently encloses the name Poetry; nor can any rule or convention
ever so absolutely obtain but some great exception may arise and disregard and
overturn it.   125

Also it must be carefully remember'd that first-class literature does not shine
by any luminosity of its own; nor do its poems. They grow of circumstances,
and are evolutionary. The actual living light is always curiously from elsewhere
—follows unaccountable sources, and is lunar and relative at the best. There
are, I know, certain controling themes that seem endlessly appropriated to the   130
poets—as war, in the past—in the Bible, religious rapture and adoration—al-
ways love, beauty, some fine plot, or pensive or other emotion. But, strange as it
may sound at first, I will say there is something striking far deeper and
towering far higher than those themes for the best elements of modern song.

Just as all the old imaginative works rest, after their kind, on long trains of   135
presuppositions, often entirely unmention'd by themselves, yet supplying the
most important bases of them, and without which they could have had no reason
for being, so "Leaves of Grass," before a line was written, presupposed some-
thing different from any other, and, as it stands, is the result of such presupposi-
tion. I should say, indeed, it were useless to attempt reading the book without   140
first carefully tallying that preparatory background and quality in the mind.
Think of the United States to-day—the facts of these thirty-eight or forty
empires solder'd in one—sixty or seventy millions of equals, with their lives,
their passions, their future—these incalculable, modern, American, seething
multitudes around us, of which we are inseparable parts! Think, in comparison,   145
of the petty environage and limited area of the poets of past or present Europe,
no matter how great their genius. Think of the absence and ignorance, in all

age of Francis Bacon and Shakspere. Indeed, when we pursue it, what growth or
advent is there that does not date back, back, until lost—perhaps its most tantalizing
clues lost—in the receded horizons of the past?

expanding frontier, in the American earth, and in the democracy of the common man
and natural faith.

87. My verses] This entire paragraph foreshadows those changes in poetry which,
by 1925, fulfilled Whitman's prophecy that "the poetic genius must emigrate" into
"a new area" of reality, of "ultimate vivification" of the new knowledge of man, so-
ciety, and the "objective universe."

cases hitherto, of the multitudinousness, vitality, and the unprecedented stimu-
lants of to-day and here. It almost seems as if a poetry with cosmic and dynamic
150   features of magnitude and limitlessness suitable to the human soul, were never
possible before. It is certain that a poetry of absolute faith and equality for the
use of the democratic masses never was.

In estimating first-class song, a sufficient Nationality, or, on the other hand,
what may be call'd the negative and lack of it, (as in Goethe's case, it sometimes
155   seems to me,) is often, if not always, the first element. One needs only a little
penetration to see, at more or less removes, the material facts of their country
and radius, with the coloring of the moods of humanity at the time, and its
gloomy or hopeful prospects, behind all poets and each poet, and forming their
birth-marks. I know very well that my "Leaves" could not possibly have
160   emerged or been fashion'd or completed, from any other era than the latter half
of the Nineteenth Century, nor any other land than democratic America, and
from the absolute triumph of the National Union arms.

And whether my friend claim it for me or not, I know well enough, too, that
in respect to pictorial talent, dramatic situations, and especially in verbal melody
165   and all the conventional technique of poetry, not only the divine works that
to-day stand ahead in the world's reading, but dozens more, transcend (some of
them immeasurably transcend) all I have done, or could do. But it seem'd to me,
as the objects in Nature, the themes of æstheticism, and all special exploitations
of the mind and soul, involve not only their own inherent quality, but the
170   quality, just as inherent and important, of *their point of view*,* the time had
come to reflect all themes and things, old and new, in the lights thrown on them
by the advent of America and democracy—to chant those themes through the
utterance of one, not only the grateful and reverent legatee of the past, but the
born child of the New World—to illustrate all through the genesis and ensemble
175   of to-day; and that such illustration and ensemble are the chief demands of
America's prospective imaginative literature. Not to carry out, in the approved
style, some choice plot of fortune or misfortune, or fancy, or fine thoughts, or
incidents, or courtesies—all of which has been done overwhelmingly and well,
probably never to be excell'd—but that while in such æsthetic presentation of
180   objects, passions, plots, thoughts, &c., our lands and days do not want, and
probably will never have, anything better than they already possess from the
bequests of the past, it still remains to be said that there is even towards all
those a subjective and contemporary point of view appropriate to ourselves
alone, and to our new genius and environments, different from anything
185   hitherto; and that such conception of current or gone-by life and art is for us the
only means of their assimilation consistent with the Western world.

Indeed, and anyhow, to put it specifically, has not the time arrived when, (if
it must be plainly said, for democratic America's sake, if for no other) there
must imperatively come a readjustment of the whole theory and nature of

---

* According to Immanuel Kant, the last essential reality, giving shape and
10n   significance to all the rest.

Poetry? The question is important, and I may turn the argument over and 190
repeat it: Does not the best thought of our day and Republic conceive of a birth
and spirit of song superior to anything past or present? To the effectual and
moral consolidation of our lands (already, as materially establish'd, the greatest
factors in known history, and far, far greater through what they prelude and
necessitate, and are to be in future)—to conform with and build on the concrete 195
realities and theories of the universe furnish'd by science, and henceforth the
only irrefragable basis for anything, verse included—to root both influences in
the emotional and imaginative action of the modern time, and dominate all that
precedes or opposes them—is not either a radical advance and step forward, or a
new verteber of the best song indispensable? 200

The New World receives with joy the poems of the antique, with European
feudalism's rich fund of epics, plays, ballads—seeks not in the least to deaden or
displace those voices from our ear and area—holds them indeed as indispensable
studies, influences, records, comparisons. But though the dawn-dazzle of the
sun of literature is in those poems for us of to-day—though perhaps the best 205
parts of current character in nations, social groups, or any man's or woman's
individuality, Old World or New, are from them—and though if I were ask'd to
name the most precious bequest to current American civilization from all the
hitherto ages, I am not sure but I would name those old and less old songs
ferried hither from east and west—some serious words and debits remain; some 210
acrid considerations demand a hearing. Of the great poems receiv'd from
abroad and from the ages, and to-day enveloping and penetrating America, is
there one that is consistent with these United States, or essentially applicable to
them as they are and are to be? Is there one whose underlying basis is not a
denial and insult to democracy? What a comment it forms, anyhow, on this era 215
of literary fulfilment, with the splendid day-rise of science and resuscitation of
history, that our chief religious and poetical works are not our own, nor adapted
to our light, but have been furnish'd by far-back ages out of their arriere and
darkness, or, at most, twilight dimness! What is there in those works that so
imperiously and scornfully dominates all our advanced civilization, and cul- 220
ture?

Even Shakespere, who so suffuses current letters and art (which indeed have
in most degrees grown out of him,) belongs essentially to the buried past. Only
he holds the proud distinction for certain important phases of that past, of being
the loftiest of the singers life has yet given voice to. All, however, relate to and 225
rest upon conditions, standards, politics, sociologies, ranges of belief, that have
been quite eliminated from the Eastern hemisphere, and never existed at all in
the Western. As authoritative types of song they belong in America just about
as much as the persons and institutes they depict. True, it may be said, the
emotional, moral, and æsthetic natures of humanity have not radically changed 230
—that in these the old poems apply to our times and all times, irrespective of

202. in the least] Read erroneously "in the last," in the first edition, *November
Boughs* (1888), in the reprint of that volume (1889) and in CPP 1888–9. Corrected
in 1889, in the first edition of *Leaves of Grass* that contained this essay.

date; and that they are of incalculable value as pictures of the past. I willingly
make those admissions, and to their fullest extent; then advance the points
herewith as of serious, even paramount importance.

235   I have indeed put on record elsewhere my reverence and eulogy for those
never-to-be-excell'd poetic bequests, and their indescribable preciousness as heir-
looms for America. Another and separate point must now be candidly stated. If I
had not stood before those poems with uncover'd head, fully aware of their
colossal grandeur and beauty of form and spirit, I could not have written
240   "Leaves of Grass." My verdict and conclusions as illustrated in its pages are
arrived at through the temper and inculcation of the old works as much as
through anything else—perhaps more than through anything else. As America
fully and fairly construed is the legitimate result and evolutionary outcome of
the past, so I would dare to claim for my verse. Without stopping to qualify the
245   averment, the Old World has had the poems of myths, fictions, feudalism,
conquest, caste, dynastic wars, and splendid exceptional characters and affairs,
which have been great; but the New World needs the poems of realities and
science and of the democratic average and basic equality, which shall be greater.
In the centre of all, and object of all, stands the Human Being, towards whose
250   heroic and spiritual evolution poems and everything directly or indirectly tend,
Old World or New.

        Continuing the subject, my friends have more than once suggested—or may
be the garrulity of advancing age is possessing me—some further embryonic
facts of "Leaves of Grass," and especially how I enter'd upon them. Dr. Bucke
255   has, in his volume, already fully and fairly described the preparation of my
poetic field, with the particular and general plowing, planting, seeding, and
occupation of the ground, till everything was fertilized, rooted, and ready to
start its own way for good or bad. Not till after all this, did I attempt any
serious acquaintance with poetic literature. Along in my sixteenth year I had
260   become possessor of a stout, well-cramm'd one thousand page octavo volume (I
have it yet,) containing Walter Scott's poetry entire—an inexhaustible mine
and treasury of poetic forage (especially the endless forests and jungles of
notes)—has been so to me for fifty years, and remains so to this day.*
        Later, at intervals, summers and falls, I used to go off, sometimes for a week
265   at a stretch, down in the country, or to Long Island's seashores—there, in the
presence of outdoor influences, I went over thoroughly the Old and New Testa-

        * Sir Walter Scott's COMPLETE POEMS; especially including BORDER MIN-
STRELSY; then Sir Tristrem; Lay of the Last Minstrel; Ballads from the German;
Marmion; Lady of the Lake; Vision of Don Roderick; Lord of the Isles;
Rokeby; Bridal of Triermain; Field of Waterloo; Harold the Dauntless; all the

        251. Old World or New] Conclusion of the first of the two divisions of this essay,
dealing in general with WW's preparation, motivation, and inspiration for *Leaves
of Grass*. The following section emphasizes certain themes, especially the theory of
man, nature, and society which this poetry embodies. For the development of each
section from earlier essays, see the footnote under the title, "A Backward

ments, and absorb'd (probably to better advantage for me than in any library or indoor room—it makes such difference *where* you read,) Shakespere, Ossian, the best translated versions I could get of Homer, Eschylus, Sophocles, the old German Nibelungen, the ancient Hindoo poems, and one or two other master- 270 pieces, Dante's among them. As it happen'd, I read the latter mostly in an old wood. The Iliad (Buckley's prose version,) I read first thoroughly on the penin- sula of Orient, northeast end of Long Island, in a shelter'd hollow of rocks and sand, with the sea on each side. (I have wonder'd since why I was not over- whelm'd by those mighty masters. Likely because I read them, as described, in 275 the full presence of Nature, under the sun, with the far-spreading landscape and vistas, or the sea rolling in.)

Toward the last I had among much else look'd over Edgar Poe's poems—of which I was not an admirer, tho' I always saw that beyond their limited range of melody (like perpetual chimes of music bells, ringing from lower *b* flat up to 280 *g*) they were melodious expressions, and perhaps never excell'd ones, of certain pronounc'd phases of human morbidity. (The Poetic area is very spacious—has room for all—has so many mansions!) But I was repaid in Poe's prose by the idea that (at any rate for our occasions, our day) there can be no such thing as a long poem. The same thought had been haunting my mind before, but Poe's 285 argument, though short, work'd the sum out and proved it to me.

Another point had an early settlement, clearing the ground greatly. I saw, from the time my enterprise and questionings positively shaped themselves (how best can I express my own distinctive era and surroundings, America, Democracy?) that the trunk and centre whence the answer was to radiate, and 290 to which all should return from straying however far a distance, must be an identical body and soul, a personality—which personality, after many considera- tions and ponderings I deliberately settled should be myself—indeed could not be any other. I also felt strongly (whether I have shown it or not) that to the true and full estimate of the Present both the Past and the Future are main considera- 295 tions.

These, however, and much more might have gone on and come to naught (almost positively would have come to naught,) if a sudden, vast, terrible, direct and indirect stimulus for new and national declamatory expression had not been given to me. It is certain, I say, that, although I had made a start before, only 300 from the occurrence of the Secession War, and what it show'd me as by flashes of lightning, with the emotional depths it sounded and arous'd (of course, I

Dramas; various Introductions, endless interesting Notes, and Essays on Poetry, 15n Romance, &c.

Lockhart's 1833 (or '34) edition with Scott's latest and copious revisions and annotations. (All the poems were thoroughly read by me, but the ballads of the Border Minstrelsy over and over again.)

Glance . . .".

273. Orient] The northermost of the two peninsulas into which Long Island di- vides at its eastern end.

299. declamatory] In the earlier contributory essays, read "poetic"; the term "declamatory" was not then disparaging.

don't mean in my own heart only, I saw it just as plainly in others, in millions)
—that only from the strong flare and provocation of that war's sights and scenes
305   the final reasons-for-being of an autochthonic and passionate song definitely
came forth.

I went down to the war fields in Virginia (end of 1862), lived thenceforward
in camp—saw great battles and the days and nights afterward—partook of all
the fluctuations, gloom, despair, hopes again arous'd, courage evoked—death
310   readily risk'd—*the cause*, too—along and filling those agonistic and lurid follow-
ing years, 1863-'64-'65—the real parturition years (more than 1776-'83) of this
henceforth homogeneous Union. Without those three or four years and the
experiences they gave, "Leaves of Grass" would not now be existing.

But I set out with the intention also of indicating or hinting some point-
315   characteristics which I since see (though I did not then, at least not definitely)
were bases and object-urgings toward those "Leaves" from the first. The word
I myself put primarily for the description of them as they stand at last, is the
word Suggestiveness. I round and finish little, if anything; and could not,
consistently with my scheme. The reader will always have his or her part to do,
320   just as much as I have had mine. I seek less to state or display any theme or
thought, and more to bring you, reader, into the atmosphere of the theme or
thought—there to pursue your own flight. Another impetus-word is Comrade-
ship as for all lands, and in a more commanding and acknowledg'd sense than
hitherto. Other word-signs would be Good Cheer, Content, and Hope.

325   The chief trait of any given poet is always the spirit he brings to the
observation of Humanity and Nature—the mood out of which he contemplates
his subjects. What kind of temper and what amount of faith report these
things? Up to how recent a date is the song carried? What the equipment, and
special raciness of the singer—what his tinge of coloring? The last value of
330   artistic expressers, past and present—Greek æsthetes, Shakspere—or in our
own day Tennyson, Victor Hugo, Carlyle, Emerson—is certainly involv'd in
such questions. I say the profoundest service that poems or any other writings
can do for their reader is not merely to satisfy the intellect, or supply something
polish'd and interesting, nor even to depict great passions, or persons or events,
335   but to fill him with vigorous and clean manliness, religiousness, and give him
good heart as a radical possession and habit. The educated world seems to have
been growing more and more ennuyed for ages, leaving to our time the inherit-

305-306. definitely came forth] This assertion may seem ambiguous; Whitman's
poetry and ideas were well defined in the three LG editions before "the direct stimu-
lus" of the Civil War. But the war had long been imminent: when the young jour-
nalist, during the Mexican War, supported "free soil"; when he opposed Northern
Democratic "hunker" politics, thus losing the editorship of the Brooklyn *Eagle* in
1848; when he realized the flimsiness of the 1850 compromises. His first LG edition
(1855), strongly depicted the outrages of slavery, and he predicted a terrible venge-

ance of it all. Fortunately there is the original inexhaustible fund of buoy-
ancy, normally resident in the race, forever eligible to be appeal'd to and
relied on.   340

As for native American individuality, though certain to come, and on a
large scale, the distinctive and ideal type of Western character (as consistent
with the operative political and even money-making features of United States'
humanity in the Nineteenth Century as chosen knights, gentlemen and warriors
were the ideals of the centuries of European feudalism) it has not yet appear'd. I   345
have allow'd the stress of my poems from beginning to end to bear upon
American individuality and assist it—not only because that is a great lesson in
Nature, amid all her generalizing laws, but as counterpoise to the leveling
tendencies of Democracy—and for other reasons. Defiant of ostensible literary
and other conventions, I avowedly chant "the great pride of man in himself,"   350
and permit it to be more or less a *motif* of nearly all my verse. I think this pride
indispensable to an American. I think it not inconsistent with obedience, hu-
mility, deference, and self-questioning.

Democracy has been so retarded and jeopardized by powerful personalities,
that its first instincts are fain to clip, conform, bring in stragglers, and reduce   355
everything to a dead level. While the ambitious thought of my song is to help
the forming of a great aggregate Nation, it is, perhaps, altogether through the
forming of myriads of fully develop'd and enclosing individuals. Welcome as
are equality's and fraternity's doctrines and popular education, a certain lia-
bility accompanies them all, as we see. That primal and interior something in   360
man, in his soul's abysms, coloring all, and, by exceptional fruitions, giving the
last majesty to him—something continually touch'd upon and attain'd by the
old poems and ballads of feudalism, and often the principal foundation of
them—modern science and democracy appear to be endangering, perhaps elimi-
nating. But that forms an appearance only; the reality is quite different. The   365
new influences, upon the whole, are surely preparing the way for grander
individualities than ever. To-day and here personal force is behind everything,
just the same. The times and depictions from the Iliad to Shakspere inclusive
can happily never again be realized—but the elements of courageous and lofty
manhood are unchanged.   370

Without yielding an inch the working-man and working-woman were to be
in my pages from first to last. The ranges of heroism and loftiness with which
Greek and feudal poets endow'd their god-like or lordly born characters—in-
deed prouder and better based and with fuller ranges than those—I was to

ance in his "Now Lucifer Was Not Dead" ("Passages Excluded From *LG* Poems").
He had, indeed, "made a start before."

313. existing] A following sentence, which concludes this paragraph in the ances-
tor essay, "How 'Leaves of Grass' Was Made," supports the footnote immediately
above with these words: "think of the book as a whirling wheel, with the War of
1861–5 as the hub on which it all concentrates and revolves."

365. quite different] The earlier essay, "How 'Leaves of Grass' Was Made," con-
tinues, more cautiously: "or involves, at most, only a passing stage."

375   endow the democratic averages of America. I was to show that we, here and
       to-day, are eligible to the grandest and the best—more eligible now than any
       times of old were. I will also want my utterances (I said to myself before
       beginning) to be in spirit the poems of the morning. (They have been founded
       and mainly written in the sunny forenoon and early midday of my life.) I will
380   want them to be the poems of women entirely as much as men. I have wish'd to
       put the complete Union of the States in my songs without any preference or
       partiality whatever. Henceforth, if they live and are read, it must be just as
       much South as North—just as much along the Pacific as Atlantic—in the valley
       of the Mississippi, in Canada, up in Maine, down in Texas, and on the shores of
385   Puget Sound.

       From another point of view "Leaves of Grass" is avowedly the song of Sex
       and Amativeness, and even Animality—though meanings that do not usually go
       along with those words are behind all, and will duly emerge; and all are sought
       to be lifted into a different light and atmosphere. Of this feature, intentionally
390   palpable in a few lines, I shall only say the espousing principle of those lines so
       gives breath of life to my whole scheme that the bulk of the pieces might as well
       have been left unwritten were those lines omitted. Difficult as it will be, it has
       become, in my opinion, imperative to achieve a shifted attitude from superior
       men and women towards the thought and fact of sexuality, as an element in
395   character, personality, the emotions, and a theme in literature. I am not going to
       argue the question by itself; it does not stand by itself. The vitality of it is
       altogether in its relations, bearings, significance—like the clef of a symphony.
       At last analogy the lines I allude to, and the spirit in which they are spoken,
       permeate all "Leaves of Grass," and the work must stand or fall with them, as
400   the human body and soul must remain as an entirety.

       Universal as are certain facts and symptoms of communities or individuals
       all times, there is nothing so rare in modern conventions and poetry as their
       normal recognizance. Literature is always calling in the doctor for consultation
       and confession, and always giving evasions and swathing suppressions in place
405   of that "heroic nudity"* on which only a genuine diagnosis of serious cases can
       be built. And in respect to editions of "Leaves of Grass" in time to come (if
       there should be such) I take occasion now to confirm those lines with the settled
       convictions and deliberate renewals of thirty years, and to hereby prohibit, as
       far as word of mine can do so, any elision of them.

410   Then still a purpose enclosing all, and over and beneath all. Ever since
       what might be call'd thought, or the budding of thought, fairly began in my
       youthful mind, I had had a desire to attempt some worthy record of that entire
       faith and acceptance ("to justify the ways of God to man" is Milton's well-
       known and ambitious phrase) which is the foundation of moral America. I felt it

20n   * "Nineteenth Century," July, 1883.

       408. thirty years] That is, since 1858, when "Sex and Amativeness" became domi-
       nant in the "Children of Adam" and "Calamus" clusters. Even to his benefactor,

all as positively then in my young days as I do now in my old ones; to formulate   415
a poem whose every thought or fact should directly or indirectly be or connive
at an implict belief in the wisdom, health, mystery, beauty of every process,
every concrete object, every human or other existence, not only consider'd from
the point of view of all, but of each.

While I can not understand it or argue it out, I fully believe in a clue and   420
purpose in Nature, entire and several; and that invisible spiritual results, just as
real and definite as the visible, eventuate all concrete life and all materialism,
through Time. My book ought to emanate buoyancy and gladness legitimately
enough, for it was grown out of those elements, and has been the comfort of my
life since it was originally commenced.   425

One main genesis-motive of the "Leaves" was my conviction (just as strong
to-day as ever) that the crowning growth of the United States is to be spiritual
and heroic. To help start and favor that growth—or even to call attention to it,
or the need of it—is the beginning, middle and final purpose of the poems. (In
fact, when really cipher'd out and summ'd to the last, plowing up in earnest the   430
interminable average fallows of humanity—not "good government" merely, in
the common sense—is the justification and main purpose of these United
States.)

Isolated advantages in any rank or grace or fortune—the direct or indirect
threads of all the poetry of the past—are in my opinion distasteful to the   435
republican genius, and offer no foundation for its fitting verse. Establish'd
poems, I know, have the very great advantage of chanting the already per-
form'd, so full of glories, reminiscences dear to the minds of men. But my
volume is a candidate for the future. "All original art," says Taine, anyhow, "is
self-regulated, and no original art can be regulated from without; it carries its   440
own counterpoise, and does not receive it from elsewhere—lives on its own
blood"—a solace to my frequent bruises and sulky vanity.

As the present is perhaps mainly an attempt at personal statement or
illustration, I will allow myself as further help to extract the following anecdote
from a book, "Annals of Old Painters," conn'd by me in youth. Rubens, the   445
Flemish painter, in one of his wanderings through the galleries of old convents,
came across a singular work. After looking at it thoughtfully for a good while,
and listening to the criticisms of his suite of students, he said to the latter, in
answer to their questions (as to what school the work implied or belong'd,) "I
do not believe the artist, unknown and perhaps no longer living, who has given   450
the world this legacy, ever belong'd to any school, or ever painted anything but
this one picture, which is a personal affair—a piece out of a man's life."

"Leaves of Grass" indeed (I cannot too often reiterate) has mainly been the
outcropping of my own emotional and other personal nature—an attempt, from
first to last, to put a Person, a human being (myself, in the latter half of the   455

Emerson, who argued against including the outspoken "Children" in LG 1860, and
to later critics, including those who "banned" the 1881 Boston edition, WW gave
substantially the same defense of these poems as he gives above.

Nineteenth Century, in America,) freely, fully and truly on record. I could not find any similar personal record in current literature that satisfied me. But it is not on "Leaves of Grass" distinctively as *literature*, or a specimen thereof, that I feel to dwell, or advance claims. No one will get at my verses who insists upon

460   viewing them as a literary performance, or attempt at such performance, or as aiming mainly toward art or æstheticism.

I say no land or people or circumstances ever existed so needing a race of singers and poems differing from all others, and rigidly their own, as the land and people and circumstances of our United States need such singers and poems

465   to-day, and for the future. Still further, as long as the States continue to absorb and be dominated by the poetry of the Old World, and remain unsupplied with autochthonous song, to express, vitalize .and give color to and define their material and political success, and minister to them distinctively, so long will they stop short of first-class Nationality and remain defective.

470   In the free evening of my day I give to you, reader, the foregoing garrulous talk, thoughts, reminiscences,

> As idly drifting down the ebb,
> Such ripples, half-caught voices, echo from the shore.

Concluding with two items for the imaginative genius of the West, when it

475   worthily rises—First, what Herder taught to the young Goethe, that really great poetry is always (like the Homeric or Biblical canticles) the result of a national spirit, and not the privilege of a polish'd and select few; Second, that the strongest and sweetest songs yet remain to be sung.

ECHOES] This group of thirteen poems was first added to LG in its tenth (1897) edition, pp. 423–430: LEAVES OF GRASS / Including / Sands at Seventy, Good-Bye My Fancy / Old Age Echoes, and a Backward Glance / O'er Travel'd Roads / By / WALT WHITMAN / Boston / Small, Maynard & Company / 1897. The English imprint was issued in London the same year by G. P. Putnam's Sons.

Old Age Echoes

An Executor's Diary Note, 1891

I said to W. W. today: "Though you have put the finishing touches on the *Leaves*, closed them with your good-by, you will go on living a year or two longer and writing more poems. The question is, what will you do with these poems when the time comes to fix their place in the volume?" "Do with them? I am not unprepared—I have even contemplated that emergency—I have a title in reserve: Old Age Echoes—applying not so much to things as to echoes of things, reverberant, an aftermath." "You have dropt enough by the roadside, as you went along, from different editions, to make a volume. Some day the world will demand to have that put together somewhere." "Do you think it?" "Certainly. Should you put it under ban?" "Why should I—how could I? So far as you may have anything to do with it I place upon you the injunction that whatever may be added to the *Leaves* shall be supplementary, avowed as such, leaving the book complete as I left it, consecutive to the point I left off, marking always an unmistakable, deep down, unobliteratable division line. In the long run the world will do as it pleases with the book. I am determined to have the world know what I was pleased to do."

Here is a late personal note from W. W.: "My tho't is to collect a lot of prose and poetry pieces—small or smallish mostly, but a few larger—appealing to the good will, the heart—sorrowful ones not rejected—but no morbid ones given."

There is no reason for doubt that "A Thought of Columbus," closing "Old Age Echoes," was W. W.'s last deliberate composition, dating December, 1891.

DIARY NOTE, 1891] Horace Traubel does not specify the date of this conversation with the poet, but obviously it resembles the almost daily notations of *With Walt Whitman in Camden* from 1888 to the end. The dating of the printed memorandum "1891" suggests relationship with the publication that year of the poet's last volume of poems.

To Soar in Freedom and in Fullness of Power.

I have not so much emulated the birds that musically sing,
I have abandon'd myself to flights, broad circles.
The hawk, the seagull, have far more possess'd me than the
        canary or mocking-bird,
I have not felt to warble and trill, however sweetly,
5   I have felt to soar in freedom and in the fullness of power, joy, volition.
    1897   *1897*

Then Shall Perceive.

In softness, languor, bloom, and growth,
Thine eyes, ears, all thy sense—thy loftiest attribute—all
        that takes cognizance of beauty,
Shall rouse and fill—then shall perceive!
    1897   *1897*

The Few Drops Known.

Of heroes, history, grand events, premises, myths, poems,
The few drops known must stand for oceans of the unknown,
On this beautiful and thick peopl'd earth, here and there a
        little specimen put on record,

POWER] In the Feinberg Collection, listed under the heading "My Poetry is more
the Poetry of Sight than Sound," is a two-page MS prose fragment in black ink
which WW had apparently intended as the beginning of a preface. From it the above
five lines, arranged as verse, were directly transcribed, no doubt by Traubel.

PERCEIVE] The MS of this poem, now in the possession of S. S. Snellenburg,
Philadelphia, was sent by Traubel, in a letter of April 16, 1908, to an autograph
collector named Sternberg (?). It contains a few more phrases, as follows, indicating
that the poet had meant to compose further lines:

                    April
                    April and May, the sunrise fresh
                    the balmy airs, the

A little of Greeks and Romans, a few Hebrew canticles, a few
     death odors as from graves, from Egypt—
What are they to the long and copious retrospect of antiquity?   5
   1897   *1897*

One Thought Ever at the Fore.

One thought ever at the fore—
That in the Divine Ship, the World, breasting Time and Space,
All Peoples of the globe together sail, sail the same voyage,
     are bound to the same destination.
   1897   *1897*

While Behind All Firm and Erect.

While behind all, firm and erect as ever,
Undismay'd amid the rapids—amid the irresistible and deadly urge,
Stands a helmsman, with brow elate and strong hand.
   1897   *1897*

A Kiss to the Bride.

Marriage of Nelly Grant, May 21, 1874

Sacred, blithesome, undenied,
With benisons from East and West,
And salutations North and South,
Through me indeed to-day a million hearts and hands,
Wafting a million loves, a million soul felt prayers;   5

KNOWN] Present location of MS unknown.

FORE] With its image of the voyage on which all peoples are bound together, this poem echoes a dominant idea in "Passage to India."

ERECT] Compare this poem with "The Pilot in the Mist"; both employ the image of the helmsman amid the rapids, and almost identical phrasing in the final lines. Compare also with line 55 of "Thou Mother with Thy Equal Brood."

BRIDE] First published in the New York *Daily Graphic*, May 21, 1874, and again in the same newspaper two days later. Nelly Grant, President Grant's daughter, married a Mr. Sartoris.

—Tender and true remain the arm that shields thee!
Fair winds always fill the ship's sails that sail thee!
Clear sun by day, and light stars at night, beam on thee!
Dear girl—through me the ancient privilege too,
10   For the New World, through me, the old, old wedding greeting:
O youth and health! O sweet Missouri rose! O bonny bride!
Yield thy red cheeks, thy lips, to-day,
Unto a Nation's loving kiss.

    1874   1897

Nay, Tell Me Not To-day the Publish'd Shame.
Winter of 1873, Congress in Session.

Nay, tell me not to-day the publish'd shame,
Read not to-day the journal's crowded page,
The merciless reports still branding forehead after forehead,
The guilty column following guilty column.

5   To-day to me the tale refusing,
Turning from it—from the white capitol turning,
Far from these swelling domes, topt with statues,
More endless, jubilant, vital visions rise
Unpublish'd, unreported.

Through all your quiet ways, or North or South, you Equal
10   States, you honest farms,
Your million untold manly healthy lives, or East or West, city or country,
Your noiseless mothers, sisters, wives, unconscious of their good,
Your mass of homes nor poor nor rich, in visions rise—
    (even your excellent poverties,)
Your self-distilling, never-ceasing virtues, self-denials, graces,
15   Your endless base of deep integrities within, timid but certain,

SHAME] First published in the New York *Daily Graphic*, March 5, 1873, this
poem was reprinted by Traubel in *The Conservator*, October, 1896. LC has five MS
pages, two of which are trial lines, three the rough draft. The Feinberg Collection
has a clipping of the *Graphic* text with corrections honored in the 1897 text. The
"publish'd shame" refers to the scandals of the Crédit Mobilier and the "Salary
Grab," an act doubling the president's salary and increasing that of other government
officials. Public indignation later forced modification.

HOURS] Many MS pages of varying sizes (LC has fifteen, Feinberg seven, and
Lion three) show that WW worked extensively upon this poem, trying and rejecting

Your blessings steadily bestow'd, sure as the light, and still,
(Plunging to these as a determin'd diver down the deep hidden waters,)
These, these to-day I brood upon—all else refusing, these will I con,
To-day to these give audience.

1873 *1897*

Supplement Hours.

Sane, random, negligent hours,
Sane, easy, culminating hours,
After the flush, the Indian summer, of my life,
Away from Books—away from Art—the lesson learn'd, pass'd o'er,
Soothing, bathing, merging all—the sane, magnetic,   5
Now for the day and night themselves—the open air,
Now for the fields, the seasons, insects, trees—the rain and snow,
Where wild bees flitting hum,
Or August mulleins grow, or winter's snowflakes fall,
Or stars in the skies roll round—   10
The silent sun and stars.

1897 *1897*

Of Many a Smutch'd Deed Reminiscent.

Full of wickedness, I—of many a smutch'd deed reminiscent
       —of worse deeds capable,
Yet I look composedly upon nature, drink day and night the
       joys of life, and await death with perfect equanimity,
Because of my tender and boundless love for him I love and
       because of his boundless love for me.

1897 *1897*

many phrases and lines—among them such title suggestions as "Notes as the wild
Bee hums," "A September Supplement," and "Latter-time Hours of a half-paralytic."
Also there is a prose MS note (Lion), apparently to be considered as a kind of gloss
upon the poem. The sentiment of the poem recalls the mood of WW's nature pieces
in *Specimen Days*, e.g., "New Themes Entered Upon" or "An Early Summer Re-
veille." Cf. also the poem "A Clear Midnight," whose second line is echoed by the
fourth line of this one.

   REMINISCENT] Although this poem first appeared in the "Old Age Echoes" of LG
1897, Dr. Bucke reprinted it two years later in his 1899 *N and F* as item 126, p. 39. MS
in Barrett.

To Be at All.

Cf. Stanza 27, "Song of Myself."

To be at all—what is better than that?
I think if there were nothing more developed, the clam in its
  callous shell in the sand were august enough.
I am not in any callous shell;
I am cased with supple conductors, all over,
5 They take every object by the hand, and lead it within me;
They are thousands, each one with his entry to himself;
They are always watching with their little eyes, from my head to my feet;
One no more than a point lets in and out of me such bliss and magnitude,
I think I could lift the girder of the house away if it lay between me and
  whatever I wanted.

1855   1897

Death's Valley.

To accompany a picture; by request. "The Valley of the Shadow of Death,"
from the painting by George Inness.

Nay, do not dream, designer dark,
Thou hast portray'd or hit thy theme entire;
I, hoverer of late by this dark valley, by its confines, having glimpses of it,
Here enter lists with thee, claiming my right to make a symbol too.
5 For I have seen many wounded soldiers die,
After dread suffering—have seen their lives pass off with smiles;
And I have watch'd the death-hours of the old; and seen the infant die;
The rich, with all his nurses and his doctors;
And then the poor, in meagerness and poverty;
10 And I myself for long, O Death, have breath'd my every breath
Amid the nearness and the silent thought of thee.

ALL] This poem also, first printed in the 1897 "Old Age Echoes," is reprinted in
Dr. Bucke's *N and F* as item 134, p. 40. Trent has the MS. A related fragment, printed
in *N and F* as item 102, p. 34, is in the Barrett Collection. Both fragments are obvi-
ously related to—indeed are rough drafts of—section 27 of "Song of Myself," as the
subhead indicates.

VALLEY] This poem was first printed in *Harper's New Monthly Magazine*, April,
1892, with the subtitle, "*To accompany a picture; by request*," and the picture itself
was reproduced on the page opposite. WW was paid $25 for the poem, and in fact, in
a letter to WW of August 28, 1889, H. M. Alden, *Harper's* editor, had suggested its
composition to accompany the picture. However, it was actually printed only in the
wake of the poet's death although WW had originally included its MS in his copy for
Good-bye My Fancy (Feinberg). Both Feinberg and Barrett have MSS. George

And out of these and thee,
I make a scene, a song (not fear of thee,
Nor gloom's ravines, nor bleak, nor dark—for I do not fear thee,
Nor celebrate the struggle, or contortion, or hard-tied knot), 15
Of the broad blessed light and perfect air, with meadows, rip-
        pling tides, and trees and flowers and grass,
And the low hum of living breeze—and in the midst God's
        beautiful eternal right hand,
Thee, holiest minister of Heaven—thee, envoy, usherer, guide at last of all,
Rich, florid, loosener of the stricture-knot call'd life,
Sweet, peaceful, welcome Death. 20

1892   1897

On the Same Picture.

Intended for first stanza of "Death's Valley."

Aye, well I know 'tis ghastly to descend that valley:
Preachers, musicians, poets, painters, always render it,
Philosophs exploit—the battlefield, the ship at sea, the myriad
        beds, all lands,
All, all the past have enter'd, the ancientest humanity we know,
Syria's, India's, Egypt's, Greece's, Rome's; 5
Till now for us under our very eyes spreading the same to-day,
Grim, ready, the same to-day, for entrance, yours and mine,
Here, here 'tis limn'd.

1892   1897

A Thought of Columbus.

The mystery of mysteries, the crude and hurried ceaseless
        flame, spontaneous, bearing on itself.

Inness, 1824–1894, was an American landscape painter famous for his romantic interpretations.

    PICTURE] The MS (Feinberg) of this eight-line passage indicates by its title—"Death's Valley"—that it was indeed probably intended for one of the stanzas, if not the first, of the preceding poem. The present title was evidently supplied by Traubel.

    COLUMBUS] The MS of this poem was printed in facsimile in *Once a Week*, July 9, 1892; and the next issue, July 16, 1892, carried Traubel's account of its composition, "Walt Whitman's Last Poem," in which he tells how the poem, written on fragments pasted on two long strips of paper, was handed to him by WW on the preceding March 16, ten days before he was to die. Some of the fragments were old envelopes whose postmarks indicate that the composition began as early as November, 1891. Complete MS in Feinberg, both rough and final drafts. The Barrett Collection has also a draft of the first six lines.

The bubble and the huge, round, concrete orb!
A breath of Deity, as thence the bulging universe unfolding!
The many issuing cycles from their precedent minute!
5   The eras of the soul incepting in an hour,
Haply the widest, farthest evolutions of the world and man.

Thousands and thousands of miles hence, and now four centuries back,
A mortal impulse thrilling its brain cell,
Reck'd or unreck'd, the birth can no longer be postpon'd:
10 A phantom of the moment, mystic, stalking, sudden,
Only a silent thought, yet toppling down of more than walls of brass or
        stone.
(A flutter at the darkness' edge as if old Time's and Space's
        secret near revealing.)
A thought! a definite thought works out in shape.
Four hundred years roll on.
15 The rapid cumulus—trade, navigation, war, peace, democracy, roll on;
The restless armies and the fleets of time following their leader
        —the old camps of ages pitch'd in newer, larger areas,
The tangl'd, long-deferr'd eclaircissement of human life and
        hopes boldly begins untying,
As here to-day up-grows the Western World.

(An added word yet to my song, far Discoverer, as ne'er before
        sent back to son of earth—
20 If still thou hearest, hear me,
Voicing as now—lands, races, arts, bravas to thee,
O'er the long backward path to thee—one vast consensus,
        north, south, east, west,
Soul plaudits! acclamation! reverent echoes!
One manifold, huge memory to thee! oceans and lands!
25 The modern world to thee and thought of thee!)

1891   1897

Other Poetic Writings

Note on the Texts

The following section includes two important categories of poetry associated with *Leaves of Grass:* (A) poems excluded from *Leaves of Grass;* (B) passages excluded from *Leaves of Grass* poems (for a list of titles, see the Table of Contents of this volume). The "excluded" poem is one which was canceled from a *Leaves of Grass* edition and not restored, or not present in the same form, in the canon of LG 1881 or LG 1891–1892; and also those poems not transferred to LG from the poet's so-called "Supplements" or supplementary volumes: *Drum-Taps;* "Songs Before Parting"; *Passage to India; As A Strong Bird on Pinions Free; Two Rivulets; November Boughs; Good-Bye My Fancy;* and *Complete Prose Works.* We have included all such poems, although they represent varying degrees of accomplishment or of substantive interest. By contrast, the second category—the "excluded passages"—represents a selection of those passages excluded from LG poems which have distinct merit and a certain independence of form and meaning. Where WW divided a poem, excluding part and preserving part in canon poems, or where parts of an excluded passage were independently dispersed for a time, we have restored the original text.

The selection was based on the same editors' collation of all texts of LG, which will appear in the Variorum Edition of *Leaves of Grass,* another volume in this edition of *The Collected Writings of Walt Whitman.* The dating of each poem and passage, together with the first note, will show its first and last appearance in an LG edition and identify the source of the text reproduced. This was usually the text of its last appearance, or its last appearance as a whole in the case of those which Whitman abbreviated, of which some survived into the canon of 1881. The date at the left, below the poem, is that of the first appearance in LG or a supplement. The date at the right is that of last appearance. A date in parenthesis at the left indicates some form of earlier publication; a parenthesis at the right indicates date of survival of some fragment of the text. The range of these dates is generally from 1855 to 1876 (several were from NB 1888 or GBF 1891). Since the poet's style, including elisions and punctuation, varied considerably during this period, we have followed in each case the form of the text in the edition from which we extracted it. An exception to this rule was our decision to ignore, with few exceptions, Whitman's numbering of lines or stanzas, which was whimsical until *LG* 1881, when he numbered only the large units, or cantos. We have numbered the lines of each passage "by fives" in the margin, as is the practice in the other categories within this edition. It was necessary to supply some titles, particularly for the excluded passages and for certain poems drawn from *LG* editions before 1867. Such titles are shown between square brackets to distinguish them from Whitman's titles.

MYTHS] Appeared in the first *Leaves of Grass* (1855), untitled, as the concluding poem; and in *LG* 1856 as "Poem of a Few Greatnesses". In *LG* 1860 ("No. 2" in a "Leaves of Grass" cluster), it was increased from sixty-seven to seventy-one lines, the present text, representing the fullest development of the poem. In 1867, with the present title, the poem was cut to forty-nine lines, perhaps in an effort to make it more objective; see the interrelated stanzas which were then discarded: lines 7–16; 60–65; and 68–71. For the last group (lines 68–71) WW substituted one line: "Has Life much purport?—Ah, Death has the greatest purport." Line 6 was altered to read: "I weather it out with you, or sink with you." Lines 28, 29, and 50 were canceled in 1867. In later editions there were minor changes in punctuation and the

POEMS EXCLUDED FROM
LEAVES OF GRASS

Great Are the Myths.

Great are the myths—I too delight in them,
Great are Adam and Eve—I too look back and accept them,
Great the risen and fallen nations, and their poets,
      women, sages, inventors, rulers, warriors, and priests.

Great is Liberty! great is Equality! I am their follower,
Helmsmen of nations, choose your craft! where you sail, I sail,   5
Yours is the muscle of life or death—yours is the
      perfect science—in you I have absolute faith.

Great is To-day, and beautiful,
It is good to live in this age—there never was any better.

Great are the plunges, throes, triumphs, downfalls of Democracy,
Great the reformers, with their lapses and screams,   10
Great the daring and venture of sailors, on new explorations.

Great are Yourself and Myself,
We are just as good and bad as the oldest and youngest or any,
What the best and worst did, we could do,
What they felt, do not we feel it in ourselves?   15
What they wished, do we not wish the same?

poem was divided into five cantos, then permanently dropped in 1881, excepting the
two couplets, lines 19–22, which became the poem, "Youth, Day, Old Age, and
Night."

    1. them] A MS (Trent) earlier than the first LG (1855) is a draft of three
stanzas (Bucke, *N and F*, No. 56), of which stanzas "1" and "3" compare closely
with the present stanzas "1" and "5." The second MS stanza reads:

    And that's so, easy enough:
    And I am no shallowpate to go about singing them above the rest and
        deferring to them;
    And they did not become great by singing and deferring.

Great is Youth—equally great is Old Age—great are the Day and Night,
Great is Wealth—great is Poverty—great is Expression—great is Silence.

Youth, large, lusty, loving—Youth, full of grace, force, fascination,
Do you know that Old Age may come after you,
20   with equal grace, force, fascination?

Day, full-blown and splendid—Day of the immense sun, action, ambition,
          laughter,
The Night follows close, with millions of suns, and
          sleep, and restoring darkness.

Wealth with the flush hand, fine clothes, hospitality,
But then the Soul's wealth, which is candor, knowl-
          edge, pride, enfolding love;
25 (Who goes for men and women showing Poverty richer than wealth?)

Expression of speech! in what is written or said, for-
          get not that Silence is also expressive,
That anguish as hot as the hottest, and contempt as
          cold as the coldest, may be without words,
That the true adoration is likewise without words, and without kneeling.

Great is the greatest Nation—the nation of clusters of equal nations.

30 Great is the Earth, and the way it became what it is;
Do you imagine it is stopped at this? the increase abandoned?
Understand then that it goes as far onward from this, as this is from the
          times when it lay in covering waters and gases, before man had ap-
          peared.

Great is the quality of Truth in man,
The quality of truth in man supports itself through all changes,
35 It is inevitably in the man—he and it are in love, and never leave each other.

The truth in man is no dictum, it is vital as eyesight,
If there be any Soul, there is truth—if there be man or woman, there is
          truth—if there be physical or moral, there is truth,
If there be equilibrium or volition, there is truth—if there be things at all
          upon the earth, there is truth.

O truth of the earth! O truth of things! I am de-
      termined to press my way toward you,
Sound your voice! I scale mountains, or dive in the sea after you.   40

Great is Language—it is the mightiest of the sciences,
It is the fulness, color, form, diversity of the earth, and of men and
      women, and of all qualities and processes,
It is greater than wealth—it is greater than build-
      ings, ships, religions, paintings, music.

Great is the English speech—what speech is so great as the English?
Great is the English brood—what brood has so vast
      a destiny as the English?   45
It is the mother of the brood that must rule the earth with the new rule,
The new rule shall rule as the Soul rules, and as the
        love, justice, equality in the Soul, rule.

Great is Law—great are the old few landmarks of the law,
They are the same in all times, and shall not be disturbed.

Great are commerce, newspapers, books, free-trade, railroads, steamers,
      international mails, telegraphs, exchanges.   50

Great is Justice!
Justice is not settled by legislators and laws—it is in the Soul,
It cannot be varied by statutes, any more than love,
      pride, the attraction of gravity, can,
It is immutable—it does not depend on majorities—majorities or what not
      come at last before the same passionless and exact tribunal.

For justice are the grand natural lawyers and perfect
      judges—it is in their Souls,   55
It is well assorted—they have not studied for noth-
      ing—the great includes the less,
They rule on the highest grounds—they oversee all
      eras, states, administrations.

The perfect judge fears nothing—he could go front to front before God,
Before the perfect judge all shall stand back—life and death shall stand
      back—heaven and hell shall stand back.

60 Great is Goodness!
    I do not know what it is, any more than I know what
            health is—but I know it is great.

    Great is Wickedness—I find I often admire it, just as
            much as I admire goodness,
    Do you call that a paradox? It certainly is a paradox.

    The eternal equilibrium of things is great, and the
            eternal overthrow of things is great,
65 And there is another paradox.

    Great is Life, real and mystical, wherever and whoever,
    Great is Death—sure as Life holds all parts together,
            Death holds all parts together,
    Death has just as much purport as Life has,
    Do you enjoy what Life confers? you shall enjoy what Death confers,
70 I do not understand the realities of Death, but I know they are great,
    I do not understand the least reality of Life—how then
            can I understand the realities of Death?

    (1855) 1860   1860 (1876)

        Poem of Remembrances
        for a Girl or a Boy of These States.

    You just maturing youth! You male or female!
    Remember the organic compact of These States,
    Remember the pledge of the Old Thirteen thenceforward to the rights,
            life, liberty, equality of man,
    Remember what was promulged by the founders, ratified by The States,
            signed in black and white by the Commissioners, and read by
            Washington at the head of the army,
5   Remember the purposes of the founders,—Remember Washington;
    Remember the copious humanity streaming from every
            direction toward America;

    STATES] Originally a poem of forty-three lines in LG 1856, with the present title;
    reappeared in LG 1860 as "Chants Democratic—6," increased by the addition of the
    present first line. In LG 1867 WW excluded the present passage of twenty-one lines
    and retained the second section (twenty-three lines) under the new title, "Think of the
    Soul" (1867–1876), which is reproduced immediately below. The excluded passage,
    as shown above, has a certain unity and meaning worthy of attention. The consecutive

Remember the hospitality that belongs to nations
        and men; (Cursed be nation, woman, man, without hospitality!)
Remember, government is to subserve individuals,
Not any, not the President, is to have one jot more than you or me,
Not any habitan of America is to have one jot less than you or me.   10

Anticipate when the thirty or fifty millions, are to become the hundred, or
        two hundred millions, of equal freemen and freewomen, amicably
        joined.

Recall ages—One age is but a part—ages are but a part;
Recall the angers, bickerings, delusions, superstitions,
        of the idea of caste,
Recall the bloody cruelties and crimes.

Anticipate the best women;   15
I say an unnumbered new race of hardy and well-defined women are to
        spread through all These States,
I say a girl fit for These States must be free, capable,
        dauntless, just the same as a boy.

Anticipate your own life—retract with merciless power,
Shirk nothing—retract in time—Do you see those
        errors, diseases, weaknesses, lies, thefts?
Do you see that lost character?—Do you see decay, consumption, rum-
        drinking, dropsy, fever, mortal cancer or inflammation?   20
Do you see death, and the approach of death?

  (1856) 1860   1860

Think of the Soul.

Think of the Soul;
I swear to you that body of yours gives proportions to
        your Soul somehow to live in other spheres;
I do not know how, but I know it is so.

reading of this and the following "Think of the Soul" reproduces the entire 1860 text
except that the serial numbers preceding stanzas have been canceled.
    SOUL] Originally the last nine stanzas of "Poem of Remembrances . . . ," 1856
(q.v., immediately preceding), these twenty-three lines were preserved in the 1867
edition, from which the earlier portion of the original poem was excluded. In the
1867 edition this poem, without title, became No. 1 of the poem cluster entitled

Think of loving and being loved;
I swear to you, whoever you are, you can interfuse yourself with such
     things that everybody that sees you shall look longingly upon you.

Think of the past;
I warn you that in a little while others will find their
     past in you and your times.

The race is never separated—nor man nor woman escapes;
All is inextricable—things, spirits, Nature, nations, you
     too—from precedents you come.

Recall the ever-welcome defiers, (The mothers precede them;)
Recall the sages, poets, saviors, inventors, lawgivers, of the earth;
Recall Christ, brother of rejected persons—brother of slaves, felons, idiots,
     and of insane and diseas'd persons.

Think of the time when you were not yet born;
Think of times you stood at the side of the dying;
Think of the time when your own body will be dying.

Think of spiritual results,
Sure as the earth swims through the heavens, does every
     one of its objects pass into spiritual results.

Think of manhood, and you to be a man;
Do you count manhood, and the sweet of manhood, nothing?

Think of womanhood, and you to be a woman;
The creation is womanhood;
Have I not said that womanhood involves all?
Have I not told how the universe has nothing better
     than the best womanhood?

  (*1856*) *1867*   *1876*

"Leaves of Grass." In 1868 it was included as "Links" in Rossetti's English edition.
With the present title and only a few changes, principally in punctuation, the poem
was retained in the editions of 1871–1872 and 1876, before being excluded from the
1881 edition. The text is that of the last edition, 1876.
    12. diseas'd] Originally, "diseased"; the elision appeared from 1867 to 1876.
    13. not] Originally, "you was not"; corrected in fourth edition, 1872.

Respondez!

RESPONDEZ! Respondez!
(The war is completed—the price is paid—the title is
        settled beyond recall;)
Let every one answer! let those who sleep be waked! let none evade!
Must we still go on with our affectations and sneaking?
Let me bring this to a close—I pronounce openly for
        a new distribution of roles;   5
Let that which stood in front go behind! and let that which was behind
        advance to the front and speak;
Let murderers, bigots, fools, unclean persons, offer new propositions!
Let the old propositions be postponed!
Let faces and theories be turn'd inside out! let mean-
        ings be freely criminal, as well as results!
Let there be no suggestion above the suggestion of drudgery!   10
Let none be pointed toward his destination! (Say! do
        you know your destination?)
Let men and women be mock'd with bodies and mock'd with Souls!
Let the love that waits in them, wait! let it die, or pass
        still-born to other spheres!
Let the sympathy that waits in every man, wait! or let
        it also pass, a dwarf, to other spheres!
Let contradictions prevail! let one thing contradict another! and let one
        line of my poems contradict another!   15
Let the people sprawl with yearning, aimless hands! let their tongues be
        broken! let their eyes be discouraged! let none descend into their
        hearts with the fresh lusciousness of love!
(Stifled, O days! O lands! in every public and private corruption!
Smother'd in thievery, impotence, shamelessness, mountain-high;
Brazen effrontery, scheming, rolling like ocean's waves
        around and upon you, O my days! my lands!

RESPONDEZ!] Appeared initially as "Poem of the Propositions of Nakedness" in
LG 1856, and in the 1860 edition without title, as number five of the "Chants
Democratic and Native American." Entitled "Respondez," it appeared in all later
editions until 1876, the source of this text. Of the eleven lines gained by revision, the
most striking were lines 2 and 17–19, which reflected the Civil War and the postwar
corruptions which WW excoriated the same year in the prose of *Democratic Vistas*
(1871). Excluding the poem as a whole in 1881, the poet transposed several lines to
other poems. Compare "Respondez," lines 6–8, 65, and 66 with "Reversals"; and
compare lines 22, 44, and 46 with "Transpositions."

For not even those thunderstorms, nor fiercest light-
20   nings of the war, have purified the atmosphere;)
—Let the theory of America still be management, caste, comparison!
        (Say! what other theory would you?)
Let them that distrust birth and death still lead the rest! (Say! why
        shall they not lead you?)
Let the crust of hell be neared and trod on! let the days be darker than the
        nights! let slumber bring less slumber than waking time brings!
Let the world never appear to him or her for whom it was all made!
Let the heart of the young man still exile itself from the heart of the old
        man! and let the heart of the old man be exiled from that of the
25   young man!
Let the sun and moon go! let scenery take the applause of the audience!
        let there be apathy under the stars!
Let freedom prove no man's inalienable right! every one who can
        tyrannize, let him tyrannize to his satisfaction!
Let none but infidels be countenanced!
Let the eminence of meanness, treachery, sarcasm, hate, greed, indecency,
        impotence, lust, be taken for granted above all! let writers, judges,
        governments, households, religions, philosophies, take such for
        granted above all!
30   Let the worst men beget children out of the worst women!
Let the priest still play at immortality!
Let death be inaugurated!
Let nothing remain but the ashes of teachers, artists, moralists, lawyers,
        and learn'd and polite persons!
Let him who is without my poems be assassinated!
Let the cow, the horse, the camel, the garden-bee—let the mud-fish, the
        lobster, the mussel, eel, the sting-ray, and the grunting pig-fish—
        let these, and the like of these, be put on a perfect equality with man
35   and woman!
Let churches accommodate serpents, vermin, and the corpses of those who
        have died of the most filthy of diseases!
Let marriage slip down among fools, and be for none but fools!
Let men among themselves talk and think forever obscenely of women! and
        let women among themselves talk and think obscenely of men!
Let us all, without missing one, be exposed in public, naked, monthly, at
        the peril of our lives! let our bodies be freely handled and examined
        by whoever chooses!

50. smouchers] Cf. "to smouch"—to gouge, to take unfair advantage. Colloquial

Let nothing but copies at second hand be permitted to exist upon the earth! 40
Let the earth desert God, nor let there ever henceforth
  be mention'd the name of God!
Let there be no God!
Let there be money, business, imports, exports, custom, authority, prec-
  edents, pallor, dyspepsia, smut, ignorance, unbelief!
Let judges and criminals be transposed! let the prison-keepers be put in
  prison! let those that were prisoners take the keys! (Say! why might
  they not just as well be transposed?)
Let the slaves be masters! let the masters become slaves! 45
Let the reformers descend from the stands where they are forever
  bawling! let an idiot or insane person appear on each of the stands!
Let the Asiatic, the African, the European, the American, and the Aus-
  tralian, go armed against the murderous stealthiness of each other!
  let them sleep armed! let none believe in good will!
Let there be no unfashionable wisdom! let such be
  scorn'd and derided off from the earth!
Let a floating cloud in the sky—let a wave of the sea—let growing mint,
  spinach, onions, tomatoes—let these be exhibited as shows, at a
  great price for admission!
Let all the men of These States stand aside for a few smouchers! let the
  few seize on what they choose! let the rest gawk, giggle, starve,
  obey! 50
Let shadows be furnish'd with genitals! let substances
  be deprived of their genitals!
Let there be wealthy and immense cities—but still through any of them,
  not a single poet, savior, knower, lover!
Let the infidels of These States laugh all faith away!
If one man be found who has faith, let the rest set upon him!
Let them affright faith! let them destroy the power of breeding faith! 55
Let the she-harlots and the he-harlots be prudent!
    let them dance on, while seeming lasts!
    (O seeming! seeming! seeming!)
Let the preachers recite creeds! let them still teach
  only what they have been taught!
Let insanity still have charge of sanity!
Let books take the place of trees, animals, rivers, clouds!
Let the daub'd portraits of heroes supersede heroes! 60
Let the manhood of man never take steps after itself!

Let it take steps after eunuchs, and after consumptive and genteel persons!

Let the white person again tread the black person under his heel! (Say! which is trodden under heel, after all?)

Let the reflections of the things of the world be studied in mirrors! let the things themselves still continue unstudied!

65   Let a man seek pleasure everywhere except in himself!

Let a woman seek happiness everywhere except in herself!

(What real happiness have you had one single hour through your whole life?)

Let the limited years of life do nothing for the limitless years of death! (What do you suppose death will do, then?)

    1856   *1876*

[*In the New Garden*].

In the new garden, in all the parts,

In cities now, modern, I wander,

Through the second or third result, or still further, primitive yet,

Days, places, indifferent—though various, the same,

5   Time, Paradise, the Mannahatta, the prairies, finding me unchanged,

Death indifferent—Is it that I lived long since?

        Was I buried very long ago?

For all that, I may now be watching you here, this moment;

For the future, with determined will, I seek—the woman of the future,

You, born years, centuries after me, I seek.

    1860   *1860*

[*Who Is Now Reading This?*].

Who is now reading this?

May-be one is now reading this who knows some wrong-doing of my past life,

GARDEN] This poem appeared only in the third edition, LG 1860, identified as number "11" of the fifteen untitled poems comprising the section then called "Enfans d'Adam." All the others survived in the "Children of Adam" cluster, or elsewhere. "In the New Garden," however, in part resembles the first poem of the final "Children of Adam." That fine poem, called "To the Garden of the World" (*q.v.*) represents the "first man, Adam" with his Eve at the beginning; the present poem sees an Adam ever new but "primitive yet," in the "new garden," in "modern" cities, seeking the Eve "of the future."

THIS] The first and only publication of this interesting poem occurred in

Or may-be a stranger is reading this who has secretly loved me,
Or may-be one who meets all my grand assumptions
    and egotisms with derision,
Or may-be one who is puzzled at me.   5

As if I were not puzzled at myself!
Or as if I never deride myself! (O conscience-struck! O self-convicted!)
Or as if I do not secretly love strangers! (O tenderly,
    a long time, and never avow it;)
Or as if I did not see, perfectly well, interior in
    myself, the stuff of wrong-doing,
Or as if it could cease transpiring from me until it must cease.   10

1860   *1860*

[*I Thought That Knowledge Alone Would Suffice*].

Long I thought that knowledge alone would suffice
    me—O if I could but obtain knowledge!
Then my lands engrossed me—Lands of the prairies, Ohio's land, the
    southern savannas, engrossed me—For them I would live—I would
    be their orator;
Then I met the examples of old and new heroes—I heard of warriors,
    sailors, and all dauntless persons—And it seemed to me that I too
    had it in me to be as dauntless as any—and would be so;
And then, to enclose all, it came to me to strike up the songs of the New
    World—And then I believed my life must be spent in singing;
But now take notice, land of the prairies, land of
    the south savannas, Ohio's land,   5
Take notice, you Kanuck woods—and you Lake Huron—and all that with
    you roll toward Niagara—and you Niagara also,
And you, Californian mountains—That you each and all find somebody
    else to be your singer of songs,

LG 1860, where it was without title, numbered "16" in the "Calamus" cluster. The present copy omits the stanza numbering.

    SUFFICE] Appeared only in LG 1860, untitled, but numbered "8" in the cluster entitled "Calamus." It is associated with another new poem of 1860, "Once I passed Through a Populous City" (*q.v.*), which is more intense and stylistically impressive. In the MS version (*ca.* 1859) both poems refer to the lover as a man. Before publication, Whitman changed the lover to a woman in the other poem, which held its place into the final LG 1891–2. The present poem WW canceled in his "Blue Copy" LG 1860. (See Bowers, p. 64 and p. 80.)

For I can be your singer of songs no longer—One who loves me is jealous
of me, and withdraws me from all but love,
With the rest I dispense—I sever from what I thought would suffice me,
for it does not—it is now empty and tasteless to me,
I heed knowledge, and the grandeur of The States,
10   and the example of heroes, no more,
I am indifferent to my own songs—I will go with him I love,
It is to be enough for us that we are together—We never separate again.

1860   1860

[Hours Continuing Long].

Hours continuing long, sore and heavy-hearted,
Hours of the dusk, when I withdraw to a lonesome and unfrequented spot,
seating myself, leaning my face in my hands;
Hours sleepless, deep in the night, when I go forth, speeding swiftly the
country roads, or through the city streets, or pacing miles and miles,
stifling plaintive cries;
Hours discouraged, distracted—for the one I cannot content myself with-
out, soon I saw him content himself without me;
Hours when I am forgotten, (O weeks and months are
5   passing, but I believe I am never to forget!)
Sullen and suffering hours! (I am ashamed—but it
is useless—I am what I am;)
Hours of my torment—I wonder if other men ever
have the like, out of the like feelings?
Is there even one other like me—distracted—his
friend, his lover, lost to him?
Is he too as I am now? Does he still rise in the morning, dejected, thinking
who is lost to him? and at night, awaking, think who is lost?
Does he too harbor his friendship silent and endless?
10   harbor his anguish and passion?
Does some stray reminder, or the casual mention of a name, bring the fit
back upon him, taciturn and deprest?

LONG] This was published, without title, as number "9" in the "Calamus" cluster
of LG 1860. It was not reprinted in subsequent editions, but among the "Calamus"
poems it is a striking expression of Whitman's theme of "comradeship."
END] Appeared only in LG 1860, as number "20" of twenty-four untitled poems of
the cluster entitled "Leaves of Grass."

Does he see himself reflected in me? In these hours,
    does he see the face of his hours reflected?

1860   *1860*

[*So Far, and So Far, and On Toward the End*].

So far, and so far, and on toward the end,
Singing what is sung in this book, from the irresistible impulses of me;
But whether I continue beyond this book, to maturity,
Whether I shall dart forth the true rays, the ones that wait unfired,
(Did you think the sun was shining its brightest?   5
No—it has not yet fully risen;)
Whether I shall complete what is here started,
Whether I shall attain my own height, to justify these, yet unfinished,
Whether I shall make THE POEM OF THE NEW WORLD, transcending all
    others—depends, rich persons, upon you,
Depends, whoever you are now filling the current Presidentiad, upon you,   10
Upon you, Governor, Mayor, Congressman,
And you, contemporary America.

1860   *1860*

Thoughts—1: Visages.

Of the visages of things—And of piercing through
    to the accepted hells beneath;
Of ugliness—To me there is just as much in it as there is in beauty—And
    now the ugliness of human beings is acceptable to me;
Of detected persons—To me, detected persons are not, in any respect,
    worse than undetected persons—and are not in any respect worse
    than I am myself;
Of criminals—To me, any judge, or any juror, is equally criminal—and
    any reputable person is also—and the President is also.

1860   *1867*

VISAGES] First appeared in *LG* 1860; reprinted in *LG* 1867 without change, un-
titled, as number "1" in the cluster of seven poems entitled "Thoughts." In the London
selected edition by W. M. Rossetti (*Poems by Walt Whitman*, 1868) it was entitled
"Visages" and printed without verbal change. It was excluded from the later editions.
The MS (Huntington) lacks the last line.

Leaflets.

What General has a good army in himself, has a good army;
He happy in himself, or she happy in herself, is happy.

  (1860) 1867   *1867*

Thoughts—6: "Of What I Write."

Of what I write from myself—As if that were not the resumé;
Of Histories—As if such, however complete, were
        not less complete than the preceding poems;
As if those shreds, the records of nations, could possibly
        be as lasting as the preceding poems;
As if here were not the amount of all nations, and of all the lives of heroes.

  1860   *1876*

Says.

1

I say whatever tastes sweet to the most perfect person, that is finally right.

2

I say nourish a great intellect, a great brain;
If I have said anything to the contrary, I hereby retract it.

LEAFLETS] Appeared independently only once, in LG 1867, with the present title, filling out the blank end of page 284. Earlier, in LG 1860, it was lines 4–5 of "Debris" (*q.v.*), a poem which appeared as a whole only in that edition.

THOUGHTS] Appeared in LG 1860, and, without alteration in LG 1867, without title as number "6" among the seven poems of a cluster entitled "Thoughts." Separately entitled "Thought" and slightly revised in editions from 1871 to 1876, the source of the present text. MS in Huntington.

  1. resumé] So in WW's text.

SAYS] Appeared in LG 1860 with the present text and title. Again entitled "Says" in 1867, it was cut from twenty-six to fifteen lines, retaining stanzas 1, 5, 7, and 8.

3

I say man shall not hold property in man;
I say the least developed person on earth is just as important and sacred
    to himself or herself, as the most developed person is to himself or
    herself.   5

4

I say where liberty draws not the blood out of
    slavery, there slavery draws the blood out of liberty,
I say the word of the good old cause in These States,
    and resound it hence over the world.

5

I say the human shape or face is so great, it must never be made ridiculous;
I say for ornaments nothing outre can be allowed,
And that anything is most beautiful without ornament,   10
And that exaggerations will be sternly revenged in your own physiology,
    and in other persons' physiology also;
And I say that clean-shaped children can be jetted and conceived only
    where natural forms prevail in public, and the human face and form
    are never caricatured;
And I say that genius need never more be turned to romances,
(For facts properly told, how mean appear all romances.)

6

I say the word of lands fearing nothing—I will have no other land;   15
I say discuss all and expose all—I am for every topic openly;

If these stanzas alone are compared with the complete text, one sees that Whitman, after the Civil War and the publication of his *Drum-Taps*, rejected the passages dealing with slavery and reform, thus heightening in the remaining stanzas the theme of the dignity and potentialities of the democratic individual, already emphasized in stanza 5 by direct quotation from the last fifteen lines of paragraph 20 of his Preface to LG 1855, his first manifesto on this subject. In the intensified version, the poem, now entitled "Suggestions," appeared in LG 1871, 1872, and for the last time in 1876, with the alteration of the epanaphora of initial phrases from "I say" (as above) to "That," or (in lines 13, 23, and 26) "And that."

    9. outre] *Sic*. Appears without accent also in Preface 1855; corrected in 1867.

I say there can be no salvation for These States without innovators—
     without free tongues, and ears willing to hear the tongues;
And I announce as a glory of These States, that they respectfully listen
     to propositions, reforms, fresh views and doctrines, from successions
     of men and women,
Each age with its own growth.

7

I have said many times that materials and the Soul
20   are great, and that all depends on physique;
Now I reverse what I said, and affirm that all depends
     on the æsthetic or intellectual,
And that criticism is great—and that refinement is greatest of all;
And I affirm now that the mind governs—and that
     all depends on the mind.

8

With one man or woman—(no matter which one—
     I even pick out the lowest,)
25 With him or her I now illustrate the whole law;
I say that every right, in politics or what-not, shall be eligible to that one
     man or woman, on the same terms as any.

1860   *1867 (1876)*

Apostroph.

O mater! O fils!
O brood continental!
O flowers of the prairies!
O space boundless! O hum of mighty products!
5 O you teeming cities! O so invincible, turbulent, proud!
O race of the future! O women!
O fathers! O you men of passion and the storm!
O native power only! O beauty!

APOSTROPH] First appeared in the third edition, *LG* 1860, as the introductory
poem of the section entitled "Chants Democratic and Native American," of which the
remaining twenty-one poems were identified only by numerals. In the succeeding
issue, 1867, the poem as a whole was replaced by a condensed and improved version

O yourself! O God! O divine average!
O you bearded roughs! O bards! O all those slumberers!   10
O arouse! the dawn-bird's throat sounds shrill! Do
      you not hear the cock crowing?
O, as I walk'd the beach, I heard the mournful notes foreboding a
      tempest—the low, oft-repeated shriek of the diver, the long-lived
      loon;
O I heard, and yet hear, angry thunder;—O you
      sailors! O ships! make quick preparation!
O from his masterful sweep, the warning cry of the eagle!
(Give way there, all! It is useless! Give up your spoils;)   15
O sarcasms! Propositions! (O if the whole world
      should prove indeed a sham, a sell!)
O I believe there is nothing real but America and freedom!
O to sternly reject all except Democracy!
O imperator! O who dare confront you and me?
O to promulgate our own! O to build for that which builds for mankind!   20
O feuillage! O North! O the slope drained by the Mexican sea!
O all, all inseparable—ages, ages, ages!
O a curse on him that would dissever this Union for any reason whatever!
O climates, labors! O good and evil! O death!
O you strong with iron and wood! O Personality!   25
O the village or place which has the greatest man or
      woman! even if it be only a few ragged huts;
O the city where women walk in public processions in
      the streets, the same as the men;
O a wan and terrible emblem, by me adopted!
O shapes arising! shapes of the future centuries!
O muscle and pluck forever for me!   30
O workmen and workwomen forever for me!
O farmers and sailors! O drivers of horses forever for me!
O I will make the new bardic list of trades and tools!
O you coarse and wilful! I love you!
O South! O longings for my dear home! O soft and sunny airs!   35
O pensive! O I must return where the palm grows
      and the mocking-bird sings, or else I die!

of the concluding nineteen lines, which appeared in a new position as "Leaves of
Grass: 1" (cf. "O Sun of Real Peace" below). Another derivative, not previously
published, "O Brood Continental," appears among uncollected poems in this edition.
    19. imperator] The Latin word for "emperor" also meant "commander" or "con-
queror."

O equality! O organic compacts! I am come to be your born poet!
O whirl, contest, sounding and resounding! I am
          your poet, because I am part of you;
O days by-gone! Enthusiasts! Antecedents!
40   O vast preparations for These States! O years!
O what is now being sent forward thousands of years to come!
O mediums! O to teach! to convey the invisible faith!
To promulge real things! to journey through all The States!
O creation! O to-day! O laws! O unmitigated adoration!
45   O for mightier broods of orators, artists, and singers!
O for native songs! carpenter's, boatman's, plough-
          man's songs! shoemaker's songs!
O haughtiest growth of time! O free and extatic!
O what I, here, preparing, warble for!
O you hastening light! O the sun of the world will ascend, dazzling, and
          take his height—and you too will ascend;
50   O so amazing and so broad! up there resplendent, darting and burning;
O prophetic! O vision staggered with weight of light!
          with pouring glories!
O copious! O hitherto unequalled!
O Libertad! O compact! O union impossible to dissever!
O my Soul! O lips becoming tremulous, powerless!
55   O centuries, centuries yet ahead!
O voices of greater orators! I pause—I listen for you!
O you States! Cities! defiant of all outside authority! I spring at once into
          your arms! you I most love!
O you grand Presidentiads! I wait for you!
New history! New heroes! I project you!
60   Visions of poets! only you really last! O sweep on! sweep on!
O Death! O you striding there! O I cannot yet!
O heights! O infinitely too swift and dizzy yet!
O purged lumine! you threaten me more than I can stand!
O present! I return while yet I may to you!
65   O poets to come, I depend upon you!

          1860   *1860 (1876)*

47. extatic] So spelled in both versions.
PEACE] Whitman revised and reorganized the last nineteen lines of "Apostroph"
(see above) to form the thirteen lines of this poem, titled "O hastening light," in
LG 1867. In LG 1871 it appeared in a new cluster, "Marches now the War Is Over,"
whose motivation—the end of the war—WW emphasized by adding the last half
of line 7, by giving the poem its present title, and by using the same phrase in
the opening line. The present text is that of 1876, the poem's last appearance.

O Sun of Real Peace.

O sun of real peace! O hastening light!
O free and extatic! O what I here, preparing, warble for!
O the sun of the world will ascend, dazzling, and take his height—and you
      too, O my Ideal, will surely ascend!
O so amazing and broad—up there resplendent, darting and burning!
O vision prophetic, stagger'd with weight of light! with pouring glories!   5
O lips of my soul, already becoming powerless!
O ample and grand Presidentiads! Now the war, the war is over!
New history! new heroes! I project you!
Visions of poets! only you really last! sweep on! sweep on!
O heights too swift and dizzy yet!   10
O purged and luminous! you threaten me more than I can stand!
(I must not venture—the ground under my feet men-
      aces me—it will not support me:
O future too immense,)—O present, I return, while yet I may, to you.

  (1860) 1867   1876

To You.

Let us twain walk aside from the rest;
Now we are together privately, do you discard ceremony;
Come! vouchsafe to me what has yet been vouchsafed
      to none—Tell me the whole story,

2. extatic] So spelled in "Apostroph." See above.

YOU] Twelve years after its first appearance, WW transformed this poem
emotionally by the insertion in 71 PI and 76 TR of the present fourth line, in which
the "talk of death" concentrates and defines a spiritual value. Without this line, in
the 1860 version, the proposed sharing of confidences suggests a somewhat gross
familiarity. The MS (Barrett) has the four-line version shown as the second of the
two stanzas of a poem entitled "To You." Each appeared separately with this title
in LG 1860, printed in reverse order on p. 403 concluding the cluster, "Messenger
Leaves." The other poem, now the familiar couplet entitled "To You" among the
LG "Inscriptions," simply declared that passing strangers should talk freely together.
The present poem did not appear in 76 PI. It reappeared only in the revised edition
of *Passage to India*, a supplement in LG 1872 and TR 1876. The contents list in some
copies ignored this poem ending p. 114. WW did not include it in the final selection
of 1881, and it has not been revived.

Let us talk of death—unbosom all freely,
5   Tell me what you would not tell your brother, wife, husband, or physician.
  (1860) 1872   1876

Now Lift Me Close.

Now lift me close to your face till I whisper,
What you are holding is in reality no book, nor part of a book;
It is a man, flush'd and full-blooded—it is I—*So long!*
—We must separate awhile—Here! take from my lips this kiss;
5   Whoever you are, I give it especially to you;
So long!—And I hope we shall meet again.
  1860   1867 (1876)

To the Reader at Parting.

Now, dearest comrade, lift me to your face,
We must separate awhile—Here! take from my lips this kiss;
Whoever you are, I give it especially to you;
So long!—And I hope we shall meet again.
  (1860) 1871   1876

CLOSE] This poem, not previously collected, first appeared as a poem of six lines in LG 1860, identified only as "24," the last in the cluster, "Leaves of Grass." In the same edition appeared the extensive "So Long," which broadly echoes the six-line poem. In the 1867 edition, "Now Lift Me Close" was the terminal poem of the "Leaves of Grass," while "So Long" terminated the entire volume, at the end of "Songs before Parting," the last of three supplements of recent poems. Although in lines 53–69 "So Long" expresses something of the same idea as "Now Lift Me Close," the latter, in its six-line concentration, gives the effect of an independent identity. In LG 1871, it was dropped in favor of "So Long"; but see a four-line derivative, "To the Reader at Parting," immediately below.

PARTING] This previously uncollected poem was a refinement of "Now Lift Me Close" (*q.v.*, above), which was excluded from LG 1871. The revised text significantly canceled the previous lines 2 and 3, which had identified the "book" with the "man" (poet). Now the relationship with the reader recalls the subtlety of meeting and parting expressed earlier in "Out of the Rolling Ocean, the Crowd" (1865). "To the Reader at Parting" appeared as the penultimate poem in the new volume, *Passage to India*, in 1871. LG 1871 ended with "So Long!" In LG 1872, both poems appeared, each in the same relative place, since the volume included the "Passage to

Debris.

*

He is wisest who has the most caution,
He only wins who goes far enough.

*

Any thing is as good as established, when that is
    established that will produce it and continue it.

*

What General has a good army in himself, has a good army;
He happy in himself, or she happy in herself, is happy,   5
But I tell you you cannot be happy by others, any more than you can beget
    or conceive a child by others.

*

Have you learned lessons only of those who admired you, and were tender
    with you, and stood aside for you?

India" supplement. In 1881 the supplements were consolidated with LG, and "To the
Reader at Parting" was excluded in favor of "So Long!" as the terminating poem.

    DEBRIS] As a single poem of sixty lines "Debris" appeared only in LG 1860. In
1867 and later issues, the poet excluded the poem as a whole, but extracted certain
passages and stanzas as separate poems or parts of new poems. In the present text we
see again the entire collage of associated ideas, epigrams, characters, and events—
with the poet present as commentator, producing the tonal and emotional unity of a
single composition. The thirty totally discarded lines included, among other good
things, the elusive and genuine lyric (lines 39–43) "I will take an egg out of the
robin's nest." Whitman thought so well of this poem that his memorandum on the
margin of the revised "Blue Book" copy of 1860, p. 424, read "with Religious Leaves
of Grass," referring to his dream of a second volume of *Leaves.* An epigram (lines
4 and 5) appeared separately as "Leaflets" (*q.v.*) in LG 1867 and was then excluded.
Seven of the passages extracted from "Debris" survived in the final poems of LG, as
follows:

        Lines 7–8: cf. "Stronger Lessons" in Sands at Seventy.
        Lines 10–18 cf. "Yet, Yet, Ye Downcast Hours" (lines 5–13).
        Lines 19–20: cf. "Offerings."
        Lines 21–24: cf. "Visor'd."
        Lines 34–35: cf. "Beautiful Women."
        Lines 52–56: cf. "Not the Pilot."
        Lines 57–60: cf. "As if a Phantom Caress'd Me" (lines 2–5).

Have you not learned the great lessons of those who rejected you, and
    braced themselves against you? or who treated you with contempt,
    or disputed the passage with you?
Have you had no practice to receive opponents when they come?

      *

10   Despairing cries float ceaselessly toward me, day and night,
The sad voice of Death—the call of my nearest
      lover, putting forth, alarmed, uncertain,
This sea I am quickly to sail, come tell me,
Come tell me where I am speeding—tell me my destination.

      *

I understand your anguish, but I cannot help you,
I approach, hear, behold—the sad mouth, the look
15   out of the eyes, your mute inquiry,
Whither I go from the bed I now recline on, come tell me;
Old age, alarmed, uncertain—A young woman's
      voice appealing to me, for comfort,
A young man's voice, *Shall I not escape?*

      *

A thousand perfect men and women appear,
Around each gathers a cluster of friends, and gay
20   children and youths, with offerings.

      *

A mask—a perpetual natural disguiser of herself,
Concealing her face, concealing her form,
Changes and transformations every hour, every moment,
Falling upon her even when she sleeps.

      *

25   One sweeps by, attended by an immense train,
All emblematic of peace—not a soldier or menial among them.

*

One sweeps by, old, with black eyes, and profuse white hair,
He has the simple magnificence of health and strength,
His face strikes as with flashes of lightning whoever it turns toward.

*

Three old men slowly pass, followed by three others, and they by three
      others,   30
They are beautiful— the one in the middle of each
      group holds his companions by the hand,
As they walk, they give out perfume wherever they walk.

*

Women sit, or move to and fro—some old, some young,
The young are beautiful—but the old are more beautiful than the young.

*

What weeping face is that looking from the window?   35
Why does it stream those sorrowful tears?
Is it for some burial place, vast and dry?
Is it to wet the soil of graves?

*

I will take an egg out of the robin's nest in the orchard,
I will take a branch of gooseberries from the old bush
      in the garden, and go and preach to the world;   40
You shall see I will not meet a single heretic or scorner,
You shall see how I stump clergymen, and confound them,
You shall see me showing a scarlet tomato, and a
      white pebble from the beach.

*

Behavior—fresh, native, copious, each one for himself or herself,
Nature and the Soul expressed—America and free-
      dom expressed—In it the finest art,   45

In it pride, cleanliness, sympathy, to have their chance,
In it physique, intellect, faith—in it just as much as to manage an army or
      a city, or to write a book—perhaps more,
The youth, the laboring person, the poor person, rivalling all the rest—
      perhaps outdoing the rest,
The effects of the universe no greater than its;
For there is nothing in the whole universe that can be more effective than
50   a man's or woman's daily behavior can be,
In any position, in any one of These States.

      *

Not the pilot has charged himself to bring his ship into port, though beaten
      back, and many times baffled,
Not the path-finder, penetrating inland, weary and long,
By deserts parched, snows chilled, rivers wet, perseveres till he reaches
      his destination,
More than I have charged myself, heeded or unheeded, to compose a free
55   march for These States,
To be exhilarating music to them, years, centuries hence.

      *

I thought I was not alone, walking here by the shore,
But the one I thought was with me, as now I walk by the shore,
As I lean and look through the glimmering light—
      that one has utterly disappeared,
60 And those appear that perplex me.

    1860   1860 (1881)

[States!]

States!
Were you looking to be held together by the lawyers?
By an agreement on a paper? Or by arms?

STATES] This poem as a whole (fifteen stanzas, forty-two lines) appeared only
once, in LG 1860, "Calamus—5," the text shown here without the initial stanza
numerals. However, WW extracted from it materials for two poems of the final LG:
in *Drum-Taps* (1865), "Over the Carnage Rose Prophetic a Voice" (cf. "States,"

Away!
I arrive, bringing these, beyond all the forces of courts and arms,   5
These! to hold you together as firmly as the earth itself is held together.

The old breath of life, ever new,
Here! I pass it by contact to you, America.

O mother! have you done much for me?
Behold, there shall from me be much done for you.   10

There shall from me be a new friendship—It shall be called after my name,
It shall circulate through The States, indifferent of place,
It shall twist and intertwist them through and around each other—Compact
      shall they be, showing new signs,
Affection shall solve every one of the problems of freedom,
Those who love each other shall be invincible,   15
They shall finally make America completely victorious, in my name.

One from Massachusetts shall be a comrade to a Missourian,
One from Maine or Vermont, and a Carolinian and an Oregonese, shall
      be friends triune, more precious to each other than all the riches of
      the earth.
To Michigan shall be wafted perfume from Florida,
To the Mannahatta from Cuba or Mexico,   20
Not the perfume of flowers, but sweeter, and wafted beyond death.

No danger shall balk Columbia's lovers,
If need be, a thousand shall sternly immolate themselves for one,
The Kanuck shall be willing to lay down his life for the Kansian, and the
      Kansian for the Kanuck, on due need.

It shall be customary in all directions, in the houses and streets, to see
      manly affection,   25
The departing brother or friend shall salute the remaining brother or
      friend with a kiss.

lines 1–2, 14–25, and 31–35); and in *LG* 1867, "A Song," later, the stirring "For You
O Democracy" (*cf.* "States," last three stanzas, lines 36–42). Both new poems
reflected the poet's Civil War experience. Before the war, the parent poem gener-
alized the democratic idealism; both postwar revisions emphasized the comradeship
engendered by the war.

There shall be innovations,
There shall be countless linked hands—namely, the Northeasterner's and
 the Northwesterner's, and the Southwesterner's, and those of the
 interior, and all their brood,
These shall be masters of the world under a new power,
30 They shall laugh to scorn the attacks of all the remainder of the world.

The most dauntless and rude shall touch face to face lightly,
The dependence of Liberty shall be lovers,
The continuance of Equality shall be comrades.

These shall tie and band stronger than hoops of iron,
35 I, extatic, O partners! O lands! henceforth with the love of lovers tie you.

I will make the continent indissoluble,
I will make the most splendid race the sun ever yet shone upon,
I will make divine magnetic lands.

I will plant companionship thick as trees along all the rivers of America,
 and along the shores of the great lakes, and all over the prairies,
40 I will make inseparable cities, with their arms about each other's necks.

For you these, from me, O Democracy, to serve you, ma femme!
For you! for you, I am trilling these songs.

 1860   1860 (1881)

Thoughts—2: "Of Waters, Forests, Hills."

Of waters, forests, hills,
Of the earth at large, whispering through medium of me;

 35. extatic] Misspelled throughout *LG* 1860.
 39. companionship] In a footnote to "Democratic Vistas" (*CPW*, p. 247) WW
wrote that "fervid comradeship [will] counterbalance and offset . . . our mate-
rialistic and vulgar American democracy. . . . I say democracy infers such loving
comradeship as its most inevitable twin or counterpart."
 THOUGHTS] "Thoughts—2" and "Thoughts—4" (which follows) each lost its
separate identity after *LG* 1867. They are here reproduced in the original text of *LG*
1860, where they appeared among the seven untitled poems of the cluster called
"Thoughts." Of these, "3," "5," and "7" survived in the final edition without sub-
stantial change. "Thoughts, 1" and "6," excluded from *LG*, are both included
above. But in *LG* 1871 appeared a seven-line poem entitled "Thoughts," of
which the first stanza was the first line of "Thoughts—4" (*q.v.* below) and
the second stanza was the entire original text of "2" as given above. In 1881
Whitman revised this as a five-line stanza by discarding the first two lines of

Of vista—Suppose some sight in arriere, through the formative chaos,
    presuming the growth, fulness, life, now attained on the journey;
(But I see the road continued, and the journey ever continued;)
Of what was once lacking on the earth, and in due time has become
    supplied—And of what will yet be supplied,   5
Because all I see and know, I believe to have purport
    in what will yet be supplied.

1860   1867 (1881)

Thoughts—4: "Of Ownership . . .".

Of ownership—As if one fit to own things could not at pleasure enter upon
    all, and incorporate them into himself or herself;
Of Equality—As if it harmed me, giving others the same chances and
    rights as myself—As if it were not indispensable to my own rights
    that others possess the same;
Of Justice—As if Justice could be any thing but the same ample law, ex-
    pounded by natural judges and saviours,
As if it might be this thing or that thing, according to decisions.

1860   1867 (1881)

Bathed In War's Perfume.

Bathed in war's perfume—delicate flag!
(Should the days needing armies, needing fleets, come again,)
O to hear you call the sailors and the soldiers! flag like a beautiful woman!

"Thoughts—2." See "Thoughts" in the cluster "By the Roadside." MS in Huntington.
    3. arriere] Given without accent in all editions.
    THOUGHTS] See footnote for "Thoughts—2" just preceding. When Whitman in
1871 transferred to that poem the first line of "Thoughts—4," he temporarily set
aside the remnant of this poem. In 1881 he recovered two small epigrams, each
entitled "Thought" in the new cluster of the *Leaves* called "By the Roadside." Lines
3 and 4 became the second poem of that cluster entitled "Thought"; line 2 became the
third so named (see LG text above).
    PERFUME] First appeared in 1865, in *Drum-Taps*, where it was identical with
the present text except for the absence of the second line. It reappeared in the "Drum-
Taps" section of LG 1867; in Rossetti's English edition of 1868 it was entitled "The
Flag." In LG 1871 Whitman added the second line and made this the title poem of a
cluster of seven poems saluting the flag, which appeared with several other retrospec-
tive clusters of poems following the "Drum-Taps" cluster. As a seven line poem,
without further change, it persisted in LG 1872 and 1876, but not in later editions.

O to hear the tramp, tramp, of a million answering
     men! O the ships they arm with joy!
5 O to see you leap and beckon from the tall masts of ships!
O to see you peering down on the sailors on the decks!
Flag like the eyes of women.

1865   *1876*

Solid, Ironical, Rolling Orb.

Solid, ironical, rolling orb!
Master of all, and matter of fact!—at last I accept your terms;
Bringing to practical, vulgar tests, of all my ideal dreams,
And of me, as lover and hero.

1865   *1876*

Up, Lurid Stars!

Up, lurid stars! martial constellation!
Change, tattered cloth—your silver group withdrawing;
Bring we threads of scarlet, in vacant spots resetting,
    Thirty-four stars, red as blood.

5 World, take good notice! the silver group has vanished;
Notice clustering now, as coals of molten iron,
Time, warning baleful, off these western shores,
    Thirty-four stars, red as blood.

(*1865*)   *1865* (*1881*)

ORB] First appeared in *Drum-Taps* (1865); reappeared without change of text or title in all successive editions of LG before the 1881 edition, from which it was excluded. After the 1867 edition, it was removed from the "Drum-Taps" cluster and appeared in the fifth cluster of "Leaves of Grass" poems, which emphasized the nature of experience.

STARS] The present text, not before published, is related to the five-line poem, "World Take Good Notice," in *Drum-Taps* (1865), which is an intensified version of the same idea and symbol. The version shown here is transcribed from an unpublished MS (Feinberg). An earlier or more primitive MS (Yale) was reproduced in facsimile by J. H. Johnston in *Century Magazine*, 2nd ser., XLIX (1911), 532; reprinted in Emory Holloway's Inclusive LG, Notes, p. 652. The Johnston text is also in two stanzas, but the refrains are comparatively more crude, the phrasing less finished, and the wording more remote from the final choice. Comparison with "World Take Good Notice" (LG text) may be rewarding.

ME] Appeared in *Sequel to Drum-Taps* (1865–1866), p. 17; reprinted in the same position in LG 1867; excluded from later editions.

Not My Enemies Ever Invade Me.

Not my enemies ever invade me—no harm to my pride from them I fear;
But the lovers I recklessly love—lo! how they master me!
Lo! me, ever open and helpless, bereft of my strength!
Utterly abject, grovelling on the ground before them.

1865–1866   *1867*

This Day, O Soul.

This day, O Soul, I give you a wondrous mirror;
Long in the dark, in tarnish and cloud it lay—But the
       cloud has pass'd, and the tarnish gone;
. . . Behold, O Soul! it is now a clean and bright mirror,
Faithfully showing you all the things of the world.

1865–1866   *1876*

When I Read the Book.

When I read the book, the biography famous;
And is this, then, (said I,) what the author calls a man's life?
And so will some one, when I am dead and gone, write my life?
(As if any man really knew aught of my life;
As if you, O cunning Soul, did not keep your secret well!)   5

1867   *1867 (1881)*

soul] First published in *Sequel to Drum-Taps* (1865–1866), p. 19, this poem
appeared in the same position, unaltered, among the poems of the "Drum-Taps"
group in LG 1867. It was not included in LG 1871, but incorporated in the new
volume of that year, *Passage to India* (p. 119). It survived in the *Passage to India*
supplements—in LG 1872 and in *Two Rivulets* (1876), the companion volume to LG
1876. The poem was excluded from LG 1881 but it is related in idea with "My
Picture-Gallery," which then appeared. Both resemble in phraseology a passage in
MS (*ca.* 1855); see below in "Uncollected Poems"—"Pictures," lines 10–11.

book] In 1871 the poet took the poem above from the "Leaves of Grass" section
of the 1867 edition, in which it first appeared (p. 268), and included it among a new
group of "Inscriptions," then numbering nine small poems, which he placed at the
front of the 1871 volume. Dropping line 5, the last line of the original poem above, he
replaced it with three lines (see the ninth Inscription). If the new poem was a
better inscription, the earlier was a poem in which genuine power and insight were
concentrated in the last line.

Lessons.

There are who teach only the sweet lessons of peace and safety;
But I teach lessons of war and death to those I love,
That they readily meet invasions, when they come.

1871   1871

Ashes of Soldiers: Epigraph.

Again a verse for sake of you,
You soldiers in the ranks—you Volunteers,
Who bravely fighting, silent fell,
To fill unmention'd graves.

1871   1876

One Song, America, Before I Go.

One song, America, before I go,
I'd sing, o'er all the rest, with trumpet sound,
For thee—the Future.

I'd sow a seed for thee of endless Nationality;
5   I'd fashion thy Ensemble, including Body and Soul;
I'd show, away ahead, thy real Union, and how it may be accomplish'd.

(The paths to the House I seek to make,
But leave to those to come, the House itself.)

LESSONS] Appeared in the volume, *Passage to India* (1871), p. 116. It was
absent from issues of that volume bound in as supplements to LG 1872 and *Two
Rivulets* (1876); it was not included in the final collection of LG 1881.
    EPIGRAPH] No epigraph originally preceded "Ashes of Soldiers," then entitled
"Hymn of Dead Soldiers," in *Drum-Taps* (1865) and in the "Drum-Taps" supple-
ment, LG 1867. In the new volume, *Passage to India* (1871), this epigraph appeared
in italics above the poem, now revised, entitled "Ashes of Soldiers" and employed as
title poem for a cluster of memorial poems. The epigraph remained in the "Passage
to India" supplements of 1872 and 1876 but was canceled when "Ashes of Soldiers"
was included with the poems finally selected for LG 1881.
    GO] One of two prefatory poems in *As a Strong Bird on Pinions Free* (1872),
WW's poem for the Dartmouth College Commencement, June 26, 1872. The volume

Belief I sing—and Preparation;
As Life and Nature are not great with reference to the Present only,   10
But greater still from what is yet to come,
Out of that formula for Thee I sing.

1872   1876

Souvenirs of Democracy.

The business man, the acquirer vast,
After assiduous years, surveying results, preparing for departure,
Devises houses and lands to his children—bequeaths
    stocks, goods—funds for a school or hospital,
Leaves money to certain companions to buy tokens,
    souvenirs of gems and gold;
Parceling out with care—And then, to prevent all cavil,   5
His name to his testament formally signs.

But I, my life surveying,
With nothing to show, to devise, from its idle years,
Nor houses, nor lands—nor tokens of gems or gold for my friends,
Only these Souvenirs of Democracy—In them—in
    all my songs—behind me leaving,   10
To You, whoever you are, (bathing, leavening this leaf especially with my
    breath—pressing on it a moment with my own hands;
—Here! feel how the pulse beats in my wrists!—
    how my heart's-blood is swelling, contracting!)
I will You, in all, Myself, with promise to never desert you,
To which I sign my name,

Walt Whitman

1872   1876 (1881)

became a Supplement in *Two Rivulets* (1876). The Commencement poem was
revised under the title, "Thou Mother with Thy Equal Brood" (*q.v.* above) in LG
1881, including a fundamental revision (in stanza 1) of the present poem, given
here in its original form and separate identity. Cf. "Souvenirs of Democracy."

DEMOCRACY] Cf. footnote to "One Song, America, Before I Go," immediately
above. This was the second of the two inscription poems to *As a Strong Bird on
Pinions Free*, the volume of 1872 and the supplement of 1876. In LG 1881, "My
Legacy" appeared as an avatar of this poem, in a revision essentially changing the
motivation (*q.v.*). Reducing the poem by four lines, the poet canceled out the
bequest of himself—with the theatrical signature in facsimile—and made his legacy
only "a bundle of songs . . . of camps and soldiers."

From My Last Years.

From my last years, last thoughts I here bequeath,
Scatter'd and dropt, in seeds, and wafted to the West,
Through moisture of Ohio, prairie soil of Illinois—through
      Colorado, California air,
For Time to germinate fully.

1876   *1876*

In Former Songs.

In former songs Pride have I sung, and Love, and passionate, joyful Life,
But here I twine the strands of Patriotism and Death.

And now, Life, Pride, Love, Patriotism and Death,
To you, O FREEDOM, purport of all!
5   (You that elude me most—refusing to be caught in songs of mine,)
I offer all to you.

2

'Tis not for nothing, Death,
I sound out you, and words of you, with daring tone—embodying you,
In my new Democratic chants—keeping you for a close,
10 For last impregnable retreat—a citadel and tower,
For my last stand—my pealing, final cry.

1876   *1876*

YEARS] Appeared only once, in *Two Rivulets* (1876), p. 30. MS, Feinberg. Quoted in Bucke, N, *and* F, II: 43, p. 67.

SONGS] Appeared only once, in *Two Rivulets* (1876), p. 31.

SHIP] In *LG* 1876, four "intercalations," as WW called them, were clippings from galley sheets pasted on blank end pages of some early issues and printed in the same position in later impressions of this edition. Only one survived in *LG* 1891–2 ("When the Full-Grown Poet Came," *q.v.* above). "The Beauty of the Ship" (*LG* 1876, p. 247) appeared before publication in a preview of the forthcoming volumes (*LG* and *TR*); this resembles WW's style and was published in the New York *Daily Tribune*, February 19, 1876. However, this poem and "After an Interval"—another "intercalation" which follows below—were excluded in later editions. The fourth "intercalation," "As In a Swoon" (*q.v.*, below) appeared again in *GBF* (1891), not in *LG*. But it was among poems WW included in *Complete Prose Works* (1892).

INTERVAL] See note, "The Beauty of the Ship," immediately above. "After an

The Beauty of the Ship.

When, staunchly entering port,
After long ventures, hauling up, worn and old,
Batter'd by sea and wind, torn by many a fight,
With the original sails all gone, replaced, or mended,
I only saw, at last, the beauty of the Ship.   5

1876   *1876*

After an Interval.

(Nov. 22, 1875, midnight—Saturn and Mars in conjunction.)

After an interval, reading, here in the midnight,
With the great stars looking on—all the stars of Orion looking,
And the silent Pleiades—and the duo looking of Saturn and ruddy Mars;
Pondering, reading my own songs, after a long interval,
        (sorrow and death familiar now,)
Ere closing the book, what pride! what joy! to find them,   5
Standing so well the test of death and night!
And the duo of Saturn and Mars!

1876   *1876*

Two Rivulets.

Two Rivulets side by side,
Two blended, parallel, strolling tides,
Companions, travelers, gossiping as they journey.

Interval" was another of the "intercalations" in LG 1876, pasted on the blank end of
page 369 in early issues and printed in the same position in later impressions. It also
appeared earlier in a preview of the forthcoming editions (presumably written by
WW) in the New York *Daily Tribune*, February 19, 1876, but it was not included in
LG editions after 1876.
   3. Mars] On Whitman's strict observation of this conjunction, Joseph Beaver
says (*Walt Whitman—Poet of Science*, 1951, p. 30): "Whitman had been watching
the two bodies draw nearer together . . . *The Nautical Almanac* lists the phe-
nomenon at 10:45 P.M. on November 21 . . . November 22 was the day that
began" as the poet watched. Praised as a naturalist by his friend, the naturalist
Burroughs, Whitman knew that the ancients regarded Saturn as the grave patron of
the sowing, Mars as god of war, Orion as the man-shaped constellation who slew
Artemis for violating the chaste Aurora, and the Pleiades as seven sisters of whom
one was hidden in shame for having loved a mortal.
   RIVULETS] Appeared only once, in the miscellany, *Two Rivulets* (1876), twin-

For the Eternal Ocean bound,
5   These ripples, passing surges, streams of Death and Life,
Object and Subject hurrying, whirling by,
The Real and Ideal,

Alternate ebb and flow the Days and Nights,
(Strands of a Trio twining, Present, Future, Past.)

10 In You, whoe'er you are, my book perusing,
In I myself—in all the World—these ripples flow,
All, all, toward the mystic Ocean tending.

(O yearnful waves! the kisses of your lips!
Your breast so broad, with open arms, O firm, expanded shore!)
       1876   *1876* (*1881*)

Or from That Sea of Time.

1

Or, from that Sea of Time,
Spray, blown by the wind—a double winrow-drift of weeds and shells;
(O little shells, so curious-convolute! so limpid-cold and voiceless!
Yet will you not, to the tympans of temples held,
5   Murmurs and echoes still bring up—Eternity's music, faint and far,
Wafted inland, sent from Atlantica's rim—strains for the
        Soul of the Prairies,

Whisper'd reverberations—chords for the ear of the West,
        joyously sounding

born with a new edition of *LG*, in uniform binding. In *Two Rivulets*, selected prose
essays alternated with clusters of poems not yet incorporated in *LG*. Lines 4 and 5 of
the poem served as epigraph on the title page, and the whole poem captioned the first
cluster of fourteen new or recent poems. "Two Rivulets" suggested Whitman's
commingled prose and verse themes, in unity with all things "for the eternal ocean
bound." A version of the tercet of the present poem, lines 10–12, and also passages
from another "excluded" poem, "Or From That Sea of Time," appear in "As Con-
sequent," a later poem of genuine power, to which Whitman gave the first place in
the new cluster of "Autumn Rivulets" in *LG* 1881. Quoted before publication in a
preview of the new volumes (probably by WW) in New York *Daily Tribune*,
February 19, 1876.

    TIME] Appeared in the volume *Two Rivulets* (1876), p. 16. See footnote above
for the poem "Two Rivulets," from which, as from the present poem, the poet
incorporated lines in the new poem, "As Consequent," which appeared in *LG* 1881

Your tidings old, yet ever new and untranslatable;)
Infinitesimals out of my life, and many a life,
(For not my life and years alone I give—all, all I give;)   10
These thoughts and Songs—waifs from the deep—here, cast high and dry,
Wash'd on America's shores.

2

Currents of starting a Continent new,
Overtures sent to the solid out of the liquid,
Fusion of ocean and land—tender and pensive waves,   15
(Not safe and peaceful only—waves rous'd and ominous too,
Out of the depths, the storm's abysms—Who knows whence?
          Death's waves,
Raging over the vast, with many a broken spar and tatter'd sail.)

    1876   *1876 (1881)*

As in a Swoon.

As in a swoon, one instant,
Another sun, ineffable, full-dazzles me,
And all the orbs I knew—and brighter, unknown orbs;
One instant of the future land, Heaven's land.

    1876   *1891 (1892)*

[Last Droplets].

Last droplets of and after spontaneous rain,
From many limpid distillations and past showers;

and survived into the final edition. That poem comprised twelve lines of new composi-
tion, followed by the motivating tercet from "Two Rivulets" and the entire eighteen
lines of the present poem, with slight verbal alterations. However, Whitman reversed
the order of stanzas, making the first stanza of the present poem the last stanza of the
new poem (*q.v.*).

    2. winrow-drift] Corrected in 1881, windrow-drift.

    SWOON] Appeared first in LG 1876, pasted on the blank end of page 207 in
some early copies; and printed in the same location in the later issue. It did not re-
appear in LG 1881. It was included in *Good-Bye My Fancy* (1891), but not when
that supplement was added to LG 1891–2. In the same year WW included it
among the few poems which he preserved in *Complete Prose Works 1892*. See note,
"The Beauty of the Ship," above.

    DROPLETS] This quatrain concluded the second paragraph of the poet's light-
hearted "Preface Note" to *Good-Bye My Fancy* (1891)—a "little cluster," he wrote,

(Will they germinate anything? mere exhalations as they all are—
        the land's and sea's—America's;
Will they filter to any deep emotion? any heart and brain?)

1891   *1891*

Ship Ahoy!

In dreams I was a ship, and sail'd the boundless seas,
Sailing and ever sailing—all seas and into every port, or out
        upon the offing,
Saluting, cheerily hailing each mate, met or pass'd, little or big,
"Ship ahoy!" thro' trumpet or by voice—if nothing more, some
        friendly merry word at least,
5   For companionship and good will for ever to all and each.

1891   *1891 (1892)*

For Queen Victoria's Birthday.

*An American arbutus bunch to be put in a little vase on
the royal breakfast table, May 24th, 1890.*

Lady, accept a birth-day thought—haply an idle gift and token,
Right from the scented soil's May-utterance here,
(Smelling of countless blessings, prayers, and old-time thanks,) *
A bunch of white and pink arbutus, silent, spicy, shy,
From Hudson's, Delaware's, or Potomac's woody banks.

1891 (1892)

* NOTE.—Very little, as we Americans stand this day, with our sixty-
five or seventy millions of population, an immense surplus in the treasury, and
all that actual power or reserve power (land and sea) so dear to nations—very
little I say do we realize that curious crawling national shudder when the "Trent
affair" promis'd to bring upon us a war with Great Britain—follow'd unques-
tionably, as that war would have, by recognition of the Southern Confederacy

of what "during the last two years I have sent out . . . , certain chirps . . . which
now I may as well gather and put in fair type while able to see . . . , for here I am
(each successive fortnight getting stiffer and stuck deeper) much like some hard-
cased dilapidated grim ancient shell-fish or time-banged conch . . . ." The poem
did not appear in the "Annex," "Good-Bye My Fancy," in *LG* 1891–2.

AHOY] First appeared in *Good-Bye My Fancy* (1891), p. 28, the poet's last
volume of miscellaneous prose and poetry. It was not among the poems which also
appeared in the "Good-Bye My Fancy," annex to *LG* 1891–1892. However, it was one
of a few poems reprinted in *CPW* (1892).

BIRTHDAY] Although Whitman's footnote to this poem (*q.v.*) reveals his ap-
preciation of Queen Victoria's presumed foresight, he did not include this tribute
among the poems from the 1891 *Good-Bye My Fancy* which made up the final

from all the leading European nations. It is now certain that all this then inevitable train of calamity hung on arrogant and peremptory phrases in the prepared and written missive of the British Minister, to America, which the Queen (and Prince Albert latent) positively and promptly cancell'd; and which her firm attitude did alone actually erase and leave out, against all the other official prestige and Court of St. James's. On such minor and personal incidents (so to call them,) often depend the great growths and turns of civilization. This moment of a woman and a queen surely swung the grandest oscillation of modern history's pendulum. Many sayings and doings of that period, from foreign potentates and powers, might well be dropt in oblivion by America—but never *this*, if I could have my way.   W. W.

L of G.

Thoughts, suggestions, aspirations, pictures,
Cities and farms—by day and night—book of peace and war,
Of platitudes and the commonplace.

For out-door health, the land and sea—for good will,
For America—for all the earth, all nations, the common people,   5
(Not of one nation only—not America only.)

In it each claim, ideal, line, by all lines, claims, ideals temper'd;
Each right and wish by other wishes, rights.

  1891   *1891 (1892)*

After the Argument.

A group of little children with their ways and chatter flow in,
Like welcome, rippling water o'er my heated nerves and flesh.

  1891   *1891 (1892)*

"Annex" to LG the same year. It was reproduced, however, in the CPW (1892). It appeared first in Philadelphia *Public Ledger*, May 22, 1890.

L OF G] The poet's apostrophe to his book appeared in his last collection of new work, *Good-Bye My Fancy* (1891), and was collected, along with the prose of this volume, in CPW (1892). It was not among the poems of this volume that appeared in the concluding annex of LG 1891–1892. MS, Feinberg Collection.

ARGUMENT] Appeared with other poems at the blank end of a prose piece on page 44 of *Good-Bye My Fancy* (1891), and again on the corresponding page of CPW (1892); not included in LG 1891–1892. MS in Feinberg Collection. First appeared in *Lippincott's Magazine*, March, 1891, with three poems retained in GBF Annex of LG—"Sounds of the Winter," "Sail out for Good, Eidólon Yacht," and "The Unexpressed."

For Us Two, Reader Dear.

Simple, spontaneous, curious, two souls interchanging,
With the original testimony for us continued to the last.

1891   1891 (1892)

DEAR] Appeared with other poems at the blank end of a prose piece on page 44 of
Good-Bye My Fancy (1891) and on the corresponding page of CPW (1892); not
included in LG 1891–2. MS in Feinberg Collection.

VERSES] Originally the concluding stanza of "Song of the Answerer," which
appeared without title in LG 1855, as "Poem of the Poet" in LG 1856, and "Leaves
of Grass—3" in LG 1860, the source of the present text. These lines, discarded in
LG 1867, epitomize one of Whitman's fundamental ideas. In LG 1881, "Song of

PASSAGES EXCLUDED FROM
LEAVES OF GRASS POEMS

[*The Writer of Melodious Verses*].

Do you think it would be good to be the writer of melodious verses?
Well, it would be good to be the writer of melodious verses;
But what are verses beyond the flowing character you could have? or be-
      yond beautiful manners and behavior?
Or beyond one manly or affectionate deed of an apprentice-boy? or old
      woman? or man that has been in prison, or is likely to be in prison?

1855   1860

[*This Is the Breath for America*].

This is the breath for America, because it is my breath,
This is for laws, songs, behavior,
This is the tasteless water of Souls—this is the true sustenance.

This is for the illiterate, and for the judges of the Supreme Court, and for
      the Federal capitol and the State capitols,
And for the admirable communes of literats, com-
      posers, singers, lecturers, engineers, and savans,   5
And for the endless races of work-people, farmers, and seamen.

1855   1860

the Answerer" was completed by the addition of canto II, formerly an LG poem,
"The Indications" (see note, "Song of the Answerer").

AMERICA] First appeared in LG 1855, p. 24, as a five-line stanza following that
text now represented in canto 17, line 360, of "Song of Myself" (then untitled). It
reappeared in the same relative position in LG 1856 ("Poem of Walt Whitman, An
American") and finally in LG 1860 ("Walt Whitman," stanzas 83 and 84), the
source of the present six-line text—in which the first line was reconstructed as two.

[*Élèves I Salute You!*].

I see the approach of your numberless gangs—I see
    you understand yourselves and me,
And know that they who have eyes and can walk are
    divine, and the blind and lame are equally divine,
And that my steps drag behind yours, yet go before them,
And are aware how I am with you no more than I am with everybody.

   1855   1860

[*Old Forever New Things*].

Flour-works, grinding of wheat, rye, maize, rice—the barrels and the half
    and quarter barrels, the loaded barges, the high piles on wharves
    and levees,
Bread and cakes in the bakery, the milliner's ribbons, the dress-maker's
    patterns, the tea-table, the home-made sweetmeats;
Cheap literature, maps, charts, lithographs, daily and weekly newspapers,
The column of wants in the one-cent paper, the news
    by telegraph, amusements, operas, shows,
The business parts of a city, the trottoirs of a city when thousands of well-
5   dressed people walk up and down,
The cotton, woolen, linen you wear, the money you make and spend,
Your room and bed-room, your piano-forte, the stove and cook-pans;

SALUTE YOU] This title was the initial line of the passage in *LG* 1860, the source of this text. It was permanently retained, but in *LG* 1867 the other four lines were replaced by a single new line which foreshadowed and linked with the substance of the following passage, now canto 39 of "Song of Myself." The original passage, here restored, compactly suggested Whitman's persistent belief in the breeding of human values in humble origins, and it illustrated a familiar role in which the poet-prophet addressed "students" (here élèves—the French word appeared without accents in some *LG* texts).

THINGS] In the first *LG* 1855 edition. the untitled "A Song for Occupations" immediately followed the incomparable initial poem, "Song of Myself," which it resembled in its familiar spirit and its emphasis on the bountiful common life, found especially in its first title (*LG* 1856), "Poem of the Daily Work of the Workmen and Workwomen of these States." After 1860 the revisions introduced a more formal spirit reflected in new titles emphasizing the class, "Workingmen," and their "Occupations." Among exclusions in *LG* 1867 was a section of eighty consecutive lines which, in the last edition, would have stood between lines 3 and 5 of canto 5 (*q.v.*). The unit of nine lines here extracted, with their effective free association of what WW, in the beginning of the entire passage, had called the "old forever new things," conveyed the living sense of a way of life now lost.

The house you live in, the rent, the other tenants, the deposit in the savings-
      bank, the trade at the grocery,
The pay on Seventh Day night, the going home, and the purchases; . . .

   1855   *1860*

[*The Teeming Mother of Mothers*].

Her daughters, or their daughters' daughters—who
      knows who shall mate with them?
Who knows through the centuries what heroes may come from them?

In them, and of them, natal love—in them that
      divine mystery, the same old beautiful mystery.
Have you ever loved the body of a woman?
Have you ever loved the body of a man?   5

Your father—where is your father?
Your mother—is she living? have you been much with her? and has she
      been much with you?

   1855   *1860*

[*This Is Mastering Me*].

O Christ! This is mastering me!
Through the conquered doors they crowd. I am possessed.

What the rebel said, gayly adjusting his throat to the rope-noose,
What the savage at the stump, his eye-sockets empty,
      his mouth spirting whoops and defiance,

MOTHERS] In LG 1855 to 1860, this passage appeared after what is now line 3, canto 8 of "I Sing the Body Electric." The theme of inherited maternal responsibility for the race had been stated above; the present lyrical recapitulation was eroded by revisions in 1867 and 1881 to a remnant of lines 4 and 5. The text is "Enfans d'Adam—3," stanzas 28–30 (LG 1860), with the omission of the irrelevant last line.

ME] These lines from page 80–81, LG 1860, followed the present canto 36, line 944 of "Song of Myself" (then "Walt Whitman"). They served to epitomize the poet's compassionate involvement in the episodes of human fortitude and faith portrayed in the previous three cantos. In LG 1867 WW excluded all except the first two lines, which now became the opening of canto 37. In LG 1881 he replaced the rhetorical first line with one more appropriate and retained the significant second line, which was added in LG 1860, the source of the present text.

5 What stills the traveller come to the vault at Mount Vernon,
 What sobers the Brooklyn boy as he looks down the shores of the Wall-
   about and remembers the Prison Ships,
 What burnt the gums of the red-coat at Saratoga
   when he surrendered his brigades,
 These become mine and me every one—and they are but little,
 I become as much more as I like.

 1855   *1860* [*1867*]

[*O Hot-Cheek'd and Blushing*].

O hot-cheek'd and blushing! O foolish hectic!
O for pity's sake, no one must see me now! my clothes
   were stolen while I was abed,
Now I am thrust forth, where shall I run?

Pier that I saw dimly last night, when I look'd from the windows!
Pier out from the main, let me catch myself with you,
5   and stay—I will not chafe you,
I feel ashamed to go naked about the world.

 6. Wallabout] See "The Wallabout Martyrs," WW's poem dealing with these victims of the American Revolution (*LG*, "Sands at Seventy").
 7. the red-coat] British General John Burgoyne (1722–1792), having gallantly fought his way down the Hudson Valley, was not supported midway, as promised, by Howe's army from New York; the surrender terms (October 17, 1777) at Saratoga provided that he and his army be withdrawn from the war.
 BLUSHING] This poem and the next, "Now Lucifer Was Not Dead," appeared in the first edition of *LG* as cantos in "The Sleepers." They remained in the same positions, with slight alterations, in all *LG* editions before 1881. In *LG* 1876, the source of the present text, the cantos of the present poem were numbered "7" and "8" (stanzas 21–24). They gave the homogeneous impression of an independent poem following the present first canto of "The Sleepers" (*q.v.*). From the beginning "The Sleepers" was one of WW's greatest reflective poems, imbued with a mystic vision of man and nature, in language and idea uniquely his own. By contrast, both the "Lucifer" poem (see below) and the present one are violent although powerful lyrics. Whitman must have felt strongly their impropriety in the context to exclude them after twenty years, but why he did not then retain these little masterpieces as independent poems remains a puzzle. "O Hot-Cheek'd and Blushing" represents a high order of symbolism, with a compelling psychological movement, from the dream fantasy of being denuded in public to the symbolic suggestion of a sexual act. This poem deserves close study.
 2. abed] In the preceding passage of "The Sleepers" the bardic narrator is a participant; beginning his journey into night, he says, "I dream . . . all the dreams of the other dreamers."
 4. Pier] At night the deserted wooden piers of the harbor of Brooklyn and New York—and often the waters beneath them—became hiding places.
 8. laps] In its primitive use, the "lap" of a garment was the skirt or coat-tail which covered the sitting person from belly to knee; hence, "to lap" was to conceal or even (of a child) "to cuddle."

I am curious to know where my feet stand and what this is flooding me,
    childhood or manhood—and the hunger that crosses the bridge be-
    tween.

The cloth laps a first sweet eating and drinking,
Laps life-swelling yolks—laps ear of rose-corn, milky and just ripen'd;
The white teeth stay, and the boss-tooth advances in darkness,   10
And liquor is spill'd on lips and bosoms by touching
    glasses, and the best liquor afterward.

1855   *1876*

[*Now Lucifer Was Not Dead*].

Now Lucifer was not dead—or if he was, I am his sorrowful terrible heir;
I have been wrong'd—I am oppress'd—I hate him that oppresses me,
I will either destroy him, or he shall release me.

Damn him! how he does defile me!
How he informs against my brother and sister, and
    takes pay for their blood!   5

      9. rose-corn] The erotic symbols in the closing lines are among Whitman's most striking. Cf. the small, rosy ear of the popcorn, then familiar.
      10. stay] In the context of the passage—to support or to remain steadfast, or to wait. Compare "white teeth" with "boss-tooth" below.
      10. boss-tooth] As compared with the factually descriptive term, "white teeth," note that "boss" originally designated a swelling or extension of an internal organ; later, any protuberance of "embossed" book covers, metal ornaments, armor, etc. Whitman also used the vernacular sense: the "boss" workman, who commands. Cf. "ear of rose-corn," line 9.
      DEAD] This poem, like "O Hot-Cheek'd and Blushing" (*q.v.* above), was retained in "The Sleepers" without significant verbal change from the first *LG* edition until 1876, the source of the present text, which was then the whole of canto 14, following what is now canto 6 of "The Sleepers" (see *LG* above). "Lucifer" represents the height of Whitman's lyric invective. The poet speaking is not "simple separate" Whitman, but the voice of a bard, hurling maledictions against the oppressors of a people. Lucifer is traditionally the personification of evil and the symbol of "fallen" man; specifically, as Venus the morning star before sunrise, this "light-bringer" fell from heaven. The prophet Isaiah authorized the western literary tradition of the fallen archangel banished by God; he further identified a Babylonian ruler destroyed by the wrath of God for persecuting His people: "How art thou fallen from Heaven, O Lucifer, son of the morning! how art thou cut down to the ground, which didst weaken the nations" (Isaiah XIV:12). Evidently Whitman's ballad-like initial phrase, "Now Lucifer was not dead," recalls Isaiah's double meaning, which he specifically directed against the supporters of slavery, for whom the lurking power of avenging justice was biding its time to strike (lines 7–8).
      1. Lucifer] The Latin name ("Light-bearer") defined his earliest mythical function as the morning star; but see the note above for the function of the myths of the fallen one.
      2. oppresses me] Four pieces of MS (Virginia) showing revisions of this passage before *LG* 1855, strengthen its interpretation as an invective against slavery.

How he laughs when I look down the bend, after the
    steamboat that carries away my woman!

Now the vast dusk bulk that is the whale's bulk, it seems mine;
Warily, sportsman! though I lie so sleepy and slug-
    gish, the tap of my flukes is death.

1855   *1876*

[*Invocation: To Workmen and Workwomen*].

Come closer to me;
Push close, my lovers, and take the best I possess;
Yield closer and closer, and give me the best you possess.

This is unfinish'd business with me—How is It with you?
5   (I was chill'd with the cold types, cylinder, wet paper between us.)

Male and Female!
I pass so poorly with paper and types, I must pass with
    the contact of bodies and souls.

American masses!
I do not thank you for liking me as I am, and liking the touch of me—I
    know that it is good for you to do so.

1855   *1876*

Fragment 146 shows almost the final development of the first two stanzas. It begins
significantly, "Black Lucifer," comparing the outcast angel with the degraded race.
Fragment 144 identifies the poem with the voice of the unfranchised Negro: "I am a
curse: a negro thinks me / You cannot speak for yourself, negro / I dart like a snake
from your mouth." The Negro cries: "Iron necklace and red sores of the shoulders I
do not mind / Hopple at the ankle will not detain me." He calls vengeance down from
heaven—"Topple upon him, Light! for you seem to me all one lurid curse!" However
the MS does not show the terrifying malediction of the last stanza of this poem, repre-
senting one of Whitman's most powerful expressions (cf. note below on line 7, "the
whale's bulk"). In his transcription of Fragment 147 (N *and* F, 42, line 2), Bucke
erroneously reports "defile" as "defy."
    7. Whale's bulk] The Old Testament suggests an inherent natural avenger, a
principle of retributive justice, or the "wrath of God"; these are represented as
mammoths resembling the hippopotamus (behemoth, Job 40:15–24), or dragons, or
whales, among them leviathan, of whom Job said, "When he raiseth himself . . . he
maketh the sea to boil like a pot." Cf. Melville's *Moby Dick* (1851), four years
earlier than *LG*; and see Job 3:8; Psalm 74:14; and Isaiah 27:1.
    INVOCATION] This passage served to introduce "A Song for Occupations" under
various titles in every *LG* edition through *LG* 1876. In the first (1855) edition the

[*Facts Showered Over with Light*].

An American literat fills his own place,
He justifies science—did you think the demon-
    strable less divine than the mythical?
He stands by liberty according to the compact of
    the first day of the first year of These States,
He concentres in the real body and soul, and in the pleasure of things,
He possesses the superiority of genuineness over fiction and romance,   5
As he emits himself, facts are showered over with light,
The day-light is lit with more volatile light—the
    deep between the setting and rising sun goes deeper many fold,
Each precise object, condition, combination, process, exhibits a beauty—the
    multiplication-table its, old age its, the carpenter's trade its, the
    grand-opera its,
The huge-hulled clean-shaped Manhattan clipper
    at sea, under steam or full sail, gleams with unmatched beauty,
The national circles and large harmonies of gov-
    ernment gleam with theirs,   10
The commonest definite intentions and actions with theirs.

1856   *1856*

poem appeared (pp. 56–64) untitled, as the second in the volume. In *LG* 1881 WW gave the poem its final title, and replaced this initial salutation by three lines empha- sizing the "eternal meanings of the trades and tools." By contrast these canceled lines expressed the poet's comradely identification with workingmen, although in *LG* 1860 he inserted two exclamations, "Male and Female!" and "American masses!" em- phasizing the broad and impersonal intention of his fervent words.

LIGHT] This passage appeared once only, in the first edition of "By Blue On- tario's Shore" (*LG* 1856) in the present canto 10 following line 17. Like other parts of the poem, this resembles, in its last eight lines, the phraseology of the "Preface" of *LG* 1855 (cf. the ninth paragraph before the end). It is a unified ex- pression of a fundamental idea in *LG*, but it enlarges the central theme, the poet, to the man of letters in general (see note, "literat"). The parent poem, entitled "Poem of the Many in One" in *LG* 1856, appeared in all later *LG* editions, with concurrent alterations and two changes of title before 1881.

1. literat] A learned person, a man of letters, presumably a writer of prose. Cf. Latin, *litteratus*, anglicized as "literatus"—and note Poe's popularization of the plural form in *The Literati of New York City* (1846). An acceptable English substitute was the noun "literate"; hence Whitman's "literat" was not entirely new coinage. He used as plural both "literats" and "literati."

[*Language for America*].

Language-using controls the rest;
Wonderful is language!
Wondrous the English language, language of live men,
Language of ensemble, powerful language of resistance,
5   Language of a proud and melancholy stock, and of all who aspire,
Language of growth, faith, self-esteem, rudeness, justice, friendliness,
      amplitude, prudence, decision, exactitude, courage,
Language to well-nigh express the inexpressible,
Language for the modern, language for America.

   1856   *1856*

[*His Shape Arises*].

His shape arises,
Arrogant, masculine, näive, rowdyish,
Laugher, weeper, worker, idler, citizen, countryman,
Saunterer of woods, stander upon hills, summer
    swimmer in rivers or by the sea,
Of pure American breed, of reckless health, his body perfect, free from
    taint from top to toe, free forever from headache and dyspepsia,
5   clean-breathed,
Ample-limbed, a good feeder, weight a hundred and eighty pounds, full-
    blooded, six feet high, forty inches round the breast and back,
Countenance sun-burnt, bearded, calm, unrefined,

AMERICA] This passage, like "Facts Showered Over With Light" (*q.v.* above, and see note) appeared only once, in the first version of "By Blue Ontario's Shores," in *LG* 1856. This also was a separate and homogeneous section, and it followed the passage just mentioned after an interval of five lines, at a point which would occur between canto 10 and canto 11 in the final *LG* text. The passage gains interest from Whitman's persistent concern with the power of language and the development of an American speech. The gist of it was expressed in prose in the Preface to *LG* 1855, the third paragraph from the conclusion.

ARISES] The *LG* 1856 "Broad-Axe Poem" and *LG* 1860 "Chants Democratic—2" concluded with stanzas 33 and 34—these eighteen lines and a following group of eleven. In *LG* 1867, in "Song of the Broad-Axe," stanza 33, the present text, was

Reminder of animals, meeter of savage and gentleman on equal terms,
Attitudes lithe and erect, costume free, neck gray
    and open, of slow movement on foot,
Passer of his right arm round the shoulders of his
    friends, companion of the street,   10
Persuader always of people to give him their sweetest
    touches, and never their meanest,
A Manhattanese bred, fond of Brooklyn, fond of Broadway, fond of the
    life of the wharves and the great ferries,
Enterer everywhere, welcomed everywhere, easily understood after all,
Never offering others, always offering himself, corrob-
    orating his phrenology,
Voluptuous, inhabitive, combative, conscientious, alimentive, intuitive, of
    copious friendship, sublimity, firmness, self-esteem, comparison,
    individuality, form, locality, eventuality,   15
Avowing by life, manners, works, to contribute illus-
    trations of results of The States,
Teacher of the unquenchable creed, namely, egotism,
Inviter of others continually henceforth to try their strength against his.

1856   *1860*

[*A Thought of the Clef of Eternity*].

What can the future bring me more than I have?
Do you suppose I wish to enjoy life in other spheres?

I say distinctly I comprehend no better sphere than this earth,
I comprehend no better life than the life of my body.

excluded (between the concluding cantos, 11 and 12). The passage gains in in-
terest as an unmistakable self-portrait.

    ETERNITY] This passage gives the impression of being an independent poem, but
in LG 1856 the present nineteen-line text was the first "movement" (lines 4–22) of a
thirty-four-line poem (finally titled, "On the Beach at Night Alone," 1871). The ex-
clusion of this passage reduced the parent poem in LG 1867 to fifteen lines (finally
fourteen in LG 1881)—an objective treatment of the "similitude" which "interlocks"
all existence, past, present, and eternal. By comparison the present poem is subjective,
representing the poet's faith in individual survival coexistent in an eternity of other
experience. The poem is here preserved with the strangeness and strength which
characterized its last appearance as part of "Leaves of Grass—12" in LG 1860.

5 I do not know what follows the death of my body,
   But I know well that whatever it is, it is best for me,
   And I know well that whatever is really Me shall live
         just as much as before.

   I am not uneasy but I shall have good housing to myself,
   But this is my first—how can I like the rest any better?
10 Here I grew up—the studs and rafters are grown parts of me.

   I am not uneasy but I am to be beloved by young and
         old men, and to love them the same,
   I suppose the pink nipples of the breasts of women with whom I shall sleep
         will touch the side of my face the same,
   But this is the nipple of a breast of my mother, always near and always
         divine to me, her true child and son, whatever comes.

   I suppose I am to be eligible to visit the stars, in my time,
   I suppose I shall have myriads of new experiences—and that the experience
15   of this earth will prove only one out of myriads;
   But I believe my body and my Soul already indicate those experiences,
   And I believe I shall find nothing in the stars more majestic and beautiful
         than I have already found on the earth,
   And I believe I have this night a clew through the universes,
   And I believe I have this night thought a thought of the clef of eternity.

   1856   *1860 (1881)*

[*What Do You Hear, Walt Whitman?*].

I hear the inimitable music of the voices of mothers,
I hear the persuasions of lovers,

10. studs and rafters] This homely phrase for the framework of a human body reminds us that the poet in his youth worked with his father as a house-builder.
12. touch the side of my face] In 1856 read: "taste the same to my lips." Nursing mothers learn that the suckling babe will first seek the nipple with its cheek. This was then nursery folklore; now it is established in pediatrics as the "rooting complex," described by C. A. and M. M. Aldrich (*ca.* 1938).
19. clef] As a music lover Whitman uses the word strictly, as an indication or sign of the precise "tonality" (here, "meaning") of eternity. Cf. the phrase, "a clew through the universe," just above.
HEAR] These lines on things heard were among those of the present canto 3 of "Salut Au Monde" in its first edition, LG 1856 ("Poem of Salutation"). In that and other early editions the poem was not strictly a global courtesy or salutation from the "new" continent to older and disparate cultures—as it was in the final revision, LG 1881, of which the penultimate lines read: "Toward you all, in America's name, / I raise high the perpendicular hand." The majority of the excluded lines expressed the

I hear quick rifle-cracks from the riflemen of East
     Tennessee and Kentucky, hunting on hills, . . .
I hear the Virginia plantation chorus of negroes,
     of a harvest night, in the glare of pineknots,
I hear the strong baritone of the 'long-shore-men of Manahatta,—I hear
     the stevedores unlading the cargoes, and singing,   5
I hear the screams of the water-fowl of solitary northwest lakes,
I hear the rustling pattering of locusts, as they strike the grain and grass
     with the showers of their terrible clouds, . . .
I hear the bugles of raft-tenders on the streams of Canada . . .

1856   *1876*

[*You Dumb Beautiful Ministers*].

We descend upon you and all things—we arrest you all;
We realize the soul only by you, you faithful solids and fluids;
Through you color, form, location, sublimity, ideality;
Through you every proof, comparison, and all the sug-
     gestions and determinations of ourselves.

1856   *1876*

[*Which Are My Miracles?*].

What shall I give? and which are my miracles?

Realism is mine—my miracles—Take freely,
Take without end—I offer them to you wherever your
     feet can carry you, or your eyes reach. . . .

poet's appreciation of things American. The present passage, a group of associated
aural images, constituted eight of the original sixteen lines between the present lines
3 and 11 of canto 3. Line 7 still remains in *LG*, but its locusts were expatriated to
Syria. This was the most impressive of the excluded passages, excepting the almost
unsurpassed transposition from canto 7, in *LG* 1881, "A Paumanok Picture."

MINISTERS] This quatrain appeared in the first edition of "Crossing Brooklyn
Ferry," *LG* 1856, then entitled "Sun-Down Poem." The passage introduced the
section of eleven lines concluding the poem, later treated as a separate canto which in
LG 1876 was numbered 12. The cantos were then consolidated, this passage was
dropped, and the remaining seven lines concluded canto 9, still the last. The passage
here reproduced appeared with only minor punctuation changes, from the beginning
until 1876, the source of this text. The point of these lines is associated with "the im-
palpable sustenance of me from all things" (line 6 of the poem). Cf. Emerson's "Each
and All."

MIRACLES] Twelve lines pruned from the original thirty-five of "Miracles"
(*q.v.*), then entitled "Poem of Perfect Miracles" in *LG* 1856. The resulting concen-

Or whether I go among those I like best, and that
    like me best—mechanics, boatmen, farmers,
5 Or among the savans—or to the soiree—or to the opera,
Or stand a long while looking at the movements of machinery,
Or behold children at their sports,
Or the admirable sight of the perfect old man, or the perfect old woman,
Or the sick in hospitals, or the dead carried to burial,
10 Or my own eyes and figure in the glass; . . .

Every spear of grass—the frames, limbs, organs, of
    men and women, and all that concerns them,
All these to me are unspeakably perfect miracles.

  1856   *1876*

[*You Who Celebrate Bygones!*].

But now I also, arriving, contribute something: . . .
Advancing, to give the spirit and the traits of new
    Democratic ages, myself, personally,
(Let the future behold them all in me—Me, so puzzling and contradictory
    —Me, a Manhattanese, the most loving and arrogant of men;)
I do not tell the usual facts, proved by records and documents,
What I tell, (talking to every born American,) requires no further proof
    than he or she who will hear me, will furnish, by silently meditating
5   alone; . . .

tration of the remaining twenty-three lines intensified the effect of "Miracles." The
first three lines, which introduced the original poem, were verbally improved, then
dropped after *LG* 1867—the textual source for the present reading. Lines 4 to 10
followed the present line 14 of "Miracles" and the concluding couplet followed line
20; they remained without essential change until canceled in *LG* 1881.

    5. savans] WW seemingly preferred this vernacular form of "savants."
    5. soiree] Cf. "soirée," French term for an evening reception or party.
    BYGONES] First a thirteen-line poem in *LG* 1860, No. 10 in the cluster, "Chants
Democratic"; in *LG* 1867 given its final title, "To a Historian," in the supplement,
"Songs Before Parting," where it was shortened by the exclusion of the present six
lines (originally 4, 6 to 9, and 11). As the fifth of the "Inscriptions," the parent poem
appeared in all later editions. The original distribution of the excluded lines was such
that they represent a generalization of the whole poem, but the intimacy of their tone
did not accord with Whitman's effort during this period to assume the communal
objectivity of the national bard.

I illuminate feelings, faults, yearnings, hopes—I
      have come at last, no more ashamed nor afraid . . .

1860   *1860*

[*Creations for Strong Artists*].

There they stand—I see them already, each poised and in its place,
Statements, models, censuses, poems, dictionaries, biographies, essays,
      theories—How complete! How relative and interfused! No one
      supersedes another;
They do not seem to me like the old specimens,
They seem to me like Nature at last, (America has
      given birth to them, and I have also;)
They seem to me at last as perfect as the animals,
      and as the rocks and weeds—fitted to them,   5
Fitted to the sky, to float with floating clouds—to
      rustle among the trees with rustling leaves,
To stretch with stretched and level waters, where ships silently sail in the
      distance.

1860   *1860*

[*Readers to Come*].

Indeed, if it were not for you, what would I be?
What is the little I have done, except to arouse you?

ARTISTS] "Laws for Creations" (*q.v.*) emphasizes Whitman's organic theory of
the creative artist and his artifact. In the original eighteen-line version (LG 1860,
"Chants Democratic—13"), lines 6 to 12 shown above perhaps overemphasized the
created work instead of the creative act, which was the central idea. They were ex-
cluded in LG 1867. Considered independently, they seem a unified statement of the
concept that the artifact is to be organically related to the form of nature originally
observed by the artist, and in the transcendental sense, that all natural facts are
"interfused."

  COME] Seven lines, of the sixteen in "Poets To Come," when it first appeared in
LG 1860 as "Chants Democratic—14," p. 186. In LG 1867, where the parent poem was
given its present title, these lines were omitted (following the present line 4),
evidently to clarify or intensify the meaning. The parent poem, which became one
of the "Inscriptions" in 1881, now gives the impression of a salute to "poets to
come," for whom this author left "a few indicative words." The two excluded stanzas,
however, emphasize the emotional condition of WW poignantly destined to speak on
winds of time to ears unborn.

I depend on being realized, long hence, where the broad fat prairies spread,
    and thence to Oregon and California inclusive,
I expect that the Texan and the Arizonian, ages hence, will understand me,
I expect that the future Carolinian and Georgian will understand me and
5   love me,
I expect that Kanadians, a hundred, and perhaps many hundred years
    from now, in winter, in the splendor of the snow and woods, or on
    the icy lakes, will take me with them, and permanently enjoy them-
    selves with me.

Of to-day I know I am momentary, untouched—I
    am the bard of the future. . . .

    1860   1860

[*O Bitter Sprig!*].

O bitter sprig! Confession sprig!
In the bouquet I give you place also—I bind you in,
Proceeding no further till, humbled publicly,
I give fair warning, once for all.

5 I own that I have been sly, thievish, mean, a prevaricator, greedy, derelict,
And I own that I remain so yet.

What foul thought but I think it—or have in me the
    stuff out of which it is thought?
What in darkness in bed at night, alone or with a companion?

    1860   1860

SPRIG!] These eight lines were the first three stanzas of "You Felons on Trial in
Courts" in its first appearance as No. 13 in the cluster, "Leaves of Grass" in LG 1860.
In LG 1867 this passage was excluded and the remaining sixteen lines (reorganized
as fifteen) were retained without significant change. The version of the poem
retained is somewhat less specifically confessional, but each conveys a psychological
compulsion having some religious interest, adroitly expressed.
    DEPARTURE] "As the Time Draws Nigh," called "To My Soul" when it first
appeared in LG 1860, concluded with this stanza of thirteen lines, of which only four
lines, the second and the last three, fundamentally revised, were reflected in the final
text. In LG 1867 it was entitled "As Nearing Departure" (now a nine-line poem)

[*Nearing Departure*].

O Soul!
Then all may arrive but to this;
The glances of my eyes, that swept the daylight,
The unspeakable love I interchanged with women,
My joys in the open air—my walks through the Mannahatta,   5
The continual good will I have met—the curious
        attachment of young men to me,
My reflections alone—the absorption into me from the landscape, stars,
        animals, thunder, rain, and snow, in my wanderings alone,
The words of my mouth, rude, ignorant, arrogant—my many faults and
        derelictions,
The light touches, on my lips, of the lips of my comrades, at parting,
The tracks which I leave, upon the side—walks and fields,   10
May but arrive at this beginning of me,
This beginning of me—and yet it is enough, O Soul,
O Soul, we have positively appeared—that is enough.

1860   *1860 (1881)*

[*Let None Be Content with Me*].

Yet not me, after all—let none be content with me,
I myself seek a man better than I am, or a woman better than I am,
I invite defiance, and to make myself superseded,
All I have done, I would cheerfully give to be trod under foot, if it might
        only be the soil of superior poems.

in the supplement, "Songs Before Parting." In 1871 it appeared with its present
title and eight-line text, and with new punctuation in 1881. The complete last stanza
in the 1860 version, given above, has independent vitality and interest.

    ME] These stanzas first appeared in "So Long!"—a new poem concluding LG
1860 and all later LG editions. In the poem's second edition, LG 1867, Whitman
divided the text by cantos, excluding from the first canto stanzas 4 and 5 and 7 to 9
as given here, exuberantly introducing two themes—progress and individualism—
expressed with more emotional propriety in later passages.

    5. for good] Then quite prevalently used in the vernacular sense, meaning
"finally" or "completely"; e.g., "he quit school for good."

5 I have established nothing for good,
   I have but established those things, till things farther onward shall be
           prepared to be established,
   And I am myself the preparer of things farther onward. . . .

   Once more I enforce you to give play to yourself—and not to depend on me,
           or on any one but yourself,
   Once morè I proclaim the whole of America for each
           individual, without exception.

   As I have announced the true theory of the youth,
10   manhood, womanhood, of The States, I adhere to it;
   As I have announced myself on immortality, the body,
           procreation, hauteur, prudence,
   As I joined the stern crowd that still confronts the President with menacing
           weapons—I adhere to all,
   As I have announced each age for itself, this moment I set the example.

   I demand the choicest edifices to destroy them;
15 Room! room! for new far-planning draughtsmen and engineers!
   Clear that rubbish from the building-spots and the paths!

       1860   1860

           [*Realities, the Visions of Poets*].

   For we support all, fuse all,
   After the rest is done and gone, we remain;
   There is no final reliance but upon us;
   Democracy rests finally upon us, (I, my brethren, begin it,)
   And our visions sweep through eternity.

       1860   1876

       POETS] In LG 1881, the final text of the reflective "As I Walked These Broad
   Majestic Days," WW excluded the last stanza. This passage, in all editions since the
   poem first appeared (LG 1860, "Chants Democratic—21") had functioned to elabo-
   rate the preceding idea that, among the modern realities, "the visions of poets" were
   still "the most solid." The text is that of 1876.
       FINAL] Originally stanza 31 in "A Word Out of the Sea" (LG 1860; in 1871
   entitled "Out of the Cradle, Endlessly Rocking") this passage, excepting the first
   two lines, was discarded in LG 1881. Critics wonder why Whitman canceled these
   impressive lines and they speculate on the actuality of the "well-beloved." (See Allen,
   Handbook, 142–143.) Comparing the excluded passage with the remaining twenty-

[*Give Me the Clue . . . the Word Final*].

O give me the clue! (it lurks in the night here somewhere;)
O if I am to have so much, let me have more!
O a word! O what is my destination? (I fear it is henceforth chaos;)
O how joys, dreads, convolutions, human shapes, and all
      shapes, spring as from graves around me!
O phantoms! you cover all the land and all the sea!   5
O I cannot see in the dimness whether you smile or frown upon me;
O vapor, a look, a word! O well-beloved!
O you dear women's and men's phantoms!

  1860   *1876*

[*Orators Fit for America*].

. . . . O I see arise orators fit for inland America;
And I see it is as slow to become an orator as to become a man;
And I see that all power is folded in a great vocalism.

Of a great vocalism, the merciless light thereof shall
      pour, and the storm rage,
Every flash shall be a revelation, an insult,   5
The glaring flame on depths, on heights, on suns, on stars,
On the interior and exterior of man or woman,
On the laws of Nature—on passive materials,
On what you called death—(and what to you therefore was death,
As far as there can be death.)   10

  1860   *1876*

---

two lines which conclude the poem, one remembers the poet's two companions "under the dusky cedars" ("When Lilacs Last in the Dooryard Bloom'd," canto 14): one, the "thought of death"—the immediate shock—as in the present lines the dread of "destination" and "chaos"; and the other, "the sacred knowledge," able to "fuse the song" of "two together" and "death." The poem was included in the 1871 *Passage to India* volume and supplements to LG 1872 and TR 1876, source of the present text.

AMERICA] These stanzas in the 1876 text were the peroration concluding "Chants Democratic—12" in LG 1860. They were not retained by WW when, in 1881, he used the four preceding stanzas of the poem as canto 1 of "Vocalism," whose second canto was also an 1860 poem, numbered "21" in a "Leaves of Grass" cluster. "To Oratists" in LG 1876 is the source of the present text.

[*Epigraph: A Carol of Harvest*].

A song of the good green grass!
A song no more of the city streets;
A song of farms—a song of the soil of fields.

A song with the smell of sun-dried hay, where the
      nimble pitchers handle the pitch-fork;
5 A song tasting of new wheat, and of fresh-husk'd maize.

  1871   *1876*

[*With Additional Songs Every Spring*].

(With additional songs—every spring will I now strike
      up additional songs,
Nor ever again forget, these tender days, the chants of
      Death as well as Life;) . . .

To tally, drenched with them, tested by them,
Cities and artificial life, and all their sights and scenes,
5 My mind henceforth, and all its meditations—my recitatives,
My land, my age, my race, for once to serve in songs,
(Sprouts, tokens ever of death indeed the same as life,) . . .

  1871   *1876*

HARVEST] "A Carol of Harvest for 1867" appeared in *Passage to India* (1871) and remained in that collection when it was bound in as a supplement to LG 1872 and TR 1876. In these editions the two stanzas above introduced the poem in the manner of an epigraph (though not so designated). The poems of this supplement were redistributed in various parts of LG 1881, and the "Carol" appeared as "The Return of the Heroes," without this preliminary song.

SPRING] "Warble for Lilac Time" appeared in the first edition of *Passage to India* (1871) and in the later PI supplements of LG and TR. In LG 1881 the final text (*q.v.*) omitted the present stanzas after lines 21 and 24, respectively. The charming parent poem dealt entirely with the memorial significance of the lilac (Lincoln) and the shy preparations made by the gradual spring to celebrate love by

[*Aroused and Angry*].

Aroused and angry,
I thought to beat the alarum, and urge relentless war:
But soon my fingers fail'd me, my face droop'd, and I resign'd myself,
To sit by the wounded and soothe them, or silently watch the dead.

1871   1876 (1881.)

this crowning luxuriance. However, the rejected lines reproduced above deserve attention as an expression of Whitman's compulsion to compare nature's life and death with mankind's artifices.

ANGRY] The 1865 *Drum-Taps*, which had been a supplement in some issues of LG 1867, was incorporated as a cluster in the *Leaves* of 1871. Whitman then inserted this epigraph in italics beneath the boldface heading, "Drum-Taps." Without change it reappeared in LG 1872 and 1876, the present text. In 1881 the poet interpolated this passage into "The Wound-Dresser," another poem in the "Drum-Taps" cluster, combining the four lines into three (lines 4–6), printed in roman between parentheses without verbal changes. The original epigraph is worth recovering as a lyrical epitomy of a major phase of WW's experience of the war.

Uncollected Poems

Pictures.

In a little house pictures I keep, ¶ many pictures
    hanging suspended—It is not a fixed house,
It is round—it is but a few inches from one side of it to the other side,
But behold! it has room enough—in it, hundreds and thousands,—all the
    varieties;
—Here! do you know this? This is cicerone himself;
And here, see you, my own States—and here the world itself,
    $\genfrac{}{}{0pt}{}{\text{bowling}}{\text{rolling}}$ through the air;

5

And there, on the walls hanging, portraits of women and men, carefully
    kept,
This is the portrait of my dear mother—and this of my father—and these
    of my brothers and sisters;
This, (I name every thing as it comes,) This is a beautiful statue, long
    lost, dark buried, but never destroyed—now found by me, and
    restored to the light;
There five men, a group of sworn friends, stalwart, bearded, determined,
    work their way together through all the troubles and impediments
    of the world;

PICTURES] Text first published in Emory Holloway's "Whitman's Embryonic
Verse," SWR, x (July, 1925) 28–40. Reprinted, with introduction and notes by
Holloway, as *Pictures: An Unpublished Poem* (New York, The June House; London,
Faber & Gwyer, 1927). MS: Yale.

The faded and battered twenty-nine-page notebook in which these lines were en-
tered in ink, with penciled emendations, is an important preliminary, a kind of aus-
pice of LG 1855, some of whose lines are here in rough draft. In its leaves the poet
recorded the experience of his days and especially of his reading in phrases that
had not achieved the rhythmic power to come, but which nevertheless reveal the
poetic process, its pictures (images) being stored in the gallery of his mind.

Underneath the title, centered on the first page of the notebook, the poet added in
pencil: "Break all this into several 'pictures.' Walt Whitman." He persisted in such
exercises after the appearance of LG 1855, as a number of fragments indicate (see

And that is a magical wondrous mirror—long it lay clouded, but the
    cloud has passed away,   10

It is now a clean and bright mirror—it will show you all you can con-
    ceive of, all you wish to behold;

And that is a picture intended for Death—it is very beautiful—(what
    else is so beautiful as Death?)

There is represented the Day, full of effulgence—full of seminal lust
    and love—full of action, life, strength, aspiration,

And there the Night, with mystic beauty, full of love also, and full of
    greater life—the Night, showing where the stars are;

There is a picture of Adam in Paradise—side by side with him Eve, (the
    Earth's bride and the Earth's bridegroom;)   15

There is an old Egyptian temple—and again, a Greek temple, of white
    marble;

There are Hebrew prophets chanting, rapt, extatic—and here is Homer;

Here is one singing canticles in an unknown tongue, before the Sanskrit
    was,

And here a Hindu sage, with his recitative in Sanskrit;

And here the divine Christ expounds eternal truth—expounds the Soul,   20

And here he appears en-route to Calvary, bearing the cross—See you,
    the blood and sweat streaming down his face, his neck;

And here, behold, a picture of once imperial Rome, full of palaces—
    full of masterful warriors;

And here, the questioner, the Athenian of the classical time—Socrates,
    in the market place,

(O divine tongue! I too grow silent under your elenchus,

(O you with bare feet, and bulging belly! I saunter along, following you,
    and obediently listen;)   25

And here Athens itself,—it is a clear forenoon,

---

below). In 1861 "Pictures" was to be a poem in the projected but never published
Banner at Daybreak (Allen, 267); and many years later in *The American* for
October 30, 1880, WW published "My Picture-Gallery" (reprinted in LG 1881),
whose six lines are a redaction of the first lines of the notebook, constituting an
eloquently simple statement about his poetic storehouse that had served him so well.
See also "Pictures" (Hanley MS) among the "Unpublished Poems."

    1. many] The paragraph symbol is WW's own, later inserted in the MS,
perhaps to indicate a new line at this point.

    4. cicerone] A guide for sightseers.

    17. Homer] Compare this and the following four lines with "Salut au Monde,"
lines 37–40.

    24. elenchus] A syllogism that refutes a proposition by proving the opposite.
Note a close variant of lines 23–25 in the fragments following the poem.

Young men, pupils, collect in the gardens of a favorite master, waiting for him.

Some, crowded in groups, listen to the harangues or arguments of the elder ones,

Elsewhere, single figures, undisturbed by the buzz around them, lean against pillars, or within recesses, meditating, or studying from manuscripts,

Here and there, couples or trios, young and old, clear-faced, and of perfect
30   physique, walk with twined arms, in divine friendship, happy,

Till, beyond, the master appears advancing—his form shows above the crowd, a head taller than they,

His gait is erect, calm and dignified—his features are colossal—he is old, yet his forehead has no wrinkles,

Wisdom undisturbed, self-respect, fortitude unshaken, are in his expression, his personality;

Wait till he speaks—what God's voice is that, sounding from his mouth?
35 He places virtue and self-denial above all the rest,

He shows to what a glorious height the man may ascend,

He shows how independent one may be of fortune—how triumphant over fate;

—And here again, this picture tells a story of the Olympic games,

See you, the chariot races? See you, the boxers boxing, and the runners running?

See you, the poets off there reciting their poems and tragedies, to crowds
40   of listeners?

—And here, (for I have all kinds,) here is Columbus setting sail from Spain on his voyage of discovery;

This again is a series after the great French revolution,

This is the taking of the Bastile, the prison—this is the execution of the king.

This is the queen on her way to the scaffold—those are guillotines;

But this opposite, (abruptly changing,) is a picture from the prison-ships
45   of my own old city—Brooklyn city;

And now a merry recruiter passes, with fife and drum, seeking who will join his troop;

And there is an old European martyrdom—See you, the cracking fire— See the agonized contortions of the limbs, and the writhing of the lips! See the head thrown back;

45. prison-ships] WW referred to these prison ships in the 1855 version of section 37, "Song of Myself." See also "The Wallabout Martyrs" in the group "Sands at Seventy."
54. observant and singing] Clearly, a picture of the poet himself.

And here is a picture of triumph—a General has returned, after a
    victory—the city turns out to meet him,
And here is a portrait of the English king, Charles the First, (are you
    a judge of physiognomy?)
And here is a funeral procession in the country,   50
A beloved daughter is carried in her coffin—there follow the parents
    and neighbors;
And here, see you—here walks the Boston truckman, by the side of his
    string-team—see the three horses, pacing stately, sagacious, one
    ahead of another;
—And this—whose picture is this?
Who is this, with rapid feet, curious, gay—going up and down Man-
    nahatta, through the streets, along the shores, working his way
    through the crowds, observant and singing?
And this head of melancholy Dante, poet of penalties—poet of hell;   55
But this is a portrait of Shakespear, limner of feudal European lords
    (here are my hands, my brothers—one for each of you;)
—And there are wood-cutters, cutting down trees in my north east
    woods—see you, the axe uplifted;
And that is a picture of a fish-market—see there the shad, flat-fish, the
    large halibut,—there a pile of lobsters, and there another of oysters;
Opposite, a drudge in the kitchen, working, tired—and there again the
    laborer, in stained clothes, sour-smelling, sweaty—and again black
    persons and criminals;
And there the frivolous person—and there a crazy enthusiast—and there
    a young man lies sick of a fever, and is soon to die;   60
This, again, is a Spanish bull-fight—see, the animal with bent head,
    fiercely advancing;
And here, see you, a picture of a dream of despair, (—is it unsatisfied
    love?)
Phantoms, countless, men and women, after death, wandering;
And there are flowers and fruits—see the grapes, decked off with vine-
    leaves;
But see this!—see where graceful and stately the young queen-cow
    walks at the head of a large drove, leading the rest;   65
And there are building materials—brick, lime, timber, paint, glass, and
    iron, (so now you can build what you like;
And this black portrait—this head, huge, frowning, sorrowful—is Luci-
    fer's portrait—the denied God's portrait,

59. criminals] Compare this and the following line with *N and F*, 1, item 16.
67. Lucifer's portrait] This and the following three lines are early workings of
the ideas that went into the making of "Chanting the Square Deific," and, among
"Passages Excluded" above, see "Now Lucifer Was Not Dead."

(But I do not deny him—though cast out and rebellious, he is my God
 as much as any;)

And again the heads of three other Gods—the God Beauty, the God
 Beneficence, and the God Universality, (they are mine, also;)

And there an Arab caravan, halting—See you, the palm trees, the
70 camels, and the stretch of hot sand far away;

And there are my woods of Kanada, in winter, with ice and snow,

And here my Oregon hunting-hut, See me emerging from the door,
 bearing my rifle in my hand;

But there, see you, a reminiscence from over sea—a very old Druid,
 walking the woods of Albion;

And there, singular, on ocean waves, downward, buoyant, swift, over
 the waters, an occupied coffin floating;

And there, rude grave-mounds in California—and there a path worn in
75 the grass,

And there hang painted scenes from my Kansas life—and there from
 what I saw in the Lake Superior region;

And here mechanics work in their shops, in towns—There the car-
 penter shoves his jack-plane—there the blacksmith stands by his
 anvil, leaning on his upright hammer;

This is Chicago with railroad depots, with trains arriving and departing
 —and, in their places, immense stores of grain, meat, and lumber;

And here are my slave-gangs, South, at work upon the roads, the women
 indifferently with the men—see, how clumsy, hideous, black, pout-
 ing, grinning, sly, besotted, sensual, shameless;

And this of a scene afar in the North, the arctic—those are the corpses
 of lost explorers, (no chaplets of roses will ever cap their icy graves
 —but I put a chaplet in this poem, for you, you sturdy English
80 heros;)

But here, now copious—see you, here, the Wonders of eld, the famed
 Seven,

The Olympian statue this, and this the Artemesian tomb,

Pyramid this, Pharos this, and this the shrine of Diana,

These Babylon's gardens, and this Rhodes' high-lifted marvel,

85 (But for all that, nigh at hand, see a wonder beyond any of them,

73. Druid] Compare line 95, "Salut au Monde."
77. hammer] The phrases describing manual labor become much more vivid in
"Song of Myself," as Holloway has noted.
78. lumber] Compare this line with line 6, "Mediums."
95. Iroquois] Compare line 48 "Our Old Feuillage."

Namely yourself—the form and thoughts of a man,

A man! because all the world, and all the inventions of the world are but the food of the body and the soul of one man;)

And here, while ages have grown upon ages,

Pictures of youths and greybeards, Pagan, and Jew, and Christian,

Some retiring to caves—some in schools and piled libraries,　　　　90

To pore with ceaseless fervor over the myth of the Infinite,

But ever recoiling, Pagan and Jew and Christian,

As from a haze, more dumb and thick than vapor above the hot sea;

—And here now, (for all varieties, I say, hang in this little house,)

A string of my Iroquois, aborigines—see you, where they march in single file, without noise, very cautious, through passages in the old woods;　　95

　　Picture

O a husking-frolic in the West—see you, the large rude barn—see you, young and old, laughing and joking, as they husk the ears of corn;

And there in a city, a stormy political meeting—a torch-light procession —candidates avowing themselves to the people;

And here is the Lascar I noticed once in Asia—here he remains still, pouring money into the sea, as an offering to demons, for favor;

And there, in the midst of a group, a quell'd revolted slave, cowering,

See you, the hand-cuffs, the hopple, and the blood-stain'd cowhide;　　100

And there hang, side by side, certain close comrades of mine—a Broadway stage-driver, a lumberman of Maine, and a deck-hand of a Mississippi steamboat;

And again the young man of Mannahatta, the celebrated rough,

(The one I love well—let others sing whom they may—him I sing for a thousand years!)

And there a historic piece—see you, where Thomas Jefferson of Virginia sits reading Rousseau, the Swiss, and compiling the Declaration of Independence, the American compact;

And there, tall and slender, stands Ralph Waldo Emerson, of New England, at the lecturer's desk lecturing,　　105

And there is my Congress in session in the Capitol—there are my two Houses in session;

96. husking-frolic] Compare line 755, "Song of Myself."

102. rough] In the 1855 version of line 497, "Song of Myself," the poet was to refer to himself as "Walt Whitman, an American, one of the roughs, a kosmos."

105. lecturing] This line was added in pencil on the opposite blank page of the notebook. WW had heard Emerson lecture, as he noted in "Old Actors, Singers, Shows, etc. in New York," *Prose Works*, ii, 697, Coll W.

And here, behold two war-ships, saluting each other—behold the smoke,
    bulging, spreading in round clouds from the guns and sometimes
    hiding the ships;

And there, on the level banks of the James river in Virginia stand the
    mansions of the planters;

And here an old black man, stone-blind, with a placard on his hat, sits
    low at the corner of a street, begging, humming hymn-tunes nasally
    all day to himself and receiving small gifts;

And this, out at sea, is a signal-bell—see you, where it is built on a reef,
110   and ever dolefully keeps tolling, to warn mariners;

And this picture shows what once happened in one of Napoleon's greatest
    battles,

(The tale was conveyed to me by an old French soldier,)

In the height of the roar and carnage of the battle, all of a sudden, from
    some unaccountable cause, the whole fury of the opposing armies
    subsided—there was a perfect calm,

It lasted almost a minute—not a gun was fired—all was petrified,

115 It was more solemn and awful than all the roar and slaughter;

—And here, (for still I name them as they come,) here are my timber-
    towers, guiding logs down a stream in the North;

And here a glimpse of my treeless llanos, where they skirt the Colorado,
    and sweep for a thousand miles on either side of the Rocky Moun-
    tains;

And there, on the whaling ground, in the Pacific, is a sailor, perched at
    the top-mast head, on the look out,

(You can almost hear him crying out, *There-e-'s white water*, or *The-e-re's
    black skin;*)

But here, (look you well,) see here the phallic choice of America, a full-
120   sized man or woman—a natural, well-trained man or woman

(The phallic choice of America leaves the finesse of cities, and all the
    returns of commerce or agriculture, and the magnitude of geog-
    raphy, and achievements of literature and art, and all the shows of
    exterior victory, to enjoy the breeding of full-sized men, or one full-
    sized man or woman, unconquerable and simple;)

—For all those have I in a round house hanging—such pictures have I—
    and they are but little.

For wherever I have been, has afforded me superb pictures,

121. phallic choice] This line sums up the theme of the "Children of Adam" group
of *LG*, and in the notebook WW—as if anticipating its potentiality—had penciled the

And whatever I have heard has given me perfect pictures,
And every hour of the day and night has given me copious pictures,   125
And every rod of land or sea affords me, as long as I live, inimitable
    pictures.

1924   1927

[*Miscellaneous Fragments for "Pictures"*].

And there a ship, long in a foreign port—but now, see you?
She is now ready to leave for home—
Short stay a-peak is her anchor,
See the pleased looks of the sailor men;

—MS: Feinberg.

And here a tent and domestic utensils of the primitive Chippewa, the
    red-faced aborigines,
See you, the tann'd buffalo hides, the wooden dish, the drinking vessels
    of horn;

—MS: Feinberg.

In the gymnasium leaping and lifting from
And here arguing the questioner in the classical time—Socrates in the
    market place
(O divine tongue! I too grow silent under your elenchus!
O bare feet! O bulging belly! I saunter along by you and listen only.

—MS: Yale.

See—there is Epicurus—see the old philosoph in a porch teaching
His physique is full—his voice clear and sonorous—his phrenology per-
    fect,
He calls around him his school of young men—he gathers them in the
    street, or saunters with them along the banks of the river, arguing.

—N and F, I, 139; MS: U of P.

direction: "take this out a ¶ by itself."
    126. pictures] In N and F, I, item 26, WW has the line, "And to me each acre of
the land and sea exhibits marvellous pictures."

[*All that We Are*].

All that we are—the solid and liquid we are, we have advanced to,
We have advanced from what was our own cohesion and our own for-
      mation
We advance to just as much more, and just as much more.
Times suffices, and the laws suffice.—

5   Send any or all,—no matter what,
We have places for any and all—good places
We receive them, we have made preparation,
We have not only made preparation for a few developed persons
We have made preparation for undeveloped persons also

10   We effuse spirituality and immortality
We put a second brain to the brain,
We put second eyes to the eyes and second ears to the ears,
Then the drudge in the kitchen—then the laborer in his stained clothes—
      then the black person, criminals, barbarians—are no more inferior
      to the rest,
The frivolous and the blunderer are not to be laughed at as before,
The cheat, the crazy enthusiast, the unsuccessful man, come under the
15   same laws as any.—

1899   *1899*

[*I Am the Poet*].

I am the poet of reality
I say the earth is not an echo

ARE] Published, *N and F*, I: 14, 15, and 16, p. 12. MS: Trent. These fifteen lines
are written on a single sheet of yellow paper, showing many corrections in pencil and
ink, and although Dr. Bucke printed them as three separate pieces, they possess an
unmistakable unity of theme—both the eligibility and the promise of every soul. This
is the poet's most persistent note. The last three lines are variants of lines 59 and 60
of the pre-1855 notebook, "Pictures" (*q.v.*), thus attesting early composition.

POET] Published, *UPP*, II, pp. 69–70. MS: LC Whitman, No. 80. These lines are
written in pencil on two pages of WW's earliest extant notebook, dated 1847. The
bracketed last two lines are lightly canceled in the MS. The first line is affirmed by
line 483, "Song of Myself": "I accept Reality and dare not question it." Although
they are but part of a remarkable outpouring which is a main source of the first

Nor man an apparition;
But that all the things seen are real,
The witness and albic dawn of things equally real   5
I have split the earth and the hard coal and rocks and the solid bed of
  the sea
And went down to reconnoitre there a long time,
And bring back a report,
And I understand that those are positive and dense every one
And that what they seem to the child they are   10
[And the world is no joke,
Nor any part of it a sham]

 1921   1921

[O I Must Not Forget!].

O I must not forget!
To you I reach friendlily—

O I must not forget
To you I adhere!—

I do not flatter—I am not polite—but I adhere to you   5
Baffled, exiled, ragged, gaunt.

 1899   1899

[Love Is the Cause of Causes]

Love is the cause of causes,
Out of the vast, first Nothing

edition of LG, these lines have an effect of unity, of a finished poem.
  FORGET!] Published, N and F, I: 124, p. 39. MS: Barrett. Six untitled penciled
lines on a scrap of blue paper, probably composed before 1860, for in both diction
and concept they are remindful of the phrasing of such early poems as "Starting from
Paumanok" and "Song of the Open Road," and indeed they could serve as a motto or
epigraph for the latter.
  CAUSES] Published in "A Whitman Manuscript" by Emory Holloway, The
American Mercury, III (December, 1924), 475–480. MS: Lion. These eight lines
were inscribed in pencil on one page of a twenty-four page notebook with brown
paper covers, which may be dated 1853–1855. On an earlier page the poet had put
the same reflection in a prose paragraph with much the same phraseology, whose
stately rhetoric is still far from the rhythms of "Song of Myself."

The ebbless and floodless vapor from the nostrils of Death,
It asked of God with undeniable will,
5   Something to satisfy itself—
By then Chaos was staid with
And duly came from them a brood of beautiful children
Whom we call the laws of nature

     1924   *1924*

[*I Last Winter*].

I last winter observed the Snow on a spree with the north west wind;
And it put me out of conceit of fences and imaginary lines.—

     1899   *1899*

[*I Cannot Be Awake*].

I cannot be awake, for nothing looks to me as it did before,
Or else I am awake for the first time, and all before has been a mean sleep.

     1899   *1899*

Light and Air!

Nothing ugly can be disgorged—
Nothing corrupt or dead set before them,
But it becomes translated or enclothed
Into supple youth or a dress of living richness
5   spring gushing out from under the roots of an old tree
barn-yard, pond, yellow-jagged bank with white pebblestones

WINTER] Published, *N and F*, I: 105, p. 35. MS: Berg. Two untitled lines in ink with penciled corrections on a small scrap of paper. In the MS "north west wind" is substituted for "Wild Drake," which is the "wood-drake" observed by the poet in line 237 of "Song of Myself." Probably composed about 1855.

I CANNOT] Published, *N and F*, I: 170, p. 49. MS: unavailable. This exceptionally sharp epigram is a poem in itself.

AIR!] Published, *N and F*, I: 32, p. 16; also in facsimile, p. 45. *Catalogue of the Whitman Collection*, Duke University Library, 1945. MS: Trent. Given its own title by the poet, this composition is in effect a complete poem; and although the last six lines do not begin with capitals, their line structure is unmistakable. The references to pismire, wren, running blackberry, and cow crunching the grass relate the piece to lines 664–668, sec. 31 of "Song of Myself," but its theme is closer to the poem "This

timothy, sassafras, grasshopper, pismire, rail-fence
rye, oats, cucumbers, musk-melons, pumpkin-vine, long string of running
      blackberry—
regular sound of the cow crunching the grass—
the path worn in the grass—katy-did, locust, tree-toad, robin—wren—   10
   1899   *1945*

[*Of Your Soul*].

Of your soul I say truths to harmonize, if any thing can harmonize you,
Your body to me is sweet, clean, loving, strong, I am indifferent how it
      appears to others or to yourself,
Your eyes are more to me than poems, your lips do better than play music,
The lines of your cheeks, the lashes of your eyes, are eloquent to me,
The $\frac{\text{hold}}{\text{gripe}}$ of your hand is richer than riches.—   5
   1899   *1899*

[*What the Sun*].

What the sun and sky do to the senses
What the landscape and waters, hills free vistas to the eye
He has done to the soul
$\frac{\text{Though}}{\text{While}}$ ever the best remains untold
$\frac{\text{Though}}{\text{While}}$ the secret and the solving still are hidden   5
   1948   *1948*

Compost," a resemblance accented by the fact that in Bucke's transcript, it is
preceded by a line not now in the MS:

      Under this rank coverlid stretch the corpses of young men.

   SOUL] Published, *N and F*, I: 58, p. 26. MS: Barrett. These five fine lines are
written in ink on a small yellow scrap of paper. Complete in effect, they have the
directness and simplicity of the poet's most vigorous period—the middle or late
1850's.

   SUN] Published, *Wake 7* (Autumn, 1948), 18. MS: Barrett. This composition,
scribbled in pencil on a single leaf, is—despite its lack of punctuation and alternative
readings—a complete and striking reflection upon one of the attributes of the poet—
such as WW catalogued in his 1855 Preface.

[*Have You Supplied*].

Have you supplied the door of the house where the old one decayed away,
    and do not see that you also want your foundation and the roof?
Have you put only doors and windows to the house where they were
    crumbled?
Do you not see that the roof is also crumbled and this day, this night,
    may fall in ruins about your heads?
Do you not see that the old foundation beams of the floor have rotted
    under your feet, and who knows when they may break?

1899   *1899*

[*I Do Not Expect*].

I do not expect to see myself in present magazines, reviews, schools,
    pulpits and legislatures—but presently I expect to see myself in
    magazines, schools and legislatures—or that my friends after me
    will see me there.

1899   *1899*

Scantlings.

White, shaved, foreign, soft-fleshed, shrinking,
Scant of muscle, scant of love-power,
Sant [*sic*] of gnarl and knot, modest, sleek in costumes,
Averse from the wet of rain, from the fall of snow, from the grit of the
    stones and soil,

SUPPLIED] Published, N *and* F, 1: 171, p. 49. MS: Berg. These four lines in ink
are so crowded and intricately revised on a small scrap of paper that Bucke's
transcription mistakes the first line for two. Composition is probably early. For
another line possibly intended for this composition, see "The power by which . . ."
among the "Fragments" of this edition.

    I do not expect] Published, N *and* F, 1: 93, p. 32. MS unavailable.

SCANTLINGS] Published, N *and* F, 1: 20, p. 13. MS: Trent. These six lines, writ-
ten in pencil on a small piece of paper, are headed by WW's own title, and there
seems no question that they were intended as a complete poem, investing with vivid
phrasing the scorn that the poet also expressed in line 1079 of "Song of Myself" about

A pretty race, each one just like hundreds of the rest,   5
A Race of scantlings from the strong growth of America.

1899   *1899*

Poem of Existence.

We call one the past, and we call another the future
But both are alike the present
It is not the past, though we call it so,—nor the future, though we call it so,
All the while it is the present only—both future and past are the present
    only.—

The curious realities now everywhere—on the surface of the earth,—in
    the interior of the earth   5
What is it? Is it liquid fire? Are there living creatures in that? Is it
    fire? solid? Is there not toward the core, some vast strange stifling
    vacuum?—Is there anything in that vacuum? any kind of curious
    flying or floating life with its nature fitted?

The existence on the innumerable stars, with their varied degrees of
    perfection, climate, swiftness
—Some probably are but forming, not so advanced as the earth—(Some
    are no doubt more advanced—

There is intercommunion
One sphere cannot know another sphere,   10
(Communion of life is with life only, and of what is after life
(Each sphere knows itself only, and cannot commune beyond itself,
Life communes only with life,
Whatever it is that follows death.

1899   *1945*

the "little plentiful manikins." This composition, no doubt, belongs to the same
period. "Scantlings," familiar to WW's experience in carpentry, are small uprights
used in house framing.
    EXISTENCE] Published, *N and F*, I: 46, p. 21; also in facsimile, p. 53, *Catalogue
of the Whitman Collection,* Duke University Library, 1945. MS: Trent. This
composition was written in ink on a single sheet in such a way as to suggest four
distinct paragraph or stanzaic structures rather than conventional line arrangement.
Yet it is indeed a poem, as the title—WW's own—declares, each part setting forth its
own theme—the "present only" of time, the reality of the earth's interior, the exist-
ences on the stars, and the intercommunion of life. The date of writing is probably in
the early 1850's.

[*Until You Can Explain* . . .].

Priests!
Until you can explain a paving stone, do not try to explain God:
Until your creeds can do as much as apples and hen's eggs, let down
    your eyebrows a little,
Until your Bibles and prayer-books are able to walk like me,
5   And until your brick and mortar can procreate as I can,
I beg you, Sirs, do not presume to put them above me.
    1899   1899

[*Remembrances*].

Remembrances I plant American ground with,
Lessons to think, I scatter as they come
I perceive that myriads of men and women never think
I perceive that ere visible effects can come, thought must come
I perceive that sages, poets, inventors, benefactors, lawgivers are only
5   those who have thought,
That maugre all differences of ages and lands they differ not,
That what they leave is the common stock of the race.
    1899   1899

Thought.

Of that to come—Of experiences—Of vast unknown matter and qualities
    lying inert—much doubtless more than known matter & qualities,
Of many a covered embryo, owner and foetus—of the long patience
    through millions of years—of the slow formation,

EXPLAIN] Published, N and F, I: 89, p. 32. MS: Feinberg. The reader will note a similarity of theme between these lines and the concluding lines (144–151) of "A Song for Occupations." Both passages make a contrast between life and non-life, between the inanimate and the organic. Yet the above lines seem complete in themselves, a full poem, and may have been so intended. Their composition probably belongs to the period of the first edition—the middle 1850's.

REMEMBRANCES] Published, N and F, I: 3, p. 9. MS: Trent. These seven lines, written in pencil on a small sheet of ruled paper, are probably of early composition because on the verso is a list of rivers and cities of Europe (N and F, IV: 11) one of the many notes the poet jotted down as preparation for his enterprise. The fourth line is lightly canceled in the MS, but still legible.

THOUGHT] Published, N and F, I: 150, p. 45. MS: Trent. Although the essential theme of these four lines—the miracle of evolution—relates them closely to section 44 of "Song of Myself," particularly lines 1154–1169, they are of later origin. They are

Of countless germs waiting the due conjunction, the arousing touch,
Of all these tending fluidly and duly to myself, and duly and fluidly to
    reappear again out of myself.—

   1899   *1899*

To the Future.

I see in you, as in the air, a divine volume, a thousand unformed poems,
    just indicated, waiting for me and The States,—no one preferred
    to ano[ther]
For I am the equal friend of each of The States, and I am the Poet of all,
Shall I wrest from you the thousand poems?
Shall I make the idiomatic book of my land?
Shall I yet finish the divine volume   5
I know not whether I am to finish the divine volume,
I shall go forth through the world. I shall traverse The States—But I
    cannot tell whither, or how long,—
Therefore I put upon record that I am well aware what floats suspended
    in you, you future, as qualities float suspended in the air.

   1959   *1959*

To an Exclusive.—.

Your tongue here? Your feet haunting The States?
But I also haunt The States, their born defender—I, determined brother
    of low persons and rejected and wronged persons—espouser of
    unhelped women,
From this hour sleeping and eating mainly that I wake and be muscular
    for their sakes,

written in pencil on the back of a partially clipped proof sheet of *LG* 1856, containing
the beginning of "Sun-Down Poem" ("Crossing Brooklyn Ferry"). In effect the lines
compose an entity, and WW supplies the title.

    FUTURE] Published and edited in Roger Asselineau's "Three Uncollected
'Leaves of Grass,'" *HLQ*, XXII (May, 1959), 255–256. MS: Huntington. This poem
is written in ink, with ink corrections, on the back of a single sheet of pink paper
which contains a rough draft of the 1860 "To a Common Prostitute." The composition
of both poems, then, may be assigned to the period between *LG* 1856 and *LG* 1860.
Another link is that the seventh line of "To the Future" is a version of the present
fourth line of the 1860 "As the Time Draws Nigh." Both poems express poignantly
great ambition and momentary, but profound, uncertainty. The same note is also
most movingly struck in the great terminal poem of 1860, "So Long!"

    EXCLUSIVE] Published, *N* and *F*, I: 60, p. 26; also, Bowers, p. 259. MS: Barrett.
These lines were written in ink on two leaves of pink paper, the title being centered

Training myself in the gymnasium for their sakes, and acquiring a ter-
     rible voice for their sakes.—
5 Rapacious! I take up your challenge!
I fight, whether I win or lose, and hereby pass the feud to them that
     succeed me;
And I charge the young men that succeed me to train themselves and
     acquire terrible voices for disputes of life and death—and be ready
     to respond to whatever needs response,
For I prophecy that there will never come a time, North or South, when
     the rapacious tongue will not be heard, each age in its own dialect.·

1899   *1955*

As of Forms.—.

Their genesis, all genesis,
They lost, all lost—for they include all.—

The earth and every thing in it,
The wave, the snake, the babe, the landscape, the human head,
Things, faces, reminiscences, presences, conditions, thoughts—tally and
5   make definite a divine indistinct, spiritual delight in the Soul.—

Of the arts, as music, poems, architecture, outlines, and the rest, they are
     in their way to provoke this delight out of the soul,
They are to seek it where it waits—for I see that it always patiently
     waits.—

Have you sought the inkling?
Have you wandered after the meanings of the earth? You need not
     wander:
10 Behold those forms.—

1899   *1955*

and underlined at the top of the first. The poet is challenging the rapacious, the
exclusive by championing the wronged and the rejected—a role vehemently, even
exultantly undertaken in the poems of the 1850's. The probable period of composition
is between 1856 and 1860.

     FORMS] Published, *N and F*, I: 59, p. 26; also Bowers, p. 258. MS: Barrett. This
poem was evidently composed by WW as one of the group of sixty-eight to seventy
poems he worked upon in the summer of 1857 to realize his plan of having at least
one hundred poems for his third edition. The surviving MS shows that it may have
been rejected, for unlike the other poems in its group, it was left unnumbered; and
later Dr. Bucke, finding it among WW's papers, printed it in his collection of
fragments. The MS evidence does not support the once-held theory that this poem is
an early draft of the poem "Germs" (1860), to whose thought it bears only a general

[*To This Continent*].

To this continent comes the offspring of the other continents,
And these poems are both offspring and fathers of superior offspring
And from these poems launches the same spirit that launched those ships,
    cities congress and the menaces that confront the President,
And these are for the lands.—

To the new continent come the offspring of the rest of the continents to
    bear offspring,   5
And these poems are both offspring and parents of superior offspring.
  1899   *1899*

[*The Divinest Blessings*].

The divinest blessings are the commonest—bestowed everywhere,
And the most superb beauties are the cheapest the world over.
  1899   *1899*

Thought.

Of recognition—Come, I will no more trouble myself about recogni-
    tion—
I will no longer look what things are rated to be, but what they really
    are to me.
  1899   *1899*

similarity in that both remark upon the spiritual significance of creation.

CONTINENT] Published, *N and F*, I: 94 and 95, p. 32. MS: Barrett. Written in black ink on two scraps of paper—one carrying the first four lines, and the other the last two, which are evidently a redaction of the first two lines. Bucke prints them as separate fragments in reverse order, but evidently they constitute a single pronouncement. Composition is probably between 1856 and 1860.

BLESSINGS] Published, *N and F*, I: 172, p. 49. MS: Unavailable. The phrase "blessings steadily bestow'd" is in WW's 1873 poem, "Nay, Tell Me Not Today the Publish'd Shame," but these two lines are probably much earlier, remindful of the epigrams of the 1860 "Debris" or "Says."

THOUGHT] Published, *N and F*, I: 80, p. 30. MS: Trent. The title is WW's own, and under it the two lines are written in ink, with much revision, on a small scrap of

[*What Would It Bring You*].

What would it bring you to be elected and take your place in the capitol?
I elect you to understand yourself: that is what all the offices in the
    republic could not do.

1899   *1899*

The Two Vaults.

Subject—Poem

—The vault at Pfaffs where the drinkers and laughers meet to eat and
    drink and carouse
While on the walk immediately overhead pass the myriad feet of Broad-
    way
As the dead in their graves are underfoot hidden
And the living pass over them, recking not of them,
5 Laugh on laughers!
Drink on drinkers!
Bandy the jest!
Toss the theme from one to another!
Beam up—Brighten up, bright eyes of beautiful young men!
Eat what you, having ordered, are pleased to see placed before you—
10   after the work of the day, now, with appetite eat,
Drink wine—drink beer—raise your voice,
Behold! your friend, as he arrives—Welcome him, where, from the
    upper step, he looks down upon you with a cheerful look
Overhead rolls Broadway—the myriad rushing Broadway
The lamps are lit—the shops blaze—the fabrics vividly are seen through
    the plate glass windows

---

paper. The composition probably belongs to the period when the poet was writing
"Thoughts" for *LG* 1860.

    YOU] Published, *N and F*, I: 82, p. 30. MS: Berg. These two lines, inaccurately
transcribed by Dr. Bucke, are on a small scrap of paper. Obviously, they are a
complete "Thought," such as those of *LG* 1860, and were probably composed at the
same time. The sentiment is illustrative of WW's untiring interest in private as well
as public character.

    VAULTS] Published, *UPP*, II, pp. 92–93. MS: LC *Whitman*, No. 93. These lines
were written, partly in pencil, partly in ink, on five pages of a green paper notebook
of 1861–1862. Lines 13–16 are badly smudged but readable. No doubt they were

The strong lights from above pour down upon them and are shed out-
    side,   15
The thick crowds, well-dressed—the continual crowds as if they would
    never end
The curious appearance of the faces—the glimpse just caught of the eyes
    and expressions, as they flit along,
(You phantoms! oft I pause, yearning, to arrest some one of you!
Oft I doubt your reality—whether you are real—I suspect all is but a
    pageant.)
The lights beam in the first vault—but the other is entirely dark   20
In the first

    1921   *1921*

Two Antique Records.

Two antique records there are—two religious platforms—
On the first one, stands the Greek sage, the classic masterpiece of virtue—
Eternal conscience is there—doubt is there—philosophy, questioning, rea-
    soning is there.
On the second stands the jew the Christ, the Consolator . . .
There is love, there is drenched purity . . . there, subtle, is the unseen
    Soul, before which all the goods and greatnesses of the world be-
    come insignificant: 5
But now a third religion I give . . . I include the antique two . . .
    I include the divine Jew, and the Greek sage—
More still—that which is not conscience, but against it—that which is not
    the Soul I include
These and whatever exists, I include—I surround all, and dare not ex-
    clude one.

    1921   *1921*

written on the spot—in Pfaff's, a basement restaurant at 653 Broadway, much
frequented in mid-century by writers, especially the group associated with the
Saturday Press. See Allen, 228–231. The poem, breaking off with an unfinished line,
is more than descriptive; it broods on appearance and reality, and confronts careless
life with waiting death. Note the symbolism of the "two vaults."

    RECORDS] Published, *UPP*, II, pp. 91–92. MS: LC *Whitman*, No. 91. These lines
are written in pencil on two pages of a black leather-covered notebook of sixty-
nine pages, of whose contents only this poem is printed in Holloway's *UPP*. Internal
evidence dates the poem as 1860–1861. It bears obvious relation to "Chanting the
Square Deific," which WW was to publish in "Sequel to Drum-Taps" five years
later.

O Brood Continental.

O brood continental!
O you teeming cities! invincible, turbulent, proud!
O men of passion & the storm! O all you slumberers!
Arouse! arouse! the dawn-bird's throat sounds shrill!
Arouse! as I walk'd the beach, I heard the mournful notes foreboding
     a tempest!
The low, oft-repeated shriek of the diver, the long-lived loon, I heard;
I heard, & yet hear, angry thunder:—O sailors! O ships! make quick
     preparation!
O from his masterful sweep, the warning cry of the eagle!
—Give way there all! it is useless—give up your spoils!

1928   *1928*

Kentucky.

Kentucky—young son of Virginia
Son of the noblest parent,—more faithful
—Virginia gave us Washington, and gave us, you

Land of the pleasant valleys! son of Virginia O could you know
With what anxious eyes from Manhattan we watch'd you,
How we said, questioning, Lo, the mother forgets herself—but would you
     forget her?
How, when the stars in our heaven—when the silver brothers on the blue
How the hearts throb

CONTINENTAL] Published, Furness, 84. MS: LC Whitman, No. 1. Furness
surmised that this poem was later incorporated in the 1860 "Apostroph," but the
truth is, interestingly, the reverse. (See Arthur Golden, "A Note on a Whitman Holo-
graph Poem," PBSA, Vol. 55 (3rd quarter, 1961), 233–236. Golden's examination
of WW's revisions in the "Blue Copy" LG 1860 demonstrates that "O Brood Con-
tinental" is actually a fair copy of the revisions the poet had made for the first fifteen
lines of "Apostroph," the prior composition. The MS, neatly drafted and titled by
WW, was evidently prepared for separate publication.
    7. quick preparation] Inaccurately transcribed by Furness as "a quick prepara-
tion."
    KENTUCKY] Published both in an arranged text by James E. Miller, Jr., and in
literal transcription from the MS by William White, *Prairie Schooner*, XXXII (Fall

These hearts that throb in the North—how
Land of the centre—blind where the heart of the continent beats—O
    could you really know   10
These hearts that throb in Manhattan,
Son of Virgin[ia]

A young son of Virginia,
Your mother forgets herself a while—but you do not forget her;
Where you come, true to your own bright star, in the equal brothers, the
    silver brother of the blue,   15
Where you come, advancing with sinewy tendons, drest in your hunting
    shirt, with your rifle on your shoulder

Son of Virginia, in the land of hunters,
Land of sweet waters and offspring
Land of the sons of the mother Virginia
Land of the pleasant valleys and sweet-tasting rivers   20
Land of hunters—O could you know
How with anxious eyes from Manhattan we watch'd you

O Land of the pleasant valleys and sweet-tasting rivers—O that you saw
These eyes that from island Manhattan so anxiously watch'd you.
O that you knew what ears waited to hear you, sons of hunters!   25

When the North felt the artery uncut
Then we knew the stars
Then we,—then America looking again at the sons of Virginia, and fields
    of the same,
Saw it was idle
Then she saw, without frowns, certain offspring of Virginia   30

1958), 172–178. MS: Feinberg. Although in essence complete, this poem was
composed in rough draft on seven separate work sheets, which show three different
starts. How WW would have finally ordered the parts cannot be known; hence the
present order is necessarily provisional. The composition may be dated as 1861
because on the back of one of the work sheets is a first draft by WW of a letter of
that year concerning his brother, Jesse. This is, of course, the year when Kentucky
wavered between secession and loyalty to the Union, an issue to be fully decided for
the North only after a brief invasion late in the year by the Confederacy. With its
occasionally powerful phrasing and characteristic idiom, the poem seems to have
been destined for *Drum-Taps*, but WW could go no further. The only omission in
this transcription is the repetition, set down three times, of the title, "Kentucky."
Other repetitions, obvious as the poem stands, would undoubtedly have disappeared
in a final draft.

And now she gazed content, on a battle-field in Virginia
And she frown'd no more on certain offspring

—And then, as to you Virginia, why will you strive against me, (we seem'd
    to hear America say.)
For more than I can conquer you you have provided me to conquer
    yourself,
35 For you provided me Washington, and have provided me these also.
O that you knew the angry and bitter tears shed at the North,
And the heart full of love and noble pride—full of brotherhood.
O that you knew the real heart of the North.

Son of hunters! Son of the pleasant valleys and sweet-tasting rivers!
Son of Virginia! would that you knew our joy in you today reflecting
40   America's joy! anxiously waited,
O that you saw these million eyes of Manhattan!
Would that you knew how we felt, when the answer came to America's
    listening ears—
When she heard the sound of your sonorous cry as it rose clear and
    shrill, wafted across the Ohio;—
When she saw you, advancing, with sinewy tendons, drest in your hunt-
    ing shirt, with your rifle on your shoulder

For do you, our American Mississippi carry the muttering news down
45   swiftly with your running waters:—do not fail,
And do you whisper them low, O river—whisper them at night without
    fail wherever, in passing, you touch the shores on the east and on
    the west
Carry them on and on, you flowing daughter—carry them to the sea—
    pour them with your stream into the sea
And do you carry them swiftly to the whole world, you sea.

1958   *1958*

BARDS] Published, *UPP* II, p. 91. MS: LC Whitman, 89, described by Holloway
as an "old leather-bound notebook" containing the date June 26, 1859, and a pasted-
in photograph of an unidentified young woman. Since this notebook is now missing,
the MS cannot be checked, and the transcript is that of its first publication. Although
lines 8 and 9 were to become, slightly altered, the two opening lines of the 1860 poem
"That Shadow My Likeness," the MS can hardly be regarded as the original draft of
that poem, which is much simpler, as well as superior, and not concerned, as this is,
with the image of the "bard of Democracy."

To the Prevailing Bards.

Comrades! I am the bard of Democracy
Others are more correct and elegant than I, and more at home in the
parlors and schools than I,
But I alone advance among the people en-masse, coarse and strong
I am he standing first there, solitary chanting the true America,
I alone of all bards, am suffused as with the common people.   5
I alone receive them with a perfect reception and love—and they shall
receive me.
It is I who live in these, and in my poems,—O they are truly me!
But that shadow, my likeness, that goes to and fro seeking a livelihood,
chattering, chaffering,
I often find myself standing and looking at it where it flits—
That likeness of me, but never substantially me.   10

1921   1921

[The Long, Long Solemn Trenches].

The long, long solemn trenches,
Has anyone thought who has stood in one of those trenches, what a
measureless history it held?
What a stately poem and mighty and awful hymn it held?
What a history there holds in the crumbling contents of trenches?
What a poem beyond all ever written or chanted?   5

1960   1960

[There Rises in My Brain].

There rises in my brain the thought of graves—
    to my lips a word for dead soldiers
The Dead we left behind—there they lie, embedded low, already fused
by Nature

TRENCHES] Published, *Walt Whitman's Civil War* (1960) by Walter Lowen-
fels, p. 13. MS: Feinberg. These five lines, complete in themselves, may be part of a
projected longer poem on trenches, for accompanying the MS fragment is another,
on which is a list of cities to be cited in such a poem: "Fredricksburg, Vicksburgh,
trenches of Petersburgh & Richmond, Gettysburgh."
    BRAIN] Published, *Walt Whitman's Civil War* (1960) by Walter Lowenfels, p.
322. MS: Feinberg. In sentiment and theme, these eight lines are so closely related to
the *Drum-Taps* "Ashes of Soldiers" that they may constitute a trial passage for this
poem. However, they are in themselves an effective entity. Composed 1861–1865.

Through broad Virginia's soil, through Tennessee—
5 The Southern states cluttered with cemeteries
the borders dotted with their graves—the Nation's dead.
Silent they lie—the passionate hot tears have ceased to flow—
time has assuaged the anguish of the living.

1960   1960

Ship of Libertad.

Blow mad winds!
Rage, boil, vex, yawn wide, yeasty waves
Crash away—
Tug at the planks—make them groan—fall around, black clouds—clouds
    of death

5 Welcome the storm—welcome the trial—let the waves
Why now I shall see what the old ship is made of
Any body can sail with a fair wind, or a smooth sea

Why now I shall know whether there is anything in you, Libertad,
I shall see how much you can stand
10 Perhaps I shall see the crash—is all then lost?

Come now we will see what stuff you are made of Ship of Libertad
Let others tremble and turn pale—let them   ?
I want to see what   ?   before I die,
I welcome the menace—I welcome thee with joy

15 What then? Have those thrones there stood so long?
Does the Queen of England represent a thousand years?

LIBERTAD] Published, Furness, p. 84. MS: LC Whitman, No. 91. Obviously in rough draft, this poem was composed in pencil on six pages of a black leather notebook of 114 pages, belonging to the period 1860–1861. The intended order of the six stanzas, a page to each, is difficult to determine, but their structure is unmistakable although the Furness transcript, which is incomplete, fails to indicate the stanzaic division. The question marks in the lines are the poet's own. The composition is an early attempt at the "Ship of State" theme in the months when the nation was deeply imperiled. The Spanish word "Libertad" (Liberty or Freedom) is, of course, a favorite borrowing, occurring many times in LG.

CAMPAIGNS] Published, UPP, II, p. 101. MS: Morgan. These lines, on a single sheet, were originally titled by the first line, which the poet canceled for the present title. The year of repulses may well have been 1862, the disastrous campaigns being

And the Queen of Spain a thousand years?
And you

Ship of the World—Ship of Humanity
—Ship of the ages   20
Ship that circlest the world
Ship of the hope of the world—Ship of Promise

1928   *1928*

After Certain Disastrous Campaigns.

Answer me, year of repulses!
How will the poets, of ages hence, look back to you & to me also?
What themes will they make out of you, O year? (themes for

> ironical
> sarcastic laughter?)

What are the proofs to be finally shown out of you?
Are they not to be shown with pride as by bards descended from me?
      my children?   5
Are they really failures? are they sterile incompetent yieldings after all?
Are they not indeed to be victorious shouts from my children?

1921   *1921*

Sights—The Army Corps, Encamped on the War Field.

The cluster of tents—the brigades and divisions
The shelter tents—the peep through the open entrance flap—the debris
      around
The balloon up for reconnoisances

---

those of McClellan, who was halted by Lee until the battle of Antietam, September 17, 1862. Or possibly the year may have been 1863 when Lee and Jackson pushed northward until Lee was halted at Gettysburg, July 1–3. In any event the poem obviously belongs to the period when WW was writing the compositions that were to make *Drum-Taps* (1865). The MS contains a number of revisions, its final, amended version being honored here.

FIELD] Published, Glicksberg, 124–125. MS: LC Whitman, 94. These lines were scribbled in an important notebook of 1862–1863 in which WW kept record of many military actions to be reported both in his newspaper dispatches (see "Fifty-First New York City Veterans," UPP, II, 37–41, and Glicksberg, 63–83) and in his *Drum-Taps* poems (note particularly "The Artilleryman's Vision" and "A March in the Roads Hard-Prest, and the Road Unknown"). The notebook is missing from the

The sights of the hospital tent—the pale-faced wounded—the men lying
    flat on the ground, on the pine boughs,
5 The shebangs of branches,—the fires built
The men emerging from their tents in the gray of the morning
The great camp of army corps, the divisions, the brigades and camps of
    the regiments
The sound of the drums—the different calls, the assembly, the early rev-
    eille, the tattoo at night, & the dinner call, etc.
The rows of tents, the streets through them
10 The squads out on the open ground going through their evolutions
The long trains of baggage wagons—the huge clouds of smoke rising
    over the tents
The ambulances—

1933   *1933*

Sonnet

Inscription, to precede Leaves
of Grass, when finished.

I for the old round earth,
The World, ever varied and new, and the father of the new,
The Kronos, huge, harsh, and brown-skinn'd—thence from eternal roots,
These Leaves utter—these, full of life, infolding all life.
By the heat of the sun—by ice and rain and air, through general nature
5   ripen'd,
Electric, repellent enough—But be not you too soon repell'd.
—Does the sane and rocky Earth, the foot cutting Kronos, repel you?

LC collection, but the MS of this poem is given in facsimile by Glicksberg, opposite
page 125. It is "skeletal," as Glicksberg notes, but sufficiently developed to give a
unified impression.
    5. shebangs] It is characteristic of WW to use this now-familiar slang term,
meaning "affair" or "contrivance." The word is a variant of "shebeen," an Anglo-
Irish term for a house where liquor is sold without license.
    SONNET] Published and edited, in Roger Asselineau's "Three Uncollected
'Leaves of Grass,'" *HLQ*, XXII (May, 1959), 257–258. MS: Huntington. "Sonnet" is
a generic term with WW, meaning a lyric of indeterminate length, even though this
piece happens to be fourteen lines. The subtitle, "Inscription, to precede Leaves of
Grass, when finished," reminds us that the poet's introductory poem to LG 1867 is an
"Inscription," and that, beginning with LG 1867, his opening cluster of poems is
called "Inscriptions" in all succeeding editions. This "sonnet" is, like the other
inscriptions, an announcement: the poet's acceptance of the "World, ever varied and
new," from the beginnings as symbolized by Kronos (in Greek mythology the Titan
who overthrew his father Uranus and was in turn dethroned by his son Zeus) to the

Is not the Earth free, wicked, terrible, full of deserts?
Think you the fertile oases only are beautiful and mean something?
Do you suppose wickedness also does not mean something?   10
—Of those, with the rest, having come, I do not reject them—these I
    infold:
The same Old Man, composite am I—the same old body and soul,
The divine average—the great pride of man in himself, bad and good.
The combined purports of both are infolded in my following songs.

1959   *1959*

While the Schools and the Teachers Are Teaching.

While the schools and the teachers are teaching after their kind,
Some, obedience to look to the protection of the laws,
Some, to assert a sovereign and God, over all, to rely on,
Some, enjoining to build outside forts and embankments;
Solitary, I here, I to enjoin for you whoever you are you to build inside,
    invisible forts,   5
Counseling every man and woman to become the fortress, the lord and
    sovereign, of himself or herself,
To grow through infinite time finally to be a supreme God himself or
    herself,
Acknowledging none greater, now or after death, than himself or herself.

1959   *1959*

present utterance of his "Leaves" infolding all life. This acceptance embraces, as central to the poet's philosophy, both the wicked and the good—both making up the "divine average," a key phrase in LG. The MS is in ink on two leaves of lined paper, with numerous penciled revisions; its composition was probably in the mid-1860's.

3. Kronos] This symbol of primal creation appears both in the 1855 "Song of Myself," now at line 1029, and the 1865–1866 "Chanting the Square Deific," line 7.

TEACHING] Published and edited by Roger Asselineau, in "Three Uncollected 'Leaves of Grass,'" *HLQ*, XXII (May, 1959) 259. MS: Huntington. Written on the same size of ruled paper and with the same sort of emendation in pencil and ink as its accompanying MS "sonnet," "Inscription, to precede Leaves of Grass . . . ," this piece is obviously an independent composition belonging to the same period. Its forthright counsel is Emersonian self-reliance carried to its furthermost reach. In "lord . . . of himself" WW, interestingly enough, is borrowing a phrase already made illustrious by English poets—among them, Sir Henry Wotton, Dryden, and Byron. The final line is an echo of line 1271 of "Song of Myself."

[*Two Elegies on Lincoln*].

UNVEIL THY BOSOM, FAITHFUL TOMB.
[April 1865]

Unveil thy bosom, faithful tomb,
Keep on—the precious gifts grow plentiful,
Thy soil, O land, indeed grows rich.

[THOU WEST THAT GAVE'ST HIM TO US]

Thou West that gave'st him to us,
That rear'dst him on thy ample prairie, and on the breasts of thy fresh
    rivers:
This day we return to thee bearing his body.

1959   *1962*

April 1865.

I heard
    The blue birds singing
I saw the yellowish green where it covered the willows
I saw the eternal grass springing up
The light of the sun on the bay—the ships, dressed with

LINCOLN] Published in facsimile, opposite pages xxv and xliii in *Drum-Taps*,
Facsimile Edition, ed. by F. DeWolfe Miller (Gainesville, Fla., 1959). Printed in
Harold W. Blodgett's "A Poet's Hero," *Symposium*, I (Spring 1962), 29. MS:
Feinberg. The first of these poems, whose title and bracketed date are WW's own, is
written in ink on a small scrap of paper. It is not "Early lines for 'Lilacs . . . ,'" as
suggested in its facsimile publication, but a rejected attempt to compose a burial
lyric immediately upon the news of Lincoln's assassination—an attempt in which the
poet succeeded with his "Hush'd be the Camps To-day," hastily inserted into *Drum-
Taps* while it was still in press. The second poem, untitled, is still another attempt,
composed on the verso of a scrap of paper bearing the MS lines of the first stanza of
the *Drum-Taps* poem, "Beat! Beat! Drums!" The second elegy is happier in its
imagery than the first, but both are moving in their directness and simplicity, though
unfulfilled.

I saw in the distant city the gala flags flying 5
I saw on the ships the profusion of colors
I knew of the fete, the feasting
—Then I turned aside & mused on the unknown dead
I thought of the unrecorded, the heroes so sweet & tender
The young men 10
The returned—but where the unreturned
I thought of the unreturned, the sons of the mothers.

1933 *1933*

beauty

series of comparisons.

not the beautiful youth with features of bloom & brightness

but the bronzed old farmer & father

not the soldiers trim in handsome uniforms marching off to sprightly
music with measured step

but the remnant returning thinned out,

not the beautiful flag with stainless white, spangled with silver & gold 5

But the old rag just adhering to the staff, in tatters—the remnant of
many battle-fields

not the beautiful girl or the elegant lady with ? complexion,

1865] Published, Glicksberg, 128. MS: LC Whitman, 105. This transcript follows the Glicksberg text, the MS now being unavailable because the 1865 Washington hospital notebook in which it was composed is missing from the LC collection. Although WW may have intended to extend the poem beyond these twelve or so lines, some of which are incomplete, they do suggest a certain completeness in themselves. Compare with "The Return of the Heroes" in LG.

BEAUTY] Published, Furness, pp. 51–52. MS: Feinberg. These lines are written in ink on the last three pages of an eighteen-page notebook with the name "Penitenzia" on the cover—a name repeated on an accompanying notebook of six pages. Both notebooks carry rough-draft lines and jottings for what may have been intended as a single poem under the title "Penitenzia." However, these ten "series of comparisons" constitute an entity in themselves. At the top of the first page WW had written, "good to bring in *lecture* or *reading*." Internal evidence suggests that the notebooks belong to the period between LG 1867 and LG 1871.

But the mechanic's wife at work or the mother of many children, middle-
  aged or old

Not the vaunted scenery of the tourist, picturesque,

But the plain landscape, the bleak sea shore, or the barren plain, with the
10   common sky & sun,—or at night the moon & stars.

  1925   *1928*

[*Mask with Their Lids*].

Mask with their lids thine eyes, O Soul!
The standards of the light & sense shut off
To darkness now retiring, inward from abysms,
The objective world behind thee left,
5 How curious, looking thence, appears the world, appear thy comrades,
Appears aloof thy life, each passion, each event.
And this thy visage [of thyself]?

  1928   *1928*

Starry Union.

See! see! see! where how the sun is beaming!
See! see! see! all the bright stars gleaming!
North or South in order moving,

LIDS] Published, Furness, p. 191. MS: Feinberg. These lines are written in the
second of the two "Penitenzia" notebooks (see note on the poem, "Beauty"); and they
constitute, as here printed, the first finally-amended version, for the Furness tran-
script includes some canceled lines and erroneous readings. The draft is preceded by
several pages of trial phrases, and one prose note of particular interest: "Let the
piece 'Droop-droop thine eyes, O Soul'—convey the idea of a trance, yet with all the
senses alert—only a state of high exalted musing—the tangible & material with all its
shows—the objective world suspended or surmounted for a while & the powers in
exaltation freedom, vision—yet the *senses* not lost or contemn'd—Then chant, cele-
brate the unknown, the future hidden spiritual world—the real reality." Date of
composition, about 1870.

    UNION] Published, *UPP*, II, p. 101. MS: Morgan. Five lines in ink on a single
sheet, with penciled revisions, plus a sixth line in pencil, this passage may have been
intended as a stanza for the longer poem, "Hands Round," below. Holloway surmises
that it may have been designed as a song for the cluster, "Marches Now the War Is
Over," which first appeared in *LG* 1871. Note the employment of rhyme and meter as

All including, folding, loving
Union all! O its Union all!   5

O its all for each & each for all!
                one,   one

1921   1921

Hands Round.

[See!] see! where the sun is beaming!
See! see! see! all the bright stars, gleaming!
See by day how the sun is beaming
See by night all the far stars gleaming
What the charm of Power unbroken?   5
What the spell of ceaseless token?
? O its hand in hand, & a Union of all
What Columbia's? friendliest token?
'Tis the hands we take for the Union of all
Here's mine—give me thine—for the Union of all   10
What Columbia's friendliest token?
All hands round for the Union all!
Here's mine—give me thine—for the Union all

Stars up above in eternal lustre
Stars of the States in a compact clustre   15
Clasping, holding, earthward, heavenward
Circling, moving, roundward & onward
All hands round for the Union all
Here's mine—give me thine—for the Union all

if the piece were to be a marching song of comparatively conventional pattern, perhaps prepared for the Centennial Celebration of 1876. Actually, at least six MSS are extant in five different collections. Two—this one (Morgan) and "Hands Round" (Trent)—are here printed as "Uncollected Poems"; two—one with the same title (Hanley) and "What the Word of Power" (Yale)—in our "Unpublished Poems"; two outlines for poems of kindred intent in LC Whitman—one (No. 111) printed by Furness, p. 206, the other (No. 230), unpublished; not in our "Fragments."

ROUND] Published, *FCI*, pp. 14–16. MS: Trent. These thirty-one lines, roughly arranged with considerable revision in four stanzas, are composed in ink on two sheets of green paper. Editors Gohdes and Silver note their obvious relation to the Morgan MS "Starry Union," and also to the "Comrades All (Hand-in-hand for once)," fragment printed by Furness, p. 206, from WW's lost Reading Book (LC Whitman, No. 111). For further relationships, see note on "Starry Union," the preceding poem. Its composition probably belongs to the year 1876, and the poem is no doubt designed as a rally poem for the Centennial. Its employment of regular rhyme and meter is, of course, exceptional.

20 Red, white, blue, to the westward
    Red, white, blue, with the breezes waving
    All combining, folding, loving,

    Northward, Southward, Westward moving
    O its all hands round for the Union all
25 Here's mine—give me thine—for the Union all
    Clasping, circling earthward, heavenward!
    Onward! onward! onward! onward!
    Stars for the sky in an eternal lustre
    Stars for the earth in a compact clustre
30 Then our hands here we give for the Union all!
    O its all hand round—and each for all!

        1949   *1949*

        Wood odors.

    Morning after a night-rain
    The fresh-cool summer-scent
    Odors of pine and oak
    The shade.

5   Wandering the negligent paths—the soothing silence,
    The stillness and the veiled
    The myriad living columns of the temple
    The holy Sabbath morning

    Incense and songs of birds in deep recesses
10 But most the delicate smells fitting the soul
    The sky aloft, seen through the tree-tops

    All the young growth & green maturity of May
    White laurel-blossoms within reach, wood-pinks, below-overhead, stately
        tulip-trees with yellow cup-shaped flowers,

        WOOD ODORS] Published, *Harper's Magazine*, CCXXI (December, 1960), 43. MS:
Livezey Collection, University of California. These lines, neatly transcribed in pencil,
with few emendations, on two lined notebook pages, were composed at the time the
poet was jotting down observations for the "Nature" notes of *Specimen Days and
Collect* (1882–1883)—a record, among much else, of the summer days he spent on
Timber Creek at the Stafford farm in New Jersey in the mid-1870's. It may be

The meow meo-o-w of the cat-bird, cluck of robin, gurgle of thrush delicious

Over and under these, in the silence, delicate wood-odors   15
Birds flitting through the trees
Tangles of old grape-vines.
    1960   1960

argued that the lines are not a poem at all, but rather a listing of descriptive phrases such as WW wrote in his *Days* (see David Goodale, "Wood Odors," *WWR*, VIII, (March, 1962, 17). But it is also true that the form of the MS itself suggests planned poetic pattern with its differentiated lines and stanzas. As Rena V. Grant remarks in her footnote to the *Harper's Magazine* publication, its composition is remindful of "a skillful vers libre excursion into the realm of organic form."

Unpublished Poems

A Soul Duet.
A Dialogue between Pleasure and the Soul.

Come O my soul and let us take
    An evening walk becoming thee
But whither dost thou choose we shall bend our course
    Or to pleasant paths or to Calvary

5 O Calvary is a mountain high
    Tis a dreadful road for a youth like me
To eat or to drink would more suit my taste
    Far better than Mount Calvary

There is no time so good as [?]
10   To ascend this mountain you can see
When old age comes on with its great load of [?]
    How then can you climb Mount Cal [vary?]

For I'd rather have peace and enjoy life's ease
    Than to be persuaded thus by thee
15 And I have heard them say there are lions in the way
    And they lurk in the passage to Calvary

DUET] MS: Hanley. Unmistakably in WW's hand, this composition harks back, both in theme and in treatment, to the journalist of the 1840's who wrote such effusions as "Fame's Vanity" or "The Playground"—see *The Early Poems and the Fiction* (Brasher, 1963)—and it must be assigned to the same period. It is written on five tattered strips pasted on dark-brown wrapping paper, and composed and amended in brown ink, black ink, purple crayon, and pencil. The many variants indicate much uncertainty in composition, an alternative title being "Climbing Mount Calvary." The hackneyed subject, the conventional structure, the expected phrasing are all related to a popular tradition: the contest between body and soul, which in

Yes tis a straight and narrow road
   And lions lurk there for their [?]
But you shall have a guard, the angel [?]
   Shall conduct you over Cal [vary]   20

No, No I abide in the pleasant plain
   With my gay companions here to be,
I must tarry awhile in the joys of the world
   Before I climb Mount Calvary

Your gay companions ere long will be gone   25
   Short sighted ones, could they but see
But if ever you're to stand on Canaan's happy land
   You must travel up the mountain Calvary

Alas! I know what to do
   You greatly have alarmed me   30
I'm sure I'm going on till I fear I am undone
   Lord help me to climb Mount Calvary
   (*ca. 1840*)

To the Poor—.

I have my place among you
Is it nothing that I have preferred to be poor—rather than to be rich?
The road to riches is easily open to me,
But I do not choose it
I choose to stay with you.—   5
   (*ca. 1847–1855*)

American literature goes back to Anne Bradstreet's "The Flesh and the Spirit" (1678), and before that to many homilies of medieval Christianity.

    POOR] MS: Feinberg. These lines, with title, are scribbled in pencil at the foot of one of two large sheets covered on both sides with prose notes on the Greek dramatists, the old Jersey prison ship, descriptions of birds, moral observations, and other miscellany, probably set down between 1847 and 1855. In none of his LG poems does WW so specifically vow himself to poverty, although he often expresses his sympathy for the poor; in line 15 of the 1855 "Great Are the Myths," later rejected, he asks:

      Who goes for men and women showing Poverty richer than wealth?

Pictures.

Lo! on a flat road runs a train'd runner, with muscular legs and thighs.—
He is thinly clothed,—he leans forward as he runs, with closed fists, and
    arms partially raised.
Lo! over the breast of the sea speeds a ship, under full sail—whitish gray,
    with her black hull underneath, she bends slightly sideways—a
    pennant is flying aloft—the waves seem to press forward—they
    topple and frolic with falling foam.
Lo! the woodcutter cutting down trees in the north-east woods in Wis-
    consin.
5   See you the attitude—see you the muscular limbs and the axe uplifted.
    (*ca. 1855*)

Broadway, 1861.

The sights now there
The splendid flags flying over all the stores
(The wind sets from the west—the flags are out stiff and broad—you
    can count every star of the thirty-four—you can count the thirteen
    stripes.)
The regiments arriving and departing,
5   The Barracks—the soldiers lounging around,
The recruiting band, preceded by the fifer—
The ceaseless din
    (*1861*)

PICTURES] MS: Hanley. This MS, whose five lines are written in ink with
penciled revisions on a small single sheet, may well be a trial exercise for the
composition, "Pictures," to which the poet devoted an entire pre-1855 notebook. (See
"Uncollected Poems.") The fourth line—about the woodcutter—is very close to line
57 of the notebook; the "ed" verbal ending in both this MS and the notebook is not
yet contracted to "'d; the script in both has the same characteristics generally—all of
which leads to the supposition that the two have approximately the same date, some
time between 1847 and 1855.

    1861] MS: Berg. These lines were written in ink on a single sheet under WW's
own title, which sets the place and time. Like the two poems following, "I Too Am
Drawn . . ." and "I Have Lived . . . ," which were composed on the verso of the
same sheet, this poem is closely related to the opening poem of *Drum-Taps*, "First O
Songs for a Prelude," in its theme of the arousing of the energies of the great
city—and of the nation—to the war.

    DRAWN] MS: Berg. Written in ink on the verso of the "Broadway, 1861" MS,

[*I Too Am Drawn*].

I too am drawn:
Come, since it must be so—away from all parlors and offices!
Form the camp—plant the flag-staff in the middle—run up the flag on the
    halyards!
Unlimber the cannon—but not for mere salutes, for courtesy,
We will want something, henceforth, besides powder and wadding.   5

(*1861*)

[*I Have Lived*].

I have lived forty years and seen only the soldiers the amateurs
I have heard from the cannon only courteous salutes
Now when I see the soldiers parading, I look on no longer in apathy

(*1861*)

[*I Stand and Look*].

I stand and look in the dark under a cloud,
But I see in the distance where the sun shines,
I see the thin haze on the tall white steeples of the city,—
I see the glistening of the waters in the distance.

(*ca. 1861–1865*)

these lines, without title, give a unified impression by themselves, although it is
possible that they may have been intended as a further stanza for the first poem. Both
poems are related in spirit and occasion to "Beat! Beat! Drums!" as is also "I Have
Lived . . . ," the poem following.

LIVED] MS: Berg. These lines are scribbled in penciled rough draft, without
title, just below the draft of "I Too Am Drawn" on the verso of the "Broadway, 1861"
MS. They may have been intended simply as additional lines for a single composi-
tion. An alternative reading of the first line is:

We have seen only the soldiers the amateurs

LOOK] MS: LC Whitman, No. 91. These lines are entered in pencil on one page of
a sixty-nine-page black leather notebook of 1860–1861. As an exercise in objective
description, they are remindful of such *Drum-Taps* vignettes as "The Torch," "The
Ship," and "A Farm Picture." The poem is remarkable for economy of expression, the
scene itself complex but the impression fully rendered.

Of My Poems.

All the others were singing the distinctions, and what was to be preferred.
Therefore I thought I would sing a song of inherent qualities in a man,
    indifferent whether they are right or wrong.

  (*ca. 1860–1861*)

My Own Poems.

Aye, merchant, thou hast drawn a haughty draft
Upon the centuries yet to come
Yet hitherto unborn—the Americas of the future:
The trick is . . . *Will they pay?*

  (*ca. 1860?*)

Of the Democratic Party 58–59–60.

They think they are providing planks of platforms on which they shall
    stand—
Of those planks it would be but retributive justice to make them coffins—

  (*ca. 1860*)

POEMS] MS: LC Whitman, No. 91. This two-line jotting was entered in pencil on
one page of the sixty-nine-page black leather notebook of 1860–1861. One of WW's
many announcements of intent, it could have fitted easily among the "Says" of LG
1860.

OWN POEMS] MS: LC Whitman, No. 228. This rough draft, in pencil with ink
revisions, is on a single small scrap. It is impossible to date it, but WW began to
make such epigrammatic pronouncements or "inscriptions" about his poetic role with
his third edition—LG 1860.

58–59–60] MS: Trent. These two lines, under WW's title, are written in pencil
on the verso of a scrap of prose jottings on the geography and population of Europe.
Compare with "To a President" and "To the States: To Identify the 16th, 17th, or
18th Presidentiad," which are also scornful pronouncements on the maneuverings of
a Democratic Party organization which WW had rejected. See also the prose jere-
miad, "The Eighteenth Presidency!"

[*To What You Said*].

To

What you said, passionately clasping my hand, this is my answer:

Though you have strayed hither, for my sake, you can never belong to me, nor I to you,

Behold the customary loves and friendships—the cold guards,

I am that rough and simple scornful person

I am he who kisses his comrade lightly on the lips at parting, and I am one who is kissed in return,   5

I introduce that new American salute

Behold love choked, correct, polite, always suspicious

Behold the received models of the parlors—What are they to me?

What to these young men that travel with me?

(*ca. 1860*)

[*While Some I So Deeply Loved*].

While some I so deeply loved (dear child, who stopt so often by you?, remember you me?

Remember you who kissed you while you lay so pale & lonesome in your cots?)

While those I knew, now dead, lie buried in their graves, unrecognized,

While the world of appearance & mirth goes on & goes on,

While so soon what is past forgotten, & the waves wash the imprints off the sand,   5

In nature's reverie sad, returning

(*1864*)

SAID] MS: Feinberg. This poem is written in pencil on the verso of page 30 (WW's numbering) of the sixty-three-page rough draft of *Democratic Vistas*. (See item 37 of the Feinberg Exhibition Catalog, Detroit, 1955.) Considerably amended, the reading is nevertheless clear in its final form. Unmistakably a "Calamus" poem in sentiment, it was probably composed at about the same time as the others, 1857–1860. When the poet came to compose his 1871 *Democratic Vistas*, he followed his customary frugal practice of using whatever bits of paper were at hand, this MS page being among them.

LOVED] MS: Yale. These lines are written in ink with penciled corrections on the verso of an MS Civil War note, dated December 23, 1864, about a recruit, Frank Lester, whose mother had called on the poet. The fifth and sixth lines are variants of lines 21 and 22 of the *Drum-Taps* poem, "The Wound-Dresser." Although this MS is, in effect, complete, it may well be a passage of an intended longer poem for *Drum-Taps*, perhaps another version of "The Wound-Dresser."

Reminiscences. 64

—I saw the bloody holocaust of the Wilderness & Manassas
I saw the wounded & the dead, & never forget them
(Ever since have they been with me—they have fused ever since in my
  poems:—)
They are here forever in my poems
5 How quick forgotten
  (*ca. 1864*)

[*Disease and Death*].

Not mere results of sin and law alone,
Sometimes I see in ye, Disease and Death!
The fear of evolution, knowledge, growth,
Reaching beyond the bounds—and so cut short.
  (*ca. 1872*)

Starry Union.

See by day
See! see! see! how the sun is blazing
See! see! see! all the bright stars shining

REMINISCENCES] MS: Huntington. This poem is a scrawl on one of ten pages of
hospital notes, otherwise prose, which the poet jotted down in 1862–1864. The title
and the line structure are WW's own; for similar poetical jottings on battle scenes
(the material to be perfected for *Drum-Taps*), see Glicksberg, pp. 121–128. The
figure 64, which is without apostrophe, may refer to the year 1864, since the bloody
Battle of the Wilderness took place in early May of that year when Grant crossed the
Rapidan and engaged Lee's forces—the beginning of his campaign against Rich-
mond. "Manassas" (or Second Bull Run) refers to the battle of August 29–30, 1862,
when Lee and Jackson badly defeated the army of General Pope along Warrenton
Pike, Virginia.
    DEATH] MS: Huntington. Originally, this reflection was three penciled lines—
the second, third, and fourth—then another line was added in ink, tentatively
canceled, and finally transposed to the top to become the poem's opening line. The
composition is without title and undated. It may belong to the early 1870's, for line
113 of the 1872 Dartmouth Commencement poem "Thou Mother with Thy Equal
Brood" may reflect its purport if "thee" and "ye" are both the poet's land:

See by day the great bright sun blazing
See by night all the stars a-shining,   5
Shining, shining, ever shining.
The sun holding the stars
God holding the suns
As the Union holds the States
As the suns hold the stars   10
As the Power holds the Suns
All free yet all held inseparably
O by day comes the sun all blaz [ing]
O by night come the stars all shin [ing]

　　(ca. 1876)

[What the Word of Power].

What the word of power unbroken?
What the charm of heaven's own token
On & ever on from the Eastward
On & ever on to the westward
Union all! O its [sic] Union all!   5
O its [sic] all for each, & each for all!

　　(ca. 1876)

"In many a smiling mask death shall approach, beguiling thee, thou in disease
　　shalt swelter,"

UNION] MS: Hanley. With the same title as the Morgan MS, printed in *UPP*, II,
101, and now in the present section of "Uncollected Poems," this composition is
obviously part of the general effort most fully represented in the "Hands Round" MS
of the Trent Collection, also in the "Uncollected Poems." Written in black ink on a
tattered white sheet, and with penciled additions, it is probably an earlier draft of the
Morgan MS, which in turn may be a revised stanza of the longer Trent MS.
Compare with "What the Word of Power," below. Two MSS poem outlines of
kindred theme are in the LC holdings. One is transcribed by Furness, p. 206 (LC
Whitman, No. 111); the other (LC Whitman, No. 230) is unpublished. The probable
date is 1876 since all these "Union" paeans are evidently inspired by the Centennial.
POWER] MS: Yale. These six lines, in ink with penciled corrections, bear
obvious relation to other MSS which are parts of an attempted poem celebrating the
Union, probably designed for the Centennial of 1876. See "Starry Union" and
"Hands Round" among the "Uncollected Poems," also a second "Starry Union" in the
"Unpublished Poems," the fragment printed by Furness, 206, and the unpublished
fragment, LC Whitman, 230. The title is supplied.

Last Words.

As to yet one more seance (doubtless the last)
Recapitulating the same old themes—the emotional, the moral, the heroic,
By head and heart of me—by voice and pen—addressing old, old words,
To you here reading—Union, Equality, Love,
5   To you America, beginning, middle, end.

(1889)

[Glad the Jaunts for the Known].

Glad the jaunts for the known,
Trusting the unknown future,
With good heart, love, remembrance,
I finishing my three score and ten,
5   Giving this book to you
Sign with love my name

(1888–1889)

Champagne in Ice.

No use to argue temperance, abstinence only,
I've had a bad spell 40 hours, continuous

WORDS] MS: Feinberg. The MS materials for this poem are composed on five
different pages made from the backs of letter sheets and split envelopes, bearing
various dates in the year 1889. Two pages contain working notes and phrases only,
the other three rough drafts, of which the one here printed is in the last, amended
form. Since the poem remained unpublished, we may infer that the poet did not
achieve the form he wanted. He did publish certain other late attempts to review his
basic themes: cf. "A Carol Closing Sixty-Nine," "L. of G.'s Purport," and "Now
Precedent Songs, Farewell."
   1. seance] By this word WW probably meant "mystical illumination."
   KNOWN] MS: LC Whitman, No. 32. Written and revised in pencil on the back of a
letter to WW from James Gordon Bennett, editor of the New York *Herald*, dated
January 23, 1888. Much revised, even in its rough draft, this piece is nevertheless
complete as a sentiment to accompany an autographed book. Since the poet is
finishing his "three score and ten," the book may well be the 1888 *Complete Poems
and Prose* in one volume, or possibly the 1889 *LG*. The intended recipient is uniden-
tified.
   ICE] MS: Lion. Although these lines may be called a "poem" only by courtesy,
they are both in form and intent an affecting and poetic note of thanks. In pencil
with inked revisions on a single small sheet, they must have been composed in the
poet's final days of invalidism. The MS was sent to Oscar Lion with the following
letter:

'Till now a heavy bottle of good champagne wine in my thirst,
Cold and tart-sweet drink'd from a big white mug half fill'd with ice,
It is started me in stomach and in head,   5
As I slowly drink, thanking my friend,
Feeling the day, and in myself, freedom and joy.

   (*ca. 1891–1892*)

To the Soul.

All is for thee
Life and Death are for thee
The Body too is for thee

   (*n.d.*)

[*Two Little Buds*].

Two little ? human Buds.
One less, one larger, here we humbly place:
Quickly decayed on earth:
But now they bloom in God's immortal garden.

   (*ca. 1870*)

     Dear Mr. Lion—Here's a bit of autobiography been havened on the
     floor of three twenty eight for a while and then drifted into sight again
     at my home today. Like it?

     Sept. 14—1942   Anne Traubel

Anne Traubel was Horace Traubel's widow; "three twenty eight" was then the num-
ber of the poet's house on Mickle Street, Camden.

    SOUL] MS: LC Whitman, No. 229. Three lines in pencil under WW's title on a
single sheet. Perhaps the poet had intended to go further. At the upper right corner
of the MS he has penciled the one word: "crude."

    BUDS] MS: Berg. These four lines are written in ink on a small scrap of paper,
which is accompanied by another scrap, the top of a piece of letter-head stationery of
the Attorney General's Office, on which is scribbled, in the same ink and script, the
tag:

              A youth beloved by all
              And in whom there was no guile.

Since this is obviously quoted, the question arises: may not the "Buds" verses also be
quoted, rather than composed? The question mark before "human" is WW's own.

[*Sunrise*].

Darkies looking at the sun as it rose, a round red glistening ball through
 the vapory morning
"Don't it look pretty?" said one.
"Yes, said the other, but it looks mighty *ambitious*
 (*n.d.*)

SUNRISE] MS: Feinberg. Written on a small scrap of paper with black ink,
untitled, and in rough draft, this composition is just an anecdote—a "memo." But it
has point, and WW gave it his customary form. The MS cannot be dated.

SESOSTRIS] Published, N and F, I: 31, pp. 15–16. MS: unavailable. Sesostris:
legendary king of Egypt, considered to belong to the 19th dynasty and sometimes
identified with Rameses II. According to Herodotus and Strabo, Sesostris conquered
the whole known world. WW's description may be derived from his reading of Sir
John Gardiner Wilkinson's *Manners and Customs of the Ancient Egyptians* (1836–
1840). See Stovall, "Notes on Whitman's Reading," *AL*, XXVI (November, 1954),

Uncollected Manuscript Fragments

[*Sesostris*].

Advance shapes like his shape—the king of Egypt's shape,
Shapes that tally Sesostris—gigantic in stature, wholesome, clean-eyed,
Six feet ten inches tall—every limb, every part and organ in proportion—
    strong, bearded, supple,
Conqueror of two continents in nine years,
Lover most of those that repelled him sternest—builder to them of phallic
    memorials,
Ruler wisely and friendly for sixty-two years—accepter of all religions
    —preferer of none,
Freer of slaves—divider among them of homesteads—maker of farmers.

5

After Death.

Now when I am looked back upon, I will hold levee,
I lean on my left elbow—I take ten thousand lovers, one after another, by
    my right hand.—

[*America*].

No Homer, Shakspere, Voltaire
No palaces, Kings' palaces nor courts,
Nor armies on the land, nor navies on the sea,

347. Also it is to be remembered that in the 1850's WW frequented Dr. Henry
Abbott's Egyptian Museum at 659 Broadway, New York. Cf. the "shapes" image in
"Song of the Broad-Axe."

DEATH] Published, *N and F*, I: 91, p. 32. MS: Barrett. In the MS fragment the
phrase "After death" is centered as a title. The Bucke transcription is slightly
inaccurate.

AMERICA] Unpublished. MS: Feinberg. These phrases are written in pencil in
this order under WW's own title on a sheet torn from the top of a larger sheet.
Evidently they are rough drafts toward the beginning lines of a poem.

But countless living equal men
Average   free

America to the Old World Bards.

Be thy task for once to thank in my name, the old world Bards
And be thy task to speak in my name to preserve the antique poems
Let them pass through
Let the phantoms walk the roads of thy soul
5   Call up the pale great
Let the procession pass—let the shadow walk through the very soul

[American Air].

American air I have breathed, breathe henceforth also of me,
American ground that supports me, I will support you also.

[War].

Armies & navies pass on the surface baleful
War & the passions of war pass on
War & the angry fight pass
War & the frantic tempers of men rage out their time & depart—
5   But we never depart

[As Nature].

As nature, inexorable, onward, resistless, impassive, amid the screams
        and din of disputants, so America.

BARDS] Unpublished. MS: LC Whitman, No. 117. These six lines are penciled on
two pages of a five-page notebook. In two further pages of jottings and phrases, the
poet advises himself that they are to be a first stanza or canto, to be followed by a
"strong Invocation." The sense of the opening lines seems to be that America is
herself addressing the poet concerning the Old World bards. The title is the poet's
own.
    AMERICAN] Published, N and F, I: 21, p. 13. MS: Barrett. Conceivably, this is a
complete poem, but the MS shows two more phrases below the line, indicating that it
was probably intended for further development.
    ARMIES & NAVIES] Unpublished. MS: Hanley. Written in pencil, these phrases
on war are a poem outline, rather than a rough draft of the poem itself.
    AS NATURE] Published, N and F, I: 101, p. 34. MS: unavailable.
    AS THE TURBULENCE] Published, N and F, I: 18, p. 13. MS: Berg. The Bucke

We Are.

As the turbulence of the expressions of the earth—as the great heat and
the great cold—as the soiledness of animals and the bareness of
vegetables and minerals
No more than these were the roughs among men shocking to me

[*As to You*].

As to you, if you have not yet learned to think, enter upon it now,
Think at once with directness, breadth, aim, conscientiousness—
You will feel a strange pleasure from the start, and grow rapidly each
successive week.

[*As We Are*].

As we are content and dumb the amount of us in men and women is
content and dumb,
As we cannot be mistaken at last, they cannot be mistaken.

? *Ashes of Roses.*

Dust of the dead—
Ashes of blue & grey,
Ashes of battle-pits
Solemn & strange cement—

transcript does not reproduce the "We are" which the poet had added above the first
line, greatly improving its sense.

AS TO YOU] Published, *N and F*, I: 73, p. 29. MS: Barrett. The last line of this
trenchant counsel is canceled in the MS, but rightly preserved by Bucke, who
transcribes it as part of a larger fragment, which begins with two lines now existing
as a separate MS. See "Who wills . . . ," below.

AS WE ARE] Published, *N and F*, I: 12, p. 11. MS: Barrett. This gnomic saying is
the poet's expression of faith in the intuitional, of which the "we" of the poem are the
agents.

ROSES] Unpublished. MS: Feinberg. On each of two leaves the poet inscribed
lines under the title (the question mark is his own), followed by a note in prose. The
whole is an undated poem outline, bearing a close relationship to the *LG* poem,
"Ashes of Soldiers."

5   Not a crop grows hence in the fields of north or south
     Nor moisture of the river, nor falling rain

Decoration day May 30. The *dust* & *debris* below in all the cemeteries not only in Virginia & Tennessee but *all through the land*   The names of the flowers   lilacs roses early lilies   the colors, purple & white & yellow & red   the graves   *Ashes of Armies   The Unknown   Army-Ashes*   The dust of each fused in the dust of each—(i.e. the rebel & the Union)

The Body—.

———

Why what do you suppose is the Body?
Do you suppose this that has always existed—this meat, bread, fruit, that
     is eaten, is the body?
No, those are visible parts of the body, materials that have existed in
     some way for billions of years—now entering into the form of the
     body
? But there is the real body too, not visible.

[*Can ?*].

Can ? make me so exuberant, yet so faintish?
The rage of an unconquerable fierceness is conquered by the touch [of
     the] tenderest hand
I cannot be awake, for nothing looks to me as it did before,
Or else I am awake for the first time, and all before has been a mean
     sleep.

BODY] Published, N and F, I: 118, pp. 37–38; and 169, p. 49. MS: Trent.
Inadvertently the MS was twice transcribed, and with slight inaccuracy, by Bucke.
In a marginal note on the MS leaf, the poet instructed himself, "make this more
rhythmic." The question mark before the last line is WW's own. The fragment is
perhaps related to the LG poem, "I Sing the Body Electric."
    CAN ?] Published, N and F, I: 116, p. 37. MS: Barrett. The question mark after
"Can" in the first line of this interesting fragment is the poet's own—proposing, in
effect, a riddle for the reader. The two words supplied in the second line are in the
Bucke transcript.

[*Decoration Day*].

Lay on the graves of all dead soldiers
Wreaths of roses and branches of palms,

Not for the dead alone—for meanings, indications
All wars, contentions past, tokens reciprocal, over the north, and over
    the South
One day, at least, hot passions laid—peace—brotherhood uprisen,   5
We joining proud, remembering thankful, sorrowing

[*Divine Is the Person*].

Divine is the $_{body}^{person}$—it is all—it is the soul also
How can there be immortality, except through mortality?
How can the ultimate realities of visible things be visible?
How can the real body ever die and [?]

Ebb and Flood Tides.

Advancing, retreating, and hand in hand
Duly with rhythmic steps turning and mouths to the right or the left
    reverting
You chorus of brothers, and sisters
Moving forever round the circles of the earth

DECORATION DAY] Unpublished. MS: Feinberg. The penciled MS shows these to
be trial lines in very rough draft, with the title "Decoration Day" half way down the
leaf rather than in position. Cf. the last four stanzas of "Ashes of Soldiers."

DIVINE] Unpublished. MS: Barrett. A small scrap, with lines much worked
over, this MS is related to the fragment "The Body," as both are to "I Sing the Body
Electric" and to "Song of Myself," especially sections 24–25.

TIDES] Unpublished. MS: Feinberg. Although these are trial lines, much revised
and amended, a distinguished image emerges, and the lyric achieves a kind of
completion.

[*The Epos of a Life*].

The Epos of a life I sing—varied the road, the way by farm & hum of
    city, & frequent trackless wild—by river, lake, & ocean—by shows
    of peace & war;
Him of The Lands, identical, I sing, along the single thread, so inter-
    spersed,

[*The Grappler*].

the grappler with his
grappling irons—I
see him ahold of
the long handles—
working them deep in
the water, carefully
feeling

5

[*Have I Refreshed*].

Have I refreshed and elevated you?
Though I have uttered no word about your particular employment, have
    you received from me new and valuable hints about your employ-
    ment?
Have you gone aside after listening to me, and created for yourself?
Have I proved myself strong by provoking strength out of you?

    LIFE] Unpublished. MS: Feinberg. Written in pencil with many corrections and
cancellations. Undoubtedly in trial form, still the lines convey vitality and a sense of
completion.
    THE GRAPPLER] Unpublished. MS: LC Whitman, 91. This is a jotting in a
leather-bound notebook of 1860–1861 which contains a miscellany of drawings,
prose, and verse. Although WW did not use this particular line in LG, it could well
have been a part of canto 5 of "A Song for Occupations," where the grappler is listed
(line 114).
    HAVE I REFRESHED] Published, *N and F*, I: 78, p. 30. MS: Barrett. Although

[*Hear My Fife!*].

Hear my fife!—I am a recruiter
Come, who will join my troop?

[*I Have Appeared*].

I have appeared among you to say that what you do is right, and what
    you affirm is right;
But that they are only the alphabet of right.—
And that you shall use them as beginnings and first attempts—
I have not appeared with violent hands to pull up by the roots any thing
    that has grown,
Whatever has grown, has grown well—
Do you fancy there is some water in the semen of the perpetual copulation   5
Do you suppose the laws might be reformed and rectified?

[*Immortality*].

How can there be immortality except through mortality?
How can the ultimate reality of visible things be visible?
How can the real body ever die?

[*I Admire*].

I admire a beautiful woman . . . I am easy about who paints her por-
    trait.
Poet go!
I am ready to swear never to write another word.

the poet did not see fit to print these lines, their sentiment is basic in LG.
    HEAR MY FIFE!] Published, N and F, I: 29, p. 15. MS: Barrett. Cf. line 46 of
the uncollected poem, "Pictures," in which the poet does not identify himself as the
recruiter.
    I HAVE APPEARED] Unpublished. MS: Feinberg. These lines, preceded by prose
jottings, apparently unrelated, are penciled on a fragment that definitely seems to be
pre-1855. Interestingly, they constitute a primitive, early form of the passage in
canto 22 of "Song of Myself," lines 464–469.
    IMMORTALITY] Published, N and F, I: 168, p. 48. MS: unavailable.
    I ADMIRE] Published, N and F, I: 182, p. 81. MS: unavailable.

[*I Am a Look*].

I am a look—mystic—in a trance—exaltation.
Something wild and untamed—half savage.
Common things—the trickling sap that flows from the end of the manly
maple.

[*I Am a Student*].

I am a student, free of a Library,—it is limitless and eternally open to me;
The books are written in numberless tongues, always perfect and alive,—
They do not own the library who buy the books and sell them again,
I am the owner of the library, for I read every page, and enjoy the mean-
ing of the same

[*I Am Become*].

I am become the poet of babes and little things.
I descend many steps—I go backward primeval
I retrace steps oceanic—I pass around not "merely my own kind," but
all the objects I see.—

[*I Am Not Content*].

I am not content now with a mere majority . . . . I must have the love
of all men and all women,
If there be one left in any country who has no faith in me, I will travel
to that country, and go to that one.

I AM A LOOK] Published, *N and F*, I: 135, p. 40. MS: unavailable. WW uses the
"trickling sap" metaphor in line 537, "Song of Myself."
I AM A STUDENT] Published, *N and F*, I: 110, p. 36. MS: Barrett. In several *LG*
poems, e.g., lines 14–20, "Song of Myself," and line 20, "Thou Mother with Thy
Equal Brood," the indoor library is a symbol of book experience in contrast with
nature's experience.
I AM BECOME] Published, *N and F*, I: 103, p. 35. MS: Barrett. The Bucke
transcript does not indicate the "quote" in the third line. Cf. canto 44, "Song of
Myself," lines 1148 ff.
I AM NOT CONTENT] Published, *N and F*, I: 151, p. 45. MS: Trent. In transcrib-

[*I Am That Halfgrown Angry Boy*].

I am that halfgrown angry boy, fallen asleep,
The tears of foolish passion yet undried upon my cheeks.

Years with all their events pass for me,
Some are spent in travel—some in the usual hunt after fortune.

I pass through the travels and fortunes of thirty years, and become old,   5
Each in its due order comes and goes,
And then a message for me comes.
The

[*I Know Many Beautiful Things*].

I know many beautiful things about men and women,
But do not know anything more beautiful than to be freehanded and
        always go on the square.

I see an aristocrat;
I see a smoucher grabbing the good dishes exclusively to himself and
        grinning at the starvation of others as if it were funny,
I gaze on the greedy hog; he snorts as he roots in the delicate greenhouse.   5
How those niggers smell!
Must that hod-boy occupy the same stage with me?
Doth the dirt doze and forget itself?
And let tomatoes ripen for busters and night walkers,
And do no better for me—   10
Who am a regular gentleman or lady,
With a stoop and a silver door-plate and a pew in church?

ing, Bucke included at the end of the second line the words—"and stand upright
before him"—which are canceled in the MS, with the period after "one."

    I AM] Published, *N and F*, I: 137, p. 41. MS: Trent. Possibly pre-1855 verse, for
on the verso of the MS is a holograph of unpublished journalistic prose. Furthermore,
the sentimental phrasing of the first two lines is almost exactly duplicated in a story
fragment (*CW*, IX, 146) belonging in mood to the fiction of the 1840's.

    I KNOW] Published, *N and F*, I: 36, pp. 17–18. MS: unavailable. A rough
draft—perhaps only a poem outline, certainly not a complete poem. The highly
idiomatic and concrete diction, the satiric vehemence suggest composition in the
early or middle 1850's.

And is the day here when I vote at the polls,
One with the immigrant that last August strewed lime in my gutter?
15 One with the thick-lipped black?

And can dew wet the air after such may be elected to Congress,
And make laws over me?
Have you heard the gurgle of gluttons perfectly willing to stuff themselves
While they laugh at the good fun of the starvation of others,
20 But when the gaunt and the starved awkwardly come for their slices
The quiet changes to angry hysterics.

It is for babies to lift themselves out of the . . .
I go not with the babies who . . .

I am none of the large baby sort;
I have no wish to lift myself above breathing air, and be specially eminent
25   or attractive;
I am not quite such a fool as that,
I remain with people on average terms—
I am too great to be a mere leader.

[*I Know That Amativeness*].

I know that amativeness is just as divine as spirituality—and this which
        I know I put freely in my poems.
I know that procreation is just as divine as spirituality—and this which
        I know I put freely in my poems.

[*I Shall Venerate*].

I shall venerate hours and days and think them immeasurable hereafter;
I am finding how much I can pass through in a few minutes.

AMATIVENESS] These two lines, separately transcribed in N *and* F, I, as 132,
p. 40, and 175, p. 49 respectively, have obvious association as one composition. No
doubt the two MSS, now untraced, were somehow disjoined.
  I SHALL VENERATE] Published, N *and* F, I: 107, p. 35. MS: unavailable. WW
was fond of the dialectal word "limpsey" (weak), sometimes using the alternative
spelling, "limpsy."
  I SUBJECT] Published, N *and* F, I: 79, p. 30. MS: Barrett. This dictum could
stand as a small poem by itself, but it was probably intended, judging from the MS
leaf, as part of a larger composition.

I was a good friend to all things before,
But now what I was seems to me limpsey and little.

[*I Subject All the Teachings*].

I subject all the teachings of the schools, and all dicta and authority to
the tests of myself
And I encourage you to subject the same to the tests of yourself—and
to subject me and my words to the strongest tests of any

[*In American Schools*].

In American schools sit men and women—
Schools for men and women are more necessary than for children.

[*I'll Trace This Garden*].

1

I'll trace this garden oer & oer
Meditate on each sweet flower
Thinking of each happy hour

2

Some say my love is gone to France

3

I'll sell my frock—I'll sell my where   5

IN AMERICAN SCHOOLS] Published, *N and F*, 1: 49, p. 23. MS: unavailable. As
one-time schoolmaster, as journalist, and as poet, WW's interest in education was un-
remitting. See Florence Bernstein Freedman's *Walt Whitman Looks at the Schools*
(1950).
GARDEN] Unpublished. MS: Feinberg. Since WW wrote these experimental
ballad lines on letterhead of the Attorney-General's Office, Washington, where he
was first employed July 1, 1865, the MS can be roughly dated. But this verse is most
atypical of WW's poems of the period. One can only surmise that either the poet was
recalling a ballad he had heard, or that he was trying his own hand. He never
lost—even after 1855—a fondness for occasional practice of conventional patterns.

4

I wish I was on yonder hill
It's there I'd sit & cry my fill
So every tear should turn a mill

5

I'll dye my dress—I'll dye it red
10   Over the world I'll beg my bread
My parents dear shall think me dead

[*It Were Easy to be Rich*].

It were easy to be rich owning a dozen banks
But to be rich

It was easy to grant offices and favor being President
But to grant largess and favor

5   It were easy to be beautiful with a fine complexion and regular features
But to be beautiful

It were easy to shine and attract attention in grand clothes
But to outshine?   in sixpenny muslin

[*Life, Light*].

Life light and the in-bound tides
? only only through ye,

IT WERE EASY] Published, *UPP*, II: 72. MS: LC Whitman, 80. Like the uncol-
lected poem "I am the poet of reality," this is winnowed from the important 1847 note-
book, the lines penciled on a single leaf. Still a fragment, still in outline, the piece has
begun to achieve concise form.

LIFE, LIGHT] Unpublished. MS: LC Whitman, 119. These trial phrases are
written in purple pencil on two lined notebook pages. It is impossible to date them,
although in mood they belong to the poems of the "Sea-Drift" cluster.

LIVING BULBS] Published, *N and F*, I: 136, p. 41. MS: Trent. These two lines in
pencil on a small piece of paper remind us that in his 1855 Preface the poet spoke of
the compact shape of melons, that in "Song of Myself," line 1296 he wrote of the "the

Through death and waning day and the ebb's depletion
Life, light, and the inbound tides

[*Living Bulbs*].

Living bulbs, melons with polished rinds smooth to the reached hand
Bulbs of life, lilies, polished melons, flavored for the mildest hand that
    shall reach.

[*Nor Humility's Book*].

Nor humility's book nor the book of despair nor of old restrictions;
Book of a new soldier, bound for new campaigns;
Book of the sailor that sails the sea stormier, vaster than any.

[*O I See Now*].

(O I see now that I have the make of materialism and things,
And that intellect is to me but as hands, or eyesight, or as a vessel,

[*Osirus*].

Osirus—to give forms.
I am he who finds nothing more divine than simple and natural things
    are divine.

polish'd breast of melons." And in a prose fragment (N and F, IV: 41) is a sentence
closely echoing the first line of this fragment: "Sweet-gum, bulb, and melons with
bulbs grateful to the hand."

    NOR HUMILITY'S BOOK] Published, N and F, I: 51, p. 23. MS: unavailable.
This fragment could stand by itself as a poem, and may have been intended as such,
but it seems more likely that the three lines are part of an unfinished composition.

    O I SEE] Published, N and F, I: 24, p. 14. MS: Trent. These verses are written in
pencil at the foot of a prose passage on the same theme. See N and F, III: 26. The MS
is a single sheet—a single composition, both prose and verse.

    OSIRUS] Published, N and F, I: 2, p. 9. MS: unavailable. Properly, "Osiris,"
Egyptian god of the lower world, mentioned by WW in line 1030, "Song of Myself."

[*The Poet Is a Recruiter*].

The poet is a recruiter
He goes forth beating
the drum,—O, who
will not join his troop?

[*The Power by Which*].

The power by which the carpenter plumbs his house is the same power
    that dashes his brains out if he fall from the roof.—

[*Prince of Wales*].

Prince of Wales in New York 1860
The Good Queen's Eldest Son
One rapid look I gave and saw
The Queen's Son
5 A fair youth
In the barouche drawn by the champing horses
Pass'd a fair youth with downcast eyes

[*A Procession Without Halt*].

A procession without halt,
Apparent at times and hid at times

RECRUITER] Unpublished. MS: LC Whitman, No. 83. This little fragment is
penciled in this form at the foot of a page of a small notebook belonging to the period
1854–1855. Cf. the fragment, "Hear my fife," above.

THE POWER BY WHICH] Published, N and F, I: 84, p. 31. MS: Berg. It is possible
that the poet intended to add this single-line fragment to the composition, "Have you
supplied . . . " See Uncollected Poems. Both deal with carpentry or home-building
as symbolic of life-building.

PRINCE OF WALES] Unpublished. MS: LC Whitman, No. 92. This impression is
entered on a page of a Brooklyn-Washington notebook of 1860–1864. The Prince of
Wales, who visited New York City on October 11, 1860, was saluted by WW in the

Rising the rising grounds in relief against the clear sky lost in the hollows, stretched interminably over the plains,

No eye that ever saw the starting—no eyes that ever need wait for the ending

Where any one goes, however ahead, the rest duly coming, however far behind,   5

Marches a marching procession

[*Remember If You Are Dying*].

Remember if you are dying, that you are dying, . . . is it so, then?

If it be so, I bring no shuffling consolation of doctors and priests,

I tell the truth . . . I tell with unvarying voice.—

[*Sanity and Ensemble*].

Sanity and ensemble characterize the great masters,

Innocence and nakedness are resumed,

Theories of the special depart as dreams,

Nothing happens, or ever has happened, or ever can happen, but the vital laws are enough,

None were or will be hunted, none were or will be retarded.   5

A vast, clear scheme, each learner learning it for himself,

Taking men, women, laws, the earth, and the things of the earth as they are,

Starting from one's-self and coming back to one's-self,

Looking always toward the poet,

Seeing all tend eternally toward happiness,   10

What is narrower than gravitation, light, life, of no account,

poem "Year of Meteors," line 11, with words probably suggested by this notebook entry.

A PROCESSION] Published, N and F, I, No. 22, p. 13. MS: Bayley. "All is a procession," said WW (line 89, "I Sing the Body Electric"), and the image, a great favorite, occurs many times in LG. These lines, however, are a poem outline rather than a fragment that has actually kindled into poetry.

REMEMBER] Published, N and F, I: 19, p. 13. MS: Barrett. The sentiment of this verse fragment is basic in LG, and in effect it is a complete poem in itself.

SANITY AND ENSEMBLE] Published, N and F, I: 28, p. 15. MS: U of P. Probably not a poem, but an outline of ideas to be expanded into a poem that never got written, although the mood faintly suggests "A Song of the Rolling Earth."

What is less than the sure formation of density, or the patient upheaving
    of strata, of no account,
What is less than that which follows the thief, the liar, the glutton, the
    drunkard, through this experience, and doubtless afterwards, that
    too of no account.
What does not satisfy each one and convince each one—that too is of no
    account.

[*Shall We Sky-lark*].

Shall we sky-lark with God
The poet seems to say to the rest of the world
Come, God and I are now here
What will you have of us

[*Ships Sail upon the Waters*].

Ships sail upon the waters,—some arriving others departing
Ten thousand cities rich, learned, populous cities—they have grown or
    certainly to grow
The States spread amply—old states and new states—they front on the
    two seas—they are edged or cleft by the Mississippi,
Congress is in session in the Capitol, or will be in session the appointed
    time,
See the President is menaced face to face by the common people, for his
5   derelictions.

The Soul's Procession.

The idea—after carrying the Soul   through all experiences   tableaux
    situations   sufferings   heroism *especially at Sea* wrecks   storms
    picture of a ship in a storm at sea

SHALL WE SKY-LARK] Published, *UPP*, II, p. 83. MS: LC Whitman No. 85. These
four lines are penciled on one page of a twenty-three-page notebook belonging to the
late 1840's or early 1850's when *LG* 1855 was in gestation.

SHIPS SAIL] Published, *N and F*, I: 77, p. 30. MS: Barrett. In effect a complete
poem, but the MS, without title on a single sheet, and much worked over, gives the
impression of being a fragment of a larger whole.

SOUL'S PROCESSION] Unpublished. MS: Barrett. A thirteen-page notebook whose
cover is inscribed by the poet with the above title, underlined. Within are a number
of prose jottings such as the first sentence of this composition. Then some of the

The Soul then stalks on by itself
Swims on—sails on like a sufficient splendid solitary ship by itself—
     There is space enough—
There are the orbs of the worlds in space with ample room enough
& there are the orbs of souls also swimming in space   5
Each one composite in itself
And the spirit of God holding them together
The orbs as the suns & worlds swim in space,
But the Souls swim in the Spirit of God in greater space

[*Spirituality, the Unknown*].

Spirituality, the unknown, the great aspirations of the soul, the idea of
     justice, divinity, immortality.

[*That Is Profitable*].

                         great to you
That is profitable which you carry with you after death
I will carefully earn riches to be carried with me after the death of my
     body
I will . . . . .

[*These Are the Caravan*].

These are the caravan of the desert—the close of the day—the encamp-
     ment and the camels.

jottings break into rhythmic trial lines, as above. The whole constitutes an interesting
early working upon a theme which is central in the poet's vision, and to which he
gave expression many times—most notably in "Passage to India."

     SPIRITUALITY] Published, N and F, I: 127, p. 39. MS: unavailable. A line
summing up meaning and intention.

     THAT IS PROFITABLE] Unpublished. MS: Feinberg. This interesting reflection
is penciled in regular line formation on a page of a substantial 212-page notebook
which, by internal evidence, can be dated as belonging to the period 1856–1857.

     THESE ARE] Published, N and F, I: 92, p. 32. MS: unavailable.

Proem.

These are the sights that I have absorbed in Manhattan Island, and in
all These States,
These are the thoughts that have come to me—some have come by night,
and some by day, as I walked,

I know that Personality is divine, and gives life and identity to a man or
woman—And I know that egotism is divine,
I know that the woman is to be equal to the man. And I know that there
is to be nothing excepted,

[*Undulating, Swiftly Merging*].

Undulating, swiftly merging from womb to birth, from birth to fullness
and transmission, quickly transpiring—
Conveying the sentiment of the mad, whirling, *fullout* speed of the
stars, in their circular orbits.

[*What, Think You*].

What, think you, does our Continent mean in reference to our race? I say
it means with radical and resistless power to assert the *Individual*
—raise a refuge strong and free for practical average use, for man
and woman:
That will America build and curiously looking around writes thereof a
poem thereof.

PROEM] Published, *N and F*, I: 33, p. 16. MS: Trent. A fragment penciled on a
piece of ruled paper with the poet's own title at the top, suggesting that these four
lines are the beginning passage of a prefatory poem.

UNDULATING] Published, *N and F*, I: 164, p. 48. MS: unavailable.

WHAT, THINK YOU] Published, *N and F*, I: 163, p. 48. MS: unavailable. This
sentiment would have interested Alexis de Tocqueville who, in his *Democracy in
America* (1835, 1840), remarked: "I readily admit that the Americans have no poets;
I cannot allow that they have no poetic ideas."

WHO WILLS] Published, *N and F*, I: 73, pp. 28–29. MS: Barrett (lines 1–2 and

[*Who Wills with His Own Brain*].

Who wills with his own brain, the sweet of the float of the earth descends
      and surrounds him,
If you be a laborer or apprentice or solitary farmer, it is the same

Have you known that your limbs must not dangle?
Have you known that your hands are to grasp vigorously?
You are also to grasp with your mind vigorously   5

Remember how many pass their whole lives and hardly once think and
      never learned themselves to think,
Remember before all realities must exist their thoughts.

As to you, if you have not yet learned to think, enter upon it now,
Think at once with directness, breadth, aim, conscientiousness,
You will find a strange pleasure from the start and grow rapidly each
      successive week.   10

[*Why Should I Subscribe*].

Why should I subscribe money to build some hero's statue?
That butcher boy is just as great a hero
He does not know what fear is.

[*Will You Have the Walls*].

Will you have the walls of the world with the air and the fringed clouds?
The Poet says God and me, What do you want from us? Ask and maybe
      we will give it you.
The Soul addresses God as his equal—as one who knows his greatness
      —as a younger brother.

8–10); MS of lines 3–7 unavailable. The first two lines are now a separate fragment
as are also lines 8–10. See "As to you . . . ," above. The entire composition, as
transcribed here and in N and F, constitutes an incomplete poem, of which other
parts may have been lost or never written.

    WHY SHOULD I] Published, N and F, I: 108, p. 35. MS: unavailable.

    WILL YOU HAVE] Published, N and F, I: 76, p. 29. MS: unavailable. Probably
composed in the early 1850's, for the sentiment is like that of "Song of Myself"—such
lines as:

        And I know that the hand of God is the promise of my own,
        And I know that the spirit of God is the brother of my own,

[The Woman That Sells].

The woman that sells candies and apples, at the street-stand,
The boy crying his newspapers in the morning.

[Poetic Lines in 1855–1856 Notebook].

Cursed is that age or nation that does not realize itself, and esteem itself
Wretched is that man who does not esteem himself

—page 9.

Of me the good comes by wrestling for it,
I am not he bringing ointments and soft wool for you,
I am he with whom you must wrestle. . . . I am
The good of you is not in me. . . . the good of you is altogether in
      yourself.
I am the one who indicates, and the one who provokes
      and tantalizes

—page 28.

I believe whatever happens I shall not forget this earth,
I believe I shall walk and walk among men and women.—
Wherever I go I believe I shall often return
There are many words and deeds that will happen that will allure me,
Where any one thinks of me or wishes me that will allure me,
Where the happy young husband and wife are, and the happy old hus-
      band and wife are, will allure me

—page 33.

Where the great renunciation is made in secret, that will allure me,
Where personal love reaches toward me, that will allure me. . . . to the
      prisoner in his cell, or the slave, or the solitary sick person, it will
      certainly allure me,

THE WOMAN THAT SELLS] Published, N and F, I: 67, p. 28. MS: unavailable.
These lines could have been intended for canto 15, "Song of Myself," which so
brilliantly details the sight and show of daily actions in America.

1855–1856 NOTEBOOK] Published, An 1855–56 Notebook Toward the Second
Edition of Leaves of Grass, edited by Harold W. Blodgett (1959). MS: Feinberg.

I do not know what is waiting for me to be—
But I know that I shall be in great form and nature
I cannot prove it to you or any one. . . . but I know it is so.

—page 35.

What the earth is and where the earth is [?]
Not more spiritual, not more divine and beautiful than this earth

—page 45.

I have all lives, all effects, all hidden invisibly in myself. . . . they
        proceed from me

—page 94.

Although most of the poetry entries in this important ninety-eight-page notebook are
trial lines and phrases toward the second edition (LG 1856), those here printed were
never used in any LG poem. A few of them are so distinguished—for example those
on page 33 of the notebook—that it is hard to understand why the poet never pub-
lished them. He could be prodigal.

Prefaces

PREFACE 1855] Whitman has not generally been credited with having written prose of a power commensurate with his poetry. However, the Preface to the first edition of *Leaves of Grass* is prose of noteworthy power and intellectual persuasiveness, with a corresponding stylistic authority. It is in fact one of the important landmarks of American literary criticism and it has continued to exert an influence on modern literature. Further comment on this preface will be found in the Introduction to the present volume. "Preface 1855" was collected with other prose works in SDC 1882, in CPP 1888, and CPW 1892. The two London reprints of this Preface (1868 and 1881) do not concern us here. The revisions, of which the bulk were made in *Specimen Days and Collect*, represented changes in Whitman's practices with respect to punctuation and other conventions, but a more important alteration was the cancellation of a number of passages which decreased the essay in bulk by about one-third. The shorter version of "Preface 1855" appears in CPW, and in Coll W: *Prose Works 1892*, Vol. II. The footnotes here, for the first edition, indicate passages canceled in later editions of the Preface, including lines which were translated into certain new poems, principally in LG 1856 and LG 1860. Poems significantly affected by such transfers are "By Blue Ontario's Shore," the most noteworthy, and also "Song of Prudence," "Song of the Answerer," "To You, (whoever you are)," "Tests," "Perfections," "Says," and "A Child's Amaze." See also the footnotes for the texts of these poems. Phrases or ideas from twenty-two of the twenty-four original paragraphs of the "Preface 1855" appear in the poems. See further, *Prose Works 1892*, Vol. II, and see Willie T. Weathers, "Whitman's Poetic Translations in his 1855 Preface," AL XIX, 1947, 21–40. The Variorum Edition of LG, edited by the present editors in *Collected Writings*, records all phrases transferred from this Preface to the poems.

Preface 1855—Leaves of Grass, *First Edition*

America does not repel the past or what it has produced under its forms or amid other politics or the idea of castes or the old religions. . . . accepts the lesson with calmness . . . is not so impatient as has been supposed that the slough still sticks to opinions and manners and literature while the life which served its requirements has passed into the new life of the new 5 forms . . . perceives that the corpse is slowly borne from the eating and sleeping rooms of the house . . . perceives that it waits a little while in the door . . . that it was fittest for its days . . . that its action has descended to the stalwart and wellshaped heir who approaches . . . and that he shall be fittest for his days. 10

The Americans of all nations at any time upon the earth have probably the fullest poetical nature. The United States themselves are essentially the greatest poem. In the history of the earth hitherto the largest and most stirring appear tame and orderly to their ampler largeness and stir. Here at last is something in the doings of man that corresponds with the broadcast doings of the day and 15 night. Here is not merely a nation but a teeming nation of nations. Here is action untied from strings necessarily blind to particulars and details magnificently moving in vast masses. Here is the hospitality which forever indicates heroes. . . . Here are the roughs and beards and space and ruggedness and nonchalance that the soul loves. Here the performance disdaining the trivial 20 unapproached in the tremendous audacity of its crowds and groupings and the push of its perspective spreads with crampless and flowing breadth and showers its prolific and splendid extravagance. One sees it must indeed own the riches of the summer and winter, and need never be bankrupt while corn grows from the

---

1. America] Lines 1–10, cf. "By Blue Ontario's Shore," 51–57.
1. what it has] Later editions read: "what the past has."
4. slough] Later editions read: "not impatient because the slough."
9. wellshaped] Later editions read: "well-shaped."
11. of all nations] Lines 11–23, cf. "By Blue Ontario's Shore," 58–65.
16. nation of nations] The sentence ending here was omitted in later editions.
18. in vast masses] Later editions omit "vast."
18. forever] Later editions read "for ever."
20. that the soul loves.] This sentence was omitted in later editions.

25 ground or the orchards drop apples or the bays contain fish or men beget
children upon women.

Other states indicate themselves in their deputies. . . . but the genius of
the United States is not best or most in its executives or legislatures, nor in its
ambassadors or authors or colleges or churches or parlors, nor even in its
30 newspapers or inventors . . . but always most in the common people. Their
manners speech dress friendships—the freshness and candor of their physi-
ognomy—the picturesque looseness of their carriage . . . their deathless at-
tachment to freedom—their aversion to anything indecorous or soft or
mean—the practical acknowledgment of the citizens of one state by the citizens
35 of all other states—the fierceness of their roused resentment—their curiosity
and welcome of novelty—their self-esteem and wonderful sympathy—their sus-
ceptibility to a slight—the air they have of persons who never knew how it felt
to stand in the presence of superiors—the fluency of their speech—their delight
in music, the sure symptom of manly tenderness and native elegance of
40 soul . . . their good temper and openhandedness—the terrible significance of
their elections—the President's taking off his hat to them not they to him—these
too are unrhymed poetry. It awaits the gigantic and generous treatment worthy
of it.

The largeness of nature or the nation were monstrous without a correspond-
45 ing largeness and generosity of the spirit of the citizen. Not nature nor swarm-
ing states nor streets and steamships nor prosperous business nor farms nor
capital nor learning may suffice for the ideal of man . . . nor suffice the poet.
No reminiscences may suffice either. A live nation can always cut a deep mark
and can have the best authority the cheapest . . . namely from its own soul.
50 This is the sum of the profitable uses of individuals or states and of present
action and grandeur and of the subjects of poets.—As if it were necessary to trot
back generation after generation to the eastern records! As if the beauty and
sacredness of the demonstrable must fall behind that of the mythical! As if men
do not make their mark out of any times! As if the opening of the western
55 continent by discovery and what has transpired since in North and South
America were less than the small theatre of the antique or the aimless sleep-
walking of the middle ages! The pride of the United States leaves the wealth
and finesse of the cities and all returns of commerce and agriculture and all the

30. common people.] In the later editions the remainder of this paragraph is
omitted, but the 1855 phrase, "common people," was extended by the words: "south,
north, west, east, in all its States, through all its mighty amplitude."

31. manners speech] Lines 30–40, cf. "By Blue Ontario's Shore", 95–98.

44. The largeness] Does not begin a paragraph in the later editions, but runs on
without interruption after line 30, "common people," where the previous paragraph
was cut.

44. of nature or] Omitted in the later texts.

45-46. Not nature . . . states] Later editions read: "Not swarming states."

51. subjects of poets.—] In the later editions the four following sentences ending

magnitude of geography or shows of exterior victory to enjoy the breed of
fullsized men or one fullsized man unconquerable and simple.   60

The American poets are to enclose old and new for America is the race of
races. Of them a bard is to be commensurate with a people. To him the other
continents arrive as contributions . . . he gives them reception for their sake
and his own sake. His spirit responds to his country's spirit. . . . he incarnates
its geography and natural life and rivers and lakes. Mississippi with annual   65
freshets and changing chutes, Missouri and Columbia and Ohio and Saint
Lawrence with the falls and beautiful masculine Hudson, do not embouchure
where they spend themselves more than they embouchure into him. The blue
breadth over the inland sea of Virginia and Maryland and the sea off Massa-
chusetts and Maine and over Manhattan bay and over Champlain and Erie and   70
over Ontario and Huron and Michigan and Superior, and over the Texan and
Mexican and Floridian and Cuban seas and over the seas off California and
Oregon, is not tallied by the blue breadth of the waters below more than the
breadth of above and below is tallied by him. When the long Atlantic coast
stretches longer and the Pacific coast stretches longer he easily stretches with   75
them north or south. He spans between them also from east to west and reflects
what is between them. On him rise solid growths that offset the growths of pine
and cedar and hemlock and liveoak and locust and chestnut and cypress and
hickory and limetree and cottonwood and tuliptree and cactus and wildvine and
tamarind and persimmon. . . . and tangles as tangled as any canebrake or   80
swamp. . . . and forests coated with transparent ice and icicles hanging from
the boughs and crackling in the wind. . . . and sides and peaks of moun-
tains. . . . and pasturage sweet and free as savannah or upland or
prairie. . . . with flights and songs and screams that answer those of the
wildpigeon and highhold and orchard oriole and coot and surf-duck and   85
redshouldered-hawk and fish-hawk and white-ibis and indian-hen and cat-owl
and water-pheasant and qua-bird and pied-sheldrake and blackbird and mock-
ingbird and buzzard and condor and night-heron and eagle. To him the heredi-
tary countenance descends both mother's and father's. To him enter the
essences of the real things and past and present events—of the enormous   90
diversity of temperature and agriculture and mines—the tribes of red abo-
rigines—the weatherbeaten vessels entering new ports or making landings on

"the middle ages!" (line 57) are between parentheses.

55. transpired since] In later texts, "since" is cancelled.

59. the breed of] In later texts read: "the sight and realization of full-sized
men" etc.

61. The American poets] Lines 61–68 and 88–89, 581–585, cf. "By Blue Ontario's
Shore," 66–76.

62. Of them a bard] In later texts the following forty-eight lines are omitted,
ending at line 110, "lips cease."

74. Atlantic coast] Lines 74–110, cf. "By Blue Ontario's Shore," 77–94 and
99–106.

rocky coasts—the first settlements north or south—the rapid stature and muscle
—the haughty defiance of '76, and the war and peace and formation of the
constitution. . . . the union always surrounded by blatherers and always calm
and impregnable—the perpetual coming of immigrants—the wharf hem'd cities
and superior marine—the unsurveyed interior—the loghouses and clearings
and wild animals and hunters and trappers. . . . the free commerce—the
fisheries and whaling and golddigging—the endless gestation of new states—the
convening of Congress every December, the members duly coming up from all
climates and the uttermost parts. . . . the noble character of the young me-
chanics and of all free American workmen and workwomen. . . . the general
ardor and friendliness and enterprise—the perfect equality of the female with
the male. . . . the large amativeness—the fluid movement of the population—
the factories and mercantile life and laborsaving machinery—the Yankee swap
—the New-York firemen and the target excursion—the southern plantation
life— the character of the northeast and of the northwest and southwest—slav-
ery and the tremulous spreading of hands to protect it, and the stern opposition
to it which shall never cease till it ceases or the speaking of tongues and the
moving of lips cease. For such the expression of the American poet is to be
transcendant and new. It is to be indirect and not direct or descriptive or epic.
Its quality goes through these to much more. Let the age and wars of other
nations be chanted and their eras and characters be illustrated and that finish
the verse. Not so the great psalm of the republic. Here the theme is creative and
has vista. Here comes one among the wellbeloved stonecutters and plans with
decision and science and sees the solid and beautiful forms of the future where
there are now no solid forms.

Of all nations the United States with veins full of poetical stuff most need
poets and will doubtless have the greatest and use them the greatest. Their
Presidents shall not be their common referee so much as their poets shall. Of all
mankind the great poet is the equable man. Not in him but off from him things
are grotesque or eccentric or fail of their sanity. Nothing out of its place is good
and nothing in its place is bad. He bestows on every object or quality its fit
proportions neither more nor less. He is the arbiter of the diverse and he is the
key. He is the equalizer of his age and land. . . . he supplies what wants
supplying and checks what wants checking. If peace is the routine out of him
speaks the spirit of peace, large, rich, thrifty, building vast and populous cities,
encouraging agriculture and the arts and commerce—lighting the study of
man, the soul, immortality—federal, state or municipal government, marriage,

110. For such the expression of] In later texts, read: "The expression of."
111. transcendant] Lines 111–117, cf. "By Blue Ontario's Shore," 119–126.
115. has vista] The passage that follows, originally 33 lines in length, ending
"draw blood" (line 135), is omitted in later editions.
118. States] Lines 118–120, cf. "By Blue Ontario's Shore," 132–133.
121. equable man] Lines 120–135, and 139–148, cf. "By Blue Ontario's Shore,"
137–153.
135–136. he never stagnates] Later texts read: "the great poet never."

health, freetrade, intertravel by land and sea. . . . nothing too close, nothing   130
too far off . . . the stars not too far off. In war he is the most deadly force of
the war. Who recruits him recruits horse and foot . . . he fetches parks of
artillery the best that engineer ever knew. If the time becomes slothful and
heavy he knows how to arouse it . . . he can make every word he speaks draw
blood. Whatever stagnates in the flat of custom or obedience or legislation he   135
never stagnates. Obedience does not master him, he masters it. High up out of
reach he stands turning a concentrated light . . . he turns the pivot with his
finger . . . he baffles the swiftest runners as he stands and easily overtakes and
envelops them. The time straying toward infidelity and confections and persi-
flage he withholds by his steady faith . . . he spreads out his dishes . . . he   140
offers the sweet firmfibred meat that grows men and women. His brain is the
ultimate brain. He is no arguer . . . he is judgment. He judges not as the
judge judges but as the sun falling around a helpless thing. As he sees the
farthest he has the most faith. His thoughts are the hymns of the praise of
things. In the talk on the soul and eternity and God off of his equal plane he is   145
silent. He sees eternity less like a play with a prologue and denouement. . . .
he sees eternity in men and women . . . he does not see men and women as
dreams or dots. Faith is the antiseptic of the soul . . . it pervades the com-
mon people and preserves them . . . they never give up believing and expect-
ing and trusting. There is that indescribable freshness and unconsciousness   150
about an illiterate person that humbles and mocks the power of the noblest ex-
pressive genius. The poet sees for a certainty how one not a great artist may be
just as sacred and perfect as the greatest artist. . . . . . The power to destroy
or remould is freely used by him but never the power of attack. What is past is
past. If he does not expose superior models and prove himself by every step he   155
takes he is not what is wanted. The presence of the greatest poet conquers . . .
not parleying or struggling or any prepared attempts. Now he has passed that
way see after him! there is not left any vestige of despair or misanthropy or
cunning or exclusiveness or the ignominy of a nativity or color or delusion of
hell or the necessity of hell. . . . . and no man thenceforward shall be de-   160
graded for ignorance or weakness or sin.

The greatest poet hardly knows pettiness or triviality. If he breathes into
any thing that was before thought small it dilates with the grandeur and life of
the universe. He is a seer. . . . he is individual . . . he is complete in him-
self. . . . the others are as good as he, only he sees it and they do not. He is   165
not one of the chorus. . . . he does not stop for any regulation . . . he is the

140. by his steady faith] Later texts omit "his." The passage following, ending
"dreams or dots" (line 148), is omitted in the later editions.
153. The power] In later texts a new paragraph begins here.
154. by him] In later texts read: "by the greatest poet."
154. never the power] In later texts read: "seldom the power."
162. The greatest poet] No paragraph break occurs here in later texts (cf. line
153, note).
163. any thing] In later texts, read: "anything."

president of regulation. What the eyesight does to the rest he does to the rest.
Who knows the curious mystery of the eyesight? The other senses corroborate
themselves, but this is removed from any proof but its own and foreruns the
170 identities of the spiritual world. A single glance of it mocks all the investigations
of man and all the instruments and books of the earth and all reasoning. What
is marvellous? what is unlikely? what is impossible or baseless or vague? after
you have once just opened the space of a peachpit and given audience to far and
near and to the sunset and had all things enter with electric swiftness softly and
175 duly without confusion or jostling or jam.

The land and sea, the animals fishes and birds, the sky of heaven and the
orbs, the forests mountains and rivers, are not small themes . . . but folks
expect of the poet to indicate more than the beauty and dignity which always
attach to dumb real objects . . . . they expect him to indicate the path be-
180 tween reality and their souls. Men and women perceive the beauty well enough
. . probably as well as he. The passionate tenacity of hunters, woodmen, early
risers, cultivators of gardens and orchards and fields, the love of healthy women
for the manly form, seafaring persons, drivers of horses, the passion for light
and the open air, all is an old varied sign of the unfailing perception of beauty
185 and of a residence of the poetic in outdoor people. They can never be assisted by
poets to perceive . . . some may but they never can. The poetic quality is not
marshalled in rhyme or uniformity or abstract addresses to things nor in
melancholy complaints or good precepts, but is the life of these and much else
and is in the soul. The profit of rhyme is that it drops seeds of a sweeter and
190 more luxuriant rhyme, and of uniformity that it conveys itself into its own roots
in the ground out of sight. The rhyme and uniformity of perfect poems show the
free growth of metrical laws and bud from them as unerringly and loosely as
lilacs or roses on a bush, and take shapes as compact as the shapes of chestnuts
and oranges and melons and pears, and shed the perfume impalpable to form.
195 The fluency and ornaments of the finest poems or music or orations or recita-
tions are not independent but dependent. All beauty comes from beautiful blood
and a beautiful brain. If the greatnesses are in conjunction in a man or woman it
is enough . . . . the fact will prevail through the universe . . . . but the
gaggery and gilt of a million years will not prevail. Who troubles himself about
200 his ornaments or fluency is lost. This is what you shall do: Love the earth and
sun and the animals, despise riches, give alms to every one that asks, stand up

168. corroborate] Lines 168–175, cf. "Tests," 4–5.
180. souls] Lines 176–199, cf. "Song of the Answerer" (the poet) who serves others
by indicating "the path between reality and their souls". Lines transferred from the
present essay are found in the second canto of the poem: see notes below, lines
329, 336, 606. Further detail on "the Answerer" appears in the note to that poem.
193. or roses] In later texts, read: "and roses."
200. Love the earth] Lines 200–215, cf. "By Blue Ontario's Shore," 235–247.
206.–207. read these . . . life,] This clause is omitted from the later editions.
212. always ready ploughed] In later editions, read: "already plough'd."
219. balks] In later editions read "baulks"; both spellings are correct.

for the stupid and crazy, devote your income and labor to others, hate tyrants, argue not concerning God, have patience and indulgence toward the people, take off your hat to nothing known or unknown or to any man or number of men, go freely with powerful uneducated persons and with the young and with 205 the mothers of families, read these leaves in the open air every season of every year of your life, re-examine all you have been told at school or church or in any book, dismiss whatever insults your own soul, and your very flesh shall be a great poem and have the richest fluency not only in its words but in the silent lines of its lips and face and between the lashes of your eyes and in every motion 210 and joint of your body. . . . . The poet shall not spend his time in unneeded work. He shall know that the ground is always ready ploughed and manured . . . . others may not know it but he shall. He shall go directly to the creation. His trust shall master the trust of everything he touches . . . . and shall master all attachment. 215

The known universe has one complete lover and that is the greatest poet. He consumes an eternal passion and is indifferent which chance happens and which possible contingency of fortune or misfortune and persuades daily and hourly his delicious pay. What balks or breaks others is fuel for his burning progress to contact and amorous joy. Other proportions of the reception of 220 pleasure dwindle to nothing to his proportions. All expected from heaven or from the highest he is rapport with in the sight of the daybreak or a scene of the winter woods or the presence of children playing or with his arm round the neck of a man or woman. His love above all love has leisure and expanse . . . . he leaves room ahead of himself. He is no irresolute or suspicious lover . . . he is 225 sure . . . he scorns intervals. His experience and the showers and thrills are not for nothing. Nothing can jar him . . . . suffering and darkness cannot— death and fear cannot. To him complaint and jealousy and envy are corpses buried and rotten in the earth . . . . he saw them buried. The sea is not surer of the shore or the shore of the sea than he is of the fruition of his love and of 230 all perfection and beauty.

The fruition of beauty is no chance of hit or miss . . . it is inevitable as life . . . . it is exact and plumb as gravitation. From the eyesight proceeds another eyesight and from the hearing proceeds another hearing and from the voice proceeds another voice eternally curious of the harmony of things with 235 man. To these respond perfections not only in the committees that were sup-

222. a scene] In later editions read: "the scenes."
230. he is of the fruition] Erroneously printed "he is the fruition," in SDC 1882 and later editions.
232. hit or miss] In later texts read: "miss or hit."
232. is inevitable] Later editions read: "is as inevitable."
233. eyesight] Lines 233–236, cf. "Assurances," 7.
236. perfections] The poem, "Perfections," an epigram, reflects the idea at large in ll. 236–247 and 264–269.
236. To these respond] This sentence was omitted in later texts.

posed to stand for the rest but in the rest themselves just the same. These
understand the law of perfection in masses and floods . . . that its finish is to
each for itself and onward from itself . . . that it is profuse and impartial
. . . that there is not a minute of the light or dark nor an acre of the earth or
sea without it—nor any direction of the sky nor any trade or employment nor
any turn of events. This is the reason that about the proper expression of beauty
there is precision and balance . . . one part does not need to be thrust above
another. The best singer is not the one who has the most lithe and powerful
organ . . . the pleasure of poems is not in them that take the handsomest
measure and similes and sound.

Without effort and without exposing in the least how it is done the greatest
poet brings the spirit of any or all events and passions and scenes and persons
some more and some less to bear on your individual character as you hear or
read. To do this well is to compete with the laws that pursue and follow time.
What is the purpose must surely be there and the clue of it must be there
. . . . and the faintest indication is the indication of the best and then be-
comes the clearest indication. Past and present and future are not disjoined but
joined. The greatest poet forms the consistence of what is to be from what has
been and is. He drags the dead out of their coffins and stands them again on
their feet . . . . he says to the past, Rise and walk before me that I may
realize you. He learns the lesson . . . . he places himself where the future
becomes present. The greatest poet does not only dazzle his rays over character
and scenes and passions . . . he finally ascends and finishes all . . . he
exhibits the pinnacles that no man can tell what they are for or what is beyond
. . . . he glows a moment on the extremest verge. He is most wonderful in
his last half-hidden smile or frown . . . by that flash of the moment of parting
the one that sees it shall be encouraged or terrified afterward for many years.
The greatest poet does not moralize or make applications of morals . . . he
knows the soul. The soul has that measureless pride which consists in never
acknowledging any lessons but its own. But it has sympathy as measureless as
its pride and the one balances the other and neither can stretch too far while it
stretches in company with the other. The inmost secrets of art sleep with the
twain. The greatest poet has lain close betwixt both and they are vital in his
style and thoughts.

238–239. that its . . . itself] Clause omitted in later texts.
240–241. earth or sea] Later texts read "earth and sea," (note added comma).
246. and similes and sound] Later texts omit "and similes."
265. measureless pride] Lines 265–268, cf. "Song of Prudence," 43–45, a direct
borrowing; cf. note on "perfections," above. See line 507 note, for all borrowings in
"Prudence."
266. lessons but] In later texts, "lessons or deductions but."
276. insousiance] In later texts correctly spelled, "insouciance."
283. greatest poet] In later texts, "great."
289. sooth] Spelled correctly, "soothe," in the later editions. Lines 288–293 parallel
the idea of "Song of Myself." Section 19, lines 382–388.

The art of art, the glory of expression and the sunshine of the light of letters is simplicity. Nothing is better than simplicity . . . . nothing can make up for excess or for the lack of definiteness. To carry on the heave of impulse and pierce intellectual depths and give all subjects their articulations are powers neither common nor very uncommon. But to speak in literature with the perfect 275 rectitude and insousiance of the movements of animals and the unimpeachableness of the sentiment of trees in the woods and grass by the roadside is the flawless triumph of art. If you have looked on him who has achieved it you have looked on one of the masters of the artists of all nations and times. You shall not contemplate the flight of the graygull over the bay or the mettlesome action of 280 the blood horse or the tall leaning of sunflowers on their stalk or the appearance of the sun journeying through heaven or the appearance of the moon afterward with any more satisfaction than you shall contemplate him. The greatest poet has less a marked style and is more the channel of thoughts and things without increase or diminution, and is the free channel of himself. He swears to his art, I 285 will not be meddlesome, I will not have in my writing any elegance or effect or originality to hang in the way between me and the rest like curtains. I will have nothing hang in the way, not the richest curtains. What I tell I tell for precisely what it is. Let who may exalt or startle or fascinate or sooth I will have purposes as health or heat or snow has and be as regardless of observation. What I 290 experience or portray shall go from my composition without a shred of my composition. You shall stand by my side and look in the mirror with me.

The old red blood and stainless gentility of great poets will be proved by their unconstraint. A heroic person walks at his ease through and out of that custom or precedent or authority that suits him not. Of the traits of the brother- 295 hood of writers savans musicians inventors and artists nothing is finer than silent defiance advancing from new free forms. In the need of poems philosophy politics mechanism science behaviour, the craft of art, an appropriate native grand-opera, shipcraft, or any craft, he is greatest forever and forever who contributes the greatest original practical example. The cleanest expression is 300 that which finds no sphere worthy of itself and makes one.

The messages of great poets to each man and woman are, Come to us on equal terms, Only then can you understand us, We are no better than you, What we enclose you enclose, What we enjoy you may enjoy. Did you suppose

294. unconstraint] Lines 293–294 and 297–300, cf. "By Blue Ontario's Shore," 221–223.

296. of writers] In later texts, "of first class writers," (note comma). In his revisions, WW restored some of the commas experimentally excluded in his earlier prose.

298. behaviour] Spelled "behavior" in later editions; both are correct.

299. forever and forever] In later editions, "for ever and ever."

302. great poets] In later texts, "great poems."

303. Only then] In 1882, read "only." The capital letter beginning each of a succession of clauses was an early experiment. In 1881 Whitman restored the small initial letter in most cases.

304. enclose . . . enclose] In later texts, spelled "inclose."

305 there could be only one Supreme? We affirm there can be unnumbered Su-
premes, and that one does not countervail another any more than one eyesight
countervails another . . and that men can be good or grand only of the con-
sciousness of their supremacy within them. What do you think is the grandeur
of storms and dismemberments and the deadliest battles and wrecks and the
310 wildest fury of the elements and the power of the sea and the motion of nature
and of the throes of human desires and dignity and hate and love? It is that
something in the soul which says, Rage on, Whirl on, I tread master here and
everywhere, Master of the spasms of the sky and of the shatter of the sea,
Master of nature and passion and death, And of all terror and all pain.

315 The American bards shall be marked for generosity and affection and for
encouraging competitors . . They shall be kosmos . . without monopoly or
secresy . . glad to pass any thing to any one . . hungry for equals night and
day. They shall not be careful of riches and privilege . . . . they shall be
riches and privilege . . . . they shall perceive who the most affluent man is.
320 The most affluent man is he that confronts all the shows he sees by equivalents
out of the stronger wealth of himself. The American bard shall delineate no
class of persons nor one or two out of the strata of interests nor love most nor
truth most nor the soul most nor the body most . . . . and not be for the
eastern states more than the western or the northern states more than the
325 southern.

Exact science and its practical movements are no checks on the greatest
poet but always his encouragement and support. The outset and remembrance
are there . . there the arms that lifted him first and brace him best . . . .
there he returns after all his goings and comings. The sailor and traveler . .
330 the anatomist, chemist, astronomer, geologist, phrenologist, spiritualist, mathe-
matician, historian and lexicographer are not poets, but they are the lawgivers of
poets and their construction underlies the structure of every perfect poem. No
matter what rises or is uttered they sent the seed of the conception of it . . . of
them and by them stand the visible proofs of souls . . . . . always of their
335 fatherstuff must be begotten the sinewy races of bards. If there shall be love and

---

305. Supreme] Lines 304–308, cf. "By Blue Ontario's Shore," 25–26.
308. grandeur of storms] Lines 308–314, cf. "To You, (whoever you are)," 42–43.
The entire poem is motivated by this paragraph—see lines 6–17 and 33–38.
312. Rage on, Whirl] In later texts, "whirl."
314. death, And of] In later texts, "death, and."
316. kosmos] In later texts, "Kosmos," but WW was not consistent in capitalizing
this word.
317. secresy] Correctly spelled as "secrecy" in later texts.
317. any thing] In later texts read: "anything."
324. eastern states . . . western] In later texts, "Eastern" and "Western"; so the
initial capital for "Northern" and "Southern" in next line, and in general when
signifying a region.
328. brace him] In later texts, "braced him."
329. sailor] Lines 329–332, cf. "Song of the Answerer," 73–74.

content between the father and the son and if the greatness of the son is the exuding of the greatness of the father there shall be love between the poet and the man of demonstrable science. In the beauty of poems are the tuft and final applause of science.

Great is the faith of the flush of knowledge and of the investigation of the 340
depths of qualities and things. Cleaving and circling here swells the soul of the poet yet it president of itself always. The depths are fathomless and therefore calm. The innocence and nakedness are resumed . . . they are neither modest nor immodest. The whole theory of the special and supernatural and all that was twined with it or educed out of it departs as a dream. What has ever 345
happened . . . . what happens and whatever may or shall happen, the vital laws enclose all . . . . they are sufficent for any case and for all cases . . . none to be hurried or retarded . . . . any miracle of affairs or persons inadmissible in the vast clear scheme where every motion and every spear of grass and the frames and spirits of men and women and all that concerns them are 350
unspeakably perfect miracles all referring to all and each distinct and in its place. It is also not consistent with the reality of the soul to admit that there is anything in the known universe more divine than men and women.

Men and women and the earth and all upon it are simply to be taken as they are, and the investigation of their past and present and future shall be unintermitted and shall be done with perfect candor. Upon this basis philosophy 355
speculates ever looking toward the poet, ever regarding the eternal tendencies of all toward happiness never inconsistent with what is clear to the senses and to the soul. For the eternal tendencies of all toward happiness make the only point of sane philosophy. Whatever comprehends less than that . . . whatever is 360
less than the laws of light and of astronomical motion . . . or less than the laws that follow the thief the liar the glutton and the drunkard through this life and doubtless afterward . . . . . . or less than vast stretches of time or the slow formation of density or the patient upheaving of strata—is of no account. Whatever would put God in a poem or system of philosophy as contending 365
against some being or influence is also of no account. Sanity and ensemble

334-5. always of their fatherstuff] This phrase and the remainder of the sentence canceled in later texts.
336. greatness . . . son] Lines 336–339, cf. "Song of the Answerer," 69–70.
338. are the tuft] In later texts, "are henceforth the tuft."
342. it president] Correctly, in later texts, "is president."
344. supernatural] Later texts read: "The whole theory of the supernatural."
347. enclose all . . . they] Later texts read: "inclose all. They . . . ."
347. sufficent] Corrected in later texts: "sufficient."
348. miracle] Later texts read: "any special miracle."
351. perfect miracles] Lines 345–352 (see also lines 238–241, cf. "Miracles," 15–20. The poem originally contained other lines from the same locations but these were excluded in 1881.
354. are simply to be taken] Later texts cancel "simply."
357. toward the poet] Later texts read "towards."
365. put God in] Lines 365–366, cf. "A Child's Amaze," 2–3.

characterise the great master . . . spoilt in one principle all is spoilt. The great master has nothing to do with miracles. He sees health for himself in being one of the mass . . . . he sees the hiatus in singular eminence. To the
370 perfect shape comes common ground. To be under the general law is great for that is to correspond with it. The master knows that he is unspeakably great and that all are unspeakably great . . . . that nothing for instance is greater than to conceive children and bring them up well . . . that to be is just as great as to perceive or tell.

375   In the make of the great masters the idea of political liberty is indispensible. Liberty takes the adherence of heroes wherever men and women exist . . . . but never takes any adherence or welcome from the rest more than from poets. They are the voice and exposition of liberty. They out of ages are worthy the grand idea . . . . to them it is confided and they must sustain it. Nothing has
380 precedence of it and nothing can warp or degrade it. The attitude of great poets is to cheer up slaves and horrify despots. The turn of their necks, the sound of their feet, the motions of their wrists, are full of hazard to the one and hope to the other. Come nigh them awhile and though they neither speak or advise you shall learn the faithful American lesson. Liberty is poorly served by men whose
385 good intent is quelled from one failure or two failures or any number of failures, or from the casual indifference or ingratitude of the people, or from the sharp show of the tushes of power, or the bringing to bear soldiers and cannon or any penal statutes. Liberty relies upon itself, invites no one, promises nothing, sits in calmness and light, is positive and composed, and knows no discouragement.
390 The battle rages with many a loud alarm and frequent advance and retreat . . . . the enemy triumphs . . . . the prison, the handcuffs, the iron necklace and anklet, the scaffold, garrote and leadballs do their work . . . . the cause is asleep . . . . the strong throats are choked with their own blood . . . . the young men drop their eyelashes toward the ground when they pass
395 each other . . . . and is liberty gone out of that place? No never. When liberty goes it is not the first to go nor the second or third to go . . it waits for all the rest to go . . it is the last. . . When the memories of the old martyrs are faded utterly away . . . . when the large names of patriots are laughed at in the public halls from the lips of the orators . . . . when the boys are no
400 more christened after the same but christened after tyrants and traitors instead . . . . when the laws of the free are grudgingly permitted and laws for informers and bloodmoney are sweet to the taste of the people . . . . when I and you walk abroad upon the earth stung with compassion at the sight of

373. that to be] In later texts, *be* (in italics).

375. Liberty] Lines 375–381, cf. "By Blue Ontario's Shore," 154–156.

376. men and women] Later texts read: "man and woman."

381. degrade it] The passage following, ending "part of the earth" (line 422), is omitted from the later texts, but thirty of the originally sixty-four lines were transposed; see note, line 384.

384. Liberty] Lines 381–398, revised and condensed, appear in the same order in "To A Foil'd European Revolutionaire," lines 1–8, 14–16, and 19–24. Lines 419–422

numberless brothers answering our equal friendship and calling no man master
—and when we are elated with noble joy at the sight of slaves . . . . when the 405
soul retires in the cool communion of the night and surveys its experience and
has much extasy over the word and deed that put back a helpless innocent
person into the gripe of the gripers or into any cruel inferiority . . . . when
those in all parts of these states who could easier realize the true American
character but do not yet—when the swarms of cringers, suckers, doughfaces, 410
lice of politics, planners of sly involutions for their own preferment to city
offices or state legislatures or the judiciary or congress or the presidency, obtain
a response of love and natural deference from the people whether they get the
offices or no . . . . when it is better to be a bound booby and rogue in office at
a high salary than the poorest free mechanic or farmer with his hat unmoved 415
from his head and firm eyes and a candid and generous heart . . . . and when
servility by town or state or the federal government or any oppression on a large
scale or small scale can be tried on without its own punishment following duly
after in exact proportion against the smallest chance of escape . . . . or rather
when all life and all the souls of men and women are discharged from any part 420
of the earth—then only shall the instinct of liberty be discharged from that part
of the earth.

As the attributes of the poets of the kosmos concentre in the real body and
soul and in the pleasure of things they possess the superiority of genuineness
over all fiction and romance. As they emit themselves facts are showered over 425
with light . . . . the daylight is lit with more volatile light . . . . also the
deep between the setting and rising sun goes deeper many fold. Each precise
object or condition or combination or process exhibits a beauty . . . . the
multiplication table its—old age its—the carpenter's trade its—the grand-opera
its . . . . the hugehulled cleanshaped New-York clipper at sea under steam 430
or full sail gleams with unmatched beauty . . . . the American circles and
large harmonies of government gleam with theirs . . . . and the commonest
definite intentions and actions with theirs. The poets of the kosmos advance
through all interpositions and coverings and turmoils and stratagems to first
principles. They are of use . . . . they dissolve poverty from its need and 435
riches from its conceit. You large proprietor they say shall not realize or
perceive more than any one else. The owner of the library is not he who holds a
legal title to it having bought and paid for it. Any one and every one is owner of
the library who can read the same through all the varieties of tongues and
subjects and styles, and in whom they enter with ease and take residence and 440

compare with the poem, lines 25–26. Fifteen lines of the poem, most importantly
the last eight, were new composition.

423–4. body and soul and] The later texts omit "and soul."

426–7. also the deep] The later texts omit "also."

430. hugehulled cleanshaped] The later texts read "huge-hull'd clean-shap'd."

439. library] After "library" the later texts read: "(indeed he or she alone is
owner,) who."

440. with ease] Later texts omit the next clause "and take . . . maternity."

force toward paternity and maternity, and make supple and powerful and rich
and large. . . . . These American states strong and healthy and ac-
complished shall receive no pleasure from violations of natural models and must
not permit them. In paintings or mouldings or carvings in mineral or wood, or
in the illustrations of books or newspapers, or in any comic or tragic prints, or
in the patterns of woven stuffs or any thing to beautify rooms or furniture or
costumes, or to put upon cornices or monuments or on the prows or sterns of
ships, or to put anywhere before the human eye indoors or out, that which
distorts honest shapes or which creates unearthly beings or places or con-
tingencies is a nuisance and revolt. Of the human form especially it is so great it
must never be made ridiculous. Of ornaments to a work nothing outre can be
allowed . . but those ornaments can be allowed that conform to the perfect
facts of the open air and that flow out of the nature of the work and come
irrepressibly from it and are necessary to the completion of the work. Most
works are most beautiful without ornament. . . Exaggerations will be
revenged in human physiology. Clean and vigorous children are jetted and con-
ceived only in those communities where the models of natural forms are public
every day. . . . . Great genius and the people of these states must never be
demeaned to romances. As soon as histories are properly told there is no more
need of romances.

The great poets are also to be known by the absence in them of tricks and
by the justification of perfect personal candor. Then folks echo a new cheap joy
and a divine voice leaping from their brains: How beautiful is candor! All faults
may be forgiven of him who has perfect candor. Henceforth let no man of us lie,
for we have seen that openness wins the inner and outer world and that there is
no single exception, and that never since our earth gathered itself in a mass have
deceit or subterfuge or prevarication attracted its smallest particle or the faint-
est tinge of a shade—and that through the enveloping wealth and rank of a state
or the whole republic of states a sneak or sly person shall be discovered and
despised . . . . and that the soul has never been once fooled and never can be
fooled . . . . and thrift without the loving nod of the soul is only a fœtid
puff . . . . and there never grew up in any of the continents of the globe nor

442. These American] Later texts begin a new paragraph here.
445. newspapers] Later texts omit the next phrase: "or in . . . prints."
446. any thing] In later texts: "anything."
450. human form] Lines 450–460, cf. "Says" ("Excluded Poems"), 8–14. Stanza
6 ("Says," line 15) based on the idea of the next paragraph (following line 460)
praises social candor and truth as the necessary conditions for freedom; stanza 7
reflects a theme in the following text (after line 513) the social need for the prudent
governance of the mind over human choice.
458. these states] Later editions capitalize "States" whenever the word substitutes
for "United States."
459–60. told there is no more need] Later editions read: "told, no more need."
461. also to be known] Later texts omit "also."

upon any planet or satellite or star, nor upon the asteroids, nor in any part of
ethereal space, nor in the midst of density, nor under the fluid wet of the sea, nor
in that condition which precedes the birth of babes, nor at any time during the   475
changes of life, nor in that condition that follows what we term death, nor in
any stretch of abeyance or action afterward of vitality, nor in any process of
formation or reformation anywhere, a being whose instinct hated the truth.

Extreme caution or prudence, the soundest organic health, large hope and
comparison and fondness for women and children, large alimentiveness and   480
destructiveness and causality, with a perfect sense of the oneness of nature and
the propriety of the same spirit applied to human affairs . . these are called up
of the float of the brain of the world to be parts of the greatest poet from his
birth out of his mother's womb and from her birth out of her mother's. Caution
seldom goes far enough. It has been thought that the prudent citizen was the   485
citizen who applied himself to solid gains and did well for himself and his
family and completed a lawful life without debt or crime. The greatest poet sees
and admits these economies as he sees the economies of food and sleep, but has
higher notions of prudence than to think he gives much when he gives a few
slight attentions at the latch of the gate. The premises of the prudence of life are   490
not the hospitality of it or the ripeness and harvest of it. Beyond the independ-
ence of a little sum laid aside for burial-money, and of a few clapboards around
and shingles overhead on a lot of American soil owned, and the easy dollars that
supply the year's plain clothing and meals, the melancholy prudence of the
abandonment of such a great being as a man is to the toss and pallor of years of   495
moneymaking with all their scorching days and icy nights and all their stifling
deceits and underhanded dodgings, or infinitessimals of parlors, or shameless
stuffing while others starve . . and all the loss of the bloom and odor of the
earth and of the flowers and atmosphere and of the sea and of the true taste of
the women and men you pass or have to do with in youth or middle age, and the   500
issuing sickness and desperate revolt at the close of a life without elevation or
naivete, and the ghastly chatter of a death without serenity or majesty, is the
great fraud upon modern civilization and forethought, blotching the surface
and system which civilization undeniably drafts, and moistening with tears the

462. Then folks] The later editions omit the two clauses beginning here and
ending "beautiful is candor."

470. been once] In later editions, "once been."

473. satellite] Later editions omit five phrases, beginning with "or star" and ending
with "wet of the sea."

476. of life] Later editions omit the clause which follows: "nor in . . . death."

477. or action afterward] Later texts omit "afterward."

487. family] Later texts read, "and for his family," (note comma).

493. a lot] A small parcel or allotment of land; not as in the vernacular sense,
"a great deal."

502. naivete] Correctly in later texts, "naïveté"; immediately following, WW in-
serted new copy in parentheses: "(even if you have achiev'd a secure 10,000 a year,
or election to Congress or the Governorship,) . . . ."

505　immense features it spreads and spreads with such velocity before the reached
kisses of the soul. . . Still the right explanation remains to be made about
prudence. The prudence of the mere wealth and respectability of the most
esteemed life appears too faint for the eye to observe at all when little and large
alike drop quietly aside at the thought of the prudence suitable for immortality.

510　What is wisdom that fills the thinness of a year or seventy or eighty years to
wisdom spaced out by ages and coming back at a certain time with strong
reinforcements and rich presents and the clear faces of wedding-guests as far as
you can look in every direction running gaily toward you? Only the soul is of
itself . . . . all else has reference to what ensues. All that a person does or

515　thinks is of consequence. Not a move can a man or woman make that affects him
or her in a day or a month or any part of the direct lifetime or the hour of death
but the same affects him or her onward afterward through the indirect lifetime.
The indirect is always as great and real as the direct. The spirit receives from
the body just as much as it gives to the body. Not one name of word or

520　deed . . not of venereal sores or discolorations . . not the privacy of the
onanist . . not of the putrid veins of gluttons or rumdrinkers . . . not pecu-
lation or cunning or betrayal or murder . . no serpentine poison of those that
seduce women . . not the foolish yielding of women . . not prostitution . .
not of any depravity of young men . . not of the attainment of gain by dis-

525　creditable means . . not any nastiness of appetite . . not any harshness of
officers to men or judges to prisoners or fathers to sons or sons to fathers or of
husbands to wives or bosses to their boys . . not of greedy looks or malignant
wishes . . . nor any of the wiles practised by people upon themselves . . .
ever is or ever can be stamped on the programme but it is duly realized and

530　returned, and that returned in further performances . . . and they returned
again. Nor can the push of charity or personal force ever be any thing else than
the profoundest reason, whether it bring arguments to hand or no. No specifica-
tion is necessary . . to add or subtract or divide is in vain. Little or big,
learned or unlearned, white or black, legal or illegal, sick or well, from the first

535　inspiration down the windpipe to the last expiration out of it, all that a male or
female does that is vigorous and benevolent and clean is so much sure profit to
him or her in the unshakable order of the universe and through the whole scope

　　506.　Still the right] In the later texts a new paragraph begins here, with change
of the opening phrase to "Ever the right . . ."
　　506–507. explanation . . . prudence] Lines 506–580, cf. "Song of Prudence,"
3–56. Of the 56 lines of this poem, all but the first two are borrowed, with appropri-
ate intensification, from the lines of the Preface, in approximately the same order
except that lines 43–45 of the poem reflect an earlier Preface passage, lines 265–269
(see note, line 265). The other notes citing parallel passages occur below at lines
509, 513, 529, and 570.
　　509. immortality] Lines 506–510, cf. "Song of Prudence," 3–4. See also, line 506,
note.
　　510. What is wisdom] In later editions, "the wisdom"; so also, "to wisdom" becomes
"to the wisdom," later in this sentence (cf. line 511).
　　513–14. soul . . . itself] Lines 513–521, cf. "Song of Prudence," 5–13. See also

of it forever. If the savage or felon is wise it is well . . . . if the greatest poet
or savan is wise it is simply the same . . if the President or chief justice is wise
it is the same . . . if the young mechanic or farmer is wise it is no more or   540
less . . if the prostitute is wise it is no more nor less. The interest will come
round . . all will come round. All the best actions of war and peace . . . all
help given to relatives and strangers and the poor and old and sorrowful and
young children and widows and the sick, and to all shunned persons . . all
furtherance of fugitives and of the escape of slaves . . all the self-denial that   545
stood steady and aloof on wrecks and saw others take the seats of the boats
. . . all offering of substance or life for the good old cause, or for a friend's
sake or opinion's sake . . . all pains of enthusiasts scoffed at by their neigh-
bors . . all the vast sweet love and precious suffering of mothers . . . all
honest men baffled in strifes recorded or unrecorded . . . . all the grandeur   550
and good of the few ancient nations whose fragments of annals we inherit . .
and all the good of the hundreds of far mightier and more ancient nations
unknown to us by name or date or location . . . . all that was ever manfully
begun, whether it succeeded or no . . . . all that has at any time been well
suggested out of the divine heart of man or by the divinity of his mouth or by   555
the shaping of his great hands . . and all that is well thought or done this day
on any part of the surface of the globe . . or on any of the wandering stars or
fixed stars by those there as we are here . . or that is henceforth to be well
thought or done by you whoever you are, or by any one—these singly and
wholly inured at their time and inure now and will inure always to the identities   560
from which they sprung or shall spring. . . Did you guess any of them lived
only its moment? The world does not so exist . . no parts palpable or impal-
pable so exist . . . no result exists now without being from its long antecedent
result, and that from its antecedent, and so backward without the farthest
mentionable spot coming a bit nearer the beginning than any other   565
spot. . . . . Whatever satisfies the soul is truth. The prudence of the greatest
poet answers at last the craving and glut of the soul, is not contemptuous of less
ways of prudence if they conform to its ways, puts off nothing, permits no
let-up for its own case or any case, has no particular sabbath or judgment-
day, divides not the living from the dead or the righteous from the unrighteous,   570

line 506, note.
515. of consequence] The four sentences following, originally 25 lines, ending
"returned again." (line 531), are omitted in later editions.
529–30. realized and returned] Lines 530–568, cf. "Song of Prudence," 14–42.
See also line 506, note.
531. any thing] In later editions, "anything."
538. forever] The six sentences following, originally 43 lines, ending "soul is
truth" (line 566), omitted in later editions, were merged in "Song of Prudence"
(see note, line 529–530).
567. the soul] The clause following, "is not . . . to its ways," is omitted in the
later editions.
570. divides not] Lines 570–580, cf. "Song of Prudence," 46–56. See also line
506, note.

is satisfied with the present, matches every thought or act by its correlative,
knows no possible forgiveness or deputed atonement . . knows that the young
man who composedly periled his life and lost it has done exceeding well for
himself, while the man who has not periled his life and retains it to old age in
575   riches and ease has perhaps achieved nothing for himself worth mentioning
. . and that only that person has no great prudence to learn who has learnt to
prefer real longlived things, and favors body and soul the same, and perceives
the indirect assuredly following the direct, and what evil or good he does
leaping onward and waiting to meet him again—and who in his spirit in any
580   emergency whatever neither hurries or avoids death.

The direct trial of him who would be the greatest poet is today. If he does
not flood himself with the immediate age as with vast oceanic tides . . . . .
and if he does not attract his own land body and soul to himself and hang on its
neck with incomparable love and plunge his semitic muscle into its merits and
585   demerits . . . and if he be not himself the age transfigured . . . . and if to
him is not opened the eternity which gives similitude to all periods and locations
and processes and animate and inanimate forms, and which is the bond of time,
and rises up from its inconceivable vagueness and infiniteness in the swimming
shape of today, and is held by the ductile anchors of life, and makes the present
590   spot the passage from what was to what shall be, and commits itself to the
representation of this wave of an hour and this one of the sixty beautiful
children of the wave—let him merge in the general run and wait his develop-
ment. . . . . Still the final test of poems or any character or work
remains. The prescient poet projects himself centuries ahead and judges per-
595   former or performance after the changes of time. Does it live through them?
Does it still hold on untired? Will the same style and the direction of genius to
similar points be satisfactory now? Has no new discovery in science or arrival at
superior planes of thought and judgment and behaviour fixed him or his so that
either can be looked down upon? Have the marches of tens and hundreds and
600   thousands of years made willing detours to the right hand and the left hand for
his sake? Is he beloved long and long after he is buried? Does the young man
think often of him? and the young woman think often of him? and do the
middleaged and the old think of him?

572. knows] In later texts, "and knows."

572. atonement.] This ends the paragraph in later editions, when the passage fol-
lowing, originally 13 lines ending "hurries or avoids death" (line 580), had been
merged in "Song of Prudence."

582. Oceanic tides . . .] In later editions the three following clauses are omitted,
the present sentence continuing, "if he be not himself" (line 585). For "semitic
muscle" (line 584) read "seminal muscle" as in "By Blue Ontario's Shore," line 8 of
Canto 6, which as a whole reflects the ideas of the present paragraph.

589. shape of today] In later texts, "shapes."

589. ductile anchors] cf. "A Noiseless Patient Spider," line 9.

593. Still the final test] In later editions this phrase begins a new paragraph.

A great poem is for ages and ages in common and for all degrees and
complexions and all departments and sects and for a woman as much as a man   605
and a man as much as a woman. A great poem is no finish to a man or woman
but rather a beginning. Has any one fancied he could sit at last under some due
authority and rest satisfied with explanations and realize and be content and
full? To no such terminus does the greatest poet bring . . . he brings neither
cessation or sheltered fatness and ease. The touch of him tells in action. Whom   610
he takes he takes with firm sure grasp into live regions previously unattained
. . . . thenceforward is no rest . . . . they see the space and ineffable
sheen that turn the old spots and lights into dead vacuums. The companion of
him beholds the birth and progress of stars and learns one of the meanings.
Now there shall be a man cohered out of tumult and chaos . . . . the elder   615
encourages the younger and shows him how . . . they two shall launch off
fearlessly together till the new world fits an orbit for itself and looks unabashed
on the lesser orbits of the stars and sweeps through the ceaseless rings and shall
never be quiet again.

There will soon be no more priests. Their work is done. They may wait   620
awhile . . perhaps a generation or two . . dropping off by degrees. A supe-
rior breed shall take their place . . . . the gangs of kosmos and prophets en
masse shall take their place. A new order shall arise and they shall be the priests
of man, and every man shall be his own priest. The churches built under their
umbrage shall be the churches of men and women. Through the divinity of   625
themselves shall the kosmos and the new breed of poets be interpreters of men
and women and of all events and things. They shall find their inspiration in real
objects today, symptoms of the past and future. . . . They shall not deign to
defend immortality or God or the perfection of things or liberty or the exquisite
beauty and reality of the soul. They shall arise in America and be responded to   630
from the remainder of the earth.

The English language befriends the grand American expression . . . . it
is brawny enough and limber and full enough. On the tough stock of a race who
through all change of circumstance was never without the idea of political
liberty, which is the animus of all liberty, it has attracted the terms of daintier   635
and gayer and subtler and more elegant tongues. It is the powerful language of

597. Has no new . . .] The sentence beginning here was omitted in later editions.
603. middleaged] In later texts read "middle-aged."
606. no finish] Lines 606–619, cf. "Song of the Answerer," 80–83.
610. of him tells] In later editions, read: "of him, like Nature, tells."
613. vacuums] Later editions omit the sentence following: "The companion . . .
meanings."
620. priests] Lines 620–627, cf. "By Blue Ontario's Shore," 226, and cursim,
224–230.
620. done] The two sentences following, "They may wait" to "take their place,"
are omitted in later editions.
624. his own priest.] The two sentences following, originally 5 lines ending "all
events and things" (line 627), are omitted in the later editions.

resistance . . . it is the dialect of common sense. It is the speech of the proud
and melancholy races and of all who aspire. It is the chosen tongue to express
growth faith self-esteem freedom justice equality friendliness amplitude pru-
640 dence decision and courage. It is the medium that shall well nigh express the
inexpressible.

No great literature nor any like style of behaviour or oratory or social
intercourse or household arrangements or public institutions or the treatment
by bosses of employed people, nor executive detail or detail of the army or navy,
645 nor spirit of legislation or courts or police or tuition or architecture or songs or
amusements or the costumes of young men, can long elude the jealous and
passionate instinct of American standards. Whether or no the sign appears
from the mouths of the people, it throbs a live interrogation in every freeman's
and freewoman's heart after that which passes by, or this built to remain. Is it
650 uniform with my country? Are its disposals without ignominious distinctions?
Is it for the evergrowing communes of brothers and lovers, large, well-united,
proud beyond the old models, generous beyond all models? Is it something
grown fresh out of the fields or drawn from the sea for use to me today here? I
know that what answers for me an American must answer for any individual or
655 nation that serves for a part of my materials. Does this answer? or is it without
reference to universal needs? or sprung of the needs of the less developed society
of special ranks? or old needs of pleasure overlaid by modern science and forms?
Does this acknowledge liberty with audible and absolute acknowledgment, and
set slavery at nought for life and death? Will it help breed one goodshaped and
660 wellhung man, and a woman to be his perfect and independent mate? Does it
improve manners? Is it for the nursing of the young of the republic? Does it
solve readily with the sweet milk of the nipples of the breasts of the mother of
many children? Has it too the old ever-fresh forbearance and impartiality? Does
it look with the same love on the last born and on those hardening toward
665 stature, and on the errant, and on those who disdain all strength of assault
outside of their own?

The poems distilled from other poems will probably pass away. The coward
will surely pass away. The expectation of the vital and great can only be
satisfied by the demeanor of the vital and great. The swarms of the polished
670 deprecating and reflectors and the polite float off and leave no remembrance.

646. amusements] The words which follow, "or the costumes of young men," are
omitted from the later texts.
652. proud beyond] In later editions an added comma modifies the meaning: "well
united, proud, beyond the old models," (cf. "well-united").
654. an American must] In later editions read: "an American, in Texas, Ohio,
Canada, must."
655. Does this answer?] The eight clauses following, originally nine lines, ending
"improve manners?" (line 661), are omitted in the later editions.
662. solve] cf. "dissolve," not present but inevitably suggested. In the context of
the entire paragraph the solution in "the sweet milk . . . of the mother of many
children" is the ideas of nature and liberty.
663. many children?] The six sentences following were omitted from the later

America prepares with composure and goodwill for the visitors that have sent word. It is not intellect that is to be their warrant and welcome. The talented, the artist, the ingenious, the editor, the statesman, the erudite . . they are not unappreciated . . they fall in their place and do their work. The soul of the nation also does its work. No disguise can pass on it . . no disguise can con-   675
ceal from it. It rejects none, it permits all. Only toward as good as itself and to-ward the like of itself will it advance half-way. An individual is as superb as a nation when he has the qualities which make a superb nation. The soul of the largest and wealthiest and proudest nation may well go half-way to meet that of its poets. The signs are effectual. There is no fear of mistake. If the one is true   680
the other is true. The proof of a poet is that his country absorbs him as affec-tionately as he has absorbed it.

Prefatory Letter to Ralph Waldo Emerson
Leaves of Grass *1856*

> To Emerson's letter in praise of *Leaves of Grass*, Whitman replied
> a year later, in an "open letter" (published but not sent) which was
> virtually a preface to his *Leaves of Grass* of 1856, where it appeared in
> the Appendix following Emerson's letter, below:

EMERSON TO WHITMAN, 1855

Concord, Massachusetts, *21 July, 1855.*

DEAR SIR—I am not blind to the worth of the wonderful gift of "LEAVES OF GRASS." I find it the most extraordinary piece of wit and wisdom that America has yet contributed. I am very happy in reading it, as great power makes us happy. It meets the demand I am always making of what seemed the sterile and stingy nature, as if too much handiwork, or too much lymph in the tempera-   5
ment, were making our western wits fat and mean.

texts—originally 13 lines, including the first six lines of the new paragraph, ending "leave no remembrance" (line 670) But see note, line 667.

667. poems distilled] Lines 667–682, cf. "By Blue Ontario's Shore," 213–219.

671. America prepares] In the later texts, the last paragraph of the Preface begins here, the earlier lines having been transferred (see note, lines 663 and 667).

673. erudite . . they are not] In later editions, "erudite, are not."

675. does its work.] The sentence following is omitted from the later texts.

677. the like of itself] The preceding phrase in later editions reads: "Only toward the like of itself."

679–80. that of its poets.] In the later editions, the Preface ends here; the following four sentences were excluded.

1. Dear Sir: Whitman's text of this letter shows two negligible departures

I give you joy of your free and brave thought. I have great joy in it. I find incomparable things said incomparably well, as they must be. I find the courage of treatment which so delights us, and which large perception only can inspire.

10   I greet you at the beginning of a great career, which yet must have had a long foreground somewhere, for such a start. I rubbed my eyes a little, to see if this sunbeam were no illusion; but the solid sense of the book is a sober certainty. It has the best merits, namely, of fortifying and encouraging.

I did not know until I last night saw the book advertised in a newspaper that

15   I could trust the name as real and available for a post-office. I wish to see my benefactor, and have felt much like striking my tasks, and visiting New York to pay you my respects.

R. W. EMERSON.

WHITMAN TO EMERSON, 1856

Brooklyn, *August, 1856.*

Here are thirty-two Poems, which I send you, dear Friend and Master, not having found how I could satisfy myself with sending any usual acknowledgment of your letter. The first edition, on which you mailed me that till now unanswered letter, was twelve poems—I printed a thousand copies, and they

5   readily sold; these thirty-two Poems I stereotype, to print several thousand copies of. I much enjoy making poems. Other work I have set for myself to do, to meet people and The States face to face, to confront them with an American

in punctuation from the MS (Feinberg). We have allowed these accidentals to stand as in Whitman's text. It is not entirely clear that the MS intends a third paragraph beginning at "I greet," but logic is on the side of retaining it. In all cases, Emerson writes the ampersand instead of spelling "and," but we follow Whitman's text in this respect, and also in showing the place and date on one line, without abbreviation and with standard punctuation.

The open letter to Emerson, which Whitman included in his second LG edition (1856), may be regarded as a preface to that edition. It is astonishing that it has not before been presented in this capacity. Excepting the brief, epistolary address to Emerson at the beginning and end, in its magnitude and style this is evidently intended for an essay; its substance is purposefully related to the poems of the volume. Whitman included this letter, which Emerson had not seen, in the Appendix, where also, and without Emerson's authorization, he associated it with the now-famous letter which Emerson had sent him a year before on reading Whitman's gift copy of the first LG volume. In fact, Whitman had already made public Emerson's letter of praise by joyfully showing it to friends, by allowing Dana, the editor, to publish it without consulting Emerson in the New York *Tribune*, and by pasting clippings of the letter in presentation copies of LG to Longfellow and others. Finally, on the spine of the 1856 volume, he displayed Emerson's golden words, "I greet you at the beginning of a great career." Despite its familiarity, we have let Emerson's letter stand as it was in the 1856 edition, preceding Whitman's "Letter to Ralph Waldo Emerson." This preface-letter is a penetrating and vivacious statement of Whitman's objectives as poet in his first phase of creativity, and of his theories of man, nature, and democratic society. It is also his best statement of his demand for

rude tongue; but the work of my life is making poems. I keep on till I make a
hundred, and then several hundred—perhaps a thousand. The way is clear to
me. A few years, and the average annual call for my Poems is ten or twenty   10
thousand copies—more, quite likely. Why should I hurry or compromise? In
poems or in speeches I say the word or two that has got to be said, adhere to the
body, step with the countless common footsteps, and remind every man and
woman of something.

Master, I am a man who has perfect faith. Master, we have not come   15
through centuries, caste, heroisms, fables, to halt in this land today. Or I think
it is to collect a ten-fold impetus that any halt is made. As nature, inexorable,
onward, resistless, impassive amid the threats and screams of disputants, so
America. Let all defer. Let all attend respectfully the leisure of These States,
their politics, poems, literature, manners, and their free-handed modes of train-   20
ing their own offspring. Their own comes, just matured, certain, numerous and
capable enough, with egotistical tongues, with sinewed wrists, seizing openly
what belongs to them. They resume Personality, too long left out of mind.
Their shadows are projected in employments, in books, in the cities, in trade;
their feet are on the flights of the steps of the Capitol; they dilate, a larger,   25
brawnier, more candid, more democratic, lawless, positive native to The States,
sweet-bodied, completer, dauntless, flowing, masterful, beard-faced, new race of
men.

Swiftly, on limitless foundations, the United States too are founding a
literature. It is all as well done, in my opinion, as could be practicable. Each   30
element here is in condition. Every day I go among the people of Manhattan
Island, Brooklyn, and other cities, and among the young men, to discover the

"an avowed, empowered, unabashed development of sex. The only salvation" against
the threatening deterioration of democratic individualism and society was for the
creative artist and thinker to combat the prevailing "infidelism" by asserting "the
eternal decency of the amativeness of Nature, the motherhood of all."

1. thirty-two poems] I.e., twelve from the 1855 first edition and twenty new
poems in *LG* 1856.

5. readily sold] The facts are not entirely ascertainable, and variously re-
ported (See C. J. Furness, *Introduction*, *Leaves of Grass*, *1855*, New York, 1939;
and Allen, pp. 150–154). Whitman plausibly told Traubel in 1888 that when he
wrote to Emerson many copies had been consigned to dealers but sales reports had
not been made. It is likely that from 800 to 1000 copies were printed, of which about
300 were cloth-bound; that very few were sold; that copies were given to influential
writers and reviewers, and the rest "remaindered" unbound or in paper covers. The
rarity of the 1856 edition does not suggest that "several thousand" copies were run
off, even from stereotype plates.

8. rude tongue] Whitman's mission called him to the public forum but his
efforts, early and late, were not successful. Some critics find the effects of oratory
in his written style.

10–11. twenty thousand] He should have known that only Longfellow among
American poets then approached these sales figures.

15. Master] Cf. first paragraph. The term, as applied to the teacher, writer,
or artist, did not suggest servility. Emerson was indeed the "Master" of the school
of literary idealism; perhaps WW is too lavish, but see the last two paragraphs of
the letter.

spirit of them, and to refresh myself. These are to be attended to; I am myself more drawn here than to those authors, publishers, importations, reprints, and so forth. I pass coolly through those, understanding them perfectly well, and that they do the indispensable service, outside of men like me, which nothing else could do. In poems, the young men of The States shall be represented, for they out-rival the best of the rest of the earth.

The lists of ready-made literature which America inherits by the mighty inheritance of the English language—all the rich repertoire of traditions, poems, histories, metaphysics, plays, classics, translations, have made, and still continue, magnificent preparations for that other plainly signified literature, to be our own, to be electric, fresh, lusty, to express the full-sized body, male and female—to give the modern meanings of things, to grow up beautiful, lasting, commensurate with America, with all the passions of home, with the inimitable sympathies of having been boys and girls together, and of parents who were with our parents.

What else can happen The States, even in their own despite? That huge English flow, so sweet, so undeniable, has done incalculable good here, and is to be spoken of for its own sake with generous praise and with gratitude. Yet the price The States have had to lie under for the same has not been a small price. Payment prevails; a nation can never take the issues of the needs of other nations for nothing. America, grandest of lands in the theory of its politics, in popular reading, in hospitality, breadth, animal beauty, cities, ships, machines, money, credit, collapses quick as lightning at the repeated, admonishing, stern words, Where are any mental expressions from you, beyond what you have copied or stolen? Where the born throngs of poets, literats, orators, you promised? Will you but tag after other nations? They struggled long for their literature, painfully working their way, some with deficient languages, some with priest-craft, some in the endeavor just to live—yet achieved for their times, works, poems, perhaps the only solid consolation left to them through ages afterward of shame and decay. You are young, have the perfectest of dialects, a free press, a free government, the world forwarding its best to be with you. As justice has been strictly done to you, from this hour do strict justice to yourself. Strangle the singers who will not sing you loud and strong. Open the doors of The West. Call for new great masters to comprehend new arts, new perfections, new wants. Submit to the most robust bard till he remedy your barrenness. Then you will not need to adopt the heirs of others; you will have true heirs, begotten of yourself, blooded with your own blood.

With composure I see such propositions, seeing more and more every day of the answers that serve. Expressions do not yet serve, for sufficient reasons; but that is getting ready, beyond what the earth has hitherto known, to take home the expressions when they come, and to identify them with the populace of The States, which is the schooling cheaply procured by any outlay any

48. The States] Presumably, "to The States."

number of years. Such schooling The States extract from the swarms of re- 75
prints, and from the current authors and editors. Such service and extract are
done after enormous, reckless, free modes, characteristic of The States. Here
are to be attained results never elsewhere thought possible; the modes are very
grand too. The instincts of the American people are all perfect, and tend to
make heroes. It is a rare thing in a man here to understand The States. 80

All current nourishments to literature serve. Of authors and editors I do not
know how many there are in The States, but there are thousands, each one
building his or her step to the stairs by which giants shall mount. Of the
twenty-four modern mammoth two-double, three-double, and four-double cylin-
der presses now in the world, printing by steam, twenty-one of them are in 85
These States. The twelve thousand large and small shops for dispensing books
and newspapers—the same number of public libraries, any one of which has all
the reading wanted to equip a man or woman for American reading—the three
thousand different newspapers, the nutriment of the imperfect ones coming in
just as usefully as any—the story papers, various, full of strong-flavored ro- 90
mances, widely circulated—the one-cent and two-cent journals—the political
ones, no matter what side—the weeklies in the country—the sporting and
pictorial papers—the monthly magazines, with plentiful imported feed—the
sentimental novels, numberless copies of them—the low-priced flaring tales,
adventures, biographies—all are prophetic; all waft rapidly on. I see that they 95
swell wide, for reasons. I am not troubled at the movement of them, but greatly
pleased. I see plying shuttles, the active ephemeral myriads of books also,
faithfully weaving the garments of a generation of men, and a generation of
women, they do not perceive or know. What a progress popular reading and
writing has made in fifty years! What a progress fifty years hence! The time is 100
at hand when inherent literature will be a main part of These States, as general
and real as steam-power, iron, corn, beef, fish. First-rate American persons are
to be supplied. Our perennial materials for fresh thoughts, histories, poems,
music, orations, religions, recitations, amusements, will then not be
disregarded, any more than our perennial fields, mines, rivers, seas. Certain 105
things are established, and are immovable; in those things millions of years
stand justified. The mothers and fathers of whom modern centuries have come,
have not existed for nothing; they too had brains and hearts. Of course all
literature, in all nations and years, will share marked attributes in common, as
we all, of all ages, share the common human attributes. America is to be kept 110
coarse and broad. What is to be done is to withdraw from precedents, and be
directed to men and women—also to The States in their federalness; for the
union of the parts of the body is not more necessary to their life than the union
of These States is to their life.

A profound person can easily know more of the people than they know of 115
themselves. Always waiting untold in the souls of the armies of common people,
is stuff better than anything that can possibly appear in the leadership of the
same. That gives final verdicts. In every department of These States, he who

travels with a coterie, or with selected persons, or with imitators, or with
120 infidels, or with the owners of slaves, or with that which is ashamed of the body
of a man, or with that which is ashamed of the body of a woman, or with any
thing less than the bravest and the openest, travels straight for the slopes of
dissolution. The genius of all foreign literature is clipped and cut small, com-
pared to our genius, and is essentially insulting to our usages, and to the organic
125 compacts of These States. Old forms, old poems, majestic and proper in their
own lands here in this land are exiles; the air here is very strong. Much that
stands well and has a little enough place provided for it in the small scales of
European kingdoms, empires, and the like, here stands haggard, dwarfed,
ludicrous, or has no place little enough provided for it. Authorities, poems,
130 models, laws, names, imported into America, are useful to America today to
destroy them, and so move disencumbered to great works, great days.

Just so long, in our country or any country, as no revolutionists advance,
and are backed by the people, sweeping off the swarms of routine representa-
tives, officers in power, book-makers, teachers, ecclesiastics, politicians, just so
135 long, I perceive, do they who are in power fairly represent that country, and
remain of use, probably of very great use. To supersede them, when it is the
pleasure of These States, full provision is made; and I say the time has arrived
to use it with a strong hand. Here also the souls of the armies have not only
overtaken the souls of the officers, but passed on, and left the souls of the officers
140 behind out of sight many weeks' journey; and the souls of the armies now go
en-masse without officers. Here also formulas, glosses, blanks, minutiæ, are
choking the throats of the spokesmen to death. Those things most listened for,
certainly those are the things least said. There is not a single History of the
World. There is not one of America, or of the organic compacts of These
145 States, or of Washington, or of Jefferson, nor of Language, nor any Dictionary
of the English Language. There is no great author; every one has demeaned
himself to some etiquette or some impotence. There is no manhood or life-
power in poems; there are shoats and geldings more like. Or literature will be
dressed up, a fine gentleman, distasteful to our instincts, foreign to our soil.
150 Its neck bends right and left wherever it goes. Its costumes and jewelry prove
how little it knows Nature. Its flesh is soft; it shows less and less of the
indefinable hard something that is Nature. Where is any thing but the shaved
Nature of synods and schools? Where is a savage and luxuriant man? Where is
an overseer? In lives, in poems, in codes of law, in Congress, in tuitions,

137. the time has arrived] The period since 1847 had been increasingly char-
acterized by the futile effort to balance slavery and free-soil forces; by the dis-
ruption of the Democratic Party, which lost WW his editorship of the Brooklyn
Eagle; by the Mexican War, desperate compromises, the fateful treachery of the
Kansas-Nebraska legislation, the resulting "bloody Kansas" strife, and the generally
weak, vacillating leaders at Washington.

168–169. in the Presidency] "rascal and thief" could have been Whitman's terms
for several recent presidents. However Franklin Pierce, president since 1853, the

theatres, conversations, argumentations, not a single head lifts itself clean out, with proof that it is their master, and has subordinated them to itself, and is ready to try their superiors. None believes in These States, boldly illustrating them in himself. Not a man faces round at the rest with terrible negative voice, refusing all terms to be bought off from his own eye-sight, or from the soul that he is, or from friendship, or from the body that he is, or from the soil and sea. To creeds, literature, art, the army, the navy, the executive, life is hardly proposed, but the sick and dying are proposed to cure the sick and dying. The churches are one vast lie; the people do not believe them, and they do not believe themselves; the priests are continually telling what they know well enough is not so, and keeping back what they know is so. The spectacle is a pitiful one. I think there can never be again upon the festive earth more bad-disordered persons deliberately taking seats, as of late in These States, at the heads of the public tables—such corpses' eyes for judges—such a rascal and thief in the Presidency.

Up to the present, as helps best, the people, like a lot of large boys, have no determined tastes, are quite unaware of the grandeur of themselves, and of their destiny, and of their immense strides—accept with voracity whatever is presented them in novels, histories, newspapers, poems, schools, lectures, every thing. Pretty soon, through these and other means, their development makes the fibre that is capable of itself, and will assume determined tastes. The young men will be clear what they want, and will have it. They will follow none except him whose spirit leads them in the like spirit with themselves. Any such man will be welcome as the flowers of May. Others will be put out without ceremony. How much is there anyhow, to the young men of These States, in a parcel of helpless dandies, who can neither fight, work, shoot, ride, run, command—some of them devout, some quite insane, some castrated—all second-hand, or third, fourth, or fifth hand—waited upon by waiters, putting not this land first, but always other lands first, talking of art, doing the most ridiculous things for fear of being called ridiculous, smirking and skipping along, continually taking off their hats—no one behaving, dressing, writing, talking, loving, out of any natural and manly tastes of his own, but each one looking cautiously to see how the rest behave, dress, write, talk, love—pressing the noses of dead books upon themselves and upon their country—favoring no poets, philosophs, literats here, but dog-like danglers at the heels of the poets, philosophs, literats, of enemies' lands—favoring mental expressions, models of gentlemen and ladies, social

instrument of the proslavery party's treacherous compromises (see note, line 137), was supplanted in June 1856 as the Democratic candidate by James Buchanan, whose platform promised even stronger support of the proslavery policies. In this letter of August, 1856, WW could have been referring to either or both. In *The Eighteenth Presidency*, Whitman's unpublished campaign pamphlet, he excoriated the current and gigantic corruptions but did not openly support any candidate. Those "corpse's eyes," the "judges," he had just accused of conniving to subvert the penalties for the slave-traders of New York City in an article (*Life Illustrated*, August 2). See Allen, pp. 191–199.

habitudes in These States, to grow up in sneaking defiance of the popular
substratums of The States? Of course they and the likes of them can never
justify the strong poems of America. Of course no feed of theirs is to stop and be
made welcome to muscle the bodies, male and female, for Manhattan Island,
195 Brooklyn, Boston, Worcester, Hartford, Portland, Montreal, Detroit, Buffalo,
Cleaveland, Milwaukee, St. Louis, Indianapolis, Chicago, Cincinnati, Iowa
City, Philadelphia, Baltimore, Raleigh, Savannah, Charleston, Mobile, New
Orleans, Galveston, Brownsville, San Francisco, Havana, and a thousand equal
cities, present and to come. Of course what they and the likes of them have been
200 used for, draws toward its close, after which they will all be discharged, and not
one of them will ever be heard of any more.

America, having duly conceived, bears out of herself offspring of her own
to do the workmanship wanted. To freedom, to strength, to poems, to personal
greatness, it is never permitted to rest, not a generation or part of a generation.
205 To be ripe beyond further increase is to prepare to die. The architects of These
States laid their foundations, and passed to further spheres. What they laid is a
work done; as much more remains. Now are needed other architects, whose
duty is not less difficult, but perhaps more difficult. Each age forever needs
architects. America is not finished, perhaps never will be; now America is a
210 divine true sketch. There are Thirty-Two States sketched—the population
thirty millions. In a few years there will be Fifty States. Again in a few years
there will be A Hundred States, the population hundreds of millions, the
freshest and freest of men. Of course such men stand to nothing less than the
freshest and freest expression.

215 Poets here, literats here, are to rest on organic different bases from other
countries; not a class set apart, circling only in the circle of themselves, modest
and pretty, desperately scratching for rhymes, pallid with white paper, shut off,
aware of the old pictures and traditions of the race, but unaware of the actual
race around them—not breeding in and in among each other till they all have
220 the scrofula. Lands of ensemble, bards of ensemble! Walking freely out from
the old traditions, as our politics has walked out, American poets and literats
recognize nothing behind them superior to what is present with them—recog-
nize with joy the sturdy living forms of the men and women of These States, the
divinity of sex, the perfect eligibility of the female with the male, all The States,
225 liberty and equality, real articles, the different trades, mechanics, the young
fellows of Manhattan Island, customs, instincts, slang, Wisconsin, Georgia, the
noble Southern heart, the hot blood, the spirit that will be nothing less than
master, the filibuster spirit, the Western man, native-born perceptions, the eye
for forms, the perfect models of made things, the wild smack of freedom,

209. America is not finished] It is often overlooked that Whitman's poetic vision
of America was prophetic and that (see lines 132–271) he was at the same time
deeply disturbed by the immediate corruption and violent actualities of public life
and by the psychic immaturity in private life which seemed to determine the course
of this disastrous mid-century in America.

California, money, electric-telegraphs, free-trade, iron and the iron mines—   230
recognize without demur those splendid resistless black poems, the steam-ships
of the sea-board states, and those other resistless splendid poems, the loco-
motives, followed through the interior states by trains of rail-road cars.

A word remains to be said, as of one ever present, not yet permitted to be
acknowledged, discarded or made dumb by literature, and the results apparent.   235
To the lack of an avowed, empowered, unabashed development of sex, (the only
salvation for the same,) and to the fact of speakers and writers fraudulently
assuming as always dead what every one knows to be always alive, is attribut-
able the remarkable non-personality and indistinctness of modern productions
in books, art, talk; also that in the scanned lives of men and women most of   240
them appear to have been for some time past of the neuter gender; and also the
stinging fact that in orthodox society today, if the dresses were changed, the
men might easily pass for women and the women for men.

Infidelism usurps most with fœtid polite face; among the rest infidelism
about sex. By silence or obedience the pens of savans, poets, historians, biog-   245
raphers, and the rest, have long connived at the filthy law, and books enslaved
to it, that what makes the manhood of a man, that sex, womanhood, maternity,
desires, lusty animations, organs, acts, are unmentionable and to be ashamed
of, to be driven to skulk out of literature with whatever belongs to them. This
filthy law has to be repealed—it stands in the way of great reforms. Of women   250
just as much as men, it is the interest that there should not be infidelism about
sex, but perfect faith. Women in These States approach the day of that organic
equality with men, without which, I see, men cannot have organic equality
among themselves. This empty dish, gallantry, will then be filled with some-
thing. This tepid wash, this diluted deferential love, as in songs, fictions, and so   255
forth, is enough to make a man vomit; as to manly friendship, everywhere
observed in The States, there is not the first breath of it to be observed in print. I
say that the body of a man or woman, the main matter, is so far quite unex-
pressed in poems; but that the body is to be expressed, and sex is. Of bards for
These States, if it come to a question, it is whether they shall celebrate in poems   260
the eternal decency of the amativeness of Nature, the motherhood of all, or
whether they shall be the bards of the fashionable delusion of the inherent
nastiness of sex, and of the feeble and querulous modesty of deprivation. This is
important in poems, because the whole of the other expressions of a nation are
but flanges out of its great poems. To me, henceforth, that theory of any thing,   265
no matter what, stagnates in its vitals, cowardly and rotten, while it cannot
publicly accept, and publicly name, with specific words, the things on which all
existence, all souls, all realization, all decency, all health, all that is worth being

237. of sex] For comment on the importance of the following discourse, see first
note above, and see Introduction to this volume.

246. books enslaved] I.e., by laws censoring literature; in 1881 Whitman's final
revision of the canon *LG* was to be withdrawn in Boston as the result of Com-
stockery.

here for, all of woman and of man, all beauty, all purity, all sweetness, all
270   friendship, all strength, all life, all immortality depend. The courageous soul,
for a year or two to come, may be proved by faith in sex, and by disdaining
concessions.

     To poets and literats—to every woman and man, today or any day, the
conditions of the present, needs, dangers, prejudices, and the like, are the
275   perfect conditions on which we are here, and the conditions for wording the
future with undissuadable words. These States, receivers of the stamina of past
ages and lands, initiate the outlines of repayment a thousand fold. They fetch
the American great masters, waited for by old worlds and new, who accept evil
as well as good, ignorance as well as erudition, black as soon as white, foreign-
280   born materials as well as home-born, reject none, force discrepancies into
range, surround the whole, concentrate them on present periods and places,
show the application to each and any one's body and soul, and show the true use
of precedents. Always America will be agitated and turbulent. This day it is
taking shape, not to be less so, but to be more so, stormily, capriciously, on
285   native principles, with such vast proportions of parts! As for me, I love scream-
ing, wrestling, boiling-hot days.

     Of course, we shall have a national character, an identity. As it ought to be,
and as soon as it ought to be, it will be. That, with much else, takes care of
itself, is a result, and the cause of greater results. With Ohio, Illinois, Missouri,
290   Oregon—with the states around the Mexican sea—with cheerfully welcomed
immigrants from Europe, Asia, Africa—with Connecticut, Vermont, New
Hampshire, Rhode Island—with all varied interests, facts, beliefs, parties,
genesis—there is being fused a determined character, fit for the broadest use for
the freewomen and freemen of The States, accomplished and to be accom-
295   plished, without any exception whatever—each indeed free, each idiomatic, as
becomes live states and men, but each adhering to one enclosing general form of
politics, manners, talk, personal style, as the plenteous varieties of the race
adhere to one physical form. Such character is the brain and spine to all,
including literature, including poems. Such character, strong, limber, just,

PREFACE 1872] Appeared in *Specimen Days and Collect*, as PREFACE, 1872,/
to "*As a Strong Bird on Pinions Free*,"/(*now "Thou Mother with thy Equal Brood*,"
in *permanent ed'n*); so also in later collections, CPP, and CPW. The volume of
1872 contained six smaller poems besides the title poem, which WW read, on the
invitation of the students, at the Dartmouth Commencement, June 26, 1872. This
Preface is especially interesting because it discloses that WW then felt that he
had perhaps accomplished what he intended in *Leaves of Grass* and that he pro-
posed a second, companion volume, to deal poetically with "democratic nationality"
—to which this title poem, at least, might ultimately belong (see further, editors'
footnotes below). He included the entire volume as one of the supplements bound
up in his miscellany, *Two Rivulets* (1876). The present text is that of 1872. Many
revisions appear in the SDC text, which was newly stereotyped, nearly all of them
in punctuation and typography, including the reduction of capital letters, and the
normalizing of the ampersand and points of suspension. The present footnotes show

open-mouthed, American-blooded, full of pride, full of ease, of passionate   300
friendliness, is to stand compact upon that vast basis of the supremacy of
Individuality—that new moral American continent without which, I see, the
physical continent remained incomplete, may-be a carcass, a bloat—that newer
America, answering face to face with The States, with ever-satisfying and
ever-unsurveyeable seas and shores.   305

Those shores you found. I say you have led The States there—have led Me
there. I say that none has ever done, or ever can do, a greater deed for The
States, than your deed. Others may line out the lines, build cities, work mines,
break up farms; it is yours to have been the original true Captain who put to sea,
intuitive, positive, rendering the first report, to be told less by any report, and   310
more by the mariners of a thousand bays, in each tack of their arriving and
departing, many years after you.

Receive, dear Master, these statements and assurances through me, for all
the young men, and for an earnest that we know none before you, but the best
following you; and that we demand to take your name into our keeping, and that   315
we understand what you have indicated, and find the same indicated in our-
selves, and that we will stick to it and enlarge upon it through These States.

WALT WHITMAN.

Preface 1872—As a Strong Bird on Pinions Free

The impetus and ideas urging me, for some years past, to an utterance,
or attempt at utterance, of New World songs, and an epic of Democracy,
having already had their published expression, as well as I can expect to give it,
in LEAVES OF GRASS, the present and any future pieces from me are really but
the surplusage forming after that Volume, or the wake eddying behind it. I   5
fulfilled in that an imperious conviction, and the commands of my nature as
total and irresistible as those which make the sea flow, or the globe revolve. But
of this Supplementary Volume, I confess I am not so certain. Having from early
manhood abandoned the business pursuits and applications usual in my time

only the verbal or other alterations affecting meaning or emphasis. A collation of
all texts, in *Prose Works 1892*, Vol. II of the present *Collected Writings*, shows that
later editions of this Preface were printed from the SDC plates, without change, in
SDC Glasgow (1883), CPP, and CPW.

3. published] In SDC and later collections, read "publish'd." During the later
period, Whitman's revisions and new composition showed a characteristic elision
of the unvoiced "e" in the terminal "ed" of past-tense verbs and verbals (cf. first
footnote above).

8. not so certain] I.e., whether this 1872 volume was "surplusage" of LG
(considered as completed) or whether it foreshadowed a new companion volume
on "democratic nationalism" (cf. the last two paragraphs of this Preface). Actually,
Passage to India (1871) was his last distinguished addition to the *Leaves*, of which
the poems then in print included almost all WW's destined major work. His physical
decline and diminution of creative power began with his stroke of paralysis and
his mother's death (1873). See note below on "any thing further."

10 and country, and obediently yielded myself up ever since to the impetus men-
tioned, and to the work of expressing those ideas, it may be that mere habit has
got dominion of me, when there is no real need of saying any thing further.
. . . But what is life but an experiment? and mortality but an exercise? with
reference to results beyond. And so shall my poems be. If incomplete here, and
15 superfluous there, *n'importe*—the earnest trial and persistent exploration shall
at least be mine, and other success failing, shall be success enough. I have been
more anxious, anyhow, to suggest the songs of vital endeavor, and manly
evolution, and furnish something for races of outdoor athletes, than to make
perfect rhymes, or reign in the parlors. I ventured from the beginning, my own
20 way, taking chances—and would keep on venturing.

I will therefore not conceal from any persons, known or unknown to me,
who take interest in the matter, that I have the ambition of devoting yet a few
years to poetic composition. . . . The mighty present age! To absorb, and
express in poetry, any thing of it—of its world—America—cities and States—
25 the years, the events of our Nineteenth Century—the rapidity of movement—the
violent contrasts, fluctuations of light and shade, of hope and fear—the entire
revolution made by science in the poetic method—these great new underlying
facts and new ideas rushing and spreading everywhere;—Truly a mighty age!
As if in some colossal drama, acted again like those of old, under the open sun,
30 the Nations of our time, and all the characteristics of Civilization, seem hurry-
ing, stalking across, flitting from wing to wing, gathering, closing up, toward
some long-prepared, most tremendous denouement. Not to conclude the infinite
scenas of the race's life and toil and happiness and sorrow, but haply that the
boards be cleared from oldest, worst incumbrances, accumulations, and Man
35 resume the eternal play anew, and under happier, freer auspices. . . . To me,
the United States are important because, in this colossal drama, they are unques-
tionably designated for the leading parts, for many a century to come. In them
History and Humanity seem to seek to culminate. Our broad areas are even now
the busy theatre of plots, passions, interests, and suspended problems, compared
40 to which the intrigues of the past of Europe, the wars of dynasties, the scope of
kings and kingdoms, and even the development of peoples, as hitherto, exhibit
scales of measurement comparatively narrow and trivial. And on these areas of
ours, as on a stage, sooner or later, something like an *eclaircissement* of all the
past civilization of Europe and Asia is probably to be evolved.

12. any thing further] He added a few major poems—e.g., "Song of the Redwood
Tree," "Prayer of Columbus," and numerous small but genuine lyrics; also, in 1881,
his final revision and reorganization of the LG poems added much to the meaning of
the work as a whole. Thereafter he revised and collected his prose works and added
one master work, "A Backward Glance . . ." (*q.v.*, above).
    33. scenas] Latin: scenes. Cf. line 29, "colossal drama . . . like those of old."
    34. incumbrances] Then an allowable spelling.
    38. seek to culminate] WW's faith in the "manifest destiny" of the United States
was fortified by his acceptance of the ancient and persistent dogma that in the

The leading parts. . . . Not to be acted, emulated here, by us again, that   45
role till now foremost in History—Not to become a conqueror Nation, or to
achieve the glory of mere military, or diplomatic, or commercial superiority—
but to become the grand Producing Land of nobler Men and Women—of
copious races, cheerful, healthy, tolerant, free—To become the most friendly
Nation, (the United States indeed,)—the modern composite Nation, formed   50
from all, with room for all, welcoming all immigrants—accepting the work of
our own interior development, as the work fitly filling ages and ages to come;—
the leading Nation of peace, but neither ignorant nor incapable of being the
leading Nation of war;—not the Man's Nation only, but the Woman's Nation—
a land of splendid mothers, daughters, sisters, wives.   55

Our America to-day I consider in many respects as but indeed a vast
seething mass of *materials*, ampler, better, (worse also,) than previously known
—eligible to be used to carry toward its crowning stage, and build for good the
great Ideal Nationality of the future, the Nation of the Body and the Soul,*—no
limit here to land, help, opportunities, mines, products, demands, supplies,   60
&c.;—with (I think) our political organization, National, State, and Municipal,
permanently established, as far ahead as we can calculate—but, so far, no
social, literary, religious, or esthetic organizations, consistent with our politics,
or becoming to us—which organizations can only come, in time, through native
schools or teachers of great Democratic Ideas, Religion—through Science,   65
which now, like a new sunrise, ascending, begins to illuminate all—and through
our own begotten Poets and Literatuses. . . . (The moral of a late well-
written book on Civilization seems to be that the only real foundation-walls and
basis—and also *sine qua non* afterward—of true and full Civilization, is the
eligibility and certainty of boundless products for feeding, clothing, sheltering   70
every body—perennial fountains of physical and domestic comfort, with inter-

* The problems of the achievement of this crowning stage through future first-
class National Singers, Orators, Artists, and others—of creating in literature an
imaginative New World, the correspondent and counterpart of the current Scientific
and Political New Worlds—and the perhaps distant, but still delightful prospect,
(for our children, if not in our own day,) of delivering America, and, indeed, all   5n
Christian lands everywhere, from the thin, moribund, and watery, but appallingly
extensive nuisance of conventional poetry—by putting something really alive and
substantial in its place—I have undertaken to grapple with, and argue, in DEMO-
CRATIC VISTAS.

perpetual changes there is a selection of the good, which perhaps spirals toward an
ultimate perfection. See, especially, the "crowning stage" (two paragraphs below)
and WW's note thereon.
    48. Producing Land] The initial capital for emphasis was generally absent in
later editions.
    58. toward] Later texts read "towards."
    65. Ideas] Later texts omit "native schools or teachers of."
    69. basis] Later texts read "bases."
    71. every body] Corrected in *SDC* to "everybody."

communication, and with civil and ecclesiastical freedom;—and that then the
esthetic and mental business will take care of itself. . . . Well, the United
States have established this basis, and upon scales of extent, variety, vitality,
75   and continuity, rivaling those of Nature; and have now to proceed to build an
Edifice upon it. I say this Edifice is only to be fitly built by new Literatures,
especially the Poetic. I say a modern Image-Making creation is indispensable to
fuse and express the modern Political and Scientific creations—and then the
Trinity will be complete.)

80   When I commenced, years ago, elaborating the plan of my poems, and
continued turning over that plan, and shifting it in my mind through many
years, (from the age of twenty-eight to thirty-five,) experimenting much, and
writing and abandoning much, one deep purpose underlay the others, and has
underlain it and its execution ever since—and that has been the Religious
85   purpose. Amid many changes, and a formulation taking far different shape
from what I at first supposed, this basic purpose has never been departed from
in the composition of my verses. Not of course to exhibit itself in the old ways,
as in writing hymns or psalms with an eye to the church-pew, or to express
conventional pietism, or the sickly yearnings of devotees, but in new ways, and
90   aiming at the widest sub-bases and inclusions of Humanity, and tallying the
fresh air of sea and land. I will see, (said I to myself,) whether there is not, for
my purposes as poet, a Religion, and a sound Religious germenancy in the
average Human Race, at least in their modern development in the United
States, and in the hardy common fibre and native yearnings and elements,
95   deeper and larger, and affording more profitable returns, than all mere sects or
churches—as boundless, joyous, and vital as Nature itself—A germenancy that
has too long been unencouraged, unsung, almost unknown. . . . With Sci-
ence, the Old Theology of the East, long in its dotage, begins evidently to die
and disappear. But (to my mind) Science—and may be such will prove its
100   principal service—as evidently prepares the way for One indescribably grander
—Time's young but perfect offspring—the New Theology—heir of the West—
lusty and loving, and wondrous beautiful. For America, and for to-day, just the
same as any day, the supreme and final Science is the Science of God—what we
call science being only its minister—as Democracy is or shall be also. And a
105   poet of America (I said) must fill himself with such thoughts, and chant his best
out of them. . . . . . And as those were the convictions and aims, for good or

77. Image-Making] In view of the twentieth century changes in the understand-
ing and use of image, myth, and symbol "to fuse and express" society and science,
WW's statement is farsighted.

79. Trinity] Later texts read "trinity."

86. what I at first supposed] The persistent supposition that WW consciously
foreshadowed the ultimate *Leaves of Grass* in LG 1855 he several times denied, as
here.

104. only its minister] It was also an idea of contemporary European and New
England transcendentalism that science (or "knowing") in its general sense, was

bad, of LEAVES OF GRASS, they are no less the intention of this Volume. As there can be, in my opinion, no sane and complete Personality—nor any grand and electric Nationality, without the stock element of Religion imbuing all the other elements, (like heat in chemistry, invisible itself, but the life of all visible life,) so there can be no Poetry worthy the name without that element behind all. . . . . . The time has certainly come to begin to discharge the idea of Religion, in the United States, from mere ecclesiasticism, and from Sundays and churches and church-going, and assign it to that general position, chiefest, most indispensable, most exhilarating, to which the others are to be adjusted, inside of all human character, and education, and affairs. The people, especially the young men and women of America, must begin to learn that Religion, (like Poetry,) is something far, far different from what they supposed. It is, indeed, too important to the power and perpetuity of the New World to be consigned any longer to the churches, old or new, Catholic or Protestant—Saint this, or Saint that. . . . It must be consigned henceforth to Democracy *en masse*, and to Literature. It must enter into the Poems of the Nation. It must make the Nation.

The Four Years' War is over—and in the peaceful, strong, exciting, fresh occasions of To-day, and of the Future, that strange, sad war is hurrying even now to be forgotten. The camp, the drill, the lines of sentries, the prisons, the hospitals,—(ah! the hospitals!)—all have passed away—all seem now like a dream. A new race, a young and lusty generation, already sweeps in with oceanic currents, obliterating that war, and all its scars, its mounded graves, and all its reminiscences of hatred, conflict, death. So let it be obliterated. I say the life of the present and the future makes undeniable demands upon us each and all, South, North, East, West. . . . To help put the United States (even if only in imagination) hand in hand, in one unbroken circle in a chant—To rouse them to the unprecedented grandeur of the part they are to play, and are even now playing—to the thought of their great Future, and the attitude conformed to it—especially their great Esthetic, Moral, Scientific Future, (of which their vulgar material and political present is but as the preparatory tuning of instruments by an orchestra,)—these, as hitherto, are still, for me, among my hopes, ambitions.

LEAVES OF GRASS, already published, is, in its intentions, the song of a great composite *Democratic Individual*, male or female. And following on and

110

115

120

125

130

135

140

only a minister to "the supreme . . . Science of God," since the "All"—the macrocosm—contains every microcosm (cf. Emerson's poem, "Each and All"). It is in this sense that WW's "underlying" purpose was religious, and that he distrusted the specialized clerical authority of ecclesiastical creeds (see below, same paragraph).

128. lusty generation] The standard "Author's Edition" of *Two Rivulets*, 1876, reads "living generation." The limited "Centennial Edition" of that issue reads "lusty," as in the present first edition text. So also do all later collections—*SDC*, *CPP*, and *CPW*.

amplifying the same purpose, I suppose I have in my mind to run through the chants of this Volume, (if ever completed,) the thread-voice, more or less audible, of an aggregated, inseparable, unprecedented, vast, composite, electric
145 *Democratic Nationality.*

Purposing, then, to still fill out, from time to time through years to come, the following Volume, (unless prevented,) I conclude this Preface to the first installment of it, pencilled in the open air, on my fifty-third birth-day, by wafting to you, dear Reader, whoever you are, (from amid the fresh scent of the
150 grass, the pleasant coolness of the forenoon breeze, the lights and shades of tree-boughs silently dappling and playing around me, and the notes of the cat-bird for undertone and accompaniment,) my true good-will and love.

Washington, D. C., May 31, 1872. W. W.

Preface 1876—Leaves of Grass *and* Two Rivulets

At the eleventh hour, under grave illness, I gather up the pieces of Prose and Poetry left over since publishing, a while since, my first and main Volume, LEAVES OF GRASS—pieces, here, some new, some old—nearly all of them (sombre as many are, making this almost Death's book) composed in by-gone
5 atmospheres of perfect health—and, preceded by the freshest collection, the little TWO RIVULETS, and by this rambling Prefatory gossip,* now send them out, embodied in the present Melange, partly as my contribution and outpouring

---

* This Preface is not only for the present collection, but, in a sort, for all my writings, both Volumes.

2n. In later editions this information appears beneath the title.

147. the following Volume] I.e., a suggested companion work to *LG* (see above footnote on the phrase, "not so certain").

148. installment] Read "instalment" in *SDC, CPP,* and *CPW.*

PREFACE 1876] Simply "Preface" when the essay first appeared in *Two Rivulets* (1876), this title was enlarged in later collections (*SDC, CPP,* and *CPW*) to read, PREFACE, 1876/*to the two-volume Centennial Edition/of L. of G. and "Two Rivulets."* Note WW's 1876 assignment of the Preface to both volumes in his first footnote (*q.v.*). Both *LG* and *TR* in 1876 were designated, on the title page, as "Author's Edition." "About two hundred copies" of each volume (Goldsmith and Wells) were differently bound and further identified as the "Centennial Ed'n 1876" by the gold-stamped label on the spine. Numerous alterations in the Preface appear in *SDC* (1882) text, which was then reproduced in the later collections. The alterations in *SDC* were largely the reduction of capitals and other mechanical changes. Only verbal changes and such others as may affect the interpretation are shown in the present footnotes. A collation based on the final edition appears in *Prose Works 1892,* Vol. II of the present *Collected Writings.*

4. Death's book] In the 1872 Preface (*q.v.*) WW proposed writing a book

to celebrate, in some sort, the feature of the time, the first Centennial of our New World Nationality—and then as chyle and nutriment to that moral, Indissoluble Union, equally representing All, and the mother of many coming Centennials. 10

And e'en for flush and proof of our America—for reminder, just as much, or more, in moods of towering pride and joy, I keep my special chants of Death and Immortality† to stamp the coloring-finish of all, present and past. For

---

† PASSAGE TO INDIA.—As in some ancient legend-play, to close the plot and the hero's career, there is a farewell gathering on ship's deck and on shore, a loosing of hawsers and ties, a spreading of sails to the wind—a starting out on unknown seas, 5n to fetch up no one knows whither—to return no more—And the curtain falls, and there is the end of it—So I have reserv'd that Poem, with its cluster, to finish and explain much that, without them, would not be explain'd, and to take leave, and escape for good, from all that has preceded them. (Then probably *Passage to India*, and its cluster, are but freer vent and fuller expression to what, from the first, and 10n so on throughout, more or less lurks in my writings, underneath every page, every line, every where.)

I am not sure but the last enclosing sublimation of Race or Poem is, What it thinks of Death. . . . . . . After the rest has been comprehended and said, even the grandest—After those contributions to mightiest Nationality, or to sweetest Song, 15n or to the best Personalism, male or female, have been glean'd from the rich and varied themes of tangible life, and have been fully accepted and sung, and the pervading fact of visible existence, with the duty it devolves, is rounded and apparently completed, it still remains to be really completed by suffusing through the whole and several, that other pervading invisible fact, so large a part, (is it not the largest 20n part?) of life here, combining the rest, and furnishing, for Person or State, the only permanent and unitary meaning to all, even the meanest life, consistently with the dignity of the Universe, in Time. . . . . . As, from the eligibility to this thought, and the cheerful conquest of this fact, flash forth the first distinctive proofs of the Soul, so to me, (extending it only a little further,) the ultimate Democratic purports, 25n the ethereal and spiritual ones, are to concentrate here, and as fixed stars, radiate hence. For, in my opinion, it is no less than this idea of Immortality, above all other

---

on the democratic society as a companion poem to LG. In the present essay (paragraph 8) he writes, "I only wish I were a younger and fresher man, to attempt the enduring Book . . . about it." After years of mounting infirmities, he now observes that the unwritten book was foreshadowed in LG and is represented by such prose works as *Democratic Vistas* (1871) in the present collection of TR. The "dual forms" of prose and poetry in the collection correspond with certain subjects—"Politics for one, and for the other, the pensive thought of Immortality" —the latter to be found in the "Passage to India" poems, a section of TR. Gay W. Allen observes (*The Solitary Singer*, 462–466) that the dualism of this book appears in the "two rivulets" of alternating prose and verse; in the conceptual duality of life—death, mortality—immortality, time—eternity, the present—the historical past. However, this polarity is resolved in the "Calamus" motivation, which unites poet and reader and the common people of disparate countries. The dualism extends formally to this Preface, of which the text emphasizes the nature of the life and social changes of WW's times, while the footnotes, almost the same in bulk, provide a corresponding running commentary on the purports of *Leaves of Grass*.

6. and . . . gossip*] This phrase and its corresponding footnote were excluded from later editions, in which there appeared the enlarged title shown in the note on title, above.

15 terminus and temperer to all, they were originally written; and that shall be
their office at the last.

For some reason—not explainable or definite to my own mind, yet secretly
pleasing and satisfactory to it—I have not hesitated to embody in, and run
through the Volume, two altogether distinct veins, or strata—Politics for one,
20 and for the other, the pensive thought of Immortality. Thus, too, the prose and
poetic, the dual forms of the present book. . . . . . The pictures from the
Hospitals during the War, in *Memoranda*, I have also decided to include.
Though they differ in character and composition from the rest of my pieces, yet
I feel that that they ought to go with them, and must do so. . . . . The
25 present Volume, therefore, after its minor episodes, probably divides into these
Two, at first sight far diverse, veins of topic and treatment. One will be found in
the prose part of Two Rivulets, in *Democratic Vistas*, in the Preface to *As a
Strong Bird*, and in the concluding Notes to *Memoranda* of the Hospitals. The
other, wherein the all-engrossing thought and fact of Death is admitted, (not for
30 itself so much as a powerful factor in the adjustments of Life,) in the realistic

ideas, that is to enter into, and vivify, and give crowning religious stamp, to De-
mocracy in the New World.

30n It was originally my intention, after chanting in Leaves of Grass the songs
of the Body and Existence, to then compose a further, equally needed Volume,
based on those convictions of perpetuity and conservation which, enveloping all
precedents, make the unseen Soul govern absolutely at last. I meant, while in a sort
continuing the theme of my first chants, to shift the slides, and exhibit the problem
35n and paradox of the same ardent and fully appointed Personality entering the sphere
of the resistless gravitation of Spiritual Law, and with cheerful face estimating
Death, not at all as the cessation, but as somehow what I feel it must be, the entrance
upon by far the greatest part of existence, and something that Life is at least as much
for, as it is for itself.
40n But the full construction of such a work (even if I lay the foundation, or give
impetus to it) is beyond my powers, and must remain for some bard in the
future. The physical and the sensuous, in themselves or in their immediate con-
tinuations, retain holds upon me which I think are never entirely releas'd; and those
holds I have not only not denied, but hardly wish'd to weaken.
45n Meanwhile, not entirely to give the go-by to my original plan, and far more to
avoid a mark'd hiatus in it, than to entirely fulfil it, I end my books with thoughts,
or radiations from thoughts, on Death, Immortality, and a free entrance into the
Spiritual world. In those thoughts, in a sort, I make the first steps or studies
toward the mighty theme, from the point of view necessitated by my foregoing
50n poems, and by Modern Science. In them I also seek to set the key-stone to my
Democracy's enduring arch. I re-collate them now, for the press, (much the same, I
transcribe my *Memoranda* following, of gloomy times out of the War, and Hospitals,)
in order to partially occupy and offset days of strange sickness, and the heaviest
affliction and bereavement of my life; and I fondly please myself with the notion of

39n. The paragraph break does not occur in later editions.
51n–52n. This parenthetical clause does not appear in later editions.

21. dual] See "dualism," note above on "Death's book."
21. The pictures] This sentence and the next were excluded in WW's later col-
lections.
25. present] In WW's later collections, "present," was dropped before "Volume,"
because obviously irrelevant.

pictures of *Memoranda*, and the free speculations and ideal escapades of *Passage to India*.

Has not the time come, indeed, in the development of the New World, when its Politics should ascend into atmospheres and regions hitherto unknown—(far, far different from the miserable business that of late and current years passes under that name)—and take rank with Science, Philosophy and Art? . . . . Three points, in especial, have become very dear to me, and all through I seek to make them again and again, in many forms and repetitions, as will be seen: 1. That the true growth-characteristics of the Democracy of the New World are henceforth to radiate in superior Literary, Artistic and Religious Expressions, far more than in its Republican forms, universal suffrage, and frequent elections, (though these are unspeakably important) . . . . . . 2. That the vital political mission of The United States is, to practically solve and settle the problem of two sets of rights—the fusion, thorough compatibility and junction of individual State prerogatives, with the indispensable necessity of centrality and Oneness—the National Identity power—the sovereign Union,

leaving that cluster to you, O unknown Reader of the future, as 'something to remember me by,' more especially than all else. Written in former days of perfect health, little did I think the pieces had the purport that now, under present circumstances, opens to me.

[As I write these lines, May 31, 1875, it is again early summer—again my birth-day—now my fifty-sixth. Amid the outside beauty and freshness, the sunlight and verdure of the delightful season, O how different the moral atmosphere amid which I now revise this Volume, from the jocund influences surrounding the growth and advent of LEAVES OF GRASS. I occupy myself, arranging these pages for publication, still envelopt in thoughts of the death two years since of my dear Mother, the most perfect and magnetic character, the rarest combination of practical, moral and spiritual, and the least selfish, of all and any I have ever known—and by me O so much the most deeply loved . . . . and also under the physical affliction of a tedious attack of paralysis, obstinately lingering and keeping its hold upon me, and quite suspending all bodily activity and comfort . . . . I see now, much clearer than ever—perhaps these experiences were needed to show—how much my former poems, the bulk of them, are indeed the expression of health and strength, and sanest, joyfulest life.]

Under these influences, therefore, I still feel to keep *Passage to India* for last words even to this Centennial dithyramb. Not as, in antiquity, at highest festival of Egypt, the noisome skeleton of Death was also sent on exhibition to the revellers, for zest and shadow to the occasion's joy and light—but as the perfect marble statue of the normal Greeks at Elis, suggesting death in the form of a beautiful and perfect young man, with closed eyes, leaning on an inverted torch—emblem of rest and aspiration after action—of crown and point which all lives and poems should steadily have reference to, namely, the justified and noble termination of our identity, this grade of it, and outlet-preparation to another grade.

69n. I see] The following sentence, concluding the paragraph, does not appear in later editions.

36. and Art] The previous passage, thirteen lines in the first edition from "One will be found," line 26, to "Philosophy and Art," were omitted in the later texts. The canceled proposal that democracy must ultimately sublimate "politics" at the level of "science, philosophy, and art," emphasized in other passages of the essay, may be thought to reflect his motivation for the second, unwritten book.

relentless, permanently comprising all, and over all, and in that never yielding
an inch . . . . then 3d. Do we not, amid a general malaria of Fogs and
Vapors, our day, unmistakably see two Pillars of Promise, with grandest,
50 indestructible indications—One, that the morbid facts of American politics and
society everywhere are but passing incidents and flanges of our unbounded
impetus of growth—weeds, annuals, of the rank, rich soil—not central, endur-
ing, perennial things?—The Other, that all the hitherto experience of The
States, their first Century, has been but preparation, adolescence—and that
55 This Union is only now and henceforth (*i. e.* since the Secession war) to enter on
its full Democratic career?

Of the whole, Poems and Prose, (not attending at all to chronological order,
and with original dates and passing allusions in the heat and impression of the
hour, left shuffled in, and undisturb'd,) the chants of LEAVES OF GRASS, my
60 former Volume, yet serve as the indispensable deep soil, or basis, out of which,
and out of which only, could come the roots and stems more definitely indicated
by these later pages. (While that Volume radiates Physiology alone, the present
One, though of the like origin in the main, more palpably doubtless shows the
Pathology which was pretty sure to come in time from the other.)

65 In that former and main Volume, composed in the flush of my health and
strength, from the age of 30 to 50 years, I dwelt on Birth and Life, clothing my
ideas in pictures, days, transactions of my time, to give them positive place,
identity—saturating them with that vehemence of pride and audacity of freedom
necessary to loosen the mind of still-to-be-form'd America from the accumulated
70 folds, the superstitions, and all the long, tenacious and stifling anti-democratic
authorities of the Asiatic and European past—my enclosing purport being to
express, above all artificial regulation and aid, the eternal Bodily Character of
One's-Self.*

* LEAVES OF GRASS.—Namely, a Character, making most of common and
normal elements, to the superstructure of which not only the precious accumulations
of the learning and experiences of the Old World, and the settled social and
85n municipal necessities and current requirements, so long a-building, shall still
faithfully contribute, but which, at its foundations and carried up thence, and
receiving its impetus from the Democratic spirit, and accepting its gauge, in all
departments, from the Democratic formulas, shall again directly be vitalized by the

102n–103n. This parenthetical clause does not appear in later editions.
107n. follow'd] This phrase between dashes is not present in later editions.

53–54. The States] Misspelled as "Sates" in all later collections.
64. Pathology] One might find the pathological in several of these works: "Dem-
ocratic Vistas" (1871), containing a blistering attack on the postwar corruption
of personality and politics in the "gilded age"; "Preface, 1872," containing com-
ments on the unrealized cultural potentialities of the United States; and "Memo-
randa During the War" (1875–1876), notes on battlefront scenes, hospital service,
and the dead.
73. One's-Self] In the later texts the clause reads: "the eternal bodily composite,

The varieties and phases, (doubtless often paradoxical, contradictory,) of the two Volumes, of LEAVES, and of these RIVULETS, are ultimately to be considered as One in structure, and as mutually explanatory of each other—as the multiplex results, like a tree, of series of successive growths, (yet from one central or seed-purport)—there having been five or six such cumulative issues, editions, commencing back in 1855 and thence progressing through twenty years down to date, (1875–76)—some things added or re-shaped from time to time, as they were found wanted, and other things represt. Of the former Book, more vehement, and perhaps pursuing a central idea with greater closeness—join'd with the present One, extremely varied in theme—I can only briefly reiterate here, that all my pieces, alternated through Both, are only of use and value, if any, as such an interpenetrating, composite, inseparable Unity. 85

Two of the pieces in this Volume were originally Public Recitations—the College Commencement Poem, *As a Strong Bird*—and then the *Song of the Exposition*, to identify these great Industrial gatherings, the majestic outgrowths of the Modern Spirit and Practice—and now fix'd upon, the grandest of them, for the Material event around which shall be concentrated and celebrated, (as far as any one event can combine them,) the associations and practical proofs of the Hundred Years' life of the Republic. The glory of Labor, and the bringing together not only representatives of all the trades and products, but, fraternally, of all the Workmen of all the Nations of the World, (for this is the Idea behind the Centennial at Philadelphia,) is, to me, so welcome and inspiring a theme, that I only wish I were a younger and a fresher man, to attempt the enduring Book, of poetic character, that ought to be written about it.

The arrangement in print of TWO RIVELETS—the indirectness of the name itself, (suggesting meanings, the start of other meanings, for the whole Vol- 100

perennial influences of Nature at first hand, and the old heroic stamina of Nature, the strong air of prairie and mountain, the dash of the briny sea, the primary antiseptics—of the passions, in all their fullest heat and potency, of courage, rankness, amativeness, and of immense pride. . . . . . Not to lose at all, therefore, the benefits of artificial progress and civilization, but to re-occupy for Western tenancy the oldest though ever-fresh fields, and reap from them the savage and sane nourishment indispensable to a hardy nation, and the absence of which, threatening to 95n

125n. curtain.] The parenthetical matter ends here in later editions.
139n. For genius] The sentence beginning here does not appear in later editions.

cumulative natural character of one's self."
74. The varieties] Beginning with this phrase, three successive paragraphs, ending with the words, "allows them," were excluded in the later editions. Evidently, much of this had relevance primarily in context with the *TR* volume. However, three ideas have general interest: that his poetry and prose works correspond in a "composite, inseparable Unity"; that the ordinary people of all lands have a common interest; and that his poetry was experimental, under the "irresistible urge" of spiritual dictation.

ume)—are but parts of the Venture which my Poems entirely are. For really
they have all been Experiments, under the urge of powerful, quite irresistible,
perhaps wilful influences, (even escapades,) to see how such things will eventu-
ally turn out—and have been recited, as it were, by my Soul, to the special
105　　　audience of Myself, far more than to the world's audience. [See, further on,

become worse and worse, is the most serious lack and defect to-day of our New
World literature.
　　　Not but what the brawn of LEAVES OF GRASS is, I think, thoroughly spirit-
ualized everywhere, for final estimate, but, from the very subjects, the direct
100n　　effect is a sense of the Life, as it should be, of flesh and blood, and physical
urge, and animalism. . . . . . . While there are other themes, and plenty of
abstract thoughts and poems in the Volume—While I have put in it (supple-
mented in the present Work by my prose *Memoranda*,) passing and rapid but
actual glimpses of the great struggle between the Nation and the Slave-power,
105n　　(1861–'65,) as the fierce and bloody panorama of that contest unroll'd itself—
While the whole Book, indeed, revolves around that Four Years' War, which,
as I was in the midst of it, becomes, in *Drum-Taps*, pivotal to the rest entire—fol-
low'd by *Marches now the War is Over*—and here and there, before and after-
ward, not a few episodes and speculations—*that*—namely, to make a type-portrait
110n　　for living, active, worldly, healthy Personality, objective as well as subjective,
joyful and potent, and modern and free, distinctively for the use of the United
States, male and female, through the long future—has been, I say, my general
object. (Probably, indeed, the whole of these varied songs, and all my writings,
both Volumes, only ring changes in some sort, on the ejaculation, How vast, how
115n　　eligible, how joyful, how real, is a Human Being, himself or herself.)
　　　Though from no definite plan at the time, I see now that I have uncon-
sciously sought, by indirections at least as much as directions, to express the
whirls and rapid growth and intensity of the United States, the prevailing tendency
and events of the Nineteenth Century, and largely the spirit of the whole current
120n　　World, my time; for I feel that I have partaken of that spirit, as I have been
deeply interested in all those events, the closing of long-stretch'd eras and ages, and,
illustrated in the history of the United States, the opening of larger ones. (The
death of President Lincoln, for instance, fitly, historically closes, in the Civilization
of Feudalism, many old influences—drops on them, suddenly, a vast, gloomy, as it
125n　　were, separating curtain. The world's entire dramas afford none more indicative—
none with folds more tragic, or more sombre or far spreading.)
　　　Since I have been ill, (1873–74–75,) mostly without serious pain, and with
plenty of time and frequent inclination to judge my poems, (never composed with
eye on the book-market, nor for fame, nor for any pecuniary profit,) I have felt
130n　　temporary depression more than once, for fear that in LEAVES OF GRASS the *moral*
parts were not sufficiently pronounc'd. But in my clearest and calmest moods I have
realized that as those LEAVES, all and several, surely prepare the way for, and
necessitate Morals, and are adjusted to them, just the same as Nature does and is,
they are what, consistently with my plan, they must and probably should be.
135n　　. . . . . . (In a certain sense, while the Moral is the purport and last intelligence
of all Nature, there is absolutely nothing of the moral in the works, or laws, or
shows of Nature. Those only lead inevitably to it—begin and necessitate it.)
　　　Then I meant LEAVES OF GRASS, as published, to be the Poem of Identity, (of
Yours, whoever you are, now reading these lines). . . . . . For genius must re-
140n　　alize that, precious as it may be, there is something far more precious, namely,
simple Identity, One's-self. A man is not greatest as victor in war, nor inventor or
explorer, nor even in science, or in his intellectual or artistic capacity, or exemplar

161n. readers,] This parenthetical phrase is not present in later editions.
167n. expression.] The present paragraph ends here in later editions, thus excluding
the more personal interpretation of the "Calamus" motif in favor of the social role

Preface of *As a Strong Bird*, &c., 1872.] Till now, by far the best part of the whole business is, that, these days, in leisure, in sickness and old age, my Spirit, by which they were written or permitted erewhile, does not go back on them, but still and in calmest hours, fully, deliberately allows them.

Estimating the American Union as so far and for some time to come, in its *110*

in some vast benevolence. To the highest Democratic view, man is most acceptable in living well the average, practical life and lot which happens to him as ordinary farmer, sea-farer, mechanic, clerk, laborer, or driver—upon and from which position *145n* as a central basis or pedestal, while performing its labors, and his duties as citizen, son, husband, father and employed person, he preserves his physique, ascends, developing, radiating himself in other regions—and especially where and when, (greatest of all, and nobler than the proudest mere genius or magnate in any field,) he fully realizes the Conscience, the Spiritual, the divine faculty, cultivated well, ex- *150n* emplified in all his deeds and words, through life, uncompromising to the end —a flight loftier than any of Homer's or Shakspere's—broader than all poems and bibles—namely, Nature's own, and in the midst of it, Yourself, your own Identity, body and soul. (All serves, helps—but in the centre of all, absorbing all, giving, for your purpose, the only meaning and vitality to all, master or mistress of all, under *155n* the law, stands Yourself.) . . . . . To sing the Song of that divine law of Identity, and of Yourself, consistently with the Divine Law of the Universal, is a main inten- tion of those Leaves.

Something more may be added—for, while I am about it, I would make a full confession. I also sent out Leaves of Grass to arouse and set flowing in men's *160n* and women's hearts, young and old, (my present and future readers,) endless streams of living, pulsating love and friendship, directly from them to myself, now and ever. To this terrible, irrepressible yearning, (surely more or less down under- neath in most human souls,)—this never-satisfied appetite for sympathy, and this boundless offering of sympathy—this universal democratic comradeship—this old, *165n* eternal, yet ever-new interchange of adhesiveness, so fitly emblematic of America—I have given in that book, undisguisedly, declaredly, the openest expression. . . . . . . Poetic literature has long been the formal and conventional tender of art and beauty merely, and of a narrow, constipated, special amativeness. I say, the subtlest, sweetest, surest tie between me and Him or Her, who, in the pages of *170n* *Calamus* and other pieces realizes me—though we never see each other, or though ages and ages hence—must, in this way, be personal affection. And those—be they few, or be they many—are at any rate *my readers*, in a sense that belongs not, and can never belong, to better, prouder poems.

Besides, important as they are in my purpose as emotional expressions for *175n* humanity, the special meaning of the *Calamus* cluster of Leaves of Grass, (and more or less running through that book, and cropping out in *Drum-Taps*,) mainly resides in its Political significance. In my opinion it is by a fervent, accepted development of Comradeship, the beautiful and sane affection of man for man, latent in all the young fellows, North and South, East and West—it is by this, *180n* I say, and by what goes directly and indirectly along with it, that the United States of the future, (I cannot too often repeat,) are to be most effectually welded to- gether, intercalated, anneal'd into a Living Union.

Then, for enclosing clue of all, it is imperatively and ever to be borne in mind that Leaves of Grass entire is not to be construed as an intellectual or scholastic *185n* effort or Poem mainly, but more as a radical utterance out of the abysms of the Soul, the Emotions and the Physique—an utterance adjusted to, perhaps born of, Democracy and Modern Science, and in its very nature regardless of the old conven- tions, and, under the great Laws, following only its own impulses.

emphasized in the following paragraph.
186n. abysms of the Soul] omitted in later editions.
188n. Modern Science] Later editions read "the Modern".

yet formative condition, I therefore now bequeath Poems and Essays as nutriment and influences to help truly assimilate and harden, and especially to furnish something toward what The States most need of all, and which seems to me yet quite unsupplied in literature, namely, to show them, or begin to show
115 them, Themselves distinctively, and what They are for. For though perhaps the main points of all ages and nations are points of resemblance, and, even while granting evolution, are substantially the same, there are some vital things in which this Republic, as to its Individualities, and as a compacted Nation, is to specially stand forth, and culminate modern humanity. And these are the very
120 things it least morally and mentally knows—(though, curiously enough, it is at the same time faithfully acting upon them.)

I count with such absolute certainty on the Great Future of The United States—different from, though founded on, the past—that I have always invoked that Future, and surrounded myself with it, before or while singing my
125 Songs. . . . (As ever, all tends to followings—America, too, is a prophecy. What, even of the best and most successful, would be justified by itself alone? by the present, or the material ostent alone? Of men or States, few realize how much they live in the future. That, rising like pinnacles, gives its main significance to all You and I are doing to-day. Without it, there were little meaning in
130 lands or poems—little purport in human lives. . . . . . . All ages, all Nations and States, have been such prophecies. But where any former ones with prophecy so broad, so clear, as our times, our lands—as those of the West?)

Without being a Scientist, I have thoroughly adopted the conclusions of the great Savans and Experimentalists of our time, and of the last hundred years,
135 and they have interiorly tinged the chyle of all my verse, for purposes beyond. Following the Modern Spirit, the real Poems of the Present, ever solidifying and expanding into the Future, must vocalize the vastness and splendor and reality with which Scientism has invested Man and the Universe (all that is called Creation,) and must henceforth launch Humanity into new orbits, conso-
140 nant with that vastness, splendor, and reality, (unknown to the old poems,) like new systems of orbs, balanced upon themselves, revolving in limitless space, more subtle than the stars. Poetry, so largely hitherto and even at present wedded to children's tales, and to mere amorousness, upholstery and superficial rhyme, will have to accept, and, while not denying the Past, nor the Themes of
145 the past, will be revivified by, this tremendous innovation, the Kosmic Spirit,

111. Poems] Later texts omit "therefore now" after "I" and read, simply: "I bequeath poems . . ."

132. our times, our lands] WW perhaps reflects the current philosophical adherence to the theory of human progress and the belief in the "Manifest Destiny" of the United States; so also in "Preface, 1872" (q.v., text and editorial comment).

156. Chemistry] Cf. the previous paragraph. WW's interest in the developing concepts of science is reflected in LG (See Joseph Beaver, *Walt Whitman, Poet of*

which must henceforth, in my opinion, be the background and underlying impetus, more or less visible, of all first-class Songs.

Only, (for me, at any rate, in all my Prose and Poetry,) joyfully accepting Modern Science, and loyally following it without the slightest hesitation, there remains ever recognized still a higher flight, a higher fact, the Eternal Soul of Man, (of all Else too,) the Spiritual, the Religious—which it is to be the greatest office of Scientism, in my opinion, and of future Poetry also, to free from fables, crudities and superstitions, and launch forth in renewed Faith and Scope a hundred fold. To me, the worlds of Religiousness, of the conception of the Divine, and of the Ideal, though mainly latent, are just as absolute in Humanity and the Universe as the world of Chemistry, or any thing in the objective worlds. To me, 150 155

> The Prophet and the Bard,
> Shall yet maintain themselves—in higher circles yet,
> Shall mediate to the Modern, to Democracy—interpret yet to them,   160
>   God and Eidólons.

To me, the crown of Savantism is to be, that it surely opens the way for a more splendid Theology, and for ampler and diviner Songs. No year, nor even century, will settle this. There is a phase of the Real, lurking behind the Real, which it is all for. There is also in the Intellect of man, in time, far in prospective recesses, a judgment, a last appellate court, which will settle it. 165

In certain parts, in these flights, or attempting to depict or suggest them, I have not been afraid of the charge of obscurity, in either of my Two Volumes— because human thought, poetry or melody, must leave dim escapes and outlets —must possess a certain fluid, aerial character, akin to space itself, obscure to those of little or no imagination, but indispensable to the highest purposes. Poetic style, when address'd to the Soul, is less definite form, outline, sculpture, and becomes vista, music, half-tints, and even less than half-tints. True, it may be architecture; but again it may be the forest wild-wood, or the best effects thereof, at twilight, the waving oaks and cedars in the wind, and the impalpable odor. 170 175

Finally, as I have lived in fresh lands, inchoate, and in a revolutionary age, future-founding, I have felt to identify the points of that age, these lands, in my recitatives, altogether in my own way. Thus my form has strictly grown from my purports and facts, and is the analogy of them. . . . . . . Within my 180

Science, 1951). In the present paragraph and the following, his belief that science must seek the humanistic sanction may have relevance to the condition of the twentieth century.

168. obscurity] Many of the powerful images of *LG* have a meaningful obscurity: the rediscovery of his poetry by American poets early in the present century probably encouraged their inclination toward a heightened intensity and subtlety of imagery.

174. effects] Properly, "effect"; corrected in later texts.

time the United States have emerg'd from nebulous vagueness and suspense, to
full orbic, (though varied) decision—have done the deeds and achiev'd the
triumphs of half a score of centuries—and are henceforth to enter upon their
real history—the way being now, (*i. e.* since the result of the Secession War,)
185   clear'd of death-threatening impedimenta, and the free areas around and ahead
of us assured and certain, which were not so before—(the past century being
but preparations, trial-voyages and experiments of the Ship, before her starting
out upon deep water.)

In estimating my Volumes, the world's current times and deeds, and their
190   spirit, must be first profoundly estimated. Out of the Hundred Years just
ending, (1776–1876), with their genesis of inevitable wilful events, and new
introductions, and many unprecedented things of war and peace, (to be realized
better, perhaps only realized, at the remove of another Century hence)—Out of
that stretch of time, and especially out of the immediately preceding Twenty-
195   Five Years, (1850–75,) with all their rapid changes, innovations, and audacious
movements—and bearing their own inevitable wilful birth-marks—my Poems
too have found genesis.

W. W.

192. introductions] *SDC* and later texts read: "wilful events, and new experiments
and introductions, . . ."
196. my Poems] *SDC* and later texts read: "the experiments of my poems . . ."
Cf. previous note; in 1882 these alterations suggest his continuing sense of the
"experimental" nature of his poetry.

CHRONOLOGY
OF WALT WHITMAN'S LIFE AND WORK

1819	Born May 31 at West Hills, near Huntington, Long Island.
1823	May 27, Whitman family moves to Brooklyn.
1825–30	Attends public school in Brooklyn.
1830	Office boy for doctor, lawyer.
1830–34	Learns printing trade.
1835	Printer in New York City until great fire August 12.
1836–38	Summer of 1836, begins teaching at East Norwich, Long Island; by winter 1837 - 38 has taught at Hempstead, Babylon, Long Swamp, and Smithtown.
1838–39	Edits weekly newspaper, the *Long Islander*, at Huntington.
1840–41	Autumn, 1840, campaigns for Van Buren; then teaches school at Trimming Square, Woodbury, Dix Hills, and Whitestone.
1841	May, goes to New York City to work as printer in *New World* office; begins writing for the *Democratic Review*.
1842	Spring, edits a daily newspaper in New York City, the *Aurora;* edits *Evening Tattler* for short time.
1845–46	August, returns to Brooklyn, writes for *Long Island Star* from September until March.
1846–48	From March, 1846, until January, 1848, edits Brooklyn *Daily Eagle;* February, 1848, goes to New Orleans to work on the *Crescent;* leaves May 27 and returns *via* Mississippi and Great Lakes.
1848–49	September 9, 1848, to September 11, 1849, edits a "free soil" newspaper, the Brooklyn *Freeman*.
1850–54	Operates printing office and stationery store; does free-lance journalism; builds and speculates in houses.
1855	Early July, *Leaves of Grass* is printed by Rome Brothers in Brooklyn; father dies July 11; Emerson writes to poet on July 21.
1856	Writes for *Life Illustrated;* publishes second edition of *Leaves of Grass* in summer and writes "The Eighteenth Presidency!"
1857–59	From spring of 1857 until about summer of 1859 edits the Brooklyn *Times;* unemployed winter of 1859 - 60; frequents Pfaff's bohemian restaurant.
1860	March, goes to Boston to see third edition of *Leaves of Grass* through the press.
1861	April 12, Civil War begins; George Whitman enlists.

1862   December, goes to Fredericksburg, Virginia, scene of recent battle
            in which George was wounded, stays in camp two weeks.

1863   Remains in Washington, D. C., working part-time in Army Pay-
            master's office; visits soldiers in hospitals.

1864   June 22, returns to Brooklyn because of illness.

1865   January 24, appointed clerk in Department of Interior, returns
            to Washington; meets Peter Doyle; witnesses Lincoln's second
            inauguration; Lincoln assassinated, April 14; May, *Drum-Taps* is
            printed; June 30, is discharged from position by Secretary James
            Harlan but re-employed next day in Attorney General's office;
            autumn, prints *Drum-Taps and Sequel*, containing "When Lilacs
            Last in the Dooryard Bloom'd."

1866   William D. O'Connor publishes *The Good Gray Poet*.

1867   John Burroughs publishes *Notes on Walt Whitman as Poet and
            Person;* July 6, William Michael Rossetti publishes article on Whit-
            man's poetry in London *Chronicle;* "Democracy" (part of *Demo-
            cratic Vistas*) published in December *Galaxy*.

1868   Rossetti's *Poems of Walt Whitman* (selected and expurgated) pub-
            lished in England; "Personalism" (second part of *Democratic Vis-
            tas*) in May *Galaxy;* second issue of fourth edition of *Leaves of
            Grass*, with *Drum-Taps and Sequel* added.

1869   Mrs. Anne Gilchrist reads Rossetti edition and falls in love with
            the poet.

1870   July, is very depressed for unknown reasons; prints fifth edition of
            Leaves of Grass, and *Democratic Vistas* and *Passage to India*, all
            dated 1871.

1871   September 3, Mrs. Gilchrist's first love letter; September 7, reads
            "After All Not to Create Only" at opening of American Institute
            Exhibition in New York.

1872   June 26, reads "As a Strong Bird on Pinions Free" at Dartmouth
            College commencement.

1873   January 23, suffers paralytic stroke; mother dies May 23; unable
            to work, stays with brother George in Camden, New Jersey.

1874   "Song of the Redwood-Tree" and "Prayer of Columbus."

1875   Prepares Centennial Edition of *Leaves of Grass* and *Two Rivulets*
            (dated 1876).

1876   Controversy in British and American press over America's neglect
            of Whitman; spring, meets Harry Stafford, and begins recuperation
            at Stafford farm, at Timber Creek; September, Mrs. Gilchrist ar-
            rives and rents house in Philadelphia.

1877   January 28, gives lecture on Tom Paine in Philadelphia; goes to
            New York in March and is painted by George W. Waters; during
            summer gains strength by sun-bathing at Timber Creek.

1878   Spring, too weak to give projected Lincoln lecture, but in June
            visits J. H. Johnston and John Burroughs in New York.

1879   April to June, in New York, where he gives first Lincoln lecture,
            and says farewell to Mrs. Gilchrist, who returns to England; Sep-
            tember, goes to the West for the first time and visits Colorado; be-

cause of illness remains in St. Louis with his brother Jeff from
October to January.

1880   Gives Lincoln lecture in Philadelphia; summer, visits Dr. R. M.
Bucke in London, Ontario.

1881   April 15, gives Lincoln lecture in Boston; returns to Boston in
August to read proof of *Leaves of Grass*, being published by
James R. Osgood; poems receive final arrangement in this edition.

1882   Meets Oscar Wilde; Osgood ceases to distribute *Leaves of Grass*
because District Attorney threatens prosecution unless the book is
expurgated; publication is resumed in June by Rees Welsh in Phila-
delphia, who also publishes *Specimen Days and Collect;* both books
transferred to David McKay, Philadelphia.

1883   Dr. Bucke publishes *Walt Whitman*, a critical study closely "edited"
by the poet.

1884   Buys house on Mickle Street, Camden, New Jersey.

1885   In poor health; friends buy a horse and phaeton so that the poet
will not be "house-tied"; November 29, Mrs. Gilchrist dies.

1886   Gives Lincoln lecture four times in Elkton, Maryland, Camden,
Philadelphia, and Haddonfield, New Jersey; is painted by John
White Alexander.

1887   Gives Lincoln lecture in New York; is painted by Thomas Eakins.

1888   Horace Traubel raises funds for doctors and nurses; *November
Boughs* printed; money sent from England.

1889   70th birthday, proceedings published in *Camden's Compliments*.

1890   Writes angry letter to J. A. Symonds, dated August 19, denounc-
ing Symonds's interpretation of "Calamus" poems, claims six
illegitimate children.

1891   *Good-Bye My Fancy* is printed, and the "death-bed edition" of
Leaves of Grass (dated 1891 - 2).

1892   Dies March 26, buried in Harleigh Cemetery, Camden, New Jersey.

Whitman on His Art

Comments, 1855–1892

In his published Prefaces to *Leaves of Grass*, in a number of unpublished Introductions, in *Democratic Vistas*, in various pieces collected in the *Complete Prose Works* (1892), and above all in "A Backward Glance O'er Travel'd Roads," Whitman set forth his convictions about the nature and purpose of his poetry.

The most important of these pronouncements are a basic part of this edition. Less formal—but no less revealing—are the notes and observations with which the poet constantly reviewed his poetic strategy, sometimes addressing himself in private diary entries, sometimes confiding opinions on his work to his trusted friends. A selection follows.

My poems when complete should be a *unity*, in the same sense that the earth is, or that the human body, (senses, soul, head, trunk, feet, blood, viscera, man-root, eyes, hair) or that a perfect musical composition is.

Great constituent elements of my poetry—Two, viz: Materialism —Spirituality—The Intellect is what is to be the medium of these and to beautify and make serviceable there.[1]

To change the book—go over the whole with great care—to make it more intensely the poem of *Individuality*—addressed more *distinctly to the single personality listening to it*—ruling out, perhaps, some parts that stand in the way of this—cull out the egot[istic] somewhat.[2]

---

[1] *Notes and Fragments*, ed. R. M. Bucke (Folcroft, Pa.: Folcroft Press, 1899), Part II, item 1, p. 55. Undated; probably written in 1855–56.
[2] Quoted in Emory Holloway, "Notes from a Whitman Student's Scrapbook," *American Scholar*, II (1933), 274. Quoted from an undated MS scrap; probably written in 1856.

In future *Leaves of Grass. Be more severe* with the final revision of the poem, nothing will do, not one word or sentence that is not *perfectly clear*—with positive purpose—harmony with the name, nature, drift of the poem. Also *no ornaments*, especially *no ornamental adjectives*, unless they have come molten hot, and imperiously prove themselves. *No ornamental similes at all—not one: perfect transparent clearness* sanity, and health are wanted—*that* is the *divine style*—O if it can be attained—[3]

Make *the Works*—Do not go into criticisms or arguments at all. Make full-blooded, rich, natural *works*. Insert natural things, indestructibles, idioms, characteristics, rivers, states, persons, etc. Be full of *strong, sensual germs*.[4]

Sat. June 21 [1856]

It seems to me quite clear and determined that I should concentrate my powers [on] *Leaves of Grass*—not diverting any of my means, strength, interest to the construction of anything else—of any other book.[5]

Feb. 25, '57. Dined with Hector Tyndale. Asked H. T. where he thought I needed particular attention to be directed for my improvement—where I could especially be bettered in my poems. He said: "In massiveness, breadth, large sweeping effects, without regard to details.—As in the Cathedral at York (he said) I came away with great impressions of its largeness, solidity, and spaciousness, without troubling myself with its parts."

Asked F. Le B. same question, viz: What I most lacked. He said: "In *euphony*—your poems seem to me to be full of the raw material of poems, but crude, and wanting finish and rhythm."

Put in my poems: *American things, idioms, materials, persons, groups, minerals, vegetables, animals, etc.*[6]

---

[3] *Notes and Fragments*, Part II, item 55, p. 69. Undated.
[4] *Notes and Fragments*, Part II, item 16, p. 57. In footnote Bucke says, "Written about 1856."
[5] *Notes and Fragments*, Part III, item 22, p. 84.
[6] *Notes and Fragments*, Part III, item 151, p. 126.

The Great Construction of the New Bible. Not to be diverted from the principle object—the main life work—the three hundred and sixty-five.—It ought to be ready in 1859 (June '57).[7]

It may be Drum-Taps may come out this winter, yet, (in the way I have mentioned in times past.) It is in a state to put right through, a perfect copy being ready for the printers—I feel at last, & for the first time without any demur, that I am satisfied with it— content to have it go to the world verbatim & punctuation. It is in my opinion superior to Leaves of Grass—certainly more perfect as a work of art, being adjusted in all its proportions, & its passion having the indispensable merit that though to the ordinary reader let loose with wildest abandon, the true artist can see it is yet under control. But I am perhaps mainly satisfied with Drum-Taps because it delivers my ambition of the task that has haunted me, namely to express in a poem (& in the way I like, which is not at all by directly stating it) the pending action of this *Time & Land we swim in*, with all their large conflicting fluctuations of despair & hope, the shiftings, masses, & the whirl & deafening din, (yet over all, as by invisible hand, a definite purport & idea)—with the unprecedented anguish of wounded & suffering, the beautiful young men, in wholesale death & agony, everything sometimes as if in blood color, & dripping blood. The book is therefore unprecedently sad, (as these days are, are they not?)—but it also has the blast of the trumpet, & the drum pounds & whirrs in it, & then an undertone of sweetest comradeship & human love, threading its steady thread inside the chaos, & heard at every lull & interstice thereof—truly also it has clear notes of faith & triumph.[8]

No one of the Themes generally considered as the stock fit for or motif for poetry is taken by W. W. for his foundation. No romantic occurrence, nor legend, nor plot of mystery, nor sentimentaliz- ing, nor historic personage or event, nor any woven tale of love, ambi- tion or jealousy is in his work. The usual dominant requirements— beauty, art, hero and heroine, form, meter, rhyme, regularity, have not only not been the laws of its creation but might almost seem at first glance to have never been suspected by the author. Thus compared

---

[7] *Notes and Fragments*, Part I, item 14, p. 57.
[8] Letter to William Douglas O'Connor, January 6, 1865. In *The Correspond- ence of Walt Whitman*, ed. Edwin H. Miller (New York: New York Uni- versity Press, 1961–), vol. I, *1842–1867* (1961), pp. 246–247.

with the rich ornamentation of the plots and passions of the best other poems, the palace hall, the velvet, the banquet, the master-pieces of paintings and statues, the costly vessels and furnishings, the melody, the multitudinous wealth of conceit, trope, incident, florid and dulcet versification and the much elaborated beauty of the accepted poets, there is something in Leaves of Grass that seems singularly simple and bare . . .

Indeed, the qualities which characterize "Leaves of Grass" are not the qualities of a fine book or poem or any work of art but the qualities of a living and full-blooded man, amativeness, pride, adhesiveness, curiosity, yearning for immortality, joyousness and sometimes uncertainty. You do not read, it is someone that you see in action, in war, or on a ship, or climbing the mountains, or racing along and shouting aloud in pure exultation.

A certain vagueness almost passing into chaos (it remains to be acknowledged) is in a few pieces or passages; but this is apparently by the deliberate intention of the author.[9]

. . . I have just concluded a contract with J. R. Osgood and Co of Boston for the publishing of my poems complete in one volume, under the title of "Walt Whitman's Poems" (the old name of "Leaves of Grass" running through the same as ever)—to be either a $2. book or a $2.50 one—if the former, I to have 25 cts royalty, if the latter, 30 cts)—The proposition for publication came from them. The bulk of the pieces will be the same as hitherto—only I shall secure now the consecutiveness and *ensemble* I am always thinking of—Book will probably be out before winter.[1]

Even as a boy, I had the fancy, the wish, to write a piece, perhaps a poem, about the seashore—that suggesting, dividing line, contact, junction, the solid marrying the liquid—that curious, lurking something (as doubtless every objective form finally becomes to the subjective spirit) which means far more than its mere first sight, grand as that is—blending the real and ideal, and each made portion of the other. Hours, days, in my Long Island youth and early manhood, I haunted the shores of Rockaway or Coney Island, or away east to

[9] *Notes and Fragments*, Part II, item 38, pp. 63–64. An omitted sentence— "W. W. is now fifty-two years old"—dates this passage as written in 1871.
[1] Letter to John Burroughs, June 17, 1881. In *The Correspondence of Walt Whitman*, vol. III, *1876–1885* (1964), pp. 230–231.

the Hamptons or Montauk. Once, at the latter place (by the old light-house, nothing but sea-tossings in sight in every direction as far as the eye could reach), I remember well, I felt that I must one day write a book expressing this liquid, mystic theme. Afterward, I recollect, how it came to me that instead of any special lyrical or epical or literary attempt, the seashore should be an invisible *influence*, a per-vading gauge and tally for me, in my composition. (Let me give a hint here to young writers. I am not sure but I have unwittingly followed out the same rule with other powers besides sea and shores—avoiding them, in the way of any dead set at poetizing them, as too big for formal handling—quite satisfied if I could indirectly show that we have met and fused, even if only once, but enough—that we have really absorbed each other and understand each other.)

There is a dream, a picture, that for years at intervals (sometimes quite long ones, but surely again, in time) has come noiselessly up before me, and I really believe, fiction as it is, has entered largely into my practical life—certainly into my writings, and shaped and colored them. It is nothing more or less than a stretch of interminable white-brown sand, hard and smooth and broad, with the ocean perpetually, grandly, rolling in upon it, with slow-measured sweep, with rustle and hiss and foam, and many a thump as of low bass drums. This scene, this picture, I say, has risen before me at times for years. Sometimes I wake at night and can hear and see it plainly.[2]

"I have found the law of my own poems," was the unspoken but more and more decided feeling that came to me as I pass'd, hour after hour, amid all this grim yet joyous elemental abandon—this plentitude of material, entire absence of art, untrammel'd play of primitive Nature—the chasm, the gorge, the crystal mountain stream, repeated scores, hundreds of miles—the broad handling and absolute uncramped-ness—the fantastic forms, bathed in transparent browns, faint reds and grays, towering sometimes a thousand, sometimes two or three thousand feet high—at their tops now and then huge masses pois'd and mixing with the clouds, with only their outlines, hazed in misty lilac, visible. ("In Nature's grandest shows," says an old Dutch writer, an ecclesiastic, "amid the ocean's depth, if so might be, or countless worlds rolling above at night, a man thinks of them, weighs all, not

2 "Sea-shore Fancies," in *Prose Works 1892*, ed. Floyd Stovall (New York: New York University Press, 1963–64), vol. I, *Specimen Days* (1963), pp. 138–139.

for themselves or the abstract, but with reference to his own person-
ality, and how they may affect him or color his destinies.")[3]

The *worry* of Ruskin—he has at various times sent to me for six
sets of my ($10, two Vol.) centennial Edition—& sent the money for
them—with *Leaves of Grass* is that they are too *personal*, too emo-
tional, launched from the fires of *myself*, my spinal passions, joys,
yearnings, doubts, appetites etc etc.—which is really what the book is
mainly for, (as a type however for those passions, joys, workings etc
in all the race, at least as shown under modern & especially American
auspices)—Then I think he winces at what seems to him the *Demo-
cratic* brag of L. of G.—I have heard from R several times through
English visitor friends of his—It is quite certain that he has intended
writing to me at length—& has doubtless made draughts of such
writing—but defers & *fears*—& has not yet written—R like a true
Englishman evidently believes in the high poetic art of (only) making
abstract works, poems, of some fine plot or subject, stirring, beautiful,
very noble, completed within their own centre & radius, & nothing to
do with the poet's special personality, nor exhibiting the least trace of
it—like Shakespere's great unsurpassable dramas. But I have dashed at
*the greater drama going on within myself & every human being—that
is what I have been after—*[4]

Well—the lilt is all right: yes, right enough: but there's some-
thing anterior—more imperative. The first thing necessary is the
thought—the rest may follow if it chooses—may play its part—but
must not be too much sought after. The two things being equal I
should prefer to have the lilt present with the idea, but if I got down
my thought and the rhythm was not there I should not work to secure
it. I am very deliberate—I take a good deal of trouble with words: yes,
a good deal: but what I am after is the content not the music of words.
Perhaps the music happens—it does no harm: I do not go in search
of it.[5]

[3] "An Egotistical 'Find,'" in *Specimen Days*, pp. 210–211.
[4] Letter to William Douglas O'Connor, October 7, 1882. In *The Correspond-
ence of Walt Whitman*, vol. III, *1876–1885* (1964), p. 307.
[5] Conversation with Horace Traubel, Wednesday, May 16, 1888. Quoted in
Traubel, *With Walt Whitman in Camden*, I (Boston: Small, Maynard,
1906), 163.

My last, my final, my conclusive, message (conclusive for me) is in A Backward Glance: the steel of its strength is there—the screw-point—the heart-spot of it, too—is there, in that, where I say, 'But it is not in Leaves of Grass distinctly as *literature* or a specimen'—and so on (you remember the passage): that's me—the last of me if not the first—doctrine or no doctrine, Bucke or no Bucke. Taking it in that spirit—freely, bravely, according to its design—with that paragraph and others closely connected—you will see that all my parts cohere—that there are no loose joints: one reason explains all: Leaves of Grass—(intact, unbroken, not a comma removed) from first to last—from the very earliest poems to the very latest—from Starting from Paumanok to Sands at Seventy.[6]

There is a tally-stamp and stage-result of periods and nations, elusive, at second or third hand, often escaping the historian of matter-of-fact—in some sort the nation's spiritual formative ferment or chaos —the getting in of its essence, formulating identity—a law of it, and significant part of its progress. (Of the best of events and facts, even the most important, there are finally not the events and facts only, but something flashing out and fluctuating like tuft-flames or eidólons, from all.) My going up and down amidst these years, and the impromptu jottings of their sights and thoughts, of war and peace, have been in accordance with that law, and probably a result of it. . . . In certain respects, (emotionality, passions, spirituality, the invisible trend,) I therefore launch forth the divisions of the following book as not only a consequent of that period and its influences, but in one sort a History of America, the past 35 years, after the rest, after the adjuncts of that history have been studied and attended to.[7]

As I conclude . . . the interrogative wonder-fancy rises in me whether (if it be not too arrogant to even state it,) the 33 years of my current time, 1855–1888, with their aggregate of our New World doings and people, have not, indeed, created and formulated the foregoing leaves—forcing their utterance as the pages stand—coming actually from the direct urge and developments of those years, and not from any individual epic or lyrical attempts whatever, or from my pen or

[6] Conversation with Horace Traubel, Monday, September 10, 1888. Quoted in Traubel, *With Walt Whitman in Camden*, II (New York: Daniel Appleton, 1908), 297.
[7] "Note at Beginning," in *Complete Poems & Prose, 1855–1888.*

voice, or any body's special voice. Out of that supposition, the book might assume to be consider'd an autochthonic record and expression, freely render'd, of and out of these 30 to 35 years—of the soul and evolution of America—and of course, by reflection, not ours only, but more or less of the common people of the world. . . . In another sense (the warp crossing the woof, and knitted in,) the book is probably a sort of autobiography; an element I have not attempted to specially restrain or erase. . . .[8]

I will not reject any theme or subject because the treatment is too personal. As my stuff settles into shape, I am told (and sometimes myself discover, uneasily, but feel all right about it in calmer moments) it is mainly autobiographic, and even egotistic after all— which I finally accept, and am contented so.[9]

[8] From "Note at End," in *Complete Poems & Prose, 1855–1888*, pp. 141–142.
[9] From "Memoranda," in *Good-Bye My Fancy* (Philadelphia: David McKay, 1891), p. 45.

A Whitman Manuscript

These manuscript pages are, respectively, the tenth and thirteenth (pages eleven and twelve being torn out) and the fourteenth and fifteenth pages of a small red 1855–1856 notebook of ninety-eight ruled pages, now in the Feinberg Collection. Among numerous Whitman notebooks, it is of particular importance, for in it the poet entered ideas, phrases, and lines for the poems of the 1855 and 1856 editions of *Leaves of Grass*. (See *An 1855–56 Notebook Toward the Second Edition of Leaves of Grass*, ed. Harold W. Blodgett [Carbondale: Southern Illinois University Press, 1959]).

On page 10 Whitman jotted six lines from which he developed the second section, lines 6–19, of "Crossing Brooklyn Ferry," and on page 13 he composed five lines which are the first form of lines 27–30 in the third section of the poem. Note that "glistening" is a revision for the cancelled "bright," that "high up" is a revision for "thus afar afar off," and that there are other cancellations as well. Compare the MS lines with those of the text. Both pages are cancelled by a vertical line, Whitman's customary device for indicating that he had used the passage in *Leaves of Grass*.

I have looked toward the Latin by, to notice the airing ships. So I have looked on the white sails of the the sloops it [...]

She never better principle throng't all my poems — (Besides novels, compositions of my sort)

Present my great characters, good liors, Characters,

Present the best phases of Character, that are one, than a woman is eligible to present noble phases of character to young men

Illustration

I must combine the tenderness and travelling sympathetic meaning of Jean Paul with the strength of Homer and the perfect reason of Shakespeare.

Criticism

WALT WHITMAN

Leaves of Grass: A Volume of Poems Just Published†

To give judgment on real poems, one needs an account of the poet himself. Very devilish to some, and very divine to some, will appear the poet of these new poems, the "Leaves of Grass;" an attempt, as they are, of a naive, masculine, affectionate, contemplative, sensual, imperious person, to cast into literature not only his own grit and arrogance, but his own flesh and form, undraped, regardless of models, regardless of modesty or law, and ignorant or silently scornful, as at first appears, of all except his own presence and experience, and all outside the fiercely loved land of his birth, and the birth of his parents, and their parents for several generations before him. Politeness this man has none, and regulation he has none. A rude child of the people! —No imitation—No foreigner—but a growth and idiom of America. No discontented—a careless slouch, enjoying today. No dilettante democrat—a man who is art-and-part with the commonalty, and with immediate life—loves the streets—loves the docks—loves the free rasping talk of men—likes to be called by his given name, and nobody at all need Mr. him—can laugh with laughers—likes the ungenteel ways of laborers—is not prejudiced one mite against the Irish—talks readily with them—talks readily with niggers—does not make a stand on being a gentleman, nor on learning or manners—eats cheap fare, likes the strong flavored coffee of the coffee-stands in the market, at sunrise— likes a supper of oysters fresh from the oyster-smack—likes to make one at the crowded table among sailors and work-people—would leave a select soiree of elegant people any time to go with tumultuous men, roughs, receive their caresses and welcome, listen to their noise, oaths, smut, fluency, laughter, repartee—and can preserve his presence perfectly among these, and the like of these. The effects he produces in his poems are no effects of artists or the arts, but effects of the original eye or arm, or the actual atmosphere, or tree, or bird. You may feel the unconscious teaching of a fine brute, but will never feel the artificial teaching of a fine writer or speaker.

† Unsigned review by Whitman, *"Leaves of Grass:* A Volume of Poems Just Published," in the *Brooklyn Daily Times*, September 29, 1855. This text was first collected by Whitman's literary executors in the miscellany *In Re Walt Whitman* (1893).

Other poets celebrate great events, personages, romances, wars, loves, passions, the victories and power of their country, or some real or imagined incident—and polish their work and come to conclusions, and satisfy the reader. This poet celebrates natural propensities in himself; and that is the way he celebrates all. He comes to no conclusions, and does not satisfy the reader. He certainly leaves him what the serpent left the woman and the man, the taste of the Paradisaic tree of the knowledge of good and evil, never to be erased again.

What good is it to argue about egotism? There can be no two thoughts on Walt Whitman's egotism. That is avowedly what he steps out of the crowd and turns and faces them for. Mark, critics! Otherwise is not used for you the key that leads to the use of the other keys to this well-enveloped man. His whole work, his life, manners, friendships, writings, all have among their leading purposes an evident purpose to stamp a new type of character, namely his own, and indelibly fix it and publish it, not for a model but an illustration, for the present and future of American letters and American young men, for the south the same as the north, and for the Pacific and Mississippi country, and Wisconsin and Texas and Kansas and Canada and Havana and Nicaragua, just as much as New York and Boston. Whatever is needed toward this achievement he puts his hand to, and lets imputations take their time to die.

First be yourself what you would show in your poem—such seems to be this man's example and inferred rebuke to the schools of poets. He makes no allusions to books or writers; their spirits do not seem to have touched him; he has not a word to say for or against them, or their theories or ways. He never offers others; what he continually offers is the man whom our Brooklynites know so well. Of pure American breed, large and lusty—age thirty-six years, (1855,)—never once using medicine—never dressed in black, always dressed freely and clean in strong clothes—neck open, shirt collar flat and broad, countenance tawny transparent red, beard well-mottled with white, hair like hay after it has been mowed in the field and lies tossed and streaked—his physiology corroborating a rugged phrenology—a person singularly beloved and looked toward, especially by young men and the illiterate—one who has firm attachments there, and associates there —one who does not associate with literary people—a man never called upon to make speeches at public dinners—never on platforms amid the crowds of clergymen, or professors, or aldermen, or congressmen— rather down in the bay with pilots in their pilot-boat—or off on a cruise with fishers in a fishing-smack—or riding on a Broadway omnibus, side by side with the driver—or with a band of loungers over the open grounds of the country—fond of New York and Brooklyn—fond of the life of the great ferries—one whom, if you should meet, you need not expect to meet an extraordinary person—one in whom you will see the singularity which consists in no singularity—whose contact is no dazzle or fascination, nor requires any deference, but has the easy fascination of what is homely and accustomed—as of something you knew before, and was waiting for—there you have Walt Whitman, the begetter of a new offspring out of literature, taking with easy nonchalance the chances of its present reception, and, through all misunderstandings and distrusts, the chances of its future reception—preferring always to speak for himself rather than have others speak for him.

EDWARD EVERETT HALE

Leaves of Grass: Brooklyn, 1855†

Everything about the external arrangement of this book was odd and out of the way. The author printed it himself, and it seems to have been left to the winds of heaven to publish it. So it happened that we had not discovered it before our last number, although we believe the sheets had then passed the press. It bears no publisher's name, and, if the reader goes to a bookstore for it, he may expect to be told at first, as we were, that there is no such book, and has not been. Nevertheless, there is such a book, and it is well worth going twice to the bookstore to buy it. Walter Whitman, an American,—one of the roughs,—no sentimentalist,—no stander above men and women, or apart from them, —no more modest than immodest,—has tried to write down here, in a sort of prose poetry, a good deal of what he has seen, felt, and guessed at in a pilgrimage of some thirty-five years. He has a horror of conventional language of any kind. His theory of expression is, that, "to speak in literature with the perfect rectitude and *insouciance* of the movements of animals, is the flawless triumph of art." Now a great many men have said this before. But generally it is the introduction to something more artistic than ever,—more conventional and strained. Antony began by saying he was no orator, but none the less did an

† From the *North American Review*, LXXXII (January, 1856), 275–277.

oration follow. In this book, however, the prophecy is fairly fulfilled in the accomplishment. "What I experience or portray shall go from my composition without a shred of my composition. You shall stand by my side and look in the mirror with me."

So truly accomplished is this promise,—which anywhere else would be a flourish of trumpets,—that this thin quarto deserves its name. That is to say, one reads and enjoys the freshness, simplicity, and reality of what he reads, just as the tired man, lying on the hillside in summer, enjoys the leaves of grass around him,—enjoys the shadow,—enjoys the flecks of sunshine—not for what they "suggest to him," but for what they are.

So completely does the author's remarkable power rest in his simplicity, that the preface to the book—which does not even have large letters at the beginning of the lines, as the rest has—is perhaps the very best thing in it. We find more to the point in the following analysis of the "genius of the United States," than we have found in many more pretentious studies of it.

"Other states indicate themselves in their deputies, but the genius of the United States is not best or most in its executives or legislatures, nor in its ambassadors or authors or colleges or churches or parlors, nor even in its newspapers or inventors;—but always most in the common people. Their manners, speech, dress, friendships;—the freshness and candor of their physiognomy, the picturesque looseness of their carriage, their deathless attachment to freedom, their aversion to everything indecorous or soft or mean, the practical acknowledgment of the citizens of one State by the citizens of all other States, the fierceness of their roused resentment, their curiosity and welcome of novelty, their self-esteem and wonderful sympathy, their susceptibility to a slight, the air they have of persons who never knew how it felt to stand in the presence of superiors, the fluency of their speech, their delight in music (the sure symptom of manly tenderness and native elegance of soul), their good temper and open-handedness, the terrible significance of their elections, the President's taking off his hat to them, not they to him,—these too are unrhymed poetry. It awaits the gigantic and generous treatment worthy of it."

The book is divided into a dozen or more sections, and in each one of these some thread of connection may be traced, now with ease, now with difficulty,—each being a string of verses, which claim to be written without effort and with entire *abandon*. So the book is a collection of observations, speculations, memories, and prophecies, clad in the simplest, truest, and often the most nervous English,—in the midst of which the reader comes upon something as much out of place as a piece of rotten wood would be among leaves of grass in the meadow, if the meadow had no object but to furnish a child's couch. So slender is the connection, that we hardly injure the following scraps by extracting them.

"I am the teacher of Athletes;
He that by me spreads a wider breast than my own, proves the width of my own;
He most honors my style who learns under it to destroy the teacher;
The boy I love, the same becomes a man, not through derived power, but in his own right,
Wicked rather than virtuous out of conformity or fear,
Fond of his sweetheart, relishing well his steak,
Unrequited love, or a slight, cutting him worse than a wound cuts,
First-rate to ride, to fight, to hit the bull's-eye, to sail a skiff, to sing a song, or to play on the banjo,
Preferring scars, and faces pitted with small-pox, over all latherers and those that keep out of the sun."

Here is the story of the gallant seaman who rescued the passengers on the San Francisco: —

"I understand the largest heart of heroes,
The courage of present times and all times;
How the skipper saw the crowded and rudderless wreck of the steamship, and death chasing it up and down the storm,
How he knuckled tight, and gave not back one inch, and was faithful of days and faithful of nights,
And chalked in large letters on a board, 'Be of good cheer, we will not desert you';
How he saved the drifting company at last,
How the lank, loose-gowned women looked when boated from the side of their prepared graves,
How the silent old-faced infants, and the lifted sick, and the sharp-lipped, unshaved men;
All this I swallowed, and it tastes good; I like it well, and it becomes mine:
I am the man, I suffered, I was there."

Claiming in this way a personal interest in every thing that has ever happened in the world, and, by the wonderful sharpness and distinctness of his imagination, making the claim effective and reason-

able, Mr. "Walt. Whitman" leaves it a matter of doubt where he has
been in this world, and where not. It is very clear, that with him, as
with most other effective writers, a keen, absolute memory, which takes
in and holds every detail of the past,—as they say the exaggerated
power of the memory does when a man is drowning,—is a gift of his
organization as remarkable as his vivid imagination. What he has
seen once, he has seen for ever. And thus there are in this curious
book little thumb-nail sketches of life in the prairie, life in California,
life at school, life in the nursery,—life, indeed, we know not where
not,—which, as they are unfolded one after another, strike us as real,
—so real that we wonder how they came on paper.

For the purpose of showing that he is above every conventional-
ism, Mr. Whitman puts into the book one or two lines which he would
not address to a woman nor to a company of men. There is not any-
thing, perhaps, which modern usage would stamp as more indelicate
than are some passages in Homer. There is not a word in it meant to
attract readers by its grossness, as there is in half the literature of the
last century, which holds its place unchallenged on the tables of our
drawing-rooms. For all that, it is a pity that a book where everything
else is natural should go out of the way to avoid the suspicion of being
prudish.

GEORGE SAINTSBURY

Leaves of Grass†

Several years have now passed since Walt Whitman's poetical
works and claims were first brought before the notice of Englishmen
of letters, yet it is more than doubtful whether, even among this class,
there is any clear and decided view of his merits to be found prevailing.
His poems have suffered the usual fate of such abnormal productions;
it has been considered that admiration of them must be a kind of volun-
tary eccentricity, a gratuitous flourish in the face of respectability and
orthodoxy. And it cannot be denied that he has not altogether escaped

† From *The Academy* (London), October 10, 1874, pp. 398–400. George
Saintsbury, Professor of Literature at Edinburgh from 1895 to 1915, had a
well-established critical reputation when he wrote this review. (References
are to the 1871 edition.)

that worst of all calamities to a literary man, the admiration of the in-
competent. It is true that he has been praised, with discrimination as
well as with emphasis, by Mr. Swinburne; but unfortunately Mr.
Swinburne's praise is mainly a passport to the favour of those who
would be likely to appreciate Whitman without any passport at all.
The testimony of his other panegyrists has been not a little weakened:
in some by supposed national or political prejudices; in others, as al-
ready mentioned, by notorious literary incompetence.

It is very much to be hoped that the publication of this new
edition of the 'Leaves of Grass' may be the occasion of a deeper and
wider study of the American poet, a study which may be carried on
purely as a matter of literature, and not with any lurking intention to
illustrate preconceived ideas as to the merits or demerits of Walt
Whitman's principles, practice, or mode of expression.

The volume now before us is very different in outward appear-
ance from the edition of fourteen years ago, which has so long caught
the eye by its dissimilarity to its brother occupants of the bookshelf.
The old cloth boards, deeply and mystically stamped with strange
emblems, have given way to an outer coat of sober and decent green
suitable to any modern English poem. Thick paper and bold type have
yielded to the exigencies of increased matter. The very titles of some
of the poems have made concessions to conventionality. "Enfants
d'Adam" have transplanted themselves into plain English; "Proto-Leaf"
has disappeared from the contents; and "A Boston Ballad the 78th year
T. S.," which used to excite vague and uncomfortable chronological
uncertainties, has become, to the great solace of the reader, "A Boston
Ballad, 1854." Altogether the book might seem to a too-fanciful critic
to have abandoned, at least in externals, its former air of youthful and
exuberant provocation, and to demand, more soberly if not less confi-
dently, the maturer consideration of the student of letters.

But it is still as ever far more easy to argue for or against the book
than to convey a clear account of it to persons not acquainted with it.
Although the contents are divided and subdivided by the headings
which the author has prefixed, yet these headings convey but little
idea of what comes under them, sometimes indeed have very little
reference to it. Nor is the connection of the different divisions of the
work and their interdependence more obvious. It may be easy to ex-
plain the meaning of "Children of Adam," of "Passage to India," and
some others; but what shall we make of "Calamus," or of 'Leaves of
Grass' itself? For the answers we must refer the reader to the book
that it may give its own reply.

Moreover, the poet has in this edition availed himself of the incorporation of "Drumtaps" and other recently published matter, to dispose the whole contents of the volume in a new order, and to make many additions, alterations, and transpositions in individual poems. These changes are for the most part, as it appears to us, decided improvements, and the whole work possesses at present a unity and a completeness which are no small advantage. There are few poets who require to be studied as a whole so much as Walt Whitman—quotations and even tolerably extensive selections will not do—and it is a great gain to be directed by the author himself as to the order in which he would have us conduct the study.

It is not difficult to point out the central thesis of Walt Whitman's poetical gospel. It is briefly this: the necessity of the establishment of a universal republic, or rather brotherhood of men. And to this is closely joined another, or rather a series of others, indicating the type of man of which this universal republic is to consist, or perhaps which it is to produce. The poet's language in treating the former of these two positions is not entirely uniform; sometimes he speaks as of a federation of nations, sometimes as if mankind at large were to gravitate towards the United States, and to find in them the desired Utopia. But the constitution of the United States, at least that constitution as it ought to be, is always and uniformly represented as a sufficient and the only sufficient political means of attaining this Utopia, nay, as having to some extent already presented Utopia as a fact. Moreover, passing to the second point, the ideal man is imaged as the ideal Yankee, understanding that word of course as it is understood in America, not in Europe. He is to be a rather magnificent animal, almost entirely uncultured (this is not an unfair representation, although there are to be found certain vague panegyrics on art, and especially on music), possessing a perfect *physique*, well nourished and clothed, affectionate towards his kind, and above all things firmly resolved to admit no superior. As is the ideal man, so is the ideal woman to be. Now it may be admitted frankly and at once, that this is neither the creed nor the man likely to prove attractive to many persons east of the Atlantic. If it be said that the creed is a vague creed, and the man a detestable man, there will be very little answer attempted. Many wonderful things will doubtless happen "when," as the poet says, "through these States walk a hundred millions of superb persons;" but it must be allowed that there is small prospect of any such procession. One is inclined for very many sound reasons, and after discarding all prejudices, to opine that whatever salvation may await the world may possibly come from quarters other than from America. Fortunately, however, admiration for a creed is easily separable from admiration for the utterance and expression of that creed, and Walt Whitman as a poet is not difficult to disengage from Walt Whitman as an evangelist and politician. The keyword of all his ideas and of all his writings is universality. His Utopia is one which shall be open to everybody; his ideal of man and woman one which shall be attainable by everybody; his favourite scenes, ideas, subjects, those which everybody, at least to some extent, can enjoy and appreciate. He cares not that by this limitation he may exclude thoughts and feelings, at any rate phases of thought and feeling, infinitely choicer and higher than any which he admits. To express this striving after universality he has recourse to methods both unusual and (to most readers) unwelcome. The extraordinary jumbles and strings of names, places, employments, which deface his pages, and which have encouraged the profane to liken them to auctioneers' catalogues or indexes of encyclopædias, have no other object than to express this universal sympathy, reaching to the highest and penetrating to the lowest forms of life. The exclusion of culture, philosophy, manners, is owing also to this desire to admit nothing but what is open to every human being of ordinary faculty and opportunities. Moreover it is to this that we may fairly trace the prominence in Whitman's writings of the sexual passion, a prominence which has given rise, and probably will yet give rise, to much unphilosophical hubbub. This passion, as the poet has no doubt observed, is almost the only one which is peculiar to man as man, the presence of which denotes virility if not humanity, the absence of which is a sign of abnormal temperament. Hence he elevates it to almost the principal place, and treats of it in a manner somewhat shocking to those who are accustomed to speak of such subjects (we owe the word to Southey) *enfarinhadamente*. As a matter of fact, however, the treatment, though outspoken, is eminently "clean," to use the poet's own word; there is not a vestige of prurient thought, not a syllable of prurient language. Yet it would be a great mistake to suppose that sexual passion occupies the chief place in Whitman's estimation. There is according to him something above it, something which in any ecstasies he fails not to realize, something which seems more intimately connected in his mind with the welfare of mankind, and the promotion of his ideal republic. This is what he calls "robust American love." He is never tired of repeating "I am the poet of comrades"—Socrates himself seems renascent in this apostle of friendship. In the ears of a world (at least on this side the Atlantic) incredulous of such things, he reiterates the expressions of Plato to Aster, of Socrates respecting Charmides, and in this respect fully justifies (making allowance for altered manners) Mr. Symonds' assertion of his essentially Greek character, an assertion which most students of Whitman will heartily endorse. But we must again repeat that it is not so much in the matter as in the manner of his Evangel that the strength of Whitman lies. It is impossible not to notice his exquisite descriptive faculty, and his singular felicity in its use. Forced as he is, both by natural inclination and in the carrying out of his main idea, to take note of "the actual earth's equalities," he has literally filled his pages with the song of birds, the hushed murmur of waves, the quiet and multiform life of the forest and the meadow. And in these descriptions he succeeds in doing what is most difficult, in giving us the actual scene or circumstance as it impressed him, and not merely the impression itself. This is what none but the greatest poets have ever save by accident done, and what Whitman does constantly and with a sure hand. "You shall," he says at the beginning of his book:

"You shall no longer take things at second or third hand, nor look through the eyes of the dead, nor feed on the spectres in books:

'You shall not look through my eyes either, nor take things from me:

"You shall listen to all sides and filter them from yourself."

But affluent as his descriptions are, there are two subjects on which he is especially eloquent, which seem indeed to intoxicate and inspire him the moment he approaches them. These are Death and the sea. In the latter respect he is not, indeed, peculiar, but accords with all poets of all times, and especially of this time. But in his connection of the two ideas (for the one always seems to suggest the other to him), and in his special devotion to Death, he is more singular. The combined influence of the two has produced what is certainly the most perfect specimen of his work, the "Word out of the Sea" (in this edition it has, we are sorry to see, lost its special title, and become the first merely of "Sea-Shore Memories"). Unfortunately it is indivisible, and its length precludes the possibility of quotation. But there is another poem almost equally beautiful, which forms part of "President Lincoln's Burial Hymn," and for this space may perhaps be found: —

"DEATH-CAROL.

Come, lovely and soothing Death,
Undulate round the world serenely arriving, arriving,
In the day, in the night, to all, to each,
Sooner or later, delicate Death.

Prais'd be the fathomless universe,
For life and joy, and for objects and knowledge curious;

And for love, sweet love. But praise! praise! praise!
For the sure-enwinding arms of cool-enfolding Death.

Dark Mother, always gliding near, with soft feet,
Have none chanted for thee a chant of fullest welcome?
Then I chant it for thee—I glorify thee above all;
I bring thee a song that when thou must indeed come, come un-
       falteringly.

Approach, strong Deliveress!
When it is so—when thou hast taken them, I joyously sing the
       dead,
Lost in the loving, floating ocean of thee,
Laved in the flood of thy bliss, O Death.

From me to thee glad serenades,
Dances for thee I propose, saluting thee—adornments and feast-
       ings for thee;
And the sights of the open landscape and the high spread sky are
       fitting,
And life and the fields and the huge and thoughtful night.

The night, in silence under many a star;
The ocean-shore, and the husky whispering wave whose voice
       I know;
And the soul turning to thee, O vast and well-veiled death,
And the body gratefully nestling close to thee.

Over the tree-tops I float thee a song!
Over the rising and sinking waves—over the myriad fields and
       the prairies wide;
Over the dense-packed cities all and the teeming wharves and
       ways,
I float this carol with joy, with joy to thee, O Death!"

It is easy enough to connect this cultus of Death, and the pantheism
which necessarily accompanies it, with the main articles of Whitman's
creed. Death is viewed as the one event of great solemnity and im-
portance which is common to all—the one inevitable, yet not common-
place incident in every life, however commonplace; and, further, it
must not be overlooked that Death is pre-eminently valuable in such a
system as this, in the capacity of reconciler, ready to accommodate
all difficulties, to sweep away all rubbish. The cheeriest of optimists
with the lowest of standards cannot pretend to assert or expect that

everyone will live the ideal life—but Death pays all scores and obliterates all mistakes.

There remains, however, still to be considered a point not least in importance—the vehicle which Whitman has chosen for the conveyance of these thoughts. He employs, as most people know who know anything at all about him, neither rhyme nor even regular metre; the exceptions to this rule occurring among his more recent poems are few and insignificant. A page of his work has little or no look of poetry about it; it is not, indeed, printed continuously, but it consists of versicles, often less in extent than a line, sometimes extending to many lines. Only after reading these for some time does it become apparent that, though rhyme and metre have been abandoned, rhythm has not; and, moreover, that certain figures and tricks of language occur which are generally considered more appropriate to poetry than to prose. The total effect produced is dissimilar to that of any of the various attempts which have been made to evade the shackles of metre and rhyme, while retaining the other advantages of poetical form and diction. Whitman's style differs very much from that of such efforts as Baudelaire's 'Petits Poèmes en Prose,' for from these all rhythm, diction, and so forth not strictly appropriate to prose is conscientiously excluded. It is more like the polymeters of the poet's namesake Walt in Richter's 'Flegeljahre,' except that these latter being limited to the expression of a single thought are not divided into separate limbs or verses. Perhaps the likeness which is presented to the mind most strongly, is that which exists between our author and the verse divisions of the English Bible, especially in the poetical books, and it is not unlikely that the latter did actually exercise some influence in moulding the poet's work. It is hard to give a fair specimen of it in the way of quotation—that already given is not representative, being too avowedly lyrical—and the rhythm is as a rule too varying, complex, and subtle to be readily seized except from a comparison of many instances. Perhaps, however, the following stanza from "Children of Adam" may convey some idea of it:—

> "I have perceived that to be with those I like is enough;
> To stop in company with the rest at evening is enough;
> To be surrounded by beautiful, curious, breathing, laughing flesh
>   is enough;
> To pass among them, or touch any one, or rest my arm ever so
>   lightly round his or her neck for a moment—what is this
>   then?
> I do not ask any more delight—I swim in it as in a sea.
> There is something in staying close to men and women, and

> looking on them, and in the contact and odour of them, that
> pleases the soul well;
> All things please the soul—but these please the soul well."

It will be observed that the rhythm is many-centred, that it takes fresh departures as it goes on. The poet uses freely alliteration, chiasmus, antithesis, and especially the retention of the same word or words to begin and end successive lines, but none of these so freely as to render it characteristic. The result, though perhaps uncouth at first sight and hearing, is a medium of expression by no means wanting in excellence, and certainly well adapted for Whitman's purposes. Strange as it appears to a reader familiarised with the exquisite versification of modern England or France, it is by no means in disagreeable contrast therewith, being at least in its earlier forms (for in some of the later poems reminiscences of the English heroic, of Longfellow's hexameters, and even of Poe's stanzas occur) singularly fresh, light, and vigorous. Nor should the language pass unmentioned—for though of course somewhat Transatlantic in construction and vocabulary, it is not offensively American. The chief blemish in the eyes of a sensitive critic is an ugly trick of using foreign words, such as "Libertad" for liberty, "*habitan* of the Alleghanies," to become *élève* of mine," "with reference to *ensemble*," and so forth; but even this does not occur very frequently. Few books abound more in "jewels five words long;" it is hardly possible to open a page without lighting upon some happy and memorable conceit, expression, thought, such as this of the grass:

> "It is the handkerchief of the Lord;
> A scented gift and remembrance designedly dropt,
> Bearing the owner's name someway in the corners, that we may
> see and remark, and say Whose?"

Or this of children's love to a father:

> "They did not love him by allowance, they loved him with
> personal love."

Or again of the grass:

> "And now it seems to me the beautiful uncut hair of graves."

Such in matter and in manner are Walt Whitman's 'Leaves of Grass,' and there only remains to be added one recommendation to their study. The book, aggressive and vainglorious as it seems, is in reality remarkably free from vituperativeness of tone. Hardly to some "eunuchs, consumptive and genteel persons" is strong language used,

and after all it rests with every reader whether he chooses to class
himself with these. Amid all the ecstatic praise of America there is no
abuse of England; amid all the excitement of the poems on the War
there is little personal abuse of the Secessionists. No Englishman, no
one indeed, whether American or Englishman, need be deterred from
reading this book, a book the most unquestionable in originality, if
not the most unquestioned in excellence, that the United States have
yet sent us.

WILLIAM DEAN HOWELLS

[Whitman in Retrospect]†

Mr. Walt Whitman calls his latest book *November Boughs*, and
in more ways than one it testifies and it appeals beyond the letter to the
reader's interest. For the poet the long fight is over; he rests his cause
with what he has done; and we think no one now would like to consider
the result without respect, without deference, even if one cannot ap-
proach it with entire submission. It is time, certainly, while such a
poet is still with us, to own that his literary intention was as generous
as his spirit was bold, and that if he has not accomplished all he in-
tended, he has been a force that is by no means spent. Apart from the
social import of his first book ("without yielding an inch, the working-
man and working-woman were to be in my pages from first to last"),
he aimed in it at the emancipation of poetry from what he felt to be
the trammels of rhyme and metre. He did not achieve this; but he
produced a new kind in literature, which we may or may not allow to
be poetry, but which we cannot deny is something eloquent, suggestive,
moving, with a lawless, formless beauty of its own. He dealt literary
conventionality one of those blows which eventually show as internal
injuries, whatever the immediate effect seems to be. He made it possible
for poetry hereafter to be more direct and natural than hitherto; the
hearing which he has braved nearly half a century of contumely and
mockery to win would now be granted on very different terms to a
man of his greatness. This is always the way; and it is always the

† From William Dean Howells, "Editor's Study," *Harper's Monthly*,
LXXVIII (February, 1889) 488–492. Howells, in his ninth year as editor
of *Harper's*, was the foremost critical voice in the American literary world.
Although he could not honestly recognize Whitman as a major poet, he had
liked him for many years (see *Literary Friends and Acquaintances* [1900],
pp. 73–76).

way that the reformer (perhaps in helpless confession of the weakness
he shares with all humankind) champions some error which seems as
dear to him as the truth he was born to proclaim. Walt Whitman was
not the first to observe that we are all naked under our clothes, but he
was one of the greatest, if not the first, to preach a gospel of nudity;
not as one of his Quaker ancestry might have done for a witness
against the spiritual nakedness of his hearers, but in celebration of the
five senses and their equal origin with the three virtues of which the
greatest is charity. His offence, if rank, is quantitatively small; a few
lines at most; and it is one which the judicious pencil of the editor will
some day remove for him, though for the present he "takes occasion
to confirm those lines with the settled convictions and deliberate re-
newals of thirty years." We hope for that day, not only because it will
give to all a kind in poetry which none can afford to ignore, and which
his cherished lines bar to most of those who read most in our time and
country, but because we think the five senses do not need any celebra-
tion. In that duality which every thoughtful person must have noticed
composes him, we believe the universal experience is that the beast
half from first to last is fully able to take care of itself. But it is a vast
subject, and, as the poet says, "it does not stand by itself; the vitality
of it is altogether in its relations, bearings, significance." In the mean
while we can assure the reader that these *November Boughs* are as
innocent as so many sprays of apple blossom, and that he may take the
book home without misgiving.

We think he will find in reading it that the prose passages are,
some of them, more poetic than the most poetic of the rhythmical
passages. "Some War Memoranda," and "The Last of the War Cases"
—notes made twenty-five years ago—are alive with a simple pathos and
instinct with a love of truth which recall the best new Russian work,
and which make the poet's psalms seem vague and thin as wandering
smoke in comparison. Yet these have the beauty of undulant, sinuous,
desultory smoke forms, and they sometimes take the light with a
response of such color as dwells in autumn sunsets. The book is well
named *November Boughs:* it is meditative and reminiscent, with a sober
fragrance in it like the scent of fallen leaves in woods where the leaves
that still linger overhead,

> "Or few, or none, do shake against the cold—
> Bare ruined choice where late the sweet birds sang." [1]

1. Howells misquotes the passage from Shakespeare's Sonnet 73, which reads:

> . . . or none, or few, do hang
> Upon those boughs which shake against the cold,
> Bare ruin'd choirs where late the sweet birds sang.

It is the hymn of the runner resting after the race, and much the same as he chants always, whether the race has been lost or won.

II.

"To get the final lilt of songs;
To penetrate the inmost lore of poets; to know the mighty ones—
Job, Homer, Æschylus, Dante, Shakespeare, Tennyson, Emerson;
To diagnose the shifting, delicate tints of love and pride and
     doubt; to truly understand,
To encompass these, the last keen faculty and entrance price,
Old age, and what it brings from all its past experiences"—

this is now the "good gray poet's" aspiration, and he throws it "out at the object," as Matthew Arnold says, with the syntactical incompleteness of a sigh. It is the mood and the manner of several other lyrical passages in the book, and is more important only because it bears incidentally upon the question lately asked by Mr. Edmund Gosse, "Has America produced a poet?" Mr. Gosse says he asks it rather in compliance with an editorial wish than from his own impulse, and certainly he asks it with all the grace and gentleness inseparable from his literature. In answering it negatively he confines himself to poets no longer alive, and so no longer susceptible to hurts of pride or vanity. At the same time he intimates that if it were a question of living poets it could not be a question at all; or, if he does not intimate this, he leaves the living poets to infer it from the kindness of the terms he uses toward them. He names Chaucer, Spenser, Shapespeare, Milton, Dryden, Pope, Gray, Burns, Wordsworth, Coleridge, Byron, Shelley, and Keats as the British worthiest; and he asks, "What dead American is worthy to join the twelve, and make an Anglo-Saxon's baker's dozen?" He thinks none, and he gives his reasons: perfectly good reasons for those who are already of his opinion; charming reasons for all; courteous reasons, respectful, even reverential reasons, but carrying conviction to no contrary mind. This is in the nature of things; for as no one can say what poetry is, so no one can say who is a poet. One may quite easily defy Mr. Gosse to say what touch in all Dryden thrills and lifts like many touches in Emerson. One may challenge him to prove the art of Pope finer than the art of Longfellow, or bid him show where and how Burns is better than Bryant. But at the end of the ends the case is what it was: he remains as unpersuaded as you do. Still, as true Americans, and as the most provincial people on the planet in certain respects, we could not leave the case as it was. One of the literary newspapers invited a symposium of American authors to sit upon Mr. Gosse and his reasons, and they all, or nearly all, declared that Emerson was worthy to be the baker's dozenth: there might be doubts about Longfellow, or there might be doubts about Bryant, but there could not be any doubt about Emerson. The verdict was interesting as a proof that Emerson holds the first place in the critical esteem of those among us best fitted to judge him; but it seems odd that at a feast where there were so many living poets (whose worthiness Mr. Gosse refused to question) none was found ready to sacrifice either his brother or himself, and so provide an immortal thirteenth on on the spot.

Walt Whitman's Career†

I

The old poet who for so many years has made the public his confidant during the slow stages of his departure from the world is now at rest.

To the last he expressed himself in verse after that fashion which he elaborated about the middle of the century, and which far more than the two or three indecencies he printed, set against him the prigs and the narrow-minded among literary folk. As in religion so in literature, one must genuflect and cross one's self in orthodox fashion or submit to anathema.

In his slender volume of verse and prose issued this year by David McKay in Philadelphia, Walt Whitman bade his strange, unromantic and yet imposing Muse farewell:

> "Good-bye, my Fancy.
> Farewell, dear mate, dear love.
> I'm going away I know not where.
> Or to what fortune, or whether I may ever see you again.
> So good-bye, my Fancy.
> Now for my last—let me look back a moment.
> The slower, fainter ticking of the clock is in me.
> Exit, nightfall, and soon the heart-thud stopping."

† Obituary in the *New York Times*, Sunday, March 27, 1892.

This is from what he called the second annex to "Leaves of Grass," for the old poet was by nature more prone than any to linger over what he felt to be his masterpiece and add to it touch after touch. With the artist this tendency is fatal, because the touch falls direct on the canvas or marble, but with the poet, especially a poet so little careful of rhyme and rhythm as Whitman, it makes less trouble; one can always go back to the original edition to find the work free from afterthoughts. With Whitman, indeed, inspiration did not come with a rush; he brooded on his matter, perhaps because of a defective early education, which made him a laborious composer, but the very efforts which he made to overcome his disadvantage of training brought him in the end to a pitch of originality attained by few poets of the century.

In the passing away of a writer whom his admirers loved to call the Good Gray Poet the City of New York has lost the most remarkable literary character since Washington Irving. If his merits are not conceded so generally as are those of Irving, it may be said that his was much the more singular character and career, and that while Irving followed close on English precedents in prose literature, Whitman struck out a path for himself in verse. As to originality, Poe is his only rival. Both formed other writers. Poe left his mark on Frenchmen like Baudelaire and Scotchmen like Robert Louis Stevenson. Whitman had the honor of causing Alfred Lord Tennyson to change his style late in life, as appears from the Jubilee Ode published in honor of Queen Victoria in 1887. Among those of little note whom he influenced was the unfortunate Ada Isaacs Menken, whose slender volume of verse is full of Whitmanisms.

Whitman was a New York poet in more ways than one. His ancestry was half Dutch, half English; his birthplace Long Island; his home for many years alternately Brooklyn or New York, and his heart at all times was centered on our great, vibrating hive of a city. But New York never cared for Walt Whitman or bought his books or read them. Probably very few New-Yorkers have seen the poem which speaks of

> "Manhattan streets with their powerful throbs, with the beating
>   drums, as now
> The endless, noise chorus, the rustle and clank of muskets, (even
>   the sight of the wounded,)
> Manhattan crowds, with their turbulent musical chorus, with
> varied chorus and light of the sparkling eye.
> Manhattan faces and eyes forever for me."

And the reason was that Whitman, whose smooth early verses had pleased the crude, literary tastes of the readers of newspapers in the early half of the century, sprang with a bound far beyond their comprehension when he learned to disdain the fetters of ordinary rhythm and the chains of rhyme. He was a descendant of the Netherlanders, a people who produced in Rembrandt an artist who displeased the citizens of Amsterdam just as soon as he carried the use of dark backgrounds and powerful contrasts of black and yellow to the perfection which now enchants amateurs.

II

Born at West Hills, L.I., in a farmhouse within sight and sound of the ocean, on the 31st of May, 1819, Walter Whitman received a strain of Holland blood from his mother and of English from his father, who was a carpenter and housebuilder when not attending to his farm. In 1823 the Whitmans moved to Brooklyn, and in 1832 the boy was taken from school and put in the office of a lawyer, then in that of a physician and finally into a printing office to do errands and odd jobs. There he set type, an accomplishment that stood him in stead all his life, for it gave him the chance to reach the ear of the public again and again when no publisher would issue his poems. In 1836 he was still with the *Long Island Patriot* of Brooklyn, but in the following year, perhaps realizing that his education was very deficient, he began to teach school, thus getting an opportunity to learn something while posing as an instructor. After two years of this he started at Huntington, L.I. a paper called the *Long Islander*, which has had as long a life as its founder.

Two years later he was in New York on the *Aurora*, a sheet that made itself greatly hated by the more respectable citizens. In 1847 and 1848 he edited the Brooklyn *Eagle*, but quarreled with the proprietor during the following year on politics, and accepted an offer to work on the staff of a paper just started in New Orleans—the *Crescent*. With his brother Jefferson he traveled slowly by canal and river, seeing much of New York, Lower Canada, and the States on the Mississippi. Returning to Brooklyn in 1851, he started the *Freeman* as a weekly, and next year became a carpenter and undertook the building of houses. During his trips to the West and South he had begun to question the ordinary forms of literature, and by 1854 had already struck the peculiar vein which delights a comparative few, is not understood by the multitude and proves a stumbling block to those who feel strongly on the subject of convention in literary and social matters.

Whitman seems to have been profoundly shocked by the hypocrisy that obtains in men and women, of our race and time, and the revulsion immediately showed itself in his style. From a dry, anxious, and colorless versification he turned to a turgid, warm, overloaded method, in which he sought to unite the best of prose and poetry, retaining the elasticity of prose, and yet not losing all the artificial helps of verse. In so doing rhyme had to be sacrificed and rhythm changed to a largely unconventional movement, which has been aptly likened to Wagner's music.

III

The enormous size of the Union and the crude, turbulent life, the Commonwealth growing like magic along the tremendous waterways of North America fired his imagination. He appeared in his new phase —as champion of democracy and disinterested lover of all mankind— in the year 1855, when a slim, small quarto called "Leaves of Grass," appeared in New York, including but twelve poems. Needless to say that it was published and to a large extent printed by himself, though the name of A. H. Rome appears as publisher. The next edition was in 1856, with 384 pages, 16mo, and thirty-two poems, and the third in 1860, with 456 duodecimo pages. This was his creative period, during which his ideas, not fully understood by himself, were in embryo, waiting for the intellectual shock caused by the rebellion to give them maturity.

Whitman's first two editions were hardly noticed; the third was published at Boston by Eldridge & Co., a reputable firm, and had friends to back it; a London edition was issued by the Longmans. But the outbreak of the rebellion gave little leisure for literary quarrels. True to the gospel he had begun to preach, and with too much Quaker blood in his veins to enlist as a soldier, sympathizing deeply with the spirit of the people in the first years of the war, Whitman in 1862 left New York to nurse and help in all possible ways the sick and wounded in the hospitals in and about Washington. He has left the record of his ministrations in later editions of "Leaves of Grass," but more particularly in the prose "Memoranda During the War," published in "Two Rivulets," (Author's Edition, Camden, N.J., 1876).

Personal friends of Whitman who knew him in Washington during the war, where he held clerkships in the Department of the Interior and the Attorney General's office, speak of him as a good comrade, who seemed a trifle anxious to make himself conspicuous by a peculiar dress—broad hat, flannel shirt exposing the breast, and semi-military cloak. These peculiarities may be set down to his lack of a sense of the ridiculous, to his profound seriousness as regards himself—to his egotism, in short—rather than a purpose to attract attention.

But there was also in his mind the same impulse to throw aside clothes as well as conventions which appeared in the old gymnosophists, in Fourier, in the artist-poet William Blake. Whitman sang his own body and liked to speak of the nude; he had a fixed idea found in all ages and most races that the hairy breast is the breast of a powerful man and that the power in a man, or the brute in him, deserves more admiration than is quite compatible with Christian dogmas. It must be remembered that when he sang thus the literary ideals of the United States ran toward pallor, stooping shoulders, and a minute learning in the classical tongues. In these days of athletics his deification of the body would have caused much less scandal.

The dismay which such utterances cast among cultivated men brought up under the eye of the clergy, among college professors and bardlets gazing over at the British Islands, among the fastidious and romantic who fed on Tennyson and Wordsworth and swooned at the sound of an Americanism, may well be left to the imagination. Whitman is still reviled by these and their like.

> "Has any supposed it lucky to be born?
> "I hasten to inform him or her it is just as lucky to die, and I know it."

These brave sentences were penned by Whitman years ago, and now he has experienced the other end of that chain of circumstances which we call life, that chain which he tried to understand in its entirety, every link of it, and to express in the prose poems called "Leaves of Grass," "Two Rivulets," and "Passage to India." It need not be inferred that a man of so great vitality as his ever wished to die while any portion of that magnificent health his parents gave him remained in his veins. Those sentences reflect the titanic optimism of the man and form part of the consoling spirit that breathes through all he wrote. An egotist, and boastful of his egotism, he sang:

> "I will effuse egotism and show it underlying all—and I will be the bard of the personality.
> "And I will show of male and female that either is but the equal of the other.

"And sexual organs and acts do you concentrate in me—for I
am determined to tell, with courageous clear voice, to prove
you illustrious.

"And I will show that there is no imperfection in the present—
and can be none in the future.

"And I will show that whatever happens to anybody it may be
turned to beautiful results—and I will show that nothing
can happen more beautiful than death.

"And I will thread a thread through my poems that time and
events are compact.

"And that all things of the universe are perfect miracles, each
as profound as any."

IV

Nor did Whitman confine himself to a theoretical egotism in his
writings, but liked the incense of public recognition so well that his
dress and behavior on the street often appeared to be calculated to
insure conspicuousness, but, as we have seen, this petty vanity was
apparent rather than actual. In his intercourse with men and women
he impressed his own personality at all times, often rousing great
affection, and in many cases lifelong friendships resulted long before
he reached that mellow patriarchal stage with which the present gen-
eration is familiar.

His odd dress—wide open flannel shirt, wide trousers, broad-
brimmed soft hat, and thick stick—prejudiced against him many
persons who thought that he was merely a vain fellow who sought
notoriety at any cost. Many, also, who took the trouble to read his
verse were repelled by the apparent lawlessness of versification and
the tremendous heaping up of epithets, repetitions, and eccentric
grammar. And of those who condoned or enjoyed these oddities a
goodly part fell away when they came to read the passages in which
Whitman contends like an inspired physiologist for the beauty and
dignity, nay, the poetry, of functions and organs not mentioned save in
medical works.

Whitman's great strength and his great weakness was gen-
eralization. He strikes it in the first lines of "Leaves of Grass:"

"One's self I sing—a simple, separate person:
Yet utter the word Democratic, the word En masse."

and is at pains to talk often of the "ensemble" and to use other French
words (ma femme, feuillage, repondez, delicatesse, melange) with a

freedom that did not please scholars at all, since English is entirely
equal to the expression he sought. He wrestled with the big common-
place world of the United States, and managed, after his own strange
fashion, to express its grandeur. But even the United States was too
restricted a theme for him. He tried to express the human being inside
and out, body, brains, and soul, and in the ardor of his composition
found the shackles of rhyme and rhythm, sometimes of reason also, too
strict for what he wished to say. Hence the quaint form of his poetic
speech, the lists of qualities and attributes, organs and functions, tools,
instruments, and things used in the trades and other occupations of
man.

He was orbic, and wished to embrace everything in the mirror of
his verse like those spheres of polished metal that stand on lawns. Like
them he succeeded in being a curiosity while he lived rather than the
mirror which people are in the habit of consulting. His very power
oppressed him. Ill-digested and shapeless as his work is compared to
the poetry of the great bards of the past, Whitman resembled one of
those poets of medieval Ireland who were crammed with a large amount
of ill-assorted knowledge and turgid in rhetoric, but filled with the
truest poetic flame and really appreciated only by the extremely naive
on the one hand, and on the other by people of the widest sympathies,
the deepest knowledge, and the keenest critical faculty. We may liken
him to such poets as were found in Ireland by Edmund Spenser in the
sixteenth century, whose songs, when duly translated for him into
English, compelled his admiration.

V

But while these bards, of course, sang of old heroes and the tribal
chief of the day who had most distinguished himself in wars and cattle
spoils, Whitman was under the influence of his own land and century.
While he was a young man the ideas of Jean Jacques Rousseau and
Fourier were still agitating people in the United States. Whitman is
not without traces of their influence, but other circumstances helped to
mold him. His attitude toward religion when it can be detected is
distinctly Quakerish, that is to say, opposed to ecclesiastical control and
in favor of great individual liberty with a corresponding equality be-
tween the sexes.

The inchoate aspirations after freedom, the rude, unmannerly,
boisterous behavior of youth, the tremendous reaching out after some
nebulous but gigantic ideal of the future which characterized the town
populace of these States up to the time that the civil war made blood

to flow and brought Americans to their bearings are reflected, wonderfully reflected, in the greater part of "Leaves of Grass." But that book also contains the close of the epoch in the war fever of 1861, and here again Whitman responded to the national movement with the section called "Drum Taps," in which will be found lyrics of surpassing dignity, beauty, and thrilling grandeur, bearing that stamp of simplicity which is beyond all praise.

Whitman's bigness of heart is not merely claimed in a hundred poems, but shown in many moving passages, such as that describing the body of a fallen woman in the Morgue. The love of man for man, as well as man for woman, forms a striking element in his chaotic creed; but, indeed, with Whitman, love reaches out beyond humanity and embraces the cosmos with the same passionate affection with which he regards a blade of grass. Probably the citizens who chase dollars in New York are the human beings for whom he could cherish the greatest contempt, yet he says,

> "The little plentiful manikins, skipping around in collars and
>   tail'd coats,
> I am aware who they are—(they are positively not worms and
>   fleas)
> I acknowledge the duplicates of myself—the weakest and shallow-
>   est is deathless with me."

In this passage he reached as near humor as he ever did, but according to his own view of things exhibits therein the catholicity of his benevolence toward all.

Critics may say that in absence of humor Whitman showed weakness, but such generalizations are not good for much. He took himself with immense seriousness. But had he not done so—would we have had thoughts so profound, a picture of the great bulk of Americans so interesting, verses expressed in such a novel and often effective form? Assuredly not. We would have missed the stimulus which lurks quite as much in the extraordinary and, to some minds, extravagantly dull method of his expression as in the ideas themselves, which are difficult enough to seize.

Ralph Waldo Emerson, for example, was in many ways the exact opposite of Whitman, yet, on closer analysis, there are larger likenesses than dissimilarities between the two. Both were optimists of the most exaggerated kind. Whitman took his favorable view of life, mankind, the future from the signs of vigor, advance, wealth, and populousness about him. Emerson had, perhaps, a harder task to be optimistic beneath the whining tone of Cambridge and the glacial air of Boston, and rightly saved his soul by keeping to his Concord home. But Emerson also gained a hearing, quite as narrow and scholarly as Whitman's, by the way, by an odd versification and no little obscurity of expression. Both were misunderstood and little read, finding appreciation quicker in Canada and in England than in their own land, but both earned the title first applied to Emerson, that of Great American. And Emerson was one of the first to appraise Whitman at his true value.

VI

Since the rebellion Walt Whitman has occupied a strange position in letters and caused a little war of pens more than once across the Atlantic. He contracted hospital malaria at Washington which in 1873 brought on a paralytic attack, from which he was long in recovering. But as early as 1864 the portions of his poems which were thought by many indecent got him into trouble. Secretary Harlan removed him from his clerkship while he was at work on one of his noblest efforts, "President Lincoln's Funeral Hymn," a most exquisite piece, beginning "When lilacs last in the dooryard bloomed."

Never chary of crying out when assailed, the poet was soon comforted by another appointment in the Attorney General's office.

In 1865, 1867, and 1870 he reprinted "Leaves of Grass," continually adding, classifying, and changing the contents to suit his widening ideas. In 1868 a great honor befell him in the appearance at London of "Walt Whitman's Poems," edited by W. M. Rossetti, many of the crudest expressions being suppressed. Robert Buchanan also appeared as his champion in essays published that year. These were echoes in approval of the ardent praise of John Burroughs: "Notes on Walt Whitman, as Poet and Person," and "The Good Gray Poet: a Vindication," by W. D. O'Connor, because readers of that edition could not see why people in America were outraged. His enemies were strong enough, however, to stop the publication of his complete poems in 1881 by the Osgoods on a threat of prosecution.

From 1855, when his first venture appeared, Whitman was attacked in the public press on the score of immorality. He clung to the idea of "telling all" and was not disheartened by the assaults of those who disbelieve in calling a spade a spade. In 1870 appeared the "Passage to India," poems, and "Democratic Vistas," prose. In 1871 a long poem, justly censured for interminable lists of objects, such as machines, tools, &c. was prepared for and delivered at the opening of the American Institute in New York, and he also published what was afterward christened "Song of the Exposition."

Till 1873, when he was paralyzed, he retained his second clerk-ship at Washington, and after recovery (1879) traveled in Colorado, Kansas, and Missouri. In 1880 he made a visit to Canada where Dr. Maurice Bucke proved not only a friend, but a champion, in a pub-lished biography of the poet. After the Osgood firm declined to go on with the printing of "Leaves of Grass," Whitman took the stereotyped plates and began to publish for his own account at Camden. Sometimes for a year or two together he disposed of a respectable number of volumes at high prices. Occasional magazine articles helped him also, but the report went abroad that he was in dire necessity and it roused much ill feeling in England, where it was charged that Americans neglected their greatest literary man since Emerson out of prudery and inability to appreciate his worth. Whatever truth there was in these charges, the fact of Whitman's extreme poverty was never proved. On the contrary, he lived frugally, but well, surrounded by friends and admirers. In late years sums of money have been raised for him in New York, Philadelphia, Glasgow, and other places, to make his end more comfortable.

It is impossible to forecast what Whitman's place in American literature is going to be. For one thing he represents, as no college graduate and scholarly man has hitherto, the great bulk of the Nation educated in common schools. Yet hitherto he has been the scholar's delight, and the people will have none of him, unless it be a jewel from "Drum Taps," or a rhapsody entirely free from physiological theories like that beginning, "Out of the cradle endlessly rocking," a threnody on a forsaken mocking bird, which ranks with the greatest productions of genius in English.

At any rate, posterity is not going to judge him as harshly as some of the virtuous of to-day have done, for how can the men of the future fail to be won over by a man who believes so rapturously in the essential goodness of all created things—even of that pit, the soul of man! In one of the notes which run as the subsidiary stream in small type at the foot of the pages of "Two Rivulets," the poet, apparently staggered at the attempt to understand himself or his real object, haz-ards this opinion (it is in the preface): "Probably, indeed, the whole of these varied songs, and all my writings, both volumes, only ring changes in some sort on the ejaculation, How vast, how eligible, how joyful, how real, is a Human Being, himself or herself!"

HAVELOCK ELLIS

Whitman†

"Whatever tastes sweet to the most perfect person, that is finally right"—this, it has been said, is the maxim on which Whitman's morality is founded, and it is the morality of Aristotle. But no Greek ever asserted and illustrated it with such emphatic iteration.

From the days when the Greek spirit found its last embodiment in the brief songs, keen or sweet, of the "Anthology,"[1] the attitude which Whitman represents in the "Song of Myself" has never lacked representatives. Throughout the Middle Ages those strange haunting echoes to the perpetual chant of litany and psalm, the Latin student-songs, float across all Europe with their profane and gay paganism, their fresh erotic grace, their "In taberna quando sumus," their "Ludo cum Cæcilia," their "Gaudeamus igitur."[2] In the sane and lofty sensuality of Boccaccio, as it found expression in the history of Alaciel and many another wonderful story, and in Gottfried of Strasburg's[3] assertion of human pride and passion in "Tristan and Isolde," the same strain changed to a stronger and nobler key. Then came the great wave of the Renaissance through Italy and France and England, filling art and philosophy with an exaltation of physical life, and again later, in the movements that center around the French Revolution, an exaltation of arrogant and independent intellectual life. But all these manifestations were sometimes partial, sometimes extravagant; they were impulses of the natural man surging up in rebellion against the dominant Christian temper; they were, for the most part consciously, of the nature of reactions. We feel that there is a fatal lack about them which Christianity would have filled; only in Goethe is the antagonism to some extent reconciled. Beneath the vast growth of Christianity, for ever exalting

---

† From Havelock Ellis, *The New Spirit* (1890), pp. 107–125. This excerpt comprises most of the third and the entire fourth section of a five-part essay on Whitman.
[1] The Greek Anthology is a collection of thousands of epigrammatic poems in Greek literature, ranging from the seventh century B.C. to the tenth century A.D. [*Editors*].
[2] Respectively, "When we are in the tavern," "I sport with Cecilia," "Let us therefore rejoice" [*Editors*].
[3] A thirteenth-century poet now remembered for his version in Middle High German, c. 1210, of the familiar Tristram and Isolde legend [*Editors*].

the unseen by the easy method of pouring contempt on the seen, and still ever producing some strange and exquisite flower of *ascêsis*—some Francis or Theresa or Fénelon[4]—a slow force was working underground. A tendency was making itself felt to find in the theoretically despised physical—in those every-day stones which the builders of the Church had rejected—the very foundation of the mysteries of life; if not the basis for a new vision of the unseen, yet for a more assured vision of the seen.

No one in the last century expressed this tendency more impressively and thoroughly, with a certain insane energy, than William Blake—the great chained spirit whom we see looking out between the bars of his prisonhouse with those wonderful eyes. Especially in "The Marriage of Heaven and Hell," in which he seems to gaze most clearly "through narrow chinks of his cavern," he has set forth his conviction that "first the notion that man has a body distinct from his soul is to be expunged," and that "if the doors of perception were cleansed, everything would appear to man, as it is, infinite." This most extraordinary book is, in his own phraseology, the Bible of Hell.

Whitman appeared at a time when this stream of influence, grown mighty, had boldly emerged. At the time that "Leaves of Grass" sought the light Turgenev was embodying in the typical figure of Bassaroff[5] the modern militant spirit of science, positive and audacious—a spirit marked also, as Hinton[6] pointed out, by a new form of asceticism, which lay in the denial of emotion. Whitman, one of the very greatest emotional forces of modern times, who had grown up apart from the rigid and technical methods of science, face to face with a new world and a new civilization, which he had eagerly absorbed so far as it lay open to him, had the good inspiration to fling himself into the scientific current, and so to justify the demands of his emotional nature; to represent himself as the inhabitant of a vast and coordinated cosmos, tenoned and mortised in granite:

> "All forces have been steadily employed to complete and delight
> me,
> Now on this spot I stand with my robust soul."

[4] Francis: St. Francis of Assisi (1182–1226); Theresa: St. Theresa (1515–1582), Spanish Carmelite nun; Fénelon: a French prelate and writer (1651–1715) [*Editors*].
[5] The youthful revolutionary hero of Turgenev's novel *Fathers and Sons* (1862) [*Editors*].
[6] James Hinton (1822–1875), English sociologist, author of *Philosophy and Religion* (1881) and other books [*Editors*].

That Whitman possessed no trained scientific instinct is unquestionably true, but it is impossible to estimate his significance without understanding what he owes to science. Something, indeed, he had gained from the philosophy of Hegel—with its conception of the universe as a single process of evolution, in which vice and disease are but transient perturbations—with which he had a second-hand acquaintance that has left distinct, but not always well assimilated, marks on his work; but, above all, he was indebted to those scientific conceptions which, like Emerson, he had absorbed or divined. It is these that lie behind "Children of Adam."

This mood of sane and cheerful sensuality, rejoicing with a joy as massive and calm-eyed as Boccaccio's, a moral-fibered joy that Boccaccio never knew, in all the manifestations of the flesh and blood of the world—saying, not: "Let us eat and drink, for to-morrow we die," but, with Clifford: "Let us take hands and help, for this day we are alive together"[7]—is certainly Whitman's most significant and impressive mood. Nothing so much reveals its depth and sincerity as his never-changing attitude towards death. We know the "fearful thing" that Claudio, in Shakespeare's play, knew as death:

> "to die and go we know not where;
> To lie in cold obstruction and to rot;
> . . . . to be worse than worst
> Of those that lawless and uncertain thoughts
> Imagine howling!"

And all the Elizabethans in that age of splendid and daring life—even Raleigh and Bacon—felt that same shudder at the horror and mystery of death. Always they felt behind them some vast medieval charnel-house, gloomy and awful, and the sunniest spirits of the English Renaissance quail when they think of it. There was in this horror something of the child's vast and unreasoned dread of darkness and mystery, and it scarcely survived the scientific and philosophic developments of the seventeenth century. Whitman's attitude is not the less deep-rooted and original. For he is not content to argue, haughtily indifferent, with Epicurus and Epictetus, that death can be nothing to us, because it is no evil to lose what we shall never miss. Whitman will reveal the loveliness of death. We feel constantly in "Leaves of Grass" as to some extent we feel before the "Love and Death" and some other pictures of

---

[7] William Kingdon Clifford (1845–1879), English mathematician, author of *Elements of Dynamics* (1879–1887) [*Editors*].

one of the greatest of English artists. "I will show," he announces, "that nothing can happen more beautiful than death." It must not be forgotten that Whitman speaks not merely from the standpoint of the most intense and vivid delight in the actual world, but that he possessed a practical familiarity with disease and death which has perhaps never before fallen to the lot of a great writer. At the end of the "Song of Myself" he bequeaths himself to the dust, to grow from the grass he loves:

> "If you want me again, look for me under your bootsoles,
> You will hardly know who I am or what I mean,
> But I shall be good health to you nevertheless,
> And filter and fiber your blood."

And to any who find that dust but a poor immortality, he would say with Schopenhauer, "Oho! do you know, then, what dust is?" The vast chemistry of the earth, the sweetness that is rooted in what we call corruption, the life that is but the leavings of many deaths, is nobly uttered in "This Compost," in which he reaches beyond the corpse that is good manure to sweet-scented roses, to the polished breasts of melons; or again, in the noble elegy, "Pensive on her dead gazing," on those who died during the war. In his most perfectly lyrical poem, "Out of the Cradle endlessly rocking," Whitman has celebrated death—"that strong and delicious word"—with strange tenderness; and never has the loveliness of death been sung in a more sane and virile song than the solemn death-carol in "When Lilacs last in the Dooryard bloomed":

> "Dark mother, always gliding near with soft feet,
> Have none chanted for thee a chant of fullest welcome?
> Then I chant it for thee, I glorify thee above all,
> I bring thee a song, that when thou must indeed come, come
>   unfalteringly.
>   *   *   *   *   *
> "Over the tree-tops I float thee a song,
> Over the rising and sinking waves, over the myriad fields and
>   the prairies wide,
> Over the dense-packed cities all and the teeming wharves and
>   ways,
> I float this carol with joy, with joy to thee, O Death."

Whitman's second great thought on life lies in his egoism. His intense sense of individuality was marked from the first; it is emphatically asserted in the "Song of Myself"—

"And nothing, not God, is greater to one than one's self is"—

where it lies side by side with his first great thought. But even in the "Song of Myself" it asserts a separate existence:

> "This day before dawn I ascended a hill and looked at the crowded heaven,
> And I said to my spirit, *When we become the enfolders of those orbs and the pleasure and knowledge of everything in them, shall we be filled and satisfied then?*
> And my spirit said, *No, we but level that lift to pass and continue beyond.*"

In the end he once, at least, altogether denies his first thought; he alludes to that body which he had called the equal of the soul, or even the soul itself, as excrement:

> "Myself discharging my excrementitious body to be burned, or reduced to powder, or buried,
> My real body doubtless left to me for other spheres."

The first great utterance was naturalistic; this egoism is spiritualistic. It is the sublime apotheosis of Yankee self-reliance. "I only am he who places over you no master, owner, better, God, beyond what waits intrinsically in yourself." This became the dominant conception in Whitman's later work, and fills his universe at length. Of a God, although he sometimes uses the word to obtain emphasis, he at no time had any definite idea. Nature, also, was never a living vascular personality for him; when it is not a mere aggregate of things, it is an order, sometimes a moral order. Also he wisely refuses with unswerving consistency to admit an abstract Humanity; of "man" he has nothing to say; there is nothing anywhere in the universe for him but individuals, undying, everlastingly aggrandizing individuals. This egoism is practical, strenuous, moral; it cannot be described as religious. Whitman is lacking—and in this respect he comes nearer to Goethe than to any other great modern man—in what may be possibly the disease of "soul," the disease that was so bitterly bewailed by Heine. Whitman was congenitally deficient in "soul"; he is a kind of Titanic Undine.[8] "I never had any particular religious experiences," he told Bucke, "never felt the need of spiritual regeneration"; and although he describes himself as "pleased with the earnest words of the sweating Methodist preacher, impressed seriously at the camp-meeting," we know what weight to give to this utterance when we read elsewhere, of animals:

[8] Female water sprite familiar in European folklore [*Editors*].

"They do not sweat and whine about their condition,
They do not lie awake in the dark and weep for their sins,
They do not make me sick discussing their duty to God,
Not one is dissatisfied, not one is demented with the mania of
    owning things,
Not one kneels to another, nor to his kind that lived thousands of
    years ago,
Not one is respectable or unhappy over the whole earth."

We may detect this lack of "soul" in his attitude towards music;
for, in its highest development, music is the special exponent of the
modern soul in its complexity, its passive resignation, its restless mysti-
cal ardors. That Whitman delighted in music is clear; it is equally
clear, from the testimony of his writings and of witnesses, that the
music he delighted in was simple and joyous melody as in Rossini's
operas; he alludes vaguely to symphonies, but

"when it is a grand opera,
Ah, this indeed is music—this suits me."

That Whitman could have truly appreciated Beethoven, or understood
Wagner's "Tannhäuser," is not conceivable.

With Whitman's egoism is connected his strenuousness. There is
a stirring sound of trumpets always among these "Leaves of Grass."
This man may have come, as he tells us, to inaugurate a new religion,
but he has few or no marks upon him of that mysticism—that Eastern
spirit of glad renunciation of the self in a larger self—which is of the
essence of religion. He is at the head of a band of sinewy and tan-
faced pioneers, with pistols in their belts and sharp-edged axes in their
hands:

"And he going with me leaves peace and routine behind him,
And stakes his life to be lost at any moment."

This strenuousness finds expression in the hurried jolt and bustle
of the lines, always alert, unresting, ever starting afresh. Passages of
sweet and peaceful flow are hard to find in "Leaves of Grass," and the
more precious when found. Whitman hardly succeeds in the expression
of joy; to feel exquisitely the pulse of gladness a more passive and
feminine sensibility is needed, like that we meet with in "Towards
Democracy";[9] we must not come to this focus of radiant energy for
This egoism, this strenuousness, reaches at the end to heights of

[9] A book of poems (1883) by Edward Carpenter (1844–1929), an English
author much influenced by Whitman [Editors].
repose or consolation.

sublime audacity. When we read certain portions of "Leaves of Grass" we seem to see a vast phalanx of Great Companions passing for ever along the cosmic roads, stalwart Pioneers of the Universe. There are superb young men, athletic girls, splendid and savage old men—for the weak seem to have perished by the roadside—and they radiate an infinite energy, an infinite joy. It is truly a tremendous diastole of life to which the crude and colossal extravagance of this vision bears witness; we weary soon of its strenuous vitality, and crave for the systole of life, for peace and repose. It is not strange that the immense faith of the prophet himself grows hesitant and silent at times before "all the meanness and agony without end," and doubts that it is an illusion and "that may-be identity beyond the grave a beautiful fable only." Here and again we meet this access of doubt, and even amid the faith of the "Prayer of Columbus" there is a tremulous, pathetic note of sadness.

Yet there is one keen sword with which Whitman is always able to cut the knot of this doubt—the sword of love. He has but to grasp love and comradeship, and he grows indifferent to the problem of identity beyond the grave. "He a-hold of my hand has completely satisfied me." He discovers at last that love and comradeship—adhesiveness—is, after all, the main thing, "base and finale, too, for all metaphysics"; deeper than religion, underneath Socrates and underneath Christ. With a sound insight he finds the roots of the most universal love in the intimate and physical love of comrades and lovers:

> "I mind how once we lay, such a transparent summer morning,
> How you settled your head athwart my hips and gently turned
>   over upon me,
> And parted the shirt from my bosom-bone, and plunged your
>   tongue to my bare-stript heart,
> And reached till you felt my beard, and reached till you held my
>   feet.
> "Swiftly arose and spread around me the peace and knowledge
>   that pass all the argument of the earth,
> And I know that the hand of God is the promise of my own,
> And I know that the spirit of God is the brother of my own,
> And that all the men ever born are also my brothers, and the
>   women my sisters and lovers,
> And that a kelson of the creation is love."

IV

This "love" of Whitman's is a very personal matter; of an abstract Man, a *solidaire* Humanity, he never speaks; it does not appear ever to have occurred to him that so extraordinary a conception can be formulated; his relations to men generally spring out of his relations to particular men. He has touched and embraced his fellows' flesh; he has felt throughout his being the mysterious reverberations of the contact:

> "There is something in staying close to men and women and
>   looking on them, and in the contact and odor of them, that
>   pleases the soul well,
> All things please the soul, but these please the soul well."

This personal and intimate fact is the center from which the whole of Whitman's morality radiates. Of an abstract Humanity, it is true, he has never thought; he has no vision of Nature as a spiritual Presence; God is to him a word only, without vitality; to Art he is mostly indifferent; yet there remains this great moral kernel, springing from the sexual impulse, taking practical root in a singularly rich and vivid emotional nature, and bearing within it the promise of a city of lovers and friends.

This moral element is one of the central features in Whitman's attitude towards sex and the body generally. For the lover there is nothing in the loved one's body impure or unclean; a breath of passion has passed over it, and all things are sweet. For most of us this influence spreads no farther; for the man of strong moral instinct it covers all human things in infinitely widening circles; his heart goes out to every creature that shares the loved one's delicious humanity; henceforth there is nothing human that he cannot touch with reverence and love. "Leaves of Grass" is penetrated by this moral element. How curiously far this attitude is from the old Christian way we realize when we turn to those days in which Christianity was at its height, and see how Saint Bernard with his mild and ardent gaze looked out into the world of Nature and saw men as "stinking spawn, sacks of dung, the food of worms."

But there is another element in Whitman's attitude—the artistic. It shows itself in a two-fold manner. Whitman came of a vigorous Dutch stock; these Van Velsors from Holland have fully as large a part in him as anything his English ancestry gave him, and his Dutch race shows itself chiefly in his artistic manner. The supreme achievement in art of the Dutch is their seventeenth century painting. What marked those Dutch artists was the ineradicable conviction that every action, social or physiological, of the average man, woman, child, around them might be, with love and absolute faithfulness, phlegmatically set forth. In their heroic earthliness they could at no point be repulsed; color and light may aureole their work, but the most commonplace things of Nature shall have the largest nimbus. That is the temper of Dutch art throughout; no other art in the world has the same characteristics. In the art of Whitman alone do we meet with it again, impatient indeed and broken up into fragments, pierced through with shafts of light from other sources, but still constant and unmistakable. The other artistic element in Whitman's attitude is modern; it is almost the only artistic element by which, unconsciously perhaps, he allies himself to modern tradition in art instead of breaking through them by his own volcanic energy—a curious research for sexual imagery in Nature, imagery often tinged by bizarre and mystical color. Rossetti occasionally uses sexual imagery with rare felicity, as in "Nuptial Sleep":

> "And as the last slow sudden drops are shed
> From sparkling eaves when all the storm has fled,
> So singly flagged the pulses of each heart."

With still greater beauty and audacity Whitman, in "I sing the body electric," celebrates the last abandonment of love:

> "Bridegroom night of love working surely and softly into the
>   prostrate dawn,
> Undulating into the willing and yielding day,
> Lost in the cleave of the clasping and sweet-fleshed day."

Or, again, in the marvelously keen "Faces"—so realistic and so imaginative—when the "lily's face" speaks out her longing to be filled with albescent honey. This man has certainly felt the truth of that deep saying of Thoreau's, that for him to whom sex is impure there are no flowers in Nature. He cannot help speaking of man's or woman's life in terms of Nature's life, of Nature's life in terms of man's; he mingles them together with an admirably balanced rhythm, as in "Spontaneous Me." All the functions of man's or woman's life are sweet to him because they bear about them a savor of the things that are sweet to him anywhere in the world,

> "Of the smell of apples and lemons, of the pairing of birds,
> Of the wet of woods, of the lapping of waves."

Sometimes when he is on this track he seems to lose himself in mystic obscurity; and the words in which he records his impressions are mere patches of morbid color.

There is a third element in Whitman's attitude. It is clear that he had from the outset what may be vaguely called a scientific purpose in that frank grasp of the body, which has a significance to be measured by the fierce opposition it aroused, and by the tenacity with which, in the latest volume of his old age, "November Boughs," he still insists that the principle of those lines so gives breath to the whole scheme that the bulk of the pieces might as well have been left unwritten were those lines omitted. He has himself admirably set this forth in "A Memorandum at a Venture" in "Specimen Days and Collect." In religion and politics we have after a great struggle, gained the priceless possibility of liberty and sincerity. But the region of sex is still, like our moral and social life generally, to a large extent unreclaimed; there still exist barbarous traditions which medieval Christianity has helped to perpetuate, so that the words of Pliny regarding the contaminating touch of a woman, who has always been regarded as in a peculiar manner the symbol of sex—"Nihil facile reperiabatur mulierum profluvio magis monstrificum"[1]—are not even yet meaningless. Why should the sweetening breath of science be guarded from this spot? Why should not "freedom and faith and earnestness" be introduced here? Our attitude towards this part of life affects profoundly our attitude towards life altogether. To realize this, read Swift's "Strephon and Chloe," which enshrines, vividly and unshrinkingly, in a classic form, a certain emotional way of approaching the body. It narrates the very trivial experiences of a man and woman on their bridal night. The incidents are nothing; they are perfectly innocent; the interesting fact about them is the general attitude which they enfold. The unquestioning faith of the man is that in setting down the simple daily facts of human life he has drowned the possibilities of love in filth. And Swift here represents, in an unflinchingly logical fashion, the opinions, more or less realized, more or less disguised, of most people even to-day. Cannot these facts of our physical nature be otherwise set down? Why may we not "keep as delicate around the bowels as around the head and heart?" That is, in effect, the question which, in "A Memorandum at a Venture," Whitman tells us that he undertook to answer. This statement of it was probably an afterthought; else he would have carried out his attempt more thoroughly and more uncompromisingly.

For I doubt if even Whitman has fully realized the beauty and purity of organic life; the scientific element in him was less strong than the moral, or even the artistic. While his genial poetic manner of grasping things is of prime importance, the new conceptions of purity are founded on a scientific basis which must be deeply understood. Swift's morbid and exaggerated spiritualism, a legacy of medievalism—and the ordinary "common-sense" view is but the unconscious shadow of medieval spiritualism—is really founded on ignorance, in other words, on the traditional religious conceptions of an antique but still surviving barbarism.

[1] The quotation, from Pliny the Elder's *Natural History*, Book 7, chapter 15, is slightly garbled. It means "Nothing could easily be found that is more remarkable than the monthly flux of women" [*Editors*].

From our modern standpoint of science, opening his eyes anew, the wonderful cycles of normal life are for ever clean and pure, the loathsomeness, if indeed anywhere, lies in the conceptions of hypertrophied and hyperæsthetic brains. Some who have striven to find a vital natural meaning in the central sacrament of Christianity have thought that the Last Supper was an attempt to reveal the divine mystery of food, to consecrate the loveliness of the mere daily bread and wine which becomes the life of man. Such sacraments of Nature are everywhere subtly woven into the texture of men's bodies. All loveliness of the body is the outward sign of some vital use.

Doubtless these relationships have been sometimes perceived and their meaning realized by a sort of mystical intuition, but it is only of recent years that science has furnished them with a rational basis. The chief and central function of life—the omnipresent process of sex, ever wonderful, ever lovely, as it is woven into the whole texture of our man's or woman's body—is the pattern of all the process of our life. At whatever point touched, the reverberation, multiplexly charged with uses, meanings, and emotional associations of infinite charm, to the sensitive individual more or less conscious, spreads throughout the entire organism. We can no longer intrude our crude distinctions of high and low. We cannot now step in and say that this link in the chain is eternally ugly and that is eternally beautiful. For irrational disgust, the varying outcome of individual idiosyncrasy, there is doubtless still room; it is incalculable, and cannot be reached. But that rational disgust which was once held to be common property has received from science its death-blow. In the growth of the sense of purity, which Whitman, not alone, has annunciated, lies one of our chief hopes for morals, as well as for art.

BARRETT WENDELL

Walt Whitman†

Until 1855, when the first edition of "Leaves of Grass" appeared in a thin folio, some of which he set up with his own hands, Whitman had not declared himself as a man of letters. From that time to the end

† From Barrett Wendell, *The Literary History of America* (New York, 1900), pp. 466–479.

he was constantly publishing his eccentric poetry, which from time to time he collected in increasing bulk under the old title. He published, too, some stray volumes of prose,—"Democratic Vistas," and the like. Prose and poetry alike seem permeated with a conviction that he had a mission to express and to extend the spirit of democracy, which he believed characteristic of his country. To himself, then, he seemed the inspired prophet of an America which he asserted to be above all things else the land of the people; few men have ever cherished a purpose more literally popular. His fate has been ironic. Though even in his lifetime he became conspicuous, it is doubtful whether any man of letters in his country ever appealed less to the masses. He was a prophet of democracy, if you like; but the public to which his prophecy made its way was at once limited, fastidiously overcultivated, and apt to be of foreign birth.

Beyond question Whitman had remarkable individuality and power. Equally beyond question he was among the most eccentric individuals who ever put pen to paper. The natural result of this has been that his admirers have admired him intensely; while whoever has found his work repellent has found it irritating. Particularly abroad, however, he has attracted much critical attention; and many critics have been disposed to maintain that his amorphous prophecies of democracy are deeply characteristic of America. The United States, they point out, are professedly the most democratic country in the world; Whitman is professedly the most democratic of American writers; consequently he must be the most typical.

The abstract ideal of democracy has never been better summed up than in the well-known watchwords of republican France: Liberty, Equality, Fraternity. Disguised and distorted though these words may have been by a century of French Revolutionary excess, there is no denying that they stand for ideals essential noble and inspiring. What is more, these ideals, which everywhere underlie the revolutionary spirit, have consciously influenced the nineteenth century on both sides of the Atlantic. * * *

Now, Walt Whitman's gospel of democracy certainly included liberty and laid strong emphasis on fraternity. He liked to hail his fellow-citizens by the wild, queer name of "camerados," which, for some obscure reason of his own, he preferred to "comrades." The ideal which most appealed to him, however, was that of equality. Though he would hardly have assented to such orthodox terms, his creed seems to have been that, as God made everything, one thing is just as good as another. There are aspects in which such a proposition seems analogous to one which should maintain a bronze cent to be every whit as good as a gold eagle because both are issued by the same government from the same mint. At best, however, analogies are misleading arguments; and people who share Whitman's ideal are apt to disregard as superstitious any argument, however impressive, which should threaten to modify their faith in equality. It is a superstition, they would maintain, that some ways of doing things are decent and some not; one way is really just as good as another. It is a superstition that kings, nobles, and gentlemen are in any aspect lovelier than the mob. It is a superstition that men of learning are intellectually better than the untutored. It is a superstition which would hold a man who can make a chair unable consequently to make a constitution. It is a superstition that virtuous women are inherently better than street-walkers. It is a superstition that law is better than anarchy. There are things, to be sure, which are not superstitions. Evil and baseness and ugliness are real facts, to be supremely denounced and hated; and incidently, we must admit, few arraignments of the vulgarity and materialism which have developed in the United States are more pitiless than those which appear in Whit-man's "Democracy Vistas." The cause of these hurtful things, however, he is satisfied to find in the traces of our ancestral and superstitious devotion to outworn ideals of excellence. We can all find salvation in the new, life-saving ideal of equality. Let America accept this ideal, and these faults will vanish into that limbo of the past to which he would gladly consign all superstitions. Among these, he logically, though reluctantly, includes a great part of the poetry of Shakspere; for Shakspere, undoubtedly a poet, was a poet of inequality, who repre-sented the people as a mob. For all his genius, then, Shakspere was an apostle of the devil, another lying prophet of the superstition of excel-lence.

Even though excellence be a wicked and tyrannical ideal, however, democratic prophecy does not forbid the whole world equally to im-prove. Equalisation need not mean the reducing of all that is admirable to the level of what is base. It may just as well mean the raising of much that is base towards the height of what is admirable. The super-stition which has worked most sordid evil is that which denies human equality. Retract the denial, then; let human beings be equal, and the force which has most distorted mankind shall cease working. Then all alike may finally rise, side by side, into an equality superior to what has gone before. The prophets of equality are so stirred by dreams of the future that they half forget the horrors of present or past; and among prophets of equality Walt Whitman has the paradoxical merit of eminence.

Now, this dogma of equality clearly involves a trait which has not yet been generally characteristic of American thought or letters,—a complete confusion of values. In the early days of Renaissance in New England, to be sure, Emerson and the rest, dazzled by the splendours of that new world of art and literature which was at last thrown open, made small distinction between those aspects of it which are excellent and those which are only stimulating. At the same time they adhered as firmly as the Puritans themselves to the ideal of excellence; and among the things with which they were really familiar they pretty shrewdly distinguished those which were most valuable, either on earth or in heaven. With Walt Whitman, on the other hand, everything is confused.

Take, for example, a passage from his "Song of Myself," which contains some of his best-known phrases[1] * * *

Here is perhaps his best-known phrase, "the beautiful uncut hair of graves." Here are other good phrases, like "the faint red roofs of mouths." Here, too, is undoubtedly tender feeling. Here, into the bargain, is such rubbish as "I guess it is the handkerchief of the Lord,"— who incidentally uses perfumery,—and such jargon as "Kanuck, Tuckahoe, Congressman, Cuff." In an inextricable hodge-podge you find at once beautiful phrases and silly gabble, tender imagination and insolent commonplace,—pretty much everything, in short, but humour. In America this literary anarchy, this complete confusion of values, is especially eccentric; for America has generally displayed instinctive common-sense, and common-sense implies some notion of what things are worth. One begins to see why Whitman has been so much more eagerly welcomed abroad than at home. His conception of equality, utterly ignoring values, is not that of American democracy, but rather that of European. His democracy, in short, is the least native which has ever found voice in his country. The saving grace of American democracy has been a tacit recognition that excellence is admirable.

In temper, then, Walt Whitman seems less American than any other of our conspicuous writers. It does not follow that in some aspects he is not very American indeed. Almost as certainly as Hawthorne, though very differently, he had the true artistic temperament; life moved him to moods which could find relief only in expression. Such a temperament would have expressed itself anywhere; and Whitman's would probably have found the most congenial material for expression in those European regions which have been most disturbed by French Revolutionary excess. He chanced, however, to be born, and to attain the maturity which he awaited before he began to publish, in unmingled American surroundings. As obviously as Hawthorne's experi-

[1] See lines 99–130 [*Editors*].

ence was confined to New England, Whitman's was confined to that of the lower classes in those regions which were developing into modern New York.

Whoever remembers the growth of this region will remember what sometimes seemed the ugliest thing to the eye, the most overwhelmingly oppressive to any instinct of taste, the most sordidly hopeless atmosphere possible to human experience. Now, Whitman, we remember, came to his maturity within scent of the East River; and certainly the East River, separating New York and Brooklyn, was at that time the spot of spots where life seemed most material, most grindingly distant from ideal beauty. Yet the contemplation of this very East River evoked from Whitman the poem which sometimes seems his most nearly beautiful. [See] the last stanza of his "Crossing Brooklyn Ferry"² * * *

The eight preceding stanzas are very like this,—confused, inarticulate, and surging in a mad kind of rhythm which sounds as if hexameters were trying to bubble through sewage. For all these faults, Whitman has here accomplished a wonder. Despite his eccentric insolence both of phrase and of temper you feel that in a region where another eye would have seen only unspeakable vileness, he has found impulses which prove it, like every other region on earth, a fragment of the divine eternities. The glories and beauties of the universe are really perceptible everywhere; and into what seemed utterly sordid Whitman has breathed ennobling imaginative fervour. Cultured and academic folk are disposed to shrink from what they call base, to ignore it, to sneer at it; looking closer, Whitman tells us that even amid base things you cannot wander so far as to lose sight of the heavens, with all their fountains of glorious emotion.

But what is this emotion? Just here Whitman seems to stop. With singular vividness, and with the unstinted sympathy of his fervent faith in equality, he tells what he sees. Though often his jargon is amorphously meaningless, his words are now and again so apt as to approach that inevitable union of thought and phrase which makes lasting poetry. When he has reported what he sees, however, utterly confusing its values, he has nothing more to say about it. At most he leaves you with a sense of new realities concerning which you must do your thinking for yourself.

* * *

Even in [the] bits * * * which come so much nearer form than is usual with Whitman, one feels his perverse rudeness of style. Such eccentricity of manner is bound to affect different tempers in different

² Lines 101–132 [*Editors*].

ways. One kind of reader, naturally eager for individuality and fresh glimpses of truth, is disposed to identify oddity and originality. Another kind of reader distrusts literary eccentricity as instinctively as polite people distrust bad manners. In both of these instinctive re- actions from such a method of address as Whitman's there is an element of truth. Beyond doubt, eccentric masters of the fine arts give rise to perverse eccentricity in imitators. Browning and Carlyle, to go no further, have bred in brains feebler than their own much nonsensical spawn; and so has Walt Whitman. But some artists of great power prove naturally unable to express themselves properly. Their trouble is like a muscular distortion which should compel lameness, or a vocal malformation which should make utterance hoarse or shrill. So there have been great men, and there will be more, whom fate compels either to express themselves uncouthly or else to stay dumb. Such a man, great or not, Whitman seems to have been. Such men, greater than he, were Carlyle and Browning. The critical temper which would hold them perverse, instead of unfortunate, is mistaken.

On the other hand, that different critical temper which would welcome their perversities as newly revealed evidences of genius is quite as mistaken in another way. If any general law may be inferred from the history of fine arts, it is that any persistent school of expres- sion must be articulate. In any art, of course, vital expression must be spontaneous; academic training, dogmatic routine, has never originated much that is worth while. The nobler works of art, however, which have maintained themselves as permanent parts of the great structure of human expression, have form. Their lasting vitality comes partly from the fact that their makers have spontaneously obeyed natural laws which may be generalised into academic principles. The develop- ment of human expression seems like the growth of a tree. The same vital force which sends the trunk heavenward, puts forth branches, and from these in turn sends forth twigs and leaves; but the further they stray from the root, the weaker they prove. The trunk lives, and the greater branches; year by year, the lesser twigs and leaves wither. Now, eccentricity of manner, however unavoidable, is apt to indicate that art has strayed dangerously far from its vital origin. Oddity is no part of solid artistic development; however beautiful or impressive, it is rather an excrescent outgrowth, bound to prove abortive, and at the same time to sap life from a parent stock which without it might grow more loftily and strongly.

Walt Whitman's style is of this excrescent, abortive kind. Like Carlyle's or Browning's, it is something which nobody else can imitate with impunity; and so, like theirs, it is a style which in the history of literature suggests a familiar phase of decline. That it was inevitable you will feel if you compare "Ethiopia Saluting the Colours" or "My Captain" with the unchecked perversities of Whitman's verse in general. The "Song of Myself," or "Crossing Brooklyn Ferry," which we may take as generally representative of his work, are so recklessly misshapen that you cannot tell whether their author was able to write with amenity. When you find him, however, as in those lesser pieces, attempting technical form, you at once feel that his eccentricity is a misfortune, for which he is no more to blame than a lame man for limping, or a deaf and dumb for expressing emotion by inarticulate cries. The alternative would have been silence; and Whitman was enough of a man to make one glad that he never dreamed of it.

In this decadent eccentricity of Whitman's style there is again something foreign to the spirit of this country. American men of letters have generally had deep artistic conscience. This trait has resulted, for one thing, in making the short story, an essentially organic form of composition, as characteristic of American literature as the straggling, inorganic three volume novel is of English. Now and again, to be sure, American men of letters have chosen to express themselves in quite another manner. They have tried to reproduce the native dialects of the American people. This impulse has resulted in at least one masterpiece, that amazing Odyssey of the Mississippi to which Mark Twain gave the fantastic name of "Huckleberry Finn." As we remarked of the "Biglow Papers," however, this "dialect" literature of America often proves on analysis more elaborately studied than orthodox work by the same writers. Neither the "Biglow Papers" nor "Huckleberry Finn" could have been produced without an artistic conscience as strenuous as Irving's, or Poe's, or Hawthorne's. The vagaries of Walt Whitman, on the other hand, are as far from literary conscience as the animals which he somewhere celebrates are from unhappiness or respectabilitiy. Whitman's style, then, is as little characteristic of America as his temper is of traditional American democracy. One can see why the decadent taste of modern Europe has welcomed him so much more ardently than he has ever been welcomed at home; in temper and in style he was an exotic member of that sterile brotherhood which eagerly greeted him abroad. In America his oddities were more eccentric than they would have been anywhere else.

On the other hand, there is an aspect in which he seems not only native but even promising. During the years when his observation was keenest, and his temper most alert, he lived in the environment from which our future America seems most likely to spring. He was born and grew up, he worked and lived, where on either side of the East River the old American towns of New York and Brooklyn were developing into the metropolis which is still too young to possess ripe traditions. In full maturity he devoted himself to army nursing,— the least picturesque or glorious, and the most humanely heroic, service which he could have rendered his country during its agony of civil war. In that Civil War the elder America perished; the new America which then arose is not yet mature enough for artistic record. Whitman's earthly experience, then, came throughout in chaotic times, when our past had faded and our future had not yet sprung into being. Bewildering confusion, fused by the accident of his lifetime into the seeming unity of a momentary whole, was the only aspect of human existence which could be afforded him by the native country which he so truly loved. For want of other surroundings he was content to seek the meaning of life amid New York slums and dingy suburban country, in the crossing of Brooklyn Ferry, or in the hospitals which strove to alleviate the drums and tramplings of civil war. His lifelong eagerness to find in life the stuff of which poetry is made has brought him, after all, the reward he would most have cared for. In one aspect he is thoroughly American. The spirit of his work is that of world-old anarchy; its form has all the perverse oddity of world-old abortive decadence; but the substance of which his poems are made—their imagery as distinguished from their form or their spirit—comes wholly from our native country.

In this aspect, then, though probably in no other, he may, after all, throw light on the future of literature in America. As has been said before, "He is uncouth, inarticulate, whatever you please that is least orthodox; yet, after all, he can make you feel for the moment how even the ferry-boats plying from New York to Brooklyn are fragments of God's eternities. Those of us who love the past are far from sharing his confidence in the future. Surely, however, that is no reason for denying the miracle that he has wrought by idealising the East River. The man who has done this is the only one who points out the stuff of which perhaps the new American literature of the future may in time be made."

BASIL DE SELINCOURT

The Form: Constructive Principles†

Our understanding of Whitman's form is incomplete till we see what it excludes; for a thing has no positive if it has no negative qualities. Of course the idea of *Leaves of Grass* was to be all-inclusive; the poem was conceived in a spirit of universal hospitality, and such a spirit would be unfavourable to conscious method of any kind, would be likely to pride itself on having none. But this more or less inevitable pose must not bluff the critic. The form of a work which aims at impressing us with the spiritual coherence of all things may well share the elusiveness of its theme and be as inapprehensible as life itself. Yet unless some connecting thread, however fine, holds its divergences in a unity, the aim is unaccomplished.

Form in verse means, as a rule, metre. Whitman felt rightly that no metre or combination of metres could serve the peculiar purpose he had in view. At the same time he was not averse, as we have seen, to the introduction of metrical fragments here and there, and even shows a partiality for jingling effects. If we are right in thinking that he made a mistake in this, we have only to analyse the grounds on which our judgment rests, and we shall find the principle of exclusion which we are looking for.

But first let us note that the mistake itself was of secondary importance. The primary requisite for the form of *Leaves of Grass* was that its spaciousness should be recognised and that the composer should write to scale. No one afflicted with sensitiveness about the minor literary proprieties would have been likely to rise to the careless amplitude of manner necessary to the filling of so gigantic a mould. We recognise this easily enough if we compare the master with his followers, the originator with the mimics. The normal writer of Whitmanesque verse feels in every line the influence of the metre he has dispensed with and exhibits the affectations of a disdainful culture. But Whitman, like all who bring a revelation through art, is faithful to

† From Basil De Selincourt, *Walt Whitman*, *A Critical Study* (London, 1914; New York: Russell & Russell, 1965), pp. 94–118.

nature, and his method turns upon the discovery of nature in what had seemed unnatural. He aimed at being himself in his poetry, and this required him to stand out as poetry personified in solitary relief against the whole poetic achievement of the past. He seemed to ask less than others of the Muse. It devolved upon him to give more. Choosing informality, he chose in effect a form which permitted him no concealment, no breathing-space. We cannot wonder if he did not stay to consider what his ideals denied to him; his task was to be ready with what they exacted. Only the intrusion, the conspicuous and abiding presence of matter inconsistent with the common forms could justify his departure from them.

Yet if he rather transcends than refuses metre, it is not the less true that recognisably metrical lines are out of keeping with the spirit of his poetry. His lines are not metrical; what are they, then? We glanced earlier at an objection often taken to the form of *Leaves of Grass* to the effect that it has a spurious emotionality; that the line-system has the same relation to poetry as the habitual use of italics has to prose. The objection, we think, is inapplicable; but obviously the presentment of a composition in lines is meaningless and otiose, unless the lines have some common measure and are identities in nature as well as in name.

The identity of the lines in metrical poetry is an identity of pattern. The identity of the lines in *Leaves of Grass* is an identity of substance; and this is in effect by far the subtler and more exacting condition of the two. Tyrannous spontaneity allows the poet so little respite that every line must, as it were, contain his personality in the germ. Whitman himself never, I think, formulated this demand, and in the course of his work he frequently overrides it. But it is a natural deduction from his admitted principles. He looked upon each of his poems as the leaf or branch of a tree. The line is to the poem what the poem is to the work as a whole. To say this is to say that certain forms are excluded, that certain kinds of line will not do.

A quotation from early manuscript passages written before Whitman had quite found his bearings will show better than anything else what his form rejects and why. Among the variorum readings given in the third volume of the Camden Edition of the collected works (p. 128) we find the following: —

> There is no word in my tongue,
> No array, no form of symbol,
> To tell his infatuation
> Who would define the scope and purpose of God.

Readers familiar with *Leaves of Grass* will at once feel a want of equivalence in these four lines; and what does the sensation point to if not to the presence of equivalence in Whitman's lines generally? Each true line of Whitman's comes to us, as I have said, floated separately on an independent breath. Like the sea-waves to which he himself so often compared them, his lines are not less recognisably units because of their variable shapes and sizes. And in the third of those quoted above, some principle of equivalence is violated. It is violated, therefore it exists. The words "to tell his infatuation" are merely transitional; they explain what precedes, prepare for what follows, and offer the mind no substantial resting place. The passage as it continues becomes still more instructive: —

Mostly this we have of God: we have man.
Lo, the Sun:
Its glory floods the moon,
Which of a night shines in some turbid pool,
Shaken by soughing winds;
And there are sparkles mad and tossed and broken,
And their archetype is the sun.

Of God I know not;
But this I know;
I can comprehend no being more wonderful than man;
Man, before the rage of whose passions the storms of heaven
        are but a breath;
Before whose caprices the lightning is slow and less fatal;
Man, microcosm of all Creation's wildness, terror, beauty and
        power,
And whose folly and wickedness are in nothing else existent.

The weakness here is quite as obvious, if not quite so transparent. In the first passage one of the lines was like a plank bridging a chasm over which the reader walked insecurely, feeling as if there were nothing under him. Here the effect is of a succession of stepping-stones. The lines are independent, but then are discontinuous. And the reason soon appears. The observations of the first stanza are not really made for their own sake; they are made with a purpose: in fact, in order to prepare us for a simile. Even their independence, therefore, is apparent rather than real. It is not independence; it is insulation. The turbid pool, the soughing winds, do not appear before us substantively; they are counted out like symbols, and each has its stage in the process of ethical deduction in which the simile is applied. The lines that hold them are, in fact, dependencies; they are not full lines; they demand their unit of attention from us and do not satisfy it.

It is to the junction in them of these two seemingly incompatible qualities, continuity and independence, that Whitman's mature lines owe their integrity, and it is this that dictates their behaviour in company, so to speak, explaining the shape of the poems, their formal development, and the difficulties and resources of the craftsman. The line is a personality, the poem is a battalion, the book is an army. To illustrate the point, let us quote a paragraph in full: —

> Here is the efflux of the soul,
> The efflux of the soul comes from within through embower'd gates, ever provoking questions,
> These yearnings why are they? these thoughts in the darkness why are they?
> Why are there men and women that while they are nigh me the sunlight expands my blood?
> Why when they leave me do my pennants of joy sink flat and lank?
> Why are there trees I never walk under but large and melodious thoughts descend upon me?
> (I think they hang there winter and summer on those trees and always drop fruit as I pass;)
> What is it I interchange so suddenly with strangers?
> What with some driver as I ride on the seat by his side?
> What with some fisherman drawing his seine by the shore as I walk by and pause?
> What gives me to be free to a woman's and man's goodwill? what gives them to be free to mine?

The importance of continuity to the form is displayed at once here in that *epanaphora*, that taking up of words or phrases, which is a pronounced characteristic of the style of *Leaves of Grass*. Each line hangs by a loop from the line before it. The motion is like the motion of walking; we continually catch up our foremost foot and take a half step beyond. It is of course the substantial self-sufficiency of the lines that necessitates this interlocking. And their equivalence turns upon their relation to a progressive, an accumulating idea. For example, the repetition of such a phrase as "the efflux of the soul," though it lengthens the line in which it occurs, does nothing to help that line to take us further; it has a different function; it joins the line more closely to its predecessor than the pronoun "it" would do and, by demanding less attention from the reader, decreases the weight of the line, thus actually preserving the equivalence it seems at first sight to impair.

In what sense, then, finally are the lines

> Here is the efflux of the soul

and

> The efflux of the soul comes from within through embower'd gates, ever provoking questions,

equivalent lines? We have seen that their equivalence is in their content; to say this is to say it is in their context also—that it depends upon their association together. They have not the equivalence that two lines of blank verse have and which they have equally whether they stand next to one another or not. The second is equivalent to the first only as consequent upon it. In the first, an image is, as it were, posited: the conception of the soul as a radiating centre. In the second, the same image is elaborated. Suppose then that for the second line, stumbled at first sight by its length and complexity, we substitute

> The efflux of the soul comes from within through embower'd gates,

and stop there, we shall find, not only that the line has lost poetry, but that it has lost equilibrium also. Why is this? Surely because, in the line as Whitman wrote it, we take the phrase

> comes from within through embower'd gates

transitionally, and because it is when so taken that its true value appears. If we emphasise it, as would be necessary were it to stand alone, we lose its suggestiveness and go searching for some precise significance which we do not find. But if we pass by way of it to the words

> ever provoking questions

and look to them for the first purpose of the line, the phrase falls into its relative place with beautiful accuracy. Is it because the gates are embowered that the questions are provoked? This, or something like it, gives the line, no doubt, its coherence of idea. But the point is that a mystical and an everyday expression have been weighed together and that their effect is felt in their juxtaposition. We weigh them in this way together because they are placed before us as constituents of a single line; and, having so weighed them, we find that the momentum set up by

> Here is the efflux of the soul

is preserved and carried one stage further. The equivalence of the two
lines is thus an equivalence of movement and of weight.

The problem of each succeeding line will be the same; to preserve
the movement, to advance it by a stage and to maintain equilibrium in
the advance. Reading to the end of the paragraph with this idea in
view, we shall find that each line solves the problem in its own way.
One has an element of surprise, another brings us into closer contact
with the object, a third has its expanding generalisation, a fourth its
illuminating detail; and the line in parenthesis is especially noticeable,
niched there like some light obstacle in flowing water and revealing
the current which it checks. To put the matter in general terms: the
constitution of a line in *Leaves of Grass* is such that, taken in its
context, the poetic idea to be conveyed by the words is only perfectly
derivable from them when they are related to the line as a unit; and the
equivalence of the lines is their equivalent appeal to our attention as
contributors to the developing expression of the poetic idea of the
whole.

Thus the progress of Whitman's verse has much in common with
that of a musical composition. For we are carrying the sense of past
effects along with us more closely and depending more intimately upon
them than is possible in normal verse. What we can achieve at any
point of our structure depends upon the trains of association we have
set up, the number of balls we have kept spinning, the speed and
quality of movement we have attacked or attained. And just as the
context limits, so it also lays its claim upon us. For if no line can do
more than maintain and add its unit to the general flow, none may do
less. And just as in music, so here; it is impossible to lay down any
rule for the maintenance of equivalence of effect, for the retaining of
attention and accumulation of interest to the close. The condition of
the effect that we are to produce now is the effect we have produced
up to now; it lies with the modifications we have produced in our
hearer's receptivity, the anticipations we have formed there. Here a
fortissimo seems necessary; but its place is taken perhaps by a *pianis-
simo*, perhaps by a silence, and the effect is sustained. There we have
a *diminuendo;* its point lies in the *crescendo* that preceded it; and
behold! while the sound lessens, the meaning grows. Throughout, the
test is whether the emotional pitch propounded is maintained, whether
the piece continues to expand in significance as it expands in volume.

Perhaps it is because the significance of words accumulates faster
than that of notes of music that frequent division into paragraphs be-

comes necessary, and also the frequent interpolation of parenthetical reflections. We go back and begin again where we began before in order, not that we may travel the same route a second time, but that we may travel to the same goal by a neighbouring route: —

> Allons ! whoever you are come travel with me !
> Traveling with me you find what never tires.

> The earth never tires,
> The earth is rude, silent, incomprehensible at first, Nature is rude and incomprensible at first.
> Be not discouraged, keep on, there are divine things well envelop'd,
> I swear to you there are divine things more beautiful than words can tell.

> Allons ! we must not stop here,
> However sweet these laid-up stores, however convenient this dwelling we cannot remain here,
> However shelter'd this port and however calm these waters we must not anchor here,
> However welcome the hospitality that surrounds us we are permitted to receive it but a little while.

These lines exhibit splendidly the alternating *crescendo* and *diminuendo* spoken of above. In "Traveling with me you find what never tires" we come immediately to a climax; there is no carrying the idea further; we must have a line of silence and start afresh. "The earth never tires" takes up the idea again, and in a sense is an addition to it; but it is a concessive, an explanatory addition; it is a concrete example and suggestion, and, as such, is taken as platform for a new "flight into the wordless." The poet soars, using a marked *crescendo*, which comes freely because the theme is simple. The line "I swear to you" is an easy and yet an enjoyable *fortissimo*. Again there is a pause; and then a new theme develops (the transitoriness of life on earth), needing tenderer handling; and so we have the deliberate and delicious *diminuendo* which brings the paragraph to a close.

The use of parenthesis is a recurring feature of Whitman's technique, and no explanation of his form can be adequate which does not relate this peculiarity to the constructive principles of the whole. He frequently begins a paragraph or ends one with a bracketed sentence, or begins or ends some section of a poem with a bracketed paragraph, sometimes even begins or ends a poem parenthetically. Thus the *Song of the Exposition* opens with the beautiful aside: —

(Ah little recks the laborer,
How near his work is holding him to God.
The loving Laborer through space and time.)

and the last piece in *Calamus* significantly closes:—

Be it as if I were with you. (Be not so certain but I am now with
you.)

This persistent bracketing falls well into the scheme we have laid
down of independent units that serve an accumulating effect. The
bracket, one need not remark, secures a peculiar detachment for its
contents; it also, by placing them outside the current and main flow
of the sense relates them to it in a peculiar way. And although for the
time being the flow is broken, it by no means follows, as we saw, that
our sense of the flow is broken; on the contrary, it is probably en-
hanced. We look down upon the stream from a point of vantage and
gauge its speed and direction. More precisely, the bracket opening
a poem or paragraph gives us, of course, the idea which that whole
poem or paragraph presupposes, while the closing bracket gives the
idea by which what precedes is to be qualified and tempered. We have
thus as it were a poem within a poem; or sometimes, when a series of
brackets is used, we have a double stream of poetry, as in *By Blue
Ontario's Shore* where the waters blend and yet remain discriminate,
a deeper and more personal current of feeling persisting under the
strength and buoyant onrush of the surface. All this carries out and
amplifies the peculiar formal significance of *Leaves of Grass*, with
its strange submission of words to unfamiliar musical associations.
Continuity and independence being Whitman's opposing principles
of composition, independence emerges in the bracket into relative
prominence. The disjunctive spirit of language asserts itself; literature
contemplates music.

But the analogy with music is still unexhausted. Not only is the
method of progression similar, the means of progression have also
much in common. The chief difference between musical and verbal
expression, as a rule, is that words, carrying each their modicum of
meaning, have done their part when they have delivered it, while
notes, being meaningless except in combination, develop new mean-
ings by presenting a single combination in varying contexts or with
varying accompaniment. In fact, repetition, which the artist in
language scrupulously avoids, is the foundation and substance of
musical expression. Now Whitman, for reasons we have touched on,
uses words and phrases more as if they were notes of music than any

other writer. As we shall see elsewhere, it was to him part of the virtue and essence of life that its forms and processes were endlessly reduplicated; and poetry, which was delight in life, must somehow, he thought, mirror this elemental abundance. Language generally expects us, when an object has been mentioned, to hold that object in view until all that has to be said about it has been said. But the object, if it were actually before us, would continue to assert itself in a thousand ways, and its persistency—its refusal, as it were, to believe that it can be monotonous to us—is its reality, and if its reality, then surely its poetry also.

> You have waited, you always wait, you dumb, beautiful
> ministers,
> We receive you with free sense at last, and are insatiate hence-
> forward.

Why should not words imitate things and keep up the same patient knocking at the mind's doors until we genuinely admit them?

The meaning of repetition lies of course in the fact that it is impossible to have the same experience twice. If there is to be value in the repeating over and over of some form of words, there must be something in them or in their varying contexts to enable the mind to pass from a first to a second impression of them, and from a second to a third and a fourth, feeling at each stage that more is added in discovery than is lost through the trouble of treading the old path. Words, we must recollect, are partly vehicles of truth, partly vehicles of emotion; they may exhibit a simple relation or suggest a complex one. Now the more complex the relation suggested, the more familiar we must be with the words that suggest it if we are to profit by every breath of suggestion they contain. We have only to grasp the sense of a geometrical proposition and we have done with the words of it; we have no disposition to say them over. But the words of a poem we often learn by heart and repeat them to ourselves as we might repeat a prayer. We are conscious that they proceed out of a certain state of feeling which we desire to enter into and to make our own; to enter into a state we must become familiar with it as an experience; and so we repeat the poem over and over to ourselves, at each repetition experiencing more intimately and more profoundly the spiritual state reflected in it. The poem thus becomes less and less a form of words to us and more and more a key to life. The reason is that the disposition of the words demands from the mind that is to understand them a corresponding disposition. They emanate from and represent a har-mony into which we enter only by reproducing it in our own being.

What applies to our deliberate repetition of a poem to ourselves can be applied to the handling of a poem by its composer if he so chooses. His object is not to state truths but to convey feelings; and the feeling with which we hear a certain form of words may well depend precisely upon the fact that we are not hearing it for the first time, the feeling itself changing and developing as its occasion is repeated. Lyric poetry acknowledges the virtue of repetition in the refrain, which, though in the main a concession to the forms of the musical accompaniment, has its value in reviving and sustaining the implied emotional mood.

But there is a further point. A truth necessarily continues true. Of an emotion our chief test is the degree to which it admits of constancy; feelings are habitually proved and established by a frequent reiteration of the expression of them. Now poetry gives us this assurance as a rule by the elevation of manner, the unified tone, the remoteness, which are in themselves evidence of sustained feeling, being unattainable without it. Repetition (with certain exceptions irrelevant here) is thus more otiose in poetry than in prose. For the web of expression is more tightly woven, every word has full force, and a higher concentration is demanded of the reader who is to assimilate the mood. The poem does not so much rise to a certain altitude, as exist there; and the danger is not that we may doubt the emotion, but that we may fail to recognise the objects to which it attaches—a failing which sometimes extends beyond a poet's readers to the poet himself.

Now the absence of recognised formalities which is characteristic of *Leaves of Grass* robs language of these high-pitched associations, and obliges us to interpret it in accordance with the dictates of mere common sense. When Whitman bids us

Behold this compost, behold it well,

we know that if we take up a handful of garden soil and turn it over in our hands, we shall be quite in the spirit of his intention. It was one of his ideals in poetry not to lose sight of these everyday simplicities. Yet a form or style which begins from and reverts to such simplicities must forge instruments of some kind to carry it from the simplicities to the profundities. Poetic exaltation is not the less necessary because it is not presupposed. And of Whitman's instruments for obtaining it, repetition—repetition of forms, of phrases, of themes—is perhaps the chief. It is not only that it assists him, as we have seen, to carry out the principle of accumulating weight, his first law of construction. It is also that by it he brings home to us the increasing value for emotion of expressions the value of which, at first hearing, seemed to lie in their very divorce from it, in their cool substantiality. His most astonishing effects are thus often produced by means least compatible with ordinary poetry, the means, like the effects they serve, being peculiarly his own. *Crossing Brooklyn Ferry* is perhaps the greatest and boldest example of them: —

> Flood-tide below me! I see you face to face!
> Clouds of the west—sun there half an hour high—I see you
>   also face to face!

Beginning thus with the common attitude to common objects, we find ourselves gradually, as it were, intermingled with them and caught up through the medium of the poet's interpretation into the sentiment and atmosphere they create: —

> Ah! what can ever be more stately and admirable to me than
>   mast-hemm'd Manhattan?
> River and sunset and scallop-edg'd waves of flood-tide?

Without losing touch with our own experience, we make a passage from natural to impassioned vision. We do more than read poetry. We feel it in its process and formation; not lifted into another world, but acquainted with the deepening and extending vistas of the world we live in: —

> Flow on, river! flow with the flood-tide, and ebb with the ebb-
>   tide!
> Frolic on, crested and scallop-edg'd waves!
> Gorgeous clouds of the sunset! drench with your splendor me,
>   or the men and women generations after me!
> Cross from shore to shore, countless crowds of passengers!
> Stand up, tall masts of Mannahatta! stand up, beautiful hills of
>   Brooklyn! . . .
> You have waited, you always wait, you dumb, beautiful ministers,
> We receive you with free sense at last, and are insatiate hence-
>   forward.
> Not you any more shall be able to foil us, or withhold yourselves
>   from us,
> We use you, and do not cast you aside—we plant you per-
>   manently within us,
> We fathom you not—we love you—there is perfection in you
>   also,
> You furnish your parts toward eternity,
> Great or small, you furnish your parts toward the soul.

There is in this a living presentment of the condition out of which all poetry springs. It is sometimes made a criticism of Whitman that, instead of writing poetry, he writes about it and tries to explain what it is. Often he does so; but often when he seems to be doing so, he is in reality doing much more. He is communicating not merely a poem, an example of poetry, but the spiritual attitude, which if we can assimilate it, will make use according to our measure poets ourselves. No process of explanation serves here. It is work for the greatest of poets in their moments of greatest inspiration. *Crossing Brooklyn Ferry* is such a 'poem of poetry'; it summarises experiences, offers a new key to that dark door, would endow us with a new experiencing faculty. A purpose so sublime may well have demanded this strange blend of the ecstasies of music, the exactitudes of speech.

It will be pertinent to observe, finally, that Whitman has discovered and elaborated in *Leaves of Grass* a form for which other poets seem to have searched in vain. What after all was Goethe seeking for in those splendid lyrics *Prometheus*, *Ganymed* and their like, if not some principle of equivalence for his lines which would be independent of metrical ties or would at least enable him to override them? Such a lyric as *Prometheus* has of course a sustained exaltation of manner, a conciseness of symbolic allusion, which Whitman never aims at and which, even if he had aimed at it, he probably could not have compassed. But considering it on its formal side only, may we not attribute to the lack of Whitman's 'substantial equivalence' that element of trickery or experimentation which the lines seem so often to display? The poet halts, as it were, between two principles, only half conscious of their antagonism, with the result that justice is done to neither: —

> Ihr nähret kummerlich
> Von Opfersteuern
> Und Gebetshauch
> Eure Majestät,
> Und darbtet, wären
> Nicht Kinder und Bettler
> Hoffnungsvoller Thoren.

Irony towers here, and it is piled up on something like the substantial principle, until at the word 'wären' the spell is broken, and we revert to measurement by syllables. The next stanza: —

> Da ich ein Kind war,
> Nicht wusste wo aus noch ein,

> Kehrt' ich mein verirrtes Auge
> Zur Sonne, als wenn drüber wär'
> Ein Ohr, zu hören meine Klage,
> Ein Herz, wie mein's,
> Sich des Bedrängten zu erbarmen.—

exhibits precisely those faults of which Whitman was sensitive in his first drafts for *Leaves of Grass*. The actual line division is not the real one. There is an inherent discrepancy between the style and the form. Exactly the same defect appears in the English imitations of Goethe to which Matthew Arnold was so much addicted. Some of his best thought is to be found in work which he has thrown into this irregular recitative; but the poetic result is, by general admission, unsatisfactory. Sometimes his themes are Whitmanesque:—

> They see the Scythian
> On the wide steppe, unharnessing
> His wheel'd house at noon.
> He tethers his beast down, and makes his meal,
> Mare's milk, and bread
> Baked on the embers: all around . . .

Such a passage as this fails, again, precisely for lack of any determining principle in the lines, anything to assure us that, in the absence of metrical regularity, they do not simply begin and end at haphazard. Mere variableness is not only unpleasing but unintelligible. In order that change should have a meaning, we must have with it an instrument for measuring it, a standard to which it may be applied. Whitman makes an original contribution to poetic craft in that he discovers and exhibits a new standard, a new basis for variation. The freedom of his lines is pleasurable to us and conveys an intelligible impression only in so far as we instinctively recognise the common principle they exemplify, and measure them by tacit reference to it.

VAN WYCK BROOKS

The Precipitant†

Whitman—how else can I express it?—precipitated the American character. All those things that had been separate, self-sufficient, incoördinate—action, theory, idealism, business—he cast into a crucible; and they emerged, harmonious and molten, in a fresh democratic ideal, based upon the whole personality. Every strong personal impulse, every coöperating and unifying impulse, everything that enriches the social background, everything that enriches the individual, everything that impels and clarifies in the modern world owes something to Whitman. And especially of those American writers who have written preëminently for young men—and which has not?—Whitman alone, it seems to me, has pitched his tone to the real spring of action in them.

All this indicates a function quite different from that of a poet in any but the most radical and primitive sense of the word (the sense in which it was held by Whitman himself), a man, that is to say, who first gives to a nation a certain focal centre in the consciousness of its own character. Virgil did this, Mazzini did this, Björnson did this; and it was the main work of Whitman to make fast what he called "the idea and fact of American Totality," an idea and fact summed up with singular completeness in his own character and way of life. Emerson before him had provided a kind of skeleton outline; but what Emerson drew in black and white Whitman filled in with colour and set in three dimensions.

A *focal centre*—that is the first requisite of a great people. And by this I do not mean the sense of national or imperial destiny which has consolidated the great temporal powers of history. I mean that national "point of rest," to adopt a phrase in which Coleridge indicated that upon which the harmony of a work of art is founded and to which everything in the composition is more or less unconsciously referred; that secure and unobtrusive element of national character, taken for granted, and providing a certain underlying coherence and background of mutual understanding which Rome, for example, had in

† From *Three Essays on America* by Van Wyck Brooks. Copyright 1934 by E. P. Dutton & Co., Inc. Renewal 1955 by Van Wyck Brooks. Published by E. P. Dutton & Co., Inc., and used with their permission.

everything the name of Cato called up, or England in her great remembered worthies, or the elder Germany in Martin Luther. "National culture," to speak in the dialect of our own time, is only the perhaps too-conscious equivalent of this element in which everything admirably characteristic of a people sums itself up, which creates everywhere a kind of spiritual team-work, which radiates outward and articulates the entire living fabric of a race.

For us, it seems to me, Whitman laid the cornerstone of a national ideal capable in this way of releasing personality and of retrieving for our civilization, originally deficient in the richer juices of human nature, and still further bled and flattened out by the "machine process," the only sort of "place in the sun" that is really worth having.

But at this point one has to discriminate. The social ideal of Whitman is essentially a collection of raw materials, molten and malleable, which take shape only in an emotional form. This emotional attitude is at bottom the attitude of a perfectly free personality, naturally affirmative, naturally creative; the rude material of right personal instinct, which is, however, antecedent to the direction personality is to adopt and to the ideas that are to inform it.

To ignore this distinction, as most of the direct disciples of Whitman have done, is to go wrong utterly. And in fact Whitman himself ignored the distinction, and himself went wrong. Perfectly right in all his instincts, perfectly right so long as he kept to the plane of instinct, he was lost on the plane of ideas. He lacked a sure sense of his own province and limitations. Influenced no doubt by his disciples, he began in later years to assume functions not properly his own, and the greatness and sweetness of his character were increasingly marred by much pomposity and fatuousness. He was led to speak not as a poet but as an authority, the painful results of which may be seen in his newspaper interviews.

All this was probably inevitable. Whitman's instinct was to affirm everything, to accept everything, to relish the personal and human elements in everything. For himself he accepted "sustenance, clothing, shelter and continuity." As regards the world, he was equally catholic and passive. Soldiers being the strapping upright animals they are, he accepts armies because armies breed them. He enjoys an old restaurateur because he knows how to select champagne, likes to look at nursemaids because they are so trim and wholesome and at fashionable women because they are so pretty and gay, likes money because of a certain strength it implies and business because it is so active, nimble and adventurous. On the plane of instinct, where he properly belongs, he is right in each case: on the plane of ideas, the practical effect is that, in accepting everything, he accepts the confusion of things and the *fait accompli.*

It is, in fact, the simple corollary of his thorough-going mood of affirmation on the personal, instinctive, emotional plane, that his ideas should be perfectly conventional. In ideas he is just an old-fashioned Jacksonian democrat. Except for a certain amount of uncommonly vigorous criticism, of the stock type, on American abuses, he never questions the old institutions. He takes for granted "the unform'd and nebulous state of many things, not yet permanently settled, but agreed on all hands to be the preparations of an infinitely greater future." He talks the greatest amount of nonsense about the "feudalism" of a contemporary Europe whose typical artists have been men like Tolstoy, Dostoevski, Millet, Thomas Hardy. He is never able to release himself from the vicious comparative; he is morbid about geography. Not being satisfied by the greatness of anything as a positive fact, he has to prove its greatness by belittling something else. A fertile plain strikes him at once as more fertile than any other plain on earth, a grand scene "outvies all the historic places of note," an American general is more of a general than Napoleon, an American poem has to be better than any poem hitherto.

All this is just what Bryant used to say—it is just our fun. And the funniest thing of all, from this point of view, is to find Whitman solemnly posed, as he records it, before a vast canvas twenty feet by twelve, representing "Custer's Last Rally," the work of one John Mulvany; finding its "physiognomy realistic and Western," with an "almost entire absence of the stock traits of European war pictures," and recommending that it be sent to Paris "to show Messieur Crapeau [*sic*] that some things can be done in America as well as others." A scene that demonstrates once for all that Whitman was never intended to be an authority, even on democracy.

An opportunity, and in certain respects also a faculty, Whitman had, in his own time and place, very similar to those of Montaigne. I mean by this, on the one hand, a malleable and still incoherent race to be interpreted to itself, to be articulated, to be brought into focus, and on the other a temperament typical of that race, a range of sympathy coincidental with it, and a power of revealing and in a sense fixing the racial norm. "I look within myself, I am only concerned with myself, I reflect on myself, I examine myself, I take pleasure in myself," said Montaigne; and all France for the first time saw itself in a looking-glass and fell together in a common discipline.

The raw materials of a racial norm Whitman provided; but—and in this he resembled Emerson—he was too passive to go further. He assembled in himself and his writings the characteristics of America—with him originated the most contagious, the most liberating, the most unifying of native impulses; but he failed to react upon them, to mould them, and to drive them home. He had no ideas, and he was satisfied to have none. He lacked, above all, intensity. He was too complacent. He was incapable of discipline and he did not see that discipline is, for Americans, the condition of all forward movement.

But the conventionality of Whitman's intellectual equipment is not, for us, a necessary part of the personal attitude which he originated. History is filled with instances of men who, having been called upon to originate fresh points of view, have had, in order to establish these points of view, to adopt a severely conventional position towards most of the phenomena of their time. Each of these men has had his disciples in the letter and his disciples in the spirit—Martin Luther, for example, especially in questions economic and social. The direct and immediate children of Luther, those who have laid apostolic hands on one another from generation to generation, are simply the bourgeoisie of the world; but the true Lutherans are those who, in every age, have thought keenly and honestly and independently and have, in so doing, contributed stone by stone to the great catholicism of the future. So also with Whitman and the children of Whitman. It was inevitable, in the America of his time, that he should have been so much of an outrageous egoist (consider the provocation!), inevitable that he should, in Emerson's phrase, have swallowed the universe like a cake, inevitable that he should have been undiscriminating, confused and a little fatuous. To affirm sufficiently, he had to affirm everything.

We are in a different position, and we have different responsibilities. On the philosophical side, the simple doctrine of evolution, in its crude form the last word in Whitman's cosmos, has been refined and ripened. Above all, we have no excuse not to see that affirmation, in the most real sense, proceeds to a certain extent through rejection, by merely dropping off most of the old clothes that Whitman found quite good enough. To keep these old clothes, to affirm that since everything is good they must be good also, to embroider them and make them over and stalk about in them, loudly affirming one's own ego and the indiscriminate grandeur of all creation, with particular reference to the Whole Crowd of Good Americans—all this is not to continue and to reaffirm the right Whitmanian tradition; but it is, in a way, to have the sanction of Whitman's own character and experience, and it is, above all, to do what the typical contemporary Whitmanian does.

In some way—and primarily by returning upon Whitman as

Whitman returned upon Emerson, not, as in that case, by adding emotion to intellect, but by adding intellect to emotion—the social ideal the raw materials of which have been provided by Whitman must be formulated and driven home.

JOHN COWPER POWYS
Walt Whitman†

I want to approach this great Soothsayer from the angle least of all profaned by popular verdicts. I mean from the angle of his poetry. We all know what a splendid heroic Anarchist he was. We all know with what rude zest he gave himself up to that "Cosmic Emotion," to which in these days the world does respectful, if distant, reverence. We know his mania for the word "en masse," for the words "ensemble," "democracy" and "libertad." We know his defiant celebrations of Sex, of amorousness, of maternity; of that Love of Comrades which "passeth the love of women." We know the world-shaking effort he made—and to have made it at all, quite apart from its success, marks him a unique genius!—to write poetry about every mortal thing that exists, and to bring the whole breathing palpable world into his Gargantuan Catalogues. It is absurd to grumble at these Inventories of the Round Earth. They may not all move to Dorian flutes, but they form a background—like the lists of the Kings in the Bible and the lists of the Ships in Homer—against which, as against the great blank spaces of Life itself, "the writing upon the wall" may make itself visible.

What seems much less universally realized is the extraordinary genius for sheer "poetry" which this Prophet of Optimism possessed. I agree that Walt Whitman's Optimism is the only kind, of that sort of thing, that one can submit to without a blush. At least it is not indecent, bourgeois, and ill-bred, like the fourth-hand Protestantism that Browning dishes up, for the delectation of Ethical Societies. It is the optimism of a person who has seen the American Civil War. It is the

† From *Visions and Revisions* (New York: G. A. Shaw, 1915; London, Macdonald, 1955), pp. 281–289. Reprinted by permission of Macdonald & Co., Ltd., and the estate of the late John Cowper Powys.

optimism of a man who knows "the Bowery," and "the road," and has had queer friends in his mortal pilgrimage.

It is an interesting psychological point, this difference between the "marching breast-forward" of Mrs. Browning's energetic husband, and the "taking to the open road" of Whitman. In some curious way the former gets upon one's nerves where the latter does not. Perhaps it is that the boisterous animal-spirits which one appreciates in the open air become vulgar and irritating when they are practised within the walls of a house. A Satyr who stretches his hairy shanks in the open forest is a pleasant thing to see; but a gentleman, with lavender-colored gloves, putting his feet on the chimney-piece is not so appealing. No doubt it is precisely for these Domestic Exercises that Mr. Chesterton, let us say, would have us love Browning. Well! It is a matter of taste.

But it is not of Walt Whitman's Optimism that I want to speak; it is of his poetry.

To grasp the full importance of what this great man did in this sphere one has only to read modern "libre vers." After Walt Whitman, Paul Fort, for instance, seems simply an eloquent prose writer. And none of them can get the trick of it. None of them! Somewhere, once, I heard a voice that approached it; a voice murmuring of

"Those that sleep upon the wind,
And those that lie along in the rain,
Cursing Egypt—"

But that voice went its way; and for the rest—what banalities! What ineptitudes! They make the mistake, our modern free-versifiers, of thinking that Art can be founded on the Negation of Form. Art can be founded on every other Negation. But not on that one—never on that one! Certainly they have a right to experiment; to invent—if they can— new forms. But they must invent them. They must not just arrange their lines *to look like poetry*, and leave it at that.

Walt Whitman's New Form of Verse was, as all such things must be, as Mr. Hardy's strange poetry, for instance, is, a deliberate and laborious struggle—ending in what is a struggle no more—to express his own personality in a unique and recognisable manner. This is the secret of all "style" in poetry. And it is the absence of this labour, of this premeditated concentration, which leads to the curious result we see on all sides of us, the fact, namely, that all young modern poets *write alike*. They write alike, and they *are* alike—just as all men are like all other men, and all women like all other women, when, without the "art" of clothing, or the "art" of flesh and blood, they lie down side by side in the free cemetery. The old poetic forms will always have their place. They can never grow old-fashioned; any more than Pisanello, or El Greco, or Boticelli, or Scopas, or any ancient Chinese Painter, can grow old-fashioned. But when a modern artist or poet sets to work to create a new form, let him remember what he is doing! It is not the pastime of an hour, this. It is not the casual gesture of a mad iconoclast breaking Classic Statues into mud, out of which to make goblins. It is the fierce, tenacious, patient, constructive work of a lifetime, based upon a tremendous and overpowering Vision! Such a vision Walt Whitman had, and to such constant inspired labour he gave his life—notwithstanding his talk about "loafing and inviting his soul"!

The "free" poetry of Walt Whitman obeys inflexible, occult laws, the laws commanded unto it by his own creative instinct. We need, as Nietzsche says, to learn the art of "commands" of this kind! Transvaluers of old values do not spend all their time sipping absinthe. Is it a secret still, then, the magical unity of rhythm, which Walt Whitman has conveyed to the words he uses? Those long, plangent, wailing lines, broken by little gurgling gasps and sobs; those sudden thrilling apostrophes and recognitions; those long-drawn flute-notes; those resounding sea-trumpets; all such effects have their place in the great orchestral symphony he conducts!

Take that little poem—quite spoiled before the end by a horrible bit of democratic vulgarity—which begins:

"Come, I will build a Continent indissoluble;
I will make the most splendid race the sun ever shone upon—"

Is it possible to miss the hidden spheric law which governs such a challenge? Take the poem which begins:

"In the growths, by the margins of pond-waters—"

Do you not divine, delicate reader, the peculiar subtlety of that reference to the rank, rain-drenched *anonymous weeds*, which every day we pass in our walks inland? A botanical name would have driven the magic of it quite away.

Walt Whitman, more than anyone, is able to convey to us that sense of the unclassified pell-mell, of weeds and stones and rubble and wreckage, of vast, desolate spaces, and spaces full of débris and litter, which is most of all characteristic of your melancholy American landscape, but which those who love England know where to find, even among our trim gardens! No one like Walt Whitman can convey to us the magical *ugliness* of certain aspects of Nature—the bleak, stunted, God-forsaken things; the murky pools where the grey leaves fall; the dead reeds where the wind whistles no sweet fairy tunes; the unspeakable margins of murderous floods; the tangled sea-drift, scurfed with scum; the black sea-winrow of broken shells and dead fishes' scales; the roots of willow trees in moonlit places crying out for demon-lovers; the long, moaning grass that grows outside the walls of prisons; the leprous mosses that cover paupers' graves; the mountainous wastes and blighted marshlands which only unknown wild-birds ever touch with their flying wings, and of which madmen dream—these are the things, the ugly, terrible things, that this great optimist turns into poetry. "Yo honk!" cries the wild goose, as it crosses the midnight sky. Others may miss that mad-tossed shadow, that heart-breaking defiance —but from amid the drift of leaves by the roadside, this bearded Fakir of Outcasts has caught its meaning; has heard, and given it its answer.

Ah, gentle and tender reader; those whose heart, it may be has never cried all night for what it must not name, did you think Swinburne or Byron were the poets of "love"? Perhaps you do not know that the only "short story" on the title-page of which Guy de Maupassant found it in him to write *that word* is a story about the wild things we go out to kill?

Walt Whitman, too, does not confine his notions of love to normal human coquetries. The most devastating love-cry ever uttered, except that of King David over his friend, is the cry this American poet dares to put into the heart of "a wild-bird from Alabama" that has lost its mate. I wonder if critics have done justice to the incredible genius of this man who can find words for that aching of the soul we do not confess even to our dearest? The sudden words he makes use of, in certain connections, awe us, hush us, confound us, take our breath,—as some of Shakespeare's do—with their mysterious congruity. Has my reader ever read the little poem called "Tears"? And what *purity* in the truest, deepest sense, lies behind his pity for such tragic craving; his understanding of what love-stricken, banished ones feel. I do not speak now of his happily amorous verses. They have their place. I speak of those desperate lines that come, here and there, throughout his work, where, with his huge, Titanic back set against the world-wall, and his wild-tossed beard streaming in the wind, he seems *to hold open* by main, gigantic force that door of hope which Fate and God and Man and the Laws of Nature are all endeavoring to close! *And he holds it open!* And it is open still. It is for this reason— let the profane hold their peace!—that I do not hesitate to understand very clearly why he addresses a certain poem to the Lord Christ!

Whether it be true or not that the Pure in Heart see God, it is certainly true that they have a power of saving us from God's Law of Cause and Effect! According to this Law, we all "have our reward" and reap what we have sown. But sometimes, like a deep-sea murmur, there rises from the poetry of Walt Whitman a Protest that *must* be heard! Then it is that the Tetrarchs of Science forbid in vain "that one should raise the Dead." For the Dead are raised up, and come forth, even in the likeness wherein we loved them! If words, my friends; if the use of words in poetry can convey such intimations as these to such a generation as ours, can anyone deny that Walt Whitman is a great poet?

Deny it, who may or will. There will always gather round him— as he predicted—out of City-Tenements and Artist-Studios and Factory-Shops and Ware-Houses and Bordelloes—aye! and, it may be, out of the purlieus of Palaces themselves—a strange, mad, heart-broken company of life-defeated derelicts, who come, not for Cosmic Emotion or Democracy or Anarchy or Amorousness, or even "Comradeship," but for that touch, that whisper, that word, that hand outstretched in the darkness, which makes them *know*—against reason and argument and all evidence—that they may hope still—*for the Impossible is true!*

D. H. LAWRENCE

Whitman†

Whitman is the greatest of the Americans. One of the greatest poets of the world, in him an element of falsity troubles us still. Something is wrong; we cannot be quite at ease in his greatness.

This may be our own fault. But we sincerely feel that something is overdone in Whitman; there is something that is too much. Let us get over our quarrel with him first.

All the Americans, when they have trodden new ground, seem to have been conscious of making a breach in the established order. They have been self-conscious about it. They have felt that they were

† From *Nation & Athenaeum*, XXIX (July 23, 1921), 616–618. Reprinted by permission of the *New Statesman*, London. This essay is the forerunner of Lawrence's chaper on Whitman in *Studies in Classic American Literature*.

trespassing, transgressing, or going very far, and this has given a certain stridency, or portentousness, or luridness to their manner. Perhaps that is because the steps were taken so rapidly. From Franklin to Whitman is a hundred years. It might be a thousand.

The Americans have finished in haste, with a certain violence and violation, that which Europe began two thousand years ago or more. Rapidly they have returned to lay open the secrets which the Christian epoch has taken two thousand years to close up.

With the Greeks started the great passion for the ideal, the passion for translating all consciousness into terms of spirit and ideal or idea. They did this in reaction from the vast old world which was dying in Egypt. But the Greeks, though they set out to conquer the animal or sensual being in man, did not set out to annihilate it. This was left for the Christians.

The Christians, phase by phase, set out actually to *annihilate* the sensual being in man. They insisted that man was in his reality *pure spirit*, and that he was perfectible as such. And this was their business, to achieve such a perfection.

They worked from a profound inward impulse, the Christian religious impulse. But their proceeding was the same, in living extension, as that of the Greek esoterics, such as John the Evangel or Socrates. They proceeded, by will and by exaltation, to overcome *all* the passions and all the appetites and prides.

Now, so far, in Europe, the conquest of the lower self has been objective. That is, man has moved from a great impulse within himself, unconscious. But once the conquest has been effected, there is a temptation for the conscious mind to return and finger and explore, just as tourists now explore battlefields. This self-conscious *mental* provoking of sensation and reaction in the great affective centres is what we call sentimentalism or sensationalism. The mind returns upon the affective centres, and sets up in them a deliberate reaction.

And this is what all the Americans do, beginning with Crêvecœur, Hawthorne, Poe, all the transcendentalists, Melville, Prescott, Wendell Holmes, Whitman, they are all guilty of this provoking of mental reactions in the physical self, passions exploited by the mind. In Europe, men like Balzac and Dickens, Tolstoi and Hardy, still act direct from the passional motive, and not inversely, from mental provocation. But the æsthetes and symbolists, from Baudelaire and Maeterlinck and Oscar Wilde onwards, and nearly all later Russian, French, and English novelists set up their reactions in the mind and reflect them by a secondary process down into the body. This makes a vicious living and a spurious art. It is one of the last and most fatal effects of ideal-

ism. Everything becomes self-conscious and spurious, to the pitch of
madness. It is the madness of the world of to-day. Europe and America
are all alike; all the nations self-consciously provoking their own pas-
sional reactions from the mind, and *nothing* spontaneous.

And this is our accusation against Whitman, as against the others.
Too often he deliberately, self-consciously *affects* himself. It puts us
off, it makes us dislike him. But since such self-conscious secondariness
is a concomitant of all American art, and yet not sufficiently so to pre-
vent that art from being of rare quality, we must get over it. The ex-
cuse is that the Americans have had to perform in a century a curve
which it will take Europe much longer to finish, if ever she finishes it.

Whitman has gone further, in actual living expression, than any
man, it seems to me. Dostoevsky has burrowed underground into the
decomposing psyche. But Whitman has gone forward in life-knowl-
edge. It is he who surmounts the grand climacteric of our civilization.

Whitman enters on the last phase of spiritual triumph. He really
arrives at that stage of infinity which the seers sought. By subjecting
the *deepest centres* of the lower self, he attains the maximum conscious-
ness in the higher self: a degree of extensive consciousness greater,
perhaps, than any man in the modern world.

We have seen Dana and Melville, the two adventurers, setting out
to conquer the last vast *element*, with the spirit. We have seen Melville
touching at last the far end of the immemorial, prehistoric Pàcific
civilization, in "Typee." We have seen his terrific cruise into uni-
versality.

Now we must remember that the way, even towards a state of
infinite comprehension, is through the externals towards the quick.
And the vast elements, the cosmos, the big things, the universals, these
are always the externals. These are met first and conquered first. That
is why science is so much easier than art. The quick is the living being,
the quick of quicks is the individual soul. And it is here, at the quick,
that Whitman proceeds to find the experience of infinitude, his vast
extension, or concentrated intensification into Allness. He carries the
conquest to its end.

If we read his pæans, his chants of praise and deliverance and
accession, what do we find? All-embracing, indiscriminate, passional
acceptance; surges of chaotic vehemence of invitation and embrace,
catalogues, lists, enumerations. "Whoever you are, to you endless an-
nouncements. . . ." "And of these one and all I weave the song of
myself." "Lovers, endless lovers."

Continually the one cry: I am everything and everything is me. I
accept everything in my consciousness; nothing is rejected:—

"I am he that aches with amorous love:
Does the earth gravitate? does not all matter, aching, attract
all matter?
So the body of me to all I meet or know."

At last everything is conquered. At last the lower centres are conquered. At last the lowest plane is submitted to the highest. At last there is nothing more to conquer. At last all is one, all is love, even hate is love, even flesh is spirit. The great oneness, the experience of infinity, the triumph of the living spirit, which at last includes everything, is here accomplished.

It is man's accession into wholeness, his knowledge in full. Now he is united with everything. Now he embraces everything into himself in a oneness. Whitman is drunk with the new wine of this new great experience, really drunk with the strange wine of infinitude. So he pours forth his words, his chants of praise and acclamation. It is man's maximum state of consciousness, his highest state of spiritual being. Supreme spiritual consciousness, and the divine drunkenness of supreme consciousness. It is reached through embracing love. "And whoever walks a furlong without sympathy walks to his own funeral dressed in his own shroud." And this supreme state, once reached, shows us the One Identity in everything, Whitman's cryptic *One Identity*.

Thus Whitman becomes in his own person the whole world, the whole universe, the whole eternity of time. Nothing is rejected. Because nothing opposes him. All adds up to one in him. Item by item he identifies himself with the universe, and this accumulative identity he calls Democracy, En Masse, One Identity, and so on.

But this is the last and final truth, the last truth is at the quick. And the quick is the single individual soul, which is never more than itself, though it embrace eternity and infinity, and never *other* than itself, though it include all men. Each vivid soul is unique, and though one soul embrace another, and include it, still it cannot *become* that other soul, or livingly dispossess that other soul. In extending himself, Whitman still remains himself; he does not become the other man, or the other woman, or the tree, or the universe: in spite of Plato.

Which is the maximum truth, though it appears so small in contrast to all these infinites, and En Masses, and Democracies, and Almightynesses. The essential truth is that a man is himself, and only himself, throughout all his greatnesses and extensions and intensifications.

The second truth which we must bring as a charge against

Whitman is the one we brought before, namely, that his Allness, his One Identity, his En Masse, his Democracy, is only a half-truth—an enormous half-truth. The other half is Jehovah, and Egypt, and Sennacherib: the other form of Allness, terrible and grand, even as in the Psalms.

Now Whitman's way to Allness, he tells us, is through endless sympathy, merging. But in merging you must merge away from something, as well as towards something, and in sympathy you must depart from one point to arrive at another. Whitman lays down this law of sympathy as the one law, the direction of merging as the one direction. Which is obviously wrong. Why not a right-about-turn? Why not turn slap back to the point from which you started to merge? Why not *that* direction, the reverse of merging, back to the single and overweening self? Why not, instead of endless dilation of sympathy, the retraction into isolation and pride?

Why not? The heart has its systole diastole, the shuttle comes and goes, even the sun rises and sets. We know, as a matter of fact, that all life lies between two poles. The direction is twofold. Whitman's *one direction* becomes a hideous tyranny once he has attained his goal of Allness. His One Identity is a prison of horror, once realized. For identities are manifold and each jewel-like, different as a sapphire from an opal. And the motion of merging becomes at last a vice, a nasty degeneration, as when tissue breaks down into a mucous slime. There must be the sharp retraction from isolation, following the expansion into unification, otherwise the integral being is overstrained and will break, break down like disintegrating tissue into slime, imbecility, epilepsy, vice, like Dostoevsky.

And one word more. Even if you reach the state of infinity, you can't sit down there. You just physically can't. You either have to strain still further into universality and become vaporish, or slimy: or you have to hold your toes and sit tight and practise Nirvana; or you have to come back to common dimensions, eat your pudding and blow your nose and be just yourself; or die and have done with it. A grand experience is a grand experience. It brings a man to his maximum. But even at his maximum a man is not more than himself. When he is infinite he is still himself. He still has a nose to wipe. The state of infinity is *only* a state, even if it be the supreme one.

But in achieving this state Whitman opened a new field of living. He drives on to the very centre of life and sublimates even this into consciousness. Melville hunts the remote white whale of the deepest passional body, tracks it down. But it is Whitman who captures the whale. The pure sensual body of man, at its deepest remoteness and intensity, this is the White Whale. And this is what Whitman captures.

He seeks his consummation through one continual ecstacy: the ecstacy of *giving himself*, and of being taken. The ecstacy of his own reaping and merging with another, with others; the sword-cut of sensual death. Whitman's motion is always the motion of *giving himself:* This is my body—take, and eat. It is the great sacrament. He knows nothing of the other sacrament, the sacrament in pride, where the communicant envelops the victim and host in a flame of ecstatic consuming, sensual gratification, and triumph.

But he is concerned with others beside himself: with woman, for example. But what is woman to Whitman? Not much? She is a great function—no more. Whitman's "athletic mothers of these States" are depressing. Muscles and wombs: functional creatures—no more.

> "As I see myself reflected in Nature,
> As I see through a mist, One with inexpressible completeness,
>   sanity, beauty,
> See the bent head, and arms folded over the breast, the Female
>   I see."

That is all. The woman is reduced, really, to a submissive function. She is no longer an individual being with a living soul. She must fold her arms and bend her head and submit to her functioning capacity. Function of sex, function of birth.

> "This, the nucleus—after the child is born of woman, man is
>   born of woman,
> This is the bath of birth, the merge of small and large, and the
>   outlet again—"

Acting from the last and profoundest centres, man acts womanless. It is no longer a question of race continuance. It is a question of sheer, ultimate being, the perfection of life, nearest to death. Acting from these centres, man is an extreme being, the unthinkable warrior, creator, mover, and maker.

And the polarity is between man and man. Whitman alone of all moderns has known this positively. Others have known it negatively, *pour épater les bourgeois.* But Whitman knew it positively, in its tremendous knowledge, knew the extremity, the perfectness, and the fatality.

Even Whitman becomes grave, tremulous, before the last dynamic truth of life. In *Calamus* he does not shout. He hesitates: he is reluctant, wistful. But none the less he goes on. And he tells the mystery of manly love, the love of comrades. Continually he tells us the same truth: the new world will be built upon the love of comrades, the new great dynamic of life will be manly love. Out of this inspiration the creation of the future.

The strange Calamus has its pink-tinged root by the pond, and it sends up its leaves of comradeship, comrades at one root, without the intervention of woman, the female. This comradeship is to be the final cohering principle of the new world, the new Democracy. It is the cohering principle of perfect soldiery, as he tells in "Drum Taps." It is the cohering principle of final *unison* in creative activity. And it is extreme and alone, touching the confines of death. It is something terrible to bear, terrible to be responsible for. It is the soul's last and most vivid responsibility, the responsibility for the circuit of final friendship, comradeship, manly love.

> "Yet, you are beautiful to me, you faint-tinged roots, you make
>   me think of death;
> Death is beautiful from you (what, indeed, is finally beautiful
>   except death and love?).
> I think it is not for life I am chanting here my chant of lovers, I
>   think it must be for death.
> For how calm, how solemn it grows to ascend to the atmosphere
>   of lovers;
> Death or life, I am then indifferent, my soul declines to prefer
>   (I am not sure but the high soul of lovers welcomes death
>   most),
> Indeed, O death, I think now these leaves mean precisely the
>   same as you mean—"

Here we have the deepest, finest Whitman, the Whitman who knows the extremity of life, and of the soul's responsibility. He has come near now to death, in his creative life. But creative life must come near to death, to link up the mystic circuit. The pure warriors must stand on the brink of death. So must the men of a pure creative nation. We shall have no beauty, no dignity, no essential freedom otherwise. And so it is from Sea-Drift, where the male bird sings the lost female: not that she is lost, but lost to him who has had to go beyond her, to sing on the edge of the great sea, in the night. It is the last voice on the shore.

> "Whereto answering, the sea
> Delaying not, hurrying not,
> Whispered me through the night, very plainly before daybreak,

Lisp'd to me the low and delicious word death,
And again death, death, death, death,
Hissing melodious, neither like the bird nor like my aroused
    child's heart,
But edging near as privately for me rustling at my feet,
Creeping thence steadily up to my ears and laving me softly all
    over,
Death, death, death, death, death—"

What a great poet Whitman is: great like a great Greek. For him the last enclosures have fallen, he finds himself on the shore of the last sea. The extreme of life: so near to death. It is a hushed, deep responsibility. And what is the responsibility? It is for the new great era of mankind. And upon what is this new era established? On the perfect circuits of vital flow between human beings. First, the great sexless normal relation between individuals, simple sexless friendships, unison of family, and clan, and nation, and group. Next, the powerful sex relation between man and woman, culminating in the eternal orbit of marriage. And, finally, the sheer friendship, the love between comrades, the manly love which alone can create a new era of life.

The one state, however, does not annul the other: it fulfils the other. Marriage is the great step beyond friendship, and family, and nationality, but it does not supersede these. Marriage should only give repose and perfection to the great previous bonds and relationships. A wife or husband who sets about to annul the old, pre-marriage affections and connections ruins the foundations of marriage. And so with the last, extremest love, the love of comrades. The ultimate comradeship which sets about to destroy marriage destroys its own *raison d'être*. The ultimate comradeship is the final progression from marriage; it is the last seedless flower of pure beauty, beyond purpose. But if it destroys marriage it makes itself purely deathly. In its beauty, the ultimate comradeship flowers on the brink of death. But it flowers from the root of all life upon the blossoming tree of life.

The life-circuit now depends entirely upon the sex-unison of marriage. This circuit must never be broken. But it must be still surpassed. We cannot help the laws of life.

If marriage is sacred, the ultimate comradeship is utterly sacred, since it has no ulterior motive whatever, like procreation. If marriage is eternal, the great bond of life, how much more is this bond eternal, being the great life-circuit which borders on death in all its round. The new, extreme, the sacred relationship of comrades awaits us, and the future of mankind depends on the way in which this relation is entered upon by us. It is a relation between fearless, honorable, self-responsible men, a balance in perfect polarity.

The last phase is entered upon, shakily, by Whitman. It will take us an epoch to establish the new, perfect circuit of our being. It will take an epoch to establish the love of comrades, as marriage is really established now. For fear of going on, forwards, we turn round and destroy, or try to destroy, what lies behind. We are trying to destroy marriage, because we have not the courage to go forward from marriage to the new issue. Marriage must never be wantonly attacked. *True* marriage is eternal; in it we have our consummation and being. But the final consummation lies in that which is beyond marriage.

And when the bond, or circuit of perfect comrades is established, what then, when we are on the brink of death, fulfilled in the vastness of life? Then, at last, we shall know a starry maturity.

Whitman put us on the track years ago. Why has no one gone on from him? The great poet, why does no one accept his greatest word? The Americans are not worthy of their Whitman. They take him like a cocktail, for fun. Miracle that they have not annihilated every word of him. But these miracles happen.

The greatest modern poet! Whitman, at his best, is purely himself. His verse springs sheer from the spontaneous sources of his being. Hence its lovely, lovely form and rhythm: at the best. It is sheer, perfect, *human* spontaneity, spontaneous as a nightingale throbbing, but still controlled, the highest loveliness of human spontaneity, undecorated, unclothed. The whole being is there, sensually throbbing, spiritually quivering, mentally, ideally speaking. It is not, like Swinburne, an exaggeration of the one part of being. It is perfect and whole. The whole soul speaks at once, and is too pure for mechanical assistance of rhyme and measure. The perfect utterance of a concentrated, spontaneous soul. The unforgettable loveliness of Whitman's lines!

"Out of the cradle endlessly rocking."

Ave America!

LEWIS MUMFORD

High Noon†

"He that by me spreads a wider breast than my own proves the width of my own." So Walt Whitman chanted in the Song of Myself; and in the greatness of Whitman the genius of Emerson was justified. Walt Whitman was a cosmos: he was inclusive where Emerson and Thoreau were restrictive: he was sensual and jolly where they were refined and taut: he identified himself with the mere bulk and vastness of the American continent, and, with a tremendous appetite for the actual, entered into the experience of the pioneer, the roadhand, the mechanic, the woodman, the soldier, the farmer. In some remote Dutch ancestor of Whitman's one figures the men and women of Franz Hals's portraiture, people large, lusty, loving, men who like their sweetheart and their steak, women who give themselves to love as the flower bows to the weight of the bee. With Emerson, to repeat the obvious, one surveys the world from a glacial summit: the air is rarefied, and at the distance even the treacherous places in the land-scape seem orderly and innocent. With Whitman one sees the heights from the bosom of the valley: the "unseen is proved by the seen, till that becomes unseen, and receives proofs of its own."

Whitman absorbed so much of the America about him, that he is more than a single writer: he is almost a literature. Pushing his way like some larval creature through one husk after another, through the hard shell of Puritanism, in which he wrote Temperance Tracts, through the shell of republicanism in which he glorified all the new political institutions, through the flimsy casement of romantic poetry, iridescent with cheap colors and empty rhymes, Whitman finally achieved his own metamorphosis, and emerged, with dripping wings, into the untempered mid-day of the American scene. The stages of this metamorphosis have created contradictions in Whitman's work; and if we are to appreciate his full achievement, we must be ready to throw aside the vestiges of his larval state.

First, there was in Whitman a certain measure of the political

† From Lewis Mumford, *The Golden Day* (New York: Boni & Liveright, 1926; W. W. Norton, 1934), pp. 121–128. Reprinted by permission of the author and the publisher.

religiosity of Joel Barlow and Philip Freneau. Political nationalism, in
certain aspects of Whitman's thought, assumed a mystical beauty and
centrality: he wrote about the United States as if they were the tissue
of men's eternal desires—as if the robbery of Mexican territory, for
example, could be justified to the Mexicans as well as the Americans
by the inevitable drag of our Manifest Destiny. Here Whitman was
confusing spiritual with temporal dominion. He had conceived new
spiritual patterns, appropriate to the modern, which were to be ful-
filled in the America of his dreams; and it was hard to resist identi-
fying this hope of a wider America with the expansionist activities of
political bandits. In this mood, to speak frankly, Whitman ranted.

Nevertheless, when one sums up Whitman's observations upon
the Union and upon the political state of the country, no one surely
ever ranted with so many reservations; and it is unfair to take the
bombastic lines out of the context that perpetually qualifies them. The
political reality that was so precious to Whitman was only a means
of permitting the growth of "superb persons," and a life, "copious,
vehement, spiritual, bold." Moreover, between the Walt Whitman who
wrote the original Leaves of Grass, and the defeated and paralyzed
man who lingered on through the Gilded Age, there is a difference;
and by 1879 Whitman had come to realize that his democracy was one
that had been based on free land and equal opportunity to use it, and
that failure was beginning to threaten the political structure. "If the
United States," he wrote, "like the countries of the Old World, are also
to grow vast crops of poor, desperate, dissatisfied, nomadic, miserably
waged populations, such as we see looming upon us of late years—
steadily, even if slowly, eating into them like a cancer of lungs or
stomach—then our republican experiment, notwithstanding all its sur-
face-successes, is at heart an unhealthy failure. . . ." That was not all.
"By the unprecedented open-up of humanity enmasse in the United
States in the last hundred years, under our institutions, not only the
good qualities of the race, but just as much the bad ones, are prom-
inently brought forward. Man is about the same, in the main, whether
with despotism or whether with freedom."

That saving and irrefragable common sense was what ballasted
all of Whitman's hopes and expectations. He lived to see the America
he dreamed of undermined and rotten: he saw the Kings of Iron and
Oil and Cotton supplant not merely the older ones who ruled by divine
right but the new one elected quadrennially by the people: he saw the
diverse but well-mixed America of his youth give way to the America
of the melting pot, which neither welded the old nationalities nor had
the spiritual power to create a new one: he saw the sickly barbers
and perfumers of the New York literary schools of the forties turn

into the gentlemanly tailors who cut their stories and their thoughts to fit the fat paunches of the middle classes in the seventies: he saw all this, and denied nothing. No critic ferreted out the weaknesses and pettinesses of America with a surer nose than Whitman tracked them down in his Democratic Vistas: what could be said against his dream, Whitman said, with the staunch candor of a friend. But his thought and his vision were unshaken; the promise of America had not disappeared. If it was absent from the immediate scene, it had nevertheless taken form in his poems; and his poems were still waiting to shape a new America.

In Leaves of Grass Whitman had fulfilled Emerson in more ways than either of them suspected. There are passages of Emerson's prose which have, potentially, the prosody of Whitman; but whereas Emerson's poems, at their best, remain fragmentary and broken, because the meaning was somehow always warping the metes and measures Emerson respected and clung to, in Whitman, at his best, these new thoughts find their own beat, and become poetry of the first rank. Whitman had discovered Emerson's inner form in creating his own. He himself had stammered and stuttered so long as he kept to the old metres: his early work was weak and sentimental because he had nothing to say within the bounds of those previous culture-molds which Whitman tagged as "feudal." New streams of thought and experience were confluent in Whitman: the *Weltanschauung* of Hegel, precursor of the evolutionists, who saw the world as a continual becoming, and both the bad and the good as part of the total meaning of the universe; the electric doctrine of Emerson, which bade every man find his own center and every institution to answer up for its results in one's own life; the unstratified society of America, where the bus driver was as good as the next man, and the private soldier as great as the statesman whose policies reduced him to a pawn; the cleansing operations of science, which confronted every variety in thought, and made no more distinction between the clean and the unclean, the minute and the immense, than some indifferent deity, for whom the fall of a gnat and the fall of an Empire are of precisely the same importance. Out of the discussions of the Fourierists, and the societies of Free Lovers, and women who pressed for the political and social emancipation of their sex, as well as out of his own capacious adventures, Whitman got the courage to deal with the varieties of sexual experience, too: in the Children of Adam and Calamus he brushed past the nice restraints of Emerson—who "held his nose" at its passages— and Thoreau, who, like Natty Bumpo and Paul Bunyan, averted himself from any passion more intense than friendship.

Whitman took in the quaker, the puritan, the cosmopolitan, the

pioneer, the republican; and what came out in his poems was none of
these things: it was a new essence; none of the ordinary labels de-
scribed it. It had the smell of reality which was science; it had the
largeness of comprehension which was philosophy; and it had the
doubts, searchings, quests, achievements, and consummations which
are the stuff of life itself. Whitman found no need to add an extra
dimension to his experience: to transcribe for him was in the highest
sense to *translate*. Whatever tended to create full-bodied and full-
minded men and women tended toward enlarging the significance of
every single activity, no matter how base or minute. The veil of ap-
pearance was as mysterious and beautiful as anything behind the veil.
Perhaps it was all Maya, all illusion; or perhaps life was like a set of
Chinese boxes: one removed the outer box of appearance, and dis-
covered another box—appearance. What of it? A single blade of grass
was enough to confound all the atheists; and whatever else the uni-
verse might hold, he reckoned that there was no sweeter meat than
that which clung to his own bones. Such faith does not need external
props and certitudes: it mocks at the testimony of bibles, for it is itself
the source of such testimony.

People have hesitated to call Whitman's poems poetry; it is useless
to deny that they belong to sacred literature. If the Leaves of Grass are
not poetry, it is only because not every generation endows us with
such a poet.

VERNON LOUIS PARRINGTON

Afterglow of the Enlightenment: Walt Whitman†

If the philosophy of the Enlightenment[1] was fast disintegrating
in the America of 1870, it still numbered its picturesque followers
who sought to leaven the age with the social spirit of an earlier
generation. It was a noble bequest—this gift of the French thinkers

† Excerpted from Vernon Louis Parrington, "Afterglow of the Enlighten-
ment: Walt Whitman," in *Main Currents in American Thought*, vol. III,
pp. 69–86. Copyright 1930 by Harcourt Brace Jovanovich; renewed 1958
by Vernon Louis Parrington, Jr.; Louise P. Tucker; Elizabeth P. Thomas.
Reprinted by permission of the publisher.
[1] The eighteenth-century philosophical movement characterized by the ra-
tionalism of such figures as Voltaire and Diderot in France, Pope and Hume
in England, and Franklin and Paine in America [*Editors*].

—with its passion for liberty, its faith in man, its democratic program. From that great reservoir had come pretty much all that was generously idealistic and humanitarian in the life of the two preceding generations. Its persuasive idealism had woven itself so closely into the fabric of national thought that our fathers had come to believe that America was dedicated in a very special sense to the principles of a free society. The democratic movement returned to it constantly to refresh its strength and take new bearings. At every great crisis the familiar pronouncement of the Declaration of Independence had been confidently appealed to in furtherance of social justice. And now in the days of an acquisitive individualism, when idealism was begging alms in the marketplace, it still threw flashes of romantic splendor on the crude American scene. Old Peter Cooper[2] still dreamed his dreams of social justice after eighty years had passed over his head; and Thaddeus Stevens,[3] grown crabbed and surly from bitter struggles, mutely testified to his passionate equalitarianism on the day of his burial. But it was Walt Whitman in his den at Camden—culturally and in the things of the spirit countless leagues removed from Boston—who was the completest embodiment of the Enlightenment—the poet and prophet of a democracy that the America of the Gilded Age was daily betraying.

In his somewhat truculent pose of democratic undress Whitman was a singular figure for a poet, and especially an American poet. The amplitude and frankness and sincerity of his rich nature were an affront to every polite convention of the day. Endowed with abundant sensuousness and catholic sympathies, he took impressions as sharply as wax from the etcher's hand; and those impressions he transcribed with the careful impartiality of the modern expressionist. His sensitive reactions to experience were emotional rather than intellectual. A pagan, a romantic, a transcendentalist, a mystic—a child of the Enlightenment yet heeding the lessons of science and regarding himself as a realist who honored the physical as the repository of the spiritual—to an amazing degree he was an unconscious embodiment of American aspiration in the days when the romantic revolution was at flood tide. His buoyant nature floated easily on the turbulent stream of national being, and his songs were defiant chants in praise of life—strong, abundant, procreative—flowing through the veins of America. . . .

* * *

[2] Peter Cooper (1791–1883) was a New York inventor and philanthropist, founder of Cooper Union [Editors].
[3] Thaddeus Stevens (1792–1868), U.S. representative from Pennsylvania, was a prominent abolitionist [Editors].

So it was as a revolutionary that Whitman began his work; and a revolutionary he remained to the end, although in his last years he chose to call himself an evolutionist. A born rebel, he was always preaching the gospel of rebellion. "I am a radical of radicals," he said late in life, "but I don't belong to any school."[4] It was this revolutionary spirit that made him the friend of all rebellious souls past and present. "My heart is with all you rebels—all of you, today, always, wherever: your flag is my flag,"[5] he said to a Russian anarchist; and it was this sympathy that enabled him to understand Fanny Wright and Tom Paine and Priestley, who "have never had justice done them."[6] "The future belongs to the radical," and so Leaves of Grass—he says in "Starting from Paumanok"—"beat the gong of revolt." Conventional law and order he frankly despised and those individuals who sought their own law and followed it awoke his admiration. Thoreau's "lawlessness" delighted him—"his going his own absolute road let hell blaze all it chooses." It is a coward and a poltroon who accepts his law from others—as true of communities as it is true of individuals. He was a good Jeffersonian in his fear of Federalistic consolidation that must put an end to local rights and freedoms.

> To the States or any one of them, or any city of the States, *Resist much, obey little,*
> Once unquestioning obedience, once fully enslaved,
> . . . no nation, state, city of this earth, ever afterward resumes its liberty.[7]
> I am for those that have never been master'd,
> For men and women whose tempers have never been master'd,
> For those whom laws, theories, conventions can never master.[8]

This is the spirit of the radical forties when men were prone to repudiate their allegiance to the political state; when left-wing Abolitionists were dissolving the Union by resolutions; and transcendentalists were proclaiming the doctrine of nullification of unrighteous law. It had come out of the Jacksonian upheaval, but it was daily discovering fresh sanctions as the anarchistic premises of the Enlightenment were more adequately explored and the revolutionary spirit of Europe broke

[4] Quoted in Horace Traubel, *With Walt Whitman in Camden*, I (Boston: Small, Maynard, 1906), 215.
[5] *Ibid*, p. 65.
[6] *Ibid*, pp. 74–80.
[7] "To the States," lines 1–3.
[8] "By Blue Ontario's Shore," lines 288–290.

in upon America. During these turbulent years Whitman's great plan was in gestation, but before *Leaves of Grass* came to print in the first slender edition of 1855 other influences had been at work, confirming his earlier views, endowing them with lyric passion and expanding them into a grandiose whole. Those influences would seem to have been the fervid emotionalism of the fifties, the monistic idealism of the transcendental school, and the emerging scientific movement. On the whole perhaps it was the first, with its vague and expansive Utopianism, that bit most deeply, stimulating his rich pagan nature to unconventional frankness and encouraging him to throw off the inhibitions of a Puritan ethicism that held American thought in narrow bondage. The rude and ample liberalisms that so shocked his early readers were in no sense peculiar to Whitman, despite common opinion, but the expression of the surging emotionalism of the times, and *Leaves of Grass*, can best be understood by setting its frank paganism against the background of the lush fifties.

* * *

But pagan though he was in his deeper nature, a child of the emotional fifties, he was a transcendentalist also and his democratic philosophy, as it took shape, bears unmistakable marks of the New England school, supplemented perhaps by Quakerism. His well-known comment, "I was simmering and simmering; it was Emerson brought me to boil," suggests much, and in particular that the Enlightenment as it had come to him through the Jeffersonian heritage was supplemented and spiritualized by the Enlightenment as it had taken special form in passing through the transcendental mind. To this latter source must be traced the philosophic monism that served to draw his speculations together—a mystic sense of the divine oneness of life that took his major postulates in golden hands and fused them into a single spiritual whole. Thus instructed the "great Idea, the idea of perfect and free individuals," became curiously Emersonian in all its amplifications. There is the same glorification of consciousness and will, the same exaltation of the soul, the same trust in the buried life that men call instinct, the same imperious call to heed the voice of innate Godhood; and round and about this "perfect and free individual" is a mystical egocentric universe wherein the children of men may luxuriate in their divinity. The body is excellent as the soul is excellent; away, therefore, with all shamefacedness—the mean secretiveness, the putting of fingers to the lips in presence of the naked, the lies in presence of open palpable fact! For if this be indeed God's universe, and He is in and through it all, the children of Adam may stand in His presence unafraid—nay, rather with pride in their own excellence.

"I exist as I am, that is enough," for "Divine am I inside and out, and I make holy whatever I touch or am touch'd from."

Whitman not only accepted Emerson with ungrudging loyalty but he dwelt much with Hegel[9] and the German idealists, and with their help he penetrated curiously to the core of things, discovering there an inner spiritual reality that is the abiding substance behind the external manifestation. He had come upon food to sustain his faith in presence of the mean and base that compassed him about, and the puzzling contradictions of life no longer troubled him. If man be perfectible, if he be indeed a child of God though still in his infancy, how glorious must be the future toward which he is pressing! The evil will pass and the good remain.

> Roaming in thought over the Universe, I saw the little that is
>   Good steadily hastening towards immortality,
> And the vast all that is call'd Evil I saw hastening to merge
>   itself and become lost and dead.[1]

When he turned from the oracular utterance of *Leaves of Grass* to sober exposition, he phrased it thus:

> There is, apart from more intellect . . . a wondrous some-
> thing that realises without argument . . . an intuition of the
> absolute balance, in time and space, of the whole of this multi-
> farious, mad chaos of fraud, frivolity, hoggishness—this revel of
> fools, and incredible make-believe and general unsettledness, we
> call the *world;* a soul-sight of that divine clue and unseen thread
> which holds the whole congeries of things, all history and time,
> and all events however trivial, however momentous, like a leash'd
> dog in the hands of the hunter.[2]

To discover this divine clue and be drawn by the unseen thread into the orbit of things, to suffer the Me—the "human identity of under-standing, emotions, spirit"—to fuse with the Not Me—"the whole of the material, objective universe and laws, with what is behind them in time and space"—became therefore for Whitman the grand ob-jective of man's life and effort. This for him was the sum and sub-stance of religion, which was no other than the binding of the in-

---

[9] Georg Wilhelm Hegel (1770–1831) was a German philosopher whose idealistic dialectic Whitman liked to take into account. See his poem "The Base of All Metaphysics" [*Editors*].
[1] "Roaming in Thought." The subtitle of this poem, here quoted in its entirety, is : (After reading Hegel) [*Editors*].
[2] Whitman, *Prose Works 1892*, ed. Floyd Stovall, vol. I, *Specimen Days* (New York: New York University Press, 1963), pp. 257–258 [*Editors*].

dividual back upon the whole. "A vast similitude interlocks all." And
so from his conception of social solidarty he went forward to the
conception of spiritual solidarity, and discovered religion to be the
crown and glory of the "American Idea." Walt Whitman and America
were to be the prophets of religion. "Easily at home in a natural world
of prodigious brightness and scale, he . . . saw 'the most splendid
race the sun ever shone upon,' and was urging the life of instinct and
impulse. Love was the key—taking form and in 'Starting from Pauma-
nok' he asserted his Love, Democracy, Religion—a new religion." His
message was purpose.

> The soul,
> Forever and forever—longer than soil is brown and solid—longer
> than water ebbs and flows.

> I will make the poems of materials, for I think they are to be the
> most spiritual poems,
> And I will make the poems of my body and of mortality,
> For I think I shall then supply myself with the poems of my soul
> and of immortality.

> I will make a song for these States that no one State may under
> any circumstances be subjected to another State,
>   .   .   .   .   .   .
> I will sing the song of companionship,
>   .   .   .   .   .   .
> I will write the evangel-poem of comrades and of love,
>   .   .   .   .   .   .
> I am the credulous man of qualities, ages, races,
> I advance from the people in their own spirit,
>   .   .   .   .   .   .
> I, too, following many and follow'd by many, inaugurate a re-
> ligion, . . .
>   .   .   .   .   .   .
> Each is not for its own sake,
> I say the whole earth and all the stars in the sky are for re-
> ligion's sake.

> I say no man has ever yet been half devout enough,
> None has ever yet adored or worship'd half enough,
> None has begun to think how divine he himself is, and how
> certain the future is.

> I say that the real and permanent grandeur of these States must
> be their religion,

Otherwise there is no real and permanent grandeur;

. . . .

My comrade!
For you to share with me two greatnesses, and a third one rising
    inclusive and more resplendent,
The greatness of Love and Democracy, and the greatness of
    Religion.[3]

But this new religion of the mystical Whitman, in harmony with
post-transcendental thought, was deeply impregnated with the spirit of
science. He was in the very fullness of his powers when the conception
of evolution came to him and he greeted it gladly, weaving it into all
his thinking and discovering in it a confirmation of his idealistic philos-
ophy. It was the evolution of Herbert Spencer, it must be remembered,
that Whitman accepted—teleological, buoyantly optimistic, dominated
by the conception of progress, shot through with the spirit of the
Enlightenment; and such an evolution was a confirmation and not a
denial of his transcendental premises. It supplemented rather than
contradicted the tenets of his faith. Like Emerson as he saw the bounds
of the material universe slowly pushed back by science he discovered
amidst the constant change the presence of growth, development, the
natural passage from the simple to the complex; and like Theodore
Parker[4] he felt that this slow unfolding was no other than the un-
folding of God, making Himself evident and unmistakable to man.
Evolution was God's great plan. "The law over all, the laws of laws,
is the law of successions," he was persuaded; "for what is the present
after all but a growth out of the past?" But noble as is the evidence of
God's work discoverable by science, the soul is not content to rest with
such evidence; it must seek out the reality behind the manifestation;
and for this work the poet alone is fitted. The poet must complete the
work of the scientist. The noble "Passage to India" is a lovely chant of
human progress, the adventurous soul conquering the earth; but it
must not pause there; it must seek God through the universe until it
finds Him, and "Nature and Man shall be disjoin'd and diffused no
more," and "All these hearts as of fretted children shall be sooth'd."

Bathe me O God in thee, mounting to thee,
I and my soul to range in range of thee.[5]

[3] "Starting from Paumanok," lines 69–74, 86, 92, 95–96, 102, 105–111,
131–133.
[4] Boston Unitarian and reformer (1810–1860) [*Editors*].
[5] "Passage to India," lines 192–193.

It was in this profoundly religious spirit that Whitman accepted science, built it into his poetry, rested confidently upon it; and it is this spirit that explains his formal statement in the "Song of Myself."

> I accept Reality and dare not question it,
> Materialism first and last imbuing.
>
> Hurrah for positive science! long live exact demonstration!
> Fetch stonecrop mixt with cedar and branches of lilac,
> This is the lexicographer, this the chemist, this made a grammar
>   of the old cartouches,
> These mariners put the ship through dangerous unknown seas,
> This the geologist, this works with the scalpel, and this is the
>   mathematician.
>
> Gentlemen, to you the first honors always!
> Your facts are useful, and yet they are not my dwelling,
> I but enter by them to an area of my dwelling.[6]

Equipped with such a philosophy and supported by such a faith Whitman accepted the twin duties laid upon him: to make clear to America her present failure in the great adventure—how far she had fallen short hitherto of any adequate democratic reality; and to mark out afresh the path to the Canaan of democratic hopes—reviving the early hopes of the Enlightenment and drawing in lovelier colors the democratic Utopia dreamed of for a hundred years. To be both critic and prophet—that he conceived to be his mission, a mission that he was faithful to for upwards of forty years. For the first duty he was admirably equipped. No other knew this America so intimately or so broadly—had penetrated so lovingly to the common heart and read so clearly its secret hopes and fears. That America was not yet a democracy—was very far indeed from a democracy—that it was a somewhat shoddy *bourgeois* capitalistic society shot through with cant and hypocrisy and every meanness, he saw with calm, searching eyes. No contemporary critic, not Godkin,[7] not Emerson, saw more clearly the unlovely reality or dealt with it more scathingly, not only in *Leaves of Grass* but especially in his prose writings and in casual talk. Amongst scores of such passages a single one must serve for illustration.

> I say that our New World democracy, however great a success in uplifting the masses out of their sloughs, in materialistic

---

[6] "Song of Myself," lines 483–492.
[7] Edwin Lawrence Godkin (1831–1902), American editor and founder of *The Nation* [*Editors*].

development, products, and in a certain highly-deceptive superficial popular intellectuality, is, so far, an almost complete failure in its social aspects, and in really grand religious, moral, literary, and esthetic results. . . . Shift and turn the combinations of the statement as we may, the problem of the future of America is in certain respects as dark as it is vast. Pride, competition, segregation, vicious wilfulness, and license beyond example, brood already upon us. Unwieldy and immense, who shall hold in behemoth? who bridle leviathan? Flaunt it as we choose, athwart and over the roads of our progress loom huge uncertainty, and dreadful threatening gloom. It is useless to deny it: Democracy grows rankly up the thickest, noxious, deadliest plants and fruits of all—brings worse and worse invaders—needs newer, larger, stronger, keener compensations and compellers. Our lands embracing so much . . . hold in the breast that flame also, capable of consuming themselves, consuming us all. . . . Even today, amid these whirls, incredible flippancy, and blind fury of parties, infidelity, entire lack of first-rate captains and leaders, added to the plentiful meanness and vulgarity of the ostensible masses—that problem, the labor question, beginning to open like a yawning gulf, rapidly widening every year—what prospect have we? We sail a dangerous sea of seething currents, cross and under-currents, vortices,— all so dark and untried.[8]

As a realist Whitman granted the worst charges of the critics of democracy, but he probed deeper and brought other facts to light that modified the equation. It was the difficult question the old Federalists had posed and that Carlyle had lately revived—the question, is not this meanness inseparable from democracy? is not your people in fact a great beast, requiring the lash and the curb? It was the crux of the long debate over democracy and to it Whitman gave anxious and frequent consideration. In fighting the battle of 1790 over again, like Jefferson he rested his case on the native integrity and measureless potentiality of the "bulk-people"—they are the deep soil from which spring the abundant fruits and flowers of civilization. Gentle-nurtured folk do not understand this—they do not like the rank qualities of vital being. Matthew Arnold "always gives you the notion that he hates to touch the dirt—the dirt is so dirty! But everything comes out of the

8 Whitman, *Prose Works 1892*, ed. Floyd Stovall (New York: New York University Press, 1963–64), vol. II, *Collect and Other Prose* (1964), pp. 370, 422 [*Editors*].

dirt—everything: everything comes out of the people . . . not university people, not F.F.V. people: people, people, just people!" In the rude, vital, natural man is the inexhaustible wellspring of good and evil; "He's got it all . . . not only the cruel, beastly, hoggish, cheating, bedbug qualities, but also the spiritual—the noble—the high-born"; in "some ways" he is a "devil of a fellow," but he is not "all devil or even chiefly devil." And because he is not chiefly devil such love and beauty and justice and comradeship as there is in the world, such progress in civilization as has been made hitherto, have been possible— how otherwise? If he has journeyed thus far out of the primeval slime, what bounds shall be set to his eventual journeyings? Why put out one's eyes with a mere handful of years?

So Whitman projected his democratic commonwealth far into the future; he would not have us believe that it had been realized here in America. Political democracy, the struggle for political rights that had engaged America hitherto, was only negative, a necessary preliminary to the ultimate reality. "I submit," he said, "that the fruition of democracy, on aught like a grand scale, resides altogether in the future," and its realization depends upon the use to which the people put their freedom. If from it emerges a proud and self-conscious individualism— "the quality of Being, in the object's self, according to its own central idea and purpose, and of growing therefrom and thereto—not criticism by other standards, and adjustments thereto"—then democracy on a grand scale will be possible and the self-reliant citizen will take his place in a free creative society. The ideal of the growing man, and the ideal of the perfect State—broadly social rather than narrowly political —these were his twin ideals; and the tie that is to bind men together in spontaneous solidarity is love. How characteristic is his sketch of the perfect city, and how deeply saturated with the Enlightenment! There is wanting only a physiocratic economics to make it perfect.

A great city is that which has the greatest men and women,
. . . .
Where the city stands with the brawniest breeds of orators and
    bards,
Where the city stands that is belov'd by these, and loves them in
    return and understands them,
Where no monuments exist to heroes but in the common words
    and deeds,
Where thrift is in its place, and prudence is in its place,
Where the men and women think lightly of the laws,

Where the slave ceases and the master of slaves ceases,
Where the populace rise at once against the never-ending audac-
    ity of elected persons,

.   .   .   .

Where outside authority enters always after the precedence of
    inside authority,
Where the citizen is always the head and ideal, and President,
    Mayor, Governor and what not, are agents for pay,
Where children are taught to be laws to themselves, and to
    depend on themselves,
Where equanimity is illustrated in affairs,

.   .   .   .

Where the city of faithfulest friends stands,
Where the city of the cleanliness of the sexes stands,

.   .   .   .

There the great city stands.[9]

Individualism, solidarity—on such strong bases he erected his ideal democracy, and the heaven-reaching temple will be overlaid with the rich arts and graces of a civilization worthy at last of the name. Such was the Enlightenment as it came to flower in the passionate idealism of Walt Whitman—a dream that was mocked and flouted and nullified by the Drews and Fisks and Goulds[1]—the "hoggish, cheating, bedbug qualities" of a generation that scorned him for a beast. Even his stout faith was shaken at times by the infidelities of the Gilded Age. He was troubled by the gap that opened between the free individual and the perfect State. "I seem to be reaching for a new politics—for a new economy," he confessed in 1888; "I don't quite know what, but for something."[2] Although he protested, "The older I grow . . . the more I am confirmed in my optimism, my democracy," he projected his hopes farther into the future. He sympathized with the socialists but he was not one of them. His revolutionary ardor abated and he preferred in later years to call himself an evolutionist.[3] "Be radical—be radical," he said to Traubel, "be not too damned radical."[4] With his catholic sympathies that refused all bitterness he could not be a partisan—"after

[9] "Song of the Broad-Axe," lines 108, 115–121, 123–126, 130–131, 134.
[1] Daniel Drew (1797–1879), Jay Gould (1836–1892), and James Fisk (1834–1872) were American speculators of the post–Civil War era, which Parrington had dubbed "The Great Barbecue" [*Editors*].
[2] Traubel, I, 101.
[3] *Ibid*, 193, 216.
[4] *Ibid*, 223.

the best the partisan will say something, something better will be said by the man."[5]

So in the twilight of the romantic revolution Whitman quietly slipped away. The great hopes on which he fed have been belied by after events—so his critics say; as the great hopes of the Enlightenment have been belied. Certainly in this welter of today, with science become the drab and slut of war and industrialism, with sterile money-slaves instead of men, Whitman's expansive hopes seem grotesque enough. Democracy may indeed be only a euphemism for the rulership of fools. Yet in a time of huge infidelities, in the dun breakdown and disintegration of all faiths, it is not wholly useless to recall the large proportions of Walt Whitman, his tenderness, his heartiness, his faith, his hope. There was in him no weak evasion, no sniveling over the shards of the goodly vessel broken at the well, but even when "old, alone, sick, weak-down, melted-worn with sweat," a free and joyous acceptance of life.

> Thanks in old age—thanks ere I go,
> For health, the midday sun, the impalpable air—for life, mere life,
>
> .   .   .   .
>
> For all my days—not those of peace alone—the days of war the same,
> For gentle words, caresses, gifts from foreign lands,
> For shelter, wine and meat—for sweet appreciation,
>
> .   .   .   .
>
> For beings, groups, love, deeds, words, books—for colors, forms,
> For all the brave strong men—devoted, hardy, men—who've forward sprung in freedom's help, all years, all lands,
> For braver, stronger, more devoted men—(a special laurel ere I go, to life's war's chosen ones,
> The cannoneers of song and thought—the great artillerists—the foremost leaders, captains of the soul:)
> As soldier from an ended war return'd—As traveler out of myriads, to the long procession retrospective,
> Thanks—joyful thanks!—a soldier's, traveler's thanks.[6]

A great figure, the greatest assuredly in our literature—yet perhaps only a great child—summing up and transmitting into poetry all the passionate aspirations of an America that had passed through the

[5] *Ibid*, 363.
[6] "Thanks in Old Age," lines 1–2, 4–6, 9–14.

romantic revolution, the poet of selfhood and the prophet of brother-hood, the virile man and the catholic lover—how shall Walt Whitman become dumb or cease to speak to men unless the children of those who are now half-devil and half-God shall prove to be wholly devil—or wholly moron?

HENRY ALONZO MYERS

Whitman's Conception of the Spiritual Democracy, 1855–1856†

I

Although more than forty years have passed since Walt Whitman's death, his message has not yet become a part of our national cultural heritage. This loss to America is attributable to the failure of the average reader, and of many critics, to grasp the essential significance, the permanent element, in his writings. The literature of comment and controversy accumulated in his name has sometimes replaced old misinterpretations with new ones; more often it has perpetuated the good gray nonsense of tradition. Whitman's recent fame, like his earlier infamy, has been founded on the sands of changing literary and social conventions, for his notoriety has become fame only as the customs which he ignored have gone out of fashion; and his work, sometimes vilified, sometimes appreciated, has frequently been understood in its relations to other things rather than in its own inner meaning.

It has been his fate to be used as a means rather than to be considered as an end; his effigy, not the true Whitman, served as a central figure in two bloodless civil wars, fought for emancipation from the old literary forms and from the conceptions of sex current in the nineteenth century. A new and an incidental Whitman has been revealed with each change in popular interest, and the true Whitman, who might otherwise have been found in the text of his writings, has been obscured by the smoke of battle raised by his self-appointed disciples. Whitman remains, abroad and at home, the poet of political

† From *American Literature*, VI (November, 1934), 239–246. Copyright 1934 by Duke University Press and reprinted by permission of the publisher. (References to Whitman's texts have been changed to reflect the page numbers in the Norton Critical Edition.)

democracy and social freedom, the advocate of certain strange personal modes of behavior, in spite of the fact that a sober analysis of *Leaves of Grass* proves that the Whitman of 1855, convinced that he had a large mission to fulfill, brought to world literature a new and profound interpretation of life in terms of an inner, spiritual democracy, an interpretation which has often been so completely overlooked that Whitman's brief period of fame as the poet of adolescent America, already past its zenith, seems to approach decline. Nor will he remain the poet of the present and of the future as well as of the past, unless we turn our attention to this spiritual democracy, realizing that he is the poet, not of a social and economic period, but of an America that never dies.

Although few have yet shown an understanding of Whitman's mission and fulfillment, the better part of the appreciation of his work has been based on a true feeling, an intuitive grasp, of his meaning. Emerson, in view of his lack of warmth toward the reformers of society, could hardly have greeted him warmly, as he did, at the beginning of a great career which was to consist merely of conflicts with convention. Nor could merely accidental elements in his writings have attracted Thoreau, Burroughs, Garland, Tennyson, and Swinburne, who were often repelled by his eccentricities and drawn back only by a feeling of his intrinsic greatness. This feeling indeed has doubtless haunted a host of other commentators, who, through their inability to express in rational discourse the deep meaning which they feel in Whitman's poetry, have been reduced from the position of critics to the level of the aesthetic chatterboxes who must express themselves by such banalities as Homeric or Cosmic.

It may well be that the correct interpretation of Whitman will eventually owe more to the frank opposition to the poet expressed by certain critics than to the often inchoate exposition of his admirers. Certainly, we can take no better starting-point than the question raised over thirty years ago by John Jay Chapman, a question he obviously thought only an idiot could answer in the affirmative: "Can the insulting jumble of ignorance and effrontery, of scientific phrase and French paraphrase, of slang and inspired adjective, which he [Whitman] puts forward with the pretence that it represents thought, be regarded, from any possible point of view, as a philosophy, or a system, or a belief?"[1] This question, since it immediately challenges the essential Whitman, is quite properly the question to have in mind throughout our undertaking.

[1] John Jay Chapman, *Emerson and Other Essays* (New York, 1898), p. 120.

If we call to mind Bacon's maxim that truth comes out of error more rapidly than out of confusion, we find further help in Santayana's *Interpretations of Poetry and Religion*. There we learn that Whitman "basked in the sunshine of perception and wallowed in the stream of his own sensibility," that for him the world "has no inside," and that in his works "it is a phantasmagoria of continuous visions, vivid, impressive, but monotonous and hard to distinguish in memory."[2] We are indebted to the discrimination which Santayana brought to his task, for these statements are not confusion, but error; they are the exact opposites of the truth, and, as such, they point to the truth as clearly as ever error can.

We have then before us the very questions appropriate to our undertaking. What was Walt Whitman's mission? How did he fulfil it? Is it true that his world has no inside?

Let us first examine the inside of Walt Whitman's world. Most rationalists agree that the inside of the world of appearances or perceptions is not something that would prove tangible if we could reach it, like the kernel of a nut; they believe that the inside of a world of perceptions, always in a state of flux, must be some principle of permanence, for instance, a law or laws. Taking a typical list of perceptions from Walt Whitman, we find the poet looking through them to something akin to the inside of the rationalist's world.

> The sharp-hoofed moose of the north, the cat on the house-sill,
>   the chickadee, the prairie-dog . . .
> I see them and myself the same old law.[3]

Or turning to the pages of "To Think of Time," we find that Whitman is quite as much given to listing the conceptions which make up the inside of his world as to listing the perceptions of the outside.

> The law of the past cannot be eluded!
> The law of the present and future cannot be eluded!
> The law of the living cannot be eluded—it is eternal!
> The law of promotion and transformation cannot be eluded!
> The law of heroes and good-doers cannot be eluded!
> The law of drunkards, informers, mean persons, cannot be
>   eluded![4]

These verses are in themselves sufficient to show that Whitman lived in a world having an inside as well as an outside, and that he

[2] George Santayana, *Interpretations of Poetry and Religion* (New York, 1900), p. 180.
[3] "Song of Myself," lines 249, 252, 1856 text.
[4] "To Think of Time," lines 81–86, 1856 text.

recognized the importance of his inner world. Indeed, we shall find that this world is uppermost in his thought, that it is the very reason and justification for the presentation of a world of experience.

His method of communicating this world is that of giving selected pictures from his own experience. In this method he has the greatest confidence; although he speaks again and again of "the same old law" which he finds in his own experience, the thought of systematically formulating this law never occurs to him. He furnishes us with the materials; we must see the law as he has seen it, feel it as he has felt it. As he tells us in the preface to *November Boughs* (1888), his purposes were always implicit rather than explicit. "After completing my poems," he says, "I am curious to review them in the light of their own (at the time unconscious, or mostly unconscious) intentions, with certain unfoldings of the thirty years they seek to embody."[5] And as we read the two important prefaces to his poems (of 1855 and 1888), we realize that these purposes never became explicit in his mind, that he could never formulate them systematically. For this he had no gift; when he tries to tell us in prose what his purposes are, he is apt to overlook the significance of his own verses: his attempt at explanatory prose simply becomes more poetry, as is evident from the ease with which he recast the 1855 preface into three new poems a year later.

In 1855 indeed he was able to sum up his notion of the function of the poet, although he was unable to develop his statement sufficiently to make it clear. "Of all mankind," he wrote, "the great poet is the equable man. Not in him but off from him things are grotesque or eccentric or fail of their sanity. Nothing out of its place is good and nothing in its place is bad. He bestows on every object or quality its fit proportions neither more nor less." [6] This, which might pass for an expression of democracy or mere indolence, rightly understood is not far from the genius attributed to Sophocles, "who saw life steadily and saw it whole." The right interpretation of this conception of the great poet's function shows us something far different from a desire to bask in perceptual sunshine; we detect a yearning to get beyond the evaluations of finite existence and to apprehend the perfection of everything in its place. For who has come closer to Spinoza's *intellectualis amor Dei* than has Whitman in the 1855 preface? "The known universe," he says, "has one complete lover and that is the greatest poet. He consumes an eternal passion and is indifferent which chance happens and

[5] Whitman, "A Backward Glance O'er Travel'd Roads," in *Leaves of Grass: Comprehensive Reader's Edition*, ed. Harold W. Blodgett and Sculley Bradley (New York: W. W. Norton & Co., 1968), p. 562, *q.v.* above [*Editors*].
[6] Whitman, "Preface 1855," in *Leaves of Grass: Comprehensive Reader's Edition*, p 712, *q.v.* above [*Editors*].

which possible contingency of fortune or misfortune and persuades
daily and hourly his delicious pay."[7] Certainly, if the world of Whitman
has no inside, the world of Spinoza is equally vacuous. But, as we shall
see, Whitman's world has an inside warmer in human values than the
cold necessity which lies at the heart of Spinoza's.

The importance of the inner world to Whitman is apparent in
the fact that he has gone beyond the middle of the 1855 preface before
he turns aside to discuss, as a secondary topic, political liberty and
equality. It is made further apparent when we note the contrast between
the just equality of men proclaimed as an *eternal law* in his poetry and
the political inequality discovered by his sober and critical analysis of
the American experiment in *Democratic Vistas*. In the preface (1855)
Whitman insists again and again that the perfect poet will find all
beings equal in his eyes, *not in society*, but in the inner world. In order
to discover this equality the poet must pierce through the surface to
the inside. "The poets of as kosmos advance through all interpositions
and coverings and turmoils and stratagems to first principles."[8] The
first principle of equality is to be seen first by the poet (Whitman in
this preface compares the poetic faculty to clear vision). He retained
this conception of the poet's function in looking back over his com-
pleted work. "Whatever may have been the case in years gone by, the
true use for the imaginative faculty of modern times is to give ultimate
vivification to facts, to science, and to common lives, endowing them
with glows and glories and final illustriousness which belong to every
real thing, and to real things only."[9] This preoccupation with first prin-
ciples, this yearning to see all things as they really are, this earnest
exhortation to pierce all outward coverings and turmoils is the keynote
in the preface to the poetry of a barbarian wallowing in the stream of
his own sensibility, a barbarian whose world "has no inside"!

But when we examine the poetry itself, especially the poems of
1855 and 1856, we are grateful to Santayana for turning our attention
to the inside of Whitman's world. We rub our eyes. Why have we so
long missed this plainly written message?

II

Giving up the notion that the Civil War brought Whitman to
poetic maturity, let us consider the poems in the 1855 edition in their
proper order, holding in mind Whitman's contention that the poet's

[7] *Ibid.*, p. 715, above [*Editors*].
[8] *Ibid.*, p. 721, above [*Editors*].
[9] "A Backward Glance O'er Travel'd Roads," p. 564, above [*Editors*].

function is to see things clearly and to reveal that *eternal* equality of beings which may be known by seeing each thing in its place and as it really is. Here, if anywhere, we shall find the immediate result of that mental simmering which had recently been brought to a boil.

The first poem, "Walt Whitman," long famous as the anthem of provincial egotism, proves a perfect expression of the transcendentalist's method of belief, just as *Cogito, ergo sum* is the starting-point of Descartes's method of doubt. In the attempt to see things as they really are, what is more natural than that the poet, like the philosopher, should start with what is nearest at hand, himself? The poem is a progressive attempt to define or understand one real thing, Walt Whitman.

"What is a man anyhow? What am I? What are you?"[1] The answer is well known to anyone who has read the poem. A man is not something small, contained within an impermeable shell, and set off against a world order.

> I pass death with the dying, and birth with the new-washed babe,
> and am not contained between my hat and boots. . . .[2]

Who is Walt Whitman? He is infinite; he is of the past and of the present and future, of the old and of the young; his personality admits no barriers; he sees through good and evil, through space and time. He pervades everything, becomes everything; he has died a thousand deaths; he has carefully considered you before you were born. He will admit no limitations.

This splendid poem proceeds in the most concrete manner imaginable through great sweeping enumerations of the things with which Whitman identifies himself, not by logical argument, but by a sympathy and understanding which have seldom been equaled. It is splendid poetry; at the same time it comes very close to the most famous philosophical theories of what the self is or ought to be. Putting this imaginative insight into matter-of-fact terms, we find that for Whitman a man is not an empty something that has experiences; a man is rather the sum total of his experiences. A man is as unlimited as his experience; in thought he is the whole world; everything comes within his experience; in thought he is the whole world; everything that comes within his experience is a part of him, and even things of which he is not explicitly or immediately aware, the past and the future, are also parts of him. "The world," said Schopenhauer, "is my idea." Were we

---

[1] "Song of Myself," line 391.
[2] "Song of Myself," line 133.

looking for terms to explain Spinoza's notion of the ideal self or Hegel's notion of the escape from the state of isolation and "unhappy consciousness" by identification of self with reality, we should not need to change any term in Whitman's conception.

Emerson wrote in his diary (1840): "In all my lectures, I have taught one doctrine, namely, the infinitude of the private man."[3] Whitman very probably took over this idea from Emerson without being consciously aware of it; he derived the spirit rather than a formal doctrine from the master, and he embodied this spirit according to his own peculiar talents. It emerges as the infinite and self-contained person, who is the sum total of his experiences. Such is the conception which Whitman sets over against the "featherless biped" of the logicians and the "political animal" of those whose world has a social surface but no inside.

Thus the idea of an unlimited personality is the first principle of *Leaves of Grass*. It is accompanied at every point by the further principle of equality, for it is not only Walt Whitman who is an unlimited, all-embracing personality. The very opening verses make this assertion:

> I celebrate myself,
> And what I assume you shall assume;
> For every atom belonging to me, as good belongs to you.[4]

Taken out from the poetry and set up as theory, the grounds on which he asserts this equality are not illogical. Equality exists only in a world of unlimited personalities. How can one unlimited personality be either more or less than another? This argument, expressed in accordance with his method, may be found in the verses made out of the 1855 preface:

> Have you thought there could be but a single Supreme?
> There can be any number of Supremes—one does not countervail
>   another any more than one eye-sight countervails another,
>   or one life countervails another.[5]

Undoubtedly this concept of equality had its origin in the surface world of American democracy, where it had been an ideal since the Declaration of Independence. But with Whitman equality is much more than a political ideal; it is an *eternal fact* in the real world of unlimited personalities; it is a great first principle.

---

[3] *Emerson's Journals*, ed. E. W. Emerson and R. W. Forbes (New York, 1911), V, 380.
[4] "Song of Myself," lines 1–3.
[5] "By Blue Ontario's Shore," lines 24–25.

> In all people I see myself—none more, and not one a barleycorn
>   less,
> And the good or bad I say of myself, I say of them.[6]

Equality of this kind, a real equality between unlimited personalities, is discovered only by piercing through the coverings and turmoils to the insides of beings. Out of the American democracy of 1855, Walt Whitman constructed an inner complement to the outer world, a spiritual democracy governed by two principles, one the unlimited individual, the other the equality of individuals. Finding these principles in the poems is not a matter of judiciously choosing apt quotations; on the contrary, there is nothing in the 1855 and 1856 *Leaves* which does not follow *a priori* from them. Once they are clearly grasped, we soon find that each verse contributes something to them, that each verse is an attempt to read these inner principles through the maze and confusion of life on the surface. Once we grasp the true nature of these principles, realizing that they are, secondarily slogans of the social democracy, we no longer see Walt Whitman's poems as a mere catalogue of perceptions, nor as a mere satisfaction in his own sensibility; moreover, we discover that many of his themes, which have hitherto seemed related only to his eccentricities, are direct consequents of these principles. * * *

CESARE PAVESE

Whitman—Poetry of Poetry Writing†

Too often, it seems to me, the image of Walt Whitman which commentators have before their eyes is that of a bearded centenarian intent on contemplating a butterfly and gathering into his mild eyes the final serenity of all the joys and miseries of the universe. It may be the fault of the photograph which all the definitive editions of *Leaves*

---

[6] "Song of Myself," lines 401–402.
† From *Walt Whitman Abroad*, ed. Gay Wilson Allen (Syracuse, N.Y.: Syracuse University Press, 1955), pp. 189–197. Originally published in Cesare Pavese, *La litteratura americana e altri saggi* (Turin: Einaudi, 1951). The English translation is by Roger Asselineau. Reprinted by permission of the editor and the translator. (References to Whitman's texts have been changed to reflect the page numbers in the Norton Critical Edition.)

of Grass authorized by Bucke, Harned, and Traubel, his literary executors, bear on the frontispiece; or of the myth of a stately prophet, almost a thaumaturge, which his enthusiastic disciples have created; or of his being considered as the unconscious third member of the triad Tolstoy-Hugo-Whitman which for a time obsessed all minds. Though definitively destroyed by the works mainly of English and French critics, the legend of Walt Whitman as a seer, an illuminee, the founder of new religions, the image of Walt Whitman as a handsome white-bearded old man has persisted and unconsciously influences the preferences of readers—and thus the opinion is too wide-spread nowadays that the true, the great Walt is, if not exactly the personality of the last effete sections of Leaves of Grass ("Sands at Seventy"; "Goodbye, My Fancy"; "Old Age Echoes"), at least the man who wrote the short pieces on friendship ("Calamus"), the vigorous and tender war-vignettes entitled "Drum-Taps" and the fugitive visions contained in "Whispers of Heavenly Death." The comparison of a white-bearded Walt Whitman with the poems of "Calamus," composed between thirty-five and forty, which vibrate with such youthful health and self-confidence, will seem strange. And it is well known that poetry is neither youth nor old age; it is simply poetry. But I am not speaking of these sections of Leaves of Grass precisely in this way to disparage them. I am only saying that the commentators of Whitman who tend to reduce all his works *merely* to these pages devoted to impressions or vignettes run the risk of falsifying and minimizing to no inconsiderable extent the unique originality of the poet and even ultimately the vignettes themselves. For, in this way, the poetry of mature inspiration, even though it has produced the short poems of "Calamus," has also given rise after all to something like the long Songs which constellate the first two editions of Leaves of Grass. These should not be judged by the same standard as the effete and disconnected garrulity (the judgment is Walt Whitman's own)[1] of an old age which, we may now say, was not quite Olympian.

Indeed, people frequently forget something which is quite obvious: that when the "sage of Camden" gave the definitive form to the book of his whole life in the 1881 edition—the seventh one—he was merely verifying and concluding at seventy-two years of age the results of a work which he had conceived dimly for the first time at thirty and already completed for the greater part at forty-eight in the 1867 edition —the fourth one. And what Walt Whitman's superb manhood was, that manhood during which he meditated and translated his book into ac-

[1] See "Queries to my Seventieth Year" [Editors].

tions, whoever has not understood it through his poems, may realize it by looking at the photograph which Whitman himself, when he was not yet the "sage of Camden," placed at the beginning of the future "Song of Myself" in 1855, in the first edition of *Leaves of Grass*. A giant with a worker's shirt open at the neck and a thick beard; all his life is concentrated in two mysterious eyes which at times really look quite tender—I believe someone has called this photograph that of a "rowdy." But, whether we like it or not, the Walt Whitman of almost all the *Leaves of Grass* that counts, is this one—at least for those who can understand him.

In spite of the scepticism that has become widespread as the result of a legitimate reaction against the uncritical canonization of the "seer," it can be maintained with good arguments that Walt Whitman has always worked consciously, with a clear critical sense. And it is only natural, for it would be necessary otherwise to turn Walt Whitman, an earthly-minded man and a keen user of the file if ever there was one, into the antipathetic figure of an ecstatic idler into whose ears from time to time a demon whispers his songs. *The Magnificent Idler*[2] is precisely the title of a lively biography in novel form, devoted to him by Cameron Rogers, the scholar who to date, I think, has best understood the poet, precisely because he has not attempted to dissert in a rhetorical manner about the catalogues and the vignettes, the psychic and internal rhymes, his homosexuality or his magnetism and such trifles, but has soundly recreated his man, attributing to him gestures, words, moods, which any unassuming reader can glimpse in the poems. And an idler Walt Whitman truly was in the sense in which every poet is an idler when instead of working he prefers to go for a walk, ruminating and twisting in his mind his future lines or "verses" with much fatigue and the rare joys which compensate for that fatigue. An idler [he was] as regards ordinary kinds of work, because he had other work to do which robbed him of all other interests and perhaps even of some of his sleep. But these things Valéry-Larbaud has already said and very well indeed.[3]

Instead of this, it is important to emphasize that Walt Whitman knew what he was doing and that, when all is said and done—like every artist who achieves something, Walt Whitman ruminated, twisted, lived, *willed* his something, and that, if some of his theoretical pretensions have proved wrong or ill-founded in the long run in the light of our present age, the same thing has happened and keeps hap-

[2] See Cameron Rogers, *The Magnificent Idler: The Story of Walt Whitman*, 1926 [*Editors*].
[3] See Valéry-Larbaud, *Oeuvres Choisies de Walt Whitman*, 1930 [*Editors*].

pening not only to all artists, but also to all men. And if before such
a sentence as: "Isolated advantages in any rank or grace or fortune—
the direct or indirect threads of all the poetry of the past—are in my
opinion distasteful to the republican genius and offer no foundation for
its fitting verse,"[4] anyone will observe that these are things which
should not be said, even in jest, we can answer that it was above all by
means of thoughts of this kind that Walt Whitman managed to clarify
and delimit the proper "poetic matter" and that in any case, immediately
after this heretical sentence, he takes pleasure in relating an anecdote
he had read in his youth—which anecdote will also show how in the old
days when theoreticians were still disputing on *genres* and schools,
artists knew where they stood regarding all these things. Rubens said
to his students before a picture of uncertain authorship: "I do not
believe the artist, unknown and perhaps no longer living, who has
given the world this legacy, ever belonged to any school, or ever
painted anything but this one picture, which is a personal affair—a
piece out of a man's life."[5] And, reporting these words when almost
seventy, Walt Whitman knew what he was saying—knew, if ever any
man in America did, what was a work made out of the whole existence
of one man.

It would be easy, however, by compiling a list of gnomic passages
gleaned from the numerous prefaces, explanations, glosses and mem-
oires with which the volume of his *Prose Works* is crowded, to throw
a paradoxical light on many aspects chosen among the gaudiest of
Whitman's predications, and unsuspected consequences would result
from it—consequences unsuspected not only by the author.

Walt Whitman said: "Our fundamental want today in the United
States, with closest, amplest reference to present conditions, and to the
future, is of a class, of native authors, literatuses, far different, far
higher in grade than any yet known, sacerdotal, modern, fit to cope
with our occasions, lands, permeating the whole mass of American
mentality, taste, belief, breathing into it a new breath of life . . .
affecting politics far more than the popular superficial suffrage, with
results inside and underneath the elections of Presidents or Congresses
—radiating, begetting appropriate teachers, schools, manners, and, as
its grandest result, accomplishing . . . a religious and moral character
beneath the political and productive and intellectual bases of the
States."[6] It should be noted that this is one of his great obsessions; there

---

[4] "A Backward Glance O'er Travel'd Roads," p. 573, above [*Editors*].
[5] See note 4 [*Editors*].
[6] Whitman, *Prose Works 1892*, ed. Floyd Stovall (New York: New York
University Press, 1963–64), vol. II, *Collect and Other Prose* (1964), p. 365.

are traces of it at the very beginning of the volume of his *Prose Works*. If then we put side by side with it the companion obsession whose singularity nobody has yet noticed: the story of the world seen only through its supreme literary manifestations, through the great national poems, and if we recall his naturalistic habit of declaiming in the open air, which frightened the seagulls of Coney Island, as he has described it himself, or entertained the omnibus-drivers of Broadway at the expense of Homer, Shakespeare, Aeschylus, Ossian and other immortals, we shall find it easy to build up on documents such a paradoxical theory of the Whitman phenomenon as we mentioned above. To the aforesaid poems—the contemporaries, Walter Scott and Alfred Tennyson were counted, like Ossian, as great national poets—we must add the numerous magazines of the time, Emerson, natural history books, encyclopaedias, melodramas, and we shall have all the apparent, exterior culture of Walt Whitman.

And then, in conclusion, we shall say that Walt Whitman wanted to do for America what the various national poets have done in their day for their own people. Walt Whitman is quite obsessed with this romantic idea which he was the first to transplant to America; he sees America and the world only in relation to the poem which will express them in the XIXth century and in comparison with this nothing else matters. He it is, the great primitive, the fierce enemy of all literature that deprives nature of its sponaneity—he it is who, in a supreme lament on the extinction of the red race, has said: "(No picture, poem, statement passing down to the future) . . ."[7]

Walt Whitman lived out the idea of this mission so intensely that, though not avoiding the fatal failure of such a design, he yet avoided through it the failure of his work. He did not write the primitive poem of which he dreamed, but the poem of that dream. He did not succeed in his absurd attempt to create a poetry adapted to the democratic and republican world and to the character of the newly discovered land—because poetry is one—but as he spent his life repeating this design in various forms, he made poetry out of this very design, the poetry of the discovery of a world new in history and of the singing of it. To put the apparent paradox in a nutshell, he wrote poetry out of poetry-writing.

But we have said, Walt Whitman worked consciously and with a certain critical sense. And it would seem from this essay on poetic art that he certainly was not the best historian of his own work. The case is complex at this stage. Walt Whitman deceived himself about the

---

[7] "Yonnondio," line 8 [*Editors*].

scope, the effects, and the meaning of *Leaves of Grass;* we might even say that he raved about such matters. But it is quite another matter with the essence and nature of his book and I cannot bring myself to believe that a poet, and especially a poet like Walt Whitman, who undertakes to renovate the expression and the spirit of the taste of his time, if he succeeds in producing something vital, should fail to know afterwards how it is done, in other words that he should fail to know why he has written in this way rather than in that way and on this rather than on that. Especially Walt Whitman, I repeat, who has not even the ambiguous halo of a very young poet to protect himself, but at thirty, after trying various trades, after pitiful attempts at short-story writing and journalism, put together a hundred pages or so after working at it for at least four years, and slowly evolved, developed, enriched, modified it in an indefatigable search for a better expression of his thought. Anyone reflecting upon it without knowing the work would find it quite natural for Walt Whitman to have indulged in doctrinal idiosyncrasies. But there remains the problem that while none of those who shared his culture has been able to draw from it anything but collections of medieval ballads or hymns to progress, Walt Whitman has worked the miracle of *Leaves of Grass*, through it or in spite of it.

And anyone who knows how to read will soon discover in the *Prose Works* certain protests, certain assertions, certain intuitions (for lack of a better word) which are definitely among the best passages of all Whitman's erratic critical essays. Let us think, for instance, of the serenity with which the poet analyzes the reasons and motives of his book in the already quoted *A Backward Glance o'er Travel'd Roads.* The first thing he says about it is this: ". . . a feeling or ambition to articulate and faithfully express in literary or poetic form, and uncompromisingly, my own physical, emotional, moral, intellectual, and aesthetic Personality in the midst of, and tallying, the momentous spirit and facts of its immediate days, and of current America—and to exploit that Personality, identified with place and date, in a far more candid and comprehensive sense than any hitherto poem or book." [8] At bottom, after the usual absurd expositions of the truly democratic nature of *Leaves of Grass*, there recurs as a conclusion the idea that the book is not the expression of an imaginary world, or a gallery of detached figures (the vignettes), but a Person, a sensibility, living in the real world. "*Leaves of Grass* indeed (I cannot too often reiterate) has mainly been the outcropping of my own emotional and other personal nature—an

[8] "A Backward Glance O'er Travel'd Roads," p. 563, above [*Editors*].

attempt, from first to last, to put *a Person*, a human being (myself in the latter half of the Nineteenth Century, in America) freely, fully and truly on record."[9] This idea, besides its critical bearing on Walt Whitman's work, is of singular historical importance, because there appeared with it for the first time in America the problem which in the twentieth century all American artists have again tried to solve. However one may define it, there is something eternal and ever new about this problem. While a European artist, belonging to the Old World, will maintain that the secret of art is to build up a more or less imaginary world, to deny reality in order to replace it by a much more significant one, an American of the recent generations will tell you that his ideal is to reach the true nature of things, to see things with virgin eyes, to attain that "ultimate grip of reality"[1] which alone is worth acquiring. A kind of conscious adaptation of the self to the world and to America. It is therefore fair to recognize that Walt Whitman has not only been the first to evince in his work this tendency of the national culture, but has also discovered it within himself and formulated it with a great critical clarity that few of his commentators have been able to attain.

If I do not believe that the *form* of Walt Whitman's poetry consists of a series of small pictures remarkable for their gracefulness, as many commentators have declared or suggested, I do not believe either that the architecture of the whole book is in any way effective, contrary to what Walt and his disciples always thought.

The small pictures, or vignettes, would be those short impressionistic poems—or fragments of poems—in which a figure, a scene, a thought or a landscape is fixed in its essential lines: and they also had the defect of multiplying pitilessly as he grew older on account of the half-ridiculous, half-pitiful mania of the "sage of Camden" for seeing in every small thing the symbol of his vast system and to express it in a parallel, an image, or a description. Yet, in a nature like this, which had a tendency to prophesy, the vignette, in which he was generally so skilled, rather took the form of an apologue or exemplification justified by the whole of his doctrine and of his book. But more recent critics who have rightly rejected his prophetic pretensions, have merely deprived the vignettes of their support and meaning, reducing them to miserable fragments, and completely destroying the perspective, because it has naturally be-

[9] *Ibid.*, pp. 573–574 [*Editors*].
[1] The phrase is Sherwood Anderson's in *Dark Laughter*, but the general idea can be verified only by studying extensively all the vast field of North American experiments in poetry during the last thirty years.

come the fashion to consider best among the vignettes the more melo-
dramatic of them, like "O Captain! My Captain!," "Come up from the
Fields, Father," and "The Singer in Prison."

The extreme justification of the vignettes, which consisted of
the architectural design of *Leaves of Grass*, represents—as all may
see—the translation into art of the prophetic impulse, the practical
purpose of the book, in the same way as the bold architecture of the
Divine Comedy. Yet, as the architecture of *Leaves of Grass* is made
up of less appreciated philosophical material, or as it bears little
resemblance to a cathedral, or for some other reason, there has been
less hostility towards it than towards that of the *Divine Comedy*,
and the boldest are finally those who accept it, claiming as an ex-
cuse that, all things considered, the order of the poems is in its es-
sential lines the chronological order of their composition,[2] and so
the matter ceases to be worth examining.

Thus we must dismiss the vignettes—the effete or modest im-
pressions as well as the descriptive passages of the long "Songs"—
and the structure of the book—a useless hierarchy imposed on iden-
tical pages of argument or passion—but where then shall we find
Walt Whitman's form?

Let us pause to consider a poem, a long poem I should say, the
hardest piece of *Leaves of Grass*, the "Song of Myself." As early as
the first edition this "Song" stood out as the main poem of the book
though without a title as yet, and it shared the fortune of the rest of
the book, undergoing changes, corrections, suppressions and addi-
tions of all kinds. In 1881 we find it in its definitive form, with
fifty-two sections, enormous even by comparison with the poems of
the first brood "aux titres immenses, les mastodontes et les iguano-
dons de la création whitmanienne."[3] This, "Song of Myself" is, as
it were, the quintessence of *Leaves of Grass*: one can find in it all
the themes, the profound with the simple, contained in Whitman's
poetry.

One of the interesting points about it is that just as the whole
book is worthless as far as the structure is concerned, so this poem
could bear, without any harmful consequences, long suppressions or
additions or transfers, which is precisely what the author has done

---

[2] See the chapter "Plan" in Basil De Sélincourt's *Walt Whitman, A Critical
Study* (London, 1914; New York: Russell & Russell, 1965) pp. 164–187
[*Editors*].
[3] ". . . of the immense titles, the mastodons and iguanodons of Whitman's
creations," Valéry Larbaud, *Oeuvres Choisies de Walt Whitman*, (1930),
p. 32.

or would have gone on doing if he had not been prevented by the accidental occurrence of old age and death. Do we mean by this that the worth of the poem lies in the fragmentary pictures in which some realistic description holds the attention? Not at all, though there are in it passages which can be neglected and others which can be counted among the one hundred best pages of the poetry of all times.

Let us begin with the meter. It is a waste of time—and I have wasted a lot myself—to go through the *Prose Works* of the good gray poet with the hope of extracting from *Specimen Days*, from his experiences as a wound-dresser during the Civil War and his happy holidays as a nudist in the solitude of Timber Creek, pages, fragments, vignettes comparable to similar themes in *Leaves of Grass* and apt to show conclusively that there is no difference between his prose and his poetry. No one admires more than I do the artistic prose of Walt Whitman, but it is further necessary to point out that it was almost all written after the Civil War, during his illness, when his beard was already at least grizzly. I have already shown how, from then on, Walt Whitman brooded rather long over his poems and, though he discovered the new vein which we might call "contemplative" [cf. all *Leaves of Grass* from *Autumn Rivulets* (1881) to *Old Age Echoes* (posthumous)], yet in that Indian summer of the impressions, thoughts, revealing comparisons and endless flowering of his vignettes, in spite of numerous new qualities, there is lacking the vigor and the thrill which transfigured even the most allegorical or dogmatic pages of the first *Leaves of Grass*. Almost all his poems from *Autumn Rivulets* (which he began to compose as early as 1865) to his death, would gain in immediacy, clarity, and power by being written in prose. And the prose passages which accompany them, are indeed undoubtedly preferable. On the contrary, in what he wrote before *Whispers of Heavenly Death* (1871), who wants to read, or even remembers nowadays, his few prose writings? There are therefore two parts in Whitman's work: his poetry and his prose, and there is between his poetry and his prose a fundamental difference which cannot be ignored, for it would amount to confounding, among other things, what Walt Whitman himself differentiated with such care.

RANDALL JARRELL

Some Lines from Whitman†

Whitman, Dickinson, and Melville seem to me the best poets of the 19th Century here in America. Melville's poetry has been grotesquely underestimated, but of course it is only in the last four or five years that it has been much read; in the long run, in spite of the awkwardness and amateurishness of so much of it, it will surely be thought well of. (In the short run it will probably be thought entirely too well of. Melville is a great poet only in the prose of *Moby Dick*.) Dickinson's poetry has been thoroughly read, and well though undifferentiatingly loved—after a few decades or centuries almost everybody will be able to see through Dickinson to her poems. But something odd has happened to the living changing part of Whitman's reputation: nowadays it is people who are not particularly interested in poetry, people who say that they read a poem for what it says, not for how it says it, who admire Whitman most. Whitman is often written about, either approvingly or disapprovingly, as if he were the Thomas Wolfe of 19th Century democracy, the hero of a de Mille movie about Walt Whitman. (People even talk about a war in which Walt Whitman and Henry James chose up sides, to begin with, and in which you and I will go on fighting till the day we die.) All this sort of thing, and all the bad poetry that there of course is in Whitman—for any poet has written enough bad poetry to scare away anybody—has helped to scare away from Whitman most "serious readers of modern poetry." They do not talk of his poems, as a rule, with any real liking or knowledge. Serious readers, people who are ashamed of not knowing all Hopkins by heart, are not at all ashamed to say, "I don't really know Whitman very well." This may harm Whitman in your eyes, they know, but that is a chance that poets have to take. Yet "their" Hopkins, that good critic and great poet, wrote about Whitman, after seeing five or six of his poems in a newspaper review: "I may as well say what I should not otherwise have said, that I always knew in my heart Walt Whitman's mind to be more

† From Randall Jarrell, *Poetry and the Age* (New York: Alfred A. Knopf, 1953), pp. 112–120, 131–132. Copyright 1952, 1953 by Randall Jarrell. Reprinted by permission of Alfred A. Knopf, Inc.

like my own than any other man's living. As he is a very great scoundrel this is not a very pleasant confession." And Henry James, the leader of "their" side in that awful imaginary war of which I spoke, once read Whitman to Edith Wharton (much as Mozart used to imitate, on the piano, the organ) with such power and solemnity that both sat shaken and silent; it was after this reading that James expressed his regret at Whitman's "too extensive acquaintance with the foreign languages." Almost all the most "original and advanced" poets and critics and readers of the last part of the 19th Century thought Whitman as original and advanced as themselves, in manner as well as in matter. Can Whitman really be a sort of Thomas Wolfe or Carl Sandburg or Robinson Jeffers or Henry Miller—or a sort of Balzac of poetry, whose every part is crude but whose whole is somehow great? He is not, nor could he be; a poem, like Pope's spider, "lives along the line," and all the dead lines in the world will not make one live poem. As Blake says, "all sublimity is founded on minute discrimination," and it is in these "minute particulars" of Blake's that any poem has its primary existence.

To show Whitman for what he is one does not need to praise or explain or argue, one needs simply to quote. He himself said, "I and mine do not convince by arguments, similes, rhymes,/ We convince by our presence." Even a few of his phrases are enough to show us that Whitman was no sweeping rhetorician, but a poet of the greatest and oddest delicacy and originality and sensitivity, so far as words are concerned. This is, after all, the poet who said, "Blind loving wrestling touch, sheath'd hooded sharp-tooth'd touch"; who said, "Smartly attired, countenance smiling, form upright, death under the breast-bones, hell under the skull-bones"; who said, "Agonies are one of my changes of garments"; who saw grass as the "flag of my disposition," saw "the sharp-peak'd farmhouse, with its scallop'd scum and slender shoots from the gutters," heard a plane's "wild ascending lisp," and saw and heard how at the amputation "what is removed drops horribly in a pail." This is the poet for whom the sea was "howler and scooper of storms," reaching out to us with "crooked inviting fingers"; who went "leaping chasms with a pike-pointed staff, clinging to topples of brittle and blue"; who, a runaway slave, saw how "my gore dribs, thinn'd with the ooze of my skin"; who went "lithographing Kronos . . . buying drafts of Osiris"; who stared out at the "little plentiful mannikins skipping around in collars and tail'd coat,/ I am aware who they are, (they are positively not worms or fleas)." For he is, at his best, beautifully witty: he says gravely, "I find I incorporate gneiss, coals, long-threaded moss, fruits, grain, esculent roots,/ And

am stucco'd with quadrupeds and birds all over"; and of these quad-
rupeds and birds "not one is respectable or unhappy over the whole
earth." He calls advice: "Unscrew the locks from the doors! Unscrew
the doors from their jambs!" He publishes the results of research:
"Having pried through the strata, analyz'd to a hair, counsel'd with
doctors and calculated close,/ I find no sweeter fat than sticks to my
own bones." Everybody remembers how he told the Muse to "cross
out please those immensely overpaid accounts,/ That matter of Troy
and Achilles' wrath, and Aeneas', Odysseus' wanderings," but his ac-
count of the arrival of the "illustrious emigré" here in the New World
is even better: "Bluff'd not a bit by drainpipe, gasometer, artificial
fertilizers,/ Smiling and pleas'd with palpable intent to stay,/ She's
here, install'd amid the kitchenware." Or he sees, like another
Breughel, "the mechanic's wife with the babe at her nipple inter-
ceding for every person born,/ Three scythes at harvest whizzing in a
row from three lusty angels with shirts bagg'd out at their waists,/
The snag-toothed hostler with red hair redeeming sins past and to
come"—the passage has enough with not only (in Johnson's phrase) to
keep it sweet, but enough to make it believable. He says:

> I project my hat, sit shame-faced, and beg.

> Enough! Enough! Enough!
> Somehow I have been stunn'd. Stand back!
> Give me a little time beyond my cuff'd head, slumbers, dreams,
>   gaping,
> I discover myself on the verge of a usual mistake.

There is in such changes of tone as these the essence of wit. And
Whitman is even more far-fetched than he is witty; he can say about
Doubters, in the most improbable and explosive of juxtapositions: "I
know every one of you, I know the sea of torment, doubt, despair and
unbelief./ How the flukes splash! How they contort rapid as lightning,
with splashes and spouts of blood!" Who else would have said about
God: "As the hugging and loving bed-fellow sleeps at my side through
the night, and withdraws at the break of day with stealthy tread,/
Leaving me baskets cover'd with white towels, swelling the house with
their plenty"?—the Psalmist himself, his cup running over, would have
looked at Whitman with dazzled eyes. (Whitman was persuaded by
friends to hide the fact that it was God he was talking about.) He says,
"Flaunt of the sunshine I need not your bask—lie over!" This unusual
employment of verbs is usual enough in participle-loving Whitman,
who also asks you to "look in my face while I snuff the sidle of evening,"

or tells you, "I effuse my flesh in eddies, and drift it in lacy jags." Here are some typical beginnings of poems: "City of orgies, walks, and joys. . . . Not heaving from my ribb'd breast only. . . . O take my hand Walt Whitman! Such gliding wonders! Such sights and sounds! Such join'd unended links. . . ." He says to the objects of the world, "You have waited, you always wait, you dumb, beautiful ministers"; sees "the sun and stars that float in the open air,/ The apple-shaped earth"; says, "O suns— O grass of graves— O perpetual transfers and promotions,/ If you do not say anything how can I say anything?" Not many poets have written better, in queerer and more convincing and more individual language, about the world's *gliding wonders:* the phrase seems particularly right for Whitman. He speaks of those "circling rivers the breath," of the "savage old mother incessantly crying,/ To the boy's soul's questions sullenly timing, some drown'd secret hissing"— ends a poem, once, "We have voided all but freedom and our own joy." How can one quote enough? If the reader thinks that all this is like Thomas Wolfe he *is* Thomas Wolfe; nothing else could explain it. Poetry like this is as far as possible from the work of any ordinary rhetorician, whose phrases cascade over us like suds of the oldest and most-advertised detergent.

The interesting thing about Whitman's worst language (for, just as few poets have ever written better, few poets have ever written worse) is how unusually absurd, how really ingeniously bad, such language is. I will quote none of the most famous examples; but even a line like O *culpable! I acknowledge. I exposé!* is not anything that you and I could do—only a man with the most extraordinary feel for language, or none whatsoever, could have cooked up Whitman's worst messes. For instance: what other man in all the history of this planet would have said, "I am a habitan of Vienna"? (One has an immediate vision of him as a sort of French-Canadian halfbreed to whom the Viennese are offering, with trepidation, through the bars of a zoological garden, little mounds of whipped cream.) And *enclaircise* —why, it's as bad as *explicate!* We are right to resent his having made up his own horrors, instead of sticking to the ones that we ourselves employ. But when Whitman says, "I dote on myself, there is that lot of me and all so luscious," we should realize that we are not the only ones who are amused. And the queerly bad and merely queer and queerly good will often change into one another without warning: "Hefts of the moving world, at innocent gambols silently rising, freshly exuding,/ Scooting obliquely high and low"—not good, but *queer!*—suddenly becomes, "Something I cannot see puts up libidinous prongs,/ Seas of bright juice suffuse heaven," and it is sunrise.

But it is not in individual lines and phrases, but in passages of some lengths, that Whitman is at his best. In the following quotation Whitman has something difficult to express, something that there are many formulas, all bad, for expressing; he expresses it with complete success, in language of the most dazzling originality:

> *The orchestra whirls me wider than Uranus flies,*
> *It wrenches such ardors from me I did not know I possess'd them,*
> *It sails me, I dab with bare feet, they are lick'd by the indolent*
> *   waves,*
> *I am cut by bitter and angry hail, I lose my breath,*
> *Steep'd amid honey'd morphine, my windpipe throttled in fakes*
> *   of death,*
> *At length let up again to feel the puzzle of puzzles,*
> *And that we call Being.*

One hardly knows what to point at—everything works. But *wrenches* and *did not know I possess'd them;* the incredible *it sails me, I dab with bare feet; lick'd by the indolent; steep'd amid honey'd morphine; my windpipe throttled in fakes of death*—no wonder Crane admired Whitman! This originality, as absolute in its way as that of Berlioz' orchestration, is often at Whitman's command:

> *I am a dance—play up there! the fit is whirling me fast!*
> *I am the ever-laughing—it is new moon and twilight,*
> *I see the hiding of douceurs, I see nimble ghosts whichever way*
> *   I look,*
> *Cache and cache again deep in the ground and sea, and where*
> *   it is neither ground nor sea.*
> *Well do they do their jobs those journeymen divine,*
> *Only from me can they hide nothing, and would not if they*
> *   could,*
> *I reckon I am their boss and they make me a pet besides,*
> *And surround me and lead me and run ahead when I walk,*
> *To lift their cunning covers to signify me with stretch'd arms*
> *   and resume the way;*
> *Onward we move, a gay gang of blackguards! with mirth-*
> *   shouting music and wild-flapping pennants of joy!*

If you did not believe Hopkins' remark about Whitman, that *gay gang of blackguards* ought to shake you. Whitman shares Hopkins' passion for "dappled" effects, but he slides in and out of them with ambiguous swiftness. And he has at his command a language of the calmest and most prosaic reality, one that seems to do no more than present:

The little one sleeps in its cradle.

*I lift the gauze and look a long time, and silently brush away
flies with my hand.*

*The youngster and the red-faced girl turn aside up the bushy
hill,*

I peeringly view them from the top.

The suicide sprawls on the bloody floor of the bedroom.

*I witness the corpse with its dabbled hair, I note where the
pistol has fallen.*

It is like magic: that is, something has been done to us without our
knowing how it was done; but if we look at the lines again we see
the *gauze, silently, youngster, red-faced, bushy, peeringly, dabbled*—
not that this is all we see. "Present! present!" said James; these are
presented, put down side by side to form a little "view of life," from
the cradle to the last bloody floor of the bedroom. Very often the
things presented form nothing but a list:

The pure contralto sings in the organ loft,

*The carpenter dresses his plank, the tongue of his foreplane
whistles its wild ascending lisp,*

*The married and unmarried children ride home to their Thanks-
giving dinner,*

The pilot seizes the king-pin, he heaves down with a strong arm,

*The mate stands braced in the whale-boat, lance and harpoon are
ready,*

The duck-shooter walks by silent and cautious stretches,

The deacons are ordain'd with cross'd hands at the altar,

*The spinning-girl retreats and advances to the hum of the big
wheel,*

*The farmer stops by the bars as he walks on a First-day loafe
and looks at the oats and rye,*

The lunatic is carried at last to the asylum a confirm'd case,

*(He will never sleep any more as he did in the cot in his mother's
bed-room;)*

The jour printer with gray head and gaunt jaws works at his case,

*He turns his quid of tobacco while his eyes blur with the manu-
script,*

The malform'd limbs are tied to the surgeon's table,

What is removed drops horribly in a pail; . . .

It is only a list—but what a list! * * *

They might have put on his tombstone WALT WHITMAN: HE HAD
HIS NERVE. He is the rashest, the most inexplicable and unlikely—the
most impossible, one wants to say—of poets. He somehow *is* in a class
by himself, so that one compares him with other poets about as readily
as one compares *Alice* with other books. (Even his free verse has a
completely different effect from anybody else's.) Who would think of
comparing him with Tennyson or Browning or Arnold or Baudelaire?
—it is Homer, or the sagas, or something far away and long ago, that
comes to one's mind only to be dismissed; for sometimes Whitman *is*
epic, just as *Moby Dick* is, and it surprises us to be able to use
truthfully this word that we have misused so many times. Whitman *is*
grand, and elevated, and comprehensive, and real with an astonishing
reality, and many other things—the critic points at his qualities in
despair and wonder, all method failing, and simply calls them by
their names. And the range of these qualities is the most extraordinary
thing of all. We can surely say about him, "He was a man, take him
for all in all. I shall not look upon his like again"—and wish that
people had seen this and not tried to be his like: one Whitman is
miracle enough, and when he comes again it will be the end of the
world.

I have said so little about Whitman's faults because they are
so plain: baby critics who have barely learned to complain of the
lack of ambiguity in *Peter Rabbit* can tell you all that is wrong with
Leaves of Grass. But a good many of my readers must have felt
that it is ridiculous to write an essay about the obvious fact that
Whitman is a great poet. It is ridiculous—just as, in 1851, it would
have been ridiculous for anyone to write an essay about the obvious
fact that Pope was no "classic of our prose" but a great poet. Critics
have to spend half their time reiterating whatever ridiculously obvious
things their age or the critics of their age have found it necessary to
forget: they say despairingly, at parties, that Wordsworth is a great
poet, and *won't* bore you, and tell Mr. Leavis that Milton is a great
poet whose deposition *hasn't* been accomplished with astonishing
ease by a few words from Eliot. . . . There is something essentially
ridiculous about critics, anyway: what is good is good without our
saying so, and beneath all our majesty we know this.

Let me finish by mentioning another quality of Whitman's—
a quality, delightful to me, that I have said nothing of. If some day
a tourist notices, among the ruins of New York City, a copy of
Leaves of Grass, and stops and picks it up and reads some lines in it,
she will be able to say to herself: "How very American! If he and his

country had not existed, it would have been impossible to imagine them."

RICHARD VOLNEY CHASE

One's Self I Sing†

The main item of the 1855 edition of *Leaves of Grass* was, of course, "Song of Myself," the profound and lovely comic drama of the self which is Whitman's best poem and contains in essence nearly all, yet not quite all, there is to *Leaves of Grass*. The comic spirit of the poem is of the characteristic American sort, providing expression for a realism at once naturalistic and transcendental, for the wit, gaiety, and festive energy of all good comedy, and also for meditative soliloquy, at once intensely personal and strongly generic.

One circumstance that contributes to the general spontaneity of "Song of Myself" is, in fact, Whitman's unsuccessful attempt to be an Emersonian or Wordworthian moralist. In his preface, he wrote that "of all mankind the poet is the equable man. Not in him but off from him things are grotesque or eccentric or fail of their sanity . . . He is the arbiter of the diverse and he is the key. He is the equalizer of his age and land." Whitman tries, indeed, to install himself in his poem on this high moral ground: he will, he says, first regenerate himself by leaving the fallacious artificialities of modern life and getting back to fundamentals; then, having perfected himself as the norm, he will summon all the world to him to be freed of its abnormalities. But although in the poem the self remains pretty much at the center of things, Whitman finds it impossible to accept the idea that it is a norm. To the sententious prophet who "promulges" the normative self, the comic poet and ironic realist keep introducing other, disconcertingly eccentric selves.

Who goes there? hankering, gross, mystical, nude. . . .

Whoever he is, he is not in a position to utter morality. The self in this poem *is* (to use Lawrence's phrase) "tricksy-tricksy"; it does

† From Richard Volney Chase, *Walt Whitman Reconsidered* (New York: William Sloane Associates, 1955), pp. 58–66, 72–73, 81–82. Copyright 1955 by Richard Chase. Reprinted by permission of William Morrow and Company, Inc.

"shy all sorts of ways" and is finally, as the poet says, "not a bit tamed," for "I too am untranslatable." So that as in all true, or high, comedy, the sententious, the too overtly insisted-on morality (if any) plays a losing game with ironical realism. * * *

"I resist anything better than my own diversity," says Whitman, and this is the characteristic note of "Song of Myself." * * * If one finds "Song of Myself" enjoyable at all, it is because one is conscious of how much of the poem, though the feeling in many of its passages need not perhaps have been comic at all, nevertheless appeals to one, first and last, in its comic aspect. The poem is full of odd gestures and whimsical acts; it is written by a neo-Ovidian poet for whom self-metamorphosis is almost as free as free association, who can write "I am an old artillerist" or "I will go to the bank by the wood, and become undisguised and naked" as easily as he can write:

> Askers embody themselves in men and I am embodied in them,
> I project my hat, sit shame-faced, and beg.

The sense of incongruous diversity is very strong in "Song of Myself," and although one does not know how the sly beggar projecting his hat or the martial patriot is transformed into the "acme of things accomplish'd," and "encloser of things to be" who suddenly says:

> I find I incorporate gneiss, coal, long-threaded moss, fruits, grains, esculent roots,
> And am stucco'd with quadrupeds and birds all over,

one is nevertheless charmed with the transformation.

Whitman conceives of the self, one might say, as James conceives of Christopher Newman in *The American*—as having the "look of being committed to nothing in particular, of standing in an attitude of general hospitality to the chances of life." In other words, the "self" who is the protagonist of Whitman's poem is a character portrayed in a recognizable American way; it illustrates the fluid, unformed personality exulting alternately in its provisional attempts to define itself and in its sense that it has no definition. The chief difference between "Song of Myself" and *The American* is, of course, the difference between the stages on which Whitman and James allow the self to act, James confining the action to his international scene and Whitman opening his stage out into an eventful universe which is a contradictory but witty collocation of the natural and the transcendent, the imperfect and the utopian, the personal and the generic—a dialectic world out of whose "dimness opposite equals advance" and in which there is "always a knit of identity" but "always distinction."

The very scope of Whitman's universe and the large freedom he assumes to move about in it allowed him to appropriate new areas of experience and thus to make of "Song of Myself" the original and influential poem it is. For one thing, this is the first American poem to invade that fruitful ground between lyric verse and prose fiction that so much of modern poetry cultivates, and one may suppose that "Song of Myself" has had at least as much effect on the novel as, let us say, *Moby Dick* or *The Golden Bowl* have had on poetry. The famous lines in Section 8 are, at any rate, both "imagistic" and novelistic:

> The little one sleeps in its cradle;
> I lift the gauze and look a long time, and silently brush away
>   flies with my hand.
> The youngster and the red-faced girl turn aside up the bushy
>   hill;
> I peeringly view them from the top.
> The suicide sprawls on the bloody floor of the bedroom;
> I witness the corpse with its dabbled hair, I note where the
>   pistol has fallen.

It is probably true that more than anyone else, more than Blake or Baudelaire, Whitman made the city poetically available to literature:

> The blab of the pave, tires of carts, sluff of boot-soles, talk of
>   the promenaders,
> The heavy omnibus, the driver with his interrogating thumb,
>   the clank of the shod horses on the granite floor . . .

Such lines as these have been multitudinously echoed in modern prose and poetry, they have been endlessly recapitulated by the journey of the realistic movie camera up the city street. One might argue that Whitman's descriptions of the city made possible T. S. Eliot's *Waste Land*. The horror of Eliot's London, as of Baudelaire's "*cité pleine de rêves*," is unknown in *Leaves of Grass*, but was not Whitman the first poet, so to speak, who put real typists and clerks in the imaginary city?

There can be no doubt that "Song of Myself" made sex a possible subject for American literature, and in this respect Whitman wrought a great revolution in, for example, his beautiful idyllic scene in which the "handsome and richly drest" woman imagines herself to join the "twenty-eight young men" who "bathe by the shore." In such a passage as this (as Henry Adams was to point out) American literature was moving toward the freedom and inclusiveness that came more naturally to Europeans—to Flaubert, or Chekhov, whose panoramic novelette

The Steppe includes a similarly idyllic scene of bathing and sexuality. It is sex, too, although of an inverted kind, that allows Whitman to write the following unsurpassable lines in which love is at once so sublimely generalized and perfectly particularized:

> And [I know] that a kelson of the creation is love,
> And limitless are leaves stiff or drooping in the fields,
> And brown ants in the little wells beneath them,
> And mossy scabs of the worm fence, and heap'd stones, elder,
>   mullein and poke-weed.

No summary view of "Song of Myself" would be complete without reference to the elegiac tone of the concluding lines. If, as we have been saying, Whitman's poem is remarkable for its gross inclusive scope, his elegiac verse is a great act of discrimination and nicety. Where else, in the generally grandiose nineteenth-century melodrama of love and death shall we find anything like the delicate precision of these incomparable lines?[1]

As every poet does, Whitman asks us provisionally to accept the imagined world of his poem. It is a fantastic world in which it is presumed that the self can become identical with all other selves in the universe, regardless of time and space. Not without precedent in Hindu poetry, this central metaphor is, as an artistic device, unique in American literature, as is the extraordinary collection of small imagist poems, versified short stories, realistic urban and rural genre paintings, inventories, homilies, philosophizings, farcical episodes, confessions, and lyric musings it encompasses in "Song of Myself." Yet as heavily taxing our powers of provisional credence, as inventing a highly idiosyncratic and illusory world, "Song of Myself" invites comparison with other curious works of the American imagination— *Moby Dick*, let us say, and *The Scarlet Letter* and *The Wings of the Dove*. It is of the first importance at any rate to see that Whitman's relation of the self to the rest of the universe is a successful aesthetic or compositional device, whatever we may think of it as a moral assertion.

If we look at Whitman's implicit metaphor more closely, we see that it consists in the paradox of "identity." The opening words of *Leaves of Grass*, placed there in 1867, state the paradox:

> One's-self I sing, a simple separate person,
> Yet utter the word Democratic, the word En-Masse.

[1] See lines 1334–1346, p. 89, above [*Editors*].

In more general terms the opening lines of "Song of Myself" state the same paradox:

> I celebrate myself and sing myself;
> And what I assume you shall assume;
> For every atom belonging to me, as good belongs to you.

Both politically and by nature man has "identity," in two senses of the word: on the one hand, he is integral in himself, unique, and separate; on the other hand, he is equal to, or even the same as, everyone else. Like the Concord transcendentalists, Whitman was easily led in prophetic moods to generalize the second term of the paradox of identity beyond the merely human world and with his ruthless equalitarianism to conceive the All, a vast cosmic democracy, placid, without episode, separation or conflict, though suffused, perhaps, with a bland illumination. More than anything else, it is this latter tendency which finally ruined Whitman as a poet, submerging as it did, his chief forte and glory—his entirely original, vividly realistic presentation of the comedy and pathos of "the simple separate person."

What finally happens is that Whitman loses his sense that his metaphor of self vs. en-masse is a *paradox*, that self and en-masse are in dialectic opposition. When this sense is lost the spontaneously eventful, flowing, and largely indeterminate universe of "Song of Myself" is replaced by a universe that is both mechanical and vaguely abstract. Whatever, in this universe, is in a state of becoming is moving toward the All, and the self becomes merely the vehicle by which the journey is made.

In some of his best as well as in some of his worst poems, Whitman actually conceives of the self as making a journey—for example, "Song of the Open Road," "Crossing Brooklyn Ferry," and "Passage to India." In others the self journeys, as it were, not forward and outward but backward and inward, back to the roots of its being, and discovers there a final mystery, or love, comradeship, or death—for example, the *Calamus* and *Sea Drift* poems. (Notably among the latter are "Out of the Cradle Endlessly Rocking" and "As I Ebb'd with the Ocean of Life".) In "Song of Myself," however, the self is not felt to be incomplete; it has no questing odyssey to make. It stands aggressively at the center of things, "Sure as the most certain sure, plumb in the uprights, well entretied, braced in the beams." It summons the universe, "syphons" universal experience through its dilating pores, calls "anything back again when I desire it." Or the self imagines itself to be infinitely expandable and contractible (like the web of the spider in Whitman's little poem called "A Noiseless Patient

Spider"), so that there is no place where at any moment it may not be, no thing or person with whom it may not merge, no act in which it may not participate. Of great importance is the fact that most of "Song of Myself" has to do not with the self searching for a final identity but with the self escaping a series of identities which threaten to destroy its lively and various spontaneity. This combination of attitudes is what gives "Song of Myself" the alternately ecstatic and gravely musing, pastoral-godlike stability one feels at the center, around which, however, the poet is able to weave the most astonishing embellishments of wit and lyric song.

This is perhaps a valid way of feeling the sifting modes of sensibility in the poem. Yet it would be wrong to attribute any clear cut structure to "Song of Myself." "The United States themselves are essentially the greatest poem," wrote Whitman in his preface. A Jacksonian Democrat, Whitman was not an admirer of federal unity, either in a nation or a poem. He was content to make his poem a loose congeries of states and half-settled territories. He was content that his poem should mirror that "freshness and candor of . . . physiognomy," that "picturesque looseness of carriage," and that "deathless attachment to freedom" which, in his preface, he attributed to his countrymen. His style would be organic; he would "speak in literature with the perfect rectitude and insouciance" of animals and growing things. Although capable of finely pictorial images, Whitman composed more by ear than by eye, and his ear being attuned to music of the looser, more variable sort, such as the Italian operas, he strung his poems together on a free melodic line and by means of motifs, voices, recapitulations, recitatives, rests, *crescendi* and *diminuendi*.

* * *

Considered as a comic poem, "Song of Myself" combines Dionysian gaiety and an impulse toward verbal artificiality with the tone and cultural presuppositions of American humor—a striking feat of hybridization certainly, yet no more so than that which produced *Moby Dick*. The intention here is not to deny the justice of Emerson's remark that Whitman's poem was "a remarkable mixture of the *Bhagvatgeeta* and the *New York Herald*" or of the voluminous but one-sided academic scholarship which, following Emerson's remark, has regarded "Song of Myself" as an amalgam of Oriental philosophy and American realism. The intention is rather to shift the ground of discourse toward a more strictly literary view—the view which Emerson also adumbrated in his remark that the first edition of *Leaves of Grass* was an "extraordinary piece of wit and wisdom."

In 1889 Whitman said to his Camden friends, "I pride myself on being a real humorist underneath everything else" and when it was

suggested that he might after all go down in history as a "comedian"
he replied that one "might easily end up worse." He will certainly
not go down in history as, purely and simply, a comedian. But humor
was always a strong part of his sensibility, and it is difficult to see
how it ever came to be a cliché about Whitman that "he had no
sense of humor." There is substantial evidence that in his early life his
mind turned naturally toward comic writing. Much of his newspaper
work, particularly the "Sun-Down Papers From the Desk of a School-
master," which he wrote for the *Long Island Democrat* and the
sketches he did for the New Orleans *Crescent* (1848) show that he had
mastered at least the easier tricks of the native folk humor. * * *

One may even suppose that future readers may find Whitman
more relevant to their vital concerns than the tragic moralists among
our American writers. Of these tragic moralists, with their pastoral
legend, Cooper may seem the first and Hemingway the last. Yet Whit-
man may be regarded as more modern than Hemingway. For was it
not Whitman who first sought out the grounds on which in the midst
of our urban modernization the individual with all his dilemmas and
aspirations can exist, whereas Hemingway still clings to a version
of nineteenth-century romanticism which in Melville and Mark Twain
was already nostalgic? The future reader may not think it an extreme
case if someone should remark to him that Whitman's utopian rejec-
tion of society is under modern conditions the necessary first step
toward the preservation of what is vital in society and the revitalization
of what is not, and, furthermore, that despite his intellectual short-
comings, despite even the final disappearance of his idealism into
the All, Whitman knew more of the homely root facts of the life of
modern society than did Melville or Mark Twain, and that at his best
his vision stubbornly began and ended with these root facts.

GAY WILSON ALLEN

Walt Whitman: "Cosmos-Inspired"†

Whitman delineated his poetic role most clearly—or at least
most vividly—in the Preface to his first edition of *Leaves of Grass*,

† From Gay Wilson Allen, "Walt Whitman: 'Cosmos-Inspired,' " in *New
World Writing: 8* (New York: New American Library, 1955), pp. 273–280.
Copyright 1955 by Gay Wilson Allen. Reprinted by permission of New

and it was both cosmological and national. Cosmologically, the poet that Whitman wanted to be was the "one complete lover" of the known universe, i.e., of the natural order of existence, and out of his love for the physical world he could intuit the spiritual world which gives life and existence to the physical. This love and intuition enabled the poet to acquire the "wisdom" which we have already noticed, wisdom which defies adequate translation into words, but in passage after passage Whitman reveals his conviction that in the eternal scheme of creation each part, regardless of how seemingly trivial, is equally important and equally immortal. In fact, he believes that there is no actual termination of existence of any kind—no death—only change. What is called "death," therefore, is no more to be feared than birth, for both are merely stages in the everlasting cycles of life.

Consequently Whitman's poems are filled with symbols of resurrection, from fish eggs to sprouting grass and Adam propagating the human race.

> I believe a leaf of grass is no less than the journey-work of
>   the stars,
> And the pismire is equally perfect, and a grain of sand, and
>   the egg of the wren,
> And the tree-toad is a chef-d'oeuvre for the highest,
> And the running blackberry would adorn the parlors of
>   heaven, . . .

Whitman worships the human body not only because every man or woman is the son or daughter of God (one of the tenets in his "new" religion) but also because it ferries the seeds of life, so that each person bridges, potentially at least, past and future generations. The act of procreation he describes as

> Parting track'd by arriving, perpetual payment of perpetual
>   loan,
> Rich showering rain, and recompense richer afterward.
>
> Sprouts take and accumulate, stand by the curb prolific and vital,
> Landscapes projected masculine, full-sized and golden.

The poet, too, is a propagator, and Whitman often uses sexual imagery to describe his function, begetting a new race on women fit for conception. And this is not inconsistent with his role as cultural time-binder, conserving the knowledge and experience of past genera-

---

American Library and Gay Wilson Allen. This selection comprises the last three of a five-section essay.

tions and by his imaginative intuition drawing upon the future, thereby making both past and future present and available to his readers:

> Without effort, and without exposing in the least how it is done, the greatest poet brings the spirit of any or all events and passions and scenes and persons, some more and some less, to bear on your individual character as you hear or read. To do this well is to compete with the laws that pursue and follow Time. What is the purpose must surely be there and the clue of it must be there— and the faintest indication is the indication of the best, and then becomes the clearest indication. Past and present and future are not disjoin'd but join'd. The greatest poet forms the consistence of what is to be, from what has been and is. He drags the dead out of their coffins and stands them again on their feet. He says to the past, Rise and walk before me that I may realize you. He learns the lesson—he places himself where the future becomes the present.[1]

The poet capable of performing these miracles would have to be "great" indeed, and Whitman calls him not only a poet of the cosmos but himself a "kosmos" [Whitman's preferred spelling], that is, a symbolical microcosm of the macrocosm. By the magic of sympathetic identification the symbolical "I" can range back and forth in time and space, thus in a sense annihilating time and space. Whitman's poems are suffused with "cosmic emotion" when he images the evolutionary processes which have culminated in his own birth and personal identity in the present physical world—see section 44 of "Song of Myself."

> *All forces have been steadily employ'd to complete and delight*
> *me,*
> *Now on this spot I stand with my robust soul.*

Here Whitman drew simultaneously upon both mysticism and contemporary science. As a mystic he intuited "the kelson of the universe" to be love, and he trusted the "Faithful and friendly . . . arms" of nature that had carried and guided him to the present moment of human existence, but scientific theory (in astronomy, biology, and geology, all of which he studied in books, lectures, and journalistic popularizations) enabled him to visualize his evolutionary origin:

---

[1] Quoted from 1882 revised version of 1855 preface.

My feet strike an apex of the apices of the stairs,
On every step bunches of ages, and larger
        bunches between the steps,
All below duly travel'd, and still I mount and mount.

. . . .

Cycles ferried my cradle, rowing and rowing
        like cheerful boatmen,
For room to me stars kept aside in their own rings,
They sent influences to look after what was to hold me.

Before I was born out of my mother generations guided me,
My embryo has never been torpid, nothing could overlay it.

Thus through the lyric "I" of "Song of Myself," speaking for
the human race from its faint inception to its future culmination,
Whitman can prophesy:

The past and present wilt—I have fill'd them, emptied them,
And proceed to fill my next fold of the future.

The cosmic poet and the national poet would seem logically to
be at opposite extremes of the literary spectrum, but Whitman was
more successful in fusing the two than might be expected; though when
we consider the national temper of the American people in the 1850's
his achievement is not so surprising. From the early Puritans the young
nation had inherited the belief that God had ordained a special,
fortunate destiny for it. The Puritans intended the Theocratic State of
Massachusetts to be God's Own Government on earth, and the
successes of the American people in their two wars with England had
increased their confidence in a Providential destiny. After the acquisi-
tion of the vast territories in the regions of Oregon and California,
just nine years before Whitman published his first *Leaves of Grass,*
the possibilities for future growth and development fairly staggered
their imagination. They shared William Cullen Bryant's vision of the
"Mother of a Mighty Race":

Oh mother of a mighty race,
Yet lovely in thy youthful grace!
The elder dames, thy haughty peers,
Admire and hate thy blooming years.

. . . .

They know not, in their hate and pride,
What virtues with thy children bide;

. . . .
There's freedom at thy gates and rest
For Earth's down-trodden and opprest,
A shelter for the hunted head,
For the starved laborer toil and bread,
    Power, at thy bounds,
Stops and calls back his baffled hounds.

Despite the fact that slavery still existed in the United States, Whitman continued to harbor this national dream, this idealistic hope in 1855. He was well aware that slavery was a great evil, and in newspaper editorials and articles, he had angrily denounced the political corruption of all existing political parties in the late 1840's and 1850's. In 1856, in a political tract called "The Eighteenth Presidency!," he admitted that, "At present, the personnel of the government of these thirty millions, in executives and elsewhere, is drawn from limber-tongued lawyers, very fluent but empty feeble old men, professional politicians" and rarely from "the solid body of the people." In this tract he even predicted a civil war if the slave-owners continued to dominate the national legislature and the judiciary. But he still had faith in the innate goodness of human nature and the common people.

When he wrote his 1855 Preface, Whitman was not narrowly provincial or chauvinistic. Although he believed that most nations had failed to provide a society worthy of humanity, he did not reject or undervalue their contributions:

America does not repel the past, or what it has produced under its forms, or amid other politics, or the idea of castes, or the old religions—accepts the lesson with calmness—is not impatient because the slough still sticks to opinions and manners and litature, while the life which served its requirements has passed into the new life of the new forms—perceives that the corpse is slowly borne from the eating and sleeping rooms of the house—perceives that it waits a little while in the door—that it was fittest for its days—that its action has descended to the stalwart and well-shaped heir who approaches—and that he shall be fittest for his days.[2]

The idea of building on the past Whitman never rejected, and his ideal nation was always something to be achieved in the

[2] Quoted from 1882 revised version.

future. He was never smugly complacent about present conditions. He did say in the 1855 Preface, "Here at last is something in the doings of man that corresponds with the broadcast doings of the day and night." But in the same paragraph he showed that what he meant was that nature had made unprecedented development possible: "One sees it must indeed own the riches of the summer and winter, and need never be bankrupt while corn grows from the ground, or the orchards drop apples, or the bays contain fish, or men beget children upon women." In the next paragraph Whitman stated his main theme: "The largeness of the nation, however, were monstrous without a corresponding largeness and generosity of the spirit of the citizen."

As late as 1874, in "Song of the Redwood-Tree," Whitman re-asserted his belief that on the North American continent, with its abundant and unexhausted natural resources, a new society could arise "proportionate to Nature." But it was not material prosperity, mere wealth or power, or world-domination, that he expected:

> But more in you than these, lands of the Western shore,
> (These but the means, the implements, the standing-ground,)
> I see in you, certain to come, the promise of thousands of years,
>   till now deferr'd,
> Promis'd to be fulfill'd, our common kind, the race.

This same thought Whitman had already treated in "Passage to India" (1868–71), in which he presented the functions of the poet as that of humanizing the discoveries and inventions of science:

> Then not your deeds only O voyagers, O scientists and inventors,
>   shall be justified,
> All these hearts as of fretted children shall be sooth'd,
> All affection shall be fully responded to, the secret shall be told,
> All these separations and gaps shall be taken up and hook'd
>   and ink'd together,
> The whole earth, this cold, impassive, voiceless earth, shall be
>   completely justified,
> Trinitas divine shall be gloriously accomplish'd and compacted
>   by the true son of God, the poet,
> (He shall indeed pass the straits and conquer the mountains,
> He shall double the cape of Good Hope to some purpose,)
> Nature and Man shall be disjoin'd and diffused no more,
> The true son of God shall absolutely fuse them.

It is now abundantly obvious that Walt Whitman's greatest am-bition was to be a moral leader, but he hoped to initiate and exert this leadership through his poems, and he ended his 1855 Preface with this test: "The proof of a poet is that his country absorbs him as affectionately as he has absorbed it." Judged by this standard, he failed dismally, as he himself admitted in 1888 in "A Backward Glance o'er Travel'd Roads." Except for a few American readers here and there, he first gained significant acceptance in England among the literary elite.

Today most literary historians and critics in the United States rank Whitman as the greatest poet America has yet produced, but it has taken a long time for him to win this recognition, and the victory is far from complete even yet. During the past decade or two the most fashionable poetic style in English and American literature has been close-textured, unimpassioned, hard, cold, and ironic. Whitman's emotional, expansive style has not appealed to the disciples of Ezra Pound and T. S. Eliot. Yet these two masters did not really reject Whitman, however difficult at times they found it to come to terms with him. As early as 1909 Pound recorded in an essay only recently published, "I think we have not yet paid enough attention to the deliberate artistry of the man, not in details but in the large." Pound thought himself to be "more in love with beauty," but confessed "a lesser vitality," and credited Whitman with being "The first great man to write in the language of his people," even as Dante did. In a poem called "A Pact," written in 1913, Pound declared: "I make a truce with you, Walt Whitman—/I have detested you long enough." From time to time he broke the truce, but Pound continued to believe that "Whitman's faults are superficial, he does convey an image of his time, he has written *histoire morale* as Montaigne wrote the history of his epoch."

Eliot has made few public statements about Whitman, but in 1927 in reviewing Emory Holloway's biography he compared the American poet and Tennyson, and subsequently in an open letter he called Whitman "a great master of versification, though much less reliable than Tennyson." He did not care for Whitman's social, religious, or moral ideas, but said he deserved to be remembered as "a verse maker." Edith Sitwell, however, in *The American Genius, an Anthology of Poetry and Some Prose* (1951), compares Whitman to Blake, and reminds us that both poets "were born at the time when their characteristics were most needed": Blake during an age of stultifying materialism; Whitman "after a time of vague misty abstractions," and he made it his mission "to lead poetry back to the 'divine original, concrete.'" This mission he did not accomplish during his lifetime, but his influence continues to live, and will probably increase as his poems become more widely read and understood.

The understanding is as important as the reading, for no poet of his century has been more often caricatured and distorted, and un-

intentionally by himself and his friends as well as his enemies. Further-
more, Whitman can be embarrassing even to his admirers. He not
only personified *the self* in himself, but actually exploited his person-
ality in a [most] relentless, indiscriminate, and sometimes almost un-
scrupulous manner. Such conduct alienated most educated people of
his own literary generation. Today the "genteel" authors whom the
nineteenth-century readers admired, to the exclusion of Whitman, are
in low repute, but this reversal has not sufficiently erased the public
suspicion that a poet who exploited his own eccentricities must have
been a fake.

Some of Whitman's self-exploitation cannot be easily excused,
and it is all the more regrettable because he misjudged and distorted
his own poems. He was not strongest in his most personal poems, such
as parts of "Starting from Paumanok," or his sentimental pleas to his
reader to forget that he was holding a book instead of a human being
who invited kisses and caresses. Nor is Whitman strongest in his
most doctrinaire poems—those in which he preaches—states general
principles in abstract language instead of appealing to the senses
through vivid, concrete imagery. "Salut au Mond!" is almost as tire-
some as the doctrinal sections of "Starting from Paumanok," but its
final goal is a poetic expression of an ambition both personal and
cosmic:

> My spirit has pass'd in compassion and determination around
>   the whole earth,
> I have look'd for equals and lovers and found them ready for me
>   in all lands,
> I think some divine rapport has equalized me with them.

This vision was "cosmic" because Whitman believed it to be in
harmony with the underlying structure of the universe. Hart Crane,
the aborted follower of Whitman in the twentieth century, was right
when he declared a quarter of a century ago: "He, better than any
other, was able to coordinate those forces in America which seem
most intractable, fusing them into a universal vision which takes on
additional significance as time goes on."

WILLIAM CARLOS WILLIAMS

An Essay on *Leaves of Grass*†

LEAVES OF GRASS! It was a good title for a book of poems, especially for a new book of American poems. It was a challenge to the entire concept of the poetic idea, and from a new viewpoint, a rebel viewpoint, an American viewpoint. In a word and at the beginning it enunciated a shocking truth, that the common ground is of itself a poetic source. There has been inklings before this that such was the case in the works of Robert Burns and the poet Wordsworth, but in this instance the very forms of the writing had been altered: it had gone over to the style of the words as they appeared on the page. Whitman's so-called "free verse" was an assault on the very citadel of the poem itself; it constituted a direct challenge to all living poets to show cause why they should not do likewise. It is a challenge that still holds good after a century of vigorous life during which it has been practically continuously under fire but never defeated.

From the beginning Whitman realized that the matter was largely technical. It had to be free verse or nothing with him and he seldom varied from that practice—and never for more than the writing of an occasional poem. It was a sharp break, and if he was to go astray he had no one but himself to blame for it. It was a technical matter, true enough, and he would stick it out to the end, but to do any more with it than simply to write the poems was beyond him.

He had seen a great light but forgot almost at once after the first revelation everything but his "message," the idea which originally set him in motion, the idea on which he had been nurtured, the idea of democracy—and took his eye off the words themselves which should have held him.

The point is purely academic—the man had his hands full with the conduct of his life and couldn't, if they had come up, be bothered with other matters. As a result, he made no further progress as an

† First published in *Leaves of Grass: One Hundred Years After*, ed. Milton Hindus (Stanford University Press, 1955). Copyright 1955 by Florence H. Williams. Reprinted by permission of New Directions Publishing Corp., agents for Mrs. William Carlos Williams.

artist but, in spite of various topical achievements, continued to write with diminishing effectiveness for the remainder of his life.

He didn't know any better. He didn't have the training to construct his verses after a conscious mold which would have given him power over them to turn them this way, then that, at will. He only knew how to give them birth and to release them to go their own way. He was preoccupied with the great ideas of the time, to which he was devoted, but, after all, poems are made out of words not ideas. He never showed any evidence of knowing this and the unresolved forms consequent upon his beginnings remained in the end just as he left them.

Verses, in English, are frequently spoken of as measures. It is a fortunate designation as it gives us, in looking at them, the idea of elapsed time. We are reminded that the origin of our verse was the dance—and even if it had not been the dance, the heart when it is stirred has its multiple beats, and verse at its most impassioned sets the heart violently beating. But as the heart picks up we also begin to count. Finally, the measure for each language and environment is accepted. In English it is predominantly the iambic pentameter, but whether that is so for the language Whitman spoke is something else again. It is a point worth considering, but apart from the briefest of notices a point not to be considered here. It may be that the essential pace of the English and the American languages is diametrically opposed each to the other and that that is an important factor in the writing of their poetry, but that is for the coming generations to discover. Certainly not only the words but the meter, the measure that governed Whitman's verses, was not English. But there were more pressing things than abstract discussions of meter to be dealt with at that time and the poet soon found himself involved in them.

Very likely the talk and the passionate talk about freedom had affected him as it had infected the French and many others earlier. It is said that, when as a young man he lived in New Orleans, he had fallen in love with a beautiful octoroon but had allowed his friends and relatives to break up the match. It is possible that the disappointment determined the pattern of his later rebellion in verse. Free verse was his great idea! *Versos sueltos* the Spanish call them. It is not an entirely new idea, but it was entirely new to the New York Yankee who was, so to speak, waiting for it with open arms and an overcharged soul and the example of Thomas Jefferson to drive him on.

But verse had always been, for Englishmen and the colonials that imitated them, a disciplined maneuver of the intelligence, as it is today, in which measure was predominant. They resented this American with his new idea, and attacked him in a characteristic way—*on moral grounds*. And he fell for it. He had no recourse but to defend himself and the fat was in the fire. How could verse be free without being immoral? There is something to it. It is the same attack, with a more modern tilt to it, that undoubtedly bothers T. S. Eliot. He is one of the best informed of our writers and would do us a great service, if free verse—mold it as he will—is not his choice, to find us an alternative. From the evidence, he has tried to come up with just that, but up to the present writing he has not brought the thing off.

The case of Mr. Eliot is in this respect interesting. He began writing at Harvard from a thoroughly well-schooled background and produced a body of verse that was immediately so successful that when his poem *The Waste Land* was published, it drove practically everyone else from the field. Ezra Pound, who had helped him arrange the poem on the page, was confessedly jealous. Other American poets had to take second place. A new era, under domination of a return to a study of the classics, was gratefully acknowledged by the universities, and Mr. Eliot, not Mr. Pound, was ultimately given the Nobel Prize. The drift was plainly away from all that was native to America, Whitman among the rest, and toward the study of the past and England.

Though no one realized it, a violent revolution had taken place in American scholarship and the interests from which it stemmed. Eliot had completely lost interest in all things American, in the very ideology of all that America stood for, including the idea of freedom itself in any of its phases. Whitman as a symbol of indiscriminate freedom was completely antipathetic to Mr. Eliot, who now won the country away from him again. The tendency toward freedom in the verse forms, which seemed to be thriving among American poets, was definitely checked and the stage was taken over for other things. I shall never forget the impression created by *The Waste Land*. it was as if the bottom had dropped out of everything. I had not known how much the spirit of Whitman animated us until it was withdrawn from us. Free verse became overnight a thing of the past. Men went about congratulating themselves as upon the disappearance of something that had disturbed their dreams; and indeed it was so—the dreams of right-thinking students of English verse had long been disturbed by the appearance among them of the horrid specter of Whitman's free verse. Now it was as if a liberator, a Saint George, had come just in the nick of time to save them. The instructors in all the secondary schools were grateful.

Meanwhile, Mr. Eliot had become a British subject and removed himself to England where he took up residence. He became a member of the Church of England. He was determined to make the break with America complete, as his fellow artist Henry James had done before him, and began to publish such poems as *Ash Wednesday* and the play *Murder in the Cathedral*, and the *Four Quartets*. Something had happened to him, something drastic, something to do, doubtless, with man's duty and his freedom in the world. It is a far cry from this to Whitman's thought of man as a free agent. The pendulum had gone the full swing.

It is inevitable for us to connect the happenings in the world generally with what takes place in the poem. When Mr. Eliot quit writing, when he quit writing poems, it looked as if he had got to a point where he had nowhere else to turn, and as if in his despair he had given up not only the poem but the world. A man as clever and well informed as he was had the whole world at his feet, but the only conclusion that he reached was that he wanted none of it. Especially did he want none of the newer freedom.

Not that he didn't in his verse try it on, for size, let us say, in his later experiments, particularly in *Four Quartets*, but even there he soon came to the end of his rope. The accented strophe he had definitely given up, as Wagner in the prelude to *Parsifal* had done the same, but to infer from that fact that he had discovered the freedom of a new measure was not true. It looked to me, at least, as if there were some profound depth to his probing beyond which he dared not go without compromising his religious faith. He did not attempt it. It is useful to record the limits of his penetration and the point at which he gave up his attempts to penetrate further. Just how far shall we go in our search for freedom and, more importantly, how shall our efforts toward a greater freedom be conditioned in our verses? All these decisions, which must be reached in deciding what to do, have implications of general value in our lives.

The young men who are students of literature today in our universities do not believe in seeking within the literary forms, the lines, the foot, the way in which to expand their efforts to know the universe, as Whitman did, but are content to follow the theologians and Mr. Eliot. In that, they are children of the times; they risk nothing, for by risking an expanded freedom you are very likely to come a cropper. What, in the words of Hjalmar Ekdal in *The Wild Duck*, are you going to invent?

Men, offering their heads, have always come up with new proposals, and the world of events waits upon them, and who shall say whether it were better to close one's eyes or go forward like Galileo to the light or wait content in the darkness like the man in the next county? Whitman went forward to what to him seemed desirable, and so if we are to reject him entirely we must at least follow him at the start to find out what his discoveries were intended to signify and what not to signify.

Certainly, we are in our day through with such loose freedom as he employed in his verses in the blind belief that it was all going to come out right in the end. We know now that it is not. But are we, because of that, to give up freedom entirely? Merely to put down the lines as they happen to come into your head will not make a poem, and if, as happened more than once in Whitman's case, a poem result, who is going to tell what he has made? The man knew what he was doing, but he did not know all he was doing. Much still remains to discover, but that freedom in the conduct of the verses is desirable cannot be questioned.

There is a very moving picture of Whitman facing the breakers coming in on the New Jersey shore, when he heard the onomatopoeic waves talk to him direct in a Shakespearean language which might have been Lear himself talking to the storm. But it was not what it seemed; it was a new language, an unnamed language which Whitman could not identify or control.

For as the English had foreseen, this freedom of which there had been so much talk had to have limits somewhere. If not, it would lead you astray. That was the problem. And there was at about that time a whole generation of Englishmen, prominent among whom was Frank Harris, whom it did lead astray in moral grounds, just as there were Frenchmen at the time of the French Revolution who were led astray and are still being led astray under the difficult conditions that exist today. It is the reaction against such patterns of thought that moved Eliot and that part of the present generation which is not swallowed up by its fascination with the scene which draws them to Paris whenever they get the opportunity to go there. For in your search for freedom—which is desirable—you must stop somewhere, but where exactly shall you stop? Whitman could not say.

To propose that the answer to the problem should lie in the verse itself would have been to those times an impertinence—and the same would be the case even now. The Greeks had their Dionysia in the spring of the year, when morals could be forgotten, and then the control of life resumed its normal course. In other words, they departmentalized their lives, being of an orderly cast of mind, but we do not lend ourselves easily to such a solution. With us it is all or nothing, provided we are not caught at it. Either we give ourselves to a course of action or we do not give ourselves. Either we are to be free men or not free men—at least in theory. Whitman, like Tom Paine, recognized no limits and that got him into trouble.

But the waves on the Jersey shore still came tumbling in, quieting him as their secret escaped him, isolating him and leaving him lonesome—but possessed by the great mystery which won the world to his side. For he was unquestionably the child of the years. What was the wave that moved the dawning century also moved him and demanded his recognition, and it was not to be denied. All the discoveries and inventions which were to make the twentieth century exceed all others, for better or worse, were implicit in his work. He surpassed the ritualistic centuries which preceded him, just as Ehrlich and Koch and finally Einstein were to exceed Goethe. It was destined to be so, and the New World of which he was a part gave him birth. He had invented a new way of assaulting fate. "Make new!" was to him as it was to Pound much later on an imperious command which completely controlled him.

If he was to enlarge his opportunity he needed room, in verse as in everything else. But there were to be no fundamental changes in the concepts that keep our lives going at an accepted pace and within normal limits. The line was still to be the line, quite in accord with the normal contours of our accepted verse forms. It is not so much that which brought Whitman's verse into question but the freedom with which he laid it on the page. There he had abandoned all sequence and all order. It was as if a tornado had struck.

A new order had hit the world, a relative order, a new measure with which no one was familiar. The thing that no one realized, and this includes Whitman himself, is that the native which they were dealing with was no longer English but a new language akin to the New World to which its nature accorded in subtle ways that they did not recognize. That made all the difference. And not only was it new to America—it was new to the world. There was to be a new measure applied to all things, for there was to be a new order operative in the world. But it has to be insisted on that it was not disorder. Whitman's verses seemed disorderly, but ran according to an unfamiliar and a difficult measure. It was an order which was essential to the new world, not only of the poem, but to the world of chemistry and physics. In this way, the man was more of a prophet than he knew. The full significance of his innovations in the verse patterns has not yet been fully disclosed.

The change in the entire aesthetic of American art as it began to differ not only from British but from all the art of the world up to this time was due to this tremendous change in measure, a relative measure, which he was the first to feel and to embody in his works. What he was leaving behind did not seem to oppress him, but it oppressed the others and rightly so.

It is time now to look at English and American verse at the time Whitman began to write, for only by so doing can we be led to discover what he did and the course that lay before him. He had many formidable rivals to face on his way to success. But his chief opponent was, as he well knew, the great and medieval Shakespeare. And if any confirmation of Shakespeare's sacrosanct position in the language is still sought it is easily to be obtained when anything is breathed mentioning some alteration in the verse forms which he distinguished by using them. He may be imitated as Christopher Fry imitates him, but to vary or depart from him is heresy. Taken from this viewpoint, the clinical sheets of Shakespeare as a writer are never much studied. That he was the greatest word-man that ever existed in the language or out of it is taken for granted but there the inquiry ends.

Shakespeare presented Whitman with a nut hard to crack. What to do with the English language? It was all the more of a problem since the elements of it could not be presented at all or even recognized to exist. As far as the English language was concerned, there was only to use it and to use it well according to the great tradition of the masters.

And indeed it was a magnificent tradition. At the beginning of the seventeenth century it had reached an apogee which it had, to a great extent, maintained to the present day and of which it was proud and jealous. But when Shakespeare wrote, the laurels were new and had so recently been attained and had come from such distinguished achievements that the world seemed to pause for breath. It was a sort of noon and called for a halt. The man himself seemed to feel it and during an entire lifetime did no more than develop to the full his talents. It was noon sure enough for him, and he had only to stretch out in the sun and expand his mood.

Unlike Whitman, he was or represented the culmination of a historic as well as literary past whose forms were just coming to a head after the great trials which were to leave their marks on the centuries. There had been Chaucer, but the language had come of age since then as had the country. Now America had been discovered and the world could not grow much larger. Further expansion, except in a limited degree, was unlikely, so that the poet was left free to develop his world of detail but was not called upon to extend it. More was not necessary than to find something to do and develop it for the

entire span of a long life. But as always with the artist, selection was
an important point in the development.

For instance, as his sonnets show, Shakespeare was an accom-
plished rhymer, but he gave it up early. The patches of heroic couplet
which he wrote for the Players in *Hamlet* are among the best examples
of that form. Yet his main reliance was on blank verse—though he did,
on occasion, try his hand at a triple accent which he rejected without
more than a thought. The demands of the age called for other things
and he was, above everything else, a practical man.

Practicing for so long a time upon the iambic pentameter, he had
the opportunity to develop himself prodigiously in it. Over the years
he shows a technical advance, a certain impatience with restraint in
his work which makes it loose and verges more toward the conforma-
tion of prose. There is a great difference between Shakespeare's earlier
and later work, the latter being freer and more natural in tone.

A feeling for prose began to be felt all through his verse. But at
his death the form began to lapse rapidly into the old restrictions. It
got worse and worse with the years until all the Elizabethan tenor had
been stripped away, or as Milton phrased it speaking of his illustrious
predecessor:

> Sweetest Shakespeare, Nature's child,
> Warbled his native woodnotes wild.

With Milton came Cromwell and the English Revolution, and Shake-
speare was forgotten, together with the secrets of his versification, just
as Whitman today is likely to be forgotten and the example of his
verses and all that refers to him.

The interest that drove Whitman on is the same one that drove
Shakespeare at the end of his life in an attempt to enlarge the scope of
written verse, to find more of expression in the forms of the language
employed. But the consequences of such experimentation are always
drastic and amount in the end to its suppression, which in the person
of a supreme genius is not easy.

From what has been said thus far, you can see why it is im-
possible to imitate Shakespeare; he was part of a historic process which
cannot repeat itself. All imitations of the forms of the past are mean-
ingless, empty shells, which have merely the value of decorations. So
that, if anything is now to be created, it must be in a new form. Whit-
man, if he was to do anything of moment, could not, no matter how
much he may have bowed down to the master, imitate him. It would
not have had any meaning at all. And his responsibility to the new
language was such that he had no alternative but to do as it bade him.

Though he may not have known it, with Whitman the whole spirit of the age itself had been brought under attack. It was a blind stab which he could not identify any more than a child. How could he, no matter how acute his instincts were, have foreseen the discoveries in chemistry, in physics, in abnormal psychology, or even the invention of the telephone or the disclosure of our subterranean wealth in petroleum? He knew only, as did those who were disturbed by his free verse, that something had occurred to the normal structure of conventional aesthetic and that he could not accept it any longer. Therefore, he acted.

We have to acknowledge at once in seeking a meaning involving the complex concerns of the world that the philosophic, the aesthetic, and the mechanical are likely to stem in their development from the same root. One may be much in advance of the other in its discoveries, but in the end a great equalizing process is involved so that the discovery of the advance in the structure of the poetic line is equated by an advance in the conception of physical facts all along the line. Man has no choice in these matters; the only question is, will he recognize the changes that are taking place in time to make the proper use of them? And when time itself is conceived of as relative, no matter how abstruse that may sound, the constructions, the right constructions, cannot be accepted with a similar interpretation. It may take time to bring this about, but when a basic change has occurred in our underlying concern it brooks no interference in the way it will work itself out.

Whitman didn't know anything about this, nor does Mr. Eliot take it into his considerations nor Father Merton either, but if they had to construct a satisfactory poetic line it had and still has to be done according to this precept. For we have learned, if we have learned anything from the past, that the principles of physics are immutable. Best, if you do not approve of what writing has become, to follow in Mr. Eliot's footsteps.

For it is important to man's fate that these matters be—if anything is important to man's fate in this modern world. At least, you cannot retrace steps that have been taken in the past. And you don't know, you simply do not know, what may come of it. No more than Whitman knew what his struggle to free verse may have implied and may still imply for us no matter how, at the moment, the world may have forsaken him. The books are not closed even though the drift in the tide of our interest may at the moment be all the other way. It cannot so soon have reversed itself. Something is still pending, though the final shape of the thing has not yet crystallized. Perhaps that is the reason

for the regression. There are too many profitable leads in other asso-
ciated fields of the intelligence for us to draw back now.

Where have the leads which are *not* aesthetic tended to take us in
the present country? By paying attention to detail and our telescopes
and microscopes and the reinterpretations of their findings, we realize
that man has long since broken from the confinement of the more rigid
of his taboos. It is reasonable to suppose that he will in the future, in
spite of certain setbacks, continue to follow the same course.

Man finds himself on the earth whether he likes it or not, with
nowhere else to go. What then is to become of him? Obviously we
can't stand still or we shall be destroyed. Then if there is no room for
us on the outside we shall, in spite of ourselves, have to go *in:* into the
cell, the atom, the poetic line, for our discoveries. We have to break
the old apart to make room for ourselves, whatever may be our tragedy
and however we may fear it. By making room within the line itself
for his inventions, Whitman revealed himself to be a worthy and cou-
rageous man of his age and, to boot, a farseeing one.

IWAO MATSUHARA

Walt Whitman in Japan†

To deal with Whitman is to remind all of us once again, though
sadly, of the truth of an old saying that a prophet is not without honor
save in his own country. For, at the time when Whitman first published
his *Leaves of Grass* at his own expense, who recognized his greatness
as a poet, besides Emerson, among the literary men of his country?
Whitman was little read and likewise little appreciated not only in
his life time but also for so many years after his death in the land
that had given birth to him, while other countries in the world, notably
France and Japan, acclaimed him as the greatest of all poets of
democracy. In 1900, or forty-five years after the publication of the
first edition of the *Leaves*, Wendell in his *Literary History of America*

† From Iwao Matsuhara, "Walt Whitman in Japan: From the First Intro-
duction to the Present," *Thought Currents in English Literature* (Tokyo)
XXIX (January, 1957). Included in this selection are the introductory three
pages and the concluding section. Reprinted by permission of Mrs. Matsu-
hara.

speaks of Whitman as being an un-American, whose ideas of equality are not of America but of France. Even in the Twenties the most popular poet of democracy in America was not Whitman but Longfellow. Lately the Whitman enthusiasts of this country as well as those of other countries have no doubt rejoiced with what seems to be a definitive biography of Whitman in *The Solitary Singer* by Gay Wilson Allen. But the wonder is that it has taken so long as one hundred years after the first edition of the *Leaves* for a country in the West, with the keenest of critical minds and the best of modern facilities and equipment, to clarify the biological facts of the poet, for, according to Malcolm Cowley, "this is not the final book on Whitman, even for the present generation," and at least two books should be written: one would be a critical discussion of him as a poet, and the other a selection of his best poems.[1] One might have felt, though vaguely, of Whitman's certain source of poetical inspirations or of peculiar rhythms in the vocal song or opera, which has come to light only lately through the publication of *Whitman and Opera* by Robert Faner. One may marvel at the interest that the Westerners show in facts or at their ability of finding and gathering facts whether in history or contemporary life; they are always concerned with the factual above all else in one's life as well as in a nation's. This is no doubt their strength, but, at the same time, it may be regarded as their weakness. Is it not because the biological facts of a poet always loom so prodigiously large over his ideas or feelings that the critics often fail to separate the two, or to evaluate adequately his poetic ideas or ideals as such or apart from the actual facts in his life? Whitman has been denounced and abused by not a few critics in his country as being sensual, pagan, abnormal, or what not, and even to this day he is regarded as "the most difficult of poets (to understand) for Americans."[2] Is this not largely because not only his readers but also his critics fail to distinguish what is imaginary from what is actual in the poet whose intense imagination and almost universal sympathy find no parallel among other poets, or are unable to appreciate the ideal "Walt" apart from the actual Walter Whitman after all?

So strange may it seem to some Westerners that such a country as Japan whose history of Western thought and culture is no more than a century old, and in the minds of whose people still linger shadows of feudalism, has welcomed Whitman as the greatest of

[1] Malcolm Cowley: "Walt Whitman, Champion of America," in the *New York Times Review*, Feb. 6, 1955.
[2] Waldo Frank: "With a Voice as Big as America," in the *New York Times Book Review*, July 3, 1955.

poets of democracy or hailed him as the emancipator of mankind as well as the bearer of a new Gospel even from the days when the poet was living to this. Some may suppose that this is due to the racial traits of the people, which are, as a rule, so fanciful or whimsical as to be attracted by anything new in the West, whether in politics, literature, or science, as the political events of this country in the past several decades clearly testify: the country has been swayed by some political theories of the West; it has swung from the extreme left-wing or communism to the equally extreme right-wing or totalitarianism, or from militarism to the idea of peace at any cost or without any provision for its national defense. This tendency is especially noticeable in its modern writers, who are always attracted by some fashionable literary ideologies in the West, and their literature at best is an imitation of a foreign literature whether it is Russian, French, English, or American. * * *

Contrary to what the name of this present era or Showa is purported to signify—clearness and harmony—the nation has had to wage the greatest of wars and to suffer in consequence the worst in her history, and so supposedly the age of Whitman in this country has made no great strides as has been expected. And since the space allotted for this article has almost been taken up, the account of Whitman in this era must be as brief as possible.

Of many articles on Whitman that have appeared during this present era, the most curious is a serial one that the *Daichōwa* (the Great Harmony) printed from May to July in the 2nd year of Showa (1927). The writer is a reputed artist as well as a poet, Kōtaro Takamura, who translated and published the *Specimen Days* in the 10th year of Taisho (1921). In some of these articles Takamura conjectures that Whitman's father had a venereal disease and among his offspring Jesse had epilepsy and Edward was an idiot. The *Eigo no Kenkyu* (the Study of English) devoted its October number of the 4th year of Showa (1929) to Whitman, in which are found various phases of the poet's life and work discussed by writers, mostly professors of colleges, and Whitman bibliography in Japan given for the first time. The monthly that was founded for the purpose of study in Blake and Whitman in February of the 6th year of Showa (1931) under the editorship of Muneyoshi Yanagi and Bunsho Jugaku and continued for two years shows that some scholars have found the spiritual kinship of these two poets as well as an Oriental point of view they have proposed to themselves in their study. One of the interesting articles in its numbers contains a letter of Emory Holloway addressed to Shigetaka Naganuma. The *Gakuto* (the Light on Learning), a monthly on books, published by Maruzen Company, has had many articles on Whitman in its issues since the 28th year (1953). The most memorable of them all is the Whitman exhibition held at this company in July of the same year by some top Whitman enthusiasts in this country. A catalogue for the exhibition was issued on the occasion, which contains, besides articles on Whitman and his bibliography in Japan, the Message for Walt Whitman Exhibition by John M. Allison, American Ambassador to Japan. The *Eigo Seinen* (the Rising Generation), a monthly for the study of English and literature, printed "Sōseki and Whitman" in its July number of the 30th year (1955), to which it has already been referred.

Among the books that have been published during this era, devoting wholly or partly to Whitman, first mention should be made of *Amerika Bungaku* (American Literature) by Matsuo Takagaki, which saw light in the 3rd year of Showa (1928). Takagaki belongs to the pioneers in this field of study. In this book the author discusses Whitman in one chapter with Lanier, and lays emphasis on the organic rhythm of the former poet. Takagaki has also written of Whitman's influence on Chesterton's prose in his *Kikaijidai no Bungaku* (Literature in the Age of Mechanism), which was published in the following year. Chesterton's appreciation of Whitman, he says, is not due to his own discovery but to the spirit or trend of the time. As is natural with a classically minded scholar or professor, Sōfu Taketomo has not much to do with Whitman, only lays his emphasis on the position the poet holds in American literature in the section called "American Poets" in his *Eibungaku Ron* (Essays on English Literature), published in the same year. *Whitman's Poems, Selected with Introduction and Notes*, by Takeshi Funahashi, published in the following year, was not the first of its kind, as *Whitman's Political Works Selected* by T. Arishima was published in the 8th year of Taisho (1919), but it shows that the editor by this time had become fully sympathetic with the poet. The 7th year of Showa or 1932 witnessed the publication of *Whitman Zakko* (Whitman Miscellanies). The author is Takashige Naganuma, who has devoted many years to the study of Whitman and has written frequently on the poet. The interesting sections of the book may be those that deal with the origin of the *Leaves*, Whitman's early poems and novels, and the list of books on and by the poet in the author's possession. Soon after this publication, this author began to translate Whitman's poems and completed the same in two volumes in the 25th year of Showa (1950). Whitman as a critic is for the first time noted by Gen Sakuma in his *Amerika Hihyo no Kenkyu* (A Study of American Criticism), published in the 10th year of Showa (1935).

In the next two years there appeared two works on Whitman, namely, *Walt Whitman* by Takashi Sugiki and *Whitman no Shin Kenkyu* (A New Study of Walt Whitman) by Yasuji Shimizu. The former deals with the life and the work of Whitman and is helpful as an introductory to the study of the poet, while the latter is chiefly a study of ideas of the poet, the most interesting part being the sections that deal with the poet's source in the Oriental ideas.[3] The reader of Whitman may find a curious work in *Whitman Sanbi* (In Praise of Whitman), a fictional biography of the poet by Shichiro Nagami, one of the editors of the *Study of English*, published in the 16th year or 1941. Takeshi Saito's *Amerika Bungaku Shi* (A Historical Survey of American Literature), published in the same year, contains a brief life sketch of and some criticism on Whitman. In the former a rumor that the poet has had children is regarded as a fact, and in the latter the poet is said to have been of "once-born mind" and "not twice-born mind." Whitman is treated as one of one hundred masterpieces by Yasuo Yamato in his *Eibei Bungaku Gaikan* (The Masterpieces of English and American Literature), published in the 23rd year (1948), which young students may find useful as an informative book. Whitman's ideal of democracy and its significance in this new age are dealt with by Shōtaro Ojima in *Amerika no Bungaku to Kyoiku* (American Literature and Education), published in the 24th year (1949). Whitman as the last of American Renaissance is discussed in Masaru Shiga's *Amerika Bungaku no Seicho* (The Growth of American Literature), which is the latest of his several works on similar subjects, published in the 29th year (1954). Though a popular book and by no means a scholarly work, Mitsuru Ishii's *Amerika Bungaku Yūran* (A Tour Through American Literature), published in the same year, has many interesting references to Whitman. The author is well known as a collector of books on Whitman and has often written of the poet.

The postwar years have witnessed, besides new editions or reprints of translations of Whitman's poems, such as Tomita's, Shiratori's, and Arishima's, two new versions of his selected poems by Kinju Kiguchi and Masao Yaku (in the 24th year or 1949) and by Akira Asano (in the 25th year or 1950), and another of his complete poems by Shigetaka Naganuma (in the same year).

Among other translations mention should be made of Masaru Shiga's version of *Democratic Vistas*, which appeared in the 28th year or 1953, and Kinichi Ishikawa's translation of *The Times of Melville and Whitman* by Van Wyck Brooks, which was published in the

---

[3] The work was published posthumously in 1937.

29th year or 1954. One thing more to be added as an observation of these postwar years is this, that students and scholars in this country have come to be really interested in American literature for the first time in history, especially the younger generation has been roused in the serious study of great writers in that land, as is shown by the number of graduation theses of students in universities and colleges, which increases as years go on. And Whitman has a prominent place among them.

However unfortunate the late war may have been for this country, its result has been not without some benefits to its people: for one thing they have really come to know the U.S. and its people through direct contacts with many experts and eminent men in every field of activities in that land. There have been not a few American scholars and professors of universities who have come to this country to lecture on their literature through the invitations of various institutions in this country. And as far as Whitman is concerned, there have been three notable lectures or speeches made by American professors in the past three years, namely, Prof. Leon Howard, of California University at Los Angeles, on "The Long Foreground of Whitman's *Leaves of Grass*," delivered before a group of university or college professors of American literature at the special meeting of American Seminar in the Tokyo University, July 14, 1954; Dr. Robert A. Jelliffe, Exchange Visiting Lecturer at Kobe Jogakuin, on "Whitman One Hundred Years Later," addressed to members of the America-Japan Society, May 27, 1955; and Prof. Gay Wilson Allen, of New York University, "On Whitman," given at the Tokyo American Cultural Center, July 25, 1955.

The interest that has prompted me to pen this essay is what in Whitman has really appealed to the intellectuals and literati of this land, or whether rightly or wrongly understood, to what extent they have accepted or rejected the poet in the past sixty-five years. Obviously, the initial difficulty to be encountered in such an attempt lies in obtaining necessary materials for the subject, which are not available in one library or two. I am indebted to the materials or literature of Whitman Mr. Koichi Kodama gathered for the thesis he has written at my suggestion on the same subject, though from a different point of view, without access to which this would not have been written. Another difficulty is to do justice to the words and phrases to be quoted, for all the literature except Lafcadio Hearn's is written in Japanese. All translators realize the difficulty of translating Japanese into English, for in some cases it is well-nigh impossible to translate, not only because of great differences in the expression between the two languages but also because of vagueness in some Japanese words, which may be the beauty of the language, but, at the same time, is its fundamental weakness. To what extent I have succeeded in this attempt is not for me to say. Then, I am well aware of what is most desirable of this essay, or a full account of the influence of Whitman on the poets of this country, but this is beyond the scope of the present essay as it would make another story of or essay on the poet. If this essay with all its shortcomings were to contribute toward the mutual understanding of the two nations, the United States and Japan, I should be amply rewarded in the attempt, for such understanding is essential for the peace and welfare not only of the two peoples but of the world at large. All this might have been said at the outset of this essay, but is there any great difference whether stated in the prologue or in the epilogue anyway?

MALCOLM COWLEY

[Hindu Mysticism and Whitman's "Song of Myself"]†

One reason among others why "Song of Myself" has been widely misprized and misinterpreted, especially by scholars, is that they have paid a disproportionate share of attention to its sources in contemporary culture. Besides noting many parallels with Emerson, they have found that it reflected a number of popular works and spectacles. Among these are Italian opera (notably as sung at the Astor Place Theatre in the great season of 1852–1853, when "Alboni's great self" paid her long and only visit to New York); George Sand's novel, *The Countess of Rudolstadt*, which presented the figure of a wandering bard and prophet (as well as another of her novels, *The Journeyman Joiner*, in which the hero was a carpenter and a proletarian saint); Frances Wright's then famous defense of Epicurean philosophy, *A Few Days in Athens;* the Count de Volney's *Ruins*, predicting the final union

† From Cowley's "Introduction" to *Leaves of Grass* (New York: Viking Press, 1959), section 2, pp. x–xiv, and section 4, pp. xx–xxvi. Copyright © 1959 by The Viking Press, Inc. Reprinted by permission of The Viking Press, Inc.

of all religions; Dr. Abbott's Egyptian Museum, on Broadway; O. M. Mitchel's book, *A Course of Six Lectures on Astronomy*, as well as other writings on the subject; and a number of essays clipped from the English quarterly reviews, of which the poet seems to have been a faithful reader. All these works and shows had a discernible influence on Whitman, but when they are listed with others and discussed at length they lead to one of the misconceptions that are the professional weakness of scholars. They tempt us to conclude that "Song of Myself" was merely a journalist's report, inspired but uneven, of popular culture in the 1850s. It was something more than that, and something vastly different from any of its literary sources.

I might suggest that the real nature of the poem becomes clearer when it is considered in relation to quite another list of works, even though Whitman had probably read none of them in 1855. Most of them he could not have read, because they were not yet written, or not published, or not translated into English. That other list might include the *Bhagavad-Gita*, the *Upanishads*, Christopher Smart's long crazy inspired poem *Jubilate Agno*, Blake's prophetic books (not forgetting *The Marriage of Heaven and Hell*), Rimbaud's *Illuminations*, *The Chants of Maldoror*, and Nietzsche's *Thus Spake Zarathustra*, as well as *The Gospel of Sri Ramakrishna* and a compendious handbook, *The Philosophies of India*, by Heinrich Zimmer (New York, 1951). I am offering what might seem to be a curious list of titles, but its double purpose is easy to explain. "Song of Myself" should be judged, I think, as one of the great inspired (and sometimes insane) prophetic works that have appeared at intervals in the Western world, like *Jubilate Agno* (which is written in a biblical style sometimes suggesting Whitman's), like the *Illuminations*, like *Thus Spake Zarathustra*. But the system of doctrine suggested by the poem is more Eastern than Western, it includes notions like metempsychosis and karma, and it might almost be one of those *Philosophies of India* that Zimmer expounds at length.

What is extraordinary about this Eastern element is that Whitman, when he was writing the poems of the first edition, seems to have known little or nothing about Indian philosophy. It is more than doubtful that he had even read the *Bhagavad-Gita*, one of the few Indian works then available in translation. He does not refer to it in his notebooks of the early 1850s, where he mentions most of the books he was poring over. A year after the first edition was published, Thoreau went to see him in Brooklyn and told him that *Leaves of Grass* was "Wonderfully like the Orientals." Had Whitman read them? he asked. The poet answered, "No: tell me about them." He seems to have taken advantage of Thoreau's reading list, since words from the Sanskrit (notably "Maya" and "sudra") are used correctly in some of the poems written after 1858. They do not appear in "Song of Myself," in spite of the recognizably Indian ideas expressed in the poem, and I would hazard the guess that the ideas are not of literary derivation. It is true that they were vaguely in the air of the time and that Whitman may have breathed them in from the Transcendentalists or even from some of the English quarterly reviewers. It also seems possible, however, that he reinvented them for himself, after an experience similar to the one for which the Sanskrit word is samadhi, or absorption.

What it must have been was a mystical experience in the proper sense of the term. Dr. Richard Maurice Bucke, the most acute of Whitman's immediate disciples, believed that it took place on a June morning in 1853 or 1854. He also believed that it was repeated on other occasions, but neither these nor the original experience can be dated from Whitman's papers. On the other hand, his notebooks and manuscripts of the early 1850s are full of sidelong references to such an experience, and they suggest that it was essentially the same as the illuminations or ecstasies of earlier bards and prophets. Such ecstasies consist in a rapt feeling of union or identity with God (or the Soul, or Mankind, or the Cosmos), a sense of ineffable joy leading to the conviction that the seer has been released from the limitations of space and time and has been granted a direct vision of truths impossible to express. As Whitman says in the famous fifth chant of "Song of Myself":

> Swiftly arose and spread around me the peace and joy and
>   knowledge that pass all the art and argument of the earth;
> And I know that the hand of God is the elderhand of my own,
> And I know that the spirit of God is the eldest brother of my
>   own,
> And that all the men ever born are also my brothers . . . and
>   the women my sisters and lovers.

It is to be noted that there is no argument about the real occurrence of such ecstasies. They have been reported, sometimes in sharp detail, by men and women of many different nations, at many historical periods, and each report seems to bear a family resemblance to the others. Part of the resemblance is a feeling universally expressed by mystics that they have acquired a special sort of knowledge not learned from others, but directly revealed to the inner eye. This supposed knowledge has given independent rise to many systems of philosophy or cosmology, once again in many different cultures, and once again there is or should be no argument about one feature of almost all the systems or bodies of teaching: that they too have a family resemblance, like the experiences on which they are based. Indeed, they hold so many principles in common that it is possible for Aldous Huxley and others to group them all together as "the perennial philosophy."

The arguments, which will never end, are first about the nature of the mystical state—is it a form of self-hypnosis, is it a pathological condition to be induced by fasting, vigils, drugs, and other means of abusing the physical organism, or is it, as Whitman believed, the result of superabundant health and energy?—and then about the source and value of the philosophical notions to which it gives rise. Do these merely express the unconscious desires of the individual, and chiefly his sexual desires? Or, as Jungian psychologists like to suggest, are they derived from a racial or universally human unconscious? Are they revelations or hallucinations? Are they supreme doctrines, or are they heretical, false, and even satanic? They belong in the orthodox tradition of Indian philosophy. In Western Christianity, as also in Mohammedianism, the pure and self-consistent forms of mysticism are usually regarded as heresies, with the result that several of the medieval mystics were burned at the stake (though Theresa of Avila and John of the Cross found an orthodox interpretation for their visions and became saints).

Whitman cannot be called a Christian heretic, for the simple reason that he was not a Christian at any stage of his career, early or late. In some of the poems written after the Civil War, and in revisions of older poems made at the same time, he approached the Christian notion of a personal God, whom he invoked as the Elder Brother or the great Camerado. But then he insisted—in another poem of the same period, "Chanting the Square Deific"—that God was not a trinity but a quaternity, and that one of his faces was the "sudra face" of Satan. In "Song of Myself" as originally written, God is neither a person nor, in the strict sense, even a being; God is an abstract principle of energy that is manifested in every living creature, as well as in "the grass that grows wherever the land is and the water is." In some ways this God of the first edition resembles Emerson's Oversoul, but he seems much closer to the Brahman of the *Upanishads*, the absolute, unchanging, all-enfolding Consciousness, the Divine Ground from which all things emanate and to which all living things may hope to return. And this Divine Ground is by no means the only conception that Whitman shared with Indian philosophers, in the days when he was writing "Song of Myself."

*   *   *

It is in the eighth sequence, which is a sermon, that Whitman gives us most of the doctrines suggested by his mystical experience, but they are also implied in the rest of the poem and indeed in the whole text of the first edition. Almost always he expresses them in the figurative and paradoxical language that prophets have used from the beginning. Now I should like to state them explicitly, even at the cost of some repetition.

Whitman believed when he was writing "Song of Myself"—and at later periods too, but with many changes in emphasis—that there is a distinction between one's mere personality and the deeper Self (or between ego and soul). He believed that the Self (or atman, to use a Sanskrit word) is of the same essence as the universal spirit (though he did not quite say it *is* the universal spirit, as Indian philosophers do in the phrase "Atman is Brahman"). He believed that true knowledge is to be acquired not though the senses or the intellect, but through union with the Self. At such moments of union (or "merge," as Whitman called it) the gum is washed from one's eyes (that is his own phrase), and one can read an infinite lesson in common things, discovering that a mouse, for example, "is miracle enough to stagger sextillions of infidels." This true knowledge is available to every man and woman, since each conceals a divine Self. Moreover, the divinity of all implies the perfect equality of all, the immortality of all, and the universal duty of loving one another.

Immortality for Whitman took the form of metempsychosis, and be believed that every individual will be reborn, usually but not always in a higher form. He had also worked out for himself something approaching the Indian notion of karma, which is the doctrine that actions performed during one incarnation determine the nature and fate of the individual during his next incarnation; the doctrine is emphatically if somewhat unclearly stated in a passage of his prose introduction that was later rewritten as a poem, "Song of Prudence." By means of metempsychosis and karma, we are all involved in a process of spiritual evolution that might be compared to natural evolution. Even the latter process, however, was not regarded by Whitman as strictly natural or material. He believed that animals have a rudimentary sort of soul ("They bring me tokens of myself"), and he hinted or surmised, without directly saying, that rocks, trees, and planets possess an identity, or "eidólon," that persists as they rise to higher states of being. The double process of evolution, natural and spiritual, can be traced for ages into the past, and he believed that it will continue for ages beyond ages. Still, it is not an eternal process, since it has an ultimate goal, which appears to be the reabsorption of all things into the Divine Ground.

Most of Whitman's doctrines, though by no means all of them, belong to the mainstream of Indian philosophy. In some respects he went against the stream. Unlike most of the Indian sages, for example, he was not a thoroughgoing idealist. He did not believe that the whole world of the senses, of desires, of birth and death, was only maya, illusion, nor did he hold that it was a sort of purgatory; instead he praised the world as real and joyful. He did not despise the body, but proclaimed that it was as miraculous as the soul. He was too good a citizen of the nineteenth century to surrender his faith in material progress as the necessary counterpart of spiritual progress. Although he yearned for ecstatic union with the soul or Oversoul, he did not try to achieve it by subjugating the senses, as advised by yogis and Buddhists alike; on the contrary, he thought the "merge" could also be achieved (as in chants 26–29) by a total surrender to the senses. These are important differences, but it must be remembered that Indian philosophy or theology is not such a unified structure as it appears to us from a distance. Whitman might have found Indian sages or gurus and even whole sects that agreed with one or another of his heterodoxies (perhaps excepting his belief in material progress). One is tempted to say that instead of being a Christian heretic, he was an Indian rebel and sectarian.

Sometimes he seems to be a Mahayana Buddhist, promising nirvana for all after countless reincarnations, and also sharing the belief of some Mahayana sects that the sexual act can serve as one of the sacraments. At other times he might be an older brother of Sri Ramakrishna (1836–1886), the nineteenth-century apostle of Tantric Brahmanism and of joyous affirmation. Although this priest of Kali, the Mother Goddess, refused to learn English, one finds him delivering some of Whitman's messages in—what is more surprising—the same tone of voice. Read, for example, this fairly typical passage from *The Gospel of Sri Ramakrishna*, while remembering that "Consciousness" is to be taken here as a synonym for Divinity:

> The Divine Mother revealed to me in the Kali temple that it was She who had become everything. She showed me that everything was full of Consciousness. The Image was Consciousness, the altar was Consciousness, the water-vessels were Consciousness, the doorsill was Consciousness, the marble floor was Consciousness—

all was Consciousness. . . . I saw a wicked man in front of the
Kali temple; but in him I saw the Power of the Divine Mother
vibrating. That was why I fed a cat with the food that was to be
offered to the Divine Mother.

Whitman expresses the same idea at the end of chant 48, and in
the same half-playful fashion:

Why should I wish to see God better than this day?
I see something of God each hour of the twenty-four, and each
    moment then,
In the faces of men and women I see God, and in my own face in
    the glass;
I find letters from God dropped in the street, and every one is
    signed by God's name,
And I leave them where they are, for I know that others will
    punctually come forever and ever.

Such parallels—and there are dozens that might be quoted—are
more than accidental. They reveal a kinship in thinking and experience
that can be of practical value to students of Whitman. Since the Indian
mystical philosophies are elaborate structures, based on conceptions
that have been shaped and defined by centuries of discussion, they
help to explain Whitman's ideas at points in the first edition where he
seems at first glance to be vague or self-contradictory. There is, for
example, his unusual combination of realism—sometimes brutal realism
—and serene optimism. Today he is usually praised for the first, blamed
for the second (optimism being out of fashion), and blamed still more
for the inconsistency he showed in denying the existence of evil. The
usual jibe is that Whitman thought the universe was perfect and was
getting better every day.

It is obvious, however, that he never meant to deny the existence
of evil in himself or his era or his nation. He knew that it existed in his
own family, where one of his brothers was a congenital idiot, another
was a drunkard married to a streetwalker, and still another, who had
caught "the bad disorder," later died of general paresis in an insane
asylum. Whitman's doctrine implied that each of them would have
an opportunity to avoid those misfortunes or punishments in another
incarnation, where each would be rewarded for his good actions. The
universe was an eternal becoming for Whitman, a process not a
structure, and it had to be judged from the standpoint of eternity.
After his mystical experience, which seemed to offer a vision of eter-
nity, he had become convinced that evil existed only as part of a

universally perfect design. That explains his combination of realism and optimism, which seems unusual only in our Western world. In India, Heinrich Zimmer says, "Philosophic theory, religious belief, and intuitive experience support each other . . . in the basic insight that, fundamentally, all is well. A supreme optimism prevails everywhere, in spite of the unromantic recognition that the universe of man's affairs is in the most imperfect state imaginable, one amounting practically to chaos."

Another point explained by Indian conceptions is the sort of democracy Whitman was preaching in "Song of Myself." There is no doubt that he was always a democrat politically—which is to say a Jacksonian Democrat, a Barnburner writing editorials against the Hunkers, a Free Soiler in sympathy, and then a liberal but not a radical Republican. He remained faithful to what he called "the good old cause" of liberty, equality, and fraternity, and he wrote two moving elegies for the European rebels of 1848. In "Song of Myself," however, he is not advocating rebellion or even reforms. "To a drudge of the cottonfields," he says, "or emptier of privies I lean. . . . on his right cheek I put the family kiss"; but he offers nothing more than a kiss and an implied promise. What he preaches throughout the poem is not political but religious democracy, such as was practiced by the early Christians. Today it is practiced, at least in theory, by the Tantric sect, and we read in *Philosophies of India:*

> All beings and things are members of a single mystic family
> (*kula*). There is therefore no thought of caste within the Tantric
> holy "circles" (*cakra*). . . . Women as well as men are eligible
> not only to receive the highest initiation but also to confer it in the
> role of guru. . . . However, it must not be supposed that this in-
> difference to the rules of caste implies any idea of revolution within
> the social sphere, as distinguished from the sphere of spiritual
> progress. The initiate returns to his post in society; for there too
> is the manifestation of Sakti. The world is affirmed, just as it is—
> neither renounced, as by an ascetic, nor corrected, as by a social
> reformer.

The promise that Whitman offers to the drudge of the cottonfields, the emptier of privies, and the prostitute draggling her shawl is that they too can set out with him on his perpetual journey—perhaps not in their present incarnations, but at least in some future life. And that leads to another footnote offered by the Indian philosophies: they explain what the poet meant by the Open Road. It starts as an actual

road that winds through fields and cities, but Whitman is doing more
than inviting us to shoulder our duds and go hiking along it. The real
journey is toward spiritual vision, toward reunion with the Divine
Ground; and thus the Open Road becomes Whitman's equivalent for
all the other roads and paths and ways that appear in mystical teach-
ings. It reminds us of the Noble Eightfold Path of the Buddhists, and
the Taoist Way; it suggests both the *bhakti-marga* or "path of devotion"
and the *karma-marga* or "path of sacrifice"; while it comes closer to
being the "big ferry" of the Mahayana sect, in which there is room
for every soul to cross to the farther shore. Whitman's conception,
however, was even broader. He said one should know "the universe
itself as a road, as many roads, as roads for traveling souls."

I am not pleading for the acceptance of Whitman's ideas or for
any other form of mysticism, Eastern or Western. I am only suggesting
that his ideas as expressed in "Song of Myself" were bolder and more
coherent than is generally supposed, and philosophically a great deal
more respectable.

V. K. CHARI

Whitman and Indian Thought†

On reading the first edition of the *Leaves of Grass*, Thoreau re-
marked that the book was "wonderfully like the Orientals." Emerson
found in it a curious mixture of the *Bhagavad-Gita* and the New York
Herald. Since then scholars, both Western and Indian, have steadily
attested to the striking resemblances in Whitman's poetry to the ancient
Hindu teachings. Recent research on Whitman, both Indian and Ameri-
can, has confirmed these resemblances. Whitman, along with his
Transcendentalist companions, has come to be studied more and more
in the light of Vedantic thought. But the absence of any established
evidence that Whitman studied the Hindu books has remained a serious
hurdle in Whitman research. Even Whitman's published notebooks and
manuscripts do not seem to throw much light on Whitman's Indian
sources. Professor Gay Wilson Allen, who besides being an authority

† From the *Western Humanities Review*, XIII (1959), 291–297. Reprinted
by permission of the *Western Humanities Review*.

on Whitman has had the good fortune of inheriting some valuable manuscript material from the Furness Collection, says in his recent monumental Whitman biography: "Whether Whitman had read any Oriental literature . . . the most diligent search of scholars has not yet determined."[1]

Whitman's references to India are altogether of a superficial nature, and his poem "Passage to India," which might have been the only direct evidence of Whitman's enthusiasm for India, reveals no precise knowledge about India and is the least Indian of his poems. But then it is to be wondered how without reading the Hindu books Whitman came unwittingly to exhibit such marked affinities with Hindu Vedantic thought. Romain Rolland, who doubted the Indian origin of Whitman's inspiration, was quick to perceive these affinities; but he attributed the poet's mystical experiences to his own subjective realization and partly to the predilections of his background and culture. Rolland's appraisal of Whitman completely underrates the importance of the role of books in the making of the poet. That Whitman was an indefatigable reader and that he passed through a long period of self-instruction before "making" his poems is clear from his preparatory reading and thought. Books had a great deal more importance in Whitman's mental growth than has generally been estimated. They clarified his native visions and confirmed his intuitions; further they opened out to him new horizons of experience. The range of Whitman's knowledge was extraordinary to judge from his manuscript notebooks. Moreover, the comprehensive duties of an editor compelled him to read almost all important publications of his time and review them in his papers. Thus all the contemporary journalistic literature, the best plays, operas, sermons, lectures and articles were accessible to him.

In the years during which the *Leaves* were in the making there was a considerable vogue in America for Hindu religious ideas, particularly through the enthusiasm of the New Englanders. And the English and American periodicals of the time contained much Vedantic material, through the interest created in it by the "Roy" literature. Miss Adrienne Moore in her interesting study[2] has shown how Rammohan Roy was the medium through which Hindu philosophy of the Advaitic (non-dualistic) Vedantic brand reached New England and how he was influential in stirring in the American mind an interest in Indian thought. Whitman, who read almost everything that came his way, could not have escaped some contact with these ideas, though here we

[1] Gay Wilson Allen, *The Solitary Singer* (New York, 1955), p. 141.
[2] Adrienne Moore, *Rammohan Roy and America* (Calcutta, 1942).

are up against a difficulty in making a positive affirmation. Whitman's knowledge of the Vedanta, if he possessed any knowledge of it at all, may have been indirect, derived through the Transcendentalists, and mainly through the writings of Emerson, which surely influenced him during his formative years.

Both Emerson and Whitman felt the need for a new, impersonal "doctrine of the soul." Hence they were attracted to the German doctrines of Self and Emerson took avidly to the Neo-Platonic conception of the Oversoul and the more strikingly developed doctrine of Self in the Atman-Brahman concept of the *Gita* and the *Katha Upanishad*. Emerson's contact with Indian literature probably began during his Harvard days as suggested by his reading lists and marginalia, and he probably gathered a fairly intimate acquaintance with Indian thought even before he published the first of his writings in 1836. This probability is considerably strengthened by internal evidences. Traces of Hindu influence can be discovered in *Nature*, the essays on "Oversoul," "Spiritual Laws," "Intellect," and "Compensation," besides the more deeply Indian of his essays, "Plato," which contains the kernel of Emerson's orientalism. The theme of these essays is the spiritual oneness of Being and intuitive identity, of which the poem "Brahma" is the classic expression. In his essay on "Intellect" Emerson develops systematically a theory of "intellectual intuition" which bears a close resemblance to the Vedantic doctrine. Emerson's essays might have been a channel through which Indian ideas were transmitted to Whitman. It is a significant fact that Whitman reviewed Emerson's "Spiritual Laws" in 1847, and passages in that essay affirming the identity of spiritual being and those that say that the soul is the "one Bottom," the identity underlying differences, that "it is only the finite that has wrought and suffered, the infinite lies stretched in smiling repose," might have aided his spiritual "conversion." The year 1847–48 was crucial in Whitman's spiritual development as it marked the culmination of a long process of subconscious incubation. In that year Whitman experienced a remarkable accession of power, a new birth. Whitman recorded this in his manuscript notebook for 1847–48, which contains a clear, though half-articulate, adumbration of the "Song of Myself."

Whether impelled by native or foreign influences or by his own innate disposition, Whitman came to express in his poems a body of mystical beliefs which are also the fundamental assumptions of the Hindu Advaita Vedanta. The *Leaves of Grass* is to be studied and understood rather as a body of mystical verse comparable to the apocalyptical utterances of the *Upanishads* and the *Gita* than as a finished work of art. In respect to some of his fundamental beliefs Whitman

approximates the Advaita Vedantic philosophy. In fact, the affinities
are so deep that Whitman's writing lend themselves to a consistent
interpretation in the light of the Vedanta. Whitman, like the Vedantist,
recognizes intuition, a form of supra-sensuous, supra-rational mode of
knowing-by-being or knowledge through self-immediacy. The Tran-
scendentalists found out the inadequacy of the rational approach and
turned to intuition as a real source of knowledge. In this they could
have been aided by Neo-Platonic conceptions and by Schelling's idea of
immediate cognition. But it was in the Vedantic philosophy that one
came across a systematic and comprehensive doctrine of "intellectual
intuition."[3]

Emerson had a deep distrust of human thought and protested
against its exclusive sway in life: "What help from thought? Life is
not dialectics." Emerson believed that thought works a division between
man and the world, and causes an internal fissure. Thought being
dualistic by nature cannot take us beyond differences. There is an inner
nature in thought, "the felt unity," which is the immediate centre of all
mediate experience. This inner nature of thought is the Self which is
identical with Reality. This principle of unity is the indifference-point
of subject and object and can be known in a state of pure immediacy.
Such is the central doctrine of the Vedanta, Whitman calls this faculty
the "soul-sight" or the "root-centre" of the mind. Emerson calls it the
"intellect receptive" which is a unitive, non-dualistic vision, that gives
us a "perception of identity" by establishing the "union of the knower
with the things known." The intellect is an integral vision of the whole.
"The intellect is a whole and demands integrity in every work," says
Emerson; "we live in succession, in division, in parts, in particles; we
see the world piece by piece." "While the world will be whole and re-
fuses to be disparted, we seek to act partially, to sunder, to appropri-
ate." Whitman realized the intuitive identity of the universe and rose
to the conception of an absolute Being or Substance, which is at once
the support and essence of the world.

> Ethereal, pervading all. . . .
> Essence of forms, life of the real identities, permanent,
>   positive. . . .
> I, the general soul. . . .[4]

This soul is the "only certainty" and "final substance." Emerson speaks
of "the aboriginal abyss of real Being" which lies "under all this running

---

[3] "Intellectual" because it is a knowing function, *jñāna;* "intuition" because
it is immediate.
[4] "Chanting the Square Deific," lines 41–44.

sea of circumstance."[5] The thought of the Oversoul as the substratum of the universe is common to Emerson and Whitman. For Whitman this oversoul or "Kosmic spirit" is no other than one's own self. In the "Song of Myself" is expressed this cosmic vision, the exalted sense of mystic self-expansion which is the highest achievement of the intuitional sense. As a result of this cosmic consciousness the poet, freed of all impediments, becomes perfectly fluid and diaphanous and reflects within himself the cosmic existence. In an attempt to embrace the Infinite, Whitman goes on endlessly inventorying; and his catalogues emphasize the spiritual unity of the world, not its multiplicity. In Whitman's paradoxical style (reminiscent of Emerson's "Brahma" and the verses of the *Gita*) opposites constantly meet and dissolve; all tends to the dissolution of distinctions. Santayana's criticism that with Whitman the surface is absolutely all and that for him the world has no inside is unjustified, for Whitman's vision not only embraces the All but penetrates beneath the surface to "the depths of qualities and things," to "first principles."

> Only the kernel of every object nourishes;
> Where is he who tears off the husks for you and me?
> Where is he that undoes stratagems and envelopes for you and
>   me. . . .[6]

> I fly those flights of a fluid and swallowing soul,
> My course runs below the surroundings of plummets.[7]
> I force surfaces and depths also. . . .[8]

The "intellect," in the words of Emerson, "pierces the form" and penetrates the material husks of reality to its core. "It is an organ for burrowing," says Thoreau. To Whitman as to Emerson subject-object differences are not real. Whitman often expresses the consciousness that all is one and all is self. "All these I feel or am." The mystic's unifying vision obliterates distinctions and attains at-oneness with the All, *Sarvātmatva*. This vision emancipates the poet from the attachment to the particular and the finite and leads to a remarkable enlargement of sympathies. Whitman's love is largely anonymous in character and he sings of human beings in the mass. It has been stated that Whitman's attempt to see life without distinctions results in formlessness in his poetry. "Sing me the universal," Whitman says to his muse. He sets

[5] "Compensation."
[6] "Song of the Open Road," lines 88–90.
[7] "Song of Myself," lines 800–801.
[8] *Ibid.*, line 988.

to himself an unlimited subject whereas particular things are the stuff of poetry. But where Whitman has lost as a poet he has gained as a mystic. For, in escaping the particular he has escaped the binding quality of things, of *nāmarūpa*, or name and form. He has, according to the Vedantist, attained *Mōksa* or release.

From this supreme realization emerges the Transcendental Self, the immutable identical substance underneath the changing world of phenomena. In his essay "Oversoul" Emerson develops the concept of a transcendental self, the soul within man, the vast spiritual background and the substratum of all functions and states of consciousness. The resemblance between this idea and the Upanishadic concept of *Atman-Brahman* is unmistakable. Whitman is conscious of himself as two, as "my soul and I." Emerson speaks of the "distinction of the outer and the inner self; the double consciousness that within this erring passionate mortal self sits a supreme calm immortal mind. . . ." Thoreau too is aware of "a certain doubleness by which I can stand as remote from myself as from another . . ." a "spectator sharing no experience . . . that is no more I than it is you." Beneath the flood of "ego" phantoms is the true self, "the background of our being" which is the self of all. Whitman calls this "the mystical identity, the real Me or You." This self is not to be identified with the not-self, the name and form. Ignorance or *Avidya* consists in the superposition of the not-self on the Self (*Ātmani anātmādhyāsa*). Discrimination between the two is the starting point as well as the end of all knowledge. Whitman conceives of his role as that of a spectator unattached to actions and their consequences, sharing all experience, yet detached from it, standing apart and watching the masquerade of life:

> . . . depressions and exaltations
> Battles, the horrors of fratricidal war, the fever of doubtful news,
>   the fitful events;
> These come to me days and nights and go from me again,
> But they are not the Me myself.
> Apart from the pulling and hauling stands what I am,
> Stands amused, complacent, compassionating, idle, unitary . . .
> Both in and out of the game and watching and wondering at it.[9]

This self is the transcendental witness in us, the spectator (*Sāksi*) or detached percipience. The *Upanishad* describes two birds perching on the self-same tree, one of which feeds on the delicious fruit, while the other, not tasting of it, looks on. Whitman sits and looks out on the

---

[9] "Song of Myself," lines 71–79.

world of misery, evil, and suffering with supreme indifference and detachment. This distinction between his real nature, the "mystical identity the real I or You or Me"[1] and the phenomenal strata of his mind is constant in Whitman. And this self being the very root is also the self of all. Hence does Whitman "celebrate myself and sing myself" and assume that "every atom belonging to me as good belongs to you." Whitman's self is not the dialectical being of the Germans, torn by an inner differentiation and caught in an endless web of relationships. It is not the many-in-one of Hegel but an "identity" transcending the relational existence:

> To these proud laws of the air, the water and ground, proving
>   my interior soul impregnable,
> And nothing exterior shall ever take command of me.[2]

Emerson says: "There is a deeper fact in the soul than compensation, to wit its own nature. The soul is not a compensation, but a life. The soul is."[3] Whereas the world is governed by the laws of compensation, the soul is independent of such laws and subsists in its own right; it follows out its own laws and standards and is never the object of external will. The self thus separated from the phenomenal modes is neither like the *Pour-soi* of the Existentialists, which constitutes itself by self-negation, but is felt as a being in its plenitude, positive and self-certain.

> To feel the puzzle of puzzles
> And that we call Being.[4]

As a result of this self-realization Whitman experiences an inner liberation, a release from all earthly ballasts:

> . . . loos'd of limits and imaginary lines,
> Going where I list, my own master total and absolute,
> . . . divesting myself of the holds that would hold me.[5]

In a process of dynamic self-expansion Whitman's soul, like the *Viswarupa* (Cosmic Form) of the *Gita*, enters into all and becomes all. "The universe is in myself; it shall pass through me as a procession." He contains multitudes and contradicts himself, for he has known the

---

[1] See "I Sit and Look Out."
[2] "A Song of Joys," lines 137–138.
[3] "Compensation."
[4] "Song of Myself," lines 609–610.
[5] "Song of the Open Road," lines 53–54, 57.

underlying identity of things. He transcends all ethical distinctions and stands indifferent like the seer in the *Upanishads*.

> Apart from right, apart from the unright,
> Apart from both what has been done and what has not been done
> Untouched by good and untouched by evil.

In what might be a close echo of the above passage from the *Upanishad* Whitman says:

> Evil propels me and reform of evil propels me, I stand indifferent.[6]

He is freed from all dualities and tensions of body and soul, of matter and spirit.

> Clear and sweet is my soul, clear and sweet is all that is not my soul.[7]

While Carlyle remained a "sick soul" haunted by the spectre of world-destruction, while Emerson suffered from congenital low-spirits, and while Thoreau's mind in spite of its remarkable peace and poise bristled with criticisms and negations, Whitman showed a complete accord with existence and gave an unqualified approval to everything. He feels an ineffable sense of fruition and fullness:

> I am satisfied, I see, dance, laugh, sing.[8]

Whitman has been blamed for his incapacity to portray evil and human suffering. But the poems of Whitman do not purport to portray evil; they express rather this exalted vision of a mystic.

ROGER ASSELINEAU

[The "Plan" for *Leaves of Grass*]†

* * * The book is too often studied as a unit and critics tend to forget that it represents forty years of assiduous experimentation, that

---

[6] "Song of Myself," line 465.
[7] *Ibid*, line 52.
[8] *Ibid*, line 59.
† From Roger Asselineau, *The Evolution of Walt Whitman: The Creation of a Personality*, trans. Roger Asselineau and Richard P. Adams (Cam-

Whitman was thirty years old when he began, and that he was an old man when he stopped. They also forget that during the same period of time the United States made the transition from a rural to an industrial civilization after a terrible civil war. Whitman's book is therefore the fruit of a long life and the mirror of a crucial period of American history.[1] To use another image, it is not a plain of uniform nature and origin, but a plateau where layers of different geological periods have been brought to the surface by various upheavals and later eroded. It is true that Whitman wanted us to consider only the final result, that is to say, the text of 1892. He said so in a note prefixed to the "deathbed" edition:

> As there are now several editions of L. of G., different texts and dates, I wish to say that I prefer and recommend this present one, complete, for future printing, if there should be any; a copy and fac-simile, indeed, of the text of these 438 pages.[2]

And Horace L. Traubel reports that he once said:

> So far as you may have anything to do with it I place upon you the injunction that whatever may be added to the *Leaves* shall be supplementary, avowed as such, leaving the book complete as I left it, consecutive to the point I left off, marking always an unmistakable, deep down, unobliteratable division line. In the long run the world will do as it pleases with the book. I am determined to have the world know what I was pleased to do.[3]

Surely he has a right to try to impose a version to which he did his best to give a definitive structure, but we also have a right, which he recognized, to prefer a different approach, to try to rediscover behind the completed façade which he has left us the living presence of the author who slowly built up this work.

Here a problem arises: had Whitman conceived the definitive plan of *Leaves of Grass* as it appeared in the "deathbed" edition before 1855? He said so in 1881. For, when the 1881 edition was published, he declared to a Boston reporter:

---

bridge: The Belknap Press of Harvard University, 1960), pp. 5–13. Copyright 1960 by the President and Fellows of Harvard College. Reprinted by permission of the publisher. (References to Whitman's prose works have been changed to reflect the page numbers in the Norton Critical Edition.)

[1] "My book and I—what a period we have presumed to span! those thirty years from 1850 to '80—and America in them!" "A Backward Glance o'er Travel'd Roads," p. 565, above [*Editors*].

[2] Printed on verso of title page of *LG* 1891–92.

[3] "An Executor's Diary Note," 1891, p. 575, above [*Editors*].

It is now, I believe, twenty-six years since I began to work upon the structure; and this edition will complete the design which I had in mind when I began to write. The whole affair is like one of those old architectural edifices, some of which were hundreds of years in building, and the designer of which had the whole idea in mind from the first. His plans are pretty ambitious, and as means or time permits, he adds part after part, perhaps at quite wide intervals. To a casual observer it looks in the course of its construction odd enough. Only after the whole is completed one catches the idea which inspired the designer, in whose mind the relation of each part to the whole had existed all along. That is the way it has been with my book. It has been twenty-six years building. There have been seven different hitches at it. Seven different times have parts of the edifice been constructed sometimes in Brooklyn, sometimes in Washington, sometimes in Boston, and at other places. The book has been built partially in every part of the United States. And this edition is the completed edifice.[4]

As early as 1876 he had stated in an interview with one J.B.S. of the New York *World*: "I set out with a design as thoroughly considered as an architect's plan for a cathedral."[5]

What do these assertions mean? At first glance they are at least surprising. The book gives the impression, not of having developed harmoniously over the years, but of having undergone a series of Protean metamorphoses. A quick look at the different editions is enough to show this. The text of 1855 is a river of lava. Some of the poems in it, particularly the one which later became "Song of Myself," are interminable. They are not differentiated by titles, they are all indiscriminately called "Leaves of Grass." In 1856 the work was enriched with a large number of short pieces, and this time all the poems had titles. But it is only in 1860 that we find the first attempt at organization; most of the short poems now are grouped in sections with titles, but within each section, the poems lose their individuality; instead of titles they bear only numbers, as one numbers the panels of a frame house before taking it to pieces and moving it to another location. In 1867 the aspect of the book once more changed completely. Titles reappeared, each poem had its own, but now the sections in their turn lost their individuality. Except for "Children of Adam" and "Calamus" they were undifferentiated and all called "Leaves of Grass"; a partial return to the uniformity of the first edition. In 1871 the poems devoted

---

[4] *Boston Globe*, August 24, 1881.
[5] *New York World*, May 21, 1876.

to the Civil War were finally incorporated in the book. They formed three groups interpolated among the existing sections, thus introducing an element of diversity and also giving the collection a sort of skeleton. The edition of 1876 consisted for its part of two volumes, but the first merely reproduced the edition of 1871. For the new poems were not yet part and parcel of *Leaves of Grass* proper. They were relegated to the second volume and mingled with pieces of prose. It was only in 1881 that they were allowed a place in the collection. Is it not altogether remarkable that from 1867, that is to say, precisely from the time Whitman tried to give his book a little order, he was unable immediately to incorporate the poems which he wrote? If he had really had a plan in mind, it would have been easy for him to find a place for each of them. Even if we concede that the Civil War surprised him and upset his projects, how can we explain his failure to include in *Leaves of Grass* the poems which in 1876 he was constrained to keep apart provisionally in the miscellaneous volume entitled *Two Rivulets*? Why, moreover, did he not announce his design in the 1855 preface? And, if he had a plan from the beginning, why is it that he continued until 1881 to change the order and the titles of the various poems? Why did his book begin to be organized only in 1860 (and even then not tightly)? As a matter of fact, in 1857, commenting in a letter on the 1860 edition which was almost ready, he made this very revealing statement:

> It is, I know Well enough, that *that* must be the *true Leaves of Grass*—and I think it has an aspect of completeness, and makes its case clearer.—The old poems are all retained.—The difference is in the new character given to the mass, by the additions.[6]

According to this, he had as early as 1857 the impression that the edifice was finished. But can we even speak of an edifice? He was so reluctant to give his work an architectural aspect that he used a word as little suggestive of order and harmony as "mass" to describe the material of the volume to come. Besides, he made no allusion to any changes in structure; the difference he found between the two volumes was mainly quantitative; if the new edition was to produce a different impression, it would not be owing to a different arrangement, but to added material.

Several years later, on May 31, 1861, to be precise, he noted in

---

[6] Letter to Sara Tyndale, dated Brooklyn, July 20, 1857. In *The Correspondence of Walt Whitman*, ed. Edwin H. Miller (New York: New York University Press, 1961–), vol. I, *1842–1867* (1961), p. 44.

the rough draft of a preface which he never had occasion to publish: "The paths to the house are made—but where is the house itself? At most only indicated or touched."[7] Could he say more frankly that there was no order in the work which he thus submitted to the reader and that he had not followed any plan? However he went on in these terms: "Nevertheless, as while we live some dream will play its part, I keep it in my plan of work ahead to yet fill up these *Whisperings*, (if I live & have luck) somehow proportionate to their original design."[8]

Thus, at the very time when he seemed to recognize that there was no trace of a plan in his *Leaves of Grass*, once more he asserted that he had one in his head. What precisely did he mean by "plan"? The interview which he gave in 1876 to the New York *World*, from which I have already cited a passage, may be of some help. For here he said among other things:

> I set out to illustrate, without any flinching, actual humanity. I proposed to myself a series of compositions which should depict the physical, emotional, moral, intellectual and spiritual nature of a man.
>
> —That man being yourself?
>
> —That man for purposes of illustration, being myself . . . You can see I had first to deal with the physical, the corporal, the amative business—that part of our nature which is developed so strongly between the ages of 22 and 35. It is that part of my endeavor which caused most of the harsh criticism, and prevented candid examination of the ensuing stages of the design.[9]

We may compare this declaration with the one he made the same year in the Preface to *Two Rivulets*:

> It was originally my intention, after chanting in *Leaves of Grass* the songs of the Body and Existence, to then compose a further, equally needed Volume, based on those convictions of perpetuity and conservation which, enveloping all precedents, make the unseen Soul govern absolutely at last. I meant, while in a sort continuing the theme of my first chants, to shift the slides, and exhibit the problem and paradox of the same ardent and fully appointed Personality entering the sphere of the resistless gravitation of Spiritual Law, and with cheerful face estimating Death,

[7] *Walt Whitman's Workshop*, ed. C. J. Furness (Cambridge: Harvard University Press, 1928), p. 135.
[8] *Ibid.*
[9] See note 5 [Editors].

not at all as the cessation, but as somehow what I feel it must be, the entrance upon by far the greatest part of existence, and something that Life is at least as much for, as it is for itself. . .

Meanwhile, not entirely to give the go-by to my original plan, and far more to avoid a mark'd hiatus in it, than to entirely fulfil it, I end my books with thoughts, or radiations from thoughts, on Death, Immortality, and a free entrance into the Spiritual world. In those thoughts, in a sort, I make the first steps or studies toward the mighty theme, from the point of view necessitated by my foregoing poems, and by Modern Science. In them I also seek to set the key-stone to my Democracy's enduring arch.[1]

It is clear then that if Whitman had a plan in mind from the beginning, it was a singularly vague one—not a detailed and rigorous scheme with logical articulations clearly marked, but only two or three very general ideas which he proposed to develop. In other words, from the beginning, he knew where he was going and what he wanted, what great themes he was going to treat: the body, then the spiritual life, and then, by a natural progression, death and immortality, and finally, man no longer alone but in society, which for him was, of course, a democratic society. But he had no idea of the way in which he was to organize this rich material and compose his book. Only the goal toward which he was heading was fixed; the ways which he would take to attain it changed constantly, as his gropings and the frequent revisions he made in his poems indicate. In fact he admitted in the Preface of 1872:

When I commenced, years ago, elaborating the plan of my poems, and continued turning over that plan, and shifting it in my mind through many years, (from the age of twenty-eight to thirty-five,) experimenting much, and writing and abandoning much, one deep purpose underlay the others, and has underlain it and its execution ever since—and that has been the Religious purpose. Amid many changes, and a formulation taking far different shape from what I had first supposed, this basic purpose has never been departed from in the composition of my verses.[2]

It would therefore be more proper to speak of germs than of a plan. The word "plan" implies an architectural structure. But, as the evidence given above has shown, and as the detailed study of the dif-

[1] "Preface 1876," q.v. above [Editors].
[2] "Preface 1872," q.v. above [Editors].

ferent editions will prove, *Leaves of Grass* was not really constructed.
Whitman allowed his book to grow within his mind little by little
with an organic and almost vegetable growth. (In this sense the title
of his book was particularly happy.) He did not intervene except to
preserve a certain cohesion, a unity more organic than logical, which
he defined himself in the "Notes on the Meaning and Intention of
Leaves of Grass" published after his death by Richard Maurice Bucke:
"My poems when complete should be *a unity*, in the same sense that
the earth is, or that the human body, (senses, soul, head, trunk, feet,
blood, viscera, man-root, eyes, hair) or that a perfect musical composi-
tion is."[3]

Or again, as John Burroughs said in his *Notes on Walt Whitman*,
Leaves of Grass is "a series of growths, or strata, rising or starting
out from a settled foundation or centre and expanding in successive
accumulations."[4]

This comparison with the formation of a tree trunk is perhaps
a little stiff, but at least it takes account of the instinctive, non-logical
character of the development of *Leaves of Grass*. On the contrary,
Oscar L. Triggs misses the point badly when he maintains that "*Leaves
of Grass* has a marked tectonic quality. The author, like an architect,
drew his plans, and the poem, like a cathedral long in building, slowly
advanced to fulfilment. Each poem was designed and written with refer-
ence to its place in an ideal edifice."[5] Nothing could be more false, as
we have seen. Such order as can be found in the later editions was im-
posed from the outside; it represents an intervention posterior to the
act of creation.

At the beginning, then, Whitman had no plan; only a group of
fairly general themes. It could hardly have been otherwise, given the
subject which he had chosen. He was trying to express the inexpressible,
an impossible task, never-ending, always to be resumed. He wanted his
poems joyously to proclaim their "tidings old, yet ever new, untrans-
latable."[6]

He set off bravely in search of a new *Weltanschauung* that would
be in harmony with the needs of his democratic and scientific century:

> . . . it is imperatively and ever to be borne in mind that
> *Leaves of Grass* entire is not to be construed as an intellectual or

---

[3] *Notes and Fragments*, ed. R. M. Bucke (London, 1899), p. 55.
[4] *Walt Whitman's Workshop*, pp. 9–10.
[5] Whitman, *Complete Writings* (New York: G. P. Putnam's Sons, 1902),
X, 101.
[6] "Or from That Sea of Time," line 8.

scholastic effort or Poem mainly, but more as a radical utterance
out of the abysms of the Soul, the Emotions and the Physique—
an utterance adjusted to, perhaps born of, Democracy and Modern
Science . . .[7]

Though from no definite plan at the time, I see now that I
have unconsciously sought by indirections at least as much as
directions, to express the whirls and rapid growth and intensity
of the United States, the prevailing tendency and events of the
Nineteenth Century, and largely the spirit of the whole current
World, my time . . .[8]

Therefore he was only gradually aware of all the implications of
his work:

. . . I set out with the intention also of indicating or hinting
some point-characteristics which I since see (though I did not
then, at least not definitely) were bases and object-urgings toward
those "Leaves" from the first.[9]

This was hardly a rational process, or one that could be defined in
rational terms. However, his subject being otherwise impossible to
grasp, it was the only method that offered itself to him. Anyhow, he
did not believe that anyone could ever succeed in pressing more closely
into the mystery which lies at the heart of things.

The best poetic utterance, after all, can merely hint, or re-
mind, often very indirectly, or at distant removes. Aught of real
perfection, or the solution of any deep problem, or any completed
statement of the moral, the true, the beautiful, eludes the greatest,
deftest poet—flies away like an always uncaught bird.[1]

Though the fowler in the course of successive editions tried to tighten
the meshes of his net, he could never succeed in catching the bird.

Consequently, because of the fleeting nature of the subject and
the peculiar progress of a way of thinking that proceeded by successive
approximations, Leaves of Grass was slowly shaped by the interaction
of two different processes, the one of instinctive growth and the other
of rational and deliberate construction. * * *

---

[7] "Preface 1876," q.v. above [Editors].
[8] Ibid., q.v. above [Editors].
[9] "A Backward Glance o'er Travel'd Roads," q.v. above [Editors].
[1] Whitman, November Boughs (1888), p. 56.

KARL SHAPIRO

The First White Aboriginal†

D. H. Lawrence has more in common with Walt Whitman than with any other man, and it was Lawrence who called Whitman the first white aboriginal. Coming from Lawrence, who felt unable to pay an unequivocal compliment, the epithet was the highest praise. Lawrence's quest was for the aboriginal, the pure energy of the soul. Being an Englishman, he fled from the white man and his white religions and the terrible whiteness of consciousness (which he called mentality) and raced with all his strength to the dark races and beyond, to the blood religions, the spirit of the serpent, and all that. Lawrence made a magnificent leap across civilization into the aboriginal darkness. He is one of the supreme heretics of white, modern civilization. And so for him to bless Walt with the title of the first white aboriginal is a matter of tremendous import. Lawrence is one of the great spirits of our age, as Whitman is, although from Lawrence stems a good deal of the negativity of modern intellectual life. From Whitman stems much of what there is of the opposite. Lawrence sprang from a modern industrial hell which he never forgave and was never far enough away from to understand. Whitman did not have to spring; he sprouted, he vegetated, he loafed out of nowhere into the role of prophet and seer. At a single stroke, apparently without preparation, he became the one poet of America and Democracy. He is the one mystical writer of any consequence America has produced; the most original religious thinker we have; the poet of the greatest achievement; the first profound innovator; the most accomplished artist as well—but nobody says this nowadays. For in the twentieth century Walt Whitman is almost completely shunned by his fellows. He has no audience, neither a general audience nor a literary clique. Official criticism ignores him completely; modern neo-classicism, as it calls itself, acknowledges him with embarrassment. (Ezra Pound "forgives" Whitman because "he broke the new wood," meaning he broke iambic pentameter.) And scholars nowadays, happily

† From James E. Miller, Jr., Karl Shapiro, and Bernice Slote, *Start with the Sun: Studies in Cosmic Poetry* (Lincoln: University of Nebraska Press, 1960), pp. 57–70. Copyright 1960 by University of Nebraska Press. Reprinted by permission of the publisher.

confused by the scholarly complexities of contemporary poets, look upon Walt as a grand failure and an anachronism.

Lawrence, in his search around the world for a pure well of human energy, acknowledged Whitman with love. It is a rare thing for Lawrence. He says:

> Whitman, the great poet, has meant so much to me. Whitman, the one man breaking a way ahead. Whitman, the one pioneer. And only Whitman. No English pioneers, no French. No European pioneer-poets. In Europe the would-be pioneers are mere innovators. The same in America. Ahead of Whitman, nothing. Ahead of all poets, pioneering into the wilderness of unopened life, Whitman. Beyond him, none. His wide, strange camp at the end of the great high-road. And lots of new little poets camping on Whitman's camping ground now. But none going really beyond.

But at this point Lawrence changes his tune and explains how Whitman failed. He says that Whitman fell into the old fallacy of Christian love, confusing his great doctrine of Sympathy with Love and Merging. Nothing was more loathsome to the puritanical Lawrence than Merging, and when Whitman merged Lawrence disgorged. How Lawrence longed to merge! And how the mere shake of the hand horrified him! Lawrence in thousands of passages obsessively records his tabu against touching. *Noli me tangere!* It is the opposite of Whitman's obsession *for* touching:

> Is this then a touch? quivering me to a new identity,
> Flames and ether making a rush for my veins,
> Treacherous tip of me reaching and crowding to help them,
> My flesh and blood playing out lightning to strike what is hardly
>   different from myself,
> On all sides prurient provokers stiffening my limbs,
> Straining the udder of my heart for its withheld drip,
> Behaving licentious toward me, taking no denial,
> Depriving me of my best as for a purpose,
> Unbuttoning my clothes, holding me by the bare waist. . . .

(This is the passage in "Song of Myself" which, after a parenthesis— "What is less or more than a touch?"—leads into "I think I could turn and live with animals, they're so placid and self-contain'd,/I stand and look at them long and long." It is one of the greatest moments of poetry.)

Lawrence, with his deep love of animals and his irritable suspicion of mankind, was the inferior of Whitman. Whitman had the natural love of man which Lawrence, rightly, called American. Lawrence was fascinated, hypnotized, and slightly sick in the stomach. Lawrence says if Walt had known about Charlie Chaplin he would have assumed one identity with him too. What a pity, Lawrence sneers. He'd have done poems, paeans, and what not, Chants, Songs of Cinematernity. "Oh, Charlie, my Charlie, another film is done—"

But in the end Lawrence gives in; he knows a kindred spirit when he sees one. He looks down his nose at Whitman's paeans upon Death— Lawrence, who is one of the true poets of Death—and then adds:

> But the exultance of his message still remains. Purified of MERGING, purified of MYSELF, the exultant message of American Democracy, of souls in the Open Road, full of glad recognition, full of fierce readiness, full of joy of worship, when one soul sees a greater soul.
> The only riches, the great souls.

This is the last line of Lawrence's book called *Studies in Classic American Literature*, and I submit that it is a fine concession to be wrung from Lawrence, the archetype of tortured modern man, the man without heroes. Lawrence and Whitman are two modern poets with the deepest concern for mankind, the farthest insight, the widest sympathy, the simplest and best expression. They are scriptural writers in the long run, despising professionalism and current fashions. But Lawrence fails to do more than pose the problem of modern civilization versus the individual intelligence. He has no answer. He half invents fascism; he is torn between the image of the free natural male (the father who is always leaving home to become a gipsy) and the image of the leader, the aristocrat. He had it both ways: he remains unresolved. But he also had the vision. He became, in effect, an American, an American among Red Indians and rattlesnakes, close to that darker America betrayed by the white religions, Mexico, which he also loved. But it was Whitman's America that he held out for, "the true democracy [as Lawrence said], where soul meets soul, in the open road. Democracy. American democracy where all journey down the open road. And where a soul is known at once in its going." Strange words coming from the author of *Kangaroo* and *The Plumed Serpent*.

Lawrence suffers somewhat the fate of Whitman today. He is declassed. He enjoys a kind of underground popularity among writers, but he is outside the pale of the Tradition. He is too violent, too special, too original. And he is too outspoken. But Lawrence could never survive within a tradition, any more than Whitman. He has, at his best, a style so lean it matches the burnt-away clean language of prophets.

Most of Lawrence's disciples, it seems to me, misunderstand him; but at least he has disciples. Whitman has no disciples and practically no living literary reputation. He is only a name.

What has happened to Whitman in the century since *Leaves of Grass* was published? It matters very little what happened historically. There were the usual false praises and the usual false deprecations, and enough of the true acclaim to give us faith in the history of criticism. There has never been anything we could call popularity for Whitman. Publishers are inclined to prepare elaborate editions of *Leaves of Grass*, in the same way that they release erotic editions of the Song of Songs: in a wrong-headed way, it is a compliment to Whitman. But the famous minds of the present century have not closed with Whitman, in my opinion. And the leading poets of the twentieth century have coolly and with relentless deliberation suppressed Whitman and kept him from exerting his force. Any Whitman advocate of great talent, for example Hart Crane, is forced to apologize for this allegiance before he is admitted to the company of moderns. There is no question that an Act of Exclusion has been in perpetual operation against Whitman since 1855 and is carried on today by the leading "classicists" of English and American poetry. Walt just won't do. He is vulgar; he is a humbug; he copies the names of rivers out of the sixth-grade geography book; he is an optimist; he is unlettered; he is a theosophist; he abhors institutions; he is auto-erotic; he loves everybody; he is a Rotarian; he goes to the opera; he can't distinguish between good and evil; he has no sense of humor; he cannot solve his own paradox about the greatness of the individual and the greatness of the En-Masse; he has no style—etc., etc.

All such accusations are true, and one could multiply them for pages and pages. Yet in the last analysis, they do not matter. Emerson saw humor in Whitman, though he called it wit. But Whitman thought he was writing a kind of bible. And it is the biblical quality of Whitman (as with Lawrence) that is so offensive to lovers of literature. What insolence! they say, and they are right. For neither Whitman nor Lawrence were "writers"; they were prophets. Literature makes it its business to stone prophets.

Whitman is indeed full of humbug, as when he talks about his experiences as a wound-dresser.

One night in the gloomiest period of the war, in the Patent Office hospital in Washington city, as I stood by the bedside of a Pennsylvania soldier, who lay, conscious of quick approaching death, yet perfectly calm, and with noble, spiritual manner, the veteran surgeon, turning aside, said to me, that though he had witness'd many, many deaths of soldiers, and had been a worker at Bull Run, Antietam, Fredericksburg, etc., he had not seen yet the first case of man or boy that met the approach of dissolution with cowardly qualms or terror. . . . Grand, common stock! to me the accomplish'd and convincing growth, prophetic of the future; proof . . . of perfect beauty, tenderness and pluck, that never feudal lord, nor Greek, nor Roman breed, yet rival'd. Let no tongue ever speak disparagement of the American races, north or south. . . .[1]

This sounds like Churchill at his worst.

It does not seem to me that Whitman is a complicated case of poor manners, confusions, and paradoxes; of philosophical muddle and literary naïveté; of good intentions, high passages, and bad dreary bogs. But even if I exaggerate his achievement, I maintain that he is the one and only poet of America who has ever attempted to adumbrate the meaning of America. The twentieth-century American poet avoids this commitment, by and large: he considers it fitting and proper to take refuge in History against the horrors of progress; or in pure dialectic; or in the catacombs of established faith; or, failing that, in what is called the Language. Whitman's vision has degenerated into a thing called the Language; that is, the American Language, the natural nonhieratic language out of which a mythos might germinate. But Whitman contended that the mythos was at hand. He defined it; he sang it; he argued it; he poured it out. To no avail.

Twentieth-century poetry is a poetry of perfections. It is the least spontaneous poetry since—whatever date for the birth of artificiality you call to mind. It is the pride of twentieth-century poetry that even Yeats was brought to heel by critics who called for a "hard brittle technique." It is the pride of twentieth-century poetry that one publishes a poem once a decade. It is the boast of our poetry that it is impersonal, and that it can mean more or less what you think it means, and be right in the bargain. Whitman subscribed to—in a sense he invented—the philosophy of personalism. Lawrence too spoke with his own mouth and took the consequences. It was not for either to duck back into the Tradition. Yet Whitman did not repudiate the past; nor did he look with any pleasure upon the present, the America of a hundred years ago. He wrote in *Democratic Vistas:*

Never was there . . . more hollowness at heart than at present, and here in the United States. Genuine belief seems to

---

[1] All of the prose quotations from Whitman in this essay are found in "Democratic Vistas," one of Whitman's prefaces [*Editors*].

have left us. The underlying principles of the States are not
honestly believ'd in. . . . The spectacle is appalling. We live
in an atmosphere of hypocrisy throughout. The men believe not
in the women nor the women in the men. A scornful supercilious-
ness rules in literature. The aim of all the littérateurs is to find
something to make fun of. A lot of churches, sects, etc., the most
dismal phantasms I know, usurp the name of religion. . . . The
depravity of the business classes of our country is not less than
has been supposed, but infinitely greater. The official services of
America, national, state, and municipal, in all their branches and
departments, except the judiciary, are saturated in corruption,
bribery, falsehood, maladministration; and the judiciary is tainted.
. . . In business (this all-devouring modern word, business),
the sole object is, by any means, pecuniary gain. . . . I say that
our New World democracy . . . is, so far, an almost complete
failure in its social aspects, and in really grand religious, moral,
literary, and aesthetic results. . . .

Whitman sees the corruption and persists in his faith that the
principle of democracy will overrule the corrupt. Let us call it the
romantic position. But Whitman (like Jefferson) does not feel that
the written word of democratic principle is sacrosanct. He goes to the
heart of the matter. Man must do good, he says, because that is his
ultimate nature. The man who falls a prey to corruption, dandyism,
superficiality, selfishness, is a fallen man. Whitman despises him. He
believes it natural to be pure: nature purifies. He has a kind of worship
of chemistry, shared by his countrymen, an animal faith in the god
of the sun and the god of water. It is precisely his contempt for ideas of
sin and evil which places him among the great teachers of mankind.

What chemistry!
That the winds are really not infectious,
That this is no cheat, this transparent green-wash of the sea which
    is so amorous after me,
That it is safe to allow it to lick my naked body all over with its
    tongues,
That it will not endanger me with the fevers that have deposited
    themselves in it,
That it is all clean forever and forever,
That the cool drink from the well tastes so good,
That blackberries are so flavorous and juicy. . . .
That when I recline on the grass I do not catch any disease . . .

He did not have a simple faith in the frontiers of knowledge; on the contrary, he held a limited belief in physical achievements.

> Not you alone proud truths of the world,
> Not you alone ye facts of modern science,
> But myths and fables of eld, Asia's, Africa's fables,
> The far-darting beams of the spirit, the unloos'd dreams,
> The deep diving bibles and legends,
>
> . . . . .
>
> You too with joy I sing.

America to Whitman was not a laboratory, but a place in the journey of mankind where the best in man might flower. America was not the goal; it was a bridge to the goal. In "Passage to India" he says of Columbus:

> (Ah Genoese thy dream! thy dream!
> Centuries after thou art laid in thy grave,
> The shore thou foundest verifies thy dream.)

But the dream is not satisfying enough. We must steer for the deepest waters and take passage to the skies themselves. We must go where mariner has not yet dared to go, risking the ship, ourselves, and all. It is not a geographical poem or a historical poem, although when Whitman talks about the Atlantic cable and its eloquent gentle wires, he sounds silly. But the physical achievement is his symbol of not progress but goodness. It is axiomatic to Whitman that we shall lay cables, build the Union Pacific Railroad, and fly airships to Jupiter. That is the childlike and wonderful faith of the ordinary modern man who is not thrown into reverse by the terror of it all. Whitman is not even talking about that. It is the twentieth-century "classical" poet who is materialistic and who writes scathing books of poems against the electric toaster. For Whitman says in the same poem that the seas are already crossed, weathered the capes, the voyage done. Everything is known already. The advancement of man physically seems to him good but only a trifle. What really concerns him is that man shall explore the soul.

> Passage indeed O soul to primal thought,
> Not lands and seas alone, thy own clear freshness,
> The young maturity of brood and bloom,
> To realms of budding bibles.
>
> . . . . .
>
> Back, back to wisdom's birth, to innocent intuitions,
> Again with fair creation.

Whitman is a mystic and he admits it. This is one more reason for his unpopularity. The best modern poets are allowed to admire a mystic but aren't allowed to be one. Whitman is too close for comfort. Furthermore, he had no theology worth sorting out, except a kind of Quakerism, and religion wasn't his concern. Man was his concern. And not American man. Whitman is not only the first white aboriginal; he is the first American; or that may be the same thing. When I read Whitman, good or bad, I always feel that here is first and foremost an American. I feel that the fundamental religiosity of Whitman plus the contempt for religion is American.

Whitman dissociated himself from mere poets and other writers. Who touches his book touches a man, he said in "Song of Myself":

> I do not despise you priests, all time, the world over,
> My faith is the greatest of faiths and the least of faiths,
> Enclosing worship ancient and modern and all between ancient
>   and modern,
> Believing I shall come again upon the earth after five thousand
>   years,
> Waiting responses from oracles, honoring the gods, saluting the
>   sun,
>   . . . . .
> Helping the llama or brahmin as he trims the lamps of the idols,
> Dancing yet through the streets in a phallic procession, rapt and
>   austere . . .

and so on, down to the Mississippi Baptists with the jerks and spasms.

Whitman is too faithful in his belief in man to lay down the rules for a creed. It is unnecessary. If man is of Nature, and Nature is good, good will triumph. Evil is the failure of man to be as good as he can. For man to become all that is utterly possible is divine. And as every man is divine, inside and out, even the lowest are divinities. What is commonly looked down on nowadays in Whitman's talks about the divine average, is the average. Whitman would have emphasized the *divine*, rather than the average. Each person to him possessed divinty, and to repudiate that divinity was criminal. It is the god in each man and woman (which Lawrence called the Holy Ghost) that we can communicate with. I have rapport with you (Whitman's hieratic termi-nology is always couched in some kind of American French)—I have rapport with you because my divinity, my true personality, has a mouth to speak with. My lower self cannot speak; it can only commit acts of instinct. Yet there is a hierarchy of acts. Each thing to its nature:

(The moth and the fish-eggs are in their place.

The bright suns I see and the dark suns I cannot see are in their place,

The palpable is in its place and the impalpable in its place.)

And Whitman says he is not stuck up and is in his place. Being "in place," of course, is not humility; nor is it a sign of any known orthodoxy.

Whitman asserts his divinity and he cannot evade it, despite a passing show of humility. He has the vision of himself as well in the scale of things. But he acknowledges the god in oneself; and here he makes a break with conventional poetry and conventional thought which is the core of his philosophy.

Divine am I inside and out, and I make holy whatever I touch or am touch'd from.

It is Whitman's creed of the equality of the body and the soul. The body is not cursed; it is the miraculous materialization of the soul. The origin of this body-soul Whitman does not explain; he merely states that it is holy and the holy of holies. If he can find any object of worship more worthy than another it shall be his body or a part of his body. And while he is doting on himself he slips without warning into sun-worship, nature-worship, love-worship, and then back to himself. It goes like this:

If I worship one thing more than another it shall be the spread of my own body, or any part of it,

Translucent mould of me it shall be you!

Shaded ledges and rests it shall be you!

Firm masculine colter it shall be you!

Whatever goes to the tilth of me it shall be you!

You my rich blood! your milky stream pale strippings of my life!

Breast that presses against other breasts it shall be you!

My brain it shall be your occult convolutions!

Root of wash'd sweet-flag! timorous pond-snipe! nest of guarded duplicate eggs! it shall be you!

Mix'd tussled hay of head, beard, brawn, it shall be you!

Trickling sap of maple, fibre of manly wheat, it shall be you!

Sun so generous it shall be you!

Vapors lighting and shading my face it shall be you!

You sweaty brooks and dews it shall be you!

Winds whose soft-tickling genitals rub against me it shall be you!

Broad muscular fields, branches of live oak, loving lounger in
    my winding paths, it shall be you!
Hands I have taken, face I have kiss'd, mortal I have ever
    touch'd, it shall be you.
I dote on myself, there is that lot of me and all so luscious.

He begins with his own corpus, which he finds so luscious; he
forgets himself and begins looking around the park, then he recalls
the amorous uses of parks; and after a breath, he comes back to him-
self and "the lot of him." It is all very simple but it is anything but
trivial. If you read on and on you see that Whitman is not talking
about himself at all and acting like a baby discovering its toes—but
that is the superficial trick of it; he is talking about the primal dis-
covery of self. He is talking about consciousness in the only way it can
be talked about: physically. I do not think for a second that Whitman
was either narcissistic or egomaniac; he was trying to obliterate the
fatal dualism of body and soul. All this monotony about keeping as
clean around the bowels ("delicate" was the word he used) as around
the heart and head is not a swipe at Victorian convention; it was his
way of acknowledging the physicality of the soul, or the spirituality
of the body. Lawrence shied away; and most American writers in
more or less the same puritan tub get the backwash of revulsion about
this physical "obsession" of Whitman's.

But this is only the beginning. Whitman wanted first to create
the full individual, the full person, and this he did by tearing away
the draperies. His wish was to form the complete person, the free
man, the man free in himself, *in order to put this free man into the
world*. The dialectical conflict in Whitman, as in everyone else I
suppose, is the free individual versus the crowd of mankind. The
twentieth-century poet slinks into his study and says, No crowds for
me. But Whitman took it on. He is the only modern poet who has
the courage to meet the crowd. And, falling back into his demotic
French, he delivers the abstraction En-Masse. "Endless unfolding of
words of ages! / And mine a word of the modern, the word En-Masse."
This becomes one of the most ridiculed passages in Whitman, in which
he drunkenly chants: "Hurrah for positive science! long live exact
demonstration!" and "Gentlemen, to you the first honors always!" But
these funny passages of Whitman, I must repeat, are there, not be-
cause he is a fool, but because he has the courage of his convictions.
For just after this idiotic hurrahing for exact demonstration comes
another of the great bursts of poetry, the one beginning "Walt Whit-
man, a kosmos, of Manhattan the son, / Turbulent, fleshy, sensual, eat-

ing, drinking, and breeding. . . ." (Whitman is always aware of the comic possibilities of his position like most prophets. Imagine the jokes that Jesus told!) The balanced man, the free man, the man who meets his potentiality, is a fit man for the new world, the democracy he envisions.

> The purpose of democracy [says Whitman is prose] . . . is, through many transmigrations and amid endless ridicules, arguments, and ostensible failures, to illustrate, at all hazards, this doctrine or theory that man, properly train'd in sanest, highest freedom, may and must become a law, and series of laws, unto himself, surrounding and providing for, not only his own personal control, but all his relations to other individuals, and to the State; and . . . *this*, as matters now stand in our civilized world, is the only scheme worth working from, as warranting results like those of Nature's laws, reliable . . . to carry on themselves.

The concept of En-Masse is not absurd and not laughable, as other expressions of his certainly are, such as Democracy, Ma Femme. But even Whitman's tendency to view Democracy as feminine is penetrating. He would not be surprised to discover in modern America that woman is slightly out of harness; he would approve it. Whitman was the first great American feminist.

A great poet is not merely a poet of his nation but a poet of all peoples. Whitman, who had little enough reward for his book, and has little enough today, looked beyond literature and beyond the greatness of art. His true personality went out beyond America, beyond religions, and even beyond mankind. His poems about the self and the mass of America were written before the Civil War, but the war between the North and South brought everything home to Whitman. His vision might well have been destroyed, but with his natural passion for unity he embarked on a new discovery, not of the body and soul, or rapport, or the En-Masse, but of the exploration of Death. Whitman had always believed in Death as the purposeful continuity of existence, but he had had no significant experience of it. One can barely imagine what the Civil War was to Whitman, this fanatically intense American, this New World man, the first white aboriginal, with his lusty physical joy of life, his love of comrades, his genius for poetry, and his natural mysticism. Whitman was stricken by the War but he was recreated by it. Columbus had been a rather nebulous hero; Lincoln was the reincarnation of the American god to him. Half of Whitman's great poetry is war poetry and poetry upon Lincoln and his death, and death poetry, though it cannot all be dated from the War. Whitman accepted death as he did sex and otherness, self and not-self. The War returned to him the particularity of death, and it produced in him not bitterness but love. He triumphed over it. He saw beyond history and beyond America. But what he saw was with the American vision: in Whitman's dialectic, you do not give up the past for the vision: the past is of the vision as much as the future. In the open air "a great personal deed has room" and it is such a deed that seizes upon the hearts of the whole race of man. And this deed is not discovery or triumph or a formula of belief: it is the giving oneself—the Whitman in oneself—to the other, the comrade. Whitman knew that giving in the past had always been a form of taxation and protection. This new kind of giving is reckless and mystical, differing from the old giving because Whitman gives body and soul without sacrificing one to the other. Whitman is no humanist and no ordinary libertarian but a seer who dreams of free individuality in a world of free souls. The open road may be a commonplace symbol, but it is a deliberate symbol, and it stands for an actuality. That actuality is America as Whitman sees America in himself. The anti-Whitman party of our time is an attempt, of course, to deny the vision of the new world with its physical materialism, experimentalism, and the whole concept of man for the world. It turns out that Whitman is not for the "people" and not for the impressively learned poets of our time. He is for man who begins at the beginning— all over again. There is more to poetry than books, he says in "Song of the Open Road."

> I think heroic deeds were all conceiv'd in the open air, and all
>   free poems also,
> I think I could stop here myself and do miracles . . .
> Here a great personal deed has room . . .
> Here is realization . . .
> Here is adhesiveness . . .
> Do you know what it is as you pass to be loved by stran-
>   gers? . . .
> These are the days that must happen to you:
> You shall not heap up what is call'd riches . . .
> What beckonings of love you receive you shall only answer with
>   passionate kisses of parting,
> You shall not allow the hold of those who spread their reach'd
>   hands toward you.
> Allons! after the great Companions, and to belong to them!

They too are on the road—they are the swift and majestic men—
          they are the greatest women . . .
They go! they go! I know that they go, but I know not where
          they go,
But I know that they go toward the best—toward something
          great.

It is all there: the greatness of the body and the greatness of the
soul; the touching of the world and the heroism of departure; the
magnificent motion of death; the expanding cycle of consciousness; the
essential holiness of all things. And always at the center, the self,
the moment of incarnation, the Walt Whitman of oneself. The
aboriginal or, if you like, the American.

The power of Whitman in the world is incalculable. In litera-
ture it has long been calculated as nothing. It is because of poets
like Whitman that literature exists, but it is always literature that
determines to exterminate its Whitmans, its Blakes, its Lawrences,
its Henry Millers. The probability is that Whitman will never be
"accepted" as one of the great writers of mankind; acceptance is
always a function of the writers who assume the power of literature,
for whatever reasons, and who make literature one of the arms of the
law. Because Whitman is beyond the law of literature, and beyond all
law, he is condemned to extinction from generation to generation.
Whitman is one of those poets who hate religion and who eventually
become a religion. To prevent this happening is forever the mission
of his best disciples.

BERNICE SLOTE

Start with the Sun†

In all periods when man finds himself alien to the whole, a lost
cousin of the universe in which he has been displayed by his own
mind's discoveries, he must make some effort to redefine himself.

† From James E. Miller, Jr., Karl Shapiro, and Bernice Slote, *Start with the
Sun: Studies in Cosmic Poetry* (Lincoln: University of Nebraska Press,
1960), pp. 229–238. Copyright 1960 by University of Nebraska Press. Re-
printed by permission of the publisher.

We say it is now that man is in trouble (though "now" may be
in the eternal present). "Vitally, the human race is dying," wrote
D. H. Lawrence in his 1930 *A Propos of Lady Chatterley's Lover.*
"It is like a great uprooted tree, with its roots in the air. We must
plant ourselves again in the universe." One solution for man's sepa-
rateness is the theme of those we call life-writers—principally Walt
Whitman, D. H. Lawrence, Hart Crane, Dylan Thomas—those who
have a sense of the cosmos and who in their art perform the ritual of
union. What they say in their work is a recognized primitive truth,
though often expressed with symbolic complexity: that man may find
himself both human and divine as he returns to touch the earth with
awareness and love, and joins the sun's creative stream. "Start with
the sun," said Lawrence as his conclusion to *Apocalypse*, "and the rest
will slowly, slowly happen." That is, start with the elements, with the
first principle of creation, with the knowing eye of the creative self.

The poetry which starts with the sun—the "life-poetry"—makes
two great affirmations: connection and creation, and these squarely in
the face of man's increasing terror at the loss of humanity and his
bewilderment at the absence of God. The sense of humanity is best
realized by *connection*, when man knows his own identity within the
circle of the cosmos. The sense of divinity is found in *creation*, in the
germinal sun of each beginning. To make these affirmations was Whit-
man's profound intention in *Leaves of Grass*. How he and other poets
after him viewed nature and man and art will indicate more of the
unity of their work.

Whitman was a preacher of sorts, and his recurring text was
unity, or the theme of cosmic connections. Here the poet may say:
I am part of all, or I am like all other forms, or I *am* all. All objects
of the universe have reference to the soul, said Whitman. That we are
part of the living incarnate cosmos was the great text of D. H.
Lawrence to the very end, as he finally wrote in *Apocalypse:* "I am part
of the sun as my eye is part of me. That I am part of the earth my feet
know perfectly, and my blood is part of the sea." In all life is the "same
old law," said Whitman. "The force that through the green fuse drives
the flower/Drives my green age," wrote Thomas. One name for all,
said Hart Crane:

> I dreamed that all men dropped their names, and sang
> As only they can praise, who build their days
> With fin and hoof, with wing and sweetened fang
> Struck free and holy in one Name always.

In Whitman's vision-poems man is even more wildly identified with every other man and animal and object. "We two, how long we were fool'd," he wrote:

> Now transmuted, we swiftly escape as Nature escapes,
> We are Nature, long have we been absent but now we return,
> We become plants, trunks, foliage, roots, bark,

and we are fishes, hawks, clouds, seas—"We are snow, rain, cold, darkness, we are each product and influence of the globe." This is the incantation of man's union with all of life. But even death has its position. Whitman marveled at the chemistry of the earth which makes spring out of compost. To be the earth and the sea is in the death-life cycle of Thomas's lines on the burning death of a child—death in which one must "enter again the round/Zion of the water bead/And the synagogue of the ear of corn."

The aim of the poetry of connections is outlined in one of Whitman's last poems ("As They Draw to a Close") in which he states the intentions of his songs: to introduce man through the fusion of Space and Time and "the flowing eternal identity" to Nature which encompasses all these and God—"to the joyous electric all," and even to an exultation in Death, which is also part of the scheme. The very bigness of this program did not bother Whitman, for the point was simple: wholeness and unity—or as man we die, and die in ourselves, if we are out of the rhythm of our natural home. The result of conscious and emotional attachment is freedom: "Me imperturbe, standing at ease in Nature." Only the planted tree has the power of the new leaf and the growing branch.

If the theme of life-poetry is first of all the wholeness of man and nature, its characteristic image and symbol will be taken from the archetypal rhythms of birth, death, and renewal; from the elements of water and earth, fire and air; from the alternation of day and night. It will use the old emotionally charged myths of Adam and the ark; of Dionysus and Persephone; of wine, the tree, the phoenix, the fish; of the zodiac and all weathers. Because the poet feels the natural world to be live, though not sentient, man may find his union in the sense of something beyond and before the reason—germ, sea, sun, touch, force, pulse—perhaps Thomas's "elementary town" in "Twenty-Four Years." He goes *in* to night, womb, seed; but he must be prepared to go outward as well as inward. Whitman, for example, sees the universe itself as a road for traveling souls in "Song of the Open Road." He is imaginatively at home in space with sun and stars, exuberantly

> Speeding with tail'd meteors, throwing fire-balls like the rest,
> Carrying the crescent child that carries its own full mother in
> its belly,

and, he continues in "Song of Myself," "I tread day and night such roads." In another line of that poem Whitman chants, "I ascend from the moon, I ascend from the night." Lawrence's lines in his last, unfinished "Prayer" are similar:

> Give me the moon at my feet
> Put my feet upon the crescent, like a Lord!

Such images become the sacred objects of man's ritual of celebration in the natural world. They remind him that he, too, is in the rhythmic design.

Another way of preserving the concept of man's cosmic nature is in the ancient dual glass of macrocosm and microcosm, in which the universe is body, and man is a universe compact. Whitman's "Out from Behind this Mask," a poem to confront a portrait, gives the most complete statement of the microcosm:

> Out from behind this bending rough-cut mask,
>
> . . . . .
>
> This heart's geography's map, this limitless small continent, this
> soundless sea;
> Out from the convolutions of this globe,
> This subtler astronomic orb than sun or moon, than Jupiter,
> Venus, Mars,
> This condensation of the universe, (nay here the only universe,
> Here the idea, all in this mystic handful wrapt) . . . .

These lines sound Elizabethan. One is reminded therefore that the idea of man as the universe condensed appears in many other times and kinds of poetry. The difference is that what may in some poetics be a manner, or a conceit, is organic metaphor in the Whitman kind of verse. It is almost less metaphor than literal belief. With Dylan Thomas, for example, nature habitually operates in sexual forms, beginning with the implied fecundity of the "torrent salmon sun" of the "Prologue" to his *Collected Poems* (see also "In the Beginning" and "My World is Pyramid"). This is not a mirror of the world, but the world as it is. Conversely, the body of man is made up of natural forces ("Light Breaks Where No Sun Shines"):

> Dawn breaks behind the eyes;
> From poles of skull and toe the windy blood
> Slides like a sea. . . .

In other poems he uses the "seashell flesh," the "other sun" of the blood, "thunderclapping eyes," "weather in the flesh and bone," and reverses the images to those of man in nature, as in the lines from "In Country Sleep":

> the vein of birds in the winged, sloe wrist
> Of the wood! Pastoral beat of blood through the laced leaves!

The complete chain of images to and from man is suggested in elemental terms, as Thomas in "Especially When the October Wind" describes man "caught by the crabbing sun" and walking "on fire," casting his "shadow crab upon the land." But the focus can be reversed: man also throws his shadow shape into the sky. The myth of the man in the stars, the astrological macrocosm, is familiar in cosmic poetry. Thomas's sonnets of "Altarwise by Owl-Light" have their exegesis in the zodiac, according to Elder Olson in *The Poetry of Dylan Thomas*.[1] That Lawrence also used the Kabbalistic myth of the offspring of the stars, the children of Adam, is pointed out in *D. H. Lawrence and the Body Mystical* by Frederick Carter,[2] with whom Lawrence began the work which resulted in *Apocalypse*. And may not Whitman's "Children of Adam" poems refer obliquely to the descent through the body of what Carter calls that great original "Father of Men, the great protoplasm Adam," and the possible journey back to the beginning? The life-poets have generally told a universal story—the saga (in Thomas's phrase) from mermen to seraphim.

To start with the sun means also to start from beginnings. It means, in life-poetry, the theme of creation. And creation begins first of all with direct personal involvement. Out of yourself and nobody else, said Whitman, must come the recognition of life:

> Stop this day and night with me and you shall possess the origin
> of all poems,
> You shall possess the good of the earth and sun, (there are mil-
> lions of suns left,)
> You shall no longer take things at second or third hand, nor
> look through the eyes of the dead, nor feed on the spectres
> in books,
> You shall not look through my eyes either, nor take things from
> me,
> You shall listen to all sides and filter them from your self.

[1] Elder Olson, *The Poetry of Dylan Thomas* (Chicago: The University of Chicago Press, 1955), pp. 64–86.
[2] Frederick Carter, *D. H. Lawrence and the Body Mystical* (London: Denis Archer, 1932), pp. 21–25.

The journey in Time and Space must be a firsthand affair. He is lucky who knows where he is, who absorbs and returns directly, who is "the caresser of life wherever moving." If he senses the mystery ("alive in the waters and singingbirds" as Thomas described in "Poem in October"), he will also find a greater mystery, even a divinity in himself. Whitman suggests in many ways the divinity of man. Visually, he draws the halo—"no head without its nimbus of gold-color'd light" ("To You"). In "A Song for Occupations" he reverses the source of divine knowledge: bibles and religions "have all grown out of you";

> It is not they who give the life, it is you who give the life,
> Leaves are not more shed from the trees, or trees from the earth,
>   than they are shed out of you.

But the chief sign of man's divinity is his power to create. In this he is as good as God, and as responsible, Whitman says in "Laws for Creations."

God is sometimes identified with the life-force, and so symbolized by the sun as the pulse or force of creation, the power which orders the cosmos. Whitman's lines in "Passage to India" condense these uses of the sun-symbol:

> O Thou transcendent,
> Nameless, the fibre and the breath,
> Light of the light, shedding forth universes, thou centre of them,
>
> . . . .
>
> Thou pulse—thou motive of the stars, suns, systems,
> That, circling, move in order, safe, harmonious,
> Athwart the shapeless vastnesses of space. . . .

Lawrence sometimes thought of the physical sun, or light, as simply a part of the whole process of becoming (perhaps you and I and the sun, in the plasm of life, have created each other). But there is also a greater mystery, an interior light. In "Space," Lawrence speaks of a cosmic, wild heart

> that sends pulses even through me;
> and I call it the sun;
> and I feel aristocratic, noble, when I feel a pulse go through me
> from the wild heart of space, that I call the sun of suns.

Both Lawrence and Whitman used images of the revealed and the unknown (or dark) creative forces. Whitman in "Song of Myself" described this mysterious order: "The bright suns I see and the dark suns I cannot see are in their place." The sun finds its human evidence in the creative mind and the creative body; thus the importance of the sexual symbols used so frequently by both Lawrence and Thomas. All signs of power and growth in nature become sacred revelations. Crane thus presents in "Lachrymae Christi" a Dionysian Christ in the resurrection of spring, and Lawrence's terms of the primitive "mana" and "demiurge" emphasize the God-power in nature and the pulse of creative life which is the symbolic sun.

At this point in the literature of physical mysticism there is a turn in the idea of creator and creation. Though it is not unusual to think of God as the life-force, the pulse of creation, it is here that a special significance is given to the object itself. For the *object*, which is the incarnation of the divine impulse, may precede the *idea* of creation and be therefore the god himself. So the mystery is truly alive in the water and the singing birds. Whitman's constant invocations to object and person, to every body and leaf, are not accidents in his poetics. For in "Song of the Open Road," it is "you objects that call from diffusion my meanings and give them shape!" Lawrence's dramatic version of this idea is in "Red Geranium and Godly Mignonette." God did not plan these things; no one could have thought of them.

> But imagine, among the mud and the mastodons
> god sighing and yearning with tremendous creative yearning,
>   in that dark green mess
> oh, for some other beauty, some other beauty
> that blossomed at last, red geranium, and mignonette.

Thus the creator (God or the poet) is in some great channel of heat and movement and desire, and is seen only in the body of what has appeared. God is both the urge and the object. In some of Lawrence's loveliest lines (in "The Body of God"),

> There is no god
> apart from poppies and the flying fish,
> men singing songs, and women brushing their hair in the sun.

To start with the sun is to start also with the creative, divine object, the physical world of the real poems—"what we call poems being merely pictures," said Whitman in "Spontaneous Me." To him, the real poems were in "The loving day, the mounting sun, the friend I am happy with," and in all human, physical nature. Perhaps the best statement of the intention of the life-poet is in the little-known lines of Whitman's "Debris":

I will take an egg out of the robin's nest in the orchard,
I will take a branch of gooseberries from the old bush in the
    garden, and go and preach to the world;
You shall see I will not meet a single heretic or scorner,
You shall see how I stump clergymen, and confound them,
You shall see me showing a scarlet tomato, and a white pebble
    from the beach.

What kind of poetry will come out of this emphasis on the creativeness and continuity of life? In the first place, man and all other physical forms will be the vocabulary of the poet—a kind of earth-language. Whitman made this very explicit in passages in "A Song of the Rolling Earth":

A song of the rolling earth, and of words according,
Were you thinking that those were the words, those upright
    lines? those curves, angles, dots?
No, those are not the words, the substantial words are in the
    ground and sea,
They are in the air, they are in you.

Human bodies are words, he says—and all the elements:

Air, soil, water, fire—those are words,
I myself am a word with them—my qualities interpenetrate with
    theirs—my name is nothing to them,
Though it were told in the three thousand languages, what would
    air, soil, water, fire, know of my name?

       .   .   .   .   .

I swear I begin to see little or nothing in audible words,
All merges toward the presentation of the unspoken meanings of
    the earth,
Toward him who sings the songs of the body and of the truths
    of the earth,
Toward him who makes the dictionaries of words that print
    cannot touch.

Some of the most vivid expressions of earth-language are in Thomas, perhaps because he is closer to the ancient Druidic lore of the first alphabet found in the shapes of twigs and trees. He uses the calligraphy of leaves in "A Winter's Tale," and in "Altarwise by Owl-Light" has one very compact passage:

Now stamp the Lord's Prayer on a grain of rice,
A Bible-leaved of all the written woods
Strip to this tree: a rocking alphabet,

Genesis in the root, the scarecrow word,
And one light's language in the book of trees.

"Especially When the October Wind" is a language-poem on the substance of poetry: "syllabic blood," the "wordy shapes of women," the "vowelled beeches," "water's speeches," and the "dark-vowelled birds." The real poem finds the grammar to release the meaning implicit in man and the body of the world.

The poem is another object in a world of forms. The art of its creation is sometimes minimized if one looks at the rolling, seemingly diffuse lines of Whitman and Lawrence, or the density of language in Crane and Thomas. Why is one not more compact? Why is the other not more clear? (Why is Whitman's scarlet tomato not Lawrence's red geranium?) It is true that Lawrence emphasized the pulse and flow of open rhythms; Thomas said that his poems were "hewn."[3] But however the shape of the lines may differ, or the speed of articulation vary (as some poets work faster than others, so imagery may flash on the mind's screen by either slow motion or a high-speed projector), the one principle in common to all the poets who emphasize the life-process is freedom—or spontaneity, movement, scope. Whitman and Lawrence give the effect of a large, open, living flow in their prosody. Crane in his "condensed" and Thomas in his "compressed" poems also give the effect of daring and freedom in the way their images generate and fuse into a sometimes bewildering but actually organic stream. They skyrocket, though in different landscapes. Poetry is an artful earth in either form; it has the effect, not the actuality of freedom and the raw uncolored stuff. Though a poem may seem roughly free and simple on the surface, its sophistication may be in some interior logic—like Whitman's hinge of the hand that puts to scorn all machinery. Lesser poets and imitators of poets are likely to rely on the effect only. They end with exclamation without intention, with a line like a throw-away bottle. The real poem in Whitman's tradition is itself an earth-language. It too is an object, a form, an element. It has order and rhythm like the total cosmos. As life itself is always in movement, this kind of poem leads to unquietness, not completion. The true poems, said Whitman in "Song of the Answerer," are not the finish but the outset:

They bring none to his or her terminus or to be content and
full,

[3] Henry Treece, *Dylan Thomas* (London: Lindsay Drummond Ltd., 1949), p. 141.

Whom they take they take into space to behold the birth of
    stars, to learn one of the meanings,
To launch off with absolute faith, to sweep through the cease-
    less rings and never be quiet again.

Never to be quiet again—this means that the true poem has in it
the spark of creative power, that its physical form is creative as well
as created. The poem is a process of creation which is never still in
any real imagination.

Start with the sun, said Lawrence. Perhaps one begins and ends
with genesis: As Thomas said of his own art, the poet writes "for the
lovers, their arms/Round the griefs of the ages." It was Whitman's
hope that life would be made evident, incarnate, in his own leaves
and that they would transmit the creative sun: "Thou orb aloft
full-dazzling!" he began his bardic invocation, "Strike through these
chants." Writers in the Whitman tradition make the strongest affirma-
tion possible: that we do not live by either illusion or disillusion; that
no life is cheap or need be separate; that in the earth we may grow
into possibilities; that we take nothing secondhand. To be absorbed
directly out of the self and directly with the earth in the pulse of
creation is no mean aim for a writer. Such an ideal, seriously practiced,
might change the face of poetry in any period. Start with the sun:
Perhaps then we may be absolved from the poetry of mirrors.

DENIS DONOGHUE

Walt Whitman†

"Connoisseur of Chaos" is an elegant dialogue by Wallace
Stevens that holds aboriginal experience at the safe distance of
contemplation. The first voice says that the law of inherent opposites,
of essential unity, is "as pleasant as port." The contrast of life and
death is "pretty," presumably because it is suavely contained in the
essential unity. "The squirming facts exceed the squamous mind,"
yes, but nevertheless "relation" appears and expands, and as April
comes to summer, it seems good. The second voice speaks with

† From Denis Donoghue, *Connoisseurs of Chaos* (New York: Macmillan,
1965), pp. 23–41. Copyright 1965 by Denis Donoghue. Reprinted by per-
mission of The Macmillan Company.

distaste of an order too fixed, too "Plantagenet," and conjures a pensive man, a man of saving grace, the grace of imagination:

> The pensive man . . . He sees that eagle float
> For which the intricate Alps are a single nest.[1]

If the pensive man is the "man-hero" of Stevens' "Notes toward a Supreme Fiction," we are at the center of Stevens' world, his "*fluent mundo*." There is no better place from which to view the athletic *mundo* of Walt Whitman, because Stevens gives us all the terms we need, and his fluency shows us how much sweat and spirit Whitman had to expend before an American poet could deploy those terms with such control, such elegance. I have in mind such terms as chaos, order, the great disorder which is itself an order, "relation," "the pensive man." Whitman wielded all these, or their rugged equivalents, and he had to press them into being before Stevens could put them on show, like Yeats' circus animals. Whitman's version of Stevens' pensive man, for instance, is the "equable man" invoked in the preface to the first edition of *Leaves of Grass* and again in "By Blue Ontario's Shore," and in both cases identified with "the poet," a generic figure, master of the intricate Alps. And if we need Whitman's tone of voice to shape the meaning of the phrase, we have it: "Now there shall be a man cohered out of tumult and chaos." The man thus cohered is not Whitman himself or any particular man, not even Lincoln, but a man still in vision, in prophecy. Whitman sees him whenever he looks into the middle distance or enters a brown study. Once, for Edward Dowden's benefit, he described the "spine or verteber principle" of *Leaves of Grass* as "a model or ideal (for the service of the New World & to be gradually absorbed in it) of a complete healthy, heroic, practical modern Man."[2] Indeed, the best way to read *Leaves of Grass* is to consider it Whitman's notes toward a supreme fiction; the supreme fiction that in Whitman and Stevens is Man.

I have no wish to force upon Whitman and Stevens a congruity foreign to their tempers. Indeed, Whitman's shadow falls more directly upon the poems of Ezra Pound and William Carlos Williams than upon Stevens' philosophical discriminations. So we will not push the association too far. But even the differences between the two poets are vivid. Stevens' poems press toward a moment of stillness in which perception

---

[1] *Collected Poems of Wallace Stevens* (London: Faber & Faber, 1955), p. 215.
[2] Walt Whitman, *Correspondence*, Vol. II, *1868–1875*, ed. Edwin Haviland Miller (New York: New York University Press, 1961), p. 154.

is acute and all the harmonies sing. I think of this as Stevens' answer to that quite different stillness in T. S. Eliot's poems in which the poet, like a celebrant priest, hands over his individuality to the ritual of the sacrifice, and the result is a calm of self, all stillness, all repose. Whitman is not interested in such "moments," either Eliot's or Stevens', nor is he interested in the spectacular moments of Hart Crane or Marius the Epicurean. He demands that the continuities shall flow all the time, not merely at Key West but wherever a man happens to be. The peaks of feeling do not satisfy him; he wants the whole landscape, nothing less. Hence the defining "figure" of Whitman's mind is the equals sign—equals, not plus or minus. Where the New England Fathers set up a covenant with God, based on severance and inequality, Whitman set up a covenant with nature, governed by the energy that makes all things equal. If he found two things traditionally considered enemies, he would declare their identity, or at least make them friends in a larger community. Ideally, A is A and B is B, and in the flow of energy A equals B.

This explains why Whitman was never troubled by the problem that confronted every major Romantic poet—the nature of the self. He does not hunt and trail and worry the problem, as Coleridge does, or Keats, Byron, Wordsworth, even Emerson. He would never have written a poem like Coleridge's "Frost at Midnight," never have tried to write Wordsworth's *Prelude*, because Wordsworth and Coleridge in those poems are vexed by question marks, plus and minus signs, and Whitman's act of faith has erased these as impertinent. For him life is —in Yeats' phrase—"the fire that makes all simple"; simple because equal. He would speak of "the old knot of contrarieties," but he was always sure he could open it. (At least until the Civil War; later he would tell a different story.)

Hence he begins by saying, Let x equal the self. Then x equals A plus B plus C plus D plus E, and so on, where each letter stands for a new experience contained and possessed, and the self is the sum of its possessions. This is the law of Whitman's lists. If you say that the self—x—is the sum of its possessions, A, B, C, D, and so on, then the more you add to the right-hand side of the equation, the more you enrich the left, and you do this without bothering about the "nature" of the x. You assume, as most Romantic poets did, that the self is not at any moment fixed, complete, or predetermined, and then you are free to develop or enlarge it at any time by adding to its experience. * * *

Whitman was thrilled and sometimes dazzled by the felicities of his equation. He never lost faith in it; and if he questioned it, notably

in "As I Ebb'd with the Ocean of Life," the question merely testifies
to the power of the sea as a symbol of "merging" and obliteration, one
of the perennial temptations of American literature. In one of the
recurrent "moments" of American literature the imagination confronts
reality in the guise of a poet gazing at the sea. The imperious singer
in Stevens' "The Idea of Order at Key West" walks by the sea and
partly invents it with her song. But whether she invents it or discovers
it, she will master it, because she stands and walks and sings for
Wallace Stevens, not another poet. Whitman is more representative
of American experience when the sea throws down a challenge to his
selfhood that he is not sure he can survive, and in one of his rare
and extreme moments he says:

> O baffled, balk'd, bent to the very earth,
> Oppress'd with myself that I have dared to open my mouth,
> Aware now that amid all that blab whose echoes recoil upon
> me I have not once had the least idea who or what I am,
> But that before all my arrogant poems the real Me stands yet
> untouch'd, untold, altogether unreach'd . . .[3]

The sea is Stevens' reality, and Whitman's too, and for once
in this extreme moment Whitman fears that the sea has obliterated
all the dense particulars of reality on which his equation depends—
and then there is nothing but the void. In *Sea-Drift* he will be his own
man again, but only when he has settled and populated the sea with
ships and sea captains and swimmers and a child and her father
walking on the beach at night, feeling the "vast similitude" that
"interlocks all." The equation is, in the nick of time, verified.

But it is verified. In the essay "Experience" Emerson says that
one of the consequences of the Fall of Man is that the Me is utterly
separated from the Not-Me. But Whitman disposes of the problem
briskly by declaring that the Me is simply the sum of the Not-Me it
contains. And he implies, of course, that it is the part of prudence as
well as faith to make that sum as large as possible. One should keep
adding to the self as Whitman kept adding to *Leaves of Grass*, thereby
gaining the best of all possible worlds, being and becoming. Any
experience genuinely assimilated adds to what Whitman calls "the
Me myself." Hence he will say, "The press of my foot to the earth
springs a hundred affections," and again, "Is this then a touch? . . .

---

[3] Whitman, *Complete Poetry and Selected Prose*, ed. James E. Miller, Jr.
(Boston: Houghton Mifflin, 1959), p. 197. All verse quotations, unless
otherwise specified, are from this edition.

quivering me to a new identity . . ." The equation would also allow for the incorporation of any and every kind of experience. There would be no problem, for instance, in the rivalry of poet and scientist, one of the issues warily touched in Wordsworth's great *Preface*. Whitman can bring science into the equation simply by calling it, as he does in the preface of 1872, "a new sunrise." He can therefore avoid the slough of self-pity that we call "romantic irony." And he can evade one of the perennial problems, that of appearance and reality, simply by declaring their identity. He would never have said, as Stevens did, "Let be be finale of seem." Whitman wants the whole opera, not just the finale, so he declares that what seems is, here and now, and is good. Freed from metaphysical embarrassments, Whitman could devote himself to his equations, collecting experiences as the dominant culture of his day collected material possessions, and—in a sense—for "similar" reasons: because the verification of the self depended upon an exhibited affluence, perhaps even upon conspicuous waste. T. S. Eliot has spent many years persuading us that our possessions are vulgar, ephemeral. Hence we attend to him as we listen to our consciences, and no more frequently. Whitman spent most of his life sponsoring an affluent society, with this admonition, that our possessions should include sympathies, accords, pleasures, marriages, pains, passions, the sun and the stars as well as gadgets. But judged simply as an esthetic—though how simple is that?—Whitman's creed was uncannily faithful to the dominant metaphors of his place and time. He did not repudiate the metaphors; he thought they were excellent and would serve every occasion, if only you worked them hard enough, put everything in, material and spiritual.

Because his equations were designed to include everything, like and unlike, city and country, they could also include evil. It was William James, I think, who brought into critical currency the notion that Whitman lacked a sense of evil. In a lecture of 1895 he spoke of "our dear old Walt Whitman's works" as the handbook of that "temperamental optimism" that is "incapable of believing that anything seriously evil can exist."[4] What James started Yeats continued, in a famous passage in *A Vision*. But it will not do. No one will ask Whitman to speak like Saint Augustine, Kierkegaard, or that accomplished neo-Augustinian of our own day, Graham Greene. But it is willful to argue that Whitman was blind to evil or that he felt it sluggishly. Some of the most haunting passages in "Song of Myself" are appre-

---

[4] William James, *The Will To Believe* (New York: Dover Publications, n.d.), pp. 32 ff.

hensions of sickness and pain, "the silent old-faced infants and the lifted sick." It is not that Whitman was insensitive to the pain of others, but—I concede only this—that he was a little too ready to assimilate this pain to the genial law of his own equation. * * *

If Whitman's equations can include evil, they should have no difficulty with death. Sometimes he euphemistically translates death to read "immortality," as in the last lines of "To Think of Time," which read in the first version:

> I swear I think there is nothing but immortality!
> That the exquisite scheme is for it, and the nebulous float is for it, and the cohering is for it,
> And all preparation is for it . . . and identity is for it . . . and life and death are for it.[5]

And generally Whitman assumes that death merely inaugurates a new cycle of life and is therefore not a thing to fear or bewail. There were moments in which, like many nineteenth-century poets and dramatists, he was more than half in love with easeful death. Several passages, even in *Sea-Drift*, sound like program notes to Wagner's *Tristan*, the motif being "the low and delicious word Death," whispers of heavenly death. But for the most part death and evil are contained in the expanding self, the x, and therefore "justified."

Given the primary equation by which the self is identified with the sum of its contents, Whitman goes on to declare other equations, especially where the old orthodoxies luxuriated in antagonism—soul and body, for instance, which in Whitman's animal faith are distinct but without difference. He would eliminate the distinction with an equation, thus earning D. H. Lawrence's celebrated praise. Throughout *Leaves of Grass* this equation persists, and Whitman returns to assert it several times in *A Backward Glance*. "Behold, the body includes and is the meaning, the main concern, and includes and is the soul," he says in "Starting from Paumanok," and again, in effect, in *Children of Adam* and "Song of Myself." A later poet, W. B. Yeats, in at least one of his moods would present the fullness of being as "a perfectly proportioned human body" in splendid animation, and he would point to certain passages in Dante for theory and to "certain beautiful women" for proof. The same hope would send Yeats into the theater and toward certain spectacularly theatrical poems, poems all gesture

---

[5] See the first edition, reprinted with an introduction by Malcolm Cowley (New York: Viking Press, 1959), p. 104. Later Whitman changed "death" to "materials." See *Complete Poetry and Selected Prose*, p. 308.

and nonchalance. Yeats would bring his thought to drama, to crisis. But Whitman was not content with a few fine crises. The electrical body would have to certify the soul at all times, and he would "sing" it to encourage it to do so. Where Dante had behind him the doctrine and incitement of the Incarnation, the word made flesh, Whitman had only the prompting of his own animal faith. But for him it was, of course, enough. This is why, discussing Yeats, we constantly need terms drawn from the theater; but these are useless in reading Whitman. In Whitman—both in our reading and his writing—the relevant terms are those that define the entire range of experience centered on the body. Above all, Whitman needs terms that evade the importunities of an arrogant and jealous consciousness, because he is honorbound to dissolve the old dichotomies of soul and body, mind and matter, consciousness and experience. In short, he needs all those words that are themselves equals signs, terms that denote the intersection of subject and object, the Me and the Not-Me. In a long list the central term is "contact."

From the first page of the first edition of *Leaves of Grass* this word reverberates through the poems and prose. "I am mad for it to be in contact with me," he says of the atmosphere, and in "A Song for Occupations," I pass so poorly with paper and types . . . I must pass with the contact of bodies and souls." *Children of Adam* is virtually a tone poem on contact. And even when the key terms are more general, they are acceptable to Whitman only if they can prove their origin in bodily experience; many are phrenological terms. He chooses words like *inhale, adhere, respiration, adhesiveness, meeting, inspiration, acceptation, realization, give, receive, press, swallow.* * * *

When Whitman in the third stanza of "I Sing the Body Electric" confronts an old man and enters the meaning of his existence, we can almost foretell that the last grace of the encounter will be a touching, a contact, not just a "seeing":

> When he went with his five sons and many grandsons to hunt or
>   fish, you would pick him out as the most beautiful and
>   vigorous of the gang,
> You would wish long and long to be with him . . . you would
>   wish to sit by him in the boat, that you and he might
>   touch each other.

Emerson would worry because objects can touch each other only at one point. Whitman did not worry. One point was enough; you had only to ensure that there would be, always, one. * * *

A life of such continuous intimacy, a life of contact, is Whitman's

ideal human image. It will blur the distinction between man and
God, thus setting up yet another equation, the largest in intention.
Whitman effects this equation in "A Song of Joys" and celebrates it
in "Song at Sunset":

> To be this incredible God I am!
> To have gone forth among other Gods, these men and women
>   I love!

This divinity flows and sanctifies, by contact, everything it sees, hears,
touches, tastes, or smells; it is Whitman's version of the laying on of
hands. Stevens will say, "God and the human imagination are one,"
and he will offer as proof the extreme reaches of his own perception.
But this is not Whitman's faith. Stevens is convinced that man is God
to the degree of his vision, his perception, his visual imagination.
Whitman is convinced that man is God to the latitude of his contact.
In Whitman's heaven we communicate by touch. In "Song of the
Redwood-Tree" the new earth and the new heaven are one, an earthly
paradise of contact, silent because it is itself the ultimate poem that
renders all lesser poems redundant. Kenneth Burke says that man
craves images of "perfection," is "rotten with perfection." Whitman
claimed, in the world of experience, everything, simply—like moun-
taineers possessing themselves of Everest—because it was there. If it
existed, Whitman had to touch it; if it was possible, it was for that
very reason a necessity, a compulsion. And because the limits of the
possible and the actual must coincide, and this requires extreme pres-
sure of invocation, he must command the High Style, almost the
Sublime.

The sources of this compulsion—much more than a "vision" of
life—are not at all clear. Whitman found a few of the signposts he
needed in Emerson, and he pursued them far beyond the point at
which Emerson elected to rest. He picked up a certain spirit of the
age from the German idealists by way of Coleridge and the transcen-
dentalists. A few echoes of Oriental lore reached him from Thoreau.
From Hegel he took the consolation of historical approval. His debts
to Carlyle and the American poets he favored are another story, and
hardly an exciting one. But in fact his own native temper, I think,
dictated most of his lines. * * *

Indeed, one of the notable things in Whitman is his attempt to
draw a little of the old meaning of the word "nature" into the new
romantic ethos of plenitude. Sometimes he speaks of nature, ad-
mittedly, when he has in mind only daffodils and the great outdoors,

but more often—as in "Song of Myself"—nature means "the perfect fitness and equanimity of things," and it will certainly include what he calls, in the original preface, "the eternal tendencies of all toward happiness." Nature is the principle of energy allowing that a thing shall be itself. After this the thing can be implicated in hundreds of relationships; and these in turn will depend for their vitality upon the original blessing of identity. Nature is, to use Yeats' terms on another occasion, "self-creating, self-delighting," and as Whitman says in "Myself and Mine":

> Let others finish specimens, I never finish specimens,
> I start them by exhaustless laws as Nature does, fresh and
>   modern continually.

In short, nature is the principle that exhibits itself in being, delights in plentitude, and reconciles difference. It is the new decorum.

Hence the proper attitude, the secular equivalent of religious piety, is Emerson's "nonchalance." When the principle of energy is diffused through all things and courses through an individual man, the proof is ease, grace, tact. In "One Hour to Madness and Joy" Whitman invokes it: "To find a new unthought-of nonchalance with the best of Nature." This nonchalance will, of course—like Stevens' Supreme Fiction—give pleasure; and it is part of Whitman's morality to disengage the pleasure principle from an antecedent scruple. In his world the principle of pleasure is verified by the energy that animates it, and it is therefore, in the easiest of his translations, "good." When Yeats thought of nonchalance and praised it—as he often did —he took the word from Castiglione's *sprezzatura* and borrowed its air of high breeding, aristocratic hauteur, a handsome spread of civility and splendor. But just as Whitman celebrates the average and calls it divine, so also he commandeers a traditional aristocratic term and hands it over to his new democratic man. And one of the promises he makes on these ceremonial occasions is that the democratic man of nonchalance will be released from the current obsession with time and transience. It is the part of faith and prudence to accept the flow of time, to set aside the "quest for permanence." If Saturday is succeeded by Sunday, this is the natural course and order of things and not at all an instance of what Samuel Beckett, glossing Proust, will call "the poisonous ingenuity of Time in the science of affliction." Stevens is again the poet who has most vividly acknowledged the natural course of things, and he has done something to liberate us from our bondage to Grecian urns and the idiom of bangs and whimpers. In this he stands with Whitman, and, if anything, more firmly, because the Whitman of the later poems sometimes slipped back into the feeling that, alas, death's the end of all. But both poets find, even in the shadow of time and death, that unities are still possible. Each poet goes his own way, singing unities of self in quite different terms. But they share the basic feeling. Whitman's nonchalant hero will not always satisfy Stevens, even when the hero walks among his peers with superb presence in "Song of the Answerer," and finds gratifying harmonies in "Song of the Rolling Earth." It isn't characteristic of Stevens to celebrate the glamorous resources of ordinary people—their nonchalance—as he did, for once, in the poem "Ordinary Women."

We are concerned with the nature of Whitman's poetry in its most characteristic phases, in the years before the war. After the war, as students of Whitman agree, there is a notable change. Whitman's "bumps" would persist, his cast of mind would remain substantially what it had always been, he would make the same demands upon himself and others. But most of the demands would be frustrate and the great equations would not, finally, work out. It was too late to change, and there were no kindly spirits to bring him, as they would bring Yeats, new metaphors, new analogies. Postwar America disappointed Whitman precisely because it failed to live up to the demands of the old metaphors—demands of tact and grace. He would still try to "humanize" the new world with the old familial metaphors; he would try to hold the new fact close to the old value. And he would resist as long as possible the feeling that the new world of "things" was hostile to the freedom of man. A naturalistic philosophy was already audible that would seal man's faith, his obliteration beneath the mountains of alien things. But Whitman would resist. He would insist and then hope and finally pray that products are not hostile to their producers, nature is not hostile to man's purposes. But it was to be a rear-guard action, as "Song of the Exposition" makes clear, and more and more the rueful note would win out, the old equations now subverted by the new mathematics. And when fact split apart from value, when relation was impossible, then of course the grammar of contact was impossible too. It was the only grammar Whitman knew, the only grammar certified by the human body. Once this failed, a genuine culture was impossible, a culture, that is, based on the "daily toils" of all the people, the nature of human sympathies, the axioms of the body. If man is cut adrift from nature, the next step is the separation of man from man—no contact. Some poets can bear this; a few thrive on it; and some, like Emily Dickinson, have their own resources of metaphor that allow them to proceed. But the destitution of Whitman's later poetry arises from the gap between the old metaphors and the new facts; and Whitman could fill the gap only with petulance, the tone of the broken sage.

ANTHONY BURGESS

The Answerer†

British musicians have been better Whitman publicists than British men of letters. Whitman, a hard poet to quote (as Uncle Ponderevo admits in *Tono-Bungay*), was learned by heart by thousands of provincial choral singers—those who tackled Delius's *Sea Drift*, Vaughan Williams's *A Sea Symphony*, Holst's *Dirge for Two Veterans*, eventually Bliss's *Morning Heroes*. Because Whitman, like the Bible, seemed to stand on the margin of art, composers saw that they could add some art to him. More than that, he was democratic, even sweaty, and the right librettist for a musical renaissance that turned against the Mendelssohnian salons and went to the sempiternal soil. Whitman's free verse (not *vers libre*, a very salony thing) was a corrective to the four-square folkiness that bedevilled so many rural rhapsodies and even *The Planets*, but his rhythms were lyrical or declamatory, not—like Eliot and Pound (who eventually made a pact with Whitman, having 'detested him long enough')—muffled, arhetorical, conversational.

Whitman's verse-technique is still of interest to the prosodist. His basic rhythm is an epic one—the Virgilian dactyl-spondee—and his line often hexametric:

> I perceive that the ghastly glimmer is noonday sunbeams reflected,
> And debouch to the steady and central from the offspring great and small.

He sometimes sounds like Clough's *Amours de Voyage*, though it would be hard to imagine a greater disparity of tone and attitude than

† From *Urgent Copy* (New York: W. W. Norton & Co., 1968), pp. 48–53. Originally appeared in *The Spectator*. Reprinted by permission of the publisher and the author.

that which subsists between these two Victorians. Nevertheless, both Clough and Whitman saw that the loose hexameter could admit the contemporary and sometimes the colloquial:

> I too am not a bit tamed, I too am untranslatable,
> I sound my barbaric yawp over the roofs of the world.
> I bequeath myself to the dirt to grow from the grass I love,
> If you want me again look for me under your boot-soles.

When Whitman becomes 'free,' it is as though he justifies truncation or extension of the basic hexameter by some unspoken theory of a line-statement or line-image. Flouting classical procedure in refusing to allow any spill-over from line to line, he invokes a tradition older than Virgil—that of Hebrew poetry. British composers, their noses well-trained, sniffed the Bible in Whitman:

> If you would understand me go to the heights or water-shore,
> The nearest gnat is an explanation, and a drop or motion of
> waves a key.

There are passages of Whitman, as of Blake, which have a ring of something from the Apocrypha. This is appropriate for the age of the American Vision which produced him, or which he—and President Lincoln and Mrs. Beecher Stowe—helped to produce.

Whitman's verse-style is so consistent (he only very rarely tried strophic forms and was not happy in them) that any volume of his can encompass single-line 'inscriptions' as well as poems as long as 'Song of Myself': chippings and totempoles attest the one tree. There is never any sense of the fragmentary, since—as his overall title indicates—if he is to present the American plain he must do so through its constituent blades, leaves and clumps. He has only one subject—acceptance of the life-death cycle and reverence for it—and, since he uses an invariable technique, *Leaves of Grass* has a unity to be found in few other poets' collected volumes. The consistency of subject-matter and rhythm is also in the language. This is an idiosyncratic compound of the colloquial, the technical (but to admit the colloquial has always been to admit the technical) and the traditionally 'poetic.' The latter sometimes comes out in otiose eye-contractions like 'ebb'd' and 'walk'd' and 'seiz'd'; sometimes in inversions that deliberately point the dactylic rhythm ('I sing the body electric'), most often in the drawing on the common stockpot of the nineteenth century ('. . . for well dear brother I know, /If thou wast not granted to sing thou would'st surely die'). Some of his loan-words—'allons,' 'eleve,' 'eidolons,' 'camerado'—are there to internationalise his material. In 'To Foreign Lands' he says:

> I heard that you ask'd for something to prove this puzzle the
>   New World,
> And to define America, her athletic Democracy,
> Therefore I send you my poems that you behold in them what
>   you wanted.

But Whitman's aim is rather to present a universal democratic vista in terms of the American myth. The America of his poems sometimes seems as symbolic as that of Blake, and the bearded figure that strides across it with a big hello—the Answerer, all things to all men—is as much a home-made archetype as the Giant Albion.

What makes Whitman antipathetic to many Europeans is his quality of uncompromising acceptance. We take it for granted that the poet should be sick, and it is the convention to sneer at the eupeptic and wince at the possessor of the loud voice, blessing his friend in the morning. 'The disease of modern life' that Matthew Arnold tried to diagnose turned into health when it crossed the Atlantic. Whitman seems to advocate anarchy, telling the States: 'Resist much, obey little, /Once unquestioning obedience, once fully enslaved'; like Blake, he accepts an antinomian universe: 'I am not the poet of goodness only, I do not decline to be the poet of wickedness also . . . Evil propels me and reform of evil propels me, I stand indifferent'; he welcomes Darwinianism, science, technology. More than anything, he is a flesh-glorifier—pagan rather than on the muscular-Christian pattern of Charles Kingsley:

> Walt Whitman, a kosmos, of Manhattan the son,
> Turbulent, fleshy, sensual, eating, drinking and breeding . . .
> I believe in the flesh and the appetites,
> Seeing, hearing, feeling, are miracles, and each part and tag of
>   me is a miracle.

Browning, too, glorified the flesh but only by first making it remote, pushing it back into an Italian painting or an imagined song of David. Whitman's carnality is here-and-now stuff, taking place under the sun in Kansas or Wisconsin or on fish-shaped Paumanok.

It is a sensuality omnifutuant rather than (what John Addington Symonds thought it might be) 'homo-erotic.' Whitman was always quick to assert his heterosexuality and boast of his illegitimate off-spring: one has no reason to disbelieve him. But the mythical Answerer he makes of himself has to be androgynous. The volume of poems called *Calamus* rejoices in male love, but it is not a collection of love poems in the conventional sense. It is as if Whitman were looking for erotic symbols of an asexual union. After celebrating

> two simple men I saw today on the pier in the midst of the crowd, parting the parting of dear friends,
> The one to remain hung on the other's neck and passionately kiss'd him,
> While the one to depart tightly prest the one to remain in his arms,

Whitman gives us a poem saying:

> I believe the main purport of these States, is to found a superb friendship, exalté, previously unknown,
> Because I perceive it waits, and has been always waiting, latent in all men.

The juxtaposition is not accidental.

As one of the nineteenth-century innovators, Whitman can be ranked with Hopkins: Hopkins himself was aware of an affinity, though he did not relish it (he asked Bridges if Whitman had written anything like 'Harry Ploughman' and said that he would be sorry if he had). Whitman's vocabulary is very wide (though not from delving into the recherché so much as admitting a new—much wider than Tennysonian—subject-matter) and his rhetorical sweep is symphonic. One of the most important of his innovations—reviled in his day as a barbarism—is the rhetorical catalogue, the enumeration in line after long line of visual phenomena, either taken from the natural world or the man-made. It required courage to list at enormous length rather than to take the conventional path of generalisation, but the courage has been posthumously rewarded. The catalogues of 'Song of Myself' are magnificent; the unremitting detail of 'Drum Taps' makes it probably the finest long war-poem of all time. Perhaps only an American poet could see the rhetorical possibilities of this enumerative technique; the immense plurality of the United States is made for this kind of celebration, and even a plain roll-call ('Mississippi with bends and chutes, /And my Illinois fields, and my Kansas fields, and my fields of Missouri . . .') can lift the heart without much help from a poet. America herself dictated the technique to a man passionately in love with America. It is, of course, a technique that looked forward to the epic cinema of Griffiths, poetry derived from the juxtaposition of visual images.

The America that Whitman presented in his poems was a vision-

ary country, built in an epic fantasia on the theme "E Pluribus Unum.'
Such an America, roamed by the linker, the joiner-of-hands, the
Answerer, who says 'indifferently and alike *How are you friend?* to
the President at his levee and . . . *Good-day my brother*, to Cudge
that hoes in the sugar-field,' never existed and never could. Men are
meaner and less forgivable than Whitman was willing to see, and
perhaps his democratic vistas fill too many modern Americans with
discomfort, making them shut their eyes to his greatness. It is dif-
ferent for scholars, of course: this new edition of *Leaves of Grass*[1] is
one of the most beautiful books to have come recently out of America,
and the editors have lavished great industry on its preparation. Also,
which is right for this poet, much love.

KENNETH REXROTH

Walt Whitman†

Our civilization is the only one in history whose major artists
have rejected its dominant values. Baudelaire, Mallarmé, Rimbaud,
Stendhal, Flaubert, Dostoevsky, Melville, Mark Twain—all are self-
alienated outcasts. One nineteenth-century writer of world importance
successfully refused alienation, yet still speaks significantly to us—
Walt Whitman, the polar opposite of Baudelaire.

Most intellectuals of our generation think of America as the
apotheosis of commercial, competitive, middle-class society. Because
Whitman found within it an abundance of just those qualities that it
seems today most to lack, the sophisticated read him little and are
inclined to dismiss him as fraudulent or foolish. The realization of the
American Dream as an apocalypse, an eschatological event which
would give the life of man its ultimate significance, was an invention
of Whitman's.

Other religions have been founded on the promise of the Com-
munity of Love, the Abode of Peace, the Kingdom of God. Whitman
identified with his own nation-state. We excuse such ideas only when

[1] *Leaves of Grass: A Comprehensive Reader's Edition*, ed. Harold W. Blodgett
and Sculley Bradley (New York: New York University Press, 1965).
† From Kenneth Rexroth, "Classics Revisited XXXV," *Saturday Review*,
September 3, 1966. Reprinted by permission of the author.

they began 3,000 years ago in the Levantine desert. In our own time
we suspect them of dangerous malevolence. Yet Whitman's vision
exposes and explodes all the frauds that pass for the American Way
of Life. It is the last and greatest vision of the American potential.

Today, when many intellectuals and politicians hold each other in
supreme contempt, few remember that America was founded by, and
for three generations ruled by, intellectuals. As they were driven from
power in the years before the Civil War their vision of a practicable
utopia diffused out into society, went underground, surfaced again in
cooperative colonies, free-love societies, labor banks, vegetarianism,
feminism, Owenites, Fourierists, Saint-Simonians, anarchists, and
dozens of religious communal sects. Whitman was formed in this
environment. Whenever he found it convenient he spoke of himself as
a Quaker and used Quaker language. Much of his strange lingo is not
the stilted rhetoric of the self-taught, but simply Quaker talk. Most
of his ideas were commonplaces in the radical and pietistic circles and
the Abolition Movement. This was the first American Left, for whom
the Civil War was a revolutionary war and who, after it was over,
refused to believe that it was not a won revolution.

Unfortunately for us, as is usually the case in won revolutions,
the language of the revolutionists turned into a kind of newspeak.
The vocabulary of Whitman's moral epic has been debauched by a
hundred years of editorials and political speeches. Still, there are two
faces to the coin of newspeak—the counterfeit symbol of power and
the golden face of liberty. The American Dream that is the subject of
Leaves of Grass is again becoming believable as the predatory society
that intervenes between us and Whitman passes away.

Walt Whitman's democracy is utterly different from the society
of free rational contractual relationships inaugurated by the French
Revolution. It is a community of men related by organic satisfactions,
in work, love, play, the family, comradeship; a social order whose es-
sence is the liberation and universalization of selfhood. *Leaves of
Grass* is not a great work of art just because it has a great program,
but it does offer point-by-point alternatives to the predatory society, as
well as to the systematic doctrine of alienation from it that has de-
veloped from Baudelaire and Kierkegaard to the present.

In all of Whitman's many celebrations of labor, abstract relations
are never mentioned. Money appears to be scorned. Sailors, carpenters,
longshoremen, bookkeepers, seamstresses, engineers, artists—all seem
to be working for "nothing," participants in a universal creative effort
where each discovers his ultimate individuation. The day's work over,
they loaf and admire the world on summer hillsides, blowing on leaves

of grass, or strolling the quiet First-Day streets of Manhattan, arms about one another's broad shoulders, or making love in religious ecstasy. Unlike almost all other ideal societies, Whitman's utopia, which he calls "These States," is not a projection of the virtues of an idealized past into the future, but an attempt to extrapolate the future into the American present. His is a realized eschatology.

The Middle Ages called hope a theological virtue. They meant that, with faith and love, hope was essential to the characteristic being of mankind. Now hope is joy in the presence of the future in the present. On this joy creative effort depends, because creation relates past, present, and future in concrete acts that result in enduring objects and experiences. Beyond the consideration of time, Whitman asserts the same principle of being, the focusing of the macrocosm in the microcosm, or its reverse, which is the same thing, as the source of individuation. Again and again he identifies himself with a transfigured America, the community of work in love and love in work, this community with the meaning of the universe, the vesture of God, a great chain of being which begins, or ends, in Walt Whitman, or his reader—Adam-Kadmon who contains all things—ruled in order by love.

Whitman's philosophy may resemble that of the *Upanishads* as rewritten by Thomas Jefferson. What differentiates it is the immediacy of substantial vision, the intensity of the wedding of image and moral meaning. Although Whitman is a philosophical poet, almost always concerned with his message, he is at the same time a master of Blake's "minute particulars," one of the clearest and most dramatic imagists in literature.

Not the least element of his greatness is his extraordinary verse. He was influenced, it is true, by Isaiah, Ossian, and all the other sources discovered by scholarship. His poetry has influenced all the cadenced verse that has come after it. Yet, in fact, there has never been anything like Whitman's verse before or since. It was original and remained inimitable. It is the perfect medium for poetic homilies on the divinization of man.

Only recently it was fashionable to dismiss Whitman as foolish and dated, a believer in the myth of progress and the preacher of an absurd patriotism. Today we know that it is Whitman's vision or nothing.

"Mankind, the spirit of the Earth, the paradoxical conciliation of the element with the whole and of unity with multitude—all these are called utopian, and yet they are biologically necessary. For them to be incarnated in the world all we may need is to imagine our power of

loving developing until it embraces the total of man and of the earth."
So said Teilhard de Chardin. Or, as Whitman says in the great
mystical poems which are the climax of his book, contemplation is
the highest form and the ultimate source of all moral activity because
it views all things in their timeless aspect, through the eyes of love.

HORACE M. KALLEN

Of Love, Death, and Walt Whitman†

It is conventional for poets of the Great Tradition to chant of
love and death, for the philosophers to talk about them and for priests
to exploit them. Love and death are the points of no return in Every-
man's history, the moments of truth in the human condition. From
love and death grow the meanings of churchmen's rites and roles and
symbols, the dogmas of theologians, the doctrines of philosophers.
Love and death are that in the life of mankind which sustains a
perhaps never-to-be-quieted solicitude to save man the sinner and
sufferer from the annihilation which is death by means of the creation
that is love—by means of love, to conquer death which, but for love,
God's or man's, is man's destiny. The Tradition celebrates a perfect
heavenly love which transfigures, and overcomes as it transfigures,
the dangerous earthly one whose beginning is lust and whose end is
death. The Tradition proclaims and celebrates the immortality of the
human self. Its priests are trained to instruct the self in a way of life
which shall prepare it for the happy life it shall lead when it is dead.
Its poets are inspired to envision and disclose this after-life. Its theo-
logians and, with almost no exception, its philosophers, devise proof
after changing proof that mankind live this life when they are dead.

But the children of the new time and the new world whose
boundaries have been stretched beyond measure by science, whose
uncontainable forces have been contained and subdued to the service
of man by man's mechanical inventions, the children of the world
which Walt Whitman foresaw and prophesied the coming of, no
longer believe as their forbears believed that love conquers death.
They no longer reverence and fear the priest for the power of his

† From the *Walt Whitman Review* (Wayne State University Press), XV, 3
(September, 1969), 171–180. Reprinted by permission of Wayne State Uni-
versity Press.

rites and incantations. They no longer are reassured by the theologian's dogmas nor convinced by the philosopher's dialectic. Indeed theologians have themselves become insecure spirits with the most daring among them announcing the death of God, while philosophers argue on anxious and afraid, having come to see death naked, and invincible to love, and man thus reduced to a futility, a meaningless nothing, a living absurdity, born only to die. Philosophers now see man's existence as but hopeless and lonely struggling against death, and the idea of immortality as a suicidal self-deception.[1] And the poets, the playwrights, the painters, all the *avant garde* of the arts, take up this 'absurd' to embelish, to glorify and to sanctify. By canonizing, they endow the proclaimed meaningless with meanings which displace without replacing those that their forbears bet their lives on. The self-chosen frontiersmen of the spirit of the age are said to have become paganized. But they have not become pagan as the pagans were pagan. If their paganism is not a sham, it is an illusion.

For there was that in the authentic pagan spirit which responded to the poet, the man of art, as Heaven's chosen voice, which held the priest with his wizardry in small esteem. We recognize it in the tale which Homer tells of Odysseus and a priest and a poet on their knees before him begging for their lives. The hero spares the poet and without hesitation kills the priest. Priests had powers that frightened, but who was ever afraid of a poet, whose powers had been poured into him by the gods? Odysseus, impervious to the priest, stood in awe of the poet. Plato was also in awe of men inspired by the gods; he would not have any such inspired soul intruding upon the good order, the safety, the certainty of his perfect society, the Republic.

Whether because of irresistible intuition, or for other causes which the learned in Whitman can elaborate, Walt Whitman had mightily this pagan sense of the primacy of the poet. In 'The Song of the Answerer' he yet again repristinated the immemorial Homeric perception of the authentic poet as he is—numinous, holy, truly revealing to man what man is, and what is man's destiny.

> A man is a summons and a challenge,
> (It is vain to skulk—do you hear that mocking and laughter?
> Do you hear the ironical echoes?)

[1] This, the God-rejecting priestcraft of Russian Communism have sardonically translated into Communist truth. They have used the knowledges and knowhow of science as means in the practice of the mortician's art to embalm and enshrine the ever-disintegrating yet still undisintegrated body of dead Lenin so that daily thousands of pilgrims may come to view and reverence it. To Whitman, Lenin's corpse could be but 'good manure.'

A man is a summons and a challenge whom the poet's poems . . .

> prepare for death, yet they are not the finish, but rather the
> outset.
> They bring none to his or her terminus or to be content and full,
> Whom they take they take into space to behold the birth of stars
> to learn one of the meanings.
> To launch off with absolute faith, to sweep through the ceaseless
> rings and never be quiet again.

So, the true poet's poems, preparing for death, invite and spur on the living of life.

This conviction of Whitman's that the true poet's vocation is a summons and a challenge answering to all human challenges and answers is, of course, of Whitman's essence. But his answer to the summons and challenge of death is no longer the answer of the first of his leaves of grass, of his 'Song of Myself.' There the young man not yet thirty presents himself, not as an immortal soul temporarily inhabiting a mortal body and struggling to live on in a world of incalculable diversities, ineffably lonely and alone, needing, calling for, companionship. Although the personal pronoun *I* flashes by like telegraph poles seen from a moving train, their role is like that of the conjunction *and*. They bring into the foreground and join together one after another, persons and places, thoughts and things, each a singular and momentary presence, present but not-to-be-accounted-for.

Call what you like the abstractions—Emersonian, pantheist, transcendentalist, or what have you—wherewith Whitman enjoyed himself *en philosophe*; as a poet, he was an empiricist and a radical one. He spoke his moods, his perceptions, his aspirations and reflections as they came, uttering each without prejudice, for its concrete uniqueness, and all for the concrete uniqueness of their successions. And so he presented the singularities of death. Of course, those singularities, like all others, clashed as singularities must. Their contradictions are natural events of the ongoing flux of diversification and contradiction which is existence, and why should the moments of death be otherwise? So, in one place Whitman declares:

> The smallest sprout shows that there is really no death
> And if ever there was, it led forward life, and does not wait at
> the end to arrest it,
> And ceased the moment life appeared.

In another:

I am not an earth nor an adjunct of an earth,
I am the mate and companion of people, all just as immortal and
    fathomless as myself,
They do not know how immortal; but I know.

And in a third:

I sound triumphal drums for the dead . . . I fling through my
    embouchures the loudest and gayest music to them,
Vivas to those who have failed, and to those whose war-vessels
    sank in the sea.
And to all generals who lost that lost engagement, and all over-
    come heroes, and the numberless unknown heroes equal to
    the greatest heroes known.

And in a fourth:

And I know that I am deathless.
I know this orbit of mine cannot be swept by a carpenter's
    compass,
I know that I shall not pass like a child's carlicue cut with a
    burnt stick at night : . .

My foothold is tenoned and mortised in granite
I laugh at what you call dissolution,
And I know the amplitude of time.
I am the poet of common sense and of the demonstrable and of
    immortality.

And in a fifth:

And I say to mankind, Be not curious about God
For I who am curious about each am not curious about God
(No array of terms can say how much I am at peace about God
    and about death).

And in a sixth:

And as to you, death, and your bitter hug of mortality, it is idle
    to try to alarm me. . . .
And as to you, corpse, I think you are good manure but that
    does not offend me
I smell the white roses sweet-scented and growing
I reach to the leafy lips . . . I reach to the polished breasts of
    melons.

And as to you, life, I reckon you are the leavings of many deaths
No doubt I have died myself many tens of thousands times
before . . .

O suns . . . O grass of graves . . . O perpetual transfer and
promotion . . . if you do not say anything how can I say
anything?

And a seventh:

There is that in me . . . I do not know what it is but I know
it is in me.

Do you see, O my brothers and sisters
It is not chaos or death . . . it is form and union and plan
. . . it is eternal, it is happiness.

Yet, over the dead of a naval battle the poet mourns

These so . . . these irretrievable!

Tradition, I believe, mistakenly interprets Whitman's cameos of
non-selective singularity on the principle of the Brahmin's *tat svam
asi* (I am that). I believe, however, that the poet keeps saying of
each person or thing or event he experiences, 'There,' not '*but* for
the grace of God' rather, '*with* the grace of God, go I.' If, then, I
am that as death, it is only because I don't ever die, because I am
the Proteus who forever returns, and 'I bequeath myself to the dirt
to grow from the grass I love.' Youthful George Santayana, although
appreciative of the tradition, condemns this poetic radical empiricism
of Whitman's as barbarian, and his poems the poems of 'a man who
regards his passions as their own excuse for being, who does not
domesticate them either by understanding their cause or by con-
centring their ideal goal.'

But here, I can't help thinking, Santayana misses the inwardness
of Whitman. For here, neither can I help thinking, Whitman un-
covers his awareness of how pervasive, how present, singularity and
difference are. All his self-identifications with the multitudinous unique-
ness whose aggregation add up into his universe serve only to affirm
those identities; affirm them as if they were their own causes and
their own goals, even as Whitman felt himself to be.

I exist as I am, that is enough
If no other in the world be aware I sit content
And if each and all be aware I sit content.

And if he is stopped—

> it is enough, O soul—O soul, we have positively appeared; that
> is enough.

These last verses could lead one to take Whitman for an existentialist, modern style, since the ultimate object of contemporary existentialist faith is the indefeasible singularity of each existent. But if Whitman is so taken, he must be taken without the anxiety that is the source, the drive of life, to the existentialist schools—the anxiety which for them names the inescapable struggle of the living, who, as living die, not to die. Once Whitman did experience an anxiety—he called it *the terrible doubt of appearances*—the doubt that man's hoped-for immortality might be merely a 'may-be,' the doubt that all else could be anything else than a 'may-be.' But then comes true friendship and saves from doubt. It restores certainty, brings security, stands as the base of all metaphysics, and can be and is had with each and every being, all unique, all their singular selves whether as objective, past or present outward fact or as subjective inward remembrance or fantasy:

> When he whom I love travels with me or sits a long while
>   holding me by the hand,
> When the subtle air, the impalable, the sense that words and
>   reason hold not, surround us and pervade us
> Then I am charged with untold and untellable wisdom I am
>   silent. I require nothing further
> I cannot answer the question of appearances or of identity beyond the grave
> But I walk or sit indifferent, I am satisfied.
> He ahold of my hand has completely satisfied me.

In the same vein our Answerer replies to philosophers and churchmen. Deep beneath their creeds and codes, their doctrines and disciplines, there lives, he tells them,

> The dear love of man for his comrade, the attraction of friend
>   to friend,
> Of the well-married husband and wife, of children for parents,
>   Of city for city and land for land.

The doubt stays with him. He continues aware of uncertainty, and the anguish of it is still not quenched. His counter to it could well be interpreted as the last bastion of existentialism:

Do I contradict myself?
Very well then . . . I contradict myself;
I am large . . . I contain multitudes.

May I repeat, multitudes all different from one another, all unique and all equal in this poet's sight, as their comings and goings join them together to be the universe.

And now I turn to still another, the last, the subtlest, the most acceptable, of Whitman's envisionments of death. Some existentialist utterances about life and death might be taken for resonances of this one of Whitman's, even though they approach death 'in fear and trembling.' The most sonant of them argue and preach jeremiads over 'the years of the modern' whose talliers they are, the years that Whitman chanted a paean to, a paean and prophecy of human progress *en masse*, in equal liberty to form a free society of free men, performing, performing, leaving behind them the performed for 'the unperformed more gigantic than ever.' The talliers of these years of the modern lived and suffered, still live and suffer as who does not, evil times. These years are years of the greatest, the bloodiest wars that mankind ever waged; years of infinite inhumanity of man to man; years when cruelty and killing became articles of faith and ways of life in every land; years of the sadist believing with invincible belief that his faith and works would bring him and his kind their true deserts—the never-yet-attained life more abundant in peace and glory as masters of the world.

Some who became existentialists bet their own lives on resisting this evil; the most celebrated is French Jean Paul Sartre; others saw in the evil the purpose of an ultimate good; the most celebrated of these is German Martin Heidegger; others rejected it and fled it; the most celebrated of these is German Karl Jaspers. All became aware that death was the ultimate issue of their lives, their doom to be averted or advanced. One needs 'courage to be,' urged German Paul Tillich, a foe of the cannibal forces which turned his native land and his fellow countrymen into an abomination unspeakable. One needs courage to be because to be, is to be the fear of extinction, to be the 'existential anxiety' which is the inwardness of living on. Except to French Gabriel Marcel, who clung to the soul and the Otherworld where it would live on when it had died in this one, death was, to the authentic existentialists, at once present menace and future extinction. They have written that the sense of this, the idea of it, is substance of man's substance; that it works toward the shaping of the actual human career; that against it not even the illusion of immortality serves as an effective barrier. Death is nothingness. Death is not-to-be, and man, Sartre argues, 'wants only one thing—to be.' To be is to be free, 'for man is condemned to be free' and necessary death is alienation from freedom—the last absurdity of a nauseous world of absurdities.

Says Heidegger: I am born to die. Death is what awaits me, awaits me, yet it isn't life, so only renders life a thing of anxiety. Maybe, if I don't fight death, if instead of always struggling to prevent it, I accept it and take it resolutely into myself, I can achieve a certain anxiety-beset 'freedom to death,' I can encounter death with an armed joy.

Both Sartre and Heidegger, and others like Karl Jaspers and even French Algerian Camus, developed each, a personal dialectic that should, if not dissipate man's fear of death, at least reconcile him to it. Yet, Jaspers discloses, no mode of philosophizing can do this. 'If, as Socrates had suggested, to philosophize is to learn how to die, this . . . is actually the condition of the good life. To learn to live and to learn how to die are one and the same thing.'

But knowing this is not the same as wanting to die, as cherishing and welcoming death, although enjoying life. Our Mark Twain, no existentialist, was a spirit of this kind. He eulogized death many times in his pleasant life. I cite but two. Recalling the day that his daughter Jean had died, he wrote: 'She has been enriched with the most precious gift of all—that gift which makes all other gifts mean and poor—death. I have never wanted any released friend of mine restored to life since I reached manhood.' In *Letters from Earth* our greatest humorist has Satan write to him correspondence in heaven: 'Life was not a valuable gift, but death was. Life was a fever-dream— the heaviest curse devisable by divine ingenuity, but death was sweet, death was gentle, death was kind, death healed the bruised spirit and the broken heart and gave them rest and forgetfulness, death was man's best friend; when man could endure life no longer, death came and set him free.'

Imagine a dialogue on death between our existentialists, Mark Twain and Walt Whitman, the Answerer.

Whitman and Twain had both lived out our Civil War—the war fought, as Abraham Lincoln told the American mourners assembled at Gettysburg, to determine whether any nation conceived in liberty and dedicated to the proposition that all men are created equal could long endure. For Whitman, his role in the war was as momentous as Sartre's in the war against the form of ultimate evil we call Hitlerism. The commander-in-chief of freedom's army became for Whitman, beyond anything a flag could be, the precious symbol of the American

Idea, ever thrusting forward to establish as living fact the equal freedom and fellowship of all mankind. 'Here,' Whitman had written long before, 'here is not merely a nation but a teeming nation of nations.' America is the race of races. Its poet must be the voice and oracle of their diversity: 'The genius of the United States is not best or at most, save always in the common people—their deathless attachment to freedom—the air they have of persons who never knew how it felt to stand in the presence of superiors.' Elsewhere our Good Gray Poet had written, 'The noble soul rejects any liberty or privilege or wealth that is not open to every other man on the face of the earth.' On the battlefields and in the hospitals of the Civil War, Whitman had come face to face with this nobility; he had suffered with its champions and victims the costs of it, and he had grown into a reverent love of Abraham Lincoln as their incarnation, their sacrificial avatar. The war's wounded and killed, Lincoln's murder, led to the last, the most meaningful turn in Whitman's sense of the relation in life between love and death with which, I have suggested, Whitman might engage in a dialogue with Mark Twain and the existentialists, setting his new assurance beside the humorist's exaltation of death and the existentialists' equilibrations and assuagements.

'When Lilacs Last in the Dooryard Bloom'd' gives the poet's final envisionment of the place of death in life, its final expression. He is mourning for murdered Lincoln and for all who gave their lives that the nation might live. He is himself living out his loss in his mourning. He has heard a solitary thrush and calls out:

> Song of the bleeding throat,
> Death's outlet song of life, (full well dear brother I know,
> If thou was not granted to sing thou would'st surely die.)

And as he mourns his threnody, laying his sprig of lilac on his great Captain's coffin, he would lay that first bloom of spring on very death itself:

> For fresh as the morning, thus would I chant a song for you O
>   sane and sacred death.

And he learns how, from the lone thrush singing, now to sing a song for now sane and sacred death, is to celebrate all life and living, all persons and places, it is to bring pictures of bourgeoning life 'to adorn the burial house of him I love.' The poet now knows that it is in the processional of life that he knows 'death, its thought and the sacred knowledge of death.' Walking now with the thought and knowledge of death for companions, he reaches the thrush that must sing so that it should not die:

> And the voice of my spirit tallied the song of the bird.

> Come lovely and soothing death,
> Undulate round the world, serenely arriving, arriving,
> In the day, in the night, to all, to each,
> Sooner or later delicate death.

> Prais'd be the fathomless universe,
> For life and joy, and for objects and knowledge curious,
> And for love, sweet love—but praise! praise! praise!
> For the sure-enwinding arms of cool-enfolding death.

> Dark mother always gliding near with soft feet,
> Have none chanted for thee a chant of fullest welcome?
> Then I chant it for thee, I glorfy thee above all,
> I bring thee a song that when thou must indeed come, come un-
>   falteringly.

> Approach strong deliveress,
> When it is so, when thou hast taken them I joyously sing the
>   dead,
> Lost in the loving floating ocean of thee,
> Laved in the flood of thy bliss O death.

> From me to thee glad serenades,
> Dances for thee I propose saluting thee, adornments and feast-
>   ings for thee,
> And the sights of the open landscape and the high-spread sky
>   are fitting,
> And life and the fields, and the huge and thoughtful night.

> The night in silence under many a star,
> The ocean shore and the husky whispering wave whose voice I
>   know,
> And the soul turning to thee O vast and well-veil'd death,
> And the body gratefully nestling close to thee.

> Over the tree-tops I float thee a song,
> Over the rising and sinking waves, over the myriad fields and
>   the prairies wide,
> Over the dense-pack'd cities all and the teeming wharves and
>   ways,
> I float this carol with joy, with joy to thee O death.

Such now was, to Walt Whitman, the living inwardness of death. Whenever and however death happens, it is self-consummation, it is climax. It is life living itself out, using itself up, converting to joy of life all the fears, the dread and anxiety over loss, defeat, tragedy that so largely flow together in our awareness of death. What requires that men should feel, that, because there is death, because we don't stay alive when we are dead, life is absurd and not worth living? Or that death is absurd because life is worth living? The present age, remembering only the recent past, revolted by its own traits, appalled by its anticipation of the future, could, if they listened, perhaps find a challenging consolation in the words that Mr Holmes addressed on Memorial Day, 1895, to his fellow veterans of the Civil War come together to remember their dead:

> I do not know what is true. I do not know the meaning of the universe. But in the midst of doubt, in the collapse of creeds, there is one thing I do not doubt, and that is that the faith is true and adorable which leads a soldier to throw away his life in obedience to a blindly accepted duty, in a cause which he little understands, in a plan of campaign of which he has no notion, under tactics of which he does not see the use.

Then let them also turn to Walt Whitman, recalling the same tragedies that Holmes recalled. Holmes' challenging consolation could become triumphant insight if they let themselves share with the poet his adult realization that living and dying are an identical process, that we begin to die when we begin to live, that we stop dying when we stop living, that death may be as lovely and soothing, as sane and sacred and joyous as life, once they recognize it. They might even float carols of their own with joy, with joy to thee, O death.

Such is the kindest and wisest word of the Answerer to all who fearing death and disillusioned about immortality, also fear life. In another place, 'Song of the Open Road,' he calls to them and to all:

> Allons! through struggles and wars!
> The goal that was named cannot be countermanded.
> Have the past struggles succeeded?
> What has succeeded? yourself? your nation? Nature?
> Now understand me well—it is provided in the essence of things
>   that from any fruition of success, no matter what, shall
>   come forth something to make a greater struggle necessary.

This sequence in which dying is the process of living and living the process of dying, is the substance of existence. It makes the interval between birth from what we were not, and death whereby at last we become again the naught we were. There is no cure for birth or death, George Santayana advises, save to enjoy the interval of existing. To enjoy it, Walt Whitman declares, is to die living and live dying, by loving.

HAROLD W. BLODGETT

The Critical Response

Although the need to advance his own cause sometimes led Whitman to project the image of the neglected poet, he candidly admitted in later days that, considering the provocation, he had fared well in the reception of *Leaves of Grass*. And indeed the poet is fortunate who can, in Melville's phrase, evoke the shock of recognition in the mind of an Emerson, a Thoreau, a Dana, or a Hale. It could be argued that Whitman did not really have to write reviews of his own to set himself forward as "an American bard at last!" But possessed with his dream of creating a new poetry for a great democratic society, he could forego no seemingly persuasive means to find his readers. We may consider now that he need not have worried, for almost from the inception of the *Leaves* he was to draw impressive advocacy. But when he first began what was to become an intricate and laborious process of putting before the public successive and expanded printings of his book, the prospect must have seemed at times to be lonely— even desperate.

Yet commentators appeared quickly. Not all were friendly; some were mocking or hostile, a few were penetrating, but the sheer aggregate of their writings began to attest to the significance of a new voice. A sort of campaign ensued. At home, John Burroughs, Moncure Conway, William Douglas O'Connor, among others, wrote on Whitman, not as literary critics in any sense, but as disciples or propagandists. Abroad, respectful and critical attention came early from distinguished writers—among them William Michael Rossetti in England, 1867; Ferdinand Freiligrath in Germany, 1868; Edward Dowden in Ireland, 1871; Mme. Blanc (Thérèse Bentzon) in France, 1872. They were to be followed by such names as George Saintsbury in 1874; James Thomson, 1874; Robert Louis Stevenson, 1879; and John Addington Symonds, 1887.

Much of this earlier criticism had to do with the poet's purely aesthetic qualifications or with the question of the man himself. Was he an artist at all? Was he actually the mystifying lover and compeller of the *Leaves*? But the less immediate questions went directly to issues which Whitman himself emphasized. Was he indeed the poet of democracy, and if so, what claim does democracy have to be able to produce a great literature? Does Whitman speak for nationalism—for the aggrandizement of the States and the glorification of the American man? Or is his vision truly that of the internationalist who speaks for the globe and the human family? Was he merely dealing in the materials of poetry, quite unable, despite noble intentions, to create and control great imaginative expression? Was he a fraud, or a rare spirit? All these questions were proposed while Whitman was still living, and they emerged in a context of controversy, for the poet's personal supporters, regarding themselves as beleaguered, found it difficult, if not impossible, to be objective.

For some years after Whitman's death and well into the next century, the academic world, by and large, refused to recognize him, and Barrett Wendell's characterization of his craft as "hexameters trying to bubble through sewage" was praised for its wit. There were admirable exceptions, of course, but in school readers he was usually represented only by "O Captain! My Captain!" and in the public regard he was filed as America's "good gray poet," useful for editorial and patriotic reference, but not requiring to be read. But this insensibility was soon to change. Bliss Perry published a scholarly and balanced biography in 1906, and perceptive appraisals were presently available from other critics—among them Francis B. Gummere, John A. Macy, and Basil De Selincourt. In 1915 Van Wyck Brooks brilliantly presented Whitman as the "precipitant" of the American character. Whitman had come into his own, but American complacency could still be sharply cut by Bernard Shaw's remark in 1922, on the occasion of the thirtieth anniversary of Whitman's death: "Whitman is a classic, not a best seller. Curious that America should be the only country in which this is not as obvious as the sun in the heavens."

However, the usually percipient Shaw spoke for the past, not the future. It is obvious that Whitman is indeed a classic, but equally obvious that he has now become a staple—and stable—commodity on the market. At the present moment—without citing statistics—*Leaves of Grass* is available in many forms and editions, commanding an unfaltering response from the common reader as well as the college student, who, though he may purchase Whitman as a text, is likely to keep his *Leaves* not out of compulsion but for love. And Whitman's poetry and prose is in the world market as well, with more than fifty different translations in foreign tongues, according to a recent estimate.

Walt Whitman has traveled a long road since in the 1850's he forlornly wrote a manuscript note calling for "a poem which more familiarly addresses those who will, in future ages, understand me. (Because I write with reference to being far better understood then I can possibly be now.)" In the years following the 1922 anniversary observance, D. H. Lawrence acutely demonstrated that he was one of the understanders, a searching critic both praising and scolding the one he loved. Another was Emory Holloway, who, with later scholars —notably Clifton Joseph Furness—began to make available the rich materials of Whitman's workshop—his notebooks and early drafts There were, of course, fluctuations in this irresistible tide of expanding recognition. For example, the formulations of the "New Criticism," prominent in the thirties, found Whitman's optimism distressing, his use of abstractions inexact, his attitude of acceptance repellent. The "new critics" preferred poetry to be muted, ironic, and—if possible— ambiguous. Whitman did not belong to this company even though Randall Jarrell insisted on pointing out his extraordinary poetic power.

It seems clear now that response to Whitman is no longer engaged with what was once a relevant question: Is he a great poet? Its engagement is rather with questions of how and in what ways his greatness is manifested, and with its limitations, and its particular strength. An increasing number of examinations both of the man Whitman and of his poetry (the two subjects really cannot be separated) are now revealing fresh insights and suggesting new areas. A notable emphasis in recent criticism is upon the sheer joy of being that Whitman would confer, his offering of a poetry of passionate life, a new paganism, a worship of the sun. We find Anthony Burgess remarking that Whitman has only one subject, really—acceptance of the life-death cycle and reverence for it. We see that Karl Shapiro, himself a poet in the Whitman tradition, recognizes in his great predecessor an overriding intuition for "the essential holiness of things." All this is remindful of Wallace Stevens' vision of Whitman "walking along a ruddy shore . . . Nothing is final, he chants. No man shall see the end./His beard is of fire and his staff is a leaping flame."

But there are other strong revelations of quite a different sort in Whitman criticism, and what seems of paramount importance in these days of violence, political confusion, and dangerous rivalries is its emphasis upon the poet's vision of an ideal democratic society. Whitman could not foresee such twentieth-century developments as the sharp urbanization of population, the mechanization of industry by computer, the paralysis of traffic saturation, the appalling insistence of television—above all the threat of an energy capable of total global annihilation. No nineteenth-century figure could—with the possible exception of the sardonic Henry Adams, who bridged the two centuries. But Whitman had a great gift beyond such prophecy—a powerful apprehension that grasped the central human need: the experience of spiritual strength, the expenditure of love. This need is now finding expression in the studies that are hailing a new consciousness in young America, demanding the restoration of "the non-material elements of man's existence." This is a return to Whitman, a renewal of the hope he had affirmed in the brief prefatory note of his 1888 English edition of *Democratic Vistas:* "I think Literature—a new, superb, democratic literature—is to be the medicine and lever, and (with Art) the chief influence in modern civilization." One is reminded of a remark attributed to General de Gaulle by André Malraux: "Perhaps politics is the art of putting daydreams in their place. Nothing serious can be done if you bow to daydreams. But how can anything great be done without them?" Does Walt Whitman furnish the means of greatness? Recent critical response seems, with excitement, to explore this possibility.

Selected Bibliography

BIBLIOGRAPHIES AND EDITIONS

The most complete current bibliographical listing for Whitman is "Whitman: A Current Bibliography," by William White, published quarterly (March, June, September, December) in the *Walt Whitman Review* (Wayne State University Press), since March–June, 1956. See also the quarterly "Current Bibliography" in *American Literature* (Duke University Press); the annual compilation "MLA International Bibliography," published each spring as a supplement of *PMLA* by the Modern Language Association; and the annual survey *American Literary Scholarship* (Duke University Press). Further bibliographical listings, in order of publication, are:

Holloway, Emory, and Saunders, Henry S. "A Bibliography of Walt Whitman." In *The Cambridge History of American Literature*, ed. W. P. Trent et al., I, 551–581. New York: G. P. Putnam's Sons, 1918.

Wells, Carolyn, and Goldsmith, Alfred F. *A Concise Bibliography of the Works of Walt Whitman.* Boston: Houghton Mifflin, 1922.

Allen, Gay Wilson. *Twenty-Five Years of Walt Whitman Bibliography, 1918–1942.* Boston: F. W. Faxon, 1943.

Johnson, Thomas H. "Walt Whitman." In *Literary History of the United States*, ed. R. E. Spiller et al., III, 759–768. New York: Macmillan, 1948.

Miller, Edwin Haviland and Rosalind S. *Walt Whitman's Correspondence—A Checklist.* New York: New York Public Library, 1957.

Allen, Gay Wilson. "A Check List of Whitman Publications, 1945–1960. In *Walt Whitman as Man, Poet, and Legend*, pp. 179–244. Carbondale: Southern Illinois University Press, 1961.

White, William. "Walt Whitman's Journalism: A Bibliography." *Walt Whitman Review*, XIV, 3 (September, 1968).

This selective bibliography is exclusive of the almost innumerable editions of Whitman's separate titles. The two editions of his collected works are: *The Complete Writings of Walt Whitman*, ed. Richard Maurice Bucke, Thomas B. Harned, and Horace Traubel, 10 vols. (New York: G. P. Putnam's Sons, 1902), and *The Collected Writings of Walt Whitman* (New York: New York University Press, 1961–); under the general editorship of Gay Wilson Allen and Sculley Bradley, in 17 volumes, of which 9 have been published: *The Correspondence*, ed. Edwin Haviland Miller, 5 vols. (1961–1969); *Prose Works 1892*, ed. Floyd Stovall, 2 vols. (1963–1964); *The Early Poems and the Fiction*, ed. Thomas Brasher (1963); *Leaves of Grass: Comprehensive Reader's Edition*, ed. Harold W. Blodgett and Sculley Bradley (1965; reprinted, New York: W. W. Norton, 1968).

BIOGRAPHIES

Bucke, Richard Maurice. *Walt Whitman.* Philadelphia: David McKay, 1883.

Bliss, Perry. *Walt Whitman: His Life and Work.* Boston: Houghton Mifflin, 1906.

Holloway, Emory. *Whitman: An Interpretation in Narrative.* New York: Alfred A. Knopf, 1926.

Catel, Jean. *Walt Whitman: La Naissance du Poète.* Paris: Les Éditions Rieder, 1929.

Fausset, Hugh l'Anson. *Walt Whitman: Poet of Democracy.* London: Jonathan Cape, 1942.

Canby, Henry S. *Walt Whitman, An American; A Study in Biography.* Boston: Houghton Mifflin, 1943.

Allen, Gay Wilson. *The Solitary Singer: A Critical Biography of Walt Whitman.* New York: Macmillan, 1955.

Asselineau, Roger. *The Evolution of Walt Whitman.* 2 vols. Cambridge: The Belknap Press of Harvard University, 1960–1962. Originally published as *L'Évolution de Walt Whitman.* Paris: Didier, 1954.

CRITICAL STUDIES

De Selincourt, Basil. *Walt Whitman: A Critical Study.* London: Martin Secker, 1914.

Bailey, John C. *Walt Whitman.* New York: Macmillan, 1926.

Arvin, Newton. *Whitman.* New York: Macmillan, 1938.

Matthiessen, F. O. "Only a Language Experiment." In *American Renaissance,* pp. 517–625. New York: Oxford University Press, 1941.

Allen, Gay Wilson. *Walt Whitman Handbook.* Chicago: Packard, 1946.

Schyberg, Frederik. *Walt Whitman.* Translated from the Danish by Evie Allison Allen. New York: Columbia University Press, 1951.

Chase, Richard. *Walt Whitman Reconsidered.* New York: William Sloan, 1955.

Hindus, Milton, ed. *"Leaves of Grass" One Hundred Years After.* Stanford: Stanford University Press, 1955.

Miller, James E., Jr. *A Critical Guide to "Leaves of Grass."* Chicago: University of Chicago Press, 1957.

Allen, Gay Wilson. *Walt Whitman as Man, Poet, and Legend.* Carbondale: Southern Illinois University Press, 1961.

Lewis, R. W. B., ed. *The Presence of Walt Whitman.* New York: Columbia University Press, 1962.

Miller, Edwin Haviland. *Walt Whitman's Poetry: A Psychological Journey.* New York: New York University Press, 1968.

RELATED STUDIES AND SOURCES

Bucke, Richard Maurice, ed. *Notes and Fragments Left by Walt Whitman.* London: Talbot, 1899.

Traubel, Horace. *With Walt Whitman in Camden.* 5 vols. Vol. I, Boston: Small, Maynard, 1906; vol. II, New York: Daniel Appleton, 1908; vol. III, New York: Mitchell Kennerley, 1914; vol. IV, ed. Sculley Bradley, Philadelphia: University of Pennsylvania Press, 1953; vol. V, ed. Gertrude Traubel, Carbondale: University of Southern Illinois Press, 1964.

Cleveland, Rodgers, and Black, John, eds. *The Gathering of the Forces.* 2 vols. New York: G. P. Putnam's Sons, 1920. (Whitman's newspaper pieces in *The Brooklyn Daily Eagle,* 1846–1847.)

Holloway, Emory, ed. *The Uncollected Poetry and Prose of Walt Whitman.* 2 vols. Garden City, N.Y.: Doubleday, Page, 1921.

Clifton, Joseph Furness. *Walt Whitman's Workshop.* Cambridge: Harvard University Press, 1928.

Barrus, Clara. *Whitman and Burroughs, Comrades*. Boston: Houghton Mifflin, 1931.

Bychowski, Gustav. "Walt Whitman: A Study in Sublimation." *Psychoanalysis and the Social Sciences*, III (1951), 223–261.

Bowers, Fredson, ed. *Whitman's Manuscripts: "Leaves of Grass"* (1860). Chicago: University of Chicago Press, 1955.

Eby, Edwin Harold, ed. *A Concordance of Walt Whitman's "Leaves of Grass" and Selected Prose Writings*. Seattle: University of Washington Press, 1955.

Pearce, Roy Harvey, ed. *Whitman: A Collection of Critical Essays*. Englewood Cliffs, N.J.: Prentice-Hall, 1962.

Chari, V. K. *Whitman in the Light of Vedantic Mysticism*. Lincoln: University of Nebraska Press, 1964.

Waskow, Howard J. *Whitman: Explorations in Form*. Chicago: University of Chicago Press, 1966.

Golden, Arthur, ed. *Whitman's: "Blue Book."* 2 vols. New York: New York Public Library, 1967.

Index of Titles

Norton Critical Editions

CRANE   *The Red Badge of Courage*   edited by Donald Pizer   *Third Edition*

DARWIN   *Darwin*   selected and edited by Philip Appleman   *Second Edition*

DEFOE   *A Journal of the Plague Year*   edited by Paula R. Backscheider

DEFOE   *Moll Flanders*   edited by Edward Kelly

DEFOE   *Robinson Crusoe*   edited by Michael Shinagel   *Second Edition*

DICKENS   *Bleak House*   edited by George Ford and Sylvère Monod

DICKENS   *David Copperfield*   edited by Jerome H. Buckley

DICKENS   *Hard Times*   edited by George Ford and Sylvère Monod   *Second Edition*

DICKENS   *Oliver Twist*   edited by Fred Kaplan

DONNE   *John Donne's Poetry*   selected and edited by Arthur L. Clements   *Second Edition*

DOSTOEVSKY   *The Brothers Karamazov*   (the Garnett translation)   edited by Ralph E. Matlaw

DOSTOEVSKY   *Crime and Punishment*   (the Coulson translation)   edited by George Gibian   *Third Edition*

DOSTOEVSKY   *Notes from Underground*   translated and edited by Michael R. Katz

DREISER   *Sister Carrie*   edited by Donald Pizer   *Second Edition*

Eight Modern Plays   edited by Anthony Caputi

ELIOT   *Middlemarch*   edited by Bert G. Hornback

ELIOT   *The Mill on the Floss*   edited by Carol T. Christ

ERASMUS   *The Praise of Folly and Other Writings*   translated and edited by Robert M. Adams

FAULKNER   *The Sound and the Fury*   edited by David Minter   *Second Edition*

FIELDING   *Joseph Andrews with Shamela and Related Writings*   edited by Homer Goldberg

FIELDING   *Tom Jones*   edited by Sheridan Baker   *Second Edition*

FLAUBERT   *Madame Bovary*   edited with a substantially new translation by Paul de Man

FORD   *The Good Soldier*   edited by Martin Stannard

FRANKLIN   *Benjamin Franklin's Autobiography*   edited by J. A. Leo Lemay and P. M. Zall

GOETHE   *Faust*   translated by Walter Arndt, edited by Cyrus Hamlin

GOGOL   *Dead Souls*   (the Reavey translation)   edited by George Gibian

HARDY   *Far from the Madding Crowd*   edited by Robert C. Schweik

HARDY   *Jude the Obscure*   edited by Norman Page

HARDY   *The Mayor of Casterbridge*   edited by James K. Robinson

HARDY   *The Return of the Native*   edited by James Gindin

HARDY   *Tess of the d'Urbervilles*   edited by Scott Elledge   *Third Edition*

HAWTHORNE   *The Blithedale Romance*   edited by Seymour Gross and Rosalie Murphy

HAWTHORNE   *The House of the Seven Gables*   edited by Seymour Gross

HAWTHORNE   *Nathaniel Hawthorne's Tales*   edited by James McIntosh

HAWTHORNE   *The Scarlet Letter*   edited by Seymour Gross, Sculley Bradley, Richmond Croom Beatty, and E. Hudson Long   *Third Edition*

HERBERT   *George Herbert and the Seventeenth-Century Religious Poets*   selected and edited by Mario A. DiCesare

HERODOTUS   *The Histories*   translated and selected by Walter E. Blanco, edited by Walter E. Blanco and Jennifer Roberts